BEST PRACTICES
IN SCHOOL PSYCHOLOGY

DATA-BASED AND COLLABORATIVE DECISION MAKING

BEST PRACTICES
IN SCHOOL PSYCHOLOGY

DATA-BASED AND COLLABORATIVE
DECISION MAKING

EDITED BY
PATTI L. HARRISON & ALEX THOMAS

From the NASP Publications Board Operations Manual

The content of this document reflects the ideas and positions of the authors. The responsibility lies solely with the authors and editors and does not necessarily reflect the position or ideas of the National Association of School Psychologists.

Published by the National Association of School Psychologists

Copies may be ordered from:
NASP Publications
4340 East West Highway, Suite 402
Bethesda, MD 20814
301-657-0270
301-657-3127, fax
866-331-NASP, Toll Free
e-mail: *publications@naspweb.org*
www.nasponline.org/publications

Best Practices in School Psychology: Data-Based and Collaborative Decision Making
ISBN: 978-0932955-53-1 (print)

Best Practices in School Psychology (4-book series)
ISBN: 978-0-932955-52-4 (print), ISBN: 978-0-932955-51-7 (electronic)

Printed in the United States of America

20 10 9 8 7 6

Table of Contents

Introduction 1

Introduction and Framework

1   The National Association of School Psychologists Model for Comprehensive and Integrated School
    Psychological Services. 9
    Rhonda J. Armistead and Diane L. Smallwood

2   Problem-Solving Foundations for School Psychological Services 25
    Kathy Pluymert

3   A Comprehensive Framework for Multitiered Systems of Support in School Psychology 41
    Karen Callan Stoiber

4   The Evolution of School Psychology: Origins, Contemporary Status, and Future Directions 71
    James E. Ysseldyke and Daniel J. Reschly

Data-Based Decision Making and Accountability

5   Best Practices in Problem Analysis 87
    Theodore J. Christ and Yvette Anne Arañas

6   Best Practices in Data-Analysis Teaming 99
    Joseph F. Kovaleski and Jason A. Pedersen

7   Best Practices in Universal Screening 121
    Craig A. Albers and Ryan J. Kettler

8   Best Practices in Facilitating and Evaluating the Integrity of School-Based Interventions 133
    Andrew T. Roach, Kerry Lawton, and Stephen N. Elliott

9   Best Practices in Diagnosis of Mental Health and Academic Difficulties in a Multitier
    Problem-Solving Approach 147
    Frank M. Gresham

10 Best Practices in Curriculum-Based Evaluation 159
    Kenneth W. Howell and John L. Hosp

11 Best Practices in Curriculum-Based Evaluation in Early Reading. 171
    Michelle K. Hosp and Kristen L. MacConnell

12 Best Practices in Written Language Assessment and Intervention 187
    Christine Kerres Malecki

13 Best Practices in Instructional Assessment of Writing 203
    Todd A. Gravois and Deborah Nelson

14 Best Practices in Mathematics Assessment and Intervention With Elementary Students 219
    Ben Clarke, Christian T. Doabler, and Nancy J. Nelson

15 Best Practices in Mathematics Instruction and Assessment in Secondary Settings 233
    Yetunde Zannou, Leanne R. Ketterlin-Geller, and Pooja Shivraj

16 Best Practices in Neuropsychological Assessment and Intervention 247
    Daniel C. Miller and Denise E. Maricle

17 Best Practices in Play Assessment and Intervention 261
    Lisa Kelly-Vance and Brigette Oliver Ryalls

18 Best Practices in Conducting Functional Behavioral Assessments 273
    Mark W. Steege and Michael A. Scheib

19 Best Practices in Rating Scale Assessment of Children's Behavior 287
    Jonathan M. Campbell and Rachel K. Hammond

20 Best Practices in Can't Do/Won't Do Academic Assessment 305
    Amanda M. VanDerHeyden

21 Best Practices in Clinical Interviewing Parents, Teachers, and Students 317
    James J. Mazza

22 Best Practices in Identification of Learning Disabilities 331
    Robert Lichtenstein

23 Best Practices in the Assessment and Remediation of Communication Disorders 355
    Melissa A. Bray, Thomas J. Kehle, and Lea A. Theodore

24 Best Practices in Multimethod Assessment of Emotional and Behavioral Disorders 367
    Stephanie H. McConaughy and David R. Ritter

25 Best Practices in the Assessment of Youth With Attention Deficit Hyperactivity Disorder Within a
    Multitiered Services Framework 391
    Renée M. Tobin, W. Joel Schneider, and Steven Landau

26 Best Practices in Early Identification and Services for Children With Autism Spectrum Disorders 405
    Ilene S. Schwartz and Carol A. Davis

27 Best Practices in Assessment and Intervention of Children With High-Functioning Autism Spectrum
    Disorders 417
    Elaine Clark, Keith C. Radley, and Linda Phosaly

28 Best Practices in Writing Assessment Reports 433
    Robert Walrath, John O. Willis, and Ron Dumont

Consultation and Collaboration

29 Best Practices in School Consultation 449
    William P. Erchul and Hannah L. Young

30 Best Practices in School-Based Problem-Solving Consultation: Applications in Prevention and
    Intervention Systems 461
    Thomas R. Kratochwill, Margaret R. Altschaefl, and Brittany Bice-Urbach

31 Best Practices in Behavioral/Ecological Consultation 483
    Tammy L. Hughes, Jered B. Kolbert, and Laura M. Crothers

32 Best Practices in School-Based Mental Health/Consultee-Centered Consultation by School Psychologists 493
Jonathan Sandoval

33 Best Practice in Instructional Consultation and Instructional Consultation Teams 509
Sylvia Rosenfield

34 Best Practices in Facilitating Consultation and Collaboration With Teachers and Administrators . 525
Robin S. Codding, Lisa M. Hagermoser Sanetti, and Florence D. DiGennaro Reed

35 Best Practices in School Psychologists' Promotion of Effective Collaboration and Communication Among School Professionals 541
Tanya L. Eckert, Natalie Russo, and Bridget O. Hier

36 Best Practices as an Internal Consultant in a Multitiered Support System 553
Kathy McNamara

37 Best Practices in Implementing School-Based Teams Within a Multitiered System of Support . . . 569
Matthew K. Burns, Rebecca Kanive, and Abbey C. Karich

38 Best Practices in Providing Inservices for Teachers and Principals 583
Laura M. Crothers, Jered B. Kolbert, and Tammy L. Hughes

39 Best Practices in Establishing Effective Helping Relationships 595
Julia E. McGivern, Corey E. Ray-Subramanian, and Elana R. Bernstein

Index 617

Best Practices in School Psychology: Series List 633

Introduction

BEST PRACTICES IN SCHOOL PSYCHOLOGY: OVERVIEW OF THE SERIES

Best Practices in School Psychology is the sixth iteration of an intraprofessional collaborative effort to provide a single source for contemporary knowledge about many valued topics within school psychology. It has been more than 30 years since the first edition of *Best Practices in School Psychology* was published. In those 30 years and six editions, there have been substantial changes in the quantity of chapters, range of topics, and intended outcomes of school psychology services. However, the purpose of all editions of *Best Practices in School Psychology*, including the current edition, has remained constant over the years: to provide the current, relevant, and valued information necessary for competent delivery of school psychological services. Thus, chapters across editions have focused on *practices* by school psychology practitioners. Although chapters are not intended to be detailed reviews of research, research documentation is included in the chapters to provide an evidence-based foundation for recommended best practices.

This edition of *Best Practices in School Psychology* is designed to be a comprehensive resource, allowing readers to refer to chapters in the process of gaining information about specific, important professional practice topics and updating readers about contemporary techniques and methods. The primary target audience is school psychology practitioners who provide services in school settings, as was the case for previous editions. Similarly, the chapters may provide useful resources for other school-based professionals, as well as those who provide services to children in other settings. *Best Practices* also may serve as a helpful supplement for graduate courses when used in conjunction with primary course textbooks. As a compilation of best practices on major topics, *Best Practices in School Psychology* will assist school psychology practitioners, graduate students, interns, faculty, and others by providing readings on many specific areas of interest.

The content in this edition of *Best Practices in School Psychology* is expanded from earlier editions to include a broader range of topics, with considerable attention to multitiered, problem-solving, and evidence-based approaches for the delivery of effective school psychology services. The school psychology services outlined in this edition focus on improving student outcomes through data-based and collaborative activities in schools. Chapters emphasize prevention and intervention efforts for both student-level and systems-level services that recognize the importance of culture and individual differences across students, families, schools, and communities.

This edition of *Best Practices* was developed over 5 years, with multiple focus groups consisting of practitioner school psychologists, as well as graduate students and faculty, assisting the editors with organization and new topics for chapters to represent current and future needs. In addition, chapter authors and reviewers identified additional chapter topics.

The result is that this edition is organized a bit differently than previous editions. This edition is a four book series, with each book corresponding to one of the four interrelated components of the broad framework of the 2010 National Association of School Psychologists (NASP) *Model for Comprehensive and Integrated School Psychological Services* (i.e., the NASP Practice Model; see http://www.nasponline.org/standards/2010standards/2_PracticeModel.pdf): (a) *practices that permeate all aspects of service delivery*, including data-based and collaborative decision making; (b) *student-level services*, including instructional and academic supports and social and mental health services; (c) *systems-level services*, including school-wide learning practices, preventive and response services, and family–school collaboration; and (d) *foundations* of school psychological services, including diversity, research and program evaluation, and legal/ethical/professional practices.

About half of the chapters in this edition are updates of chapters included in earlier editions, and the other half focus on new and topical issues of importance in contemporary school psychology. Although it is impossible to include chapters for *all* areas of relevance to school psychology, it is hoped that the resulting 150 chapters provide a good representation of major services and issues in the field.

Organizational Framework of the Series

Each of the four books in the series has two or three separate sections corresponding to the specific domains of school psychology established in the 2010 NASP Practice Model. The titles of the four books and of the sections within each are outlined below:

1. *Best Practices in School Psychology: Data-Based and Collaborative Decision Making*

   Introduction and Framework
   Data-Based Decision Making and Accountability
   Consultation and Collaboration

2. *Best Practices in School Psychology: Student-Level Services*

   Interventions and Instructional Support to Develop Academic Skills
   Interventions and Mental Health Services to Develop Social and Life Skills

3. *Best Practices in School Psychology: Systems-Level Services*

   School-Wide Practices to Promote Learning
   Preventive and Responsive Services
   Family–School Collaboration Services

4. *Best Practices in School Psychology: Foundations*

   Diversity in Development and Learning
   Research and Program Evaluation
   Legal, Ethical, and Professional Practice

Chapter Structure

Typically, chapters include the following components, which provide readers with a predictable chapter structure:

Overview. Includes a definition and history of the topic and may provide situations for which a practicing school psychologist may wish to consult the chapter. This section orients the reader to the major issues, characteristics, and needs related to a chapter topic. It is introductory and establishes the context for the information presented.

Basic Considerations. Provides background information, research, training, experience, equipment, and other basics that school psychologists should know to effectively deal with the topic.

Best Practices. The heart and most extensive part of a chapter. Authors were asked to provide best practices and to include options and perspectives so that school psychologists can mesh their professional orientation with other successful possibilities.

Summary. A synopsis of the topic, which includes a brief review and discussion of the best practices.

References. Publications and resources that support the chapter authors' information. Authors were asked to not make exhaustive lists, because chapters are intended to focus on evidence-based practices and not simply present a compilation of research.

Unlike previous editions of *Best Practices*, the current edition does not include Annotated Bibliographies at the end of each chapter. Instead, readers have online access to each chapter's Annotated Bibliography on the NASP website (http://www.nasponline.org/publications). Annotated Bibliographies include articles, books, Web-based information, and other resources suggested by authors of each chapter for follow-up reading to gain a more detailed view of best practices for the topic discussed in a chapter.

It is our hope that this edition of *Best Practices in School Psychology* will support current and future school psychologists in their ongoing quest for improved procedures and practices and the acquisition of professional skills needed to enhance students' success in their schools, homes, and communities.

INTRODUCTION TO THE BOOK: BEST PRACTICES IN SCHOOL PSYCHOLOGY: DATA-BASED AND COLLABORATIVE DECISION MAKING

This book includes three sections of chapters about school psychology practices that permeate all aspects of service delivery, including an introduction and framework, data-based decision making and accountability, and consultation and collaboration.

Introduction and Framework

The first section of this book includes four introductory chapters that provide the framework for the delivery of school psychology services, as well as for the sixth edition of *Best Practices in School Psychology*. The chapters provide a panoramic view of contemporary school psychology and are relevant for all other chapters in the four books. Topics include the 2010 NASP *Model for Comprehensive and Integrated School Psychological Services,* problem-solving foundations, multitiered systems of support, and the evolution of advances and future needs in school psychology.

Data-Based Decision Making and Accountability

Chapters in this section focus on the Data-Based Decision Making and Accountability domain of the 2010 NASP *Model for Comprehensive and Integrated School Psychological Services.* This domain represents practices that permeate all activities of school psychology service delivery (see http://www.nasponline.org/standards/2010standards/2_PracticeModel.pdf, p. 4):

> School psychologists have knowledge of varied models and methods of assessment and data collection methods for identifying strengths and needs, developing effective services and programs, and measuring progress and outcomes. As part of a systematic and comprehensive process of effective decision making and problem solving that permeates all aspects of service delivery, school psychologists demonstrate skills to use psychological and educational assessment, data collection strategies, and technology resources and apply results to design, implement, and evaluate response to services and programs. Examples of professional practices associated with data-based decision making and accountability include the following:
>
> * School psychologists use a problem-solving framework as the basis for all professional activities.
> * School psychologists systematically collect data from multiple sources as a foundation for decision making and consider ecological factors (e.g., classroom, family, community characteristics) as a context for assessment and intervention in general and special education settings.
> * School psychologists collect and use assessment data to understand students' problems and to select and implement evidence-based instructional and mental health services.

- School psychologists, as part of an interdisciplinary team, conduct assessments to identify students' eligibility for special education and other educational services.
- School psychologists use valid and reliable assessment techniques to assess progress toward academic and behavioral goals, to measure responses to interventions, and to revise interventions as necessary.
- School psychologists assist with design and implementation of assessment procedures to determine the degree to which recommended interventions have been implemented (i.e., treatment fidelity).
- School psychologists use systematic and valid data collection procedures for evaluating the effectiveness and/or need for modification of school-based interventions and programs.
- School psychologists use systematic and valid data collection procedures to evaluate and document the effectiveness of their own services.
- School psychologists use information and technology resources to enhance data collection and decision making.

Consultation and Collaboration

Chapters in this section focus on the Consultation and Collaboration domain of the 2010 NASP *Model for Comprehensive and Integrated School Psychological Services*. This domain represents practices that permeate all activities of school psychology service delivery (see http://www.nasponline.org/standards/2010standards/2_PracticeModel.pdf, pp. 4–5):

School psychologists have knowledge of varied models and strategies of consultation, collaboration, and communication applicable to individuals, families, groups, and systems and methods to promote effective implementation of services. As part of a systematic and comprehensive process of effective decision making and problem solving that permeates all aspects of service delivery, school psychologists demonstrate skills to consult, collaborate, and communicate effectively with others. Examples of professional practices associated with consultation and collaboration include the following:

- School psychologists use a consultative problem-solving process as a vehicle for planning, implementing, and evaluating academic and mental health services.
- School psychologists effectively communicate information for diverse audiences, such as parents, teachers and other school personnel, policy makers, community leaders, and others.
- School psychologists consult and collaborate at the individual, family, group, and systems levels.
- School psychologists facilitate communication and collaboration among diverse school personnel, families, community professionals, and others.
- School psychologists function as change agents, using their skills in communication, collaboration, and consultation to promote necessary change at the individual student, classroom, building, and district, state, and federal levels.
- School psychologists apply psychological and educational principles necessary to enhance collaboration and achieve effectiveness in provision of services.

ACKNOWLEDGMENTS

It is fascinating to compare the assembling and publication of this sixth edition of *Best Practices in School Psychology* with the circumstances surrounding the first edition. The comparison highlights the growth and diversity of the profession, the organizational vitality and commitment of NASP, and the increasing influence and importance of school psychologists during the intervening 30+ years.

In 1982, when work began on the first edition, NASP had 7,500 members (2014 membership exceeds 25,000), and training, field placement, practice, and credentialing standards for school psychology were at a much earlier stage of development. For the first edition of *Best Practices*, the acknowledgments section thanked six individuals who assisted in reviewing the 39 chapters and in typesetting—yes, literally setting type of the text. Selection of font style and size, space between lines, paper stock, cover art, selection of the printer, obtaining copyright, design of shipping cartons, method of shipping, cost, and the like were made by the coeditors, and communications with authors and reviewers were primarily by U.S. mail along with occasional phone calls. Three thousand copies of the first edition of *Best Practices* were printed and then trucked to, stored at, and eventually distributed from a school psychologist's garage in Connecticut. The introductory price to members, including shipping, was $22. Times change.

For this sixth edition of *Best Practices*, there are hundreds of people to thank and acknowledge. First, the approximately 300 authors of our 150 chapters spread across four books deserve our gratitude. We appreciate the dedication, enthusiasm, and efforts of this highly talented group.

In addition to our editorial review, an earnest effort was made to have each chapter peer-reviewed by at least three school psychologists (two current practitioners and a university- or other non-school-based school psychologist). We must heartily thank the reviewers who read first drafts, provided important feedback to authors, and shared their suggestions for improvement of the chapters. Once these reviews were received, the reviewed chapters were forwarded to the author along with copies of comprehensive reviewer notations and editor comments. It was a time-consuming process for the reviewers, and our authors' final manuscripts substantially benefited from these extensive reviewer efforts. Reviewers who contributed to this edition, and who receive our appreciation, are:

Melinda Adkins	Ronald S. Palomares	Candis Hogan
Elsa Arroyos	Anna M. Peña	Susan Jarmuz-Smith
Barry Barbarasch	Madi Phillips	Rita Lynne Jones
Brian J. Bartels	Pamela M. Radford	Regina K. Kimbrel
John Biltz	Alecia Rahn-Blakeslee	Misty Lay
Alan Brue	Tracy Schatzberg	Mary Levinsohn-Klyap
Elliot J. Davis	Nicole Skaar	Monica McKevitt
Bill Donelson	Marlene Sotelo-Dynega	Katherine Mezher
Amy N. Esler	Vicki Stumme	Sara Moses
René Fetchkan	Jackie Ternus	Mary Alice Myers
Beth Glew	Lori Unruh	Ed O'Connor
Bryn Harris	Ellie L. Young	Leslie Z. Paige
Denise Hildebrand	Ashley Arnold	Shamim S. Patwa
Daniel Hyson	Michelle S. Athanasiou	Debbie Phares
Jessica (Dempsey) Johnston	Susan Bartels	E. Jeanne Pound
Cathy Kennedy-Paine	Jill Berger	Stephanie Rahill
Laurie McGarry Klose	Brandee Boothe	Nancy Peña Razo
Brian Leung	Kelly R. Swanson Dalrymple	Margaret Sedor
Jane Lineman-Coffman	Emma Dickinson	Carole A. Sorrenti
Courtney L. McLaughlin	Katie Eklund	Patricia Steinert-Otto
Dawn Miller	Pam Fenning	James M. Stumme
Karin Mussman	Marika Ginsburg-Block	Lynne Ostroff Thies
Karen O'Brien	Julie Hanson	Nate von der Embse
Rivka I. Olley	Jasolyn Henderson	

This sixth edition of *Best Practices* is the first edition that does not include Jeff Grimes as coeditor. Jeff worked with Alex Thomas as coeditor of all previous editions and made many contributions to the framework and content of *Best Practices* editions over the years. Further, Jeff has been a long-time leader in school psychology, and our field has benefitted greatly from his commitment, wisdom, and vision. We thank Jeff for all he has done for *Best Practices* and school psychology.

The efforts of Mike Schwartz have proved invaluable to the completion of this edition. Mike Schwartz has been the copyeditor for every chapter in this and in the last two editions of *Best Practices*. He read and reread each of the chapters and contributed substantive comments and perspectives in addition to making sure that references were properly cited, tenses agreed, tables aligned, verbs and nouns were compatible, and ideas remained focused. We thank him for his talent and good humor.

The look and feel of this edition, and the consistency and ease of reference, is due to the metadiligent efforts of Linda Morgan, NASP Director of Production. She actively participated in the myriad details associated with this work and took the lead in the design and presentation. Additionally, she fact checked and triple fact checked every reference and citation. NASP is fortunate to have her talents, and this edition of *Best Practices* is richer due to her involvement.

There are other people at the NASP national office who quietly and competently worked to enhance this edition of *Best Practices*. We thank Brieann Kinsey, Manager of Editorial Production, for her time fact checking, proofreading, and ensuring that what was printed was accurate and consistent with the overall "feel" of the publication. We also thank Denise Ferrenz, Director of Publications, for dealing with the multitude of planning, publication, and marketing considerations associated with a project of this magnitude.

Alex Thomas
Patti Harrison

EDITOR NOTE

Authors were invited to write chapters for this edition of *Best Practices* because of their expertise and experience in a specific topic. In a number of cases, these authors have written other publications or developed resources on the same topic and reference these materials in their *Best Practices* chapters. Therefore, authors were instructed to include a disclosure statement at the end of their *Best Practices* chapters, in line with the 2010 NASP *Principles for Professional Ethics*, Standard III.V.6 (see http://www.nasponline.org/standards/2010standards/1_%20Ethical%20Principles. pdf), which requires school psychologists to disclose financial interests in resources or services they discuss in presentations or writings.

Disclosure. Alex Thomas and Patti Harrison have financial interests in publications they coauthored or coedited and that are referenced by authors of several chapters in this edition of *Best Practices in School Psychology*. These include, for Alex Thomas, previous editions of *Best Practices in School Psychology* and, for Patti Harrison, *Contemporary Intellectual Assessment: Theories, Tests, and Issues; Adaptive Behavior Assessment System;* and *ABAS-II: Clinical Use and Interpretation.*

Section 1
Introduction and Framework

1 The National Association of School Psychologists Model for Comprehensive and Integrated School Psychological Services

Rhonda J. Armistead
Charlotte-Mecklenburg (NC) Schools
Diane L. Smallwood
Philadelphia College of Osteopathic Medicine

The National Association of School Psychologists (NASP) *Model for Comprehensive and Integrated School Psychological Services* (NASP Practice Model; NASP, 2010a) represents NASP's official policy regarding the delivery of comprehensive school psychological services. The NASP Practice Model is intended to be used in conjunction with the NASP *Standards for Graduate Preparation of School Psychologists* (NASP, 2010e), *Standards for the Credentialing of School Psychologists* (NASP 2010d), *and Principles for Professional Ethics* (NASP, 2010c) to provide a unified set of national principles that guide graduate education, credentialing, professional practices, and ethical behavior of school psychologists. The NASP Practice Model, which was adopted by the NASP Delegate Assembly in 2010, is intended to educate the profession and the public regarding appropriate professional practices and to stimulate the continued development of school psychology as a profession. Moreover, this edition of *Best Practices in School Psychology* uses the NASP Practice Model as an organizing framework for presenting current best practices within all of the domains of school psychological services.

This chapter describes the development of the NASP Practice Model, summarizes professional practices and organizational principles considered essential to comprehensive school psychological services, and emphasizes its critical role as a vehicle for communicating information about what services might reasonably be expected to be available from most school psychologists.

Finally, strategies to promote the NASP Practice Model's adoption at national, state, and local levels are suggested.

OVERVIEW

NASP first established standards for the graduate preparation and credentialing of school psychologists more than 40 years ago. Since that time, NASP has utilized its governance structure to develop and adopt policy documents pertaining to the graduate preparation, credentialing, ethics, and professional practices of school psychologists.

The four NASP policy documents provide a unified set of national principles that guide graduate education and credentialing in school psychology and serve as the basis for ethical and professional behavior of school psychologists. These four documents define contemporary school psychology, promote appropriate and effective school psychological services for all children and youth, and provide a foundation for the future of school psychology.

The NASP Practice Model provides school psychologists, educators, and consumers with a guide for excellence in school psychological services. The NASP Practice Model is aligned with standards for graduate preparation and credentialing of school psychologists and describes the services that typically would be provided by school psychologists, as well as the organizational conditions needed to support the delivery of effective school psychological services. Although there is no question that there is substantial variability among school psychologists with regard to levels of training, years of experience, and specific professional competencies, graduate education programs that are consistent with national standards prepare school psychologists to have at least entry-level skills in each of the domains described by the NASP Practice Model.

As an introduction to this edition of *Best Practices*, this chapter will describe the significance of the NASP Practice Model and the rationale and processes used to inform its development. The chapter will place the NASP Practice Model within the context of educational reform and summarize empirical support for the domains and the organizational principles relative to improving the outcomes for schools, families, and students. Suggested practices for the NASP Practice Model's use by school psychologists, supervisors, graduate education programs, and state associations will be described.

BASIC CONSIDERATIONS

The 2000 revision of the standards documents marked the initiation of a 10-year review and revision cycle for NASP standards. Prior to that time, the four standards documents were developed and revised as individual policy statements that addressed critical aspects of the school psychology profession. Beginning in 2000, however, the standards documents were reviewed and revised as an integrated set of principles that are interrelated and united in their purpose of advancing consistency in graduate preparation, credentialing, ethics, and professional practices in school psychology.

The 2010 NASP Practice Model is the most recent revision of the *Standards for the Provision of School Psychological Services*, which was first adopted by NASP in 1978, with later revisions in 1984, 1992, 1997, and 2000. Throughout all of the updates, the purpose of the document has been to define excellence in the practice of school psychology and to educate both professionals and consumers regarding appropriate professional practices. In 2000, the title of the *Standards for the Provision of School Psychological Services* was changed to the *Guidelines for the Provision of School Psychological Services* (NASP, 2000a) to reflect the differences in the enforceability of standards in graduate preparation and credentialing versus in practice settings.

The NASP program approval process and the National School Psychology Certification Board provide vehicles for requiring standards in graduate programs and credentialing, at least for NASP-approved school psychology graduate programs and for school psychologists holding the Nationally Certified School Psychologist (NCSP) credential. Because there is no comparable mechanism for enforcing standards for professional practice, it was thought more appropriate to view the practice document as a set of guidelines that define best practices for the profession rather than as enforceable standards.

NASP has created a national model for the practice of school psychology with its 2010 NASP Practice Model. The NASP Practice Model is closely aligned with the standards for graduate preparation and credentialing, and it translates the knowledge and skills required of school psychologists into statements of what school psychologists routinely do to address the diverse needs of children, families, and schools.

Visions of the Future in School Psychology

School Psychology: A Blueprint for Training and Practice is a series of documents first published in 1984 and revised in 1997 and 2006 (Ysseldyke, Reynolds, & Weinberg, 1984; Ysseldyke et al., 1997; Ysseldyke et al., 2006). These works, authored by a small but influential group of school psychologists, attempted to build upon the collective foundations of knowledge discussed via the professional "futures" conferences dating from Boulder in 1949 through the 2002 online conference on the Future of School Psychology.

Blueprints I, II, and *III* have had significant impact on NASP standards, particularly the official NASP *Standards for Graduate Preparation of School Psychologists*. The *Blueprint* series were visionary documents designed to reflect "exemplars of successes and promising trends in today's schools and the school psychology specialty" as a means of forecasting the training and practice needs of school psychologists (Ysseldyke et al., 2006, p. 39).

By examining circumstances within education and emerging factors in society, *Blueprint* framers were able to propose changes and correct limitations of previous versions. The *Blueprint* envisioned that in order for school psychologists to be instrumental in improving the academic and social–emotional outcomes of children, domains of competencies were needed. The *Blueprint* also recognizes that school psychologists must be involved in helping systems build and sustain their capacity for fostering and developing the essential academic and social competencies for students. School psychologists, as systems consultants, were meant to ensure that the individual components of systems would work together so that optimal outcomes would be achieved. These concepts figure prominently in the 2010 NASP Practice Model.

Whereas the *Blueprints* represent an "expert" perspective, the NASP standards were developed using consensus building among all involved stakeholders. Moreover, the NASP standards reflect official policy of the Association, as adopted through a formal vote by the NASP Delegate Assembly. Nevertheless, the *Blueprints* have influenced a vision for school psychology, and each revision has contributed to subsequent development of the standards documents.

School psychology is represented by multiple organizations that serve various constituencies within the field of school psychology, including NASP, Division 16 of the American Psychological Association, and Trainers of School Psychologists as well as other smaller organizations. Over the past 10 years, these organizations have collaborated on conferences and other projects to bring together school psychologists around the world to talk about the shape of school psychology going forward into the future. The first conference on the future of school psychology was held in Indianapolis in 2002, with Internet-based participation by hundreds of school psychologists at other remote locations around the world. The proceedings of the 2002 Multisite Conference on the Future of School Psychology were published in a joint issue of the *School Psychology Review* and the *School Psychology Quarterly* (Sheridan & D'Amato, 2004).

An online Conference on the Future of School Psychology took place in the fall of 2012, providing an opportunity for school psychologists to discuss critical issues facing the profession and to consider how our collective resources can best support children, families, and schools (http://www.indiana.edu/~futures/). The three online sessions are fully archived, allowing the keynote presentations and panel discussions to be available to vast audiences of practitioners, university faculty, graduate students, and other interested parties. Perhaps the greatest message inherent in the mission and operations of the 2012 Conference on the Future of School Psychology is the importance of collaboration and shared data-driven decision making in creating a future in which school psychological services are an integral part of student support systems throughout the world.

Development of the NASP Standards Documents

Each revision of the NASP standards involves an extensive process of landscape assessment, involving reviews of current legislation, regulations, best practices and future directions in psychology and education, and consideration of feedback from stakeholders within school psychology (e.g., practitioners, trainers, graduate students, affiliated state associations, related school psychology organizations) as well as external stakeholder groups such as parents, teachers, and other professional associations. The development of the 2010 NASP standards, including the NASP Practice Model, started in April 2007, 3 years prior to adoption by the NASP Delegate Assembly in March 2010.

The standards revision process began with a Web-based survey soliciting feedback on the existing 2000 standards. It resulted in more than 2,700 responses. Multiple focus groups were held during NASP conventions and governance meetings.

Finally, a public comment period from February to April 2009 allowed all stakeholders, both internal and external to the field, to provide feedback regarding final drafts of the four sets of standards.

Three different groups were involved in producing the final versions of the standards. Writing teams developed drafts, reviewed and assimilated comments and suggestions, and then sought feedback from a development group consisting of leaders from NASP and other school psychology organizations. A reaction group comprising members of stakeholder groups and the general public reviewed final drafts. Approximately 500 responses were considered by the writing teams during the public comment period. Final drafts of the standards were also presented and debated twice by the NASP Delegate Assembly before the final vote.

Given this comprehensive development and review process, the NASP Practice Model and the other standards documents clearly reflect a consensus perspective on contemporary best practices in school psychology.

Rationale for the NASP Practice Model

Since their inception more than 40 years ago, the NASP standards have had a progressively positive impact upon the field of school psychology and have contributed to substantial consistency today in the preparation and credentialing of school psychologists across the United States.

According to Waldron and Prus (2006), 68% of reviewed programs were NASP approved, meaning that a peer review had judged them to be consistent with 2000 NASP *Standards for Training and Field Placement Programs* (NASP, 2000c) during the period 2001–2005.

The percentage of school psychologists with specialist level (defined by 60 or more graduate semester hours in school psychology) or higher preparation has remained relatively stable and at approximately 80% for about 20 years (Castillo, Curtis, & Gelley, 2012). The NASP (2000b) *Standards for the Credentialing of School Psychologists* have been widely accepted as well. More than 30 states now use NASP credentialing standards to qualify school psychologists as professionals.

So, this question needs consideration: Since NASP has set standards for the provision of school psychological services for more than 40 years, why do the roles of school psychologists continue to vary significantly from one school district to the next and from one state to another?

The most recent national survey data report that school psychologists are employed in greater numbers and are accessible to more students and schools, but the availability of comprehensive services as envisioned by the practice standards remains largely unattained (Castillo et al., 2012).

Why a National Model of School Psychological Services Is Needed

When the NASP standards revision workgroup met in 2007 and 2008 to review the feedback regarding the 2000 standards and considered the contemporary and anticipated psychological needs of children and families, several possible advances for service delivery emerged. Discrete domains of knowledge and skills had been articulated by leaders throughout the 1990s and early 2000s, yet there was a perceived need to describe the roles of school psychologists in a way that integrated their many competencies into a framework for effective service delivery.

In addition, survey responses indicated that the 2000 *Guidelines for the Provision of School Psychological Services* (NASP, 2000a) were not widely used as a basis for creating and implementing effective systems for the delivery of school psychological services. Because earlier iterations of the practice standards were considered advisory, in practical terms they appeared to have minimal impact on the perceived role of school psychologists, as evidenced by their adoption into state regulations as definitions for school psychology practice or by changes in job descriptions.

A fundamental goal in development of the NASP Practice Model was to produce a user-friendly document that could be a valuable resource to audiences both within and outside of the school psychology professional community. The idea of a *model* emerged as a means for

verbally and visually describing the services that school psychologists can provide. Moreover, it was recognized that a model should also emphasize the need for organizational conditions to support comprehensive school psychological services.

The 2010 NASP Practice Model translates the knowledge base and skills of school psychology into a set of professional practices associated with 10 domains of practice. While each domain delineates a discrete set of knowledge and skills, the NASP Practice Model also reflects the integration of these competencies into a cohesive framework of services.

It is the integration envisioned in the NASP Practice Model that has the potential for the greatest impact on students and schools. Thus, domains such as Data-Based Decision Making and Accountability along with Consultation and Collaboration are essential to all student-level services as well as to systems-level services.

Communicating the Value of School Psychological Services

The importance of the NASP Practice Model for communicating the services that might be expected of a school psychologist is not trivial. To achieve the goal of ensuring widespread accessibility to school psychological services, decision makers and consumers, including boards of education, school administrators, teachers and other educators, families, and the public, must understand the importance of these services for the successful educational outcomes for all children. A coherent model that translates the standards for graduate preparation and credentialing into examples of what school psychologists actually do at the individual, classroom, and systems levels serves this purpose.

Although school psychologists historically have been associated with psychoeducational assessment and special education services, school psychologists' roles have been expanding for several decades (Curtis, Lopez, et al., 2008; Castillo et al., 2012). Although school psychologists continue to spend the majority (58%) of their time engaged in special-education-related activities, 2009–2010 national survey data indicate that school psychologists report spending up to 20% of their time in delivering services intended to improve academic or social–emotional outcomes for students (Castillo et al., 2012). The data also support the conclusion that school psychologists provide student-level and system-wide services consistent with the NASP Practice Model. However, the types of practices vary. For example, 25% of school psychologists' time is devoted to developing and delivering intensive interventions, whereas only 8% of their time is spent developing interventions for general education (Castillo et al., 2012).

Contemporary Context for School Psychology

As the standards revision process began, members of all of the writing teams met jointly to consider the impact of contextual factors on the practice of school psychology. These included the current emphasis on accountability for the academic progress of all students in K–12 schools, as well as the increasingly diverse student population with respect to ethnic, linguistic, and economic backgrounds. Children's social and emotional wellness and the importance of schools for the accessibility of mental health services were also critical issues. The writing teams also considered numerous trends, such as utilizing population-based prevention methods and the necessity of evidence-based interventions. The following sections provide a brief overview of how these influenced the development of the NASP Practice Model.

Accountability in service delivery.

The trend toward performance-based accountability for school psychologists in training was evident in earlier versions of NASP's standards. The 1994 NASP *Standards for Training and Field Placement Programs in School Psychology* for the first time required programs to demonstrate how to ensure that all program graduates were able to demonstrate positive, measurable change in the educational or mental health status of children and youth. The performance-based nature of the NASP graduate preparation standards is now reflected in the requirements for national certification in school psychology.

Currently, demonstration of positive, measurable outcomes for children and youth is a requirement for obtaining the NCSP credential, whether the evidence is completing a NASP-approved program or submitting case study evidence to the National School Psychology Certification Board. Similarly, the NASP Practice Model emphasizes that data-based decision making and accountability competencies permeate the services of school psychologists. Within each domain for student- or systems-level services, there is the expectation that school psychologists use data to select evidence-based interventions or programs and evaluate the effectiveness of these decisions.

By 2010, the movement toward performance-based accountability, which began in the 1990s, had developed into an almost exclusive focus upon outcomes-based accountability for schools and school personnel. As Curtis (2000) predicted, school psychologists are being called upon to evaluate, modify, and demonstrate the effectiveness of their own performance. This context was an important one for developing the NASP Practice Model as a cohesive framework for delivery of school psychological services. Thus, the NASP Practice Model has potential for becoming the basis of state and district efforts to develop instruments for personnel appraisal.

Improving educational outcomes.

School psychologists whose practice is consistent with the NASP Practice Model have the potential to make substantial contributions to school improvement efforts. Research on educational outcomes over the past 30–40 years has provided a considerable amount of evidence about conditions that support student learning. Many of these studies emphasize three major influences on learning: school-level factors, teacher-level factors, and student-level factors (e.g., Marzano, 2003; Bryk, Sebring, Allensworth, Luppescu, & Easton, 2010). School psychologists have much to offer with regard to each of these factors.

Marzano (2003) identified five specific school-level factors that influence learning outcomes: a guaranteed and viable curriculum, challenging goals and effective feedback, parent and community involvement, a safe and orderly environment, and collegiality and professionalism. School psychologists can make significant contributions to school planning teams in each of these areas. With a knowledge base in both education and psychology, school psychologists understand the importance of a strong curriculum for all students and have knowledge of how to design effective instructional strategies to ensure that all students find success in learning. In addition, school psychologists can facilitate positive home–school relationships that also are essential to school success. School psychologists work with other educators to help create safe and supportive learning environments in which all students can achieve and feel connected to others. Finally, the work ethic of school psychologists is grounded in collaborative and collegial relationships with other educators, community leaders, and families.

As consultants and colleagues, school psychologists work with teachers to solve individual and classroom problems with learning and behavior. Research has shown that teacher-level factors, including use of instructional strategies, classroom management skills, and design of classroom curriculum, can have powerful effects on student learning (Marzano, 2003). Using a collaborative problem-solving approach, school psychologists can help teachers implement effective classroom management strategies and implement instructional strategies to meet the needs of diverse learners.

School psychologists also have expertise in addressing a variety of student-level factors, including academic engagement, motivation, and cognitive and learning abilities. Through both direct and indirect services, school psychologists provide academic and emotional supports to students and teachers, increasing the probability that successful learning outcomes will be attained (Durlak, Weissberg, Dymnicki, Taylor, & Schellinger, 2011).

Evidence-based practice in school psychology. School psychology has long been considered a science-based profession, and school psychologists are usually trained as scientist practitioners. Although practitioners have applied the scientific method while studying problems in natural settings, many preconceptions persist, that the medical model attributes learning and behavioral problems to traits residing within a person. In schools, students are routinely in groups, and problems often need to be addressed at the group or classroom level rather than by singling out individual students as the focus of interventions. The NASP Practice Model reflects a shift from an emphasis on individuals to a systems-level orientation using problem-solving processes for groups of students (e.g., see Pluymert, Chapter 2).

Values underlying the NASP Practice Model. The 2010 NASP standards documents reflect a set of six principles about the nature of school psychological services and the importance of these services to the well-being and academic success of all students. These principles assert that school psychologists (a) have a knowledge base in both psychology and education; (b) use effective strategies and skills to help students succeed academically, socially, behaviorally, and emotionally; (c) use their knowledge and skills to create safe, supportive, fair, and effective learning environments for all students; (d) demonstrate knowledge and skills relevant to the work that they do; (e) ensure that their professional practices reflect understanding and respect for human diversity and social justice; and (f) integrate knowledge and skills across all domains of practice to deliver a comprehensive range of services that result in direct and measurable outcomes for children, families, and schools.

Because the NASP Practice Model is based upon the needs of schools, families, and students and is organized in a way to best meet those needs, it allows flexibility for agencies and professionals to develop policies and organizational structures to support practitioners' providing a comprehensive range of services. However, it is important to note that the 10 domains of professional practice outline services that a school psychologist should be capable of delivering at a basic level, that is, as a beginning practitioner given sufficient organizational support. School psychologists' competencies will range from basic level to expert. The NASP Practice Model does not differentiate services based on graduate preparation (e.g., doctoral or specialist level) or amount of experience.

For optimal implementation, the NASP Practice Model recommends that schools provide necessary infrastructure in terms of appropriate numbers of school psychologists and support for professional practice. These recommendations are outlined in the Organizational Principles section of the NASP Practice Model.

Model for Comprehensive and Integrated School Psychological Services

The various aspects of school psychological services are depicted graphically in Figure 1.1 and can be described in this way:

> School psychologists provide effective services to help children and youth succeed academically, socially, behaviorally, and emotionally. School psychologists provide direct educational and mental health services for children and youth, as well as work with parents, educators, and other professionals to create supportive learning and social environments for all children. School psychologists apply their knowledge of both psychology and education during consultation and collaboration with others. They conduct effective decision making using a foundation of assessment and data collection. School psychologists engage in specific services for students, such as direct and indirect interventions that focus on academic skills, learning, socialization, and mental health. School psychologists provide services to schools and families that enhance the competence and well-being of children, including promotion of effective and safe learning environments, prevention of academic and behavior

Figure 1.1. NASP Model for Comprehensive and Integrated School Psychological Services

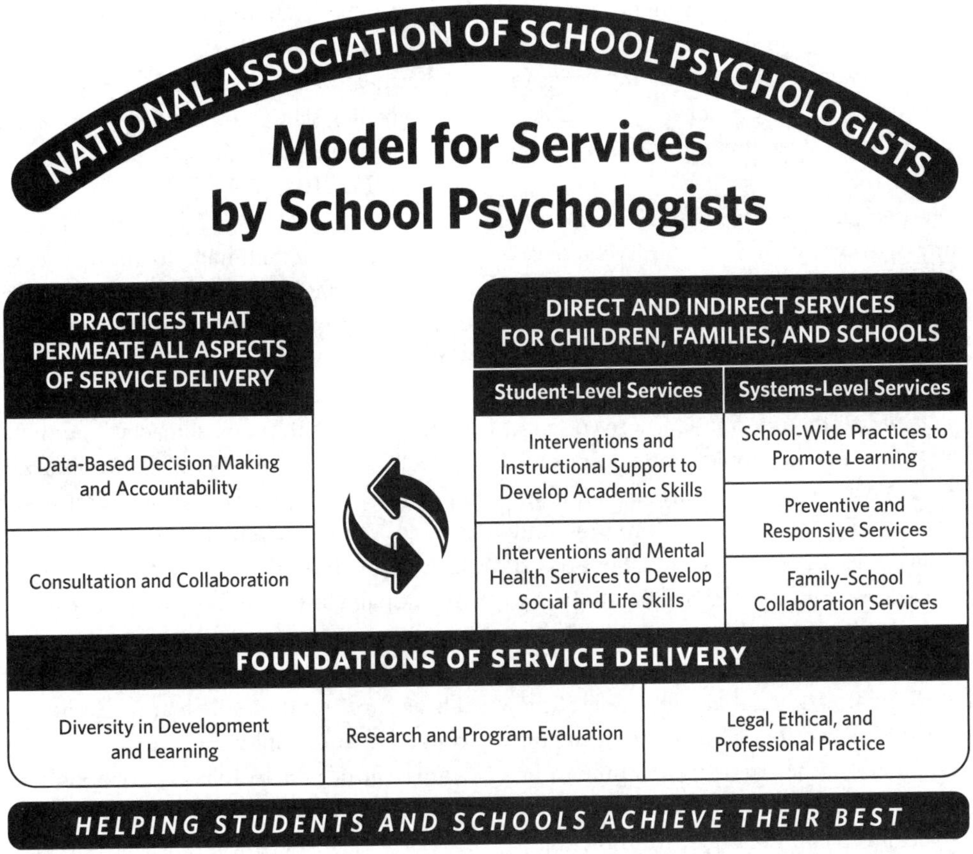

Note. From "Model for Comprehensive and Integrated Psychological Services, NASP Practice Model Overview" [Brochure], by National Association of School Psychologists, 2010, Bethesda, MD: National Association of School Psychologists. Copyright 2010 by National Association of School Psychologists. Reprinted with permission.

problems, response to crises, and improvement of family–school collaboration. The key foundations for all services by school psychologists are understanding of diversity in development and learning; research and program evaluation; and legal, ethical, and professional practice. (NASP, 2010a, p. 1)

The NASP Practice Model comprises two major sections, one describing professional practices of school psychologists and the other describing a set of organizational principles for supporting comprehensive school psychological services. The Professional Practices section presents examples of typical activities of school psychologists in each of 10 domains of school psychology practice. The Organizational Principles section describes the organizational framework necessary for effective delivery of school psychological services for children, families, and schools.

Professional Practices

Practices That Permeate All Aspects of Service Delivery

Data-Based Decision Making and Accountability
School psychologists have knowledge of varied models and methods of assessment and data collection methods for identifying strengths and needs, developing effective services and programs, and measuring progress and outcomes. As part of a systematic and comprehensive process of effective decision making and problem solving that permeates all aspects of service delivery, school psychologists demonstrate skills to use psychological and educational assessment, data collection strategies, and technology resources and apply results to design, implement, and evaluate response to services and programs. (NASP, 2010a, p. 4)

As practitioners, school psychologists use a problem-solving framework as the basis for all professional activities. They use their skills in assessment and data collection to gather information that is needed to make decisions about how to address the educational needs of students and to determine the level of progress that is made in response to instructional and behavioral interventions.

Data-based decision making is one of the cornerstones of school psychology practice, and school psychologists are knowledgeable about a variety of methods to collect, analyze, and apply data in their efforts to support students, families, and schools. As practitioners, school psychologists conduct assessments of individual learning and behavior, and utilize the information derived from those assessments to plan and implement appropriate educational and behavioral interventions. In addition, school psychologists assist in monitoring progress and evaluating the outcomes associated with school-based programs and services (e.g., see Roach, Lawton, & Elliott, Chapter 8).

Contemporary approaches to school-based assessment go well beyond the traditional norm-referenced individual tests of intellectual functioning and academic achievement, although such instruments continue to be core components of almost every school psychology practitioner's repertoire. With the 2004 reauthorization of the Individuals with Disabilities Education Act, there has been a shifting emphasis, away from traditional ability–achievement discrepancy models of eligibility determination for learning disabilities and toward a problem-solving orientation, using a response-to-intervention (RTI) approach to identifying students who require special educational programs and services. Consequently, not only must school psychologists now have strong knowledge of traditional measurement procedures, but they also must have a high level of proficiency in assessment strategies and techniques associated with the RTI approach. The NASP Practice Model emphasizes multitiered systems of service delivery and the use of an overarching problem-solving framework to define educational concerns, develop and implement data-driven intervention plans, and evaluate effectiveness of educational programs and services (see Stoiber, Chapter 3).

Consultation and Collaboration

School psychologists have knowledge of varied models and strategies of consultation, collaboration, and communication applicable to individuals, families, groups, and systems and methods to promote effective implementation of services. As part of a systematic and comprehensive process of effective decision making and problem solving that permeates all aspects of service delivery, school psychologists demonstrate skills to consult, collaborate, and communicate effectively with others. (NASP 2010a, p. 4)

Although the ultimate focus of the work done by school psychologists is directed toward improving educational outcomes for children and youth, much of their time is spent interacting with other adults. Thus, school psychologists engage in a variety of problem-solving tasks with parents, teachers, and other educators, as well as community-based professionals. Their skills in effective techniques for consultation and collaboration enable school psychologists to facilitate changes in instructional approaches and behavioral supports at individual, classroom, and systems levels.

Schools are complex systems in which individuals carry out their responsibilities within a team framework. There are grade-level teams, building-based intervention teams, child study teams, and crisis response teams, all of which utilize a collaborative approach to addressing school-based issues. School psychologists can provide leadership in these group tasks, based upon their skills in communication and collaboration as well as their training and expertise in the problem-solving model.

Direct and Indirect Services for Children, Families, and Schools: Student-Level Services

Interventions and Instructional Support to Develop Academic Skills

School psychologists have knowledge of biological, cultural, and social influences on academic skills; human learning, cognitive, and developmental processes; and evidence-based curricula and instructional strategies. School psychologists, in collaboration with others, demonstrate skills to use assessment and data collection methods and to implement and evaluate services that support cognitive and academic skills. (NASP, 2010a, p. 5)

As consultants with extensive knowledge of human learning and cognition, school psychologists work collaboratively with teachers and administrators to ensure that all students have access to high-quality evidence-based instruction. School psychologists are in a position to link teachers and other educators with research about educational interventions that work, as well as information about how to address barriers to learning.

School psychologists are highly skilled in the process of systematic problem solving and can guide teachers through an analysis of students' academic and behavioral problems that will lead to the development and implementation of effective intervention plans at the individual, group, and systems levels. In addition, school psychologists work with teachers and administrators to monitor implementation of intervention plans and to collect and analyze data related to student outcomes.

Interventions and Mental Health Services to Develop Social and Life Skills

School psychologists have knowledge of biological, cultural, developmental, and social influences on behavior and mental health; behavioral and emotional impacts on learning and life skills; and evidence-based strategies to promote social–emotional functioning and mental health. School psychologists, in collaboration with others, demonstrate skills to use assessment and data collection methods and to implement and evaluate services that support socialization, learning, and mental health. (NASP, 2010a, p. 5)

To learn efficiently, students also must experience an optimal amount of success in their personal and social functioning. Consequently, school psychologists, in collaboration with parents and other school personnel, identify factors that support the development of effective skills in behavioral self-control, affective regulation, and interpersonal functioning. School psychologists are well prepared to assist schools in planning, implementing, and evaluating the effectiveness of programs and services that support the social and emotional well-being of all students.

Research has shown that students who participate in school-based social and emotional learning programs are likely to show improved academic performance (Durlak et al., 2011). School psychologists have valuable expertise to contribute to school and district efforts to support the social and emotional needs of all students. Working with teachers, administrators, and parents, school psychologists can play an active role in development of effective social–emotional learning programs.

Direct and Indirect Services for Children, Families, and Schools: Systems-Level Services

School-Wide Practices to Promote Learning

School psychologists have knowledge of school and systems structure, organization, and theory; general and special education; technology resources; and evidence-based school practices that promote learning and mental health. School psychologists, in collaboration with others, demonstrate skills to develop and implement practices and strategies to create and maintain effective and supportive learning environments for children and others. (NASP, 2010a, p. 6)

In order to work effectively within educational settings, school psychologists must understand and apply theories of organizational development and systems-level change (Curtis, Castillo, et al., 2008). It is not sufficient to know *what* to do to address various problems of learning and behavior. School psychologists must also know *how* to facilitate change at individual, group, and systems levels in order to implement programs and services that will enhance students' performance in academic and social contexts.

School psychologists work with other school personnel to identify and address needs of schools and systems with regard to academic, social, behavioral, and emotional outcomes for all students. This could include positive behavioral support programs, social–emotional learning programs, and universal screening programs, as well as multitiered systems of intervention for academic and behavioral problems.

Preventive and Responsive Services

School psychologists have knowledge of principles and research related to resilience and risk factors in learning and mental health, services in schools and communities to support multitiered prevention, and evidence-based strategies for effective crisis response. School psychologists, in collaboration with others, demonstrate skills to promote services that enhance learning, mental health, safety, and physical well-being through protective and adaptive factors and to implement effective crisis preparation, response, and recovery. (NASP, 2010a, p. 6)

In educational settings, school psychologists can address academic and mental health issues most appropriately and effectively within a multilevel framework of prevention and intervention. At the universal level, programs and services address the entire school population, with the goal of establishing academic, social, and emotional competence in all members of the school community.

Family–School Collaboration Services

School psychologists have knowledge of principles and research related to family systems, strengths, needs, and culture; evidence-based strategies to support family influences on children's learning and mental health; and strategies to develop collaboration between families and schools. School psychologists, in collaboration with others, demonstrate skills to design, implement, and evaluate services that respond to culture and context and facilitate family and school partnerships and interactions with community agencies for enhancement of academic and social–behavioral outcomes for children. (NASP, 2010a, p. 7)

A substantial body of research has shown conclusively that student outcomes are improved through consistent and effective partnerships between families and schools (Christenson & Reschly, 2010; Esler, Godber, & Christenson, 2008). School psychologists typically are in a position to facilitate positive working relationships between school personnel and family members.

Foundations of School Psychological Service Delivery

Diversity in Development and Learning

School psychologists have knowledge of individual differences, abilities, disabilities, and other diverse characteristics; principles and research related to diversity factors for children, families, and schools, including factors related to culture, context, and individual and role differences; and evidence-based strategies to enhance services and address potential influences related to diversity. School psychologists demonstrate skills to provide effective professional services that promote effective functioning for individuals, families, and schools with diverse characteristics, cultures, and backgrounds and across multiple contexts, with recognition that an understanding and respect for diversity in development and learning and advocacy for social justice are foundations for all aspects of service delivery. (NASP, 2010a, p. 7)

School psychologists recognize that understanding the cultural context in which learning and behavior occur is a vital aspect of identifying and addressing educational needs. Successful service delivery rests on the ability of school personnel to select specific interventions that are likely to result in positive outcomes with particular individuals. Appropriate selection of such interventions cannot take place without consideration of cultural factors that may interact with other variables to facilitate or detract from the desired outcomes.

As a result of NASP's standards for graduate education, school psychologists are well prepared to understand the importance of values, beliefs, traditions, customs, and parenting styles of the children and families they serve. Furthermore, their training has placed emphasis on the need to explore the impact of their own culture on interactions with others and to take all of these factors into account when planning and delivering services to children, families, and schools.

Research and Program Evaluation

School psychologists have knowledge of research design, statistics, measurement, varied data collection and analysis techniques, and program evaluation sufficient for understanding research and interpreting data in applied settings. School psychologists demonstrate skills to evaluate and apply research as a foundation for service delivery and, in collaboration with others, use various techniques and technology resources for data collection, measurement, and analysis to support effective practices at the individual, group, and/or systems levels. (NASP, 2010a, p. 8)

With a federal legislative mandate to ensure the use of research-based instructional strategies (the 2002 No Child Left Behind Act), school personnel must pay attention to key principles for translating research into practice. School psychologists not only must acquire knowledge about empirically supported interventions, but also must gain an understanding of how to apply research findings to specific classroom contexts. School psychologists can assist teachers and other school personnel in collecting and interpreting ongoing progress monitoring data to evaluate growth of individual students as well as to evaluate effectiveness of programs and services.

The term *program evaluation* often evokes images of large-scale multifaceted grant projects with teams of external evaluators. In fact, the principles and techniques of program evaluation are equally applicable to monitoring implementation and measuring effects of school-based interventions for individual students and small groups, as well as for class- and district-wide programs. School psychologists can play a key role in designing and carrying out systematic data collection procedures to evaluate school-based programs.

Legal, Ethical, and Professional Practice

School psychologists have knowledge of the history and foundations of school psychology; multiple service models and methods; ethical, legal, and professional standards; and other factors related to professional identity and effective practice as school psychologists. School psychologists demonstrate skills to provide services consistent with ethical, legal, and professional standards; engage in responsive ethical and professional decision making; collaborate with other professionals; and apply professional work characteristics needed for effective practice as school psychologists, including respect for human diversity and social justice, communication skills, effective interpersonal skills, responsibility, adaptability, initiative, dependability, and technology skills. (NASP, 2010a, p. 8)

The practice of school psychology is heavily influenced by federal and state legislation and regulations. In addition, case law at all levels has delineated principles for meeting the educational needs of children within the mandate of a free and appropriate public education for all children. School psychologists often are the primary advocates for the educational and legal rights of children and families in school settings and must work with other school personnel to ensure that all students receive appropriate programs and related services.

As noted by Prasse (2008), professional standards, including ethical codes, do not have the same legal weight as laws and regulations, but they are critical as consensual beliefs about best practices and appropriate conduct for professionals. Generally, school psychologists who practice in accordance with professional standards will also meet the obligations outlined in educational regulations and legislation.

Organizational Principles

The NASP Practice Model is framed by six organizational principles that reflect broad organizational principles of effective schools. These principles are summarized next.

Principle 1: Organization of Service Delivery

School psychological services are provided in a coordinated, organized fashion and are delivered in a manner that ensures the provision of a comprehensive and seamless continuum of services. Services are delivered in accordance with a strategic planning process that considers the needs of consumers and utilizes an evidence-based program evaluation model. (NASP, 2010a, p. 9)

School psychological services are best planned and delivered using a strategic planning process wherein a plan is developed based upon a systematic assessment of students and families in the local community. Seven standards describe the values and organization needed to ensure coordinated, equitable, and needs-based services.

Principle 2. Climate

It is the responsibility of the school system to create a climate in which school psychological services can be delivered with mutual respect for all parties. Employees have the freedom to advocate for the services that are necessary to meet the needs of consumers and are free from artificial, administrative, or political constraints that might hinder or alter the provision of appropriate services. (NASP, 2010a, p. 9)

Schools, like all work places, should attend to the suitability of the work place for its employees. Four standards for a positive, professional work environment are outlined under this principle.

Principle 3. Physical, Personnel, and Fiscal Support Systems

School systems ensure that (a) an adequate recruitment and retention plan for employees exists to ensure adequate personnel to meet the needs of the system; (b) all sources of funding, both public and private, are used and maximized to ensure the fiscal support necessary to provide adequate services; (c) all employees have adequate technology, clerical services, and a physical work environment; and (d) employees have adequate personnel benefits necessary to support their work, including continuing educational professional development. (NASP, 2010a, p. 10)

Implementation of the NASP Practice Model is predicated upon adequate staffing and fiscal support for school psychologists. This principle articulates four essential supports needed to implement comprehensive school psychological services. For example, when school psychologists are fully implementing the NASP Practice Model, the ratio of students to school psychologists should not exceed 500–700 students to each school psychologist.

Principle 4. Professional Communication

School systems ensure that policies and practices exist that result in positive, proactive communication among employees at all administrative levels of the organization. (NASP, 2010a, p. 10)

School psychologists are often responsible for maintaining confidential and sensitive oral and written communications when conducting their work on behalf of students and families. Four standards address how schools can ensure that professional communications are protected.

Principle 5. Supervision and Mentoring

The school system ensures that all personnel have levels and types of supervision and/or mentoring adequate to ensure the provision of effective and accountable services. Supervision and mentoring are provided through an ongoing, positive, systematic, collaborative process between the school psychologist and a school psychology supervisor or other school psychology colleagues. This process focuses on promoting professional growth and exemplary professional practice leading to improved performance by all concerned, including the school psychologist, supervisor, students, and the entire school community. (NASP, 2010a, p. 11)

Professional support and oversight for school psychologists exists on a continuum, beginning during graduate preparation and extending to the end of one's career. Principal 5 describes the nature and extent of supervision and mentoring that is appropriate for stages of practice. Evaluation and accountability for school psychological services are central tenets.

Principle 6. Professional Development and Recognition Systems

Individual school psychologists and school systems develop professional development plans annually. The school system ensures that continuing

professional development of its *Model for Comprehensive and Integrated School Psychological Services* personnel is both adequate for and relevant to the service delivery priorities of the school system. School systems recognize the need for a variety of professional development activities. (NASP, 2010a, p. 11)

A career in school psychology must involve life-long professional growth and responsiveness to the students, families, and schools within one's professional community. Standards for the administrative support of continuing professional development and its application in practice are described under this principle.

BEST PRACTICES FOR ADOPTING AND PROMOTING THE NASP PRACTICE MODEL

In the contemporary world of sound bites and Twitter messages, effectively communicating the link between what school psychologists are trained to do and how school psychological services can improve the academic and social outcomes for students has been an elusive goal. One goal for the 2010 NASP Practice Model is to communicate what services school psychologists are trained to do but are not always permitted to do in all school districts. Another important goal for the NASP Practice Model is to improve outcomes for students and schools by aligning practice with training and research, to promote comprehensive services, and to improve the quality and consistency of services available to all students. The NASP Practice Model has the potential to achieve these goals only if school psychologists advocate for its adoption at the state and local level.

NASP as an organization has become skilled at developing professional standards and the related messages, resource materials, and tools for promoting these standards, but these alone will not improve the ratio of school psychologists to students or expand the breadth of school psychological services available in schools. It will take influencing policy makers at all levels—federal, state, and local—to adopt policies that support academic and mental health supports for students.

The benefits of the NASP Practice Model to the profession are inextricably linked to the ways the model helps schools meet the demands of educational reform and 21st-century education. The NASP Practice Model at its core reflects a school psychologist who has the skills to apply the scientific method to study problems but also knows how to do it within an applied setting (Tilly,

2008). Within the current emphasis on educational outcomes, school psychology will increasingly be held accountable for conducting only those practices that will result in positive outcomes for students. The following advocacy actions, if implemented, could achieve the goals of the NASP Practice Model.

Practitioners

School psychology practitioners are in the best position to articulate the benefits of the NASP Practice Model for students and schools. Activities for implementing the model at the local level include the following:

- Link the goals of school improvement planning with the NASP Practice Model when talking with district or building administrators (e.g., link school psychological services with district goals to reduce bullying or increase reading proficiency).
- Make targeted presentations to school boards, district administrators, or principals, connecting the needs of schools with the role of the school psychologist and the NASP Practice Model's recommendations.
- Use the NASP Practice Model as an organizing framework when orienting school administrators about the skills of school psychologists and the types of student and school issues they can expect school psychologists to address or provide services for.
- Advocate for an appropriate student–school psychologist ratio as defined by the NASP Practice Model with policy makers within the district.
- Advocate for implementing the NASP Practice Model with parent groups by conducting a presentation to parents showing how their concerns are those school psychologists have knowledge and skills to address.
- Reference the NASP Practice Model during all district communications involving school psychologists. For example, when programs or initiatives are highlighted, identify the relevant domain of practice.
- Self-evaluate the effectiveness of your practice, using the NASP Practice Model as a benchmark for comprehensiveness.
- Identify goals for professional growth plans using the domain competencies within the model.
- Plan continuing professional development as guided by the NASP Practice Model.
- Evaluate job openings and district progressiveness according to the comprehensiveness of their school psychological services and the degree to which the organizational principles are met.

Supervisors of School Psychologists

Supervisors of school psychologists are in a position to ensure that the organizational principles outlined in the NASP Practice Model are in place. Specific advocacy actions that can be implemented by school psychology supervisors include the following:

- Evaluate the alignment of current professional practices within a district with the expectations of the NASP Practice Model, also taking into consideration the NASP *Principles for Professional Ethics*
- Assess the degree to which the system is effective in addressing barriers to learning and suggest improvements based upon the NASP Practice Model
- Evaluate the needs of school psychologists (e.g., ratios, supervision, technology, and other supports) using the Organizational Principles of the model
- Refer to the NASP Practice Model when revising district policies for student support services and advocate for a student–school psychologist ratio consistent with the model
- Evaluate candidates for employment utilizing competencies consistent with the NASP Practice Model (e.g., utilize the NASP Practice Model when interviewing and ask questions regarding skills and experiences referencing the domains)
- Organize coaching, mentoring, and professional development around the domains of practice
- Incorporate the NASP Practice Model when developing personnel evaluation processes or appraisal instruments for school psychologists (NASP, 2012)

Graduate Education Programs

Graduate educators and graduate students will find numerous benefits of the NASP Practice Model and can facilitate its adoption with the following activities:

- When recruiting candidates and developing program descriptions, use the NASP Practice Model to describe the preparation one will receive in school psychology and the role school psychologists will have in employment
- Evaluate potential internship sites against the NASP Practice Model, especially utilizing the organizational principles
- Organize the program curriculum around the NASP Practice Model and ensure that student performance is assessed in each of the practice domains

State School Psychology Associations

There are large-scale benefits of moving the NASP Practice Model into state policy. State regulations supporting the NASP Practice Model can promote more equitable practice across school districts within a state. By establishing professional expectations, there is greater potential for promoting positive outcomes for children and schools. State associations can engage in the following activities to promote the model:

- Promote the NASP Practice Model on state association websites and feature it in newsletter articles that show state examples of the NASP Practice Model implementation
- Organize state association professional development around identified needs and long-term objectives consistent with the NASP Practice Model
- Compare a state's existing definitions and standards for school psychology practice with the NASP Practice Model to determine recommendations for revisions to state regulations
- Advocate for an appropriate student–school psychologist ratio as defined by the NASP Practice Model with state policy makers such as the state board of education or state legislators
- Reference the NASP Practice Model in all promotional efforts such as school psychology awareness activities, state or local resolutions, professional presentations, or awards
- Utilize the NASP Practice Model when involved in state policy development for initiatives such as multitiered systems of support, school-based mental health, or other school improvement initiatives

Since its adoption in 2010, NASP leaders have actively promoted the NASP Practice Model and have strategically developed materials and resources to help the profession understand its benefits and implications of its adoption. The NASP Practice Model has already become an important framework for other NASP initiatives such as the school psychology demographic survey conducted in 2010, the NASP self-assessment tool for continuing professional development, and this edition of *Best Practices*.

SUMMARY

The NASP Practice Model is the official position of NASP regarding the delivery of school psychological services by school psychologists. It is aligned with the standards for school psychology training and credentialing and supports the ethical behavior of effective school psychologists. The NASP Practice Model delineates the competencies and services of school psychologists across 10 domains of practice and describes the integration of these competencies into a cohesive framework within which services should be provided. The NASP Practice Model also includes the organizational support and infrastructure, such as an appropriate ratio of school psychologists to students, that is necessary for implementing the comprehensive model. The NASP Practice Model represents the contemporary context of school psychology and is an important tool for communicating the relevance of school psychological services to successful educational outcomes for students.

The goals of the NASP Practice Model are to promote consistency of practice among school psychologists and to inform policy makers about characteristics of effective and high-quality school psychological services. The model was developed to meet the needs of schools, families, and students, and it allows flexibility for schools and professionals to develop local policies and structures while also providing sufficient content to ensure the most appropriate utilization of school psychologists.

For school psychologists, the NASP Practice Model is suitable for advocating and communicating about school psychological services, is a sound framework for developing job descriptions and personnel appraisal measures, and should prove to be useful for assessing continuing professional development needs.

More information can be found at the NASP Practice Model Resource (http://www.nasponline.org/standards/practice-model/Implementation-and-Promotion-Resources.aspx), which includes a NASP Practice Model brochure suitable for distribution; a brief PowerPoint overview of the NASP Practice Model with helpful resources for describing and promoting the model; an advocacy roadmap to assist school psychologists in assessing school and student needs and to determine how these could be addressed by implementation of the NASP Practice Model; and NASP Practice Model domain pages that compile NASP policy and resource documents (position papers, fact sheets, policy briefs), published articles from *Communiqué*, *School Psychology Review*, *School Psychology Forum*, *Principal Leadership* (NASSP), as well as professional development resources such as webinars, archived workshops, and trainings in the NASP Online Learning Center.

REFERENCES

Bryk, A. S., Sebring, P. B., Allensworth, E., Luppescu, S., & Easton, J. Q. (2010). *Organizing schools for improvement: Lessons from Chicago.* Chicago, IL: University of Chicago Press.

Castillo, J. M., Curtis, M. J., & Gelley, C. (2012). School psychology 2010–Part 2: School psychologists professional practices and implications for the field. *Communiqué, 40*(8), 4–6.

Christenson, S. L., & Reschly, A. L. (Eds.). (2010). *Handbook of school-family partnerships.* New York, NY: Routledge.

Curtis, M. J. (2000). Commentary on Swerdlik and French: The preparation of school psychologists for the twenty-first century. *School Psychology Review, 29,* 589–590.

Curtis, M. J., Castillo, J. M., & Cohen, R. C. (2008). Best practices in system-level change. In A. Thomas & J. Grimes (Eds.), *Best practices in school psychology V* (pp. 887–902). Bethesda, MD: National Association of School Psychologists.

Curtis, M. J., Lopez, A. D., Castillo, J. M., Batsche, G. M., Minch, D., & Smith, J. C. (2008). The status of school psychology: Demographic characteristics, employment conditions, professional practices, and continuing professional development. *Communiqué, 36*(5), 27–29.

Durlak, J. A., Weissberg, R. P., Dymnicki, A. B., Taylor, R. D., & Schellinger, K. B. (2011). The impact of enhancing students' social and emotional learning: A meta-analysis of school-based universal interventions. *Child Development, 82,* 405–432, doi: 10.1111/j.1467-8624.2010.01564.x

Esler, A. N., Godber, Y., & Christenson, S. L. (2008). Best practices in supporting school–family partnerships. In A. Thomas & J. Grimes (Eds.), *Best practices in school psychology V* (pp. 917–936). Bethesda, MD: National Association of School Psychologists.

Marzano, R. J. (2003). *What works in schools: Translating research into action.* Alexandria, VA: Association for Supervision and Curriculum Development.

National Association of School Psychologists. (2000a). *Guidelines for the provision of school psychological services.* Bethesda, MD: Author.

National Association of School Psychologists. (2000b). *Standards for the credentialing of school psychologists.* Bethesda, MD: Author.

National Association of School Psychologists. (2000c). *Standards for training and field placement programs in school psychology.* Bethesda, MD: Author.

National Association of School Psychologists. (2010a). *Model for comprehensive and integrated school psychological services.* Bethesda, MD: Author. Retrieved from http://www.nasponline.org/standards/2010standards/2_PracticeModel.pdf

National Association of School Psychologists. (2010b). *Model for comprehensive and integrated psychological services, NASP Practice Model overview* [Brochure]. Bethesda, MD: Author. Retrieved from http://www.nasponline.org/standards/practice-model/Practice_Model_Brochure.pdf

National Association of School Psychologists. (2010c). *Principles for professional ethics.* Bethesda, MD: Author. Retrieved from http://www.nasponline.org/standards/2010standards/1_%20Ethical%20Principles.pdf

National Association of School Psychologists. (2010d). *Standards for the credentialing of school psychologists.* Bethesda, MD: Author. Retrieved from http://www.nasponline.org/standards/2010standards/2_Credentialing_Standards.pdf

National Association of School Psychologists. (2010e). *Standards for graduate preparation of school psychologists.* Bethesda, MD: Author. Retrieved from http://www.nasponline.org/standards/2010standards/1_Graduate_Preparation.pdf

National Association of School Psychologists. (2012). A framework for the personnel evaluation of school psychologists utilizing the NASP Practice Model. *Communiqué, 41*(3), 26–27.

Pluymert, K. (2014). Problem-solving foundations for school psychological services. In P. Harrison & A. Thomas (Eds.), *Best practices in school psychology: Data-based and collaborative decision making* (pp. 25–40). Bethesda, MD: National Association of School Psychologists.

Prasse, D. P. (2008). Best practices in school psychology and the law. In A. Thomas & J. Grimes (Eds.), *Best practices in school psychology V* (pp. 1903–1920). Bethesda, MD: National Association of School Psychologists.

Roach, A. T., Lawton, K., & Elliott, S. N. (2014). Best practices in facilitating and evaluating the integrity of school-based interventions. In P. Harrison & A. Thomas (Eds.), *Best practices in school psychology: Data-based and collaborative decision making* (pp. 133–146). Bethesda, MD: National Association of School Psychologists.

Sheridan, S. M., & D'Amato, R. C. (2004). Partnering to chart our futures: *School Psychology Review* and *School Psychology Quarterly* combined issue on the Multisite Conference on the Future of School Psychology. *School Psychology Review, 33,* 7–10.

Stoiber, K. C. (2014). A comprehensive framework for multitiered systems of support in school psychology. In P. Harrison & A. Thomas (Eds.), *Best Practices in school psychology: Data-based and collaborative decision making* (pp. 41–70). Bethesda, MD: National Association of School Psychologists.

Tilly, W. D., III. (2008). The evolution of school psychology to science-based practice: Problem solving and the three-tiered model. In A. Thomas & J. Grimes (Eds.), *Best practices in school psychology V* (pp. 17–36). Bethesda, MD: National Association of School Psychologists.

Waldron, N., & Prus, J. (2006). *A guide for performance-based assessment, accountability, and program development in a school psychology training program* (2nd ed.). Bethesda, MD: National Association of School Psychologists. Retrieved from http://www.nasponline.org/standards/approvedtraining/perfassess.pdf

Ysseldyke, J. E., Burns, M., Dawson, P., Kelley, B., Morrison, D., Ortiz, S., … & Telzrow, C. (2006). *School psychology: A blueprint for training and practice III.* Bethesda, MD: National Association of School Psychologists. Retrieved from http://www.nasponline.org/resources/blueprint/FinalBlueprintInteriors.pdf

Ysseldyke, J. E., Dawson, P., Lehr, C., Reschly, D., Reynolds, M., & Telzrow, C. (1997). *School psychology: A blueprint for training and practice II.* Bethesda, MD: National Association of School Psychologists. Retrieved from http://www.nasponline.org/resources/blueprint/blue2.pdf

Ysseldyke, J. E., Reynolds, M., & Weinberg, R. A. (1984). *School psychology: A blueprint for training and practice.* Minneapolis, MN: National School Psychology Inservice Training Network, University of Minnesota.

2 Problem-Solving Foundations for School Psychological Services

Kathy Pluymert

Community Consolidated School District 15, Palatine, IL

OVERVIEW

Data-based problem solving is emerging as one of the most important practices in school reform efforts. Public education systems are becoming more adept at using data in continuous improvement cycles as they strive to meet increased societal demands for improved performance (Bernhardt, 2009; Goldring & Berends, 2009; http://www.keysonline.org/about/csi.html). School psychologists must have substantial expertise in understanding the data-based problem-solving process, and in applying these skills in their work settings, if they are to serve in meaningful roles in school improvement and in ensuring positive outcomes for all students.

The purpose of this chapter is to examine data-based problem solving as it applies to all aspects of school system functioning. The data-based problem-solving process uses data to identify and analyze why problems are happening, to create viable changes to improve system performance that result in improved student outcomes, and to monitor system and student outcomes over time. Many of the examples used in this chapter apply data-based problem solving to individual student needs. The chapter also illustrates the process using larger contexts of district-level and building-level problem solving. The important point here is that whether a district is evaluating student math performance across grade levels in response to a new curriculum adoption, or a school-based team is evaluating the reading performance of an individual struggling reader in third grade, the problem-solving process is the same. For the purposes of this chapter, *data-based problem solving* is operationally defined as using data within a well-defined, systematic problem-solving process to make decisions about continuously improving educational

programs and services. Data-based problem solving is a continuous improvement cycle that begins with collecting and analyzing data targeted to understand student academic and behavioral skill needs. The data for large groups, small groups, and individual students are reviewed to clarify why problems are occurring. Evidence-based interventions are implemented to address identified needs. Outcome data are monitored to determine the success of these interventions on student achievement and behavior, and changes are made if data suggest that desired outcomes have not been met.

For the process to be effective it must occur within the context of a school system dedicated to continuous improvement by professionals who use data for self-reflection and who understand how the school's internal practices have an impact on student educational and mental health outcomes. Given the critical role of data-based problem solving within school systems, school psychologists must be self-reflective professionals who have solid skills in both implementing and facilitating the data-based problem-solving process if they are to serve in meaningful positions now and in the future.

Data-Based Problem Solving and School Reform

Data-based problem solving is critical in meeting today's stakeholder demands for increased accountability from public institutions. In the field of education, this public sentiment is reflected in increasingly specific accountability for student-based outcomes in legislation that regulates assessment and funding for U.S. public schools. To respond to these demands, school systems have rallied to improve their ability to use data to inform practice and to demonstrate positive student outcomes.

Legislative Accountability Measures

The most influential piece of legislation in this regard is the 2001 reauthorization of the Elementary and Secondary Education Act (ESEA), commonly known as No Child Left Behind (NCLB). NCLB defines success as 100% of students meeting a state-defined level of academic proficiency by 2014. It requires that schools examine annual student performance data in grades 3–12 as measured by a state-developed and administered standardized achievement test. It also created serious penalties for schools that were not able to reach the lofty and inflexible standards set within the legislation. In an attempt to improve educational outcomes for subgroups of students who have historically not met performance benchmarks, the law holds schools specifically account-able for the performance of subgroups of students who were especially at risk for underachievement, including students from low-income families, students who have identified disabilities and need special education, racial and ethnic minorities, and students who are learning to speak English. These subgroups were disaggregated from the general school population, and schools were held accountable for 100% of these populations meeting the same benchmark standards at the same rate and same time as their grade-level peers who do not face these risk factors.

Although NCLB had noble aspirations, particularly in its focus on social justice and equality of educational outcomes for underresourced students, the concept that 100% of students can achieve an arbitrary universal benchmark within the same specified time frame is prima facie absurd. While it is a reasonable expectation that virtually all students can meet basic academic proficiency standards over time, the psychometric realities of individual differences alone would indicate that it is not true that all students will reach proficiency at the same rate. One unintended negative consequence of NCLB is that states have set a low bar for achievement benchmarks in order to meet NCLB accountability standards. As a result, the public is given a disingenuous report of student proficiency (Cronin, Dahlin, Adkins, & Kingsbury, 2007).

Given the realities of attempting to implement the requirements of NCLB, there is a push for a more realistic conceptualization of student achievement that moves away from a static 100% of students achieving a benchmark at the same time to accountability models based on student growth. Growth models are more reflective of how children and adolescents actually learn, grow, and progress to mastery. An additional benefit of growth models is that schools account for growth in all students, both those who are at risk and those who are in need of accelerated programming, rather than focusing on benchmarks alone.

There is a growing consensus within education that changes are needed when ESEA is reauthorized. As of 2014, two very different points of view are reflected in proposed changes in ESEA. One model focuses on student growth while the other continues the state-determined level of accountability and many of the harsh provisions of NCLB. Politics aside, most educators agree that one of the most important recommended changes is that student outcomes and school efficacy should be examined using student growth rather than a static benchmark as the accountability standard. A promising indicator of this potential change is the U.S. Department of Education (2011) report on a study of a variety of growth models currently used by states to investigate the viability, strengths, and weaknesses of these models (Blagg, 2011). School psychologists need to become proficient in understanding growth models for groups and for individual students and are encouraged to engage in a meaningful way in this important policy development.

The conversation about how schools demonstrate positive outcomes for students is critical for school psychologists. The expectation that all students can meet benchmark proficiency standards over time is a school-wide conversation that involves every professional in the system and is the bottom line in school improvement efforts. School psychologists can play an important part in the dialogue, which extends far beyond whether or not a specific student has a disability or is eligible for special education. The push for data-based accountabi-lity has huge implications for why many schools are reallocating rich resources, such as the skill sets of school psychologists, away from focusing primarily on admin-istering psychological tests to individual students to active data collection and analysis that directly informs improvements needed in instructional planning. Many schools are asking school psychologists to serve on teams that work primarily within extant data sets or naturally occurring situations examining school-based skills. School psychologists have much to offer school-based and district-level teams, using their skills as psychologists and as educators to add value to team functioning in data-based problem solving, the primary focus of which is improved student performance reflected in outcome data.

Professional Associations in Education

The increasing emphasis on data-based problem solving is evident in multiple professional groups, including teachers unions such as the National Education Association (n.d.), school administrator groups such as American Association of School Administrators (n.d.), and curriculum specialists groups such as the Association for Supervision and Curriculum Development (2012), that have offered models for data-based decision making. Within the field of school psychology, the National Association of School Psychologists (NASP) *Model for Comprehensive and Integrated School Psychology Services* (NASP, 2010) emphasizes data-based problem solving, assessment, statistics, and psychometrics. Coursework and requisite field placements in preservice education provide an exceptionally good foundation for school psychologists to take the opportunity to play a meaningful role in school improvement. Although the problem-solving model focuses on teams of professionals working together, the process also emphasizes the importance of each team member using his or her unique professional skills to add to the team process (Bahr & Kovaleski, 2006). Being a data coach is one example of a specific role for which school psychologists are well prepared (Love, Stiles, Mundry, & DiRanna, 2008).

Data-Based Problem Solving With Fidelity

School improvement using data-based problem solving is a dynamic, iterative process that requires systems to evolve over time in response to identified student needs. Data-based problem solving requires that school systems, school-based teams, and individual school-based professionals engage in self-reflective practice (York-Barr, Sommers, Ghere, & Montie, 2006). Identifying innovations and implementing and evaluating educational practice are processes that should show continuous improvement in both outcomes and process as measured by fidelity to research-based practices. To a large extent, the focus of problem-solving efforts needs to be on what the school as a system and the adults in the school setting need to do differently to facilitate student success (Batsche et al., 2005; Sugai et al., 2010).

Reflective practice also serves as a catalyst for professional development for school psychologists, as it provides ongoing opportunities to understand how they can improve their skills in using and applying data-based problem solving (Harvey & Struzziero, 2008). School psychologists often serve their teams by identifying research-based interventions or solutions to systems problems. School psychologists need to continuously develop new knowledge to add to the repertoire of solutions from which the group can draw, providing an important resource that adds value to teams on which they serve. Given the applied research settings of schools, it is often only through attempting an innovation and reviewing its positive and negative effects that the system is able to identify successful interventions for the setting. School psychologists are well prepared to do this kind of work and can improve their skills through professional development related to the contexts of these emerging demands.

BASIC CONSIDERATIONS

School psychology literature is rich with resources on data-based problem solving. As more school systems move to use of a multitiered systems of support model (MTSS; sometimes called response to intervention [RTI]) for service delivery, school psychologists need to understand the use of a variety of formal and nonstandardized data collected by teachers and school administrators to evaluate programs and to make decisions about individual students. In addition, ongoing professional development in areas such as curriculum, instruction, and formative and summative classroom-based assessment that are used regularly by teachers and administrators are an important supplement to an existing knowledge base that school psychologists bring to their employment setting.

Historical Perspectives of Problem Solving

Data-based problem solving has long been identified as a best practice in the field of school psychology. School psychology has historically been closely aligned with a scientist–practitioner model (Barlow, Hayes, & Nelson, 1984; Raimy, 1950). Language identifying data-based problem solving as an important role for school psychologists appears as early as 1960 in the Association for Supervision and Curriculum Development journal *Educational Leadership* (Gray, 1960). In the 1970s, school psychology literature and practice models that emphasize teams of professionals, including school psychologists utilizing school-based problem solving to facilitate student success, began to appear more frequently (Deno & Mirkin, 1977). In the 1980s, innovations such as collaborative consultation and other indirect service delivery models and intervention teams emerged that helped students before special education services (Chalfant & Pysh, 1989; Graden, Zins, & Curtis, 1988; Reschly, 1988; Rosenfield, 1991). School psychologists played a leading role when RTI emerged in the late 1990s and early 2000s. School psychologists were the primary authors of key policy documents such as *Response to Intervention: Policy Considerations and Implementation*, one of the most widely cited and seminal publications on RTI implementation (Batsche et al., 2005).

Contemporary School Psychology Practice

Data-based problem solving has always been a critical skill set for school psychologists, but the way in which data-based decision making has been practiced within schools has changed significantly, most notably with respect to the nature of the data schools use for problem solving. A recent review of topics covered in NASP publications such as *Communiqué* and *School Psychology Review* and in the fourth and fifth editions of *Best Practices in School Psychology* shows a shift in school-based practice for many school psychologists. Many of the changes are related to increased implementation of RTI or the MTSS model in public schools.

A growing number of school psychologists are moving away from using individually administered psychological assessment instruments as primary data sources in their daily work in data-based decision making. School psychologists are increasingly working as active participants in an indirect service delivery model as a member of a school-based team. These multidisciplinary teams use a variety of data, most often data that are either extant academic performance data or student behavioral data, to identify, develop, and evaluate instructional outcomes and interventions.

For school psychologists who work in a system more closely aligned to special education service delivery, it is important to remember that NCLB accountability legislation requires schools to demonstrate that all students in special education must be progressing in the general education curriculum. Except for students with severe disabilities, students are assessed using grade-level academic performance measures. As a result, program evaluation data for students in special education should be closely aligned with outcomes that are the same as those of students in general education programs. School psychologists serving students in special education need to understand a variety of data such as classroom-based formative assessments, intervention-based mastery measures, progress monitoring using curriculum-based measures, and high-stakes achievement tests used by teachers and school administrators for program evaluation. If school psychologists

are to stay viable within the changing landscape of schools, then it is critical that school psychologists are fluent in using data that teachers and administrators use to make decisions about both individual students and program efficacy.

Assets in Professional Advocacy

In order for school psychologists to play an important role in data-based problem solving and evaluation of student outcomes, school psychologists need to demonstrate to school administrators and policy makers that they have a set of knowledge and skills that can be applied to school-based problem solving at multiple levels of the school organization that goes beyond those of a special education teacher, social worker, or administrator. When competition for resources results in questions about which members of the team are most needed to accomplish data analysis for problem solving, it is critical professional advocacy for school psychologists to be able to demonstrate that they can meet the needs of the school in ways that are unique and add value to the school community (Thomas, Pluymert, & Armistead, 1998). The NASP website is rich with materials related to the NASP Practice Model (NASP, 2010) and related professional advocacy materials that offer many illustrations and applications that highlight the unique and versatile contributions of school psychologists (http://www.nasponline.org).

School psychologists' skill sets that are most closely aligned to the current data-based problem-solving model and practices include expertise in psychometrics, application of statistics to decision-making models, systematic classroom observation, functional assessment of behavior-applied research methodology, and program evaluation. These skills are vitally important to data-based problem solving but are typically not a strong part of preservice training or experience of teachers or school administrators. School psychologists can serve school districts and building-based teams by evaluating published research findings to identify appropriate interventions.

School psychologists have skills to assist teachers through collaborative consultation to apply principles of human learning, child and adolescent development, executive functioning skills, and social–emotional factors to student learning and classroom management. School psychologists, compared to many other mental health providers in schools, can provide school-based mental health services, with the added benefit of also having training and experience in program evaluation to demonstrate measurable outcomes for these mental health services.

Finally, school psychologists are well positioned to provide teams and teachers with support in intervention implementation. School psychologists are wise consumers of research in choosing interventions that would have evidence of potential success with a targeted problem. An additional tangible benefit school psychologists have in providing support in using research-based interventions is that some of the most complex problems in intervention implementation are treatment integrity, data collection, and data analysis. Unless fidelity aspects of intervention implementation are systematically assessed, positive results sometimes do not occur because the interventions are not delivered as designed. Fidelity in intervention delivery and data collection is needed to ensure that decisions will be made on the basis of data collected rather than speculation (Fixsen, Naoom, Blase, Friedman, & Wallace, 2005). School psychologists can serve teams in facilitating conversations about fidelity and outcomes that can be examined for clues about reasons that an intervention may or may not be yielding desired results.

Additional Professional Development

School psychologists who do not have specific undergraduate or graduate preparation in teaching or curriculum and instruction would be prudent to seek professional development in curriculum, instruction, and various models of formative and summative evaluation currently being used in schools. This working knowledge would add significant value to a school psychologist's existing skill set. Expertise in these areas is needed to provide sufficient background to be informed contributors during problem-solving conversations about how well suited core instructional programming is for students served by the school and the goodness of fit of interventions chosen to supplement the existing curriculum.

One of the most sweeping changes in U.S. education occurred in 2012 as most states adopted the Common Core State Standards (National Governors Association Center for Best Practices & Council of Chief State School Officers, 2010). The Common Core State Standards will be the foundation for most states' high-stakes assessments beginning in 2014. These assessments are currently under development by two consortia that were funded by federal grants to develop new kinds of interactive and standards-based assessments. The Smarter Balanced Assessment Consortium (http://www.smarterbalanced.org) and the Partnership for Assessment of College and Careers (http://www.parcconline.org) are two consortia that school psychologists should be following to become familiar with the nature of these new assessments. The adoption of these new standards and related assessments presents an unprecedented opportunity for school psychologists to (a) help their school systems understand how these new assessments relate to testing systems that are familiar to schools and (b) provide meaningful consultation in understanding how to apply this developing methodology to data-based decision-making processes in schools.

Finally, school psychologists can add value to the school team if they have a strong understanding of organizational behavior components in systems change. School psychologists can provide support and leadership to their peers as the team moves from one service delivery model to another. It is also important to attend to the personal social–emotional ramifications of transitions and change for teachers and administrators, and to help schools attend to these in a way that facilitates personal and organizational adaptive functioning (Bridges, 2009).

BEST PRACTICES IN PROBLEM SOLVING

Data-based problem solving requires the systematic use of a process that includes problem identification, problem analysis, plan development, and plan evaluation. There are four basic questions that form the essential components of data-based problem solving: What is the problem (problem identification)? Why is it happening (problem analysis)? What should be done about it (plan development)? Did it work (plan evaluation)?

Problem Identification

The first step in problem solving involves developing a clear, measurable, and operational definition of the problem. A well-defined problem clarifies the nature, magnitude, and context of the problem in observable terms. Creating an operational definition of the problem serves to develop consensus about the nature of the problem and helps the team understand the scope of the problem and see the conditions in which the problem occurs. When developing the problem statement, teams should use information that is readily observable, is easily obtainable, and occurs naturally in the school setting to maximize the efficacy of the problem-solving process. The data that school teams use in problem identification should define the problem in terms that teachers and parents readily understand (Tilly, 2008). A well-crafted problem definition clearly targets what the student should be doing when the problem is solved.

Is There a Problem?

An important first task is to use data to determine whether or not the concern presented represents a real problem. At times, a problem is actually a function of the perceptions and experiences of the individual who reports the problem. In an example that is familiar to school psychologists who serve high-achieving schools, where typical students' academic scores fall at the 70th percentile on a nationally normed test, a student who scores at the 50th percentile might be brought to the attention of the team for problem solving and potential intervention because the teacher sees the student's classroom performance as substantially below his or her peers. The classroom teacher can be provided with instructional coaching to provide differentiated instruction to facilitate growth for this student, since the student's academic performance alone does not warrant consideration for intervention. The school psychologist can provide assistance in helping the teacher put his or her initial perception of the problem into context through a broader peer comparison standard than an individual classroom alone would offer.

Is the Problem That Is Presented the Right Problem to Solve?

It is important for the team to be sure that addressing the problem as presented is the best way to address an underlying concern. There are times when teachers, parents, or students perceive a situation as an individual student problem when, in fact, the identified issue is representative of a larger issue. This point can be illustrated in a situation in which a novice kindergarten teacher reported to a school psychologist that a student frequently misbehaved. In order to collect baseline data and to create context for the reported problem, the school psychologist completed a classroom observation. Baseline data for the frequency of the target student's noncompliance were collected and compared to the rates of these same behaviors in other students in the classroom. While the student data showed noncompliance, the target student's rate of compliance was not significantly different from that of several other students in the class. There were actually three other students who were noncompliant more often than the targeted

student. To provide additional context on the classroom environment and instruction, there was no well-defined organizational system in the classroom for use of materials, and there were no readily apparent alternative activities for students to choose when their work was completed. An additional consideration for the team was that there were some unrealistic expectations on the part of the novice teacher for how long young children should be seated and expected to work independently. The problem was reconceptualized as a classroom-level problem that resulted in a set of classroom-based consultations to change the new teacher's classroom management strategies and to teach students classroom behavioral expectations in the context of developmentally appropriate expectations that resulted in improvements for the whole class.

What Is the Magnitude of the Problem?

To provide a comprehensive problem definition, the team needs to examine the difference in performance between the problem situation and some target that would represent desired performance. Identifying the difference between the two is often referred to as *gap analysis* during problem identification.

The team must answer two questions: (a) What is the individual (or group) expected to do? (b) What is the individual (or group) actually doing? Defining the difference between target student (or group) performance and expected performance provides a measure of the problem. Defining the expected performance also provides the team with a target that can be used to identify when the problem is resolved.

The team needs to collect or use existing baseline data to measure and understand the parameters of the difference and to determine how big of a gap there is between current and desired performance. Data comparison gives the team a sense of the magnitude of the problem. The gap analysis data help the team understand the intensity of intervention needed and a reasonable time frame in which a solution can be expected.

Examples of well-defined problem statements might be: (a) John correctly identifies 8 letter sounds while his peers identify 21.1 sounds. (b) Sally's most recent RIT score on the NWEA *Measures of Academic Progress* in fall 2012 as a seventh grader was 201. The average (mean) score for a seventh grader in the fall is 216.3 (using 2011 national norms). Her score is more comparable to a typical fourth-grade fall RIT score performance in the national norm group. (c) Fred handed in 50% of assigned homework this past quarter. His peers handed in an average of 90% of assigned homework in the same quarter.

Problem Analysis

The second step in data-based problem solving is to create a hypothesis about why the problem is occurring. A clear understanding of the problem's cause leads to successful solutions (Burns & Gibbons, 2008; Christ, Burns, & Ysseldyke, 2005). The team considers a variety of factors that would lead to increasing the likelihood that the correct hypothesis is chosen. These factors include differentiating between whether the problem is a skill problem versus a performance problem, determining situations in which the problem is most likely and least likely to occur, and identifying the most salient factors that are contributing to the problem. The team then generates the most plausible and alterable hypotheses and collects additional data as needed to validate or refute the chosen hypotheses.

Is It a Skill Problem or Performance Problem?

One of the first questions that a team asks in hypothesis generation is often conceptualized in terms of whether a student "can't do" or "won't do" a skill or perform a task. In other words, the team needs to determine if the problem is the result of a student needing to develop a new skill, to use a skill that is already mastered in a new setting, or apply the skill to a new or more complicated task. In some situations this could involve a student's choice to engage in a behavior.

Generally speaking, the default assumptions should be that a student does not have the desired skill and the skill should be taught. An important caveat for teams to remember in answering this question is that some performance deficits are actually skill deficits. A student may have learned a skill but not understand when the skill is to be applied or not be able to generalize the skill to a new setting. The student may need explicit instruction, scaffolding, or supported practice to apply a skill to a new situation.

Teams should examine data about when the problem occurs and when it does not. If the problem occurs across settings, it is more likely to be a skill deficit that would require that a student or group needs to be explicitly taught the new skill. If the problem occurs in some settings, or in some conditions, the situation may be one in which additional practice, scaffolding, changing of certain elements of the environment, or differential reinforcement could improve the students' performance in an unfamiliar or more complex setting.

Are There Sufficient Data to Confirm or Refute the Proposed Hypothesis?

What evidence is there to confirm that the root cause the team has chosen is correct? In the case of an individual student, the team may need to collect additional baseline data to be sure that the problem is framed accurately. Information collected might include additional setting-specific observations, curriculum-based measurement data, or counts of behavioral events. The data should be examined in the context of the curriculum, instruction, and environmental factors that could have an impact on performance or contribute to the problem in some way. The team should consider whether or not there are clues about what has proven to be effective and not effective in changing behavior and facilitating learning on the basis of the student's past performance and response to other interventions.

During problem analysis, the team uses the operational definition of the problem in the context of other relevant data as a guide to complete a root cause analysis. There are a variety of specific methodologies that teams can use to ensure that their efforts are getting to the correct hypothesis about why the problem is occurring. Some examples of formal tools for teams to consider would include: five whys (keep asking "why" until the team comes to a basic reason for the problem), appreciation (keep asking "so what?" until the team comes to a basic reason for the problem), or cause-and-effect diagrams using fishbone or other similar diagramming methods to document potential causes to clarify possible hypotheses (e.g., MindTools, Baldridge).

Is the Hypothesis Related to Alterable Factors Within the School's Control?

When teams are choosing among hypotheses to explain problems in student performance it is important to consider which hypotheses seem most promising for choosing or creating interventions. Teams are well advised to consider only those hypotheses for which they can reasonably create interventions that can be completed within the context of the school. School staff cannot create viable interventions that relate to factors in which the school has limited or no control of variables (Florida ESE Personnel Development Support Project, 2011). An example might be a student who frequently does not complete homework because he or she has to care for younger siblings in the evening. The school cannot necessarily create an intervention to change the family's need for evening child care or the resources to provide the care. The school can, however, create a supportive, regular, and structured environment during the school day that provides an opportunity for the student to complete homework. Homework can be differentiated for this student to allow the student the needed educational experiences while taking his or her life situation outside of school into consideration. The school can also create communication mechanisms with the family to provide additional support in long-term assignments and other homework that could require family involvement on weekends or that could involve other available adults or community resources.

Is There Sufficient Expertise on the Team?

Problem-solving teams can competently analyze student performance only if the team includes professionals who have significant knowledge in the domain in which the problem exists and have expertise to generate hypotheses, as well as viable and effective interventions. More than any other component of problem solving, problem analysis requires team members to have broad and deep knowledge about relevant aspects of the problem. For example, it is not possible to competently analyze the function of a behavior problem if no one on the team has expertise in student behavior and mental health (Sugai, et al., 2010).

There may be situations in which a team needs to go outside of its regular membership to find needed expertise. This is particularly important when the identified problem involves the needs of a student who is from a different language or cultural group in order to be sure that cultural, social, and linguistic factors are considered. The team may need to seek the input of a second language specialist to answer questions about how the student's acquisition of English language skills has an impact on the student's performance. To ensure that issues of equity and cultural factors are considered, the team may have specific questions about how well the student functions within the context of his or her native language and culture. An individual who has knowledge of a child's native language or culture can provide consultation to the team to put concerns into a cultural context (Walker Tileston, 2011). Students who come from other countries, who come from educational systems that are very different from U.S. schools, whose education was interrupted, or who are underschooled relative to their chronological age or perhaps never attended school, have unique issues that need to be considered in developing hypotheses. These situations are occurring with relative frequency as the population becomes more diverse and immigrants are moving to geographic locations that have not to this point seen substantial growth in diversity among their residents (Annie E. Casey Foundation, 2013).

Plan Development

The third step in data-based problem solving is to develop a plan to close the gap between current and desired performance. The team needs to develop a decision rule to serve as the operational definition of what desired performance would be if the problem is solved. Next, an intervention is identified to address the problem that is specifically related to the team's hypothesis about why the problem is occurring. The intervention should have reasonable evidence of being successful in closing the gap between the current performance and the desired level of performance for a comparable group of students. There should be a plan in place to regularly monitor both implementation fidelity and student outcomes in response to the intervention. Finally, the school must be able to support the implementers to ensure that interventions are provided with integrity.

What Is the Goal?

The problem-solving team needs to develop a goal statement that represents a viable solution and that clearly defines closing the gap between actual performance and desired performance. The solution should delineate what the school or group (or student) needs to do that it is not currently doing. This working definition serves as a decision rule for the team to evaluate the success of the intervention.

When the problem is one of inappropriate or maladaptive behavior, it is important that the team define the solution in terms of a student engaging in a replacement behavior. School psychologists understand from behavioral theory that it is not sufficient to stop an undesirable behavior. The unwanted behavior needs to be replaced with a more adaptive behavior. An example that teachers and parents easily understand is the situation in which a person who needs to change behavior to achieve a healthy weight cannot just stop eating altogether, as this does not represent a realistic solution to the problem. The solution is to establish the replacement behavior of eating a specified quantity of healthy foods every day.

Goal statements must be written as a measurable statement of expected outcomes.
Writing a goal that is well defined, measurable, and observable provides the team with identifiable markers

to know whether or not the desired outcome has been accomplished. It also provides a metric by which the team can begin to examine progress toward the desired outcome. Examples of an individual student behavior goal could include staying seated or completing work for a desired percentage of time, reading a grade-level passage at a given rate, or completing a series of calculations correctly. Examples of measurable and specific goals for a grade level might include, for example, that 85% of second graders will read 90 words correctly in a minute on a second-grade passage by May 1 or that 90% of fifth graders will have zero office disciplinary referrals in the course of the first semester.

A priori decision-making rules serve as a standard to measure whether or not the intervention is successful and guide the team in determining how well the student or group is responding to interventions. An example of a measurable goal for a system-wide problem might be determining a desired curriculum-based measurement score based on benchmarking data that can be used for program evaluation (Shinn, 2010). An example of a measurable goal for an individual student could be mastery of a sequence of successive replacement behaviors that represent increased approximations of desired behaviors.

Develop an effective intervention plan.
When developing a viable intervention plan, several factors need to be considered: (a) evidence that the intervention is effective for the problem, (b) treatment acceptability, (c) data collection planning, and (d) resource allocation that provides sufficient support to the individual who is responsible for implementing the intervention (Fixsen et al., 2005; Schulte, Easton, & Parker, 2009).

Several reputable organizations offer resources that can be used to find viable interventions. Some of these include the What Works Clearinghouse (http://ies.ed. gov/NCEE/wwc/), the Center on Instruction (http://www.centeroninstruction.org), the Center for Effective Collaboration and Practice (http://cecp.air.org), the Florida Center for Reading Research (http://www.fcrr. org), and Best Evidence Encyclopedia (http://www. bestevidence.org).

Consider treatment acceptability.
It is important for teams to be flexible, creative, and resourceful to identify interventions seen as viable by those who will be implementing the intervention (Nastasi, 2000). Factors that can influence the acceptability of the intervention include (a) whether the implementer of the intervention sees it as something that can be done in a way that can

be streamlined into already existing routines and (b) whether the implementer considers whatever support is provided as sufficient to implement the intervention successfully. While there are formal measures of treatment acceptability, in the time constraints of applied settings of schools, problem-solving teams can use collaborative and honest consensus-building conversations to ensure that those who are implementing the intervention see the plan as doable.

How outcome data will be collected.
Determining a plan for data collection is easier when goals are well defined using observable outcomes. If the goal is specific and measurable, then the nature of data that are collected to measure outcomes follows directly from the goal. Data collection is facilitated by keeping the process simple and time efficient, and by using naturally occurring and readily available resources and methods. Data that are easy to collect and record increase the likelihood that the data will be collected as planned. It is critical that teams think through the pragmatics of data collection and plan this aspect of implementation carefully. Again, the team members who will be collecting the data need to see the data collection plan and methods as viable. Data collection can become unreliable if team expectations are unrealistic. Sometimes, teachers or other implementers such as paraprofessionals do not collect data because they do not have the skills, time, or willingness to collect the data. School psychologists or other team members can offer practical support by training and/or by collecting, recording, analyzing, or graphing data for the team.

How implementation integrity will be ensured.
Choosing and planning the intervention require that the team discusses specific logistics of intervention design and implementation to ensure that the intervention can be implemented with integrity. The key factor in successful intervention outcomes is that the intervention is implemented as designed. Unfortunately, this aspect of intervention development and delivery can be the most difficult part of determining why the intervention may or may not have succeeded (Hardcastle & Justice, 2008). While school settings present many intervening variables that cannot be controlled when implementing interventions, careful attention to treatment integrity can increase the team's confidence in the intervention process and results.

The team should discuss and carefully plan strategies to be used, materials needed, when and how often the intervention will occur, who will implement the intervention, where the plan will be implemented, and when it will begin. Factors to discuss include how difficult the program is to implement, how much change is required to implement the program, whether or not the school has sufficient infrastructure to implement the intervention, and if the intervention is sufficiently comprehensive to address the complexity of the problem (Fixsen et al., 2005).

Teams should carefully consider the use of data collection in the process of intervention implementation to evaluate treatment fidelity. Fidelity measures can include checklists that teachers may use for self-monitoring or, when feasible, observational checklists that provide the implementer with feedback. Many curricula and intervention programs come with fidelity tools that an observer can use to provide an assessment of fidelity through walk-throughs or self-checks.

Teams can also complete a task analysis of the steps needed to provide the intervention with integrity and use this to create a simple checklist. Gawande (2009) offers compelling reasons from a variety of professions about the way in which the use of a simple checklist increases fidelity to practice. Checklists can make a substantial difference in the quality of the intervention by ensuring the implementer's attention to necessary details that can result in the difference between success and failure for an intervention. Team members charged with monitoring fidelity need to carefully attend to factors that may be compromising treatment integrity and provide coaching and support, or modify the plan, while maintaining the treatment integrity beyond scheduled meeting times.

Ensure adequate intervention supports and resources. The team must work diligently with individuals implementing the intervention to determine how much and what kind of support the implementers need to provide the intervention as designed. Carefully planning supports offered to those implementing the intervention can significantly increase treatment integrity. The team needs to examine a variety of assets in the school that can be brought to address the situation. Both direct support in delivering the interventions and indirect supports to provide assistance to those who work directly with students should be considered.

One of the most important direct service considerations is dedicated time to implement the interventions. Scheduling the intervention and determining who will provide it are often significant barriers. Some teams can capture time by stopping current practices or interventions that are not resulting in student growth, and

replacing these with the targeted interventions. Creative use of human resources such as paraprofessionals, specialists, peer tutors, or community volunteers can be viable means to successfully implement interventions. It is important for the team to think outside typical roles of professionals to provide supports (VanDerHeyden & Burns, 2010).

Specific hands-on intervention delivery supports that school psychologists may be able to provide include creating or collecting materials needed; ensuring that needed materials are available and easily accessible; developing data collection sheets; and entering, analyzing, or graphing data. In some cases, practical assistance such as finding tangible reinforcers for teachers to use can be a much appreciated gesture that increases the teacher's willingness to provide the reinforcement with integrity.

In addition to support in delivering the intervention itself, school psychologists can provide consultative support to those implementing the interventions. Some indirect services to support intervention fidelity include supports that are considered coaching. Coaching is a critical support for the person implementing interventions, particularly if the implementer is not experienced in the intervention. Coaching supports might include providing direct instruction and modeling, providing written resources, observing the intervention and providing feedback, and graphing and interpreting data collected (Annenberg Institute for School Reform, 2004; Knight, 2011).

In addition to formal coaching structures, school psychologists can provide additional support via regular informal consultation and collaborative conversations with those implementing the intervention outside of scheduled meetings. These can provide impromptu opportunities for immediate troubleshooting. It is good practice to meet with a teacher implementing an intervention within a day or two of the start of an intervention, and then a week later to discuss the intervention implementation. The meetings can be as simple as hallway conversations to check in with the implementer. If a difficulty is identified during this simple follow-up, then more intensive consultation or formal coaching can be scheduled to tweak implementation to increase fidelity.

Schedule regular progress reviews. In order to make data-based decisions, the team needs to review intervention data at regular intervals. Generally speaking, a rule of thumb is that intervention outcomes and progress should be reviewed every 6–8 weeks, or more frequently if the intervention is more intense. The team needs to allow a long enough time to give the intervention adequate time to work, but not so long that an intervention that is not working goes on too long. The reality of time constraints and scheduling demands can sometimes result in a team not meeting to follow up to see how the intervention is going. Unless teams are diligent about reviewing data and monitoring progress (Shinn, 2010), programs and interventions become part of the school fabric without benefit of understanding the benefits and limitations of the programs.

A vital team practice to ensure that progress is monitored at regular intervals is for the team to plan follow-up team meetings at the time of the problem-solving meeting to create the first follow-up review and at regular intervals thereafter. It is important for the team to put follow-up meeting dates on the school or team meeting calendar and on the team meeting documentation forms. In addition, a team facilitator or administrator needs to be assigned to schedule and hold follow-up team meetings to review data.

Plan Evaluation

The fourth step in data-based problem solving is to use outcome and fidelity data to determine whether or not the intervention has resulted in a reduction in the performance gap and a resolution of the problem. The basic question the team asks at this juncture in the process is if the plan worked. To answer this question, the team reviews data collected on progress toward the stated goal, the level of current discrepancy from the desired outcome, and the level of resources needed to maintain or increase student outcome based on progress monitoring data.

Plan Is Successful

If the intervention is successful, the student (or group) reached the criteria (decision rule) set by the team as the goal for the intervention outcome. The team can choose to either decrease the intensity of the intervention or discontinue the intervention. If the students have mastered a skill and no longer need an intervention, it may be a good idea to continue to collect progress monitoring data, even if at a reduced level of frequency, to ensure that the students continue to make progress at the same level or rate and have generalized the skill enough to perform it independently. Another alternative is to teach students to monitor their own progress. If the student is successful

after a predetermined interval of data collection, the intervention can be discontinued. If the student performance decreases, the level of support can be increased until performance improves.

Some experts consider the best measure of intervention efficacy to include continued progress monitoring when an intervention is discontinued to see if a student needs the supports of the intervention to make progress. If the student does not continue to make progress, the intervention is reintroduced to see if progress resumes. Riley-Tillman and Burns (2009) offer a variety of single-case design models to use to determine individual student RTI for teams to consider. Carefully designed data analysis is in the best interest of students when high-stakes decisions, including special education entitlement, are under consideration.

Plan Is Not Successful

If, on the other hand, the outcome data do not meet the standard for success, the team needs to ask additional questions to determine the best course of action to create a plan to improve the outcome. The team should closely examine how close the student's performance approximated the desired performance to determine the next steps. If the student made no progress at all, the team may need to cycle through the entire problem-solving process to be sure that the correct problem was identified, or that the correct hypothesis was chosen, to explain the reason for the discrepancy.

If the student makes limited progress but does not meet the decision rule for success, the team will want to consider one of several options. One important question would be whether the intervention was delivered as designed. Many of the supports suggested in the previous section may need to be reconsidered or provided to facilitate increased intervention fidelity. A second question might be if the intervention itself is powerful enough to provide needed support, particularly if the problem is such that the student is still significantly discrepant from his or her peer group. The team may need to intensify some component of the intervention (e.g., increase time or frequency of the intervention) or may need to consider a more intensive intervention. Another possible solution might be to add another layer of support in order to provide a more intensive intervention plan. Finally, the team may decide that the initial goal was too ambitious and that successive approximations with intermediate goal setting needs to be used to allow the student to eventually reach the desired outcome.

Data-Based Problem-Solving Model Applied to MTSS

A data-based problem-solving approach looks at school resources as flexible and considers creative allocations of both professional and financial resources to focus on risk reduction and early intervention in all areas of student functioning that facilitate school success (Batsche et al., 2005). Services are delivered on a continuum that begins with large group instruction (usually within the general education context), and may include any number of supports added together to facilitate student growth. While RTI has been the term of art used to describe this service delivery model, more recently the model is being referred to as MTSS. The reason behind this change in language is at least in part because MTSS is a good descriptor of the school-based model for service delivery that provides students with a continuum of services that are layers of service supports. The words *response to intervention* sometimes has the connotation of a series of discrete interventions that students do not "respond to" until they get to the place of qualifying for special education. The relationship between RTI and MTSS language and the context is well articulated by Walker and Shinn (2010).

Using the MTSS service delivery structure as a model, the next sections describe probable data-based problem-solving conversations and issues to consider within the context of each of the three tiers, or levels of intensity of service delivery. Each level of service uses the same approach or process for data-based problem solving, but the scale of the problem, the nature of the data, and the variability of factors that can have an impact on outcomes are different. Thus, problem solving at each level of service delivery has a bit of a different focus to questions that the team may ask during problem solving.

Problem Solving in Tier 1

The foundation for good student outcomes is a strong universal system that provides core instruction and prevention-oriented programming that result in at least 80% of students reaching benchmarks for academic achievement and behavior. The data are collected at various levels within a school system including district, individual school building, and grade level. The data used for this level of analysis would typically include high-stakes, state-administered, standardized academic proficiency tests; norm-referenced

tests of the district's choosing; universal screening measures for academics; or school-wide discipline data. Many schools are developing and using common formative assessments as an additional way to assess whether or not students are meeting grade-level benchmarks associated with Common Core State Standards.

In order to ensure good decision making, wise administrators and school psychologists understand the validity within each measure and relationships across measures so that data are triangulated. Schools should also look at information that examines systems and processes of school functioning that are related to these outcome measures. This information would include a variety of sources of information beyond assessment measures about why a problem might exist, including information about how well or how often classrooms are implementing core curriculum with fidelity; how well teachers adhere to best practices in instruction; and whether or not teams meet as planned to consider student data, including error analysis of formative assessment to improve instruction and of how well curriculum, instruction, and assessments are aligned. In order to facilitate reliable data-based decision making, the data should be accurate and part of efficient systems in which the data are easy to collect and enter into systems that provide easy and quick access to information (Jimerson, Burns, & VanDerHeyden, 2007; Merrell & Buchanan, 2006).

Systems-level problem solving would look at underlying systems issues in core curriculum, instruction, and school-wide discipline and classroom management systems that would offer district and school teams the opportunity to develop hypotheses about needed changes. Systems-level changes could range from large decisions like the adoption of a reading series better suited to the student population to smaller-scale changes like providing targeted professional development on differentiated instruction or student engagement for teachers.

Questions to Ask for Tier 1 Data Analysis

Data to be collected and analyzed to evaluate universal/Tier 1 systems should primarily include considerations in the areas of core instruction, curriculum, and school and classroom environment in addition to factors related to students. The Florida Multi-Tiered System of Support Network (http://www.florida-rti.org) offers a number of suggestions for questions in the areas of instruction, curriculum, environment, and learner that teams should consider.

What Kind of Data Should Be Collected to Solve Problems at Tier 1

Data sources could include direct observation, walk-throughs, interviews, curriculum maps, surveys, attendance, tardies, and office disciplinary referrals. The data can be disaggregated to consider different performance levels for subgroup and grade-level data for academic and behavior/discipline to ensure that the school data do not show different patterns that might indicate the need for different approaches or that could uncover disproportionality in discipline or in underachievement. Grade-level teams in particular may find that reviews of classroom-based formative assessments, error analysis of student work, and lesson plans yield good information about student progress in the core curriculum and excellent information that is directly applicable to informing instruction.

Problem Solving in Tier 2

Schools can expect that somewhere in the range of 10–15% of students will need to have some additional supports beyond those that are available through the core curriculum or universal support systems to meet academic and behavioral benchmarks. It is critical for schools to use decision rules for identifying students in need of supplemental interventions based on desired outcomes, community standards, and available resources (Shinn, 2010; Burns & Gibbons, 2008).

Schools use the same kinds of data for Tier 2 data conversations as are used in Tier 1 problem solving. In addition, evaluating outcomes for Tier 2 services would typically include mastery measures or formative/summative assessments specifically designed for interventions being used, diagnostic tools for the purpose of identifying skills that need additional instruction or support to be mastered, and progress monitoring measures that are not sensitive to practice effects. The data analysis would identify specific skills in which students need additional support. Careful examination of the data would also assist in providing clues that would help the team identify empirically supported interventions or supports (Cates, Blum, & Swerdlik, 2011).

Questions to Ask for Tier 2 Data Analysis

Questions that teams need to ask when engaging in data-based problem solving at the secondary or Tier 2 level of service delivery are more targeted and complex and require more frequent review. Schools that have

efficient MTSS in place look for Tier 2 interventions that are connected directly to the core instructional program. These supplemental interventions are specifically targeted to increase student academic engaged time in content and skills that have been identified as priorities (Johnson, 2011).

Kincaid (2012) suggests that problem solving at Tier 2 requires that teams consider multifaceted and complex aspects of why students are not successful. Data are collected more frequently given the intensity of programming. Generally speaking, Tier 2 teams examine small group data for program evaluation and to identify students who may need more intensive supports.

Problem Solving in Tier 3

Data-based problem-solving questions that tertiary teams address shift from looking at groups of students to focusing on interventions designed for individual students or very small groups that need intensive instruction and supports or students whose academic needs are so significant that they need targeted core replacement. The questions to be answered about tertiary supports is how much and what kinds of support does this student need to be successful both academically and behaviorally. The problem-solving process at the tertiary level considers data about student outcomes that examine the intensity of service delivery needed to result in improved performance for students who are not successful with multiple layers of good core instruction and targeted group interventions. Many schools consider Tier 3 services to include entitlement to special education, and questions about eligibility should focus on specific special education services needed to close the gap between student performance and benchmark grade-level performance.

Since data analysis at the tertiary level is usually for an individual student, data can be more unique to a specific problem, and need to be collected more frequently given the intensity of the intervention. Specific questions about student RTI often requires a solid understanding of analysis of data using single-case design methods (Riley-Tillman & Burns 2009). The questions that need to be answered by a problem-solving team would include those related to the student's current performance in comparison to his or her peer group, the amount of the discrepancy between the student and his or her peers, and the intensity and layers of interventions needed to result in student progress (Shinn, 2007).

SUMMARY

Data-based problem solving is a team-based process that uses information within a well-defined, systematic problem-solving process to make decisions about continuously improving educational programs and services. Data-based problem solving includes the process of collecting and analyzing data to understand student academic and behavioral skill needs (for large groups, small groups, and individuals), investigating and applying research-based interventions, monitoring the success of these interventions on student achievement and behavior in the school setting, and making needed changes to improve performance. There are four basic questions that form the essential components of data-based problem solving: What is the problem (problem identification)? Why is it happening (problem analysis)? What should be done about it (plan development)? Did it work (plan evaluation)? The field of education recognizes data-based problem solving as a key tool for school improvement.

Data-based problem solving has long been identified as a best practice in the field of school psychology. That said, the way in which data-based decision making has been practiced within the field has changed significantly for many school psychologists, most notably with respect to the nature of the data school psychologists use for problem solving. School psychologists are increasingly functioning as members of school-based teams using authentic or extant data to consider student outcomes at the district, school, and grade levels. Data-based problem solving is a best practice in ensuring that all aspects of schooling result in positive outcomes for all students. Consequently, school psychologists must have substantial expertise in understanding the data-based problem-solving process and in applying these skills in their work settings if they are to continue to serve an important role in facilitating success for all students.

REFERENCES

American Association of School Administrators. (n.d.). *Closing the gap: Turning SIS/LMS data into action.* Alexandria, VA: Author. Retrieved from http://www.aasa.org/ClosingtheGap.aspx

Annenberg Institute for School Reform. (2004). *Instructional coaching.* Providence, RI: Author.

Annie E. Casey Foundation. (2013). *2013 Kids Count data book.* Baltimore, MD: Author. Retrieved from http://datacenter.kidscount.org/files/2013KIDSCOUNTDataBook.pdf

Association for Supervision and Curriculum Development. (2012). *ASCD school improvement tool.* Alexandria, VA: Author. Retrieved from http://sitool.ascd.org

Bahr, M., & Kovaleski, J. (2006). The need for problem-solving teams. *Remedial and Special Education, 27,* 2–5.

Barlow, D. H., Hayes, S. C., & Nelson, R. O. (1984). *The scientist practitioner: Research and accountability in clinical and educational settings.* New York, NY: Pergamon.

Batsche, G., Elliot, J., Graden, J., Grimes, J., Kovaleski, J., & Prasse, D. (2005). *Response to intervention: Policy considerations and implementation.* Alexandria, VA: National Association of State Directors of Special Education.

Bernhardt, V. L. (2009). *Data, data everywhere: Bringing all the data together for continuous improvement.* Larchmont, NY: Eye on Education.

Blagg, D. (2011). *Growth and consequences: Will NCLB give way to growth models?* Cambridge, MA: Harvard Graduate School of Education. Retrieved from http://www.gse.harvard.edu/news-impact/2011/01/growth-and-consequences-will-nclb-give-way-to-growth-models/#ixzz28YhMfjSk

Bridges, W. (2009). *Managing transitions* (3rd ed.). Cambridge, MA: Da Capo Lifelong.

Burns, M. K., & Gibbons, K. A. (2008). *Implementing response to intervention in elementary and secondary schools.* New York, NY: Routledge.

Cates, G., Blum, C., & Swerdlik, M. (2011). *Effective RTI training and practices.* Champaign, IL: Research Press.

Chalfant, J., & Pysh, M. (1989). Teacher assistance teams: Five descriptive studies on 96 teams. *Remedial and Special Education, 10*(6), 49–58.

Christ, T., Burns, M., & Ysseldyke, J. (2005). Conceptual confusion within response-to-intervention vernacular: Clarifying meaningful differences. *Communiqué, 34*(3), Retrieved from http://www.nasponline.org/publications/cq/cq343rti.aspx

Cronin, J., Dahlin, M., Adkins, D., & Kingsbury, G. G. (2007). *The proficiency illusion.* Washington, DC: Thomas B Fordham Institute.

Deno, S., & Mirkin, P. (1977). *Data-based program modification.* Minneapolis, MN: Leadership Training Institute for Special Education.

Fixsen, D. L., Naoom, S. F., Blase, K. A., Friedman, R. M., & Wallace, F. (2005). *Implementation research: A synthesis of the literature* (FMHI Publication #231). Tampa, FL: Louis de la Parte Florida Mental Health Institute, University of South Florida.

Florida ESE Personnel Development Support Project. (2011). *Guiding tools for instructional problem solving.* Tallahassee, FL: Florida Center for Interactive Media, Florida State University. Retrieved from http://www.florida-rti.org/_docs/GTIPS.pdf

Gawande, A. (2009). *The checklist manifesto: How to get things right.* New York, NY: Metropolitan Books.

Goldring, E. B., & Berends, M. (2009). *Leading with data pathways to improve your school.* Thousand Oaks, CA: Corwin Press.

Graden, J., Zins, J., & Curtis, M. (Eds.). (1988). *Alternative education delivery systems: Enhancing instructional options for all students.* Washington, DC: National Association of School Psychologists.

Gray, S. W. (1960). Broader role for school psychologists. *Educational Leadership, 17,* 226–252.

Hardcastle, B., & Justice, K. (2008). Integrity of intervention implementation. In S. Fernley, S. LaRue, & J. W. Norlin (Eds.), *What do I do when: The answer book on RTI* (vol. 2, pp. 11:11–11:12). Horsham, PA: LRP.

Harvey, V. S., & Struzziero, J. A. (2008). *Professional development and supervision of school psychologists* (2nd ed.). Thousand Oaks, CA: Corwin Press.

Johnson, E. (2011). *How to develop an effective Tier 2 system*. Washington, DC: RTI Action Network. Retrieved from http://www.rtinetwork. org/essential/tieredinstruction/tier2/how-to-develop-an-effective-tier-2-system

Jimerson, S., Burns, M., & VanDerHeyden, A. (Eds.). (2007). *Handbook of response to intervention: The science and practice of assessment and intervention*. New York, NY: Springer.

Kincaid, D. (2012, June). *Blending academic and behavioral response to intervention*. Paper presented at the Illinois Positive Behavior Interventions and Supports Network Summer Leadership Conference, Rosemont, Illinois.

Knight, J. (2011). *Unmistakable impact*. Thousand Oaks, CA: Corwin.

Love, N., Stiles, K. E., Mundry, S., & DiRanna, K. (2008). *The data coach's guide to improving learning for all students*. Thousand Oaks, CA: Corwin Press.

Merrell, K., & Buchanan, R. (2006). Intervention selection in school-based practice: Using public health models to enhance systems capacity of schools. *School Psychology Review, 35*, 167–180.

Nastasi, B. (2000). School psychologists as healthcare providers in the 21st century: Conceptual framework, professional identity, and professional practice. *School Psychology Review, 29*, 540–554.

National Association of School Psychologists. (2010). *Model for comprehensive and integrated school psychological services*. Bethesda, MD: Author. Retrieved from http://www.nasponline.org/standards/2010standards/2_PracticeModel.pdf

National Education Association. (n.d.). *The KEYS-CSI model*. Washington, DC: Author. Retrieved from http://www.keysonline.org/about/csi.html

National Governors Association Center for Best Practices & Council of Chief State School Officers. (2010). *Common Core State Standards*. Washington, DC: Author.

Raimy, V. C. (Ed.). (1950). *Training in clinical psychology*. Englewood Cliffs, NJ: Prentice-Hall.

Reschly, D. (1988). Special education reform: School psychology revolution. *School Psychology Review, 17*, 459–475.

Riley-Tillman, T., & Burns, M. (2009). *Evaluating educational interventions*. New York, NY: Guilford Press.

Rosenfield, S. (1991). Developing school-based consultation teams: A design for organization change. *School Psychology Quarterly, 7*, 27–46.

Schulte, A., Easton, J., & Parker, J. (2009). Advances in treatment integrity research: Multidisciplinary perspectives on the conceptualization, measurement, and enhancement of treatment integrity. *School Psychology Review, 38*, 460–475.

Shinn, M. (2007). Identifying students at risk, monitoring performance, and determining eligibility within response to intervention: Research on educational need and benefit from academic intervention. *School Psychology Review, 36*, 601–617.

Shinn, M. (2010). Building a scientifically based data system for progress monitoring and universal screening across three tiers, including RTI using curriculum-based measurement. In M. Shinn & H. Walker (Eds.), *Interventions for achievement and behavior problems in a three-tier model including RTI* (3rd ed.). Bethesda, MD: National Association of School Psychologists.

Sugai, G., Horner, R. H., Algozzine, R., Barrett, S., Lewis, T., Anderson, C., … Simonsen, B. (2010). *School-wide positive behavior support: Implementers' blueprint and self-assessment*. Eugene, OR: University of Oregon.

Thomas, A., Pluymert, K., & Armistead, L. (1998). *Practical strategies to expand services to children and families*. Bethesda, MD: National Association of School Psychologists.

Tilly, W. D., III. (2008). The evolution of school psychology to science-based practice. In J. Grimes & A. Thomas (Eds.), *Best practices in school psychology V* (pp. 17–36). Bethesda, MD: National Association of School Psychologists.

U.S. Department of Education Office of Planning. (2011). *Final report on the evaluation of the growth model pilot project*. Washington, DC: Author.

VanDerHeyden, A. M., & Burns, M. (2010). *Essentials of response to intervention*. Hoboken, NJ: Wiley.

Walker, H., & Shinn, M. (2010). Systemic, evidence-based approaches for promoting positive student outcomes within a multitier framework: Moving from efficacy to effectiveness. In M. Shinn & H. Walker (Eds.), *Interventions for achievement and behavior problems in a three-tier model including RTI* (3rd ed.). Bethesda, MD: National Association of School Psychologists.

Walker Tileston, D. (2011). *Closing the RTI gap: Why poverty and culture count*. Bloomington, IN: Solution Tree Press.

York-Barr, J., Sommers, W., Ghere, G. S., & Montie, J. (2006). *Reflective practice to improve schools* (2nd ed.). Thousand Oaks, CA: Corwin Press.

3

A Comprehensive Framework for Multitiered Systems of Support in School Psychology

Karen Callan Stoiber
University of Wisconsin–Milwaukee

OVERVIEW

Across most states and school districts, there is increasing recognition of the importance of multitiered models of service delivery. Inherent to a multitiered model is the provision of high-quality instruction to all students through the use of evidence-based practices and supplemental differentiated support within a positive school culture. Another key concept in multitiered service delivery is that the intensity of intervention should be matched to the severity of the concern, with the focus and intensity of support increasing as a student progresses from one tier to the next higher tier (Gresham, 2007). The intended result of multitiered intervention progression is a validated, data-based approach to understanding students' needs and a description of what promotes or inhibits their academic and social performance. This expanded understanding is used by school psychologists and other school personnel in planning next steps within a comprehensive services system. In a multitiered model, students exhibiting learning or behavioral difficulties can receive immediate support to ensure their academic growth and competence development without a special education label.

Multitiered instructional and service delivery approaches are described in the literature using various terms, such as multitiered prevention model, multitiered intervention services, multitiered differential instruction, or multitiered systems of support. For the purposes of this chapter, multitiered systems of support (MTSS) will be used because it connotes a comprehensive, unified approach that reflects the roles and functions of school psychologists in supporting prevention, intervention, and instruction, both directly and indirectly. More specifically, school psychologists may function in MTSS as leaders, collaborative partners, interventionists, data-based decision makers, consultants, or coaches. In addition, the construct *system of support* has broad application for school psychologists in addressing both academic and social–behavioral concerns. The shift in schools toward adopting and adapting multitiered models is consistent with the current emphasis in education on prevention and early intervention and the use of problem-solving and data-based practices to guide instructional and intervention decisions. In addition, MTSS corresponds with the National Association of School Psychologists (NASP) *Model for Comprehensive and Integrated School Psychological Services* (NASP, 2010), also known as the NASP Practice Model, which represents the official policy of NASP on the delivery of school psychological services.

This chapter begins with an overview of origins and definitions of multitiered models, specifically, response to intervention (RTI) and positive behavioral support (PBS). Next, the construct of MTSS is presented, followed by the rationale for a comprehensive and integrated multitiered system of support model in school psychology. Then a description of universal, targeted, and intensive strategies corresponding to each tier in MTSS is provided, with particular attention to considerations pertinent for school psychologists. This section is followed by an explanation of key components leading to successful implementation of MTSS. A discussion of the roles, responsibilities, and functions of school psychologists within a multitiered services framework, including their work across a variety of levels—systems, school-wide, classroom, and individual student—also occurs in the section on the key components of MTSS.

This comprehensive and integrated conceptualization of multitiered service delivery is intended to provide a broad structure on which more specific components are described with greater depth and detail in other chapters in this edition of *Best Practices*.

The shift toward schools embracing RTI and PBS models was initiated, at least in part, with federal policy demanding educational reform. Since the National Commission on Excellence in Education (1983) published *A Nation at Risk*, the educational community has been nudged to rethink schooling practices so as to ensure high-quality instruction for all students. The widespread demand for school reform was further endorsed when Congress passed the 2002 No Child Left Behind Act (NCLB) and the 2004 Individuals with Disabilities Education Improvement Act (IDEIA), which highlighted attention on racial disparities in special education decisions. Whereas NCLB pushed school districts and schools to implement programs proven to be effective based on scientific evidence, IDEIA further specified "incentives for whole-school approaches, scientifically based early reading programs, positive behavior interventions and supports, and early intervening services to reduce the need to label children as disabled in order to address the learning and behavioral needs of such children" (IDEIA, 2004, p. 4).

RTI and PBS emerged as reasonable solutions for responding to at least six big issues related to academic achievement and/or social–behavioral concerns in U.S. schools. These issues are (a) children enter school with varying degrees of readiness, which can place them on a trajectory of school failure if not addressed early; (b) recognition of increasing numbers of students not attaining expected proficiency levels, particularly reading and mathematics; (c) documentation of problems with IQ–achievement discrepancy criteria for determining learning disability, and that such testing provided limited instructionally useful information; (d) knowledge of evidence-based early interventions reducing at-risk children's literacy and social–emotional and behavioral difficulties; (e) overrepresentation of ethnic minority children classified as requiring special education; and (f) evidence of special education being more costly though not necessarily more effective, as relatively few children exit and no clear special education practice is linked to those who exit.

Most agree that the combination of a national plea for excellence and equity in U.S. education along with legislative changes linked to NCLB and IDEIA provided a strong impetus for schools to adopt RTI and PBS approaches. It also is noteworthy, however, that these directives promoted, if not mandated, systemic approaches that coordinate general and special education services into an integrated and comprehensive system. Most descriptions of RTI and PBS, nonetheless, have conceptualized these models as separate systems of service delivery, or view PBS as being a component of RTI (Burton et al., 2012; McIntosh, Brown, & Borgmeier, 2008), with a few noteworthy exceptions (see, e.g., Adelman & Taylor, 2012; Lane, Menzies, Kalberg, & Oakes, 2012).

Thus, despite the current movement toward multitiered instruction and intervention approaches, little educational or school psychology literature has specifically addressed the roles, functions, or activities of school psychologists within a comprehensive, unified, and integrated multitiered model of service delivery. The lack of attention to comprehensive models of MTSS in school psychology literature is striking in contrast to the immense attention given to these two educational change initiatives—RTI and PBS—as they both incorporate multitiered service delivery systems. The school psychology literature contains extensive discussion of RTI frameworks as well as specific recommendations for school psychologists' implementation of technical aspects related to it (Glover & DiPerna, 2007; O'Connor & Freeman, 2012). Further, school psychology is viewed as taking a lead role in constructing a knowledge base regarding RTI procedures and practices even though it is mostly aligned with general education. A recent search of EBSCO by Johnston (2011) for *response to intervention* or *RTI* in the title, for example, indicated a ratio of school psychology authors to regular education authors of at least 15 to 1. Also worth noting is that scholars in school psychology (i.e., Jimerson, Burns, & VanDerHeyden, 2007) are credited with editing the first handbook on RTI, with the majority of chapter authors affiliated with school psychology.

Similarly, the topic of PBS has emerged during the past decade as an important area of practice for school psychologists (Crone & Horner, 2003). In particular, the use of functional assessment (Jones & Wickstrom, 2010; Stoiber & Gettinger, 2011; Ysseldyke & Christenson, 2002) and school-wide PBS (McIntosh, Reinke, & Herman, 2010) or positive behavioral interventions and supports has received attention in the school psychology literature as practical and potentially evidence-based PBS approaches. These variations of PBS models have been shown to be effective when research-based strategies are embedded, address aspects of the school environment, and target students' strengths and needs in improving student behavior and school outcomes. Further, the involvement of school psychologists as leaders, change agents, and consultants in facilitating PBS has been linked to its successful implementation (George, White, & Schlaffer, 2007). Similar to RTI models, PBS ascribes to proactive prevention and intervention strategies to meet students' needs rather than what some may view as traditional, wait-to-fail methods.

Definitional Features of RTI, PBS, and MTSS

While RTI and PBS commonly incorporate a multitiered or MTSS approach to modifying or supplementing instruction or interventions to be more responsive to students' needs, the terms RTI, PBS, and MTSS are not synonymous. That is, even though RTI and PBS hold many practical ramifications for the roles and activities of school psychologists, including their functioning related to assessment, consultation, and intervention, they do not constitute the same practices. For school psychology to move toward a more comprehensive and integrated system of multitiered service delivery, it is useful to examine definitions and concepts linked to RTI and PBS, including how they are distinguished and fit within MTSS, as a basis for defining and designing a comprehensive model of MTSS.

Defining Features of RTI

Various definitions of RTI are available in the literature, with Burns and VanDerHeyden (2006) providing the following description: "RTI is the systematic use of assessment data to most efficiently allocate resources in order to enhance learning for all children" (p. 3). Although their definition is cited frequently in the school psychology literature (Jimerson et al., 2007; O'Connor & Freeman, 2012), one concern with this definition and others that emphasize the role of "assessment data" is that such descriptions can be interpreted as depicting RTI mostly being about identification rather than about prevention and improving instruction. Also notable is the existence of various conceptualizations and approaches to RTI, and the legislation driving it does not specify any particular model. Rather, the federal government has specified that districts and states should be given considerable leverage in how approaches are implemented so as to reflect the unique needs of the community (Wixson, 2011). As Wixson points out, it is important to realize that RTI models that have become most widely implemented were not mandated, nor do they necessarily embrace the most useful or feasible approaches.

Although RTI has roots as an optional approach to identifying students with learning disabilities, its impact on intervention selection and impetus for educational change is much broader (Hawkins, Barnett, Morrison, & Musti-Rao, 2010; Sansosti & Noltemeyer, 2008). As noted by Hawkins et al. (2010), a defining characteristic of RTI is the decision-making component being informed not only by early screening and assessment but by "outcomes of empirically defensible prevention programs and sequences of interventions as the database for service delivery determination" (p. 25). As such, defining RTI as "the practice of providing high-quality instruction and interventions matched to student need, monitoring progress frequently to make decisions about changes in instruction or goals, and applying child response data to important educational decisions" (Batsche et al., 2005) has advantages because of its focus on instruction and on matched interventions. Yet this definition of RTI also fails to incorporate attention to how RTI should inform us about the "outcomes of empirically defensible prevention programs" and how such outcomes need to be evaluated relative to the context and conditions of the current learning environment. In this regard, it is suggested that definitions of RTI should focus on scientific or evidence-based knowledge as a core component. Nonetheless, both of the above definitions of RTI embrace rethinking how we use early intervention assistance and data to formulate the most effective instruction and services a student receives. Thus, they propel a major change in the way schools identify and support students with learning challenges. Both definitions of RTI are applauded for having moved the professions of school psychology and education in a positive, proactive direction.

Defining Features of PBS

PBS, or positive behavioral interventions and supports, has been defined as a practical approach to addressing problem behavior by focusing on contextual aspects surrounding such behavior (Dunlap, Carr, Horner, Zarcone, & Schwartz, 2008; Stoiber & Gettinger, 2011). The term PBS will be used here. However, the constructs PBS and positive behavioral interventions and supports are viewed as interchangeable, as they appear in the literature with generally consistent characteristics. Similar to RTI, PBS is based on a problem-solving model that aspires to provide a range of prevention and intervention approaches that are applied systematically based on students' demonstrated needs. PBS also aims to target and prevent inappropriate and disruptive behaviors through implementing effective and responsive teaching and behavioral management strategies so as to improve the overall social climate of the school as well as learner conditions for all students (Sugai & Horner, 2010). Although no one model of PBS emerges as being applied universally or viewed as the gold standard, multicomponent, differentiated instruction at the system, classroom, and individual student levels is inherent in PBS frameworks.

School-wide PBS is the application of PBS that incorporates a continuum of behavior support strategies implemented across the entire school using a tiered services model. Tiers typically include school-wide social instruction (Tier 1), targeted strategies for students who have been identified as at risk for serious behavioral difficulties (Tier 2), and intensive interventions for students who demonstrate significant behavior problems or disabilities (Tier 3).

Stoiber and Gettinger (2011) have suggested that multitiered PBS approaches should emphasize prevention and intervention strategies for all students in all settings in an effort to promote children's development of social competence and resilience rather than viewing PBS as a strategy aimed at reducing problem behavior or as reserved for intensive interventions. For example, Stoiber and Gettinger (2011) have suggested function-linked assessment as beneficial in designing positive support plans across tiered levels. Specifically, Stoiber and Gettinger recommend the use of a three-pronged preventive–teaching–alternative response set of strategies (see also Fox, Dunlap, Hemmeter, Joseph, & Strain, 2003) to meet the needs of all children, including those with challenging behaviors, in the regular classroom environment whenever possible. Preventive strategies are designed to buffer against or eliminate setting conditions or triggers that set off the problem behavior, teaching strategies help students learn and develop competencies that serve as alternatives to the problem behavior, and alternative response strategies are designed to alter prior responses or consequences that have been maintaining the problem behavior.

Through the implementation of PBS, children with challenging behavior who received strategies that are preventive, teach competencies, and are altered so as to be responsive rather than reactive or punishing were shown to learn and demonstrate social behaviors and competencies similar to children who teachers regard as typical in their development (Gettinger & Stoiber, 2006; Stoiber & Gettinger, 2011). This work is an example of how an evidence-based practice such as functional assessment has application in selecting and differentiating intervention strategies at all levels and thus should

not be reserved for use solely at the upper tiers. If we truly intend for the first tier to be preventive, general education teachers can benefit from tools such as functional assessment to assist them in making sound instructional decisions and data-informed plans for all learners.

Ramifications of RTI and PBS as Separate Integrated Initiatives

RTI and PBS offer equally important opportunities for improving education. Yet until recently RTI and PBS have typically been conceptualized as unique or distinct initiatives that involve separate roles and activities for school psychologists. The discrete, as opposed to unified, depiction of the academically focused RTI and the behaviorally focused PBS is striking because both models incorporate screening, progress monitoring, and data-based decision making to allow for early identification and movement within a multitiered prevention and intervention system. To enhance implementation, both RTI and PBS require administrative support and a systems-level perspective that focus on ways schools can be altered systematically to influence and improve student outcomes. RTI and PBS also address racial, cultural, linguistic, and socioeconomic disparities in achievement outcomes and aim to reduce the over-representation of children of color in special education (Santamaria, 2009). Thus, RTI and PBS both represent leading models for educational change and school improvement in the United States. For this reason alone it is essential to consider how school psychologists can be most efficient and effective in their implementation of RTI and PBS by conceptualizing both through an integrated multitiered service delivery lens.

One of the major pitfalls of viewing RTI and PBS as distinct practice entities rather than as a comprehensive and integrated service delivery system is that such a conceptualization can result in splitting personnel and limited resources between the two initiatives. This division may lead to a breakdown in communication and collaboration among key players, reduce the shared knowledge and understanding within the school community, and duplicate procedures and processes. Of even greater concern is that such a split could result in neither initiative being implemented effectively, or one or both criticized as failing to work. In contrast, a broad multitiered model holds the potential to incorporate both RTI and PBS in a balanced and cohesive framework along with other relevant school improvement and reform initiatives, such as those aimed at addressing racial disparities in special education.

Thus, the intent of this chapter is to provide a model of MTSS for school psychologists to address a full range of academic, behavioral, and social needs among children and families. At the core of this vision is the belief that in embracing a systemic approach in school psychology that combines a foci on achievement and mental health our profession will not only continue to be involved in the conversation on school improvement, but lead it in meaningful ways.

MTSS Defined and Conceptualized

Conceptualized as a broad and inclusive instructional intervention and positive support model, MTSS has the primary goal of optimizing schooling outcomes for all students, particularly those students who are likely to not keep pace in developing competencies commensurate with their peers without differentiated strategies and early intervening services. The following definition of MTSS is suggested, which is adapted based on work of various leaders in multitiered service delivery: MTSS refers to a multicomponent, comprehensive, and cohesive school-wide and classroom-based positive support system through which students at risk for academic and behavioral difficulties are identified and provided with evidence-based and data-informed instruction, support, and intervention (e.g., Adelman & Taylor, 2012; Denton, 2012; McIntosh, Chard, Boland, & Horner, 2006).

MTSS is framed within the contextual features that are emphasized in PBS with explicit attention to environmental, ecological, and the larger community such as home–school relations, school climate, and school personnel knowledge and skills. These contextual factors are viewed as affecting how students' needs are manifested and how well the system (e.g., school, teachers, school psychologists, and other school personnel) responds in the provision of support. MTSS also reflects the RTI principle of being a "fluid and flexible continuum of services through system-level implementation" (Kupzyk, Daly, Ihlo, & Young, 2012, p. 221). The multiple contextual factors affecting the quality and types of services provided within an MTSS model are illustrated in Figure 3.1. The proffered conceptualization represents not only a reframing of educational change, but rather a transformation in the way school professionals, classrooms, schools, and systems function. By addressing academic and behavior outcomes in an integrated organizational schema, both become salient within the school structure.

In this model, the knowledge, skills, understandings, and decision making of school-based practitioners, including school psychologists, interface with resources available in the school and the school implementation climate. The more distal influences, such as whether the school is situated in an urban or suburban community or the level of home–school collaboration, can interface with proximal factors such as teacher knowledge or level of leadership an administrator, school psychologist, or professional learning community provides in the implementation of MTSS. Obviously, whether and how receptive school personnel embrace a comprehensive system of support varies, which in turn has an impact on which early interventions are applied, for whom they are selected, and whether they are implemented successfully, both at the individual and system levels.

At a proximal level, school psychologists and other essential school personnel are viewed as having a direct and critical role in facilitating MTSS as implementers. As seen in Figure 3.1 and described in detail in a later section, successful implementation of MTSS at all levels hinges on six key components: differentiated instruction; screening, assessment, and progress monitoring; prevention and intervention focus; intervention fidelity; evidence-based practices; and professional development. School psychologists can empower teachers to be instructional leaders through their application of MTSS key components such as progress monitoring, differentiated instruction, and evidence-based practices. As educators become more knowledgeable and observe an increase in student performance levels, it is expected to enhance their and other school personnel's acceptance and commitment to MTSS.

School psychologists also can collaborate with administrators and other educators in designing the professional development component of an MTSS program and ensuring that it includes a continuing support component. The degree and level of buy-in by teachers, staff, and parents, as well as site-based administrative support, are among the most potent determiners of high-quality and sustained use of effective instructional and positive support practices (Gettinger & Stoiber, 2006, 2012; Kratochwill, Volpiansky, Clements, & Ball, 2007). Thus, the conceptualization of MTSS as involving multifaceted distal and proximal influences—including the child's family and teachers along with the child's ethnic and cultural background and community, district, and school philosophies and resources—also depicts school psychologists as holding a crucial role.

Table 3.1 provides a list of the resources and elements linked to the implementation of MTSS. Rather than viewing RTI and PBS as distinct initiatives that address

Figure 3.1. A Conceptual Model of Multitiered Systems of Support

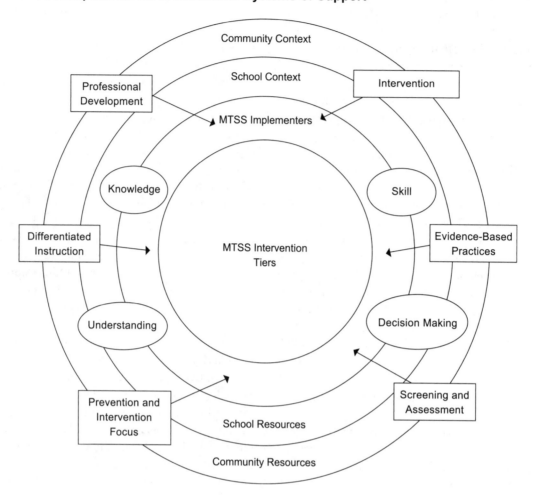

either academic or social–behavioral concerns, MTSS is an integrated system of classroom and school-wide learning and behavioral supports that are informed effectively through early identification and assessment. The impetus for MTSS is to ensure that schools not only more effectively and efficiently address problems early after onset, but can prevent many from occurring through a better developed, interconnected organizational structure for delivering school services. The above conceptualization of MTSS is intended, thus, to foster a structure that emphasizes high-quality instruction, prevention, and intervention within the context of integrated support systems.

Advantages of MTSS

One of the key advantages of a comprehensive and integrated multitiered model is that it harnesses and focuses the importance of getting it right because it permeates all aspects of the school. No longer do school staff and parents wonder whether there exists a greater

emphasis on targeting social competence or the number of students inappropriately referred for disability determination (Lane et al., 2012). Rather it should be known by all that the primary goal is to support students in a combined, comprehensive, cohesive manner. A combined, comprehensive, cohesive focus addresses and supports all students behaviorally, socially, and academically. Support for an integrated MTSS approach stems from the demonstrated positive effects noted for school-based prevention curricula designed to promote children's social and emotional competence (i.e., social–emotional learning) on children's academic outcomes (Durlak, Weissberg, Dymnicki, Taylor, & Schellinger, 2011).

One example of an integrated MTSS approach whereby both academic and behavior supports are provided for all students is the Michigan Integrated Behavior and Learning Support Initiative (Michigan Department of Education, 2012). Schools participating in the Michigan Initiative are demonstrating in the first

Table 3.1. Multitiered System of Support Model: Facilitating Elements

- Effective core curriculum and positive behavior instruction matched to state/district learner goals and expectations
- Coordinated and aligned system of effective prevention, intervention, and support
- Clearly articulated interventions that can be arranged on a continuum of intensity and level of support that fit the school context
- A broad and diverse range of evidence-based prevention strategies, teaching strategies, and alternative response strategies that school personnel have training and practice in implementing
- Meaningful and important goals, objectives, and/or benchmarks representing reading, mathematics, and social competence and mental health wellness
- Brief, repeatable, formative assessment of progress toward benchmark goals that is sensitive to intervention
- Integrated, flexible general and special education service delivery to provide intervention of increasing intensity and with increased opportunities for practice and learning
- Differentiated instructional strategies that provide effective intervention to students at risk early to prevent more severe difficulties
- Decision procedures that are reliable and valid and that can mobilize intensive prevention resources very early before serious learning difficulty and/or social–behavioral problem behavior occurs
- District and/or school-wide collaborative process and procedures to coordinate resources within school and community context to accomplish tiered prevention needs
- Carefully designed and ongoing professional development that incorporates consultation and coaching to ensure that instruction/intervention at all levels is high quality, delivered with fidelity, and evaluated to be consistent with evidence-based and empirically validated processes and programs

2 years of implementation, on average, a 26% reduction in identifying students with special education needs and a 21% reduction in referrals. Schools achieve the best results when the implementation of evidence-based practices occurs with fidelity, resulting in office discipline referrals decreasing, on average, 10% per year and the students reaching state-level reading assessment standards increasing, on average, 5% every year (Hartsell & Hayes, 2012). These results support the contention of the Michigan Initiative that as students engage in less disruptive behaviors the capacity of schools to address instructional needs increases.

The fact that students' academic performance such as reading failure has been shown to be related to school dropout (Alliance for Excellent Education, 2002), delinquency (Center on Crime, Communities, and Culture, 1997), and, sadly, suicide (Daniel et al., 2006) also provides support for adopting integrated multitiered services. In addition, there exists evidence that many students who receive services at more advanced tier levels for academic concerns exhibit behavioral issues as well, with interventionists at this level struggling and needing support to manage these students' behavior (Denton, 2012; Pyle & Vaughn, 2012). Although there are discrepant perspectives regarding whether more academic or behavioral concerns are brought to collaborative problem-solving and/or Individualized Education Program teams, evidence suggests notable overlap in the academic performance and behavioral support needs of students who receive services under the emotional or behavioral disorders category and

under the learning disabilities/mild mental retardation/intellectual disabilities category (Nelson, Benner, Lane, & Smith, 2004).

Further, although the evidence is not conclusive, some researchers report that the academic performance levels of students with learning and emotional disabilities are comparable (Lane et al., 2012). Perhaps the rationale for school psychology to use a comprehensive and integrated framework is best captured in the words of state-level department of education personnel who summarized a major concern voiced in school improvement efforts: "We hear from all of the districts that one of the things they are having a hard time doing is braiding work that they do around different initiatives together" (Quigley, 2012, p. 2). MTSS responds to such a petition by integrating efforts to target learning and academic outcomes and at the same time effectively promoting students' social competence, positive mental health, and resilience.

BASIC CONSIDERATIONS

Although multitiered models are evolving, the number of tiers in a multitiered model generally ranges from two to four or more, with a three-tiered system that parallels a public health prevention model being most common (Burton et al., 2012). The three tiers are often called primary or universal (Tier 1), secondary or targeted (Tier 2), and tertiary or intensive (Tier 3). The tiers of instruction/intervention are usually differentiated based on multiple criteria, with instruction and support becoming more intensive as students move to higher tiers. Increased intensity typically involves using more systematic, explicit, and supplemental instruction; designing smaller and more homogeneous groupings of students; and expanding the dosage (i.e., amount and frequency) of supplemental instruction (Denton, 2012; Wanzek & Vaughn, 2011). Dosage of interventions also may vary based on the intent of the intervention or recommendations of publishers of intervention programs. The use of progress-monitoring procedures to facilitate decision making should be used especially at the Tier 2 and Tier 3 levels, with Tier 2 students typically requiring less monitoring (e.g., weekly or biweekly) than students at Tier 3 (e.g., twice a week or more).

Key features of primary, secondary, and tertiary tiers in multitiered school-based services are provided below, along with important considerations for instructional differentiation and for the role of school psychologists. Because descriptions of multitiered instruction are the most prevalent in the area of reading, it is drawn upon for the purpose of providing academically focused examples. Tier 1 is viewed as foundational within MTSS. Thus it is suggested that Tier 1 be aligned with state standards and incorporate state assessment measures. Given that the majority of academic and behavioral problems can be prevented through comprehensive services at the universal level, more resources and attention should be provided at this tier.

Tier 1: Universal

Tier 1 represents the largest level, which is the core instructional or social–behavioral program. Tier 1 is universal, at the class, school, or district level, and intended to incorporate sound, empirically derived curriculum and instruction. As such, Tier 1 aims to have an impact on the greatest number of students by meeting 80–90% of their needs through valid instructional, classroom managerial, prevention, and school-wide programs. A considerable body of evidence suggests that for most students, including those who are at risk for learning or behavioral difficulties, quality evidence-based classroom instruction will be sufficient. Importantly, for Tier 1 to meet the needs of 80–90% of students, schools must carefully match the academic curriculum or social–behavioral program core content and goals to the majority of their students' level of performance.

Schools may most readily meet the requirement of high-quality, evidence-based instruction by implementing a core curriculum or program that is considered to be evidence based and addresses key learner goals. With regard to academic instructional strategies, reading emerges as the area in which there exists solid research-based curriculum and knowledge. Among the criteria to consider in designing and providing targeted instruction and interventions are the five key elements identified by the National Reading Panel (2000) as essential for reading success: (a) phonemic awareness, (b) phonics, (c) reading fluency, (d) vocabulary, and (e) reading comprehension. It should be noted that these five elements serve as a template in designing intervention plans to meet students' needs and in evaluating the focus and outcomes of reading interventions across all tiers.

When schools do not adopt a published evidence-based curriculum program, teachers have greater responsibility in ensuring that students have had adequate opportunities to learn critical content. Nonetheless, teachers typically will need to make adjustments with published programs, and school psychologists can play an essential role in this regard at Tier 1. More specifically, although effective Tier 1 instruction usually provides the necessary foundation for most students to be successful, teachers typically need to adapt or supplement core curricula to meet the diverse needs of children.

Considerations for School Psychologists

At Tier 1, school psychologists may serve as an important resource at the planning level and provide input in the selection and identification of (a) quality evidence-based core classroom instruction and (b) universal screening measures and procedures to identify students at risk for academic and mental health difficulties. In terms of Tier 1 implementation, school psychologists can assist teachers in effectively differentiating instruction and in using screening and assessment data to inform instructional decisions, such as forming small, flexible groups of students with similar learning needs or difficulties.

School psychologists might also help with identifying students' instructional needs and corresponding supportive instructional strategies that can promote or better accommodate students' learning. For example, some students will require repeated exposure to new content as it may be introduced using the core curriculum at a rapid rate and not provide enough opportunities for practice for struggling learners (Denton, 2012). Alternately, more advanced enrichment-type materials need to be available for higher achieving students. For educators working with younger students, teaching staff should incorporate these more challenging-type activities in conjunction with daily instructional activities such as center time. Regardless of students' grade level, teachers should guide higher performing students in selecting these materials so as to extend and optimize their skill development. Here an important role of school psychologists that can be overlooked is not only to encourage teachers to provide enrichment materials, but to facilitate teachers' guiding of advanced students in pursuing more challenging curricula materials. Because teacher attention is easily pulled to address the needs of students who are performing below expected levels or who are exhibiting challenging behaviors, the learning needs of more advanced students can be easily disregarded but also should be addressed in a multitiered model (Reis, McCoach, Little, Muller, & Kaniskan, 2011).

While adequate exposure to high-quality instruction and critical core curriculum may be more easily understood and applied with regard to academic achievement, a universally applied social–behavioral curriculum should likewise be evident and integrated into Tier 1. Some leaders in PBS have suggested the following core elements of PBS: school-wide expectations, rules, and procedures along with explicit lessons specifying how they are taught (Sugai & Horner, 2010). Table 3.2 provides an overview of commonly used universal PBS practices and indicators and is provided as a summary to use in ensuring that essential elements are being implemented. As such, the practice of teaching and supporting students occurs through core components, including (a) define and post behavioral expectations and rules, (b) teach behavioral expectations, (c) provide a reward system for appropriate behavior, (d) develop a continuum of consequences for problem behavior, and (e) collect continuous behavioral data and use them for decision making. Although schools may launch PBS by clarifying and posting behavioral expectations in corridors and classrooms, it is recommended that all of the elements of positive support noted in Table 3.2 occur.

Another essential aspect of Tier 1 is the use of environmental support and classroom management strategies that facilitate a positive school climate and the development of positive social competencies. It would be difficult, if not impossible, to determine whether a student requires more targeted or intensive intervention unless the school and classroom are conducive and responsive learning settings. Ysseldyke and Christenson (2002) identified 12 types of classroom support-for-learning factors: classroom environment, instructional match, instructional expectations, instructional presentation, academic engaged time, progress monitoring, relevant practice, adaptive instruction, informed feedback, student understanding, motivational factors, and cognitive emphasis. School psychologists can assist educators in examining the extent to which such instructional factors are being implemented effectively by using a developed measure such as Ysseldyke and Christenson's (2002) Functional Assessment of Academic Behavior. Another method for examining quality of instruction or adherence to an established set of instructional expectations is to conduct a classroom practices walk-through, which examines key instructional features. Table 3.3 features characteristics of evidence-based and differentiated instruction that could be adapted for use as indicators or items on this type of measure.

A variety of social–emotional learning programs for preschool through elementary school (see, e.g., selected programs listed on http://www.casel.org or http://www.ctclearinghouse.org; PATHS, Second Step, Strong Kids/Strong Start/Strong Teens, Social Decision Making/Problem Solving Program) also are available for

Table 3.2. Positive Behavior Support Indicators

- Classroom rules are defined for each of the school-wide expectations and are posted in classrooms.
- Classroom routines and procedures are explicitly identified for activities where problems often occur (e.g., entering class, asking questions, sharpening pencil, using restroom, during dismissal).
- Expected behavior routines in the classroom and school building are taught.
- Positive acknowledgment of students demonstrating adherence to classroom rules and routines occurs more frequently than reprimanding inappropriate behaviors.
- Procedures exist for tracking classroom positive behaviors and challenging behaviors.
- Classrooms have a range of consequences and interventions for problem behavior that are documented and consistently delivered.
- Schools prioritize the provision of prevention and intervention strategies and programs for students identified as at risk or as prone to problem behaviors.
- Classroom teachers and school staff report being knowledgeable and supported in implementing prevention and intervention approaches.

Table 3.3. Key Characteristics of Evidence-Based and Differentiated Instruction and Intervention

- Instruction is explicit whereby key concepts are taught purposefully.
- Instruction is targeted at important content and behavioral objectives that students need to learn.
- Instructional formats promote active student involvement and many ways to be engaged or reengaged, and to respond, including the use of motivation and self-regulation strategies.
- Instruction progresses logically with a focus on easier to more challenging skills.
- Key skills and competencies are delineated and modeled so that students are not left to infer what constitute essential concepts, how they look, or what they mean.
- Instruction provides many as well as extended opportunities for students to engage in guided and independent practice, with both corrective and positive feedback.
- Mastery of key academic skills and social competencies is monitored carefully so that reteaching, instructional modeling, and increased learning opportunities occur as needed.
- A variety of small group instruction is used in which students are grouped based on a variety of indicators (particular skill development, need, interest).
- Key learning goals, objectives, expectations, and/or standards are posted on students' desks or the board as well as in school corridors.
- Intensive interventions are available, which clearly and ostensibly target areas requiring remediation.
- Intensive interventions occur early and without delay for those students with the lowest performance levels in an effort to close the gap with typically developing students.

Note. Based on information from Denton (2012), Gettinger and Stoiber (2008, 2012), and Stoiber and Gettinger (2011).

implementation at the foundational tier level. Most social–emotional learning programs incorporate a strengths-based view of the child and thus emphasize prevention and ecological perspectives in favor of targeting child-focused deficit factors. Regardless of whether a school adopts a structured set of guidelines or a packaged social–emotional learning program, school psychologists can assist by ensuring that high-quality screening for mental health needs and teaching of appropriate behavior are delivered effectively to all students at the universal or primary instructional level.

Tier 2: Targeted

Tier 2 serves a smaller grouping of students who are thought to require more help, time, or support that increases in intensity or magnitude. Tier 2 interventions are often referred to as strategic, targeted, or supplemental. They are not intended to replace the core program or curricula, but rather to enhance and supplement students' learning. Further, Tier 2 interventions may be delivered following standard protocols for instructional interventions that permit increased practice opportunities for skill development (e.g., mathematics, reading, or social skills) or selected evidence-based intervention/instruction in small groups. The content of Tier 2 instruction should be yoked to the core curriculum or instruction covered for the class or grade level in the regular education setting, but with the addition of more exposure, more time, and more opportunities to learn. Based on a review of Tier 2

instruction, Gersten et al. (2009) found that for Tier 2 literacy instruction to be effective, it should target key skills for which students require additional support, occur three to five times weekly in 20- to 40-minute sessions, and provide multiple practice opportunities with teacher feedback. Tier 2 instruction should begin as soon as possible after students have been identified as performing below grade-level expectations, with implementation typically occurring for a minimum of 6–10 weeks, with some students requiring 10–20 weeks or more (Denton, 2012; Fletcher, Denton, Fuchs, & Vaughn, 2005). Both behaviorally and academically focused Tier 2 interventions involve supplemental curricula and/or approaches. As such, an important mantra of Tier 2 should be "supplement, supplement, supplement!" (Ball & Trammell, 2011, p. 507).

Importantly, Tier 2 instruction does not necessarily require a specially designed Tier 2 curriculum program, as some classroom teachers may be able to deliver Tier 2 instruction using off-the-shelf programs available in the school or a computer-based program. However, it should not be expected that teachers or learning specialists will naturally know how to conduct Tier 2 interventions, and they may benefit from explicit curricular materials that specify activities and strategies for adapting instructional content or teaching specific content, such as vocabulary words (Gettinger & Stoiber, 2008, 2012). Regardless of the Tier 2 type curriculum used, the second tier often requires a reallocation of teaching personnel resources, a different instructional design, and/or a well-designed set of focused strategies.

Considerations for School Psychologists

School psychologists can assist in providing consultation and offering assistance in the implementation of Tier 2 interventions with teachers either individually or at collaborative team meetings. Even when schools have adopted a specific Tier 2 level curriculum or intervention program, school psychologists can help promote its effectiveness by providing support or feedback to teaching staff regarding evidence-based approaches or strategies. To be helpful in this role, school psychologists should (a) help identify the targeted area of concern; (b) assist in selecting evidence-based interventions or strategies to address the targeted concern; (c) facilitate conducting, understanding, and interpreting progress monitoring and outcome data; and (d) follow up in determining next steps given the results from the progress monitoring and outcome data.

In the area of literacy, for example, several effective teaching strategies are supported by research to help students develop core reading skills at preschool through secondary levels. There is support for several reading strategies: explicit modeling and teaching, targeted instruction, daily review, teaching for generalization, use of repeated readings, guided and independent practice, monitoring student learning, and multiple opportunities for practice (Denton, 2012; Jones, Yssel, & Grant, 2012). However, at the secondary level, the focus shifts to remediation and content recovery, with the goal of helping students to pass core courses/exams and to graduate (Coyne, Capozzoli, Ware, & Loftus, 2010; Pyle & Vaughn, 2012). Coyne and colleagues developed a multitiered approach for at-risk adolescents that targeted vocabulary development. Their supplemental Tier 2 vocabulary intervention incorporated an explicit focus on targeted vocabulary words coupled with multiple opportunities for practice and immediate feedback. Coyne et al. (2010) noted improved learning of the targeted vocabulary words for the at-risk students as well as for their peers. Struggling adolescents also benefit from instructional methods and intervention approaches that integrate a focus on motivation and more complex word study (e.g., multisyllabic, vocabulary words linked to subject content). There also is support for a multicomponent reading intervention that targets multiple skill areas (e.g., phonics, vocabulary, reading comprehension) as potentially beneficial with upper-elementary, middle-school, and high-school–age students who struggle in reading (Canter, Klotz, & Cowan, 2008; Kamil et al., 2008). Though the knowledge base on Tier 2 interventions with English language learners is somewhat limited, support exists for focusing more on their oral language skills, including vocabulary development, and providing extended opportunities for practicing learned words in communicating and in listening activities.

At Tier 2, social–behavioral programs may focus greater attention to teaching school-wide behavioral expectations to at-risk groups on students in small groups. Here the school psychologist can support teachers by making sure that students receive frequent recognition and positive consequences for meeting expectations and that they have opportunities to practice competencies such as engaging peers appropriately, taking turns when talking, giving compliments, or using strategies such as Stop and Think to resist criticizing or bullying others. Tier 2 strategies are indicated for students who benefit from more frequent and contingent behavioral feedback or more explicit focus on keystone social competencies such as anger-control or friendship-making skills. Implementation of a check-in/check-out program such as the Behavior Education Program (Crone, Horner, & Hawken, 2004) is one strategy that has been shown to work effectively in connecting with at-risk students.

Gettinger and Stoiber (2006) and Stoiber (2004) have suggested that to determine the focus of interventions such as those implemented in Tier 2, it is important to target high-priority behavioral concerns and to attempt to integrate them within academically focused activities when feasible. In designing the intervention, school psychologists and other support personnel should consider the following: (a) incorporate goals for changing behavior that the students are capable of learning or adapting, (b) focus on developing key competencies that likely have powerful effects on adjustment or on access behaviors that allow entry to beneficial environments, (c) select chosen interventions corresponding to the child's needs as opposed to the practitioner's intervention preferences or biases, (d) emphasize simplicity as it usually promotes intervention integrity and efficiency, and (e) work toward getting all involved adults to scaffold and support the behavior. One useful strategy during collaborative teams is for school psychologists to use the above list as a guide during the team meetings. The school psychologist might use such a guide to monitor the meeting process so as to ensure each item is addressed effectively.

School psychologists may employ approaches such as functional assessment to design more targeted interventions such as affect awareness or anger management strategies that use information including the reason or intents underlying the student's behavior. Functional assessment also can be helpful in determining how teachers and staff might alter their responses so they do not trigger or provide consequences that inadvertently reward inappropriate behaviors in individual students or groups of students. Several curricula targeting social–behavioral concerns in the schools can be adapted and are applicable for second tier interventions (e.g., Steps to Respect, Resolving Conflict Creatively Program). Similar to academically focused Tier 2 interventions, packaged programs are not required, and decisions to adopt them should be based on implementation factors including ease of use, costs, available resources, and feasibility.

School psychologists, for example, can help schools and educators select targeted social competence goals and subgoals for individuals or groups of students to achieve. The Tier 2 program, for example, could focus on three major social competence goals based on the work of Stoiber and Kratochwill (2002b) that are highlighted in Table 3.4: (a) emotion regulation and self-control skills, (b) social awareness and group participation/cooperation skills, and (c) responsible social decision making and life choices. As shown in Table 3.4, each major social competence goal includes subgoals that can be used to guide particular skills that might be the focus for a student or group of students to develop. School psychologists could help teachers determine which goals and subgoals are most appropriate for a student or group of students and also assist them in designing methods for monitoring and interventions aimed at facilitating students' development of the selected social competencies.

Tier 3: Intensive

Tier 3 contains the most intensive magnitude of intervention, with these interventions being the more individualized, customized, and aligned with a student's identified needs. In many school settings, Tier 3 may be delivered one-on-one or in small groups to the approximately 1–5% of students who do not sufficiently benefit from the first two tiers. However, the percentage of students who require the more intensive tiered intervention will vary depending upon the criteria and

Table 3.4. Key Social Competence Goals and Subgoals

Social Competence Goal 1: Emotion Regulation and Self-Control Skills

The child is able to recognize and has a sense of personal responsibility for his or her own feelings, thoughts, actions, and reactions in human emotion and interpersonal social interactions.

- Can recognize, identify, and communicate one's feelings and thoughts
- Is flexible and can adapt to changing and challenging environments and events
- Shows responsibility in making choices that lead to productive, positive social outcomes
- Demonstrates perseverance in problem solving and persistence in managing challenges, disappointments, and failures
- Can identify being upset or angry and control this emotion in interpersonal interactions with peers or adults

Social Competence Goal 2: Social Awareness and Group Participation/Cooperation Skills

The child will develop understanding of social relationships and group cooperation skills, including understanding of others' feelings, friendship making, adapting and working cooperatively in groups, and finding solutions to conflicts.

- Can recognize and identify feeling in others and shows concern for others' social and emotional needs
- Initiates healthy interpersonal relationships and is accepted by peers and adults
- Maintains and sustains trusting social relationships with peers and adults in diverse interpersonal and learning environments
- Engages in productive conflict resolutions, including providing and accepting constructive feedback
- Works cooperatively with others as a partner or in a team or small group and participates appropriately in a large group
- Negotiates and accepts personal compromises in interpersonal situations when reasonable

Social Competence Goal 3: Responsible Social Decision Making and Life Choices

The child will develop ethical and responsible ways in making decisions so as to function positively and effectively in school, home, and community settings.

- Sets personal goals for accomplishing activities or performing social, learning, or work-related tasks
- Chooses friends who are task oriented and demonstrate motivation to perform school tasks well
- Shows motivation to learn and do well in school, home, and community settings
- Recognizes and resists people or situations that are potentially unsafe
- Takes leadership in modeling appropriate behavior or setting a positive environment

Note. From *Outcomes: Planning, Monitoring, Evaluating* by K. C. Stoiber and T. R. Kratochwill, 2002. San Antonio, TX: PsychCorp/Pearson Assessment. Copyright 2001 by NCS Pearson, Inc. Adapted with permission.

decision rules set. Whether and how the specific strategies or approaches used in Tiers 2 or 3 differ from those in Tier 1 depend on how a state, district, and/or school have conceptualized multitiered services.

Tier 3 is differentiated from lower tiered intervention in several ways. Tier 3 is intensive, strategic, and supplemental instruction and/or intervention and often considerably longer in duration than the 6–20 weeks of supplemental instruction provided in Tier 2. In addition, Tier 3 is specifically designed and customized small-group or individualized instruction that is extended beyond the time allocated for Tier 1 and Tier 2. Intensive Tier 3 interventions usually differ significantly from Tiers 1 and 2 in terms of the resources/support needed, time required, amount of professional involvement beyond the classroom teacher, and other factors necessary for facilitating progress. Further, the dosage and duration of a Tier 3 intervention may vary based on grade level. At the secondary level, for example, some students may require and benefit from multiple years of intensive intervention and remediation (Pyle & Vaughn, 2012). In this respect, the application and duration of intensive intervention can be fundamentally different for secondary students than for elementary-level students.

Tier 3 strategies designed to address social–emotional and behavioral concerns typically are most effective when they occur within school-wide PBS approaches that include intensive interventions for students who require a high level of specialized support (Bradshaw, Mitchell, & Leaf, 2010). Such interventions may be designed based on functional assessments to determine individualized strategies to teach functionally equivalent replacement or alternative behaviors, extinguishing problem behaviors by strengthening the contingencies between behavior and positive consequences, and, if necessary, applying negative consequences to eliminate extremely disruptive and/or potentially harmful behavior (see Stoiber, 2004; Stoiber & Gettinger, 2011). There also is support for conducting interventions at the third tier with small groups of students who require intensive and customized instruction and practice to focus on improving targeted social competencies, such as learning not to disrupt, tease, or annoy others deliberately, or replacing whining, crying, and complaining with constructive comments and interpersonal communication (Sugai & Horner, 2008, 2009).

Considerations for School Psychologists

Implementation of Tier 3 should constitute a real and significant change in the support and services a student receives as part of the decision-making process and,

ultimately, education process. As such, school psychologists can serve an important role in consulting with teachers and other personnel to determine the focus, content covered, and strategies implemented in Tier 3. As students who receive higher intensity interventions are more likely to exhibit both academic and social–emotional and behavioral difficulties (Lane et al., 2012; Bradshaw, Koth, Thornton, & Leaf, 2010), school psychologists can be especially helpful, as clear-cut answers rarely exist regarding which intervention will prove most effective. It may be necessary to explore multicomponent customized strategies aimed at enhancing student motivation, especially when students demonstrate little or no growth.

In designing interventions at Tier 3, school psychologists can review the goals and subgoals suggested for designing Tier 2 interventions in Table 3.4. Owing to the severity and/or intensity of social–behavioral difficulties students at the Tier 3 level typically encounter, they may benefit from interventions stemming from several of the possible subgoals for improving behavior listed in Table 3.4. Thus, it is suggested school psychologists collaborate with the classroom teacher in selecting the goals/subgoals that present as the top one or two behaviors to address. More specifically, in selecting goals or subgoals, they should consider which ones would likely lead to the most productive outcomes in terms of preventing the student from requiring special education or a more restrictive classroom. Here the school psychologist may especially want to be aware of keystone behaviors that lead to enhanced social competence and capacity of reduce escalating, highly disruptive, and/or physically harmful behaviors. School psychologists also should consider selecting behaviors that would help reduce the level of support the student needs to function without special education services. It can be helpful to use a structured assessment or monitoring system to determine the prioritized behavior such as the Social Competence Performance Checklist (Stoiber, 2004).

It is likely that owing to the severity of the challenging behavior the student will require a multicomponent support plan that includes clearly specified preventative, teaching, and altered response-type strategies. In designing the positive support plan it is suggested that multiple components be included to address the multiple reasons linked to the behavior of concern. For example, a student with severe aggressive tendencies or anger control issues will benefit from both teacher-taught and peer-mediated conflict resolution and negotiation strategies that include training in communication, mediation, assertiveness, and de-escalation for the target student and teachers and peers involved in the intervention. At Tier 3 it is highly recommended that school psychologists use structured approaches such as functional assessments to develop individualized strategies and use available resources on evidence-based intervention strategies (see Stoiber, 2004; Vannest, Reynolds, & Kamphaus, 2008). Data collection regarding whether and how the intervention is working should be done on a regular basis and may be required on a daily basis depending on the selected goal and severity of the student concern. Data-based decisions regarding next steps for students in Tier 3 should be conducted for individual students who may be served in small groups or instructed one-on-one.

School psychologists can also advise educational personnel regarding decision rules for entering and exiting Tier 3 instruction and/or intervention. Generally there are four ways that students enter higher intensity intervention (Pyle & Vaughn, 2012; Vaughn et al., 2011):

- Student has participated in two rounds of Tier 2 instruction/intervention and has not made sufficient progress even after adjustments in intervention strategies.
- Student has received only one round of Tier 2 instruction/intervention, but shows a marked lack of progress; further Tier 2 instruction is deemed insufficient to put the student back on track.
- Student has received less than one round of Tier 2 instruction, but more intensive intervention is indicated to accelerate skill development and prevent the student from becoming more difficult to remediate.
- Student had previously received Tier 3 instruction and has exited and then reentered Tier 3 as needed.

School psychologists can be very helpful not only in helping define the level of intervention intensity required for the child to improve or perform at expected levels but also in determining student eligibility for special education. Based on an MTSS model, a child is identified as having a disability when (a) preintervention and postintervention performance has not changed significantly despite implementation of a validated intervention or (b) intensive intervention beyond general education was required for the child to respond at an expected level of performance (National Association of State Directors of Special Education & Council of Administrators of Special Education, 2006). It should be

noted that students at all age levels (preschool, elementary, secondary), including those with significant delays or difficulties in learning and behavior, can learn and demonstrate learning abilities and skills similar to higher performing children when provided with appropriate, differentiated, and intentional instruction (Coyne et al., 2010; Denton, 2012; Gettinger & Stoiber, 2012). Thus, school psychologists' actions and activities at all intervention levels should aim to optimize a student's success, not to label or classify them.

BEST PRACTICES IN FACILITATING MTSS

School psychologists are viewed as valuable and essential contributors, if not leaders, in the implementation of multitiered services in the schools. Table 3.5 provides a summary of considerations for school psychologists in their implementation of MTSS at Tiers 1, 2, and 3. Clearly, the reasons in support of a comprehensive and integrated perspective aimed at aligning multitiered services are complex and, thus, require a multifaceted approach as specified in Table 3.5. The translation of ideological support inherent in MTSS into practice requires well-delineated expectations and well-defined skill sets. Because school psychologists bring broad and integrated training experiences, including particular competencies in assessment, instruction, consultation, prevention, and intervention design, they hold a central role in the implementation of MTSS. In view of the assumption that a multitier approach should be used to efficiently differentiate and improve instruction for all students, it is important to examine what schools, school psychologists, and other school personnel need to get right to perform MTSS effectively.

Although no absolutes exist in how to implement MTSS, there is a knowledge base accruing on key characteristics to improve learner outcomes. These essential characteristics include (a) differentiated instruction; (b) screening, assessment, and progress monitoring; (c) prevention and intervention focus; (d) intervention fidelity; (e) evidence-based practices; and (f) professional development. Suggested roles of school psychologists related to each of these six characteristics are summarized in Table 3.6. The conceptualization of MTSS presented in Figure 3.1 depicts these six components as influencing the context and quality of multitiered services. The components provided in Figure 3.1 also highlight ways school psychologists can and should make critical contributions in ensuring that MTSS not only is implemented, but is done systematically.

Table 3.5. Considerations for School Psychologists in MTSS Implementation at Tiers 1, 2, and 3

Tier 1

- Assist in the selection and identification of quality evidence-based core classroom instruction and social–emotional learning programs.
- Help select and implement universal screening measures and procedures to address academic and social–behavioral development, such as standardized measure of reading comprehension and measures or structure for screening students for mental health and/or social–behavioral needs.
- Promote effective differentiation of instruction and behavioral support, including forming small groups or customizing strategies, based on screening and progress monitoring data.
- Maximize opportunities for struggling learners to be provided with repeated exposure to new content and to practice new skills.
- Guide higher performing students to enrichment and more challenging learning content and activities.
- Help develop and establish a school-wide positive behavior system that includes (a) defining, posting, and teaching expectations for positive behavior; (b) establishing a reward system; (c) providing a continuum of consequences for problem behavior; and (d) collecting continuous and meaningful social–behavioral data to use in decision making.
- Facilitate selection and use of environmental support and classroom management strategies.
- Assist in developing and/or conducting walk-through evaluations of core academic content, key teaching strategies, and social–emotional learning experiences in classrooms.
- Support school-based professional development.

Tier 2

- Guide, monitor, and follow up on collaborative team decisions to ensure students receive appropriate intervention strategies.
- Provide consultation to teachers and parents, which includes offering support or feedback regarding effective implementation of evidence-based approaches or strategies.
- Support teachers in using effective teaching strategies, such as explicit modeling and teaching of key content and skills, targeted instruction, daily review, teaching for generalization, use of repeated readings, guided and independent practice, and multiple opportunities for practice.
- Provide resources and support teachers in selecting and implementing specific evidence-based social–emotional and behavioral programs and strategies, such as check-in/check-out, peer tutoring, friendship making, and antibullying.
- Assist teachers and schools in selecting and implementing progress monitoring measures to determine student performance related to core academic and social–behavioral skills.
- Help teachers differentiate teaching approaches, including varying pace to respond to students' needs, varying groupings to increase opportunities to respond and receive feedback, and varying content to increase generalization and learning of key skills and knowledge.
- Coach teachers in their instruction of keystone social competencies: (a) emotion regulation and self-control skills, (b) social awareness and group participation/cooperation skills, and (c) responsible social decision making and life choices.
- Facilitate all school staff involvement in scaffolding and supporting expected student learning behaviors throughout the school setting.

Tier 3

- Advise educational personnel regarding decision rules for entering and exiting Tier 3 instruction and/or intervention.
- Facilitate the design of customized small-group or individualized instruction/interventions matched to student needs based on adequate progress monitoring data.
- Ensure that intensive, strategic, and supplemental instruction and/or intervention occurs for a sufficient duration (a minimum of 10–20 weeks) with longer duration often required for students at the secondary level.
- Use structured approaches such as functional behavioral assessments to develop individualized positive support plans that incorporate targeted and intensive approaches including teacher-taught conflict resolution and negotiation, functional communication, peer mediation, anger control, and de-escalation strategies.
- Foster use of intervention strategies to counter students' potential severe aggressive tendencies and promote a safe school environment by enhancing student development of social competencies and reduction of highly disruptive and/or physically harmful behaviors.
- Ensure regular and sufficient data collection on intervention effectiveness and efficiency corresponding to targeted goals and severity of the student concern.
- Provide professional training to staff on intervention programs and strategies, progress monitoring, and the use of data to inform and alter instructional interventions.

Table 3.6. Roles of School Psychologists to Improve Learner Outcomes Within MTSS

High-Quality Differentiated Instruction

Focus consultation and classroom environmental change on…
- More opportunities and time to learn by using strategies such as repeated reading and reteaching
- Increase student engagement by matching instructional level to student learner capacity and needs, by keeping content relevant, and by fostering interest through novel content and diverse teaching strategies
- Incorporate small-group instruction to extend and expand curriculum and match pace, type and level of content covered, and dosage and duration of instruction/intervention to learner's needs

Meaningful Assessment, Screening, and Progress Monitoring

Facilitate identifying and monitoring student needs early and efficiently by helping schools…
- Determine which state standards, district benchmarks, or classroom-based indicators will be used to assess representative academic and social–emotional/behavioral competencies
- Select key learner benchmarks and cutoff scores used to indicate adequate performance or progress and assist with standardizing such measures if needed
- Specify decision rules based on performance and/or proficiency levels for indicating that the student is exceeding, meeting, or not meeting expected academic and social–emotional/behavioral standards and benchmarks

Identifying and Selecting Prevention and Intervention Programs and Strategies

Promote adapting and adopting prevention and intervention by helping teachers, parents, and collaborative teams…
- Specify prioritized goal for changing or improving academic and/or social outcomes that the student can learn
- Focus on key competencies likely to have the most potent impact on the student's adjustment or access to beneficial environments
- Implement selected strategies and programs in multiple settings by various adults and/or peers through scaffolding and supporting the student's positive development and motivation to be productive

Intervention Fidelity

Assist with examining, understanding, and promoting fidelity at the school, classroom, and teacher/parent level by…
- Acting as an implementation coach by extending and repurposing consultative activities and practices
- Targeting teaching and learning practices that have a long-range impact on improving academic and behavioral competencies in students, such as use of peer tutoring or other peer-mediated strategies or student self-regulation approaches
- Providing constructive feedback on specific elements of prevention and intervention implementation, such as methods used in engaging students, reteaching key concepts, and differentiating or supplementing lesson content
- Promoting a sense of teacher ownership of the intervention program through helping teachers learn appropriate strategies and adapt features to their classroom environment
- Fostering a positive culture for productive interactions between the implementation coach and implementer

Identifying, Selecting, Translating, and Evaluating Evidence-Based Practices

Facilitate adoption, implementation, examination, and evaluation of evidence-based practices by …
- Comparing and examining the characteristics of the empirical study to the current student population including social–economic background, ethnicity, and community setting
- Selecting measures and incorporating formative and summative data collection to demonstrate effectiveness and promote staff buy-in
- Establishing socially and empirically valid outcomes based on reliable and feasible measures that fit the context and constitute a level of proficiency yoked to present classroom norms and indicators
- Using outcome data to focus and refine implementation of preventive, alternative, and responsive strategies by explicitly linking them to important indicators, such as improved achievement or school climate

Professional Development

Initiate, maintain, and sustain multitiered service delivery by …
- Specifying essential functions and tasks needed to implement and support comprehensive MTSS aimed at addressing barriers to student learning and responsive teaching
- Identifying a school-based leader/coordinator and school personnel to serve on the MTSS professional learning community or working group to carry out central activities
- Helping establish goals, activities, and time lines for implementing MTSS
- Determining how methods for ensuring MTSS will be deemed as successful and how adaptations will be made if data or staff endorse the need for change in implementation practices
- Making sure that at least 90% of school staff demonstrate knowledge and skills needed to implement Tier 1, Tier 2, and Tier 3 instruction and interventions
- Facilitating provision of mentoring and coaching throughout implementation, especially during early implementation, to promote intervention fidelity

High-Quality Differentiated Instruction

Instruction that is differentiated emerges as a hallmark of MTSS. Yet controversy surrounds how to do differentiation so that it has a high probability of helping the most students be successful learners. Importantly, differentiated instruction should occur at all tiers, including Tier 1, despite evidence that differentiation tends to be limited at this level (Reis et al., 2011). Particular attention needs to be given to differentiation strategies at the first tier for at least three reasons: (a) schools typically place their greatest emphasis on the universal level because it has an impact on the largest number of students and can have the most robust effects; (b) the first tier is the level at which schools initiate implementation of MTSS, making success at this level critical for continued commitment and refinement during implementation; and (c) attention should be given to teacher and peer interactions, culturally responsive implementation of instruction, and other classroom climate factors at Tier 1 because they can have an impact on subgroup biases, such as race and ethnicity. When such biases occur, they can lead to inappropriate decisions to advance a student to a higher tier.

At Tier 1 the degree of differentiation should match the instructional needs of the majority of students being served in the particular school or classroom context. That is, rather than the expected 80% of students being on track in meeting instructional goals, schools serving high-risk populations may have an inverted pyramid with 50% or more of the students requiring support beyond the standard curriculum. For example, Gettinger and Stoiber (2008) noted in their study involving more than 300 urban Head Start children that these preschoolers performed on average one standard deviation below the mean on a standardized measure of receptive vocabulary. VanDerHeyden, Snyder, Broussard, and Ramsdell (2007) observed a parallel pattern of low performance with an at-risk population of students, reporting 81% of participants scoring below the mean (with 50% scoring more than one standard deviation) on a standardized preschool readiness scale. Thus, especially when serving students in high-poverty, high-risk contexts, the mantra of "differentiate, differentiate, differentiate" applies to all tiers, including the universal-level tier.

Role of the School Psychologist
School psychologists can lend essential assistance by helping plan and design systematic and strategic methods of instructional differentiation (see Table 3.6). One pedagogical strategy in which differentiation should occur across all tiers is offering more opportunities and time to learn. That is, the core curriculum is taught and retaught, or taught with more examples and opportunities to practice covered concepts for students needing greater support. Educationally disadvantaged students and those from culturally diverse backgrounds, in particular, may benefit from differentiated instruction. Differentiated instruction is considered a culturally responsive strategy to narrow the achievement gap through appropriate academic assistance (Santamaria, 2009). Another strategic tool based on the principles extending opportunities to learn is the use of repeated reading, which can be differentiated at all tiers and with all age groups. For preschool children, repeated reading may be implemented in the form of exposing children to repeated storybook reading, both in large instruction and as part of small group instruction at Tier 1 and higher tiers (Gettinger & Stoiber, 2012). Systematic application of repeated reading may be used with older students through the use of rereading passages to improve both reading fluency and reading comprehension (Jones et al., 2012).

Regardless of the lesson content or instructional grouping, effective differentiated instruction should attend to student engagement. Researchers have demonstrated that increased engagement is connected to increased levels of student achievement, motivation, and interest in tasks (Adelman & Taylor, 2006). The provision of a broad range of learning activities matched to students' needs and skills enhances the likelihood of the students being engaged learners. Although student engagement is essential at all tiers in multitier services, it may be more prone to get lost at Tier 1 due to higher student-to-teacher ratios and whole group instruction being more common. With regard to development of core academic skills, researchers and practitioners have evidenced students' declining interests and engagement in literacy and reading in recent years, which may be due to a mismatch between the needs of diverse learners in the classroom and the instructional content and opportunities available to them (Reis et al., 2011). In addition, engagement is a key concern at the secondary level, when students may become less motivated to succeed or to learn content. Thus, when the goal is to improve student behavior and academic outcomes, Adelman and Taylor's (2006) emphatic plea, "It's not about controlling behavior; it's about engaging and reengaging students in learning" (p. 49), applies across age levels. The findings of Doll et al. (2005) are noteworthy here. They reported that teachers referring students to collaborative teams often have limited instructional knowledge or expertise regarding more complex instructional strategies. School psychologists thus can be especially helpful by having and providing expertise in areas such as instructional match and motivational strategies.

Another differentiated instruction strategy is the use of flexible grouping. Students may work in large groups, centers, small groups, pairs, or individually. School psychologists can lend support in the use of small groups, which also can and should be implemented at all multitier levels. There is evidence supporting small group instruction as being equally or more effective than one-on-one tutoring (Denton, 2012). Small groups are an excellent format to extend and expand on the curriculum and to match the pace and level of exposure required for students to learn effectively. In forming groups, the group should be small enough so that every child has plenty of opportunities to respond, but large enough so that there are plenty of different responses from children, allowing for both peer interaction and immediate teacher feedback. Group size should reflect participating learners' needs and be monitored and adjusted based on skill levels. In addition, grouping should not be limited to selection of homogeneous skill-level groups. Rather, small groups should include heterogeneous grouping to address student diversity and to foster a culturally responsive approach (i.e., incorporates strategies and supports student diversity in terms of prior knowledge and experiences and linguistic and learner differences). Cooperative groups are one grouping strategy aimed at enabling students to work together while addressing the different ways that students learn. Cooperative groups allow students to work in heterogeneous groups in which students learn to share perspectives, viewpoints, and approaches to learning. Cooperative groups can promote the development of social interaction skills and active student participation, which are linked to academic achievement and motivation to learn (Santamaria, 2009).

The size of instructional groups in Tiers 1, 2, and 3 typically will differ based on students' age and grade level. At Tier 2, for example, small groups may consist of two to four students at the early childhood and primary levels, with research supporting supplemental interventions conducted in small groups for these ages of students being as effective as when delivered individually (Denton, 2012). Tier 2 small groups of 5–10 students may occur at the middle school level, whereas larger groups of 10–15 students are appropriate at the high school secondary level (Pyle & Vaughn, 2012). However, as students require more intensive and concentrated interventions at the tertiary tier, the suggested size

decreases to one to three students at the preschool and kindergarten level, two to four at elementary level, and a maximum of five students at the middle and high school level.

Although the issue of group size in multitiered interventions needs further study to determine which teacher-to-student ratios are most effective, a recent study indicated that a computer-assisted small-group tutoring program that was implemented with struggling readers at the primary grades in high-poverty schools was as effective as one-to-one tutoring and more efficient in serving many more struggling readers (Chambers et al., 2011). Another investigation examining the issue of group size and the relationship between teacher-to-student ratios (one-to-one, one-to-two, one-to-three, and one-to-five) in multitiered interventions for struggling readers in the first grade found no significant differences in the various group size conditions (Schwartz, Schmitt, & Lose, 2012). However, there was some indication of a reduction in literacy performance as the size of the small group increased, suggesting both individual and small group instruction may be most beneficial for reducing achievement gaps among the beginning readers most at risk. Because Tiers 1 and 2 typically occur within the regular education classroom, staff involvement in its implementation needs to be efficient and manageable. Tier 2 and 3 interventions may be provided outside of the classroom, and the instructors can be teachers or other educational specialists such as learning specialists, behavior interventionists, instructional coaches, or special educators. No matter what intervention level, the instructor should be trained in the content domain delivered (e.g., reading, mathematics, social–behavioral learning), as domain-specific knowledge is foundational for accurate differentiation.

Other decision-making aspects regarding instructional grouping include determining specific content or skills to cover, the dosage (time spent each day or week), and the duration of the intervention. By design, Tier 2 and Tier 3 small group interventions should be more intensive with a concentrated focus and implemented for the length of time required to produce positive results. In terms of intervention dosage, students typically receive daily 30–40 minutes of supplemental instruction in Tier 2 small group instruction. Students at Tier 3 may receive an additional 20- to 30-minute intervention session three or more times per week (Gresham, 2007). To determine the duration of Tier 2 or 3 interventions, there is support for evaluating progress after 10, 20, and 30 weeks of instruction using the benchmark and assessment criteria established for exiting an intervention tier. With regard to the length of intervention for reading difficulties, some evidence indicates that subsequent to receiving daily 30-minute intervention in small groups, approximately 25% met criteria after 10 weeks of intervention, another 25% at 20 weeks, an additional 25% after 30 weeks (approximately the entire school year), and 25% never met the criteria (Denton, 2012).

School psychologists can be helpful in assisting teachers and schools in determining clear procedures and documentation regarding whether and how students are responding to the intervention. In particular, it is important to ensure that the overall process of providing supplemental intervention occurs using high standards and that there is appropriate communication with key stakeholders, including administrators and parents, so as to minimize misunderstandings regarding implementation dosage decisions. In addition, school psychologists can assist in facilitating procedural integrity to ensure that the overall process and steps taken in intervention treatment and decision making were followed consistently (Nellis, 2012).

Meaningful Assessment, Screening, and Progress Monitoring

As noted in the above section, one of the challenges in providing differentiated instruction within a multitiered model is identifying which students should receive what types of support, for how long, and under what conditions. Teaching and learning is most effective when teachers are able to assess students' current level of behavioral and/or academic functioning, and use this information to facilitate students' advancement to higher levels of performance along with a better match of opportunities to learn. To implement multitiered services effectively, assessment and progress monitoring data are necessary to determine whether students are making appropriate progress toward instructional and/or intervention goals. Further, outcome evaluation is required to examine whether these students attain expected outcomes on standardized tests of achievement in core content areas. If a high percentage of students perform below expected levels on standardized tests, it is questionable whether high-quality instruction has occurred. The legislation and statutes underlying multitiered service delivery, such as RTI and PBS, do not mandate any specific assessment or screening procedures per se. However, data-based documentation of repeated assessments of achievement occurring at

reasonable intervals is required in RTI. Some individuals have noted that approaches to RTI may place an emphasis on measurement because it is viewed as primarily a strategy to replace IQ discrepancy identification and to reduce the number of students identified as learning disabled (Johnston, 2011).

Such a measurement emphasis, even when viewed as a strategy aimed at guaranteeing appropriate instruction, may end up heavily focused on standardization across screening and progress monitoring procedures, and, unfortunately, the field has not arrived at a consensus on the gold standard for determining what represents an adequate intervention response (Barth et al., 2008; Denton, 2012). For example, although measures of oral reading fluency in connected text are well recognized as highly predictive of reading comprehension for young readers (Fuchs, Fuchs, Hosp, & Jenkins, 2001), there are questions regarding the reliability of repeated oral reading fluency measurement because the forms may not be statistically equated. In addition, as the profession has moved toward using standardized oral reading fluency measures, they can no longer be considered as truly "curriculum based" as they do not come directly from the curricula content that the student learned.

One typical approach to examine intervention response in reading is to use a student's postintervention performance in a domain of interest (i.e., reading comprehension, oral reading fluency) in relation to predetermined benchmarks based on national, local, or classroom norms. Barth et al. (2008) have cautioned against the use of a cut point on a specific measure because scores tend to fluctuate above and below set thresholds with repeated testing. Further, they noted that single "[t]est performance cannot be the sole determinant of special education status. It would be tragic if the determination of responder status became formulaic and was used in schools in the same way as approaches based on ability–achievement discrepancy" (p. 305). There is an obvious need for more information on the consequences of applying various cut-score criteria, and whether such approaches should be used separately or in combination with other approaches, when determining adequate instructional response at each level.

Similar to attempts being made to increase standardization of screening and progress monitoring methods, schools may favor using standard intervention packages so as to standardize instruction and intervention practices. When such packages fail, the student is considered the source of the problem (i.e., a nonresponder, treatment resister) because the instruction/intervention has been proven to be effective (at least in some settings, though not necessarily the setting in which it was implemented). Unfortunately, such a perspective does not use assessment and progress monitoring as a means to examine contextual variables that may contribute to whether and how the intervention is working. A parallel case can be made when a single indicator, such as the number of office referrals/detentions, is used to determine the effectiveness of PBS. First, office referrals/detentions provide a negative indicator of the school or district, as opposed to a positive indicator of the school climate. Second, office referrals/detentions provide little information regarding what needs to be changed or adjusted in the school environment to produce improved success and learning for all students, including those prone to having behavioral difficulties and obtaining office referrals/detentions. In summary, although assessment and progress monitoring exist as a key component within a tiered school-based prevention model, clearer specifications are needed regarding how the results from monitoring of progress should be used to alter instruction and/or intervention goals.

Role of the School Psychologist

Adjustments or instructional modifications aim to meet student needs at the individual, group, class, or system level. These accommodations can occur best when based on data obtained from early screening, assessment, and progress monitoring. Typically screening and progress monitoring results are used along with other child learning and response indicators to make important educational decisions, including which instructional accommodations or what level of tiered instruction or support may be beneficial for a student or group of students. In a more integrative MTSS approach, optimal instructional and behavioral strategies include a focus on context, including qualities of learning and teaching, with such contextual knowledge informing instruction and intervention decision making (see Figure 3.1).

In determining which students may benefit from differentiated instruction/intervention, it is important to address this question: What do we expect all students to do or know, based on state standards, district benchmarks, or classroom-based indicators on select measures? Whereas the state standards and district-level benchmarks may be set, school psychologists can play an important role at the school or classroom level in determining what indicators would be used. Indicators are defined as representative academic and social–emotional–behavioral competencies used to measure progress toward the benchmarks and standards. For

example, in the area of reading, oral fluency or reading comprehension may be selected as the key indicators, with proficiency levels specified for each grade. In applying state standards, school psychologists can also assist in establishing standardized benchmarks for indicating adequate performance or progress on outcome measures at the district level or school level, such as students performing above the 25th percentile on norm-referenced reading or mathematics assessments, and students performing at or below the 25th percentile are candidates for more intensive intervention. Those same benchmark cutoffs (e.g., 25%) could also be applied in determining whether the intervention was successful for a specified tier or whether a student should advance or exit a tier (Denton, 2012).

The decision rules used for determining whether and which level of intervention a student receives may need to be adjusted based on the average performance and proficiency levels observed for a school or district. That is, if only 20% of students in a school are meeting the state-level standard for proficiency on a mathematics or reading outcome measure, applying a decision rule of all students below the 25% level on the measure as meeting criteria for more intense interventions would not be reasonable. There also should be a direct link between the progress monitoring measures and indicators and the decision rules used to determine whether students are meeting, not meeting, or exceeding expected academic and social–emotional and behavioral standards and benchmarks.

As school psychologists are often perceived by other school personnel as being leaders regarding the issues of assessment, screening, and progress monitoring, it is especially critical that the profession be knowledgeable in areas such as which criteria should be used in establishing cutoff levels or decision rules based on school-, district-, or state-level measures. In this respect, school psychologists can be instrumental in facilitating the selection and use of academic and social–behavioral indicators in guiding critical decisions in the implementation of MTSS. Specifically, these can be decisions regarding (a) who may benefit from either further formative or diagnostic assessment and interventions and (b) when students should exit to either more or less intense instruction and/or interventions.

Identifying and Selecting Prevention and Intervention Programs and Strategies

School-based prevention and intervention generally refer to programs, practices, or strategies intended to increase skills, competencies, or outcomes of children or families in targeted areas (see Forman et al., 2013; Stoiber & DeSmet, 2010). Several groups have established criteria for reviewing the effectiveness of prevention and intervention programs and practices such as the Promising Practices Network (http://www.promisingpractices.net), the Collaborative for Academic, Social, and Emotional Learning (http://www.casel.org), and the federally funded initiative What Works Clearinghouse (http://ies.ed.gov/ncee/wwc/).

More specifically, Promising Practices provides descriptions and applications of intervention strategies for addressing academic concerns (e.g., Peer-Assisted Learning Strategies) and for developing social–emotional and behavioral competencies (e.g., Social Decision Making/Problem Solving, the Good Behavior Game). Promising Practices also presents overviews of specific intervention programs designed to improve academic outcomes (e.g., Reading Recovery) and social–emotional–behavioral issues (Life Skills Training, Second Step Violence Prevention). Similarly, the What Works Clearinghouse provides reviews of academic and behavioral programs for implementation in the schools that include evidence ratings regarding the level of research to support practices on a variety of topics (e.g., dropout prevention, reducing behavior problems in the elementary school classroom, improving adolescent literacy, effective literacy and English language instruction for English language learners). The Collaborative for Academic, Social, and Emotional Learning provides a guide for selecting programs based on extensive research and analysis. The guide highlights more than 20 universal school-based social and emotional learning programs intended for all students that can be delivered by existing school staff.

Role of the School Psychologist

School psychologists assume a pivotal role in the selection of prevention and intervention within MTSS (see Stoiber & DeSmet, 2010, for more information on intervention planning, selection, and monitoring). To define the focus of the intervention, it is important to target high-priority academic or behavioral concerns. Once the focus of the prevention or intervention has been determined, the following features might be considered: (a) specify goals for changing behavior that the child is capable of learning or adopting, (b) focus on key competencies that likely have powerful effects on adjustment or on access behaviors that allow entry to beneficial environments, (c) make sure chosen interventions correspond to the child's needs as opposed to the

practitioner's intervention preferences or biases, (d) emphasize simplicity as it usually promotes intervention integrity and efficiency, and (e) work toward getting all involved adults to scaffold and support the academic performance or behavior (Stoiber, 2004). There is some evidence that prevention and intervention work best when strategies for addressing academic and social–behavioral concerns converge. In designing interventions, support also exists to examine potential ecological change variables that are alterable as opposed to targeting child-based deficits. In this regard, teachers and interventionists are encouraged to first look at instructional and ecological factors as a source of the problem prior to viewing the student as the source (McIntosh et al., 2008; Ysseldyke & Christenson, 2002).

In identifying and selecting appropriate interventions, school psychologists can readily access information offered on websites such as those listed above. Interventions are selected within an MTSS framework by gathering relevant information on the ecology of the classroom, including instructional and supportive learning components (e.g., teacher behavior, task demands, grouping strategies) along with the student's instructional needs. The approach of first looking at instruction as the potential source of the problem prior to looking at the student is particularly applicable to the design of interventions targeting social–emotional and behavioral concerns. School personnel are better able to explain student response to instruction/intervention through examining the relationship between the student's behavior and environmental events that are linked to the occurrence or nonoccurrence of a student's performance behavior. To make informed decisions about instruction and intervention effectiveness, school psychologists can assist either directly or indirectly in evaluation practices within the current setting. One way that school psychologists can assist is through the use of intervention fidelity measures.

Intervention Fidelity

Intervention fidelity (also known as treatment integrity) measures are used to examine whether an intervention is being implemented as intended and planned. In general, high intervention fidelity is associated with better student performance outcomes (Durlak & Dupre, 2008), which provides support for the use of fidelity measures to improve implementation of multitiered prevention and intervention components. It is well known that individual teachers within their classrooms have the greatest impact on whether and how well a school reaches a high level of implementation, which ultimately should facilitate desired outcomes (Denton, 2012). Several leaders in multitiered service delivery have noted that we cannot assume that carefully articulated instructional programs and intervention strategies, even when accompanied with high-quality professional development, will lead to school personnel carrying out instructional and behavioral interventions as intended (Kratochwill et al., 2007; Sanetti & Kratochwill, 2009). Rather, the content and skills taught in professional development frequently are not well generalized from training to implemented classroom or school-wide practices (Denton, 2012). Further, practitioners may adapt interventions for various reasons such as for efficiency, simplicity, experience, intuition, and resource availability (Lilienfeld, Ammirati, & David, 2012). Thus, one widespread suggestion for improving the implementation of multitiered services is to measure the fidelity of implementation and to provide ongoing support based on indicators from implementing these measures.

Role of the School Psychologist

School psychologists can assist with examining, understanding, and promoting fidelity in MTSS by measuring implementation of school-wide and classroom-level strategies, and providing feedback to teams and school personnel. Acting as an implementation coach is conceptualized as an extension of consultation practices typically performed by school psychologists. Table 3.7

provides an overview of the purpose and types of activities corresponding to the role of MTSS implementation coach.

In the application of MTSS, school psychologists may promote some types of adaptations (e.g., deciding size of groups or most important social–behavioral competencies to target) to ensure a sense of ownership among school personnel, which could be beneficial. In this respect, it is important to understand deviations or adjustments of an intervention to determine what types facilitate or hinder the success of MTSS. With knowledge of how intervention adaptations have an impact on outcomes, school psychologists can assist in determining whether the use of local school-site modifications are effective by documenting and evaluating their impact. Many evidence-based instructional and intervention programs include fidelity measures that can be rated based on observations conducted in the school or classroom. Intervention fidelity can be checked by developing measures that capture the key elements of the intervention program (e.g., see Tables 3.2, 3.3, and 3.4). The methods of checking fidelity are well aligned with an evidence-based practices framework, which is discussed next.

Evidence-Based Practices

In the past decade and a half there has been a strong focus in education and psychology on research evidence

Table 3.7. Intervention Fidelity Classroom Coach: Role and Functions

- Facilitate teacher awareness and self-monitoring of their behaviors, skills, competencies, and attitudes.
- Target specific teacher practices known to promote children's development of academic skills and/or social–behavioral competencies. These will likely change with different curricula content or as the teacher develops and implements particular strategies. Practices may be drawn directly from fidelity measures included in an instructional or intervention program or from a design based on school-wide or classroom-level goals. For example, in fostering literacy, target methods for teaching vocabulary or for promoting reading comprehension. In facilitating social competence, target the use of peer tutoring or student self-regulation.
- Provide classroom-based feedback in the application of concepts and practices emphasized in professional development practices. For example, provide feedback on establishing a positive classroom environment, on using small-group instruction, or on differentiating and supplementing lesson content.
- Provide constructive opportunities for teachers to reflect on their practices via examination of real-life context probes and questions (may use video of their instruction to facilitate teacher reflection).
- Increase the teacher's motivation to improve and change instructional behaviors and attitudes actively by discussing any barriers that may interfere with making suggested changes in practice and, ultimately, to improve his or her instruction and interactions with children.
- Collect data on the way that teachers implement expected instructional practices (treatment integrity), and use this information as feedback and to illustrate their performance in the classroom.
- Respond to any questions the teacher might have regarding implementation of multitiered services in the school.
- Model and guide teachers in their implementation of the differentiating instruction and interventions at each tier level.
- Support specific goals or activities stemming from a prior professional development session, such as promoting student engagement or using progress-monitoring data to inform instructional decisions.
- Support teacher use of progress monitoring, both for data collection and for instruction decisions.
- Support teacher autonomy and professionalism.

supporting what works to improve outcomes of school-based services for children and families. Growth in the quantity of research and policies on evidence-based practice has resulted in various resources available on numerous websites (e.g., What Works Clearinghouse; Promising Practices Network; Blueprints for Healthy Youth Development, http://www.colorado.edu/cspv/blueprints) as well as a multitude of criteria and definitions regarding what qualifies as evidence. Although a variety of definitions exist on what qualifies as evidence in evidence-based practices, most definitions incorporate statistically significant results, solid research design, and high-quality outcome measures. For a number of years, successful implementation of evidence-based programs has been associated with improved academic and social–behavioral outcomes (see Kratochwill & Stoiber, 2000; Stoiber & Kratochwill, 2000, 2002a; Weist, 1997). Despite this knowledge base, researchers have substantiated that evidence-based prevention and intervention programs are frequently implemented unsuccessfully, with limited treatment integrity, or with poor quality (Chitiyo, May, & Chitiyo, 2012; Langley, Nadeem, Kataoka, Stein, & Jaycox, 2010). Further, while a plethora of core and supplemental programs may exist for purchase and use in schools, many do not have a sound research base that supports their effectiveness. The noted gap between a knowledge base of evidence-based interventions, along with the occurrence of some schools adopting programs without a strong empirical basis, presents a disconnect with national policies and federal mandates urging schools to implement evidence-based prevention and early intervention services in conjunction with multitiered models.

A movement emphasizing the use of evidence-based practices reflects the recognition that few evidence-based interventions have been tested and applied within the contexts of schools, and that when evidence-based interventions have been implemented in the schools the evidence base is questionable (Stoiber & DeSmet, 2010). For example, although there is research to support the efficacy of school-wide PBS resulting in a reduction in challenging behavior (Bradshaw, Mitchell, & Leaf, 2010) and in promoting positive academic outcomes (Horner et al., 2009), a recent review that examined the evidence of these school-based programs identified only 2 of the 10 studies as meeting criteria (Chitiyo et al., 2012). Reflected in the construct of evidence-based practices is recognition that schools can have unique qualities and diverse ecological features and may not resemble the laboratory-type or specific context features in which an evidence-based intervention was found to produce successful outcomes. Because the evidence base even for widely distributed approaches such as school-wide PBS is not yet well established (Chitiyo et al., 2012), it is highly recommended that school psychologists play an active role in the ongoing evaluation of MTSS and related practices in their schools. An evidence-based practice approach has broader application in actual schools and classrooms as it includes prevention and intervention strategies that are based on scientific principles and empirical studies and use data-based decision making in the setting in which they are implemented (Stoiber & DeSmet, 2010). In an evidence-based practices framework, a scientific basis informs practice, and practice outcomes inform scientific knowledge and ongoing and future school-based decision making. Such an approach ensures that the empirical knowledge base is combined with practice-based wisdom and efficiency.

Role of the School Psychologist

As practitioners engaged in evidence-based practices, school psychologists identify and select prevention/intervention programs not only by examining the program's empirical basis, but also by attending to how well the ecological features associated with the development of an intervention, such as student demographics, community type, and school resources, are matched to the particular school situation or individual student characteristics in which it will be applied. Similarly, school psychologists who embrace an evidence-based practice approach would test and evaluate whether and how a particular set of prevention and intervention strategies is working by applying data-based approaches for systematically planning, monitoring, and evaluating outcomes of their own service delivery. School psychologists can be an excellent resource by facilitating the use of methods such as calculating Reliable Change Index or effect size methods to examine outcomes based on observational data, rating scale data, or benchmark scaling (Stoiber & Gettinger, 2011; Stoiber, Gettinger, & Fitts, 2007). In this regard, instruction or interventions are not considered evidence based in practice unless they are shown to produce positive outcomes for the student, group of students, or school setting they were designed to help. From such a perspective, when an intervention is not successful, the first place to examine as the source of difficulty should be the instruction or intervention strategy, rather than assuming it lies with the student.

The school psychologists' role in facilitating evidence-based practices is multifaceted. Their involvement includes identifying and selecting prevention and intervention programs and strategies along with facilitating the use of assessment and progress monitoring, either directly or indirectly, to improve teaching, instruction, and interventions. An evidence-based approach is especially indicated with MTSS due to a general lack of evidence for using particular interventions with particular children in particular contexts. In addition, we do not know whether all components of an evidence-based intervention are required to yield effective results, or which components are most essential with various populations of students (Berkel, Mauricio, Shoenfelder & Sandler, 2011; Stoiber & Kratochwill, 2002a).

For example, there is considerably less information available on effective reading instruction for English language learners and few investigations of evidence-based interventions have been conducted in the schools with diverse populations or in urban settings. Similarly, some well-known evidence-based interventions may have been validated with primarily Caucasian students in a suburban school setting or implemented with resources such as graduate students, causing them to be less relevant for ethnic minorities in urban settings or unfeasible in a typical school. Thus an evidence-based intervention may need to be altered with an emphasis on some components more than others based on the characteristics of the student population and type of setting (e.g., urban versus suburban, Caucasian student population versus ethnic minorities, large district versus small district). In addition, some literature indicates that when innovations, such as multitiered models, are adapted locally they have a greater likelihood of being sustained (Berkel et al., 2011). As educators witness the positive outcomes associated with their data-informed practice they are more likely to sustain it. Because MTSS is viewed as comprehensive, school psychologists' use of evidence-based practices would occur at all multitiered levels (district, school, classroom, and individual student).

To evaluate and make decisions within an evidence-based practices framework, the school psychologist or members of the intervention team should establish socially and empirically valid outcomes that can be measured repeatedly and reliably across the duration of the intervention. This step requires the school psychology practitioner and/or team to know and understand educational benchmarks that are validated in relation to long-term outcomes. For example, if a norm-referenced indicator such as reading comprehension at the 35th percentile is selected as the outcome, it should be known whether this constitutes the level of proficiency needed for a child to effectively function in the current and future general education classrooms (Denton, 2012).

Obviously, establishing appropriate benchmarks for the social–behavioral domain can be more difficult because grade-level standards are less available. For this reason, practitioners may benefit from resources such as the Functional Assessment and Intervention System (Stoiber, 2004) or Outcomes: Planning, Monitoring, Evaluating (Stoiber & Kratochwill, 2002b), which include goals, subgoals, and benchmarks for targeting social–behavioral competence that have been socially validated by educators. Evidence-based programs such as Strong Kids/Strong Teens, Second Step: A Violence Prevention Curriculum, and Steps to Respect also can be used as a resource in developing outcome goals in the social–behavioral domain. By incorporating evidence-based practices within MTSS, schools and school psychologists can focus and refine their use of preventive, alternative, and responsive services and, ultimately, improve outcomes linked to teaching, instruction, and interventions at their school sites.

Professional Development

Given the breadth and complexity of successful implementation of MTSS, it is not surprising that professional development is recognized as vital for success at all stages in the process of implementing systems change, that is, initiating, maintaining, and sustaining multitiered services. Professional development emerges as an essential, if not crucial, element in MTSS as it ensures that the prior five components are of high quality. Table 3.8 provides an overview of specific content and structures to consider when planning, designing, and conducting professional development activities. One of the first challenges to educational reform efforts such as those inherent in MTSS is that professionals within the school system must develop and operate on the same page, with shared meaning, goals, and responsibility. Professional development should emphasize strategies, skills, and dispositions aimed at building capacity at the individual professional, school, and system levels. The need for focused training is especially important for successful implementation of MTSS because it has been identified along with lack of administrative support and limited resources as the top reason interfering with the success of school change initiatives (Jones et al., 2012). In addition, professional development has been linked to promoting the application of differentiated evidence-based and empirically validated procedures, processes, and programs, with

Table 3.8. Professional Development Focus and Activities to Promote Successful MTSS

Initiate MTSS with the teacher and staff buy-in. Facilitate and explore discussion on the following questions:
- What are the major barriers to learning and teaching, school-wide and in classrooms?
- What is the school doing to address the major barriers to learning and teaching, school-wide and at the classroom level?
- How well does the school address barriers to learning and teaching, school-wide and at the classroom level?
- Who provides student and learning supports school-wide and in the classroom?
- How can efforts be unified to support students, learning, and teaching, school-wide and at the classroom level?
- How can multitiered systems of support be embedded into the school culture and be maintained and sustained over time?

Implement MTSS by organizing and specifying the following:
- Identify essential functions and tasks needed to implement and support a comprehensive multitiered system of support to address barriers to student learning and teaching.
- Designate a coordinator of the multitiered initiative with strong leadership and in-depth knowledge of multitiered components.
- Identify school personnel to serve on the MTSS professional learning community or an MTSS working group that will work in conjunction with the MTSS coordinator in carrying out central activities, such as constructing the content and schedule of professional development.
- Plan and commit to, at minimum, biweekly meetings of the MTSS coordinator and the professional learning community.
- Establish goals, activities, and timelines for implementing MTSS.
- Determine how multitiered instruction/interventions will be deemed to be effective and successful.
- Select assessment and progress monitoring tools and processes to be used to identify instructional and intervention needs.
- Consider methods to maximize parent and teacher support in MTSS processes and procedures.

Maintain and sustain MTSS by:
- Aligning resources and key personnel with strategic goals linked to the implementation of MTSS.
- Providing ongoing support and continuous improvement through the use of fidelity checks linked to MTSS implementation coaching. Make sure coaching is perceived as supportive as opposed to evaluative.
- Fostering staff buy-in by making adjustments and adaptations based on process feedback.
- Facilitating increased opportunities for school personnel to examine data linked to MTSS.
- Strengthening and empowering all MTSS participants through the use of effective "solution finding" sessions that build on lessons learned through implementation of MTSS.

Note. Based on information from Adelman and Taylor (2012) and Sansosti and Noltemeyer (2008).

instructional and intervention fidelity (Gettinger & Stoiber, 2012; Kratochwill et al., 2007). Capacity building is best facilitated through improving relationships and developing key knowledge and competencies in a collaborative manner, as opposed to a top-down reform (Sansosti & Noltemeyer, 2008).

Role of the School Psychologist

School psychologists bring a unique skill set to MTSS as they are prepared to assume a variety of roles involving collaboration with both educators and administrators: problem solving, consultation, and intervention planning. An underlying assumption of multitiered practices is that educational professionals are able (a) to accurately identify which students will struggle to learn or behave appropriately; (b) to implement instructional and intervention strategies effectively; (c) to monitor so that reteaching, differentiated instruction, or behavioral supports are provided as needed; and (d) to remediate concerns through targeted intervention strategies. It also is assumed that students will be provided with an adequate opportunity to learn academically, socially, and behaviorally. Yet there exists considerable evidence that teachers struggle in differentiating instruction and in implementing intervention strategies with integrity (Jones et al., 2012; Kratochwill et al., 2007). Thus, despite elements such as differentiation being viewed as a hallmark of multitiered services and suggested widely as an appropriate response to meeting diverse learner needs, implementation continues to be very limited (Latz, Speirs Neumeister, Adams, & Pierce, 2009).

A recent study by Al Otaiba et al. (2011) demonstrated the effectiveness of professional development conditions aimed at helping staff differentiate Tier 1 reading instruction based on student literacy and language performance indicators. They incorporated detailed instruction in technologies and software for individualizing student instruction and using assessment to inform instruction coupled with biweekly in-classroom coaching support. This and other studies by Al Otaiba et al. (2011) suggest that professional development leads not only to teachers implementing small-group instruction, but also to teachers delivering significantly more differentiated small-group instruction that was associated with improved reading outcomes for students, including students from culturally diverse backgrounds.

While there are other examples of schools and districts that have solved the challenges of implementing multitiered services, many school personnel remain perplexed as to what specific content and practices should occur at each tier level, which measures and criteria should be used to monitor and examine progress, and how to translate research evidence in selecting and implementing interventions. Thus, collaboration and team participation are critical at all stages of professional development: planning, implementing, and providing ongoing support for MTSS activities. In particular, ongoing implementation support in the form of performance feedback has been linked to greater intervention fidelity (Codding, Livanis, Pace, & Vaca, 2008), and emerges as important for the success of MTSS. Performance feedback typically consists of providing the teacher or other implementer with graphed intervention fidelity data accompanied by written recommendations for improving the focus and accuracy of their implementation.

With regard to determining the focus of professional development, school psychologists would benefit from being reflective practitioners who examine their own knowledge, skills, understanding, and decision-making capacities related to MTSS. Though the field of school psychology is credited as having a dominant voice in the multitiered procedures and processes linked to RTI and PBS, some educators have argued that school psychologists typically have little knowledge of the instructional content or subject matter (e.g., reading) implemented within tiered models (Johnston, 2011). Further, school psychologists have indicated minimal knowledge of reading assessment and interventions (Nelson & Machek, 2007), and less knowledge in mathematics assessment and intervention (Stoiber & Vanderwood, 2008). In addition, school psychologists may not fully understand the intricacies involved in getting MTSS right without being fully engaged in the implementation of key components, such as differentiating instruction, designing interventions, or monitoring students' responses. Thus, it is important for school psychologists to be aware of what they know and what they do not know in the operations of MTSS. As Bernhardt and Hebert (2011) have noted, we must focus on continuous improvement and get it right if we are to get major systems change initiatives right. Further, they argue that if you do it right, all involved will participate in continuous improvement processes. Thus, to do MTSS right, school psychologists must commit to being an integral part of the continuous learning and improvement process.

SUMMARY

Many compelling reasons exist for rethinking educational service delivery and eligibility decision making. Perhaps most essential is the failure of prior traditional general and special education methods to produce optimal results. Multitiered intervention progression occurring within a positive support-based school climate is a validated, data-based approach to addressing students' needs. MTSS represents a comprehensive and cohesive approach aimed at improving educational outcomes of all students, including high-achieving and at-risk students. Piecemeal attempts to implement initiatives incorporating multitiered services, most notably RTI and PBS separately, may not lead to the long-term benefits of a more integrative MTSS. An organizational framework for conceptualizing MTSS, with particular attention to the role and function of school psychologists, is provided. Doing MTSS right should mean real change in the type and quality of educational services a student receives at each tiered level.

Successful implementation of MTSS will require integration of differentiated instruction and interventions within general education, a reallocation of resources, collaboration at the individual and team levels, and new professional development and training initiatives. The more cohesive and integrated the support system, the better school psychologists will be at addressing a broad range of academic, behavioral, and social concerns manifested in diverse learner populations. To accomplish this important goal, school psychologists must also hold an integral and well-respected role within such a system. School psychologists can contribute to MTSS by helping facilitate the six key components considered essential for its success: differentiated instruction; screening, assessment, and progress monitoring; prevention and intervention focus; intervention fidelity; evidence-based practices; and professional development. Although there is no single right way to put MTSS into action, these six components are viewed as critical in the pathway to optimal implementation. School psychologists may benefit from reflecting on how their role interfaces with these six implementation factors.

As school psychologists consider their roles and functions within MTSS, they will likely need to rethink their practice and ways to balance prior demands and expectations with the unique opportunities and functions linked to MTSS. School psychologists also are encouraged to examine how MTSS is derived in their district and school settings and, importantly, how they can facilitate its being applied successfully. Only by doing so and by making comprehensive, multitiered service delivery a priority can school psychologists advocate effectively for the necessary and efficient implementation of a broad range of prevention and intervention activities. Fragmented approaches to address students' academic and mental health needs will likely yield outcomes that are less than optimal. Such outcomes can no longer be acceptable.

AUTHOR NOTE

Disclosure. Karen Callan Stoiber has a financial interest in books she authored or coauthored referenced in this chapter.

REFERENCES

Adelman, H. S., & Taylor, L. (2006). *The implementation guide to student learning supports.* Thousand Oaks, CA: Corwin.

Adelman, H. S., & Taylor, L. (2012). Mental health in schools: Moving in new directions. *Contemporary School Psychology, 16*, 9–18. Retrieved from http://www.smhp.psych.ucla.edu/pdfdocs/contschpsych.pdf

Al Otaiba, S., Connor, C. M., Folsom, J. S., Greulich, L., Meadows, J., & Li, Z. (2011). Assessment data-informed guidance to individualize kindergarten reading instruction: Findings from a cluster-randomized control field trial. *Elementary School Journal, 111*, 535–560. doi:10.1086/659031

Alliance for Excellent Education. (2002). *Every child a graduate: A framework for excellent education for all middle and high school students.* Washington, DC: Author. Retrieved from http://www.all4ed.org/files/archive/publications/EveryChildAGraduate/every.pdf

Ball, C. R., & Trammell, B. A. (2011). Response-to-intervention in high-risk preschools: Critical issues for implementation. *Psychology in the Schools, 48*, 502–512. doi:10.1002/pits.20572

Barth, A. E., Stuebing, K. K., Anthony, J. L., Denton, C. A., Mathes, P. G., Fletcher, J. M., & Francis, D. J. (2008). Agreement among response to intervention criteria for identifying responder status. *Learning and Individual Differences, 18*, 296–307.

Batsche, G., Elliot, J., Graden, J. L., Grimes, J., Kovaleski, J. F., Prasse, D., ... Tilly, W. D., III. (2005). *Response to intervention: Policy considerations and implementation.* Alexandria, VA: National Association of State Directors of Special Education.

Berkel, C., Mauricio, A. M., Schoenfelder, E., & Sandler, I. N. (2011). Putting the pieces together: An integrated model of program implementation. *Prevention Science, 12*, 23–33. doi:10.1007/s11121-010-0186-1

Bernhardt, V. L., & Hebert, C. L. (2011). *Response to intervention and continuous school improvement: Using data, vision and leadership to design,* implement, and evaluate a school-wide prevention system. New York, NY: Eye on Education.

Bradshaw, C. P., Koth, C. W., Thornton, L. A., & Leaf, P. J. (2010). Altering school climate through school-wide positive behavioral interventions and supports: Findings from a group-randomized effectiveness trial. *Prevention Science, 10*, 100–115.

Bradshaw, C. P., Mitchell, M. M., & Leaf, P. J. (2010). Examining the effects of school-wide positive behavioral interventions and supports on student outcomes: Results from a randomized controlled effectiveness trial in elementary schools. *Journal of Positive Behavioral Interventions, 12*, 161–179.

Burns, M. K., & VanDerHeyden, A. M. (2006). Using response to intervention to assess learning disabilities: Introduction to the special series. *Assessment for Effective Intervention, 32*, 3–5.

Burton, D., Kappenberg, J., Ax, E. E., Begley, L., Burke, L., Crandall, A. B., ... McPherson, S. (2012). *The complete guide to RTI: An implementation toolkit.* Thousand Oaks, CA: Corwin.

Canter, A., Klotz, M. B., & Cowan, K. (2008). Response to intervention: The future for secondary schools. *Principal Leadership, 8*(6), 12–15.

Center on Crime, Communities, and Culture. (1997). *Education as crime prevention* (Occasional Paper Series No. 2). New York, NY: Author. Retrieved from http://www.ncjrs.gov/App/Publications/abstract.aspx?ID=172486

Chambers, B., Slavin, R. E., Madden, N. A., Abrami, P., Logan, M. K., & Gifford, R. (2011). Small-group, computer-assisted tutoring to improve reading outcomes for struggling first and second graders. *Elementary School Journal, 111*, 625–640. doi:10.1086/659035

Chitiyo, M., May, M. E., & Chitiyo, G. (2012). An assessment of the evidence base for school-wide positive behavior support. *Education and Treatment of Children, 35*, 1–24.

Codding, R. S., Livanis, A., Pace, G. M., & Vaca, L. (2008). Using performance feedback to improve treatment integrity of class-wide behavior plans: An investigation of observer reactivity. *Journal of Applied Behavior Analysis, 41*, 417–422. doi:10.1901/jaba.2008.41-417

Coyne, M. D., Capozzoli, A., Ware, S., & Loftus, S. (2010). Beyond RTI for decoding: Supporting early vocabulary development within a multitier approach to instruction and intervention. *Perspectives on Language and Literacy, 93*, 498–520.

Crone, D. A., & Horner, R. H. (2003). *Building positive behavior support systems in schools: Functional behavioral assessment.* New York, NY: Guilford Press.

Crone, D. A., Horner, R. H., & Hawken, L. S. (2004). *Responding to problem behavior in schools: The behavior education program.* New York, NY: Guilford Press.

Daniel, S. S., Walsh, A. K., Goldston, D. B., Arnold, E. M., Reboussin, B. A., & Wood, F. B. (2006). Suicidality, school dropout, and reading problems among adolescents. *Journal of Learning Disabilities, 39*, 507–514. doi:10.1177/00222194060390060301

Denton, C. A. (2012). Response to intervention for reading difficulties in the primary grades: Some answers and lingering questions. *Journal of Learning Disabilities, 45*, 232–243.

Doll, B., Haack, K., Kosse, S., Osterloh, M., Siemers, E., & Pray, B. (2005). The dilemma of pragmatics: Why schools don't use quality team consultation practices. *Journal of Educational & Psychological Consultation, 16*, 127–155. doi:10.1207/s1532768xjep

Dunlap, G., Carr, E. G., Horner, R. H., Zarcone, J. R., & Schwartz, I. S. (2008). Positive behavior support and applied behavior analysis: A familial alliance. *Behavior Modification, 32*, 682–698.

Durlak, J. A., & Dupre, E. P. (2008). Implementation matters: A review of research on the influence of implementation on program outcomes and the factors affecting implementation. *American Journal of Community Psychology, 41*, 327–350. doi:10.1007/s10464-008-9165-0

Durlak, J. A., Weissberg, R. P., Dymnicki, A. B., Taylor, R. D., & Schellinger, K. B. (2011). The impact of enhancing students' social and emotional learning: A meta-analysis of school-based universal interventions. *Child Development, 82*, 405–432.

Fletcher, J. M., Denton, C. A., Fuchs, L., & Vaughn, S. R. (2005). Multi-tiered reading instruction: Linking general education and special education. In S. O. Richardson & J. W. Gilger (Eds.), *Research-based education and intervention: What we need to know* (pp. 21–43). Baltimore, MD: International Dyslexia Association.

Forman, S. G., Shapiro, E. S., Codding, R. S., Gonzales, J. E., Reddy, L. A., Rosenfield, S. A., … Stoiber, K. C. (2013). Implementation science and school psychology. *School Psychology Quarterly, 28*, 77–100. doi:10.1037/spq0000019

Fox, L., Dunlap, G., Hemmeter, M. L., Joseph, G. E., & Strain, P. S. (2003). The teaching pyramid: A model for supporting social competence and preventing challenging behavior in young children. *Young Children, 58*(4), 48–52.

Fuchs, L. S., Fuchs, D., Hosp, M. K., & Jenkins, J. R. (2001). Oral reading fluency as an indicator of reading competence: A theoretical, empirical, and historical analysis. *Scientific Studies of Reading, 5*, 239–256. doi:10.1207/S1532799XSSR0503_3

George, M. P., White, G. P., & Schlaffer, J. J. (2007). Implementing school-wide behavior change: Lessons from the field. *Psychology in the Schools, 44*, 41–51. doi:10.1002/pits.20204

Gersten, R., Compton, D., Connor, C. M., Dimino, J., Santoro, L., Linan-Thompson, S., & Tilly, W. D., III. (2009). *Assisting students struggling with reading: Response to intervention and multi-tier intervention for reading in the primary grades.* Washington, DC: Institute of Education Sciences, U.S. Department of Education.

Gettinger, M., & Stoiber, K. C. (2006). Functional assessment, collaboration, and evidence-based treatment: An experimental analysis of a team approach for addressing challenging behavior. *Journal of School Psychology, 44*, 231–252.

Gettinger, M., & Stoiber, K. (2008). Applying a response-to-intervention model for early literacy development among low-income children. *Topics in Early Childhood Special Education, 27*, 198–213.

Gettinger, M., & Stoiber, K. C. (2012). Curriculum-based early literacy assessment and differentiated instruction with high-risk preschoolers. *Reading Psychology, 33*, 11–36. doi:10.1080/02702711.2012.630605

Glover, T. A., & DiPerna, J. C. (2007). Service delivery for response to intervention: Core components and directions for future research. *School Psychology Review, 36*, 526–540.

Gresham, F. M. (2007). Evolution of the response-to-intervention concept: Empirical foundations and recent developments. In S. R. Jimerson, M. K. Burns, & A. M. VanDerHeyden (Eds.), *Handbook of response to intervention: The science and practice of assessment and intervention* (pp. 10–24). New York, NY: Springer. doi:10.1007/978-0-387-49053-3_2

Hartsell, K., & Hayes, S. (2012). Spotlight on MiBLSi. *Spotlight Briefs, 2*(1), 1–5.

Hawkins, R., Barnett, D. W., Morrison, J. Q., & Musti-Rao, S. (2010). Choosing targets for assessment and intervention: Improving important student incomes. In R. A. Ervin, G. Peacock, E. Daly, & K. Merrell (Eds.), *The practical handbook of school psychology. Effective practices for the 21st century* (pp. 13–30). New York, NY: Guilford Press.

Horner, R. H., Sugai, G., Smolkowski, K., Eber, L., Nakasato, J., Todd, A. W., & Esperanza, J. (2009). A randomized, wait-list controlled effectiveness trial assessing school-wide positive behavior support in elementary schools. *Journal of Positive Behavior Interventions, 11*, 133–144.

Individuals with Disabilities Education Improvement Act of 2004, Pub. L. No. 108-446. (2006).

Jimerson, S., Burns, M., & VanDerHeyden, A. (Eds.). (2007). *Handbook of response to intervention: The science and practice of assessment.* New York, NY: Springer.

Johnston, P. H. (2011). Response to intervention in literacy: Problems and possibilities. *Elementary School Journal, 111*, 511–534. doi:10.1086/659030

Jones, K. M., & Wickstrom, K. F. (2010). Using functional assessment to select behavioral interventions. In R. Ervin, G. Peacock, E. Daly, & K. Merrell (Eds.), *Practical handbook of school psychology* (pp. 192–210). New York, NY: Guilford Press.

Jones, R., Yssel, N., & Grant, C. (2012). Reading instruction in Tier 1: Bridging the gaps by nesting evidence-based interventions within differentiated instructions. *Psychology in the Schools, 49*, 210–218. doi:10.1002/pits.21591

Kamil, M. L., Borman, G. D., Dole, J., Kral, C. C., Salinger, T., & Torgesen, J. (2008). *Improving adolescent literacy: Effective classroom and intervention practices: A practice guide* (NCEE #2008-4027). Washington, DC: National Center for Education Evaluation and Regional Assistance, U.S. Department of Education. Retrieved from http://ies.ed.gov/ncee/wwc

Kratochwill, T. R., & Stoiber, K. C. (2000). Empirically supported interventions and school psychology: Conceptual and practice issues: Part II. *School Psychology Quarterly, 15*, 233–253.

Kratochwill, T. R., Volpiansky, P., Clements, M., & Ball, C. (2007). Professional development in implementing and sustaining multitier prevention models: Implications for response to intervention. *School Psychology Review, 36*, 618–631.

Kupzyk, S., Daly, E. J., III, Ihlo, T., & Young, N. D. (2012). Modifying instruction within tiers in mutitiered intervention programs. *Psychology in the Schools, 49*, 219–230.

Lane, K. C., Menzies, H. M., Kalberg, J. R., & Oakes, U. B. (2012). A comprehensive, integrated three-tier model to meet students' academic, behavioral, and social needs. In K. R. Harris, S. Graham, & T. Urdan (Eds.), *APA educational psychology handbook* (Vol. 3, pp. 551–581). Washington, DC: American Psychological Association.

Langley, A. K., Nadeem, E., Kataoka, S. H., Stein, B. D., & Jaycox, L. H. (2010). Evidence-based mental health programs in schools: Barriers and facilitators of successful implementation. *School Mental Health, 2*, 105–113. doi:10.1007/s12310-010-9038-1

Latz, A. O., Speirs Neumeister, K. L., Adams, C. M., & Pierce, R. L. (2009). Peer coaching to improve classroom differentiation: Perspectives from Project CLUE. *Roeper Review, 31,* 27–39.

Lilienfeld, S. O., Ammirati, R., & David, M. (2012). Distinguishing science from pseudoscience in school psychology: Science and scientific thinking as safeguard against human error. *Journal of School Psychology, 50,* 7–36. doi:10.1016/j.jsp.2011.09.006

McIntosh, K., Brown, J. A., & Borgmeier, C. J. (2008). Validity of functional behavior assessment within an RTI framework: Evidence and future directions. *Assessment for Effective Intervention, 34,* 6–14.

McIntosh, K., Chard, D. J., Boland, J. B., & Horner, R. H. (2006). Demonstration of combined efforts in school-wide academic and behavioral systems and incidence of reading and behavior challenges in early elementary grades. *Journal of Positive Behavior Interventions, 8,* 146–154.

McIntosh, K., Reinke, W. M., & Herman, K. E. (2010). School-wide analysis of data for social behavior problems: Assessing outcomes, selecting targets for intervention, and identifying need for support. In G. G. Peacock, R. A. Ervin, E. J. Daly, & K. W. Merrell (Eds.), *The practical handbook of school psychology* (pp. 135–156). New York, NY: Guilford Press.

Michigan Department of Education. (2012). *Integrated Behavior and Learning Support Initiative expands support around the state: MiBLSi supports student success.* Lansing, MI: Author.

National Association of School Psychologists. (2010). *Model for comprehensive and integrated school psychological services.* Bethesda, MD: Author. Retrieved from http://www.nasponline.org/standards/2010standards/2_PracticeModel.pdf

National Association of State Directors of Special Education & Council of Administrators of Special Education. (2006). *Response to intervention. NASDE and CASE White Paper on RTI.* Alexandria, VA: Author.

National Commission on Excellence in Education. (1983). *Report of the National Commission on Excellence in Education.* Washington DC: Author.

National Reading Panel. (2000). *Teaching children to read: An evidence-based assessment of the research literature on reading and its implications for reading instruction.* Bethesda, MD: National Institute for Literacy.

Nellis, L. M. (2012). Maximizing the effectiveness of building teams in response to intervention implementation. *Psychology in the Schools, 49,* 245–256.

Nelson, J. R., Benner, G. J., Lane, K., & Smith, B. W. (2004). Academic achievement of K–12 students with emotional and behavioral disorders. *Exceptional Children, 71,* 59–73.

Nelson, J. M., & Machek, G. R. (2007). A survey of training, practice, and competence in reading assessment and intervention. *School Psychology Review, 36,* 311–327.

O'Connor, E. P., & Freeman, E. (2012). District-level considerations in supporting and sustaining RTI implementation. *Psychology in the Schools, 49,* 297–310. doi:10.1002/pits.21598

Pyle, N., & Vaughn, S. (2012). Remediating reading difficulties in a response to intervention model with secondary students. *Psychology in the Schools, 49,* 273–284. doi:10.1002/pits.21593

Quigley, R. K. (2012, Spring/Summer). Deconstructing disproportionality and building positive behavior support. *Learning Connections,* pp. 1–2. Retrieved from http://news.education.wisc.edu/news-publications/newsletter

Reis, S. M., McCoach, D. B., Little, C. A., Muller, L. M., & Kaniskan, R. B. (2011). The effects of differentiated instruction and enrichment pedagogy on reading achievement in five elementary schools. *American Educational Research Journal, 48,* 462–501.

Sanetti, L. H., & Kratochwill, T. R. (2009). Toward developing a science of treatment integrity: Introduction to the special series. *School Psychology Review, 38,* 445–459.

Sansosti, F. J., & Noltemeyer, A. (2008). Viewing response-to-intervention through an educational change paradigm: What can we learn? *California School Psychologist, 1355*–1366.

Santamaria, L. J. (2009). Culturally responsive differentiated instruction: Narrowing gaps between best pedagogical practices benefiting all learners. *Teacher College Record, 111,* 214–224.

Schwartz, R. M., Schmitt, M. C., & Lose, M. K. (2012). The effect of teacher-student ratio on early intervention outcomes. *Elementary School Journal, 112,* 547–567.

Stoiber, K. C. (2004). *Functional Assessment and Intervention System.* San Antonio, TX: PsychCorp/Pearson Assessment.

Stoiber, K. C., & DeSmet, J. (2010). Guidelines for evidence-based practice in selecting interventions. In R. Ervin, G. Peacock, E. Daly, & K. Merrell (Eds.), *Practical handbook of school psychology* (pp. 213–234). New York, NY: Guilford Press.

Stoiber, K. C., & Gettinger, M. (2011). Functional assessment and positive support strategies for promoting resilience: Effects on teachers and high-risk children. *Psychology in the Schools, 48,* 686–706.

Stoiber, K., Gettinger, M., & Fitts, M. (2007). Functional assessment and positive support strategies: Case illustration of process and outcomes. *Early Childhood Services, 1,* 165–179.

Stoiber, K. C., & Kratochwill, T. R. (2000). Empirically supported interventions and school psychology: Rationale and methodological issues: Part 1. *School Psychology Quarterly, 15,* 75–105.

Stoiber, K. C., & Kratochwill, T. R. (2002a). Evidence-based interventions in school psychology: Conceptual foundations of the procedural and coding manual of Division 16 and the Society for the Study of School Psychology Task Force. *School Psychology Quarterly, 17,* 233–253.

Stoiber, K. C., & Kratochwill, T. R. (2002b). *Outcomes: Planning, Monitoring, Evaluating.* San Antonio, TX: PsychCorp/Pearson Assessment.

Stoiber, K. C., & Vanderwood, M. (2008). Traditional service delivery vs. problem-solving consultative models: Urban school psychologists' use, needs, and priorities. *Journal of Educational and Psychological Consultation, 18,* 264–292.

Sugai, G., & Horner, R. H. (2008). What we know and need to know about preventing problem behavior in schools. *Exceptionality, 16,* 67–77.

Sugai, G., & Horner, R. H. (2009). Responsiveness-to-intervention and school-wide positive behavior supports: Integration of multi-tiered system approaches. *Exceptionality, 17,* 223–237.

Sugai, G., & Horner, R. (2010). School-wide positive behavior supports: Establishing a continuum of evidence-based practices. *Journal of Evidence-Based Practices for Schools, 11,* 62–83.

VanDerHeyden, A. M., Snyder, P. A., Broussard, C., & Ramsdell, K. (2007). Measuring response to early literacy intervention with preschoolers at risk. *Topics in Early Childhood Special Education, 27,* 232–249.

Vannest, K. J., Reynolds, C. R., & Kamphaus, R. W. (2008). *Intervention guide*. Minneapolis, MN: Pearson.

Vaughn, S., Wexler, J., Roberts, G., Barth, A. E., Cirino, P. T., Romain, M., ... Denton, C. A. (2011). The effects of individualized and standardized interventions on middle school students with reading disabilities. *Exceptional Children, 77*, 391–407.

Wanzek, J., & Vaughn, S. (2011). Is a three-tier reading intervention model associated with reduced placement in special education? *Remedial and Special Education, 32*, 167–175.

Weist, M. D. (1997). Expanded school mental health services: A national movement in progress. *Advances in Clinical Child Psychology, 19*, 319–352.

Wixson, K. (2011). A systematic view of RTI research: Introduction to the special issue. *Elementary School Journal, 111*, 503–510. doi:10.1086/659029

Ysseldyke, J. E., & Christenson, S. L. (2002). *FAAB: Functional Assessment of Academic Behavior*. Longmont, CO: Sopris West.

4

The Evolution of School Psychology: Origins, Contemporary Status, and Future Directions

James E. Ysseldyke
University of Minnesota
Daniel J. Reschly
Vanderbilt University (TN)

OVERVIEW

Since the 1970s, we have had the opportunity to witness a struggle between two competing paradigms and have contributed to a major paradigm shift in school and other areas of applied psychology as well as in general and special education. The shift has been from a focus on inputs and professional processes to an increasing emphasis on outcomes and benefits to students/clients. School psychology has changed from a model of practice in which the indications of high-quality services ranged from the assessments given, insightful interpretations, and general prescriptions for classification and placement to the delivery of a multitiered system of supports (MTSS) emphasizing prevention, early identification and treatment, and intensive evidence-based interventions.

The paradigm shift has a rich and deep foundation in research, public policy, law, and practice. In this chapter we review the foundations for the paradigm shift, major influences on the shift, and the kinds of changes that have taken place in school psychology training; examine current practices; and discuss probable future developments.

FOUNDATIONS FOR THE SCHOOL PSYCHOLOGY PARADIGM SHIFT

One easily overlooked foundation for the paradigm shift is the extraordinary growth of the number of school psychologists since the 1970s, establishing the resources to develop a broad range of psychological services in

multitiered support systems. School psychology grew from approximately 10,000 to more than 32,000 practitioners employed in public schools from 1977 to 2010, an increase of 220%. Much of this increase is attributable to the rise in special education funding and the federal maintenance-of-effort requirements that protect special education funding at the state level (Parrish & Harr-Robins, 2011). The enormous growth also is a testament to the work of school psychologists, which has been seen as highly valuable by general and special education administrators. The national ratio of students to school psychologists has changed over this period from about 4,000:1 to 1,500:1 (see Figure 4.1).

Although the work of several pioneers could be cited as exemplifying the contrasting models, we focus on two: Cronbach (1957), who contrasted psychological models for the delivery of services and described short-run empiricism, a foundation for current problem solving; and Bijou (1968, 1970), who focused on environmental conditions that could be changed to enhance academic and behavioral competencies. Several scholar-practitioners in school psychology and related areas were insightful translators of the basic work of Cronbach and particularly of Bergan (Bergan, 1977; Bergan & Kratochwill, 1990) and Deno (Deno, 1985; Deno & Mirkin, 1977). Bergan's behavior consultation, the fundamental model for a wide range of problem-solving applications in school psychology today, combined applied behavior analysis and instructional science to the solution of problems at individual, group, and

Figure 4.1. Growth of School Psychology 1977 (*N* = 9,950) to 2010 (*N* = 32,984)

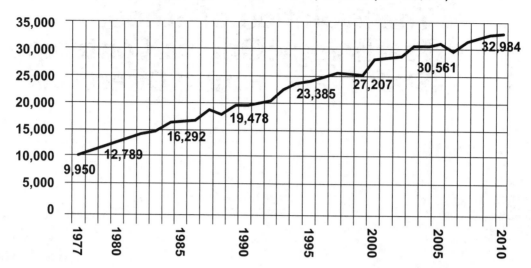

Note. Based on information compiled from public data available from annual reports to Congress from the U.S. Office of Special Education Programs.

systems levels. Deno's work on problem solving and applications of behavior assessment to academic skills in the form of curriculum-based measurement (CBM) markedly improved the measurement of the effects of academic interventions and, indirectly, behavioral interventions. The early work led to what we now observe and label either response to intervention (RTI) or MTSS.

Correlational Model

The correlational model emphasizes assessment of the natural variations among people in cognitive abilities and physical and social–emotional domains. Studies are completed to determine the extent to which measures of individual differences (abilities, psychological or hypothetical cognitive processes, and personality) are correlated with actual educational achievement and behavior. If there are significant relationships (correlations) between these natural variations and performance, it is assumed that increased efficiency and enhanced overall performance can be produced by differential selection, treatment, or placement.

The correlational model attempts to advance human welfare by selecting the right persons for different training programs, instructional interventions, or careers and by matching persons to programs where they can be successful and productive. Individual differences are seen as relatively unchangeable, and the main outcome is to fit persons to existing programs. The traditional school psychology model of refer–test–place is consistent

with the correlational science of attempting to place students in special education programs best suited to their abilities and needs.

Experimental (Problem-Solving) Model

In the experimental model the focus is on competence enhancement, and the fundamental aim is to create higher levels of performance through (a) discovering the best interventions and (b) implementing and disseminating the best interventions. Different treatments or interventions are contrasted carefully so that causal statements can be made about which had the highest average effects for groups of participants or, in single-subject designs, for individuals. Careful control of experimental conditions is extremely important so that valid comparisons can be made between the treatments. The experimental model is applied today in a variety of school psychology services that frequently use time series analysis data to design and evaluate individual, group, and system interventions. Changing performance is the goal, not fitting students to treatments that are intended to match their abilities or cognitive processes.

Bijou's Early Work

On September 1, 1968, Sidney Bijou delivered an invited address titled "What Psychology Has to Offer Education—Now" to the Division of School Psychologists' meeting at the 76th annual convention of the American Psychological Association (APA). The address was 17 years prior to publication of the first edition of *Best Practices in School Psychology* and predated the formation of the National Association of School Psychologists. Later published in the *Journal of Applied Behavior Analysis* (Bijou, 1970), Bijou's paper is one of several seminal papers in our field and provides a part of the context for this opening chapter. Bijou argued that the "great majority" and "large minority" of psychologists were focused on the mind, on collecting facts about the abilities of the child along with advancing promising theories of personality development, socialization, and psychopathology. These psychologists were focused on issues of prediction, coping, and defending. Bijou described a third group of psychologists, those he labeled "the small minority," offering a set of concepts and principles derived exclusively from experimental research; that is, a methodology for applying the concepts and principles directly to teaching practices, a research design that deals with changes in the individual child rather than drawing inferences from group averages, and a philosophy of science focused on observable accounts of relationships between individual behaviors and their determining conditions. Bijou argued that this small minority offered to education an experimental science of behavior, a problem analysis and problem-solving methodology akin to the approach advocated by Cronbach and seen in practice in contemporary problem-solving and experimental approaches.

The offer of Bijou's small minority was for a psychology focused on experimental methodologies rather than correlational findings, and one in which research was focused on identification of functional relationships. As we begin this chapter we find ourselves asking: "What does *school* psychology have to offer education—now," and arguing that the response to that question has changed since the 1970s in ways Bijou envisioned and in what we refer to as a "paradigm shift." At the same time we recognize that the correlational model lives on strongly in the continued effort to identify ways in which scores on aptitude measures interact with treatments to produce differential outcomes for students.

Aptitude by Treatment Interactions

The aptitude by treatment interaction (ATI) approach involves the study of (a) differences among treatments, (b) aptitude differences among persons, and (c) interaction of aptitudes and treatments. Based on the interactions, individuals would be assigned to treatments that would produce the best results. Cronbach (1957) suggested that "[f]or any potential problem there is

some best group of treatments to use and some best allocation of persons to treatments (p. 680). The educational application suggested by Cronbach, greater emphasis on individual prescriptions, was the basis for diagnostic–prescriptive teaching and much of school psychology since the 1970s. He wrote: "We should *design* treatments, not to fit the average person, but to fit groups of students with particular aptitude patterns. [W]e should seek out the aptitudes which correspond to (interact with) modifiable aspects of the treatment" (p. 681).

ATI Failure and Short-Run Empiricism

ATI is one of the most attractive ideas in all of basic and applied psychology (Arter & Jenkins, 1977; Dunn & Dunn, 2001; Fuchs, Hale, & Kearns, 2011). Despite many efforts since the 1960s, the promise of ATI as a model for practice has not been realized. By the 1970s Cronbach's frustration with ATI as a basis for applied psychology was palpable. He wrote, "Once we attend to interactions, we enter a hall of mirrors that extends to infinity" (Cronbach, 1975, p. 119). In the years between 1957 and 1975, Cronbach and his colleagues conducted many studies in which attempts were made to identify interactions of aptitudes and treatments. The results were negative. The hypothesized interactions usually did not occur. When the rare finding of a statistically significant interaction did occur, the interactions were weak, unpredictable, unstable across replications, and impossible to apply to practical situations. Generally, significant interaction effects, when they existed then and now, were for prior achievement within the domain of behavior that was the dependent variable in the ATI experiments. For example, prior achievement in mathematics interacts with the level and kind of math instruction that is most effective (Rittle-Johnson, Star, & Durkin, 2009). This kind of interaction is not at all what Cronbach had in mind originally nor what is claimed by contemporary advocates of aptitude by treatment interactions with hypothetical cognitive or psychological processing constructs (e. g., Hale, Kaufman, Naglieri, & Kavale, 2006).

In place of aptitude by treatment interaction, Cronbach suggested context-specific evaluation and short-run empiricism: "One monitors responses to the treatment and adjusts it" (Cronbach, 1975, p. 126). The use of short-run empiricism (problem solving), the application of MTSS, and the selection of behavior change or instructional design principles from the available literature are the contemporary applications of Cronbach's conclusions about correlational and experimental models and ATI-based practice.

Despite decades of research undermining the claims of ATI advocates, contemporary school psychology practice continues to reflect elements of the correlational model with assumptions of ATI relationships. Current practices consistent with this theme focus on cognitive processing, particularly constructs such as working memory, executive functions, and planning. Naturally occurring variations in these and other cognitive processes are used in one of three ways in current school psychology practice: (a) processing variations and deficits are seen as important to the identification of specific learning disabilities (SLD; Fuchs et al., 2011; Hale et al., 2006), (b) processing deficits are used as targets for interventions such as teaching working memory skills or executive functioning processes, and (c) attempts are made to match instruction to cognitive processing strengths to attain improved results.

Little is added to SLD identification using processing strengths and weaknesses since nearly all students, including normal achievers, show strengths and weaknesses over a large battery of intellectual, achievement, and processing tests. Therefore, cognitive strengths and weaknesses do not and cannot distinguish normal from struggling readers. The second use has not been validated due to difficulty in changing processing abilities beyond the stimulus materials used in instruction; that is, alleged improvements do not transfer to other stimulus materials and do not improve academic learning. Finally, no new evidence of ATI exists using the more recent cognitive processes; that is, no evidence exists that improved learning and achievement are produced by matching instructional methods to cognitive processes such as working memory, executive functioning, and planning.

Some contemporary scholars advance the importance of maintaining a processing orientation of SLD (Fuchs et al., 2011), perhaps to ensure some consistency with the federal definition of SLD (34 CFR 300.9). However, even advocates of a cognitive processing orientation acknowledge that the use of cognitive processing either to teach the processes or in ATI matching is not supported by research. Specifically, Fuchs et al. (2011) concluded:

> Scientific evidence does not justify practitioners' use of cognitively focused instruction to accelerate the academic progress of low-performing children with or without apparent cognitive deficits and an SLD label. At the same time, research does not support "shutting the door" on the possibility that cognitively focused interventions may *eventually*

[emphasis added] prove useful to chronically nonresponsive students in rigorous efficacy trials. (p. 102)

The ATI story has not changed since the 1970s. Processing variables may *eventually* prove useful, but they are not currently valid bases for identifying SLD, informing instruction about what to teach, or designing instructional methods, conclusions consistent with those early findings (e.g., Hammill & Larsen, 1974; Ysseldyke, 1971). The question for school psychologists is: To what extent should current services to students be based on currently unvalidated models that eventually may be useful? Our answer is that current use of cognitive processing assessments and interventions are a waste of valuable time and resources.

Problem Solving: RTI

Implementation of problem-solving RTI is accomplished through the creation of multitiered systems that integrate general, remedial, and special education into a single seamless system of educational intervention. The key processes are the use of student RTI as the foundation for all decisions, single-subject designs with time series analysis graphs to assess progress, CBM and behavioral assessment sensitive to growth, empirically validated academic and behavioral interventions, and functional academic and behavioral analysis. The roots of this movement are well established in the history of school psychology (Bergan, 1977; Deno & Mirkin, 1977). Successful models and applications at the state and local levels exist as models for expanded implementation (National Association of State Directors of Special Education, 2005; Reschly & Bergstrom, 2009). The conditions that prompted the paradigm shift are discussed in the next section.

CONTEXTUAL FACTORS IN THE SCHOOL PSYCHOLOGY PARADIGM SHIFT

The school psychology paradigm shift is based on unresolved achievement and behavioral challenges in general, remedial, and special education; research illustrating that improved academic and behavioral outcomes are attainable through evidence-based interventions; policy recommendations from prestigious national organizations, including issuance of *School Psychology: A Blueprint for Training and Practice* and NASP Practice Model documents; and legal changes at the national, state, and local levels.

Contemporary Challenges

Perhaps the most pervasive influence on the paradigm shift is the demand for better results across educational systems and the recognition that previously separated systems of general, remedial, and special education must be integrated more effectively to use resources efficiently and improve outcomes. The paradigm shift depends heavily on research-based academic and behavioral interventions that to date frequently are *not* taught in teacher education programs (Smartt & Reschly, 2007; Walsh, Glaser, & Wilcox, 2006), nor routinely implemented with good treatment fidelity in school psychology practice (Flugum & Reschly, 1994; Telzrow, McNamara, & Hollinger, 2000). Policy analyses and legal requirements (Elementary and Secondary Education Act [ESEA], the 2002 No Child Left Behind Act [NCLB], Individuals with Disabilities Education Act [IDEA]) increasingly demand accountability for results, with strong emphasis on implementation of empirically validated interventions and progress monitoring with changes in interventions that are not meeting goals. For example, NCLB used the phrase "scientifically-based instruction" 183 times along with specifying the criteria for being scientifically based and emphasizing particularly its application in reading instruction. IDEA incorporated by reference the tenets of ESEA and NCLB. Both of the key federal laws (IDEA and ESEA) are overdue for reauthorization in mid-2013. However, there is no suggestion that the accountability expectations in either law will be significantly changed.

Educational Achievement

Many policy makers, business leaders, and government officials believe that current levels of educational achievement in U.S. schools do not meet contemporary or future needs for a highly skilled and well-informed populace. Results are especially disappointing for students with at-risk characteristics, especially the combination of minority status and poverty, and students with disabilities (Aud, Fox, & KewalRamani, 2010; Barton & Coley, 2010; National Assessment of Educational Progress, 2011). In Figure 4.2 we show the percentage of students in the various ethnic groups, students with disabilities, and students of poverty status who performed at the below basic, basic, and proficient levels on 2011 National Assessment of Educational Progress Reading and Math. One can note the significant disparity among groups.

Reading or mathematics competence at a below basic level at fourth or eighth grade has several significant implications including (a) high likelihood of poor reading and mathematics competencies at school completion and in adulthood, (b) increased difficulty with school subjects that require basic reading and math skills and with coping with increasing demands at fourth grade and beyond to use reading and math as a means of learning, (c) increased risk for identification with a high-incidence disability, (d) increased risk of school dropout, (e) increased risk of delinquency and law violations, (f) limited vocational and career opportunities, and (g) increased risk of unemployment during the adult years. Indeed, Aud, Fox, and KewekRamani (2010) and Barton and Coley (2010)

Figure 4.2. National Assessment of Educational Progress Reading and Math by Group

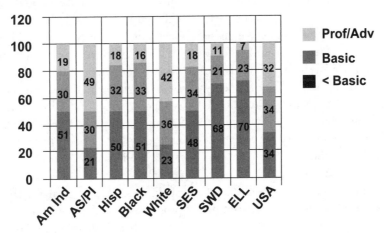

Note. USA = Summary for all U.S. groups; ELL = English language learner; SWD = students with disabilities; SES = socioeconomic status as determined by eligibility for free or reduced-cost school lunch; Hisp = Hispanic; AS/PI = Asian/Pacific Islander; Am Ind = American Indian/Alaska Native; < Basic = less than basic level of performance.

document poorer educational and career outcomes for groups that have a high proportion of students performing at a below basic level in reading and mathematics, including dropout rates, post-high school participation in educational and career opportunities, poorer incomes, higher unemployment, and higher incarceration rates. The increased risk of poor outcomes represented by poor education achievement at the fourth- and eighth-grade levels has vast implications for individuals, groups, and general well-being of society.

The vast majority of students in special education programs have significant reading problems. Reading deficits are the single most frequent reason for referral for special education eligibility consideration (Fletcher et al., 2002). Similar concerns exist in other subject areas, including mathematics and science where achievement levels of students with disabilities and children with at-risk characteristics are markedly below U.S. population averages. Furthermore, U.S. students at all levels of achievement obtain lower scores than comparable students from other economically developed nations on the 2007 Trends in International Math and Science Study (Mullis, Martin, & Foy, 2008). Clearly, there is tremendous pressure on schools and teachers that is created by the fact that the United States is the only nation with a dual focus on educational excellence *and* equity.

Expensive Educational Programs With Equivocal Results

The modern accountability movement has its origins in the 1983 *A Nation at Risk* report, which lamented the low level of achievement of U.S. students relative to those in some other countries. The context in 1984 was the perception of a declining U.S. economy that could not compete successfully with other nations, particularly Japan. The cause of the 1980s economic malaise according to *A Nation at Risk* was the country's low educational standards and achievement. Here is an irony. Over the next two decades, the U.S. economy became the most efficient in the world. Has anyone heard a politician, a public intellectual, or even an educator who attributed the extraordinary improvement in U.S. economic productivity to the public schools? No, probably not. Here is the lesson. Societal problems often are attributed to failings of education. However, schools rarely are credited with causing or contributing significantly to societal and economic advances.

In the mid-1990s federal policy emphasizing greater accountability was significantly advanced after Congress examined the results of the Title I program, established

originally by ESEA. In the early to mid-1990s Congress learned that despite 30 years of funding including billions of dollars, no significant benefits were identified in several Title I evaluations. These findings led to a debate over whether to abolish the program or to increase accountability mechanisms to achieve better results. The result was a marked increase in accountability provisions, primarily in general education and increasingly in special education.

Special education results for students with high-incidence disabilities are equivocal despite substantially greater resources, estimated at about 1.9 times the per student costs in general education (Parrish & Harr-Robins, 2011). High-incidence disabilities including SLD, speech–language impairments, emotional–behavioral disorders, intellectual disabilities, and other health impaired constitute the vast majority of students with disabilities and are a major focus of school psychologists. Students in these categories typically are not identified until school entrance when poor performance in learning, behavior, or both results in teacher referral, determination of disability status, and need for special education. According to several meta-analyses, the overall effects of special education identification and placement are equivocal for high-incidence disabilities (Burns & Ysseldyke, 2009; Kavale, 2005; Kavale & Forness, 1999; Morgan, Frisco, Farkas, & Hibel, 2010). The results of special education, despite significantly larger per student expenditures, are not impressive, particularly for special education self-contained classes (Kavale & Forness, 1999). Although effective special education interventions exist that produce good results (e.g., direct instruction, progress monitoring with formative evaluation, strategy instruction), these interventions are underused and are often poorly implemented (Kavale, 2005). Special education for children with low-incidence and multiple disabilities has been much more effective and is not discussed here.

The achievement test results presented in Figure 4.2 also document unequivocally the achievement gaps between groups in the nation. The achievement gaps are related to minority disproportionality in special education (Donovan & Cross, 2002), a problem that has existed in U.S. schools for more than a century (Dunn, 1968; Kodel, 2002), often leading to close scrutiny of a school psychologist's work regarding the diagnosis of disabilities. Recent analyses show that the assessment procedures used by school psychologists are not the principal cause of minority disproportionality in special education, accompanied by a much greater emphasis on general education problem solving, prevention, and early identification/treatment (Reschly, 2009). IDEA established enhanced regulations prohibiting "significant" disproportionality that have not worked effectively, leading to the likelihood that Congress will establish additional requirements to ameliorate minority disproportionality in the pending IDEA reauthorization.

Three Blueprints on the Future of Training and Practice in School Psychology

Since 1984 three *Blueprints* have been written outlining the future of training and practice in school psychology (Ysseldyke, Reynolds, & Weinberg, 1984; Ysseldyke, Dawson, et al., 1997; Ysseldyke et al., 2006). Each of the *Blueprint* documents (the first developed by the National School Psychology Inservice Training Network at the University of Minnesota and the latter two commissioned by the National Association of School Psychologists [NASP]) outlined domains of competence for the practice of school psychology and provided a stimulus for discussion and debate about future directions for the profession. *Blueprint II* generated open discussion and was adopted as an official policy of NASP in July 1997. In addition, the NASP training standards used *Blueprint II* as a template, adding technology as a separate domain. *Blueprint II* became a template for organization of the annual NASP meeting and for issuance of continuing education units as part of the Nationally Certified School Psychologist program. *Blueprint III* became an organizational template for *Best Practices in School Psychology V* (Thomas & Grimes, 2008). Beginning with *Blueprint I*, university school psychology training programs structured their training standards and competencies around the domains of competence outline in the *Blueprints*. They refined them (and new programs added them) with the issuance of each of the *Blueprint* documents.

In 2010 NASP issued the *Model for Comprehensive and Integrated School Psychological Services*, a model specifying 10 domains of competence that are practically and functionally the equivalent of the 11 domains specified in *Blueprint III*. It serves as a guide to organization and delivery of school psychological services at all levels. The model is designed to be used in conjunction with the NASP *Standards for Graduate Preparation of School Psychologists*, *Standards for the Credentialing of School Psychologists*, and *Principles for Professional Ethics* to guide training and ethical practice.

Research Support for Evidence-Based Practice

Empirically validated interventions and behavioral interventions are the foundations for the paradigm shift described in this chapter. Several researchers have conducted meta-analyses looking at effect sizes for specific interventions. Effect sizes related to these interventions are summarized in Figure 4.3. An effect size from a meta-analysis is the average impact of an intervention compared to a control group stated in terms of standard deviation (SD) units across a large number of studies conducted by independent scholars. Interventions with substantial effect sizes (e.g., > 0.5 SD) generally produce practically significant benefits. In contrast to the effect sizes in Figure 4.3, the effect sizes for traditional special education placements on achievement are in the range of 0.0–0.3 SD (Kavale & Forness, 1999). Effect sizes for aptitude by treatment interactions and training hypothetical psychological processes generally are in this same range (0.0–0.3 SD) (Burns & Ysseldyke, 2009; Kavale, 2005; Kavale & Forness, 1999).

Hattie (2009) produced a synthesis of more than 800 meta-analyses identifying educational approaches that work to advance educational achievement. These meta-analyses show that many instructional practices are superior to others, that there is a science of instruction that can be communicated to others and applied more broadly. Unfortunately,

[i]n the field of education one of the most enduring messages is that "everything seems to work." It is hard to find teachers who say they are "below average" teachers, and everyone (parent, politician, school leader) has a reason why their particular view about teaching or school innovation is likely to be successful. (p. 1)

Hattie (2009) argues that there is a rich evidence base in education, but rarely is it used by teachers, and rarely does it lead to policy changes that have an impact on teaching. He indicates that one factor limiting translation of research to practice has been difficulty summarizing and comparing all the different types of evidence. Tyack and Cuban (1995) contend that little has changed in the practice of teaching over the past century. We have had and continue to have age-grading of students, the self-contained classroom, and division of knowledge into subjects. They argue that many innovations have been variously "welcomed, improved, deflected, co-opted, modified, and sabotaged" (p. 7) and schools have developed cultures and rules to govern the way people behave when in them.

Figure 4.3. Effect Sizes of Different Educational Intervention Principles

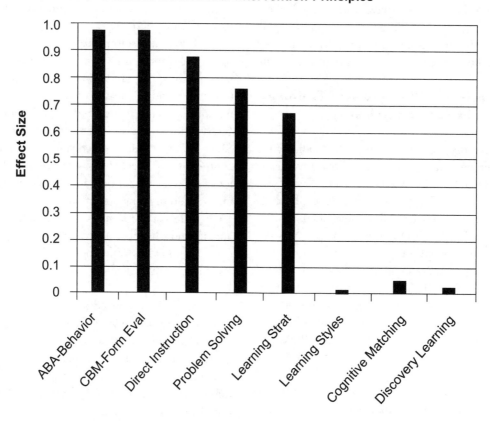

Educational Intervention

Note. ABA = applied behavior analysis; CBM = curriculum-based measurement.

Disconnected Eligibility, Intervention, and Program Evaluation Practices

Traditional classification criteria and eligibility evaluations are largely irrelevant to the development of effective special education services for students with high-incidence disabilities. Traditional eligibility evaluations focus on formulating abstract inferences from limited samples of behavior about hypothetical internal attributes (e.g., intellectual functioning, cognitive processes) that cannot be observed directly or, generally, modified significantly through known interventions. Furthermore, teachers and other school personnel need information on what and how to teach, empirically validated interventions matched to learning and behavior needs, tools to monitor progress and change instruction/intervention that is not working, benchmark data in relation to meeting state-mandated standards, and criteria to exit students from special education services. In short, traditional evaluations do not set the occasion for effective special education treatments, a serious lapse that significantly diminishes the potential benefits of special education.

Much Assessment That Does Not Matter

There are three kinds of assessments: assessments that are technically inadequate, assessments that are technically adequate and do not matter, and assessments that are both technically adequate and matter. Many of the assessment devices administered by school psychologists have been shown to be technically inadequate; that is, they do not have the necessary reliability and validity to be used in making important decisions that have a direct effect on students' life opportunities (Salvia, Ysseldyke, & Bolt, 2013). Many technically adequate assessments do not matter because they do not provide information that leads directly to implementation of interventions with known outcomes. What is needed are technically adequate assessments that lead to interventions with predictable positive outcomes.

Descriptions of changes in assessment needed to improve school psychology services and improve results appeared earlier (Reschly, 1980, 1988) and are featured prominently in the *Blueprint* documents discussed above. Assessment that matters focuses on what can be changed in the environment through instructional and behavioral interventions to produce socially valid results versus the traditional approach of attempting to assess hypothetical constructs that are inferred from behavior and largely unrelated to improved academic or behavioral results.

Dilemma of SLD

Significant changes in SLD classification practices are underway as a result of research leading to the IDEA revision of the special regulations regarding identification of SLD (34 CFR 300.309). Substantial research indicated that the requirement of a severe discrepancy between intellectual ability and academic achievement was deeply flawed due to poor stability over time (unreliability); invalid in the sense of allocating resources; and harmful by delaying treatment, especially with reading problems, to the late third or fourth grade when reading interventions are less successful and more expensive (Fletcher et al., 2002; Gresham, 2002). Alternatives to the severe discrepancy method of identifying SLD were incorporated into IDEA including RTI (Reschly & Bergstrom, 2009). The new regulations specified that state and federal authorities could not require the use of severe discrepancy and mandated that RTI had to be permitted. These changes establish the potential for profound changes in school psychologists' roles related to special education eligibility determination, from testing to find deficits in hypothetical constructs to contributing to the design, implementation, and evaluation of interventions to determine special education eligibility (as part of a comprehensive evaluation; Reschly & Bergstrom, 2009) and progress in special education.

CONTEMPORARY CHANGES IN SCHOOL PSYCHOLOGY TRAINING AND PRACTICE

In earlier editions of *Best Practices*, we (Reschly, 2008; Reschly & Ysseldyke, 2002) wrote generally about the trends in education and training of school psychologists as well as trends in practice. In this edition we focus on the major shifts that have taken place since the 1970s. We begin with the caveat that there is considerable variability among training programs and continuing education efforts and among local education agencies and state education agencies in whether and the extent to which shifts have taken place. In some settings the shifts we talk about are evident, while in others, practices look much like they did in the 1970s. In short, the shift is uneven.

In Table 4.1 we list 11 major shifts that have taken place since the 1970s. Early school psychologists functioned primarily as testers and often played the role of gatekeepers of special education. With publication of the first *Blueprint* there was a call for training and practice to reflect data-driven assessment and accountability, a domain that remained in *Blueprint II* and *III* and the current NASP Practice Model.

Assessment practices in the early years were focused on making predictions: helping decide who could and could not be successful in school, making special education eligibility decisions, and making academic tracking decisions and vocational decisions. Current decisions are directed toward enhancing individual student competence and on helping *all* students be successful in school.

Early assessment efforts were directed at describing student characteristics, strengths and weaknesses, correlates of academic difficulties, and pathology with the

Table 4.1. Major Paradigm Shifts in the Training and Practice of School Psychology Since the 1970s

From	To
Testing to identify disabilities	Assessment of environments, individuals, and systems
Making predictions about success	Enhancing outcomes across domains
Assessment of unobservable hypothetical constructs	Identification of evidence-based interventions matched to needs
Correlated constructs	Experimental, problem solving, services
Refer–test–place	RTI/MTSS applied in general, remedial, and special education
Accountability for processes/procedures	Accountability for results
Identify deficits	Identify strengths, promote resilience
Disability as a defect	Disability as a dimension of human difference
Problems as child centered	Problems as complex interactions of child, expectations, environment, and systems
Insightful test-based analyses and recommendations	Design of evidence-based interventions implemented with good fidelity and treatment integrity
Independent practice based on evaluations, reports, recommendations	Collaboration with teachers, parents, and children to design, implement, and evaluate evidence-based interventions

intended goal of problem admiration rather than problem solving. Since the passage of ESEA and IDEA, the focus has shifted to one of planning or designing evidence-based interventions. ESEA and IDEA call for accountability systems that hold states, districts, and schools accountable for student academic progress. They also call for implementation of evidence-based interventions with all students. The focus on evidence-based interventions is seen in the formation of an APA Division 16 task force on evidence-based interventions and in the work of Kratochwill and Stoiber (2000).

Early assessment and decision-making efforts were characterized by a refer–test–place model. It repeatedly has been demonstrated that most students referred for special education evaluations are in fact determined to be eligible for special education, raising major questions about the value of traditional eligibility evaluations (Algozzine, Christenson, & Ysseldyke, 1982; Ysseldyke & Algozzine, 1981; Ysseldyke, Vanderwood, & Shriner, 1997). We need practices that shift from sifting and sorting students to multitiered serving and supporting of those students.

Two decades ago if a director of special education were asked to describe the nature of his or her district's services the response would be one of outlining processes. The response would be something like: "Our population is composed of students with disabilities with the diagnoses of SLD ($N = 392$), speech/language impairment ($N = 321$), intellectual disability ($N = 47$), emotional disturbance ($N = 39$), visually impaired ($N = 10$), hearing impaired ($N = 11$), and multiple disabilities ($N = 11$). The students are served in resource rooms, self-contained classrooms, homebound settings, residential settings, and regular classrooms." ESEA and IDEA shifted the focus dramatically from processes and procedures to outcomes. The focus shifted to looking at gains in achievement over time and to nonachievement outcomes like personal responsibility and independence, contributions as citizens, getting along with one another, and so forth through standards-based instruction. The current focus is on articulation of high standards; assessments linked to standards; and holding of teachers, schools, and state education agencies accountable for student outcomes.

There has been a shift from a deficit to a resilience perspective. The large majority of school psychological practices during the last three decades of the 20th century were focused on identification of student deficits, dysfunctions, and disabilities. The focus clearly was on identification of student weaknesses for the purpose of designing instructional programs to overcome the weaknesses. During that same time frame, and more recently during the first 14 years of the 21st century, we have seen a shift to a focus on resilience, on individual strengths, and on ways to alter environmental contingencies to enhance student competence (Masten, 2001; Seligman & Czikszentmihalyi, 2000). This shift is parallel to the shift from a search for within-student pathology to problems in environmental context, and from design of programs to accommodate correlates of disability to programs for manipulating environments to remove barriers and improve the probability of success.

Especially since 2000 there has been a major shift in the attribution of problems. The correlational methodology was focused on identifying within-student deficits, disabilities, disorders, and dysfunctions. Problems consistently were attributed to single or multiple within-student factors. The large majority of current practitioners recognize the complex nature of problems and search for interactions between individuals and the environments in which they function. Focus is on assessment of learning environments (Ysseldyke & Christenson, 2002), curriculum, instruction, and instructional strategies and on the ways in which schools are organized.

There has been a significant shift in attention to matters of implementation integrity and fidelity of treatment. This shift stemmed in part from the research finding that implementation integrity was a critical variable in whether or not treatments worked (Bolt, Ysseldyke, & Patterson, 2010; Roach & Elliott, 2008). School psychologists now regularly check to see if the interventions they prescribe are implemented with fidelity by teachers. Major organizations publish implementation checklists. For example, Heartland Area Education Agency 11 in Iowa publishes implementation integrity checklists on more than 20 educational programs ranging from Read Naturally to Peer-Assisted Learning Strategies. The RTI Action Network publishes a self-assessment of problem-solving implementation and a set of RTI implementation rubrics. The National Research Center on Learning Disabilities publishes materials on fidelity of implementation.

The problems that come to the attention of today's school psychologist are complex and multifaceted. They involve an interaction of social, environmental, systems, and individual factors. The problems will not be resolved by single disciplines operating in isolation, but require multiple disciplines, working collaboratively toward solutions.

EXAMPLES FROM CURRENT PRACTICE

Many best practices are illustrated in Jimerson, Burns, and VanDerHeyden (2007). Ikeda et al. (2007) describe lessons learned using a problem-solving approach in Heartland Area Education Agency 11 in Iowa. This chapter is an integration of the many papers that have been written on the statewide model used in Iowa and describes the "whys" and "hows" of large-scale implementation. It affords the reader a very nice primer on the kinds of activities necessary to implement a problem-solving model and an analysis of the factors that make such a model effective. Especially useful is the section on the unintended consequences of changes in practice. Tucker and Sornson (2007) describe the instructional support concept with a focus on implementation with individual students, provide illustrations of how instructional support teams work on a day-to-day basis, and give evidence that the use of such support teams and an experimental model results in reduction of referrals for special education services and improved outcomes for students.

Marston, Lau, and Muyskens (2007) provide an example of implementation of the problem-solving model in the Minneapolis Public Schools. CBM data were used to monitor student progress through the curriculum and to assist teachers in data-driven decision making. The model was used to make decisions about eligibility for special education services. At the same time it was used to free up school psychologists' time to expand their role as a problem solver, as a building leader, and as a systems change facilitator. School psychologists' training in statistics and measurement, evidence-based interventions, and effective instructional strategies, behavioral consultation, and home–school collaboration helps them take a role as an effective facilitator in problem-solving model implementation.

Bollman, Silberglitt, and Gibbons (2007) illustrate the use of a systems-level organization and a multitiered problem-solving process for intervention delivery in the St. Croix River Education District in Minnesota. They describe how they have implemented system-wide, scientifically based instructional practices in reading, data-based measurement practices including CBM, and five elements of school-wide organization: continuous measurement, grade-level team meetings, flexible grouping, grade-level scheduling, and concentrated resources. They describe how they used their systems-level model to promote and enhance achievement in their district. School psychologists were involved in all aspects of planning and implementation of the model.

FUTURE DIRECTIONS

We close this chapter with a broad-lens view of what we see as some very general directions that the field is moving in, clearly more rapidly in some settings than in others.

Data-Based Decision Making and Accountability

Data-Based Decision Making and Accountability is a domain of practice in each of the three *Blueprints* and in the NASP Practice Model (NASP, 2010). It will continue to be a major domain in preparation programs and in practice. In fact, data-based decision making is an important component of activities in all of the domains in the Practice Model. School psychologists operate as scientist-practitioners, gathering data to inform the decisions they make, and gathering evidence about whether the recommendations they make lead to improved academic and mental health outcomes for students. It is expected that practicing school psychologists will be competent in gathering and using information to make decisions, and it is expected that they will remain accountable for the decisions they make.

Focus on Academic and Behavioral Instruction and Interventions

Stiggins (2002) has made an important distinction between assessment *of* learning and assessment *for* learning. He argues that assessment of learning is "built around the mistaken belief that the most important decisions are made by those program planners and policymakers whose actions affect the broadest range of classrooms and students" (p. 759). Stiggins argues that assessments of the future need to be composed of formative assessments along with involving students in the assessment process. Assessments in the future need to be intervention oriented, providing teachers with information they need to provide students with the necessary supports within MTSS. Clearly the efforts of the APA Task Force on Evidence-Based Interventions, along with increasing legal demands in new laws and legislation, will create a tremendous push for using only interventions with demonstrated research support.

The positive behavior interventions and supports (PBIS) system advocated by Sugai and Horner (2002) provides yet another clear example of future practice. According to Sugai and Simonsen (2012), PBIS is

an implementation framework that is designed to enhance academic and social behavior outcomes for all students by (a) emphasizing the use of data for informing decisions about the selection, implementation, and progress monitoring of evidence-based behavioral practices; and (b) organizing resources and systems to improve durable implementation fidelity. (Sugai & Simonsen, 2012, p. 1)

The effectiveness of PBIS is supported by a wide range of data, including a randomized controlled trial (Horner et al., 2009). Other proactive and preventive strategies also have great promise (e.g., Bradshaw, Zmuda, Kellam, & Ialongo, 2009).

Increased Use of Problem Solving and Progress Monitoring

Throughout this chapter we have talked about the promise of the problem-solving, progress-monitoring, and formative-evaluation approaches to student assessment and intervention planning. There currently are technology-enhanced systems for enabling teachers to assess students' zone of proximal development and assign work matched to student skill level. We expect to see increased use of these systems in the future.

Dissemination of Research and Online Resources

The gap between research findings and practitioner access has tightened exponentially since 1970. Numerous online sources exist for evidence-based interventions and direct assessments of academic and behavioral skills. Judicious use of these resources still is required, along with judgments about what is and is not evidence based. A significant part of graduate preparation today involves educating students (and many times senior faculty) in the use of online resources.

Improved Training of Practicing School Psychologists and Researchers

In the 1990s there were no clear directions on what school psychology training and practice ought to look like. With publication of the three *Blueprints*, direction became clearer, and both preservice and inservice training were affected. Standards for training and practice were built, and the NASP Practice Model was adopted. The current standards for both training and practice are mapped to the NASP Practice Model. Direction for accreditation, the continuing education

system, and training are clearer than ever before. We expect that over time both training and practice will reflect the NASP Practice Model and that both will be vastly improved.

School psychology has changed in positive directions that enhance the benefits of our work for children, teachers and parents, classrooms, schools, and systems. Practice today is variable as it always has been. However, the balance is shifting toward evidence-based services that focus on prevention, early identification and early treatment of problems, and, when necessary, intense interventions for children needing longer term and more complex treatments. School psychologists in the future will build on the foundations that exist today and move toward more effective services.

AUTHOR NOTE

Disclosure. James E. Ysseldyke has a financial interest in books he authored or coauthored referenced in this chapter.

REFERENCES

Algozzine, B., Christenson, S., & Ysseldyke, J. E. (1982). Probabilities associated with the referral to placement process. *Teacher Education and Special Education, 5*, 19–23.

Arter, J. A., & Jenkins, J. R. (1977). Examining the benefits and prevalence of modality considerations in special education. *Journal of Special Education, 11*, 281–298.

Aud, S., Fox, M. S., & KewalRamani, A. (2010). *Status and trends in the education of racial and ethnic groups*. Washington, DC: National Center for Education Statistics.

Barton, P. E., & Coley, R. J. (2010). *The Black-White achievement gap: When progress stopped*. Princeton, NJ: Education Testing Service.

Bergan, J. R. (1977). *Behavioral consultation*. Columbus, OH: Merrill.

Bergan, J. R., & Kratochwill, T. R. (1990). *Behavioral consultation and therapy*. New York, NY: Plenum.

Bijou, S. (1968). *What Psychology Has to Offer Education—Now!* Invited Address to Division 16 of the American Psychological Association, September 1, 1968. San Francisco, CA.

Bijou, S. (1970). What psychology has to offer education—now. *Journal of Applied Behavior Analysis, 3*, 65–71.

Bollman, K. A., Silberglitt, B., & Gibbons, K. A. (2007). The St. Croix River education district model: Incorporating systems-level organization and a multitiered problem-solving process for intervention delivery. In S. R. Jimerson, M. K. Burns, & A. M. VanDerHeyden (Eds.), *Handbook of response to intervention: The science and practice of assessment and intervention* (pp. 319–330). New York, NY: Springer.

Bolt, D., Ysseldyke, J. D., & Patterson, M. (2010). Students, teachers, and schools as sources of variability, integrity, and sustainability in implementing progress monitoring. *School Psychology Review, 39*, 612–630.

Bradshaw, C. P., Zmuda, J. H., Kellam, S. G., & Ialongo, N. S. (2009). Longitudinal impact of two universal preventive interventions in first grade on educational outcomes in high school. *Journal of Educational Psychology, 101*, 926–937.

Burns, M. K., & Ysseldyke, J. E. (2009). Prevalence of evidence-based practices in special education. *Journal of Special Education, 43*, 3–11.

Cronbach, L. J. (1957). The two disciplines of scientific psychology. *American Psychologist, 12*, 671–684.

Cronbach, L. J. (1975). Beyond the two disciplines of scientific psychology. *American Psychologist, 30*, 116–127.

Deno, S. L. (1985). Curriculum-based measurement: The emerging alternative. *Exceptional Children, 52*, 219–232.

Deno, S. L., & Mirkin, P. K. (1977). *Data-based program modification: A manual*. Minneapolis, MN: Leadership Training Institute for Special Education, University of Minnesota.

Donovan, M. S., & Cross, C. T. (2002). *Minority students in special and gifted education*. Washington, DC: National Academies Press.

Dunn, L. (1968). Special education for the mildly retarded: Is much of it justifiable? *Exceptional Children, 35*, 5–22.

Dunn, R., & Dunn, K. (2001). *Teaching elementary students through their individual learning styles: Practical approaches for grades 3–6*. Boston, MA: Allyn & Bacon.

Fletcher, J. M., Lyon, G. R., Barnes, M., Stuebing, K. K., Francis, D. J., Olson, R. K., & Shaywitz, S. E. (2002). Classification of learning disabilities: An evidence-based evaluation. In R. Bradley, L. Danielson, & D. P. Hallahan (Eds.), *Identification of learning disabilities: Research to practice* (pp. 185–250). Mahwah, NJ: Erlbaum.

Flugum, K. R., & Reschly, D. J. (1994). Prereferral interventions: Quality indices and outcomes. *Journal of School Psychology, 32*, 1–14.

Fuchs, D., Hale, J. B., & Kearns, D. M. (2011). On the importance of a cognitive processing perspective: An introduction. *Journal of Learning Disabilities, 44*, 99–104.

Gresham, F. M. (2002). Responsiveness to intervention: An alternative approach to the identification of learning disabilities. In R. Bradley, L. Danielson, & D. P. Hallahan (Eds.), *Identification of learning disabilities: Research to practice* (pp. 467–519). Mahwah, NJ: Erlbaum.

Hale, J. G., Kaufman, A. S., Naglieri, J. A., & Kavale, K. A. (2006). Implementing IDEA: Integrating response to intervention and cognitive assessment methods. *Psychology in the Schools, 43*, 753–770.

Hammill, D., & Larsen, S. (1974). The effectiveness of psycholinguistic training. *Exceptional Children, 41*, 5–14.

Hattie, J. (2009). *Visible learning: A synthesis of over 800 meta-analyses relating to achievement*. New York, NY: Routledge.

Horner, R. H., Sugai, G., Smolkowski, K., Eber, L., Nakasato, J., Todd, A. W., & Experanza, J. (2009). A randomized, wait-list controlled effectiveness trial assessing school-wide positive behavior support in elementary schools. *Journal of Positive Behavior Interventions, 11*, 133–144.

Ikeda, M. J., Rahn-Blakeslee, A., Niebling, B. C., Gustafson, J. K., Allison, R., & Stumme, J. (2007). The Heartland Area Education Agency 11 problem-solving approach: An overview and lessons learned. In S. R. Jimerson, M. K. Burns, & A. M. VanDerHeyden (Eds.), *Handbook of response to intervention: The science and practice of assessment and intervention* (pp. 255–268). New York, NY: Springer.

Jimerson, S. R., Burns, M. K., & VanDerHeyden, A. M. (2007). *Handbook of response to intervention: The science and practice of assessment and intervention*. New York, NY: Springer.

Kavale, K. A. (2005). Effective intervention for students with specific learning disability: The nature of special education. *Learning Disabilities, 13*, 127–138.

Kavale, K. A., & Forness, S. R. (1999). Effectiveness of special education. In C. R. Reynolds & T. B. Gutkin (Eds.), *The handbook of school psychology* (3rd ed., pp. 984–1024). Hoboken, NJ: Wiley.

Kodel, K. (2002). *Elizabeth Farrell and the history of special education*. Arlington, VA: Council for Exceptional Children.

Kratochwill, T., & Stoiber, K. (2000). Empirically supported interventions and school psychology: Conceptual and practical issues, Part II. *School Psychology Quarterly, 38*, 349–358.

Marston, D., Lau, M., & Muyskens, P. (2007). Implementation of the problem-solving model in the Minneapolis public schools. In S. R. Jimerson, M. K. Burns, & A. M. VanDerHeyden (Eds.), *Handbook of response to intervention: The science and practice of assessment and intervention* (pp. 279–287). New York, NY: Springer.

Masten, A. (2001). Ordinary magic: Resilience processes in development. *American Psychologist, 56*, 227–238.

Morgan, P. L., Frisco, M., Farkas, G., & Hibel, J. (2010). A propensity score matching and analysis of the effects of special education. *Journal of Special Education, 43*, 236–254.

Mullis, I. V. S., Martin, M. O., Foy, P. (with Olson, J. F., Preuschoff, C., Erberben, C., Arora, A., & Galia, J.). (2008). *TIMSS 2007 international mathematics report: Findings from IEA's trends in international mathematics and science study at the fourth and eighth grades*. Chestnut Hill, MA: TIMSS and PIRLS International Study Center, Boston College.

National Assessment of Educational Progress. (2011). *The nation's report card: Reading, math*. Washington DC: National Center for Education Statistics.

National Association of School Psychologists. (2010). *Model for comprehensive and integrated school psychological services*. Bethesda, MD: Author. Retrieved from http://www.nasponline.org/standards/2010standards/2_PracticeModel.pdf

National Association of State Directors of Special Education. (2005). *Response to intervention: Policy considerations and implementation*. Alexandria, VA: Author.

Parrish, T., & Harr-Robins, J. (2011). Fiscal policy and funding for special education. In J. M. Kauffman & D. P. Hallahan (Eds.), *Handbook of special education* (pp. 363–377). New York, NY: Routledge.

Reschly, D. J. (1980). School psychologists and assessment in the future. *Professional Psychology, 11*, 841–848.

Reschly, D. J. (1988). Special education reform: School psychology revolution. *School Psychology Review, 17*, 459–475.

Reschly, D. J. (2008). School psychology RTI paradigm shift and beyond. In A. Thomas & J. Grimes (Eds.), *Best practices in school psychology V* (pp. 3–15). Bethesda, MD: National Association of School Psychologists.

Reschly, D. J. (2009). *Prevention of disproportionate special education representation using response to intervention*. Washington DC: Learning Point Associates. Retrieved from http://inpathways.net/TQ_Issue_Paper_RTI_Disproportionality.pdf

Reschly, D. J., & Bergstrom, M. K. (2009). Response to intervention. In T. B. Gutkin & C. R. Reynolds (Eds.), *The handbook of school psychology* (4th ed., pp. 434–460). Hoboken, NJ: Wiley.

Reschly, D. J., & Ysseldyke, J. E. (2002). Paradigm shift: The past is not the future. In A. Thomas & J. Grimes (Eds.), *Best practices in school psychology IV* (pp. 3–20). Bethesda, MD: National Association of School Psychologists.

Rittle-Johnson, B., Star, J. R., & Durkin, K. (2009). The importance of prior knowledge when comparing examples: Influences on conceptual and procedural knowledge of equation solving. *Journal of Educational Psychology, 101*, 836–852.

Roach, A., & Elliott, S. N. (2008). Best practices in facilitating and evaluating intervention integrity. In A. Thomas & J. Grimes (Eds.), *Best practices in school psychology V* (pp. 195–208). Bethesda, MD: National Association of School Psychologists.

Salvia, J., Ysseldyke, J., & Bolt, S. (2013). *Assessment in special and inclusive education.* Belmont, CA: Wadsworth.

Seligman, M. E. P., & Czikszentmihalyi, M. (2000). Positive psychology [Special issue]. *American Psychologist, 55*(1).

Smartt, S. M., & Reschly, D. J. (2007). *Preparation of teachers to teach reading.* Nashville, TN: National Comprehensive Center on Teacher Quality.

Stiggins, R. (2002). Assessment crisis: The absence of assessment FOR learning. *Phi Delta Kappan, 83*, 758–765.

Sugai, G., & Horner, R. (2002). The evolution of discipline practices: School-wide positive behavior supports. *Child & Family Behavior Therapy, 24*(1–2), 23–50.

Sugai, G., & Simonsen, B. (2012). *Positive behavioral interventions and supports: History, defining features, and misconceptions.* Storrs, CT: University of Connecticut Center for Positive Behavioral Interventions and Supports.

Telzrow, C. F., McNamara, K., & Hollinger, C. L. (2000). Fidelity of problem-solving implementation and relationship to student performance. *School Psychology Review, 29*, 443–461.

Thomas, A., & Grimes, J. (Eds.). (2008). *Best practices in school psychology V.* Bethesda, MD: National Association of School Psychologists.

Tucker, J., & Sornson, R. O. (2007). One student at a time, one teacher at a time: Reflections on the use of instructional support. In S. R. Jimerson, M. K. Burns, & A. M. VanDerHeyden (Eds.), *Handbook of response to intervention: The science and practice of assessment and intervention* (pp. 269–278). New York, NY: Springer.

Tyack, D. B., & Cuban, L. (1995). *Tinkering toward utopia: A century of public school reform.* Cambridge, MA: Harvard University Press.

Walsh, K., Glaser, D., & Wilcox, D. D. (2006). *What education schools aren't teaching about reading and what elementary teachers aren't learning.* Washington DC: National Center on Teacher Quality.

Ysseldyke, J. E. (1971). Diagnostic-prescriptive teaching: The search for aptitude by treatment interactions. In L. Mann & D. Sabatino (Eds.), *The first review of special education* (Vol. 1, pp. 5–32). Philadelphia, PA: Buttonwood Farms.

Ysseldyke, J. E., & Algozzine, B. (1981). Diagnostic classification decisions as a function of referral information. *Journal of Special Education, 15*, 429–435.

Ysseldyke, J. E., Burns, M. K., Dawson, P., Kelley, B., Morrison, D., Ortiz, S., … Telzrow, C. (2006). *School psychology: A blueprint for training and practice III.* Bethesda, MD: National Association of School Psychologists.

Ysseldyke, J. E., & Christenson, S. (2002). *Functional assessment of academic behavior.* Longmont, CO: Sopris West.

Ysseldyke, J. E., Dawson, P., Lehr, C., Reschly, D., Reynolds, M., & Telzrow, C. (1997). *School psychology: A blueprint for the future of training and practice II.* Bethesda, MD: National Association of School Psychologists.

Ysseldyke, J. E., Reynolds, M. C., & Weinberg, R. A. (1984). *School psychology: A blueprint for training and practice.* Minneapolis, MN: National School Psychology Inservice Training Network.

Ysseldyke, J. E., Vanderwood, M., & Shriner, J. (1997). Changes over the past decade in special education referral to placement probability. *Diagnostique, 23*, 193–201.

Section 2
Data-Based Decision Making and Accountability

5 Best Practices in Problem Analysis

Theodore J. Christ
Yvette Anne Arañas
University of Minnesota

OVERVIEW

The purpose of this chapter is to describe the theoretical foundations and practical significance of problem analysis. While a *problem* is defined as an unacceptable discrepancy between expected and observed performance, *problem analysis* is the systematic process of assessment and evaluation to better understand the nature and possible solution for the problem. Problem analysis includes the collection, summary, and use of information to verify or reject relevant hypotheses related to both the cause and solution of a problem. Problem analysis contributes to the Data-Based Decision Making and Accountability domain in the National Association of School Psychologists (NASP) *Model for Comprehensive and Integrated School Psychological Services* (NASP, 2010), which requires that practitioners competently use assessments and data to assess and meet the needs of students.

This chapter describes the theoretical foundation of problem analysis and describes its relevance at the individual, group, and systems levels. School psychologists who are not experts in a specific content area will learn how to use a content-specific hypothesis-testing framework as a guide to formulate intervention recommendations. This chapter encourages school psychologists to seek or develop additional content-specific frameworks to organize hypothesis testing and make concrete connections to the relevant research.

BASIC CONSIDERATIONS

Problem analysis is best guided by context- and content-specific expertise. The context is often the school and classroom setting. The content is often related to academic or social–emotional skills and performance. A school psychologist who lacks expertise in either the context or content might still function as a successful problem analyst if he or she relies on science and evidence to make decisions. This section establishes that problem analysis is scientific, relies on low-level inferences, and focuses on alterable variables.

Scientific Method

An understanding and appreciation for science is inherent to problem analysis. Both the scientific method and scientific body of evidence inform problem analysis. In brief, the scientific method is the process of inquiry and discovery. The scientific body of evidence is the knowledge, interventions, and evidence-based practices that emerge from systematic research.

The steps for problem analysis are consistent with that of the scientific method. They are (a) identify a problem; (b) hypothesize likely causes; (c) select methods for assessment such as reviews, interviews, observations, and tests; (d) collect data; (e) review data; and (f) revise hypotheses regarding likely causes or, if the cause is isolated, form a hypothesized solution. Table 5.1 presents an application of the scientific method to an example of a student with a reading problem.

There are two types of hypotheses associated with problem analysis: analytic and intervention (see Table 5.2). An analytic hypothesis is developed in the second step of the scientific method and relates to the likely causes of the problem. Analytic hypotheses guide analysis with improved articulation of the purpose for data collection. That is, data are collected for a reason and analytic hypotheses define those reasons throughout problem analysis. An example of an analytic hypothesis

Table 5.1. The Six Steps of the Scientific Method and Problem Analysis

Scientific Method	Problem Analysis	Example
Observe and identify the problem of interest	Identify the problem	Teacher observes that a student is struggling in reading
Develop and identify relevant hypotheses	Hypothesize likely causes and maintaining conditions (analytic hypotheses)	*General:* • Poor instructional match • Low exposure to instruction • Poor curricular match • Need for more practice • Inaccurate critical skills • Low rate critical skills • Low motivation/incentive *Specific:* • Inaccurate performance oral reading performance • Low rate or automaticity on oral reading
Design and select procedures to test relevant hypotheses	Select methods for assessment such as reviews, interviews, observations, and tests	*General:* • Review educational records • Interview the student and teacher • Observe student performance within instructional conditions and interacting with the curriculum • Test with oral reading assessments to calculate the percent of words read correctly (accuracy) and the number of correct words per minute (rate); use vocabulary and comprehension measures as necessary • Test the student response to a targeted intervention aimed at the maintaining variable (e.g., incentivized performance, repeated practice, timed practice, instruction and curricular match)
Collect data	Collect the data	Review, interview, observe, test
Analyze and synthesize data	Review data	Synthesize the data to evaluate and address possible causes and maintain conditions so to inform intervention actions
Devise a tentative conclusion	Revise hypotheses regarding likely causes or form an hypothesized solution (intervention hypotheses)	• *Intervention:* The student requires targeted practice of vowel and consonant diagraphs to establish accuracy and automaticity for work attached and word identification • *Goal:* The student identifies four words correctly in 1 minute (35% accuracy) when presented with a list of words with vowel and consonant diagraphs; if the intervention is effective, then the student will gain three words per minute per week with increased levels of accuracy until the student reaches 65 words read correctly in 1 minute (95% accuracy)

is, "The student cannot read because he or she struggles to decode words." The second type of hypothesis is an intervention hypothesis, which is developed during the final step of the scientific method. This hypothesis relates to the likely solutions for a problem. An example of an intervention hypothesis is, "A phonics intervention will teach the student how to match sounds to letters and subsequently improve reading performance." Intervention recommendations are defined as hypotheses because problem solutions are tentative until demonstrated as effective. Intervention hypotheses

emerge from analytic hypotheses. A common error in problem analysis is omitting analytical hypothesis testing and immediately performing intervention hypothesis testing. This error frequently leads to failed intervention attempts, wasted resources, and frustrated staff.

Analytic hypotheses function to formulate and test the supposed causes of a problem. For example, there are common analytic hypotheses that should be tested when there are reading problems in a particular grade. These analytic hypotheses may address prior exposure to effective instruction, instructional match, and the

Table 5.2. Example Analytic and Intervention Hypotheses for Reading

Analytic Hypotheses	Intervention Hypotheses
There is a poor instructional match (e.g., pacing, feedback) that contributes to insufficient growth. For example: the material is presented too quickly.	If provided instruction at a slower pace with increased feedback, then the student will demonstrate more rapid growth.
There is a poor curricular match that contributes to insufficient growth. For example: level of the material is too difficult.	If provided with curriculum materials that match or more closely approximate the student's skills, then the student will demonstrate more rapid growth.
There are inaccurate critical skills (e.g., does not know letter sounds, diagraphs, or sight words) that contribute to insufficient growth.	If provided with demonstration and slow deliberate practice, then the student will demonstrate more rapid growth toward performance at 95% or greater accuracy.
There is a low performance rate on critical skills that contributes to insufficient growth. For example: accurate and slow decoding and word identification.	If provided with incrementally faster paced practice with feedback, then the student will demonstrate more rapid growth toward automatic performance.
There is a low motivation or lack of incentives that contribute to insufficient growth. For example: the student can perform when provided sufficient incentives, which might be more interesting materials, activities, or tangibles.	If provided with an incentive to improve performance, then the student will demonstrate more rapid growth toward work completion and higher levels of performance on classroom assessments.

achievement of relevant foundational skills. When formulating analytic hypotheses for academic problems, it may be helpful for school psychologists and educators to refer to a set of research- and evidence-based standards such as the Common Core State Standards (National Governors Association Center for Best Practices & Council of Chief State School Officers, 2010) for reading, mathematics, and other subjects. Finally, it might also be useful to reference hierarchies of skill development so to discern the likely sequence of skill acquisition and instruction. Such hierarchies can help to conceptualize a sequence of analytical hypotheses.

Poor instruction might have caused the problem. Deficit skills that are inconsistent with the task demands for third-grade reading might maintain the problem. The process that begins with analytic hypotheses must progress to intervention hypotheses so that problem analysis concludes with useful recommendations. Some examples are presented in Table 5.2, which illustrates how analytic hypotheses (supposed causes) are associated with intervention hypotheses (possible solutions).

It is more helpful to organize hypothesis statements into a hypothesis-testing framework, which can effectively guide the process. Figure 5.1 presents an example of a hypothesis-testing framework for reading, which incorporates some information about reading interventions from Scammaca, Vaughn, Roberts, Wanzek, and Torgesen (2007) and unpublished meetings with K. Bollman, M. C. Coolong-Chaffin, and D. Wagner (personal communication, March 21, 2013). This example is discussed in more detail in Figure 5.1 and

is only intended to serve as an illustration. We strongly encourage researchers and practitioners to develop, evaluate, and refine their own hypothesis-testing frameworks. They have the potential to both refine the analytic process for professionals and document the process, which requires substantial expertise in the content and context of school-based problems.

Levels of Inference

An *inference* is a tentative conclusion or assumption that lacks explicit support from available data. Hypotheses are inferences by definition. It is critical that problem analysts make distinctions between what is known and what is inferred or hypothesized. There are two types of approaches in making inferences: high inference and low inference. A high inference approach typically relies on theoretical, within-person constructs such as personality, psychopathology, or aptitude profiles. Such constructs are difficult to observe directly and they tend to rely on the assumption that outward behaviors are merely symptoms of an internal trait. Evidently, this approach requires a number of assumptions whose veracity is often unknown.

A low inference approach relies on direct observation of explicit behaviors and testable hypotheses. In contrast to the high inference approach, this requires relatively few untested assumptions. Examples of low inference hypotheses include (a) lack of quality instruction, (b) poor curriculum match, (c) poor instructional match, (d) insufficient opportunities for practice, (e) inaccurate critical skills, and (f) low rate

Figure 5.1. An Example of a Problem Analysis Hypothesis Framework for Reading

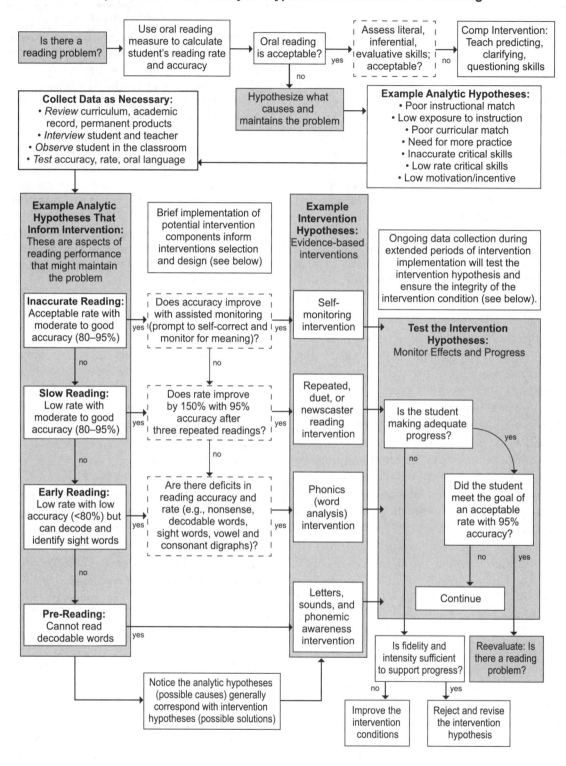

skills. These hypotheses are preferred over high inference hypotheses because they are based on testable assumptions. Thus, low-level inferences should take precedence and should be exhausted prior to the use of high-level inferences. Moreover, the most relevant analytic hypotheses and approaches will emphasize those variables that can be altered to have an impact in solving a problem. Low-level inferences and alterable hypotheses are most closely linked with successful problem solutions.

Alterable Causal and Maintaining Variables

Problem analysis aims to identify variables that both cause and maintain problems. *Causal variables* are usually historical, such as insufficient nutrition, disadvantaged experiences, or lack of prior exposure to effective instruction. *Maintaining variables* persist in the present context to influence and sustain the problem. Although there are both biological and ecological variables that interact to cause and maintain problems, the goal of analysis is to promote problem solutions rather than ruminate about unalterable conditions. Problem analysis aims to examine causal and maintaining variables that can be manipulated by an intervention team. Variables such as instruction, classroom rules, and seating arrangements are considered to be *alterable variables*. In contrast, inalterable variables are irrelevant unless they interact with the alterable variables. For example, physical impairments such as blindness or deafness are inalterable. However, such impairments might help explain why previous instruction was ineffective and consequently guide future strategies, thus interacting with alterable variables.

Alterable variables are usually in the ecology (e.g., class instruction and curriculum) and not within the learner. The learner's environment is composed of a large number of alterable variables that influence performance, such as seating arrangements and classroom rules. A problem analyst can hypothesize that the arrangement of the ecology will promote desirable outcomes and can monitor student's progress to test this hypothesis.

Characteristics of Novice and Expert Analysts

In school psychology, an effective and efficient problem analyst is expected to have context-specific expertise in instruction, curriculum, and ecological variables that interact with learner variables. A problem analyst needs content-specific expertise in reading, writing, mathematics, classroom behavior, and social development. Unfortunately, many school psychologists develop substantial expertise in test interpretation with modest knowledge of the context and content of education. For that reason, many school psychologists are novices at problem analysis because they lack domain-specific expertise (i.e., context and content knowledge).

Those with area-specific knowledge and experience are likely to employ a top-down approach to problem analysis. Experts use their content- and context-specific knowledge and experiences for problem analysis. They are more likely than novices to sample information about a problem strategically and search for familiar patterns, principles, and concepts associated with possible problem solutions. Familiarity with area-specific patterns and procedures enables experts to identify the most relevant variables, ignore trivial details, and generally combine complex patterns into meaningful chunks of information. For example, when a student is disruptive in the classroom, an expert behavior analyst is more likely to focus on the causal mechanisms and functions of the problem behavior. The expert may find that the behaviors function to access peer attention, access teacher attention, or escape task demands. When addressing a problem, the expert is likely to extract the most relevant information to analyze and represent a problem using a goal-directed, top-down approach.

In contrast, a novice is likely to rely on a bottom-up approach for problem analysis because he or she has limited knowledge and experience. The novice often focuses on the extraneous or surface-level variables associated with a problem. It is more difficult for the novice to strategically identify and attend to the most relevant information. A novice behavior analyst might focus on the topography of a target behavior or irrelevant antecedents rather than on the function of the behavior. Despite these difficulties, novice school psychologists can solve problems effectively without having content- and context-specific knowledge. They can use systematic hypothesis-testing frameworks to solve a given problem. In the example of the disruptive student, a novice problem analyst can develop a functionally based set of analytic hypotheses to guide problem analysis. These hypotheses also can yield intervention hypotheses. For example, if problem analysis supported the hypothesis that disruption functioned to escape from task demands (e.g., difficult math work), then the likely intervention hypothesis might include a replacement behavior for escape (e.g., escape cards) with modified task demands (e.g., ensure instructional match).

BEST PRACTICES IN PROBLEM ANALYSIS

The prior section established that problem analysis by school psychologists incorporates the scientific method, low levels of inference, alterable variables, and expert knowledge of both the context and content. In practice, it takes time for school psychologists to develop these skills and an appreciation of their value. Therefore, best practices in problem analysis is facilitated by selected implementation of problem analysis with a multitiered system of support. It is also facilitated by selective use of systematic hypothesis testing frameworks, which make the process explicit and enhances the potential for wide-scale implementation.

Problem Solving and Multitiered Systems of Support

A school psychologist must identify the problem, classify it, and analyze it at the systems, group, or individual level before selecting or implementing an intervention. That is, it is necessary to have information about a problem to understand why it occurs. It is a common error to select an evidence-based or a well-marketed intervention; however, this well-marketed intervention might be improperly aligned with a local problem. Evidence-based interventions work for particular populations with specified deficits. No intervention works generically to solve all problems. It is problem analysis that helps align solutions with the problem at hand.

Problem Analysis for the System, Group, and Individual

A multitiered system of support is highly inefficient if all problems are analyzed at the individual student level. It is much more efficient to evaluate the prevalence of a particular problem to align the scope of the intervention with the scope of the problem. Therefore, problem solving and problem analysis occur at the systems level so that core curriculum, instruction, and support are assessed, evaluated, and refined. It is very common for school psychologists to observe reading performance, math performance, or behavior as a prevalent problem that is best addressed with systemic changes. Those systemic changes are guided by careful analysis.

Regardless of the quality of systemic supports, some groups and individuals will require supplemental and intensive supports. Most problems in education are not individual student problems. Rather, they are typically more pervasive. Because problem analysis on the individual student level is the most inefficient use of resources, it is worthwhile to consider systemic and group analysis first and reserve individualized problem analysis for uncommon cases. The value of efficiency is consistent with the goals of working smarter, not harder; doing less, but doing it better; and doing it once, but for extended amounts of time. Problem analysis should enhance decisions about what is done, how it is done, for whom it is done, and for what reasons it is done. Ultimately, problem analysis is about an alignment of

problem characteristics with problem solutions or interventions.

Problem Analysis Precedes Standard Protocol

It is common for school psychologists to employ a standard protocol approach as part of a multitiered system of supports. This standard protocol provides a default approach to intervention for common problems. This approach is relatively easy to implement because it uses the same intervention or treatment for all students who have similar problems in a particular area (Fuchs, Mock, Morgan, & Young, 2003). Standard protocols, however, do not address individual differences and do not emphasize problem analysis. To address this gap, school psychologists can use problem analysis to refine standard protocols so that they understand the type of problems and solutions before selecting a standard intervention program. For example, students with routine deficits in early reading are likely to benefit from an evidence-based phonics intervention. Initially, that intervention must be selected or developed with problem-specific knowledge that emerges through problem analysis. After implementation and evaluation, a high quality solution is readily available in the education system. That intervention becomes standard protocol for use in the future. Thereafter, problem identification and problem analysis function to match identified problems efficiently with standardized interventions.

Theoretical Orientations Guide Systematic Hypothesis-Testing Frameworks

A variety of theoretical orientations can support hypothesis testing and support problem analysis. For instance, *developmental theories* provide information about typical development among children and can inform what kind of instruction and interventions are needed to promote learning and growth in students who are developing differently from these trajectories. Other theoretical orientations can inform interventions specifically for academic skill deficits. The *instructional hierarchy*, for example, provides a framework that postulates that skills progress in four stages: acquisition, fluency, generalization, and adaptation (Daly, Lentz, & Boyer, 1996; Haring & Eaton, 1978). An *applied behavioral analysis* orientation can be useful to develop hypotheses about which environmental events predict and maintain a target behavior, especially when a student has a performance deficit. It is also useful to guide task analysis and the construction of skills hierarchies.

Curriculum-based assessment and curriculum-based evaluation can inform problem analysis. Curriculum-based assessment is particularly relevant to problem analysis because it is used to assess students within the context of their curriculum content and learning needs (Hintze, Christ, & Methe, 2006). Curriculum-based evaluation provides an intricate hypothesis-testing framework across both academic and social skill domains such as reading, mathematics, written expression, language, social skills, and task-related behavior. The curriculum-based evaluation hypothesis-testing framework usually is presented in a series of flowcharts with corresponding decision-making rules and assumes that performance discrepancies exist because prior knowledge or skills have yet to be established. For more details about curriculum-based evaluation, see Hosp, Hosp, Howell, and Allison (2014).

Understanding the limitations of applying certain theories is important to effective problem analysis. For instance, hypotheses related to general intelligence are usually limited to diagnosing developmental disabilities, but the diagnoses are not necessarily useful in selecting instruction and interventions. The traditional framework of using test-based trait and aptitude profiles relies on high inference approaches and distal measurements and thus is not very consistent with effective problem analysis.

Development and Use of Systematic Hypothesis-Testing Frameworks

School psychologists are expected to use context- and content-specific expertise to solve academic and social behavior problems. Unfortunately, many school psychologists lack training and expertise across the many context and content domains within educational systems. The breadth and depth of academic, behavioral, and socioemotional problems that school psychologists address are substantial. Because it is not always possible to be independent experts for all the problems that might arise in schools, practitioners can develop and use content-specific systematic hypothesis-testing frameworks to address problems. Such frameworks can provide explicit guidance, particularly when a school psychologist lacks expertise in a specific content area. In problem analysis, an effective framework should (a) derive from evidence-based practices; (b) be embedded within the scientific method; (c) emphasize low inference methods of assessment and evaluation; (d) evaluate alterable causal and maintaining variables; and (e) integrate expert approaches of analysis, which embed

navigational aids so that the sequence and targets of evaluation are optimized.

Effective problem analysis seeks to establish knowledge in assessment and evaluation to optimize content-specific problem analysis. Identifying and developing explicit hypothesis-testing frameworks will contribute to establish the school psychologist as a problem analyst. There are some early examples that might inform future development, including curriculum-based evaluation and curriculum-based assessment for instructional design and applied behavior analysis. Each provides some systematic approach to assessment and evaluation to declare relevant analytic hypotheses. When a school psychologist lacks expertise, hypothesis-testing frameworks provide scaffolds and a system of support to guide analysis. Likewise, hypothesis-testing frameworks guide the identification of problem solutions. For example, deficits in a critical foundational skill area might disable learning and, thereby, establish and maintain learning problems.

Examples of Systematic Hypothesis-Testing Frameworks

There are two examples of systematic hypothesis-testing frameworks. The first was presented in Figure 5.1 and it uses oral reading assessments to illustrate a simple and familiar hypothesis-testing framework. This example begins with an oral reading assessment, such as curriculum-based measurement of oral reading (CBM-R). This is a useful starting point because many schools use CBM-R for universal screening, which is useful to identify reading problems. It is at that point that problem analysis begins with the development and consideration of relevant analytic hypotheses related to causal and maintaining variables. Some examples are listed in Figure 5.1. Data subsequently are collected from interviews, observations, tests, and reviews of extant data and evaluated to inform the use of analytic hypotheses. The figure illustrates tests of skills-based oral reading deficits. The bottom left section of that figure is intended to illustrate how the analytic hypotheses and intervention hypotheses/recommendations generally correspond, such that analytics inform interventions. The bottom right section of that figure illustrates the way in which ongoing progress monitoring functions to continually test and update the intervention hypothesis. Although this particular example lends itself to problem analysis of individual students or small groups, problem analysis often will apply to larger groups of students.

Figure 5.2. Problem Analysis at the System, Group, and Individual Levels

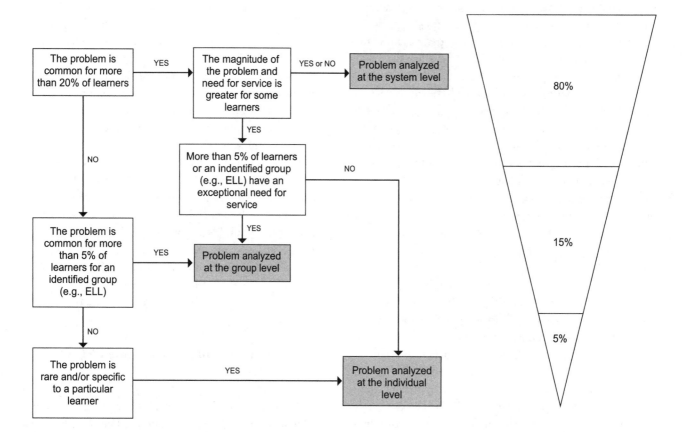

Figure 5.2 represents problem analysis for a multi-tiered system of supports. Neglecting a systems-level or group-level problem can overwhelm both problem solving and the system of supports. Problem analysis is often resource intensive and cannot be sustained if an excessive number of problems are analyzed at the individual level. It is when specific groups and learners have distinct needs relative to the local population that resources are allocated to analyze those problems. The white boxes in Figure 5.2 are hypothesis. If data support the first hypothesis in Figure 5.2, then analysis will progress to test this hypothesis: The magnitude of the problem and need for services are greater for some learners. This hypothesis is designed to provide support for groups and individuals with substantial needs. The needs of the system are established by the discrepancy between the performance of the population and some external criterion such as proficiency on a large-scale assessment in reading. The need for interventions at the group or individual level is established by the discrepancy between a learner's performance and that of the local norms for the school, district, or classroom population. Those students who are discrepant from local standards are

at even greater risk for academic failure. This is consistent with the 80–15–5 model for multilevel systems of support.

Once the scope of the problem within the population is defined at the system, group, and individual level, then the school psychologist, or problem analyst, may begin to develop hypothesis statements. Because poorly defined expectations are often the root of school-based behavior problems, the first hypothesis statement a problem analyst would ask is, "Do students know what is expected of them?" If the students clearly are aware of expectations, then the problem analyst can progress to evaluate instructional match or ecological contingencies.

If expectations were not taught and are not clearly established, then the problem analyst might recommend a remediation strategy. Expectations can be taught through explicit instruction, modeling, practice, or direct feedback. The implicit hypothesis is: If expectations are taught, then the magnitude of the problem will be reduced. This is an example of an if/then hypothesis. An if/then hypothesis establishes a tentative belief that a particular manipulation in the ecology will result in a predicted change in learner behavior. The hypothesis-testing framework is directly linked to interventions because the framework terminates with a testable hypothesis for intervention, the intervention hypothesis. The intervention itself is a hypothesis because it is a putative and testable solution to the problem. It is best practice to recognize and define recommendations for instruction and intervention as hypothetic statements. The effect of an intervention is unknown until after data are collected and evaluated.

Assessment for Problem Analysis

Assessment is a basic competency for school psychologists (NASP, 2010). Appropriate assessment data are collected using a multimethod, multidomain, and multisource approach. Figure 5.3 features a matrix that illustrates this approach. Reviews, interviews, observations, and tests serve as different assessment methods, while the instruction, curriculum, environment, and the learner represent the multiple domains (Heartland Area Education Agency 11, 2006).

It is necessary to note that problem analysis does not require that school psychologists use an exhaustive set of assessments across all methods, domains, and sources of information. Instead, assessment should generate the necessary information for answering a set of well-specified questions. The school psychologist should be able to readily respond to the question, "How will the assessment procedure answer the assessment question?" For instance, if mathematical calculation skills are a concern, then a school psychologist may ask the following two questions: (a) "Is this a skill deficit, a generalization problem, or a performance deficit?" and

Figure 5.3. Assessment: Multidomain, Multimethod, Multisource Matrix

| | | Multiple methods of assessment | | | |
		Review	Interview	Observe	Test
Multiple sources of information	Instruction	Permanent products of student work, records of prior strategies and their effects, lesson plans	Teachers, parents, paraprofessionals, administrators, and peers to describe experiences and perceptions of pace, opportunities to respond, engagement, contingencies, and activities	When and where the problem is most likely and least likely to occur	Systematic manipulations of procedures that include opportunities to respond, repeated practice, durations, contingencies, or activities
	Curriculum	Books, worksheets, software, scope, and sequence	Teachers, parents, paraprofessionals, administrators, and peers to describe content organization, difficulty, and level	When and where the problem is most likely and least likely to occur	Systematic manipulations of difficulty, stimulus, presentation, interspersed materials, and content
	Environment	Seating charts, rules, school layout	Teachers, parents, paraprofessionals, administrators, and peers to describe organization, rules, and set up	When and where the problem is most likely and least likely to occur	Systematic manipulations of praise, contingencies, escape, work, completion, criteria for success and failure, seating, and distractions
	Learner	Educational records, health records, prior tests and reports	Teachers, parents, paraprofessionals, administrators, and peers to describe observations and experiences with a specific student or group	When and where the problem is most likely and least likely to occur	

(b) "If this is a skill deficit, then which specific skills are affected?" The intensity and thoroughness of assessment will be determined, in part, by the severity and characteristics of the problem. For instance, those influences maintaining minor problems may be relatively easy to identify. Consequently, assessment and evaluation for problem analysis might be brief and relatively few cells in the matrix would be completed. In contrast, the influences maintaining severe problems— or problems that are resistant to standard protocol solutions—may be difficult to identify. In those cases, assessment for problem analysis would be more extensive and more cells in the matrix would be completed. More severe problems that establish high levels of risk or are resistant to intervention require a more extensive dataset to support problem analysis.

SUMMARY

School psychologists establish a unique and necessary niche when they engage in effective problem analysis. The field will thrive and school psychologists will become invaluable to multitiered systems of supports, which depend on effective and efficient problem solving and problem analysis. The dynamic process of problem analysis is the essential link between assessment and intervention. In this sense, problem analysts function as applied scientists in that they seek to discover the relationship between independent variables (instruction, curriculum, environment) and dependent variables (skills and behavior of the learner). The goal is to modify the conditions of the independent variables to have an impact on the state of the learner.

Problem analysis progresses from (a) a well-identified problem to (b) possible causes to (c) possible solutions to (d) a validated solution. As discussed, successful problem analysis depends on knowledge and appreciation of science as both a method and resulting body of evidence. Problem analysis progresses through steps similar to the scientific method, which includes problem identification, hypothesis development, hypothesis testing, and the generation of tentative conclusions in the form of intervention recommendations. Problem analysis also depends on the body of evidence that emerges from science. Published research and evidence-based practices is relied on to inform analytic hypothesis and intervention hypothesis development.

Problem analysis is most effective when low inference methods of assessment and interpretation that focus on the causal and maintaining variables are relied on. There are many theories and perspectives on student development. Those that are most relevant to problem analysis are immediately testable through observation of skills and behavior in the school-based setting. School psychologists and other educators often have expertise in one or more content areas, but rarely have broad and deep expertise in all domains. As discussed, the ability to identify and organize the most relevant information is an important aspect to problem analysis. Together, and for those reasons, we recommend the ongoing development and evaluation of content-specific hypothesis-testing frameworks. Although there are a few simple examples presented in this chapter, researchers and content experts must develop, evaluate, and refine frameworks that are content and context specific. These will assist the nonexpert problem analysts as they pursue intervention recommendations through problem analysis.

In practice, problem analysis is fundamental to multitiered systems of support. It helps to understand the causal and maintaining features of problems before solutions are proposed. As discussed, it also helps to understand the prevalence of problems. This understanding helps to determine whether the intervention should target the system, core supports, identifiable groups, or individuals. Multitiered systems of support are rarely sustainable if each problem is resolved at the individual student level. Many problems are common to systems and can be either prevented or resolved more efficiently at the group level.

REFERENCES

Daly, E. J., Lentz, F. E., & Boyer, J. (1996). The instructional hierarchy: A conceptual model of understanding the effective components of reading interventions. *School Psychology Quarterly, 11,* 369–386.

Fuchs, D., Mock, D., Morgan, P. L., & Young, C. L. (2003). Responsiveness-to-intervention: Definitions, evidence, and implications for the learning disabilities construct. *Learning Disabilities Research & Practice, 18,* 157–171.

Haring, N. G., & Eaton, M. D. (1978). Systematic instructional procedures: An instructional hierarchy. In N. G. Haring, T. C. Lovitt, M. D. Eaton, & C. L. Hansen (Eds.), *The fourth R: Research in the classroom* (pp. 23–39). Columbus, OH: Merrill.

Heartland Area Education Agency 11. (2006). *Program manual for special education.* Johnston, IA: Author. Retrieved from http://www.iowaideainfo.org/vimages/shared/vnews/stories/4a8b1534597fd/Special%20Education%20Procedures%20Manual%20January%202015%202013%20final.pdf

Hintze, J. M., Christ, T. J., & Methe, S. A. (2006). Curriculum-based assessment. *Psychology in the Schools, 43,* 45–56.

Hosp, J., Hosp, M., Howell, K., & Allison, R. (2014). *The ABCs of curriculum-based evaluation: A practical guide to effective decision making.* New York, NY: Guilford Press.

National Association of School Psychologists. (2010). *Model for Comprehensive and Integrated School Psychological Services.* Retrieved from http://www.nasponline.org/standards/2010standards/2_PracticeModel.pdf

National Governors Association Center for Best Practices & Council of Chief State School Officers. (2010). *Common Core State Standards for English language arts and literacy in history/social studies, science, and technical subjects.* Washington, DC: Author.

Scammaca, N., Vaughn, S., Roberts, G., Wanzek, J., & Torgesen, J. K. (2007). *Extensive reading interventions in grades K–3: From research to practice.* Portsmouth, NH: RMC Research.

6

Best Practices in Data-Analysis Teaming

Joseph F. Kovaleski
Indiana University of Pennsylvania
Jason A. Pedersen
Derry Township (PA) School District

OVERVIEW

Our chapter, "Best Practices in Data-Analysis Teaming," in *Best Practices V* (Kovaleski & Pedersen, 2008), reviewed the use of problem-solving teams from the early days of teacher assistance teams (Chalfant, Pysh, & Moultrie, 1979) through those models promulgated nationally during the 1980s and 1990s, such as instructional support teams (Kovaleski, Tucker, & Stevens, 1996), instructional consultation teams (Rosenfield & Gravois, 1996), and problem-solving teams (Graden, Casey, & Christenson, 1985). We noted that, historically, these problem-solving teams focused on individual students for the purpose of designing unique interventions that were customized to students' assessed needs. Our purpose in that chapter was to introduce readers to the use of the problem-solving process for the analysis of all students' proficiency levels and for the design of interventions that are directed at class-wide instructional changes intended to improve overall proficiency rates. We dubbed this process *data-analysis teaming* and identified its use as residing in Tier 1 of a multitiered system of supports. In doing so, we established a set of working procedures for Tier 1 teams to follow in pursuing school-wide goals.

Since the publication of that chapter, the implementation of multitiered systems of supports has expanded pervasively throughout the country, typically associated with and identified by the term *response to intervention* (RTI; Zirkel & Thomas, 2010). Although RTI stands as an alternative procedure for the identification of specific learning disabilities in the 2004 Individuals with Disabilities Education Act, it is frequently understood by practitioners to be synonymous with the multitiered system (Kovaleski & Black, 2010). Thus, both RTI and the multitiered system have been described to include those assessment and intervention procedures that are used to improve the proficiency of all students (Tier 1) and to identify specific students for scientifically based interventions at Tiers 2 and 3 (Batsche et al., 2005). It is gratifying that within this widespread implementation a number of states and local education agencies have established Tier 1 data-analysis teams as a fundamental feature of their multitiered RTI programs. For example, Pennsylvania has provided extensive training on data-analysis teams in its statewide rollout of training in its Response to Instruction and Intervention initiative. Similarly, the Minnesota Department of Education has an RTI Community of Practice group that is organized to support data-analysis teams across the state (D. M. Hyson, personal communication, March 23, 2012).

Furthermore, the practice of teams of teachers meeting to analyze various types of data to inform instruction has become widespread even when it is not explicitly associated with RTI. Schmoker (2001) was an early pioneer of training teachers to use available data to guide their instruction. Similarly, DuFour and Eaker (1998) embedded the analysis of student data by teachers in their Professional Learning Communities model. In addition, Love, Stiles, Mundry, and DiRanna (2008) published detailed operating procedures for teachers and data coaches on this topic.

Although our previous chapter (Kovaleski & Pedersen, 2008) covered operating procedures for data-analysis teams at Tier 1 of a multitiered system, it stopped short of articulating procedures for data-based decision making at Tiers 2 and 3. To address how data-analysis teams can operate at all stages of a multitier system, this chapter has three goals: (a) to update and refine the original procedures for the operation of Tier 1 data-analysis teams, (b) to articulate how data-analysis teams should operate for students needing Tier 2 and 3 supports, and (c) to provide expanded procedures for extending the deliberations of data-analysis teams to include data on student behavior.

As we describe these procedures, we envision school psychologists as active functionaries in all tiers. In the National Association of School Psychologists (NASP) *Model for Comprehensive and Integrated School Psychological Services* (NASP, 2010), the activities and roles presented in this chapter primarily pertain to the domain of Data-Based Decision Making because of its focus on the use of data to make decisions in the context of a multitiered system of service delivery. However, they also draw from other domains: Consultation and Collaboration, School-Wide Practices to Promote Learning, and Research and Program Evaluation, and have relevance to the domains for development of both academic and behavioral–affective interventions.

BASIC CONSIDERATIONS

The most essential component of a multitiered RTI system is clearly the pervasive use of data. The data streams vary from high-stakes, group-administered assessments to individually administered assessments to individual observations. The data-analysis team utilizes all of the data from various sources and levels with the goal of summarizing it in an easily understood format to inform the most accurate decision making for students.

Collecting Data

Data-analysis teams consist of teams of teachers, school psychologists, administrators, and other educators who meet to review existing data and to conceptualize how the data inform instructional decision making. Obviously then, data-analysis teams need useful and reliable data to consider. The most common sources of these data are statewide tests, universal screenings, measures used to monitor progress, and what we refer to as drill-down assessments.

Statewide Assessment Data

The most basic and readily available data are the results of statewide tests, which are required by the No Child Left Behind (NCLB) Act in grades 3–8 and at least once

from grades 10–12. Many states require testing in reading, mathematics, and content areas in multiple grades. Suffice it to say that in any given state, there is substantial information from statewide testing available to data-analysis teams, including overall scores and subskill breakdowns.

Universal Screening Data

Although statewide testing data are useful, the fact that these tests are administered on an annual basis (and typically in the spring when it is too late to adjust instruction) has induced many school districts to assess students' basic skills more frequently using universal screening techniques. These measures should have the following features:

- The assessments need to be closely linked to, or derived from, state or national standards in the curriculum area in question, or serve as indicators of student performance on those standards, as in the case of general outcome measures. For example, assessment instruments that tap the big ideas in reading are particularly useful.
- The assessments should be capable of being administered efficiently to large groups of students, either individually or in groups. For example, in some schools, teachers are responsible for administering the assessments to their students while other schools have used "SWAT teams" (school workers armed with timers; M. Ferchalk, personal communication, July 30, 2006) to assist teachers with the assessments so that loss of instructional time is minimized.
- Instruments need to be capable of being administered three or more times per school year so that students' progress can be appraised.
- Resulting data should be capable of being disaggregated for the entire group in terms of percentages of students at various attainment levels (e.g., proficient, at risk, deficient) on specific skills (e.g., phoneme segmentation) and for individual students in terms of their performance on those skills. For this reason, instruments that provide scores on individual subskills are more useful than those that provide only overall scores (e.g., composite reading or math skills).
- Measures must be sensitive to small increments of growth so that even small changes in skill levels can be detected between assessment sessions.

Current universal screening procedures include those derived from curriculum-based measurement (CBM), such as AIMSweb (Shinn & Garman, 2006), Dynamic

Indicators of Basic Early Literacy Skills (DIBELS) Next (Good & Kaminski, 2011), and Easy CBM (Alonzo, Tindal, Ulmer, & Glasgow, 2006), as well as computer-adapted assessments, such as STAR Reading (Renaissance Learning, 1996) and the Measures of Academic Progress (Northwest Evaluation Association, 2004).

In terms of universal screening for behavior, there are two complementary methods that permit users to examine school-wide data and disaggregate the data by classes, students, prosocial behaviors, and type of infraction. The first type of universal screener for behavior is based on office discipline referrals and includes platforms such as the School-Wide Information System (May et al., 2000) and Tracking Referrals, Encouragements, Notifications, Discipline, Safety (Sprick, 2011). The second source of behavioral data uses a multigate rating system, such as that employed by the Systematic Screening for Behavioral Disorders (Walker & Severson, 1992), the Social Skills Intervention System Performance Screening Guide (Elliott & Gresham, 2008b), the Behavior and Emotional Screening System (Kamphaus & Reynolds, 2007), and the Student Risk Screening Scale (Drummond, 1994). These data provide a more complete picture of the climate of a given school or grade level that is useful in intervention planning. All of these behavioral measures also provide the potential for drilling down to the classroom and student level for data-analysis teams working at Tiers 2 and 3.

Progress Monitoring Data

Frequent monitoring of student progress has been established as a critical aspect of RTI (Batsche et al., 2005). Kovaleski, VanDerHeyden, and Shapiro (2013) recommend that progress monitoring occur at least every other week at Tier 2 and weekly at Tier 3. Many of the universal screening tools described above (especially those that appraise academic skills) have applications that are useful to measure progress on a frequent basis. The consideration of progress monitoring data on individual students is a critical function of data-analysis teams to gauge the effectiveness of interventions and to make decisions about tier movement.

Drill-Down Assessments

Increasingly, data-analysis teams working at Tiers 2 and 3 desire to conduct more extensive analyses of students' specific academic skills and subskills. This approach is embodied in tactics such as curriculum-based evaluation and consists of procedures to drill down into specific academic subskills that are fundamental aspects of the terminal skill. Enhanced assessment of student behavior

is best accomplished with functional behavioral assessment procedures. The involvement of school psychologists in these drill-down assessments is particularly important as teams work to craft precise interventions based on students' specific skills.

Preparing Data Displays

An important facet of conducting effective and efficient data-analysis team meetings is the advance preparation of data displays that are user friendly. That is, teachers should be able to read and readily understand the data being presented, whether they are in the form of spreadsheets, graphs, or other formats. For Tier 1 teaming, bar graphs that depict the numbers of students who are deficient in, are developing, and have acquired the skill in question are helpful for group data. For deliberations regarding Tiers 2 and 3, it is most useful to construct data displays that include on one screen the results for all students on different measures (e.g., oral reading fluency and comprehension). All of the universal screening instruments described above are capable of providing multiple data sorts and displays. However, it is recommended that these often voluminous printouts be reserved for inspection by administrators, teachers, school psychologists, and data managers at times other than during the data-analysis team meetings. Early in the development of the process, analyzing data may be an unfamiliar activity for some staff and may seem overwhelming. Using one or two easily readable summary documents should increase the efficiency of the meetings.

It is also important for school psychologists and other personnel skilled in data analysis to train teachers to interpret data-summary documents before implementing actual data-analysis team meetings so that all participants in the meetings have a full understanding of the data and time is not lost on basic data interpretation.

Many schools rely on a data manager to access available data and prepare the displays. We have observed a number of school psychologists undertake this function, although other personnel have also stepped forward for this duty. The activity of preparing useful data displays is enhanced by the use of data warehousing, which allows for the storage and manipulation of multiple data sources (e.g., state test results, universal screening data, attendance).

BEST PRACTICES IN THE OPERATION OF DATA-ANALYSIS TEAMS

In this section, we articulate the operational procedures that data-analysis teams use for decision making. We begin by addressing some general issues that are pertinent for all team procedures, then detail procedures for team functioning at Tiers 1, 2, and 3. We conclude with recommendations about how data-analysis teaming can be evaluated for effectiveness and considerations for their use in secondary schools.

Team Membership

In our experience, data-analysis teams should include no more than six teachers. When addressing interventions at Tiers 2 and 3, team members may include special education teachers, school counselors, social workers, and behavior specialists, in addition to the general education teachers. Personnel who have special competence with students of various cultural and ethnic groups can also be regular or ad hoc members. The school principal is a critical team member for all meetings, although in large schools assistant principals may serve on the teams. Strong administrative support is thought to be a key feature of collaborative school teams (Kovaleski & Pedersen, 2008), particularly in regard to the commitment of logistic resources and the assessment of the integrity of instruction and intervention.

Because a central function of data-analysis teams is the analysis of universal screening and other student data, data-analysis teams need to include a staff member who is knowledgeable about measurement theory and the particular assessments used in the screening process. School psychologists are the ideal personnel to undertake this role, because they have extensive training and experience in these areas. Therefore, the school psychologist who serves the school should be an essential member of the data-analysis teams at all tiers. In addition, because the data gathered throughout the three-tier process may become part of the evidence for special education eligibility for some students in an RTI framework, the school psychologist also performs the role of data shaper for the data-analysis team. That is, the school psychologist not only consults with the team on effective measurement techniques for the purpose of instructional improvement, but also ensures that any data collected have the appropriate psychometric characteristics that are necessary for other important educational decisions for individual students (Kovaleski et al., 2013).

Data-analysis teams may also include staff members who have special expertise in basic skills and other subject areas. Particularly helpful are team members who are knowledgeable about the research evidence for various instructional programs and strategies, because a main purpose of data-analysis teams is identifying and implementing evidence-based practices. Finally, all teams need members who are well versed in the problem-solving process per se. Both of these needs speak to the regular involvement of school psychologists on data-analysis teams.

Frequency and Duration of Meetings

Meetings of data-analysis teams to address Tier 1 issues should occur immediately after the administration of universal screening. For most schools, universal screenings occur three times per year (early fall, midwinter, spring), although there may be informal meetings of teachers between these dates. Generally, meetings last at least an hour, but may be longer in the initial years of operation as teachers learn the data-analysis process. Meetings to discuss individual students for Tier 2 and 3 supports should be scheduled shortly after the Tier 1 data-analysis team and then a minimum of one time per month for review of progress. How school personnel find time for data-analysis teams and other meetings is a challenging, but surmountable, task. (Further information on this topic can be found at www.rti4success.org.)

Record Keeping

It is important for data-analysis teams to maintain a written record of the data analyzed and the decisions made. For data-analysis team record keeping, we have designed the Screening and Information Recording Form–Academics (Appendix A) for use with academic domains and the Screening and Information Recording Form–Behavior (Appendix B), a parallel form for addressing behavioral issues. In addition to their record-keeping function, these forms serve as de facto agendas for data-analysis team meetings. Although these forms are not designed for individual students, and therefore may not become part of an individual student's educational record, data-analysis teams need to be mindful of student confidentiality laws and regulations when using and sharing these forms.

Meeting Procedures: Tier 1

The function of the data-analysis team in Tier 1 is to review data on all students, articulate the overall level of proficiency of the group, set interim goals for the group, identify instructional strategies to address students' improvement, and plan logistics for supporting the instructional changes. In this section, specific procedures at each stage of the process are described in detail.

Review of the Data

The data to be reviewed should be disseminated to all participants by the data manager before the meeting so that they can inspect the data and prepare for the team discussion. Each data-analysis team meeting begins with a review of the data that have recently been gathered and summarized (typically universal screening results). A critical issue at this point is that the Tier 1 data-analysis team should only review data displays on groups of students (e.g., entire grade) such as those displayed in Figure 6.1, which depicts academic data from DIBELS Next, and Figure 6.2, which depicts behavioral data from the School-Wide Information System. The data-analysis team should not be presented with any displays that include data on the performance of individual students at this point in the process, because to do so

invariably leads to discussion of specific students (which is reserved for Tier 2 and 3 discussions) and away from consideration of whole-class instructional strategies.

Using the Screening and Information Recording Form–Academics (Appendix A, page 1), the facilitator asks the team to articulate the performance of the entire group of students at the grade level on the skills that are pertinent for that part of the curriculum. Performance is described as the percentage of students performing at proficient, emerging, or deficient levels. Different assessment instruments use variants of these terms, which may be preferred by teams using these instruments. For example, using the data display in Figure 6.1, the data-analysis team would describe this group of first graders as follows: 79% of the group are proficient on the DIBELS Next Phoneme Segmentation Fluency subtest, as indicated by a score of 40 or more phoneme segments per minute (psm); in 15% this skill is emerging, as indicated by scores between 25 and 39 psm; and 7% of

Figure 6.1. DIBELS Next Tier 1 Data

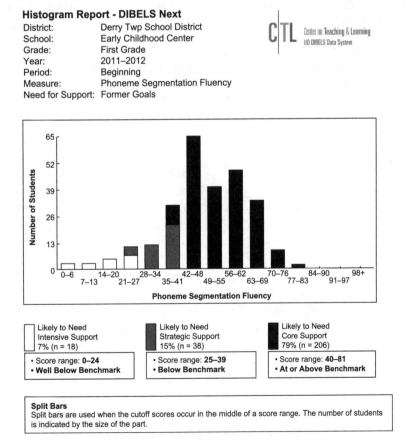

Figure 6.2. School-Wide Information System Data

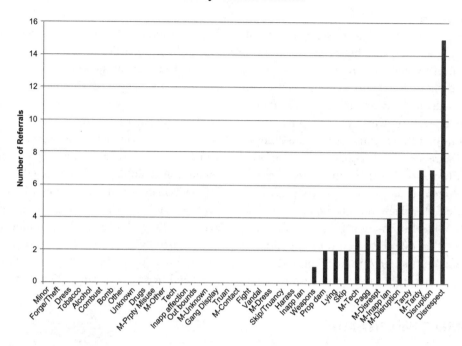

Referrals by Problem Behavior

Note. From the *School-Wide Information System* (http://www.swis.org). Copyright 2013 by Education and Community Supports. Reprinted with permission.

the students are in the deficient range for this skill as indicated by scores below 24 psm. For a grade-wide or class-wide analysis of behavior, the Screening and Information Recording Form–Behavior (Appendix B, page 1) would be used. Analyzing the data from Figure 6.2 indicates that 25% (or 15 actual incidents) of the office discipline referrals were for disrespect, 12% (7 incidents) of behaviors were disruptive in nature, with tardiness making up another 12% (7 incidents) of the office discipline referrals. Additional analysis of the behaviors can take place to determine location and time of day.

Goal Setting

Next, the data-analysis team sets a goal for the group of students in reference to the next date of assessment. This goal is described in terms of the percentage of students who the team projects can reach proficiency or target performance on the target skill or behavior by that date. Although the percentages set as interim goals (e.g., goals set in early fall for midwinter) may vary depending on the performance of the group, teams should keep in mind that the great majority of students are expected to display proficiency or the target performance on the skill or behavior by the end of the school year, especially in the early grades. For example, the data-analysis team

might project that 90% of the students would be proficient on the DIBELS Next Phoneme Segmentation Fluency subtest by the January assessment, which would be annotated on the appropriate section of the Screening and Information Recording Form–Academics (Appendix A, page 1). Additionally, the data-analysis team might also project that office discipline referrals for disrespect might be reduced to seven incidents, a 50% reduction, which would be annotated on the corresponding section of the Screening and Information Recording Form–Behavior (Appendix B, page 1).

Generation of Strategies

The next step may be the most critical one in the process. After a goal is set, the data-analysis team discusses instructional and management strategies that will help all students achieve the goal by the next benchmark assessment. The review of possible strategies should be a focused discussion of materials, instructional procedures, and organizational structures that target the specific skill or behavior. Brainstorming, as it is typically understood, is not encouraged, because it has the connotation of a free-wheeling generation of ideas that may or may not have any relevance to the target skill or may not have acceptable research support.

When data-analysis teams operate in schools that have core instructional packages that have good research support, the generation of possible strategies should match closely with procedures described for use with these materials. Data-analysis teams in schools that have less robust core curricula will likely consider materials and instructional procedures that will supplement the core curricula in areas where they do not adequately address the target skills. Unlike the interventions that are customized for individual students by data-analysis teams in later tiers, the strategies selected by Tier 1 data-analysis teams are intended to be used for all students toward the goal of proficiency for the entire group. Data-analysis teams need to consider strategies that become a regularly scheduled aspect of the daily classroom routine and result in improvements in skills for the whole class. These strategies include those used for whole-group instruction as well as those that help teachers differentiate instruction for the widely varying skill levels in any classroom. Similarly, strategies to address student behavior should be closely aligned with the overall school discipline code. For example, data-analysis teams in schools using school-wide positive behavioral supports should identify strategies that are components of this program.

Selection of Strategies

Historically, teachers in problem-solving teams chose strategies from the generated (or brainstormed) list, with teacher acceptability as a major consideration in strategy selection (Rosenfield, 1987). However, with the advent of NCLB, data-analysis teams should now analyze or filter the strategies according to the extent to which they are based on scientific evidence. The data-analysis team should appraise each generated strategy according to three criteria: (a) Does the strategy have a solid research base? (b) Are there instructional materials readily available for implementing the strategy? (c) Is the strategy relatively easy to learn and implement in the context of a general education classroom? Strategies that are selected for use by the teachers based on all three criteria are annotated in the appropriate section (page 1, Appendices A and B) of the Screening and Information Recording forms.

Planning for Implementation

An important stage of the data-analysis team process is creating a specific plan for the implementation of the selected strategies. School psychologists are well aware of the challenges faced by problem-solving teams in achieving treatment fidelity of interventions

recommended for implementation by teachers (Flugum & Reschly, 1994). This challenge is especially pertinent for data-analysis teams, as a primary intention of this process is that all teachers at a grade level will implement the selected strategies. Consequently, planning for the implementation of the selected strategies requires consideration of specific logistical and organizational aspects of implementing the strategies. Factors such as duration and frequency of the strategy, when it will occur during the school day, how the regular routine of the classroom will be altered to accommodate the change, and what supports might be needed (e.g., use of teacher aides and volunteers) should be discussed and specific steps planned to deal with these issues.

Another primary consideration is the awareness that some teachers on the data-analysis team (i.e., at that grade level) may not be familiar with a particular strategy. The data-analysis team needs to develop a plan for helping these teachers learn to deliver the strategy effectively. Tactics such as peer coaching, team teaching, modeling of strategies, and group discussions about strategy implementation should be conducted in the period of time before the next formal data-analysis team meeting. In addition, individual feedback on the teacher's level of implementation as described by Noell et al. (2005) would be a useful procedure to incorporate into the implementation plan. Either other teachers or specialists consulting with the data-analysis team (e.g., school psychologists) can meet periodically with each teacher to gauge the treatment fidelity and provide guidance to increase the match between the plan and the implementation. The assessment of instructional fidelity can also be built into school principals' routine observation of teachers.

The logistical steps to support the teachers in using the strategies as planned should be annotated on page 1 of the respective Screening and Information Recording Form (see Appendices A and B). All participants in the data-analysis team need to understand that the Strategies Selected and Logistics sections of the Screening and Information Recording forms represent a commitment of the group to implement the strategies and make the planned instructional or management changes. This level of accountability is another rationale for the active involvement (i.e., physical presence) of the school principal in these deliberations.

Supporting the Implementation

The commitment made by the team to the planned changes needs to be supported during the intermeeting period on two levels. First, the support activities annotated in the logistics section need to be faithfully delivered by the teachers as well as the other nonteaching members of the team. Second, the school principal needs to play an active role between formal meetings in setting a climate of both support and accountability by ensuring that the logistical and organizational aspects of the plan are carried out. For example, teachers may need free periods to model strategies or to coach other teachers. The school principal provides for accountability through activities such as inspecting lesson plans, checking that the strategies have been embedded into the daily instructional routine, and conducting teacher observations during periods when the selected strategies are scheduled to be used. This active involvement of the school principal sends the message that the data-analysis team process and the consequent changes to the instructional process are not optional ideas but are the vehicles by which the school stays on track in meeting its academic and behavioral goals, including those required at the state and federal levels (e.g., adequate yearly progress requirements).

Meeting Procedures: Tier 2

So far, this description of the data-analysis team process has focused on the setting of goals for entire groups of students and the design of classroom strategies that help teachers address the needs of all students in Tier 1 of a multitiered system. In this section we describe the procedures for analyzing data on individual students who are not responding at an acceptable level to the core curricula and classroom instruction in Tier 1. It should be noted that, although it is necessary to present this and the next section (Tier 3 procedures) sequentially, it should not be presumed that this ordering implies that these activities occur at different meetings. Data-analysis teams may review whole class (Tier 1) data and individual student data (Tiers 2 and 3) at the same meeting or they may choose separate (shorter) meetings to focus on Tier 1 versus Tier 2 and 3 analyses.

Review of the Data

At this point the team should focus on data displays that provide information on individual students, such as those depicted in Figures 6.3 and 6.4. The task for the data-analysis team is to identify students who exhibit similar instructional or behavioral needs as indicated by the data, and to construct groups that will receive interventions that are targeted to those needs. Generally, this process is facilitated by sorting the students from high to low on a particularly critical skill. Figure 6.3 depicts such an array of results of reading assessments, including measures of oral reading fluency, accuracy, oral reading fluency rate of improvement, and reading comprehension (STAR Reading), with the data sorted (high to low) by the students' most recent scores on oral reading fluency. Figure 6.4 depicts classroom-level behavioral data including ratings of prosocial behaviors, motivation to learn, as well as ratings of general reading and math skills. It is up to the data-analysis team to decide which available data are most relevant to display depending on grade level and instructional domain, and which particular data type is most useful for the initial review of student-specific data.

Figure 6.3. Tier 2 Academic Data

Students at Strategic in Fall	Fall ORF Score	Winter ORF Score	Reached Winter Benchmark (Target)	Reached Winter Strategic (Target)	Winter ORF Accuracy	Progress Monitoring ROI (Fall to Winter)	STAR Reading Fall Scaled Score (Target 310)
Alexis	82	109	X		99%	0.42	302
Anthony	74	105	X		99%	0.08	310
Mia	75	98	X		99%	1.82	322
Aiden	67	87		X	100%	1.47	288
Noah	56	83		X	97%	2.03	229
Madison	56	77		X	96%	1.67	307
Jayden	59	76		X	95%	2.54	196
Daniel	76	70		X	96%	1.79	295
Chloe	65	68			96%	0.9	265
Abigail	57	63			93%	-0.3	301
Luis	53	60			94%	3.8	195

Note. ORF = oral reading fluency; ROI = rate of improvement.

Figure 6.4. Tier 2 Behavioral Data

Teacher	Student	Math	Reading	Motivation	Prosocial
Smith	Samantha	4	4	2	2
	Terry	5	5	4	5
	Anna	5	5	5	4
	Micheal	5	5	2	2
	Isabella	3	4	5	5
	Paige	4	4	5	5
	Anthony	5	4	3	2
	Trent	5	5	5	4
	Mae	4	4	4	1
	Alex	4	5	5	4
	Melissa	5	5	1	1
	Jackson	5	5	2	5
	Trevor	5	5	4	4
	Hannah	5	5	4	4
	Karen	5	5	4	3
	Amelia	3	3	3	4
	Grace	5	5	5	5
	Elliot	4	4	5	5
	Alexa	3	4	3	4
	Chloe	4	4	2	2
	Lydia	5	5	5	5
	Baxter	4	2	2	3

	Total in Class	Math	Reading	Motivation	Prosocial
1s	3	0	0	1	2
2s and 3s	15	3	2	6	4

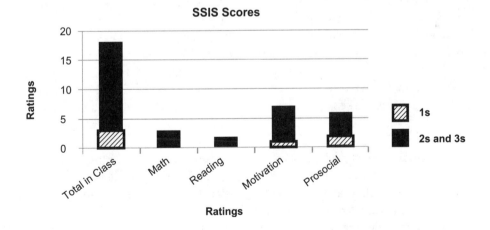

Sorting Students Into Instructional Groups

The data-analysis team next analyzes the data to identify students who have similar instructional needs, using the Screening and Information Recording forms (page 2 of Appendices A and B) to sort students into groups. The Screening and Information Recording Form–Academics (Appendix A) has been customized so that students who need instruction in reading decoding, fluency, and/or comprehension can be indicated by placing their names in the designated cells under each intervention type. Additional columns are provided for those students who might have reached the benchmark level but for whom extended progress monitoring is desired and for students who might have other needs. For example, using the data displayed in Figure 6.3, the data-analysis team might assign Noah, who has made good progress in oral reading fluency from fall to winter, but whose comprehension is still below the fall and winter STAR Reading benchmarks, into a group of students who will receive an intervention targeted to improvement of comprehension. Abigail, on the other hand, who appears to be comprehending at benchmark level on the recent (winter) administration of STAR Reading, but who has made little progress in her oral reading fluency, might be designated for an intervention that emphasizes fluency building. Anthony, who seems to be making good progress in both oral reading fluency and comprehension, might be identified for periodic progress monitoring rather than for a Tier 2 intervention group.

A similar process is used for creating intervention groups based on behavioral need. The Screening and Information Recording Form–Behavior (Appendix B) includes generic intervention groups on page 2, which can be customized based on the behavioral needs displayed by the students. In Figure 6.4, Chloe was rated as having no concerns in academic skills (rated as 4 on a scale of 4 for both reading and math), but is at risk in terms of motivation to learn and prosocial behaviors (rated as 2 on a scale of 4). There are four additional students with similar patterns of ratings for whom a group can be formed to address increasing appropriate classroom behaviors. Additionally, Chloe and her peers represented 5 of the 15 office discipline referrals for disrespect at the grade level, further indicating the need and the nature of the limited prosocial behaviors. Consequently, these students might be grouped on the Screening and Information Recording Form–Behavior for a particular group intervention for their prosocial skills.

Goal Setting

The next step is to set goals. Even though students in each group have different scores, rather than set goals for individual students, a measurable goal is set for each group and annotated in the designated section of the appropriate Screening and Information Recording Form (Appendices A and B, page 2). For example, students in the designated comprehension intervention group might have a goal to reach a score of 394 (40th percentile) on the spring administration of STAR Reading. Similarly, the goal for the aforementioned prosocial skills group might be to decrease their incidents of disrespectful behavior by 50%.

Identification of Intervention Packages

Our preference for the identification of interventions to match students' assessed needs in Tier 2 is the so-called standard-protocol approach (Vaughn & Fuchs, 2003). Standard-protocol interventions are designed to target specific skills by using research-based instructional procedures in a structured, manualized manner. This approach is based on the notion that it is most efficacious to use robust interventions to teach specific skills at a high degree of treatment integrity. At this point, a range of commercially produced standard-protocol intervention packages are available for a number of commonly identified skill deficiencies, especially in the area of reading. Additionally, there are several commercially available standard-protocol interventions for behavior (e.g., Social Skills Intervention System Class-Wide Intervention Program; Elliott & Gresham, 2008a) as well as other research-based behavioral interventions (e.g., Check-in, Check-out; Hawken & Horner, 2003) that can be employed. The data-analysis team would annotate the appropriate Screening and Information Recording Form (Appendices A and B, page 2) with the strategy (program) that best matches the students' assessed needs. Of course, it is assumed here that the school district has chosen wisely in its purchase of supplemental instructional packages and behavior change programs that can be tapped for use by data-analysis teams in individual schools.

Planning for Progress Monitoring

In the same section of the Screening and Information Recording Form (Appendices A and B, page 2), the data-analysis team annotates the particular assessment measure that will be used to monitor the progress of students in various intervention groups. The progress monitoring measure should match the skill being addressed in the intervention groups. For example, a data-analysis team might choose to use a maze assessment or a computer-adapted measure (e.g., STAR Reading) to monitor students in the aforementioned comprehension group and a CBM of oral reading fluency to monitor students in the fluency and decoding groups. For behavioral targets, behavioral assessment techniques or direct behavior ratings (Chafouleas, Riley-Tillman, & Sugai, 2007) would be indicated. In Tier 2, we recommend that students' progress be monitored at least every other week. A space to designate that frequency is available on the Screening and Information Recording Form. The involvement of school psychologists in advising data-analysis teams regarding appropriate progress monitoring procedures is particularly critical in Tiers 2 and 3.

Planning for Implementation

The data-analysis team next addresses logistical issues, such as who will implement the supplemental interventions and how the school schedule will be arranged to accommodate the interventions. Typically, the school administrators have created a functional schedule that allows for appropriate intervention time slots as well as arranged for the availability of designated personnel for conducting the interventions. In addition, procedures to monitor the fidelity of the intervention should be planned at this stage of the meeting and annotated on the Screening and Information Recording Form (Appendices A and B). The active involvement of the school principal in the data-analysis team for supporting these logistics is crucial at this point.

Meeting Procedures: Tier 3

Tier 3 data-analysis team meetings consist of data analysis and deliberations about interventions for those students who display the most significant deficiencies in the general education program. These meetings involve enhanced assessments of students' needs, customizing individual interventions while working within a standard-protocol format, and more frequent progress monitoring.

Conducting Additional Assessments

In Tier 2, the data-analysis team focused entirely on data from existing sources such as statewide test results and data from universal screenings and school-wide counts of behavior (e.g., office discipline referrals). In Tier 3, the significance of students' deficiencies calls for a more in-depth analysis (drilling down) of student functioning. As indicated earlier, procedures such as curriculum-based evaluation and instructional assessment are recommended for a more complete analysis of students' academic subskills, while functional behavioral assessment would be used for significant behavioral issues. Selecting individual students for these assessments should be based on the identification of those students who display significant deficiencies on universal screenings or on an analysis of progress monitoring data as students progress through Tier 2. Many of these assessment modalities are best handled by school psychologists.

Review of the Data

For students at the Tier 3 level, data-analysis teams should again review all existing data, including drill-down data. Figure 6.5 depicts a data set of students identified for Tier 3 supports. As is apparent, a number

Figure 6.5. Tier 3 Academic Data

Students at Intensive in Fall	Fall ORF Score	Winter ORF Score	Reached Winter Benchmark (Target 92)	Reached Winter Strategic (Target 67)	Winter ORF Accuracy	Progress Monitoring ROI (Fall to Winter)	STAR Reading Fall Scaled Score (Target 310)	STAR Reading Winter Scaled Score (Target 352)	STAR Reading Fall to Winter Student Growth Percentile
Weston	20	Moved out					85		
John	49	72			95%	3.3	175	290	66
Pedro	52	72			97%	2.24	198	304	65
Fernanda	46	62			94%	1.57	129	182	32
Devan	43	57			93%	10	186	240	33
Donovan	38	56			93%	0.34	158	211	27
Dakota	36	53			95%	0.46	130	209	44
Malik	Moved in	48			96%			112	
Marcos	30	46			90%	1.85	155	249	52
Caitlin	39	45			82%	1.64	152	185	22
Verc	Moved in	45			87%	3.21		190	
Corbin	34	37			86%	0.74	120	143	19
Eliza	22	25			78%	0.25	84	103	26
Chaz	6	10			44%	NWF	63	74	46
Alayna	5	9			50%	NWF	66	89	51

Note. ORF = oral reading fluency; ROI = rate of improvement.

of students have very deficient skills. As an example, we have selected Eliza as one of the students for whom additional assessment will be conducted. She displays very poor oral reading fluency and comprehension (STAR Reading) and minimal growth from fall to winter. On a subsequent curriculum-based evaluation, Eliza performed poorly on assessments of comprehension, oral reading fluency, and vocabulary (as expected). She also scored in the intensive range on a phonics survey, displaying poorly developed skills in decoding words with long vowels, *r*-controlled vowels, and digraphs. She also had difficulty on tasks requiring phoneme deletion and breaking words into phonemes. This drill-down analysis indicated that Eliza's reading is hampered by very deficient phonemic awareness and phonics skills. These data would be inserted in the first section of page 3 of the Screening and Information Recording Form–Academics (Appendix A).

In terms of behavior, Chloe (in Figure 6.4) was selected for additional assessment using an individual behavior rating scale (Social Skills Intervention System Teacher Rating Scale) which yields data about a student's social skills (e.g., communication skills, cooperation, assertion, responsibility, empathy, engagement, self-control) and problem behaviors (e.g., externalizing, bullying, hyperactivity/inattention, internalizing, autism spectrum). In regard to her social skills, she displayed poor cooperation, empathy, engagement, and self-control, but good communication and responsibility. On the problem behavior subscales she demonstrated higher levels of externalizing and bullying, but typical levels of hyperactivity/inattention and internalizing. Data from this assessment would be entered in the appropriate section of the Screening and Information Recording Form–Behavior (Appendix B, page 3).

Goal Setting

In Tier 3, the data-analysis team sets goals for individual students. For example, measurable goals for Eliza might be set for both phonics skills and oral reading fluency, and so annotated on the appropriate section of the Screening and Information Recording Form–Academics (Appendix A, page 3). Similarly, an individual behavioral goal would be set for Chloe and annotated on the corresponding section of the Screening and Information Recording Form–Behavior (Appendix B, page 3).

Strategy Identification

At this stage, the data-analysis team would identify customized strategies for each student based on the

student's now-expanded data profile. In the academic domain, it is likely that multiple students will display similar instructional needs, so interventions again can be delivered in groups that are designed to match those assessed needs. The difference in Tier 3 is that, while standard-protocol interventions would still be used, intervention specialists would more specifically individualize for each student within those groups. In addition, the frequency and/or duration of the intervention sessions could be increased. For behavioral issues, interventions customized to the individual student via a behavior intervention plan are often needed. Information about the identified strategies would again be annotated by the data-analysis team in the designated section on the Screening and Information Recording forms (Appendices A and B, page 3).

Planning for Progress Monitoring

Students receiving Tier 3 services require frequent progress monitoring, which we recommend to be conducted on at least a weekly basis. As described for Tier 2, the specific progress monitoring measure should match the identified concern. The plans for progress monitoring should be annotated on the Screening and Information Recording forms (Appendices A and B) in the designated section of page 3.

Planning for Implementation

As in previous tiers, the data-analysis team should also plan for logistics of the intervention and identify procedures for monitoring the fidelity of the intervention. Examining treatment integrity is most important at this stage because students in Tier 3 usually are not making adequate progress and questions will begin to emerge about whether the student should be considered for eligibility for special education. Before considering the possibility of a disabling condition, the team should ensure that students are not failing to respond to the interventions because the interventions have not been implemented with fidelity. The fidelity checks conducted at this stage need to account for not only the manualized intervention but also any customized procedures that were planned by the data-analysis team. As indicated earlier, school principals, instructional coaches, and school psychologists are likely personnel to assist with the fidelity-checking process.

Identification of Nonresponders

Students who fail to make adequate progress through three tiers of instruction and intervention and who are significantly deficient in level may need to be considered for special education eligibility. Among the indicators of the need for a comprehensive evaluation for special-education eligibility are below-basic scores on state proficiency tests, history of failure in the curriculum, the provision of targeted instructional support using research-based programs and techniques with multiple changes driven by data, and a rate of progress that is below both target and typical rates. Kovaleski et al. (2013) provide detailed procedures for determining eligibility for severe learning disabilities identification that incorporate RTI data.

Subsequent Meetings

As previously described, Tier 1 data-analysis team meetings are held approximately three times per year after each administration of universal screening. Meetings held at midyear and in spring follow the same format as the initial meeting in the fall and record the progress of the students since the last meeting based on the recently conducted universal screening results. Goals are reset to advance performance on the same measures adjusted to new benchmark levels or to performance on another measure. By analyzing students' performance on the next higher level skill, the data-analysis team evaluates the success of the strategies selected in the last meeting and decides whether to continue or expand those strategies or to generate and select new ones. This decision depends on the measured success of the strategies as reflected in the data and on the need to create new strategies based on advancing curricular expectations. Again, strategies are generated and filtered, and logistics for implementation and support are recorded in detail. Meetings of the data-analysis team to appraise the progress of students in Tiers 2 and 3 occur more frequently (e.g., monthly) so that the effects of group-based or customized interventions on the progress of individual students can be evaluated, strategies changed or adapted as needed, and students transitioned in and out of support.

Evaluation of Effectiveness

The data-analysis team process is intended to provide supports to teachers in their implementation of standards-aligned core curricula, research-based instructional strategies, and school-wide positive behavior supports through careful planning and analysis of collected data. It is expected that approximately 80% of students should reach acceptable proficiency levels (Batsche et al., 2005) with this type of support at Tier 1. Additional students should reach desired levels with intensified supports at subsequent tiers. It is important to evaluate the effectiveness of the data-analysis team process by appraising over time the percentages of students who reach proficiency on the universal screening measures used during the process as well their performance on other objective measures, such as statewide proficiency tests. In addition, the effectiveness of standard-protocol interventions used in Tiers 2 and 3 should be evaluated as to their success in improving the performance of students receiving these procedures. Similarly, the effects of data-analysis team–generated strategies on school-wide measures of behavior need to be appraised. Shapiro and Clemens (2009) described a number of procedures for analyzing and evaluating the effects of multitiered systems of support that can be used in this regard.

School psychologists can be particularly helpful in conducting these program evaluations. For example, the second author of this chapter, who serves as the school psychologist for Hershey Primary Elementary School, conducted two analyses of the results of the data-analysis team process in that school. Figure 6.6 depicts the performance of kindergarten students on the DIBELS Next Phoneme Segmentation Fluency subtest during the end-of-year (spring) assessment over a 10-year period. As indicated in the figure, the percentages of students meeting benchmark (i.e., low risk) increased progressively over the 10-year period, while the percentage of students in the at-risk level progressively decreased. Figure 6.7 provides a scatterplot of fifth-grade students' scores on the DIBELS Oral Reading Fluency subtest compared with their scores on the statewide reading test (Pennsylvania System of School Assessment). These data indicate that a high percentage of students who met the benchmark on the Oral Reading Fluency subtest on DIBELS Next scored in the proficient range on the statewide test, a finding that has been frequently replicated (e.g., Shapiro, Keller, Lutz, Santoro, & Hintze, 2006).

From these analyses it is reasonable to conclude that the combination of a robust core curriculum, universal screening, and the data-analysis team activity is helping this school meet its overall performance goals. An analysis of Figure 6.6 reveals a particularly interesting phenomenon: The scores of successive groups of kindergarten students immediately improved with the implementation of the data-analysis team process and were progressively better each year after. That is, teachers participating in data-analysis teams became increasingly better at bringing larger numbers of students to proficiency. It can be hypothesized that this

Figure 6.6. Phoneme Segmentation Fluency Data Over a 10-Year Period

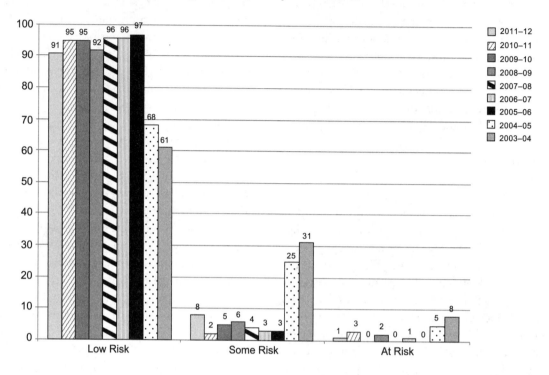

Derry Township SD: Kindergarten Spring Performance
Phoneme Segmentation Fluency Since 2002–03

Figure 6.7. Scatterplot of Oral Reading Fluency and State Testing Data

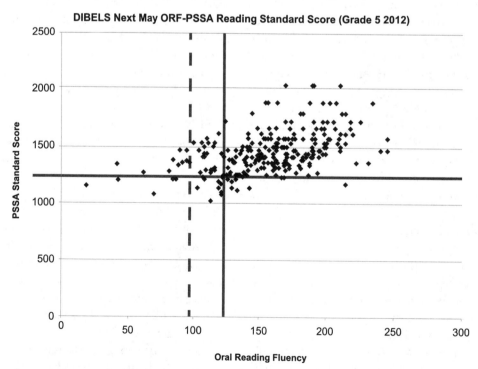

DIBELS Next May ORF-PSSA Reading Standard Score (Grade 5 2012)

Note. ORF = oral reading fluency; PSSA = Pennsylvania System of School Assessment.

effect is a function of teachers becoming increasingly selective in identifying strategies that incisively address the benchmark skills and increasingly proficient at implementing these strategies. Although further research into the data-analysis team process is needed to test this effect more rigorously, this type of analysis is representative of how school psychologists can plan and implement program evaluation procedures to determine if programs are meeting expectations.

Considerations for Secondary Schools

The data-analysis process described above is designed for both elementary and secondary schools. In secondary schools, it is recommended that data-analysis teams consist of teams of teachers who work at a particular grade level, although we have also had some success with meetings of teachers from individual departments (e.g., mathematics, English, sciences). In larger schools, multiple data-analysis teams at a particular grade level may be needed. In these cases, combining teachers who are assigned to particular groups of students is optimal. Other team members should include school principals, assistant principals, specialists, and one staff member assigned as data manager (e.g., the school psychologist). The meeting procedures follow the same format as described above.

Data considered by data-analysis teams in secondary schools should consist of periodic screening measures appropriate for those levels (e.g., Measures of Academic Progress, STAR Reading and Mathematics) as well as results of annual statewide or district-wide assessment. The data sets should include results from assessments in reading, writing, mathematics, and content subjects as available. The data sources on student behavior that have been presented previously appear to be appropriate across the K–12 grade range.

The analysis of basic-skills data by teams of teachers who teach various content subjects in secondary schools provides a special opportunity for these teachers. Because basic skills are rarely taught as separate subjects (periods) in secondary schools, the challenge of meeting adequate yearly progress goals for these skills is the shared responsibility of all of the teachers. Consequently, when strategies are generated and logistics considered, the implication is that these strategies will be implemented by all teachers across different subject areas. For example, strategies to increase the proficiency level of all students in writing would need to be implemented in social studies, sciences, English, and other subjects. For some schools, this process presents a different perspective on teaching at the secondary level, as all teachers are conceptualized as literacy teachers, regardless of their particular course assignments.

Some school psychologists have reported the use of formative assessments of students' content knowledge as well as student grades as the focus of their data-analysis teams at the secondary level. For example, secondary schools in Hudson (WI) School District are using formative content assessments to provide regular feedback on student performance to teachers (C. McIntyre, personal communication, October 31, 2012). When data-analysis teams analyze content assessments or student grades, the focus shifts from basic skill issues to the skills required to pass or excel in coursework, which opens the discussion to issues such as study skills, homework, and test taking. Using student grades in combination with data from tests of basic skill proficiency appears to be a promising approach for using data-analysis teams in secondary schools.

SUMMARY

The evolution of the problem-solving process that is a cornerstone of the practice of school psychology can be described in terms of the increased use of data to inform decision making about students. Contemporary team-based applications of problem-solving in the context of a multitiered organizational structure require the use of both academic and behavioral student data to function most effectively. With the ongoing focus on the accountability of educational entities to produce meaningful academic gains as well as to promote students' behavioral and emotional adjustment, the use of data-based procedures to guide school programs as described in this chapter should continue to be seen as essential to the achievement of these aims.

AUTHOR NOTE

Disclosure. Joseph F. Kovaleski has a financial interest in books he authored or coauthored referenced in this chapter.

REFERENCES

Alonzo, J., Tindal, G., Ulmer, K., & Glasgow, A. (2006). *easyCBM online progress monitoring assessment system.* Eugene, OR: Center for Educational Assessment Accountability.

Batsche, G., Elliott, J., Graden, J. L., Grimes, J., Kovaleski, J. F., Prasse, D., & Tilly, W. D., III. (2005). *Response to intervention: Policy considerations and implementation.* Alexandria, VA: National Association of State Directors of Special Education.

Chafouleas, S. M., Riley-Tillman, T. C., & Sugai, G. (2007). *School-based behavior assessment and monitoring for informing instruction and intervention.* New York, NY: Guilford Press.

Chalfant, J. C., Pysh, M. V., & Moultrie, R. (1979). Teacher assistance teams: A model for within-building problem solving. *Learning Disability Quarterly, 2,* 85–96.

Drummond, T. (1994). *The Student Risk Screening Scale (SRSS).* Grants Pass, OR: Josephine County Mental Health Program.

DuFour, R., & Eaker, R. E. (1998). *Professional learning communities at work: Best practices for enhancing student achievement.* Bloomington, IN: National Education Service.

Educational and Community Supports. (2013). *School-Wide Information System (SWIS).* Retrieved from http://www.swis.org

Elliott, S. N., & Gresham, F. M. (2008a). *Social Skills Improvement System (SSIS): Classwide intervention program.* Minneapolis, MN: NCS Pearson.

Elliott, S. N., & Gresham, F. M. (2008b). *Social Skills Improvement System (SSIS): Performance screening guide.* Minneapolis, MN: NCS Pearson.

Flugum, K. R., & Reschly, D. J. (1994). Prereferral interventions: Quality indices and outcomes. *Journal of School Psychology, 32,* 1–14.

Good, R. H., & Kaminski, R. (2011). *DIBELS Next assessment manual.* Eugene, OR: Institute for the Development of Educational Assessment.

Graden, J. L., Casey, A., & Christenson, S. L. (1985). Implementing a prereferral intervention system: Part I: The model. *Exceptional Children, 51,* 377–384.

Hawken, L. S., & Horner, R. H. (2003). Evaluation of a targeted intervention within a schoolwide system of behavior support. *Journal of Behavioral Education, 12,* 225–240.

Kamphaus, R. W., & Reynolds, C. R. (2007). *Behavior Assessment System for Children–Second Edition (BASC-2): Behavioral and Emotional Screening System (BESS).* Bloomington, MN: Pearson.

Kovaleski, J. F., & Black, L. (2010). Multi-tier service delivery: Current status and future directions. In T. A. Glover & S. Vaughn (Eds.), *The promise of response to intervention: Evaluating current science and practice.* New York, NY: Guilford Press.

Kovaleski, J. F., & Pedersen, J. (2008). Best practices in data analysis teaming. In A. Thomas & J. Grimes (Eds.), *Best practices in school psychology V* (pp. 115–130). Bethesda, MD: National Association of School Psychologists.

Kovaleski, J. F., Tucker, J., & Stevens, L. (1996). Bridging special and regular education: The Pennsylvania Initiative. *Educational Leadership, 53*(7), 44–47.

Kovaleski, J. F., VanDerHeyden, A., & Shapiro, E. S. (2013). *The RTI approach to evaluating learning disabilities.* New York, NY: Guilford Press.

Love, N., Stiles, K. E., Mundry, S., & DiRanna, K. (2008). *The data coach's guide to improving learning for all students.* Thousand Oaks, CA: Corwin.

May, S., Ard, W., Todd, A., Horner, R., Glasgow, A., Sugai, G., & Sprague, J. (2000). *School-Wide Information System (SWIS).* Eugene, OR: University of Oregon.

National Association of School Psychologists. (2010). *Model for comprehensive and integrated school psychological services.* Bethesda, MD: Author. Retrieved from http://www.nasponline.org/standards/2010standards/2_PracticeModel.pdf

Noell, G. H., Witt, J. C., Slider, N. J., Connell, J. E., Gatti, S. L., Williams, K. L., … Duhon, G. J. (2005). Treatment implementation following behavioral consultation in schools: A comparison of three follow-up strategies. *School Psychology Review, 34,* 87–106.

Northwest Evaluation Association. (2004). *Measures of academic progress.* Lake Oswego, OR: Author.

Renaissance Learning. (1996). *STAR Reading.* Wisconsin Rapids, WI: Author.

Rosenfield, S. (1987). *Instructional consultation.* Hillsdale, NJ: Erlbaum.

Rosenfield, S., & Gravois, T. (1996). *Instructional consultation teams: Collaborating for change.* New York, NY: Guilford Press.

Schmoker, M. (2001). *Data driven decisions to improve results* [Video]. Sandy, UT: School Improvement Network.

Shapiro, E. S., & Clemens, N. H. (2009). A conceptual model for evaluating system effects of response to intervention. *Assessment for Effective Intervention, 35,* 3–16. doi:10.1177/1534508408330080

Shapiro, E. S., Keller, M. A., Lutz, J. G., Santoro, L. E., & Hintze, J. M. (2006). Curriculum-based measures and performance on state assessment and standardized tests: Reading and math performance in Pennsylvania. *Journal of Psychoeducational Assessment, 24,* 19–35. doi:10.1177/0734282905285237

Shinn, M. R., & Garman, G. (2006). *AIMSweb.* Eden Prairie, MN: Edformation.

Sprick, R. (2011). *Tracking Referrals, Encouragements, Notifications, Discipline, Safety (TRENDS).* Eugene, OR: Pacific Northwest Publishing.

University of Oregon Center on Teaching and Learning. (2013). *DIBELS Next Tier 1 Data.* Eugene, OR: Author. Retrieved from http://dibels.uoregon.edu

Vaughn, S., & Fuchs, L. S. (2003). Redefining learning disabilities as inadequate response to instruction: The promise and potential pitfalls. *Learning Disabilities Research & Practice, 18,* 137–146. doi:10.1111/1540-5826.00070

Walker, H., & Severson, H. (1992). *Systematic screening for behavior disorders.* Longmont, CO: Sopris West.

Zirkel, P. A., & Thomas, L. B. (2010). State laws and guidelines for implementing RTI. *Teaching Exceptional Children, 43,* 60–73.

APPENDIX A. SCREENING AND INFORMATION RECORDING FORM–ACADEMICS

Tier 1 Screening and Intervention Record Form (Academics)

Date:_____   Meeting: ___Beginning ___Midyear ___End of Year   Grade:_____

Meeting Attendees	Position	Meeting Attendees	Position

Target Skill: Percentage of Students at Proficient Level Based on Benchmark/Standard

Goal for Next Quarter: Percentage of Students at Proficient Level Based on Benchmark/Standard

Strategies Selected for Implementation This Quarter (Tier 1)

Logistics for Implementation of Strategies Selected ("To do")

Tier 2–3 Screening and Intervention Record Form (Academics)

Students Identified for Tier 2–3

Decoding	Decoding & Fluency	Fluency	Fluency & Comprehension	Comprehension	Monitor	Other

Goal for Next Quarter (Tier 2)

Decoding	
Decoding/Fluency	
Fluency	
Fluency/ Comprehension	
Comprehension	

Strategies (Programs) Selected for Implementation This Quarter (Tier 2)

Group	Strategy/Program	Progress Monitoring	PM Freq.
Decoding			
Decoding/Fluency			
Fluency			
Fluency/ Comprehension			
Comprehension			

Logistics for Implementation of Strategies Selected ("To do")

Tier 3 Screening and Intervention Record Form (Academics)

Students Identified for Tier 3 (Customized Interventions)

Student Name	Assessment Measure	Score	Assessment Measure	Score	Assessment Measure	Score

Goal for Next Quarter (Tier 3)

Student Name	Goal

Strategies Selected for Implementation This Quarter (Tier 3)

Student Name	Strategies	Person Responsible	Frequency

Progress Monitoring Plan

Student Name	Measure	Person Responsible	Frequency

NEXT MEETING   Date:_____   Location:_____   Time:_____

APPENDIX B. SCREENING AND INFORMATION RECORDING FORM–BEHAVIOR

Tier 1 Screening and Intervention Record Form (Behavior)

Date:_____   Meeting: ___Beginning ___Midyear ___End of Year   Grade:_____

Meeting Attendees	Position	Meeting Attendees	Position

Target Behaviors (High Frequency Across Multiple Students)

Goals for Next Quarter: Percent Decrease in Numbers of Identified Target Behaviors

Strategies Selected for Implementation This Quarter (for Each Target Behavior)

Logistics for Implementation of Strategies Selected ("To do")

Tier 2–3 Screening and Intervention Record Form (Behavior)

Students Identified for Tier 2–3

Intervention Grouping #1	Intervention Grouping #2	Intervention Grouping #3	Intervention Grouping #4	Intervention Grouping #5	Monitor	Other

Goal for Next Quarter (Tier 2)

Intervention Grouping #1	
Intervention Grouping #2	
Intervention Grouping #3	
Intervention Grouping #4	
Intervention Grouping #5	

Strategies (Programs) Selected for Implementation This Quarter (Tier 2)

Group	Strategy/Program	Progress Monitoring	PM Freq.
Intervention Grouping #1			
Intervention Grouping #2			
Intervention Grouping #3			
Intervention Grouping #4			
Intervention Grouping #5			

Logistics for Implementation of Strategies Selected ("To do")

Tier 3 Screening and Intervention Record Form (Behavior)

Students Identified for Tier 3 (Customized Interventions)

Student Name	Assessment Measure	Score	Assessment Measure	Score	Assessment Measure	Score

Goal for Next Quarter (Tier 3)

Student Name	Goal

Strategies Selected for Implementation This Quarter (Tier 3)

Student Name	Strategies	Person Responsible	Frequency

Progress Monitoring Plan

Student Name	Measure	Person Responsible	Frequency

NEXT MEETING   Date:_____   Location:_____   Time:_____

7

Best Practices in Universal Screening

Craig A. Albers
University of Wisconsin–Madison
Ryan J. Kettler
Rutgers, The State University of New Jersey

OVERVIEW

Universal screening within educational settings is a process that generally consists of administering measures or collecting other data to allow broad generalizations to be made regarding the future performance and outcomes of all students, both at the individual level and at the group level (e.g., classroom, grade, school, and district). More specifically, universal screening procedures are designed to (a) be administered to all students; (b) identify students who are at risk of future academic, behavioral, or emotional difficulties and should thus be considered for prevention services or more intensive interventions; (c) provide data regarding the degree to which school-based academic instruction, behavioral assistance, and social–emotional programs are meeting the needs of students at the classroom, grade, school, and district levels; and (d) provide information to school psychologists and other educators about individual students' and systems' academic, behavioral, and social–emotional needs (Kettler, Glover, Albers, & Feeney-Kettler, 2014a). At the most basic level, universal screening procedures are designed to identify those students who are currently asymptomatic but who will experience difficulties at some time in the future. The data lead to inferences about future performance.

This chapter is intended to provide school psychologists with fundamental knowledge regarding how to evaluate and select universal screening procedures appropriate for use within their schools. With this information, school psychologists will be able to provide guidance to school-based teams responsible for the selection, implementation, and interpretation of universal screening procedures.

The implementation and utilization of universal screening procedures are critical components of the National Association of School Psychologists (NASP) *Model for Comprehensive and Integrated School Psychological Services* (NASP, 2010). As a critical component of the NASP domain of Data-Based Decision Making and Accountability, universal screening procedures are practices that are essentially applicable to all aspects and domains of school psychology service delivery. For example, when linked with universal instruction and supplemental intervention, universal screening is an important component for improving academic engagement and achievement, as well as facilitating effective instruction for all students from diverse educational settings. Furthermore, universal screening procedures provide data for the problem-solving process (e.g., Albers, Elliott, Kettler, & Roach, 2013), assist in decision making in multitiered models (e.g., Parisi, Ihlo, & Glover, 2014), and guide service provision to students who are language or cultural minorities (e.g., Albers, Mission, & Bice-Urbach, 2013).

School psychologists have expertise in assessment, data collection and interpretation, and evidence-based practice, and thus should serve in a leadership role in multiple aspects of universal screening, including the selection of appropriate procedures, administration of the measures when appropriate, data analysis, and interpretation. In the remainder of this chapter, we (a) examine basic considerations associated with evaluating and selecting an appropriate universal screening measure; (b) describe the broad types of universal screening procedures that are available; (c) provide an overview of best practices in universal screening; and (d) conclude with a brief example of how a school psychologist can be involved in the selection, implementation, and interpretation of universal screening practices. Considering that the appropriateness of a universal screening procedure is highly dependent on the specific conditions within a school or district, we avoid making specific recommendations for certain measures. Rather, we emphasize the critical variables to consider when examining the use of specific procedures within the local school setting.

BASIC CONSIDERATIONS

Best practices in universal screening require that school psychologists have knowledge in multiple areas: (a) the role of universal screening within prevention and early intervention models, (b) applicable psychometrics (e.g., reliability and validity, including conditional probability) and other characteristics (e.g., accessibility) associated with universal screening, and (c) the different types of universal screening approaches (e.g., broadband versus narrowband, multiple gate).

Universal Screening

Screening as a method of early identification is not a new concept in educational settings. The relatively recent emphasis in education to implement multitiered intervention has resulted in renewed and increased interest in universal screening (e.g., Donovon & Cross, 2002; Kettler, Glover, Albers, & Feeney-Kettler, 2014b), with a shift in focus from screening for identification to screening for intervention. Although there remains much to learn regarding optimal universal screening approaches, it is clear that universal screening systems need to be appropriate (e.g., compatible with local needs, aligned with constructs of interest, supported theoretically and empirically), usable (e.g., feasible, acceptable, accompanied by accommodations), technically adequate (e.g., reliable and leading to valid inferences), and determined to have outcome utility (Glover & Albers, 2007).

Prevention and early intervention programs, consistent with response-to-intervention (RTI) models, are predicated on identifying students who are in need of various intervention services as early as possible in order to minimize or even avert the pervasive negative consequences that occur as a result of academic difficulties and failure. These multitiered intervention models and the problem-solving process require a continuous review of student progress. In particular, data collection should occur to determine (a) how all students are performing academically, behaviorally, and emotionally (i.e., universal screening); (b) how students are responding to core (i.e., universal) instruction and programs (i.e., assessment and progress monitoring); and (c) how students are responding to supplemental interventions and supports (i.e., ongoing progress monitoring). Therefore, early identification is a high priority based on the assumption that behavioral and academic problems—both proximal and distal—can be averted, or least minimized, through early identification, prevention, and intervention.

Evaluating Universal Screening Procedures

Because screening is a form of assessment, guidelines for evaluating universal screening measures and procedures mirror recommendations for assessment in general. First and foremost, school psychologists should ensure that universal screening data are directly linked with intervention services. The intervention services should be supported by research and evaluation in one's own educational setting. Second, it is essential to recall that there is error in all measurement. However, we tend to tolerate greater error associated with universal screening procedures as compared to measures that are used for classification purposes. This increased tolerance is because of (a) the expectation that screeners must be more time and resource efficient and (b) the understanding that the decisions made based on data from universal screening procedure are associated with lower stakes decisions (e.g., group intervention rather than classification with a disability). Nevertheless, school psychologists must be aware of this measurement error—resulting in varying degrees of precision—when interpreting universal screening results and developing corresponding recommendations. Thus, concepts of reliability and validity, including conditional probability, are critical components to consider when providing guidance to school teams and administrators.

Reliability

Among the list of potential screening systems, indices of reliability should be compared as an indicator of how consistent the scores are. Internal consistency, test–retest reliability, and interrater reliability are all key types of evidence for the consistency of scores from screening systems. Because screening systems are preventive and brief by nature, it may be acceptable for such reliability coefficients (e.g., coefficient alpha around .80 rather than around .90) to be lower than would be acceptable for more complete assessment batteries. Once a screening system is identified as adequately reliable, the issue of the validity of inferences drawn from its scores can be addressed.

Validity

Five types of validity evidence should be considered when evaluating universal screening procedures: (a) content validity, (b) validity based on response processes, (c) internal structure validity, (d) validity based on relations to other variables, and (e) consequential validity. Content validity refers to the degree to which the content of the measure appears to reflect the dimension of interest. Validity based on response processes refers to the degree to which the respondent to a measure interprets and responds to it as intended. Internal structure validity refers to how well the relationships among parts of a test (e.g., items, subscales) match the theory on which the test is based. Validity evidence based on relations to other variables (i.e., criterion validity) refers to scores from a measure sharing positive relationships with similar variables (i.e., convergent validity), negative relationships with dissimilar variables (i.e., divergent validity), and nonrelationships with unrelated variables (i.e., discriminant validity). Relations to other variables is one of the most common types of evidence used in evaluating assessment tools in education and psychology, and is critical because we develop universal screening tools with preconceived notions regarding how they will relate to measures of other constructs (e.g., reading, motivation, and attention). The most important subtype of this evidence for universal screening systems is convergent validity, which specifically focuses on the relationship between new assessment tools and established measures of similar constructs (e.g., achievement and cognitive ability). Consequential validity evidence is a broader concern that represents an endpoint in the instrument evaluation process. It concerns larger issues such as whether the implementation of the screening system has had a net positive or net negative effect on the school system. All of these types of validity evidence are important to evaluating universal screening systems.

Validity: Conditional Probability

While test developers have historically used the Pearson correlation for quantifying evidence based on relations between scores that lie on an interval scale, knowing a specific Pearson correlation between a universal screening measure and some defined outcome measure does not provide the necessary information to guide a school psychologist in selecting an appropriate universal screening measure. Instead, a more appropriate set of indices for evaluating screening systems—based on the concept of diagnostic accuracy and known as conditional probability indices—has gained popularity for use by school psychologists.

While many screening systems may yield a score or scores that can be interpreted on an interval level, the purpose of the assessment is typically to divide examinees into two groups: (a) those in need of prevention or early intervention services and (b) those who do not need prevention or early intervention services. Conditional probability indices are a set of proportions that take into account the two dichotomies involved with each screening case. When an individual is screened, one relevant dichotomy is that the individual may or may not be identified as needing preventive intervention, and the second relevant dichotomy is that the individual may or may not actually need intervention. The first dichotomy is defined by the outcome of the screening system in question. The second dichotomy is defined by the real and true need and can never be known with certainty. The gold standard criterion, which is typically an established measure that is too long to be used universally in practice, is used in research as a proxy for reality. The cases are sorted into four categories based on the two dichotomies: a true positive (identified by the screening system and needing help in reality), a false positive (identified by the screening system but not needing help in reality), a false negative (not identified by the screening system but needing help in reality), and a true negative (not identified by the screening system and not needing help in reality).

From these four categories, numerous indices can be calculated. Sensitivity (the proportion of examinees who need help who are accurately identified) and specificity (the proportion of examinees who do not need help who are accurately not identified) are the most commonly reported. Also important to consider are positive predictive value (i.e., the proportion of examinees who are identified who actually need help) and negative predictive value (i.e., the proportion of examinees who are not identified who actually do not need help). Two other indices—important for providing the context for interpreting the aforementioned—are the hit rate (the proportion of all cases that are true positive or negative) and the base rate (the proportion of all cases that in reality need preventive intervention). Table 7.1 is a depiction of the four categories relevant to screening

Table 7.1. Conditional Probability Framework

	Reality (Truth)		
Screening System	Needs Help	Does Not Need Help	Total
Not at-risk score	False negatives (FN)	True negatives (TN)	FN + TN
At-risk score	True positives (TP)	False positives (FP)	TP + FP
Total	FN + TP	TN + FP	FN + TN + TP + FP

Note. Sensitivity = [TP / (TP + FN)]; specificity = [TN / (TN + FP)]; positive predictive value = [TP / TP + FP]; negative predictive value = [TN / (TN + FN)]; hit rate = [(TP + TN) / (FN + TN + TP + FP)]; base rate = [(TP + FN) / (FN + TN + TP + FP)].

decisions, and includes formulas to calculate the aforementioned indices.

It is important that the aforementioned indices, particularly sensitivity, specificity, negative predictive value, and positive predictive value, be reported together for the evaluation of a screening tool. The indices are interrelated in such a way that it is difficult to maximize all four. School psychologists should understand and use conditional probability indices in selecting an appropriate universal screening system, as Pearson correlations fail to provide the necessary information regarding the measure's diagnostic accuracy, which is the sine qua non of a universal screening measure. Figure 7.1 helps illustrate this potential shortcoming associated with the Pearson correlation. For example, in Figure 7.1a, the correlation between hypothetical oral reading fluency scores and scores from a hypothetical outcome measure is a perfect 1.0, and the conditional probability indices are also perfect (i.e., equal to 1.0). However, in Figure 7.1b, the correlation is large (i.e., .68), yet because of the nonnormal distribution of the scores from which most of the error is at the extremes, the conditional probability indices accurately reveal that the measure identifies students in need of intervention versus those not in need of intervention. Conversely, Figure 7.1c features a correlation of .68 with a different nonnormal distribution of scores, this time with most of the error around the cut score. The conditional probability indices in this case accurately reveal that the universal screening measure does not identify students in need of intervention. Because Pearson correlations do not capture the difference between error that is likely to affect a decision and error that is not likely to affect a decision, they are not appropriate for evaluating decision-making tools, such as universal screening instruments.

Universal Screening Approaches

In the broadest sense, universal screening procedures are intended to assess a child's likelihood of success or failure based on limited and varying amounts of information. Thus, schools have been doing screening to some degree for many years. The critical differences between screening that occurred in years past and screening in the current time period is the emphasis on the process being universal and the increased use of standardized measures and procedures. Prior to the recent increased interest in universal screening measures and approaches, general screening approaches were targeted toward students who were already raising concerns with educators. These approaches tended to consist of (a) records review; (b) observations; (c) more in-depth self-reports with the student; (d) in-depth standardized rating scales from parents, teachers, or others with direct or indirect contact with the student; (e) teacher referral; (f) interviews with parents, teachers, or others with direct or indirect contact with the student; (g) and performance on school, district, or state academic assessments. These more traditional screening measures tended to have inadequate technical properties, resulting in frequent misidentification of cases as false positives or false negatives. Furthermore, since these procedures were not conducted with all students, schools frequently failed to identify asymptomatic students who eventually experienced difficulties. Current best practice guidelines suggest that educators should use standardized procedures that are reliable and have been validated as part of the development process. Such approaches may be broadband, narrowband, and multiple gate.

Broadband Versus Narrowband

When attempting to determine what universal screening measure to select, school psychologists must consider what domain or domains are of interest. Broadband universal screening approaches are designed to assess several domains (academic issues, externalizing behaviors, and internalizing behaviors) concurrently, whereas narrowband universal screening approaches are designed to assess a specific domain (early literacy skills, basic mathematics skills, anxiety) of interest. DiPerna, Bailey, and Anthony (2014) described broadband

Figure 7.1. Scatterplots of Correlations and Conditional Probability Indices

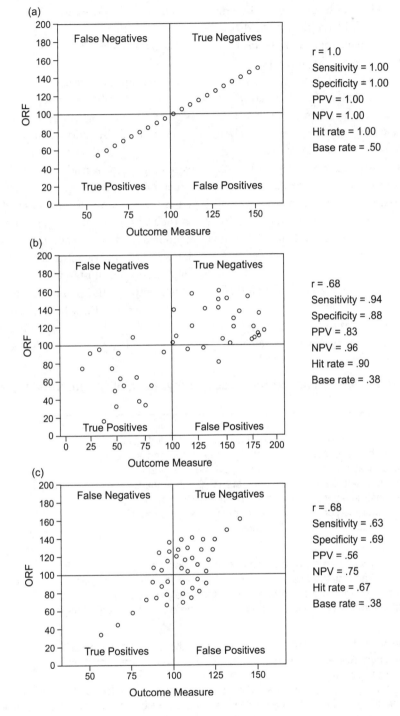

universal screening approaches as providing an efficient and broad representation of student functioning, whereas narrowband approaches provide a more in-depth assessment of specific target skills.

Multiple-Gate Approaches

Within a multiple-gate model, each sequential stage (i.e., gate) is conducted on fewer students, is more thorough,

and is increasingly accurate in identifying students at risk. These multiple-gate approaches, in which a different measure is typically used at each stage, result in a multimethod process that is consistent with best practices in assessment. An example of a multiple-gate approach could start with a teacher completing an initial screen of the whole classroom at Gate 1. This initial screen would consist of rank ordering all students in the classroom according to their frequency of disruptive behaviors. For Gate 2, the teacher would complete a standardized rating scale, such as the Behavior Assessment System for Children–Second Edition (BASC-2), for the five students ranked in Gate 1 as having the highest frequency of disruptive behaviors. Finally, Gate 3 would consist of having the school psychologist conduct a standardized observation of any student for whom the teacher's ratings on BASC-2 indicated *at-risk* or *clinically significant* scores on at least one scale. Additionally, Gate 3 could be supplemented with parental ratings on the parent form of the BASC-2. Within multiple-gate approaches, it is acceptable for the first level of screening to produce a significant number of false positives, as the more thorough second level of screening is intended to identify those students who truly do not need further assessment or intervention.

BEST PRACTICES IN UNIVERSAL SCREENING

School psychologists should consider several guidelines when examining current or new universal screening measures and procedures. Table 7.2 provides a list of these accessibility, reliability, and validity guidelines, which are also addressed in more detail below.

Selecting a Universal Screening Measure

Once existing universal screening measures and procedures are identified, the school psychologist can then begin examining whether they should be modified or supplemented by additional procedures. Christ and Nelson (2014) outline the initial questions for a school psychologist to consider when selecting a universal screening measure or system. School psychologists must determine (a) what the purpose of the measure under consideration is, including what domain is being examined and how well the measure aligns with the domain; (b) the qualifications that are necessary for someone to administer and score the measure; (c) the match between the population for whom the measure was designed and the school psychologist's population of interest; (d) whether the measure is group or individually administered; (e) what resources (e.g., personnel and

Table 7.2. Key Questions for Evaluating the Accessibility, Reliability, and Validity of a Universal Screening System

Accessibility
- Will the respondents (examinees or raters) be able to read and understand the screener?
- Does the school have the necessary infrastructure to implement the screener?
- Are fiscal resources available to purchase and support the screener?
- Will the screener be acceptable among stakeholders (e.g., students, teachers, parents)?
- Are all necessary accommodations available to implement the screener?
- Is it feasible to administer the screener in this educational environment?
- Are the rules for scoring and interpreting the screener clear?

Reliability
- Do the items fit together well (often indicated as coefficient alpha $\geqslant .80$)?
- Do scores from multiple administrations of the screener agree (positively correlate)?
- Do scores from alternate forms of the screener agree (positively correlate)?
- Do scores from multiple raters or scorers of the screener agree (positively correlate)?

Validity
- Do the items or content of the screener appear to represent the intended construct?
- Were the items or content reviewed by experts in the area of the intended construct?
- Will users respond to the screener in the intended manner?
- Does the screener agree (positively correlate) with similar measures, as intended?
- Does the screener share nonrelationships (correlations near .00) with, for example, gender, race?
- Does the screener connect to preventive interventions?
- How well does the screener predict who will have future (e.g., 3, 6, 12 months) difficulties?
- How many students does the screener misidentify (e.g., students truly at risk but identified as not being at risk, students truly not at risk but identified as being at risk)?
- Can the screener lead to changes in school-wide achievement or behavioral records?
- Can the screener lead to changes in special education placement trends?
- Have stakeholders been pleased with the change to the screener?
- Have the overall financial costs to the school been reduced by using the screener?

Note. Questions were influenced by Glover and Albers (2007), Kettler and Feeney-Kettler (2011), and Christ and Nelson (2014).

time) are necessary to administer the measure; and (f) whether appropriate technical documentation exists to support the measure's use. Additional questions for evaluating the accessibility, reliability, and validity (including predictive indices) of a universal screening measure are included in Table 7.2.

The National Center on Response to Intervention provides a thorough review of universal screening measures in the areas of literacy and mathematics (see http://www.rti4success.org/screeningTools). A significant number of measures are evaluated in terms of reliability and validity, generalizability, and efficiency, including administration and scoring time, procedures for scoring, and availability of benchmarks and norms. School psychologists are thus encouraged to consult information available on that website as a first step in examining the adequacy of their current approaches and of possible alternate approaches.

Much of the initial evidence on the accessibility, reliability, and validity of a screening system can be obtained from the technical manuals or research conducted on a screening system. However, evidence-based practice requires continuing evaluation of this evidence within the setting in which the screening system is implemented. School psychologists should continually evaluate screening systems to determine whether the psychometrics and other indices of quality hold true in their own settings. Such evidence may be collected by (a) maintaining the previous system for a year and evaluating agreement between the two, (b) calculating internal consistency for the scores obtained in practice, and (c) distributing surveys to stakeholders with questions addressing everything from accessibility to consequential validity of the new system. Collecting this evaluative evidence truly completes the cycle of evidence-based practice that is consistent with universal screening.

A critical issue in need of more consideration by researchers and practitioners alike relates to the selection of universal screening measures and procedures that are appropriate for use with all students from populations that are increasingly linguistically, culturally, and racially diverse. Variables such as limited English proficiency, types of instruction utilized within the school setting, quality of prior school experiences, attendance, and mobility are only a few of the essential variables that may have an impact on interpretation of the data that are collected (Albers et al., 2013). For example, interpretation of data collected from the universal screening of students classified as English language learners (ELLs) needs to be interpreted within

a solid understanding of specific English language proficiency levels (e.g., see Albers & Mission, 2014). Failure to do so often will result in an ELL being identified as at risk and assigned to supplemental interventions, when in reality the student is making adequate progress for a student with his or her specific level of English language proficiency.

Literacy

The literacy domain has been the most thoroughly examined over the past couple of decades. Thus, there are many universal screening options within this area, particularly for students in the earlier grades. For example, Burns, Haegele, and Petersen-Brown (2014) noted that the development of curriculum-based measurement (CBM) has advanced educators' abilities to universally screen and monitor student progress. Research conducted over multiple decades has demonstrated that CBM data are closely linked to in-class performance, are sensitive to student progress over time, are psychometrically sound, and are brief and easy to administer to a large number of students. Furthermore, the data allow teachers to compare one student's performance to the performance of other students, and also measure individual student growth. Similar advances have been made in universal screening in other academic and nonacademic areas.

One critical issue in selecting a universal screening approach for literacy is the grade range of the students to be screened, because approaches vary greatly by age. Universal screening approaches for literacy tend to be based on one or more of the five big ideas in beginning reading (i.e., phonemic awareness, alphabetic principle, accuracy and fluency with text, vocabulary, comprehension) as outlined by the National Reading Panel (National Institute of Child Health and Human Development, 2000). In early childhood literacy (i.e., preschool-age students), McConnell, Bradfield, and Wackerle-Hollman (2014) stress that universal screening measures should sample performance in the domains of oral language, alphabet knowledge and concepts about print, phonological awareness, and comprehension. Given the relative novelty of assessment approaches for preschool-age students, McConnell et al. (2014) identified three measures for consideration: (a) Get Ready to Read! Revised, (b) the CIRCLE–Phonological Awareness, Language, and Literacy System+, and (c) the Individual Growth and Development Indicators–Version 2.0.

Get Ready to Read! Revised (http://www.getreadytoread.org) is designed for use with children ages 3–6 and consists of 20 multiple-choice items that require the child to select the most appropriate answers. Items are associated with print knowledge, linguistic awareness, and emergent writing concepts. The CIRCLE–Phonological Awareness, Language, and Literacy System+ is designed for use with children ages 3.5–5 and also includes a mathematics screening component. Within the literacy area, subtests examine rapid letter naming, rapid vocabulary naming, and phonological awareness. The Individual Growth and Development Indicators–Version 2.0, designed for use with children during the year prior to entering kindergarten, examines the domains of oral language, phonological awareness, alphabet knowledge, and comprehension. School psychologists interested in learning more about these measures are encouraged to read the review provided by McConnell et al. (2014).

Universal screening and assessment in the literacy domain have received the greatest amount of attention at the early elementary grades (e.g., K–3), with limited attention at the middle and high school grade levels. Advances in CBM of early literacy performance have led to the development of the DIBELS (http://dibels. uoregon.edu/), AIMSweb (http://www.aimsweb.com), and Easy CBM (http://easycbm.com/) systems. All of these approaches screen students' skills in multiple early literacy domains, including phonological awareness, alphabetic principles, reading fluency, and reading comprehension. Early literacy measures typically include subtests relating to initial sound fluency, phoneme segmentation, letter naming fluency, letter sound fluency, nonsense word fluency, and oral reading fluency. Extending universal screening procedures for literacy to use with older elementary and middle school students typically consists of oral reading fluency measures and maze measures as indicators of reading comprehension.

Informal reading inventories, which are frequently used by educators as a form of universal screening, often have inadequate psychometric properties and insufficient evidence of diagnostic accuracy. Although there is evidence that informal reading inventories correlate with other literacy measures, significant concerns about the (a) reliability of their use, (b) linguistic differences between passages, (c) relative complexity of administering and scoring procedures, and (d) amount of time to administer the informal reading inventories suggest that alternate procedures, such as those based on CBM, are more appropriate for universal screening purposes. Similarly, many districts across the nation have started to administer the Measures of Academic Progress, which

is a computer-based adaptive assessment. Although the Measures of Academic Progress subtests are reported to have adequate psychometric information, the cost per student and the 40-minute administration time (three times per year) may be prohibitive to many districts and schools. More in-depth syntheses of universal screening literacy approaches are provided by Burns et al. (2014) and Elliott, Huai, and Roach (2007).

Mathematics

Universal screening in mathematics is beginning to gain more attention from researchers and practitioners. Universal screening in mathematics, particularly at the elementary grade levels, tends to be focused on both single proficiency domains (e.g., addition, subtraction, multiplication) and multiple proficiency domains (e.g., mathematics reasoning, word problems), whereas universal screening measures for later grades focus exclusively on multiple proficiency domains. Clarke, Haymond, and Gersten (2014) and Gersten et al. (2012) provide an in-depth review of multiple measures that can be used at different grade levels, as does the National Center on Response to Intervention. The more commonly used universal screening measures within this area include AIMSweb Math Computation Concepts and Applications, Tests of Early Numeracy (i.e., missing number, number identification, oral counting, quantity discrimination), Easy CBM, and the Measures of Academic Progress.

Social, Emotional, and Behavioral

Universal screening within the domains of social, emotional, and behavioral functioning often are in the form of broadband assessments. For example, the Social Skills Improvement System–Performance Screening Guide allows for universal screening within the areas of social behavior and academic achievement, and specific areas include reading, mathematics, motivation to learn, and prosocial behavior.

Walker, Small, Severson, and Feil (2014) provide a number of examples of multiple-gate instruments, including the Systematic Screening for Behavior Disorders, that can be used to universally screen for social, emotional, and behavioral issues. It is intended for use with elementary-age children (K–6) potentially at risk for either an externalizing (e.g., aggression, hyperactivity) or internalizing (e.g., shyness, depression) behavior disorder.

A number of other measures have evidence suggesting their appropriateness for universal screening of social, emotional, and behavioral difficulties. These include the

BASC-2 Behavioral and Emotional Screening System, the Student Risk Screening Scale, and the Strengths and Difficulties Questionnaire (see http://www.sdqinfo.com). In-depth reviews of these measures are provided by Kamphaus, Reynolds, and Dever (2014). Universal screening measures specific to mental health issues are described in detail by Levitt, Saka, Romanelli, and Hoagwood (2007) as well as by O'Connell, Boat, and Warner (2009).

Case Example

Theresa Johnson was the school psychologist at a K–5 elementary school located within a large urban school district. Approximately 3 years ago the school staff made the decision to begin implementing a multitiered intervention model within the domain of literacy. As part of this process, Ms. Johnson was charged with the task of identifying an appropriate universal screening for literacy measure for use within the school.

After reviewing multiple universal screening for literacy measures and consulting numerous resources, Ms. Johnson recommended that the school adopt the AIMSweb assessments and corresponding data management and reporting system. This recommendation was based on multiple factors, including the (a) accessibility (e.g., cost, feasibility of administration, standardized procedures) of the measures; (b) the reliability, validity, and predictive accuracy of CBM procedures as reported during the past 30 years, as well as similar evidence regarding the use of AIMSweb materials since its development; (c) the ability to use the

measures for more frequent progress monitoring of those students displaying academic difficulties; (d) the AIMSweb database, which would allow multiple individuals to enter data and allow each classroom teacher to readily access the data and corresponding reports; and (e) ability to administer AIMSweb measures for all students. Additionally, the AIMSweb database allowed for the use of multiple norms (e.g., nationwide norms, local norms) to evaluate students' performances.

The school made all of the necessary preparations (e.g., purchasing of materials and training of staff to administer measures, enter data, and interpret results) to conduct benchmarking with all students in fall, winter, and spring. Following the administration of the September (fall) benchmark, Ms. Johnson met with the school administrators and third-grade teachers to examine their data. As indicated in Figure 7.2, only 56% ($n = 28$) of the school's third-grade students performed at the average level or above on the measure of oral reading fluency, with the remaining 44% of third graders performing at the below average or well below average levels. Given the high percentage of third-grade students failing to reach the target of 77 words per minute and the high percentage of students performing below average, the third-grade team determined that they could not provide individualized supplemental interventions to each student. Rather, the data confirmed their prior concerns that the currently implemented literacy curriculum was not meeting the needs of many students. Thus, the team agreed to provide small group supplementary interventions through the remainder of the year to the students performing below

Figure 7.2. Third-Grade AIMSweb Oral Reading Fluency Scores From the Fall Benchmark Period

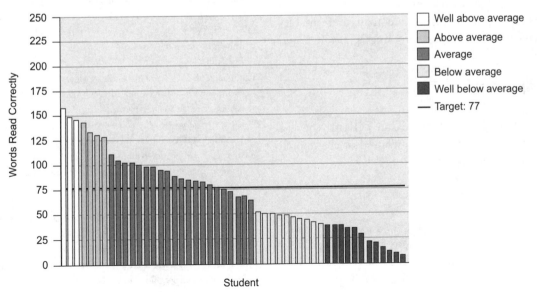

the target benchmark. To address this issue long term, the school also determined that it would explore alternative literacy curricula to implement in the next academic year.

SUMMARY

Universal screening is a scientifically based practice that involves assessing student performance and evaluating the effectiveness of instruction to identify students in need of preventive interventions. The concept of universal screening in education and related fields is not new. What is new is the increasing recognition that universal screening is a critical topic for school psychologists and other educators, not only for legal reasons, but also as best practice in providing prevention and early intervention services.

Advances in the understanding of universal screening concepts and approaches have allowed school psychologists and other educators to have access to a growing knowledge base regarding best practices in universal screening procedures across multiple domains, including academic achievement and social, emotional, and behavioral functioning. Thus, school psychologists and support personnel are able to use screening instruments with increased confidence. However, given that there are multiple approaches for conducting universal screening within each domain of interest, it is essential for school psychologists to examine which approach or approaches best fit their specific context. School psychologists are accordingly encouraged to evaluate multiple universal screening approaches on the criteria of accessibility, reliability, construct validity, and consequential validity. Science on universal screening is not yet mature, as we are only at the beginning stages of understanding the multiple components and variables that are relevant in universal screening applications and research.

AUTHOR NOTE

Disclosure. Craig A. Albers and Ryan J. Kettler have a financial interest in books they authored or coauthored that are referenced in this chapter.

REFERENCES

Albers, C. A., Elliott, S. N., Kettler, R. J., & Roach, A. T. (2013). Evaluating intervention outcomes. In R. Brown-Chidsey & K. J. Andren (Eds.), *Problem-solving based assessment for educational intervention* (2nd ed., pp. 344–360). New York, NY: Guilford Press.

Albers, C. A., & Mission, P. (2014). Universal screening of English language learners: Language proficiency and literacy. In R. J. Kettler, T. A. Glover, C. A. Albers, & K. A. Feeney-Kettler (Eds.), *Universal screening in educational settings: Evidence-based decision making for schools* (pp. 275–304). Washington, DC: American Psychological Association.

Albers, C. A., Mission, P. L., & Bice-Urbach, B. J. (2013). Considering diverse learner characteristics in problem-solving assessment. In R. Brown-Chidsey & K. J. Andren (Eds.), *Problem-solving based assessment for educational intervention* (2nd ed., pp. 101–122). New York, NY: Guilford Press.

Burns, M. K., Haegele, K., & Petersen-Brown, S. (2014). Screening for early reading skills: Using data to guide resources and instruction. In R. J. Kettler, T. A. Glover, C. A. Albers, & K. A. Feeney-Kettler (Eds.), *Universal screening in educational settings: Evidence-based decision making for schools* (pp. 171–197). Washington, DC: American Psychological Association.

Christ, T., & Nelson, P. (2014). Screening assessment: Practical and psychometric considerations. In R. J. Kettler, T. A. Glover, C. A. Albers, & K. A. Feeney-Kettler (Eds.), *Universal screening in educational settings: Evidence-based decision making for schools* (pp. 79–110). Washington, DC: American Psychological Association.

Clarke, B., Haymond, K., & Gersten, R. (2014). Mathematics screening measures for the primary grades. In R. J. Kettler, T. A. Glover, C. A. Albers, & K. A. Feeney-Kettler (Eds.), *Universal screening in educational settings: Evidence-based decision making for schools* (pp. 199–221). Washington, DC: American Psychological Association.

DiPerna, J. C., Bailey, C. G., & Anthony, C. (2014). Broadband screening of academic and social behavior. In R. J. Kettler, T. A. Glover, C. A. Albers, & K. A. Feeney-Kettler (Eds.), *Universal screening in educational settings: Evidence-based decision making for schools* (pp. 223–248). Washington, DC: American Psychological Association.

Donovan, M. S., & Cross, C. T. (2002). *Minority students in special and gifted education.* Washington, DC: National Academies Press.

Elliott, S. N., Huai, N., & Roach, A. T. (2007). Universal and early screening for educational difficulties: Current and future approaches. *Journal of School Psychology, 45,* 137–161.

Gersten, R., Clarke, B., Jordan, N. C., Newman-Gonchar, R., Haymond, K., & Wilkins, C. (2012). Universal screening in mathematics for the primary grades: Beginnings of a research base. *Exceptional Children, 78,* 423–445.

Glover, T. A., & Albers, C. A. (2007). Considerations for evaluating universal screening assessments. *Journal of School Psychology, 45,* 117–135.

Kamphaus, R. W., Reynolds, C. R., & Dever, B. V. (2014). Behavioral and mental health screening. In R. J. Kettler, T. A. Glover, C. A. Albers, & K. A. Feeney-Kettler (Eds.), *Universal screening in educational settings: Evidence-based decision making for schools* (pp. 249–273). Washington, DC: American Psychological Association.

Kettler, R. J., & Feeney-Kettler, K. A. (2011). Screening systems and decision making at the preschool level: Application of a comprehensive validity framework. *Psychology in the Schools, 48,* 430–441.

Kettler, R. J., Glover, T. A., Albers, C. A., & Feeney-Kettler, K. A. (2014a). An introduction to universal screening in educational settings. In R. J. Kettler, T. A. Glover, C. A. Albers, & K. A. Feeney-Kettler (Eds.), *Universal screening in educational settings: Evidence-based decision making for schools* (pp. 3–16). Washington, DC: American Psychological Association.

Kettler, R. J., Glover, T. A., Albers, C. A., & Feeney-Kettler, K. A. (Eds.). (2014b). *Universal screening in educational settings: Evidence-based decision making for schools.* Washington, DC: American Psychological Association.

Levitt, J. M., Saka, N., Romanelli, L. H., & Hoagwood, K. (2007). Early identification of mental health problems in schools: The status of instrumentation. *Journal of School Psychology, 45,* 163–191.

McConnell, S., Bradfield, T., & Wackerle-Hollman, A. (2014). Early childhood literacy screening. In R. J. Kettler, T. A. Glover, C. A. Albers, & K. A. Feeney-Kettler (Eds.), *Universal screening in educational settings: Evidence-based decision making for schools* (pp. 141–170). Washington, DC: American Psychological Association.

National Association of School Psychologists. (2010). *Model for comprehensive and integrated school psychological services.* Bethesda, MD: Author. Retrieved from http://www.nasponline.org/standards/2010standards/2_PracticeModel.pdf

National Institute of Child Health and Human Development. (2000). *Report of the National Reading Panel: Teaching children to read: An evidence-based assessment of the scientific research literature on reading and its implications for reading instruction.* (NIH Publication No. 004769). Washington, DC: U.S. Government Printing Office.

O'Connell, M. E., Boat, T., & Warner, K. E. (Eds.). (2009). *Preventing mental, emotional, and behavioral disorders among young people: Progress and possibilities.* Washington DC: National Academies Press.

Parisi, D. M., Ihlo, T., & Glover, T. A. (2014). Screening within a multitiered early prevention model: Using assessment to inform instruction and promote students' response to intervention. In R. J. Kettler, T. A. Glover, C. A. Albers, & K. A. Feeney-Kettler (Eds.), *Universal screening in educational settings: Evidence-based decision making for schools* (pp. 19–45). Washington, DC: American Psychological Association.

Walker, H. M., Small, J. W., Severson, H. H., Seeley, J. R., & Feil, E. G. (2014). Multiple-gating approaches in universal screening within school and community settings. In R. J. Kettler, T. A. Glover, C. A. Albers, & K. A. Feeney-Kettler (Eds.), *Universal screening in educational settings: Evidence-based decision making for schools* (pp. 47–75). Washington, DC: American Psychological Association.

8 Best Practices in Facilitating and Evaluating the Integrity of School-Based Interventions

Andrew T. Roach
Kerry Lawton
Stephen N. Elliott
Arizona State University

OVERVIEW

The purpose of this chapter is to provide a conceptual overview of the intervention integrity and possible strategies for use by school psychologists in supporting high-quality implementation of school-based interventions by teachers and other educators. Although this chapter does not explicitly address the integrity of interventions implemented by parents, family members, and other caregivers, many of the concepts and strategies are equally applicable to work with these groups.

Although most school psychologists enter the field to work with and improve the lives of children and youth, they often discover the most effective and efficient way to meet these goals is through interventions implemented by other educators (e.g., teachers, paraprofessionals, or administrators). Gutkin and Conoley (1990) referred to this situation as the "paradox of school psychology." In light of this paradox, facilitating and evaluating the implementation of teacher-mediated interventions for children is one of the most important, yet hidden, services school psychologists can provide. Concerns about the integrity with which interventions are used by teachers and other educators are fundamental to intervention effectiveness and require knowledge of assessment concepts, intervention procedures, and the application of collaborative consultation strategies.

The National Association of School Psychologists (NASP) *Model for Comprehensive and Integrated School Psychological Services* (NASP, 2010) initially introduces intervention integrity as an important element in the domain of Data-Based Decision Making and Accountability: "School psychologists assist with design and implementation of assessment procedures to determine the degree to which recommended interventions have been implemented (i.e., treatment fidelity)" (p. 4). The NASP Practice Model mentions fidelity or integrity an additional three times, endorsing it as a key consideration in providing school-based academic, behavioral, and mental health interventions.

When integrity is achieved and maintained, school psychologists' consultation and intervention efforts are more likely to achieve successful outcomes. Conversely, when integrity and implementation quality are compromised, the effectiveness of even the most thoroughly researched and carefully conceived intervention may be undermined. A review of the intervention and consultation research literature supports this asserted relationship. For example, moderate correlations ($r = .41–.58$) between the degree of integrity and measured child and adolescent outcomes have been observed by a number of researchers (Gresham, Gansle, Noell, Cohen, & Rosenblum, 1993; Noell et al., 2005).

Sanetti and Kratochwill (2009) define intervention integrity as "the extent to which essential intervention components are delivered in a comprehensive and consistent manner by an [educator] trained to deliver the intervention" (p. 448). A review of the literature in school psychology and related fields (e.g., special education, child clinical psychology, applied behavior analysis) suggests the terms *intervention* (or treatment) *integrity*, *treatment fidelity*, and *procedural reliability* are often used interchangeably to describe the same concept.

BASIC CONSIDERATIONS

Although it may be appealing to reduce integrity to a unitary, dichotomous variable (i.e., Was the intervention implemented or not?), integrity actually is multifaceted in nature, including consideration of both the content (how much) and the process (how well) of implementation. Dane and Schneider (1998) theorized that intervention integrity has five components:

- *Adherence:* Refers to how closely an educator attends to and follows the specific steps or procedures intended by the intervention's developer
- *Quality of delivery:* Includes the consideration of educators' skill, decisions, timing, choice making, and judgment in implementing an intervention
- *Program differentiation:* Refers to the degree that the proposed intervention (i.e., underlying theoretical model) differs and is distinct from other practices
- *Exposure (or dosage):* Refers to the number, length, frequency, or duration of the intervention sessions
- *Participant responsiveness:* The level of educator and student engagement in the intervention, which appears to be related to the concept of intervention acceptability

Based on their comprehensive review of research on the implementation of prevention programs, Durlak and DuPre (2008) suggested *intervention adaptation* (i.e., modifications or changes educators make to the intervention during implementation) also may merit consideration when evaluating an intervention's integrity. The inclusion of intervention adaptation in the list of considerations may surprise some readers since the field has often treated integrity and adherence as interchangeable concepts. Durlak and DuPre (2008), however, found numerous studies that demonstrated modifications made by intervention providers (e.g., teachers) improved intervention results. Moreover, they found "perfect or near-perfect implementation is unrealistic.... [Few] studies have attained levels greater than 80%" adherence (Durlak & DuPre, 2008, p. 331). Similarly, a national survey of educators implementing new interventions and instruction programs conducted by the National Diffusion Center found that more than two thirds had modified aspects of these practices, and 20% of respondents had made major changes to the new practices they adopted (Rogers, 1995).

Therefore, collaborating with teachers and other educators to modify an intervention to increase its

acceptability and facilitate its match to school and classroom contexts may be useful in promoting high-quality implementation and intervention integrity. In fact, multiple school psychology researchers have developed consultative models that emphasize collaboration among school psychologists and intervention users to create context-specific, culturally appropriate adaptations of interventions (e.g., Nastasi, Varjas, Schensul, Silva, & Ratnayake, 2000; Power et al., 2005). While allowing adaptations will generally result in decreases in educators' adherence to preplanned intervention components, encouraging their input into intervention design and implementation may produce increases in other aspects of integrity (e.g., exposure, quality, and participant responsiveness).

Relationship Between Integrity and Other Variables

In their review of integrity literature, Perepletchikova and Kazdin (2005) outlined the potential influence of intervention, educator, and student characteristics on levels of integrity. This information is summarized in Table 8.1. Clearly, one of the primary factors in promoting integrity is the acceptability of an intervention (Elliott, 1988). Teachers and other educators prefer interventions that are positive (i.e., those that increase behaviors and skills), time efficient, and minimally intrusive into their daily practice (Elliott, 1988; Elliott, DiPerna, & Shapiro, 2001; Finn, 2000). Because acceptability can influence educators' motivation and commitment to interventions, research-based strategies that are also highly acceptable to teachers and students are generally the best choices for addressing problems and concerns.

The complexity of an intervention is often negatively associated with integrity of implementation. That is, those interventions that require coordination of multiple educators (e.g., teachers, instructional aides, and specialists) use a wide variety of materials, or include numerous phases and steps are less likely to be implemented consistently and accurately (Perepletchikova & Kazdin, 2005). Conversely, novel intervention strategies that are relatively simple may be adopted by educators more easily and accurately (Rogers, 1995). Ellsworth (2000) observed "interventions that are seen as difficult to understand or adopt will diffuse more slowly, as few [educators] will voluntarily embrace change that makes their life more difficult" (p. 57). Similarly, an intervention's flexibility (i.e., its ability to be modified to different practice contexts) and compatibility with

Table 8.1. Intervention, Interventionist, and Student Characteristics That Influence Integrity

	Characteristics That Facilitate Integrity	Characteristics That Discourage Integrity
Intervention characteristics	• Acceptability of intervention • Rate of behavior change produced by intervention • Flexibility/adaptability • Compatibility with current practice	• Complexity of intervention • Multiple resources required • Time required for implementation
Interventionist characteristics	• Level of training/education • Motivation • Self-efficacy • Confidence in the intervention	• Resistance • Diversity of students worked with • Familiarity with other interventions that address the same problem
Student characteristics	• Motivation • Cooperation	• Difficult behavior or anger/hostility • Severity or duration of problem

educators' current practices and values can have an impact on integrity and implementation quality (Durlak & DuPre, 2008).

Educator characteristics also can influence levels of integrity. Highly trained individuals may be more successful at understanding and adopting unfamiliar practices. Moreover, integrity can be facilitated by educators' belief in their own skills and abilities and the likelihood that the intervention will produce positive results (Durlak & DuPre, 2008). Conversely, educators' experience with diverse populations or a wide variety of intervention options can also introduce barriers into the implementation process. When teachers' practices and beliefs are relatively established, the implementation of new strategies calls for second-order change (i.e., changes in practice that conflict with or undermine preferred materials, methods, or ways of doing things; Cuban, 1998). In light of this, educators who are untrained or less skilled may be less resistant to implementing new practices that—if paired with effective training and support—may result in greater levels of integrity (Perepletchikova & Kazdin, 2005).

School psychologists sometimes find that intervention suggestions are met with resistance, are ignored, or are implemented with low levels of commitment because they are not compatible with educators' current routines or practices (Dunst & Trivette, 1988; Elliott et al., 2001; Witt & Martens, 1988). In some cases, educators' conceptions of what is understood as good teaching may be at odds with school psychologists' interest in intervention integrity, especially if the focus of integrity evaluation is strict adherence to standardized intervention steps. For many teachers, interventions and supporting materials "manifest [themselves] as carefully organized, concrete, rigid, and well-planned units…. Teaching, on the other hand, is [viewed as] interactive, natural, and unstructured"

(O'Donnell, 2008, p. 44). Because of this, a collaborative or partnership approach to intervention design and implementation may provide school psychologists with a vehicle to facilitate integrity and implementation quality while honoring educators' professional knowledge and experiences. Research from the psychotherapy and substance abuse treatment literature makes a similar distinction between intervention providers' adherence to intervention protocols and their competence in delivering intervention strategies, suggesting the two concepts are related but distinct (Schulte, Easton, & Parker, 2009). Therefore, while attending to the adherence to intervention plans is necessary for promoting intervention integrity, school psychologists should include consideration of the other aspects of integrity in their evaluations as well.

Student characteristics can also play a role in facilitating (or discouraging) intervention integrity. Poor behavior or outright resistance to the intervention may make it difficult for teachers or other educators to implement an intervention consistently and accurately. For example, students who exhibit disruptive behavior may result in teachers omitting more challenging components of an intervention. Another possibility is that students who exhibit challenging behavior may be timed-out or suspended from classrooms or school settings, making it difficult to complete a structured program or to implement intervention strategies with any consistency. Hostility and resistance toward an intervention on the part of students may also affect educators' attitudes and commitment toward both the intervention and the student (Teyber & McClure, 2000). Conversely, students who exhibit motivation and cooperation with teachers and other educators may facilitate increased intervention integrity. In the interest of integrity, school psychologists may consider providing encouragement and support (e.g., positive behavior support [PBS] services) to establish the constructive relationships between students and educators.

Intervention Integrity's Role in Response to Intervention and Positive Behavior Support

Many school psychologists work in schools and systems where response to intervention (RTI) or PBS systems are being established and implemented. These models generally assume the presence of (or capacity to implement) effective research-based instruction and classroom management in the general education contexts as well as specific evidence-based interventions to address and remediate students' academic and behavioral difficulties. Unfortunately, without evidence that interventions are implemented with integrity, students' lack of progress may be incorrectly interpreted as nonresponsiveness, leading to more intensive and intrusive intervention supports and subsequent placement in special education. School psychologists can work with teachers and other educators to collect information on integrity information at each RTI or PBS tier, facilitating decision making about the effectiveness of intervention efforts and student progress.

BEST PRACTICES IN FACILITATING AND EVALUATING THE INTEGRITY OF SCHOOL-BASED INTERVENTIONS

To evaluate and support intervention integrity, school psychologists must operationally define the components that comprise the intervention. A checklist, ratings scale, or rubric can be developed that describes the essential components of an intervention. In some cases, school psychologists may develop an instrument that focuses solely on the presence or completion of each intervention component or step (e.g., Did the teacher have students complete the workbook exercises during the lesson? Yes or no.). Alternatively, school psychologists may decide to place the variations for each intervention component along a continuum from optimal to unacceptable practices, resulting in the development of an integrity-focused rating scale (see the example in Figure 8.1). Finally, an integrity rubric can be developed with each

Figure 8.1. Example of a Rating Scale for Evaluating Intervention Integrity

Consultee: _____ Date: _____ Consultant: _____

Response Cost Lottery

	Strongly Disagree				Strongly Agree
1. Describe system to students	1	2	3	4	5
2. Display and describe reinforcers	1	2	3	4	5
3. Place 3 x 5 card on students' desks	1	2	3	4	5
4. Card taped on three sides	1	2	3	4	5
5. Four slips of colored paper inserted (different colors for each student)	1	2	3	4	5
6. Lottery in effect for half hour	1	2	3	4	5
7. Slips removed contingent on rule violations	1	2	3	4	5
8. Teacher restates rule contingent on violation	1	2	3	4	5
9. Remaining tickets placed in box	1	2	3	4	5
10. Drawing occurs on Friday	1	2	3	4	5
11. Winner selects reinforcer on Friday	1	2	3	4	5

intervention component or element representing a rubric dimension (see the example in Figure 8.2). Variations in the components can be described in behavioral terms (i.e., behaviors that are observable and measurable or the behaviors generate a permanent product) and assigned a score for the corresponding rubric dimension.

The following three questions (adapted from Hall & Hord, 2001, p. 49) can be used to guide the

Figure 8.2. Example of a Rubric for Evaluating Intervention Integrity

	Level 3: Optimal Implementation Integrity	Level 2: Satisfactory Implementation Integrity	Level 1: Unsatisfactory Implementation Integrity
Objectives Use for Planning	Teacher uses *Intervention Resource Guide* objectives and state/district curriculum standards for planning.	Teacher uses *Intervention Resource Guide* and math textbook objectives for planning.	Teacher does not identify or use objectives for planning.
Instructional Resources Used	Instructional materials and resources include intervention program activity kits, manipulatives, games, math learning centers, calculators, computers.	Instructional materials include intervention program activity kits, textbook, worksheets.	Only the textbook and worksheets are used.
Assessment Practices	Assessment includes observation notes, open-ended questions, group projects, math journals or learning logs, graded textbook assignments and worksheets, intervention-focused tests and quizzes.	Assessment includes observation notes, graded textbook assignments and worksheets, and a combination of intervention-focused and textbook-based tests and quizzes.	Assessment includes graded textbook assignments and worksheets and textbook-based tests and quizzes.
Grouping Strategies	Teacher uses multiple grouping strategies based on interest, performance, and activity.	Teacher uses small groups to facilitate remediation of math skills.	Teacher uses only whole-group instruction.

development of integrity measures for interventions: (a) What does the intervention look like when it is in use? (b) What would I see in classrooms (or other contexts) where it is used well? (c) What will teachers (or other educators) and students be doing when the intervention is in use?

Confusion or lack of understanding about the steps and processes involved in implementation can occur when an unfamiliar intervention is implemented. School psychologists can use integrity checklists, rating scales, and rubrics to conduct observations for the purpose of identifying and addressing educators' difficulties with intervention use. In addition, teachers might use integrity self-report measures to guide their practice or to identify components for which they require additional information, training, or consultation. By monitoring and evaluating integrity, school psychologists and collaborating educators can determine which intervention components are being used successfully and which are being implemented with less consistency or success. This information can provide the impetus for consultation and professional development efforts to address the components that prove most difficult to implement.

Using Consultation to Facilitate Intervention Integrity

Because intervention integrity is a central issue in the implementation of teacher-meditated interventions, school psychologists should be familiar with and consider using consultation stages and processes in their efforts to promote integrity. Each consultation stage—initiating a consultative relationship, assessment, problem identification and goal setting, strategy selection, strategy implementation, and evaluation—can provide support for intervention integrity (Brown, Pryzwansky, & Schulte, 2006).

Establishing a positive consultative relationship provides an essential foundation for integrity by lowering the likelihood of teachers' resistance and increasing their openness and commitment to the proposed interventions (Kratochwill, Elliott, & Stoiber, 2002). Research from other fields suggests that school psychologists might facilitate changes in practice by developing reciprocal obligations with educators and relating intervention plans to their established commitments or core values (Howard, 1995; Noell et al., 2005). The assessment, problem identification, and goal setting stages of consultation are important for promoting intervention integrity. Specifically, interventions that address educators' most salient concerns are more likely to be implemented with accuracy and consistency. The foundation for intervention integrity can be established during strategy selection and implementation by attending to a variety of procedural details (Kratochwill et al., 2002): (a) identifying which individuals' are responsible for each intervention task or component, (b) acquiring or producing needed intervention resources and materials to support implementation, and (c) training and coaching educators to ensure high-quality implementation.

In preparing educators to implement novel practices, verbal explanations of the planned intervention are typically inadequate to support implementation with integrity (Reid & Parsons, 2000). Instead, school psychologists may need to provide a variety of supports to educators including (a) written instructions, (b) modeling and rehearsal of intervention strategies, and (c) in-class coaching and feedback (McGimsey, Greene, & Lutzker, 1995; Witt, VanDerHeyden, & Gilbertson, 2004).

Plan evaluation, including examination of data on student outcomes, can also provide important supporting evidence regarding treatment integrity. Examination of evaluation data with teachers may build the teachers' sense of efficacy and commitment to the intervention program or strategies. Conversely, desired outcomes that are not achieved can signal the need to reexamine data about intervention integrity to determine which components (if any) were not implemented successfully and to make plans to facilitate more accurate and competent implementation in the future. If the evaluation data suggest the intervention has not been implemented with integrity, school psychologists may need to return to previous consultation stages to troubleshoot the intervention plan (Witt et al., 2004).

Using Performance Feedback to Facilitate Integrity

Performance feedback is a process wherein a teacher's implementation efforts are monitored to determine the extent to which they are consistent with proper implementation of an intervention (Noell et al., 2005). In education settings, providing structured performance feedback is the strategy for promoting integrity with the most empirical support. In their initial investigation of performance feedback, Witt, Noell, LaFleur, and Mortenson (1997) found that without structured meetings to support teachers' implementation, intervention integrity dropped significantly within 10 days (even when teachers received intensive preintervention training).

Since this pioneering study, the positive relationship between feedback and integrity has been consistently observed across a variety of interventions and conditions.

Subsequent investigations (Mortenson & Witt, 1998; Noell, Duhon, Gatti, & Connell, 2002) have identified strategies for providing performance feedback that are likely to produce positive results. First, during each performance feedback session, the school psychologist should review data on implementation of each intervention component and/or step in order to identify areas of strength and target(s) for improvement. During this review, praise should be provided when components are implemented correctly and corrective feedback with encouragement should be provided for missed or incorrectly implemented components. After this review, the teacher should be given an opportunity to ask questions and share any concerns he or she may have about the protocol or intervention (Noell et al., 2005).

Second, performance feedback appears most effective when time-series charts are used to display treatment integrity and student progress toward intervention goals. Because student outcomes and treatment integrity are likely to be measured on different scales, presenting these data on separate charts is preferred and will help to avoid misinterpretation. These graphs can also be used to identify baseline values and benchmarks for implementation and student performance as part of a goal-setting strategy (Noell et al., 2005).

Generally speaking, observations of intervention implementation and performance feedback sessions should be conducted as frequently as possible. Although weekly feedback sessions have proven more effective than less frequent sessions or none at all, the greatest gains in integrity generally are observed when feedback is provided daily (Mortenson & Witt, 1998). If the schedule of the practicing school psychologist does not permit long-term daily observation and feedback, sessions can be scaled back to every other day, then one session per week. However, to preserve integrity during this process, scaling back from the daily sessions should only occur after the teacher achieves 100% adherence to the intervention protocol and sustains this performance for at least 3 consecutive days (Noell et al., 2005).

Using Standardized Interventions to Facilitate Integrity

Standardization, or procedural specification of an intervention, refers to the development of formal guidelines, procedural protocols, and/or manuals when the intervention is implemented. Use of a standardized intervention may have several advantages for ensuring an intervention effort's impact and effectiveness (Kratochwill & Stoiber, 2000). First, standardized interventions are often more easily disseminated to teachers and other educators. Indeed, a major shortcoming of some intervention attempts is the lack of specific procedures for training educators in their use. Thus, a standardized intervention may facilitate intervention integrity because the intervention components and the skills needed for implementation are clearly defined. Many standardized intervention programs include measures (e.g., observation protocols, checklists) that can be used to monitor intervention integrity. Practitioners can find integrity measures and support materials for a wide variety of behavioral and academic interventions at the websites for Intervention Central (http://www.interventioncentral.org) and the Heartland Area Educational Agency 11 (http://www.aea11.k12.ia. useducators/idm/checklists.html). If a standardized intervention does not include these measures, then the first step in evaluating integrity is to identify the key components of the intervention. Intervention support materials (e.g., the intervention user's guide) may include information on the intervention components that are empirically linked (via research) to the desired student outcomes (Gansle & Noell, 2007). However, we should note that published studies often report high integrity with little variability in adherence to program components, thus attenuating (i.e., weakening) the correlation between integrity and desired student outcomes (Schulte et al., 2009). Therefore, when identifying intervention components and educator behaviors to monitor during integrity evaluation, school psychologists may decide to include elements with strong theoretical links to outcomes, even if those links are not always accompanied by moderate to high correlations to outcomes and/or statistical significance in the research supporting an intervention's use. For example, general indicators of educator effectiveness (e.g., providing consistent, positive feedback or maximizing academic learning time) might be included in integrity evaluations in the absence of specific empirical support for their effect on the target intervention's effectiveness.

Considerations in Evaluating Intervention Integrity

Regardless of whether a school psychologist selects a standardized intervention protocol or develops a customized intervention in collaboration with other educators, each intervention component will need to be defined so that all observable characteristics are clearly delineated and any behaviors or products that will be considered evidence for occurrence are clearly defined (Kazdin, 2001). Using these operational definitions, the occurrence or nonoccurrence of each intervention component is recorded. From these data, two estimates of integrity—component integrity and session integrity—can be calculated and reported (Gresham, Gansle, & Noell, 1993). Component integrity is the percentage of observation sessions in which each distinct component is implemented correctly. Session integrity is the mean percentage of intervention components implemented correctly during each observation session. In addition, a global estimate of integrity should be calculated by summing the number of components implemented correctly across all observation sessions and dividing by the total number possible (Gresham, 1997).

An example of this process is illustrated in Figure 8.3, which includes an observation chart of integrity data for

Figure 8.3. Observational Data: Integrity of Direct Instruction Lesson Implementation

	Session 1 Date 1/13	Session 2 Date 1/15	Session 3 Date 1/20	Session 4 Date 1/23	Component Integrity
Teacher writes the letter on the board.	(Yes) No	(Yes) No	(Yes) No	Yes (No)	3/4 = 75%
Teacher models the sound by holding a finger under the letter and saying the sound.	(Yes) No	(Yes) No	(Yes) No	Yes (No)	3/4 = 75%
Teacher has the group repeat the letter sound in unison.	(Yes) No	(Yes) No	(Yes) No	(Yes) No	4/4 = 100%
Teacher tests understanding by asking each student to say the letter sound individually.	(Yes) No	Yes (No)	Yes (No)	(Yes) No	2/4 = 50%
Teacher corrects any student mispronunciations and has the student repeat letter sound correctly.	(Yes) No	Yes (No)	Yes (No)	(Yes) No	2/4 = 50%
Session Integrity	5/5 = 100%	3/5 = 60%	3/5 = 60%	3/5 = 60%	Global Estimate of Integrity

14/20 = 70% |

a teacher who is implementing direct instruction procedures for teaching letter–sound correspondences. The session integrity is summarized along the bottom row of the chart. These data indicate that the teacher had perfect adherence to the intervention procedure during the first session, but only 60% adherence in each of the next three sessions. Component integrity is reported in the right column of the chart. Only one component—having students repeat the letter sound as a group—was implemented in 100% of the sessions. Note that the observer wrote some additional information about the fourth intervention session that helps clarify why adherence was not achieved for one of the intervention components. The global estimate of integrity (75%) is reported in the bottom-right cell of the chart.

Benchmarks for evaluating integrity data similar to what is included in Figure 8.3 have been proposed by Perepletchikova and Kazdin (2005) and include cutoffs at 80% or above for high integrity and 50% for low integrity. In the case of the teacher in Figure 8.3, intervention integrity might be viewed as satisfactory at the global level, but consideration of the session integrity data suggests that adherence to the intervention protocol has decreased since the initial session. As such, component integrity data can be used by the school psychologist to identify potential targets for follow-up consultation and training.

Note that all three of Perepletchikova and Kazdin's (2005) criteria focus on one facet of integrity: adherence. Although gathering and analyzing data on adherence is an essential first step in evaluating intervention integrity, a number of additional questions merit consideration.

Are Intervention Components or Steps Equally Important for Intervention Effectiveness?

Each intervention component may not be necessary for an intervention to be successful, and it is unlikely that every component identified as necessary is equally important to improving student outcomes (Sanetti & Kratochwill, 2009). For example, providing immediate feedback and correction of student behavior may be more important for the success of a behavior intervention than displaying reminder posters in the classroom. In these instances, the component and session integrity estimates previously described (which consider each component equally) may lead to incorrect interpretations of integrity and its effect on outcomes. Therefore, during the operationalization phase, school psychologists should examine each intervention component

carefully, make a judgment on its relative importance, and assign it an appropriate weight (Schulte et al., 2009).

Is Quality of Implementation an Important Consideration in Evaluating Intervention Integrity?

Another important consideration during an evaluation of integrity is the competence in which the teacher implements the necessary components. Quality of implementation is a complex construct, which is unlikely to be captured using assessments intended to measure only adherence to the intervention protocol (Sanetti & Kratochwill, 2009). Although rating scales and rubrics may be used to assess competence, these measurements must adequately distinguish between degrees of teacher performance to be beneficial. Some standardized intervention programs may provide descriptions of teacher behavior that can be used to evaluate competency, but many interventions do not. Without previously established criteria on which to anchor the rating scale, the school psychologist must have an understanding of environmental, educator, and student characteristics that are important for the identified program components to have their desired effect (Sanetti & Kratochwill, 2009).

Should Direct or Indirect Measures Be Used to Evaluate Intervention Integrity?

Measures of integrity can be classified depending on whether they provide a direct or indirect assessment of educator behavior (Gresham, 1989). Direct assessments result from observation in the intervention setting (e.g., the classroom) by the school psychologist or another trained observer. These observations may occur in real time or through videoing the intervention sessions. Indirect measures of integrity typically rely on teacher self-report and are assessed most frequently through self-ratings or interview protocols (Sheridan, Swanger-Gagné, Welch, Kwon, & Garbacz, 2009). An example of a rating scale that can be completed by a teacher, school psychologist, and/or by an independent observer is included in Figure 8.1. This example refers to a response cost lottery program implemented in a classroom for a student with behavior difficulties. If a student is involved in implementing an intervention (e.g., a self-management strategy), integrity can be monitored by the student. Another form of indirect assessment of integrity is permanent product review. A permanent product is a tangible object that has been identified a priori as being sufficient evidence for implementation. For example, many standardized intervention programs include student workbooks that are completed as part of each intervention session. A school psychologist can collect and examine student workbooks to ascertain implementation progress.

Although they are expensive and may be difficult to obtain in practical settings, direct assessments are considered more reliable than indirect measures and therefore represent the gold standard for measuring integrity (Mowbray, Holter, Teague, & Bybee, 2003). Gresham et al. (1993) recommended that calculations of overall, component, and session integrity reflect direct measures, but they note indirect measures may provide additional useful information about integrity. This preference toward direct measures can be attributed, in large part, to studies documenting positive bias when teachers self-report integrity (i.e., some teachers overestimate and/or overstate their adherence to an intervention protocol; see Wickstrom, Jones, LaFleur, & Witt, 1998).

Despite this limitation, there are substantial benefits to including both indirect measures and direct measures in a system of integrity evaluation. First, as mentioned, indirect measures can serve as supplemental evidence to help ensure the accuracy of direct measures of teachers' intervention-related behavior (Jobe, 2003). Also, the use of self-reports may serve to improve integrity by providing teachers with an opportunity to identify potential barriers to successful implementation and contribute to the development of new strategies to promote an increase in fidelity (Power et al., 2005). It seems reasonable that, at a minimum, indirect measures of integrity should be collected as part of every school-based intervention effort. Best practice would include the collection of periodic direct measures (typically classroom observations) of intervention integrity. Certainly, if an intervention is being conducted as part of an RTI system or another high-stakes context, school psychologists have a responsibility to systematically collect both direct and indirect measures of integrity.

Should Integrity Measures Be Collected in Evaluations of School- and District-Wide Programs?

Because of its importance for evaluating the effectiveness of education programs, intervention integrity is addressed in the third edition of *The Program Evaluation Standards* (Joint Committee on Standards for Educational Evaluation, 2011). "Standard A4 [Explicit Program and Context Descriptions] emphasizes documenting whether treatment as implemented conforms to treatment as specified.... For treatment fidelity to be

established, the actual implemented program must be monitored and described in sufficient detail for comparison to the prescribed program" (p. 186). Research and program evaluation also is one of the 10 domains of professional practice outlined in the NASP Practice Model (NASP, 2010), meaning school psychologists should use their skills and knowledge in "data collection, measurement, analysis, accountability, and use of technology resources in evaluation of services at the individual, group, and/or systems levels" (p. 10). Documenting integrity should be an important consideration in evaluations of school- and district-wide programs designed and conducted by school psychologists.

When conducting program evaluations, monitoring integrity is essential to demonstrating a program's internal and external validity (Schlosser, 2002). Internal validity refers to the ability to conclude that implementation of an intervention or instructional program actually produced the observed outcomes. Without ascertaining the level of the integrity with which a program is carried out (or whether it was implemented at all), evaluators cannot make any meaningful conclusions about its effect. External validity is established by replication of the program. When the content and process of the intervention or instructional program is not explicitly operationalized and assessed, it is impossible to replicate the program and its observed outcomes across multiple classrooms and schools (Schlosser, 2002).

As described previously in this chapter, checklists, rating scales, or rubrics can be developed to evaluate the implementation of various program components. Once these integrity measures are developed, data collected across multiple classrooms and schools can be collected, compared, and aggregated. Analysis of these data can aid in the identification of program components that are implemented less consistently and/or less competently by participating educators. This information can guide additional professional development programming to improve the implementation quality, or inform program development and modification to improve intervention to context match.

In some practice contexts (e.g., multitiered service delivery models), school psychologists may be interested in evaluating integrity across a series of intervention programs. An option for documenting the integrity of multiple interventions is called convergent evidence scaling (CES), a method constructed for aggregating outcomes derived from multiple indexes or multiple sources of evidence about the behavior or performance of an individual or groups of individuals (see Busse,

Figure 8.4. CES Intervention Integrity Rubric

Level of Intervention Implementation Integrity	Description of Intervention Implementation Integrity	Evidence to Be Considered	CES Score
Level 5 (Highest)	All or nearly all (greater than 95%) of the intervention components were used consistently as designed and for the recommended amount of time and on the recommended schedule. Overall implementation was optimal.	• Observation form • Self-report checklist • Permanent products • Teacher interview Can provide specific scores or details from each evidence form that differentiates higher quality.	5
Level 4	81–95% of the intervention components were used as designed and the schedule and time of use were acceptable. Overall implementation was very good.	• Observation form • Self-report checklist • Permanent products • Teacher interview	4
Level 3 (Satisfactory)	75–80% of the intervention components were used as designed and the schedule and time of use were acceptable. Overall implementation was good.	• Observation form • Self-report checklist • Permanent products • Teacher interview	3
Level 2	51–74% of the intervention components were used as designed and the schedule and time of use were acceptable. Overall implementation was fair.	• Observation form • Self-report checklist • Permanent products • Teacher interview	2
Level 1 (Lowest)	Less than 50% of the intervention components were routinely used and the amount of time and schedule of implementation was erratic. Overall implementation was poor.	• Observation form • Self-report checklist • Permanent products • Teacher interview	1

Elliott, & Kratochwill, 2010; Busse, Kratochwill, & Elliott, 1999; Stoiber & Kratochwill, 2002). The CES method follows the logic of goal attainment scaling ratings and provides a common metric for aggregating data (Kiresuk, Smith, & Cardillo, 1994; Roach & Elliott, 2005).

Although CES was originally designed to integrate multiple types of treatment outcome data, it is a flexible method that can be used to integrate data regarding intervention implementation as well (Busse et al., 2010). The first challenge in using a CES method is to develop a definition of the construct (i.e., intervention integrity) being measured and the various levels or gradations of the construct that have practical significance. The second challenge is to identify the type and quality of the evidence that can be evaluated and to delineate the various levels of the construct. Once this information is established, descriptive criteria can be written to operationalize each level of the intervention integrity construct. A scoring system is designed next to quantify each of the levels, and a five-level system (where 1 represents the lowest level and 5 the highest level) is created. The final step is to establish the reliability of the resulting scores. An example of a CES intervention integrity framework is illustrated in Figure 8.4. Busse et al.'s (2010) article provides a conceptual overview of CES for those interested in using this method in their practice contexts.

SUMMARY

Planning for and evaluating intervention integrity is best practice for school psychologists who are committed to facilitating improved student outcomes. By clearly operationalizing intervention components, providing appropriate consultative support, and monitoring implementation and student progress, school psychologists can take proactive steps to ensure that students are provided with effective intervention practices. Moreover, promoting integrity is important because, as Brown-Chisdey and Steege (2005) suggest, "students and their families have the right to expect that interventions will be implemented with precision and that objective documentation will demonstrate student progress" (p. 32).

Engaging in the scope of professional behaviors necessary to facilitate and evaluate intervention integrity can be a daunting task. School psychologists must use their consultation and leadership skills to build working relationships with other educators, understand the most salient intervention targets, and identify interventions that are acceptable to teachers and also within their skill sets. Once an intervention is selected, school psychologists can provide a variety of supports (e.g., training, acquiring or creating materials, monitoring student progress) to promote initiating and sustaining implementation. To evaluate integrity, school psychologists can draw on their training in behavioral assessment and observation to develop checklists, rubrics, or rating scales, and utilize intervention permanent products and self-report measures to collect accurate and meaningful data on the implementation behaviors of teachers or educators.

In their review of implementation research, Fixsen, Naoom, Blase, Friedman, and Wallace (2005) identified the role of the implementation purveyor, who is "an individual or group of individuals representing a program or practice who actively work to implement [a] practice or program with fidelity and good effect" (p. 14). These purveyors develop practice knowledge over multiple implementation attempts, learning to anticipate practitioners' areas of challenge and needs for support. This implementation support may "engender [educators'] confidence and may lead to greater persistence to see it through when the going gets rough during the early stages of implementation" (p. 14). We believe school psychologists are uniquely qualified to serve in this capacity. With appropriate training and a commitment to facilitating and evaluating intervention integrity, school psychologists can make a positive impact on educators' implementation efforts, enhancing and advancing effective intervention practices for children and adolescents.

REFERENCES

Brown, D., Pryzwansky, W. B., & Schulte, A. C. (2006). *Psychological consultation and collaboration: Introduction to theory and practice* (6th ed.). Boston, MA: Allyn & Bacon.

Brown-Chisdey, R., & Steege, M. (2005). *Response to intervention: Principles and strategies for effective practice.* New York, NY: Guilford Press.

Busse, R. T., Elliott, S. N., & Kratochwill, T. R. (2010). Convergent evidence scaling for multiple assessment indicators: Conceptual issues, applications, and technical challenges. *Journal of Applied School Psychology, 26,* 149–161. doi:10.1080/15377901003712728

Busse, R. T., Kratochwill, T. R., & Elliott, S. N. (1999). Influences of verbal interactions during behavioral consultations on treatment outcomes. *Journal of School Psychology, 37,* 117–143. doi:10.1016/S0022-4405(98)00028-4

Cuban, L. (1998). How schools change reform: Redefining reform success and failure. *Teachers College Record, 99,* 453–477.

Dane, A. V., & Schneider, B. H. (1998). Program integrity in primary and early secondary prevention: Are implementation effects out of control? *Clinical Psychology Review, 18,* 23–45. doi:10.1016/S0272-7358(97)00043-3

Dunst, J., & Trivette, C. M. (1988). Helping, helplessness, and harm. In J. C. Witt, S. N. Elliott, & F. M. Gresham (Eds.), *Handbook of behavior therapy in education* (pp. 343–376). New York, NY: Plenum Press.

Durlak, J. A., & DuPre, E. P. (2008). Implementation matters: A review of research on the influence of implementation on program outcomes and the factors affecting implementation. *American Journal of Community Psychology, 41*, 327–350. doi:10.1007/s10464-008-9165-0

Elliott, S. N. (1988). Acceptability of behavioral treatments in educational settings. In J. C. Witt, S. N. Elliott, & F. M. Gresham (Eds.), *Handbook of behavior therapy in education* (pp. 121–150). New York, NY: Plenum Press.

Elliott, S. N., DiPerna, J. C., & Shapiro, E. (2001). *Academic intervention monitoring system*. San Antonio, TX: The Psychological Corporation.

Ellsworth, J. B. (2000). *Surviving change: A survey of educational change models*. Syracuse, NY: Clearinghouse on Information and Technology.

Finn, C. A. (2000). *Remediating behaviour problems of young children: The impact of parent treatment acceptability and the efficacy of conjoint behavior consultation and videotape therapy* (Unpublished doctoral dissertation). McGill University, Montreal, QC, Canada

Fixsen, D. L., Naoom, S. F., Blase, K. A., Friedman, R. M., & Wallace, F. (2005). *Implementation research: A synthesis of the literature*. Tampa, FL: University of South Florida, Louis de la Parte Florida Mental Health Institute, National Implementation Research Network.

Gansle, K. A., & Noell, G. H. (2007). The fundamental role of intervention implementation in assessing response to intervention. In S. Jimerson, M. Burns, & A. VanDerHeyden (Eds.), *The handbook of response to intervention* (pp. 244–251). New York, NY: Springer.

Gresham, F. M. (1989). Assessment of treatment integrity in school consultation and prereferral intervention. *School Psychology Review, 18*, 37–50.

Gresham, F. M. (1997). Treatment integrity in single-subject research. In R. D. Franklin, D. B. Allison, & D. S. Gorman (Eds.), *Design and analysis of single-case research* (pp. 93–117). Mahwah, NJ: Erlbaum.

Gresham, F. M., Gansle, K. A., & Noell, G. H. (1993). Treatment integrity in applied behavior analysis with children. *Journal of Applied Behavior Analysis, 26*, 257–263. doi:10.1901/jaba.1993.26-257

Gresham, F. M., Gansle, K. A., Noell, G. H., Cohen, S., & Rosenblum, S. (1993). Treatment integrity of school-based behavioral intervention studies: 1980–1990. *School Psychology Review, 22*, 254–272.

Gutkin, T. B., & Conoley, J. C. (1990). Reconceptualizing school psychology practice from a service delivery perspective: Implications for practice, training, and research. *Journal of School Psychology, 28*, 203–223. doi:10.1016/0022-4405(90)90012-V

Hall, G. E., & Hord, S. M. (2001). *Implementing change: Patterns, principles, and potholes*. Needham Heights, MA: Allyn & Bacon.

Howard, J. P. (1995). "Chaining" the use of influence strategies for producing compliance behavior. *Journal of Social Behavior and Personality, 10*, 169–185.

Jobe, J. B. (2003). Cognitive psychology and self-reports: Models and methods. *Quality of Life Research, 12*, 219–227. doi:10.1023/A:1023279029852

Joint Committee on Standards for Educational Evaluation. (2011). *The program evaluation standards*. Newbury Park, CA: SAGE.

Kazdin, A. E. (2001). *Behavior modification in applied settings* (6th ed.). Belmont, CA: Wadsworth.

Kiresuk, T. J., Smith, A., & Cardillo, J. E. (Eds.). (1994). *Goal attainment scaling: Applications, theory, and measurement*. Mahwah, NJ: Erlbaum.

Kratochwill, T. R., Elliott, S. N., & Stoiber, K. C. (2002). Best practices in school-based problem-solving consultation. In A. Thomas & J. Grimes (Eds.), *Best Practices in School Psychology IV* (pp. 583–608). Bethesda, MD: National Association of School Psychologists.

Kratochwill, T. R., & Stoiber, K. C. (2000). Empirically supported interventions and school psychology: Conceptual and practice issues: Part II. *School Psychology Quarterly, 15*, 233–253. doi:10.1037/h0088786

McGimsey, J. F., Greene, B. F., & Lutzker, J. R. (1995). Competence in aspects of behavioral treatment and consultation: Implications for service delivery and graduate training. *Journal of Applied Behavior Analysis, 28*, 301–315. doi:10.1901/jaba.1995.28-301

Mortenson, B. P., & Witt, J. C. (1998). The use of weekly performance feedback to increase teacher implementation of a prereferral academic intervention. *School Psychology Review, 27*, 613–627.

Mowbray, C. T., Holter, M. C., Teague, G. B., & Bybee, D. (2003). Fidelity criteria: Development, measurement, and validation. *American Journal of Evaluation, 24*, 964–981.

Nastasi, B. K., Varjas, K., Schensul, S. L., Silva, K. T., Schensul, J. J., & Ratnayake, P. (2000). The participatory intervention model: A framework for conceptualizing and promoting intervention acceptability. *School Psychology Quarterly, 15*, 207–232. doi:10.1037/h0088785

National Association of School Psychologists. (2010). *Model for comprehensive and integrated school psychological services*. Bethesda, MD: Author. Retrieved from http://www.nasponline.org/standards/2010standards/2_PracticeModel.pdf

Noell, G. H., Duhon, G. J., Gatti, S. L., & Connell, J. E. (2002). Consultation, follow up, and implementation of behavioral management interventions in general education. *School Psychology Review, 31*, 217–234.

Noell, G. H., Witt, J. C., Slider, N. J., Connell, J. E., Gatti, S. L., Williams, K. L., & Duhon, G. J. (2005). Treatment implementation following behavioral consultation in schools: A comparison of three follow-up strategies. *School Psychology Review, 34*, 87–106.

O'Donnell, C. L. (2008). Defining, conceptualizing, and measuring fidelity of implementation and its relationship to outcomes in K–12 curriculum intervention research. *Review of Educational Research, 78*, 33–84. doi:10.3102/0034654307313793

Perepletchikova, F., & Kazdin, A. E. (2005). Treatment integrity and therapeutic change: Issues and research recommendations. *Clinical Psychology: Science and Practice, 12*, 365–383. doi:10.1093/clipsy/bpi045

Power, T. J., Blom-Hoffman, J., Clarke, A. T., Riley-Tillman, T. C., Kelleher, C., & Manz, P. H. (2005). Reconceptualizing intervention integrity: A partnership-based framework for linking research with practice. *Psychology in the Schools, 42*, 495–507. doi:10.1002/pits.20087

Reid, D. H., & Parsons, M. B. (2000). Organizational behavior management in human service settings. In J. Austin & J. E. Carr (Eds.), *Handbook of applied behavior analysis* (pp. 275–294). Reno, NV: Context Press.

Roach, A. T., & Elliott, S. N. (2005). Goal attainment scaling: An efficient and effective approach to monitoring student progress. *Teaching Exceptional Children, 37*(4), 8–17.

Rogers, E. M. (1995). *Diffusion of innovations* (4th ed.). New York, NY: Free Press.

Sanetti, L. M. H., & Kratochwill, T. R. (2005). Treatment integrity assessment within a problem-solving model (pp. 304–328). In R. Brown-Chidsey (Ed.), *Problem-solving based assessment for educational interventions*. New York, NY: Guilford Press.

Sanetti, L. M. H., & Kratochwill, T. R. (2009). Toward developing a science of treatment integrity: Introduction to the special series. *School Psychology Review, 38*, 445–459.

Schlosser, R. W. (2002). On the importance of being earnest about treatment integrity. *Augmentative and Alternative Communication, 18*, 36–44. doi:10.1080/714043395

Schulte, A. C., Easton, J. E., & Parker, J. (2009). Advances in treatment integrity research: Multidisciplinary perspectives on the conceptualization, measurement, and enhancement of treatment integrity. *School Psychology Review, 38*, 460–475.

Sheridan, S. M., Swanger-Gagné, M., Welch, G. W., Kwon, K., & Garbacz, S. A. (2009). Fidelity measurement in consultation: Psychometric issues and preliminary examination. *School Psychology Review, 38*, 476–485.

Stoiber, K., & Kratochwill, T. K. (2002). *Outcomes: PME*. San Antonio, TX: The Psychological Corporation.

Teyber, E., & McClure, F. (2000). Therapist variables. In C. R. Snyder & R. E. Ingram (Eds.), *Handbook of psychological change* (pp. 62–87). New York, NY: Wiley.

Wickstrom, K. F., Jones, K. M., LaFleur, L. H., & Witt, J. C. (1998). An analysis of treatment integrity in school-based behavioral consultation. *School Psychology Quarterly, 13*, 141–152. doi:10.1037/h0088978

Witt, J. C., & Martens, B. K. (1988). Problems with problem-solving consultation: A reanalysis of assumptions, methods, and goals. *School Psychology Review, 17*, 260–275.

Witt, J. C., Noell, G. H., LaFleur, L. H., & Mortenson, B. P. (1997). Teacher use of interventions in general education settings: Measurement and analysis of the independent variable. *Journal of Applied Behavioral Analysis, 30*, 693–696. doi:10.1901/jaba.1997.30-693

Witt, J. C., VanDerHeyden, A. M., & Gilbertson, D. (2004). Troubleshooting behavioral interventions: A systematic process for finding and eliminating problems. *School Psychology Review, 33*, 363–383.

9

Best Practices in Diagnosis of Mental Health and Academic Difficulties in a Multitier Problem-Solving Approach

Frank M. Gresham
Louisiana State University

OVERVIEW

The purpose of this chapter is to present an overview of the different routes that students become eligible for special education based on whether they have low-incidence versus high-incidence disabilities. Different types of diagnostic errors that occur in determining special education eligibility (i.e., false positive and false negative diagnostic errors) will be discussed and how these errors become problematic in distinguishing between the presence or absence of special learning disabilities versus low achievement or emotional disturbance versus behavior problems will be described. The chapter concludes with a discussion of the role of response to intervention (RTI) in diagnosis in a multitier model of service delivery.

The chapter addresses school psychologists' competencies in the data-based decision making and accountability domain of the National Association of School Psychologists (NASP) *Model for Comprehensive and Integrated School Psychological Services* (NASP, 2010) as well as to the multitiered and problem-solving themes of the NASP Practice Model. This chapter will focuses on comprehensive and systematic decision making and problem solving based on a variety of data collection methods for identifying needs, planning tiered services, monitoring progress, and evaluating outcomes.

School psychologists have always been involved with the evaluation of children and youth in schools with respect to their academic skills, cognitive status, problem behaviors, and social competencies. For most children and youth, these evaluations are informal and routine, such as classwork/homework evaluations, report cards, or conduct grades. However, some students are identified as deviating from a normal course of development in areas of academic or social behavior functioning. These students may be described by teachers as "poor readers," "overactive," "noncompliant," or "slow," which often triggers a referral to school psychologists for more formal evaluations. At this point, school psychologists begin the process of diagnosis in schools.

We know that about 20% of children and youth in the United States have some type of mental health difficulty during the course of any given year and about half of all mental health difficulties in adults have an onset prior to age 14 (Kessler, Berglund, Demler, Jin, & Walters, 2005). We also know that more than one third of fourth graders do not achieve a basic level of proficiency in reading (National Assessment of Educational Progress, 2005). Research indicates that without appropriate instruction, children and youth who struggle with reading will continue to struggle throughout their school careers (Hosp & MacConnell, 2008; Juel, 1988). These data strongly suggest that school psychologists must be at the forefront of early identification and intervention with these mental health and academic difficulties.

BASIC CONSIDERATIONS

Schools supposedly qualify students for special education and related services if the students meet established criteria for a disability and demonstrate an educational need. Research reveals, however, that substantial proportions of school-identified learning disabled students fail to meet the criteria for eligibility and another proportion of students with intellectual disability are often mislabeled as having a specific learning disability (Gresham, Reschly, & Shinn, 2010). Additionally, many students who might meet established criteria for emotional disturbance either are mislabeled as learning disabled or simply go unidentified by schools (Gresham, 2005). Based on this information, it would appear that the procedures used by schools to identify students with learning and/or behavioral difficulties are often confusing, inconsistent, and perceived by some as blatantly unfair (Gresham, 2002; MacMillan & Siperstein, 2002).

There are two clearly different routes whereby children become qualified as being eligible for special education. Children diagnosed via the first route include children with sensory (deaf or blind), physical (orthopedic handicaps), medical (chronic illnesses), or intellectual (moderate–severe–profound) disability. Most, if not all, of these cases are typically diagnosed by physicians employing medical histories, physical examinations, and laboratory tests to determine the correct diagnosis. Most children with these disabilities are identified long before school entry (often at birth or shortly thereafter) and there is little disagreement among medical or educational professionals concerning the accuracy of the diagnosis (MacMillan & Siperstein, 2002). This high agreement among professionals in these cases can be explained by the fact that these children exhibit highly visible and salient characteristics about which there is little room for diagnostic error.

Children diagnosed via the second route create much more debate and disagreement among educational, psychological, and medical professionals. These children may be identified as having specific learning disabilities, mild intellectual disability, emotional disturbance, or speech/language impairments. In contrast to diagnosing children with sensory or medical disabilities, diagnosing these children with these so-called mild- or high-incidence disabilities is fraught with much diagnostic error.

There are two types of diagnostic error for these types of disabilities: *false positive errors* and *false negative errors*. A false positive error occurs when a child is identified as having a disability (e.g., specific learning disability) when in fact the child does not have the disability. A false negative error occurs when a child is mistakenly identified as not having a disability when in fact the child does have a disability.

False positive and false negative errors may also occur among the various high-incidence disability categories. For example, children meeting established criteria for intellectual disability might be incorrectly diagnosed as having a specific learning disability. In these cases, two types of diagnostic errors are made. One, the failure to identify a student as having an intellectual disability is a false negative error and two, the diagnosis of this child as having specific learning disability is a false positive error. A common error in this process occurs when school psychologists try to differentiate students with learning disabilities (discrepant low achievers) from students who are so-called garden variety low achievers (nondiscrepant low achievers). In point of fact, attempts to differentiate these two groups have been futile based on a wealth of research suggesting that these two groups are part of the same population (Francis et al., 2005; Gresham, 2002; Hoskyn & Swanson, 2000; Steubing, Barth, Weiss, & Fletcher, 2009; Steubing et al., 2002).

Differential Diagnosis of High-Incidence Disabilities

One might question the educational value of trying to differentiate among the various groups of students with so-called mild- or high-incidence disabilities such as specific learning disabilities, mild intellectual disability, or emotional disturbance. A fundamental issue is the extent to which these groups are substantially different on various important dimensions. If they are different, how do these groups differ and what are the educational implications for these students?

Categorical classification systems such as that represented in the 2004 Individuals with Disabilities Education Improvement Act (IDEIA) are based on a set of basic assumptions. These assumptions include the reliability and validity of categorical differentiation and the presumed benefits of differentiated instructional methods based on categorical distinctions and unique psychoeducational profiles of abilities. With respect to the first assumption, each disability category is presumed to be caused by some underlying within-student deficit or dysfunction (Ysseldyke & Marston, 1999). As indicated earlier, this logic makes sense and is for the most part irrefutable for students with low-incidence disabilities such as deafness, blindness, or Down syndrome. This is certainly not the case for students with high-incidence disabilities. For example, IDEIA defines a specific learning disability as a "disorder in one of more of the basic psychological processes involved in language, spoken or written.… Such term includes such conditions as perceptual disabilities, brain injury, minimal brain dysfunction, dyslexia, and developmental aphasia" (IDEIA, 2004). In an earlier definition of specific learning disabilities, the National Joint Committee on Learning Disabilities (NCJLD) stated:

> Learning disabilities is a general term that refers to a heterogeneous group of disorders manifested by significant difficulties in the acquisition or use of listening, speaking, reading, writing, reasoning, or mathematical abilities. These disorders are intrinsic to the individual, presumed to be due to central nervous system dysfunction and may occur across the lifespan. (NJCLD, 1998)

Clearly, both IDEIA and NJCLD imply that specific learning disabilities are intrinsic to the individual and are caused by some type of within-child problem. Similarly, the IDEIA definition of emotional disturbance suggests that it is a condition intrinsic to the individual and caused by within-child characteristics (Gresham, 2005). As will be discussed in the following section, what does the research evidence tell us about distinguishing children with learning disabilities from students who are simply low achievers or differentiating students with emotional disturbance from other students with behavior problems?

Differential Diagnosis of Discrepant and Nondiscrepant Low Achievement

What is the value of differentiating children who show IQ–achievement discrepancies from those children who do not show such discrepancies? In other words, is there anything unique about a group of children who show discrepant low achievement versus another group of children who might be considered nondiscrepant or so-called garden variety low achievers? Although many states no longer use IQ–achievement discrepancy to identify children with specific learning disabilities, the 2004 reauthorization of IDEIA still allows this approach as one method of identifying specific learning disabilities.

Steubing et al. (2002) conducted a meta-analysis of 46 studies that contrasted discrepant and nondiscrepant low achieving groups in behavior, achievement, and cognitive domains. Based on these 46 studies looking at 301 effects and 23,584 observations, the overall aggregated effect size was a miniscule .135. The average effect sizes within each of the domains fell in the negligible to small range. The overall aggregated effect

size within the achievement domain was -.117 and the effect size in the Behavior domain was very small ($ES = -.046$). The aggregated effect size within the cognitive domain was small ($ES = .30$). For the cognitive domain, this .30 difference is about three tenths of a standard deviation (5 points) indicating substantial overlap of discrepant and nondiscrepant groups.

Steubing et al. (2002) found that the IQ-discrepant and IQ-consistent groups were not different on the four constructs that are most closely related to reading skill and poor reading such as phonological awareness (-.13), rapid naming (-.12), verbal short-term memory (.10), and vocabulary/lexical skills (.10). In short, IQ-discrepant and IQ-consistent groups do not differ from one another in the phonological core skills that distinguish adequate from inadequate readers.

This meta-analysis calls into question the value of trying to distinguish discrepant from nondiscrepant low achievers. Consider the following hypothetical scenario: A child is referred in second grade for possible identification as having a specific learning disability in reading. A school psychologist obtains an IQ of 98 for the child and a reading score of 85. Based on these scores, the child did not meet the district's IQ–achievement discrepancy of 15 points and was not placed into special education. The child continued to struggle in reading for the next 2 years and was referred again in fourth grade for evaluation. This time, the child obtains an IQ of 96 and a reading score of 78 that exceeds the 15-point discrepancy criterion and was subsequently placed in a resource room for children with specific learning disabilities. As one might imagine, the parents of this child would understandably be upset because their child's reading difficulties were not identified and intervened upon earlier. Unfortunately, this scenario is pervasive in schools across the United States and subjects students to a wait-to-fail model of learning disability identification.

The IQ–achievement discrepancy approach to qualifying students as learning disabled has a number of conceptual and statistical drawbacks. A major controversy in discrepancy-based notions of defining learning disabilities is the central importance assigned to IQ in this process (Gresham & Witt, 1997; Steubing et al., 2009). Perhaps the most important criticism of IQ tests is that they contribute little reliable information for planning, implementing, and evaluating instructional interventions for children and youth. Moreover, according to research contrasting discrepant and nondiscrepant groups, IQ tests are not particularly useful in diagnosing and classifying students with academic learning problems in achievement, behavioral, and cognitive domains (Steubing et al., 2002). What appears to be needed is an approach to defining learning disability based on how students respond to instructional interventions rather than some arbitrarily defined discrepancy between ability and achievement.

Differential Diagnosis of Emotional Disturbance Versus Behavior Problems

Students having serious emotional, behavioral, and social difficulties present substantial challenges to schools, teachers, parents, and peers. A particularly disturbing finding is that students exhibiting severe emotional and behavioral challenges are either underserved or unserved by educational and mental health systems in the United States (Gresham, 2005). Historically, the U.S. Department of Education has estimated the prevalence rate for children and youth served as emotionally disturbed at 2% (Kauffman, 2001). However, the prevalence rate of children and youth served under the category continues to be less than 1% nationwide (U.S. Department of Education, 2011). Among the states, the category of emotionally disturbed shows the greatest variability in prevalence of any disability category (U.S. Department of Education, 2011). This large degree of variability among states is most likely due to confusion, ambiguity, and differences in definition and interpretation of emotionally disturbed.

Estimates indicate that almost 20% of school-age children and youth could qualify for a psychiatric diagnosis using criteria from the *Diagnostic and Statistical Manual of Mental Disorders* (4th ed., text rev.; DSM-IV-TR; American Psychiatric Association, 2000; Angold, 2000). Estimates have suggested that 22% of school-age children and youth have mental health problems so severe as to require attention, treatment, and supports. There is a huge disparity between the percentage of children and youth needing mental health services (more than 20%) and those actually served in special education under IDEIA.

A major challenge in the identification of students as emotionally disturbed involves a decision regarding whether emotional and/or behavioral difficulties constitute a disability. That is, when does a behavior problem become an emotional disturbance? When do social withdrawal and shyness become an anxiety disorder? When do sadness and loneliness become a major depressive disorder? When do overactivity, impulsivity, and inattention become an attention deficit hyperactivity disorder? The answer to these questions is not straightforward and ultimately involves some degree of subjective judgment. The category of emotionally disturbed describes a group of children and youth whose behavior differs from their peers more in terms of degree than in kind. Few individuals would question that children who are profoundly deaf differ in kind from their normally hearing peers in terms of hearing acuity, verbal communication skills, and receptive and expressive verbal language development. There is also little question as to what the definition of profoundly deaf is with respect to the degree of hearing loss necessary for that diagnosis (> 100 decibels, bilaterally).

The IDEIA definition of emotionally disturbed states that it is a condition characterized by one or more of the following characteristics over a long period of time and to a marked degree that adversely affects educational performance: (a) an inability to learn that cannot be explained by intellectual, sensory, or health factors; (b) an inability to build or maintain satisfactory interpersonal relationships with peers or teachers; (c) inappropriate types of behaviors or feelings under normal circumstances; (d) a general pervasive mood of unhappiness or depression; and (e) a tendency to develop physical symptoms or fears associated with personal or school problems.

The definition also includes children who are schizophrenic. The definition excludes children who are socially maladjusted, unless they are also emotionally disturbed.

A student must meet one or more of the above five criteria to qualify as emotionally disturbed and must also meet all three limiting criteria of severity, duration, and impact on school performance. These limiting criteria, however, are nebulous and subjective. Severity derives from the language "to a marked degree." Duration comes from the langue of "over a long period of time." Impact is based on the language of "adversely affects educational performance." The most controversial aspect of the emotionally disturbed definition is the social maladjustment exclusion clause (Skiba & Grizzle, 1991).

The social maladjustment exclusion clause does not allow for students to be deemed eligible as emotionally disturbed if they are socially maladjusted. They can be socially maladjusted, however, if they are also emotionally disturbed and therefore receive services. This logic is convoluted, circular, and oxymoronic. The social maladjustment clause in the emotionally disturbed definition excludes and includes a portion of students in the same sentence and directly contradicts several of the five eligibility criteria. An example is the criterion stating that emotionally disturbed is characterized by the inability to build or maintain satisfactory interpersonal relationships with peers or teachers. This criterion essentially defines the concept of social maladjustment (Walker, Ramsey, & Gresham, 2004). In short, the social maladjustment exclusion clause makes no sense in the past or current definitions of emotionally disturbed, is self-contradictory, and should be removed from the definition.

BEST PRACTICES IN DIAGNOSIS

Traditional diagnostic practices in school psychology, particularly those practices that attempt to diagnose students with specific learning disabilities or emotional disturbance, have numerous shortcomings. As discussed earlier, attempts to diagnose students with high-incidence disabilities are problematic because there is no clear, distinct gold standard that would differentiate these students into known groups. We know that it is fruitless to try to differentiate discrepant from non-discrepant low achievers based on IQ–achievement discrepancy or consistency. We also know that the current definition of emotional disturbance is fundamentally vague, inconsistent, and difficult to operationalize. One feasible solution to these problems is to adopt an RTI approach in the diagnostic process within a multitier framework of assessment, intervention, and outcome evaluation.

RTI and Diagnosis in a Multitier Approach

Diagnosis in the multitier model focuses on four things: (a) referral problem (academic, behavioral, or both), (b) environment (instructional, classroom management, and school discipline practices), (c) intensity of intervention needs (universal, selected, or intensive), and (d) intervention outcomes (immediate, intermediate, or long term). These could be restated in the language of the Bergan and Kratochwill's (1990) problem-solving stages of problem identification (the referral problem), problem analysis (the environment), plan implementation (intervention needs), and plan evaluation (the outcomes). The diagnostic process in a multitier model represents an intervention-based approach to diagnosis rather than simply classifying students as either belonging or not belonging to a particular disability category based on rather arbitrary and subjective criteria. Consistent with the organizational theme of this book, diagnosis in a multitier model takes place at each level of intervention,

universal, selected, and intensive, within both academic and behavioral systems.

RTI refers to an adequate or inadequate change in academic performance or social behavior as a function of an evidence-based intervention implemented with integrity (Gresham, 2002, 2006). There are two basic approaches to delivering interventions in an RTI model: (a) problem-solving approaches and (b) standard protocol approaches (Gresham, 2007). This chapter will focus on problem-solving RTI and will not discuss standard protocol approaches.

Problem-solving RTI can be traced back to the behavioral consultation model first described by Bergan (1977) and later revised and updated by Bergan and Kratochwill (1990). Behavioral consultation takes place in a sequence of four phases: problem identification, problem analysis, plan implementation, and plan evaluation. The goal in behavioral consultation is to define the problem in clear, unambiguous, and operational terms; to identify environmental conditions related to the referral problem; to design and implement an intervention plan with integrity; and to evaluate the effectiveness of the intervention plan. These steps in the behavioral consultation model can be restated as follows: (a) What is the problem? (b) Why is it occurring? (c) What should be done about it? (d) Did it work? Each of these problem-solving steps is described briefly in the following section.

Diagnosis of Referral Problems: Problem Identification

Problems are defined in a problem-solving approach as a discrepancy between current and desired levels of performance and as such the larger the discrepancy, the larger the problem. For example, if the current rate of oral reading fluency is 30 words read correctly per minute and the desired rate is 60 words read correctly per minute, there is a 50% discrepancy between where the student is functioning and the desired level of performance. This same logic can be applied to any type of referral problem (academic or behavioral) as the first step in a problem-solving approach.

A critical aspect of problem identification is the operational definition of the referral problem into specific, measurable terms that permit direct, objective assessment of the behavior of concern. Operational definitions are objective, clear, and complete. These definitions are objective if they can be read, repeated, and paraphrased by others. Operational definitions are clear if two or more observers of behavior are able to read the definition of behavior and use it to record and measure the occurrence and nonoccurrence of the behavior. Operational definitions are complete if they specify the boundary conditions for inclusion of behaviors in the definition and delineate those behaviors that are not part of the definition.

Operational definitions are often used to define a class of responses or a response class rather than specific behaviors. A response class is a group of behaviors that are related in some way to each other or to certain aspects of the environment. Response classes are composed of individual behaviors much like the cells comprising major organ systems in biology or atoms that make up elements in chemistry. Response classes can be defined either topographically or functionally. A topographical response class defines members of that class in terms of what the behaviors look like or their form or structure. A good example of a topographical response class is the DSM-IV-TR definition of a conduct disorder. For example, the response class of conduct disorder is made up of 15 behaviors (e.g., bullying, fighting, cruelty, stealing). These 15 behaviors form the response class of conduct disorder, but tell us nothing about the reasons these behaviors occur. Behaviors defined as being part of a functional response class occur because they serve the same function.

An essential aspect of problem identification is the determination of the type of problem the student is exhibiting. At this stage, the distinction between "can't do" and "won't do" problems becomes critical (Gresham, 1981; VanDerHeyden & Witt, 2008). Can't do problems are considered acquisition deficits, meaning that the child does not have the skill or behavior in his or her repertoire. For instance, if a child does not know the concept of regrouping in addition, then the child will fail to perform math problems that require regrouping. In this case, the acquisition deficit must be remediated by directly teaching the child the concept of regrouping in math addition problems.

Won't do problems are considered performance deficits, meaning that the child knows how to perform the behavior or skill, but does not do so. Reasons for not performing the behavior or skill may be due to the lack of opportunities to perform the skill or the lack of or low rate of reinforcement for performing a behavior. In these cases, providing multiple opportunities to perform the behavior or skill and increasing the rate of reinforcement for the behavior or skill would be the most appropriate intervention strategies. Gresham and Elliott (2007) provide an extensive discussion for this distinction in the domain of social skills, and Noell and

Witt (1999) provide empirical data on this distinction for academic difficulties.

Diagnosis of the Environment and Plan Implementation: Problem Analysis/ Intervention

After problem identification, the next step in the problem-solving process is to determine why the problem is occurring. There are a number of reasons why students exhibit academic and behavioral difficulties in school. Witt and colleagues have provided a useful set of procedures based on functional assessment of academic problems (Witt, Daly, & Noell, 2000). These authors described the five most common reasons for students' academic failure and make recommendations for interventions based on these reasons: (a) the student does not want to do the work (i.e., a won't do problem), (b) the student has not spent enough time doing the work (i.e., insufficient practice and repetition), (c) the student has not had enough assistance in doing the work (i.e., lack of instructional support), (d) the assigned activity is not teaching the student what the teacher wants to student to learn (i.e., assignment/ learning goal mismatch), and (e) the work is too difficult for the student (i.e., frustational rather than instructional level assignment). Readers should consult Witt et al. (2000) for a complete, user-friendly description of functional behavioral assessment (FBA) principles and intervention procedures for academic referrals.

Students who are chronic low achievers (i.e., the lowest of the low), particularly in reading, demonstrate extremely limited performances in the phonological core skills. Intervention efforts for these students functioning at this level must be comprehensive, systematic, intense, and consistent over a relatively long period of time. Research has shown that these interventions can be successful when delivered in a small group setting (two or three students) for periods ranging from 30 hours (Vellutino et al., 1996) to 68 hours (Torgesen et al., 2001). Even despite these intense efforts, approximately 25% of the poor reader population will not show an adequate RTI (Torgesen et al., 1999).

For social–behavioral referrals, interventions may be either nonfunction-based or function-based interventions. For universal (Tier 1) and selected (Tier 2), most referral problems do not require an FBA to design an effective intervention plan. For example, one of the most effective universal interventions for disruptive behavior in the classroom is the Good Behavior Game (Barrish, Saunders, & Wolf, 1969). The Good Behavior Game is based on an interdependent group contingency whereby the teacher divides the class into two teams, defines the response class of disruptive behavior, places a mark on the board for each team's occurrence of disruptive behavior, and rewards the team with the fewest marks on the board (e.g., free time, access to preferred activities, and so forth).

Embry (2002) conducted a comprehensive analysis of the effects on a number of outcomes. Some of the effects of the Good Behavior Game were (a) a 5% reduction in special education placement with a savings of $2–4 million per year, (b) a 2% reduction in involvement with corrections with a savings of $3–10 million per year, and (c) a 4% reduction in lifetime prevalence of tobacco use that could save states millions of dollars with the costs of tobacco-related diseases. Clearly, the Good Behavior Game functions as a so-called behavioral vaccine in which all students are administered a critical dose of the intervention that has long-term beneficial effects for the entire school population. It should be emphasized that the Good Behavior Game is a universal or Tier 1 intervention that is not based on the function of behavior.

Tier 2 or selected interventions also do not typically require an FBA to be effective. Examples of these interventions are school–home notes (Kelley, 1990), mystery motivators (Madaus, Kehle, Madaus, & Bray, 2003), positive peer reporting (Jones, Young, & Friman, 2000), and check-in/check-out adult mentoring procedures (Crone, Hawken, & Horner, 2010), to name a few. Rathvon (2008) has provided an excellent, comprehensive, and step-by-step description of many Tier 2 or selected interventions that will prove invaluable to readers of this chapter.

Students who exhibit chronic and resistant forms of problem behaviors create substantial challenges for school personnel, peers, and parents. These students constitute approximately 1–5% of the school population, are responsible for 40–50% of school behavioral disruptions, and consume 50–60% of school building and classroom resources (Sugai, Horner, & Gresham, 2002). Quite frequently, these students will require a function-based intervention to pinpoint the function or functions these behaviors serve for the student (Gresham, 2004; Gresham, Watson, & Skinner, 2001).

Function-based interventions are typically reserved to Tier 3 or intensive interventions. FBA seeks to identify the reasons or causes of students' behavior using a variety of indirect (records, interviews, and behavior ratings) and direct (systematic direct observations) assessment methods. Behavioral function is usually classified into two broad categories: positive reinforcement functions and negative reinforcement functions (see Gresham et al., 2001).

Positive reinforcement functions include social attention (from peers or teachers), access to tangibles, and access to preferred activities or automatic/sensory reinforcement (e.g., self-stimulation). Many inappropriate classroom behaviors are maintained by social attention from peers or teachers that frequently result in positive reinforcement. Other behaviors are maintained by access to tangible reinforcers. For example, bullies' behavior such as stealing other children's lunch money or athletic shoes is often maintained by access to tangible reinforcers.

Negative reinforcement functions include escape, avoidance, delay, or reduction in the magnitude of aversive stimuli (e.g., academic tasks, peers, adults, or environments). For some students, some academic activities are so aversive that students will engage in any behavior that will allow them to escape them (e.g., noncompliance or classroom disruption). Other students find school so aversive that they will engage in any behaviors that will allow them to avoid either coming to school (e.g., feigning illness) or staying in school (e.g., behaviors leading to suspension or expulsion). Several excellent texts are available that instruct school psychologists in how to conduct comprehensive FBAs for social–behavioral referrals (Umbreit, Ferro, Liaupsin, & Lane, 2007; Watson & Steege, 2012).

Diagnosis of Intervention Outcomes: Plan Evaluation

A crucial feature of the diagnostic process in a multitier model is the determination of an adequate or inadequate RTI. This process involves a set of procedures for determining that the target behaviors have been brought into functional or adequate ranges. Progression through the various levels of intervention is based on how well or how poorly students respond to interventions that have been implemented with integrity. Decisions regarding movement through the various levels must be based on continuous progress monitoring using data collected from a variety of sources (Gresham et al., 2010).

For academic referrals, adequate or inadequate RTI might be indexed to benchmark standards or normative data collected using curriculum-based measurement (CBM; Kaminski & Good, 1996; Shinn, 2010). Alternatively, school psychologists could use the criteria suggested by Fuchs and Fuchs (1997, 1998) in terms of expected growth over time as the standard for determining adequate or inadequate RTI.

Social behavior referrals present different and more challenging measurement issues for determining adequate or inadequate RTI. The most daunting challenge for this class of behaviors is that we have no well-established benchmarks or standards for social behavior similar to those that exist for academic behaviors as measured by CBM. CBM measures have been touted as general indicators of academic health (i.e., general outcome measures; Shinn, 2010). There is little consensus as to what constitutes technically adequate general outcome measures for social behavior. Table 9.1 summarizes the various methods that can be used to quantify intervention outcomes in an RTI approach to service delivery.

Despite this lack of consensus, several approaches have been recommended to quantify whether or not interventions have produced an adequate change in social behavior. The most commonly used approach for doing this in single-case designs is visual inspection of graphed data (Cooper, Heron, & Heward, 2007). Adequacy of RTI is determined by comparing baseline levels of performance to intervention levels of performance to estimate the magnitude of intervention effects. Visual inspection relies on the intraocular test of significance rather than statistical analysis ($p < .05$).

There are several advantages in using visual inspection of graphed data: (a) it does not require advanced training in complex statistical analyses, (b) it tends to identify strong effects rather than weak effects, (c) it dictates consideration of behavioral variability within baseline and intervention phases, and (d) it does not require meeting stringent statistical assumptions. The major disadvantage of visual inspection is that there are no clearly established rules or benchmarks for determining what might be considered a significant effect.

Six features of single-case design data are used to examine within- and between-phase data patterns: (a) level, (b) trend, (c) variability, (d) immediacy of effect, (e) overlap, and (f) consistency of data patterns across similar phases (Horner et al., 2005; Kratochwill et al., 2010). *Level* refers to the mean or average score within specific data phases (e.g., mean baseline phase versus mean intervention phase). *Trend* refers to the slope of the best-fitting straight line for the data within a phase (increasing or decreasing). *Variability* refers to the range or standard deviation of data around the aforementioned best-fitting straight regression line. *Immediacy of effect* refers to the change in level between the last three data points in one phase and the first three data points of the next phase (the more rapid the effect, the more convincing the inference that change was due to the intervention). *Overlap* refers to the proportion of data from one phase that overlaps with data from a previous phase (the smaller the overlap, the stronger the intervention effect). *Consistency of data patterns* across similar phases refers to the similarity of data patterns across the same phases (baseline phases and intervention phases).

Effect Size Estimates

Another way of quantifying effects in single-case designs is by using effect sizes. Effect sizes are used in meta-analysis research that integrate bodies of research by

Table 9.1. Quantification of Intervention Outcomes

Metric	Definition
Visual inspection of graphed data	Visual analysis of level, trend, variability, immediacy of effect, overlap, and consistency of data patterns
Standardized mean difference	Mean differences between treatment and control groups divided by the pooled standard deviation of treatment and control groups or the mean difference between baseline and intervention phases divided by the pooled standard deviation of baseline and intervention phases
Percentage of nonoverlapping data points	Number of data points that exceed the highest or lowest baseline data point divided by the total number of data points multiplied by 100
Percentage of all nonoverlapping data points	Percentage of data points in baseline and intervention phases compared to the proportion of overlapping data between baseline and intervention phases
Percentage change from baseline	Median data point in baseline compared to the median data point in intervention multiplied by 100
Social validation	Subjective evaluation by treatment consumers and social comparisons between target student and comparison peers

converting results of independent investigations into a common quantitative metric such as Cohen's *d* (Cohen, 1988). Cohen's *d*, known as the standardized mean difference, is calculated by subtracting the mean of the control/comparison group from the mean of the treatment group and dividing by the standard deviation of the control group (Rosenthal, 1991). The effect size is expressed as a *z* score having a mean of 0 and a standard deviation of 1.

The use of the above effect size is much less well established in single-case designs. Busk and Serlin (1992) proposed an approach for calculating effect sizes in single-case studies. The calculation of the effect size is computed by subtracting the mean of data points in the intervention phases from the mean of data points in the baseline phases and dividing by the standard deviation of the baseline phases. A major problem with this effect size estimate, however, is that it often leads to extremely large and uninterpretable effect size estimates (Parker et al., 2005).

In order to address this problem, a number of nonparametric methods have been suggested to analyze single case data. These include percentage of nonoverlapping data (PND), percentage of all nonoverlapping data (PAND), and percentage exceeding the median (PEM). PND is calculated by the number of treatment data points that exceed the highest or lowest (depending on the desired direction of change) baseline data point and dividing by the total number of data points in the treatment phase. For example, if 10 of 15 treatment data points exceed the highest baseline data point, then PND would be 67%. There are several problems with PND as an estimate of effect size. First, PND is not a true measure of treatment strength. For example, one could have high PND (>90%) with a relatively weak treatment (low baseline levels and relatively low treatment levels). Second, there is not an empirical metric to determine high, medium, or low effect sizes comparable to group design standards using effect sizes. Third, PND can be distorted by variability in baseline trends, nonorthogonal slope changes, and floor/ceiling effects (Kratochwill et al., 2010).

An alternative to PND is calculation of PAND (Parker, Hagan-Burke, & Vannest, 2007). Similar to PND, PAND reflects the data nonoverlap between phases in single-case studies, but differs in several key respects. First, PAND uses all data in baseline and treatment phases and thus avoids the criticism in PND not considering all data and including unreliable data. Second, PAND is easily translated into a phi coefficient that is a Pearson *r* for a 2 × 2 contingency table. As

such, PAND has a known sampling distribution that makes the calculation of *p* values and estimation of statistical power possible. Third, a phi coefficient can be transformed into Cohen's *d* and thus can be interpreted as a standardized mean difference effect size.

Perhaps the easiest and most relevant index to quantify the magnitude of behavior change in single-case studies is to calculate the percentage of behavior change from baseline to intervention levels of performance. This index (PEM) is calculated by taking the median data point in baseline and comparing that value to the median data point in intervention phases (Gresham, 2005). The median is used instead of the mean because it is less susceptible to outlier effects. For example, if a student's median number of negative social interactions on the playground during baseline was eight occurrences and the median number of negative social interactions during intervention was two, the PEM reduction in the target behavior would be 75%. This metric is not unlike the methods used by physicians to quantify weight loss or reductions in blood cholesterol levels. The difference is, however, that there are well-established benchmarks for ideal weights and cholesterol levels, but not for social behaviors. Also, PEM only reflects changes in the level of the target behavior and not changes in trend (slope changes across phases).

Social Validation

In addition to quantifying the effects of intervention, it is important to establish the social validity of intervention outcomes. Social validity deals with three fundamental questions faced by school psychologists: (a) What should we change? (b) How should we change it? (c) How will we know it was effective?

These three questions can be recast in terms of assessing the social significance of the goals of an intervention, establishing the social acceptability of intervention procedures by treatment consumers, and evaluating the social importance of the effects produced by the intervention (Kazdin, 1977; Wolf, 1978).

Kazdin (1977) suggested three methods for socially validating the effects of intervention. One method involves using subjective evaluations by treatment consumers to evaluate the social importance of the effects of an intervention. These subjective evaluations consist of having treatment consumers (e.g., teachers or parents) rate the qualitative aspects of the child's behavior. These global evaluations of behavior change assess how the child is functioning after the intervention to provide an overall assessment of postintervention performance.

Another method for assessing social validity is using social comparisons in which the behavior of the target child is compared to the same behavior of comparison peers in the classroom. If the intervention moves the target student's behavior into the same range of functioning as comparison peers, the intervention has produced socially valid results. Finally, combined social validation procedures can be used consisting of subjective judgments and social comparisons. More detailed presentations of the social validation process and procedures can be found in other sources (see Gresham & Lopez, 1996; Lane & Beebe-Frankenberger, 2004).

Implications of Problem-Solving Approach to Diagnosis

A major challenge in the identification of students as having so-called high-incidence disabilities involves a decision regarding whether low academic achievement or behavior problems constitute true disability. That is, at what point does low academic achievement become a specific learning disability, or at what point does a behavior problem become an emotional disturbance. The answer to these questions is not straightforward and ultimately involves some degree of subjective judgment. In the case of learning disabilities and emotional disturbance, these individuals differ from their peers more in terms of degree rather than in kind. Few professionals would disagree, for example, that individuals with profound intellectual disabilities differ in kind from their nondisabled peers and this diagnosis is virtually never questioned by the professional community. Such is not the case with high-incidence disabilities.

This chapter argued that an RTI approach to the diagnosis of these learning and behavior problems can be useful in determining the presence or absence of these high-incidence disabilities. This decision must be made at the local and individual levels by an assessment and placement team and will most certainly vary across cases and schools. The major advantage of this approach is that it moves professionals away from questionable decision-making practices (e.g., IQ–achievement discrepancy) to a data-based decision-making approach to eligibility.

SUMMARY

This chapter discussed diagnosis from the perspective of a multitier model of service delivery within the context of an RTI framework. Instead of diagnosing within-child conditions such as processing disorders in learning disabilities or underlying psychopathology in emotional disturbance, the term *diagnosis* in this approach focuses on four stages of the problem-solving approach: (a) diagnosing the problem or problem identification, (b) diagnosing why the problem is occurring or problem analysis, (c) diagnosing the correct intervention or plan design/implementation, and (d) diagnosing intervention outcomes or plan evaluation. Each of these steps in the problem-solving approach takes place at each of the three levels of intervention: universal, selected, and intensive.

In adopting the problem-solving approach to diagnosis, several important points should be considered. First, interventions designed to alter the academic and/or social behavior of students should be based on a discrepancy between current and desired levels of performance. Second, the intensity of an intervention is increased only after the student shows an inadequate response to that intervention. Third, intervention decisions are based on objective data collected continuously over time (data-based decision making). Fourth, data that are collected are well-established indicators of academic or social behavior functioning (e.g., general outcome measures). Finally, decisions about intervention intensity are based on the collection of more and more data as the student moves through each tier of intervention. RTI can and should be used by school psychologists to make important educational decisions for children and youth.

REFERENCES

American Psychiatric Association. (2000). *Diagnostic and statistical manual of mental disorders* (4th ed., text rev.). Washington, DC: Author.

Angold, A. (2000, December). *Preadolescent screening and data analysis.* Paper presented at the 2nd annual Expert Panel on Preadolescent Screening Procedures, Washington, DC.

Barrish, H., Saunders, M., & Wolf, M. (1969). Good Behavior Game: Effects of individual contingencies for group consequences on disruptive behavior in a classroom. *Journal of Applied Behavior Analysis, 2,* 119–124. doi:10.1901/jaba.1969.2-119

Bergan, J. (1977). *Behavioral consultation.* Columbus, OH: Merrill.

Bergan, J., & Kratochwill, T. (1990). *Behavioral consultation and therapy.* New York, NY: Plenum Press.

Busk, P., & Serlin, R. (1992). Meta-analysis for single-case research. In T. Kratochwill & J. Levin (Eds.), *Single-case design and analysis* (pp. 187–212). Hillsdale, NJ: Erlbaum.

Cohen, J. (1988). *Statistical power analysis for the behavioral sciences* (2nd ed.). Hillsdale, NJ: Erlbaum.

Cooper, J., Heron, T., & Heward, W. (2007). *Applied behavior analysis* (2nd ed.). Minneapolis, MN: Pearson Assessments.

Crone, D., Hawken, L., & Horner, R. (2010). *Responding to problem behavior in schools: The behavior education program.* New York, NY: Guilford Press.

Embry, D. D. (2002). The Good Behavior Game: A best practice candidate as a universal behavioral vaccine. *Clinical Child and Family Psychology Review, 5,* 273–297. doi:10.1023/A:1020977107086

Francis, D., Fletcher, J., Steubing, K., Lyon, G. R., Shaywitz, B., & Shaywitz, S. (2005). Psychometric approaches to the identification of learning disabilities: IQ and achievement scores are not sufficient. *Journal of Learning Disabilities, 38,* 98–108. doi:10.1177/00222194050380020101

Fuchs, L., & Fuchs, D. (1997). Use of curriculum-based measurement in identifying students with disabilities. *Focus on Exceptional Children, 30,* 1–16.

Fuchs, L., & Fuchs, D. (1998). Treatment validity: A unifying concept for reconceptualizing the identification of learning disabilities. *Learning Disabilities Research & Practice, 13,* 204–219.

Gresham, F. M. (1981). Social skills training with handicapped children: A review. *Review of Educational Research, 51,* 139–176. doi:10.2307/1170253

Gresham, F. M. (2002). Responsiveness to intervention: An alternative approach to the identification of learning disabilities. In R. Bradley, L. Danielson, & D. Hallahan (Eds.), *Identification of learning disabilities: Research to practice* (pp. 467–519). Mahwah, NJ: Erlbaum.

Gresham, F. M. (2004). Current status and future directions of school-based behavioral interventions. *School Psychology Review, 33,* 326–343.

Gresham, F. M. (2005). Response to intervention: An alternative means of identifying students as emotionally disturbed. *Education and Treatment of Children, 28,* 328–344.

Gresham, F. M. (2006). Response to intervention. In G. G. Bear & K. M. Minke (Eds.), *Children's needs III: Development, prevention, and intervention* (pp. 525–540). Bethesda, MD: National Association of School Psychologists.

Gresham, F. M. (2007). Evolution of the response-to-intervention concept: Empirical foundations and recent developments. In S. Jimmerson, M. Burns, & A. VanDerHeyden (Eds.), *Handbook of response to intervention: The science and practice of assessment and intervention* (pp. 10–24). New York, NY: Springer.

Gresham, F. M., & Elliott, S. N. (2007). *Social Skills Improvement System-Rating Scales.* Minneapolis, MN: Pearson Assessments.

Gresham, F. M., & Lopez, M. F. (1996). Social validation: A unifying concept for school-based consultation research and practice. *School Psychology Quarterly, 11,* 205–213. doi:10.1037/h0088930

Gresham, F. M., Reschly, D. J., & Shinn, M. (2010). RTI as a driving force in educational improvement: Research, legal, and practical perspectives. In M. Shinn & H. Walker (Eds.), *Interventions for achievement and behavior problems in a three-tier model including RTI* (pp. 47–78). Bethesda, MD: National Association of School Psychologists.

Gresham, F. M., Watson, T. S., & Skinner, C. H. (2001). Functional behavioral assessment: Principles, procedures, and future directions. *School Psychology Review, 30,* 156–172.

Gresham, F. M., & Witt, J. C. (1997). Utility of intelligence tests for treatment planning, classification, and placement decisions: Recent empirical findings and future directions. *School Psychology Quarterly, 12,* 249–267. doi:10.1037/h0088961

Horner, R., Carr, E., Halle, J., McGee, G., Odom, S., & Wolery, M. (2005). The use of single-subject research to identify evidence-based practice in special education. *Exceptional Children, 71,* 165–179.

Hoskyn, M., & Swanson, H. D. (2000). Cognitive processing of low achievers and children with reading disabilities: A selective meta-analytic review. *School Psychology Review, 29,* 102–119.

Hosp, J., & MacConnell, K. (2008). Best practices in curriculum-based evaluation in early reading. In A. Thomas & J. Grimes (Eds.), *Best practices in school psychology V* (pp. 377–396). Bethesda, MD: National Association of School Psychologists.

Individuals with Disabilities Education Improvement Act of 2004, Pub. L. No. 108–446, 20 U.S.C. 1400 et seq. (2004).

Jones, K., Young, M., & Friman, P. (2000). Increasing peer praise of socially rejected delinquent youth: Effects on cooperation and acceptance. *School Psychology Quarterly, 15,* 30–39. doi:10.1037/h0088776

Juel, C. (1988). Learning to read: A longitudinal study of 54 children from first through fourth grades. *Journal of Educational Psychology, 80,* 437–447. doi:10.1037/0022-0663.80.4.437

Kaminski, R., & Good, R. (1996). Toward a technology of assessing basic early literacy skills. *School Psychology Review, 25,* 215–227.

Kauffman, J. M. (2001). *Characteristics of emotional and behavioral disorders of children and youth* (7th ed.). Upper Saddle River, NJ: Merrill Prentice Hall.

Kazdin, A. E. (1977). Assessing the clinical or applied significance of behavior change through social validation. *Behavior Modification, 1,* 427–452.

Kelley, M. L. (1990). *School-home notes: Promoting children's classroom success.* New York, NY: Guilford Press.

Kessler, R., Berglund, P., Demler, O., Jin, R., & Walters, M. (2005). Lifetime prevalence and age-of-onset distributions of DSM-IV disorders in the National Comorbidity Survey replication. *Archives of General Psychiatry, 62,* 593–602.

Kratochwill, T. R., Hitchcock, J., Horner, R., Odom, S., Rindskopf, D., & Shadish, W. (2010). *Single-case designs technical documentation.* Retrieved from http://ies.ed.gov/ncee/wwc/documentsum.aspx?sid=229

Lane, K. L., & Beebe-Frankenberger, M. (2004). *School-based interventions: The tools you need to succeed.* Boston, MA: Pearson Education.

MacMillan, D. L., & Siperstein, G. H. (2002). Learning disabilities as operationally defined by schools. In R. Bradley, L. Danielson, & D. Hallahan (Eds.), *Identification of learning disabilities: Research to practice* (pp. 278–333). Mahwah, NJ: Erlbaum.

Madaus, M., Kehle, T., Madaus, J., & Bray, M. (2003). Mystery motivator as an intervention to promote homework completion and accuracy. *School Psychology International, 24,* 369–377. doi:10.1177/0143034303024400

National Assessment of Educational Progress. (2005). *The nation's report card: Reading.* Washington, DC: Author. Retrieved from http://nces.ed.gov/nationsreportcard/pdf/main2005/2006451.pdf

National Association of School Psychologists. (2010). *Model for comprehensive and integrated school psychological services.* Bethesda, MD:

Author. Retrieved from http://www.nasponline.org/standards/2010standards/2_PracticeModel.pdf

National Joint Committee on Learning Disabilities. (1988). *Anonymous letter to NJCLD member organizations.* Arlington, VA: Author.

Noell, G. H., & Witt, J. C. (1999). When does consultation lead to intervention implementation? Critical issues for research and practice. *The Journal of Special Education, 33,* 29–35. doi:10.1177/002246699903300103

Parker, R. I., Brossart, D. F., Vannest, K. J., Long, J. R., De-Alba, R. G., Baugh, F. G., & Sullivan, J. R. (2005). Effect sizes in single case research: How large is large? *School Psychology Review, 34,* 116–132.

Parker, R., Hagan-Burke, S., & Vannest, K. (2007). Percentage of all non-overlapping data (PAND): An alternative to PND. *The Journal of Special Education, 40,* 194–204. doi:10.1177/00224669070400040101

Rathvon, N. (2008). *Effective school interventions: Evidence-based strategies for improving student outcomes* (2nd ed.). New York, NY: Guilford Press.

Rosenthal, R. (1991). *Meta-analytic procedures for social research.* Thousand Oaks, CA: SAGE.

Shinn, M. (2010). Building a scientifically based data system for progress monitoring and universal screening across three tiers, including RTI using curriculum-based measurement. In M. Shinn & H. Walker (Eds.), *Interventions for achievement and behavior problems in a three-tier model including RTI* (pp. 259–292). Bethesda, MD: National Association of School Psychologists.

Skiba, R., & Grizzle, K. (1991). The social maladjustment exclusion: Issues in definition and assessment. *School Psychology Review, 20,* 23–28.

Steubing, K., Barth, A., Weiss, B., & Fletcher, J. (2009). IQ is not strongly related to response to reading instruction: A meta-analytic interpretation. *Exceptional Children, 76,* 31–51.

Steubing, K., Fletcher, J., LeDoux, J., Lyon, G. R., Shaywitz, S., & Shaywitz, B. (2002). Validity of IQ-discrepancy classifications in reading disabilities: A meta-analysis. *American Educational Research Journal, 39,* 469–518. doi:10.3102/00028312039002469

Sugai, G., Horner, R., & Gresham, F. M. (2002). Behaviorally effective school environments. In M. Shinn, H. Walker, & G. Stoner (Eds.), *Interventions for academic and behavior problems II: Preventive and remedial approaches* (pp. 315–350). Bethesda, MD: National Association of School Psychologists.

Torgesen, J., Alexander, A., Wagner, R., Rashotte, C., Voeller, K., & Conway, T. (2001). Intensive remedial instruction for children with severe reading disabilities: Immediate and long-term outcomes for two instructional approaches. *Journal of Learning Disabilities, 34,* 33–58. doi:10.1177/002221940103400104

Torgesen, J., Wagner, R., Rashotte, C., Rose, E., Lindamood, P., Conway, T., & Garvin, C. (1999). Preventing reading failure in young children with phonological processing disabilities: Group and individual responses to instruction. *Journal of Educational Psychology, 91,* 579–593. doi:10.1037/0022-0663.91.4.579

Umbreit, J., Ferro, J., Liaupsin, C., & Lane, K. (2007). *Functional behavioral assessment and function-based intervention: An effective practical approach.* Upper Saddle River, NJ: Pearson Education.

U.S. Department of Education. (2011). *Thirty-third annual report to Congress on implementation of Individuals with Disabilities Education Act.* Washington, DC: Author.

VanDerHeyden, A., & Witt, J. C. (2008). Best practices in can't do/won't do assessment. In A. Thomas & J. Grimes (Eds.), *Best practices in school psychology V* (pp. 131–139). Bethesda, MD: National Association of School Psychologists.

Vellutino, F., Scanlon, D., Sipay, E., Small, S., Pratt, A., Chen, R., & Denckla, M. B. (1996). Cognitive profiles of difficult-to-remediate and readily remediated poor readers: Early intervention as a vehicle for distinguishing between cognitive and experiential deficits as basic causes of specific reading disability. *Journal of Educational Psychology, 88,* 601–638. doi:10.1037/0022-0663.88.4.601

Walker, H. M., Ramsey, E., & Gresham, F. M. (2004). *Antisocial behavior in school: Evidence-based practices* (2nd ed.). Belmont, CA: Wadsworth/Thomson Learning.

Watson, T. S., & Steege, M. (2012). *Conducting school-based functional behavioral assessment: A practitioner's guide* (2nd ed.). New York, NY: Guilford Press.

Witt, J. C., Daly, E., & Noell, G. (2000). *Functional assessment: A step-by-step guide to solving academic and behavior problems.* Longmont, CO: Sopris West.

Wolf, M. M. (1978). Social validity: The case for subjective measurement or how applied behavior analysis is finding its heart. *Journal of Applied Behavior Analysis, 11,* 203–214.

Ysseldyke, J., & Marston, D. (1999). Origins of categorical special education services in schools and a rationale for changing them. In D. Rashly, W. D. Tilly, III., & J. Grimes (Eds.), *Special education in transition: Functional assessment and noncategorical programming* (pp. 1–18). Longmont, CO: Sopris West.

10

Best Practices in Curriculum-Based Evaluation

Kenneth W. Howell
Western Washington University
John L. Hosp
University of Iowa

OVERVIEW

This chapter provides an overview of curriculum-based evaluation (CBE), a systematic approach to problem solving that can help school psychologists make data-based decisions about intervention planning that focuses on improving student outcomes. A brief discussion of the terms and considerations of CBE is provided to give the background and a consistent frame of reference. The CBE process of inquiry is then presented, with explanations of each step and the decisions to be made or actions to be taken within them. Although the CBE process can be applied to social–behavioral concerns, this chapter focuses on academic problems to illustrate the process.

The information in this chapter directly addresses the domain of Data-Based Decision Making and Accountability in the National Association of School Psychologists (NASP) *Model for Comprehensive and Integrated School Psychological Services* (NASP, 2010). CBE is a structured approach to data-based decision making. In addition, the NASP Practice Model foundations of (a) diversity in development and learning; (b) research and program evaluation; and (c) legal, ethical, and professional practice are all vitally important to implementing CBE.

Assessment and evaluation have traditionally been major components of the role of the school psychologist. Surveys of NASP members typically show 50% or more of school psychologists' time is devoted to assessment (Castillo, Curtis, & Gelley, 2012). However, as evidence-based assessment and instruction practices as well as regulations regarding services to children have evolved, this role has changed. One of the biggest changes for those working with students with academic difficulties has been the shift away from an emphasis on measurement and toward a focus on problem solving so that the most likely effective intervention can be introduced. Even the most powerful intervention has limited utility when applied to a problem it is not designed to remediate.

As schools move away from traditional systems of determining placement and services to systems with a problem-solving orientation or multitiered systems of support, the use of measurement procedures that can be administered efficiently and linked directly to intervention is required. To meet these demands, school psychologists need the tools and training necessary to analyze an academic problem and link this analysis to instructional planning. School psychologists are looking for measurement and evaluation methods that will facilitate the design of interventions and complement efforts to monitor the ways students respond to these interventions. Those involved in this paradigm shift are aware that while the need to include school psychologists in evaluation has not changed, the types of measures used as well as forms of information gained have gone through significant change. In addition, the role that the school psychologist plays in the gathering and analysis of evaluation data has also shifted. For example, school psychologists are now expected to analyze data on both academic and social behaviors, participate in problem-solving teams, and use progress monitoring, as well as performance data, to assist in making and evaluating instructional recommendations.

BASIC CONSIDERATIONS

The terms *assessment, measurement,* and *evaluation* are often used in different ways by researchers, trainers, and practitioners alike. For example, the term *assessment* is used to mean (a) an instrument or tool, (b) measurement, or (c) evaluation (Hosp, 2011). Table 10.1 shows how we will be using those terms here.

School psychologists are expected to know about and use a variety of measurement and assessment tools. In current school psychology practice, many of these tools fall into the category of curriculum-based assessment (CBA). Broadly defined, CBA is the process of collecting information about skills taught in a curriculum or expected to be mastered in standards. However, as there are many ways to accomplish this goal, it is necessary to find certain attributes in a process if it is to be classified as CBA. These include use of a behavioral paradigm, direct and precise measurement, alignment with the students' learning outcomes or with standards, repeatable measurement, measurement that is sensitive to change, high content validity, and high fidelity of implementation (Shapiro, 2010). However, there is considerable debate about the exact definition of CBA as well as confusion of CBA with curriculum-based measurement (CBM), instructional assessment, progress monitoring, and CBE (Burns, MacQuarrie, & Campbell, 1999).

Within this definition of CBA, CBM is one type of CBA and typically refers to a standardized set of procedures used to measure student performance in the areas of reading, math, and written expression (Hosp, Hosp, & Howell, 2007). These standardized procedures provide useful and technically adequate directions for creating, administering, and scoring measures that have themselves been well researched and shown to be direct, precise, repeatable, sensitive to learning, and aligned with standards as well as the conditions of instruction (Deno, 2003).

CBE, the focus of this chapter, is a process of evaluation and decision making that makes extensive use of CBM and other derivations of CBA. CBE also relies on judgment, inference, and problem solving (Hosp, Hosp, Howell, & Allison, 2014). It provides a decision-making framework for thinking about the academic or social problems of students. This framework is organized around the practical and logical implications of delivering an instructional intervention within a curriculum context with established learning expectations or standards.

One component of CBE, problem solving, needs further explanation. Problem solving is generally considered to be one of the most complex cognitive operations. However, it is also something that can be taught (Pretz & Sternberg, 2005). Although many disciplines have different definitions of and approaches to problem solving, within school psychology problem solving is generally considered to have four components: problem identification, problem analysis, intervention development, and intervention implementation and evaluation (Bergen & Kratochwill, 1990). CBE uses these steps and can provide a logical approach for working within the context of educational decision making. CBE is a useful process for four reasons:

- By definition, CBE is aligned with the academic and social outcomes selected when planning an intervention.
- CBE uses CBMs (among other methods and tools). They are easily administered within classroom or applied contexts.
- CBE is flexible and formative. Within it, one-time a priori decision making is deemphasized in favor of repeated data collection and decision making across time. This allows for the precise recognition of successful interventions.
- CBE employs expert problem-solving systems through the use of field-tested formats and procedures.

Basics of CBE

It is important to know that the technology of CBE is not new (see Howell & Morehead, 1987). Important

Table 10.1. The Relations Among Measurement, Assessment, and Evaluation

Word	Definition
Evaluation	The process of using information to make decisions
Assessment	The process of collecting information about the amounts or qualities of something
Measurement	The process of determining the dimensions or limits of something in a systematic way
Tool	An instrument that can be used for one of the above processes
Inference	Arriving at a logical conclusion from a body of evidence
Judgment	Making a decision based on evidence and comparison

work pertaining to direct measurement, formative evaluation, and data-based decision making can be found in precision teaching (Kunzelmann, Cohen, Hulten, Martin, & Mingo, 1970) and data-based program modification (Deno & Mirkin, 1977).

Therefore, CBE is not the application of some unique or elaborate set of alternative measurement instruments. Rather, it is a network of curriculum-driven if–then guidelines. Each of these is attached to a question and, as such, flows as shown in the following example targeting a learner's background knowledge of computation:

- *Question 1:* Does Hubert have difficulty understanding the meaning of unfamiliar words?
- *Option 1.1:* If the answer to the question is no, then there is no need for additional questions about vocabulary.
- *Option 1.2:* If the answer to the question is yes, then additional questions are needed.

Suppose the answer is yes and Hubert has difficulty understanding the meaning of unfamiliar words. The school psychologist might ask additional questions about vocabulary such as, "Is Hubert proficient at decoding unfamiliar words?" To find out about these skills, a CBM covering decoding of unfamiliar words (typically nonwords to ensure no prior exposure) will be given and the if–then sequence is repeated. Remember, we now know Hubert has difficulty understanding the meaning of unfamiliar words:

- *Question 2:* Is Hubert proficient at decoding unfamiliar words?
- *Option 2.1:* If the answer to the question is yes, then return to higher level skills (e.g., knowledge of context clue strategies) and check those.
- *Option 2.2:* If the answer to the question is no, then the strategies for decoding unfamiliar words need to be examined.

If it is found that Hubert's decoding is adequate, then the conclusion would be to teach the context clue strategies Hubert needs to learn. Once he has learned to proficiently apply those context clue strategies, he would be ready to generalize them to a variety of unfamiliar words.

The vocabulary example provides an illustration of the format for determining what background knowledge needs to be targeted and examined and for determining what eventually needs to be taught. How efficiently and effectively this happens depends on the skills of the evaluator. Table 10.2 includes a set of rules for generating hypotheses, or assumed causes, for targeting

Table 10.2. Rules for Developing Assumed Causes

Rule	Description
Clarify the purpose.	If the purpose is to decide *what* to teach, a clear definition of what the student is expected to do and the level of proficiency expected (i.e., the standard and the criterion) are needed so that the student's performance can be compared to the criterion. If the purpose is to decide *how* to teach, data on the student's progress (or growth) and the characteristics of prior and current instruction are needed to determine how much of a change is needed and what should be changed.
Target relevant information.	Relevant information is alterable (i.e., something that can be changed through instruction or adjustments to programming), aligned with the student's needs, and essential (i.e., proficiency with a skill will be important because it serves as a prerequisite to later knowledge or skills).
Think about more than the learner.	When an individual has a problem, we often assume that is where the problem resides; however, other domains also need to be considered. The student might not be learning due to disruptive characteristics of the setting, curriculum content not aligned with his or her needs, or instruction that is not effective at producing the desired learning.
Think about types of knowledge.	Many curricular standards are based on knowledge of facts ($2 + 2 = 4$) or concepts (quantities can be combined to form new quantities), making these a frequent focus of problem solving. However, it is also important to consider knowledge of procedures (to add, start with the larger number and count up to find the sum) and metacognition (when to add, why to use the specific procedure).
Think about levels of mastery.	Another default in education has often been mastery at an accurate level (as evidenced by all those Individualized Education Program goals with 80% accuracy). However, some tasks must be mastered fluently (accurate at rate) or for generalization (in the presence of distractors or applied to new conditions).
Pick the most likely targets first.	This is the rule of parsimony, or Occam's razor. The most likely explanation for the student's lack of proficiency (i.e., the most likely solution to the problem) should be checked before going on to those that are more complex or exotic.

assessment and solving academic problems in a skillful way. Much of the CBE process hinges on the understanding and application of these rules. The if–then format becomes the carrier for the use of these rules. The process is relatively straightforward and requires answering four questions:

- *What is the problem, and why is it happening?* This is a stage of problem identification and analysis that is critical before implementing any intervention.
- *What will be done about the problem?* An intervention is developed based on the analysis of the problem.
- *Is the intervention working?* Measurement tools are selected that align most closely with the intended outcomes of the intervention. Data are used to make decisions evaluating the implementation and effectiveness of the intervention and to determine need for future intervention.
- *If the intervention is not working, then why is it not working?* This is the step where CBE is most valuable, because this is where the nature of the problem is examined and not just monitored.

BEST PRACTICE IN CURRICULUM-BASED EVALUATION

CBE is about deciding which interventions (preferably evidence based) to use and, monitoring the effectiveness of those interventions. CBE is not an instructional intervention, nor is it a measurement tool. CBE is a systematic problem-solving process for making educational decisions. The steps and procedures of CBE (and, more important, the thinking that goes along with it) can be applied to almost any educational problem in any system of delivery and at any tier of service or level of intensity. The goal of CBE is to maximize student learning through the targeted collection of useful assessment data, evaluation of student performance, and progress and application of data-based decision making.

CBE Process of Inquiry

Figure 10.1 is the flowchart for problem solving that is the CBE process of inquiry. What follows is a step-by-step discussion progressing through that process at the individual student level for an academic problem, that is, what questions need to be asked, what decisions need to be made, and what things need to be considered. This process is a heuristic overlay, meaning it can be applied

to any content area and it remains basically the same except that the skills and instruments will be different (depending on the parameters of each specific content area or the age or grade level of the student; e.g., Slentz & Hyatt, 2008). Following this presentation and examples of CBE at the student level, we discuss inclusion of CBE within multitiered systems of support and some examples of what the actions and questions would look like at other levels.

Phase 1: Fact Finding

In Phase 1, all currently known information is reviewed to determine three things: (a) how well the student should be performing or progressing (i.e., the expectation), (b) how well the student is currently performing or progressing, and (c) if there is a meaningful difference between current and expected performance or progress. If any of these three cannot be determined, additional assessment needs to be conducted to define the problem and narrow the scope of inquiry. In the language of problem solving and decision making, this is a phase that includes problem identification and validation.

Action 1.1: Concern about learning. There are many potential sources of concern about learning for students. They may come from the parent or student as well as school personnel. Often, though, the original concern presented comes from the student's teacher. It is ideal for the teacher to have evidence of this concern and some documentation for why he or she thinks this is a problem. The school psychologist can be a valuable partner at this step. Every concern should be taken seriously and run through Phase 1 as necessary. Even though not all concerns will be confirmed as problems, it is important to have a high degree of confidence in the determination of the presence or absence of a learning problem.

Action 1.2: Define the problem. In order to attempt to validate a concern as a problem, it is important to have a sufficient problem definition that can be evaluated. Therefore, it must be observable and measureable and there needs to be a meaningful standard to which to compare the student's performance. With the development of the Common Core State Standards (which have been adopted in 47 states for English language arts and/or mathematics) and the use of a common core in the remaining 3 states, at least in the areas of reading and math (and soon science), there is a consistent set of standards to which students should be compared. Problem definition is a

Figure 10.1. The CBE Process of Inquiry

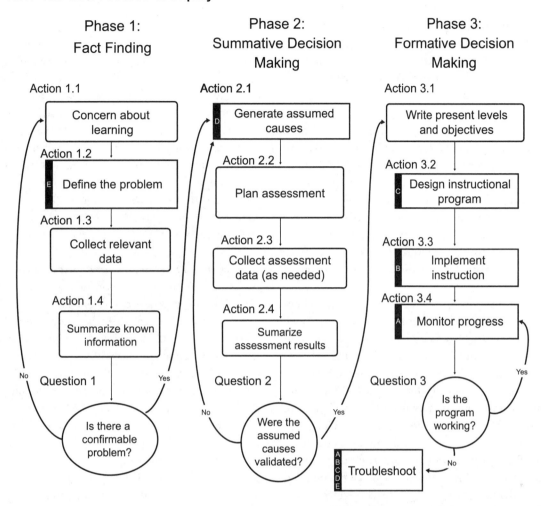

From *The ABCs of Curriculum-Based Evaluation: A Practical Guide to Effective Decision Making* by J. Hosp, M. Hosp, K. Howell, & R. Allison, 2014, New York, NY: Guilford Press. Copyright 2014 by Guilford Press. Adapted with permission.

crucial step because if it is not done accurately then all the decisions and actions that follow will be misaligned and will waste much of the school psychologist's and the child's time.

Action 1.3: Collect relevant data. This action requires consideration of the RIOT assessment procedures (Review, Interview, Observe, Test; see Hosp, 2011). Before collecting new data, existing data should be collected and examined. If there are enough data to confirm the presence of the learning problem, then no additional assessment needs to be done. If additional information is needed, then it should be quick to collect, technically adequate, and directly aligned with the hypothesized problem. General indicators and multiskill indicators are typically useful for this purpose (Hosp

et al., 2007). Class assignments or general achievement measures that sample the student's performance across a range of skills can also be useful.

Action 1.4: Summarize known information. The existing information that is collected and examined as well as the student's performance on instruments may need to be condensed so that it can be compared with his or her expected and previous performance. This is usually done in the form of scores. Both confirmatory and contradictory information should be included to determine how confident one should be with the evidence when attempting to confirm the problem.

Question 1: Can the problem be validated? This is the same as asking if the problem requires an intervention. To answer this question, the *so what* test needs to be applied. A problem fails the so what test if it is not centrally important to the student's academic success. When the intervention is not worth the effort, or would be a low priority, the problem may not be validated (we are not obligated to fix everything, only those things that are important).

An academic problem has high priority if it involves the following: (a) the standards or goals the student is expected to meet, (b) skills and knowledge that are needed to learn other important things, (c) skills that are required for access to a less restrictive setting, and (d) everyday living skills. If the answer to Question 1 is yes, then proceed to Phase 2. If the answer is no, then double check the original concern to make sure the correct one was evaluated and either conduct this phase again or discontinue the evaluation because the issue is not a priority.

A word of caution is needed here. Many school psychologists and other educators will want to move directly from Phase 1 to Phase 3. Educators want to teach or intervene and feel that time is of the essence. While intervening is important and time is precious, we can be more efficient and effective if we are planful in our approach to maximize the probability of teaching the right thing in the right way. There are not many times when you should go directly from Phase 1 to Phase 3, because if the information required to advance to Phase 3 is already known, such a detailed process as CBE would not need to be conducted in the first place. When a problem gets resolved as early as Phase 1, it means either (a) there was already good information in the system but it was not being used in a timely fashion or (b) the available information actually is not as good as anticipated and the process will return from Phase 3 shortly. Both of these are system problems, not student problems, and should signal the need for a review of the evaluation procedures at the agency (see the section on multitiered systems of support below).

Phase 2: Summative Decision Making

Once information about what the student is or is not doing is collected, the next step is to pause and figure out why. Here assessment is more targeted to check hypotheses that may explain why the student's performance is not adequate. But first the hypotheses need to be carefully generated. These possible explanations for a problem are called *assumed causes* because they must be validated or rejected through targeted assessment (then they are no longer *assumed*). The efficiency, direction, and ultimate utility of any evaluation conducted for instructional planning will depend on the quality of the assumed causes. See Table 10.3 for examples of well-aligned and misaligned assumed causes and the consequences.

Action 2.1: Generate assumed causes. For us, Action 2.1 is the most important action in the CBE problem-solving process. This is when the best thinking needs to be done. Because the hypotheses will determine the direction of all subsequent evaluation, hypotheses need to be explicit, observable, and measurable. As noted above, evaluations will only target useful variables if assumed causes that allow for this are developed (refer to Table 10.2 for the guidelines).

When developing assumed causes, evaluators examine the collected facts and use their knowledge of the learning interaction (i.e., Setting, Curriculum, Instruction, Learner [SCIL]) to determine why these facts exist. This action is often done in consultation with others or with reference materials. At this early level, any problem noted in a referral, missed item on a test, problematic observation, or troublesome interview result can be a detail that needs to be explained by generating an assumed cause. Also, the assumptions are not limited to questions about the learner as other SCIL domains should be considered.

When addressing the learner, the focus should be on whether or not the student has the background knowledge needed to succeed on the goal task. If not

Table 10.3. Comparison of the Thinking of Two School Psychologists Approaching the Same Problem

School Psychologist	Step 1: Collect Facts	Step 2: Generate Assumed Causes	Step 3: Test Assumed Causes	Step 4: Make Decisions or New Assumed Causes
1	Slow addition fact recall	Does the student have poor cognitive processing speed?	Measure of rapid automatized naming	Conclusions about things not in the curriculum
2	Slow addition fact recall	Does the student know addition facts?	Measure of addition fact proficiency	Conclusions about content that is in the curriculum (i.e., addition)

Note. From *The ABCs of Curriculum-Based Evaluation: A Practical Guide to Effective Decision Making* by J. Hosp, M. Hosp, K. Howell, & R. Allison, 2014, New York, NY: Guilford Press. Copyright 2014 by Guilford Press. Reprinted with permission.

familiar with that knowledge, begin by reviewing the state standards, curriculum checklists, status sheets, or tables of specifications. These will help define the information or skills the student most likely needs to know.

Action 2.2: Plan assessment. The assumed causes from Action 2.1 are used to form the evaluation questions and procedures: just insert the assumed causes after each stem. For example, Heloise is not progressing in spelling. The assumed cause may be that Heloise is accurate with, but not fluent in, producing common spelling patterns. Now the evaluation questions may be: Is Heloise accurate at producing common spelling patterns? Is Heloise fluent at producing common spelling patterns?

Once the evaluation questions are developed, the next step is to select or design assessment procedures that can answer the questions. The combination of evaluation questions and assessment procedures make up the assessment plan. The key to a good targeted measure is alignment. It should directly address an assumed cause (although the same procedure may address more than one assumed cause) and make use of low-inference measures (i.e., ones that employ unambiguous measurement of the skill of interest). When targeted assessments focus on the student's knowledge, they should be criterion referenced and curriculum based. This ensures that they are aligned with the standards and relate to a meaningful level of performance that defines proficient.

Action 2.3: Collect assessment data. The assumed causes from Action 2.1 are just that, assumptions. These assumptions must be validated before they can be turned into instructional recommendations. The purpose of targeted assessments is to find out if the assumptions from Action 2.1 are correct. If not, Action 2.1 is repeated.

Action 2.4: Summarize assessment results. This is similar to Action 1.4. In it, the student's targeted assessment performance is compared directly with the assumed causes listed in Action 2.1 to allow answers to Question 2 (below).

Question 2: Were the assumed causes validated? If the answer is no, then the original assumed causes did not prove to be correct, so Action 2.1 must be repeated. Take any fresh information obtained and develop new assumed causes. For example, if it was determined that Heloise was both accurate and fluent at producing common spelling

patterns, a different assumed cause for the spelling difficulty would need to be developed. Given new information that she also has difficulty copying from the board, a new assumed cause may focus on handwriting.

Phase 3: Formative Decision Making

Now that the cause of the student's difficulty has been identified and validated, it is time to plan and implement the intervention in order to remedy it. This is the phase of problem solution. It is also important to have a clear plan for evaluating the intervention plan and the student's response to it. There is no reason to monitor progress if nothing will be done when the data indicate the need for a change. Formative decision making requires more than collecting progress-monitoring data. The evaluator must look at these data and make decisions based on them.

Frequent data collection provides the school psychologist several options that are unavailable within static formats. The most obvious is that data-based decisions can be made only as frequently as data are collected. However, data collection in the form of progress monitoring is not an intervention. Progress data, like all measurement data, must be analyzed, judged, and interpreted before the evaluation process can be completed.

Action 3.1: Write present levels and objectives. When the assumed causes about learner knowledge are accurate, the results are converted into scores that summarize the student's current performance by specifically noting related skills the student can and cannot do proficiently. While having a clear statement of the student's present level of performance in the area of concern is an important component of the intervention piece of the CBE process, this can also be used as the present level of academic achievement and functional performance statement for inclusion in an Individualized Education Program (IEP). This step lists any examples of background knowledge or skills that are missing or underdeveloped as instructional goals, learning targets, or objectives on the student's instructional plan. This defines the curriculum (i.e., what is to be taught).

Action 3.2: Design the instructional program. Because information should have been collected and summarized about the instruction and setting, those findings should be included in planning the instruction. This planning process can be reviewed and updated later as data on the effectiveness of the intervention are collected. These can and should be used to adjust the instructional plan in order to maximize student learning.

Action 3.3: Implement instruction. Start teaching. Be sure to pay attention to the fidelity of implementation of the instruction. An intervention must be implemented appropriately as well as designed appropriately to ensure that it affects the intended outcomes.

Action 3.4: Monitor progress. The quality of an instructional plan is indicated by only one thing: improved student performance (i.e., progress in performance over time). After instruction has begun, data on the student's growth must be collected frequently so that trends in learning can be identified and changes in instruction, if needed, are made in a timely fashion. Visual display of data through graphing is strongly recommended. An appropriately aligned general or multiskill indicator should be used to monitor progress toward long-term goals (generally end of year or grade). This provides a broader picture of student performance and a likely more generalizable evaluation of progress. For a more proximal focus on the target skill of the intervention, subskill indicators can be used to monitor student response to that specific intervention (see Hosp et al., 2007, and Hosp & Hosp, 2012, for a discussion of general, multiskill, and subskill indicators). A combination of the two provides a more comprehensive picture of the student's progress as well as the effectiveness of the intervention.

Students with learning problems need to be monitored consistently. Once-a-week monitoring can be considered an absolute minimum for students at more intense tiers of service (Stein, 1987). This monitoring is carried out to track the impact of the instruction. The need to monitor a student's learning more frequently increases whenever (a) the magnitude of the discrepancy between the expected and actual level of performance increases, (b) the magnitude of the discrepancy between the expected and actual rate of progress increases, (c) the discrepancy is in a high-impact content area (including early literacy or numeracy as well as any area in which a deficiency can lead to risk), (d) the student's response to the intervention is insufficient, (e) the intervention plan is complex, (f) the person managing the plan is working with a large number of students, or (g) portions of the program are being delivered by someone other than the person responsible for managing the program (e.g., an instructional assistant, peer tutor, or another teacher).

Question 3: Is the program working? Review the progress monitoring data while thinking about deciding how to teach. First, decide if the student is making adequate progress. If so, then the program should be retained (although objectives should be updated as the student meets them). If progress is not adequate, then something needs to be changed.

New to the CBE process is the explicit phase of troubleshooting. As planful as the process is to identify and validate the problem and design and implement the intervention, evaluating why the intervention was not successful should be just as planful. If the answer to Question 3 was no, then retrace the steps back through the process to determine what should be revised in order to improve student learning to meet the objectives. The question at the end of each phase should serve as a self-correcting mechanism to ensure that the actions of that phase were implemented accurately, but sometimes new information comes to light that can alter the parameters of the problem or the situation.

Troubleshooting involves five main checkpoints, that is, the areas where the process is most likely to have missed the target. The checkpoints should be evaluated in order, unless there is a clear piece of information that points to an earlier point (e.g., after finding the plan was not successful, you find out that the design of the intervention did not take into consideration scheduling of specials which affects the time available to implement it).

- *Checkpoint A: Monitor progress.* Ensure that the measures selected were appropriate and that they were implemented with fidelity.
- *Checkpoint B: Implement instruction.* Ensure that the intervention was implemented with fidelity.
- *Checkpoint C: Design instructional program.* Ensure that the intervention was designed with consideration of all important characteristics and that these were aligned with, and have been validated for, the difficulty the student is experiencing.
- *Checkpoint D: Generate assumed causes.* Ensure that the assumed cause is the point in the learning progression when progress is insufficient (i.e., there are no earlier skills that are problematic).
- *Checkpoint E: Define the problem.* Ensure that the problematic area is not being affected by difficulty in another area.

The process of troubleshooting works in the opposite direction as the CBE process. In addition to the end-of-phase questions serving as a first check, procedural evaluation should work the same way as diagnostic evaluation. Instruction moves from the least complex (or foundational) skills to the most complex (or higher order) skills. Assessment starts with the most complex skill and works backward until the most advanced nonproficient skill is found. In a similar fashion, the CBE process is implemented from start to finish (although at times iteratively), but when the desired outcome is not achieved, evaluation of the process starts with the most recent component and works backward. If the process has been implemented planfully and with fidelity, then the most likely explanation for a problem is in recent actions as one has had the least time to notice a problem with them.

CBE Within a Multitier System of Supports

The descriptions and examples used up to this point have predominantly focused on decision making about intervention development and implementation for individual students with academic problems. As originally designed and developed, CBE was intended for individual teachers to use explicit and systematic methods of problem solving to plan and evaluate intervention programs for individual students. This was typically a special education teacher or school psychologist applying the process to make determinations for a student with a disability. However, individual problems do not always have individual solutions. This is one reason that multitier systems of supports have seen a great increase in use as service delivery models. Most models of multitiered systems of support incorporate a problem-solving process that makes CBE a natural fit. There are three characteristics of multitiered systems of support for which CBE provides utility: consideration of problems at multiple levels of aggregation, multiple structures for decision making, and instruction or intervention delivery at multiple tiers.

Multiple Levels of Aggregation

Because multitiered systems of support is a system-wide service delivery model rather than an instructional program, it encompasses not just individual students but groups, classrooms, grade levels, and possibly schools. It would be horribly inefficient to make every decision for each student or classroom separately when there are trends across them that can shed important light on problems and solutions. Within Phase 1 of the CBE process (fact finding), even when the target of the concern is an individual student, there are plenty of data that can and should be examined at different grouping levels. If universal screening data are available, then

whole classes and grade levels can be examined to determine whether the curriculum and instruction are generally effective. When problems are common across students within a classroom, the source might be the instruction (e.g., not enough, or not explicit enough) or the curriculum (e.g., essential skills not covered or not covered sufficiently). There may also be a setting effect (e.g., room is too hot or noisy, room layout is not conducive to the instructional methods used).

For example, Mrs. McCorkle may have concerns about Edgar's reading. He performed poorly on the universal screening test, he is not making progress, and he is starting to express his frustration. When collecting the known information, Ms. Petrillo, the school psychologist, makes a graph of the performance of all the students in Mrs. McCorkle's class. The graph shows that approximately half of the students did not meet the criterion for proficiency and that Edgar's performance is right in the middle of those who did not meet the criterion. Mrs. McCorkle is immediately worried that she needs to change her classroom instruction and starts brainstorming adjustments. Ms. Petrillo cautions her to wait until they have all the information together before making changes. Next, she graphs the screening performance of all the second graders in the school and finds that across the three classrooms only one third of the students met the criterion. Continuing the process, they, along with the other second-grade teachers and the principal, hypothesize that the classroom instruction might be fine but the curriculum does not provide enough content coverage. To validate this, they examine the curriculum in relation to the state standards and look for other resources for judging curriculum coverage. They find that although the curriculum has excellent comprehension coverage, there is little focus on word reading and decoding.

Multiple Decision-Making Structures

Individual teachers and school psychologists will always need to make decisions, but when the service delivery model is school- or district-wide, additional decision-making structures need to be in place. This is usually in the form of different types of teams for different purposes. The first level of the decision-making team is usually the grade-level team. In it, all the teachers of that grade level, with support from a school psychologist, special education teacher, or administrator, meet regularly to discuss issues that affect individual students as well as groups, classrooms, or the whole grade level. The second level is the problem-solving team. This team is often made up of teachers across grades with greater support from specialists such as the school psychologist, speech–language pathologist, and special education teacher. It is designed to address problems that are more specific to a student or small group of students.

With these different teams, CBE can be useful by providing a decision-making process that can be used with the different teams as well as individuals. Using the curriculum example above, the grade-level team can use the CBE process to identify and solve that problem. Once that problem is corrected, another can arise for a specific student. That student would then be discussed at the problem-solving team meeting. The problem-solving team uses the same process, but with a different focus, that is, more on the learner and on the interactions between the learner, and the other SCIL domains. This serves two functions: (a) some of the information gathered and generated for the grade-level team can also be used by the problem-solving team and (b) because everyone in the school is using the same process, everyone has more practice, with varied contexts, and support from others who are learning and using the same process. These are the same reasons that universal screening and core instructional programs are efficient methods.

Multiple Tiers of Instruction or Intervention

One of the hallmarks of multitiered systems of support is that instruction is delivered in tiers of service. This is a model designed to improve efficiency and outcomes by identifying students with similar needs and providing them the additional intervention they need. It proves to be a lot simpler than differentiating instruction for each student and can capitalize on the benefits of peer tutoring and modeling. The decision-making structures, in part, reflect the different tiers of intervention. Grade-level teams address issues that affect all or most of the students, while problem-solving teams address issues that affect a few students. IEP teams and individual teachers address issues that affect individual students.

Again, CBE can help streamline the processes by providing a common problem-solving framework to make decisions about the different tiers of instruction and student performance. Rather than examining the performance of an individual student, the team will want to examine the instruction provided and aggregated performance of students receiving that tier of service. For example, a grade-level team making decisions about the core instruction will examine the aggregate performance of every student in that grade. The same criterion for proficiency will be used, but the percentage of students meeting or exceeding the criterion will be examined rather than individual performance.

Determinations for more intensive tiers include smaller proportions of students but still need to aggregate the performance of all the students receiving that level of service. This will work for any level of aggregation in addition to tiers of support subgroups such as English learners, skill groups within or across classrooms, classrooms within a school, or schools within a district.

Strengths and Challenges of CBE

Given the growing use of multitiered systems of support, CBE's utility within it is an obvious strength; that is, any process, product, or strategy that does not align with common service delivery models will not be broadly useful. A second strength of CBE is improved outcomes for students. While not evidence based in the sense that it has been tested for efficacy, it is research based in that it includes components that are evidence based (National Center on Response to Intervention, 2010). Progress monitoring, formative decision making, and implementation fidelity are all essential components of CBE that have substantial evidence for improving student outcomes. Because the CBE process is not considered complete until the validated problem has been remedied, by definition improved student performance is a mandatory outcome. A third strength of CBE is that the routinization of decision-making processes has been shown to combat decision fatigue and increase accuracy and therefore effect more positive outcomes (Gawande, 2009; Groupman, 2007).

There are also challenges to CBE. Upon first implementation, the process can seem cumbersome and confusing. Novice implementers tend to focus on procedure, which makes the content more difficult to attend to. This, of course, recedes with time and practice, but with the demands placed on educators today, that change can appear too long coming. Implementing CBE as a team can help by providing a built-in support system of others who are learning the process. As one person develops expertise in an area, another may focus on a different area, and they can thereby capitalize on each other's strengths.

Another challenge to CBE is the maintenance of implementation fidelity of components. While procedural fidelity of the process as a whole is important, fidelity of implementation of the components (e.g., intervention delivery, assessment administration and scoring) is just as important. A component implemented with low fidelity will be the likely source of ineffective problem solving. Another challenge is saturation. Much information is generated in education and, when collected, it can be a lot of information to synthesize and make sense of. Conceptually, there is a point where there is enough information to maximize the probability of an accurate decision, and collecting additional information will not improve the decision accuracy. This is the point of saturation. Unfortunately, there is no metric for measuring the amount of information. If there were, then we could determine an empirical criterion for saturation. As it is, the team or individual using the CBE process also has to make the decision of when there is enough information to support a decision, disconfirming evidence has been examined but is not as strong as confirming evidence, and collecting more information will not provide additional support for the decision.

Additional Considerations

In addition to the basic considerations and best practices for implementing CBE, there are additional considerations to better align CBE with the NASP Practice Model (NASP, 2010). These are multicultural competencies and evaluation of one's effectiveness.

Multicultural Competencies Needed by School Psychologists to Implement CBE

Multicultural, or cross-cultural, competence is important to CBE. Because CBE is best used to solve complex problems, there often is not a simple solution. Culture must be considered. Knowledge or familiarity with the student and aspects of his or her culture can have a profound effect on the interpretation of pieces of information or how to collect them. This knowledge must also be applied to decision making either in the inclusion of specific information or the consideration of a problem from different perspectives.

CBE also has many commonalities with an ecological perspective and an ethnic validity model. As summarized by Miranda (in press), an ecological perspective views a student as an active participant within a connected system, similar to the consideration of the SCIL domains and their interactive effect on learning. A difference is that CBE focuses on the academic aspects whereas the traditional ecological perspective focuses on a social–cultural context and those influences on and by the student. An ethnic validity model includes a problem-solving orientation similar to CBE, but it also encompasses considerations of acceptability and teaming as core components. Both are important considerations and competencies for CBE.

How School Psychologists Can Evaluate Effectiveness in Implementing CBE

Effectiveness in implementing CBE can be evaluated in three ways: student outcomes, fidelity/accuracy, and component analysis. The first and foremost effectiveness indicator within CBE is whether the desired learning outcome was achieved. If the problem defined in Action 1.2 is no longer a problem, CBE was implemented effectively. If it is, then there may be something that could be done more effectively. The second effectiveness indicator is the frequency of the need to conduct troubleshooting. If it is necessary to troubleshoot the process every time it is implemented, then there is a problem with effectiveness. By recording where the breakdown occurs each time, the assumed cause of the ineffectiveness can be identified and an intervention planned and implemented. Third, if a particular action is a consistent source of trouble in implementation of the CBE process, then it might be necessary to conduct a more detailed analysis of that component. Observational data to record the details of implementation can be a valuable source of information. In addition, if there are fidelity checklists or protocols for that specific program or action (e.g., for a specific intervention program or strategy, for implementing progress monitoring) then they should be used.

Component analysis can also be used to evaluate efficiency in addition to effectiveness. When first implementing a strategy or process, it is common for it to take longer than once that strategy or process has been mastered (Joyce & Showers, 1995). However, once a strategy or process has been mastered, it is important to determine how it might be implemented more efficiently. Component analysis can be used to provide data on the relative time and effort that goes into various actions as well as aspects that might be adjusted to use less time and fewer resources.

SUMMARY

CBE is a systematic process of decision making in order to plan, implement, and evaluate instruction and intervention. A flowchart of the process provides a heuristic overlay that can be applied to any content area. In any area, the use of curriculum-based thinking, combined with the use of multiple data sources, leads to evaluation of great utility and precision. This utility is the product of CBE's principal assumption: Students fail at academic or social tasks because of a breakdown in the interaction among setting, curriculum, instruction, and the learner. A corollary to this is that when learner characteristics are considered, missing background knowledge is the most likely cause of failures to perform and not biological, psychological, or social disorders.

Even the most powerful intervention has limited utility when applied to the wrong objective. CBE gains much of its precision and utility from its use of targeted assessment. It is inefficient, and often unproductive, to ground an evaluation on the routine administration of a standard battery of tests. Instead, instruments should provide data to answer specific questions. Targeting unknown and relevant information differs from other models because school psychologists who use CBE think about learning problems and the process of inquiry differently. The ways school psychologists think during CBE are illustrated within the eight rules provided for developing assumed causes when selecting targets for inquiry.

CBE fits well within the current problem-solving models associated with response to intervention or multitiered systems of support. CBE is conducted to determine what to teach and how to teach it. By using the tools of analysis and problem solving illustrated in this chapter, along with a decision-making framework to guide assessment, school psychologists can play a vital role in investigating, planning for, and addressing the instructional needs of children.

AUTHOR NOTE

The authors wish to dedicate this chapter to the memory of Sharon Kurns. Sharon's work in conceptualizing and implementing CBE has been inspirational, and her guidance, support, and feedback will be greatly missed.

Disclosure. Kenneth W. Howell and John L. Hosp have a financial interest in books they authored or coauthored that are referenced in this chapter.

REFERENCES

Bergen, J., & Kratochwill, T. (1990). *Behavioral consultation and therapy.* New York, NY: Springer.

Burns, M. K., MacQuarrie, L. L., & Campbell, D. T. (1999). The difference between curriculum-based assessment and curriculum-based measurement: A focus on purpose and result. *Communiqué, 27*(6), 18–19.

Castillo, J., Curtis, M., & Gelley, C. (2012). School psychology 2010: Part 2: School psychologists' professional practices and implications for the field. *Communiqué, 40*(8), 4–6, 14–16.

Deno, S. L. (2003). Developments in curriculum-based measurement. *Journal of Special Education, 37,* 184–192. doi:10.1177/00224669030370030801

Deno, S. L., & Mirkin, P. K. (1977). *Data-based program modification: A manual.* Reston, VA: Council for Exceptional Children.

Gawande, A. (2009). *The checklist manifesto: How to get things right.* New York, NY: Metropolitan Books.

Groupman, J. (2007). *How doctors think.* Boston, MA: Houghton-Mifflin.

Hosp, J. L. (2011). Using assessment data to make decisions about teaching and learning. In K. Harris, S. Graham, & T. Urdan (Eds.), *APA educational psychology handbook* (Vol. 3, pp. 87–110). Washington DC: American Psychological Association.

Hosp, J. L., & Hosp, M. K. (2012). *Curriculum-based measurement: A teacher's guide.* Port Chester, NY: National Professional Resources.

Hosp, J. L., Hosp, M. K., Howell, K. W., & Allison, R. (2014). *The ABCs of curriculum-based evaluation: A practical guide to effective decision making.* New York, NY: Guilford Press.

Hosp, M. K., Hosp, J. L., & Howell, K. W. (2007). *The ABCs of CBM: A practical guide to curriculum-based measurement.* New York, NY: Guilford Press.

Howell, K. W., & Morehead, M. K. (1987). *Curriculum-based evaluation for special and remedial education: A handbook for deciding what to teach.* Columbus, OH: Merrill.

Joyce, B. R., & Showers, B. (1995). *Student achievement through staff development: Fundamentals of school renewal* (2nd ed.). New York, NY: Longman.

Kunzelmann, H., Cohen, M., Hulten, W., Martin, G., & Mingo, A. (1970). *Precision teaching: An initial training sequence.* Seattle, WA: Special Child Publications.

Miranda, A. H. (in press). Best practices in increasing multicultural competence. In P. Harrison & A. Thomas (Eds.), *Best practices in school psychology: Foundations.* Bethesda, MD: National Association of School Psychologists.

National Association of School Psychologists. (2010). *Model for comprehensive and integrated school psychological services.* Bethesda, MD: Author. Retrieved from http://www.nasponline.org/standards/2010standards/2_PracticeModel.pdf

National Center on Response to Intervention. (2010). *Essential components of RTI: A closer look at response to intervention.* Washington, DC: U.S. Department of Education, Office of Special Education Programs, National Center on Response to Intervention.

Pretz, J. E., & Sternberg, R. J. (2005). Unifying the field: Cognition and intelligence. In R. J. Sternberg & J. E. Pretz (Eds.), *Cognition and intelligence: Identifying the mechanisms of the mind* (pp. 306–318). New York, NY: Cambridge University Press.

Shapiro, E. (2010). *Academic skills problems: Direct assessment and intervention* (4th ed.). New York, NY: Guilford Press.

Slentz, K., & Hyatt, K. (2008). Best practices in applying curriculum-based assessment in early childhood. In A. Thomas & J. Grimes (Eds.), *Best Practices in School Psychology V* (pp. 363–376). Bethesda, MD: National Association of School Psychologists.

Stein, S. (1987). *Accuracy in predicting student reading performance based on time-series progress-monitoring data* (Unpublished doctoral dissertation), University of Oregon, Eugene, OR.

11 Best Practices in Curriculum-Based Evaluation in Early Reading

Michelle K. Hosp
Iowa Reading Research Center
Kristen L. MacConnell
The International School Nido de Aguilas

OVERVIEW

Strong literacy skills are critical to success in today's society and play an important role in both social and economic advancement (National Research Council, 1998). Being literate is crucial for obtaining an entry-level job. Statistics reveal that just 10% of today's jobs require very basic skills with less emphasis on literacy, whereas in the 1980s, 95% of jobs required those basic skills (Darling-Hammond, Barron, Pearson, & Schoenfeld, 2008). Evidence of this social and economic shift in relation to literacy can also be seen when access to information through technology is considered (e.g., computers, Internet, social networking) and how that has an impact on the work environment. Students begin their journey to obtain strong literacy skills early in their educational careers and need a variety of tools and experiences to be successful.

Since the 1970s, significant advances have been made in how to teach students to read (National Governors Association Center for Best Practices, Council of Chief State School Officers, 2010; National Reading Panel, 2000). The converging knowledge base in beginning reading provides compelling scientific evidence that students can be taught to hear the phonemes in words, to link letters to phonemes, and to transform these "… meaningless marks on paper … into something truly spectacular: language" (Shaywitz, 2004, p. 51). These building blocks to literacy are necessary and important instructional practices for achieving college- and career-ready learners.

These building blocks are included in what is known as the Common Core State Standards, published through the Council of Chief State School Officers. These standards for English language arts and literacy were designed to ensure that all students are college and career ready with their literacy skills by the end of high school (National Governors Association Center for Best Practices, Council of Chief State School Officers, 2010). The skills described in this chapter align with the foundational skills found in the standards. These foundational skills include identifying and segmenting phonemes or individual sounds in words (phonological awareness), recognizing and producing letter–sound correspondences and decoding a variety of word types (alphabetic principle), and being able to read words (e.g., sight words, word lists) and connected text fluently (i.e., accuracy and fluency; National Governors Association Center for Best Practices, Council of Chief State School Officers, 2010).

Despite the advances in scientific evidence and the adoption of the Common Core State Standards, many students in the United States experience significant difficulty learning to read. The most pervasive source of reading difficulties results from poorly developed word recognition skills (Adams, 1990). The ability to read words with accuracy and fluency is essential in achieving the ultimate goal of reading: comprehension. Therefore, instruction that focuses on how to read words is important for preventing reading difficulties. In fact, if instruction efforts occur early and are systematic, a significant number of students who would be considered at risk for identification of reading disability can catch up to their grade-level peers (Torgesen, 2000). Explicit and systematic instruction is a critical feature in the prevention of reading difficulties and holds the most power for preventing and remediating reading problems when combined with research-based reading practices.

This link between assessment and instruction is a key consideration for school psychologists. This chapter will focus on critical skills in early reading and explain how curriculum-based evaluation procedures are used to link assessment and instruction. For the purposes of this chapter, early reading is defined as the foundational skills necessary for students to learn to read in kindergarten through third grade. It is also important to note that older students who are struggling readers may be either (a) missing these foundational skills or (b) lacking proficiency with these foundational skills, and as a result are manifesting reading difficulty. School psychologists need to understand the instructional scope and sequence of skills in early reading to more effectively link assessment to instruction and to assist in the identification of missing or weak skills in older students who are struggling readers.

In the National Association of School Psychologists (NASP) *Model for Comprehensive and Integrated School Psychological Services* (NASP, 2010), the domain Data-Based Decision Making and Accountability is one of the practices that permeate all aspects of the model and links directly to curriculum-based evaluation. In addition, the curriculum-based evaluation process lends itself nicely to a multitiered model of instruction. A school psychologist can use the curriculum-based evaluation process for decision-making purposes in any tier of instruction.

BASIC CONSIDERATIONS

In order to assess early reading skills, a school psychologist must understand the basic elements of beginning reading. That is, a school psychologist must know the essential instructional skills that make up phonological awareness, the alphabetic principle, and accuracy and fluency when reading words and connected text. Further, a school psychologist should be able to identify how to prioritize skills in the early reading continuum for the purpose of selecting appropriate assessments and developing effective instruction.

To guide the school psychologist through a recommended instructional scope and sequence of early reading skills, the remainder of this section will be framed in the context of instructional blueprints for reading, referred to as *curriculum maps* (Simmons & Kame'enui, 2008). Curriculum maps are useful tools for school psychologists when consulting with teachers because they help to provide a frame of reference for discussing reading skills in relation to reading instruction.

When examining the maps (Figures 11.1–11.6) the reader will see a grid filled with instructional skills and numbers. The numbers that can be found across the top of each grid refer to the instructional month of the school year (i.e., 1 refers to the first month of school, 2 refers to the second month of school, and so on). Each map provides critical information about (a) the scope and sequence of early reading skills, (b) the points in time during the school year that specific skills should be taught (identified by an X in the shaded box), (c) recommendations for skills that should be emphasized as high-priority skills for reading instruction given limited instructional time (marked with an asterisk), and (d) suggested guidelines (represented by a number, usually quantified in rate; that is, how many phonemes/letters/sounds/words can be produced/read in 1 minute) as to how well a student should perform on these high-priority skills. The assessment data related to the suggested guidelines refer to curriculum-based measures and, more specifically, Dynamic Indictors of Basic Early Literacy Skills (DIBELS; Good & Kaminski, 2002).

Phonological Awareness

Phonological awareness is an encompassing term that includes the awareness that spoken language is broken into both larger and smaller parts (Moats, 2010; National Reading Panel, 2000). The larger parts of spoken language include skills such as understanding that sentences are made up of individual words and that words are made up of syllables. Phonemic awareness is the smaller part of phonological awareness. Phonemic awareness refers to the ability to hear and manipulate phonemes in spoken words (National Reading Panel, 2000; Vaughn & Linan-Thompson, 2004). Phonemes are the smallest unit of spoken language (Adams, 1990), typically referred to as sounds. While there are 26 letters in the English alphabet, there are roughly 41–44 different phonemes, or sounds (Honig, Diamond, & Gutlohn, 2008; National Reading Panel, 2000).

The Common Core State Standards state that students need to "demonstrate understanding of spoken words, syllables, and sounds (phonemes)" (National Governors Association Center for Best Practices, Council of Chief State School Officers, 2010, p. 15). Teaching students to hear and manipulate spoken words, syllables, and phonemes in words gives them an essential prerequisite skill for mapping sounds to printed letters and words.

School psychologists can use the curriculum maps for phonemic awareness as a consultation tool with teachers. Figures 11.1 and 11.2 display curriculum maps of phonemic awareness skills in kindergarten and first grade. Although there are different skills targeted for instruction across the two grades (kindergarten and first grade), there are specific skills that have been identified as high priorities for instruction (indicated by an asterisk). When school psychologists are consulting with teachers about instruction, the high-priority skills are the skills that are critical for reading acquisition. In kindergarten, the high-priority skills include orally blending separate phonemes, identifying the first sound in one-syllable words, and segmenting individual sounds in words. In first grade, the high-priority skills include blending three to four phonemes into a word and segmenting three to four phonemes in one-syllable words.

These high-priority skills are the skills a school psychologist would target for gathering data to guide assessment and help teachers prioritize instructional content. For example, phonemic awareness instruction should occur across kindergarten and into the first 5 months of first grade for all students. Students who are struggling with these early reading skills need to have their instruction maximized. Maximizing instruction occurs when a teacher knows which skills to target for instruction versus a teacher who decides to reteach all of the skills in the scope and sequence. A school psychologist can also use the curriculum maps to make recommendations to teachers about how students should perform on specific skills. These indicators of expected performance on high-priority skills are provided in the form of fluency rates on the curriculum maps and align with high-priority skills. For example, by the ninth month of kindergarten, a student who is on track with beginning reading skills should be able to produce 35 correct phonemes in 1 minute. Once a student can hear and manipulate the phonemes in

Figure 11.1. Mapping of Instruction to Achieve Instructional Priorities: Kindergarten

Instructional Priority: **Phonemic Awareness**	1	2	3	4	5	6	7	8	9
Focus 1: Sound and Word Discrimination									
1a: Tell whether words and sounds are same or different	X	X							
1b: Identifies which word is different		X	X						
1c: Identifies different speech sound			X	X					
Focus 2: Rhyming[c]									
2a: Identifies whether words rhyme	X								
2b: Produces a word that rhymes		X	X						
Focus 3: Blending									
3a: Orally blends syllables or onset-rimes			X	X					
*3b: Orally blends separate phonemes					X	X	X		
Focus 4: Segmentation									
4a: Claps word in sentences	X								
4b: Claps syllables in words		X	X						
4c: Says syllables				X	X				
*4d: Identifies first sound in 1-syllable words	8[a]	X	X	X	25[a]				
*4e: Segments individual sounds in words					18[b]	X	X	X	35[b]

*High-priority skill
[a]DIBELS ISF score
[b]DIBELS PSF score
[c]Optimal time for rhyme instruction not established

Note. From *Curriculum Maps: Grades K–3*, by University of Oregon Center on Teaching and Learning, 2012, Eugene, OR: University of Oregon Center on Teaching and Learning. Copyright 2012 by University of Oregon Center on Teaching and Learning. Reprinted with permission.

Figure 11.2. Mapping of Instruction to Achieve Instructional Priorities: First Grade

Instructional Priority: **Phonemic Awareness**	1	2	3	4	5	6	7	8	9
Focus 1: Sound Isolation									
1a: Identifies initial sound in 1-syllable words	X	X							
1b: Identifies final sound in 1-syllable words	X	X	X						
1c: Identifies medial sound in 1-syllable words		X	X	X					
Focus 2: Sound Blending									
*2a: Blends 3–4 phonemes into a whole word	X	X	X	X	X				
Focus 3: Sound Segmentation									
*3a: Segments 3- and 4-phoneme, 1-syllable words	35[a]								

*High-priority skill
[a]DIBELS PSF score

Note. From *Curriculum Maps: Grades K–3*, by University of Oregon Center on Teaching and Learning, 2012, Eugene, OR: University of Oregon Center on Teaching and Learning. Copyright 2012 by University of Oregon Center on Teaching and Learning. Reprinted with permission.

words, instruction should focus on mapping those phonemes to letters in the alphabet to support acquisition of the alphabetic principle.

Alphabetic Principle

Students who demonstrate strong foundational skills in phonological awareness have better odds of successfully transferring their knowledge of sounds and words to print. This awareness of letter–sound correspondence is called the alphabetic principle (Moats, 2010). The instructional method used to teach students this alphabetic understanding is commonly referred to as phonics (Adams, 1990; National Reading Panel, 2000; National Research Council, 1998). The range of skills designed to teach the alphabetic principle is very systematic. Simply stated, students must learn to map sounds to letters, to blend sounds together to read words, to automatically recognize words, and to read words in the context of connected text (Ehri, 2005). Figures 11.3 and 11.4 present curriculum maps of the alphabetic principle skills in kindergarten and first grade.

Similar to the example provided for phonological awareness above, the curriculum maps for the alphabetic

Figure 11.3. Mapping of Instruction to Achieve Instructional Priorities: Kindergarten

Instructional Priority: **Alphabetic Principle**	1	2	3	4	5	6	7	8	9
Focus 1: Letter–Sound Correspondence									
1a: Identifies letter matched to a sound	X	X	X	X	X	X			
*1b: Says the most common sound associated with individual letters			X	X	13[a]	X	X	X	25[a]
Focus 2: Decoding (Sounding Out Words)									
*2a: Blends letter sounds in 1-syllable words					13[a]	X	X	X	25[a]
Focus 3: Sight-Word Reading									
*3a: Recognizes some words by sight						X	X	X	X

*High-priority skill
[a]DIBELS NWF score

Note. From *Curriculum Maps: Grades K–3*, by University of Oregon Center on Teaching and Learning, 2012, Eugene, OR: University of Oregon Center on Teaching and Learning. Copyright 2012 by University of Oregon Center on Teaching and Learning. Reprinted with permission.

Figure 11.4. Mapping of Instruction to Achieve Instructional Priorities: First Grade

Instructional Priority: **Alphabetic Principle**	1	2	3	4	5	6	7	8	9
Focus 1: Letter and Letter Combinations									
*1a: Produces L–S correspondences (1/sec)	X	X	X						
*1b: Produces sounds to common letter combinations			X	X	X	X			
Focus 2: Decoding (Sounding Out)									
*2a: Decodes words with consonant blends		X	X	X					
*2b: Decodes words with letter combinations			X	X	X	X	X		
*2c: Reads regular 1-syllable words fluently	24[a]	X	X	X	50[a]	X	X	X	X
*2d: Reads words with common word parts				X	X	X	X		
Focus 3: Sight-Word Reading									
*3a:[a] Reads common sight words automatically	X	X	X	X	X	X	X	X	X

Instructional Priority: **Fluency**	1	2	3	4	5	6	7	8	9
Focus 4: Reading Connected Text									
*4a: Reads accurately (1 error in 20 words)				X	X	X	X	X	X
*4b: Reads fluently (1 word per 2–3 sec midyear; 1 word per sec end of year)	X	X	X	X	X	20[b]	X	X	40[b]
4c: Phrasing attending to ending punctuation						X	X	X	X
4d: Reads and rereads to increase familiarity						X	X	X	X
4e: Rereads and self-corrects while reading		X	X	X	X				

*High-priority skill
[a]DIBELS NSF score
[b]DIBELS ORF score

Note. From *Curriculum Maps: Grades K–3*, by University of Oregon Center on Teaching and Learning, 2012, Eugene, OR: University of Oregon Center on Teaching and Learning. Copyright 2012 by University of Oregon Center on Teaching and Learning. Reprinted with permission.

principal can be used when a school psychologist consults with teachers around skills associated with producing and blending letter sounds together to read words.

Accuracy and Fluency

Accuracy with reading is commonly referred to as percent correct (i.e., percentage of words read correctly or percentage of correct letter–sound correspondences produced), while fluency is viewed as the speed and ease with which a task is completed. Accuracy and fluency are critical components of reading because these skills allow students to focus on the meaning of what is read (Vaughn & Linan-Thompson, 2004). Figures 11.5 and 11.6 present curriculum maps of fluency in second and third grade.

A school psychologist who uses the curriculum maps will be able to share with teachers what skills are most critical, at what point in the year, and at which grade. All of these aspects are critical when identifying appropriate assessments and skills to focus on when using a decision-making framework such as curriculum-based evaluation.

Early Reading Assessments

The instructional scope and sequence for early reading are expansive. School psychologists can help teachers maximize instructional time by targeting high-priority skills found on the curriculum maps. For school psychologists it is important to know the general scope and sequence of literacy skills and which of those skills are critical for intervention so assessment can be directly linked to instruction. It is even more important to know which high-priority skills have reliable and valid

Figure 11.5. Mapping of Instruction to Achieve Instructional Priorities: Second Grade

Instructional Priority: **Alphabetic Principle**	1	2	3	4	5	6	7	8	9
Focus 1: Letter–Sound Knowledge									
*1a: Produces diphthongs and digraphs	X	X							
Focus 2: Decoding and Word Recognition									
*2a: Uses advanced phonic elements to recognize words	X	X	X	X					
2b: Reads compound words, contractions, possessives, inflectional endings			X	X	X	X			
*2c: Reads multisyllabic words					X	X	X		
Focus 3: Sight-Word Reading									
*3a: Reads more sight words accurately	X	X	X	X	X	X	X	X	X

Instructional Priority: **Fluency**	1	2	3	4	5	6	7	8	9
Focus 4: Reading Connected Text									
*4a: Reads 90–100 wpm	44[a]	X	X	X	68[a]	X	X	X	90[a]
4b: Reads with phrasing and expression			X	X	X				
4c: Listens to fluent oral reading and practices increasing oral reading fluency	10[b]	10	10	15	15	20	20	20	20
4d: Reads and rereads to increase familiarity	X	X	X	X	X	X	X	X	X
4e: Self-corrects word recognition errors	X	X							

*High-priority skill
[a]DIBELS NSF score
[b]Minutes of practice per day

Note. From *Curriculum Maps: Grades K–3*, by University of Oregon Center on Teaching and Learning, 2012, Eugene, OR: University of Oregon Center on Teaching and Learning. Copyright 2012 by University of Oregon Center on Teaching and Learning. Reprinted with permission.

assessments. To date, there are a variety of quality assessments for measuring these high-priority early literacy skills. These assessments serve several purposes. Each assessment that will be described below can be used to screen students' skills and monitor students' progress, and they can also serve as an outcome measure. It is important to note that the assessments were designed to serve as indicators of a student's early reading skills and were not designed to be comprehensive tests. Table 11.1 lists six measures of early reading skills that have evidence of technical adequacy. For the purpose of this chapter, the six assessments discussed come from two main sources: (a) DIBELS Next (most current edition of the DIBELS; Good & Kaminski, 2011) and (b) Word Identification Fluency and Letter–Sound Fluency (Fuchs & Fuchs, 2004). It is important to note that there are other assessments available for these same early reading skills (e.g., AIMSweb and Easy CBM offer similar measures, but the norms are each slightly different), so for consistency within this chapter, all norms and measures will be from DIBELS Next or Letter–Sound Fluency and Word Identification Fluency.

First Sound Fluency: First Sound Fluency is an individually administered, standardized assessment of phonemic awareness designed to assess a student's ability to orally produce the first sound in a word. The examiner orally presents words to the student for 1 minute and asks the student to produce the first sound in the word. For example, the examiner would say *moon*, and the student would respond /m/. The expected rate of performance for this task is 30 correct phonemes per minute by the middle of kindergarten (Good & Kaminski, 2011).

Phoneme Segmentation Fluency: Phoneme Segmentation Fluency is an individually administered, standardized assessment of phonemic awareness designed to assess a student's ability to orally segment words made up of three to four phonemes. The examiner orally presents

Figure 11.6. Mapping of Instruction to Achieve Instructional Priorities: Third Grade

Instructional Priority: **Alphabetic Principle**	1	2	3	4	5	6	7	8	9
Focus 1: Decoding and Word Recognition									
*1a: Produces common word parts	X	X							
*1b: Reads regular multisyllabic words		X	X	X	X				
1c: Reads compound words, contractions, possessives, inflectional endings		X	X	X	X	X			
1d: Uses word meaning and order in the sentence to confirm decoding efforts		X	X	X					
1e: Uses word structure knowledge to recognize multisyllabic words		X	X	X					
Focus 2: Sight-Word Reading									
2a: Increases sight words read fluently	X	X	X	X	X	X	X	X	X

Instructional Priority: **Fluency**	1	2	3	4	5	6	7	8	9
Focus 3: Reading Connected Text									
*3a: Reads 110–120 wpm	77[a]	X	X	X	92[a]	X	X	X	110[a]
3b: Reads with phrasing, expression, and inflection	X	X	X						
*3c: Increases independent reading	5[b]	10	10	15	15	20	20	25	30

*High-priority skill
[a]DIBELS NSF Score
[b]Minutes of practice per day

Note. From *Curriculum Maps: Grades K–3*, by University of Oregon Center on Teaching and Learning, 2012, Eugene, OR: University of Oregon Center on Teaching and Learning. Copyright 2012 by University of Oregon Center on Teaching and Learning. Reprinted with permission.

Table 11.1. Early Reading Skills by High Priority, Assessment, Benchmark, Time of Year, and Risk Indicator for Beginning of the Year

Critical Reading Element	High-Priority Skills	Assessment	Benchmark[a]	Time of Benchmark	Risk Indicator in Fall
Phonemic awareness	Identifies initial sounds in words	First Sound Fluency	30+ CPPM	Middle of kindergarten	<5
	Phoneme segmenting	Phoneme Segmentation Fluency	40+ CPPM	End of kindergarten	<10 (winter)
Alphabetic principle	Letter–sound	Letter–Sound Fluency	40+ CLSPM	End of kindergarten	<10
	Letter–sound correspondence	Nonsense Word Fluency, Correct Letter Sounds	58+ CLSPM	End of first grade	<18
	Blending	Nonsense Word Fluency, Whole Words Read	13+ WWRPM	End of first grade	0
Accuracy and fluency	Sight reading	Word Identification Fluency	60+ CWPM	End of first grade	<15
	Passage reading	Oral Reading Fluency	47+ CWPM	End of first grade	<16 (winter)
	Passage reading	Oral Reading Fluency	87+ CWPM	End of second grade	<37
	Passage reading	Oral Reading Fluency	100+ CWPM	End of third grade	<55

Note. CLSPM = correct letter sounds per minute; CPPM = correct phonemes per minute; CWPM = correct words per minute; WWRPM = whole words read per minute.
[a] The minimum expected score from the lowest performing student.

words to the student for 1 minute and asks the student to produce the sounds of the word. For example, the examiner would say *fish*, and the student would respond /f/ /i/ /sh/. The student can earn a score for each correct phoneme produced. The expected rate of performance for this task is 40 correct phonemes per minute by the end of kindergarten and into the beginning of first grade (Good & Kaminski, 2011).

Letter–Sound Fluency: Letter–Sound Fluency is an individually administered, standardized assessment of alphabetic principle. This assessment was designed to measure a student's ability to map sounds to letters. The examiner presents the student with a page of lower-case letters in random order. The student is instructed to produce the most common sound for as many letter sounds as possible in 1 minute. The expected rate of performance for this task is 40 correct letter sounds per minute by the end of kindergarten (Fuchs & Fuchs, 2004).

Nonsense Word Fluency: Nonsense Word Fluency is an individually administered, standardized assessment of the alphabetic principle including knowledge of letter–sound correspondences in two- and three-letter nonsense words and the ability to blend those sounds together to read nonsense words. This task measures the ability to produce or blend letters that represent their most common sound. The examiner presents the student with a page of nonsense words that follow the vowel–consonant pattern (i.e., *ot*) or the consonant–vowel–consonant pattern (i.e., *rav*). The examiner instructs the student to read as many nonsense words as possible in 1 minute. The student can earn credit for reading at either the sound level (i.e., /r/ /a/ /v/) or the word level (i.e., /rav/). Students are expected to earn a score of 58 correct letter–sound correspondences and read 13 words with automaticity in 1 minute by the end of first grade (Good & Kaminski, 2011).

Word Identification Fluency: Word Identification Fluency is an individually administered, standardized assessment of accuracy and fluency on high-frequency words from early elementary reading curricula. The examiner presents the student with a list of words and records how many words are read correctly within 1 minute. The expected rate of performance for this task is 60 correct words per minute by the end of first grade (Fuchs & Fuchs, 2004).

Oral Reading Fluency. Oral Reading Fluency, also referred to as reading curriculum-based measurement or passage reading fluency, is an individually administered, standardized assessment of accuracy and fluency in connected text. The examiner presents the student

with a reading passage and instructs the student to read the passage out loud using the student's best reading skills for 1 minute. The expected rate of performance for this task is provided in words read correctly: 47 words by the end of first grade, 87 words by the end of second grade, and 100 words by the end of third grade. Criteria for additional grades are also available (Good & Kaminski, 2011).

BEST PRACTICES IN CURRICULUM-BASED EVALUATION IN EARLY READING

Best practices in early reading involve collecting and analyzing data to make instructional decisions. Curriculum-based evaluation provides the school psychologist with a framework when consulting with teachers. When using the curriculum-based evaluation framework in the context of early reading, the assumption has been made that a student is experiencing difficulty learning with any or all of the foundational skills in reading: phonological awareness, application of the alphabetic principle, and/or accuracy and fluency with reading words or connected text (see Figure 11.7).

Phase 1: Fact Finding

Phase 1 requires the school psychologist to know the expected level of performance, know the student's current level of performance, and know if the difference between the two is meaningful. Working through Phase 1 requires (a) having a clear understanding of the potential problem, (b) making sure the information/data collected directly addresses the problem, and (c) putting it all together in order to answer this question: Is there a confirmable problem? The information required for Phase 1 relies on existing data and should not typically include the collection of additional data. In order to answer the above question four actions are taken.

Action 1.1: Be Concerned About Learning
The curriculum-based evaluation process begins when a teacher expresses concern about a student's academic progress. Typically this action occurs during Tier 1 of the multitiered model but could also happen in Tier 2 or Tier 3 if a student is not making expected progress with targeted skill instruction.

Here is an example: A second-grade teacher approaches the school psychologist in the beginning of the school year about a student named Max who is struggling with basic reading skills. The teacher explains to the school psychologist that after administering some

Figure 11.7. The Curriculum-Based Evaluation Process Flowchart

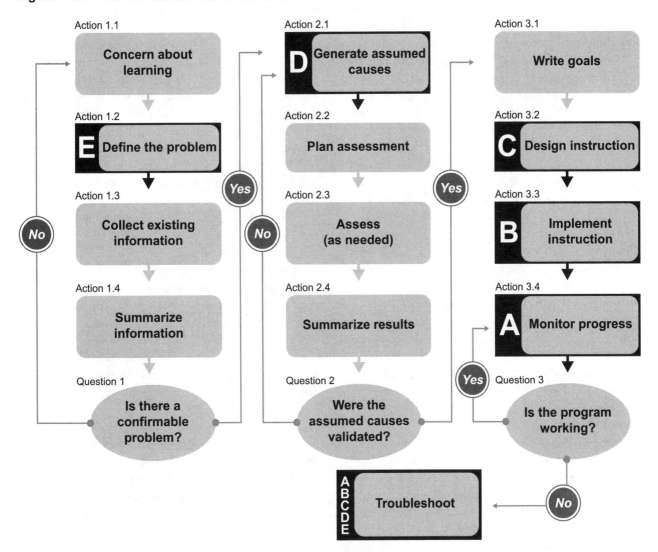

of the beginning-of-the-year assessments and after listening to Max read in class she was very concerned about Max's poor reading skills. The school psychologist determines there are multiple pieces of data that provide evidence that Max is struggling. Therefore, the school psychologist and teacher proceed with the next series of actions (Actions 1.2–1.4) to confirm the reading concern.

Action 1.2: Define the Problem

Once the teacher expresses concern about student performance, the problem needs to be clearly defined. It is the school psychologist's job to assist the teacher in narrowing down and describing the problem in observable language. Going back to the example described earlier, the teacher thinks Max has poor reading skills. The phrase the teacher used, "poor

reading skills," is not enough information to clearly define the problem. In Action 1.2 the school psychologist works with the teacher to define what Max is doing or not doing that leads the teacher to draw conclusions about Max's reading skills. Knowing what type of assessment data the teacher uses will allow the school psychologist to ask specific questions. For example, this teacher uses DIBELS Next to screen all students three times a year. The following two questions can be asked by the school psychologist: (a) Is Max able to read the second-grade Oral Reading Fluency passages with appropriate accuracy and fluency compared to the benchmark score? (b) Is Max able to show letter–sound correspondence and blend simple vowel–consonant (e.g., *it*) and consonant–vowel–consonant (e.g., *hat*) word types as measured on Nonsense Word Fluency compared to the benchmark scores? These questions start to focus on specific skills. The questions help to move away from the general issue of poor reading skills to a more focused statement about specific skills that may be contributing to or causing the student to have poor reading skills. Max's teacher can now articulate her concern more clearly to the school psychologist. Based on the questions the school psychologist asked, Max's teacher states that Max is not only reading second-grade text at a slower rate than his peers, he is also reading with less accuracy. Even more specifically, Max's teacher can now articulate that she also has concerns about his knowledge of letter–sound correspondence based on Max's performance on Nonsense Word Fluency, which was also below the benchmark for correct letter sounds and for blending whole words read. This information will be helpful in Action 1.3, which involves gathering existing data related to the problem.

Action 1.3: Gather Existing Relevant Data

The purpose of this action is to either confirm or disconfirm the presence of a problem. This action is the point in the curriculum-based evaluation process when the school psychologist would use review, interview, observations, and/or tests (i.e., RIOT) in order to obtain necessary information. The school psychologist would then review information while trying to answer the following question: Does this information provide firm proof that this student is having trouble with skills, requiring the school psychologist to move forward with the curriculum-based evaluation process, such as phonemic awareness, blending, decoding, and so on?

The school psychologist gathered information from Max's teacher and his school records to review Max's universal screening data (Oral Reading Fluency data, Nonsense Word Fluency data, and Word Identification Fluency data), teacher interview data about how Max reads aloud in class, and the teacher's permanent products like Max's writing samples and spelling tests. The school psychologist would then attempt to answer the question: Does this information provide evidence that Max is struggling with his foundational skills in reading?

Action 1.4: Summarize Known Information

At this point in Phase 1 there is a clearly defined problem statement and there are existing data to help further examine the problem. The school psychologist would summarize the information about the student using the questions from the beginning of Phase 1: (a) What is the expectation for student performance on this skill (e.g., benchmark criteria)? (b) How well is the student performing (i.e., current level of performance)?

(c) Is there a meaningful difference between expected student performance and obtained student performance (i.e., discrepancy)?

The expectations for early reading skills can be defined by looking at the benchmark criteria for each skill listed in Table 11.1. The school psychologist can use these criteria to answer the first question. For example, students who read 60 correct words in 1 minute at the end of first grade on Word Identification Fluency are considered to be on track for reading. Any student performing below this expected rate of performance needs explicit and systematic instruction in word identification skills.

The school psychologist can gather information about how well a student performs a skill by helping the teacher administer one or more of the early reading screening assessments (if these data are not already collected). How the student performs should be examined. For example, Max may read words accurately but not fluently or he might read quickly while making a lot of errors. In addition to these considerations, the school psychologist needs even more detailed information about the types of errors the student makes. Specific information regarding the types of errors is further examined in Action 2.1.

In order to answer the last question (Is there a meaningful difference between expected student performance and how well the student actually performed the skill?), a comparison needs to be made between the student's obtained score and the criteria for how well the student should be performing (i.e., the expected performance). With Max, the expected level of performance for the beginning of second grade on Oral Reading Fluency is 52 words correct with 90% accuracy, and on Nonsense Word Fluency it is 54 correct letter sounds and 13 whole words read. Max's current level of performance on Oral Reading Fluency is 34 words correct with 80% accuracy, and on nonsense word fluency it is 30 correct letter sounds and 5 whole words read. The difference between expected performance and Max's performance on Oral Reading Fluency is 18 words correct. Max's accuracy shows a 10% difference from expected performance. When examining data from Nonsense Word Fluency, the difference between the expected performance and Max's performance is 24 correct letter sounds and 8 whole words read. But is this difference meaningful? It is, because Max is below the benchmark on DIBELS Next.

A good rule of thumb for the school psychologist to follow for determining if there is a meaningful difference is to use benchmark scores on universal screening measures. The benchmark scores indicate the likelihood of a student being proficient on a meaningful outcome assessment at the end of the year. If the student is below the benchmark, then the school psychologist can assume there is a meaningful difference and steps should be taken to intervene.

Question 1: Is there a confirmable problem? Once the information is summarized from Action 1.4, the school psychologist can answer the question with either a yes or no. If a student's performance is below the benchmark, then a discrepancy exists between the expected performance and the actual performance, resulting in confirmation of a problem. When considering Max, the answer is that there is a problem. When a problem is confirmed in early reading, there should be a sense of urgency to prevent the problem from escalating, resulting in students falling significantly behind their peers. Early reading skills are the prerequisite skills necessary for becoming a fluent reader, and fluent reading not only is critical for comprehension but is essential for learning other academic content.

Once the problem is confirmed, the school psychologist should proceed to Phase 2. If the problem was not confirmed, that is, the student's performance is at or above the benchmark, then the curriculum-based evaluation process should stop and instruction should continue. It is important to note that if an initial problem was defined but not confirmed, progress monitoring is warranted. If at any time the student does not show progress with a specific skill, the curriculum-based evaluation process should be reinstated.

Phase 2: Summative Decision Making

The goal of Phase 2 is to collect additional data to determine the specific skills the student needs to be taught in order to be successful. This phase often requires conducting additional assessments and collecting additional data. The school psychologist should assist the teacher in determining if specific information has already been obtained in regard to why the student is not performing successfully with early reading skills. If this is the case, the school psychologist can proceed to Action 2.4, skipping Actions 2.1–2.3. The school psychologist is also well equipped to assist the teacher in considering other important factors that can have an impact on student learning. These additional factors include the setting, curriculum, instruction, and learner. If specific information about skills has not been obtained, then the school psychologist should proceed to Action 2.1.

Action 2.1: Generate Assumed Causes

When all data have been collected and examined, it is time to use those data to generate a hypothesis about why a student is not demonstrating certain skills related to early reading. Based on the student's performance from the early reading screeners and the school psychologist's knowledge of the scope and sequence of instructional skills (i.e., curriculum maps), statements can be made about which skills need to be taught, which skills are emerging, and which skills have been mastered. These statements lead to specific hypotheses about the student's performance. With Max, it might be hypothesized that he does not have adequate skills in decoding, and therefore he misreads many words in text. His low scores on Nonsense Word Fluency as well as Oral Reading Fluency support this hypothesis. This hypothesis can be used to help with Action 2.2, which allows the school psychologist to plan for additional assessments that focus on decoding skills.

Action 2.2: Plan the Assessment

Once a hypothesis has been generated, further assessments can be planned. When creating an assessment plan it is important to consider four assessment domains: the setting, curriculum, instruction, and learner. These domains are essential for guiding further assessment. A clear assessment plan will assist the school psychologist in maximizing the time that is spent on data collection. The main goal of Action 2.2 is to develop evaluation questions. If the assumed cause of the reading problem is that the student is not able to decode words accurately because short vowel sounds have not been mastered, then the evaluation question would ask how well the student knows sounds associated with short vowels.

Action 2.2 does not have to include a large amount of additional assessment information. Upon reviewing the student's records, the school psychologist may discover additional assessment data from previous school years. When reviewing Max's records, the school psychologist discovered additional data from screening assessments from first grade that included Nonsense Word Fluency and Word Identification Fluency. Examining these protocols revealed that while Max's knowledge of letter–sound correspondence has shown some improvement from first grade, he seems to make the same types of errors. He appears to be confusing the short /e/ and the short /i/ sounds with the long vowel sounds. Max's first-grade teacher gave him the Word Identification Fluency screener to gather more data at the end of last year and noticed that Max has a strong sight-word vocabulary. At this point, there may be enough information to be able to conclude that Max is not able to decode words accurately because he has not mastered blending words with the short /e/ and /i/ sounds.

If error patterns cannot be determined upon further review of the data collected in Phase 1, then the school psychologist should gather additional data. These data may include further observation in the classroom or administration of additional screeners in the area of concern. Because screening assessments are typically administered only once, they may not provide an adequate sample of student behavior. Having the school psychologist administer additional screeners is an efficient way to gather more data that may provide an accurate picture of a student's reading behavior.

Action 2.3: Collect Assessment Data (As Needed)

After the school psychologist examines the student's reading behavior related to specific skills, he or she can determine if additional information is needed to accurately identify why a student is not demonstrating certain skills related to early reading. Efficiency and the use of reliable and valid assessments should be a major consideration when collecting additional information. To aid the school psychologist in the next steps three options are provided.

The first option is to assess the student again on the same task but use an alternate form of the measure (i.e., equivalent but different words or sounds). If the same errors occur, then the assumed cause has been validated (i.e., the student does not know the sounds of short vowels).

The second option is to examine previous assessments or work samples for similar errors or give additional assessments that measure similar skills. For example, if the assumed cause is that the student is not able to decode words accurately because short vowel sounds have not been mastered, then this step would review other screening measures that were administered. If a screening measure were administered that measures a similar skill to Nonsense Word Fluency, such as Letter–Sound Fluency, then the student's responses on the additional measure can be examined for similar error patterns.

The third option is to create a novel assessment based on errors from previously administered assessments and work samples. For example, a list of nonsense words (based on errors from the screening assessment) and missed words reported by the teacher could be developed to assess knowledge of vowel sounds. If similar errors are present on the new list, then this error pattern indicates the student does not know short vowel sounds. It is always important to use some caution when interpreting novel assessments. The obvious problem with developing assessments is the reliability and validity

of the assessment. Once this information is collected, Action 2.4 can be implemented.

Action 2.4: Summarize Assessment Results

Now that there are sufficient data for decision making, the school psychologist can make a direct comparison between the expected level of performance and the assumed causes already identified in Action 2.1. Remember, the level of expected performance is determined based on a set of standards. These standards include the curriculum maps, which are there to guide the school psychologist's thinking about high-priority skills within the instructional scope and sequence for early reading; the Common Core State Standards; and benchmark scores or expected level of performance.

For Max, were the assumed causes validated? After reviewing error patterns from the Nonsense Word Fluency and Letter–Sound Fluency, screening data revealed that Max has mastered the short vowel sounds for /e/ and /i/ in isolation but is using the long vowel sound for /e/ and /i/ when blending simple words. The school psychologist can assist the teacher in summarizing these results, which would lead to the following statement: Max is not able to decode words accurately because the short vowel sounds for /e/ and /i/ have not been mastered in the context of reading consonant–vowel–consonant words.

Question 2: Were the assumed causes validated? The last step in Phase 2 is to answer whether the assumed causes were validated. If the assumed causes were validated, then the school psychologist can move on to Phase 3. In the case of Max, the assumed causes were validated. However, if the answer were that the data revealed that Max does know short vowel sounds, a new assumption would need to be generated to explain why Max has poor decoding skills, and the curriculum-based evaluation process would continue, returning to Action 2.1. It is important to remember that the assessment needs to match the evaluation question. The school psychologist is the link to help the teacher make sure the assessments match the area of concern.

If assumed causes are not validated, then it may be necessary for the school psychologist to (a) select different assessments or (b) review standards associated with that grade level. The additional information already gathered in Phase 2 can be reexamined to help generate new assumed causes.

Phase 3: Formative Decision Making

The goal of Phase 3 is to determine the solution that will provide the best support plan for the student. The support plan includes the content of the instruction, how the instruction will be delivered, and how the student's progress will be monitored. Each action is outlined below in Actions 3.1–3.4. Unlike Phases 1 and 2, where actions may be skipped, each action in Phase 3 is required.

Action 3.1: Write Present Levels and Goals

This action requires documenting mastered skills and determining which skills need to be taught based on an instructional scope and sequence (i.e., curriculum maps). The school psychologist can determine which skills have been mastered and which skills need to be taught by reviewing student performance on assessments as well as using information from teacher observations, work samples, and review of the essential skills on the curriculum maps. In the case of Max, when reading sounds in isolation, Max can correctly produce all short vowel sounds and all consonant sounds; however, when Max blends sounds together to read consonant–vowel–consonant words, he produces the long vowel sound for /e/ and /i/.

The school psychologist can assist in writing goals or objectives that specifically relate to the prerequisite skills associated with the area of concern. For Max, his present level of performance would be that when reading sounds in isolation Max can correctly produce all short vowel sounds and all consonant sounds. When Max blends sounds together to read consonant–vowel–consonant words, he confuses the short /e/ and /i/, producing the long vowel sound instead. The goal or objective should specifically relate to producing the short vowel sounds for /e/ and /i/ accurately and fluently when reading consonant–vowel–consonant words. Max's goal might be that when Max is presented with a page of words following the consonant–vowel–consonant word type, he will read 54 words correctly in 1 minute with 95% accuracy or greater. The necessary prerequisite skills for accomplishing this goal would be having the ability to associate the correct sound with the vowels and being able to accurately produce the sound in the context of the word. These prerequisite skills become the instructional content and lead to Action 3.2.

Action 3.2: Design Instructional Program

The instructional program should include two components: the "what" and the "when." The what refers to the specific skills that need to be taught and should be tied to the goals and objectives formulated in Action 3.1. The when relates to the sequence of skills, specifically the order in which the skills should be taught. The school psychologist should use Figures 11.1–11.6 (curriculum maps) to aid in determining what to teach and when. Additionally, the school psychologist should have an understanding of when these skills show up in the Common Core State Standards. For example, if Max is having difficulty with decoding, related to short vowel sounds, the first step would be for the school psychologist to figure out what to teach and when this instruction should occur by reviewing the scope and sequence (Figures 11.1–11.6) for the alphabetic principle in kindergarten, first, second, and third grade. In addition to these resources, the school psychologist may want to consult the book *Research-Based Methods of Reading Instruction Grades K–3* (Vaughn & Linan-Thompson, 2004). This book offers many hands-on instructional interventions with resources such as materials and clear lesson plans, as well as ideas for assessment. When the school psychologist consults with the teacher, the school psychologist can use these resources as practical tools to share.

Action 3.3: Implement Instruction

Once the issue of what to teach and when to teach is determined, Action 3.3 is conducted. This part of the instructional plan relates to the "how," which can also be defined as effective features of instruction that can be implemented regardless of the skill being taught. Good instructional practices are critical for student success. The school psychologist can assist teachers by having an idea of what principles should be followed in order to maximize instruction. These principles are outlined below and will assist school psychologists as they consult with teachers and as they conduct observations in the classroom.

- *Step 1:* Students are told what they will be learning: "Today we will learn …"
- *Step 2:* Students are told why they need to learn the skill: "This skill will help you …"
- *Step 3:* Teacher models the behavior the students need to perform: "Watch me …"
- *Step 4:* Students practice with teacher feedback: "Now you try …"
- *Step 5:* Students practice the skill with new items: "Let's try a new word …"

Telling students what they will be learning and why the skill is important assists the teacher as well as the student. Teachers have to justify why they are spending time teaching the skill. This instruction should be directly related to the students' goals and objectives. If the teacher cannot justify why the skill is being taught, then the skill might not be appropriate for instruction. Being able to clearly articulate what the lesson is about and why it is important provides a goal for each lesson. The school psychologist can help teachers understand that following these steps can maximize teaching time as it provides a clear purpose, making it easier to stay on topic.

Skills are explicitly taught in Steps 3–5 and are sometimes referred to as "I do" or modeling (Step 3), "we do" or guided practice (Step 4), and "you do" or independent practice (Step 5). These last three steps are essential for the teacher and the student. Using explicit instruction allows the teacher to demonstrate instructional understanding of skills taught as well as to demonstrate a plan to support student learning. If, for example, the school psychologist is observing instruction in a classroom and the teacher asks Max to read a word with the short vowel /e/ and he reads the word with the long /e/ sound, then it would be expected that the teacher would stop Max, say the correct sound, and have Max reread the word correctly. If the teacher either did not correct Max, had Max try again without modeling, or just told Max the answer and moved to the next word, then the school psychologist might see that Max is not receiving explicit instruction with feedback and additional opportunities to practice a skill in which he needs targeted instruction.

This information is helpful when observing and consulting with teachers. If the teacher is not providing an appropriate model (Step 3), practice with feedback (Step 4), and independent practice (Step 5), then the student is likely to perform the skill inconsistently or inaccurately. Once it has been determined what to teach, when to teach the skills, and how to teach, the next step is to make some decisions about how it is working by monitoring student progress.

Action 3.4: Monitor Progress

Monitoring student progress will lead to two decisions: (a) continue the current instructional program because student data indicate adequate growth or (b) change the instructional program because student data indicate that the student is not making adequate growth. The school psychologist can assist the teacher in determining what constitutes adequate growth. If Max is already behind his peers and his growth is commensurate with his peers, then he will never catch up. The school psychologist should encourage Max's teacher to use the end-of-year benchmark on the progress monitoring assessments at

his grade level, because this represents an adequate level of skills necessary to be on track for reading.

School psychologists should also encourage teachers to use the same measures for screening as they would for progress monitoring so that they do not have to spend time learning a new set of assessments. Monitoring student progress on identified early reading skills provides essential information about the link between assessment and instruction. This information is critical for formative decision making. Once the school psychologist has assisted the teacher in determining a meaningful goal and data have been collected and graphed toward this goal, it is time to make formative decisions.

Formative decision making guides actions regarding student performance. The school psychologist can help teachers determine when action needs to be taken. For example, if Max is receiving specific instruction to remediate his skills in early reading, and if progress monitoring data reveal that he is four consecutive data points below his goal line, then the conclusion would be that Max is not benefiting from the instruction. If nothing is done with Max's progress monitoring data, the instruction will not change and Max will not learn the needed skills. This is where the school psychologist in consultation with the teacher can help determine what changes need to be made to the instruction in order for the student to learn the skills. In this way, student performance on progress monitoring assessments is used to guide instructional decision making. Examining data and making decisions about performance leads to the final question: Is the program (i.e., instruction) working?

Question 3: Is the program working? If the data indicate that Max is making adequate progress given the instruction he is receiving, then the answer is that the program is working. However, if the answer to this question is that the program is working, it does not mean that instruction for Max never changes. It simply means that Max's skills will continue to be addressed and monitored. If progress is not adequate, the answer is that the program is not working, and the troubleshooting process begins with the school psychologist working closely with the teacher.

Troubleshooting

Troubleshooting begins by retracing the steps through the checkpoints in the process. These checkpoints are indicated by A, B, C, D, and E on the flowchart (Figure 11.7).

Checkpoint A: Monitor Progress

Checkpoint A consists of verifying that appropriate skills are being monitored and data are collected with fidelity. School psychologists can assist by observing the data collection to ensure fidelity. Many assessments come with fidelity check sheets that are easy to use. If the data are being collected with fidelity, then they move back to Checkpoint B.

Checkpoint B: Implement Instruction

School psychologists can assist by observing instruction and helping teachers determine if the instruction is implemented as it was intended. If the implementation of instruction is in good standing, then they return to Checkpoint C.

Checkpoint C: Design Instructional Program

To determine if the instructional program is designed to meet a student's learning, going back to Action 2.4 and looking at the statement about what skills the student cannot perform and why may be a good idea. School psychologists can assist by helping teachers examine the alignment between the identified needs of the student and the instructional program being implemented. If there is not a clear link between what the student's learning needs are and the instruction being provided, then the school psychologist can work with the teacher on changing the instructional program.

However, if there is alignment, then it might be that the intensity of the instruction needs to change. For example, if the student is receiving the instruction three times a week, it might be necessary to increase it to five times a week or to provide a double dose of the instruction within the same day. If expected progress is still not occurring, they should return to Checkpoint D.

Checkpoint D: Generate Assumed Causes

If the school psychologist and teacher both are confident that data were collected with fidelity, and if instruction was designed to meet the student's needs and was implemented with fidelity, and there is still little to no student progress, then it would be necessary to return to the assumed causes of why the student is not making progress. School psychologists can help the teacher by examining if there are prerequisite skills to the current instruction that might need attention. Reexamining the assumed causes provides an opportunity to focus on skills and instructional planning to meet the student's needs.

However, if it is determined that the assumed causes have been correctly identified and the student is working on the appropriate skills, then they would return to Checkpoint E, the beginning of the process.

Checkpoint E: Define the Problem

Arriving back at Checkpoint E requires revisiting the concern about learning and the definition of the problem. It could be that there are prerequisite skills that need to be addressed first, or it could be that the wrong problem was identified. School psychologists can assist teachers by going back to the curriculum maps or the Common Core State Standards and determining if the right skills have been targeted for instruction. Then the curriculum-based evaluation process would start all over again.

Additional Considerations

School psychologists might very well ask themselves if they were doing the curriculum-based evaluation correctly. Success may be judged in many ways. One way is to look at the progress monitoring data of students who have been through the curriculum-based evaluation process. If student data show greater gains after curriculum-based evaluation than before, it can be assumed that curriculum-based evaluation was implemented correctly. Another way to ensure fidelity with the process is to use the curriculum-based evaluation flowchart and overlay the observable behaviors expected at each phase. A checklist can be developed listing curriculum-based evaluation behaviors that would occur at each phase and then used to determine if the behaviors expected match what is on the checklist.

Just as important as evaluating effectiveness is making sure that appropriate multicultural considerations are implemented throughout the curriculum-based evaluation process. The school psychologist can help teachers by gathering relevant information regarding students so that everyone has a better understanding of cultural expectations. For example, if the student comes from a culture where it is customary that children do not speak in public, then it would be wrong to assume this student needs speech therapy. The school psychologist can be a great resource by talking to parents and making connections within different cultural communities that are represented in the school. This information can then be part of the curriculum-based evaluation process to show how best to assist students. When discussing student needs, the school psychologist can provide suggestions for how to address those needs while being sensitive and appropriate within the cultural experiences of the student.

SUMMARY

Best practices in early reading begin with the school psychologist having foundational knowledge about the critical elements necessary for learning to read, coupled with an understanding of how those elements fit into a systematic scope and sequence for instruction. The foundational skills for reading include phonological awareness, the alphabetic principle, and accuracy and fluency with reading words and connected text. Knowledge of what to teach and when to teach critical skills informs best practices in early reading instruction.

Curriculum-based evaluation provides a decision-making framework for linking assessment to instruction. This framework allows a school psychologist to gather and analyze information that is directly related to planning instruction. The three phases in this framework (fact finding, summative decision making, and formative decision making) allow school psychologists to make data-based decisions using reliable and valid assessments. Most important, the curriculum-based evaluation framework serves as a communication tool between teachers and school psychologists. Curriculum-based evaluation facilitates and informs conversations about specific skills that students need to be taught. Following the curriculum-based evaluation framework allows school psychologists to focus on critical skills that are important for successful reading when they are consulting with teachers or observing instruction. The curriculum-based evaluation procedures for early reading provide a curriculum map guiding the school psychologist's decisions about which assessments to use and how to integrate the assessment data to focus instruction. In addition, the curriculum-based evaluation process provides a clear direction for school psychologists who are using the multitiered model when they work with struggling readers in any tier of instruction.

REFERENCES

Adams, M. J. (1990). *Beginning to read: Thinking and learning about print.* Cambridge, MA: MIT Press.

Darling-Hammond, L., Barron, B., Pearson, P. D., & Schoenfeld, A. H. (2008). *Powerful learning: What we know about teaching for understanding.* San Francisco, CA: Jossey-Bass.

Ehri, L. (2005). Learning to read words: Theory, findings, and issues. *Scientific Studies of Reading, 9,* 167–188.

Fuchs, L. S., & Fuchs, D. (2004). *Using CBM for progress monitoring.* Retrieved from http://www.studentprogress.org/library/Training/CBM%20Reading/UsingCBMReading.pdf

Good, R. H., III., & Kaminski, R. A. (Eds.). (2002). *Dynamic Indicators of Basic Early Literacy Skills* (6th ed.). Eugene, OR: Dynamic Measurement Group.

Good, R. H., III., & Kaminski, R. A. (Eds.). (2011). *DIBELS Next assessment manual.* Eugene, OR: Dynamic Measurement Group.

Honig, B., Diamond, L., & Gutlohn, L. (2008). *Teaching reading sourcebook for kindergarten through eighth grade* (2nd ed.). Novato, CA: Arena Press.

Moats, L. (2010). *Speech to print: Language essentials for teachers.* Baltimore, MD: Paul H. Brookes.

National Association of School Psychologists. (2010). *Model for comprehensive and integrated school psychological services.* Bethesda, MD: Author. Retrieved from http://www.nasponline.org/standards/2010standards/2_PracticeModel.pdf

National Governors Association Center for Best Practices, Council of Chief State School Officers. (2010). *Common Core State Standards (English language arts and literacy).* Washington, DC: Author.

National Reading Panel. (2000). *Report of the National Reading Panel: Teaching children to read.* Bethesda, MD: Author.

National Research Council. (1998). *Preventing reading difficulties in young children.* Washington, DC: National Academies Press.

Shaywitz, S. (2004). *Overcoming dyslexia: A new and complete science-based program for reading problems at any level.* New York, NY: Knopf.

Simmons, D., & Kame'enui, E. J. (2008). *Big ideas in beginning reading: The building blocks of literacy curriculum, instruction, and assessment. Curriculum maps: Grades K–3.* Eugene, OR: University of Oregon Center on Teaching and Learning. Retrieved from http://reading.uoregon.edu/resources/downloads/bibr_curriculum_maps.pdf

Torgesen, J. (2000). Individual differences in response to early interventions in reading: The lingering problem of treatment resisters. *Learning Disabilities Research & Practice, 15,* 55–64.

Vaughn, S., & Linan-Thompson, S. (2004). *Research-based methods of reading instruction: Grades K–3.* Alexandria, VA: Association for Supervision and Curriculum Development.

University of Oregon Center on Teaching and Learning. (2012). *Curriculum maps: Grades K–3.* Eugene, OR: Author. Retrieved from https://dibels.uoregon.edu/docs/curriculum_maps.pdf

Best Practices in Written Language Assessment and Intervention

Christine Kerres Malecki
Northern Illinois University

OVERVIEW

In 2011, about one quarter of 8th and 12th graders in the United States achieved proficient (24%) or advanced (3%) levels of writing competence on the National Assessment of Educational Progress (NAEP, 2012). Half of the approximately 24,000 eighth graders and 28,000 twelfth graders reached partial proficiency with about 20% of students below basic levels of writing proficiency. Given the importance of writing skills in everyday life, it is critical that these undesirable outcomes be improved. When examining instructional practices in writing, a survey of high school teachers across the United States revealed that only half of the teachers assigned a multiparagraph writing assignment to their students in any given month (Kiuhara, Graham, & Hawken, 2009). The survey also revealed that teachers used evidence-based writing instructional practices infrequently. Thus, the nation's students are not adequately performing in writing and, not surprisingly, are not being delivered adequate instruction on nor getting adequate practice using these skills.

One reason that writing may not be getting the attention it deserves is the accountability movement. We teach what will be assessed, and often writing is not assessed. Currently, 19 states do not include writing in their K–12 statewide assessment practices. One of the reasons that states may be reluctant to assess written language is due to the more intensive processes involved in scoring these assessments. A lack of focus on assessing writing leads to less pressure to focus on writing instruction. Change is coming, however, with the majority of states in the United States having now endorsed the Common Core State Standards. The

Common Core State Standards include standards in writing and language. Although as of 2013 only 31 states assess writing as part of their typical assessment practices, with adoption of the Common Core State Standards, that number will likely get closer to 50. Educators must be prepared to assess writing and to implement best practices in writing instruction as well.

Given the leadership role that school psychologists have in guiding schools' problem solving and multitiered systems of support in schools across the country, school psychologists can play an important role in improving these outcomes, one school at a time. Through the domain of Data-Based Decision Making and Accountability in the National Association of School Psychologists (NASP) *Model for Comprehensive and Integrated School Psychological Services* (NASP, 2010), school psychologists have the knowledge, skills, and tools needed to inform assessment and intervention in the area of written expression.

Currently, teachers are often left to do what they are familiar with or to adopt buzzword curricula that may or may not have evidence for effectiveness. In this chapter, assessment and instructional strategies will be presented for school psychologists to use when working with their colleagues to improve writing assessment and intervention.

BASIC CONSIDERATIONS

Best practice in assessment and intervention in the area of written language requires the use of a problem-solving approach and the use of a multitiered model. It would be inefficient to investigate the writing difficulties of one student at a time without assessing and improving the link between assessment and instruction for all students

(Tier 1). As has become the trend in reading, this shift in practice will require school psychologists to learn about curricula and instruction in written language and to be involved at the systems level, classroom level, and individual student level. This chapter focuses on written language assessment and instruction practices that are consistent for use in multitiered systems of support and problem solving. First, efficient assessment techniques are presented that are appropriate for use for Tier 1 through Tier 3 assessment purposes, including analytical rubric approaches and curriculum-based measurement techniques in written expression. Then, the chapter will focus on providing more appropriate Tier 1 instructional methods in writing, along with suggestions and resources for supplementary interventions for struggling writers. It may be beneficial to consult the chapter on curriculum-based evaluation procedures as well as to consider elements of effective intervention across academic areas.

BEST PRACTICES IN WRITING ASSESSMENT AND INTERVENTION

Here we will discuss best practices in writing assessment and in writing intervention as well as school psychologists' evaluation surrounding written expression.

Best Practices in Writing Assessment

School psychologists can use assessment techniques in written expression that are categorized as either direct or indirect (Stiggins, 1982). The following sections will describe indirect assessment methods and direct assessment methods including holistic and analytic rubrics and curriculum-based measures.

Indirect Assessments in Standardized Tests

Indirect methods of assessment evaluate writing by having students identify correct or incorrect written language mechanics by looking at writing samples. Often these approaches use a multiple-choice or fill-in-the-blank format. Indirect methods are often used in published standardized tests of written language. This chapter will not review the most commonly used broad and specific published standardized tests. See Salvia, Ysseldyke, and Bolt (2009) for a review of an example of such measures, including the Test of Written Language–Fourth Edition, and the Oral and Written Language Scales, as well as more broad achievement tests that include written language subtests, such as the Wechsler Individual Achievement Test–Third Edition, and the

Kaufman Test of Educational Achievement–Second Edition.

Direct Assessment Using Holistic Rubrics: A Caution

Direct methods assess students' skills by having each student produce his or her own writing. That writing sample is then evaluated using tools such as rubrics or objective skill counts. Howell and Nolet (2000) discuss the writer as *author* and the writer as *secretary*. Direct methods of assessment can allow for assessing both author and secretary elements of writing, but there are challenges, particularly with assessing the author skills. Often, teachers evaluate direct methods of writing assessment by giving students a holistic score (often a letter grade) on a writing task, with that score taking into account all aspects of the writing process. Although with extensive training and practice, these ratings can be reliable, they do not provide much information about students' skills (Arter, McTighe, & Guskey, 2001); the data do not give students information on what needs improvement, nor does the information inform instructional objectives. These types of holistic ratings can be especially problematic with early writers who do not produce the volume of writing necessary for a holistic rating (McMaster & Espin, 2007). An improvement on the holistic rubric method is calculating a holistic score from a compilation of subskill ratings scored using an analytic approach (Arter et al., 2001; Culham, 2005).

Direct Assessment Through Analytic Scoring Rubrics

Using an analytic scoring rubric (Arter et al., 2001) such as the Tindal and Hasbrouck analytic scoring system (Tindal & Hasbrouck, 1991) has the advantages of stronger reliability and more information to use in determining intervention directions. Using the Tindal and Hasbrouck analytic scoring system, students' writing samples are scored on a scale from 1 to 5 on three dimensions of writing: story idea, organization and cohesion, and conventions and mechanics (see Figure 12.1 for the Tindal and Hasbrouck analytic scoring system rubric). Additionally, many educators use the 6-Trait or 6 + 1 Trait system writing approach rubrics to help students evaluate their own writing and help teachers assess writing (Graham, McKeown, Kiuhara, & Harris, 2012; Northwest Regional Educational Laboratory, 2007; Spandel, 2004). With presentation as the +1 trait, six primary traits are used and evaluated in this approach, including ideas, organization, voice, word choice, sentence fluency, and conventions.

One advantage of using analytical rubrics to assess writing is that the separate skills create a commonly used, commonly referenced list of skills that create shared understanding and vocabulary among teachers and students. It can help communicate expectations for quality writing, creates a checklist for students to use when writing, and gives teachers a uniform way to assess writing and intervene when students' writing is missing certain rubric elements (Culham, 2005). A disadvantage is that the most commonly used analytic system, 6-Trait, has had limited evidence of its reliable and valid use (Coker & Ritchey, 2010; Gansle, VanDerHeyden,

Noell, Resetar, & Williams, 2006), perhaps because the 6-Trait approach was not designed as an analytic scoring tool. The Tindal and Hasbrouck analytic scoring system, however, does have evidence for reliable use (Tindal & Hasbrouck, 1991).

Rubrics in Action

Michael is a 9-year-old boy in third grade. Imagine that Michael's mother, Ms. Johnson, is sitting in a parent–teacher conference with Michael's teacher, Ms. Bocknick. Ms. Johnson asks about Michael's writing skills, because at home he complains about writing and

Figure 12.1. Tindal and Hasbrouck Analytical Scoring System

Score	Story Idea	Organization Cohesion	Conventions Mechanics
5	• Includes characters • Delineates a plot • Contains original ideas • Contains some detail • Word choice: Contains descriptors (adverbs and adjectives) and colorful, infrequently used, and/or some long words	• Overall story is organized into a beginning, middle, and end • Events are linked and cohesive • Sentences are linked, often containing some transitions to help with organization (finally, then, next, etc.)	• Sentence structure generally is accurate • Spelling does not hinder readability • Sometimes contains dialogue • Handwriting is legible • Punctuation does not affect readability too much • Word usage generally is correct (subject, verb, object; homophone; subject–verb agreement)
4	• Includes characters, but they are not original, often coming from movies • Delineates a plot, although it is not as clear as a 5 • Contains some original ideas but it is fairly predictable • Contains some detail • Word choice: contains some descriptors (adverbs and adjectives) and some colorful, infrequently used, or long words	• Story has somewhat of a beginning, middle, and end • Events appear somewhat random, but some organization exists • Sample may contain some transitions to help with organization (finally, then, next, etc.) • Story often contains too many events, disrupting cohesion	• Sentence structure generally is accurate but not as good as a 5 • Spelling does not hinder readability too much • Sometimes contains dialogue • Handwriting is legible • Punctuation does not affect readability too much • Word usage generally is correct (subject, verb, object; homophone; subject–verb agreement)
3	• Characters are predictable and undeveloped • Plot is somewhat haphazard • May not contain original ideas • Lacks details • Word choice is somewhat predictable; contains descriptors (adverbs and adjectives)	• Somewhat of a plot exists, but story may still lack a beginning, middle, and end • Events are somewhat random • Often lacks transitions • Sometimes lacks referents	• Sentence structure has a few problems • Spelling is somewhat of a problem • May use dialogue, but does not punctuate correctly • Handwriting is legible • Punctuation is fair • Problems sometimes occur with word usage (subject, verb, object; homophone; subject–verb agreement)

Figure 12.1. Continued

Score	Story Idea	Organization Cohesion	Conventions Mechanics
2	• Includes few, if any, characters • Plot is not developed or apparent • Contains virtually no original ideas • Detail is significantly absent • Events are very predictable • Word choice is predictable, lacking descriptors (adverbs and adjectives)	• Plot lacks organization; no beginning, middle, and end • Events are random, lacking in cohesion • Lacks transitions • Often lacks referents	• Sentence structure makes the story difficult to read • Spelling makes the story difficult to read • May use dialogue, but does not punctuate correctly • Handwriting is not very legible • Punctuation is inconsistent and problematic • Word usage is problematic (subject, verb, object; homophone; subject–verb agreement)
1	• Includes few, if any, characters • Plot is nonexistent • Contains no original ideas • Detail is significantly absent • Events are few and predictable • Lacks descriptors (adverbs and adjectives)	• Plot is virtually nonexistent • Events are few and random • Lacks transitions • Lacks referents	• Sentence structure is problematic • Spelling makes the story extremely difficult to read • Handwriting is illegible, making it extremely difficult to decode • Punctuation is virtually nonexistent • Word usage is problematic (subject, verb, object; homophone; subject–verb agreement)

Note. From "Analyzing Student Writing to Develop Instruction Strategies," by G. Tindal and J. Hasbrouck, 1991, *Learning Disabilities Research & Practice*, 6, 237–245. Copyright 1991 by John Wiley & Sons. Adapted with permission.

says he is "no good at writing." Ms. Bocknick pulls out two writing samples to show his mom. Both were three-paragraph essays he worked on with a great deal of scaffolding and over the course of several days. Ms. Bocknick scored the first story using a holistic rubric on a scale of 1 (*underdeveloped*) to 5 (*fully developed*). Michael's score was a 3, indicating *partially developed*. Next, Ms. Bocknick showed Michael's mom the essay that was graded using an analytical scale, specifically the Tindal and Hasbrouck analytic scoring system. Michael scored a 5 out of 5 on story idea, a 4 out of 5 on organization and cohesion, and a 2 out of 5 on conventions and mechanics. Which of the two types of assessments likely gave Michael's mom more information about Michael's strengths and weaknesses in writing? Which scoring method likely will lead to more targeted intervention for Michael?

Direct Assessment Through Curriculum-Based Measures

Curriculum-based measurement in written expression is another direct method of assessment school psychologists

use as an objective and efficient tool for evaluating the effectiveness of written language curriculum and instruction at all levels of intensity through universal screening, benchmarking, and progress monitoring (Malecki & Jewell, 2003; McMaster & Campbell, 2008; McMaster & Espin, 2007). The benefits are the reliable and objective metrics, but the disadvantages are that these scores primarily assess writing mechanics (writer as secretary) and do not tap important writing elements such as organization, ideas, and sentence complexity (writer as author). As a general outcome measure of written expression, however, these scores have been shown to be related to overall writing quality measures (Amato & Watkins, 2011; Coker & Ritchey, 2010). The tool's utility as a general outcome measure used for screening, benchmarking, and progress monitoring, as well as the efficiency, reliability, and validity evidence for the tool warrants an extensive discussion here.

Administration and scoring of written expression curriculum-based measures.

Written expression curriculum-based measurement

involves the standardized administration of a prompt, including a picture, words to copy, or a story starter, that students respond to in writing. The typical administration used in first grade and above involves a story starter prompt, with students thinking about the prompt for 1 minute and writing for 3 minutes (see Figure 12.2). Written expression curriculum-based measures are scored using several factors. The most frequently used scoring indices are divided into three broad categories: production-dependent indices, production-independent indices, and accurate-production indices (Espin et al., 2000; Malecki & Jewell, 2003). Production-dependent indices consist primarily of how much writing a student generates (Total Words Written, Words Spelled Correctly, Correct Writing Sequences, Correct Punctuation Marks). Production-independent indices take the amount of writing the student generates out of the equation by creating percentages (Percent of Words Spelled Correctly and Percent of Correct Writing Sequences). The accurate-production indicator combines both production and accuracy (Correct Minus Incorrect Writing Sequences). See Table 12.1 for a summary of these scores and how they are calculated. More specific administration and scoring guidelines on most of these scores can be found online on many web sites, including at www.aimsweb.com and www.interventioncentral.org.

Many other scoring methods have been used in the literature, such as correct punctuation marks, number of simple sentences, correct letter sequences, and words in complete sentences (see Gansle, Noell, VanDerHeyden, Naquin, & Slider, 2002, a study that utilized and compared 14 such measures). However, this chapter is focusing on the most commonly used measures from the three categories (production-dependent, production-independent, and accurate-production indices) as well as some select new prompts and scores that have shown promise, particularly at the preschool and early elementary levels.

Written expression curriculum-based measures in preschool. Some scores are more appropriate for use at some grade levels than others. For example, at the preschool or early childhood level, measuring production is challenging. One of the few things children 3, 4, or 5 years old can be expected to do with some consistency is write their own name, but given the variability of names (i.e., Guadalupe versus Ray), it is hardly a reliable measure. Some suggest that the primary tools for assessing writing at preschool ages involve measuring the precursors to writing, such as language abilities (i.e., vocabulary) and prereading skills (Hooper, Roberts, Nelson, Zeisel, & Fannin, 2010).

Written expression curriculum-based measures in early elementary. Starting in first grade, school psychologists can use production-oriented measures with some reliability and validity. Simply the act of producing letters on a page (transcription) is related to students' beginning writing skills. Thus, having students simply produce letters such as writing the alphabet while

Figure 12.2. Standardized Administration for Written Expression Curriculum-Based Measurement

1. Select an appropriate story starter.
2. Provide the student with a pencil and a sheet of lined paper.
3. Say these specific directions to the students: "You are going to write a story. First, I will read a sentence, and then you will write a story about what happens next. You will have 1 minute to think about what you will write and 3 minutes to write your story. Remember to do your best work. If you don't know how to spell a word, you should guess. Are there any questions? [Pause.] Put your pencil down and listen. For the next minute, think about [insert story starter]."
4. After reading the story starter, begin your stopwatch and allow 1 minute for students to think. [Monitor students so that they do not begin writing.] After 30 seconds say: "You should be thinking about [insert story starter]."
5. At the end of 1 minute say: "Now begin writing." Restart your stopwatch.
6. Monitor students' attention to the task. Encourage students to work only if they are looking around or talking.
7. After 90 seconds say: "You should be writing about [insert story starter]."
8. At the end of 3 minutes say: "Stop. Put your pencil down."

Note. From "Developmental, Gender, and Practical Considerations in Scoring Curriculum-Based Measurement Writing Probes," by C. K. Malecki and J. Jewell, 2003, *Psychology in the Schools, 40*, 379–390. Copyright 2003 by John Wiley & Sons. Adapted with permission.

Table 12.1. Curriculum-Based Measurement/Written Language Scores, Definitions, and Computations

Index	Grades	Definition	Computation
Total Words Written	K–2	A count of the number of words written. A word is defined as any letter or group of letters separated by a space, even if the word is misspelled or is a nonsense word.	Total Words Written
Words Spelled Correctly	K–3	A count of the number of words that are spelled correctly. A word is spelled correctly if it can stand alone as a word in the English language.	Words Spelled Correctly
Correct Writing Sequences	3–12	A count of the correct writing sequences found in the sample. A correct writing sequence is defined as two adjacent writing units (i.e., word–word or word–punctuation) that are acceptable within the context of what is written. Correct writing sequences take into account correct spelling, grammar, punctuation, capitalization, syntax, and semantics.	Correct Writing Sequences or Total Writing Sequences minus Incorrect Writing Sequences
Percent of Words Spelled Correctly	4–12	The percentage of words in the sample that are spelled correctly.	Words Spelled Correctly/Total Words Written
Percent of Correct Writing Sequences	4–12	The percentage of correct writing sequences in the sample.	Correct Writing Sequences/ Possible Writing Sequences
Correct Minus Incorrect Writing Sequences	4–12	This measure subtracts the number of incorrect writing sequences in the sample from the total number of correct writing sequences. The number of incorrect writing sequences was calculated by subtracting the number of correct writing sequences in the sample from the total number of possible writing sequences.	Correct Writing Sequences minus Incorrect Writing Sequences or Correct Writing Sequences minus (Possible Writing Sequences minus Correct Writing Sequences)

Note. "Grades" represents the grade levels for which the scores have strongest evidence for valid and reliable use.

being timed or copying words on a page are examples of transcription. One such measure school psychologists can use is sentence copying. Typically students are given a series of pages that each have three sentences on a page. The students copy sentences that are no more than seven words under each prompt. The sentences should come from curriculum that the students are engaged with (reading materials from their reading curriculum). Words in the sentences should also have no more than seven letters. Students complete a sample sentence first and then copy the sentences for 3 minutes (Lembke, Deno, & Hall, 2003; McMaster, Du, & Petursdottir, 2009). Sentence-copy tasks have been found to have adequate reliability and validity (McMaster et al., 2011).

When moving from transcription to producing words on a page, school psychologists can give students many different types of prompts. Historically, word prompts such as story starters have been used, but for early writers, picture prompts can be more appropriate. One example of prompts used for early writers is picture-word tasks. Picture-word tasks have words and pictures presented on a page with lines next to the prompts where the students write about the word/picture prompts for 3 minutes. Typically, the writing is scored as Words Written, Words Spelled Correctly, and Correct Word Sequences. Again, reliability and validity evidence for these scores with early elementary school children has been found (McMaster et al., 2011). At the early elementary school level, giving picture, word, or sentence prompts for students to produce Total Words Written may be the least intrusive and most efficient measure for large-scale purposes. Another measure found to have promise at the early kindergarten and first-grade level is a new qualitative score that uses a sentence-writing curriculum-based measure prompt, but scores students' responses using an analytical rubric assessing response type, spelling, mechanics, grammatical structure, and relationship to prompt (Coker & Ritchey, 2010).

Written expression curriculum-based measures in middle elementary. At middle elementary, school psychologists can use these same production measures (Total Words Written, Words Spelled

Correctly, Correct Writing Sequences), production-independent measures (e.g., Percent Words Spelled Correctly, Percent Correct Writing Sequences), and accurate-production measures (e.g., Correct Minus Incorrect Writing Sequences) with confidence as valid and reliable measurements of student written expression performance (Malecki & Jewell, 2003; Videen, Deno, & Marston, 1982). That is, all of the measures show utility, and the measures are also strongly interrelated.

Written expression curriculum-based measures in later elementary. However, as students got older (fifth grade and up), the production-dependent measures became less generalizable (Jewell & Malecki, 2005). In fact, the production-dependent scores (quantity) and the production-independent scores (quality) were not correlated at the older grade levels. At least one study has suggested that even at third and fourth grade, Total Words Written may not be the best indicator of writing skills, as measured by the relationship with criterion measures (Gansle et al., 2002). These findings demonstrate that the amount a student writes is important and represents a broader picture of the students' writing skills at the lower elementary grade levels, but the quality and accuracy of students' writing are both factors that need to be considered at the upper elementary and secondary grades. Thus, at the older grade levels, research has supported the popular adage of teachers everywhere that "It doesn't matter how much you write, it is how well you write." Quality and quantity indicators are strongly related to each other at the elementary grades, but from fourth or fifth grade up (or possibly even third grade), they are no longer significantly related. This research has continued to be supported (McMaster & Campbell, 2008). Thus, educators working with individual students on written expression tasks should choose the most appropriate index based on the students' skill level.

Written expression curriculum-based measures in high school. Overall, school psychologists should consider that accurate-production measures, and perhaps all written expression curriculum-based measures, may be more valid for use with lower performing students than for higher performing students at the high school level. This would be in line with the idea of written expression curriculum-based measures being a general outcome measure of basic written language skills and not a measure designed to tap the complexities of high-quality writing at a high school level. (See Table 12.1 for tentative recommendations for score use.)

Gender differences in written expression curriculum-based measures. Gender plays an important role in individual performance on curriculum-based measures writing indices. It has been found that, generally, girls outperform boys on most of the written expression curriculum-based measures (Malecki & Jewell, 2003; McMaster & Espin, 2007). These results are consistent with the report of NAEP (2012) that found that 8th- and 12th-grade girls outperformed boys on the writing assessment. School psychologists should carefully consider these differences in writing skills between boys and girls, especially when determining discrepancies between students' skills and those of their peers when determining students' response to intervention at all tiers.

Racial and language group differences in written expression curriculum-based measures. It should also be noted that racial and cultural group differences have been found as well, with Asian students who take the NAEP assessment in 8th grade outperforming all other racial groups, and Asian, White, and biracial or multiracial students outperforming other 12th graders taking the NAEP (2012). Few studies have compared racial, ethnic, or cultural differences on written expression curriculum-based measures, but one study found that Correct Minus Incorrect Word Sequences were more related to outcome measures of writing for students learning English than for non-English-learning students (Espin et. al, 2008).

How Written Expression Curriculum-Based Measures Are Used Throughout the Multitiered Model

At all tiers, to assess how effective and efficient the general education curriculum and instruction are in a particular skill area, school psychologists need brief, reliable, and valid assessments of important skills. As discussed above, written expression curriculum-based measures meet these requirements.

Time and practical considerations in using written expression curriculum-based measures at Tier 1. Practical considerations also play a role in these decisions. Although written expression curriculum-based measures are group-administered brief assessments, scoring the writing samples takes time, specifically averaging (depending on grade level) between 22 and 31 seconds to score Total Words Written, between 25 and 37 seconds to score Words Spelled Correctly, and between 57 and 151 seconds to score Correct Writing Sequences (Gansle et al., 2002;

Malecki & Jewell, 2003). If all three scores are used, it takes between 1.5 minutes and 2.5 minutes to score one writing sample. Thus, if a school psychologist wanted to assess 60 students in each of five grades (1–5), he or she could expect it to take between 450 minutes (7.5 hours) to 750 minutes (12.5 hours) to score all of the samples. Given the time requirements, it makes sense to be more selective with what scores to use for benchmarking or screening purposes. Given the developmental considerations, it is recommended that only Total Words Written be used at the early elementary grades (1–4) and that from fifth grade up all three scores be used (and that the production-independent and accurate-production measures be calculated and recorded as well). In the example above, this would cut the scoring time to 1.5 hours for first- to fourth-grade samples and 2.5 hours for the fifth-grade sample.

Setting of benchmark targets for written expression curriculum-based measures at Tier 1.

When examining the data, it would be ideal to have research-based standards or targets on these written expression curriculum-based measures so that school psychologists can identify the percentage of students hitting the targets and can identify students not achieving that level of skill. At this time, there are no known sources that have identified a standard or criterion for successful writing on these scores. Instead, school psychologists may have to determine what standards they will use for their own population of students. This could be done via analyses to determine scores that are related to success on state tests of written language. Another approach would be to use local norms to identify how students are writing compared to his or her peers. Finally, national norms are available through AIMSweb, but caution should be used if referring to national norms. First, the national norming sample may not be reflective of any particular standard nor reflective of a school's local sample of students. However, the national norms can give some comparative information for school psychologists to use in the absence of developed standards or local norms. See Table 12.2 for a summary of comparative data available via research and AIMSweb, to be used with caution, not as standards, but as comparative data.

It should be considered that national data suggest that students are underachieving in written language (NAEP, 2012); therefore, setting a higher goal than the national 50th percentile, or at the very least getting significantly more than half of the students to achieve at that level, would be appropriate. Obviously, research to develop

solid standards on technically sound assessments that can be used to make educational decisions is sorely needed. This would also allow educators to know what scores constitute the mark for 80% of students reaching the Tier 1 benchmark.

Instructional considerations in using written expression curriculum-based measures at Tier 1.

If the levels of students' skills as represented by written expression curriculum-based measurement scores are lacking, it would be appropriate to examine the curriculum and instruction in general education (see below). In the meantime, while schools are working on improving general education curriculum and instruction in written language (see Figures 12.1 and 12.2), students in the lowest percentiles would need further, more diagnostic evaluation in written language to determine their specific skill or performance deficits. Using curriculum-based evaluation procedures would be most appropriate for this purpose of written language assessment. Once the skill or performance deficits are identified, school psychologists can recommend supplemental general education interventions that will address those deficits. Key to these interventions (addressing holes in the general education curriculum and instruction and supplementing for students when necessary) is progress monitoring. Benchmarking three times a year to monitor the general education curriculum and instruction and to check in with all students is recommended.

Use of written expression curriculum-based measures at Tier 2 and Tier 3.

A weekly or every 2 week progress monitoring schedule is crucial to monitor the progress of students receiving supplemental general education interventions and those students receiving more intensive interventions at Tier 3, which may or may not include special education services (Deno, Espin, & Fuchs, 2002). In deciding which written expression curriculum-based measures to use for progress monitoring, the same considerations described above would apply (skill level, what skill is being targeted by the intervention). School psychologists can use written expression curriculum-based measures as an effective assessment tool with which to set goals and monitor progress, because these written expression curriculum-based measures are simple and efficient, reliable and valid, and sensitive to growth over time.

Obviously, the key to effective intervention (be it general education curriculum and instruction; supplemental interventions; or intensive, individualized

Table 12.2. Compiled Means as an Example of Comparative Data on Selected Written Expression Curriculum-Based Measurement Scores From Multiple Sources (Use With Caution)

	Total Words Written	Words Spelled Correctly	Correct Writing Sequence	Percent of Words Spelled Correctly	Percent of Correct Writing Sequence	Correct Minus Incorrect Writing Sequence
	M	*M*	*M*	*M*	*M*	*M*
Grade 1						
Fall	7–8	5–6	2–5	53	22	–4
Spring	14–21	10–17	7–11	71	42	–1
Grade 2						
Fall	12–24	12–20	10–15	81	54	3
Spring	25–32	25–27	22–24	87	69	14
Grade 3						
Fall	23–36	22–32	19–28	89	70	17
Spring	34–40	33–34	30–32	91	78	22
Grade 4						
Fall	33–41	31–38	27–38	94	84	31
Spring	41–46	35–44	39–42	94	83	34
Grade 5						
Fall	37–51	37–48	35–46	94	83	37
Spring	42–67	50–65	45–63	97	86	53
Grade 6						
Fall	41–47	42–44	39–41	94	84	34
Spring	53–60	55–56	51–54	96	85	45
Grade 7						
Fall	48–54	49–55	47–49	96	84	39
Spring	58–61	56–62	53–64	96	86	46
Grade 8						
Fall	49–74	54–70	49–70	96	88	61
Spring	58–68	66–70	56–67	98	91	60

Note. Based on data from AIMSweb (2012 norms), Malecki and Jewell (2003), Mirken et al. (1981), and Shinn (1989). Data from columns 4–6 are from Malecki and Jewell (2003).

instruction) is using best practices in assessment to frequently and reliably assess skills and to adjust these interventions based on those data. In the following section is a discussion of the state of the applied research in written language intervention and its application to the multitiered framework.

Written Expression Curriculum-Based Measures in Action

Remember that it was found that Michael, the third grader in the earlier example, had difficulty in the mechanics of writing (writer as secretary) based on his analytical rubric scores. The school psychologist, Dr. Jewell, was asked to do further assessment as part of the individual problem-solving process to aid in developing potential supplemental interventions to improve Michael's writing skills. Dr. Jewell administered to Michael three curriculum-based measure writing samples over the course of 2 days in November. Dr. Jewell scored the samples using Total Words

Written (median = 40), Words Spelled Correctly (median = 21), Correct Writing Sequences (median = 13), and calculated Correct Minus Incorrect Writing Sequences (median = 13). Scores, as well as the error analysis using curriculum-based evaluation procedures, indicated that Michael's primary difficulties were spelling, capitalization at the beginning of sentences, and ending punctuation. Michael had great ideas, however, and he wrote fluently. Dr. Jewell and the team set a goal that by the end of the school year Michael would improve his spelling, capitalization, and ending punctuation, resulting in Correct Minus Incorrect Writing Sequences of 22.

Best Practices in Writing Intervention

This section will review the most up-to-date science on evidence-based effective writing intervention practices at all three tiers and will provide school psychologists with the necessary resources to share this information with teachers.

Tier 1 Intervention and the Common Core State Standards

General education curriculum and instruction is the universal intervention for students learning written language skills. It is clear that many educators are not implementing evidence-based writing instruction in their classroom practices. For example, a survey of high school teachers indicate that although teachers generally reported being aware of research-based elements of writing instruction, the teachers were infrequently using those practices in the classroom (Kiuhara et al., 2009). Worse, teachers may be using curricula or commonly accepted approaches to writing instruction that are ineffective.

The adoption of the Common Core State Standards by the majority of states in the country should help focus written language instruction by providing standards by which curriculum and instruction can be organized. The Common Core anchor standards in writing fall under four categories: (a) text, types, and purposes; (b) production and distribution of writing; (c) research to build and present knowledge; and (d) range of writing. However, tied to the writing standards are the language standards that fall under the categories of (a) conventions of standard English, (b) knowledge of language, and (c) vocabulary acquisition and usage, with a particular writing emphasis under the conventions' anchor standards. The Common Core State Standards should be kept in mind when developing writing curricula and instruction or intervention.

It is impossible to begin talking about the current state of the science in writing instruction and intervention without reviewing the broader research-based elements of effective intervention and instruction. Whether a school psychologist is consulting with teachers regarding instruction of reading skills, math skills, social skills, or physical skills, key elements of effective instruction apply. Many researchers have come to consensus on elements such as explicit instruction, scaffolded or supported instruction, opportunities to respond (practice), corrective feedback as immediate as possible, reinforcement or motivational elements, vocabulary support, and progress monitoring, with goal setting and performance feedback (see Petersen-Brown & Burns, 2011). As the literature on effective elements of writing instruction and intervention are reviewed below, these same elements will appear again and again.

Explicit instruction including self-regulated strategy instruction. Two summaries of the interventions and instructional approaches for writing skills

(Graham et al., 2012; Rogers & Graham, 2008) categorized the effective approaches under (a) explicit instruction, (b) scaffolding, (c) alternative modes of composing, and (d) other, with the vast majority of approaches falling under explicit instruction. Explicit instruction approaches include teaching students, explicitly, how to plan, draft, and revise their writing. Key to this finding is that the collection of strategies taught under the self-regulated strategy development approach (Harris & Graham, 1996) were the most effective and lasting approaches for teaching writing skills.

Self-regulated strategy development is a way to make the very abstract concepts and terms that are used to communicate about writing (brainstorm, plan, organize) concrete, clear, and accessible to all students. There are six steps in a self-regulated strategy development approach (Harris, Graham, Mason, & Friedlander, 2007):

- Stage 1: Develop students' background knowledge
- Stage 2: Discuss the strategy
- Stage 3: Model the strategy
- Stage 4: Have students memorize the strategy
- Stage 5: Support students' usage of the strategy through scaffolding
- Stage 6: Have students independently use the strategy

Scaffolded or supported instruction is clear in Stage 5. Providing students with opportunities to respond with corrective feedback is happening at Stages 4–6. Teaching the vocabulary used in the model is occurring throughout. Progress monitoring is occurring, in particular, at Stage 6. Finally, the authors of the approach recommend that enthusiasm and a supportive environment surround the approach, which maps clearly onto the motivational aspects of effective instruction (Mason, Harris, & Graham, 2011).

Self-regulated strategy development can be overwhelming because of the sheer number of different strategies that can be applied through the six-stage model. One example of a strategy is POW (P = pick my idea, O = organize my notes, W = write and say more). Although this seems like a simple mnemonic device, it is effective because it is taught systematically and explicitly through the six stages of self-regulated strategy development. Table 12.3 presents a list of the six stages of self-regulated strategy development and more examples of the strategies used as part of self-regulated strategy development.

The other strategies studied as part of the meta-analyses that fall under the explicit teaching category include teaching students to self-regulate use of

Table 12.3. Self-Regulated Strategy Development

Stages of Writing	Self-Regulation Strategies	Mnemonics
Develop background knowledge • Assess for baseline knowledge by collecting writing samples • Discuss how to write a good story and the purpose of writing • Show examples of good writing • Introduce self-regulation strategies and mnemonic devices	*Self-monitoring* • Students graph their own progress on a chart so they can see their own growth toward their goal	*Overall writing strategy* • P = pick my idea • O = organize my notes • W = write and say more
Discuss the strategy • Discuss how and when to use the different strategies • Talk about self-monitoring and goal setting • Sign contracts with the goal of learning to write independently	*Self-instructions* • Students are given a checklist with their instructions for writing: assemble materials, develop an idea, organize notes, and then write and say more	*Story writing* • POW + W = 2, H = 2 • W2 = what 2 • H2 = how 2
Model the strategy • Model the writing process, including the strategies and mnemonics, for the student • Introduce the graphic organizer, which helps to guide the student through the writing process with specific spaces for students to write notes and organize their essay before beginning to write • Introduce using positive self-statements students can use to motivate themselves	*Self-reinforcement* • Students are to create positive self-statements they can use to motivate themselves in the face of struggles such as "I just need to use my strategies and I can do a good job" or "First, I need to brainstorm my ideas"	*Story writing* • POW + C-SPACE • C = characters • S = setting • P = purpose of main characters • A = action to achieve goal • C = conclusion of action • E = emotions of character
Memorize the strategy • Students practice using the strategies and the mnemonics • Give students the graphic organizer or planning sheets so they remember to use the steps	*Metacognition* • The teacher models the thought process the students should use during the writing process and talks through the mnemonics using the Think-Aloud Procedure	*Opinion writing* • T = topic sentence • R = three or more reasons • E = ending to wrap it up • E = examine for all parts
Support the strategy • Provide scaffolding and feedback about the student's use of the strategies and the mnemonics • As students get better with using the strategies, remove the graphic organizer or planning sheets to determine if students can use the strategies and mnemonics without prompting; reintroduce them if students are not successful	*Self-Assessment* • Students use cue cards or make a checklist for students to evaluate their own writing: ▪ "Did I brainstorm my ideas first?" ▪ "Can I think of anything else?" ▪ "Did I answer the question?"	*Opinion writing* • S = suspend judgment • T = take a side • O = organize ideas • P = plan more as I write • D = develop a topic sentence • A = add supporting ideas • R = reject the other side • E = end with conclusion
Independent performance • Students are working independently with little or no support as they are using the strategies and mnemonics without prompting		*Brainstorming or planning* • P = pick goals • L = list ways to meet goals • A = (filler letter) • N = make notes • S = sequence notes *Revision* • S = does this make sense? • C = connected to my belief? • A = can I add more? • N = note errors? *Essay writing* • P = pay attention to prompt • L = list main ideas • A = add supporting ideas • N = number major points • W = work from a plan • R = remember my goals • I = include transition words • T = different sentence types • E = exciting, interesting words

Note. Based on information from Division for Learning Disabilities (2009).

strategies, teaching students to form images to facilitate creativity, teaching different types of text and how to approach writing for those purposes, and teaching spelling, handwriting, and keyboarding to facilitate writing (Graham et al., 2012; Rogers & Graham, 2008).

Other effective instructional approaches. Other instructional approaches found to be effective under scaffolding include (a) creating opportunities for collaboration in planning; (b) drafting, revising, and editing writing; (c) participating in prewriting activities; (d) assessing students' progress; and (e) setting clear and specific writing goals (Graham & Perin, 2007). More specifically, goal setting, feedback, and self-monitoring are instructional techniques that can help students be more successful with their writing skills (Graham, Harris, & Troia, 1998). Other effective approaches in the meta-analyses included allowing students to use word processing tools, increasing writing time, and using a comprehensive writing program. Note that, in general, all of the strategies listed as part of the meta-analyses are discussed here in order of effect sizes. Table 12.4 provides an overview of these research-based strategies.

Writing curricula that are most effective teach the process of writing (writer as author) and the mechanics of writing (writer as secretary) simultaneously (Graham & Harris, 2000; Howell & Nolet, 2000). For example, if a teacher were to focus on spelling, punctuation, syntax, and capitalization but did not give instruction in producing writing and did not give students time to plan and produce meaningful writing, there would be a disconnect resulting in less effective writing instruction.

Additionally, on almost every list of recommended and evidence-based practices in teaching writing is that writing should be a daily activity and there should be a writing routine as part of daily instructional time. For example, school psychologists can collaborate with teachers in planning to set aside time each day to have students write on a topic of their choice. The teacher would model the processes of writing (planning, completing planning activities, writing, editing), allow students to work on their project at whatever phase they were (planning, writing, editing), have students read each other's work and provide feedback, and celebrate the writing process as a class. It has become almost common knowledge that having students practice reading makes them more fluent readers. Unfortunately, the same principle is not as systematically applied in writing. One study found that elementary school students wrote an average of 3 hours per week, but there was a great deal of variability, with some classrooms having students writing only 30 minutes per week (Graham & Harris, 2005). It only makes sense that students will become better and more fluent writers if they have more opportunity to write and practice those skills.

Instruction at Tier 2 and Tier 3: More of the same. While improvements in core instruction are being made at Tier 1, there will be students who will require additional attention. These students may need further evaluation through curriculum-based evaluation procedures to determine what they need to be successful. This process may involve using other direct and indirect methods described earlier. Additionally, using error

---

Table 12.4. Research-Based Elements of Writing Instruction

Be explicit in the teaching of writing skills and strategies
- Teach planning, drafting, and revising skills (self-regulated strategy development; Graham et al., 2012; Rogers and Graham, 2008; see Table 12.3)
- Teach text structure and transcription (Graham et al., 2012)
- Teach creativity through imagery (Graham et al., 2012) and other prewriting activities (Graham et al., 2012; Rogers and Graham, 2008)
- Teach writing of complex sentences and paragraphs (Graham et al., 2012)

Scaffold or support learning through opportunities to respond, assessment, goal setting, and corrective feedback
- Create collaborative writing opportunities (Graham et al., 2012)
- Utilize assessment of progress, goal setting, and performance feedback (Graham et al., 2012)
- Teach word processing tools (Graham et al., 2012; Rogers and Graham, 2008)

Motivate: Make writing fun
- Use self-regulated strategy development to teach and support positive self-statements for struggling writers (Graham et al., 2012; Rogers and Graham, 2008)
- Praise writing and improvement individually (Rogers and Graham, 2008) and through group reinforcement (Graham et al., 2012)
- Post students' work in public areas (Rogers & Graham, 2008)

---

analysis procedures to further analyze the written expression curriculum-based measurement probes would be useful. With these additional data, supplementary interventions could be selected to have greater success in teaching the skills. The following are resources and examples of such interventions; however, it is important to note that, in general, the best approach is to teach students writing using the same evidence-based methods being used at Tier 1. Students needing additional support simply need more explicit instruction, more opportunities to respond, more immediate corrective feedback, more vocabulary support, more progress monitoring, and more reinforcement. There is not necessarily a magic formula for an intervention at Tier 2 and Tier 3. It is simply additional time with research-based elements of effective instruction that makes the difference.

Instructional match: It is imperative that the interventions selected for use by school psychologists and teachers match a particular student's instructional need and that it is complementary with what is happening at Tier 1. A sentence-combining strategy may have a great deal of evidence for its effectiveness, but if the student does not have the prerequisite skills needed to learn sentence combining, the intervention will not be effective. Thus, generalizations should not be made about the small sample of interventions presented in this chapter.

The first approach to finding an appropriate supplemental intervention is to examine all of the recommended elements of writing instruction discussed above. If a student is lacking in a skill served by these strategies, it may be that the student simply needs more time with that particular instructional strategy. Perhaps pairing the student with a peer and working on sentence combining is effective, but for learning to be at an appropriate rate, the student needs more time with that strategy than is built into the curriculum. However, if it appears that a truly additional, non-preexisting strategy may be called for, there are options.

There is intervention research that shows a parallel to the research on written expression curriculum-based measures related to the developmental progression of the mechanics and fluency of writing versus the process and content of writing. Specifically, for early elementary students struggling with writing, a stronger focus on handwriting and spelling instruction has been found to be more effective than writing process interventions (Graham & Harris, 2002, 2005).

Common research-based commercial interventions: Several packaged assessment and intervention materials are available that incorporate many of the recommended instructional strategies. These include the vast array of Strategic Instruction model interventions, developed by the Center for Research on Learning at the University of Kansas (commonly referred to as KU Strategies). Strategies for writing available for training and purchase include (a) Sentence Writing Strategy (Fundamentals), (b) Sentence Writing Strategy (Proficiency), (c) Paragraph Writing Strategy, (d) Theme Writing (Fundamentals), (e) Error Monitoring Strategy, and (f) InSPECT Strategy (for word processing spellcheckers). These interventions incorporate many of the elements of effective instruction (mnemonics, direct instruction of strategies), and there is evidence of the effective use of these interventions (McNaughton, Hughes, & Ofiesh, 1997; Oas, Schumaker, & Deshler, 1995). Another research-based set of intervention tools (PAL Teacher Guide) was developed and has been researched by Berninger (e.g., Berninger & Amtmann, 2003; Wong & Berninger, 2004). Finally, Anita Archer's excellent work on effective instruction applies to writing in her REWARDS Writing intervention (Archer, Gleason, & Isaacson, 2007) and in her work on effective and explicit instruction overall (Archer & Hughes, 2011).

Using mnemonic devices: The use of mnemonic devices to teach the strategies of writing is consistently recommended and commonly used and, as noted, is common in Tier 1 approaches including self-regulated strategy development (Harris & Graham, 1996). These devices range from rhymes to help students remember spelling rules (*i* before *e* except after *c*) to letter strategies to remember complex steps in writing a personal narrative (SPACE LAUNCH with the letters representing each step) or letter strategies to remember when editing (COPS; Access Center, 2013). Giving students some tools to help remember how to approach the writing process is invaluable. Without these tools, the students may be left with a blank paper, a pencil, and a sense of being overwhelmed with the task at hand.

Writing Intervention in Action

Dr. Jewell, our school psychologist, introduces Michael's teacher to a collection of research-based strategies for improving Michael's spelling, capitalization, and punctuation. All strategies follow the self-regulated strategy development stages of instruction and Archer's "I do, we do, you do" (Archer & Hughes, 2011) steps of instructional modeling and practice. For example, Dr. Jewell suggested using a copy, cover, write, and check procedure when teaching Michael to spell irregular words. Irregularly spelled words must be memorized, and the self-regulated strategy development would include helping Michael to develop background knowledge about spelling regular versus irregular words, discussing the strategy that will be taught to learn how to learn and practice irregular words, modeling the strategy, helping Michael memorize the strategy (copy, cover, write, and check), and using the "I do, we do, you do" approach to implement and practice the strategy. Similar approaches would be used for capitalization and punctuation. The school psychologist may look at screening or benchmarking data to determine if these strategies might be applied more efficiently class-wide if a majority of students were similarly struggling.

School Psychologists' Evaluation Surrounding Written Expression

School psychologists must juggle many considerations when assessing students' writing skills and when consulting with teachers on best instructional practices in written expression. Using implementation fidelity checklists can aid school psychologists in their evaluation of their own effectiveness in these pursuits. For example, when training teachers how to use written expression curriculum-based measures, school psychologists could create clear implementation checklists for teachers to use in their own self-monitoring (e.g., Did I follow standardized instructions? Am I following the assessment schedule? Did I use the correct timing?). Periodically monitoring teachers' self-monitoring can help school psychologists to know what additional training needs there might be or can alert them when assessment demands are too great for teachers. Similarly, when conducting professional development with teachers in effective instruction in writing, using implementation checklists can help teachers maintain integrity in their implementation of effective instruction and can help school psychologists know if their training and support are sufficient. Finally, school psychologists can use program evaluation and data-based decision-making skills to collect and analyze data to determine if the correct writing assessment tools are being used for the intended purposes within the school and to determine if instruction at all tiers is resulting in appropriate growth in students' writing skills over time.

SUMMARY

It is recommended that for students to be prepared to communicate in writing about all aspects of their lives, more attention should be given to instructing and assessing writing in schools. In the digital age, students are communicating in writing almost continuously, but they need instruction in the appropriate use of the English language for all of the purposes and with all the skills described as part of the Common Core in Writing and Language. To this aim, appropriate assessment tools such as psychometrically sound analytical rubrics and written expression curriculum-based measurement tools should be used to assess, monitor, and inform written language instruction at all tiers. Writing instruction should follow the essential elements of research-based instruction, including instruction that is explicit, uses scaffolding provides opportunities to respond with corrective feedback, allows for goal setting and performance monitoring, builds essential vocabulary, and is motivating. One approach to writing intervention that contains almost all of these elements is the self-regulated strategy development approach (Mason et al., 2011), including explicit instruction (Archer & Hughes, 2011), which can be used with many aspects of writing instruction across the grade levels.

REFERENCES

Access Center. (2013). *Accessing skills toward successful writing development*. Washington, DC: American Institutes for Research. Retrieved from http://www.k8accesscenter.org/training_resources/documents/WRITINGBRIEFPDF.pdf

Amato, J. M., & Watkins, M. W. (2011). The predictive validity of CBM writing indices for eighth-grade students. *The Journal of Special Education, 44*, 195–204. doi:10.1177/0022466909333516

Archer, A. L., Gleason, M. M., & Isaacson, S. (2008). *REWARDS Writing: Sentence refinement*. Longmont, CO: Sopris West.

Archer, A. L., & Hughes, C. A. (2011). *Explicit instruction: Effective and efficient teaching (What works for special-needs learners)*. New York, NY: Guilford Press.

Arter, J. A., McTighe, J., & Guskey, T. R. (2001). *Scoring rubrics in the classroom: Using performance criteria for assessing and improving student performance*. Newbury Park, CA: SAGE.

Berninger, V., & Amtmann, D. (2003). Preventing written expression disabilities through early and continuing assessment and intervention for handwriting and/or spelling problems: Research into practice. In H. Swanson, K. Harris, & S. Graham (Eds.), *Handbook of research on learning disabilities*. New York, NY: Guilford Press.

Coker, D. L., & Ritchey, K. D. (2010). Curriculum-based measurement of writing in kindergarten and first grade: An investigation of production and qualitative scores. *Exceptional Children, 76*, 175–193.

Culham, R. (2005). *6 + 1 Traits of Writing: The complete guide for the primary grades*. New York, NY: Scholastic Teaching Resources.

Deno, S. L., Espin, C. A., & Fuchs, L. S. (2002). Evaluation strategies for preventing and remediating basic skills deficits. In M. Shinn, G. Stoner, & H. Walker (Eds.), *Interventions for academic and behavior problems II: Preventive and remedial approaches* (pp. 213–241). Bethesda, MD: National Association of School Psychologists.

Division for Learning Disabilities. (2009). Self-Regulated Strategy Development (SRSD) for Writing. *Go For It, 17*, 1–4.

Espin, C., Shin, J., Deno, S., Skare, S., Robinson, S., & Benner, B. (2000). Identifying indicators of written expression proficiency for middle school students. *The Journal of Special Education, 34*, 140–153. doi:10.1177/002246690003400303

Espin, C., Wallace, T., Campbell, H., Lembke, E. S., Long, J. D., & Ticha, R. (2008). Curriculum-based measurement in writing: Predicting the success of high-school students on state standards tests. *Exceptional Children, 74*, 174–193.

Gansle, K. A., Noell, G. H., VanDerHeyden, A. M., Naquin, G. M., & Slider, N. J. (2002). Moving beyond total words written: The reliability, criterion validity, and time cost of alternative measures for curriculum-based measurement in writing. *School Psychology Review, 31*, 477–497.

Gansle, K., VanDerHeyden, A., Noell, G., Resetar, J., & Williams, K. (2006). The technical adequacy of curriculum-based and rating-based measures of written expression for elementary students. *School Psychology Review, 35*, 435–450.

Graham, S., & Harris, K. R. (2000). The road less traveled: Prevention and intervention in written language. In K. Butler & E. Silliman (Eds.), *The language learning disabilities continuum: Integration of research, technology, and education*. Mahwah, NJ: Erlbaum.

Graham, S., & Harris, K. R. (2002). Prevention and intervention for struggling writers. In M. Shinn, G. Stoner, & H. Walker (Eds.), *Interventions for academic and behavior problems II: Preventive and remedial approaches* (pp. 589–610). Bethesda, MD: National Association of School Psychologists.

Graham, S., & Harris, K. R. (2005). Improving the writing performance of young struggling writers: Theoretical and programmatic research from the Center on Accelerating Student Learning. *The Journal of Special Education, 39*, 19–33. doi:10.1177/00224669050390010301

Graham, S., Harris, K. R., & Troia, G. A. (1998). Writing and self-regulation: Cases from the self-regulated strategy development model. In D. H. Schunk & B. J. Zimmerman (Eds.), *Self-regulated learning: From teaching to self-reflective practice* (pp. 20–41). New York, NY: Guilford Press.

Graham, S., McKeown, D., Kiuhara, S., & Harris, K. R. (2012). A meta-analysis of writing instruction for students in the elementary grades. *Journal of Educational Psychology, 104*, 879–896. doi:10.1037/a0029185

Graham, S., & Perin, D. (2007). *Writing next: Effective strategies to improve writing of adolescents in middle and high schools: A report to Carnegie Corporation of New York*. Washington, DC: Alliance for Excellent Education.

Harris, K. R., & Graham, S. (1996). *Making the writing process work: Strategies for composition and self-regulation*. Cambridge, MA: Brookline Books.

Harris, K. R., Graham, S., Mason, L., & Friedlander, B. (2007). *Powerful writing strategies for all students*. Baltimore, MD: Brookes.

Hooper, S. R., Roberts, J. E., Nelson, L., Zeisel, S., & Fannin, D. K. (2010). Preschool predictors of narrative writing skills in elementary school children. *School Psychology Quarterly, 25*, 1–12. doi:10.1037/a0018329

Howell, K. W., & Nolet, V. (2000). *Curriculum-based evaluation* (3rd ed.). Belmont, CA: Wadsworth/Thomson Learning.

Jewell, J., & Malecki, C. K. (2005). The utility of CBM written language indices: An investigation of production-dependent, production-independent, and accurate-production scores. *School Psychology Review, 34*, 27–44.

Kiuhara, S. A., Graham, S., & Hawken, L. S. (2009). Teaching writing to high school students: A national survey. *Journal of Educational Psychology, 101*, 136–160. doi:10.1037/a0013097

Lembke, E., Deno, S., & Hall, K. (2003). Identifying an indicator of growth in early writing proficiency for elementary school students. *Assessment for Effective Intervention, 28*, 23–35. doi:10.1177/073724770302800304

Malecki, C. K., & Jewell, J. (2003). Developmental, gender, and practical considerations in scoring curriculum-based measurement writing probes. *Psychology in the Schools, 40*, 379–390. doi:10.1002/pits.10096

Mason, L. H., Harris, K. R., & Graham, S. (2011). Self-regulated strategy development for students with writing difficulties. *Theory Into Practice, 50*, 20–27. doi:10.1080/00405841.2011.534922

McMaster, K. L., & Campbell, H. (2008). New and existing curriculum-based writing measures: Technical features within and across grades. *School Psychology Review, 37*, 550–556.

McMaster, K. L., Du, X., & Petursdottir, A. (2009). Technical features of curriculum-based measures for beginning writers. *Journal of Learning Disabilities, 42*, 41–60. doi:10.1177/0022219408326212

McMaster, K. L., Du, X., Seungsoo, Y., Deno, S. L., Parker, D., & Ellis, T. (2011). Curriculum-based measures of beginning writing: Technical features of the slope. *Exceptional Children, 77*, 185–206.

McMaster, K., & Espin, C. (2007). Technical features of curriculum-based measurement in writing: A literature review. *The Journal of Special Education, 41*, 68–84. doi:10.1177/00224669070410020301

McNaughton, D., Hughes, C., & Ofiesh, N. (1997). Proofreading for students with learning disabilities: Integrating computer and strategy use. *Learning Disabilities Research & Practice, 12*, 16–28.

Mirken, P. K., Deno, S. L., Fuchs, L. S., Wesson, C., Tindal, G., Marston, D., & Kuehnle, K. (1981). *Procedures to develop and monitor progress on IEP goals*. Minneapolis, MN: Institute for Research on Learning Disabilities.

National Assessment of Educational Progress. (2012). *The nation's report card: Writing 2011*. Washington, DC: Author. Retrieved from http://nces.ed.gov/nationsreportcard/pdf/main2011/2012470.pdf

National Association of School Psychologists. (2010). *Model for comprehensive and integrated school psychological services*. Bethesda, MD: Author. Retrieved from http://www.nasponline.org/standards/2010standards/2_PracticeModel.pdf

Northwest Regional Educational Laboratory. (2007). *6 + 1 Trait Writing*. Portland, OR: Author. Retrieved from http://educationnorthwest.org/traits

Oas, B. K., Schumaker, J. A., & Deshler, D. D. (1995). *Learning strategies: Tools for learning to learn in middle and high schools. Secondary education and beyond: Providing opportunities for students with learning disabilities*. Pittsburgh, PA: Learning Disabilities Association of America.

Petersen-Brown, S., & Burns, M. K. (2011). Adding a vocabulary component to incremental rehearsal to enhance maintenance and generalization. *School Psychology Quarterly, 6*, 245–255.

Rogers, L. A., & Graham, S. (2008). A meta-analysis of single subject design writing intervention research. *Journal of Educational Psychology, 100*, 879–906. doi:10.1037/0022-0663.100.4.879

Salvia, J., Ysseldyke, J., & Bolt, S. (2009). *Assessment: In special and inclusive education* (11th ed.). Belmont, CA: Wadsworth.

Shinn, M. R. (Ed.). (1989). *Curriculum-based measurement: Assessing special children.* New York, NY: Guilford Press.

Spandel, V. (2009). *Creating writers through 6-Trait Writing assessment and instruction* (5th ed.). Boston, MA: Pearson Education.

Stiggins, R. J. (1982). A comparison of direct and indirect writing assessment methods. *Research in the Teaching of English, 16,* 101–114.

Tindal, G., & Hasbrouck, J. (1991). Analyzing student writing to develop instruction strategies. *Learning Disabilities Research & Practice, 6,* 237–245.

Videen, J., Deno, S., & Marston, D. (1982). *Correct word sequences: A valid indicator of proficiency in written expression* (Research Report 84). Minneapolis, MN: Institute for Research on Learning Disabilities.. doi:10.1177/00224669050380040201

Wong, B., & Berninger, V. (2004). Cognitive processes of teachers in implementing composition research in elementary, middle, and high school classrooms. In B. Shulman, K. Apel, B. Ehren, E. Silliman, & A. Stone (Eds.), *Handbook of language and literacy development and disorders* (pp. 600–624). New York, NY: Guilford Press.

13 Best Practices in Instructional Assessment of Writing

Todd A. Gravois
ICAT Resources, Inc.
Deborah Nelson
Bowie State University

OVERVIEW

With the introduction of Common Core State Standards, the continued emphasis on response to intervention (the 2004 Individuals with Disabilities Education Improvement Act), and state assessment results that are increasingly linked to classroom instruction, teachers are more than ever being called upon to effectively manage a diversity of learners with a variety of skill needs. In recognition of the amount of resources and support needed to accomplish prevailing instructional expectations, school psychologists who traditionally provide direct interventions to students outside of the classroom setting are now being charged with assisting teachers in assessing and intervening in the classroom to support the delivery of effective instruction (i.e., Tier 1). The Data-Based Decision Making and Accountability domain of the National Association of School Psychologists (NASP) *Model for Comprehensive and Integrated School Psychological Services* (NASP, 2010) reinforces the need to identify formative and summative assessment practices as a cornerstone of best practice for school psychologists. Further, school psychologists must recognize the related domain of Consultation and Collaboration if the intention is to work hand in hand with teachers to develop instructional strategies and interventions that support increased student outcomes, especially in the area of writing.

The concerns teachers face in teaching and improving students' writing performance are significant. The report of the National Assessment of Educational Progress indicated that only approximately 24% of eighth graders were considered proficient in the area of writing (National Center for Education Statistics, 2011). Given the prevalence of writing concerns, school psychologists will undoubtedly be approached by a classroom teacher, either individually or as part of a larger school-based problem-solving team, to consult and collaborate on ways to assess, identify, and intervene around a writing concern in a way that maximizes the use of data for instructional decision making.

However, the area of writing presents a challenge for teachers and for those school psychologists offering support in these situations. Since a student's writing represents a permanent product, teachers will often narrowly focus on assessing the writing product itself with a goal of gathering data solely to compare one student's performance to another. Issues such as production, fluency (e.g., correct words per minute), or accuracy (e.g., spelling, punctuation) will often become the primary focus since these areas are readily measured and can easily be compared to curricula or instructional expectations. Unfortunately, this narrow view of writing assessment neglects the interrelatedness with prerequisite reading skills that are thought to improve development of higher order, critical thinking skills, and writing itself.

Current national efforts to improve instruction and increase students' development of critical thinking skills recognize writing as a vehicle for promoting and conveying reading skills, particularly with older students (Calkins, Ehrenworth, & Lehman, 2012). The Common Core State Standards explain that all types of writing assume a level of reading skill, either for the prior knowledge needed for a writing task or in the reading skills needed to gain the content required to complete

203

the writing task. As Common Core State Standards become more embedded within the educational setting, school psychologists will be faced with the challenge of assisting an increasing number of teachers in effectively assessing and deciphering the interconnected reading and writing skills.

Further, the task of supporting improved writing performance is made more difficult by the fact that many teachers who provide instruction, especially in content areas, may not feel adequately prepared to teach writing (Graham & Harris, 2009). For example, Graham and Harris noted in a national study that those high school teachers surveyed rarely asked students to complete multiple paragraph assignments and that most writing activities were centered on short responses, completing worksheets, and making lists. They further found that writing instruction is not always delivered consistently within or across school settings nor is writing instruction always as structured by formal curricula such as with reading. When coupled with the fact that students have fewer opportunities to write and receive feedback on their writing, it is no surprise that writing concerns often appear to be complex. When hastily assessed, the result is inaccurate identification of the concern and application of less effective inerventions.

Role and Purposes of Instructional Assessment

School psychologists are faced with many choices when selecting and employing assessment techniques. Over the past 4 decades, different curriculum-based techniques have evolved as alternatives to traditional norm-referenced, standardized assessments. Techniques such as curriculum-based measurement, curriculum-based evaluation, and instructional assessment (IA) are cited in the school psychology literature as assessments that utilize curricular material to gather data about student performance. While there are similarities among the various forms of curriculum-based techniques, there are important differences in role and purpose that have been thoroughly delineated in the literature (e.g., Shapiro & Elliott, 1999; Shinn, Rosenfield, & Knutson, 1989).

The noted differences in curriculum-based techniques extend to the assessment of writing. As depicted in Table 13.1, a variety of curriculum-based techniques have been applied to the assessment of writing, each purporting different processes and foci. For example, Hasbrouck, Tindel, and Parker (1994) applied curric-

ulum-based measurement techniques to assessing writing where the use of 3-minute writing samples allowed consistent monitoring of students' progress in writing. Robinson and Howell (2008) applied curriculum-based evaluation techniques to the assessment of writing with a focus on evaluating students' performance with a goal to identify and ultimately intervene across multiple dimensions of writing. Both techniques focus on gathering data related to particular areas of writing to monitor students' progress and alert teachers to the need to vary or alter instructional programming.

Gickling and colleagues (Gravois, Gickling, & Rosenfield, 2011) have stated that instructional assessment has as its goal the gathering of assessment data for the purpose of explicitly guiding instruction and creating "the type of optimum learning conditions that are consistent with the effective teaching literature" (Gickling, Shane, & Croskery, 1989, p. 344). Hence, the first focus of IA is on using assessment for the purpose of ensuring high-quality instructional practices, after which student progress can be effectively monitored, charted, and evaluated.

Another important distinction between IA and other curriculum-based techniques is the explicit connection between reading and writing within the assessment process. Often reading and writing are treated separately in the assessment process, much like the two are treated separately in the teaching process. However, in the IA process, the assessment of students' reading performance is critical to the effective identification and analysis of presenting problems given the interwoven nature of students' reading and writing performance.

It is not possible, nor is it the intention of this chapter, to provide a detailed comparison between the various curriculum-based techniques. The point is to emphasize that each technique asserts different purposes. It is therefore the responsibility of school psychologists to distinguish between the purposes and match the appropriate assessment to the appropriate situation. The purpose of this chapter is to support school psychologists' use of IA when consulting and collaborating with classroom teachers around writing concerns in an effort to facilitate data-based decision making. This is especially important when working to support Tier 1 instructional practices (e.g., Saddler & Asaro-Saddler, 2013). The IA framework, when applied with fidelity, can be used to accurately identify and assess student skills that contribute to writing concerns and more effectively analyze the relationship among the areas of reading and writing.

Table 13.1. Curriculum-Based Techniques for Assessing Writing Concerns

Curriculum-Based Writing Assessment Technique	Major Developer	General Description	Area of Focus	Uses Curriculum Material	Instructional Level Defined	Application With Elementary and Secondary Level	Reading/Writing Relationship Assessed
Curriculum-based evaluation	Robinson & Howell (2008)	Problem-solving process; RIOT recommended; general outcome measure collection using 3-minute writing in response to prompt using a standard approach	• Writing fluency (amount of text) • Legibility (readability, handwriting) • Conventions (spelling, capitalization, punctuation) • Syntactic maturity (varied sentence lengths and types) • Semantic maturity (variety of words and vocabulary used) • Content (organization, style, cohesion) • Writing process (plans ahead, moves between stages)	Yes	No	Yes	No
Curriculum-based measurement	Hasbrouck et al. (1994)	3-minute collection using a standard approach	• Number of legible words • Total number of words written • Percentage of legible words • Correctly spelled words • Number of correct word sequences • Mean length of correct word sequences	Yes	No	Yes	No
Instructional assessment	Gravois, Gickling, & Rosenfield (2011)	Problem-solving process focusing on writing instruction and task expectations in collaboration with classroom teacher; focus on reading/writing relationship with emphasis on oral responding and student metacognitive processes with regard to writing	• Oral responding • Prior knowledge/language • Type (genre) • Written expression • Use/mechanics • Structure • Penmanship	Yes	Yes	Yes	Yes

Note. RIOT = review, interview, observe, test.

BASIC CONSIDERATIONS

Although assessment and instruction often address reading and writing as if they are two separate concerns, research results demonstrate a clear relationship between the two (e.g., Abbott, Berninger, & Fayol, 2010; Anderson & Briggs, 2011; Nelson, 2013; Fitzgerald & Shanahan, 2000). Further, Common Core State Standards discuss the need to link the assessment of writing to reading (Calkins et al., 2012). This connection is implied in the strategic alignment of the key standards so that the progression of students' reading development encapsulates the critical analysis of other authors' works. For example, Common Core State Standards four through six focus on having the student analyze the craft and structure of the authored text, and evaluate the choices made by the author in terms of vocabulary, sentence structure, and detail. More explicitly, Common Core State Standards discuss the need to assess a student's reading performance when the writing task relies on understanding of content that itself was derived from reading. This complexity of the reading and writing instruction requires an integrated assessment framework that recognizes how these two sets of skills interact in classroom-related tasks and how they have an impact on students' skill performance.

Research Relating Reading and Writing

In a review of the literature, correlations have been found among several specific components of reading and writing (Abbott et al., 2010; Nelson, 2013; Shanahan, 1984). These include the relationship between spelling and decoding, between writing performance and reading vocabulary, and between reading comprehension and writing structure and organization. Further, the acquisition of certain writing skills (e.g., planning, organization, grammar and usage, sentence and paragraph construction, and editing) have been linked to the content quality of written language products (e.g., Graham, McKeown, Kiuhara, & Harris, 2012; Rogers & Graham, 2008).

Role of Oral Responding in Writing Performance

While the Common Core State Standards also include an alignment between the standards of speaking, listening, and writing, there is limited research that supports the connection of a student's oral language with his or her writing performance. Nelson (2013) did find such a connection. In that study, students were found to use several critical oral language skills when generating a written response. In an analysis of the reading and writing performance of 105 intermediate elementary school students, results reaffirmed that the base skills of reading fluency, reading accuracy, writing fluency, spelling, grammar, mechanics, and sentence structure were related to the ability to generate an effective written response. However, an additional important finding was the unique relationship between oral responding and writing performance (Figure 13.1).

Oral responding, defined as the ability of students to provide a verbal response indicating understanding after reading an instructional-level passage, was identified as an essential skill in writing tasks that required students to

Figure 13.1. Link Between Reading, Oral Responding, and Writing

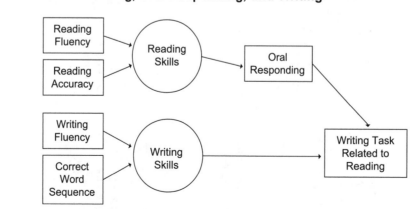

Note. Based on information from Nelson (2013).

National Association of School Psychologists

respond in writing about what was read. When analyzing writing and reading samples taken from the students, the ability to provide an oral response represented the pivotal skill in being able to generate a well-structured, organized written response indicating understanding of what was read.

To further elaborate this connection between reading and writing, if a student reads a passage of text and has difficulty generating a verbal response that would indicate an understanding at the oral level, then there is an increased likelihood that he or she will have difficulty putting that response into a cohesive and structured piece of writing. When this occurs, the teacher and school psychologist will need to collect data on the student's reading skills in order to understand the underlying reading skills required for the writing. Without doing so, the reading difficulty will be masked within the written product (e.g., it appears as if the student has difficulty writing), and writing interventions developed may not address the correct skill needs because the incorrect skill need was prioritized. On the other hand, if a student has difficulty generating a written product that does not require reading, then the need may be related to those skills pertinent to generating a written response (i.e., sentence structure, organization, spelling, mechanics). In this instance, data collection, goals, and instruction will more likely address skills of writing.

Instructional Match

As a pioneer in describing and researching the concept of instructional match, Gickling has provided a succinct review of the literature that assists in operationalizing what has now become a generally accepted and cited concept (Gickling & Havertape, 1981). The concept of instructional match refers to the existence of appropriate challenge between the salient variables that influence learning, that is, the student, instruction, and the learning task (Bloom, 1976). Creating the match remains the ultimate outcome if learning is to occur. Organizing instructional objectives and curricula materials requires an accurate assessment of the student's prior knowledge and entry skills and then strategic alignment of the instructional objectives along with the demands of the tasks. Central to this alignment is the systematic and careful introduction of appropriate challenge with regard to the instruction and task demands, that is, challenge that is not too difficult or too easy.

Appropriate Challenge

Challenge represents the point at which the curricula tasks and instructional objectives demand new and varied learning from the student. Appropriate challenge represents the point at which the new and varied learning is not so difficult as to create frustration or so easy as to illicit boredom (Poehner, 2011; Rosenfield, Gravois, & Silva, 2014; Treptow, 2006; Vygotsky, 1978). The accurate assessment of a student's prior knowledge is the foundation for determining appropriate challenge. Prior knowledge refers to the skills and experiences that a student possesses and reflects the content skills and mental schemas the student uses to connect new learning to existing knowledge (Shanahan, Fisher, & Frey, 2012).

Unfortunately, it is often difficult for teachers to determine what constitutes an appropriate level of challenge. This difficulty occurs for many reasons, including the recognition that teachers are expected to manage challenge levels for multiple students across subjects and time. However, it is also often difficult for teachers to accurately assess a student's entry skills, especially when such skills are interdependent, as in the instance of a student being asked to write in response to something he or she has read.

Challenge is contextual and is related to the type of instruction or tasks that are being presented to the student at a point in time. When the central focus is for students to read connected text, appropriate challenge is considered the point where students can accurately pronounce and identify the meaning of 93–97% of the vocabulary by sight without having to decode (Betts, 1946; Cramer & Rosenfield, 2008). When the tasks involve the practice of discrete skills (e.g., learning letters, sounds, sight words, math facts), research has found that teachers who manage the amount of challenge at a general ratio of approximately 80% known content to 20% unknown content, students are consistently able to increase the retention needed to demonstrate elevated levels of performance (MacQuarrie, Tucker, Burns, & Hartman, 2002).

Appropriate challenge can also be defined relative to the amount of new information presented during instruction as it relates to a student's working memory. Working memory refers to the capacity of individuals to attend to and manipulate new information prior to storing it in long-term memory (O'Neil & Abedi, 1996). Several characteristics, or limitations, of working memory have a direct impact on a student's ability to process information. These include (a) a limited capacity that gradually increases with age, (b) a need for rehearsal and repetition, and (c) a shutdown feature when overloaded. Violation of any of these characteristics not only has an adverse impact on the student's ability to learn and retain new information, but also contributes to partial and fragmented learning.

Origin of Challenge in Writing

When the focus is reading, the origin of challenge is largely defined as the relationship between the student's entry skills (i.e., prior knowledge) and the demands of the reading passage. Reading passages present challenge in the form of the amount and type of vocabulary, concepts, and language structure present in the reading task as they relate to the specific prerequisite skills the student brings to the situation. As such, in traditional assessment techniques (i.e., psychoeducational assessments, progress monitoring), assessment of reading focuses more on a student's interaction with the task (e.g., how fluently he or she reads the task, what he or she does when encountering an unknown word, how well he or she understands the concepts embedded in the task).

However, when writing is the area of concern, the conceptual origin of challenge shifts from the task (e.g., the reading passage) to the teacher's instructional objectives. Challenge in writing is created when the teacher communicates the type of writing expected, the audience to write for, the expected structure, and the topics that students are to write about. Depending upon the students' prerequisite skills, these objectives can be within their comfort zone or out of reach of their existing skills. Literally, the initial task of writing is a blank page that presents no challenge itself. It is not until (and how) the teacher articulates the expectations and performance objectives to the student through instruction that challenge is created.

This shift in origin of challenge being driven by the teacher, as opposed to the reading task, requires a different format, structure, and purpose of assessment when the area of concern is writing. More specifically, the focus of writing assessment becomes an equal understanding of the teacher's instructional objectives and how these are derived and communicated as much as the students' prior knowledge and entry skills to engage in writing. It demands a dialogue with the teacher to gain an understanding of the underlying concepts of an instructional match as it relates to writing (e.g., how the teacher determines how much new information will be expected from the student for the writing task). It also demands a conversation about the teacher's understanding of any prerequisite reading

required to produce the writing. All of these considerations—relationship between reading and writing, the importance of a student's oral responding, understanding of the concept of an instructional match, and the teacher's role in creating appropriate challenge—require a closer collaboration and consultation between the teacher and school psychologist when conducting instructional assessment of writing in order to maximize data-based decision making.

BEST PRACTICES IN INSTRUCTIONAL ASSESSMENT OF WRITING

IA, with its direct alignment to school curricula and the delivery of instruction, provides added value to the assessment of writing tasks, especially those that rely heavily on responding to reading texts (Gravois et al., 2011). Having access to the curricula materials that teachers are most familiar with, and from which instruction can be planned, increases the probability that school psychologists can effectively consult with teachers in a way that will result in goals and objectives aligned with the curriculum that will increase the quality of instruction and result in improved student achievement.

School psychologists should keep in mind that when considering assessment of writing, variation in student performance results from two sources. First, if writing performance requires reading and understanding a passage, then the student's ability to write will be directly affected by his or her ability to accurately read the identified passage and orally respond. In this way, difficulties with reading often manifest as difficulties with writing.

A second variation in a student's writing performance will occur if instructionally matched conditions are not present during the assessment process itself. If the school psychologist fails to create appropriate challenge during the assessment (i.e., not too difficult, not too easy), then the student will not be able to produce his or her best performance in writing. The school psychologist is required to understand where and how the challenge is created in a writing task and then manage that challenge during the assessment process itself.

Writing Dimensions

Figure 13.2 presents the dimensions of writing, and Table 13.2 summarizes each dimension. As depicted, the overarching dimensions of writing focus on students being able to convey purposefully their ideas relative to

Figure 13.2. Writing Dimensions

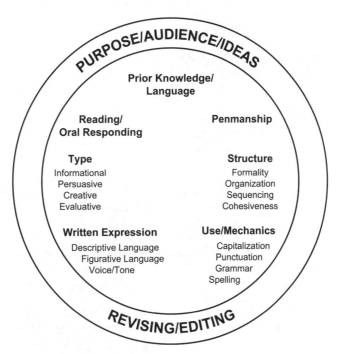

specific audiences. Likewise, proficient writing requires editing and revision as an ongoing and reflective process. Within these outer circles are the other critical dimensions that when orchestrated well represent the hallmark of good writers. These include the ability to legibly present writing so that others can read it and to structure the writing at the sentence, paragraph, and task levels. In addition, the dimensions include the ability to use appropriate spelling conventions, punctuation, and capitalization to promote better communication of the ideas that are being expressed. However, these more mechanical dimensions must interact with the ability to use expressive language and voice in a way that engages the audience to want to read the ideas. The student's ability to apply these dimensions across a series of types of writing (e.g., genres) enhances the capacity to write for different purposes and audiences. Finally, and as has been stressed throughout, the student's oral responding and reading skills represent a critical dimension of writing. Reading itself has been broken down to its own dimensions, and the reader is encouraged to revisit Gravois and Gickling (2008) as a precursor to engaging in a writing assessment.

Concept of Instructional Level in Writing

A key task of IA in writing is to identify the optimal conditions needed for writing instruction by answering five key assessment questions: (a) What does the student

know? (b) What can the student do? (c) How does the student think? (d) How does the student approach tasks that he or she is unsure of? (e) What does the teacher do?

Establishing instructional level in the writing process has a different starting point than establishing instructional level in a reading passage. In reading, instructional-level conditions are determined by the percentage of known words and unknown words in a passage and can be calculated by the school psychologist to determine whether a student can read a passage comfortably to enhance comprehension (i.e., 93–97% known). However, with writing, instructional level is established and maintained by the school psychologist, who reviews previous writing samples or constructs new writing tasks. The task can take a similar format as a classroom task that may be causing the student difficulty and require the same prerequisite skills and knowledge. Further, the task should be constructed to highlight student skill strengths and needs in a way that honors working memory and provides an appropriate level of challenge. In this respect, the school psychologist must ensure that the writing skills observed during the assessment are an accurate reflection of the student's skills and not a reflection of a misunderstanding of the task or the student being overwhelmed by the challenge inherent in the task.

In cases where the writing task is linked to reading, the concepts of instructional level must apply to both the

Table 13.2. Essential Questions Related to Writing Dimensions

Essential Dimensions	Essential Questions
Prior knowledge/language:	
Background experiences and content knowledge of concepts and topics that give meaning to a written product	Does the student have adequate language and background to convey understanding of the writing topic?
Reading/oral responding	
The ability to convey an oral understanding of what has been heard or read as a precursor to conveying written understanding	Can the student provide an oral understanding of what has been heard or read before writing?
Type	
The ability to produce the type of writing required by a task, such as persuasive, creative, technical	Does the student possess a knowledge of the type of writing required by the task?
Written expression	
The ability to use descriptive and figurative language in a way that gives voice to the written product	Can the student use adjectives, adverbs, and other vocabulary to portray a unique perspective as an author?
Use/mechanics	
The ability to convey appropriate grammar, usage, spelling, punctuation, and other language conventions in writing	Can the student generate a written product that demonstrates adequate knowledge of spelling, grammar, punctuation, etc.?
Structure	
The ability to produce a writing that addresses the topic in a logical and cohesive way	Can the student generate a written product that is sequential, is organized, flows, and makes sense?
Penmanship	
The ability to form legible letters to increase the readability of a writing product	Can the student form print or cursive letters so that the reader can decipher the writing?
Revising/editing	
The ability to improve the content quality of a writing product by addressing the usage and mechanics (editing) or by addressing the content (revising)	Does the student use specific strategies to change his or her writing to enhance readability and understanding?

reading task and the writing task used in the assessment. For this reason, the writing assessment begins with an assessment of the student's reading skills under instructional level conditions. Observing reading performance under instructional level conditions allows the school psychologist to make a determination about the student's oral responding as a precursor to assessing additional writing skills.

IA Writing Snapshot

Each interaction between the school psychologist, teacher, and student offers an opportunity to gather data related to the multiple dimensions required for successful writing (see Figure 13.1). These interactions, called IA snapshots, allow the school psychologist and teacher to identify, analyze, and ultimately prioritize areas of concern that will lead to targeted instructional

planning and monitoring. A conversation with the teacher about existing work samples represents the starting point of the snapshot. As the teacher and school psychologist gather information about the student's entry skills and prior knowledge, they can review additional work and sample the student's performance by having him or her write. During each step, the school psychologist plays an important role in helping to maintain instructional level conditions and support the teacher in continuing to make connections between the interrelated areas of writing and reading.

Step 1: Select Writing Samples

Collaboration with the teacher is an essential first step in the IA process. This collaboration allows for both the school psychologist and the teacher to develop a common picture of the student's skills. A variety of writing samples should be selected, representing a range of tasks, types of writing, and skill demands upon the student.

The reading and writing dimensions serve as a useful guide for the discussion between the teacher and school psychologist. Because of the importance of reading skills in writing tasks, and since many teachers may not be familiar with the connection between the two, it is recommended that the conversation start with the review of the reading domains (see Gravois & Gickling, 2008). In our experience, while teachers may not be familiar with this connection between reading and writing assessment, they are familiar with the instructional link, and an explanation that encompasses this viewpoint can often be effective.

Step 2: Review Writing Samples

While reviewing the writing samples, the conversation should remain focused on what the student knows and can do related to the reading and writing dimensions. It is often easy to point out all of the errors a student has made or the ways a student could improve writing. However, the first step of an IA is to help the teacher gather data on a student's prior knowledge. The school psychologist plays an important role by keeping this initial conversation focused on the critical IA questions related to each dimension. For example, the school psychologist can frame the following questions: "As we look at this piece of writing, what can the student do in terms of their word choice and descriptive language? What does this piece of writing tell us about what the student knows about the topic?"

It is not unusual for teachers to quickly revert to describing all of the areas that a student needs to improve or areas in which the student is not demonstrating curricula expectations. While it is important to know the student is not meeting grade-level expectations, such observations are less helpful in understanding where instruction should focus and how instruction should be delivered. By focusing on what a student knows and can do and understanding a student's prior knowledge and skills, the teacher and school psychologist are establishing the foundation for creating instructional level conditions later in the assessment process.

A chart categorizing what a student knows and needs is useful to organize this step of the IA process. This chart reflects the student's skills in both reading and writing. Areas observed to be things the student knows or can do are recorded and areas that require additional observation or assessment are listed as questions. Recognizing that multiple skills are required for writing,

the school psychologist and teacher should clarify or identify any writing domains—including reading—that are not represented in the samples being reviewed and make plans to review additional work or collect additional samples. As additional work samples are reviewed, a list of known skills and areas requiring additional assessment (i.e., questions) is generated and charted. This charting process has been found to be extremely helpful in systematically categorizing skills so as not to confuse or overwhelm the assessment process or the teacher.

Assessment decision 1: Is there sufficient information to adequately assess each dimension? The answer to this first decision question has implications for the identified priority, the teacher's delivery of instruction, and instructional goal setting. A misidentified or hastily identified concern can lead to a misaligned intervention. As a result, the school psychologist and teacher are cautioned to think carefully about whether the review of work samples is sufficient to gain a full picture of the student's performance as it relates to all writing dimensions, including reading and oral responding. In our experience, it is rare that these initial sample reviews provide all of the necessary information. However, teachers often feel pressure to make a decision, and it is the school psychologist's role to help see that additional data are needed to gain a full understanding of the student's skills across all dimensions of writing.

Step 3: Conduct Additional Sampling to Answer Outstanding Questions

The chart developed in Step 2 is used as a guide for additional assessment. With this guide, the school psychologist and teacher can begin to focus on outstanding questions and to gather additional data to verify needs that may not have been apparent in the initially reviewed writing samples or which may not have been obtained under instructional-level conditions (i.e., the task was too difficult for the student).

Unlike other typical writing assessments, the next step in the IA in writing is to conduct an assessment of reading in order to analyze the student's reading and oral responding under instructional level reading conditions (see Gravois & Gickling, 2008). An IA in reading will provide the school psychologist and teacher with data on the student's ability to make meaning of connected text without the barrier of writing. The IA reading assessment yields more information about the student's instructional level and performance in the critical reading dimensions. This portion of the assessment gathers the necessary information to decipher whether the student's writing difficulty may result from a reading skill difficulty (e.g., fluency, word recognition, oral responding). The inclusion of IA of reading also helps the teacher to make a direct connection between the student's reading and writing performance and, more important, helps the teacher see opportunities for instruction that complements both.

As the school psychologist and teacher sample the student's writing performance, the goal is to establish and maintain a comfort zone for the student by structuring a writing task that builds upon identified prior knowledge. The advantage of building upon the results of the reading assessment is that it allows the student to move comfortably from oral responding into written responding. For example, the school psychologist can have the student write his or her oral response or can have the student generate a written response to a teacher-generated question related to the reading. These two options mirror classroom tasks and maintain a comfort level for both the student and teacher. Likewise, the school psychologist can scribe for the student, recording the student's oral response into written work as a way to demonstrate how the student's oral language can become a written product.

Throughout this sampling, the school psychologist and teacher always attempt to build from what the student knows and can do as they gather data about other dimensions of writing. A primary goal of the IA in writing is to be able to observe and speak with the student as the student approaches a writing task. As such, it is important to sample writing in a way that allows the student to discuss his or her view of writing and of the writing task being presented. The student's explanations will vary based upon the understanding of the task, the writing process, and his or her own metacognition.

The student's performance will be influenced by exposure to appropriate challenge during previous writing instruction. If the student has been exposed to writing tasks that are too difficult, or that require skills that he or she has not been exposed to, then the student's responses will reflect this. As a result, the sampling used for the IA in writing should be designed to ensure a high chance of success by focusing on what the student knows and can do based upon previous samples and the IA in reading. The school psychologist and teacher should continue to share positive features of the student's writing specific to various writing dimensions. This feedback serves to build metacognition for students who have difficulty with writing, since they often only receive corrective feedback and are not explicitly aware of what they do well.

However, even with these efforts to maintain a comfort zone for the student during the assessment process, it is not uncommon for a student to be anxious at the thought of writing and to become tense or overwhelmed. Likewise, depending on the age of the student and the supports in place for writing in the classroom, the student may have produced only a few writing samples independently or may not know how to independently approach a writing task. Once again, the goal is to observe how the student approaches the task. The school psychologist should focus on talking through the task with the student (i.e., "What would you do first if you saw this writing activity?" "What comes next?"). An option when students are unfamiliar or overwhelmed with the actual writing is for the school psychologist to scribe while the student dictates in order to ascertain how the student would respond at the oral level with regard to the task. This maintains the student's comfort and makes explicit the connection between oral and written responding for the teacher.

The student can be asked to write and generate samples for additional assessment data to continue answering the questions generated on the original Knows, Needs, and Questions chart. Each sampling of writing should be prefaced by an explanation of what is being asked of the student and should request that the student take time to think about the task before writing. In order to present a full picture of the student's own metacognition as it relates to organizing and planning for writing, no specific graphic organizer or chart should be provided, but the student should be encouraged to take notes or jot down ideas if he or she wishes. Once finished, the student should be asked to read what he or she has written (this helps in instances where the student may have illegible handwriting) and to review the writing and make any changes (i.e., revise and edit).

The sampling step of IA is recursive and flexible. It is guided by the ability of the school psychologist and teacher to gather sufficient data to explore all of the writing dimensions. Multiple writing samples can be taken at different points in time tapping different dimensions in order to continue to answer questions listed on the Knows, Needs, and Questions chart.

Assessment decision 2: Which reading/writing dimensions need instructional support? Within the selected dimension, what will be the specific 80/20 rule for instruction? After data have been collected on the student's reading and writing skills and the relationship between those skills analyzed to determine strengths and needs, the school psychologist and teacher can begin prioritizing the appropriate concern.

As implied throughout this chapter, it is not unusual for the school psychologist and teacher to prioritize a reading concern even when the original concern was in writing. This setting of priorities is done with the understanding that the ultimate goal remains to improve the student's writing performance. That is, as skills are developed in the reading area, these will support and ultimately be applied to writing tasks. In this way, the reading skills and the accompanying writing skills can be addressed simultaneously.

When the priority concern is a specific writing dimension, the second need is to maintain an appropriate challenge during writing instruction. Without considering instructional-level conditions, a student can quickly become overwhelmed or become frustrated by the number of new skills (violating his or her working memory). Likewise, the teacher can begin to feel challenged by having to instruct too many writing dimensions at one time.

The school psychologist and teacher should work together to manage the challenge within the targeted writing dimension by employing what is called the 80/20 rule. That is, the teacher should structure instruction around the prioritized dimension by dividing the student's writing into segments. As the teacher instructs and interacts with the student around the student's writing, the teacher should narrow and focus only on 20% of the writing product, leaving the remaining 80% untouched for the moment. It is within the 20% of a student's writing that the teacher can offer targeted instruction and have the student revise or edit based upon that instruction. This does not mean targeted skills that fall within the remaining 80% of the student's writing will never be addressed. Instead, it ensures that the concerns will be addressed in a manner that will increase the likelihood of skill retention and academic and instructional success for the student and teacher.

Step 4: Match Instruction

The same care that was taken to establish and maintain instructional level conditions during assessment needs to be extended when intervening and instructing around the prioritized concerns. Classroom instruction should reflect the conditions needed for optimal teaching and learning, which includes activating prior knowledge, honoring working memory, and making connections to what is known. It is also important to maintain the connections between reading and writing in order to assist students in learning these skills in an integrated fashion.

During collaboration, school psychologists should encourage teachers to think beyond individual student needs and explore opportunities to apply strategies to groups of students or the entire class. Typically, there are multiple students with similar writing concerns, and most writing interventions can be easily adapted to the large group. Teachers are more likely to implement interventions with integrity that are applied to the whole group because of the intervention practicality and feasibility.

Regardless of the intervention chosen, there is a need to periodically reassess to adjust and fine-tune the strategies to ensure that they remain a match for the student. This constant assessment allows the teacher to decide when and whether to address other priorities, whether or not the goal for the student is appropriate, and to plan instruction that more effectively supports intervention strategies. It also supports the teacher in ensuring that the three components of instruction are being addressed in a systematic fashion. These include ensuring that students first are made aware of, and exposed to, critical skills, then are provided with adequate practice and feedback needed for accuracy and with necessary repetition for automaticity.

Assessment decision 3: What refinement needs to occur to ensure ongoing writing success? The third and final decision question for the school psychologist and teacher comes from examining the results of the teaching method put into place by the teacher. The answer to this question assists the school psychologist and teacher in identifying a workable format for monitoring progress and making any necessary adjustments to the intervention strategies to facilitate skill development.

Importance of the Decision Questions

In many alternative writing assessments, decisions about a student's skills are made largely after a cursory review of the student's writing products. However, with the IA of writing, the written product only provides one side of a multipart story with regard to the student's skills. In an effort to obtain another side of the story, it is incumbent upon the school psychologist to actually collaborate and discuss with the teacher the expectations and instructional delivery that is provided to, and for, the student. In addition, it is important to observe the student engaging in the reading and writing activities within the classroom in order to get an accurate picture of how the student integrates and applies the skills needed for the task. This observation is supplemented by conversations with the student to determine how he or she approaches the task, how he or she conceptualizes the task, and how he or she articulates the thought process that occurs as the task is completed.

As cautioned previously, it is not uncommon for teachers to misinterpret reading concerns as writing concerns because of the permanent evidence offered in writing tasks. Making decisions to prioritize skills without viewing how the student interacts with the task and obtaining a full picture of the students' reading skills is more likely to lead to interventions that are misaligned with the underlying concern. As a result, it is always recommended that school psychologists and teachers view the student's application of skills under instructional-level conditions for both reading and writing.

Interpreting the Results of the IA

Data gathered as a result of the IA in writing can yield valuable information that assists in the prioritizing of concerns, goal setting, instructional design, and progress monitoring. When the IA in reading is done as the initial step of the IA in writing, then three levels of responding are tapped: the student's oral responding after the school psychologist reads aloud to him or her as part of the reading assessment; the student's oral responding after he or she reads aloud under instructional-level conditions as part of the reading assessment; and the written response after the student reads, or responds to text, under instructional level conditions in the writing assessment.

This comprehensive picture of oral and written response within the three different contexts allows more targeted prioritizing of skill needs. For example, if the IA yields data that suggest that a student can provide an adequate oral response after the school psychologist has read text aloud (removing the barrier of word recognition and word study), but has difficulty providing an adequate oral response after he or she reads, then reading—specifically word recognition and word study skills—should be prioritized as a precursor to the expectation of the student generating a written response expressing understanding of what has been read.

The interpretation of reading and writing data collected during the assessment process should not be considered unidirectional. Reading skills are seen as contributing to writing skills and writing skills are seen as contributing to reading skills, especially with those tasks that rely heavily on reading. School psychologists should keep this in mind as interventions are designed. Ideally, interventions should be constructed so that students recognize and acknowledge that their reading texts are the products of an author's writing. Once recognized,

the student's reading text can be flexibly used as a critical tool for intervening around writing skills. The case study that follows highlights this interaction.

Case Study

The following case study captures key steps employed in the IA and details the connection between a student's reading and writing performance. Because of space limitations, not all components of the IA in writing are provided here. Instead the goal is to highlight those steps that illustrate the basic concepts of the IA process.

Step 1: Select Writing Samples
Andre's teacher was concerned with his general difficulty in creating written responses to classroom tasks and activities. His teacher described that after reading or hearing a story, Andre's oral retelling was generally better than his writing. More specifically, the teacher indicated that Andre typically spoke softly and offered a little information on his own, but would talk more if prodded or questioned. In addition, the teacher offered several samples of writing that reflected her concern.

Step 2: Review Writing Samples
The following excerpt of Andre's actual writing was taken from a language arts assignment that asked current fifth graders to write a letter to fourth-grade students. Andre wrote a total of five paragraphs with the first paragraph as follows:

> *If you want to go to fouth grade you will need to be creyatefl in you need to lisson to your teacher in pay 3D atenshain at all time and follow the rules.*

Working collaboratively, the teacher and school psychologist reviewed the sample looking for what Andre knew and could do. They noted that Andre had specific ideas he wanted to express and was correctly focused on the expected audience of fourth graders, soon to become fifth graders. His inclusion of the "3D" concept was especially important to the teacher since the class always discussed the need for students to give three dimensions of attention: eyes, ears, and body posture. The teacher was pleased that Andre attempted to use a variety of words, even those he was not completely sure of how to spell. She saw this as an important attribute since many of her students would resort to using simple words they could spell correctly. In addition, the teacher noted that while Andre used basic sentence structure of capitalization and ending punctuation, he often created run-on sentences containing too many ideas within one sentence. In further discussion, Andre's teacher indicated that he was an average reader who could typically comprehend if prodded to give more information.

Assessment decision 1: Is there sufficient information to adequately assess each dimension? At this point of reflection about Andre's reading and writing, the teacher commented that Andre's writing response actually contained more information than what she might typically observe when he gave an oral response after reading. After discussing the concern and the relationship of writing and reading performance, the school psychologist and teacher conducted an IA in reading using the peer-expected text.

Step 3: Conduct Additional Assessments to Answer Outstanding Questions

The school psychologist first read aloud to Andre and then asked him to orally retell what was read. Andre was able to retell several ideas without prompting, using two- and three-word responses. With additional prompting (e.g., who, what, where, why questions), he was able to offer more information about what was read. The teacher noted that this was a common pattern for Andre, as with most of her students. That is, when reading or being read to, students tended to give brief oral responses and required prompting and prodding to give more information. A word search of the next passage indicated that Andre knew all but two words, indicating the passage could be read at an instructional level, if not possibly an independent level.

Andre was then asked to read the identified passage. While his fluency rate was considered acceptable for a fifth grader (e.g., > 100 correct words per minute), Andre was noted not to pause at punctuation; he read in a monotone and rarely displayed voice or expression. After observing the IA in reading, and in follow-up collaboration with the school psychologist, his teacher noted how Andre's reading fluency mirrored his own writing. The teacher was especially surprised to observe the connection between Andre's reading behavior and his writing behavior. Just as he rarely used appropriate punctuation in his own writing, Andre did not seem to attend to or understand how authors used punctuation in text.

Reading-to-writing connection. In an effort to demonstrate for Andre how reading and writing skills are related, the school psychologist used sentences from

the fifth-grade peer-expected text to model how the author constructed and structured sentences. For example, the following sentence from the text was used to demonstrate for Andre how an author constructs sentences with multiple ideas (i.e., thoughts) and uses punctuation to help identify those ideas: *Mike took pictures to show his friends in class at school.*

With the teacher observing, the school psychologist discussed with Andre how authors often put multiple ideas or thoughts within one sentence. When asked how many thoughts or ideas were in the example sentence, Andre did not offer a response. The school psychologist then began to demonstrate different ideas within the sentence:

School psychologist: "'Mike took pictures.' How many thoughts?"
Andre: "One."
School psychologist: "'Mike showed his pictures to friends at school.' How many thoughts?"
Andre: "One."
School psychologist: "'Mike showed pictures in class.' How many thoughts?"
Andre: "One."
School psychologist: "'Mike showed his class at school.' How many thoughts?"
Andre: "One."

The school psychologist then returned to the original authored sentence and discussed how all of these ideas or thoughts were actually within the same sentence. The school psychologist then asked Andre how many thoughts he thought were in the original sentence, to which Andre responded, "Two." At this response, Andre was asked to read the sentence as if it contained two thoughts. He read the sentence as follows (slash marks indicate Andre's pauses when reading).

Andre: "Mike took pictures/to show his friends/in class at school."

The school psychologist then read the original sentence using the same pausing used by Andre. Andre smiled and said, "Three." At this time, the school psychologist read the sentence as follows:

School psychologist: "Mike took pictures/to show his friends in class at school."

As Andre listened, he immediately said, "Two." The school psychologist then asked the teacher to read the same sentence as if it were one idea.

Teacher: "Mike took pictures to show his friends in class at school."

With continued practice and feedback using additional sentences from the reading text, Andre was able to accurately recognize multiple ideas within various sentences. Andre was then asked to reread the entire passage. He was able to maintain the original fluency rate. However, unlike his first reading of the passage, Andre appropriately paused at punctuation and read with greater expression. The teacher was delighted to see the immediate change in Andre's reading with this brief targeted instruction. She immediately stated that most, if not all, of her students needed this same support.

Writing-to-reading connection. The school psychologists then presented Andre's original writing sample, covering the page except for the first paragraph (80/20). They discussed how Andre was now the author and he had a choice of how many thoughts he wanted to put into each of his sentences. Even before being asked to read his own writing, Andre smiled. When asked why he smiled, he said, "Too many thoughts." Asked if and how he wanted to change his sentence, the school psychologists offered to scribe. The following was Andre's response as written by the school psychologist:

> *Andre:* "If you want to go to fourth grade you will need to be creative. You need to listen to your teacher and pay 3D attention at all times. It's important to follow the rules."

Assessment decision 2: Which reading/writing dimensions need instructional support? Within the selected dimension, what will be the specific 80/20 rule for instruction? The teacher initially stated that she would have seen Andre's spelling as the major need before engaging in the IA process. However, the sampling and discussion allowed her to reflect and reorganize her own thinking about Andre's writing, in which she saw his sentence structure and punctuation as a necessary next step to becoming a better writer. She discussed that once this improved she would reassess and see if spelling might be the next area of focus.

Step 4: Match Instruction

Since the teacher was able to see the impact of using reading instruction as an effective way to develop Andre's writing skills, she immediately began outlining strategies to help Andre analyze an author's writing (i.e., sentence construction, number of ideas within each sentence, and use of punctuation). This reading and writing connection became the foundation for developing Andre's metacognition about his own writing. More important, the teacher immediately generalized this strategy as a whole class activity with Andre teaching other students how to read an author's text looking for "thoughts." Using weekly writing samples as a basis for measurement, the teacher and school psychologists were able to monitor Andre's improvement. Through this measurement they were able to document improvement in Andre's quality of reading fluency and his ability to construct and punctuate complex sentences.

SUMMARY

While the underlying principles of IA can be applied to all curriculum content areas, this chapter highlighted its unique contribution to assessing writing. The IA process applied to writing is based upon established researched principles of learning and teaching and allows school psychologists and educational professionals to gain an accurate picture of a student's prior knowledge and skills. In following the steps of IA, a school psychologist is able to select appropriate material, assess the student's performance within instructional level conditions, and identify the dimensions of writing requiring immediate support. The specificity of the results assists school psychologists, teachers, and other professionals to design, implement, and evaluate instructional strategies targeting the needed areas. Specifically, the IA process helps to more accurately prioritize a concern during the initial problem identification stage. The IA structure engages teachers in the critical reflection necessary to address the interrelated nature of writing and reading and maintains the teacher's primary role in creating challenge during writing instruction.

IA in writing is a collaborative assessment with the teacher. It requires not only that school psychologists have the content skills outlined in this chapter as they relate to conducting IAs, but also that they have the capacity to build effective collaboration centered on discussion of teachers' instruction. Both addressing the content of instructional assessment and establishing collaborative relationships with teachers will facilitate school psychologists' engagement in the meaningful work that enhances the quality of instruction students receive.

AUTHOR NOTE

Disclosure. Todd Gravois has a financial interest in books he authored or coauthored referenced in this chapter.

Todd Gravois is president and Deborah Nelson is a staff member of ICAT Resources.

REFERENCES

Abbott, E. S., Berninger, V. W., & Fayol, M. (2010). Longitudinal relationships of levels of language in writing and between writing and reading in grades 1 to 7. *Journal of Educational Psychology, 102*, 281–298.

Anderson, N. L., & Briggs, C. (2011). Reciprocity between reading and writing: Strategic processing as common ground. *The Reading Teacher, 64*, 546–549.

Betts, E. A. (1946). *Foundations of reading instruction.* New York, NY: American Book.

Bloom, B. S. (1976). *Human characteristics and school learning.* New York, NY: McGraw-Hill.

Calkins, L., Ehrenworth, M., & Lehman, C. (2012). *Pathways to the common core: Accelerating achievement.* Portsmouth, NH: Heinemann.

Cramer, K., & Rosenfield, S. (2008). Effects of degrees of challenge on reading performance. *Reading and Writing Quarterly, 24*, 199–127.

Fitzgerald, J., & Shanahan, T. (2000). Reading and writing relations and their development. *Educational Psychologist, 35*, 39–50.

Gickling, E. E., & Havertape, J. R. (1981). Curriculum-based assessment. In J. A. Tucker (Ed.), *Non-test based assessment.* Minneapolis, MN: National School Psychology Inservice Training Network, University of Minnesota.

Gickling, E. E., Shane, R. L., & Croskery, K. M. (1989). Assuring math success for low-achieving high school students through curriculum based assessment. *School Psychology Review, 18*, 344–355.

Graham, S., & Harris, K. (2009). Almost 30 years of writing research: Making sense of it all with the *Wrath of Khan. Learning Disabilities Research & Practice, 24*, 58–68.

Graham, S., McKeown, D., Kiuhara, S., & Harris, K. R. (2012). A meta-analysis of writing instruction for students in the elementary grades. *Journal of Educational Psychology, 104*, 879–896.

Gravois, T. A., & Gickling, E. E. (2008). Best practices in instructional assessment. In A. Thomas & J. Grimes (Eds.), *Best practices in school psychology V* (pp. 503–518). Bethesda, MD: National Association of School Psychologists.

Gravois, T. A., Gickling, E. E., & Rosenfield, S. (2011). *Training in instructional consultation, assessment, and teaming. Book 3: Skill sessions 4–7.* Baltimore, MD: ICAT Publishing.

Hasbrouck, J. E., Tindel, G., & Parker, R. I. (1994). Objective procedures for scoring students' writing. *Teaching Exceptional Children, 21*, 89–93.

MacQuarrie, L. L., Tucker, J. A., Burns, M. K., & Hartman, B. (2002). Comparison of retention rates using traditional, drill sandwich, and incremental rehearsal flash card methods. *School Psychology Review, 31*, 584–595.

National Association of School Psychologists. (2010). *Model for comprehensive and integrated school psychological services.* Bethesda, MD: Author. Retrieved from http://www.nasponline.org/standards/2010standards/2_PracticeModel.pdf

National Center for Education Statistics. (2011). *The nation's report card: Writing 2011* (NCES 2012–457). Washington, DC: Institute of Education Sciences, U.S. Department of Education.

Nelson, D. (2013). *Can't read or can't write: Using classroom-based measures to assess the reading writing relationship with intermediate elementary school students.* Unpublished manuscript.

O'Neil, H. F., & Abedi, J. (1996). *Reliability and validity of a state metacognition inventory: Potential for alternative assessment.* Los Angeles, CA: CRESST/University of California, Los Angeles.

Poehner, M. (2011). Frames of interaction in dynamic assessment: Developmental diagnoses of second language learning. *Assessment in Education: Principles, Policy & Practice, 18*, 183–198.

Robinson, L. K., & Howell, K. W. (2008). Best practices in curriculum-based evaluation and written expression. In A. Thomas & J. Grimes (Eds.), *Best practices in school psychology V* (pp. 439–452). Bethesda, MD: National Association of School Psychologists.

Rogers, L. A., & Graham, S. (2008). A meta-analysis of single subject design writing intervention research. *Journal of Educational Psychology, 4*, 879–906.

Rosenfield, S., Gravois, T., & Silva, A. (2014). Bringing instructional consultation to scale: Research and development of IC and IC teams (pp. 248–275). In W. Erchul & S. Sheridan (Eds.), *Handbook of research in school consultation: Empirical foundations for the field* (2nd ed.). New York, NY: Erlbaum.

Saddler, B., & Asaro-Saddler, K. (2013). Response to intervention in writing: A suggested framework for screening, intervention, and progress monitoring. *Reading and Writing Quarterly, 29*, 20–43.

Shanahan, T. (1984). Nature of the reading-writing relation: An exploratory multivariate analysis. *Journal of Educational Psychology, 76*, 466–477.

Shanahan, T., Fisher, D., & Frey, N. (2012). The challenge of challenging text. *Educational Leadership, 69*, 58–62.

Shapiro, E. S., & Elliott, S. N. (1999). Curriculum-based assessment and other performance-based assessment strategies. In C. R. Reynolds & T. B. Gutkin (Eds.), *The handbook of school psychology* (pp. 383–408). New York, NY: Wiley.

Shinn, M., Rosenfield, S., & Knutson, N. (1989). Curriculum-based assessment: A comparison of models. *School Psychology Review, 18*, 299–316.

Treptow, M. A. (2006). *Reading at students' frustrational, instructional, and independent levels: Effects on comprehension and time on-task.* Minneapolis, MN: Center for Reading Research, University of Minnesota.

Vygotsky, L. S. (1978). *Mind in society: The development of higher psychological processes.* Cambridge, MA: Harvard University Press.

14

Best Practices in Mathematics Assessment and Intervention With Elementary Students

Ben Clarke
Christian T. Doabler
Nancy J. Nelson
University of Oregon

OVERVIEW

In our chapter in *Best Practices in School Psychology V* (Clarke, Baker, & Chard, 2008) we noted, "If the lay public and educators were asked what two academic areas are most important for children to learn to be successful in school, there is little doubt a majority would say reading and mathematics . . . in that order" (p. 453), and described the built-in systems of support provided for reading instruction, including mandated time blocks, validated intervention programs, and the use of reading specialists. While we believe our observations continue to hold true, we also have seen fundamental advances in educators' awareness of the need to increase the quality of mathematics instruction and tangible advances in the tools at the disposal of all educators and school psychologists to move this effort forward.

Many of these advances arose from the publication of a number of critical documents in recent years. The National Mathematics Advisory Panel (2008) released its Foundations for Success report, which provided both an overview of the current research base and a set of critical objectives and goals to advance mathematics instruction in the United States. While singularly the National Mathematics Advisory Panel report did not carry the same weight as its corollary, the National Reading Panel report (National Reading Panel, 2000), in combination with the National Council of Teachers of Mathematics *Focal Points* (National Council of Teachers of Mathematics, 2006) and the Common Core State Standards (Common Core State Standards Initiative,

2010), the National Mathematics Advisory Panel report seemed to represent a fundamental shift in mathematics instruction. Collectively these documents have led to a narrowing of content coverage to focus on number understanding, along with critical aspects of measurement and geometry (for the elementary grades), in a coherent manner reflecting key principles within the domain of mathematical knowledge (similar to the National Reading Panel articulating the five big ideas of reading instruction). Together the National Council of Teachers of Mathematics *Focal Points*, National Mathematics Advisory Panel, and the Common Core State Standards offer a variety of vested parties, including school psychologists, a framework to begin or expand efforts to improve mathematics achievement for all students.

In part, the framework for advancing mathematics achievement will be based on similar efforts in establishing multitiered models of service delivery to deliver research-based reading instruction. Although response to intervention (RTI) was originally codified as a means to identify specific learning disabilities as a lack of response to research-based practices (such as the 2004 Individuals with Disabilities Education Act), in reality schools have implemented RTI models as a mechanism to support students across the achievement spectrum with a cascading system of tiers providing increasing support as the complexity and intensity of student need increases (Burns & VanDerHeyden, 2006; Fuchs, Fuchs, & Vaughn, 2008), with a primary goal being the prevention of long-term academic difficulties (Torgesen,

2000). As schools have implemented these systems in reading, there is a sense that reading instruction has turned the corner with emerging consensus and practice in the field reflecting research-based best practices, including an instructional focus on the five big ideas of reading (phonological awareness, alphabetic principal, accuracy and fluency with connected text, vocabulary, and comprehension) and the use of universal screeners to identify students as at risk and progress monitoring of student growth. But again, this has been primarily in the area of reading, which begs the question: What about mathematics?

From our perspective and work in the field, schools and educators are ready to implement similar models in mathematics and are looking for specific components (e.g., screeners) to integrate into already established multitiered systems of support. Because school psychologists have often played leading roles in establishing such systems in reading, it is highly likely that schools will again look to school psychologists to take a similar role as efforts in mathematics are begun. Work in implementing multitiered models of instructional support also is occurring within a significant national increase of interest in mathematics instruction. In part, this increased interest has been driven by findings that document persistently low levels of achievement on both national and international assessments of mathematics. Results from the 2011 National Assessment for Educational Progress (Aud et al., 2011) indicate that only 40% of fourth graders were deemed at or above proficient in mathematics and 18% classified as below basic. Difficulties are more pronounced for students from low-income backgrounds, ethnic minority students, and students who have been identified as learning disabled. It should be noted that although the results from the 2011 National Assessment for Educational Progress are disconcerting, they do reflect improvement from 2009 National Assessment for Educational Progress data and earlier National Assessment for Educational Progress assessments (Aud et al., 2011). Results from international studies further document the problem. Compared to counterparts across the world, U.S. students' performance falls in the lower half of the achievement spectrum, and these differences increase at the upper grade levels (Olson, Martin, & Mullis, 2008).

In part, these findings are troubling because a vast range of opportunities within academic and non-academic settings are dependent upon a fundamental understanding of mathematics. For example, within school settings a number of advanced science topics (e.g.,

physics) require a deep understanding of mathematics. Outside of school, fields with growing employment opportunities are heavily dependent upon the ability to reason with and apply mathematics (National Science Board, 2008). In an increasingly partisan political atmosphere, the importance of mathematics and mathematics education is perhaps best illustrated by almost verbatim calls from both President Bush in 2006 and President Obama in 2011 extolling the importance of mathematics and the need for a concentrated and expanded federal role increasing the nation's mathematics achievement.

The suggestions provided in this chapter align with a number of National Association of School Psychologists (NASP) *Model for Comprehensive and Integrated School Psychological Services* domains (e.g., Interventions and Instructional Support to Develop Academic Skills; NASP, 2010), but the work is driven by a continued focus of the school psychologist engaging in the practice domain of Data-Based Decision Making and Accountability. While the decisions that occur within this domain vary widely—from evaluating the progress, for example, on an at-risk student receiving a supplemental program to determining the effectiveness of a new core mathematics program for the third grade—all decisions require the skills called for with the domain. Grounding their work in this domain will enable the school psychologist to have the greatest impact on the multitude of decisions that will need to be made in order to increase the mathematics achievement of the districts, schools, and students they serve. It should also be noted that while we structure our chapter using the designations of Tier 1, Tier 2, and Tier 3, the idea of multiple-tiered systems of support and RTI is inherently complex, and no simple designation of tiers is sufficient to capture the various models that are implemented in schools today and the problem-solving approaches utilized by school psychologists. Underlying any system, however described and whatever the number of tiers, the principle of providing increasing levels of instructional support to help all children is paramount.

The purpose of this chapter is to provide a general roadmap for school psychologists toward the implementation of multitiered instructional models to help meet the goal of increasing mathematics achievement for all students. We hope to do so by suggesting specific roles for school psychologists that will be used to guide their actions in providing services in a multitier system and summarizing the critical knowledge behind this expanded role. Our chapter will attempt to highlight these new roles by providing an in-depth examination of the knowledge base that informs suggestions at each level of support.

BASIC CONSIDERATIONS

In 2008, we listed three basic considerations to guide the work of school psychologists. In this section, we will review and update those considerations. The three considerations are (a) school psychologists as assessment and instructional experts, (b) trajectories of students' mathematics learning, and (c) the limited research base in mathematics.

School Psychologists as Assessment and Instructional Experts

First, we noted the need for school psychologists to be experts on both assessment and instruction. The need for this dual expertise continues to hold true today. While there may be a number of educators who are comfortable in their understanding of reading instruction and assessment, it is highly probable that there will be relatively few who are as comfortable in the area of mathematics. For example, while it is common for schools to have specialists in reading, this is often not the case in mathematics. This gap opens the possibility that school psychologists may be asked to take on a greater role in mathematics practice.

The traditional role of school psychologists has often focused on assessment and support in this area of practice is likely to continue. Such support may range from collecting individual student data to help in instructional planning for Tier 2 and Tier 3 students to analyzing data at the group level to determine the effectiveness of school or district initiatives (e.g., evaluating the impact of a new core curricula; Gersten, Beckmann, et al., 2009). The examination of data at Tier 1 to evaluate core curricula is of particular importance. Given the large numbers of students who struggle with mathematics, it is likely that school psychologists will need to work with their school to improve the instruction provided to all students in Tier 1 and to track those efforts over time. In addition, given their expertise in working with students who are at risk or have learning disabilities, school psychologists bring a unique perspective on the types of instructional materials that are likely to provide the greatest benefit to students who have not responded to Tier 1 instruction. School psychologists can help in the selection of materials that incorporate critical design elements (e.g., explicit instructional approaches) targeting the needs of

at-risk learners. School psychologists also can bring their experience in conducting classroom observations to bear by conducting observations during mathematics instruction targeting critical teacher and student behaviors that indicate robust instructional interactions around mathematics content. We further detail these roles in later sections.

Trajectories of Students' Mathematics Learning

The second consideration we noted concerned the 5–8% of the student population who are identified as having a learning disability in mathematics and the stability of mathematics achievement over time. A number of key findings have emerged on mathematics trajectories. Using a nationally representative sample of students from the Early Childhood Longitudinal Study–Kindergarten Cohort, Morgan, Farkas, and Wu (2009) reported that students who were in the lowest 10th percentile at entrance and exit from kindergarten had a 70% chance of remaining in the lowest 10th percentile 5 years later in fifth grade. Overall mathematics achievement for these students remained two standard deviation units below students who did not demonstrate a mathematics learning disability profile in kindergarten. A number of interesting implications arise from this finding. For students identified as having a mathematics learning disability, a well-established pattern of mathematics difficulties arises early in their education, and the probability that they will break this pattern in the absence of targeted efforts is highly unlikely. This mirrors findings on the development of reading trajectories (Juel, 1988) and the resulting emphasis on prevention rather then remediation of reading difficulties. We propose that a similar tack be taken in mathematics and that school psychologists are well suited to lead this effort in large part due to the heavy reliance on early screening and detection systems that will serve as a cornerstone of identifying students in need of additional instructional assistance in mathematics.

On a positive note, findings from the same national study indicate the potential promise of positively impacting mathematics achievement earlier and mitigating long-term negative effects. In the sample of students who scored below the 10th percentile in kindergarten at entry but not at exit (i.e., a normative increase in mathematics achievement from fall to spring), it was found that only 30% of those students were below the 10th percentile in fifth grade. We believe these findings provide a compelling case for early intervention and the allocation of resources toward prevention efforts.

While we fully support early intervention, we do feel the need to exert a strong note of caution. The belief that once a student is on track he or she will remain on track is particularly tenuous in mathematics. A significant drop in overall levels of proficiency occurs in the later elementary grades, roughly corresponding to the introduction of rational numbers, resulting in a number of students who appeared to be on track beginning to struggle with mathematics. The easiest explanation is that the new content becomes too difficult for students and hence the new content is the reason for the drop in achievement. However, school psychologists should be particularly attuned to two potential pitfalls. First, instruction in the early elementary grades may have occurred without sufficient attention paid to number properties and the concepts underlying operational procedures that govern both whole and rational number systems (Wu, 1999), resulting in students demonstrating proficiency on whole number tasks but holding a superficial understanding of the underlying mathematics. Second, it may be the case that even when students have had exposure to strong instruction in whole number operations, students who are at risk may have difficulty in transferring their knowledge of key concepts to rational numbers. In either case, school psychologists should be aware of the possibilities that within the schools they serve these situations may arise and warrant systems-level changes to mathematics instruction. School psychologists can evaluate data at both a group and individual level to closely track growth across this critical transition and work with other educators to implement plans of action in case these patterns develop.

Limited Mathematics Research Base

The last consideration we noted was the relative limited research base in mathematics. And while we still recognize that research on mathematics pales in comparison to reading, there has been a gradual expansion of the research base and in particular the development of a number of curricular programs targeting the early elementary grades (e.g., Bryant et al., 2011; Clarke et al., 2011; Dyson, Jordan, & Glutting 2013; Fuchs et al., 2005). Critically, from our perspective, these programs combine an intense focus on building beginning whole number understanding with an instructional design approach that is explicit and systematic. The targeted content reflects the calls by the National Council of Teachers of Mathematics and the

Common Core State Standards, and the use of explicit and systematic design elements incorporates key findings from the research literature (National Mathematics Advisory Panel, 2008). We foresee the development of curricula programs reflecting this dual content and the design approach continuing and, it is hoped, progressing to the upper elementary grades as well.

BEST PRACTICES IN MATH ASSESSMENT AND INTERVENTIONS

Integral to the implementation of a multitiered system of academic support is the expert service that school psychologists provide to schools in assessment and instruction.

Best Practices in Tier 1

There are three major goals in the development and management of a Tier 1 system in mathematics, and school psychologists can play key roles in each of these areas. The first goal is to help schools select and implement a universal screening system to quickly gauge a student's understanding of mathematics and his or her level of risk. The use of universal screening in Tier 1 also allows school psychologists to expand their focus from the individual student to system-based service delivery, and to emphasize implementation factors associated with data-based decision making and accountability. The second goal is to help schools identify and evaluate the mathematics curriculum that will constitute their core instruction in Tier 1. Mathematics programs and materials used in Tier 1 serve as a primary vehicle for supporting students' development of mathematics proficiency. The third goal is to help schools use standardized observation protocols to determine whether students are receiving effective Tier 1 instruction in beginning mathematics. A fundamental aspect of RTI is the delivery of high-quality instruction in the general education setting. Consequently, it is necessary to make use of reliable and valid observation protocols in Tier 1 to assess system fidelity and inform decisions about instructional quality linked to student need. Together, these goals reflect the standards for practice set forth in *School Psychology: A Blueprint for Training and Practice III* (Ysseldyke et al., 2006).

Goal 1: Providing Universal Screening
Universal screening at any grade level, but especially in the early elementary grades, encourages a prevention approach to mathematics instruction and intervention.

Effective screening measures allow schools to identify those students who are potentially at risk for difficulties in mathematics. Screening for mathematics difficulty in K–1 has a specific emphasis on concepts of number and numeration. Then, in much the same way that reading assessments in upper elementary grades (i.e., grades 2–5) measure global indicators of reading proficiency such as oral reading fluency, mathematics assessments in the upper grades transition to measure more sophisticated mathematics.

In a recent synthesis of the literature base, Gersten et al. (2012) categorized screening measures into three general categories. The first category includes measures that target singular aspects of whole numbers. Measures in this category might, for example, assess students' knowledge of magnitude, strategic counting, word problem solving, or retrieval of basic number combinations. The second category includes screeners that address multiple aspects of proficiency in number. Measures that fall into this category emphasize breadth over depth of knowledge by covering a variety of related concepts and skills. Interestingly, research has found that these types of measures produce predictive validities stronger than measures that assess just one skill or concept (Gersten et al., 2012). The third category includes measures that apply a more recent approach to screening for mathematical proficiency. In this category, measures align with the grade-specific standards that students are expected to master (e.g., Common Core State Standards Initiative, 2010).

Despite this emerging research base, schools should be judicious in selecting screening systems in mathematics. School psychologists are encouraged to work with schools to carefully select screening assessment systems, and to use these types of screening measures for their intended purpose (i.e., to identify students who may benefit from additional academic support). Taking charge of efforts to implement a universal screening system entails selecting appropriate measures at each grade level and leading the school in collecting reliable and valid student data. Because screening is a preventive step, school psychologists should encourage schools to begin screening in the fall with subsequent screening data collections in the winter and spring. If overall level of performance indicates students are not on track to meet achievement objectives by the end of a specified time period (typically, the end of the school year), students may need more intensive and individualized instruction (e.g., Tier 2 or Tier 3). Administrations in the winter and spring do not serve the purpose of screening per se, but rather allow schools to reassess student skill relative to end-of-year targets and to make adjustments to student tier placements, as needed.

Unlike screening systems available in reading that use benchmark assessments to determine whether students are at risk for reading difficulties based on extensive research evidence informing the quantification of risk (i.e., cut scores), mathematics screening systems frequently rely on local or national norms to make comparisons about a student's skill relative to his or her peers. To support their use, technical information on reliability and predictive validity is often provided. However, because the decision when screening is a yes or no decision (i.e., Is the student at risk?), consideration needs to be paid to how accurately screening measures classify students as at risk or not at risk by examining the sensitivity and specificity of an instrument for specific cut scores. In other words, for a cut score indicating a student is at risk, how many students who were below the cut score were truly at risk and how many above the cut score were truly not at risk. In the absence of risk indices, it can be difficult to assess the risk level of an individual student. When selecting a screening instrument, school psychologists should consider the type of technical evidence supporting use of the instrument and should value information above and beyond predictive validity.

Currently, only a few systems are utilizing this approach. For example, the Assessing Student Proficiency in Early Number Sense (ASPENS; Clarke, Gersten, Dimino, & Rolfhus, 2012) offers the capacity to compare student performance to criterion-based standards. For example, a weighted composite score of 59 or greater on the ASPENS at the beginning of kindergarten suggests a student is on track to developing proficiency in number and numeration. Conversely, students who score less than 17 at the same time of year are unlikely to meet end-of-year grade-level expectations.

If school psychologists are working in a district or school that uses an instrument that does not provide cut scores, and thus the provision of services is a normative decision, school psychologists should be aware that the application of local norms can create instances where a student appears to be on track relative to his or her referent peer group but in reality has difficulties in mathematics when compared to students from a different school or geographical region. School psychologists need to be cognizant that student performance should be considered relative to broadly applicable standards and not local normative standards alone. For example, the school psychologist could help link local normative performance to a known critical criterion (e.g., state test performance) to examine students' performance in relation to both their local peers and to important criterion-based standards. Implementation of screening systems will require school psychologists with sophisticated levels of analysis and interpretation to lead schools in making sense of screening data and gauging student performance across time.

In contrast to other types of formative assessment, such as progress monitoring, universal screening serves as a wellness check on the mathematics health of all students and not just a sample of students. Because screening procedures involve testing all students, schools implementing universal screening will need to be prepared to carry out data collection procedures with hundreds of students and handle large sources of incoming screening data. School psychologists, as leaders in systems implementation, will need to be at the forefront of such efforts. For example, the school psychologist can play an instrumental role in helping schools manage data collection.

Once screening data have been successfully collected, school psychologists can facilitate data analysis and sharing with classroom teachers, math coaches, and interventionists. While screening is an individual decision, by collecting screening data on all students, schools also gain the ability to evaluate key aspects of their mathematics program. For example, if a school puts resources into preventing mathematics difficulties in kindergarten and first grade, over time the school psychologist should see a decrease in the number of students identified as at risk at the start of second grade. This type of effort is critical at Tier 1 because it allows a formal evaluation of how Tier 1 is working for all students. School psychologists may identify instances where large numbers of students are not responding to core or Tier 1 instruction. In those cases it is difficult to determine if students who are identified as at risk are truly at risk or if they have not been provided with effective Tier 1 instruction. In some cases, school psychologists will need to guide efforts in improving Tier 1 instruction prior to focusing on implementing intervention programs. For example, it makes little sense to focus on implementing intervention programs if 60% of the students in a grade level are identified as at risk. Tracking and evaluating screening data over time provides valuable information about how well schools are serving all students and may help schools identify targeted areas to allocate scarce resources.

At the individual student level, fall screening data should be used to determine whether students require instructional support in addition to Tier 1. For example,

if screening data suggest that a student is in need of more intense instruction, the school psychologist might recommend providing the student with Tier 2 or Tier 3 supports. A way to think about the instructional tiers is that instructional intensity is matched to student need (Baker, Fien, & Baker, 2010). That is, as student risk status increases, so too does the intensity of instruction. If a student makes inadequate progress in one instructional tier, then instructional intensity in subsequent interventions or tiers is enhanced to increase the likelihood of the student learning mathematics successfully. For example, those on track for mathematical success would continue to receive Tier 1 core instruction. Students struggling to meet grade-level expectations and in need of additional support would be placed in Tier 2 in addition to Tier 1. Those students well below grade level and in need of more differentiated and individualized instruction would be placed in Tier 3 in addition to Tier 1. In a multitiered model, it is important to think of the instructional tiers as dynamic and not as static placements. Schools should expect to transition students between tiers during the course of the school year, with the goal of moving students toward Tier 1. School psychologists need to help schools think carefully about the resources needed to maintain student progress as students transition from more intensive tiers to Tier 1, and the factors required to accelerate learning and differentiate instruction for students in Tier 2 and Tier 3.

For students in Tier 1, fall, winter, and spring screening assessments will serve as the primary mathematics data that drive instruction. For students who begin the school year on track to develop mathematical proficiency and remain on track at the winter and spring assessments, there will be little need to administer additional diagnostic tests or more frequent progress monitoring assessments that students in Tiers 2 and 3 typically require. Schools should also consider summative measures, such as end-of-year assessments, to help evaluate annual student achievement and the overall effectiveness of the mathematics system at the school and district level. Additionally, students in Tier 1 should be administered regular assessments embedded within the core mathematics program, such as mastery tests or chapter tests, to support daily adjustments to instruction. Although in-program assessments often do not demonstrate technical adequacy (i.e., reliability and validity), they do provide important information about student mastery of critical mathematics content. In essence, the initial process of screening in Tier 1 allows schools to match the intensity of assessment to the intensity of student need.

Goal 2: Ensuring High-Quality Core Instruction

A second goal of the development and management of Tier 1 instruction in mathematics that school psychologists can aid schools in accomplishing is identifying and evaluating the quality of Tier 1 mathematics curriculum. Core mathematics programs play an important role in supporting the development of students' mathematical proficiency. When well designed, a core program sets the curricular expectations of children's mathematics learning. It influences when and how well children progress through fundamental content, such as those topics identified in the Common Core State Standards (Common Core State Standards Initiative, 2010).

A coherent core mathematics program sequences topics in a fashion that adheres to the hierarchy of mathematics. For example, it will attend to the particulars of mathematics first and then progress to more advanced topics by building upon students' prior understanding. In general, a core program serves two primary purposes. First, it provides teachers with a foundation to promote important math outcomes for the majority of students, including those at risk for math difficulties. Second, it offers teachers the opportunity to reduce learning difficulties and, when necessary, increase instructional intensity for struggling students (Doabler, Fien, Nelson-Walker, & Baker, 2012).

Although most would agree with the educational importance of a coherent Tier 1 mathematics program, a growing line of curriculum evaluation research indicates that many commercially available core programs lack the instructional design principles required to meet the majority of instructional needs in Tier 1 (Bryant et al., 2008). Compounding this scarcity in available, sound curriculum materials is the shortage of evaluation procedures and tools available to school personnel for evaluating core mathematics programs. As leaders of school-wide decision-making teams, school psychologists may be called upon to work with school teams to evaluate and select instructionally sound core mathematics programs.

With this in mind, school psychologists are encouraged to reference an expanding collection of research syntheses and reports on effective mathematics instruction, such as *Foundation for Success: The Final Report of the National Advisory Mathematics Panel* (National Mathematics Advisory Panel, 2008) and the practice guide on RTI and mathematics released by the Institute of Education Sciences (Gersten, Beckmann, et al., 2009). School psychologists can also use existing evaluation instruments such as the Mathematics Curriculum Evaluation Tool (MCET; Doabler, Fein, et al., 2012). The MCET framework centers on eight instructional design principles empirically validated to improve student mathematics achievement. For example, using the MCET framework, evaluators examine core programs for opportunities built into the curriculum that support teachers in demonstrating key concepts, using representations of mathematical ideas, providing guided and independent student practice, and offering academic feedback.

In addition to supporting efforts to evaluate core programs for evidence-based instructional design principles, Tier 1 core programs should also attend to the critical content that provides the foundation for successful mathematical learning (Common Core State Standards Initiative, 2010). Critical content, or the big ideas, of early mathematics includes the foundational concepts, skills, and strategies considered necessary to achieve proficiency in more sophisticated mathematics (Coyne, Kame'enui, & Carnine, 2011). Tier 1 programs that devote significant instructional time to the big ideas of elementary mathematics provide a blueprint for meeting the instructional needs of the majority of students. To become familiar with the critical content of Tier 1, we recommend that school psychologists study the Common Core State Standards for Mathematics (Common Core State Standards Initiative, 2010) and the Learning Progressions for the Common Core State Standards for Mathematics (Institute for Mathematics and Education, 2011). In combination, these documents will serve as a valuable resource for school psychologists seeking to identify the big ideas of core mathematics instruction and support longitudinal coherence of Tier 1 curriculum.

Number sense. Experts in the area of early mathematics instruction strongly recommend having core mathematics instruction in the early grades focus on teaching early number sense. Even though the definition of number sense varies among mathematicians and researchers (Berch, 2005), most agree that it refers to having flexibility and fluidity of numbers and their corresponding mathematical representations (Berch, 2005; Gersten & Chard, 1999; National Mathematics Advisory Panel, 2008; National Research Council, 2001, 2009). Many children enter school with a firm understanding of number sense. However, a considerable number of children, particularly children from economically and educationally disadvantaged backgrounds, struggle to possess a firm understanding of number sense components. In the absence of number sense, many of these children struggle to develop the knowledge necessary to solve more complex math problems (Morgan et al., 2009).

In the early grades, informal number sense is linked to a formal understanding of whole numbers and whole number properties. As students begin to develop an initial understanding of key concepts such as counting and magnitude, they can begin to apply that understanding in increasingly sophisticated ways. For example, children can advance from basic counting (e.g., one-to-one correspondence) to the use of strategic counting to employ solution methods, such as the count-on strategy, to solve basic addition and subtraction problems (Institute for Mathematics and Education, 2011). For example, if a student has two sets of objects, five blue cubes and two yellow cubes, and is asked to tell how many objects there are altogether, the student can use the min strategy to count on from the larger set of objects to solve the problem. Students that struggle to grasp how to use efficient counting strategies tend to have difficulties in developing a robust understanding of the properties of arithmetic (e.g., commutativity and associativity of addition). Students who struggle to understand the commutative property of addition have difficulties recognizing that $a + b = b + a$. This is important because these number properties are applied to other sets of numbers (e.g., rational numbers) students encounter as they reach the upper elementary grades. Among the hallmarks of students who experience difficulty in mathematics the use of efficient and mature counting strategies is among the most prominent (Fuchs et al., 2010).

Rational numbers. Although we have primarily focused on whole number understanding, a number of students in Tier 1 begin to struggle with mathematics when rational numbers are introduced. National Assessment for Educational Progress data (Aud et al., 2011) indicate that while 39% of fourth graders are at or above proficient in mathematics, that drops to 34% by eighth grade, and it is estimated that roughly 40% of students struggle with rational number concepts. Although many of these students will require Tier 2 and Tier 3 services, the sheer number of students who struggle with rational number concepts strongly suggests that Tier 1 instruction needs to be strengthened. Implications from a limited understanding of rational numbers are profound, as eventually failure to develop rational number understanding will jeopardize the ability to access and understand increasingly advanced mathematics topics such as algebra (Milgram, 2005; National Mathematics Advisory Panel, 2008; Wu, 1999). Although school psychologists do not need to be experts in mathematics content, they should apply their knowledge of this pattern of performance and proactively engage other educators around potential solutions and track the success of those efforts by continuously examining an array of data sources for evaluating program outcomes.

Basic number operations. Across grades, school psychologists should also become aware of the importance for building fluency with basic number operations. Research suggests that automaticity of number combinations is essential for developing proficiency of multidigit whole number calculations and word problem solving (Fuchs et al., 2010; Gersten, Jordan, & Flojo, 2005). However, number combinations can be challenging for young children to solve. In fact, a converging body of evidence indicates that fluency and mastery of number combinations is one of the hallmark difficulties of students struggling to learn mathematics successfully (National Mathematics Advisory Panel, 2008). Much like the role of decoding in early literacy, automaticity with basic number combinations reduces the cognitive load of mathematical learning and thus frees the learner to attend to higher level cognitive demands, such as recognizing and using structural features to solve complex word problems (Goldman & Pellegrino, 1987; Mayer, 2009).

Goal 3: Observing Tier 1 Instruction

A third goal of a multitier model for mathematics instruction that school psychologists can facilitate is the use of standardized observation protocols to observe instruction in Tier 1 settings. Direct observation is a powerful methodology for determining whether students are receiving high-quality core mathematics instruction. In general, there are three types of observation instruments: low-inference measures, moderate-inference measures, and high-inference measures. Because school psychologists often have expertise in using a variety of assessments, including observation instruments, they can help schools select the most appropriate measure for Tier 1 observations. High-inference measures use qualitative methods such as open-ended field notes to document instructional events. Moderate-inference measures use Likert-type rating scales and rely on observer impressions to rate the quality of classroom instruction. An example of a moderate-inference measure is the Classroom Assessment Scoring System (Pianta & Hamre, 2009), which targets three domains of classroom instruction: Emotional Supports, Classroom Organization, and Instructional Supports. Low-inference observation measures use frequency estimates to capture critical components of classroom instruction. A defining characteristic of Tier 1 instruction is the instructional interactions that take place between teachers and students around core math content. Low-inference measures can document the frequency of these instructional interactions and thus provide critical information to schools about instructional quality in Tier 1.

For example, in a recent study, Doabler, Baker, et al. (in press) used a frequency count measure to observe Tier 1 instruction and found that higher rates of student practice opportunities are important for promoting student mathematics achievement. School psychologists can work with schools and teachers to use a similar observation approach to document critical instructional behaviors and interactions that are occurring in the classroom and devise ways to increase those behaviors.

Best Practices for Tier 2, Tier 3, and Beyond: Defining Supplemental Support

In the context of a multitiered system of academic support in mathematics, some students will be identified as needing mathematics intervention on the basis of normative performance on universal screening measures, and/or will struggle to achieve grade-level objectives in mathematics. These students may benefit from standardized protocol or individualized mathematics interventions in more intensive tiers of support (e.g., Tier 2, Tier 3). Concurrent with student participation in mathematics interventions, data from formative assessments should be used to facilitate instructional decision making and ensure that interventions are responsive to student need. There are three major critical practices associated with the implementation of supplemental support in a multitiered approach to mathematics intervention: (a) adopt and use a progress monitoring system to track student performance toward learning objectives over time, (b) utilize evidence-based practices in intervention delivery, and (c) collect data on intervention implementation and make adjustments to instruction as needed to ensure a good match between the intervention and student need.

Assessment in Tier 2, Tier 3, and Beyond

Formative assessment, the process of collecting data in an ongoing manner to inform instructional decisions, allows educators and school psychologists to obtain information about student performance during the learning process. Information gained from this type of assessment can be used to provide feedback to students about their performance and can support teacher decisions about instructional grouping and student

understanding of recently taught content. Research suggests that when the results of formative assessment are used by teachers to make instructional modifications and are communicated to students, student performance increases (Gersten, Chard, et al., 2009). In addition, a recent report from the Institute of Education Sciences (Gersten, Beckmann, et al., 2009) indicates that two types of formative assessment (i.e., universal screening and progress monitoring) should be components of any multitiered system of instructional support. While universal screening is a hallmark of Tier 1 implementation, progress monitoring is a key feature of implementation in Tier 2 and beyond.

Curriculum-embedded assessments. To support student learning, school psychologists can promote several types of assessments that measure the impact of Tier 2 instruction. Mastery learning, or curriculum-embedded assessments, allow interventionists to check student learning at the conclusion of individual lessons or units and support the integration of day-to-day instructional adjustments. For example, an interventionist (which could be a teacher, math specialist, or instructional assistant) teaching students how to decompose a number into 10s and 1s might provide a series of independent practice items at the end of a lesson to assess student understanding of the taught concept. If the student is unable to identify the number of 10s in teen numbers, but can do so when presented with other types of numbers, the interventionist may decide to emphasize the concept of 10s in teen numbers in the subsequent lesson. Curriculum-embedded assessments support educators in determining what adjustments to make to instruction. There is some evidence that the results of curriculum-embedded assessments are as predictive of student outcomes as the results of other types of progress monitoring assessments (Oslund et al., 2012).

Curriculum-based measurement. Curriculum-based measurement (CBM) is a second type of measure that can be used to monitor progress in Tier 2 and beyond to inform instructional decisions. Often, CBMs are brief timed measures that, in contrast to curriculum-embedded measures, generally measure skills that are more distal to the concepts taught in daily lessons. For instance, in the upper elementary grades, many CBMs focus on procedural fluency with whole number operations (i.e., some combination of addition, subtraction, multiplication, and division with whole numbers). Students receiving math intervention in the upper elementary grades may receive instruction directly targeting arithmetic operations with whole numbers; however, intervention is likely to also emphasize a number of other skills (e.g., math problem solving, rational number operations).

CBMs are intended to measure student skill in a concept believed to be predictive of mathematical proficiency (e.g., math fact fluency), and thus their use in Tier 2 and beyond serves as an indicator of student learning and supports educators in determining when to make adjustments to intervention. If a student is successful in his or her intervention program, as measured by mastery or curriculum-embedded tests, then that success should generalize to adequate growth on a more formal progress monitoring instrument.

A number of established progress monitoring systems exist in mathematics and are in use in schools and districts throughout the country. The National Center on Response to Intervention, which provides an overview of established progress monitoring systems, indicates that for progress monitoring assessments to be appropriately used to gauge student learning over time, they should demonstrate reliability and validity evidence, be sensitive to student improvement, be linked to improved student learning or teacher planning, have adequate yearly progress benchmarks, and have specified rates of improvement (National Center on Response to Intervention, 2009). Unfortunately, standards for determining mathematical gains (or lack thereof) are currently not available for many progress monitoring assessment systems. Thus, one challenge school psychologists face as they work with interventionists and data teams to interpret progress monitoring data is determining when student progress is sufficient.

It is recommended that schools use progress monitoring systems that are aligned with assessment systems adopted for universal screening for several reasons. First, because scores derived from aligned systems typically rely on the same scale, data teams can compare student performance at different points in time across measures. This comparability of scores allows for improved coordination of support services and adjustments to instruction within and across tiers. Second, it is generally more resource efficient to use the same system for universal screening and progress monitoring, because there is reduced need to provide training in administration, scoring, and interpretation for multiple assessment systems. School psychologists should lead efforts to ensure that there is alignment between screening and progress monitoring systems.

The selection of a progress monitoring system is largely dependent upon student and school need. That is, progress monitoring assessments selected for administration should assess student skill in areas where students are struggling to demonstrate proficiency. However, there are limitations in the range of skills targeted by existing systems of progress monitoring in elementary mathematics. Most progress monitoring assessments intend to document student skill in (a) early numeracy, (b) fact fluency, (c) arithmetic operations with multidigit numbers, or (d) general math concepts and applications. By coupling the use of established CBM systems with other types of data (e.g., curriculum-embedded assessment), school psychologists can support interventionists in regularly assessing student progress toward a range of learning objectives. Experts recommend that progress monitoring be conducted at least once a month to examine the progress of students receiving intervention in Tier 2 and beyond (Gersten, Beckmann, et al., 2009).

School psychologists have a vital role in helping other educators evaluate overall student response to instruction when multiple data sources can be utilized. For example, an at-risk student receiving an intervention is likely to have data on how he or she is responding to the program through curriculum-embedded assessments and progress monitoring data. In these cases, the two data sources represent a measure, the curriculum-embedded assessment, that is proximal to the intervention and a data source that is distal to the intervention and serving as a general measure of growth in mathematics (the progress monitoring measure). School psychologists will need to help educators make sense of the data collected (Gersten, Beckmann, et al., 2009).

Instruction in Tier 2, Tier 3, and Beyond

In most cases, Tier 2 instruction in mathematics occurs through the delivery of a standard protocol intervention. While the number of interventions available is increasing, very few have been evaluated by employing rigorous research methodology (Clarke, Doabler, et al., 2012). The paucity of research examining the effects of elementary mathematics interventions for students with and at risk for math difficulties underscores the challenges school psychologists face as they seek to support the implementation of evidence-based practices in schools. However, research evidence is steadily accumulating that identifies the features of instruction that are essential for building proficiency in elementary mathematics. Although it remains true that considerably less research has examined effective instructional practices in mathematics when compared to studies of reading instruction and intervention, several major themes and research findings have been identified in mathematics in the last decade that can be utilized to guide the work of school psychologists (e.g., Gersten et al., 2005; National Mathematics Advisory Panel, 2008).

Focused content. One issue plaguing mathematics instruction has been the breadth of topics covered in the mathematics curricula (Schmidt, Houang, & Cogan, 2002). While the critique of this approach as a mile wide and an inch deep is targeted at the content coverage in core or Tier 1 programs, the need for focused content is even more acute for struggling students in Tier 2 and Tier 3 intervention programs. Because these students are behind their peers, their programs need to focus on the most critical aspects of mathematics. In elementary school, this means a focus on numbers and number systems (i.e., whole and rational number systems) and the properties and operations within those systems (Gersten, Beckmann, et al., 2009; National Mathematics Advisory Panel, 2008). Other critical content for mathematics intervention recommended by experts include word problem instruction that emphasizes underlying structures of problems and includes the use of model representations and heuristics to promote generalizability of problem-solving skill across problem types (e.g., change problems, compare problems; Jitendra, DiPipi, & Perron-Jones, 2002) and fact fluency instruction that facilitates efficient recall of arithmetic facts (e.g., Fuchs et al., 2005).

When content is taught in intervention settings, experts in the fields of mathematics and education (e.g., Gersten, Beckmann, et al., 2009; National Mathematics Advisory Panel, 2008; Siegler et al., 2010) have emphasized that instruction should include multiple types of knowledge to support adequate understanding of mathematics content, that it is insufficient for instruction to focus on building either procedural knowledge or conceptual knowledge in isolation, and that the two must be integrated to support mathematical proficiency (National Mathematics Advisory Panel, 2008; Wu, 1999). To build conceptual and procedural knowledge in mathematics, strategies that allow students to grapple with content more deeply should be employed throughout instruction (e.g., concrete–representational–abstract sequences; Miller & Hudson, 2007). This may be particularly true for intervention materials that may overly rely on teaching procedures without addressing the underlying mathematics concepts. School psychologists can work with mathematics specialists to help evaluate programs to ensure the quality of content coverage and an appropriate balance between conceptual understanding and procedural knowledge.

Explicit instruction. School psychologists can also evaluate instructional programs, through curricular reviews, and the instruction provided to students, through direct observation, in terms of the level of explicit instruction. There is also strong evidence that explicit, systematic mathematics instruction can be used to effectively teach a range of learners (Gersten, Beckmann, et al., 2009) and in particular students who are at risk. Examples of explicit, systematic instruction in the context of mathematics include providing clear models for solving problems and allowing students to work with multiple representations of mathematics concepts, giving students ample opportunities to practice newly learned skills and share mathematical solutions using think-alouds, immediately and consistently providing students with feedback throughout instruction, strategically introducing new content and linking it to students' prior knowledge, and providing frequent opportunities to review content (Gersten, Beckmann, et al., 2009; National Mathematics Advisory Panel, 2008). Precision of language is also essential to support student learning in mathematics, because (a) mathematics content is vocabulary laden, (b) students may commit definitions to memory for later recall, and (c) if slightly inaccurate definitions are used, students may confuse concepts and strategy application (Ball & Bass, 2003).

Instructional intensity. Just as school psychologists play a role in supporting high-quality Tier 1 instruction, they are uniquely positioned to support the effectiveness of intervention in Tier 2 and beyond. School psychologists who are well versed in instructional design principles can utilize standardized observation protocols to assess intervention fidelity in tiers that provide supplemental academic supports. Of particular interest in Tier 2 and beyond is the notion of *instructional intensity*. As students demonstrate increased need for instructional support in mathematics (e.g., the results of screening assessments indicate widening discrepancies between student and peer performance, or students fail to respond to intervention in Tier 2), it is important to ensure that the intensity of instruction is sufficient to meet student needs. Monitoring instructional intensity is important for several reasons. For example, in a three-tiered system if a student fails to respond to Tier 2 intervention, it could be easily assumed that the student will benefit from more intensive instruction in Tier 3, but this assumption is plagued with problems. First, this assumption is predicated on the notion that Tier 3 intervention is necessarily more "intense" than Tier 2 intervention. However, in practice there are frequently few differences between Tier 2 and Tier 3 intervention in terms of typical features of intensity (e.g., duration, group size, frequency of progress monitoring). Second, there may be means for intensifying instruction in Tier 2 that can be used before the student requires Tier 3 support, thereby reserving critical school resources. Whether or not a three-tiered system is used, the idea of increasing instructional intensity as the need of the student increases serves as a valuable guideline.

School psychologists can support the process for optimizing instructional intensity within math classrooms or intervention groups in several ways. As experts in instructional design and assessment practices, school psychologists are uniquely positioned to provide interventionists with meaningful feedback about their classroom environment. Using instruments that allow for documentation of a range of features of intensity (e.g., rate of student–teacher interactions) across the range of evidence-based practices recommended by experts to improve the quality of mathematics instruction and intervention (Gersten, Beckmann, et al., 2009), school psychologists can support the effectiveness of math intervention for students with or at risk for math difficulties.

SUMMARY

The challenges of implementing multitiered systems of support in mathematics are great but also exciting. School psychologists, by virtue of their expertise in learning, instructional design, program evaluation, and assessment, have the possibility to craft a critical role in efforts to implement best practices in both the assessment and instruction of mathematics. To do so, school psychologists should lead by example in helping schools build upon existing RTI systems in reading, while recognizing that knowledge about best practices in mathematics is expanding rapidly. The school psychologist will truly need to be a scientist–practitioner staying abreast of new development in the research base and then working to transition that new knowledge into effective practices for all students. School psychologists should also be keenly aware about the context in which any reform efforts are undertaken to ensure the culture of the school and the students they serve are kept at the forefront of efforts to improve mathematics instruction and assessment. School psychologists can help build a school climate and culture that encourages all students to view success in mathematics as within their capabilities (Halpern et al., 2007).

In terms of specific practices, school psychologists will continue to have a role in the development of screening systems at Tier 1 and progress monitoring systems for at-risk students served in Tier 2 and Tier 3 settings. Building on their knowledge of observation, school psychologists can work to incorporate effective instructional practices for at-risk students in all settings, including general education.

Although not experts in mathematics content, school psychologists can work with mathematics specialists and district mathematics leaders to evaluate curricula content coverage. Doing so will ensure that the groundwork for current and future success in mathematics is strong as students advance throughout the elementary grades. School psychologists need to consistently gauge the success of their efforts by garnering feedback from colleagues and evaluating the achievement data of the schools and students they serve to determine if efforts they led are having a positive impact on achievement.

In 2001, the National Research Council (2001) stated, "All young Americans must learn to think mathematically, and they must think mathematically to learn" (p. 16). We believe the school psychologist can play a leading role in making that statement a reality.

REFERENCES

Aud, S., Hussar, W., Kena, G., Bianco, K., Frohlich, L., Kemp, J., & Tahan, K. (2011). *The condition of education 2011* (NCES 2011-033). Washington, DC: National Center for Education Statistics.

Baker, S., Fien, H., & Baker, D. (2010). Robust reading instruction in the early grades: Conceptual and practical issues in the integration and evaluation of Tier 1 and Tier 2 instructional supports. *Focus on Exceptional Children, 42*(9), 1–20.

Ball, D. L., & Bass, H. (2003). Toward a practice-based theory of mathematical knowledge for teaching. In B. Davis & E. Simmt (Eds.), *Proceedings of the 2002 annual meeting of the Canadian Mathematics Education Study Group* (pp. 3–14). Edmonton, AB, Canada: Canadian Mathematics Education Study Group.

Berch, D. B. (2005). Making sense of number sense: Implications for children with mathematical disabilities. *Journal of Learning Disabilities, 38*, 333–339. doi:10.1177/00222194050380040901

Bryant, B. R., Bryant, D. P., Kethley, C., Kim, S. A., Pool, C., & You-Jin, S. (2008). Preventing mathematics difficulties in the primary grades: The critical features of instruction in textbooks as part of the equation. *Learning Disability Quarterly, 31*, 21–35.

Bryant, D. P., Bryant, B. R., Roberts, G., Vaughn, S., Pfannenstiel, K. H., Porterfield, J., & Gersten, R. (2011). Early numeracy intervention program for first-grade students with mathematics difficulties. *Exceptional Children, 78*, 7–23.

Burns, M. K., & VanDerHeyden, A. M. (2006). Using response to intervention to assess learning disabilities: Introduction to the special series. *Assessment for Effective Instruction, 32*, 3–5.

Clarke, B., Baker, S., & Chard, D. (2008). Best practices in mathematics assessment and intervention with elementary students. In A. Thomas & J. Grimes (Eds.), *Best practices in school psychology V* (pp. 453–464). Bethesda, MD: National Association of School Psychologists.

Clarke, B., Doabler, C., Smolkowski, K., Baker, S., Fien, H., & Cary, M. S. (2012). *Examining the efficacy of a Tier 2 kindergarten mathematics intervention.* Manuscript submitted for publication.

Clarke, B., Gersten, R., Dimino, J., & Rolfhus, E. (2012). *ASPENS administrator's handbook.* Longmont, CO: Sopris West.

Clarke, B., Smolkowski, K., Baker, S. K., Fien, H., Doabler, C. T., & Chard, D. J. (2011). The impact of a comprehensive Tier 1 core kindergarten program on the achievement of students at risk in mathematics. *Elementary School Journal, 111*, 561–584. doi:10.1086/659033

Common Core State Standards Initiative. (2010). *Common Core State Standards for mathematics.* Retrieved from http://www.corestandards.org

Coyne, M., Kame'enui, E. J., & Carnine, D. (Eds.). (2011). *Effective teaching strategies that accommodate diverse learners.* Upper Saddle River, NJ: Prentice Hall.

Doabler, C. T., Fien, H., Nelson-Walker, N. J., & Baker, S. K. (2012). Evaluating three elementary mathematics programs for presence of eight research-based instructional design principles. *Learning Disability Quarterly, 35*, 200–211. doi:10.1177/0731948712438557

Doabler, C., Baker, S. K., Kosty, D., Smolkowski, K., Clarke, B., Miller, S. J., & Fien, H. (in press). Examining the association between explicit mathematics instruction and student mathematics achievement. *Elementary School Journal.*

Dyson, N. I., Jordan, N. C., & Glutting, J. (2013). A number sense intervention for low-income kindergartners at risk for mathematics difficulties. *Journal of Learning Disabilities, 46*, 166–181. doi:10.1177/0022219411410233

Fuchs, L. S., Compton, D. L., Fuchs, D., Paulsen, K., Bryant, J. D., & Hamlett, C. L. (2005). The prevention, identification, and cognitive determinants of math difficulty. *Journal of Educational Psychology, 97*, 493–513. doi:10.1037/0022-0663.97.3.493

Fuchs, D., Fuchs, L. S., & Vaughn, S. (2008). *Response to intervention: A framework for reading educators.* Newark, DE: International Reading Association.

Fuchs, L. S., Powell, S. R., Seethaler, P. M., Fuchs, D., Hamlett, C. L., Cirino, P. T., & Fletcher, J. M. (2010). A framework for remediating number combination deficits. *Exceptional Children, 76*, 135–156.

Gersten, R. M., Beckmann, S., Clarke, B., Foegen, A., March, L., Star, J. R., & Witzel, B. (2009). *Assisting students struggling with mathematics: Response to intervention (RTI) for elementary and middle schools* (Practice Guide Report No. NCEE 2009-4060). Washington, DC: U.S. Department of Education, National Center for Education Evaluation and Regional Assistance.

Gersten, R. M., & Chard, D. (1999). Number sense: Rethinking arithmetic instruction for students with mathematical disabilities. *Journal of Special Education, 33*, 18–28. doi:10.1177/002246699903300102

Gersten, R. M., Chard, D., Jayanthi, M., Baker, S. K., Morphy, P., & Flojo, J. (2009). Mathematics instruction for students with learning disabilities: A meta-analysis of instructional components. *Review of Educational Research, 79*, 1202–1242. doi:10.3102/0034654309334431

Gersten, R. M., Clarke, B., Jordan, N. C., Newman-Gonchar, R., Haymond, K., & Wilkins, C. (2012). Universal screening in mathematics for the primary grades: Beginnings of a research base. *Exceptional Children, 78*, 423–445.

Gersten, R. M., Jordan, N. C., & Flojo, J. R. (2005). Early identification and interventions for students with mathematics difficulties. *Journal of Learning Disabilities, 38*, 293–304. doi:10.1177/00222194050380040301

Goldman, S. R., & Pellegrino, J. W. (1987). Information processing and educational microcomputer technology: Where do we go from here? *Journal of Learning Disabilities, 20*, 144–154. doi:10.1177/002221948702000302

Halpern, D., Aronson, J., Reimer, N., Simpkins, S., Star, J., & Wentzel, K. (2007). *Encouraging girls in math and science* (NCER 2007-2003). Washington, DC: U.S. Department of Education, National Center for Education Research. Retrieved from http://ncer.ed.gov

Institute for Mathematics and Education. (2011). *Learning progressions for the Common Core State Standards in mathematics.* Tucson, AZ: Author. Retrieved from http://ime.math.arizona.edu/progressions/

Jitendra, A., DiPipi, C. M., & Perron-Jones, N. (2002). An exploratory study of schema-based word-problem-solving instruction for middle school students with learning disabilities: An emphasis on conceptual and procedural understanding. *Journal of Special Education, 36*, 23–38.

Juel, C. (1988). Learning to read and write: A longitudinal study of 54 children from first through fourth grades. *Journal of Educational Psychology, 80*, 437–447. doi:10.1037/0022-0663.80.4.437

Mayer, R. E. (2009). *Multimedia learning* (2nd ed.). New York, NY: Cambridge University Press.

Milgram, J. (2005). *The mathematics preservice teachers need to know.* Stanford, CA: Stanford University, Department of Mathematics. Retrieved from http://math.stanford.edu/pub/papers/milgram/FIE-book.pdf

Miller, S., & Hudson, P. (2007). Using evidence-based practices to build mathematics competence related to conceptual, procedural, and declarative knowledge. *Learning Disabilities Research & Practice, 22*, 47–57. doi:10.1111/j.1540-5826.2007.00230.x

Morgan, P. L., Farkas, G., & Wu, Q. (2009). Five-year growth trajectories of kindergarten children with learning difficulties in mathematics. *Journal of Learning Disabilities, 42*, 306–321. doi:10.1177/0022219408331037

National Association of School Psychologists. (2010). *Model for comprehensive and integrated school psychological services.* Bethesda, MD: Author. Retrieved from http://www.nasponline.org/standards/2010standards/2_PracticeModel.pdf

National Center on Response to Intervention. (2009). *Progress monitoring tools chart.* Washington, DC: Author. Retrieved from http://www.rti4success.org/progressMonitoringTools

National Council of Teachers of Mathematics. (2006). *Curriculum focal points for prekindergarten through grade 8 mathematics: A quest for coherence.* Reston, VA: Author. Retrieved from http://www.nctm.org/standards/focalpoints.aspx?id=282

National Mathematics Advisory Panel. (2008). *Foundations for success: The final report of the National Mathematics Advisory Panel.* Washington, DC: U.S. Department of Education. Retrieved from http://www2.ed.gov/about/bdscomm/list/mathpanel/report/final-report.pdf

National Reading Panel. (2000). *Report of the National Reading Panel: Teaching children to read: An evidence-based assessment of the scientific research literature on reading and its implications for reading instruction.* Washington, DC: National Institute of Child Health and Human Development.

National Research Council. (2001). *Adding it up: Helping children learn mathematics*. Washington, DC: Mathematics Learning Study Committee.

National Research Council. (2009). *Mathematics learning in early childhood: Paths toward excellence and equity*. Washington, DC: National Academies Press.

National Science Board. (2008). *Science and engineering indicators 2008* (Vol. 2). Arlington, VA: National Science Foundation.

Olson, J., Martin, M. O., & Mullis, I. V. S. (Eds.). (2008). *TIMSS 2007 technical report*. Chestnut Hill, MA: TIMSS and PIRLS International Study Center.

Oslund, E. L., Hagan-Burke, S., Taylor, A. B., Simmons, D. C., Simmons, L., Kwok, O., ... Coyne, M. D. (2012). Predicting kindergarteners' response to early reading intervention: An examination of progress-monitoring measures. *Reading Psychology, 33*, 78–103. doi:10.1080/02702711.2012.630611

Pianta, R. C., & Hamre, B. K. (2009). Conceptualization, measurement, and improvement of classroom processes: Standardized observation can leverage capacity. *Educational Researcher, 38*, 109–119. doi:10.3102/0013189X09332374

Schmidt, W., Houang, R., & Cogan, L. (2002). A coherent curriculum: The case of mathematics. *American Educator, 26*(2), 1–18.

Siegler, R., Carpenter, T., Fennell, F., Geary, D., Lewis, J., Okamoto, Y., Thompson, L., & Wray, J. (2010). *Developing effective fractions instruction for kindergarten through 8th grade: A practice guide* (NCEE 2010-4039). Washington, DC: U.S. Department of Education, National Center for Education Evaluation and Regional Assistance. Retrieved from http://ies.ed.gov/ncee/wwc/pdf/practice_guides/fractions_pg_093010.pdf

Torgesen, J. K. (2000). Individual differences in response to early interventions in reading: The lingering problem of treatment resisters. *Learning Disabilities Research & Practice, 15*, 55–64. doi:10.1207/SLDRP1501_6

Wu, H. (1999). Basic skills versus conceptual understanding. *American Educator, 23*(3), 14–19.

Ysseldyke, J., Burns, M., Dawson, P., Kelley, B., Morrison, D., Ortiz, S., ... Telzrow, C. (2006). *School psychology: A blueprint for training and practice III*. Bethesda, MD: National Association of School Psychologists. Retrieved from http://www.nasponline.org/resources/blueprint/FinalBlueprintInteriors.pdf

15

Best Practices in Mathematics Instruction and Assessment in Secondary Settings

Yetunde Zannou
Leanne R. Ketterlin-Geller
Pooja Shivraj
Southern Methodist University

OVERVIEW

Secondary mathematics often includes a series of courses that begin with Algebra I and progress through geometry, Algebra II, as well as an introduction to advanced mathematics such as trigonometry, precalculus, or statistics and probability. To gain access to these courses, Algebra I is the prerequisite (National Mathematics Advisory Panel, 2008). More than just a perfunctory obligation, Algebra I lays the foundation for success in subsequent mathematics courses by advancing students' knowledge learned in middle school—operations with rational numbers (including ratios and proportions) and simple linear equations—to solving quadratic equations and applying functional relationships. With the foundational knowledge from Algebra I in place, students can engage in more complex mathematics, including Algebra II. Students who successfully complete a minimum of Algebra II in high school have higher rates of college retention and graduation (National Mathematics Advisory Panel, 2008). Moreover, these students are better prepared to engage in college-level mathematics courses and those related to science, technology, engineering, and mathematics (Achieve, 2013a). Educational policy makers have applied these findings when setting state policies: 21 states and the District of Columbia require students to complete Algebra II to graduate from high school (Achieve, 2013b).

Although the importance of algebra cannot be overestimated, many students enter high school without the necessary prerequisite skills to be successful in algebra. On the 2011 National Assessment of Educational Progress (NAEP) in mathematics, 27% of eighth-grade students performed below the basic level of proficiency. The results are even more alarming when disaggregated: 66% of students with disabilities and 71% of English language learners scored below basic levels of proficiency in mathematics. On the algebra scale that ranges from 0 to 500, the average score for all students was 289 ($SE = 0.2$). Average scores for students with disabilities and English language learners were statistically significantly lower than other students (Hemphill & Vanneman, 2011). Because of the importance of algebra to future learning and career opportunities, coupled with assessment evidence that indicates students struggle with algebra-readiness skills and knowledge, this chapter focuses on best practices for supporting instruction and assessment in algebra.

The purpose of this chapter is to provide school psychologists working in secondary mathematics settings with the knowledge they need to effectively provide systems, teachers, and students with instructional supports as outlined in the domain of Interventions and Instructional Support to Develop Academic Skills of the National Association of School Psychologists (NASP) *Model for Comprehensive and Integrated School Psychological Services* (NASP, 2010). Specifically, we situate this discussion within the three-tiered model of instructional support, which includes high-quality core instruction, multilayered formative assessment, and evidence-based interventions for students who struggle. To improve student performance, school psychologists are expected to develop and implement evidence-based instructional strategies. Therefore, in this chapter we posit three basic considerations that support the school psychologist's ability to accurately "diagnose the conditions under which students' learning is enabled" (Tilly, 2008, p. 20) and design interventions that help students meet learning benchmarks and state standards. To begin, we provide an overview of the current standards that define the content domain in algebra, the habits of mind that students should apply to achieve success in the mathematics classroom, and the strands of mathematical proficiency, that is, the knowledge, skills, and dispositions that demonstrate understanding and fluency in the content domain. We conclude with a discussion of best practices in assessment and instruction for the school psychologist working in secondary mathematics settings. We describe the multifaceted role of the school psychologist as a leader in data-based decision making and as an instructional specialist able to apply evidence-based instructional strategies to support systems, teachers, and students in helping all students achieve. We provide practical instructional recommendations to help all students develop algebraic proficiency through high-quality core algebra instruction and interventions for students who struggle.

BASIC CONSIDERATIONS

Three basic considerations undergird the work of school psychologists working in secondary mathematics settings: Standards for Mathematical Content, Standards for Mathematical Practice, and Strands of Mathematical Proficiency. Currently, 45 states and the District of Columbia have adopted the Common Core State Standards as consistent and clear guidelines for the relevant real-world knowledge and skills in English language arts and mathematics content that students need for success in college and careers. The Common Core State Standards for Mathematics (CCSS-M) not only defines content standards for algebra and other mathematics courses from elementary to secondary school, but also identifies standards for mathematical practice—such as problem solving, reasoning and proof, communication, representation, and connections—that students are expected to develop as they engage with the mathematical content. Lastly, the CCSS-M defines what it means

for students to be mathematically proficient, possessing integrated strands of procedural fluency, conceptual understanding, and application to problem solving (National Governors Association Center for Best Practices & Council of Chief State School Officers, 2010). These basic considerations provide the school psychologist with a working understanding of what students are expected to know and be able to do, as well as the goal of mathematics instruction: proficiency. Each basic consideration is discussed in greater detail below.

Knowledge of Standards for Mathematical Content

The CCSS-M represents major shifts in the focus, coherence, and rigor of mathematics content standards across the United States. The shift in focus refers to developing greater proficiency and understanding of fewer mathematics concepts per grade. Coherence is integrated into CCSS-M by intentionally linking various concepts within each grade level and considering how to build student knowledge about those concepts over time. Rigor here refers to focusing on conceptual understanding, procedural fluency, and application to problem solving across all concepts in each grade level, and not necessarily increased problem difficulty. Students in algebra are exposed to concepts such as functions, slope and y-intercept, rate of change, linear equations, inequalities, quadratics, construction of graphs for the former topics, and analysis of those graphs. Although many of these topics may not be new to students in secondary school, the standards within them explore the topics in greater depth than in earlier grades, thereby increasing students' understanding of the concepts and how they relate to one another. For example, students in Algebra I explore the concept of creating linear models to represent data in more depth than in the eighth grade. In addition, algebra standards revisit the concept of rate of change that students encountered earlier in the curriculum. The grade-level organization of content standards from elementary through middle school emphasizes focus within the concepts covered, builds coherence between concepts across grades, and promotes rigor by providing students with opportunities to engage the same concepts in a variety of ways. At the high school level, the standards shift to college and career-readiness content that every student should know without mandating the sequence of mathematics content.

Knowledge of Standards for Mathematical Practice

In addition to specifying the mathematical content students need to know and be able to do, the CCSS-M includes Standards for Mathematical Practice that describe the habits of mind that students develop in mathematics. These standards include (a) making sense of problems and persevering in solving them, (b) reasoning abstractly and quantitatively, (c) constructing viable arguments and critiquing the reasoning of others, (d) modeling with mathematics, (e) using appropriate tools strategically, (f) attending to precision, (g) looking for and making use of structure, and (h) looking for and expressing regularity in repeated reasoning. These standards emphasize more than a superficial understanding of mathematical procedures and concepts; that is, they also target the development of students' capacity for making sense of mathematical concepts, representing mathematical ideas accurately, and communicating about mathematics.

Well-defined curricular materials should connect mathematical content standards and the Standards for Mathematical Practice to ensure students have opportunities to learn mathematics and acquire mathematical habits of mind, both necessary components of mathematical proficiency. For example, in algebra, mathematically proficient students should be able to make sense of problems by explaining relationships between equations, verbal descriptions, graphs, and tables. Furthermore, students should be able to recognize patterns in calculations and find mathematically sound shortcuts to calculations. This includes finding patterns in the simplified forms of products that form geometric sequences. For example, if students are given: $(x-1)(x+1) = x^2 + x - x - 1$, which simplifies to $x^2 - 1$, and $(x-1)(x^2 + x + 1) = x^3 + x^2 + x - x^2 - x - 1$, which simplifies to $x^3 - 1$, then students should be able to identify the pattern and determine that $(x-1)(x^3 + x^2 + x + 1)$ will result in a simplified product of $x^4 - 1$. School psychologists can consult with campus leaders and teachers to select curricular materials that incorporate focused, coherent, and rigorous content standards with the higher order mathematical processes described in the Standards for Mathematical Practice.

Knowledge of Strands of Mathematical Proficiency

Synthesizing research in mathematics education and cognitive science, the National Research Council (2001) identified five interdependent strands that constitute mathematical proficiency: (a) *procedural fluency*, the ability to perform procedures in mathematics flexibly, accurately, and efficiently; (b) *conceptual understanding*, the ability to make meaning of mathematical concepts and operations, and the relationships between them; (c) *strategic competence*, the ability to formulate, represent, and solve problems in mathematics; (d) *adaptive reasoning*, the ability to justify and explain mathematical processes; and (e) *productive disposition*, self-efficacy and an inclination to see mathematics as being useful. When solving algebraic equations, procedural fluency may involve solving an equation to determine the value of a variable using a mathematically sound process such as using inverse operations in order to isolate the variable. Students may demonstrate conceptual understanding by determining, for example, the length of a square with side, *x* + *3*, whose perimeter is 24 square units. In order to solve this problem, the student needs to understand how the side of the square relates to its perimeter. In this example, the solution is not merely the value of *x*. Upon determining the value of *x*, an additional three units must be added to determine the length of the side. Strategic competence could involve having students choose among many approaches to solve a quadratic equation, while adaptive reasoning might require students to justify their rationale for selecting one problem-solving approach over another for a given situation.

As students advance in mathematics and their network of concepts expands, the transition from arithmetic to algebra can be difficult for students who have not developed foundational understanding of arithmetic concepts and procedural fluency. Kieran (1992) found that the successful transition from using solely arithmetic to incorporating algebraic proficiency takes time and that early algebra instruction should take care to thoroughly develop students' procedural competence before providing instruction that requires students to rely solely upon a structural understanding of mathematics. Using input–output tables to work backward, identify a pattern, and create algebraic expressions that represent real-world mathematical relationships can help students begin to value algebra and see its underlying structure. We describe below how an input–output table can be used in this way. Understanding the relationship between concepts and their abstract representations, coupled with having a firm grasp of procedural fluency and strategic competence, can help students develop their ability to reason mathematically, represent situations abstractly, and maneuver flexibly in both familiar and unfamiliar mathematical terrain without resorting to memorizing endless algorithms and formulas.

Although algebra relies heavily on conceptual understanding and reasoning, strong procedural fluency associated with basic mathematical proficiency is essential for success in algebra, which allows mathematical situations to be represented abstractly and manipulated in much the same way that numbers are manipulated in arithmetic. Consider, for example, what students would need to know and be able to do in order to determine the number of comic books in a set if the number of comics books in two sets, decreased by 5, is 19. Students would need conceptual understanding to accurately interpret what they are being asked to do and to represent this situation pictorially or abstractly using, for example, a number sentence (i.e., $2 \times \square - 5 = 19$) or an equation (i.e., $2x - 5 = 19$). In addition, students would need to be able to apply their knowledge of inverse operations to solve this problem using any number of strategies, such as solving the equation by working backward with the number sentence, or making an input–output table with possible values for the number of comic books in a set to determine which value when doubled and reduced by 5 results in 19 (e.g., an input of 7 would result in 9 comic books, which is too small, whereas an input of 15 would produce an output of 25 comic books, which is too large). The ability to correctly identify the concept and develop a plan, without the accompanying ability to accurately carry out the plan—procedural fluency—will limit student success in algebra. The converse is also true. Therefore, algebraic proficiency consists of computational and procedural fluency, conceptual understanding, and the ability to utilize knowledge and skills flexibly and strategically to solve problems (Gersten, Beckmann, et al., 2009).

Cognitive research indicates that students' ability to mentally represent mathematical concepts and relationships between them relies heavily on the interconnectedness of the proficiency strands (Hiebert et al., 1997). How students learn and connect different pieces of knowledge can support or hinder their ability to understand mathematics concepts at a deep, meaningful level, as well as to use conceptual understanding to solve problems (Bransford, Brown, & Cocking, 1999). School psychologists can help educators ensure that the standards and curricular materials are robust, incorporating opportunities for all students to learn the content, cultivate mathematical habits of mind, and develop proficiency across strands. In the next section we turn to best practices in assessment and instruction for school psychologists working in secondary mathematics settings.

BEST PRACTICES IN SECONDARY MATHEMATICS

As an assessment specialist, the school psychologist plays a critical role in helping school personnel to select and administer assessments, and in ensuring that student performance data are correctly interpreted to inform instructional decisions. School psychologists provide further instructional support by incorporating all available assessment information—performance data from technically adequate formative assessments, classroom observations, student work, and psychological evaluations, to name a few—to develop instructional strategies that are designed to meet individual students' learning needs (NASP, 2010). In this section, we discuss best practices in two key areas in secondary mathematics settings: formative assessment and instruction. We focus our attention on how school psychologists can facilitate implementation of evidence-based practices in assessment and instruction in secondary settings, and how these practices can be used to make instructional decisions and develop mathematical proficiency, respectively.

Secondary mathematics instruction has been less heavily researched than that of instruction in earlier grades. Consequently, the instructional recommendations that follow rely on empirical evidence for quality algebra instruction, as well as relevant support from the literature on elementary and secondary school students who struggle in mathematics. School psychologists will draw upon their expert knowledge in designing interventions to determine how best to apply these recommendations to the specific student and learning environment in which they work and collaborate with teachers, students, and families.

Best Practices in Formative Assessment in Secondary Mathematics

Making timely and individualized educational decisions is necessary for supporting students' development of algebraic proficiency in secondary settings. Similar to other content domains, results from both formative and summative assessments in mathematics are used within a three-tiered model of support to identify students who may be at risk for not reaching expectations, determine areas of strengths and weaknesses, monitor progress through the curriculum, and evaluate students' mastery of the mathematics content. Integrating results from different assessments into a system of instructional decision making is a critical role for a school psychologist within a middle or high school mathematics classroom.

Formative assessments are designed to provide teachers with ongoing student performance data to make instructional decisions. As compared to summative assessments that are administered at the end of the learning process, formative assessments are administered before instruction begins as well as during the instructional process. Figure 15.1 illustrates how selected response and constructed response items can be used to assess student development of procedural fluency, conceptual understanding, strategic competence, and adaptive reasoning. These items are written to elicit specific information about student understanding.

Research synthesized by Gersten, Chard, et al., (2009) indicates that using formative assessments in the mathematics classroom has an impact on student achievement. Specifically, when teachers were provided with data about student progress over time, there was only a small effect on student achievement. However, this effect on achievement increased when teachers were provided with additional information to support application to instructional design and delivery decisions.

Receiving feedback from formative assessments also has an impact on students' achievement, especially when students view their own data. However, facilitating students' setting of goals from these data did not have a statistically significant effect on student outcomes (Gersten, Chard, et al., 2009). Most of these studies were conducted with younger students. Limited research is available that examines the use of formative assessments

Figure 15.1. Sample Formative Assessment Items to Assess Varying Levels of Cognitive Complexity and Possible Misconceptions

Cognitive Complexity	Example Questions	Example Student Response	Nonexample Student Response	Possible Misconception
Procedural Fluency	What is the solution to the equation $2y - 4 = 24$?	$2y - 4 + 4 = 24 + 4$ $2y = 28$ $y = 14$	$2y - 4 = 24 - 4$ $2y = 20$ $y = 10$	Student performs the same operation on both sides instead of the inverse operation to "get rid" of the constant. Student subtracts 4.
Conceptual Understanding	How many solutions does the equation $2y + 3x = 6$ have? a. One solution b. Two solutions c. No solution d. Infinitely many solutions	Infinitely many solutions	Two solutions	Student may think that each variable represents one solution. Student does not understand that the solution is an ordered pair.
Strategic Competence	Use an input–output table to find the solution to the system of equations: $y = 2$ $x + y = 2$	$y = 2$ 	x	y	 |----|----| | -1 | 2 | → | 0 | 2 | | 1 | 2 | $x + y = 2$ | x | y | |----|----| | -1 | 3 | → | 0 | 2 | | 1 | 1 | Solution: (0, 2)	$y = 2$ | y | |----| | 2 | | 2 | | 2 | $x + y = 2$ | x | y | |----|----| | -1 | 3 | | 0 | 2 | | 1 | 1 | No solution	Student may think that since there is no x value in the first equation, there is no solution. The student may not understand that $y = 2$ is a line where the x values vary but the y value does not.
Adaptive Reasoning	Why does the system of equations below have infinitely many solutions? $2y + 6x = 4$ $4y + 12x = 8$	The system of equations is true for all values of x and y OR The lines, when graphed, intersect at every single point, or are overlapping lines.	The system of equations is not true for any value of x or y OR The lines, when graphed, don't intersect at any point.	Student may struggle to interpret the meaning for this system of equations algebraically and graphically. Student confuses infinite solutions with no solution.

to support instructional decisions in middle and high school mathematics classrooms. However, promising practices are beginning to emerge that can support middle and high school teachers' instructional decision making.

Formative assessment results are used to make three types of decisions:

- *Screening decisions:* Which students are and are not on track for reaching the curricular expectations? As noted earlier, the curricular expectations extend beyond the content standards to include the levels of cognitive engagement through which students interact with the content.
- *Diagnostic decisions:* In which areas of the curriculum—content standards and cognitive engagement—is the student excelling? In which areas is the student struggling?
- *Progress monitoring decisions:* Is the student learning the material at an appropriate rate to reach the instructional goals?

For many secondary mathematics teachers, implementing formative assessments in their classroom is a novel approach to making instructional decisions. As such, they may not understand how formative assessment results aid different types of instructional decisions, how to select an appropriate instrument for making these decisions, how to interpret data to make decisions, and how to communicate these decisions to others. Because school psychologists have considerable training in these areas, the school psychologist and secondary mathematics teacher need to work collaboratively to integrate assessment knowledge with mathematics content knowledge to make the best use of formative assessment results within the classroom.

Facilitating Implementation of Formative Assessments in Secondary Mathematics Classes

School psychologists can support implementation of formative assessments in several key ways. First, within a three-tiered model of support, school psychologists need to provide teachers with the conceptual foundation for understanding the role of formative assessments within the decision-making cycle. As previously noted, many middle and high school mathematics teachers may have limited experience implementing a three-tiered model of support. Providing a clear description of how formative assessments provide information to support decision making is needed to ensure appropriate use of formative assessment data.

Second, school psychologists can provide a framework for helping teachers and administrators select relevant assessments that will be useful for informing their instruction. Although administrators may have the final decision, when mathematics becomes departmentalized at the middle and high school levels, administrators often look to the mathematics departments to make specific recommendations about which assessments to implement. However, teachers often lack fundamental understanding of measurement and assessment principles that are needed to select assessments that will lead to valid decision making (Stiggins, 1999). Without understanding the concepts of validity and reliability, teachers may lack a clear lens through which to critically evaluate the utility of various assessment tools. Because the validity of the instructional decisions relies on the quality of the results, helping teachers select appropriate assessment tools that are aligned with their intended purpose is a critical role for school psychologists.

Third, because school psychologists work within the educational system to implement a three-tiered model of support, they are well positioned to facilitate implementation and use of systems of data management and storage that extend beyond the roles and responsibilities of individual teachers. Hamilton et al., (2009) recommend developing a cohesive data management plan that establishes organizational structures and practices to support data use. Managing data from formative assessment systems is often one of the biggest barriers to implementation and use, especially for middle and high school teachers who work with large numbers of students. Data entry as well as retrieval of results should be an efficient process that reserves the majority of the teachers' time for data interpretation and implementation of instructional decisions. In fact, in a national survey probing teachers' and school districts' data use, the U.S. Department of Education (2008) reported that 37% of all responding teachers had electronic access to student achievement data. As districts or schools work to increase access as well as establish a data management plan, the school psychologist can help serve as a bridge between the district or school policies to facilitate teachers' implementation and use.

Although mathematics teachers are typically adept at interpreting information presented in graphs and tables, understanding the information as it relates to student achievement may be challenging. As such, the fourth area in which school psychologists can support teachers' use of formative assessment data is by facilitating interpretation of assessment results in relation to the intended decision. For example, mathematics teachers are well versed in interpreting data displayed in a histogram. However, when interpreting results from a universal screener that are displayed on a histogram, teachers may need additional support to understand how this presentation of data helps determine who may or may not be at risk for meeting the curricular expectations as well as to evaluate each child's relative risk status. Data-use facilitators work with educators to encourage systematic use of data, but should not be responsible for all data interpretation and analysis (Hamilton et al., 2009). A school psychologist can help build data literacy across teachers by modeling the role multiple sources of data can play in making decisions that have an impact on classroom practices.

Fifth, and finally, school psychologists can directly and indirectly support communication of assessment results. Within the educational system, school psychologists can facilitate team meetings designed to support individual students' achievement across academic subjects. Moreover, school psychologists can support teachers' dissemination of results to parents and students. Although not the direct conduit of information, school psychologists can help teachers share assessment results by providing a framework for the discussion. For example, sharing data with parents may involve the following components: (a) explain the purpose of the assessment and the decisions that will be made from the results, (b) describe the score report and the meaning of the scores (i.e., what is a scale score, grade equivalent score), (c) share the individual student's score and corroborate with additional evidence, (d) discuss the decision or action to be taken as a result of this information, and (e) describe subsequent steps in the student's educational program and how the student's progress will be evaluated. Providing teachers with a framework for discussion may help alleviate anxiety associated with sharing test results with parents.

Using Assessments to Make Formative Instructional Decisions

As discussed previously, formative assessments help teachers make screening decisions to determine who may or may not be on track for meeting the curricular expectations, diagnostic decisions to identify students' strengths and weaknesses, and progress monitoring decisions to determine if students are learning at the appropriate pace to reach their goals. Although

considerably fewer formative assessment tools are available in mathematics, several assessment systems are emerging that may support teachers' decision making. In this section, we build on school psychologists' knowledge of the uses of formative assessments to discuss relevant features and characteristics of mathematics assessment tools. The intent is not to review products that are currently available, but instead to describe characteristics that should be considered when selecting tools to implement within middle and high school mathematics classrooms.

Universal screening tools. Within the three-tiered model of support, universal screeners are implemented to help teachers identify which students are and are not on track for reaching academic benchmarks. Moreover, results can be used to identify the intensity of the support students may need to reach their goals. As such, when selecting a universal screening tool, the basic considerations of standards for mathematical content and strands of mathematical proficiency should be assessed in adequate proportions for making valid screening decisions. An alignment analysis can be conducted to determine if the test appropriately represents both the content standards and the strands of mathematical proficiency. For example, if the universal screener is intended to identify students who are at risk for not reaching the curricular expectations as specified by the CCSS-M, then the tested content should include conceptual understanding, procedural fluency, and application of the content standards while integrating the Standards for Mathematical Practice, such as modeling, reasoning, and communicating using mathematically precise language.

In addition to considering the alignment between the curricular expectations and the tested content, the cut scores that are implemented to identify students' risk status should be validated through empirical analyses to ensure that appropriate classifications are being made (Gersten, Beckmann, et al., 2009). Cut scores for universal screeners can be set using local or national normative data or empirically established criterion that are predictive of future performance. Regardless of approach, because students' scores will be evaluated against the cut score to determine their risk status, the sensitivity of these cut scores for appropriately identifying students' risk should be carefully evaluated. School psychologists can support the selection of universal screeners by supporting alignment analyses as well as examining the validity of cut scores for classification.

Diagnostic formative assessment tools.
Diagnostic formative assessments aid in instructional decision making by helping to identify students' areas of strengths and weaknesses. These should not be confused with any assessments used to make clinical diagnoses; that is, diagnostic formative assessments are used to determine in which areas of the curriculum the student is struggling, which errors the student persistently makes, and what misconceptions appear to be impeding progress. Information obtained from diagnostic formative assessments is used to determine the type of additional instructional support a student might need as well as design the content and/or delivery of intervention programs (Ketterlin-Geller & Yovanoff, 2009). Typically, this information is only warranted for students who are identified as being at risk for not meeting curricular expectations based on results from the universal screener and confirmed with other sources.

A number of tools are commercially available that are self-labeled as diagnostic formative assessments. When selecting a diagnostic formative assessment, it is important to look for tools that provide detailed information for designing supplemental instruction. In some instances, diagnostic formative assessments provide skills inventories that specify the student's level of mastery in specific knowledge and skills associated with the curricular expectations. In other cases, the results are related to the student's pathway along the learning progression toward content mastery. Although the specific type of diagnostic information varies depending upon the type of assessment selected, it is important to consider the usefulness of the information for designing supplemental instruction during the selection process. School psychologists can facilitate this process by deciphering the information presented in the diagnostic score reports to determine its instructional utility.

Progress monitoring tools. Progress monitoring plays a key role in evaluating the effectiveness of instructional decisions for supporting the academic achievement of students who were identified as at risk for not meeting curricular expectations (Gersten, Beckmann, et al., 2009). Progress monitoring assessments are administered at least monthly and results are graphed to track changes in students' performance over time. Data are evaluated to determine if the student is making adequate progress as a result of implementing instructional changes. Adequate progress is judged by comparing the rate at which the student is gaining proficiency in relation to the student's goal. Detailed decision rules can be applied.

Several key features of progress monitoring tests distinguish this assessment system from others. Specifically, students' progress is monitored using a series of tests that are consistent in difficulty and sensitive to small changes in students' knowledge and skills. Progress monitoring tests should be short in duration. In addition to being easy to administer and score, procedures for administration and scoring should be standardized to ensure reliable data across administrations.

New progress monitoring tools are emerging to support these decisions for students in middle and high school mathematics classes. Several websites have been established by the U.S. Department of Education to help educators understand the process of progress monitoring as well as select tools. The National Center on Student Progress Monitoring (http://www.studentprogress.org) provides online training opportunities as well as a number of resources. For more in-depth information, visit the Research Institute on Progress Monitoring (http://www.progressmonitoring.org). Finally, the National Center on Intensive Interventions (http://www.intensiveintervention.org) provides a listing of progress monitoring tools that have been submitted for review. In the review process, independent experts review the tools across a number of dimensions to aid in decision making.

Best Practices in Instruction in Secondary Mathematics

The school psychologist working in secondary settings should be familiar with implementing the three-tiered model of instructional support in algebra. Research that examines the relationship between instructional practices and student achievement can provide practitioners with empirical evidence to inform classroom instruction and design interventions that promote student learning at the individual, group, and systems levels (NASP, 2010). Such evidence provides a useful lens for school psychologists as they assist school personnel in implementing a three-tiered model of instructional support. In this section, we discuss best practices in algebra instruction and how these practices support the Standards for Mathematical Content, Standards for Mathematical Practice, and Strands of Mathematical Proficiency (National Governors Association Center for Best Practices & Council of Chief State School Officers, 2010). Next, we describe the role of school psychologists in supporting the implementation of high-quality, evidence-based practices in algebra within the three-tiered model of instructional support.

Evidence-Based Practices for High-Quality Algebra Instruction

Findings based on meta-analyses conducted by Gersten, Beckmann, et al. (2009); Gersten, Chard, et al. (2009); Haas (2002, 2005); Rakes, Valentine, McGatha, and Ronau (2010); and Slavin, Lake, and Groff (2009) converge to suggest that, in addition to formative assessment, the following three instructional practices, in order of convincing evidence, support students' learning of mathematics in secondary settings: (a) explicit and systematic instruction, (b) visual representation, and (c) cooperative learning. Each review also surveyed practices such as problem-based learning and technology-aided instruction. However, evidence to support the effectiveness of these practices is limited, and therefore will not be discussed in this chapter.

Explicit and systematic instruction. Explicit

and systematic instruction is characterized by the integration of several distinct instructional practices: teacher demonstration and guided practice, presentation of a range of examples, student verbalization, and corrective feedback (National Mathematics Advisory Panel, 2008). Strong evidence supports the use of explicit and systematic instruction for students with learning disabilities and those who struggle in mathematics (Gersten, Beckmann, et al., 2009). However, Gersten, Chard, et al. (2009) caution that its effectiveness with students who struggle should not be interpreted as the only effective instructional approach for these students. Ultimately, the specific instructional approach a teacher chooses will depend on many factors, such as curricular compatibility for teaching the content and student characteristics.

Success in mathematics requires students to go beyond recall and apply their understanding to new concepts. Evidence suggests that teacher demonstration—modeling a set of clearly defined steps to solve a problem or a specific problem-solving strategy through a range of representative examples that increase in difficulty—helps students who receive core instruction alone (Haas, 2002) and those who receive additional instructional supports (Gersten, Chard, et al., 2009) to develop this aspect of proficiency. When coupled with other components of explicit and systematic instruction, teacher demonstration that includes consistent and specific steps provides students with a model of precise mathematical language, accurate relationships between concepts, and appropriate use of mathematical tools. When used in conjunction with verbalization of reasoning and/or examples and nonexamples, students learn

to differentiate when a correct strategy may be more or less appropriate in comparison to others.

Gersten, Chard, et al. (2009) reported that using a sequence and range of examples to teach algebraic equations and word problems had a significant, positive impact on student achievement in secondary settings. This component of explicit and systematic instruction describes the order and variety of problems that teachers present during a lesson or set of lessons. Teachers present problems in order of increasing difficulty and model solutions for a number of different problem types related to the target concept. Based on grade-level appropriateness, a teacher may also choose to present these varying types of problems within the same lesson or across several lessons. It is important that students understand that, conceptually and structurally, the process used to solve equations is the same. However, this understanding may not come easily to students, which is why presenting students with a variety of problem types should be done systematically over time (Kieran, 1992). Kieran (1992) recommends that teachers continue to help students connect familiar arithmetic processes with new algebraic ones, and that they make the connections explicit. Haas (2005), Maccini and Gagnon (2001), and Rakes et al. (2010) also found support for using examples that are graduated in difficulty or level of abstract representation to support student learning in algebra. For example, the CCSS-M for traditional algebra courses includes solving equations and inequalities in one variable. Teachers might use a sequence of examples that range in difficulty from one to two steps, and eventually require students to combine like terms on one side of the equation before proceeding to solve it. Within multistep equations, a teacher may choose to solve simpler problems involving whole numbers before introducing problems with integers, fractional coefficients, or constants.

Student verbalizations consist of thinking aloud about their reasoning while solving mathematics problems. Students may verbalize the steps they use as they solve problems, or maybe a response to a teacher or student about their thinking. Gersten, Beckmann, et al. (2009) provide evidence to support the use of student verbalizations as a component of explicit and systematic instruction for students who struggle in elementary and middle school mathematics. When this strategy was used in conjunction with other components of explicit and systematic instruction, the effect on student achievement was even greater. Studies synthesized by Gersten, Chard, et al. (2009) and Haas (2005) also showed positive effects of student verbalizations on student achievement in secondary settings. Evidence supports the use of student verbalizations in helping students to solve word problems, but additional empirical evidence is needed to support its effect on teaching other topics in secondary mathematics. The CCSS-M and the Standards for Mathematical Practice include mathematical reasoning and expression of mathematical connections. Teachers can incorporate student verbalizations into most lessons by avoiding questions that elicit simple yes, no, or numerical answers. Instead, teachers can probe students to justify answers by asking *how* and *why* questions. Consider the expression: $2x^2 + 3xy + y^2$. *What* questions can also be appropriate to prompt student verbalization. For example, "What do you think the x and y in this expression represent?" Students' responses may reveal varying levels of conceptual understanding when multiple variables are used. Haas (2002) cites a number of nonexperimental studies that discuss students' use of written and verbal means to develop and communicate understanding of mathematical ideas.

Feedback consists of student performance data that teachers collect through formal and informal means, as well as how teachers respond to students about their learning progress. As emphasized throughout this discussion of explicit and systematic instruction, evidence supports the use of corrective feedback combined with other components to improve learning outcomes for students in secondary mathematics settings (Gersten, Beckmann, et al., 2009; Gersten, Chard, et al., 2009; Haas, 2005). Informal feedback that teachers and students receive during regular instruction may consist of a student's response to a question designed to check for understanding. If the verbalization is inaccurate, then teachers may provide corrective feedback, which models the correct process or provides students with guidance to help them develop procedural fluency and conceptual understanding. For example, according to CCSS-M, students taking algebra should be able to create equations that describe numbers or relationships. Students may be asked to write an expression that represents the cost of an item, p, in a state where sales tax is 8%. If a student writes $p + 0.08$ instead of $p + 0.08p$, then the teacher may recognize this as a common misconception that adding tax or gratuity simply means adding the percentage as a decimal constant. Core instruction that incorporates corrective feedback might include asking the student to explain his or her understanding of the similarities and differences between both expressions, followed by providing a real-world example. "If the bill at a restaurant came to $20.00, and sales tax was 8%, how would you calculate the final bill?" The teacher can model correct reasoning using verbalizations to help students compare the resulting values $20.08 and $21.60. To further check for understanding, the teacher can ask students to predict how lowering the bill or increasing the bill would affect the sales tax, if at all. This supports the students' development of other Standards for Mathematical Practice such as reasoning abstractly and constructing viable arguments.

Visual representation. The use of visual representation in mathematics instruction consists of graphical models or manipulatives such as base 10 blocks, algebra tiles, coins, and other objects to represent mathematical concepts. Evidence suggests that incorporating multiple representations into mathematics instruction can help students learn algebraic concepts and retain learning gains over time (Gersten, Chard, et al., 2009; Haas, 2002). Haas (2005) noted that the use of manipulatives, mathematical models, and multiple representations such as physical models, pictures, diagrams, graphs, tables, charts, symbols, or games to represent algebraic equations or concepts had a positive effect on student achievement. Gersten, Beckmann, et al. (2009) reported a similar effect but for students in middle school learning algebraic concepts using visual representations.

The concrete–representation–abstract instructional method incorporates visual representation and a sequenced range of examples. In this method, teachers introduce concepts using concrete objects, followed by visual representations of mathematical concepts before transitioning to the abstract representation using numbers, symbols, and variables. Similar to studies on sequence and range of examples in the preceding section, this method emphasizes the deliberate selection and sequence of examples. However, interventions related to the concrete–representation–abstract method aim to build students' facility with abstract mathematical representations, an integral part of algebraic proficiency, by developing a strong conceptual foundation first through the use of concrete and visual representations.

Visual representations in secondary mathematics instruction benefit students with learning disabilities (Gersten, Chard, et al., 2009; Maccini & Gagnon, 2000) and may help all students to develop procedural fluency and conceptual understanding (Rakes et al., 2010). Maccini and Gagnon (2000) report findings from three studies where students with learning disabilities showed significant and positive gains in being able to represent and solve problems using concrete manipulatives and semiconcrete representations. In one study, participants

Figure 15.2. Multiple Representations of the Value of 0.4

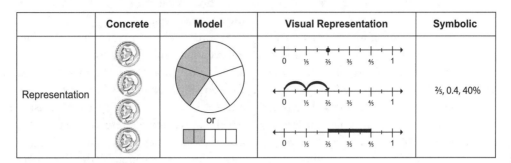

	Concrete	Model	Visual Representation	Symbolic
Representation		or		⅖, 0.4, 40%

were able to successfully represent problems abstractly and solve them using an explicit problem-solving strategy. The use of visual representations alone does not lead to academic gains (Gersten, Beckmann, et al., 2009). Researchers suggest there is a direct relationship between the level of specificity in *how* students are instructed to use visual representations and the effectiveness of this intervention (Gersten, Chard, et al., 2009).

Teacher and student use of visual representations can support the Standard of Mathematical Practice modeling with mathematics. Graphs and tables are visual representations that can help students to see the relationship between multiple mathematical representations and numeric patterns, to which they can apply arithmetic thinking to generalize mathematical relationships abstractly. In addition, visual representation can be used to help students develop conceptual understanding in algebra. For example, students can learn to use manipulatives to perform operations with polynomials (Rakes et al., 2010).

The concrete–representation–abstract method was particularly helpful in developing procedural fluency and conceptual understanding for students with learning disabilities in algebra (Maccini & Gagnon, 2000). Making the connection between multiple representations used in the concrete–representation–abstract method may help students to develop flexibility in their thinking about mathematical concepts and how best to represent them. As mentioned above, students often struggle to see the underlying structure and connectivity between multiple representations of the same content. For example, students may not recognize that the value of each representation in Figure 15.2 is the same. As such, teachers should explicitly link the visual representations to the abstract (or symbolic) notation to develop students' conceptual understanding, strategic competence, and adaptive reasoning.

Though strong evidence of effectiveness supports the use of the concrete–representation–abstract method in elementary and middle school, the findings in special education in algebra instruction suggest this model may be used to teach mathematics to high school students. However, as students develop algebraic proficiency, teachers may adjust the amount of time spent in each stage.

Cooperative learning. Cooperative learning involves peer-assisted learning with students in the same age group or across grades (Gersten, Chard, et al., 2009) and a wide range of collaborative activities that require students to work together to achieve a common goal (Haas, 2002). The effectiveness of cooperative learning varies by mathematics course, student characteristics, and whether or not peer tutors are in the same class as students being tutored. Cooperative learning that included recognizing team accomplishments and individual accountability was shown to be especially effective for improving student achievement (Haas, 2005; Slavin et al., 2009). Gersten, Chard, et al. (2009) found that cross-age tutoring in special education produced a larger effect size than same-age peer-assisted learning. Cross-age peer tutoring may be more effective than same-age tutoring because older students presumably have greater command of the concepts and therefore can provide components of explicit and systematic instruction such as demonstration, guided practice, and verbalizations that research indicates has a positive and significant effect on student outcomes (Gersten, Chard, et al., 2009; Maccini & Gagnon, 2000). Maccini and Gagnon (2000) found evidence to support the use of cooperative learning in class and across grades to promote social skills, mathematical concept and skill acquisition, and retention in students with learning disabilities and emotional disabilities in secondary settings. However, careful consideration of logistics such as time and student training may be needed to effectively incorporate peer tutoring across grades into routine class instruction.

Cooperative work may include positive interdependence, encouraging interaction, individual and group accountability, interpersonal and small-group skills, and group processing (Haas, 2005), and can complement many of the Standards for Mathematical Practice. Teachers may organize students in groups to solve novel problems, discuss possible solutions by constructing and critiquing arguments, and model mathematics after choosing the appropriate mathematical tools and strategies needed to solve the problem. Though empirical evidence in support of this practice for learning algebra and other secondary mathematics topics is limited, there may be potential to bridge the mathematical content and Standards for Mathematical Practice with the Strands of Mathematical Proficiency.

Facilitating Implementation of High-Quality Instruction in Algebra

Within the three-tiered model of instructional support, school psychologists support the implementation of high-quality instruction in several key ways. First, school psychologists are skilled at gathering and interpreting data from various sources to identify students' learning needs. In addition to student performance data from formative assessments described above, practitioners collect observational data of students in the learning environment to determine whether interventions are needed at the systems, classroom, or individual level. At the systems level, school psychologists might consider how well students perform as a group on universal screening measures and decide to observe classroom instruction to identify any environmental factors that may contribute to poor learning outcomes. Within the context of algebra, the school psychologist may look for the presence of best practices in core instruction, as noted above. For example, are both teacher and students verbalizing problem-solving strategies and steps? Both teacher and student verbalization are shown to help students develop strategic competence (the ability to identify an appropriate problem-solving strategy) and procedural fluency (the ability to employ the correct steps to solve a problem) associated with mathematical proficiency. Student verbalizations can help students to think about their thinking and solidify their understanding of procedures and concepts, while providing teachers with feedback that they can use to inform instruction (Gersten, Chard, et al., 2009; Haas, 2002). If these practices are generally absent from core

instruction, the school psychologist might recommend that such evidence-based practices be incorporated at the systems level.

Second, school psychologists design instructional interventions that address struggling students' individual learning needs and help them achieve academic goals. Consequently, school psychologists consult with teachers and students to identify specific, measureable goals for which instructional interventions are designed and against which they are evaluated. To effectively design instructional interventions, the school psychologist will incorporate knowledge of behavior and cognitive science, various types of performance data, Individualized Education Programs, the basic considerations described above, and evidence-based instructional practices. A basic understanding of algebra's cumulative nature might lead a school psychologist to design an instructional intervention that includes visual representations to help a student grasp abstract algebraic concepts. Best practices suggest that, where possible, student learning should be supported by a solid conceptual foundation that can be built using visual representations before the student to solve problems abstractly. This approach supports retention most likely as a result of the systematic development of conceptual understanding. Equipped with this knowledge, the school psychologist might design an intervention where a student who struggles with abstract concepts receives supplemental instruction that incorporates a range of examples and the concrete–representation–abstract method, with interventionists making explicit connections between the concrete, visual, and abstract representations.

Third, school psychologists also evaluate implementation fidelity of the instructional intervention and subsequent learning outcomes. Once school psychologists collect and interpret data, consult with teachers and students to identify goals, and design instructional interventions, school psychologists evaluate the effectiveness of the instructional intervention in meeting the learning goals. Assessing implementation fidelity of the intervention (How closely aligned are the prescribed changes and intervention implementation?) is an integral part of the school psychologist's role in supporting high-quality mathematics instruction. Consider, for example, that a significant number of students in one algebra class consistently respond correctly to less complex problems but struggle with more complex problems. Keeping in mind that instruction with a sequence and range of increasingly difficult problems is particularly helpful for increasing achievement for students who struggle with mathematics

Table 15.1. Sample Order of Operations Problems With Increasing Difficulty

Difficulty Level	Example	Explanation
Easy	$5 \times 2 - 3^2$	No parentheses, basic operations; modify this based on learning objectives by removing the exponent
Medium	$(8 - 9 \div 3)^2 - 4 \times 6$	Parentheses, five operations including exponents
Difficult	$7 - 2(5 + (8 \div 2 \times 4)) \div 7$	Nested parentheses, multiplication indicated by parentheses, division preceding multiplication

(Gersten, Chard, et al., 2009), the school psychologist may observe for this practice and suggest that a broader range of examples be included during core instruction. During intervention evaluation, the school psychologist collects data indicative of the level of implementation fidelity and student response to this intervention. They might observe for a specific number of problem types that range in difficulty, assess whether or not the order of examples gradually and logically increase in difficulty (see Table 15.1), and collect student work to determine if students are able to demonstrate the specified level of proficiency on difficult problems. In addition, presenting problems from least to most difficult can help students feel a sense of success. For students who struggle with mathematics, presenting a range of problem types of varying levels of difficulty, and a generous number of practice problems can help students to develop confidence in their skills and promote transfer to related problem types.

Within the three-tiered model of instructional support, the school psychologist collects a variety of data, collaborates with teachers to design instructional interventions to support student success in the content domain, and evaluates both implementation fidelity and effectiveness of the intervention. While the examples provided are not exhaustive, they are instructive for designing and evaluating instructional interventions for systems, groups, and individual students in secondary algebra settings. School psychologists are encouraged to consult with teachers to ensure that best practices in algebra instruction are incorporated into core instruction and interventions, as needed, to support academic achievement for all students.

SUMMARY

As school psychologists in secondary mathematics settings, three basic considerations form the basis for providing instructional support to help all students achieve (a) Standards for Mathematical Content, (b) Standards for Mathematical Practice, and (c) Standards of Mathematical Proficiency. To support students' success in algebra, sound mathematics curricular materials must provide students not only with opportunities to not only meet the content standards, but also with opportunities to develop the habits of mind and proficiencies that support college and career readiness. To be proficient in algebra, students must be able to integrate procedural fluency, conceptual understanding, strategic competence, and adaptive reasoning (National Research Council, 2001).

In addition to these basic considerations, school psychologists in secondary settings must be familiar with best practices in assessment and instruction in mathematics, especially algebra, in order to design and deliver instructional strategies that facilitate academic achievement for all students. It is also essential for the school psychologist to know those practices that support the development of algebra-readiness skills, such as reasoning abstractly to understand and represent mathematics flexibly. The school psychologist can support an effective instructional program in algebra in several ways. As an expert in the areas of assessment and evidence-based instruction, school psychologists are an important resource in supporting schools, teachers, and students to appropriately use formative assessments, interpret and share assessment data, design instructional interventions that meet individual learning needs and goals, and evaluate intervention effectiveness.

REFERENCES

Achieve, Inc. (2013a). *All students need advanced mathematics* Retrieved from http://www.achieve.org/math-works

Achieve, Inc. (2013b). *Americans need advanced math to stay globally competitive* Retrieved from http://www.achieve.org/math-works

Bransford, J. D., Brown, A. L., & Cocking, R. R. (Eds.). (1999). *How people learn: Brain, mind, experience, and school.* Washington, DC: National Academies Press.

Gersten, R., Beckmann, S., Clarke, B., Foegen, A., Marsh, L., Star, J. R., & Witzel, B. (2009). *Assisting students struggling with mathematics: Response to intervention (RTI) for elementary and middle schools.* (NCEE 2009-4060). Washington, DC: National Center for Education Evaluation and Regional Assistance. Retrieved from http://ies.ed.gov/ncee/wwc/publications/practiceguides/

Gersten, R., Chard, D. J., Jayanthi, M., Baker, S. K., Morphy, P., & Flojo, J. (2009). Mathematics instruction for students with learning disabilities: A meta-analysis of instructional components. *Review of Educational Research, 79*, 1202–1242.

Haas, M. (2002). *The influence of teaching methods on student achievement on Virginia's end-of-course standards of learning test for Algebra I.* (Unpublished doctoral dissertation). Virginia Polytechnic Institute and State University, Blacksburg, VA. Retrieved from http://scholar.lib.vt.edu/theses/available/etd-10062002-202857/unrestricted/HAASDISSERTATION.PDF

Haas, M. (2005). Teaching methods for secondary algebra: A meta-analysis of findings. *NAASP Bulletin, 82*(642), 24–46.

Hamilton, L., Halverson, R., Jackson, S., Mandinach, E., Supovitz, J., & Wayman, J. (2009). *Using student achievement data to support instructional decision making* (NCEE 2009-4067). Washington, DC: National Center for Education Evaluation and Regional Assistance. Retrieved from http://ies.ed.gov/ncee/wwc/publications/practiceguides/

Hemphill, F. C., & Vanneman, A. (2011). *Achievement gaps: How Hispanic and White students in public schools perform in mathematics and reading on the National Assessment of Educational Progress.* (NCES 2011-459). Washington, DC: National Center for Education Statistics, Institute of Education Sciences, U.S. Department of Education. Retrieved from http://nces.ed.gov/nationsreportcard/pdf/studies/2011459.pdf

Hiebert, J., Carpenter, T. P., Fennema, E., Fuson, K. C., Wearne, D., Murray, H., … Human, P. (1997). *Making sense: Teaching and learning mathematics with understanding.* Portsmouth, NH: Heinemann.

Ketterlin-Geller, L. R., & Yovanoff, P. (2009). Diagnostic assessments in mathematics to support instructional decision making. *Practical Assessment, Research & Evaluation, 14*(16), 1–11. Retrieved from http://pareonline.net/getvn.asp?v=14&n=16

Kieran, C. (1992). The learning and teaching of school algebra. In D. A. Grouws (Ed.), *Handbook of research on mathematics teaching and learning* (pp. 390–419). Reston, VA: National Council of Teachers of Mathematics.

Maccini, P., & Gagnon, J. C. (2000). Best practices for teaching mathematics to secondary students with special needs. *Focus on Exceptional Children, 32*(5), 1–22.

National Association of School Psychologists. (2010). *Model for comprehensive and integrated school psychological services.* Bethesda, MD: Author. Retrieved from http://www.nasponline.org/standards/2010standards/2_PracticeModel.pdf

National Governors Association Center for Best Practices & Council of Chief State School Officers. (2010). *Common Core State Standards (Mathematics).* Washington, DC: Author.

National Mathematics Advisory Panel. (2008). *Foundations for success: The final report of the National Mathematics Advisory Panel.* Washington, DC: U.S. Department of Education.

National Research Council. (2001). *Adding it up: Helping children learn mathematics.* Washington, DC: National Academies Press.

Rakes, C. R., Valentine, J. C., McGatha, M. B., & Ronau, R. N. (2010). Methods of instructional improvement in algebra: A systematic review and meta-analysis. *Review of Educational Research, 80*, 372–400.

Slavin, R. E., Lake, C., & Groff, C. (2009). Effective programs in middle and high school mathematics: A best-evidence synthesis. *Review of Educational Research, 79*, 893–911.

Stiggins, R. J. (1999). Evaluating classroom assessment training in teacher education programs. *Educational Measurement: Issues and Practice, 18*, 23–27.

Tilly, W. D., III. (2008). The evolution of school psychology to science-based practice: Problem solving and the three-tiered model. In A. Thomas & J. Grimes (Eds.), *Best practices in school psychology V* (pp. 17–36). Bethesda, MD: National Association of School Psychologists.

U.S. Department of Education. (2008). *Teachers' use of student data systems to improve instruction: 2005 to 2007.* Washington, DC: Author.

16 Best Practices in Neuropsychological Assessment and Intervention

Daniel C. Miller
Denise E. Maricle
Texas Woman's University

OVERVIEW

The purpose of this chapter is to present best practices for school psychologists associated with school-based neuropsychological assessment and intervention. Best practice in neuropsychological assessment and intervention relates to the domain of Data-Based Decision Making and Accountability within the National Association of School Psychologists (NASP) *Model for Comprehensive and Integrated School Psychological Services* (NASP, 2010). The importance of the biological bases of behavior also is addressed in the domain of Interventions and Instructional Support to Develop Academic Skills. Neuropsychological assessment is a direct student-level service designed to provide high-quality instructional support to develop academic skills.

Many school psychology training programs have limited content devoted to the biological bases of behavior, with the majority of the content contained in a standalone course or embedded within a broader review course. Since the 1990s school psychology training in the biological bases of behavior has been gradually deemphasized in the NASP *Standards for Graduate Preparation of School Psychologists* "at the same time when neuroscience and neuropsychology have revealed significant advances in our understanding of the neurobiological bases of child learning and behavior, with hundreds of relevant studies published each year" (Maricle, Miller, Hale, & Johnson, 2012, p. 72).

"The interest in the biological bases of human behavior is not new to the school psychology profession, but it is becoming more relevant to the current generation of school psychologists" (Miller, 2013, p. 2). The neuropsychological functioning of children was not emphasized in school psychology until the introduction of Public Law 94-142's definition of specific learning disabilities, when researchers began to investigate the neurobiological bases of learning disabilities. Additional focus was placed on understanding the neuropsychological functioning of children who had experienced a traumatic brain injury (TBI) after TBI became a separate disability category of the Individuals with Disabilities Education Act (IDEA) in 1990.

Since 2000, a number of factors have contributed to the need for all school psychologists to be aware of the biological and neuropsychological correlates of child disorders. These factors include the increased number of children suffering chronic medical conditions that adversely affect learning, the increased use of multiple medications to treat childhood disorders, the increase in severe behavioral disorders in the youngest of children, the rapid advances in understanding of basic cognitive processes (e.g., executive functions, working memory), and the explosion of knowledge from the neurosciences that is slowly being translated into educational practice.

Again, since 2000, strong genetic and neurobiological evidence for common neurodevelopmental disorders (e.g., autism spectrum disorders, specific learning disabilities, and attention deficit hyperactivity disorder [ADHD]) has been elucidated (Riccio, Sullivan, & Cohen, 2010). Despite these findings, many school psychologists are typically not trained to deal with the unique neuropsychological needs of these types of students. The purpose of this chapter is to introduce models for assessment and evidence-based intervention to school psychologists who are interested in applying neuropsychological principles in practice.

BASIC CONSIDERATIONS

Increasingly, neuropsychological constructs such as working memory, processing speed, and executive functions are being integrated into mainstream school psychology practice. So at a minimum, all school psychologists need to understand the contributions of these cognitive processes to academic achievement and behavior. A neuropsychological evaluation, compared to a psychoeducational evaluation, is broader in scope and focuses more on specific cognitive processes in areas such as sensorimotor skills, attentional processes, visuospatial and auditory processes, learning and memory processes, executive functions, and speed and efficiency of cognitive processing. Neuropsychological assessment may be valuable when a variety of conditions exist, such as a child who is not responding to multiple intervention strategies, a child who shows processing deficits on a traditional psychoeducational assessment, or a child who has a known or suspected neurological disorder.

Table 16.1 lists the major roles and functions for a school psychologist who has learned to integrate neuropsychological principles into practice. Table 16.2 presents a list of the advantages and limitations of applying neuropsychological principles to school psychology. A school psychologist with expertise in neuropsychology can provide neuropsychological consultations, assessments, and interventions in the schools. Neuropsychological evaluations conducted by professionals outside of the school system are often too medically oriented, with diagnoses that do not relate to IDEA special education criteria and frequently lack practical educational recommendations. A school psychologist with added expertise in neuropsychology already has the advantage of understanding school psychology practice, which typically makes his or her school neuropsychological assessments more valid and useful.

School psychologists with expertise in neuropsychology can act as important liaisons between the educational community and the medical community in planning for transitional services for children recovering from head injuries or other neurological insults. School psychologists with expertise in neuropsychology can assist school districts with other activities, such as translating medical reports for school personnel, helping teachers and parents understand the neuropsychological sequelae of neurodevelopmental, genetic, and chronic medical conditions; assisting in the design of curriculum that reflects known best practices in how learning is facilitated in the classroom; and sharing their expertise through inservice trainings for educators and parents.

Neuropsychological Assessment in the Schools

The integration of neuropsychological principles into school psychology practice is based on a qualitative understanding of brain–behavior relationships and how those relationships are manifested in everyday learning and behavior. Therefore, neuropsychological assessment is a perspective as well as a skill set. Given the breadth and depth of the knowledge base and skills required to fully integrate neuropsychological principles into school psychology practice, the training in this specialization area generally takes place at either the doctoral level or within a competency-based postgraduate training program.

Prior to the 1990s, the tests available for cognitive and neuropsychological assessment of children were, by

Table 16.1. Roles and Functions of a School Psychologist Who Applies Principles of Neuropsychology

- Provide neuropsychological assessment and intervention services to schools for students with known or suspected neurological conditions
- Assist in the interpretation of neuropsychological findings from outside consultants or medical records
- Seek to integrate current brain research into educational practice
- Provide educational interventions that have a basis in the neuropsychological or educational literature
- Act as a liaison between the school and the medical community for transitional planning for traumatic brain injury and other health impaired children and adolescents
- Consult with curriculum specialists in designing approaches to instruction that more adequately reflect what is known about brain–behavior relationships
- Conduct inservice training for educators and parents about the neuropsychological factors that relate to common childhood disorders
- Engage in evidence-based research to test for the efficacy of neuropsychologically based interventions (Miller, 2013)

Table 16.2. Advantages and Limitations of Applying Neuropsychological Principles to School Psychology

Advantages:
- Helping educators and parents understand the neurological principles underlying learning and behavior through consultation and inservice trainings
- Applying cognitive neuroscience principles to optimize the classroom learning environment
- Providing thorough assessment data that link to evidence-based interventions
- Answering the "why" question about the underlying reasons for learning difficulties, which leads to more targeted interventions
- Ensuring that there is a trained professional on staff who advocates for the application of research from neuroscience to educational practice

Limitations:
- Involves more comprehensive assessments that require more time, which may not always be available
- Requires the school psychologist to have a broader skill set or set of competencies that are not always readily available
- Requires the employer (e.g., school district) to agree to reassigned time for the school psychologist with expertise in applying neuropsychological principles in practice, which may not be feasible

today's standards, psychometrically inadequate, theoretically unsound, and frequently downward extensions of adult models. Starting in the 1990s, the psychometric and theoretical foundations of tests of cognition improved significantly. In addition, neuropsychological tests specifically designed for school-age children were introduced, beginning with tests of memory and learning (e.g., Test of Memory and Learning), then progressing to more comprehensive neuropsychology batteries (e.g., NEPSY) and specialized tests of specific cognitive processes (e.g., Delis-Kaplan Executive Function System).

A major trend in neuropsychological assessment since 2000 has been the inclusion of qualitative behaviors of a student's performance within tests, in addition to the usual quantitative scores. The emphasis on qualitative behaviors is part of a broader process assessment approach, wherein the inclusion of qualitative behaviors assists clinicians in determining the strategies a student uses to solve tasks. Several test publishers have provided base rates for common qualitative behaviors. For example, a test with such data included in the standardization will allow a practitioner to make statements such as "[a]sking for repetitions 10 times on the verbally presented material occurred with such frequency in only 3–10% of other 5 year olds in the standardization sample" (Miller, 2013, p. 33). This qualitative information can also provide a useful guide to intervention. Examples of tests that provide these base rates for qualitative behaviors include the Das–Naglieri Cognitive Assessment System, the Delis-Kaplan Executive Function System, the Wechsler Intelligence Scale for Children–Fourth Edition Integrated, and the NEPSY-II. The authors of this chapter hope that more test publishers in the future will continue to include

qualitative as well as quantitative assessment data to aid in clinical interpretation and intervention planning.

Evolution of Neuropsychologically Based Interventions in the Schools

The integration of neuropsychological principles into educational practice historically was poorly implemented. Interventions such as Doman and Delacato's perceptual–motor training for children with minimal brain dysfunction or tests such as the Illinois Test of Psycholinguistic Abilities may have had good face validity, but they did not demonstrate efficacy for treating students with perceptual–motor or language deficits. Early missteps in integrating neuropsychological principles into educational practice only reinforced the rising role of behaviorism in school psychology. Some contemporary and influential scholars still cite these early and inadequate findings as evidence for the lack of aptitude–achievement treatment effects and use those findings as the basis for current legislative changes to the definition of a specific learning disability (Reschly, Hosp, & Schmied, 2003). However, an impressive body of empirical research since the 1980s supports biological bases in the majority of childhood disorders (Riccio et al., 2010).

For many years, research in pediatric neuropsychology focused on traumatic brain injury. As a result, brain injury rehabilitation is a well-established field, and cognitive rehabilitation has a long-standing history of effective intervention for children who have sustained neurological insult. However, the use of similar rehabilitation techniques with children experiencing neurodevelopmental difficulties has not received extensive attention in the research literature, nor have school psychologists, on the whole, perceived cognitive rehabilitation/remediation to fall within the purview of their role in the schools. The overwhelming focus has been on academic remediation with little recognition or acknowledgment of the role cognition plays in learning and academic achievement. However, because cognition and neuropsychological functioning are critical to learning and cannot truly be divorced from how a child performs academically, it is imperative that research and intervention related to cognitive rehabilitation/remediation in areas such as executive functions, working memory, and processing speed be translated for use in the schools. School psychologists who apply neuropsychological principles are more likely to be familiar with the literature in these critical areas and with the research being conducted in the related fields of cognitive psychology, neuroscience, neuropsychology, developmental psychology, and educational neuroscience that would be applicable to the educational setting.

BEST PRACTICES IN APPLYING NEUROPSYCHOLOGICAL PRINCIPLES TO ASSESSMENT AND INTERVENTION

Current best practices in neuropsychological assessment, including tests of cognitive processes, demand a solid theoretical foundation to guide both assessment and intervention. Two such neuropsychological assessment models will be reviewed in this section.

Cognitive Hypothesis Testing Model

In 2004, Hale and Fiorello (Fiorello, Hale, & Wycoff, 2012) proposed a cognitive hypothesis testing (CHT) model, which is comprehensive and guides both assessment and intervention. The model integrates four components of theory, hypothesis generation, data collection, and data analysis across 13 steps (see Figure 16.1). In this model, Steps 1–5 align with traditional psychoeducational assessments, including tests of cognitive abilities and academic achievement. Steps 6–8 relate to more in-depth, targeted assessments such as tests of neuropsychological functioning (e.g., tests of learning and memory). Steps 9–13 close the loop between assessment and intervention and are consistent with Tiers 1 and 2 of a response-to-intervention (RTI) model.

If a global deficit is observed in the child's initial assessment data (Steps 1–5), a reason for the deficit is hypothesized and then further tested (Steps 6–8), and

then evidence-based interventions are designed in consultation with the teacher/parent, implemented, and monitored for effectiveness (Steps 9–13). This model provides a solid foundation for integrating multiple data sources for children who are not responding to standard interventions as a result of brain-based learning or behavior disorders (Fiorello et al., 2012).

Integrated School Neuropsychology/Cattell–Horn–Carroll Model

The school neuropsychological conceptual model was introduced by Miller in 2007 as a method of organizing school-age, cross-battery assessment data based on the underlying neuropsychological constructs being measured (Miller, 2013). This model provides interpretative structure to Steps 6–8 of the CHT model. The purposes of the school neuropsychological conceptual model are to facilitate clinical interpretation by providing an organizational framework for cross-battery assessment data, to strengthen the linkage between assessment and evidence-based interventions, and to provide a common frame of reference for evaluating the effects of neurodevelopmental disorders on neurocognitive processes.

The school neuropsychological conceptual model represents a synthesis of several theoretical and clinical approaches including Lurian theory, the process-oriented approach to assessment, neuropsychological theories (e.g., Mirsky's theory of attention, Baddeley and Hitch's theory of working memory), the cross-battery assessment approach, and Cattell–Horn–Carroll theory (Schneider & McGrew, 2012). Since 2007, the school neuropsychological conceptual model has evolved as a result of extensive usage in the field with clinical cases (Miller, 2013).

Miller introduced an updated school neuropsychological conceptual model with the major goal of further integrating school neuropsychological theories with current Cattell–Horn–Carroll theory. This integrated school neuropsychology/Cattell–Horn–Carroll model modified the classifications of the neuropsychological constructs and academic achievement areas based on current psychometric and theoretical research. This model encompasses four major broad classifications: basic sensorimotor functions, facilitators and inhibitors for cognitive processes and acquired knowledge skills, basic cognitive processes, and acquired knowledge (see Figure 16.2). All of the model classifications are influenced by each other and by social–emotional, cultural, and environmental factors.

Figure 16.1. Cognitive Hypothesis Testing Model

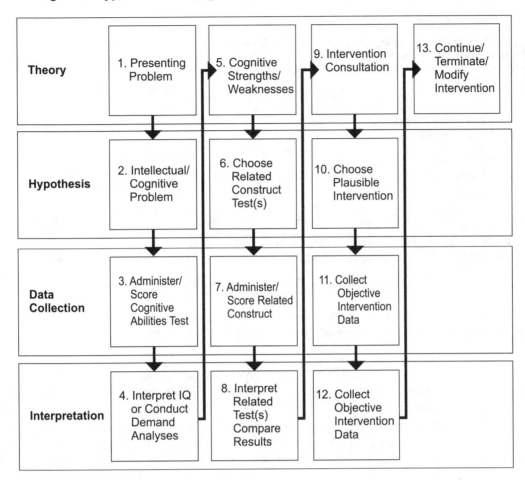

Note. From *Essentials of School Neuropsychological Assessment* (2nd ed., p. 101), by D. C. Miller, 2013, Hoboken, NJ: John Wiley and Sons. Copyright 2013 by John Wiley and Sons. Reprinted with permission.

These broad classifications are further subdivided into second-order and third-order classifications. As an example, sensorimotor tasks (broad classification) are subdivided into the second-order classifications of lateral preference, sensory functions, fine motor functions, gross motor functions, visual scanning, and qualitative behaviors. These second-order classifications can be further subdivided into third-order classifications. As an example, the second-order classification of sensory functions can be further subdivided into the third-order classifications of auditory and visual acuity, and tactile sensation and perception. See Miller (2013) for a detailed review of the integrated school neuropsychology/Cattell–Horn–Carroll model.

How the Two Models Can Be Used in Practice

A 6-year-old boy is referred for a comprehensive individual assessment because of his continued difficulties with

reading acquisition (CHT model, Step 1). A psycho-educational assessment battery is assembled that will evaluate the boy's cognitive ability and reading achievement (CHT model, Step 2). These tests are administered and interpreted (CHT model, Steps 3 and 4). A pattern of strengths and weaknesses may be identified and related to the known literature base about causal factors of reading disabilities (CHT model, Step 5). Stopping at the CHT model, Step 5, may identify the overall presence of low reading achievement but may not determine the underlying causes of the reading disorder. Using the integrated school neuro-psychology/Cattell–Horn–Carroll model, additional hypotheses are generated to identify the potential subtype of the child's reading disability (CHT model, Step 6) and to develop more specific and targeted evidence-based interventions. Based on the hypotheses generated in the CHT model, Step 6, additional neuropsychological measures are administered to the

Figure 16.2. Miller's (2013) Integrated School Neuropsychology/Cattell–Horn–Carroll Model

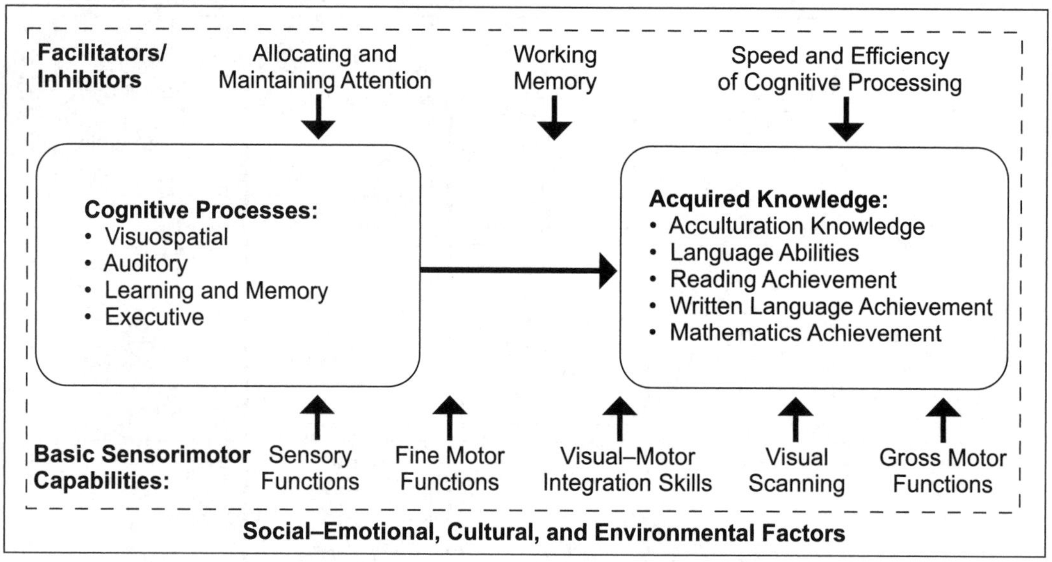

Note. From *Essentials of School Neuropsychological Assessment* (2nd ed., p. 113), by D. C. Miller, 2013, Hoboken, NJ: John Wiley and Sons. Copyright 2013 by John Wiley and Sons. Reprinted with permission.

child (e.g., tests of basic cognitive processes such as phonological processing, working memory, auditory processing, or executive functioning) and interpreted (CHT model, Steps 7 and 8). For Steps 9–13 in the CHT model, use the assessment data from Steps 1–8 to develop and monitor the effectiveness of evidence-based interventions.

School Neuropsychological Interventions

A major challenge in school psychology as a field, including the application of principles of neuropsychology, remains the continued validation of assessment data linked to evidence-based interventions (Miller, 2013). For example, school psychologists with added training in neuropsychology can identify known subtypes of learning disabilities in reading, mathematics, and writing (e.g., dysphonetic dyslexia or dysgraphia) based on a fairly high degree of scientific rigor. However, the same degree of scientific rigor is not yet as well established for the treatment efficacy of prescriptive interventions associated with these neuropsychological subtypes.

Foundations for Neuropsychological Interventions

Neuropsychology has an extensive history of school and educational applications. Although there are excellent resources on academic and psychological interventions for various childhood disabilities, few texts describe systematic and empirically supported interventions in cognitive rehabilitation/remediation. While some literature does address neuropsychological intervention, it is typically either exclusively for adults or focuses on a single disability or condition. The research linking neuroscience with educational/special educational outcomes is still very limited (Muller, 2011). Educational neuroscience research has primarily focused on identifying the parts of the brain that activate or fail to activate during different types of cognitive and academic tasks. In the realm of neuropsychologically based intervention, the cognitive domains of attention, memory, and executive functioning have been investigated the most to date.

Neuropsychologically Based Interventions for Working Memory Deficits

Research findings: Working memory has been a popular area of research and is now thought to underlie almost every aspect of academic learning. For example, Gathercole and Alloway (2004) suggest that working memory overload is responsible for working memory deficits and difficulties in learning for many children, and working memory capacity has been found to be related to reading and listening comprehension (Cain, 2006) as well as mathematics (Bull & Scerif, 2001). However, the assessment of working memory has been plagued with disagreements about the definition and operationalization of what constitutes working memory, what aspects of working memory should be assessed and in what format (e.g., visual, verbal, spatial), and what instruments or subtests within instruments reliably and validly measure working memory skills. School psychologists frequently incorporate working memory assessment into their psychoeducational assessments and interpretive reports, since many of the current instruments in use have working memory or short-term memory subtests as a component. However, many school psychologists appear to have a limited understanding of the concept of working memory, or other aspects of memory, and how or even if the measures they are using are adequately assessing working memory or other memory skills. In contrast, a school psychologist with specialty training in neuropsychology are likely to be more familiar with the neuropsychological and theoretical constructs of memory functions and to possess an understanding of how working memory relates to other cognitive processing areas, such as executive functioning or the development of academic skills. These school psychologists are also likely to have attained specialized training in assessing memory deficits using more specific or targeted instruments.

Recommendations for practice: Interventions for working memory processing deficiencies have been developed within the fields of neuropsychology, cognitive psychology, and educational psychology, and extensive applied research has documented many interventions that significantly increase the amount of information that can be stored and retrieved (Dehn, 2008). There is significant research available on the use of compensatory strategies for working memory limitations, the use of strategic processing to improve encoding and retrieval of information, and the use of neuroimaging to examine brain processes involved in learning and memory tasks. Traditionally, interventions for working memory have focused on increasing the capacity to retain information both immediately and over time. For example, Gathercole, Alloway, Willis, and Adams (2006) present research that indicates that instruction in mnemonics has proven efficacious in improving memory on a class-wide and individual basis. Although intervention has typically focused on teaching memory strategies or mnemonics, a number of other instructional approaches and interventions have been developed and are currently in use (see Dehn, 2008, for a comprehensive review).

Neuropsychologically Based Interventions for Executive Function Deficits

Research findings: The domain of executive functions has also become quite popular and has received much attention in the school psychology literature of late. School psychologists are more frequently incorporating assessment of executive functioning into their psychoeducational assessment practices, but often with little understanding of the topic or the instruments they are using to measure executive functions (Maricle, Johnson, & Avirett, 2010). Currently, there is a wide variety of theories, hypotheses, opinions, and speculation regarding executive functions. The research and literature on executive functions are still grappling with identifying a unitary definition of executive processes and their relationship to other cognitive functions. The continuing lack of consensus regarding a definition of executive functions arises in large part from trying to treat it as a single or unitary construct (Maricle, Johnson, et al., 2010; Metzler, 2007). These definitional issues contribute to multiple measurement issues, including determining which executive functions to measure and how to do so adequately. The terms for executive functions are used interchangeably and inconsistently without consensus among clinicians and researchers as to which domains constitute the critical aspects of executive functions and should be measured. Having such a broad range of skills identified as executive functioning has led to the use of many different assessment tools (Maricle, Johnson, et al., 2010). Obviously, obtaining an accurate assessment of executive functions is the key to selecting efficient, effective intervention strategies.

Recommendations for practice: Dawson and Guare (2010) provide an excellent review of interventions addressing skills such as metacognition, response inhibition, goal-directed persistence, cognitive flexibility, planning, and self-regulation that can be applied to a number of executive function deficits. Metzler (2007) also provides extensive information on interventions that can be used to address executive function deficits at a variety of levels (e.g., individual, classroom, whole school).

Neuropsychologically Based Interventions for Attentional Deficits

Research findings: Historically, children presenting with attention problems have been assessed from a behavioral perspective and have frequently been diagnosed with ADHD, attention deficit disorder (ADD), or serious emotional disturbance/disability. However, research since 2000 has provided evidence that the large majority of attention difficulties are the result of a frontal subcortical circuit disorder, which is responsible for both cognitive and behavioral characteristics commonly associated with attention disorders such as ADHD/ADD (Castellanos, Sonuga-Barke, Milham, & Tannock,

2006). These frontal subcortical abnormalities may manifest in functional cognitive impairments such as inhibitory control difficulties, problems with the regulation of attention, difficulties with vigilance or sustained attention, working memory deficits, difficulties with processing speed and cognitive efficiency, and executive function deficits such as in the area of shifting attention (see Hale, Reddy, et al., 2010, for a review).

Children with attention deficits often have significant comorbid behavioral and academic difficulties. Research has found that children with ADHD on average perform one standard deviation lower than neurotypical children on academic and cognitive measures (DuPaul, McGoey, Eckert, & VanBrakle, 2001; Mayes & Calhoun, 2006). Unfortunately, behavioral conceptualizations of attentional difficulties and the use of indirect measures such as behavior rating scales continue to dominate the field and limit the understanding of cognitive and neuropsychological functioning related to attention difficulties that is rapidly emerging.

Neuropsychological research is beginning to show that attentional problems associated with ADHD/ADD may be the result of deficits in executive functions, working memory, processing speed, and fluid reasoning (Barkley, 2012; Castellanos et al., 2006). Recent brain imaging research has consistently found evidence of reduced volume in the frontal cortex and basal ganglia structures of the right hemisphere in individuals diagnosed with ADHD in comparison with neurotypical peers and abnormal function of the dorsolateral prefrontal cortex (Dickstein et al., 2005).

Recommendations for practice: Because attention affects so many areas of academic, behavioral, and cognitive functioning, children with attention difficulties are at high risk for school failure. Therefore, recognizing the different causes of attention problems is critical for assessment and intervention (Hale, Yim, et al., 2012). Hale and colleagues go so far as to state that

> redefining ADHD as a neurobiological disorder for which cognitive and neuropsychological tests can be used to provide direct evaluation of the attention, working memory, and executive deficits displayed by children will be a critical step in advancing ADHD diagnostic and treatment practices in the years to come. (p. 698)

It would seem that moving beyond the characterization of attentional difficulties as a disruptive behavior disorder may lead to more accurate diagnosis and targeted treatment interventions. Two targeted intervention programs that have shown promise are the Pay Attention program (Thomson, Kerns, Seidenstrang, Sohlberg, & Mateer, 2001) and a cognitive remediation program developed by Butler and Copeland (2002). Both programs focus on remediating attentional skills using computer-based attentional processing programs and note improvements in their treatment groups relative to the control groups. Additionally, numerous neuropsychologically based interventions for executive functions and working memory have also been applied as interventions for attentional processing difficulties with some success.

Neuropsychologically Based Interventions for Difficulties in Reading

Research findings: Substantial research has been conducted on the neurobiological correlates of reading disability by Shaywitz and Shaywitz (2004), and neuroimaging studies have demonstrated functional differences in the brains of those identified with reading disabilities versus average readers. The research by Shaywitz and Shaywitz has focused on mapping the neural circuitry for reading. Additionally, research at the University of Washington combining brain imaging (functional magnetic resonance imaging; fMRI) and genetics has provided evidence of anomalies in brain activation associated with tasks involving phonological, orthographic, or morphological word-form storage and processing (Berninger & Holdnack, 2008). Recent evidence also suggests that attention plays a critical role in phonological processing and that the disruption of attention is a primary factor in reading disabilities (Reynolds & Besner, 2006). Additionally, fMRI studies focusing on the mechanisms of reading indicate that poor readers rely on memory rather than on an understanding of the sound–symbol relationships (Shaywitz & Shaywitz, 2011).

There is strong evidence of neural signatures and clearly defined processing deficits linked to specific learning disabilities in reading (Christo, Davis, & Brock, 2009). Subtypes of reading disabilities have been identified and general consensus has been achieved regarding their neurological correlates and characteristics. Four subtypes of reading disability are generally agreed upon: dysphonetic dyslexia, surface dyslexia, mixed dyslexia, and comprehension deficits (sometimes referred to as semantic dyslexia; Feifer, 2011b). Dysphonetic dyslexia is associated with processing of phonological and orthographic representations in the supramarginal gyrus (junction of the temporal and parietal lobes) and the inferior parietal lobule.

Dysphonetic dyslexia is characterized by the inability to use letter–sound conversion, resulting in difficulty sounding out words using the common phonological teaching methodology and in an overreliance on the visual features of the word. Auditory and phonological processing is thought to be deficient with children experiencing dysphonetic dyslexia. Surface dyslexia is associated neurologically with the left fusiform gyrus and is characterized by the overreliance on sound–symbol relationships and an inability to visualize words. Children with surface dyslexia are concentrating on the sound–symbol relationships and painstakingly decoding each word phonetically such that they do not develop word reading fluency or automaticity. Mixed dyslexia is generally considered to be a result of the inability to transfer information between the phonological and visual centers of the brain. It is a more severe form of reading disability, as it is characterized by deficits in both phonological and visual–spatial characteristics of reading. Basically, the child has no usable key to learn to read. Comprehension deficits (semantic dyslexia) are characterized by the ability to read words but difficulty comprehending or deriving meaning from written words. Individuals often make semantic errors and lack reading comprehension skills. Comprehension deficits are associated with deficits in the processing of information in white matter tracts and in the long-term storage and retrieval of acquired information. Neuropsychological research in the area of reading disabilities has primarily focused on visual processing (efficiency of the magnocellular system), temporal processing (the ability to process auditory information effectively), and phonological processing. Brain imaging has begun to establish that poor readers evidence deficits in visual processing speed, phonology, and auditory processing. Additionally, neuroimaging has been used to successfully predict who will readily respond to intervention or to determine if an intervention has been effective (Shaywitz & Shaywitz, 2011).

Recommendations for practice: Reading interventions are well established, numerous, and fairly easily located or obtained. For example, two online resources for evidence-based interventions are What Works Clearinghouse (http://ies.ed.gov/ncee/wwc/) and Best Evidence Encyclopedia (http://www.bestevidence.org). However, identifying the subtype of reading disability is critical to identifying an effective intervention. For example, a child with dysphonetic dyslexia is not likely to benefit from continued use of phonologically based interventions. Rather, the child is more likely to see response with a whole word/whole language approach. For example,

classroom-based curriculum and approaches with young children under age 7, including programs such as Fast Forward and Ladders for Literacy, have shown success. For children age 7–12, SRA Corrective Reading and Earobics II have shown promise, and for adolescents age 13 and above, the Wilson Reading Program and Read 180 have proved useful. For children with surface dyslexia, Reading Recovery, Great Leaps in Reading, and DISTAR (Reading Mastery) have a good evidence base. The Orton-Gillingham Method has shown some success with mixed dyslexia because it is a multisensory approach incorporating a number of modalities. Reading comprehension approaches such as Multipass, SQR, and Reciprocal Teaching have had some success with children experiencing comprehension deficits. The reading interventions cited above and others are reviewed by Mather and Wendling (2012). Shaywitz noted that what matters most is whether the intervention specifically relates to the child's reading difficulty and whether the intervention is applied early, often, systematically, explicitly, and consistently by a qualified teacher (Shaywitz & Shaywitz, 2011).

Neuropsychologically Based Interventions for Difficulties in Written Expression

Research findings: Written language and written language disorders have received very little attention in the research literature. Mather and Wendling (2012) noted that the writing process is very complex and involves coordination between language, thought, and motor abilities. Feifer (2011a) stated that more than any other academic skill, writing requires intact executive functions for success. Writing requires multiple executive function skills, such as attention, planning, monitoring and self-regulation, sentence generation, and long-term storage and retrieval of acquired knowledge. Imaging research has suggested that the neuroanatomical circuitry involved in writing may be dependent on the type of writing involved (Carlson, 2010). A variety of neurodevelopmental disorders may show difficulties with written language for many different reasons and with differential outcomes (Berninger, 2010).

Currently, the research would support three subtypes of writing disorders: dyslexic dysgraphias (including phonological dysgraphia, orthographic dysgraphia, mixed dysgraphia, and semantic/syntactic dysgraphia), apraxic dygraphias (including ideomotor dysgraphia, ideational dysgraphia, and constructional dysgraphia), and mechanical or motor dysgraphia (Feifer & DeFina, 2002). Apraxic and motor dysgraphias tend to be associated with traumatic or acquired brain injuries.

Phonological dysgraphia is characterized by the inability to spell words by sound, with the hallmark of this disorder being the inability to spell pseudowords or phonetically irregular words while the spelling of familiar or phonetically regular words remains intact. Individuals with this type of dysgraphia overrely on the visual features of a word and appear to memorize what the word looks like rather than being able to identify the phonemes needed to form a word. The anterior portion of the supramarginal gyrus and the posterior inferior temporal cortex are implicated in phonological dysgraphia.

Orthographic dysgraphia is characterized by the inability to see the visual symbolic representation of the word and an overreliance on the sound patterns of words. Disruptions in the angular gyrus (posterior parietal/occipital interface) appear to contribute to orthographic dysgraphia. Mixed dysgraphia is characterized by an inability to sequence letters accurately into words using either visual or sound patterns. This is a severe form of dysgraphia characterized by bizarre misspellings, omissions, additions, substitutions, and letter transpositions. The left inferior parietal lobe is considered deficient with mixed dysgraphia. Semantic/syntactic dysgraphia is the inability to master the rules of grammar and syntax. The left frontal lobe near Broca's area has been implicated in this form of dysgraphia.

Recommendations for practice: The majority of school psychologists with expertise in neuropsychology would recommend that the type of writing problem be identified prior to implementing an intervention if the intervention was expected to be effective in ameliorating the problem. Reviews of evidence-based practices in written language intervention can be found in Hooper, Knuth, Yerby, Anderson, and Moore (2009) and are available on the What Works Clearinghouse and Best Evidence Encyclopedia websites. Some evidence suggests that programs such as Spaulding Mastery, Writing to Read, Step Up to Writing, and Drag and Write are helpful in remediating the difficulties associated with phonological dysgraphia, whereas evidence suggests that Cover, Copy, Compare; the Fernald Method; or Visual Spelling may be helpful with individuals experiencing orthographic dysgraphia. Little is known about effective interventions for mixed dysgraphia, although some success with some individuals has been seen with programs such as Musical Spelling and CAST: Universal Design for Learning. CAST and Step Up to Reading have had some success with semantic/syntactic dysgraphia as well. When working memory has been implicated in writing difficulties, the use of graphic organizers, story maps, and writing wheels have shown success. Graham and Perin (2007) presented research suggesting that instruction in executive function strategies related to writing (such as strategic planning, self-regulation, and goal setting) improve writing performance. Much of the evidence-based practice would suggest that children with writing difficulties need to be explicitly taught writing skills (in other words, how to write and the strategies for successful writing).

Neuropsychologically Based Interventions for Difficulties in Mathematics

Research findings: Historically, math disorders have not received the same attention as reading or writing difficulties, and although neuropsychological explanations of, and research on, typical and atypical development of math abilities/skills has been fairly limited, it is rapidly emerging. The work of Geary (2004); Hale, Fiorello, et al. (2008); and Wilson and Dahaene (2007) has begun to establish evidence for subtypes of math disabilities. However, most of the research has been done with adults, and there is disagreement on what constitutes subtypes of math disorders in children and adolescents. Dehaene, Spelke, Pinel, Stanescu, and Tsivkin (1999); Wilson and Dahaene (2007); along with Hale and colleagues (2008) note that there are multiple cognitive and neuropsychological functions necessary for understanding mathematics with multiple neural networks involved in the processing of math tasks, depending on the specific cognitive strategies being deployed.

Recommendations for practice: The majority of intervention studies using mathematics curricula and instructional techniques have focused on regular education and typically developing students, and many of these studies do not meet minimum experimental standards for determining effectiveness of the results as reported by What Works Clearinghouse and Best Evidence Encyclopedia. Very few studies evaluating the effectiveness of math curricula and instruction have included samples of children identified with math disabilities. Interventions for remediating math difficulties appear to be more generic in nature and are not yet tied to specific math disability subtypes. Lerew (2005) proposed a model for math intervention that matches the intervention with the individual's assessed neuropsychological and mathematical deficits. Interventions for math disabilities frequently focus on skills training and explicit instruction in strategies such as self-regulation and mnemonic devices. Maricle, Psimas-Fraser, Muenke, and Miller (2010) provide a comprehensive review of assessment and intervention with math disorders from a neuropsychological perspective. Wendling and Mather (2009) also provide a review of evidence-based practices for remediating math difficulties.

Summary of Neuropsychologically Based Interventions

More research needs to be conducted that links neuroscience with educational/special educational outcomes and supports systematic empirically based neuropsychological interventions. Additionally, research on evidence-based interventions being conducted in other fields, such as cognitive psychology, neuroscience, pediatric neuropsychology, and developmental psychology, needs to be incorporated into school-based practices. Metzler (2007) notes that evidence-based interventions might occur at the level of the child or teacher, focusing on remediation or accommodation for medical, cognitive, behavioral, or social deficits, or at the system level, targeting the classroom, school, or family environment. The majority of interventions, even with the advent of RTI, are at the individual child level or the teacher or classroom level. Additionally, the difference between remediation and compensation needs to be more clearly defined.

Remediation implies a goal of correcting a deficit, whereas compensation emphasizes a need to bypass the deficit to reduce its impact on learning and academic performance. Riccio (2008) noted that neuropsychological models of intervention should be composed of methods that capitalize on individual strengths and intact functions in conjunction with compensatory strategies. Continued validation research is warranted, particularly in relation to treatment efficacy as the application of neuropsychological principles into school psychology practice becomes more commonplace.

Developmental Differences and Different Practices

The assessment instruments available today to school psychologists interested in evaluating basic neuropsychological processes have been specifically designed for school-age children and youth. This is a marked improvement over where school focused pediatric neuropsychology was prior to the 1990s, when tests were almost exclusively downward extensions of adult test batteries. Developmental differences are now accounted for by having age-matched norms for neuropsychological tests. This has been an important

evolution for the field, as the neuropsychological research has clearly established developmental trajectories for many neurodevelopmental and cognitive functions, such as executive functions, working memory, processing speed, and visual–spatial processing.

Neurocognitive development in children is dynamic, and functioning may vary depending upon ability, life circumstance, and level of support. Disruption in functioning at an early developmental stage can interfere with subsequent stages and result in a cumulative negative impact on the child's functioning. Early intervention during the course of development may be more effective in ameliorating neurocognitive deficits as a result of this plasticity of development. The evidence suggests that cognitive rehabilitation strategies may be differentially effective at different developmental stages (Limond & Leeke, 2005).

Multicultural Competencies

It is assumed that neuropsychological constructs such as sensory–motor functions, attention, memory, and executive functions are universal across cultures, class, and race. However, it is the measurement of these neuropsychological constructs among diverse individuals that represents the real challenge (Miller, 2013). The majority of neuropsychological tests are "conceived and standardized within the matrix of Western culture" (Nell, 2000, p. 3). There are very few neuropsychological tests for school-age children standardized on a variety of foreign cultures and available in other languages. Direct translation of neuropsychological tests that are still using primarily Caucasian American norm groups may result in inaccurate scores (Ortiz, Ochoa, & Dynda, 2012).

Hess and Rhodes (2005) suggested that, given the scarcity of neuropsychological measures for culturally and linguistically diverse children, the clinical interview might be the best source of information. The neuropsychological assessment of culturally and linguistically diverse populations will continue to be a challenge for school psychologists until test authors and publishers develop new measures that are ecologically valid and reliable for use with multiple populations (Miller, 2013). Research needs to be conducted to determine how individuals of diversity with and without impairment perform on the current instruments. Ultimately, school psychologists attempting to assess neuropsychological processes with students of diversity should rely more on qualitative evaluations of behaviors linked to brain functioning rather than try to use English language-based and Western culture-bound standardized tests. Regardless, school psychologists should be familiar with the tools and techniques used to identify linguistically and culturally loaded subtests within commonly used instruments, and should have an understanding of how to minimize their impact in assessment as well as how interpretations and recommendations may be affected by these variables. All school psychologists need to be cognizant of the impact that racial, ethnic, and cultural diversity have on the assessment and interpretation process.

The majority of empirically validated interventions being utilized by educational professionals are also based on middle- to upper-class European Americans and do not reflect the cultural diversity of the current school population. Although the literature supports the fact that racial and ethnic differences exist in intervention outcomes, there is a lack of data, such as base rates and treatment efficacy, which makes it difficult to estimate when, where, and how cultural differences are important. Finally, relevant to any discussion of neuropsychological assessment and intervention with children of diversity would be the intersection of limited English proficiency or bilingualism with neuropsychological functioning, assessment, and intervention.

Evaluation of Effectiveness or Outcomes

The ultimate test of the effectiveness of school psychologists applying principles of neuropsychological assessment and intervention is the positive impact these services have on the provision of a high-quality learning environment for school-age children. The goal of any school neuropsychological assessment is to specifically identify a profile of a child's neuropsychological strengths and weaknesses that can explain current academic and/or behavioral difficulties and successfully use that assessment data to guide targeted, evidence-based interventions. Objective outcome measures to monitor the effectiveness of school neuropsychological assessment services may include improvements in student learning outcomes (e.g., grades, competencies, and skills) and improvements in social–emotional functioning (e.g., adaptive behaviors and social skills).

SUMMARY

Given the advances in neuroscience and our understanding of brain–behavior relationships, it is important for school psychologists to acknowledge that various brain regions and neurocognitive constructs contribute to the multidimensional process of executing the complex skills involved in everyday behavior and academic achievement. School psychologists trained in the application of neuropsychology are best positioned to incorporate the increasingly rapid advances in neuroscience, genetics, medicine, and psychopharmacology and to translate neuropsychological theory into the educational practice. In conjunction with other professionals, school psychologists with the appropriate training in neuropsychology can apply neuroscientific knowledge to the identification, management, treatment, and eradication of learning problems in all children.

AUTHOR NOTE

Disclosure. Daniel C. Miller has a financial interest in books he authored or coauthored referenced in this chapter. He also has a financial interest in the KIDS, Inc., School Neuropsychology Post-Graduate Training Program and other online webinar continuing education opportunities.

REFERENCES

Barkley, R. A. (2012). *Executive functions: What they are, how they work, and why they evolved.* New York, NY: Guilford Press.

Berninger, V. W. (2010). Assessing and intervening with children with written language disorders. In D. C. Miller (Ed.), *Best practices in school neuropsychology: Guidelines for effective practices, assessment, and evidence-based intervention* (pp. 507–520). Hoboken, NJ: Wiley.

Berninger, V. W., & Holdnack, J. A. (2008). Nature-nurture perspectives in diagnosing and treating learning disabilities: Response to questions begging answers that see the forest and the trees. In E. Fletcher-Janzen & C. R. Reynolds (Eds.), *Neuropsychological perspectives on learning disabilities in the era of RTI: Recommendations for diagnosis and intervention* (pp. 66–79). Hoboken, NJ: Wiley.

Bull, R., & Scerif, G. (2001). Executive functioning as a predictor of children's mathematical ability: Inhibition, switching, and working memory. *Developmental Neuropsychology, 19*, 237–293.

Butler, R. W., & Copeland, D. R. (2002). Attention processes and their remediation in children treated for cancer: A literature review and the development of a therapeutic approach. *Journal of the International Neuropsychological Society, 8*, 115–124.

Cain, K. (2006). Children's reading comprehension: The role of working memory in normal and impaired development. In I. S. Pickering (Ed.), *Working memory and education* (pp. 62–91). San Diego, CA: Academic Press.

Carlson, N. R. (2010). *Physiology of behavior* (10th ed.). Boston, MA: Allyn & Bacon.

Castellanos, F. X., Sonuga-Barke, E. J., Milham, M. P., & Tannock, R. (2006). Characterizing cognition in ADHD: Beyond executive dysfunction. *Trends in Cognitive Science, 10*, 117–123.

Christo, C., Davis, J., & Brock, S. E. (2009). *Identifying, assessing, and treating dyslexia at school.* New York, NY: Springer.

Dawson, P., & Guare, R. (2010). *Executive skills in the children and adolescents: A practical guide to assessment and intervention* (2nd ed.). New York, NY: Guilford Press.

Dehaene, S., Spelke, E., Pinel, P., Stanescu, R., & Tsivkin, S. (1999). Sources of mathematical thinking: Behavioral and brain imaging evidence. *Science, 284,* 970–974. doi:10.1126/science.284.5416.970

Dehn, M. J. (2008). *Working memory and academic learning: Assessment and intervention.* Hoboken, NJ: Wiley.

Dickstein, D. P., Garvey, M., Pradella, A. G., Greenstein, D. K., Sharp, W., Castellanos, F. X., … Leibenluft, E. (2005). Neurologic examination abnormalities in children with bipolar disorder or attention deficit/hyperactivity disorder. *Biological Psychiatry, 58,* 517–524.

DuPaul, G. J., McGoey, K. E., Eckert, T. L., & VanBrakle, J. (2001). Preschool children with attention deficit/hyperactivity disorder: Impairments in behavioral, social, and school functioning. *Journal of the American Academy of Child and Adolescent Psychiatry, 40,* 508–515.

Feifer, S. (2011a). The neuropsychology of written language disorders. In A. S. Davis (Ed.), *Handbook of pediatric neuropsychology* (pp. 689–697). New York, NY: Springer.

Feifer, S. (2011b). How SLD manifests in reading. In D. P. Flanagan & V. C. Alfonso (Eds.), *Essentials of specific learning disability identification* (pp. 21–41). Hoboken, NJ: Wiley.

Feifer, S. G., & DeFina, P. A. (2002). *The neuropsychology of written language disorders: Diagnosis and intervention.* Middletown, MD: School Neuropsych Press.

Fiorello, C. A., Hale, J. B., & Wycoff, K. L. (2012). Cognitive hypothesis testing: Linking test results to the real world. In D. P. Flanagan & P. L. Harrison (Eds.), *Contemporary intellectual assessment: Theories, tests, and issues* (pp. 484–496). New York, NY: Guilford Press.

Gathercole, S. E., & Alloway, T. P. (2004). *Understanding working memory: A classroom guide.* London, UK: Medical Research Council.

Gathercole, S. E., Alloway, T. P., Willis, C., & Adams, A. M. (2006). Working memory in children with reading disabilities. *Journal of Experimental Child Psychology, 93,* 265–281.

Geary, D. (2004). Mathematics and learning disabilities. *Journal of Learning Disabilities, 37,* 4–15.

Graham, S., & Perin, D. (2007). *Writing next: Effective strategies to improve writing of adolescents in middle and high schools.* Washington, DC: Alliance for Excellent Education.

Hale, J. B., Fiorello, C. A., Dumont, R., Willis, J. O., Rackley, C., & Elliot, C. (2008). Differential ability scales: (Neuro)psychological predictors of math performance for typical children and children with math disabilities. *Psychology in the Schools, 45,* 838–858.

Hale, J. B., Reddy, L. A., Wilcox, G., McLaughlin, A., Hain, L., Stern, A., … Eusebio, E. (2010). Assessment and intervention practices for children with ADHD and other frontal-striatal circuit disorders. In D. C. Miller (Ed.), *Best practices in school neuropsychology: Guidelines for effective practices, assessment, and evidence-based intervention* (pp. 225–279). Hoboken, NJ: Wiley.

Hale, J. B., Yim, M., Schneider, J., Wilcox, G., Henzel, J. N., & Dixon, S. G. (2012). Cognitive and neuropsychological assessment of attention deficit/hyperactivity disorder. In D. P. Flanagan & P. L. Harrison (Eds.), *Contemporary intellectual assessment: Theories, tests, and issues* (pp. 687–707). New York, NY: Guilford Press.

Hess, R. S., & Rhodes, R. L. (2005). Providing neuropsychological services to culturally and linguistically diverse learners. In D. C. D'Amato, E. Fletcher-Janzen, & C. R. Reynolds (Eds.), *Handbook of school neuropsychology* (pp. 637–660). Hoboken, NJ: Wiley.

Hooper, S., Knuth, S., Yerby, D., Anderson, K., & Moore, C. (2009). A review of science supported writing instruction with implementation in mind. In S. Rosenfield & V. Berninger (Eds.), *Implementing evidence-based interventions in school settings* (pp. 49–83). New York, NY: Oxford University Press.

Lerew, C. D. (2005). Understanding and implementing neuropsychologically based arithmetic interventions. In R. C. D'Amato, E. Fletcher-Janzen, & C. R. Reynolds (Eds.), *Handbook of school neuropsychology* (pp. 758–776). Hoboken, NJ: Wiley.

Limond, J., & Leeke, R. (2005). Practitioner review: Cognitive rehabilitation for children with acquired brain injury. *Journal of Child Psychology and Psychiatry, 46,* 339–352. doi:10.1111/j.1469-7610.2004.00397.x

Maricle, D., Johnson, W., & Avirett, E. (2010). Assessing and intervening in children with executive function disorders. In D. C. Miller (Ed.), *Best practices in school neuropsychology: Guidelines for effective practices, assessment, and evidence-based intervention* (pp. 599–640). Hoboken, NJ: Wiley.

Maricle, D., Miller, D. C., Hale, J. B., & Johnson, W. L. (2012). Let's not lose sight of the importance of the biological bases of behavior. *Trainer's Forum, 31,* 71–84.

Maricle, D. E., Psimas-Fraser, L., Muenke, R. C., & Miller, D. C. (2010). Assessing and intervening with children with math disorders. In D. C. Miller (Ed.), *Best practices in school neuropsychology: Guidelines for effective practices, assessment, and evidence-based intervention* (pp. 521–549). Hoboken, NJ: Wiley.

Mather, N., & Wendling, B. J. (2012). *Essentials of dyslexia assessment and intervention.* Hoboken, NJ: Wiley.

Mayes, S. D., & Calhoun, S. L. (2006). WISC IV and WISC III profiles in children with ADHD. *Journal of Attention Disorders, 9,* 486–493.

Metzler, L. (2007). *Executive function in education: From theory to practice.* New York, NY: Guilford Press.

Miller, D. C. (2013). *Essentials of school neuropsychological assessment* (2nd ed.). Hoboken, NJ: Wiley.

Muller, E. (2011) Neuroscience and special education. *inForum.* Retrieved from http://nasdse.org/DesktopModules/DNNspotStore/ProductFiles/72_f2f7f9b7-ff92-4cda-a843-c817497e81e4.pdf

National Association of School Psychologists. (2010). *Model for comprehensive and integrated school psychological services.* Bethesda, MD: Author. Retrieved from http://www.nasponline.org/standards/2010standards/2_PracticeModel.pdf

Nell, V. (2000). *Cross-cultural neuropsychological assessment: Theory and practice.* Mahwah, NJ: Erlbaum.

Ortiz, S. O., Ochoa, S. H., & Dynda, A. M. (2012). Testing with culturally and linguistically diverse populations: Moving beyond the verbal-performance dichotomy into evidence-based practice. In D. P. Flanagan & P. L. Harrison (Eds.), *Contemporary intellectual assessment: Theories, tests, and issues* (pp. 526–552). New York, NY: Guilford Press.

Reschly, D. J., Hosp, J. L., & Schmied, C. M. (2003). *And miles to go…: State SLD requirements and authoritative recommendations.* Washington,

DC: U.S. Department of Education. Retrieved from http://www.nrcld.org/about/research/states/MilestoGo.pdf

Reynolds, M., & Besner, D. (2006). Reading aloud is not automatic: Processing capacity is required to generate a phonological code from print. *Journal of Experimental Psychology: Human Perception and Performance, 32*, 1303–1323.

Riccio, C. A. (2008). Compatibility of neuropsychology and RTI in the diagnosis and assessment of learning disabilities. In E. Fletcher-Janzen & C. R. Reynolds (Eds.), *Neuropsychological perspectives on learning disabilities in the era of RTI: Recommendations for diagnosis and intervention* (pp. 82–98). Hoboken, NJ: Wiley.

Riccio, C. A., Sullivan, J. R., & Cohen, M. J. (2010). *Neuropsychological assessment and intervention for childhood and adolescent disorders*. Hoboken, NJ: Wiley.

Schneider, W. J., & McGrew, K. S. (2012). The Cattell-Horn-Carroll Model of Intelligence. In D. P. Flanagan & P. L. Harrison (Eds.), *Contemporary intellectual assessment: Theories, tests, and issues* (pp. 99–144). New York, NY: Guilford Press.

Shaywitz, S. E., & Shaywitz, B. A. (2004). Reading disability and the brain. Educational Leadership, *61*(6), 6–11.

Shaywitz, S. E., & Shaywitz, B. A. (2011). Dyslexia. In A. S. Davis (Ed.), *Handbook of pediatric neuropsychology* (pp. 669–681). New York, NY: Springer.

Thomson, J., Kerns, K., Seidenstrang, L., Sohlberg, M., & Mateer, C. (2001). *Pay attention: A children's attention processing training program*. Wakeforest, NC: Lash and Associates.

Wendling, B. J., & Mather, N. (2009). *Essentials of evidence-based academic interventions*. Hoboken, NJ: Wiley.

Wilson, A. J., & Dehaene, S. (2007). Number sense and developmental dyscalculia. In D. Coch, G. Dawson, & K. Fischer (Eds.), *Human behavior, learning and the developing brain: Atypical development* (pp. 212–238). New York, NY: Guilford Press.

17 Best Practices in Play Assessment and Intervention

Lisa Kelly-Vance
Brigette Oliver Ryalls
University of Nebraska Omaha

OVERVIEW

School psychologists are involved with assessment and intervention services in early childhood. The challenge is to deliver developmentally appropriate services that result in valid and reliable information about a child's level of performance that lead directly to intervention. Play assessment and intervention is one option. The purpose of this chapter is to provide an overview of the most researched play assessment and intervention systems. It is beyond the scope of the chapter to train in the procedures. For that, references and links are included.

According to Piaget (1962), play is the work of children. Play is enjoyable and motivating for children and it is how they spend much of their time. Not only is play an important part of children's daily routine, it is also an indicator of their developmental levels (Eisert & Lamorey, 1996) and a context where valuable teaching and learning occurs. Indeed, play skills enhance competencies critical to academic success in schools such as reading, math, social/emotional development, and abstract thought (Singer, Golinkoff, & Hirsh-Pasek, 2006). Thus, school psychologists can and should integrate play into their assessment and intervention approaches in early childhood.

Play as an assessment and intervention context is relatively new in the field of school psychology but is increasingly popular with practitioners and researchers because of the current emphasis on ecologically valid assessments, context-based interventions, and progress monitoring. One of the powerful benefits of play assessment is that it leads directly to interventions and progress monitoring in the same play context. Play assessment has been suggested to be a multiculturally sensitive (Meisels & Atkins-Burnett, 2000) and parent friendly (Meyers, McBride, & Peterson, 1996) practice.

These characteristics make play assessment and intervention congruent with the National Association of School Psychologists (NASP) *Model for Comprehensive and Integrated School Psychological Services* (NASP, 2010), particularly Data-Based Decision Making and Accountability and Interventions and Instructional Support to Develop Academic Skills, which focus on data-based decision making and accountability and interventions that support cognitive and developmental processes. In fact, the NASP position statement on *Early Childhood Assessment* specifically states that play assessment is an appropriate approach to evaluating the needs of young children (NASP, 2009). Play assessment and intervention is also consistent with the National Association for the Education of Young Children position statement (National Association for the Education of Young Children, 2003).

Play is ubiquitous in early childhood and can be conceptualized as an activity that is not a means to an end but an end itself (i.e., play for the sake of play), is motivating to the individual, and is associated with positive emotions (Tamis-LaMonda, Uzgiris, & Bornstein, 2002). Play assessment is when play is used as the context for evaluating a child's current level of functioning and determining whether there are areas that require intervention. Play intervention is derived from a play assessment and is conducted in the play context.

For the purposes of this chapter, our focus will primarily be on assessment and intervention in the cognitive and social domain. While play assessment and intervention can be used in other domains such as communication and motor skills, it is beyond the scope and purpose of this chapter to include them.

What is important to the understanding of how play assessment and intervention came to the attention of school psychologists is the interest that basic researchers have had in the topic for decades, resulting in a vast, strong, empirical foundation (e.g., Piaget, 1962) that can be applied to the identification of children with specific intervention needs. Piaget's extensive study of how children's play changes with development is one of the earliest and arguably the most influential examples of such research. Specifically, he chronicled the change from sensorimotor to representational play. Numerous descriptions of the typical developmental progression from solitary exploration to cooperative pretend play have been well documented and empirically supported (e.g., Belsky & Most, 1981; Elder & Pederson, 1978; Fenson, 1984; Fenson & Ramsay, 1980; Lyytinen, 1991; McCune-Nicolich, 1981; Parten, 1932; Tamis-LeMonda & Bornstein, 1996).

Interest has also been stimulated by recent trends in school psychology, particularly an increased emphasis on multitiered approaches. Given the requirement of systematic, data-based practice of response to intervention (RTI), play assessment and intervention are logical choices for school psychologists working in early childhood settings and have several features that make them appealing in an RTI model of practice. The developmental sequence described in play assessment coding schemes allows school psychologists to monitor progress in a logical and empirically validated manner and data can be collected regularly and with minimal environmental modification. Play assessment is one procedure that can be integrated with other assessment approaches in a multitier model to gain a complete picture of the child's level of performance. In contrast to standardized tests that can be difficult for parents to comprehend and find useful, the information obtained from a play assessment is easy for parents to understand. Providing interventions in the play context is also a logical format, and early childhood teachers and parents of young children are arguably more likely to demonstrate treatment adherence if they find the process credible.

BASIC CONSIDERATIONS

The use of standardized tests with young children has been criticized on several fronts. These types of tests serve eligibility purposes but do not provide information about how to develop or monitor appropriate interventions, are not ecologically valid, do not assess the child in the natural context, and are a potentially unmotivating and inappropriate means of gathering valid information about a young child (Kelly-Vance & Ryalls, 2005). Further, many school psychologists have expressed misgivings about the use of tests to determine young children's current level of performance (Barnett, Macmann, & Carey, 1992) and would prefer to use alternative strategies such as play assessment (Bagnato & Neisworth, 1994).

Background

The origins of play assessment and intervention stem from psychoanalytic work with children at the turn of the twentieth century. Therapists used information from children's play to determine their mental health needs and then used the play context during therapy. This practice continues in many different therapeutic approaches (Stagnitti & Cooper, 2009). More recently, and for the reasons discussed above, school psychologists working in early childhood began using play assessment as an observational strategy in the 1980s (as discussed in Athanasiou, 2007). Linder (1990) brought even more attention to the procedures with the publication of the original play assessment model (Linder, 1993a) and her subsequent play intervention model (Linder, 1993b). Since then, school psychologists have been using play assessment and intervention, but the empirical support for its use has only recently emerged (e.g., Conner, Kelly-Vance, & Ryalls, 2014; Farmer-Dougan & Kaszuba, 1999; Kelly-Vance, Needelman, Troia, & Ryalls, 1999; Kelly-Vance & Ryalls, 2005; Kelly-Vance, Ryalls, & Gill-Glover, 2002; Mallory, Kelly-Vance, & Ryalls, 2010; Meyers et al., 1996; Sempek, Kelly-Vance, & Ryalls, 2012; Sualy, Yount, Kelly-Vance, & Ryalls, 2011). Fortunately, studies are confirming what school psychologists have known intuitively, which is that this approach is a reliable and valid means of assessing young children and determining their intervention needs. Moreover, the assessment procedures can be used regularly to monitor the progress of children receiving interventions. Interventions in the context of play are showing promise in helping children develop play skills (Conner et al., 2014; Mallory et al., 2010; O'Connor & Stagnitti, 2011; Stagnitti et al., 2011; Sualy et al., 2011).

Training

While the specific materials and procedures required for different versions of play assessment and intervention vary, all forms are similar enough that general guidelines concerning equipment and training can be provided. With regard to equipment, one of the advantages of play assessment and intervention is that no specialized materials or equipment are required. All types of play assessment and intervention involve children playing with toys, other play materials (e.g., crayons and paper), and/or nontoy objects that elicit play in a substitutive fashion. While some forms of play assessment do require a particular set of play objects (e.g., Stagnitti, Unsworth, & Rodger, 2000), others can be conducted in any toy room or early childhood classroom (e.g., Kelly-Vance & Ryalls, 2008; Linder, 2008a; Stagnitti et al., 2000) as long as the available toys are diverse enough to elicit a wide range of play behaviors, including complex pretend play, and are attractive to both boys and girls. Some specific considerations regarding toy choice will be discussed below.

Knowledge about child development in general, and the developmental course of play in particular, is necessary to effectively use play assessment and intervention approaches. Familiarity with daily routines of children from different cultures may also be necessary when interpreting play assessment results and determining interventions. A thorough understanding of the problem-solving approach used with children who have more intense needs is often necessary in utilizing play assessment to guide the intervention process. Play assessments are observational coding systems, thus some experience using such systems is beneficial. Familiarity with the specific play assessment system is obviously required, as is some training and experience identifying particular examples of success or failure or assigning specific codes to play behaviors (e.g., substitution). As with any observational coding system, such experience is necessary to ensure the reliability of the assessment across observers and across play sessions (Salvia, Ysseldyke, & Bolt, 2007). With respect to the type of training required for actual intervention implementation, an understanding of basic principles of operant conditioning, direct teaching, and best practices in working with young children is necessary.

BEST PRACTICES IN PLAY ASSESSMENT AND INTERVENTION

In this section we will review how play assessment and intervention fit into an RTI model. Three major play assessment and intervention systems will be reviewed along with consideration for selecting appropriate approaches. Finally, a case study will illustrate one example of using play assessment and intervention in an early childhood program.

Play Assessment and Intervention in an RTI System

A conceptual multitiered model of services for young children can be applied to play assessment and intervention (see Table 17.1). The first tier parallels general education in the school-aged population. In early childhood, this tier applies best to families, child-care centers, parent resource facilities, and community agencies. School psychologists and other educators can disseminate general information to parents about child development, how to observe children's play to determine where they are functioning, how to promote cognitive development through appropriate play activities, and who to contact if a child is not meeting developmental milestones. The goal at this tier is for families and early childhood caregivers to have access to the information and implement the most basic procedures of play assessment and intervention. Research indicates that mothers have a basic understanding of the order of play development but know less about specific developmental milestones in play than milestones in other domains such as language and motor development (Tamis-LeMonda, Chen, & Bornstein, 1998; Tamis-LeMonda, Shannon, & Spellman, 2002). If a parent or child care worker has concerns about a child's development, then contact can be made with the school district and Tier 2 interventions will be considered.

In Tier 2, a formal play assessment is conducted by a trained school psychologist, and the child's strengths and areas of intervention need are determined. Based on this

Table 17.1. Play Assessment and Intervention in a Three-Tiered RTI Model

	Tier 1	Tier 2	Tier 3
Assessment approach	Screening	Monthly or bimonthly	Intense frequency (weekly or more)
Intervention approach	General skills	Small groups	Small group or individual
Service delivery approach	Informational	Consultation and/or direct services	Consultation and intensive direct services
Intervention agents	Parents	Parents, teachers, child-care providers	Parents, teachers, child-care providers, special education support staff

play assessment data, interventions are then developed collaboratively with the professional(s) who conducted the play assessment and the individual(s) responsible for intervention implementation. Possible intervention providers include school psychologists, parents, preschool teachers, and child-care providers. Given their knowledge of data-based decision making and intervention development, school psychologists are an obvious choice for the role of consultant with these cases. This role includes interpreting assessment data, scripting the intervention, and monitoring the progress of the intervention. If a child is in a preschool or daycare center, then small group interventions may be appropriate and the consultant could develop a protocol for several children with similar needs. Otherwise, individual interventions may be required. Incidentally, the frequent use of individual intervention at this level contrasts what generally occurs with school-aged children where small group interventions are most common at Tier 2. In both individual and small group interventions, a goal is determined and the child's progress is regularly monitored by the service provider. At this tier, progress is determined by using a play assessment scale and periodically evaluating the child's rate of progress toward the predetermined goal(s). Because of potential for rapid change in early childhood, frequent monitoring is recommended.

Tier 3 is a more intense version of Tier 2 and may require that a child spend a trial placement in an early intervention program. The intervention is more intensely implemented, progress-monitoring data are collected more frequently, and a team of early childhood professionals should be included to consider whether the child is eligible for special education services. At both Tiers 2 and 3, a play assessment coding scheme provides a benchmark for where a child should be functioning and can help teams evaluate a child's discrepancy from peers, rate of progress, and amount of support needed to ensure progress. If the child continues to be functioning significantly below his or her peers and is not progressing at a rate that would indicate he or she may catch up, early intervention services through special education should be considered and a full evaluation conducted. The child's response to the play intervention could be a major consideration in the eligibility decision. This information can be integrated with other types of assessment and data collection to determine eligibility for early intervention services. Once in early intervention services, play assessment can be one method of monitoring the effectiveness of the child's programming.

Types of Play Assessment and Intervention

Although many forms of play assessment exist, only those with a linked intervention system will be reviewed in this section. Three linked play assessment and intervention systems currently exist. They are Transdisciplinary Play-Based Assessment and Intervention, Play Assessment and Intervention System, and Learn to Play Assessment and Intervention System. Each system and their subcomponents will be described below, including a summary of research on each system. General guidelines for conducting play assessments will then be provided and a case study demonstrating how play assessment data can be used to develop and monitor interventions in the context of play will be presented.

Transdisciplinary Play-Based Assessment and Intervention

One of the earliest and most influential play assessment and intervention systems was developed by Toni Linder in the early 1990s and was recently revised (Linder, 1990, 1993a, 2008a, 2008b, 2008c). The current system is thoroughly described in three manuals, the Transdisciplinary Play-Based Assessment-2 (TPBA-2; Linder, 2008a), Transdisciplinary Play-Based Intervention-2 (TPBI-2; Linder, 2008b), and the Administrative Guide for TPBA-2 and TPBI-2 (2008c). Her transdisciplinary approach captures the essence of collaboration in that a team of early childhood service providers and parents work together to find out information about a child's developmental levels and link them directly to interventions.

Transdisciplinary Play-Based Assessment.
The Transdisciplinary Play-Based Assessment (TPBA) is conducted in what Linder called an arena format, where individuals from various disciplines observe the child in free play and document the play behaviors. These individuals communicate their findings with one another throughout the observational period, allowing for a shared perspective on the child's skill level. General guidelines for conducting the data-gathering sessions are described in her books (Linder, 2008a, 2008b, 2008c).

Prior to the play session, the family facilitator contacts the child's family members to find out their concerns and collect preliminary information on the child's family history and current level functioning. The structure of the play assessment session takes into account any information obtained from the parents. The observational team consists of a play facilitator, who engages with the child; a family facilitator, who is responsible for discussing the process with the parent; the evaluators; and a person to operate the camera. A large play area such as a classroom is recommended for the session, but any setting with a variety of familiar and novel toys can be used. Initially, the child plays alone and no structure is imposed upon the activities. The play facilitator can participate but not initiate any of the play. Facilitation occurs in the second phase, where the play facilitator attempts to provide opportunities for the child to engage in activities that have not yet been observed that may be in the child's repertoire. This is essentially a testing phase. The goal is to observe the child's abilities in various types of play, problem solving, communication, fine and gross motor play, and preacademic skills. For the third phase, the child is then observed playing with another child and interacting with a parent or caregiver. The session ends with a snack, and feedback is provided to the parent. The entire session lasts between 60 and 90 minutes.

A major part of the Linder system is the detailed observation guidelines. She provides guidelines for four major domains: sensorimotor, emotional and social, communication, and cognitive development. The applicable ages vary but, in general, the guidelines apply to young children up to 72 months of age. Each major domain is further subdivided into more specific categories. For example, in the area of Cognitive Development, TPBA-2 provides observational guidelines for assessing performance in attention, memory, problem solving, social cognition, complexity of play, and conceptual knowledge. Observations are documented and summarized on forms provided in the TPBA-2 manual. Performance is compared to same-age peers and concerns are noted. Specific suggestions for intervention are derived from the TPBA-2 results (Linder, 2008b).

Two published studies have reported on the validity of Linder's TPBA approach. Myers et al.'s (1996) study of the social validity of TPBA found that parents and early childhood professionals preferred the TPBA process to more traditional information yielded from standardized tests. Kelly-Vance et al. (1999) found a high correlation between scores from the Bayley Scales of Infant Development-II and the cognitive development guidelines from Linder's TPBA. In addition, one unpublished dissertation examined the concurrent and content validity and the test-retest and interrater reliability of TPBA and found it adequate (Friedli as cited in Athanasiou, 2007). To date, no studies have been published examining the revised TPBA-2 since its publication in 2008.

Transdisciplinary Play-Based Intervention.

Like TPBA, Transdisciplinary Play-Based Intervention (TPBI) focuses on the sensorimotor, emotional and social, communication, and cognitive domains of development and provides strategies for facilitating development in each domain and associated subcategories. Interventions are planned and implemented in a 12-step process by the TPBI team in collaboration with parents, caregivers, and teachers. Linder and contributors have developed multiple checklists, worksheets, and rubrics to document and guide the process of intervention development and implementation. Overall, much like TPBA, the TBPI process involves multiple team members, is flexible and tailored to the abilities and needs of the child, does not require any specific materials, and can be implemented in the child's natural environment. In addition to interventions implemented in the context of play, TPBI-2 also includes interventions implemented in the context of daily living (home or classroom) and in reading and learning contexts. The nature, intensity, and duration of the interventions are determined for each child individually. Although the intervention strategies in TPBI-2 are based on standard practices, there is to date no published research documenting the effectiveness of TPBI-2, either alone or with TPBA-2 as a linked system of assessment and interaction.

Play Assessment and Intervention System

The Play Assessment and Intervention System (PLAIS) is a linked assessment and intervention system developed primarily by Kelly-Vance and Ryalls (2005, 2008). It is composed of two parts: The Play in Early Childhood Evaluation System (PIECES) and the Child Learning in Play System (CLIPS). PIECES is the assessment component and CLIPS is the intervention component. Each component is described in turn below.

Play in Early Childhood Evaluation System.

The PIECES is an assessment of cognitive development and social interaction in the context of play (Kelly-Vance & Ryalls, 2005, 2008). PIECES involves a 30-minute observation of a child engaged in free play and can be conducted in any setting with any toy set as long as the toy set is large and varied enough to elicit a wide range of behaviors. Most often, these observations take place in a classroom or child-care program during unstructured play time. No instructions are given, and the observer does not interact with the child unless the child initiates the interaction. The child can play alone or with other children. When engaged in social play, observations are made concerning the target child's ability to initiate play, play cooperatively with others, and any social behaviors that may be interfering with the child's ability to play well with others.

PIECES can be used to screen for children's needs in early childhood. Classroom observations during free play can help determine those children who demonstrate typically developing play skills and those who may need more in-depth assessment and subsequent intervention. For screening purposes, the school psychologist observes children in pretend play areas using the core subdomain (Exploratory/Pretend Play) and, once the child demonstrates age-appropriate skills in this subdomain, the child is considered competent and no further observations are needed. Thus, the observation times vary depending on how quickly the child shows age-appropriate skills. Longer observations are often needed with children who do not show age-appropriate skills and more detail is required so that interventions can be developed.

The PIECES coding guidelines are broken down into multiple subscales examining different categories of cognitive development and social interaction, although the specific subcategories differ. The PIECES coding scheme contains one core subdomain as well as several supplemental subdomains (see Table 17.2). The

Table 17.2. PIECES Core and Supplemental Subdomains

Core subdomains
Exploratory Play:
- Mouthing
- Basic Manipulation
- Single Functional Act
- Nonmatching Combination
- Similarity-Based Combination
- Functional Combination
- Matching Combination
- Complex Exploration
- Approximate Pretend Play
Simple Pretend Play:
- Self-Directed Pretending
- Object-Directed Pretending
- Other-Directed Pretending
- Substitution Pretending
- Repetitive Combinations
- Variable Combinations
- Agentive Pretending
Complex Pretend Play: Multiple-Step Sequences

Supplemental subdomains
Strategic Behavior and Problem Solving
Discrimination and Categorization
Quantities and Numbers

supplemental subdomains are adapted versions of several of Linder's TPBA (Linder, 1993) subcategories. PIECES is unique in that the item sequence that makes up the Exploratory/Pretend Play core subdomain was drawn from the extensive empirical literature on the typical development of play (Belsky & Most, 1981; Fenson, 1984; Lyytinen, 1991; Tamis-Lemonda, Bornstein, Cyphers, Toda, & Ogina, 1992). In the PIECES coding, every play behavior produced by the child can be classified on the core subdomain scale. Supplemental subdomains are reserved for specific types of behaviors (such as trial-and-error problem solving, sorting, and drawing) that may or may not occur in any given play session.

Children's cognitive level can be described by using the PIECES coding guidelines. Play behaviors are documented on the coding and summary forms developed by the authors. Specific examples of play are described and categorized into core and supplemental subdomains. The highest level of play is noted for all subdomains. In addition, school psychologists may also want to document the type of play that was seen most frequently in each subdomain. Finally, the child's level of functioning from the PIECES subdomains are compared to his or her chronological age, and discrepancies are noted and used to determine if the child requires intervention in specific areas. Observations of free play can be supplemented with interviews with parents and/or teachers when there are questions about a child's level of performance. Interventions are later targeted at the play and/or social skills found to be discrepant from peers.

PIECES has been evaluated empirically and found to have high interrater reliability (Kelly-Vance & Ryalls, 2005). In addition, this high interrater reliability was achieved with a relatively simple training procedure. That is, individuals with a background in observational techniques can be trained to accurately and reliably use these guidelines to assess play behavior with as little as a half day of training. Test–retest reliability (Kelly-Vance & Ryalls, 2005) is adequate. Because play is not facilitated and can be used with any toys or settings, this procedure can also be used with English language learners (Sempek et al., 2012) and extended for use with children with motor challenges (Kokkoni et al., 2010).

Child Learning in Play System. In PLAIS, CLIPS interventions are determined directly from the strengths and areas of need observed in the PIECES assessment and address needs in both cognitive and social domains. A problem-solving approach is used to determine the specific interventions, tailored to the particular needs of the child. Interventions can be implemented by a school psychologist or by another trained adult (i.e., teacher, parent, or caregiver; see Dempsey, Kelly-Vance, & Ryalls, 2013). Intervention approaches include direct teaching of play skills and/or social skills individually or with peers. Play skills to be taught are determined by the child's current level of functioning and, by using the developmental progression of play, selecting the next skill in this progression as the teaching target. These play skills can be taught in the natural play context or through the use of theme books (e.g., birthday party, picnic) that are read to the child and then acted out with a toy set after hearing the story. Social skills can be taught by using a social skills curriculum or the use of social stories. The skills are then generalized to the play context. Principles of operant conditioning are used, such as modeling, prompting, and reinforcement. Progress is monitored throughout the intervention.

Several published studies have documented the effectiveness of the PLAIS as a linked assessment/intervention system. Specifically, CLIPS interventions have been documented to improve the play level and/or language ability of typically developing preschoolers (Mallory et al., 2010; Conner et al., 2014), as well as preschoolers with verified speech language impairment (Sualy et al., 2011). In these studies, interventions were found to be effective when implemented one to two times a week for as little as 4–8 weeks.

Learn to Play Assessment and Intervention System

The Learn to Play program is a play assessment and intervention system developed by Karen Stagnitti (1998, 2007), an occupational therapist and specialist in early childhood intervention, and her colleagues. It is composed of three parts: the Symbolic and Imaginative Play Developmental Checklist (SIP-DC), the Child-Initiated Pretend Play Assessment (ChIPPA), and the Learn to Play intervention program. Each component is described in turn below.

Symbolic and Imaginative Play Developmental Checklist.
The SIP-DC is an observational checklist for children ages birth to 3 years that examines pretend play in six domains: play themes, sequence of play acts, object substitution, social interaction, role play, and doll/teddy play (Stagnitti, 1998). The checklist can be used for assessment and progress monitoring. It is administered by observing a child in spontaneous play

and requires a certain minimal set of common toys and objects (e.g., doll, truck, container, stick), the precise nature of which depends on the child's age. If certain behaviors are not produced spontaneously, play acts can be modeled and the child's ability to imitate can be recorded. In addition to direct observation, the SIP-DC can be used in interviews with parents, caregivers, and teachers who are familiar with the child's level of play. Currently, no published research has been done to empirically validate the SIP-DC.

Child-Initiated Pretend Play Assessment.
ChIPPA is a norm referenced standardized instrument developed in Australia and is designed to assess the spontaneous play skills of children aged 3–7 years (Stagnitti, 2007). The assessment is administered individually, takes 30 minutes or less, and can be conducted in a clinic, school, or home. To reduce outside distraction, the assessment is conducted in what they call a fort that is constructed by placing a blanket over the top of two chairs. The child and practitioner sit in the fort together. The child participates in two consecutive sessions involving different standardized toy sets. In the conventional-imaginative session, children play with a farm set that includes, for example, dolls, vehicles, and tools. Other toys may be used. In the symbolic session, children are given more generic items such as boxes, sticks, pebbles, and cloth, along with two simple cloth dolls. Play is scored to determine the elaborateness of the child's pretend play, the number and nature of object substitutions, and the amount of imitation. ChIPPA has been empirically examined in a number of published studies and appears to be psychometrically sound. Specifically, it has been found to possess good interrater and test–retest reliability (Pfeifer, Queiroz, Santos, & Stagnitti, 2011; Stagnitti & Unsworth, 2004), to have high concurrent validity when compared to social competence measures (Uren & Stagnitti, 2009), and to discriminate between typical and atypical preschoolers (Stagnitti et al., 2000). ChIPPA has also been tested cross culturally (Dender & Stagnitti, 2011; Pfeifer et al., 2011) and to measure changes in play levels in children of low socioeconomic status (Reynolds, Stagnitti, & Kidd, 2011). Finally, researchers have also begun to empirically assess play-based interventions using ChIPPA (O'Connor & Stagnitti, 2011).

Learn to Play program.
The Learn to Play program (Stagnitti, 1998) is an intervention program aimed at raising a child's level of imaginative play in the

six domains examined in the SIP-DC. The intervention program can be implemented by a practitioner, teacher, or parent. Interventions can be conducted a one-on-one or in a group setting. The Learn to Play manual includes detailed activity sheets for each of the six domains. Each activity sheet lists a goal, required materials, a description of what to do, and additional play ideas similar to the targeted activity. Activity sheets are ordered based on the typical age/level of the activity. The Learn to Play program recognizes that children may be at different levels on the different domains and allows flexibility in implementation. The specific activities implemented are chosen based on the levels of play observed in SIP-DC (or ChIPPA).

The effectiveness of ChIPPA and Learn to Play as a linked system of assessment and intervention has been documented in one empirical report (O'Connor & Stagnitti, 2011). In this study, children 5–8 years old with intellectual disabilities participated in either an intervention group or a control group. Children in the intervention group participated in the Learn to Play program for 1 hour twice a week over a 6-month period. Results indicated the children in the intervention group showed fewer play deficits, were less socially disruptive, and more socially connected after the intervention. The comparison group did not show these changes.

Additional Considerations in Play Assessment

Regardless of which form of play assessment is chosen, the setting and facilitation of play are important considerations, each of which is described below.

Setting

One of the many positive characteristics of play assessment is that it can be conducted in a variety of settings such as home, childcare, preschool, Head Start, or early intervention programs. When selecting toys for play assessment it is important to make sure that the toys are appropriate for the age, assumed developmental level, and gender of the child being assessed. While it is commonly recognized that children of different ages/ developmental levels may choose to play with different types of toys, it is important to keep in mind that boys and girls also have preferences and these preferences may have an impact on the outcome of the assessment. By 2 years of age, children display preferences for certain types of toys (O'Brien & Huston, 1985). That is, boys and girls tend to prefer to play with toys that are stereotypically consistent with their own gender. While

both boys and girls show this tendency, research has shown that this tendency is more pronounced for boys (Cherney, Kelly-Vance, Gill-Glover, Ruane, & Ryalls, 2003). Specifically, Cherney and colleagues found that while boys played with predominantly male stereotyped toys (e.g., cars, trucks), girls played predominantly with neutral toys (e.g., puzzles, a cash register). More importantly, for both boys and girls, it was found that the male stereotyped toys elicited the simplest forms of play and the female stereotyped toys (e.g., dolls and kitchen set) elicited the highest levels of play. Thus, when conducting a play assessment the school psychologist should ensure that a variety of toys that are gender appropriate are available and encourage children to play with toys that have the potential to elicit more complex forms of play.

Facilitation

Some play assessment approaches involve significant levels of facilitation and/or modeling, often requiring the reproduction of very specific play behaviors. We believe, however, best practice involves a nonfacilitated, free-play situation with minimal direction. Eliminating facilitation from the format helps ensure a more standardized session that removes facilitator bias and increases the likelihood of obtaining high levels of reliability across raters, children, and sessions. One exception to this guideline concerns questions about skills that may not have been demonstrated during the session or potentially emerging skills. It is appropriate to attempt to elicit behaviors such as drawing and/or counting that do not spontaneously occur for many children. Similarly, if there are questions about the upper limits of some emerging behaviors, then it is acceptable to attempt to elicit such behaviors, particularly when developing interventions.

Instead of facilitating play in a traditional sense, parents and play team members may participate in child-directed play and provide verbal praise (e.g., "Good job"). In addition, adults should redirect children (e.g., "What else can you play with?") who continue to play with the same toy in the same manner for 5 minutes or longer. This is an attempt to vary the play behaviors during the session but not to encourage any specific type of play.

Case Illustration

The following case illustrates the use of play assessment and intervention when working with an individual child, representing the third tier of a multitier process. Joey is

4 years, 4 months old and attends Head Start 5 days a week. His family includes his parents and an older brother who attends a different Head Start class. Joey has attended the program for 3 months, during which time he rarely was seen playing with other children.

The Head Start teacher contacted the school psychologist, Ms. Sanchez, to discuss her concerns. The teacher reported that she only sees Joey playing by himself and he usually is in the block area, computer station, or wandering.

Ms. Sanchez contacted the parents, and they agreed with the teacher report and stated they see the same behaviors at home. Joey's parents reported that Joey and his brother sometimes play together but their play is so different they end up fighting.

Ms. Sanchez then observed Joey during free play for an hour. During the first 30 minutes she conducted a play assessment using PIECES and determined Joey's highest level of play was at the self-directed pretend play level (i.e., child acts on himself or herself, such as eating from an empty spoon or combing his or her hair). Joey engaged in four play acts that were self-directed play. Other play consisted of seven similarity-based combinations (i.e., combining objects based on functional similarity) and matching combinations (performs two

or more actions with an object, such as putting balls in a shape sorter and then putting the balls in a bucket). During the PIECES observation, Ms. Sanchez also noted that a peer joined Joey twice in the block area and began building a complex structure. The peer attempted to engage Joey in building a tower but Joey remained with his own blocks and did not respond to the peer's initiation. In addition, Joey's play skills were similar in the presence versus absence of the peer. For the next 30 minutes Ms. Sanchez conducted an observation of Joey's social interactions using duration recording and found that Joey interacted with peers 3% of the time and the interactions consisted of a peer approaching him and Joey then ignoring the peer. Two additional observations resulted in similar levels of performance (see Figure 17.1). Therefore, the behavior of concern was that Joey's level of play skills was below what is expected for his age and consisted of exploratory and simple pretend play with the highest level being self-directed pretend play.

Ms. Sanchez hypothesized that Joey did not have play skills that were age appropriate and this was having an impact on his social interactions because he did not understand the play of his peers. If Joey were taught higher levels of play, then he would have more

Figure 17.1. Percentage of Time Joey Spent in Social–Interactive Play by Week

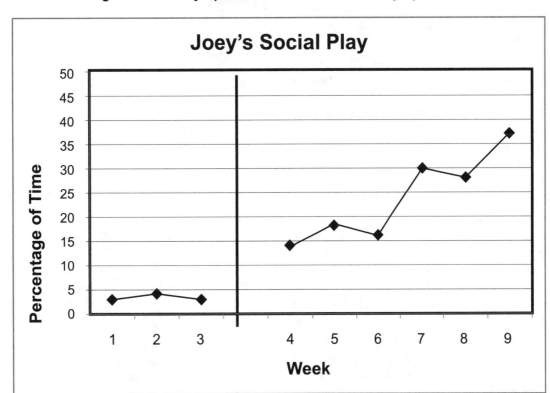

opportunities to play with peers, thus increasing his social interactions. To confirm or refute her hypothesis, Ms. Sanchez decided Joey first needed to learn play skills and then he needed help generalizing these skills to peers.

A paraprofessional (a school psychologist could also have been used) was trained to conduct the actual intervention, which consisted of the following steps:

Step 1: Select the appropriate play skill. The play skill to target was determined from Joey's highest level of play on PIECES (self-directed pretend play). The next skill in a developmental sequence of play was object-directed pretend play, so that was selected as the target skill.

Step 2: Teach the play skill. Because Joey was typically playing alone, the paraprofessional conducted these steps during that time: (a) Model the play skill. The paraprofessional modeled object-directed play with a variety of objects. (b) Prompt Joey to do the play skill. After modeling the behavior, the paraprofessional then handed Joey the toys and gave a command specific to the play skill (e.g., "Rock the baby." "Stir the soup."). If Joey did not demonstrate the requested behavior, then Step 2a would have been repeated until Joey complied. (c) Praise Joey when he demonstrated the play skill. The paraprofessional provided verbal praise for any approximation of the play behavior.

Step 3: Generalize the skill to peers. Generalization was incorporated into the daily intervention sessions. After the teaching phase, the paraprofessional guided Joey to the pretend play center where other children were playing. She gave Joey verbal instructions about how to join in the play and, when needed, reminded him of the play skills they worked on earlier. She then praised Joey for any pretend play.

The intervention was implemented daily for 30 minutes during center time. For the first 10 minutes, the paraprofessional implemented Steps 1 and 2. The last 20 minutes were spent in generalization with peers. Next, Ms. Sanchez taught Joey's parents to teach the play skills at home and asked them to help him play with his older brother.

Ms. Sanchez collected weekly data on the percentage of time Joey spent in social versus isolated play (see Figure 17.1). After 6 weeks of intervention, Ms. Sanchez conducted a 30-minute PIECES observation during which time Joey displayed 7 other-directed play acts, 8 self-directed acts, and 10 exploratory play acts. He also showed three complex play acts of sequencing two simple play acts (e.g., self-directed, other-directed) together logically. Then Ms. Sanchez observed Joey's social interactions for 30 minutes to determine the

percent of time he spent playing with peers. Results were that Joey interacted with peers during play 37% of the time. While he was not comparable to peers, he was making progress. Ms. Sanchez concluded that increasing Joey's play skills was related to improvement in his social skills.

Joey's parents met with Ms. Sanchez and the teacher and concluded that the intervention would continue at home and the teacher would prompt and reinforce Joey's play in the classroom but would not teach play skills unless needed at a future time.

SUMMARY

The existing empirical literature indicates that there are numerous benefits to using play assessment and intervention with young children. Because the assessment is conducted in the natural environment of play, it is motivating and elicits the highest level of a child's functioning. The process offers flexibility, which is critical when working with young children. The results of a play assessment lead naturally to interventions that can be implemented and monitored by many different individuals in various settings with a minimal amount of training. Research to date indicates these interventions are effective in improving the developing skills of preschool children.

REFERENCES

Athanasiou, M. S. (2006). Play-based approaches to preschool assessment. In B. A. Bracken & R. Nagle (Eds.), *Psychoeducational assessment of preschool children* (4th ed., pp. 219–238). Mahwah, NJ: Erlbaum.

Bagnato, S. J., & Neisworth, J. T. (1994). A national study of the social and treatment "invalidity" of intelligence testing for early intervention. *School Psychology Quarterly*, *9*, 81–102. doi:10.1037/h0088852

Barnett, D. W., Macmann, G. M., & Carey, K. T. (1992). Early intervention and the assessment of developmental skills: Challenges and directions. *Topics in Early Childhood Special Education*, *12*, 21–43. doi:10.1177/027112149201200105

Belsky, J., & Most, R. K. (1981). From exploration to play: A cross-sectional study of infant free play behavior. *Developmental Psychology*, *17*, 630–639. doi:10.1037/0012-1649.17.5.630

Cherney, I. C., Kelly-Vance, L., Gill-Glover, K., Ruane, A., & Ryalls, B. O. (2003). The effects of stereotyped toys and gender on play assessment in 18–47-month-old children. *Educational Psychology*, *22*, 95–106. doi:10.1080/01443410303222

Conner, J., Kelly-Vance, L., Ryalls, B., & Friehem, M. (2014). A play and language intervention for two-year-old children: Implications for improving play skills and language. *Journal of Research in Childhood Education*, *28*(2), 221–237. doi:10.1080/02568543.2014.883452.

Dempsey, J., Kelly-Vance, L., & Ryalls, B. (2013). The effect of a parent training program on children's play. *International Journal of Psychology: a Biopsychosocial Approach, 13,* 117–138. doi:org/10.72220/1941-7233.13.6

Dender, A., & Stagnitti, K. (2011). Development of the Indigenous Child-Initiated Pretend Play Assessment: Selection of play materials and administration. *Australian Occupational Therapy Journal, 58,* 34–42. doi:10.1111/j.1440-1630.2010.00905.x

Eisert, D., & Lamorey, S. (1996). Play as a window on child development: The relationship between play and other developmental domains. *Early Education & Development, 7,* 221–234. doi:10.1207/s15566935eed0703_2

Elder, J. L., & Pederson, D. R. (1978). Preschool children's use of objects in symbolic play. *Child Development, 49,* 500–504. doi:10.2307/1128716fr

Farmer-Dougan, V., & Kaszuba, T. (1999). Reliability and validity of play-based observations: Relationship between the play behavior observation system and standardized measures of cognitive and social skills. *Educational Psychology, 19,* 429–441. doi:10.1080/0144341990190404

Fenson, L. (1984). Developmental trends for action and speech in pretend play. In I. Bretherton (Ed.), *Symbolic play: The development of social understanding* (pp. 249–270). Orlando, FL: Academic Press.

Fenson, L., & Ramsay, D. S. (1980). Decentration and integration of the child's play in the second year, *Child Development, 51,* 171–178. doi:10.2307/1129604

Kelly-Vance, L., Needelman, H., Troia, K., & Ryalls, B. O. (1999). Early childhood assessment: A comparison of the Bayley Scales of Infant Development and a play-based technique. *Developmental Disabilities Bulletin, 27,* 1–15.

Kelly-Vance, L., & Ryalls, B. O. (2005). A systematic, reliable approach to play assessment in preschoolers. *School Psychology International, 26,* 398–412. doi:10.1177/0143034305059017

Kelly-Vance, L., & Ryalls, B. O. (2008). Best practices in play assessment and intervention. In A. Thomas & J. Grimes (Eds.), *Best practices in school psychology V* (pp. 549–559). Bethesda, MD: National Association of School Psychologists.

Kelly-Vance, L., Ryalls, B. O., & Gill-Glover, K. (2002). The use of play assessment to evaluate the cognitive skills of 2- and 3-year-old children. *School Psychology International, 23,* 169–185. doi:10.1177/0143034302023002909

Kokkoni, E., Dempsey, J., Harbourne, R. T., Kelly-Vance, L., Ryalls, B., & Stergiou, N. (2010, June). *Developing sitting postural control and play in children with cerebral palsy.* Poster presented at the annual meeting of the North American Society for the Psychology of Sport and Physical Activity, Tucson, AZ

Linder, T. W. (1990). *Transdisciplinary Play-Based Assessment: A functional approach to working with young children.* Baltimore, MD: Brookes.

Linder, T. W. (1993a). *Transdisciplinary Play-Based Assessment: A functional approach to working with young children* (rev. ed.). Baltimore, MD: Brookes.

Linder, T. W. (1993b). *Transdisciplinary Play-Based Intervention: Guidelines for developing a meaningful curriculum for young children.* Baltimore, MD: Brookes.

Linder, T. W. (2008a). *Transdisciplinary Play-Based Assessment-2.* Baltimore, MD: Brookes.

Linder, T. W. (2008b). *Transdisciplinary Play-Based Intervention-2.* Baltimore, MD: Brookes.

Linder, T. W. (2008c). *Administrative guide: Transdisciplinary Play-Based Assessment and Intervention-2.* Baltimore, MD: Brookes.

Lyytinen, P. (1991). Developmental trends in children's pretend play. *Child: Care, Health and Development, 17,* 9–25. doi:10.1111/j.1365-2214.1991.tb00675.x

Mallory, J. M., Kelly-Vance, L., & Ryalls, B. O. (2010). Incorporating divergent thinking into play interventions for preschool children with developmental risk factors. *International Journal of Creativity and Problem Solving, 20,* 57–71.

McCune-Nicolich, L. (1981). Toward symbolic functioning: Structure of early pretend games and potential parallels with language. *Child Development, 52,* 785–797. doi:10.2307/1129078

Meisels, S. J., & Atkins-Burnett, S. (2000). The elements of early childhood assessment. In J. P. Shonkoff & S. J. Meisels (Eds.), *Handbook of early childhood intervention* (pp. 231–257). New York, NY: Cambridge University Press.

Meyers, C. L., McBride, S. L., & Peterson, C. A. (1996). Transdisciplinary, play-based assessment in early childhood special education: An examination of social validity. *Topics in Early Childhood Special Education, 16,* 102–126. doi:10.1177/027112149601600109

National Association for the Education of Young Children. (2003). *Position statement on early childhood curriculum, assessment, and program evaluation.* Washington, DC: Author. Retrieved from http://www.naeyc.org/files/naeyc/file/positions/pscape.pdf

National Association of School Psychologists. (2009). *Early childhood assessment* [Position Statement]. Bethesda, MD: Author. Retrieved from http://www.nasponline.org/about_nasp/positionpapers/EarlyChildhoodAssessment.pdf

National Association of School Psychologists. (2010). *Model for comprehensive and integrated school psychological services.* Bethesda, MD: Author. Retrieved from http://www.nasponline.org/standards/2010standards/2_PracticeModel.pdf

O'Brien, M. O., & Huston, A. C. (1985). Development of sex-typed play behavior in toddlers. *Developmental Psychology, 21,* 866–871. doi:10.1037/0012-1649.21.5.866

O'Connor, C., & Stagnitti, K. (2011). Play, behavior, language, and social skills: The comparison of a play and a non-play intervention within a specialist school setting. *Research in Developmental Disabilities, 32,* 1205–1211. doi:10.1016/j.ridd.2010.12.037

Parten, M. (1932). Social participation among preschool children. *Journal of Abnormal and Social Psychology, 27,* 243–269. doi:10.1037/h0074524

Pfeifer, L., Queiroz, M., Santos, J., & Stagnitti, K. (2011). Cross-cultural adaptation and reliability of Child-Initiated Pretend Play Assessment (ChIPPA). *Canadian Journal of Occupational Therapy, 78,* 187–195. doi:10.2182/cjot.2011.78.3.7

Piaget, J. (1962). *Play, dreams, and imitation in childhood.* New York, NY: Norton.

Reynolds, E., Stagnitti, K., & Kidd, E. (2011). Play, language, and social skills of children attending a play-based curriculum school and a traditionally structured classroom curriculum school in low socio-economic areas. *Australian Journal of Early Childhood, 36,* 120–130.

Salvia, J., Ysseldyke, J. E., & Bolt, S. (2007). *Assessment in special and inclusive education* (10th ed.). Boston, MA: Houghton Mifflin.

Sempek, A. N., Kelly-Vance, L., & Ryalls, B. O. (2012). Cross-cultural relationship: Maternal acculturation, knowledge/beliefs on play and children's play level. *School Psychology: From Science to Practice, 5*, 12–22.

Singer, D., Golinkoff, R. M., & Hirsh-Pasek, K. (Eds.). (2006). *Play = learning: How play motivates and enhances children's cognitive and social-emotional growth.* New York, NY: Oxford University Press.

Stagnitti, K. (1998). *Learn to Play: A practical program to develop a child's imaginative play skills.* Victoria, Australia: Co-ordinates Therapy Services.

Stagnitti, K. (2007). *The Child-Initiated Pretend Play Assessment manual and kit.* Melbourne, Australia: Co-Ordinates Therapy Services.

Stagnitti, K., & Cooper, R. (2009). *Play as therapy: Assessment and therapeutic interventions.* London, UK: Jessica Kingsley.

Stagnitti, K., Malakellis, M., Kenna, R., Kershaw, B., Hoare, M., & de Silva-Sanigorski, A. (2011). Evaluating the feasibility, effectiveness and acceptability of an active play intervention for disadvantaged preschool children: A pilot study. *Australasian Journal of Early Childhood, 36*, 66–72.

Stagnitti, K., & Unsworth, C. (2004). The test-retest reliability of the child-initiated pretend play assessment. *The American Journal of Occupational Therapy, 58*, 93–99. doi:10.5014/ajot.58.1.93

Stagnitti, K., Unsworth, C., & Rodger, S. (2000). Development of an assessment to identify play behaviors that discriminate between the play of typical preschoolers and preschoolers with pre-academic problems. *Canadian Journal of Occupational Therapy, 67*, 291–303.

Sualy, A., Yount, S., Kelly-Vance, L., & Ryalls, B. O. (2011). Using a play intervention to improve the play skills of children with a language delay. *International Journal of Psychology: A Biopsychosocial Approach, 9*, 105–122.

Tamis-LeMonda, C. S., & Bornstein, M. H. (1996). Variation in children's exploratory, nonsymbolic, and symbolic play: An explanatory multidimensional framework. In C. Rovee-Collier & L. Lipsitt (Eds.), *Advances in infancy research* (pp. 37–78). Norwood, NJ: Ablex.

Tamis-LeMonde, C. S., Bornstein, M. H., Cyphers, L., Toda, S., & Ogina, M. (1992). Language and play at one year: A comparison of toddlers and mothers in the United States and Japan. *International Journal of Behavioral Development, 15*, 19–42.

Tamis-LeMonda, C. S., Chen, L. A., & Bornstein, M. H. (1998). Mothers' knowledge about children's play and language development: Short-term stability and interrelations. *Developmental Psychology, 34*, 115–124. doi:10.1037/0012-1649.34.1.115

Tamis-LeMonda, C. S., Shannon, J., & Spellmann, M. (2002). Low-income adolescent mothers' knowledge about domains of child development. *Infant Mental Health Journal, 23*, 88–103. doi:10.1002/imhj.10006

Tamis-LaMonda, C. S., Uzgiris, I. C., & Bornstein, M. H. (2002). Play in parent-child interactions. In M. H. Bornstein (Ed.), *Handbook of parenting* (2nd ed., pp. 221–242). New York, NY: Psychology Press.

Uren, N., & Stagnitti, K. (2009). Pretend play, social competence, and involvement in children aged 5-7 years: The concurrent validity of the Child-Initiated Pretend Play Assessment. *Australian Occupational Therapy Journal, 56*, 33–40. doi:10.1111/j.1440-1630.2008.00761.x

18 Best Practices in Conducting Functional Behavioral Assessments

Mark W. Steege
Michael A. Scheib
University of Southern Maine

OVERVIEW

Students' disruptive behaviors that interfere with their own, or classmates', acquisition of academic and social behaviors present challenges to professionals within schools. For example, interfering behaviors such as aggression, property destruction, threats of violence or harm, and bullying clearly violate school rules, social boundaries, and standards of acceptable behavior. Likewise, verbal and nonverbal opposition to instruction, self-injury, stereotypy, and inappropriate social behaviors interfere with students' educational progress. Historically, when students who exhibited such behaviors were referred for school psychological services, a descriptive or diagnostic approach was utilized (Betz, Alison, & Fisher, 2011). Generally, the outcome of the school psychological assessment resulted in the identification of a "disability," a determination of eligibility for services, and some form of special education placement (Steege & Pratt, 2012). In all too many cases, descriptive/diagnostic assessments became the expected role of school psychologists (Reschly, Tilly, & Grimes, 1999). Occasionally, this led to affectionate nicknames such as "Chester the tester," "Shirley, you test," and "WISC jockey."

There will always be a need for traditional assessments and classification and placement of students within special education programs (Deno, 2012). However, these assessments have limited application within a problem-solving, solution-focused model of service delivery in which school psychologists collaborate with educators and families in the design of effective interventions. Indeed, when offered the opportunity to collaborate with team members in the design of individualized interventions, school psychologists who relied on standardized assessments were often found grasping for solutions. These school psychologists often utilized an intervention selection process that was based on (a) the typography (or form) of the behaviors, (b) examples of interventions used with previous students who engaged in similar behaviors, (c) a review of research demonstrating the effectiveness of interventions with other students whose characteristics and needs were quite different from the referred student, or (d) a practitioner's philosophical orientation toward treatment (Steege & Watson, 2009). All too often the result of these practices was (a) placement in a special education program that was not truly individualized to the characteristics, learning histories, learning preferences, or therapeutic needs of the student or (b) the design of hit-or-miss interventions that were rarely effective or therapeutic.

Since the early 1980s, the limitations of the assessment placement and nonfunctional service delivery model have been extensively reviewed, resulting in an increased recognition of the need for an assessment process that goes beyond mere descriptions of interfering behaviors and diagnostic determinations to a deeper understanding of the functions of these behaviors (Steege & Watson, 2009). This assessment model is based on a theoretical framework and a firm foundation of empirical evidence showing that interventions based on the functions of behavior are more effective than those based solely on diagnostic descriptions (Betz et al., 2011). This model, in which psychologists assess interfering behaviors for the purpose of understanding why behaviors occur and then use that information to design effective interventions, is referred to as functional behavioral assessment (FBA).

The purpose of this chapter is to provide school psychologists with an introduction to and overview of best practice methods for conducting FBAs within school settings. After reading this chapter it is expected that school psychology practitioners will be able to (a) identify and describe purposes for conducting an FBA; (b) identify and describe indirect, direct descriptive, and functional analysis procedures; and (c) link results from FBAs to evidence-based and function-based interventions. It is recommended that school psychology practitioners receive supervision during their professional development in conducting and interpreting FBAs.

BASIC CONSIDERATIONS

Simply put, FBA is a process for understanding the variables that contribute to the occurrence of interfering behaviors. FBA is both a theoretical framework for understanding human behavior and a set of assessment procedures. When conducting FBAs, school psychologists identify and describe the relationships between the unique characteristics of the student and the contextual variables that motivate and reinforce behavior. FBA is a systematic process that results in the identification and description of those variables. School-based teams, using these assessment results, are able to work in concert with the student and his or her teachers, parents, and others to develop person-centered interventions that result in socially meaningful behavior change (Steege & Watson, 2009).

On a pragmatic level, the FBA process considers the goodness of fit among the student, environment, current behavioral supports, curriculum, instructional methodologies, and social relationships. For example, with a student identified with a severe emotional disability, the school psychologist may examine (a) the immediate classroom environment; (b) the student's academic, social, and behavioral strengths and weaknesses; (c) motivational variables; (d) curriculum features; (e) social variables; and (f) reinforcement contingencies. A combination of interviews, observations, rating scales, and curriculum-based assessments would constitute a comprehensive FBA with this student (Steege & Pratt, 2012).

Practice Guidelines

The National Association of School Psychologists (NASP) *Model for Comprehensive and Integrated School Psychological Services* (NASP, 2010a) is designed to be used in conjunction with the NASP *Standards for Graduate Preparation of School Psychologists* (NASP, 2010b), *Standards for the Credentialing of School Psychologists* (NASP, 2010c),

and *Principles for Professional Ethics* (NASP, 2010d) to provide a unified set of national principles that guide graduate education, credentialing, professional practice and services, and ethical behavior of effective school psychologists. There are two domains of practice in which school psychologists are encouraged to consider FBA methodologies: (a) Data-Based Decision Making and Accountability and (b) Interventions and Mental Health Services to Develop Social and Life Skills. Specifically, when conducting FBAs, school psychologists use systematic decision making to consider the antecedents, consequences, functions, and potential causes of behavioral difficulties that may impede learning or socialization. They conduct interviews and observations to collect data from multiple sources as a foundation for determination of the functions of behaviors and for the selection of interventions in general and special education settings. School psychologists then develop and implement behavior change programs at individual, group, classroom, and schoolwide levels that demonstrate the use of appropriate ecological and behavioral approaches (e.g., positive reinforcement, environmental adaptations, social skills training, and positive psychology) to student discipline and classroom management.

Paralleling the development and refinement of FBA methods has been the emergence of a problem-solving model of school psychology practice, including Deno's (1989) model. Consistent with FBA, Deno's problem-solving model emphasizes the effectiveness of going beyond a diagnostic and placement model of school psychology to a process involving a multitiered continuum of assessment, intervention, and evaluation (Steege & Pratt, 2012).

Evidence Base for FBAs

Since the 1980s, the fields of applied behavior analysis, school psychology, and special education have seen a multitude of published studies devoted to the subject of FBA (e.g., Betz et al., 2011; Kelly, LaRue, Roane, & Gadaire, 2011; Steege & Watson, 2009; Wacker, Berg, Harding, & Cooper-Brown, 2011). This body of literature has clearly demonstrated that (a) assessments of interfering behaviors need to be conducted on an individualized basis, (b) interfering behaviors occur as a result of a complex interaction between environmental and individual variables, (c) individual topographies of interfering behaviors may be maintained by multiple forms of reinforcement, and (d) interventions based on the functions of behaviors are more effective and/or more efficient than interventions based on subjective opinion or diagnostic criteria (Steege & Watson, 2009). The literature also is replete with examples of the broad application of FBA methodologies across varied disabilities (e.g., autism, behavioral impairment, emotional disability, learning disability, and intellectual disabilities), typically developing students, specific populations (e.g., early childhood, K–12, and adults), behaviors (e.g., aggression, opposition, reading errors, self-injury, stereotypy, and written language), and settings (e.g., communities, homes, hospitals, and schools; Hanley, Iwata, & McCord, 2003; Mueller, Nkosi, & Hine, 2011; Steege & Pratt, 2012).

Conceptual Foundations of FBA

Review and synthesis of this body of research has repeatedly demonstrated that in most cases disruptive behaviors are not caused by a singular controlling variable. Rather, disruptive behaviors are the result of a confluence of transient variables that interact in a dynamic fashion, with the net result being a behavioral incident (i.e., the perfect storm). When conducting an FBA, school psychologists consider each of these variables and the degree to which each variable may contribute to the occurrence of interfering behaviors. Disruptive behavior occurs within a context. There are variables that trigger the behavior (antecedents) and variables that follow and strengthen behavior (i.e., reinforcement). When conducting the FBA, the school psychologist is engaged in an investigative process of gathering information, forming tentative hypotheses, gathering more information, conceptualizing the interactions of controlling variables, and finally identifying and designing function-based interventions.

What follows is a brief description of these contributing variables as well as suggestions linking assessment results to function-based interventions. It is important to recognize that for each contributing variable there may be several function-based interventions. The selection of interventions is based on multiple factors, including the needs of the students, available resources, and expertise of interventionists (e.g., teachers, parents, educational technicians). The following examples are meant to illustrate only one or two possible solutions, thereby illustrating how the results of the FBA may inform the selection of interventions.

Antecedents of Behavior

Antecedents are variables that occur prior to and influence the occurrence of the target behavior (i.e.,

the behavior addressed by the FBA). A comprehensive FBA assesses the relative contributions of each of the following antecedent variables.

Contextual variables. This refers to the broad contexts in which interfering behaviors occur (e.g., math class or the hallway). This information is used to focus the assessment process. If disruptive behavior occurs during math, then what is going on in math class? Is the material too difficult for this student? Is the pace of instruction too fast or too slow? Knowledge of the contextual variables associated with elevated levels of interfering behaviors may also inform antecedent-based interventions (e.g., modifying or adapting the environment, instructional methods, or seating arrangement to reduce the probability of interfering behaviors).

Individual mediating variables. These include individual sensitivities or preferences that contribute to, but do not cause, occurrences of interfering behaviors. An understanding of mediating variables helps illuminate the manner in which antecedent variables evoke interfering behaviors (i.e., motivating variables). For example, a student who is sensitive to loud noises may engage in disruptive behaviors to avoid or leave the middle school cafeteria, or a student who is sensitive to corrective feedback from teachers, making errors, and has a need to be perfect may engage in disruptive behavior when individualized instructional supports are provided. Directly addressing these issues by teaching coping skills and/or by using desensitization procedures could be a component of a function-based intervention package.

Individual behavior deficits. These are student-specific academic, social, adaptive living, or communication skill deficits that contribute to occurrences of interfering behaviors. Identification of these behavior deficits highlights potential skills to teach for the purpose of developing strong repertoires of prosocial replacement behaviors. For example, a student with communication skill delays may display disruptive behavior to communicate a want or need. Addressing this deficit by teaching communication skills may decrease disruptive behaviors, or a student displaying disruptive behavior maintained by peer attention may benefit from direct social skills addressing reciprocal age-appropriate social interaction skills.

Motivating operations. This refers to variables that momentarily alter (a) the reinforcing effectiveness of other stimuli or events and (b) the frequency of behaviors that historically have been reinforced by those stimuli or events (Cooper, Heron, & Heward, 2007). Motivating operations alter the value of reinforcing consequences and thereby evoke interfering behaviors that historically have produced those consequences. As an example, the deprivation of attention for a student may increase the value of attention as a reinforcer and increase the likelihood of attention-maintained interfering behaviors. Likewise, presentation of difficult tasks to a student increases the value of task termination (negative reinforcement) and the probability of disruptive behaviors that result in escape from academic demands. Knowledge of these motivating operations enables school-based teams to implement proactive strategies to reduce the likelihood of interfering behaviors. For example, with students whose behavior is reinforced by attention, the school psychologist could develop an intervention package that includes (a) functional communication training in which the student is taught to appropriately request social interactions, (b) noncontingent reinforcement in which social attention is provided on a fixed time schedule to minimize the issue of deprivation, and (c) social attention as a reinforcement when the student displays appropriate social or academic replacement behaviors.

Discriminative stimuli. This signals the availability of reinforcement and therefore triggers interfering behaviors. Owing to a student's reinforcement history, the student may be more likely to engage in interfering behaviors in the presence of specific stimulus conditions, and, therefore, the identification of relevant discriminative stimuli is critical for planning proactive environmental modifications. Given that the majority of interfering behaviors are reinforced by the actions of others (e.g., provide attention, withdraw demands, provide tangibles), the mere presence of those individuals who provide socially mediated reinforcement may make interfering behaviors more likely to occur.

Consequences of Behavior

Reinforcing consequences are those variables that follow the target behavior and that increase the future probability of target behaviors. For example, peer attention produced by a student's off-task comments in the classroom may function as a reinforcing consequence that increases the future likelihood of those interfering behaviors. In another case, the school psychologist noticed a pattern in which a student was regularly directed to an in-school suspension area when the student was disruptive. In this case, based on prior information that indicated that there was a mismatch between the student's skills and the teacher's instruction, the school psychologist hypothesized that disruptive behavior was being reinforced by negative reinforcement (i.e., escape from difficult task demands). Identification of the reinforcing consequences that maintain interfering behaviors informs effective interventions by highlighting which consequences should be (a) withheld or minimized contingent on interfering behaviors (i.e., extinction) and (b) delivered contingent on appropriate replacement behaviors. In addition to identifying the type of reinforcement, the schedule, quality, magnitude, and timing of reinforcement are also relevant considerations. Identifying and describing these parameters of reinforcement lead to an understanding of the power or robustness of the reinforcing contingency. This information is critical in planning effective reinforcement contingencies for replacement behaviors that are likely to compete with the contingencies maintaining interfering behaviors (Steege & Pratt, 2012).

In sum, the goal of an FBA is to identify how and to what degree antecedent and consequence variables interact to produce and maintain interfering behaviors so that comprehensive, function-based intervention plans may be developed. The following section details the array of procedures available for gathering information about these variables.

BEST PRACTICES IN CONDUCTING FBAS

Just as no one experimental design is applicable to every research question and, similarly, no one medication is effective for all ailments, no one FBA assessment model is used when assessing disruptive behaviors. On a pragmatic level, the selection of FBA procedures is based on (a) form, rate, and intensity of the behavior; (b) degree of sophistication and understanding of antecedent and consequence variables of respondents (e.g., parents, teachers, behavior analysts) during interviews; (c) accuracy of previously recorded information pertaining to disruptive behaviors and/or contributing variables; (d) availability of personnel to assist with assessment protocols and data collection; and (e) competencies of evaluators in conducting various FBA methods.

Qualifications for Conducting FBAs

As with any assessment, school psychologists need to consider if they have the necessary educational preparation and professional experiences required for conducting

FBAs. At a minimum, academic preparation should include graduate-level coursework in learning theory (i.e., respondent and operating conditioning, social learning theory) and in psychological assessment (including training in conducting FBAs). School psychologists should also consider the developmental levels and cultural, ethnic, and linguistic backgrounds of referred students and the potential influences these factors may have on both occurrences of target behaviors and acceptability of function-based interventions. As with any formal assessment procedure, school psychologists should receive supervision in conducting FBAs during practica, internship, or postdegree training experiences. School psychologists trained to conduct (a) semistructured and structured clinical interviews, (b) anecdotal and systematic observations, (c) recordings of behaviors using a variety of recording procedures, (d) curriculum-based measures of academic and adaptive behaviors, (e) preference assessments, (f) basic single-case experimental designs (i.e., A/B and alternating treatments), and (g) assessments of social–emotional functioning using rating scales (parent, teacher, and self-report forms) have the prerequisite skills for conducting a comprehensive and conceptually sound FBA with most school-based referrals.

Indirect Assessment

Indirect FBA methods are characterized by the assessment of behavior based on information provided by teachers, parents, staff, and in some cases the referred person. Examples of indirect FBA procedures include record reviews, interviews, and recording forms. Steege and Watson (2009) identify, describe, and illustrate the application of several behavior analytic interview forms that are applicable to school settings. These forms could be used by school psychologists to identify antecedent and consequence variables associated with disruptive behaviors and to form tentative hypotheses about what might be triggering and reinforcing disruptive behaviors.

A word of caution here: Because of the relative efficiency and cost-effectiveness of FBAs, conducting an FBA using only indirect FBA procedures may be tempting. However, filling out a one-page form or simply conducting brief and informal interviews may not constitute a valid FBA. Indeed, such practice often results in inaccurate results, faulty hypotheses, and ineffective interventions (Steege & Watson, 2009). Unless the results of the indirect FBA are consistent across informants and the practitioner is able to form solid hypotheses regarding behavioral function, the indirect FBA may be considered only the first step in conducting a comprehensive FBA. When the practitioner is not confident about the results of an indirect FBA, and the hypotheses are tentative at best, additional assessments are necessary. In these cases, direct assessment procedures are indicated. Table 18.1 lists examples of several published indirect FBA procedures.

Direct Descriptive Assessment

Direct descriptive FBA procedures involve observing and real-time recording of interfering behaviors and associated antecedents and consequences. Direct descriptive FBA procedures involve collecting data via systematic observations of the individual within natural settings (e.g., classrooms, cafeteria, hallways, gym, playground, home). Recording procedures range from anecdotal recording (i.e., observing and writing a narrative description of behaviors and relevant variables) to the use of prescribed recording procedures. Direct descriptive FBA procedures may involve a process in which the school psychologist observes and records target behaviors as well as antecedent and consequence variables (Thompson & Borrero, 2011). There are, of course, those cases in which direct observation by the school psychologist is not possible. For example, the behavior may occur infrequently or unpredictably. In these situations it is often difficult to schedule an observation, and instead an observation

Table 18.1. Indirect FBA Methods

Method	Examples
Behavior analytic interviews	• Antecedent Variables Assessment Form; Individual Variables Assessment Form; Consequence Variables Assessment Form (Steege & Watson, 2009) • Interview Questions for Ascertaining a Positive/Negative Reinforcement Function (Cipani & Schock, 2011) • Functional Assessment Informant Record for Teachers (Edwards, 2002) • Functional Analysis Interview (O'Neill et al., 1997)
Behavior analytic rating scales	• Functional Analysis Screening Tool (Iwata & DeLeon, 1996) • Motivation Assessment Scale (Durand & Crimmins, 1988)

form completed by teachers, parents, or staff to record interfering behaviors and contextual variables could be used. For example, Cipani and Schock (2011) describe and illustrate an A-B-C (antecedent, behavior, consequence) descriptive analysis method in which, for example, teachers, parents, or paraprofessionals observe and record relevant antecedents and consequences pertaining to prespecified target behaviors.

Direct descriptive FBA procedures have two major purposes. First, they document the occurrence of interfering behaviors and associated triggers, antecedents, and consequences. Second, they measure the severity (e.g., frequency, duration, intensity) of interfering behaviors. These procedures are valuable in identifying associated contextual variables. However, just as correlation does not mean causation, association does not mean function. In order to validate hypotheses regarding functional relationships between the interfering behavior and contextual variables, a functional analysis is required. Table 18.2 lists several direct descriptive FBA procedures.

Functional Analysis

Functional analysis refers to an assessment model in which environmental events are systematically manipulated and examined within single-case experimental designs (Betz et al., 2011). Within this model, a functional relationship is said to exist when a change in one variable results in the change of a specific behavior. In other words, functional analysis procedures involve an experimental analysis of the cause–effect relationships between interfering behaviors and specific, predetermined antecedents and consequences. Functional analysis procedures include (a) the systematic manipulation of antecedent conditions (e.g., presentation of academic tasks) and/or consequence conditions (i.e., withdrawal of academic expectations/materials following disruptive behavior) as assessment trails, (b) the recording of disruptive behaviors within each trail,

and (c) the comparison of behavioral level or trends across assessment conditions.

A structural analysis is an approach to functional analysis that involves testing hypotheses about variables that appear to evoke interfering behaviors by arranging antecedent conditions and recording subsequent behaviors (Wacker et al., 2011). A consequence analysis, on the other hand, is conducted in order to confirm hypotheses about variables that appear to reinforce interfering behaviors. This approach involves arranging situations and providing specific consequences contingent on occurrences of interfering behaviors (e.g., O'Neil et al., 1997; Steege, Wacker, Berg, Cigrand, & Cooper, 1989). Both brief (Steege & Northup, 1998) and extended (e.g., Iwata, Dorsey, Slifer, Bauman, & Richman, 1982) models for conducting functional analyses also have been described. Both models involve the observation of behavior and the direct manipulation of antecedent and/or consequence variables for the purpose of empirically determining the variables that motivate and/or maintain interfering behaviors. The brief functional analysis model incorporates the same general procedures as the extended analysis, except the number and duration of assessment sessions is limited (Steege & Watson, 2009).

Although functional analysis is often the most precise and accurate method of assessing interfering behaviors, there are many situations that preclude its use. For example, functional analysis methods may be contraindicated in cases in which (a) the interfering behavior is dangerous to the individual (e.g., severe self-injury) or to others (e.g., aggression), (b) the interfering behavior is of such a low rate that observation is unlikely (e.g., high-intensity but low-rate property destruction), (c) direct observation causes the individual to inhibit his or her behavior, (d) the situation is at a point of crisis and immediate intervention is required, (e) staff members trained to complete either a brief or extended functional analysis of interfering behavior are not readily available,

Table 18.2. Direct Descriptive FBA Methods

Method	Source
Antecedent–Behavior–Consequence	Cipani & Schock (2011)
Behavioral Observation of Students in Schools	Shapiro (1996)
Conditional Probability Record	Steege & Watson (2009)
Functional Behavioral Assessment Observation Form	Steege & Watson (2009)
Functional Assessment Observation Form	O'Neill et al. (1997)
Interval Recording Procedure	Steege & Watson (2009)
Scatterplot Analysis	Touchette, MacDonald, & Langer (1985)
Direct Access Trigger Analysis Trial	Cipani & Schock (2011)
Task Difficulty Antecedent Analysis Form	Steege & Watson (2009)

and (f) the reinforcement contingencies used during the assessment process may result in an overall escalation of disruptive behaviors. Thus, many school psychologists may find that indirect and direct descriptive procedures are most appropriate for the vast majority of referrals in which an FBA is indicated (Steege & Watson, 2009).

Requirements of an FBA

As outlined in Steege and Watson (2009), the essential components of an FBA include (a) identification and description of interfering behaviors, (b) recording of current levels of occurrence of interfering behaviors, (c) identification and description of antecedent variables, (d) identification and description of reinforcing consequences and parameters of reinforcement, (e) hypothesis statement, and (f) function-based and evidence-based interventions. What follows describes the general process for conducting effective and comprehensive FBAs.

Phase 1: Identifying and describing of interfering behavior. The purpose of this initial phase is to identify those behaviors that interfere with a student's acquisition of skills or his or her performance of appropriate behaviors (i.e., academic and social) within the context of the school, home, or community setting. This is often conducted through interviews, record reviews, and direct observations. The Individualized Education Program (IEP) team needs to clearly and unambiguously define each behavior and needs to agree on an operationalized definition of each interfering behavior (i.e., define behavior in concrete terms using clear and unambiguous descriptions). A behavior has been operationalized when all IEP team members agree on the definition and are able to observe and accurately record the behavior (Steege & Watson, 2009).

Phase 2: Recording interfering behaviors. During this phase, direct observation and recording of interfering behaviors is conducted. Recording of behaviors is important because it provides the team with information about the behaviors, answering questions such as (Steege & Watson, 2009): To what degree does this behavior interfere with the student's academic or social function? What is the relative intensity of the behavior? How often does this behavior occur? Relative to FBA, recording behavior allows for an objective description of the degree to which the interfering behavior interferes with student learning and functioning. Moreover, recordings of behavior serve as a benchmark (baseline) to be used as a point of comparison

when evaluating the effectiveness of subsequent function-based interventions. There are several procedures that may be used to record behaviors (e.g., frequency, duration, intensity, performance based, partial interval, whole interval, momenta, time sampling). There is no one best procedure. Rather, the selection of behavior recording procedures depends on the dimensions of the behavior (i.e., form, presentation) and the resources (i.e., time, applicability to the setting, skills of observers/recorders).

Phase 3: Identifying and describing antecedent and consequence variables. This may involve any combination of indirect, direct, structural, and experimental analyses. The choice of procedures is determined by the target behavior (low versus high rate, mild versus severe, teacher versus peer mediated) and the skills and experience of the evaluator. This phase of the FBA process focuses on collecting and synthesizing those variables that influence the onset of the interfering behavior (i.e., antecedents) and those variables that serve to reinforce the occurrences of interfering behavior (i.e., consequences). This is where the school psychologist pulls it all together, where he or she integrates the results of assessment (i.e., indirect, direct, descriptive, structural, and/or experimental analyses). Recall the principle of interactionism, where the variables that contribute to interfering behavior interact in often complex ways to trigger and strengthen interfering behaviors. Also, these variables are not static. For example, the motivational influence of a stimulus is temporary (i.e., deprivation of attention makes attention more valuable as a reinforcer, but once attention is provided, the motivation effects are reduced). Likewise, events that follow and strengthen interfering behavior (i.e., reinforcing consequences) vary in terms of timing, amount, quality, and schedule. The goal here is to synthesize the assessment data and offer a reasonable conceptual explanation as to how these variables interact dynamically to maintain interfering behaviors.

Phase 4: Developing hypotheses. Hypotheses are position statements derived from assessment results that specify the variables that evoke, occasion, and maintain interfering behaviors. The hypothesis is a summary, comparable to diagnostic impressions, that synthesizes and conceptualizes the variables that contribute to interfering behavior. In short, it tells the school psychologist what he or she is up against and, as such, guides the selection of function-based interventions.

Table 18.3. Identification, Description, and Level of Occurrence of Kris's Behaviors

Interfering Behavior	Description	Recording Procedure	Daily Average (November 2012)	Range (November 2012)
Nonverbal opposition	A response set including one or more of the following behaviors during situations in which Kris is expected to participate in tasks/activities: head down on the table, flopping to the floor	Duration	11.4 minutes per school day	7–38 minutes/ school day
Verbal opposition	A response set including one or more of the following behaviors during situations in which Kris is expected to participate in tasks/ activities: stating "No," "Forget it," "I'm not doing that," "You've got to be kidding," "Seriously?" and then not participating in the assigned task; occurrences of target behavior separated by 15 seconds of nonoccurrence of the behavior	Frequency	25.5 occurrences per school day	6–84 occurrences per school day

Phase 5: Linking assessment data to interventions. The ultimate value of the FBA is to identify function-based interventions. When considering the elements of a behavior support plan, identifying antecedents allows modifications to be made in those variables to reduce the probability of the interfering behavior occurring. For example, identification of individual variables leads to selection of coping skills or desensitization procedures that are particular to the student, and identification of consequence variables tells what should be done to avoid reinforcing the interfering behavior and how to provide sufficient reinforcement for the replacement behavior. It is also important to take into consideration the dynamic relationship among antecedent, individual, and consequence variables. Therefore, behavior support plans need to be sensitive to interactive effects of these variables and provide for flexible delivery of intervention strategies (Steege & Watson, 2009).

Case Example

Consider the case of a sixth-grade student, Kris, who displayed disruptive behaviors within the school setting. A referral for an FBA was requested by the IEP team. The school psychologist conducted the FBA using a multisource, multisetting, and multimethod assessment model (Merrell, 2001). The school psychologist began the assessment process by conducting a record review. Next, the school psychologist conducted behavior analytic interviews with the student, school personnel (i.e., classroom teacher, paraprofessional, guidance counselor, social worker), and parents. Next, the school psychologist conducted several anecdotal observations of the student in different classroom settings and situations.

The school psychologist used information garnered from interviews and observations to operationally define disruptive behavior and designed a data collection procedure to measure levels of occurrence of behaviors. To increase the accuracy of data collection, the school psychologist provided instruction and coaching in observing and recording behavior to the classroom teacher and paraprofessional that included verbal and written explanation, demonstration, role-playing, and performance feedback. The results of the initial phases of the FBA process are illustrated in Table 18.3.

Next, based on the findings from interviews and anecdotal observations, the school psychologist conducted selected direct observations of Kris within several classroom situations (e.g., completing math worksheets, small group language arts instruction, small group math instruction, recess, completing language arts worksheets). During these observations the school psychologist used a 6-second partial interval recording procedure to measure occurrences of both nonverbal and verbal opposition. The results of direct observations are summarized in Table 18.4.

Table 18.4. Results of Direct Observation for Kris

Setting	Verbal Opposition (%)	Nonverbal Opposition (%)
Math worksheets (two observations)	14	39
Language arts small group	3	2
Math small group (two observations)	42	24
Recess	0	0
Language arts worksheets (two observations)	0	0

Table 18.5. Identification of Antecedents and Consequences for Kris

Contextual Variables	Antecedent: Unconditioned Motivating Operation	Antecedent: Conditioned Motivating Operation	Antecedent: Discriminative Stimuli	Individual Mediating Variables	Individual Behavior Deficits	Interfering Behaviors	Reinforcing Consequence	Parameters of Reinforcement
Contexts in which interfering behaviors are likely to occur	Unlearned stimulus conditions that alter the value of reinforcing consequences and the probability of interfering behaviors	Learned stimulus conditions that alter the value of reinforcing consequences and the probability of interfering behaviors	Stimuli or events that indicate the availability of reinforcing consequences for interfering behaviors	Individual sensitivities and preferences that contribute to interfering behaviors	Behavior deficits (e.g., communication, academic, and/or social skill deficits) that contribute to interfering behaviors	Behaviors that interfere with learning of self and/or others	Events that contingently follow interfering behaviors and increase the future probability of those behaviors	• Schedule • Quality • Magnitude • Timing
Individual or small group math work	Aversive internal states (e.g., anxious feelings) may increase the value of escape as a reinforcer, increase the likelihood of interfering behaviors maintained by escape, and increase the value of the reduction of aversive internal states	The presentation of math tasks predicts a worsening set of conditions, thereby increasing the value of escape and the likelihood of interfering behaviors maintained by escape	Kris's math teacher may signal the availability for escape from math-related tasks	Sensitivities to corrective feedback and vocal directives	Academic skill deficit in the area of math	• Verbal opposition • Nonverbal opposition	Negative reinforcement: avoidance of or escape from nonpreferred or challenging academic tasks, specifically math Automatic reinforcement: arousal reduction (decrease of aversive internal states)	Avoidance delivered on a continuous reinforcement schedule; produces a low-quality break immediately, but for variable durations Escape delivered on a variable ratio schedule; produces high-quality escape when preferred activities (e.g., walks outside) are offered after variable delays

Table 18.6. Functional Interventions for Kris

Contextual Variables	Antecedent: Unconditioned Motivating Operation	Antecedent: Conditioned Motivating Operation	Antecedent: Discriminative Stimuli	Individual Mediating Variables	Individual Behavior Deficits	Replacement Behavior	Extinction	Reactive Procedures
Modification of contextual variables Modify instructional curriculum Modify length of assignments Intersperse easy and difficult instructional opportunities Reinforce participation in individualized and small group settings.	Interventions addressing unlearned stimulus conditions that alter the value of reinforcing consequences and the probability of interfering behaviors Behavioral relaxation to reduce aversive internal states; therefore minimizing the effectiveness of automatic reinforcement	Interventions addressing learned stimulus conditions that alter the value of reinforcing consequences and the probability of interfering behaviors Activity schedule depicting both math tasks and reinforcers during and following math instruction Noncontingent reinforcement in the form of scheduled breaks during math instruction	Minimize the effectiveness of stimuli or events that trigger occurrences of interfering behaviors Stimulus pairing: schedule opportunities for Kris to engage in preferred activities embedding math instruction Classroom teacher to provide increased reinforcement for Kris's participation during math instruction	Minimize individual sensitivities and preferences that contribute to interfering behaviors Self-management Behavioral coaching Teach Kris future coping skills In vivo systematic desensitization procedures	Behavioral skills training to address behavior deficits (e.g., communication, academic, and/or social skill deficits) that contribute to interfering behaviors Continue with curriculum-based method probes in math Modify curriculum to appropriate instructional levels Functional communication training	Specify replacement behavior (i.e., appropriate behavior that is the logical alternative to interfering behaviors) and reinforcement procedures Increase participation in academic instruction Increase accuracy of task completion Increase functional communication skills Differential reinforcement of appropriate behaviors (DRI, DRA)	Interventions to minimize reinforcement of interfering behaviors Escape extinction: avoid providing negative reinforcement following interfering behaviors	Interventions to use in the event interfering occurs Response interruption, redirection to task, and differential reinforcement of appropriate behaviors (DRI, DRA)

Note. DRI = Differential reinforcement of incompatible behavior; DRA = differential reinforcement of alternate behaviors.

The school psychologist reviewed and analyzed the results of the interviews and observations. The synthesis of these data is summarized in Table 18.5.

Testing hypotheses. Based on the results of interviews and observations, it was hypothesized that both verbal opposition and nonverbal opposition were reinforced by negative reinforcement (i.e., avoidance of or escape from task demands, specifically math instruction and math assignments). Next, the school psychologist conducted a can't do/won't do assessment. These findings suggested that, even when highly motivated, Kris completed grade-level math problems with 25–35% accuracy. These data suggested a skill versus a performance deficit. During additional curriculum-based math assessments, Kris completed fifth-grade-level and fourth-grade-level math problems at 55% and 85% accuracy, respectively. Finally, the school psychologist observed and recorded interfering and on-task behaviors (6-second partial interval) during math instruction using fourth-grade materials. Kris was observed participating in math instruction and completing math worksheets with no occurrences of verbal or nonverbal opposition and with 89% on-task behavior.

Figure 18.1. Functional Behavioral Assessment Rating Scale–Revised

Student _____ Date of Birth_____

Grade _____School _____

FBA completed by_____

Date completed_____

Person using the FuBARS_____

Use the following rating scale to evaluate the quality of the FBA:
1. **Identification and Description of Interfering Behavior(s)**
   0 = Interfering behavior not identified
   1 = Concern is identified (e.g., acting out) but specific target behavior is not identified
   2 = Specific behavior is identified, but it is described in ambiguous and nonbehavioral terms
   3 = Behavior is identified and described in clear, unambiguous terms

2. **Current Levels of Occurrence (CLO) of Interfering Behaviors**
   0 = CLO not reported
   1 = CLO estimated
   2 = CLO reported, but CLO based on anecdotal observations
   3 = CLO reported, and CLO based on observations and recordings of the target behavior

3. **Identification and Description of Individual Mediating Variables That Contribute to the Interfering Behavior**
   0 = Mediating individual variables that contribute to interfering behavior not assessed
   1 = Mediating individual variables that contribute to interfering behavior identified
   2 = Mediating individual variables that contribute to interfering behavior identified and described
   3 = Mediating individual variables that contribute to interfering behavior identified and described, clear example provided
   NA = Individual mediating variables not applicable to interfering behavior

4. **Identification and Description of Individual Behavior Deficits**
   0 = Behavior deficits that contribute to interfering behavior not assessed
   1 = Behavior deficits that contribute to interfering behavior identified
   2 = Behavior deficits that contribute to interfering behavior identified and described
   3 = Behavior deficits that contribute to interfering behavior identified and described, clear example provided
   NA = Individual behavior deficits not applicable to interfering behavior

Figure 18.1. Continued

5. Identification and Description of Antecedent Variables: Unconditioned Motivating Operations (MOs)
0 = MOs that temporarily alter the value of a reinforcing consequence not assessed
1 = MOs that temporarily alter the value of a reinforcing consequence identified
2 = MOs that temporarily alter the value of a reinforcing consequence identified and described
3 = MOs that temporarily alter the value of a reinforcing consequence identified and described, clear example provided
NA = MOs not applicable to the interfering behavior

6. Identification and Description of Antecedent Variables: Discriminative Stimuli
0 = Discriminative stimuli that occasion interfering behavior not assessed
1 = Discriminative stimuli that occasion interfering behavior identified
2 = Discriminative stimuli that occasion interfering behavior identified and described
3 = Discriminative stimuli that occasion interfering behavior identified and described, clear example provided
NA = Discriminative stimuli not applicable to the interfering behavior

7. Identification and Description of Reinforcing Consequences and Parameters of Reinforcement
0 = Consequence variables that reinforce the occurrence of interfering behavior not assessed
1 = Consequence variables that reinforce the occurrence of interfering behavior identified
2 = Consequence variables that reinforce the occurrence of interfering behavior identified and described
3 = Consequence variables that reinforce the occurrence of interfering behavior identified and described, clear example provided
  • Schedule of Reinforcement
    0 = Schedule of reinforcing consequence not identified
    1 = Schedule of reinforcing consequence identified and described
  • Quality of Reinforcement
    0 = Quality of reinforcing consequence not identified
    1 = Quality of reinforcing consequence identified and described
  • Timing of Reinforcement
    0 = Timing of reinforcing consequence not identified
    1 = Timing of reinforcing consequence identified and described

8. Hypothesis Statement
0 = Hypothesis statement not included
1 = Hypothesis statement included, but written in ambiguous, nonbehavioral terms (e.g., motivated by frustration)
2 = Hypothesis statement written in behavioral terms, but does not consider all factors contributing to the problem behavior (e.g., only describes reinforcing contingencies and fails to mention antecedent variables)
3 = Hypothesis statement well written in behavioral terms and considers the full range of antecedent, individual, and consequence variables associated with the occurrence of the problem behavior

Linking assessment data to intervention. The results of the FBA documented that nonverbal and verbal opposition occurred within the context of math instruction. Modification of antecedents (i.e., curriculum) resulted in a marked decrease in interfering behaviors and an increase in on-task behaviors. Thus, with this FBA, modification of instructional antecedents was indicated. The can't do/won't do assessment identified Kris's preference for activities such as use of a video game console while the FBA identified negative reinforcement (i.e., breaks from tasks) as a reinforcer. Both forms of reinforcement could be used to maintain Kris's participation in math-based instruction.

Figure 18.1. Continued

9. Evidence-Based Interventions

0 = Evidence-based interventions not included

1 = Evidence-based interventions are recommended, but they are not based on empirical research

2 = Evidence-based interventions are recommended, but the research was conducted with populations that differ markedly from the individual

3 = Evidence-based interventions are recommended and have been validated with similar clinical populations as the individual

10. Function-Based Interventions

0 = Function-based interventions not included

1 = Function-based interventions are recommended, but they are not directly linked to the results of the assessments

2 = Function-based interventions are recommended, but they only address one aspect of the referral question (e.g., interventions are designed to reduce interfering behavior only, interventions focus on modifying reinforcing consequences only)

3 = Function-based interventions are recommended, and they address each of the controlling variables (e.g., discriminative stimuli, conditioned and unconditioned motivating operations, individual variables, and consequences)

Score _____   Total points possible _____

Percent score _____

Note. From *Conducting School-Based Functional Behavioral Assessments: A Practitioner's Guide* (2nd ed.), by M. W. Steege and T. S. Watson, 2009, New York, NY: Guilford Press. Copyright 2009 by Guilford Press. Adapted with permission.

Finally, the FBA identified that Kris evidenced behaviors associated with math anxiety. Instructing Kris in behavioral relaxation techniques and cueing Kris to use these strategies proactively were recommended as part of the intervention package. Table 18.6 illustrates the linkage of interventions to specific behavioral functions.

How School Psychologists Can Evaluate Their Own Effectiveness in Conducting FBAs

The Functional Behavioral Assessment Rating Scale–Revised (FuBARS-R) is used to measure the quality of FBAs (see Figure 18.1). The FuBARS-R may be used as a formative assessment to guide the FBA process or as a summative assessment tool to evaluate the completed FBA. For example, prior to conducting an FBA, the school psychologist could review the components of the FuBARS-R and use this tool to guide the assessment process. The FuBARS-R could also be used to self-evaluate a partially completed FBA and then self-correct any shortcomings. Finally, school psychologists are also encouraged to periodically use the FuBARS-R to self-evaluate completed FBAs and, presuming high levels of performance, self-reinforce their professional competency in conducting FBAs.

SUMMARY

FBA is a powerful tool for assisting school psychologists in understanding and changing interfering behaviors. Although it is legally mandated, FBA also represents a best practices approach for developing positive behavior support plans, another legally mandated procedure. The phases and procedures described herein, if implemented carefully and thoughtfully, will likely result in improved educational and social outcomes for children. Although there is considerable research that remains to be done on various aspects of the application of FBA in schools, the basic principles, methodology, and procedures are firmly grounded in both experimental and applied research.

AUTHOR NOTE

Disclosure. Mark W. Steege has a financial interest in books he authored or coauthored referenced in this chapter.

REFERENCES

Betz, A. M., Alison, M., & Fisher, W. W. (2011). Functional analysis: History and methods. In W. W. Fisher, C. C. Piazza, & H. S.

Roane (Eds.), *Handbook of applied behavior analysis* (pp. 206–225). New York, NY: Guilford Press.

Cipani, E., & Schock, K. (2011). *Functional behavioral assessment, diagnosis, and treatment: A complete system for education and mental health settings* (2nd ed.). New York, NY: Springer.

Cooper, J. O., Heron, T. E., & Heward, W. L. (2007). *Applied behavior analysis* (2nd ed.). Upper Saddle River, NJ: Pearson.

Deno, S. L. (1989). *Curriculum-based measurement and special education services: A fundamental and direct relationship* (pp. 1–17). New York, NY: Guilford Press.

Deno, S. L. (2012). Problem-solving assessment. In R. Brown-Chidsey & K. Andren (Eds.), *Assessment for intervention: A problem-solving approach* (2nd ed., pp. 10–39). New York, NY: Guilford Press.

Durand, V. M., & Crimmins, D. B. (1988). *The Motivation Assessment Scale.* Topeka, KS: Monaco & Associates.

Edwards, R. P. (2002). A tutorial for using the Functional Assessment Informant Record–Teachers (FAIR-T). *Proven Practice: Prevention and Remediation Solutions for Schools, 4,* 31–38.

Hanley, G. P., Iwata, B. A., & McCord, B. E. (2003). Functional analysis of problem behavior: A review. *Journal of Applied Behavior Analysis, 36,* 147–185.

Iwata, B. A., & DeLeon, I. G. (1996). *Functional Analysis Screening Tool (FAST).* Gainesville, FL: University of Florida, Florida Center on Self-Injury.

Iwata, B. A., Dorsey, M. F., Slifer, K. J., Bauman, K. E., & Richman, G. S. (1982). Toward a functional analysis of self-injury. *Analysis and Intervention in Developmental Disabilities, 2,* 3–20.

Kelly, M. E., LaRue, R. H., Roane, H. S., & Gadaire, D. M. (2011). Indirect behavioral assessments: Interviews and rating scales. In W. W. Fisher, C. C. Piazza, & H. S. Roane (Eds.), *Handbook of applied behavior analysis* (pp. 182–190). New York, NY: Guilford Press.

Merrell, K. W. (2001). *Helping students overcome depression and anxiety: A practical guide.* New York, NY: Guilford Press.

Mueller, M. M., Nkosi, A., & Hine, J. F. (2011). Functional analysis in public schools: A summary of 90 functional analyses. *Journal of Applied Behavior Analysis, 44,* 807–818.

National Association of School Psychologists. (2010a). *Model for comprehensive and integrated school psychological services.* Bethesda, MD: Author. Retrieved from http://www.nasponline.org/standards/2010standards/2_PracticeModel.pdf

National Association of School Psychologists. (2010b). *Standards for graduate preparation of school psychologists.* Bethesda, MD: Author. Retrieved from http://www.nasponline.org/standards/2010standards/1_Graduate_Preparation.pdf

National Association of School Psychologists. (2010c). *Standards for the credentialing of school psychologists.* Bethesda, MD: Author. Retrieved from http://www.nasponline.org/standards/2010standards/2_Credentialing_Standards.pdf

National Association of School Psychologists. (2010d). *Principles for professional ethics.* Bethesda, MD: Author. Retrieved from http://www.nasponline.org/standards/2010standards/1_%20Ethical%20Principles.pdf

O'Neill, R. E., Horner, R. H., Albin, R. W., Sprague, J. R., Storey, K., & Newton, J. S. (1997). *Functional assessment and program development for problem behavior: A practical handbook* (2nd ed.). Belmont, CA: Wadsworth.

Reschly, D. J., Tilly, W. D., III., & Grimes, J. P. (Eds.). (1999). *Special education in transition: Functional assessment and noncategorical programming.* Longmont, CO: Sopris West.

Shapiro, E. S. (1996). *Academic skills problem workbook.* New York, NY: Guilford Press.

Steege, M. W., & Northup, J. (1998). Brief functional analysis of problem behavior: A practical approach for school psychologists. *Proven Practice: Prevention and Remediation Solutions for Schools, 1,* 4–11, 37–38.

Steege, M. W., & Pratt, J. (2012). Functional behavior assessment: The cornerstone of effective problem solving. In R. Brown-Chidsey & K. J. Andren (Eds.), *Assessment for intervention: A problem-solving approach* (2nd ed., pp. 125–144). New York, NY: Guilford Press.

Steege, M. W., Wacker, D. P., Berg, W. K., Cigrand, K. K., & Cooper, L. J. (1989). The use of behavioral assessment to prescribe and evaluate treatments for severely handicapped children. *Journal of Applied Behavior Analysis, 22,* 23–33.

Steege, M. W., & Watson, T. S. (2009). *Conducting school-based functional behavioral assessments: A practitioner's guide* (2nd ed.). New York, NY: Guilford Press.

Thompson, R. H., & Borrero, J. C. (2011). Direct observation. In W. W. Fisher, C. C. Piazza, & H. S. Roane (Eds.), *Handbook of applied behavior analysis* (pp. 191–205). New York, NY: Guilford Press.

Touchette, P. E., MacDonald, R. F., & Langer, S. N. (1985). A scatter plot for identifying stimulus control for problem behavior. *Journal of Applied Behavior Analysis, 18,* 343–351.

Wacker, D. P., Berg, W. K., Harding, J. W., & Cooper-Brown, L. J. (2011). Functional and structural approaches to behavioral assessment of problem behavior. In W. W. Fisher, C. C. Piazza, & H. S. Roane (Eds.), *Handbook of applied behavior analysis* (pp. 165–181). New York, NY: Guilford Press.

Best Practices in Rating Scale Assessment of Children's Behavior

Jonathan M. Campbell
Rachel K. Hammond
University of Kentucky

OVERVIEW

Assessment of children's behavior through the use of behavior rating scales constitutes a critical source of information for practicing school psychologists. In this chapter we provide a general overview of the purpose, strengths, weaknesses, and uses of rating scale assessments of children's behavior. The role of rating scale assessment of children's behavior is also discussed with respect to two service delivery models utilized within the field, a "traditional" model of assessment and service delivery and a response-to-intervention (RTI) model of assessment and service delivery. We focus on third-party rating scales as opposed to emphasizing the role of self-report instruments and on ratings of behavior as opposed to ratings of academic functioning.

Background

For the purposes of the chapter, we define a behavior rating scale as an instrument completed by an informant, usually a teacher or parent, that provides a rating of an individual based upon observation of that individual over some extended period of time, such as a month or longer (see Martin, Hooper, & Snow, 1986, for a similar definition). Although behavior rating scales involve third-party respondent evaluations of student behavior, scales vary significantly with respect to their purpose (e.g., screening versus classification), respondents (e.g., teacher versus parent), content coverage (e.g., narrowband versus omnibus), and length (e.g., few items versus many items). Respondents familiar with the

student, typically a parent or teacher, respond to a list of items that describe the child across a variety of domains. Items sample specific, and often problematic, behaviors (e.g., "hits other children"), interaction styles (e.g., "is shy around other students"), or affective states (e.g., "is sad"). Respondents endorse items using response formats that vary slightly across scales. For example, the Child Behavior Checklist (Achenbach & Rescorla, 2001) uses a three-point scale to assess how true behavioral descriptions are for a child (e.g., *not true* to *very true*). In contrast, the Behavior Assessment System for Children–Second Edition (BASC-2; Reynolds & Kamphaus, 2004) requires respondents to rate behavior frequency using a scale that ranges from *never* to *always/ almost always*.

Rating scales also vary according to breadth of coverage. Some scales are designed to yield a comprehensive profile of a student's behavioral functioning, so-called omnibus rating scales such as the BASC-2. Other scales are designed to measure fewer aspects of behavior, such as indicators associated with attention deficit hyperactivity disorder (ADHD), so-called narrowband rating scales, such as index forms of the Conners–Third Edition (Conners, 2009). Several rating scales consist of systems of assessment by offering multiple forms appropriate for different ages (e.g., preschool or school age) for multiple respondents that yield standardized scores that can be compared.

Behavior rating scales constitute a critical source of assessment data for the purposes of behavioral assessment and have been utilized in the fields of school psychology and related professions, such as child clinical psychology, for decades. Practicing school psychologists utilize behavior rating scales routinely, with 75% of school psychologists reporting using behavior rating scales in the majority of their most recent emotional–behavioral referrals (Shapiro & Heick, 2004). Although a preferred assessment tool in responding to behavioral referrals, the future role and use of behavior rating scales may evolve in the future as RTI models are developed for student behavior.

Role of Behavior Rating Scales

The use of behavior rating scales aligns most clearly with the National Association of School Psychologists (NASP) *Model for Comprehensive and Integrated School Psychological Services* (NASP, 2010) domain of Data-Based Decision Making and Accountability. Behavior rating scale data constitute an important source of information for the three explicit goals stated in the 2010 Practice Model on data-based decision making and accountability: (a) identifying student strengths and needs, (b) developing effective services, and (c) measuring progress and outcomes. As discussed further in the chapter, behavior rating scales yield data that contribute to the goal of systematic data collection from multiple sources and across multiple contexts. Indeed, several widely used behavior rating scale systems feature multiple forms that may be completed by multiple informants to provide behavioral assessment data across various contexts. These forms may also be used to collect information from multiple informants for differing purposes, such as proactive identification of student needs and informing service delivery.

The use of behavior rating scales also contributes to school psychologists' collection and use of assessment data to understand students' behavioral adjustment and to guide selection of evidence-based interventions. Behavior rating scale data constitute a valuable source of input for school psychologists when they are operating as part of an interdisciplinary evaluation team to identify students' eligibility for school-based services. Within the context of monitoring progress, behavior rating scales may also yield useful data that contribute to understanding students' responsiveness to intervention and guiding modifications.

BASIC CONSIDERATIONS

As with any assessment procedure or specific instrument, a behavior rating scale should demonstrate satisfactory psychometric properties. With respect to internal consistency reliability, screening instruments should meet or exceed .80, and measures used for the purposes of classification should meet or exceed .90. Behavior rating scales should demonstrate evidence of temporal stability (i.e., test–retest reliability), which is of particular importance if ratings are to be used across time points to document changes in student behavior. In addition, behavior rating scales should demonstrate evidence of validity, such as criterion-related validity in instances of screening and classification. If the behavior rating scale is norm referenced, the normative sample should be contemporary, be representative of the population of interest, and be composed of age groups sufficiently large to document differences across age groups.

Psychometric Evaluation

Screening is defined as purposeful and prospective identification of disorder by use of specific instruments, procedures, or testing. The traditional process of screening involves the administration of a screening instrument to a large group of individuals and then is followed by a gold standard instrument or procedure when the screen is positive. Traditional validation of screeners typically takes the form of criterion-related (or predictive) validity with the screener serving as the predictor and the diagnostic outcome the criterion. The general model crosses the result of the screening measure (positive or negative), with the results of a gold standard diagnostic measure (positive or negative; see Figure 19.1).

Similarly, the model may compare the result of the screening measure with an outcome of interest, such as school suspension or failure to graduate. A positive screen confirmed by accurate identification is a *true positive*. A negative screen confirmed by accurate exclusion is a *true negative*. In contrast, a positive screen that is disconfirmed is a *false positive*, and a negative screen that is disconfirmed is a *false negative*.

A screener's *overall accuracy* or "hit rate" is the proportion correctly identified by the screener (see Figure 19.2 for example). A screener's *sensitivity* refers to the proportion of individuals correctly detected as having the disorder within a sample. A screener's *specificity* refers to the proportion of individuals correctly excluded as not having the disorder. A screener's *positive predictive value* refers to the proportion of individuals who screen positive who are identified with the disorder. A screener's *negative predictive value* refers to the proportion of individuals who screen negative who are excluded as

Figure 19.1 Four Categorical Outcomes for Screening Results and Diagnostic Decisions

		Diagnostic Decision or Critical Outcome (e.g., Suspension)	
		Positive	Negative
Screening Result	Positive	True positive (a)	False positive (Type I error) (b)
	Negative	False negative (Type II error) (c)	True negative (d)

Note. Sensitivity = a / (a + c); specificity = d / (b + d); positive predictive value = a / (a + b); negative predictive value = d / (c + d); false negative rate = c / (a + c); false positive rate = b / (b + d).

having the disorder. Various guidelines exist in the screening literature regarding what constitutes acceptable levels of overall test accuracy, sensitivity, specificity, positive predictive value, and negative predictive value. Carran and Scott (1992) suggest that sensitivity, specificity, and hit rate values should meet or exceed .80.

Selection of a Norm Group

Contemporary behavior rating scales often feature different norm groups for generating standard scores, and the choice of norm group will affect the normative score obtained. For example, the BASC-2 scales allow for normative scores to be calculated using a general norm sample, a clinical norm sample, and separate-sex groupings within both the general and clinical norm samples. School psychologists should consult the test manual for guidance regarding which norm group to use for their particular purpose, and the recommendations will differ across behavior rating scales. For example, authors of the BASC-2 recommend use of the general combined-sex norm group for initial identification purposes; however, clinical norms may be useful for differential diagnosis (Reynolds & Kamphaus, 2004). In contrast, authors of the Social Skills Improvement System–Rating Scale (Gresham & Elliott, 2008) recommend use of sex-specific norm groups because of consistent differences observed

between males and females in the area of social skill development. It may be beneficial to compare behavior rating scale scores across norming groups in order to better interpret elevated ratings. For example, a child's scores may not only exceed 95% of same-age peers but also exceed 86% of same-age peers with identified clinical disorders, which may support classification decision making.

Additional Considerations

In addition to psychometric considerations, other considerations, such as usability, social validity, and perceived importance from stakeholders, are of equal or perhaps greater importance. Sound psychometric evidence constitutes a minimal criterion for the use of behavior rating scales, and other considerations will necessarily facilitate or limit the usefulness of behavior rating scales within the context of school-based behavioral assessment. For example, serial readministration of teacher-rated full-length scales for the purpose of repeated screenings and progress monitoring will likely fail as an assessment practice due to resistance from teachers. It is also important to consider the role of behavior rating scales within the context of a larger behavioral assessment framework. Behavior rating scales are well suited to perform some assessment tasks and are not as suitable for others. Overall, behavior rating scales constitute one source of evidence and demonstrate

Figure 19.2 An Example of Screening 1,000 Students With a Problem Base Rate of .05

		Diagnostic Result or Critical Outcome (e.g., Suspension)		
		Disorder/Outcome	No Disorder/Outcome	
Screening Result	Positive	True Positive 40	False Positive 95	PPV 40/135 = .30
	Negative	False Negative 10	True Negative 885	NPV 855/865 = .99
		Sensitivity 40/50 = .80	Specificity 855/950 = .90	Hit rate 40 + 855/1000 = .90

Note. Sensitivity of the test is .80. Specificity of the test is .90. PPV = positive predictive value; NPV = negative predictive value.

advantages and disadvantages when compared and contrasted with other methods of behavioral assessment.

Advantages of Behavior Rating Scales

Behavior rating scales feature three distinct advantages when compared with other methods of behavioral assessment, such as direct behavioral observation. Efficiency constitutes the first advantage. Ratings are typically completed by respondents in fewer than 20 minutes and produce a great deal of information regarding the behavioral functioning of a student. The efficiency of behavior rating scale assessment is particularly valuable for detecting the presence of low-base-rate behavior, such as truancy or violent behavior, but also low frequency behavior that may be detected only after significant time investment, such as through direct

behavior observation. Behavior rating forms are also inexpensive, simple to administer and to complete, and easy to score.

Second, respondents are generally persons who are familiar with the student and have observed the student as part of the naturalistic environment (i.e., the rater is part of the observational context as opposed to entering as an outsider). The involvement of parents and teachers as respondents to behavior rating scales is important because these persons often initiate referrals for children's mental health services.

Third, behavior rating scales allow for normative comparisons between the individual being rated and an age-matched group of peers. Normative data provide useful information regarding how age-appropriate or atypical behavior may be for the individual being evaluated.

Disadvantages of Behavior Rating Scales

From a psychometric perspective, a major disadvantage of behavior rating scales is undesirable variability in ratings (e.g., Martin et al., 1986), attributable to at least four sources: (a) rater variance, (b) setting variance, (c) temporal variance, and (d) instrument variance. Rater variability is attributed to raters who observe the student in the same setting, such as a classroom, but produce different ratings. Differences across raters may arise due to response biases, such as respondents' tendencies to rate leniently or severely, proneness to use the midpoints of a scale (i.e., central tendency effect), or susceptibility to halo effects. Halo effects refers to raters' tendencies to base a behavior rating on a nonrelevant characteristic, such as a different behavior or gender.

Rater variance is not unusual for behavior rating scales, where low to moderate interrater agreement has been documented (e.g., Achenbach, McConaughy, & Howell, 1987). Interrater disagreement is moderated by several variables, such as the type of behavior being rated, with ratings of externalizing symptoms (e.g., aggression) typically reaching higher levels of agreement than internalizing symptoms (e.g., withdrawal).

Setting variance refers to variability in children's behavior according to context. Respondents familiar with the child's behavior at home may not observe problematic behavior in other contexts, such as in the educational setting. Evidence for setting variance exists by contrasting interrater reliabilities for informants across different settings. For example, interrater agreement between teachers is typically higher than interrater agreement between teachers and parents (e.g., Achenbach et al., 1987). Temporal variance refers to student behavior changes that occur over time. Therefore, the same respondent's ratings will inevitably differ across some interval of time. Instrument variance refers to differences that occur when two behavior scales designed to measure similar constructs yield different results. Interpretation is hindered when psychometrically strong scales yield differences, and the evaluator is faced with the question of which results to interpret.

Principles and Standards for Evidence-Based Assessment

The central notion of evidence-based assessment is simple: Practitioners should use assessment measures that are supported by an empirical knowledge base characterized by sound technical adequacy and carefully conducted research (Mash & Hunsley, 2005). Of course, the complexity of this goal is quickly realized when one considers the varied purposes of psychological assessment, such as those described earlier (e.g., screening or intervention monitoring). It should also be emphasized that no measure is designed to respond to all assessment purposes. Therefore, a scale might be considered an evidence-based assessment for one purpose but not for another.

The seemingly straightforward goal of establishing standards of technical adequacy for psychological instruments also becomes complex as one considers how to go about evaluating reliability evidence, validity evidence, and norming techniques. For example, an assessment measure should not simply be judged to be valid or invalid in general terms; rather, a measure may be supported as valid for specific usages, such as screening, identification, or progress monitoring. For the purposes of our chapter, we include discussion of behavior rating scales that demonstrate appropriate psychometrics and are judged to be evidence based for use by school psychologists (see Table 19.1).

Training, Experience, and Necessary Equipment

Little specialized knowledge, experience, and equipment are required for school psychologists to administer and score behavior rating scales. Across various measures, instructions to raters typically include a brief introduction to the response scale and identify a time frame for rating children's behavior, such as within the last several months. In general, respondent ratings are summed to produce an overall score of behavioral adjustment or behavioral risk that is compared with some set of normative data, whether nationally representative or locally developed.

Published behavior rating scales, such as the Achenbach System of Empirically Based Assessment (ASEBA) scales and BASC-2, are accompanied by computer scoring software to facilitate scoring and clinical interpretation. For teacher and parent respondents, no specialized experience is needed to provide behavior rating data. However, rating scales typically require some period of observation and contact with a student to produce a valid result. Rating scale instructions and items are written typically for readability at the elementary school level, although some exceptions exist (see Campbell, 2005).

School psychologists should review directions with raters and not expect that parents and teachers will fully read or understand how to accurately complete the

Table 19.1 Description of Selected Behavior Rating Scales for School-Age Children

Scale	Items	Ages	Forms	Content/Domains
Screening (Tier 1)				
BESS	27 or 30	3–18 years	Parent, teacher, self	Total T ($T \geq 71$ = risk)
BSC	12	K–8th grade	Teacher	Total raw (raw ≥ 36 = risk)
Conners 3-GI	10	6–18 years	Parent; teacher	Total, restless–impulsive, lability
Diagnosis and classification (Tier 3)				
ASEBA	120	6–18 years	Parent, teacher, self	Total, externalizing, internalizing, syndrome scales, competence scales, DSM-oriented scales
BASC-2	139–160	6–21 years	Parent, teacher, self	Validity scales, total, externalizing, internalizing, clinical scales, adaptive scales
Conners 3-Full	110 or 115	6–18 years	Parent, teacher, self	Response validity scales, DSM-IV-TR symptom scales, ADHD content, learning problems
Intervention planning (Cross-tiered purpose)				
SSIS-RS	79 or 90	3–18 years	Parent, teacher, self	Social skills, problem behavior, academic competence, validity scales
Intervention monitoring (Tiers 2 and 3)				
ASEBA BPM	19	6–18 years	Parent, teacher, self	Internalizing, externalizing, attention problems, total problems
SSIS-RS	79 or 90	3–18 years	Parent, teacher, self	Social skills, problem behavior, academic competence, validity scales

Note. BESS = Behavioral Assessment for Children–Second Edition, Behavioral and Emotional Screening System; BSC = Behavior Screening Checklist; Conners 3-GI = Conners–Third Edition, Global Index; ASEBA = Achenbach System of Empirically Based Assessment; BASC-2 = Behavioral Assessment for Children–Second Edition; Conners 3–Full = Conners–Third Edition, Full Length Scale; SSIS-RS = Social Skills Improvement System Rating Scales; ASEBA BPM = Achenbach System of Empirically Based Assessment Brief Problem Monitor; DSM = *Diagnostic and Statistical Manual*; DSM-IV-TR = *Diagnostic and Statistical Manual* (4th ed., text rev.); ADHD = attention deficit hyperactivity disorder.

forms. Further, school psychologists should discuss with parents and teachers who their comparison group should be. For example, special education teachers might rate a student compared with their caseload of students rather than with what is developmentally appropriate for behavior or social skills.

In contrast to administration and scoring, professional training is required for appropriate interpretation of behavior rating scale information. As omnibus behavior rating scales have increased in sophistication and content, school psychologists are faced with greater amounts of data. Problem solving, conceptualization, and integration of sometimes disparate data are required to render defensible interpretations of behavior rating scale data, whether generated for the purposes of screening, identification, or some other purpose. Further, the use of behavior rating scales must be considered within a larger framework of integrated behavioral assessment, which should include data collection, interpretation, and use from various techniques, such as direct behavioral observation, interviewing, and functional assessment.

BEST PRACTICES IN RATING SCALE ASSESSMENT OF CHILDREN'S BEHAVIOR

Although the guiding conceptual framework for the current NASP (2010) Practice Model is to situate school psychology practice within general-problem solving and tiered service delivery models, there is no clear consensus regarding how behavioral assessment techniques, in general, and behavior rating scales, in particular, should be used within such a framework (see Chafouleas, Volpe, Gresham, & Cook, 2010).

In the next sections, we describe two different, yet potentially complementary, models for using behavior rating scales within school settings. The first discussion is grounded in a traditional approach to the utilization of behavior rating scales that involves screening, identification, intervention planning, and intervention monitoring. The second discussion is grounded in tiered service delivery models based upon an RTI framework. The sections are organized around three general purposes of the domain of Data-Based Decision Making and Accountability in the NASP (2010)

Practice Model: (a) identifying student needs, (b) developing effective services, and (c) measuring progress and outcomes.

Traditional and Contemporary Uses of Rating Scales

Utilization of behavior rating scales within a traditional assessment paradigm involves four complementary activities: (a) screening, (b) classification, (c) intervention planning, and (d) intervention monitoring. Within the traditional model, the NASP (2010) practice goal of identifying student needs is operationalized as the use of behavior rating scales for screening and identification of student mental health needs. The NASP practice goals of data-based decision making and accountability assimilate the traditional uses of behavior rating scales. The NASP practice goal of developing effective services is operationalized as the use of behavior rating scales to assist in guiding intervention services at the level of the individual student. Finally, the NASP recommendation to measure progress and outcomes is identified at the level of the individual student as intervention monitoring.

Although in this chapter we have opted to identify this model of behavior rating scale assessment as traditional, the model should not be mistaken for a refer–test–place utilization of behavior rating scales within the larger context of behavioral assessment. Using abbreviated behavior rating scales as screeners, for example, involves proactively identifying behavioral difficulties as opposed to waiting for teacher referral to initiate intervention.

Identification of Strengths and Needs: Screening

The field has experienced a growing interest in early identification of mental health and behavioral difficulties in school-age youth. School-based screening is built on the notion that earlier identification of undetected problems will result in improved outcomes for individuals with disorders and disabilities. Various types of brief behavior rating scales have been developed and evaluated as screeners. Some exist as general mental health screeners and others are designed to identify specific concerns, such as identifying risk of self-harm, or specific disorders, such as autism. Regardless of the screening target, ideal screening instruments are those that are brief, inexpensive, and can be used by lay respondents, which makes behavior rating scales ideal choices as screeners within school settings. Screening instruments should also demonstrate strong psychometric

properties. As with any assessment procedure, screening measures should demonstrate internal consistency reliability and temporal stability reliability; that is, screeners should feature items that share some relationship with one another and produce similar results over test administrations.

Behavioral and Emotional Screening System. The Behavioral and Emotional Screening System (Kamphaus & Reynolds, 2007) is a 27-item screening measure developed from the BASC-2 (Reynolds & Kamphaus, 2004), using theoretical grounds and principal components analysis for item reduction. It features parent and teacher forms for children in preschool through grade 12 and can be completed in approximately 5–10 minutes. It also includes a self-report form for students in grades 3–12. It was normed with 12,350 individuals (3,300 students, 4,450 teachers, and 4,600 parents) from 233 cities in 40 states in the United States and yields an overall T score that is interpretable as indicating normal ($T = 20$ to 60), elevated ($T = 61–70$), or extremely elevated ($T \geq 71$) levels of risk. Across age groups, median split-half reliability is .96, test–retest reliability values range from .80 to .91, and interrater reliability ranges from .82 to .83 for parent forms and .71 to .80 on teacher forms (Kamphaus & Reynolds, 2007). Split-half reliability ranges from .90 to .93 and internal consistency is .80 for the student forms. The Behavioral and Emotional Screening System correlates negatively with achievement scores, grades, and school work habits. Test authors report good convergent and divergent validity as evidenced by appropriate correlations between the BASC-2 (e.g., Teacher Form/BASC-2 Externalizing Correlation = .79) and ASEBA (e.g., Teacher Form/ ASEBA Teacher Report Form Total Problems Scale = .76). In an independent sample of 496 rural elementary school children, King-Vogel (2010) found the teacher ratings to be predictive of office discipline referrals, suspensions, and attendance. Ratings were also predictive of reading fluency and criterion-referenced measures of math, science, and social studies. Student ratings also demonstrate good concurrent validity as evidenced by relationships with other self-report measures of behavioral adjustment (Kamphaus & Reynolds, 2007).

Behavior Screening Checklist. The Behavior Screening Checklist (Muyskens, Marston, & Reschly, 2007) is a 12-item teacher report form designed for use with grades K–8. Teachers rate student behavior in three areas: Classroom Behaviors (e.g., Follows

Directions), Externalizing Behaviors, (e.g., Physical Behavior Toward Others), and Socialization (e.g., Peer Interactions) using a 5-point scale (higher scores reflect greater risk for behavior and academic problems). It yields a total raw score that can range from 12 to 60, and a cutscore of ≥36 is recommended for identifying students at risk. It was developed and validated with 22,056 students in the Minneapolis Public School system. Internal consistency (Cronbach's α) ranged from .92 to .95 across grades, and interrater reliability is .83 for six pairs of teachers rating 143 students. Muyskens et al. (2007) found scores to be positively related to school suspensions and absences and negatively related to reading and math achievement. Males earned higher raw scores than females, and race/ethnic groups also differed. King-Vogel (2010) reported that scores were predictive of office discipline referrals, suspensions, and attendance as well as criterion-referenced reading, math, science, and social studies performance.

Conners-Third Edition ADHD Index.

Although there are several appropriate behavior rating scales that appear reliable and valid for proactive identification of varied behavioral and academic difficulties, behavior rating scales may also be used to screen for specific difficulties, such as ADHD symptomatology as illustrated by the Conners-Third Edition ADHD Index (Conners, 2009). It consists of 10-item teacher and parent forms, and items appearing on the form are those that best differentiated between individuals with ADHD from the general normative sample. Internal consistency and temporal stability reliability meet or exceed .84 for both parent and teacher rating scales. Interrater reliability is .85 for parent pairs and .85 for teacher pairs. Both parent and teacher scales were developed and initially validated with small samples of students with ADHD and matched groups. Diagnostic accuracy differed across males and females with sensitivity and specificity rates .78 or higher for both forms and positive predictive value and negative predictive value of .80 or higher across both forms.

Comments on Screening

Clearly, evidence-based behavior rating screening instruments are available for use within public school settings. However, school psychologists' proactive screening and identification efforts must be balanced with ethical, practical, and contextual considerations (see Chafouleas, Kilgus, & Wallach, 2010). For example, critical concerns exist regarding rights to privacy for students and whether different behavior rating screeners

fall under the purview of typical school assessment practice. Of those measures introduced in our contribution, the Behavior Screening Checklist would appear more aligned with typical school assessment practice when compared with the Behavioral and Emotional Screening System or Conners–Third Edition ADHD Index. Further, decisions regarding utilizing behavioral screening measures must involve input from various stakeholders, such as administrators, teachers, community, parents, and students. Consensus is also needed regarding what to screen for, whether behavioral difficulties in general or other mental health concerns, such as depression.

Most important, in our opinion, is to consider the impact of identifying mental health and behavioral problems on current service delivery capacity within schools. If behavior ratings are employed as screeners, then more children will be identified who are in need of intervention services, a number that may well overwhelm schools' capacity to respond. Chafouleas, Kilgus, et al. (2010) cogently argue, however, that coordination with community-based providers may prove a reasonable solution to this concern.

Identification of Strengths and Needs: Classification

In addition to screening, behavior rating scales offer a source of valuable information regarding the identification of student behavior needs for the purposes of diagnosis and classification. Indeed, behavior rating scales were originally developed with the purpose of diagnosis and classification in mind, particularly the venerable ASEBA. Omnibus rating scales provide school psychologists with various types of information provided from a third-party perspective, including an increased focus on identifying areas of strength and behavioral adaptation. For example, the BASC-2 scales feature summary scores that describe students' functional communication skills, social skills, and academic skills. Four omnibus behavior rating scales that meet evidence-based assessment standards are described next.

Achenbach System of Empirically Based Assessment.

The ASEBA (Achenbach & Rescorla, 2001) is composed of various forms designed for various age groups, such as preschoolers (i.e., 1.5–5 years), school-age youth, and young adults. Forms for school-age youth are designed for students between ages 6 and 18 and consist of a parent form, the Child Behavior Checklist, the Teacher Report Form, and the Youth Self-Report Form (ages 11–18). The Child Behavior

Checklist consists of seven competence domains followed by 120 problem behaviors (e.g., "cries a lot") rated on a 3-point scale (*not true, somewhat or sometimes true,* and *very true or often true*) to describe the child's behavior over a 6-month period. The teacher report form consists of four academic competence ratings followed by the same 120 problem behaviors rated on a 3-point scale, but only for a 2-month period. The Child Behavior Checklist and Teacher Report Form yield Total, Externalizing, and Internalizing T scores to describe the individual's general behavioral functioning. Both forms yield T scores for eight empirically derived scales, such as Anxious/Depressed, and Aggressive Behavior domains, as well as six rationally derived *Diagnostic and Statistical Manual* (DSM) oriented scores, such as ADHD and anxiety problems. The Child Behavior Checklist was normed with 1,753 students (52% males), and the Teacher Report Form was normed with 2,319 students (48% boys). Test authors report internal consistency reliability and temporal stability that meet or exceed .90 for Child Behavior Checklist and Teacher Report Form Total, Externalizing, and Internalizing scores; syndrome-level score internal consistency reliability and temporal stability ranged from .60 to .95 across scales; and DSM-oriented score internal consistency reliability and temporal stability ranged from .62 to .95. Syndrome and DSM-oriented scales that involve externalizing versus internalizing behavior ratings tend to yield more reliable ratings. The Child Behavior Checklist and the Teacher Report Form demonstrate content, construct, and criterion-related validity as evidenced, in part, by favorable correlations with other behavior rating scales.

Behavior Assessment System for Children– Second Edition.

Like the ASEBA scales, the BASC-2 (Reynolds & Kamphaus, 2004) consists of multiple rating forms (i.e., Parent Rating Scale, Teacher Rating Scale, and Self-Report Form) designed for use across various age groups, including preschoolers (2–5 years), children (6–11 years), and adolescents/young adults (12–21 years). The BASC-2 requires that respondents read behavioral descriptions and describe how the child has behaved "in the last several months" using a 4-point scale (*never, sometimes, often,* and *almost always*). The Teacher Rating Scale forms contain 139 items for both children and adolescents/young adults. The Parent Rating Scale forms feature 160 items for children and 150 for adolescents/young adults. All BASC-2 forms yield T scores. For the Parent Rating Scale and the Teacher Rating Scale school-age and adolescent/young adult forms, the BASC-2 yields an overall Behavior

Symptoms Index, Externalizing Problems Composite, Internalizing Problems Composite, and Adaptive Skills Composite. The Teacher Rating Scale also yields a School Problems Composite. Each composite score is composed of individual scales, such as Hyperactivity and Aggression for the Externalizing Composite and Anxiety and Depression for the Internalizing Composite.

BASC-2 also features scales designed to assess the quality of rater response, including whether there is a tendency for the rater to be excessively negative when reporting on the child's behavior. The F Index attempts to capture rater tendency to engage is an overly critical response style via calculating the number of items that were endorsed by fewer than 3% of respondents in item tryouts. Inconsistent responding is also measured through the Consistency Index by calculating the number of paired items containing similar content that are rated differently by the respondent (e.g., "Is sad" is rated as *never*, "Is not happy" is rated as *almost always*).

The Teacher Rating Scale normative sample consists of 4,650 individuals, and the Parent Rating Scale normative sample consists of 4,800 individuals that match 2001 U.S. Census data fairly well. For the Parent Rating Scale and Teacher Rating Scale forms, internal consistency reliability meets or exceeds .90 for all composite scores. Median subscale score internal consistency reliability meets or exceeds .80 for both the Parent Rating Scale and Teacher Rating Scale forms. Various types of validity evidence are provided by test authors in support of BASC-2, such as factorial validity, concurrent validity, and content validity evidence.

Conners–Third Edition, Full Form.

Although the Conners' forms (Conners, 2009) historically focus on ADHD symptomatology, we consider inclusion of the scales as omnibus scales to be appropriate because of content coverage of the measure. That is, the Conners' scales assess indicators of ADHD, but also measure comorbid problems, such as conduct disorder, and associated difficulties, such as peer and family problems. The Conners–Third Edition is a set of three forms: full-length forms, short forms, and two index forms; the ADHD Index, discussed previously; and the Global Index Form, a 10-item scale consisting of the highest loading items from previous versions of the Conners.

The Full Parent Form contains 110 items, and the Full Teacher Form contains 115 items. Both forms ask the respondent to provide a rating of behavior over the past month using a 4-point scale (*not true at all, just a little true, pretty much true,* and *very much true*). Both parent and teacher forms feature eight identical content scales, such as Inattention, Hyperactivity/Impulsivity, Defiance/Aggression, Peer Relations, and Family Relations; three validity scales; five DSM-IV-TR (*Diagnostic and Statistical Manual of Mental Disorders*, 4th ed., text rev.) Symptom Scales, among other scales. The Parent Form samples problems with home life that are not sampled with the Teacher Form. Three validity scales provide evidence regarding a raters' tendency to be overly positive, overly negative, and inconsistent.

The Full Parent Form and the Full Teacher Form were normed with 3,400 individuals ages 6–18 years stratified to match the 2000 U.S. Census on age, gender, and race/ethnicity variables. Internal consistency coefficients range from .77 to .97 for the entire sample, and temporal stability reliability ranges from .70 to .98 for a 2- to 4-week test–retest interval. Interrater reliability coefficients range from .52 to .94. The test manual reports validity evidence in the form of factor analysis, in terms of both the normative sample and a confirmatory sample. Convergent and divergent validity information is presented, as well as discriminative validity attesting to the capacity of these full forms to discriminate between youth with ADHD and other groups of individuals with learning and behavioral disorders.

Social Skills Improvement System Rating Scales.

Although not a clinical instrument per se, the Social Skills Improvement System (SSIS) Rating Scales (Gresham & Elliott, 2008) covers several domains of student functioning and warrants mention. The SSIS Rating Scales is one component of a comprehensive assessment and intervention program designed to improve students' social skills. It is designed to assess social behavior, identify specific social behavior acquisition and performance deficits, identify specific social skills strengths, and assess the presence of problem behaviors that interfere with social skills. It is based upon the Social Skills Rating System (Gresham & Elliott, 1990), which was a widely used behavior rating scale for assessment of children's social skills. The SSIS Rating Scales features three forms, including two versions of a student self-report form (ages 8–12 and ages 13–18) and two third-party scales, one for teachers and one for parents. Parent and teacher forms are appropriate for ages 3–18. The SSIS Rating Scales requires that respondents read socially skilled behavioral descriptions (e.g., "Takes turns in conversations") and problem behaviors (e.g., "Bullies others") and rate the frequency of the child's behavior over the past 2 months using a 4-point scale (*never, seldom, often,* and *almost always*). For

Social Skills items, teachers and parents rate the importance for each behavior (i.e., *not important, important,* and *critical*) to provide guidance regarding the social importance of the skill. The Teacher Form contains 83 items, and the Parent Form features 79 items. Norms were based upon 950 teachers and 2,800 parents rating students matched to 2006 U.S. Census data.

Teacher and parent forms generate Social Skills and Problem Behavior composite scores, and the Teacher Form also yields an Academic Competence composite score. The Social Skills composite is based upon seven subscales: Cooperation, Assertion, Responsibility, Self-Control, Communication, Empathy, and Engagement. The Problem Behavior composite is based upon Externalizing, Internalizing, Bullying, Hyperactivity/Inattention, and Autism Spectrum subscales. Similar to the BASC-2, it features validity indices that provide measures of respondents' response style, patterned responding, and consistency of responding. Internal consistency reliability is .94 or higher for both parent and teacher Social Skills and Problem Behavior scores, while temporal stability reliability is .82 or higher for these scales. Interrater reliability is .53 or higher for Social Skills and Problem Behavior scores across similar pairs of raters (e.g., two parents rating the same child). Concurrent validity is reported for the SSIS Rating Scales as evidenced by expected patterns of correlations, such as those with the BASC-2 and Social Skills Rating System. A unique feature is the accompaniment of a universal social behavior curriculum and a targeted intervention guide, which can be used in conjunction with the rating scales in order to monitor progress on implemented curriculum and interventions.

Best Practice Strategy for Behavior Rating Scale Use in Classification and Diagnosis

Martin et al. (1986) described an assessment strategy for school psychologists that consists of collecting behavior rating scales in a multisetting, multisource, and multi-instrument design. In this model, student behavior is rated across at least two settings (e.g., home and school), by at least two raters per each setting (e.g., mother and father; two teachers), with at least two instruments for each rater (e.g., ASEBA and BASC-2). Data are interpreted across rating scales and patterns of values deemed more reliable than any individual rating. Determining sources of rating disagreements can help to isolate situationally specific aspects of problematic social–emotional functioning. Several measures described in this chapter facilitate the process of rater comparisons by calculating interrater agreement statistics (e.g., ASEBA), plotting respondents' derived scores on a single graph (e.g., BASC-2), and grouping respondents' item-level responses by domains (e.g., SSIS Rating Scales).

School psychologists should also incorporate behavior rating scale data within a larger multimethod framework for determining appropriate classification and diagnosis of social–emotional concerns. The framework should include data collection from self-report, teacher and parent interview, behavioral observation, and other methods as appropriate, such as review of developmental history and office discipline referrals. School psychologists should include self-reports when possible, particularly when internalizing disorders, such as anxiety and depression, are under diagnostic consideration. If evaluation resulted from proactive screening, these data should also be considered within classification and diagnostic decision making. Several behavior rating scales feature potential linkages between scale results and special education eligibility categories, such as Emotional Disturbance, Other Health Impairment, and Autism (Conners, 2009).

Developing Effective Services: Intervention Planning

For contemporary behavior rating scales, there has been greater emphasis on the linkage between results and intervention than for prior versions. The linkage is due, in part, to the growing emphasis on problem-solving service delivery models within the field of school psychology. For example, the SSIS Rating Scales is considered one component of a larger tiered system of social skills development and problem behavior prevention. The SSIS Rating Scales instrument is identified as a Tier 2 procedure designed for planning social skills interventions that may be selected from materials available within the larger social skills program. Behavior rating scale assessment and intervention linkage is clear within the SSIS model, such that computer scoring software identifies a particular social skills lesson plan that aligns with the problem area identified from the rating.

Behavior rating scale data may be useful for assisting in the prioritization of targets for intervention. In the presence of significant elevations across various domains, norm-referenced scores may prove useful in targeting the problem area falling at the most extreme point and associated with the greatest impairment within the school environment. Another advantage of utilizing behavior rating scale assessment for the purpose of intervention planning is that data may be compared across settings. Discrepant ratings may guide decisions regarding where intervention should occur, such as the presence of externalizing behavior problems within the context of one classroom setting versus another.

Measuring Progress and Outcomes: Intervention Monitoring

Behavior rating scales have a long history of use for the purpose of monitoring effects of intervention, particularly for specific areas of concern, such as ADHD symptomatology (e.g., Conners' scales). Within this tradition, behavior rating scales are most typically utilized in a pre–post testing format whereby postintervention scores are compared with preintervention scores to determine if intervention has proved beneficial. Contemporary behavior rating scales feature useful programs that allow for serial ratings to be plotted and statistically compared across time points. For example, the SSIS Rating Scales features a Progress Report program that plots standard scores ($M = 100$; $SD = 15$) over time and highlights statistically significant change scores from the pretest or baseline score as well as from the preceding score ($p < .05$).

For behavior rating scales to be useful for frequent monitoring of intervention within school settings, scale length must be shortened to accommodate respondent time restrictions. As such, repeated administration of full-length behavior rating scales, such as the ASEBA or BASC-2, is unwieldy. Several contemporary brief behavior rating scales have been developed in concert with well-established measures for the purpose of monitoring students' progress within the context of an intervention.

Brief Problem Monitor. The Brief Problem Monitor (Achenbach, McConaughy, Ivanova, & Rescorla, 2011) is a 19-item behavior rating scale designed to monitor children's behavioral functioning and children's responsiveness to intervention across various settings, including schools (Achenbach et al., 2011). It yields Internalizing (e.g., fearful or anxious), Externalizing (e.g., threatens), Attention Problem (e.g., cannot concentrate), and Total Problem *T* scores. Content was derived from the full form of the ASEBA through factor analysis, item response theory, and rational item selection. The rating interval is modifiable, such that the rater is asked to provide a description of the child within (blank) days. The evaluator completes the time interval of interest by writing in the number of days in the blank space. The response scale is identical to the ASEBA parent scales. Scoring software produces both graphical displays for visual comparisons of scores across raters as well as graphed scores over a maximum of 10 ratings so that patterns of behavior rating are viewable over time.

For Total Problem scores, internal consistency reliability is .90 for the Parent Form and .92 for the Teacher Form, temporal stability is .85 for the Parent Form (8-day interval) and .93 for the Teacher Form (16-day interval). For the remaining scales, internal consistency and temporal stability meets or exceeds .80 for both parent and teacher forms. Parent–teacher interrater reliability for the Total Problem score is .33.

Conners–Third Edition Short and Global Index Forms. The Conners–Third Edition (Conners, 2009) features two behavior rating forms that may be utilized to evaluate effects of intervention over time. The Short Form consists of 45 items that sample inattention, hyperactivity/impulsivity, learning problems, and peer relationship problems, among others. The Short Form was developed with 769 parents and 744 teachers, and internal consistency and temporal stability reliability meets or exceeds .78 across both forms. Interrater reliability is .83 for pairs of parents and .77 for paired teachers. Short Form scores correlate with other behavior rating scales in expected directions, providing evidence of scale validity.

The Global Index Form is a 10-item scale developed from the highest loading items from the original Conners scales and identified by authors as a useful instrument to measure general effectiveness of an intervention. Internal consistency and temporal stability reliability are favorable with values meeting or exceeding .80 across parent and teacher forms. Interrater reliability is .80 for parent pairs and .74 for teacher pairs. Parent-rated Global Index scores correlate significantly with parent-rated BASC-2 and Child Behavior Checklist scores. Item content samples core aspects of ADHD symptomatology, such as inattention and impulsivity, as well as other affective indicators, such as quick mood changes and temper outbursts.

Modified Omnibus Rating Scales. In contrast to the field of academic monitoring, behavioral assessment practice, in general, and behavior rating scale development, in particular, have yet to identify a general outcome measure that is sufficiently flexible to capture general behavioral functioning and is sufficiently responsive to document general changes that may arise from various interventions (see Gresham et al., 2010). In an attempt to develop a behavioral general outcome measure, several authors have developed abbreviated forms based upon well-established behavior rating scales. For example, Gresham et al. (2010) developed a 12-item brief behavior rating scale from the teacher form of the Social Skills Rating System. Items were selected from a pool of 29 items that proved to be sensitive to detecting change from the First Step to Success, an early intervention program. Scale content samples eight social skills, three problem behaviors, and one rating of general academic competence. The 12-item scale shows promising internal consistency reliability (.70) and temporal stability (.71) as well as evidence of criterion-related validity.

As with other assessment purposes, school psychologists should supplement behavior rating scale data with other data sources to document the effects of an intervention. Over the short term, for example, direct behavior observation is recommended as such data are typically more sensitive to change than behavior rating scale data. Direct behavioral observation should closely align with the goals of the intervention, such as tracking changes in specified behavioral targets. Over the longer term, however, direct behavior observation is likely to prove to be difficult to sustain and other methods, such as behavior ratings, may be more feasible for documenting behavioral changes. The limitation of behavior rating scale use in documenting intervention response is the likely mismatch between the targeted goals of intervention, such as reducing out-of-seat behavior, with general ratings, such as internalizing, externalizing, and attention problems. In this instance, the behavior rating scale data will likely capture out-of-seat behavior in the externalizing summary score, but the rating of this specific behavior will be surrounded by additional measurement noise.

Case Example of Behavior Rating Scale Use From Traditional Assessment Model

Generic Elementary School adopted a proactive screening program to identify potential social–emotional and behavior difficulties exhibited by first-grade students within the first month of the school year. The school psychologist coordinated the screening program with input from first-grade teachers and school administrators. The school utilized the Behavioral and Emotional Screening System Teacher Rating scale during the screening process and used a conservative cutoff score of $T \geq 70$ as suggestive of difficulties. As a result, Generic Elementary School identified 10 first-grade students who exceeded the threshold score.

The school psychologist coordinated collection of follow-up behavior rating scales for the 10 children identified by the initial screener. The school psychologist selected the BASC-2 scales for the purpose of additional assessment to guide decision making for follow-up assessment. For one student, Brian, results of the BASC-2 scales revealed consistent and significant concerns in the areas of overactive behavior, social withdrawal, atypical social interactions, and limited functional communication skills. After reviewing the rating scale data, the school psychologist conducted additional evaluation to determine if Brian met special education eligibility criteria for autism. Additional evaluation data included classroom observation, autism-specific rating scale data from parents and teachers, as well as individual assessment with Brian. Based on the findings, Brian was found to be eligible for special education services under the category of autism. The special education team identified increased socially appropriate behavior and social approach behavior as two of several educational objectives. Intervention progress was measured by several direct behavior observations conducted by the school psychologist within the classroom and during lunch. Direct observational data were supplemented with SSIS Rating Scales parent and teacher ratings that were collected (a) 1 week prior to intervention, (b) 12 weeks after the implementation of the intervention, and (c) at the end of the school year to document short-term and long-term benefits of intervention. Results showed improvement in various aspects of social skills, particularly in the areas of social engagement, communication, and cooperation. Further, the school psychologist readministered the BASC-2 scales at the end of the school year to provide an additional comparison point for Brian's behavioral adjustment within the classroom and a home. Results from both teacher and parent ratings revealed that overactive behavior, social withdrawal, and atypical social interactions clinical scores had decreased and that ratings of Brian's functional communication skills had improved over the course of the year.

Use of Behavior Rating Scales From a Problem-Solving Model

In order to most efficiently identify student needs, develop effective services, and measure the progress based on those services, school psychologists will find that the problem-solving model aligns with effective behavior screening and assessment. Tilly (2008) defined the core questions of the basic problem-solving model: (a) Is there a problem and what is it? (b) Why is the problem happening (or problem analysis)? (c) What can be done about the problem (or intervention development)? (d) Did the intervention work?

Essentially, as noted by Chafouleas et al. (2010), school psychologists have likely been involved in team-based problem solving approaches for many years (e.g., through student assistance teams). However, this team process, regardless of intent, often has served as a precursor to special education referral or a general brainstorming strategy that had limited data to support decisions.

Further, traditional practice has led to what Walker, Severson, and Seely (2010) noted as the refer–test–place model, within which behavior ratings' main purpose was providing data for placement. Evident challenges associated with this model have been consistently noted, including overlooking those with internalizing symptoms and the potential for teacher referrals to be subjective or underrepresentative of those who are at risk (e.g., Walker et al., 2010). Moreover, this model does not utilize behavior ratings in a preventive manner; that is, school psychologists compare the rating to the norm sample and assess degree of deviance from the norm. In contrast, the problem-solving process incorporates other sources to ensure children at risk are not overlooked and utilizes data to help identify appropriate interventions and/or assessment progress made from those interventions. A problem-solving approach promotes a wider usage of behavior rating scales, specifically within the process of prevention and intervention, leading toward a more proactive role for school psychologists.

Identifying Student Strengths and Needs

Chafouleas et al. (2010) noted that the usage of defensible, data-based decision-making tools for problem solving for behavior has been delayed as compared with academics. Partially, this is because we know, for example, far less about emotional, mental health, and behavioral tools for prevention than is known about the process and components required for reading. Further, two decision-making models are promoted in the RTI literature for academic problems: standard protocol or problem-solving models (Hughes & Dexter, 2011). States have varied in their use for academic decision making in determining how students will be served once identified as being at risk (e.g., Berkeley, Bender, Peaster, & Saunders, 2009). A standard protocol approach for behavior and mental health problems would seem counterintuitive. That is, decision making regarding behavioral needs would be individualized based on a student's culture, history, and available resources, specifically through the problem-solving approach. Although the process of tiered behavior interventions is still a growing field, what is known is that mental health services and supports are needed in schools, and the early identification and prevention of problem behaviors will potentially improve student outcomes. Consequently, school psychologists are critical for systems change that uses behavior ratings are one tool that will increase the ability for individual needs to be met within a data-based decision model.

In order to identify student needs in a preventive model, RTI frameworks promote universal screening, such that all students are assessed typically three times a year and students not meeting a predetermined level would receive Tier 2 interventions. Although universal screening has been utilized effectively for academics, deployment of universal screening for various areas of behavior is not well established. Tobin, Schneider, Reck, and Landau (2008) identified a model whereby universal screening for ADHD behavior could be completed by teachers and parents. However, universal screeners are suggested for many other areas, including internalizing and externalizing behaviors, social skills, study skills, and bullying (e.g., Shinn & Walker, 2010). The implementation of multiple behavior rating screeners across domains would provide potentially valuable information. But the feasibility of such a system is questionable. Therefore, school psychologists must involve themselves in the evaluation planning process to provide input when prioritizing social behavior assessment and monitoring.

As mentioned previously, there are ethical considerations for school psychologists regarding the use of behavior rating scales as screeners. If a student is found to have elevated internalizing symptoms from a universal screening, then the first step of the problem-solving model is complete. However, not only must school psychologists score the screeners in a timely manner, but schools must have the intervention structure, resources, and professional development in place in order to respond. School psychologists also must be aware of the screener's likelihood of false positives and of the result for those who might unnecessarily be referred for intervention (see Figure 19.2). Similar concerns exist for false negatives, particularly for internalizing symptoms, which are often missed through traditional teacher referral systems.

Developing Effective Services

The problem-solving model contains the problem analysis and intervention development stages (Tilly, 2008), both of which relate to developing effective services for students. Here, a distinction is possible between behavioral- and academic-tiered intervention planning from the aforementioned standard protocol

and problem-solving models. Data obtained from universal screenings and progress monitoring tools upon identification would be considered a component of problem analysis rather than an independent source of data. For example, if a student were rated as *rarely* in his or her assigned area via the Behavior Screening Checklist, then the problem-solving team would develop specific interventions, taking into account the student's age, classroom environment, and individual preferences and skills. The previous parameters of behavior ratings, specifically being defensible, psychometrically sound, and feasible, continue to be recommended at this stage of intervention development.

Regardless of whether a student is in a tiered prevention model or has been identified as a student with a disability, utilizing behavior rating scale data is helpful for planning or revising intervention plans. Considering the complexities of a student exhibiting aggressive behaviors, for example, behavior rating scales would provide one source of information regarding the severity of the behavior as well as other potential comorbid problems (e.g., internalizing symptoms). For students in a Tier 2 or Tier 3 intervention framework, however, systematic behavior observations or a combination of such would be more appropriate due to the sensitivity and specificity of data provided. That being said, interventions developed from initial hypotheses derived from behavior ratings, for example, rather than solely from teacher report or office referrals, would likely lead to more effective services in the area of behavior.

Students not responding to Tier 2 intervention may benefit from additional behavioral assessment approaches, such as completion of a functional behavior assessment, which uses data to assist with intervention development based upon hypothesized functions of behavior. At this point in a tiered delivery system, students will have demonstrated needs requiring intensive supports and school psychologists will assist in either initiating or revising a behavior intervention plan. Behavior ratings are one piece of data that can be utilized in the functional behavior assessment, in conjunction with multiple data sources, to develop individualized interventions.

School psychologists should also consider evaluation of their own practices, and specifically should ask this one question: Are we doing what is most effective and meaningful for students? Ongoing data collection and analysis are processes that school psychologists should use to evaluate their practices, including direct interventions with students (e.g., a social skills curriculum) or consultative services from which indirect interventions were implemented. Behavior ratings allow a direct method for school psychologists to use in evaluating effectiveness of their methods and/or services.

Measuring Progress and Outcomes

Data provided from behavior rating scales can assist with identifying students in need of interventions and developing individualized plans, which can lead to measuring progress. However, the most important goal is determination of progress: Did it work?

Behavior rating scales will be one component to assist school psychologists and the team in making this decision. The format of measuring progress has received much attention in the literature and practice, particularly in the academic areas through the use of curriculum-based measurement. However, Gresham et al. (2010) noted that currently for social behaviors there is no agreed-upon form of measurement that is change sensitive and technically adequate. Yet, due to the challenges with using existing, reactive data such as office discipline referrals, a systematic process of measuring student progress and outcomes in the area of behavior has gained warranted attention.

This chapter has outlined specific rating scales that school psychologists could select for measuring progress, specifically the Brief Problem Monitor and SSIS Rating Scales. Both of these measures will help track how students respond to targeted interventions and allow the problem-solving team to evaluate whether to maintain the current plan or to modify it. Although this is a newer field of study and additional scales will continue to be developed, for many cases the SSIS Rating Scales would support the use of progress monitoring for social behavior. This process does not come without challenges as we seek measures that possess technical adequacy, treatment validity, and change sensitivity.

Teachers might not find the process of using systematic behavior ratings to systematically measure progress meaningful or worthwhile if school psychologists do not guide the problem-solving team in planning and determining whether to change or maintain interventions. At this stage, behavior-ratings-specific descriptions of behaviors would provide baseline data, which can later be used as a comparison at posttreatment. Behavior challenges warranting intervention monitoring with a high degree of specificity would not appear to benefit from the use of behavior-rating-scale data to track intervention response if the scale is not sensitive enough to track changes in targeted behaviors. For example, a behavior rating scale may not be sensitive enough to assess changes in aggression through the use of general frequency ratings (e.g., *often*, *always*). A daily frequency count of aggressive behaviors may better assess whether behavior is decreasing, maintaining, or increasing. As noted previously, a combination of behavior rating and frequent observation of targeted behaviors would be considered most effective for Tier 2 and Tier 3.

Multicultural Competencies Needed by School Psychologists

Another question for the use of behavior ratings in measuring progress and outcomes relates to the social validity and relationship to what is required within the environment. This relates to the need of school psychologists to understand the diverse population they serve. Sullivan and A'Vant (2009) indicated that "multiculturalism must move beyond basic knowledge and appreciation of diversity and cultural difference to embody *responsiveness* [sic] to difference in order to facilitate real change" (p. 1). School psychologists should, through training and experiences, increase their multicultural competence, specifically in the area of assessment, such that the practices where students continue to be overlooked or overidentified due to their cultural differences do not continue to permeate our service provision.

The multifaceted purposes outlined for behavior ratings provide a potential outlet for more multicultural competent practice. However, behavior rating scales cannot stand alone. Similar to norm-referenced tests, behavior ratings will still hold cultural loading that might or might not be sensitive to the population screened or assessed. For example, a promising screener, the Behavior Screening Checklist, was found similar to other research to identify African American and Native American students with higher scores, thus not distinguishing between behaviors potentially based on cultural or racial differences (Muyskens et al., 2007). Further, school psychologists should be aware of scales that are translated into other languages. Although this practice could be helpful, there are concerns with the process of translation as well as norming samples. There are also multiple considerations for school psychologists in regard to their ability to work with and administer behavior rating scales to families who speak a different language.

Moreover, as mentioned, caregivers and teachers might provide significantly discrepant ratings. For example, a teacher might rate a student as exhibiting a higher level of externalizing behavior than is reported at home. If a school psychologist has observed negative behaviors at school, then an immediate response might be to discount parent ratings. Given the school culture and climate, however, the student could respond differently across settings. Thus, a multiculturally competent school psychologist will consider how students' varying cultural backgrounds might have an impact on children's behavior, and ultimately how students are perceived and evaluated on behavior rating scales. School psychologists should be aware of cultural loadings in behavior rating scales and variances across students' environment that ultimately might affect how children are rated and perceived by both caregivers and teachers.

RTI Case Example

School psychologists considering incorporating behavior rating scales into an RTI framework may find this case example helpful. Let us take the example of Mark, a 7-year-old second grade student. Mark has a history of reading fluency and word reading weaknesses, and he has been receiving Tier 2 small-group reading intervention in the classroom. This year, the school district has placed an emphasis on behavior and academic RTI, and thus teachers are implementing Tier 1 social curriculum and universal screening for behavior, utilizing teacher-completed Behavior Screening Checklists. Mark's ratings fell above the predetermined cutoff score. Behaviors of concern included getting out of his seat, independent work completion, and appropriate verbal interactions with others. Thus, the problem-solving team met, reviewed records, and interviewed his parents. Concerns were confirmed for Mark, and thus the team developed an initial behavior plan, part of which the school psychologist implemented in a small group intervention using the Social Skills Improvement System intervention guide for curriculum development for Mark and three similar age male peers. To monitor progress on this intervention, the school psychologist had the teacher and parent complete the SSIS Rating Scales at baseline in support of Mark's individual plan. Then, the SSIS Rating Scales was completed monthly, and daily progress sheets were completed by the teacher to determine if progress was being made on the plan. Based on adequate progress as predetermined by the problem-solving team after 3 months of intervention, Mark would be monitored and return to Tier 1 supports in the classroom while his reading skills continued to be targeted based on limited progress. If Mark had not shown adequate progress on the identified social behaviors, then the team would have needed to investigate the intervention type and frequency and make relevant modifications.

Recent Developments

The enterprise of developing and marketing behavior rating scales has responded to the growing interest and adaptation of behavioral RTI. For example, the ASEBA scales feature a brief scale to assess RTI (Achenbach et al., 2011), the BASC-2 system of assessment includes a screening instrument, and the SSIS aligns its components with tiered intervention (e.g., the SSIS Rating Scales is described as a Tier 2 assessment). Although behavior rating scales have been modified to address changes in service delivery models, the feasibility and usability of the systems have yet to be clearly established.

The recent development and initial validation of Direct Behavior Rating scale technology also warrants mention. Christ, Riley-Tillman, and Chafouleas (2009) define a Direct Behavior Rating as "an evaluative rating that is generated at the time and place that behavior occurs by those persons who are naturally present in the context of interest" (p. 205). For example, a teacher may be asked to rate the percentage of time that a student was engaged in disruptive behavior using a scale from 0 to 100%. In such an instance, the teacher would be provided with an operational definition of disruptive behavior and provided instruction and training regarding how to use the Direct Behavior Rating. According to Direct Behavior Rating developers, Direct Behavior Ratings combine "the immediacy of systematic direct observation and the efficiency of behavior rating scales" (Christ et al., 2009, p. 201). In contrast to behavior rating scales, Direct Behavior Ratings require the respondent to rate behavior immediately after a specified period of time, thus reducing the latency between the observation and rating. Also, in contrast to behavior rating scales, Direct Behavior Ratings provide operational definitions to inform ratings, such as defining disruptive behavior as any student action that interrupts classroom instruction as opposed to a behavior rating scale stem of "is disruptive." The Direct Behavior Rating method may hold promise as a strategy to identify and operationalize a general outcome measure for progress monitoring within a tiered service delivery model.

Desirable Direct Behavior Rating characteristics are efficiency, flexibility, and repeatability, which are critical features for deployment in such a system. Direct Behavior Ratings would not supplant behavior rating scales in a larger assessment framework, but they may provide complementary information for various purposes, such as screening or intervention monitoring. More detailed information about these scales and their use can be found at http://www.directbehaviorratings.com/cms/ (Chafouleas & Riley-Tillman, 2013).

SUMMARY

Behavior rating scales are used frequently by school psychologists when evaluating social, emotional, and behavioral concerns and constitute an important source of data within the larger context of behavioral assessment. Behavior rating scales feature strengths and liabilities across various purposes of behavioral assessment, whether from a traditional assessment paradigm or a problem-solving model of service delivery. With respect to strengths, behavior rating scales allow for efficient data collection provided by respondents who observe children within naturalistic settings over a period of time. On the negative side of the ledger, behavior rating scales are susceptible to respondent perceptions and biases, such as halo effects or response tendencies that do not relate to the behavior of interest. Contemporary behavior rating scales estimate response biases through the inclusion of validity scales.

Behavior rating scales may be used for various traditional assessment purposes within school settings, such as screening, identification, intervention planning, and intervention monitoring. Behavior rating scales may also prove valuable within the context of service delivery through RTI models. Owing to cost and time efficiency, brief behavior rating scales are well suited to serve as behavioral screeners from a traditional assessment perspective, and behavior rating scales may prove amenable for adaptation as general outcome measures within the context of universal screening and progress monitoring. Behavior rating scales yield data that are relevant for the purposes of special education eligibility decision making as well as for prioritizing targets for intervention and providing useful pre–post data to assist in determining if an intervention has yielded beneficial effects. Several widely used contemporary behavior rating scales have been modified for use within a problem-solving service delivery model. However, the deployment and evaluation of behavior rating scales for this purpose have not been fully evaluated.

REFERENCES

Achenbach, T. M., McConaughy, S. H., & Howell, C. T. (1987). Child/adolescent behavioral and emotional problems: Implications of cross-informant correlations for situational specificity. *Psychological Bulletin, 101,* 213–232.

Achenbach, T. M., McConaughy, S. H., Ivanova, M. Y., & Rescorla, L. A. (2011). *Manual for the ASEBA Brief Problem Monitor.* Burlington, VT: University of Vermont, Research Center for Children, Youth, and Families.

Achenbach, T. M., & Rescorla, L. A. (2001). *Manual for ASEBA CBCL forms and profiles.* Burlington, VT: University of Vermont, Research Center for Children, Youth, and Families.

Berkeley, S., Bender, W. N., Peaster, L. G., & Saunders, L. (2009). Implementation of response to intervention: A snapshot of progress. *Journal of Learning Disabilities, 42,* 85–95.

Campbell, J. M. (2005). Diagnostic assessment of Asperger's disorder: A review of five third-party rating scales. *Journal of Autism and Developmental Disorders, 35,* 25–35.

Carran, D. T., & Scott, K. G. (1992). Risk assessment in preschool children: Research implications for the early detection of educational handicaps. *Topics in Early Childhood Special Education, 12,* 196–211.

Chafouleas, S. M., Kilgus, S. P., & Wallach, N. (2010). Ethical dilemmas in school-based behavioral screening. *Assessment for Effective Intervention, 35,* 245–252.

Chafouleas, S. M., & Riley-Tillman, T. C. (2013). *Direct Behavior Ratings.* Retrieved from http://www.directbehaviorratings.com/cms/

Chafouleas, S. M., Volpe, R. J., Gresham, F. M., & Cook, C. R. (2010). School-based behavioral assessment within problem-solving models: Current status and future directions. *School Psychology Review, 39,* 343–349.

Christ, T. J., Riley-Tillman, T. C., & Chafouleas, S. M. (2009). Foundation for the development and use of Direct Behavior Rating (DBR) to assess and evaluate student behavior. *Assessment for Effective Intervention, 34,* 201–213.

Conners, C. K. (2009). *Conners-Third Edition.* North Tonawanda, NY: Multi-Health Systems.

Gresham, F. M., Cook, C. R., Collins, T., Dart, E., Rasethwane, K., Truelson, E., & Grant, S. (2010). Developing a change-sensitive brief behavior rating scale as a progress-monitoring tool for social behavior: An example using the Social Skills Rating System: Teacher Form. *School Psychology Review, 39,* 364–379.

Gresham, F. M., & Elliott, S. N. (1990). *Social Skills Rating System.* Circle Pines, MN: American Guidance Service.

Gresham, F. M., & Elliott, S. N. (2008). *Social Skills Improvement System: Rating Scales.* Bloomington, MN: Pearson Assessments.

Hughes, C. A., & Dexter, D. D. (2011). Response to intervention: A research-based summary. *Theory Into Practice, 50,* 4–11. doi:10.1080/00405841.2011.534909

Kamphaus, R. W., & Reynolds, C. R. (2007). *BASC-2 Behavioral and Emotional Screening System manual.* Bloomington, MN: Pearson Assessments.

King-Vogel, K. R. (2010). *The use of behavioral screeners in elementary schools: Concurrent validity and concordance rates.* (Unpublished doctoral dissertation). University of Georgia College of Education, Athens, Georgia.

Martin, R. P., Hooper, S., & Snow, J. (1986). Behavior rating scale approaches to personality assessment in children and adolescents. In H. M. Knoff (Ed.), *The assessment of child and adolescent personality.* (pp. 309–352). New York, NY: Guilford Press.

Mash, E. J., & Hunsley, J. (2005). Evidence-based assessment of child and adolescent disorders: Issues and challenges. *Journal of Clinical Child & Adolescent Psychology, 34,* 362–379.

Muyskens, P., Marston, D., & Reschly, A. L. (2007). The use of response-to-intervention practices for behavior: An examination of the validity of a screening instrument. *The California School Psychologist, 12,* 31–45.

National Association of School Psychologists. (2010). *Model of comprehensive and integrated school psychological services.* Bethesda, MD: Author. Retrieved from http://www.nasponline.org/standards/2010standards/2_PracticeModel.pdf

Reynolds, C. R., & Kamphaus, R. W. (2004). *Behavior Assessment System for Children-Second edition (BASC-2).* Circle Pines, MN: American Guidance Service.

Shapiro, E. S., & Heick, P. F. (2004). School psychologist assessment practices in the evaluation of students referred for social/behavioral/emotional problems. *Psychology in the Schools, 41,* 551–561.

Shinn, M. R., & Walker, H. M. (2010). *Interventions for achievement and behavior problems in a three-tier model including RTI.* Bethesda, MD: National Association of School Psychologists.

Sullivan, A. L., & A'Vant, E. (2009). On the need for cultural responsiveness. *Communiqué, 38*(3), 8–9.

Tilly, W. D., III. (2008). The evolution of school psychology to science-based practice: Problem solving and the three-tiered model. In A. Thomas & J. Grimes (Eds.), *Best practices in school psychology V.* (pp. 17–36). Bethesda, MD: National Association of School Psychologists.

Tobin, R. M., Schneider, W. J., Reck, S. G., & Landau, S. (2008). Best practices in the assessment of children with attention deficit hyperactivity disorder: Linking assessment to response to intervention. In A. Thomas & J. Grimes (Eds.), *Best practices in school psychology V.* (pp. 617–631). Bethesda, MD: National Association of School Psychologists.

Walker, H. M., Severson, H. H., & Seeley, J. R. (2010). Universal, school-based screening for the early detection of behavioral problems contributing to later destructive outcomes. In M. R. Shinn & H. M. Walker (Eds.), *Interventions for achievement and behavior problems in a three-tier model including RTI.* (pp. 677–702). Bethesda, MD: National Association of School Psychologists.

20 Best Practices in Can't Do/Won't Do Academic Assessment

Education Research & Consulting, Inc., Fairhope, AL

OVERVIEW

The notion that students may not always display academic performance to their greatest potential is conventionally accepted and consistent with most people's everyday experiences. At any given moment in time, children's behaviors are governed by environmental events and internal states that cause them to behave predictably. When children are tired, sick, distracted, stressed, hungry, or sad they may exert less sustained effort on a difficult task. When children must choose between one task and another more appealing task, they are likely to choose the more appealing task. When children are very interested in a topic or anticipate either great reward for completing the less appealing task or great punishment for not completing the less appealing task, they are likely to overcome the desire to engage in the more appealing task and, instead, complete the less appealing task. Children in classrooms are confronted with a wide array of choices at any moment in time, and the choices they make relate predictably to and even forecast their longer term academic success.

The marshmallow studies conducted by psychologist Walter Mischel (Shoda, Mischel, & Peake, 1990) in a laboratory preschool provided a surprising window into the longer term adaptation and success of children over their schooling career. Mischel's experiments involved leaving a marshmallow on a plate in front of a 4-year-old child, telling the child that he or she could ring a bell at any time and this would cause the adult to return to the office and permit the child to eat the marshmallow right away, or the child could wait for some interval of time and instead would be given two marshmallows when the adult returned. Young children who were able to wait experienced greater schooling success over the subsequent decades. Mischel's simple experiments helped psychologists understand that the skills involved in delaying gratification, for example, could be taught and had as much to do with longer term academic achievement as intellectual ability. This finding again seems to resonate with school psychologists who are interested in not only predicting longer term achievement but also promoting and accelerating it wherever possible.

School psychologists seem to understand that achievement has a lot to do with ability, but academic achievement also has a lot to do with other skills, often referred to as executive function skills in the school psychology literature. School psychologists have certainly observed the very skilled student who struggled to complete tasks and did not finish college, just as school psychologists have observed the less skilled student who demonstrated sustained effort on less appealing tasks and attained greater academic accomplishments than the more skilled student. Hence, it is not surprising that research in positive psychology has shown that measured traits like conscientiousness and effortful attention account for standardized test score changes above and beyond measures of intelligence in some studies (Duckworth, 2011). Hattie (2009), for example, reported a moderate to large effect ($d = .48$) for motivation and concentration, persistence, and engagement on academic achievement.

Hence, the can't do/won't do assessment is a simple technique that school psychologists seem to like because it operationalizes and makes accessible information about whether or not the child's measured performance reflects the child's true skill capacity and thereby provides concrete direction for deciding what types of instructional supports will be of highest yield for that child.

305

BASIC CONSIDERATIONS

The roots of the can't do/won't do assessment can be found in early work in curriculum-based measurement (CBM) and functional academic assessment.

Roots of Can't Do/Won't Do Assessment

Deno and Mirkin (1977) asserted that the effect of an instructional strategy could not be ensured prior to its use and that any instructional strategy must be evaluated as it was implemented to verify that it improved learning. Deno and Mirkin argued that time series data (i.e., repeated measurement) on critical indices of skill development (CBM) could characterize current learning and forecast longer term learning outcomes. CBM provided school psychologists and teachers with a method to gain immediate feedback on the utility of an instructional strategy so that ineffective strategies could be replaced and yield better results for students. Lentz and Shapiro (1986) linked brief skill assessments to instructional design and explained the mechanics of data- and hypothesis-driven instruction, laying the foundation for the problem-solving model (Shinn, 1989) that is conventionally understood as the basis of multitiered models of service delivery in schools. As with many innovations in school psychology, practical field-based implementations of can't do/won't do assessment occurred simultaneously with research evaluation projects.

Development and Research Evaluation of Can't Do/Won't Do Assessment

In 1997, Joe Witt began a project designed to convert the teacher referral process into a functional analysis of children's performance in the classroom. Using the ideas and methodologies set forth in the behavior analysis literature and CBM as the primary tool for decision making, researchers and field trial participants began conducting universal screenings in elementary schools. Children who were found to be at risk during screening participated in what the research team called the skill-performance deficit assessment, which was later simplified to the can't do/won't do assessment.

The rationale for the assessment was that school psychologists needed to know whether students required performance contingencies or a skill-building intervention. In the absence of direct assessment data, adults' assumptions about the causes of poor student performance tended to be inaccurate (VanDerHeyden, Witt, & Naquin, 2003). In the framework of data-driven decision making and multitiered intervention, the can't do/won't do assessment was found to be a highly useful filter, both reducing the numbers of students needing more intensive intervention and increasing the efficacy of intervention in a large-scale way because only those students who needed skill-building intervention received it (VanDerHeyden et al., 2003; VanDerHeyden, Witt, & Gilbertson, 2007). Children whose performances were found to be sensitive to rewards were provided with a system of contingencies to encourage more stable, higher quality performance every day in the classroom. In a multitiered intervention system, this filter was important because, first, it reduced the number of students who required intensive individual intervention, thereby making intervention efforts less burdensome and ultimately more manageable and effective for schools. Second, the can't do/won't do assessment filter allowed a better match between intervention strategies and the student's needs, again paving the way for greater intervention effects.

Three studies are most pertinent as direct examinations of the empirical value of the can't do/won't do assessment. Noell et al. (1998) systematically introduced and examined the effects of instructional treatments that might increase reading performance. Treatment conditions included a contingent reward condition, which was expected to increase the performance of students whose poor performance was caused by a performance deficit (i.e., students could do the work, but they were not sufficiently motivated to do the work). Other conditions included instructional supports expected to differentially benefit students whose poor performance was caused by skill deficits (i.e., students could not do the work) and included conditions such as modeling and practice. Similarly, Daly, Martens, Hamler, Dool, and Eckert (1999) sequentially implemented contingent rewards (designed to test the effect of incentives on performance) and several instructional manipulations (e.g., easier task, supported practice completing the task) while measuring student performance using time series data. In both studies, researchers found that children responded differently to the different treatment arrangements, with some showing increased performance for rewards and others showing increased performance only with skill-building intervention.

Later, Duhon et al. (2004) extended this research by conducting a similar assessment to determine whether a student showed a performance or skill deficit and then conducting an extended intervention phase to validate the findings of the assessment. Students were exposed to an indicated and then a contraindicated intervention, based on the findings of the performance or skill deficit assessment. Specifically, those who were found to have a performance deficit were exposed to a contingency-based treatment (i.e., indicated) and a skill-building treatment without incentives (i.e., contraindicated). Students who were found to have a skill deficit were exposed to a skill-building treatment (i.e., indicated) and a contingency-based treatment (i.e., contraindicated). In all cases, the indicated treatment was more successful, validating the assessment of skill and performance deficits.

BEST PRACTICES IN CAN'T DO/WON'T DO ASSESSMENT

The can't do/won't do assessment can be used as part of a multitiered screening process, or it can be used on an individual basis to guide instruction. The can't do/won't do assessment requires 5–10 minutes to administer, depending on the content area being assessed (i.e., reading performance, writing performance). Standardized administration procedures should be followed (provided in the Appendix) and a school psychologist can conduct the assessment inside or outside of the classroom. Can't do/won't do assessments for reading must be administered individually, whereas can't do/won't do assessments for mathematics or writing may be administered individually or in small groups. The basic format is the same regardless of the academic area being assessed, and the underlying logic can be applied to many other academic and behavior targets. Typically a single trained school psychologist conducts all needed can't do/won't do assessments in a given school. There are eight steps in using the can't do/won't do assessment.

Step 1: Incorporate Can't Do/Won't Do Assessment Into an Existing Universal Screening Process

By using whatever universal screening tool and data management system is being used in a system (e.g., DIBELS), the cutscore is applied to the universal screening to determine which students are at risk. Any student performing in the risk range is then selected to participate in the can't do/won't do assessment.

Universal screening procedures can be organized to occur school-wide within a single day, and all can't do/won't do assessments can be completed approximately a week later, also usually within a single day. Research data suggest that where core instruction is adequate, universal screening may identify 15% of students for participation in the can't do/won't do assessment, and about 10% of

the screened population may demonstrate a skill deficit (a can't do problem) requiring skill-building intervention (VanDerHeyden et al., 2003; VanDerHeyden et al., 2007). To make use of the universal screening data that are already collected, the school psychologist must consider and verify the adequacy of the screening process. More information about screening can be found in Kovaleski, VanDerHeyden, and Shapiro (2013). Adequate screenings are those that contain content that is well aligned with key instructional objectives, that use materials that have been developed for and validated as screening measures, and that yield stable scores that accurately forecast longer term learning outcomes. A common error in screening is related to efficiency. Often systems administer too many screening assessments and find themselves in a sea of data, then fail to connect the data to effective follow-up actions in the school. Hence, it can be very helpful for systems to complete a screening inventory in which the data team lists all screening measures being used, specifies the purpose or the decision that will be made with each set of scores obtained from each measure, and summarizes the time and costs required to administer each measure along with the technical adequacy for each measure (see Kovaleski et al., 2013, for a sample screening inventory).

In considering the technical adequacy of potential screening measures, it is important to understand classification accuracy. For every decision that is made about risk status, the decision can be judged as correct or incorrect as compared to some more comprehensive assessment or longitudinal outcome. Classification accuracy metrics such as sensitivity and specificity tell the school psychologist how many decisions are correct and how many decisions are incorrect based on the screening measure and the screening cutscore; these data are typically reported in technical manuals for screening measures. When school psychologists understand classification accuracy, they can make thoughtful adjustments to cutscores and decision rules to permit more accurate and more efficient screening procedures and decisions. All prediction models (e.g., regression, hierarchical linear modeling) generate classification accuracy data, and fundamentally these data determine what cutscores will be used and how useful those cutscores will be for determining risk.

Step 2: Rule Out or Address Core Instructional Problems Prior to Conducting Individual Assessment

As was noted above, all screening measures have a decision rule or cutscore for determining risk. Where many students (e.g., half or more) fall into the at-risk group during screening, core instructional problems (e.g., class-wide, grade-wide, or school-wide) must be examined and addressed prior to singling out individual students for follow-up assessment and intervention. Where many students are at risk according to the screening, accurate decisions about individual students are much more likely to be incorrect than correct, and universal supplemental intervention strategies are likely to be more efficient and more effective solutions. After class-wide interventions have been conducted, students in need of small-group or individual intervention can be determined more accurately, and intervention gains can be demonstrated class-wide and even school-wide (Slavin & Lake, 2008; VanDerHeyden, McLaughlin, Algina, & Snyder, 2012). Hence, where class-wide problems are detected, class-wide intervention is recommended as a first step.

Step 3: Prepare Faculty and Parents for the Can't Do/Won't Do Assessment

Preparation for the can't do/won't do assessment can be integrated into the preparation for universal screening at the school. Schools often do a poor job of preparing teachers and parents for universal screening and multitiered intervention in the school, and this is an area in which school psychologists can play a valuable leadership role. Preparation for screening should occur well before the screening data are scored. At the beginning-of-the-year orientation the school psychologist can provide a 10-minute overview of what screening measures are used at the school and how the data will be used. School psychologists might indicate that the screening measures are intentionally brief so as not to disrupt instructional time, that the measures are meaningful indicators of important learning outcomes like learning to read, and that the purpose of the measures is to evaluate how well instructional programs are functioning overall for all students and to identify students who need supplemental support or intervention to ensure they do not fall behind. It is useful to frame the screening explicitly as a prevention activity. Parents should be told how the scores will be shared with them (see Kovaleski et al., 2013, for reproducible handouts that can be used to communicate screening results to parents).

Ongoing communication is very important if the goal of screening is to produce data that will actually be used by teachers and instructional leaders in the system. Here again, the school psychologist can play an important leadership role. Prior to screening day, the school psychologist should provide an overview for teachers to show how the data will be scored, what the scores mean, and (with graphed samples) how the data can be used to adjust the program of instruction to accelerate learning for large groups and individual children. Preparation should occur every year for screening, even in veteran sites. It is helpful to explain to teachers that class-wide problems will be addressed with class-wide interventions (if this is the case) and that individual children who are at risk during the screening will participate in the can't do/won't do assessment. Parents and teachers may have concerns about the use of rewards during assessment. The school psychologist should explain that the rewards are essential to the integrity of the assessment (the assessment cannot be conducted without rewards) and that the assessment will yield valuable information that will be used to improve learning outcomes for children. The school psychologist might explain that knowing that a child's performance can improve into the not-at-risk range to earn a reward allows the school to more effectively address the child's performance problem and may prevent a skill deficit in the future. It is important to specify that providing contingencies for stable, high-quality academic performance in the classroom can be accomplished without relying extensively on tangible rewards. For example, for children with a won't do problem, simply requiring higher quality work for the child to participate in preferred activities during the school day is often a highly effective intervention.

Step 4: Assemble Materials to Administer the Assessment

To conduct the can't do/won't do assessment, a school psychologist meets with the child or small groups of children outside of the classroom. Materials needed to conduct the assessment include a blank copy of the screening measure that was used during universal screening, the score that the student earned on the universal screening measure, a digital countdown timer, a treasure chest containing small tangible items and coupons for special privileges, scripted instructions for administering the assessment (see the Appendix), and graphing software (e.g., Excel, iSTEEP). There is no need to identify new measures for the can't do/won't do assessment. Using the screening measure is required because the screening score is the baseline against which performance with rewards will be compared. If the screening measure has been well selected (i.e., aligned with learning expectations, brief, reliable, and able to forecast future learning) and teachers have had a chance to weigh in on selection of the actual screening materials (e.g., a reading passage selected from a set of passages), then the screening measure has social validity (i.e., measures a skill that children are expected to be able to do to be successful in the instructional program and represents a skill that most children in that setting can successfully complete).

The treasure chest can be built with minimal expense (e.g., less than $100 for a school of 500 students for two screening occasions). When selecting items for the treasure chest, it is a good idea for the school psychologist to talk with teachers and students about special privileges, activities, and tangible rewards that the students would like to work for and make sure those items are included in the treasure chest. In selecting items for the treasure chest, the school psychologist should consider the age of the children. Older students often prefer items such as "get out of homework free" cards, edible items, or special in-school privileges such as passes to go to the front of the lunch line, rather than small toys. An example of what to put in the treasure chest are stickers; pencils; erasers; small toys (rubber balls, Yo-Yo, small Frisbees, noise makers, spinning tops); small puzzles; edible treats (cracker packages, candy); hairbows, plastic jewelry; coupons for special activities in class (e.g., computer game, time at the music station); and coupons for special privileges (e.g., special helper, errand runner, line leader, first in line for lunch).

Step 5: Follow Standardized Procedures

To conduct the assessment, the school psychologist or other trained adult will sit with the child or children, establish rapport, and show the child or children the treasure chest. The school psychologist should encourage the children to explore the items in the treasure chest and verify that each child sees a reward that he or she would like to work for. The idea is to identify a reward that is highly motivating to the child. If the child does not seem excited about any of the items in the treasure chest, the school psychologist should negotiate an alternative reward that the child does seem excited about. Care should be taken to minimize any embarrassment that may be caused to children who do not earn a reward (e.g., score the papers of those who have earned a reward first and allow those children to return to class so that the child who did not earn a reward can be provided with some supportive discussion, encouragement, and understanding that he or she will have an opportunity to try again during intervention). For older children enrolled in secondary settings, individual assessment is preferred. Care should also be taken to ensure that children returning to classrooms do not cause disruption to the teaching routine with any earned rewards or that children do not suffer any embarrassment by having earned or not earned a reward. One way to minimize potential embarrassment is to have children place any earned rewards in their backpacks and instruct them that they cannot be removed until they get home. It is useful to send a note home to parents explaining that small rewards may be used to maximize performance and if the parent finds one in his or the child's backpack it is because the child earned it during school.

Once the child has selected an item or activity that he or she would like to earn, then the school psychologist can administer the screening task. Following the scripted instructions, the school psychologist will administer the task and then score the measure and deliver the reward only if the child scored higher than his or her in-class screening score. Importantly, the reward should not be given if the criterion is not met. Some school psychologists use consolation rewards (e.g., a sticker) for children who do not meet the reward criterion. Depending on the purpose for which the assessment is being used, school psychologists may repeat baseline conditions (briefly withdraw contingencies) and then reinstate the reward condition to more conclusively examine the effect of incentives on performance. Another variation involves administering multiple trials at each assessment point and recording the median score for decision making. If the school psychologist is administering multiple measures, then the school psychologist will need to maximize the reward's effect on each trial using indiscriminable contingencies.

To use indiscriminable contingencies, the school psychologist might tell the child, "I am going to ask you to complete three worksheets. The last time you did this worksheet, you scored _____ (say the number) digits correct in 1 minute. Today, I'm going to give you three tries on the same worksheet. But, I am not sure which one will be scored. I am going to shuffle the papers and pick one to score when we are done. If *that* score is higher than _____ (say the number) digits correct, then you will earn the reward. So be sure to do your best work on all the worksheets." When planning for the use of rewards in an intervention program, efforts should be made to control for satiation, be acceptable for use in the classroom, promote behavioral maintenance (or treatment effects over time), and adjust the contingency to promote sustained performance score increases over time (e.g., beat the last highest score).

Step 6: Record, Summarize, and Interpret Data

Can't do/won't do scores should be graphed and interpreted for teachers. Teachers can use this information right away to require higher quality performance from students who are, in fact, capable of higher quality work than they may be demonstrating in class. Teachers and school psychologists should share scores with parents during parent–teacher conferences. Importantly, the school psychologist should briefly interpret the data for the teacher and indicate how instruction could be altered to improve student learning based on the data obtained.

In Figure 20.1, the can't do/won't do assessment was used as a larger package of a multitiered system of support or response to intervention (http://www.isteep.com/login.aspx). Here the entire class was screened using CBM for reading. After a class-wide performance problem was ruled out (i.e., class median score was in the instructional range), the lowest performing children who were also in the frustrational range were selected for the can't do/won't do assessment (Students 13, 14, and 15). Each bar in this graph shows the words read correctly per minute on a grade-level passage for each child in this second-grade class. The lowest performing students each have two bars on the graph. The first bar shows their scores during class-wide screening (29, 14, and 13 words read correctly per minute [wc/min]) and the second bar shows wc/min scores on the same passage during the can't do/won't do assessment (68, 19, and 34 wc/min). These data indicated that one student (Student 13) improved her performance above the instructional criterion when offered an incentive to beat her score. Based on these data, this student was not recommended for further skill-building intervention. Instead, teachers were provided with ideas to adjust contingencies in the classroom to require and support higher quality performance in the classroom. Two students did not improve enough to meet the instructional criterion. These students did beat their last scores and therefore earned a reward. But because the instructional criterion was not met, both students were recommended for further assessment and skill-building intervention. Within a multitiered system of supports, these students proceeded to individual intervention and demonstrated a successful response to intervention (RTI).

School psychologists may wish to conduct a more detailed analysis of the effect of incentives on performance. Figures 20.2 and 20.3 show some variations of this assessment that are more informative but more time consuming. Figure 20.2 shows that the student's academic performance is improved with the use of incentives. These data could also be evaluated in light of some benchmark criteria used by the school to determine risk status. So, for example, if the criterion used to reflect risk status was 50 digits correct per minute, then decision makers may conclude that this student should receive individual skill-building intervention combined with incentives for improved performance. If, on the other hand, the benchmark criterion used by the school was 30 digits correct per minute, then decision makers may conclude that intervention is not needed and teachers may be provided with feedback about how to obtain higher quality performance in the everyday learning environment. In the example provided in Figure 20.3, this student's performance is similar during baseline and reward conditions (i.e., performance is unimproved with the use of contingent rewards). However, instruction produces an immediate improvement in performance. Adding contingent rewards to the instruction condition does not further improve performance. Hence, school psychologists should recommend a skill-building intervention and monitor growth to determine if the intervention successfully resolves the performance problem or if additional assessments and interventions might be needed.

Step 7: Use Data for Systems-Level Problem Solving

The can't do/won't do assessment can be considered a second screening. All screening data, when adequately collected, provide information that can be used to identify patterns of performance problems within the school or school system. The school psychologist is the ideal leader to organize and guide interpretation of the data. When using the data generated from screening activities, the school psychologist must consider the adequacy of the data, note potential limitations, and caution against overinterpretation of the data. The school psychologist can examine scores to identify systemic problems (e.g., classes or grades and content areas in which many students perform in the at-risk range on the screening task). The school psychologist has ideally assisted the school to select the correct screening tasks and to consider performance in both

Figure 20.1. Reading Performance for All Students in the Class

| Frustrational | Instructional | Mastery | ■ Regular Scores | □ Can't Do/Won't Do |

Teacher A   Grade: 2   Mean: 69.73   Median: 66
Assessment Info: 11/17/2003, Class-Wide, Read Second

Words Read Correct in 1 Minute

Student 1: 127
Student 2: 108
Student 3: 108
Student 4: 106
Student 5: 98
Student 6: 79
Student 7: 68
Student 8: 66
Student 9: 65
Student 10: 62
Student 11: 52
Student 12: 51
Student 13: 29 / 68
Student 14: 14 / 19
Student 15: 13 / 34

Note. Adapted from "Best Practices in Can't Do/Won't Do Assessment," by Amanda M. VanDerHeyden and Joseph C. Witt. In *Best Practices in School Psychology V,* by A Thomas and J. Grimes, 2008, Bethesda, MD: National Association of School Psychologists. Copyright 2008 by National Association of School Psychologists. Adapted with permission.

reading and mathematics. This preparation lays the groundwork for troubleshooting the alignment of instructional actions in the classroom with an accepted set of essential learning outcomes (e.g., Common Core State Standards). Troubleshooting actions might involve adjusting the instructional calendar, providing more and/or higher quality instructional time in certain content areas, and providing a system for verifying that students are mastering key learning objectives at the expected time points. Fruitful objectives of the problem-solving activities that might be led by the school

psychologist include improving efficiency of assessment and intervention procedures, improving efficacy of intervention efforts, identifying and addressing high-yield instructional targets, and linking the needs of the system to professional development activities. These problem-solving activities require organizational buy-in and collaboration, so the activities should be discussed with data team members using the screening data as a basis for action.

Ideally, data teams meet at each grade level with the school principal, the school psychologist, and any RTI

Figure 20.2. A Student's Performance Improved With the Opportunity to Earn a Reward

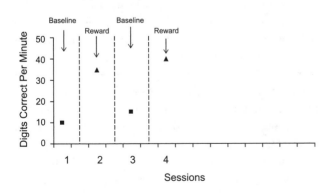

Figure 20.3. A Student's Performance Unimproved With the Opportunity to Earn a Reward

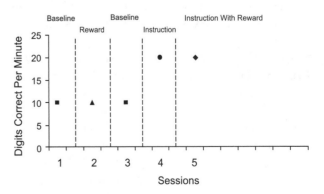

or intervention coaches or coordinators present from the school. In a small district, these meetings are highly useful for district coordinators to attend because the meetings are where instructional changes are planned and district-level coordinators can share data and strategies and provide continuity across schools.

There is no shortcut for this problem-solving process. If teachers are to use the data to change their teaching behavior in the classroom, they must understand the rationale for the change, be adequately equipped with skills and materials to make the change, and have follow-up support that considers the extent to which the change was made and the resulting improvement (or lack of improvement) in student performance.

School psychologists can also consider potential trouble spots in the system where vulnerable children are not experiencing success at the desired level. Frequently, vulnerable children include those who have recently moved into a district, who receive free or reduced lunch, and who performed in the risk range on a previous screening. The school psychologist can assist in verifying that the system plans and deploys support for these struggling children and in providing a follow-up analysis of the extent to which the support is working. The school psychologist is an ideal person to consider a helicopter view of learning and to organize data to identify targets for improvement at the systems level. Innovative leadership actions might include, for example, considering the scope of expected learning goals across multiple grade levels and of strategic actions that last more than a year to reduce the deleterious effects of between-school transitions and to promote greater learning success.

If systemic problems are not detected, then the school psychologist can meet individually with teachers to share the results of the screening and the can't do/won't do assessments. The purpose of this discussion is to (a) summarize the findings and indicate that further assessment and possibly intervention will be recommended (in the case of a can't do problem) or (b) suggest contingencies to encourage more stable, high-quality performance (in the case of a won't do problem).

Step 8: Understand the Benefits and Limitations of Can't Do/Won't Do Assessment

An interaction occurs between student proficiency, assessment task difficulty, and sensitivity of the effect of incentives on performance. Users of the can't do/won't do assessment must be aware of the potential for the assessment task to be so challenging that it cannot detect a performance deficit. When can't do/won't do assessment is used as part of the universal screening decision, this distinction is unimportant. When the assessment is used for intervention planning, measuring the effect of reduced task difficulty with and without incentives is highly relevant to intervention planning (see Figure 20.4). Consistent with its intended purpose as a simple, useful filter for decision making, caution should be taken to not overinterpret the can't do/won't do assessment. The can't do/won't do assessment does not tell an assessment team that a child's performance will never be affected by contingencies. Depending on how it is used, an assessment team likely will not be able to tell if the child's performance changed as a result of familiarity with the task or of better understanding of task directions and fewer distractions. If performance was unimproved when students were given an opportunity to earn a reward, it is possible that the assessment was not valid because the task was too challenging (i.e., the measure is not sensitive to performance change that would occur if the task had been easier) or that a different set of reward options may have produced an improvement. A simple, streamlined interpretation could be that performance was not improved despite the incentives, so a skill-building intervention should be attempted, or that performance was improved to the not-at-risk range with the use of incentives, so a skill-building intervention is not indicated and instead a system of contingencies should be tried.

Research is needed to examine the stability of performance deficits over time, their amenability to intervention, and the odds of long-term academic failure for children showing both can't do and won't do problems in their schooling career. Figures 20.5 and 20.6 provide the percentage of students overall who were found to be in the risk group on a standardized measure of achievement from the VanDerHeyden et al. (2003) dataset, the percentage of won't do cases found to be at risk, and the percentage of can't do cases or cases found to improve with incentives but not to improve sufficiently to be ruled out as a can't do problem. Interestingly, risk of failure on both measures is higher for children whose performance does not improve to the not-at-risk range for incentives. This finding is an example of the types of questions researchers might ask to quantify the utility of the assessment and its value in predicting (and ultimately bringing about intervention to reduce) the odds of longer-term failure.

School psychologists should select the assessment process that yields adequate data upon which to base a decision in the most efficient way possible. If the can't do/won't do assessment is used as part of a larger

Figure 20.4. Interaction Between Task Difficulty, Student Proficiency, and the Sensitivity of the Can't Do/Won't Do Assessment

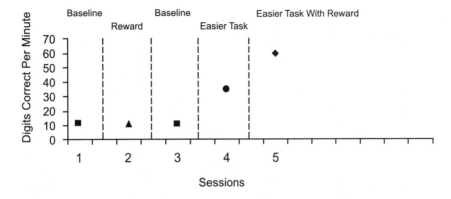

Note. From "Best Practices in Can't Do/Won't Do Assessment," by Amanda M. VanDerHeyden and Joseph C. Witt. In *Best Practices in School Psychology V*, by A Thomas and J. Grimes, 2008, Bethesda, MD: National Association of School Psychologists. Copyright 2008 by National Association of School Psychologists. Reprinted with permission.

package of an RTI model, then the brief version may be utilized efficiently and effectively (VanDerHeyden et al., 2003). If the school psychologist is conducting the assessment as part of individual intervention planning, then a more complicated analysis may be conducted (Daly et al., 1999), with the ultimate goal being to identify an intervention that will work for the child when that intervention is correctly used. Won't do behavior or performance problems cause variable performance trends and create errors in program or intervention

evaluation. Including an assessment like the can't do/won't do assessment is particularly important (and often overlooked) in research studies and program evaluation projects. Undetected performance deficits create noise in the data that can cause evaluation teams to underestimate or overestimate a program's (or an intervention's) effects. Hence, school psychologists working with systems to evaluate programs and make recommendations should consider including a direct assessment like the can't do/won't do assessment in the

Figure 20.5. Percentage of All Students, Students With a Won't Do Problem, and Students With a Can't Do or Combined Can't Do/Won't Do Problem Performing in the At-Risk Range on the Woodcock-Johnson

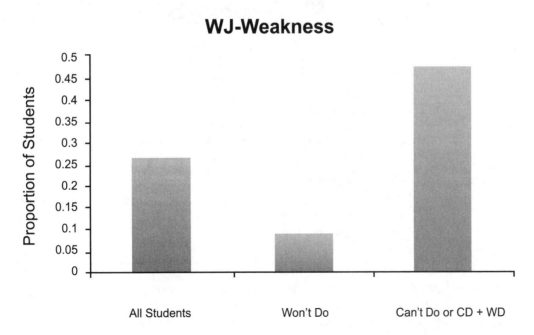

Figure 20.6. Percentage of All Students, Students With a Won't Do Problem, and Students With a Can't Do or Combined Can't Do/Won't Do Problem Performing in the At-Risk Range on the Iowa Test of Basic Skills (ITBS)

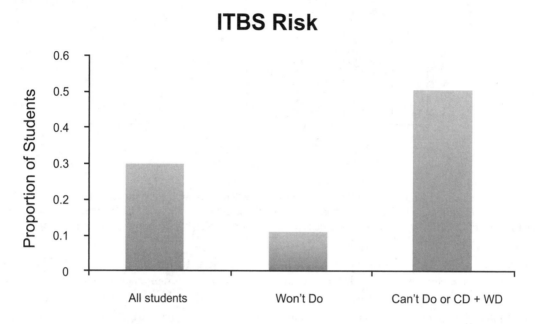

program evaluation. It is a time-efficient assessment that removes error associated with performance variability attributable to motivational variables as opposed to instruction.

SUMMARY

The can't do/won't do assessment is a time-efficient assessment that allows users to know whether a child's performance can be improved through the use of rewards and adjustment of performance contingencies or whether skill-building instruction is necessary. It is a simple behavioral concept that is useful for creating homogeneous groups of children and matching students with interventions that are likely to be effective. The assessment is recommended as a follow-up to universal screening, and results can be used to filter out children in need of performance contingencies (i.e., won't do) from those who require skill-building intervention (i.e., can't do). Use of the can't do/won't do assessment can facilitate systems-level decision making in evaluating programs of instruction because it can be used to reduce instability in student performance caused by performance deficits.

The can't do/won't do assessment is a technique that is broadly related to the ideal of creating and sustaining learning environments that assist learners to put forth their best learning effort, to demonstrate sustained attention and engagement, and to use cognitive skills to govern their choices in the classroom such that they experience longer term learning success.

AUTHOR NOTE

Disclosure. Amanda M. VanDerHeyden has a financial interest in books she authored or coauthored referenced in this chapter.

REFERENCES

Daly, E. J., III, Martens, B. K., Hamler, K. R., Dool, E. J., & Eckert, T. L. (1999). A brief experimental analysis for identifying instructional components needed to improve oral reading fluency. *Journal of Applied Behavior Analysis, 32*, 83–94. doi:10.1901/jaba. 1999.32-83

Deno, S. L., & Mirkin, P. K. (1977). *Data-based program modification: A manual.* Reston, VA: Council for Exceptional Children.

Duckworth, A. L. (2011). The significance of self-control. *Proceedings of the National Academy of Sciences, 108*, 2639–2640. doi:10.1073/pnas. 1019725108

Duhon, G. J., Noell, G. H., Witt, J. C., Freeland, J. T., Dufrene, B. A., & Gilbertson, D. N. (2004). Identifying academic skill and performance deficits: The experimental analysis of brief assessments of academic skills. *School Psychology Review, 33*, 429–443.

Hattie, J. (2009). *Visible learning: A synthesis of over 800 meta-analyses relating to achievement.* New York, NY: Routledge.

Kovaleski, J., VanDerHeyden, A., & Shapiro, E. (2013). *Comprehensive evaluation of learning disabilities: A response-to-intervention approach.* New York, NY: Guilford Press.

Lentz, F. E., & Shapiro, E. S. (1986). Functional assessment of the academic environment. *School Psychology Review, 15,* 346–357.

Noell, G. H., Gansle, K. A., Witt, J. C., Whitmarsh, E. L., Freeland, J. T., LaFleur, L. H., … Northup, J. (1998). Effects of contingent reward and instruction on oral reading performance at differing levels of passage difficulty. *Journal of Applied Behavior Analysis, 31,* 659–663. doi:10.1901/jaba.1998.31-659

Shinn, M. R. (Ed.). (1989). *Curriculum-based measurement: Assessing special children.* New York, NY: Guilford Press.

Shoda, Y., Mischel, W., & Peake, P. K. (1990). Predicting adolescent cognitive and self-regulatory competencies from preschool delay of gratification: Identifying diagnostic conditions. *Developmental Psychology, 26,* 978–986.

Slavin, R. E., & Lake, C. (2008). Effective programs in elementary mathematics: A best-evidence synthesis. *Review of Educational Research, 78,* 427–515.

VanDerHeyden, A. M., McLaughlin, T., Algina, J., & Snyder, P. (2012). Randomized evaluation of a supplemental grade-wide mathematics intervention. *American Educational Research Journal, 49,* 1251–1284. doi:10.3102/0002831212462736

VanDerHeyden, A. M., Witt, J. C., & Gilbertson, D. A. (2007). Multi-year evaluation of the effects of a response-to-intervention (RTI) model on identification of children for special education. *Journal of School Psychology, 45,* 225–256. doi:10.1016/j.jsp.2006.11.004

VanDerHeyden, A. M., Witt, J. C., & Naquin, G. (2003). Development and validation of a process for screening referrals to special education. *School Psychology Review, 32,* 204–227.

APPENDIX. INSTRUCTIONS FOR THE CAN'T DO/WON'T DO ASSESSMENT

Materials needed: probes with student's name, student's teacher's name, and date printed at the top; treasure chest.

Math

1. Greet the student by saying, "We're going to do some math today."
2. Say, "The last time you did this math worksheet, you scored _____ digits correct."
3. Say, "Today, I'm going to give you an opportunity to do this worksheet again. If you can beat your score, then you can pick anything you like from the treasure chest."
4. Show the student the treasure chest. Allow the student to briefly sample items in the treasure chest.
5. Say, "Do you see anything in there that you would like to earn?" If the student does not seem excited about any of the items in the treasure chest, you may offer free time, outside time, a visit with his or her favorite teacher, or get the student to nominate something reasonable.

6. Say, "This is a math worksheet. All of the problems are _____ (addition, subtraction, multiplication, division). When I say start, you may begin answering the problems. Start on the first problem on the left on the top row (*point to the problem*). Work across and then go to the next row. Do you have any questions?"
7. Say, "Start." Wait 2 minutes.
8. Monitor the student's performance to ensure that the student works the problems in rows and does not skip around or answer only the easy problems.
9. Say, "Stop."
10. Count the number of digits correct. If the student increased his or her score by one digit, then allow the student to select something from the treasure chest. If the student did not increase his or her score by one digit, then do not allow the student to make a selection from the treasure chest.

Writing

1. Greet the student by saying, "We're going to do some writing today."
2. Say, "The last time you wrote a story with your class, you wrote _____ words."
3. Say, "Today, I'm going to give you an opportunity to write another story. If you can write more words this time than you did last time, then you can pick anything you like from the treasure chest."
4. Show the student the treasure chest. Allow the student to briefly sample items in the treasure chest.
5. Say, "Do you see anything in there that you would like to earn?" If the student does not seem excited about any of the items in the treasure chest, you may offer free time, outside time, a visit with his or her favorite teacher, or get the student to nominate something reasonable.
6. Say, "This is a writing assignment. Turn your paper over and you will see a sentence at the top of the page. You will be writing a story using this sentence. You will have 1 minute to think about what you would like to write. Do not begin writing until I say begin. Do you have any questions?"
7. Say, "This is your think time."
8. Wait 1 minute.
9. Say, "Start." Wait 3 minutes.
10. Say, "Stop."
11. Count the number of words written. If the student increased his or her score by one digit, then allow the student to select something from the treasure

chest. If the student did not increase his or her score by one digit, then do not allow the student to make a selection from the treasure chest.

Reading

1. Greet the student by saying, "We're going to do some reading today."
2. Say, "The last time you read this story, you read _____ words correctly."
3. Say, "Today, I'm going to give you an opportunity to read this story again. If you can read more words this time than you did last time, then you can pick anything you like from the treasure chest."
4. Show the student the treasure chest. Allow the student to briefly sample items in the treasure chest.
5. Say, "Do you see anything in there that you would like to earn?" If the student does not seem excited about any of the items in the treasure chest, you may offer free time, outside time, a visit with his or her favorite teacher, or get the student to nominate something reasonable.

6. Say, "When I say start, begin reading aloud at the top of the page. Read across the page (*demonstrate by pointing*). Try to read each word. If you come to a word that you do not know, I will tell it to you. The goal is for you to read as many words as you can correctly in 1 minute. Be sure to do your best reading. Do you have any questions?"
7. Say, "Start." Allow the student to read for 1 minute. Follow along on your copy, marking the words that are read incorrectly. If the student pauses on a word, wait only 3 seconds, tell the student the word, and move on.
8. After 1 minute say, "Stop reading." Draw a vertical line after the last word read. Thank the student for reading.
9. Count the number of words read correctly and number of errors. Errors are words that are not pronounced correctly and, thus, include skipped words, mispronounced words, substitutions, and words that you have to tell the student. Additions (i.e., words the student adds to the story) are not counted as errors.

James J. Mazza
University of Washington

21 Best Practices in Clinical Interviewing Parents, Teachers, and Students

OVERVIEW

Conducting assessments is a major pillar within the framework of responsibilities that are part of a school psychologist's job (Sattler & Hoge, 2006). In fact, it would be nearly impossible for a school psychologist to function on a daily basis without utilizing either direct or indirect assessment information. Thus, school psychologists are continually updating and refining their assessment skills in order to provide the most appropriate data-based decision making in determining school-based interventions, behavioral strategies, and consultation while working with school personnel, students, and their families. The value of these skills is highlighted in the National Association of School Psychologists (NASP) *Model for Comprehensive and Integrated School Psychological Services* (NASP, 2010) and aligns with the domain of Data-Based Decision Making and Accountability. This chapter will focus on the utility of these skills through a multitiered approach with the emphasis on assessment.

The importance of conducting high-quality assessments that yield accurate information cannot be overstated. The implementation of any treatment or intervention program for students is based on an accurate assessment of the problem. Given that assessment is the foundation of the intervention process, school psychologists need to design their assessment procedures to include multiple environments (i.e., home, school, and with peers) and multiple informants (i.e., parents, teachers, and the students themselves) based on a theoretical perspective or model for integrating the assessment information. One such perspective is the ecological–transactional model (Overstreet & Mazza, 2003), which is based on Bronfenbrenner's (1977) ecological systems theory and Belsky's (1980) ecological perspectives model. The utility of the ecological–transactional model for school psychologists in regard to assessment is briefly discussed below.

The ecological–transactional model is based on Bronfenbrenner's (1977) theory and utilizes the system levels of ontogenic, microsystem, mesosystem, exosystem, and macrosystem. However, school psychologists primarily focus on the first two levels. The ontogenic level focuses on the characteristics of the child, and the microsystem level focuses on the immediate environments that encompass the child, such as school, family, and peers. The remaining levels beyond the microsystem expand to account for the system-to-system interrelationships and community to societal interactions, which tend to be outside the typical assessment practice of school psychologists.

The ecological–transactional model also integrated Belsky's (1980) ecological perspective, which focuses on the interrelationships between the ontogenic and microsystem levels, highlighting the importance of the bidirectional relationships across levels. Overstreet's and Mazza's (2003) ecological–transactional model illustrates the interconnectedness between the ontogenic and microsystem levels and addresses why assessment information that focuses on the interrelationships between the two levels is important. Thus, in order to conduct best practices in assessment, the methodology of gathering data needs to account for the bidirectional relationships among the student and his or her microsystem environments or settings. Although there are numerous assessment techniques and measures that can accomplish this task (e.g., self-report measures, behavioral observation, teacher and parent report measures), this chapter will focus on the single assessment method: the clinical interview.

The clinical interview offers one of the most powerful assessment tools within the school psychologist's arsenal (Busse & Beaver, 2000). Sattler and Mash (1998) define a clinical assessment interview as "an interview designed to obtain information about an interviewee's behavior, temperament, and personality" (p. 3). Busse and Beaver (2000) refer to interviewing as "a hallmark of assessment processes and perhaps the most common method used to obtain information to evaluate individuals" (p. 235). However, as with all assessment methods, there are strengths and weaknesses that need to be addressed. This chapter will focus on the different aspects of clinical interviewing, including the different types of clinical interviews for parents, teachers, and students. In addition, this chapter will cover topic domains for each informant, the different functions of interviewing based on a three-tiered model, interpretation of discrepant data, situation-specific interviews, and challenges of conducting clinical interviews.

BASIC CONSIDERATIONS

Before discussing the aspects of the clinical interview itself, there are several basic considerations that need to be examined before an interview should take place. First, as essential and unique as clinical interviews are in collecting data, they are only one method of a multimethod (i.e., self-report measures, direct observation, parent rating scales) comprehensive assessment. Many researchers have stressed the importance of conducting multimethod assessments across multiple environments (McConaughy, 2013; Whitcomb & Merrell, 2012). This is consistent with the ontogenic and microsystem levels of the ecological–transactional model highlighted above. With that said, it is important to examine the strengths and weaknesses of clinical interviews in the context of a multimethod assessment.

Strengths and Weaknesses of Clinical Interviews

The ability to collect data using a clinical interview has multiple benefits, especially in the context of a multi-tiered approach.

Strengths of Clinical Interviews
The clinical interview structure often allows greater flexibility than other methods for the school psychologist

to ask follow-up questions regarding the severity, frequency, and chronicity of the problem; the environment in which the situation occurs; and/or information that is not available via observation or other informant report (i.e., internalizing disorders). When information is obtained through the clinical interview process, the ability to immediately follow up and gather additional important details as they directly relate to current intervention strategies is easily facilitated. This is important when obtaining information for why a Tier 2 intervention is not working or if the level of services at Tier 3 is effective.

Along similar lines, a second benefit of using clinical interviews is being able to identify the underlying causes of behavior, such as thoughts and cognitions, that may lead to mental health problems such as anxiety or depression. It is the ability to assess the frequency and severity of the underlying causes of behavior that differentiate clinical interviewing from behavioral interviewing (Busse & Beaver, 2000). Given that anxiety and depression are the most prevalent mental health problems experienced by adolescents and children (Whitcomb & Merrell, 2012), being able to determine the frequency and severity of these underlying thoughts and cognitions is important for intervention purposes (Cook, Burns, Browning-Wright, & Gresham, 2011). Thus, clinical interviewing offers a strong tool for high-stakes data-based decision making for intervention evaluations at the Tier 3 level while also identifying co-occurring issues.

A third advantage of using clinical interviews is that it provides an opportunity to establish rapport and develop trust with the interviewee (Sattler & Hoge, 2006). Establishing rapport is often beneficial when the parent, teacher, and student are asked to implement intervention strategies based on the assessment information. Thus, the clinical interview provides an opportunity to establish a working relationship that may act as an early buy-in to subsequent interventions.

Weaknesses of Clinical Interviews
As stated above, clinical interviews are not without their challenges. One significant disadvantage of clinical interviews is their relatively low rates of reliability and validity compared to other methods, especially if the interviewer has not been trained (Sattler & Hoge 2006). Sources of error in clinical interviews include interviewee and interviewer biases, such as the attitude of the interviewee toward the interviewer and excessive or inappropriate questioning regarding a specific topic. These biases may lead to

inaccurate conclusions and thus ineffective interventions (Cook et al., 2011).

Second, cross-informant discrepancies are frequent and pose a challenge to school psychologists trying to understand the true nature of the behavioral issues involved. For example, a clinical interview with a teacher may identify attention problems as the significant student behavior problem, while a similar interview with the student's parents does not.

A third challenge is that specific informants within the interview process may be more accurate reporters than others, depending on the behavior of concern. For example, if the identified problem of the student is noncompliant and aggressive behavior, then the clinical interview with the student is likely to underreport the frequency and severity of the issues, and thus relying on the parent and teacher interviews may provide more accurate information (Whitcomb & Merrell, 2012). The opposite is likely true when the identified concern is an internalizing behavior such as depression or suicidal behavior, where the student is more likely to provide more accurate information than the parents and teachers (Mazza & Reynolds, 2008). Implications regarding cross-informant discrepancy are discussed later in this chapter.

Fourth, conducting clinical interviews is resource intensive, meaning that interviews are often conducted one-on-one and take up a substantial amount of time. Because the multitiered approach, such as response to intervention (RTI), is designed to be time efficient, the use of clinical interviews often occurs at the Tier 3 level (Cook et al., 2011). Thus, the decision to use clinical interviews needs to be balanced with the unique data from clinical interviews and the time premium of the school psychologist.

The final challenge regarding clinical interviews is the need for training. Similar to other comprehensive assessment measures, such as cognitive and academic batteries, formal training is necessary for several types of clinical interviews. This is especially true of clinical interviews that are structured and semistructured, where adhering to scoring rules applies and interrater reliability has been established with the trainer (Whitcomb & Merrell, 2012). Receiving formal training in clinical interviews that provide diagnostic classification or assessment of high-risk youth cannot be overstated, along with the ethical implications of not doing so.

Types of Clinical Interviews

There are three types of clinical interviews that are used by school psychologists: structured, semistructured, and unstructured (Whitcomb & Merrell, 2012). There are advantages and disadvantages to each type.

Structured Clinical Interviews

Structured clinical interviews are standardized methods for asking questions and subsequent follow-up questions based on the informant's responses (Whitcomb & Merrell, 2012). They were first used predominately in psychiatric settings to provide diagnostic classification, but their use has since broadened to other settings and applications (Whitcomb & Merrell, 2012). Structured clinical interviews are designed with a specific purpose (i.e., diagnosis using the *Diagnostic and Statistical Manual of Mental Disorders*, 5th ed. [DSM-5]; American Psychiatric Association [APA], 2013), are highly scripted, have scoring rules, and require extensive training. Two of the most common structured clinical interviews used with children and adolescents that school psychologists may be familiar with are the Diagnostic Interview Schedule for Children–Version IV (Shaffer, Fisher, Lucas, Dulcan, & Schwab-Stone, 2000) and the Diagnostic Interview for Children and Adolescents–IV (Reich, Welner, & Herjanic, 1999).

Advantages. There are numerous advantages to structured clinical interviews (Whitcomb & Merrell, 2012). Among the clinical interviews, they are likely to have the strongest psychometric properties in terms of reliability and validity. The highly scripted nature of the interview itself and the requirement of extensive training minimizes interviewer biases and is more likely to produce consistent administration of the interview. Second, structured clinical interviews tend to be broad based in nature, allowing for multiple diagnoses to be made that more accurately reflect the issue of comorbidity that is present among the disorders in children and adolescents (Whitcomb & Merrell, 2012). Although capturing the comorbidity of symptomatology is important, many of the structured clinical interviews have specific modules or sections that can be used if specific issues are already known and are the focus of the assessment. This ability to provide focused, structured clinical interviews reduces the time commitment for completion, which is viewed as another advantage.

Disadvantages. There are several disadvantages to structured clinical interviews. First, they require extensive training to acquire the competency or mastery level necessary to adequately use the assessment tool. Second, the administration of the interview to an informant is approximately 60–90 minutes and is time consuming (Sattler & Hoge, 2006). Maintaining a child's attention for a 60- to 90-minute structured clinical interview can prove challenging. Third, they are often used for making diagnostic decisions, whereas school psychologists tend to be focused more on intervention-based decision making that aligns with a multitiered model of services. Given the three disadvantages mentioned above, the day-to-day use of structured clinical interviews by school psychologists needs to be well thought out.

Semistructured Clinical Interviews

Semistructured clinical interviews have some standardized procedures that must be followed but also allow for flexibility for the interviewer to ask additional clarifying questions based on the informant's responses (Whitcomb & Merrell, 2012). Follow-up questions may focus on severity, frequency, and chronicity if behavioral and/or mental health issues are the focus, while other questions may focus on the effectiveness of a particular intervention when interviewing parents and/or teachers. There are numerous semistructured clinical interviews that are available for school psychologists to use, such as the Schedule for Affective Disorders and Schizophrenia–School Age–Present State Version (Ambrosini & Dixon, 1996) and the Semistructured Clinical Interview for Children and Adolescents (McConaughy & Achenbach, 2001).

Advantages. The advantages of the semistructured clinical interviews are numerous. First and foremost, compared to the structured clinical interviews, the semistructured clinical interviews are used much more frequently by school psychologists in their day-to-day schedules. Owing to their flexibility, semistructured clinical interviews can be more readily adapted for intervention-focused issues found at the higher Tier 2 and Tier 3 levels, which is where school psychologists tend to spend the majority of their time (Cook et al., 2011). Second, semistructured clinical interviews can range from broadband-type assessments such as the Semistructured Clinical Interview for Children and Adolescents (McConaughy & Achenbach, 2001) or be used to focus on very specific or narrowband, at-risk behaviors such as suicide, like the Suicidal Behavior Interview (Reynolds, 1989). Third, because semistructured clinical interviews can be narrowly focused while also providing flexibility in questioning, they are often viewed as a good assessment tool to gather more information regarding issues identified in the broad-based assessment or to revise ongoing treatment

strategies and interventions (Cook et al., 2011). Finally, semistructured clinical interviews are frequently accompanied with moderate to strong psychometric properties of reliability and validity (Whitcomb & Merrell, 2012).

Disadvantages. For all of their advantages and utility, semistructured clinical interviews also have some disadvantages. First, semistructured clinical interviews require training to become adherent to the scoring, coding, and interviewing format in regard to follow-up questions. Although training takes time and financial resources, it does help establish a mastery or competency level that increases the reliability and validity of the assessment results. Second, semistructured clinical interviews are often conducted one-on-one and vary greatly in their time to complete. Thus, school psychologists need to be strategic in their application and use. Finally, consistency across interviewers is difficult to establish, especially if training is minimal, as one interviewer may ask follow-up questions in one area while another does not (Sattler & Hoge, 2006). This disadvantage is related to the weak reliability and validity found for some semistructured clinical interviews (Sattler & Hoge, 2006).

Unstructured Clinical Interviews

Unstructured clinical interviews do not have an established format or framework. Rather, they are viewed as highly flexible and individualized to the student, situation, and intervention. Although the name implies that there is no focus or direction to the interview, it is a bit misleading. Unstructured clinical interviews remain part of the assessment battery for school psychologists when they need to identify the problem area or concern before conducting the clinical interview. Thus, the referral issue helps guide the direction and questions for the unstructured clinical interview (Busse & Beaver, 2000).

Advantages. There are several major advantages to unstructured clinical interviews. First, the school psychologist can adapt the interview to follow whatever issues arise during the interview. This type of format allows current issues or difficulties to take precedence over other standardized questions and structures. Thus, the unstructured clinical interview is individualized. Second, unstructured clinical interviews do not require formal training, which saves on time and financial resources, although it should be noted that training in how to conduct clinical interviews in general is still recommended (McConaughy, 2013). Finally, given that each unstructured clinical interview is individualized, there are cost-saving benefits for the school districts because the districts are not purchasing protocols or standardized questionnaire packets.

Disadvantages. First, the consistency of the assessment across time is problematic and is subject to the temporal events of the administrator. Thus, using findings from one unstructured clinical interview may be different than from the same interview conducted a week later due to the lack of consistency by the interviewer. Similarly, the lack of consistency across interviewers results in poor psychometric properties for the assessment measure. Finally, the results of unstructured clinical interviews across different informants are hard to compare to each other because of the lack of standardized questions being asked across informants. This disadvantage may muddy the assessment result picture rather than help clarify it.

BEST PRACTICES IN CLINICAL INTERVIEWING OF PARENTS, TEACHERS, AND STUDENTS

Before conducting best practice assessments with clinical interviews, there are several important factors that need to be addressed beyond the basic considerations of the clinical interview methodology. These factors are based on questions that school psychologists need to address before conducting their clinical interviews.

What is the referral issue or area of concern? Within the context of the ecological–transactional model, the referral issue needs to include not only the student's behavior or issues but also the different environments or microsystem levels that may be contributing to the referral issue. Furthermore, school psychologists are often presented with referral issues or concerns that have been already identified. However, there may be additional issues that are comorbid or precipitating factors that are unknown (Cook et al., 2011). Thus, the referral issue provides a starting point into the domain area that needs to be assessed and then will likely broaden to account for the interrelationships between the child and the microsystem environments. Beyond the identification of the domains, the nature of the referral issue or concern is used to help determine the weighted value of the informant's clinical interview information over others. The issue of weighting some clinical interview information over others is discussed later in this chapter.

What is the purpose of the interview? There are numerous types of clinical interviews that are designed for different purposes (McConaughy & Ritter, 2008), and the school psychologist needs to match the clinical interview with the intended purpose. The answer to this question will dictate the type of interview that may be used as well as the type of questions that will be asked. In addition, the purpose of the interview is also inclusive of the function of the interview, that is, how the information is going to be used. Some clinical interviews may be conducted to classify students into special education categories (i.e., emotional–behavioral disorder) or for making psychiatric diagnoses (i.e., depression), while other are designed to assist teachers in providing classroom-wide interventions (i.e., consultation). The structure of the clinical interview and the type of questions would be different based on the purpose.

What is the structure of the school setting? The structure of the school setting is important as it relates to the level or tier in which the problem is being identified. In using a multitiered model, such as RTI, the school psychologist is likely to be called upon when a student is experiencing a concern that has already been elevated to Tier 2 or Tier 3 (Cook et al., 2011). Determining whether the issue or concern is at Tier 2 or Tier 3 provides direction in the type of clinical interview necessary and also who the school psychologist may interview. For example, if a student at Tier 2 is shown to have motivational struggles based on the progress monitoring evaluation, a clinical interview with the general education teacher may focus on how to make revisions or adjustments to the current intervention strategy within the classroom. However, if the student is at Tier 3, then the school psychologist may conduct a thorough mental health assessment that includes a clinical interview designed to examine the student's depression and anxiety symptoms. Thus, the structure of the school setting can have an impact on the choice of informants who receive a clinical interview. This is consistent with the ecological–transactional model and the need to account for the microsystem-level environments.

What informants should be assessed using clinical interviews? The answer to this is dependent on several other questions that were stated earlier. In determining who should be assessed using clinical interviews, the school psychologist has to identify the presenting problem behavior or area of concern as well as the purpose of the clinical interview (Busse & Beaver, 2000). In most circumstances, the informants usually consist of the student, the parents, and the student's teacher (Whitcomb & Merrell, 2012). There are several important factors that also need to be considered regarding informants. First, many students have parents who live separately and thus an attempt to interview both parents should be made. In addition, some students' main caregiver is a stepparent or grandparent who would most likely represent the best informant of the student's home life (Busse & Beaver, 2000). Second, the age of the student is likely to influence the choice of the school informant. For students in elementary school, the homeroom or lead teacher would likely have the most contact with the student and have the most knowledge regarding academic issues and classroom behavior, and therefore would be identified as the teacher informant. For students in middle and high school, where students have multiple teachers, the informant may be the teacher who has the most exposure to the student, or it could be the teacher who witnesses the identified problem behaviors (Busse & Beaver).

Procedural Steps for Clinical Interviews

Once the different informants have been identified, then procedural information needs to be collected and the "pregame" plan needs to be developed before the clinical interview process begins (McConaughy, 2013; Whitcomb & Merrell, 2012). Procedural information refers to getting consent to conduct the clinical interviews. School psychologists should follow their district procedures in obtaining consent as they would for other assessment methodologies. As Busse and Beaver (2000) point out, this step should include written consent forms that are signed as a means for protecting the parents, the school psychologist, and the school. In addition, the process of getting informed consent may establish communication with the informant and build rapport, and this has been viewed as a necessary stage for the assessment process to proceed (Busse & Beaver).

A second procedural step is being proactive in determining the different types of questions or areas of information to be addressed with each informant. For example, questions regarding cooperating with peers and classroom involvement are most likely to be asked of the teacher, while questions of developmental milestones and medical history are best assessed with the parents (Whitcomb & Merrell, 2012). In addition, the pregame plan should involve preparation for addressing developmental issues (i.e., preschool or elementary children), multicultural factors, and language issues. For example, if the student informant is a first or second grader, establishing rapport before starting the assessment interview and allowing the student to have manipulatives, such as crayons and paper for drawing, are helpful in providing a more relaxed environment for the student, and this in turn increases the likelihood of getting more and accurate information (McConaughy, 2013). Thus, the pregame plan procedures are important to follow to increase the likelihood of high-quality interactions and in turn increase the validity of the clinical interview assessment information.

Conducting Clinical Interviews

Conducting clinical interviews that adhere to best practices may be dependent on various school district policies and varying roles and responsibilities that school psychologists may have within and across districts. With that said, and using the basic considerations mentioned in the last section, Table 21.1 provides a short list of what to do and what not to do regarding best practices

Table 21.1. What to Do and What Not to Do in Clinical Interviewing

What to Do	What Not to Do
• Do establish rapport	• Do not ask questions you already know the answer to
• Do explain the rules of confidentiality	• Limit the use of "wh" questions (e.g., what, why, when)
• Do sit at the level of the informant; thus, if the student is a young child, sitting at the same level as the child is important	• Do not expect children under the age of 6 to distinguish time of events
• Do use open-ended questions	• Do not use psychological jargon
• Do follow the lead of the informant	• Do not ask yes/no or closed-ended questions
• Do use your active listening skills (PACERS)	• Do not make judgments on answers
• For children, do use toys, props, or games to help them feel at ease	• Do not ask "why" questions to ascertain motives
• Do use illustrations or examples with children to help clarify a question	• Do not repeat the same question if a "silent" response is received
• Do respect the informant's defense mechanisms (i.e., silence or "I don't want to answer that question")	• Do not confront the informant

in clinical interviewing. In addition, Figure 21.1 provides a representation of the common elements found in clinical interviews as well as some of the unique domains that should be covered based on the informant. Table 21.1 and Figure 21.1 can be viewed as a complementary checklist or guideline to use in the process of conducting a clinical interview (details from each are expanded below).

The guidelines listed in Table 21.1 will become second nature after gaining some experience in conducting this type of assessment and deserve further discussion. As with other assessment methodologies, the purpose of conducting clinical interviews is to get reliable and valid information. One of the first things to do is to establish rapport with the individual before starting the interview and explain the nature of the interview, including the rules of confidentiality. In addition, there may be some initial anxiety a student or parent experiences once the interview starts, so respecting the interviewee's defense mechanisms and following his or her lead is important. Thus, if a child has a silent response to a question (i.e., defense

mechanism), there is no need to repeat the question, and it is best to simply move on to the next question. The use of open-ended questions usually provides more productive answers during the interview process while also helping the interviewee feel more at ease. On the flip side, do not ask a lot of "wh" (e.g., what, why, when) questions, because these questions can be answered with one or two words. Similarly, do not ask questions to which the answer is already known, and try to stay away from psychological jargon. When asking questions, try to remain affectively neutral, without making judgments or acting surprised regarding the answer to any question. When interviewing young children, ages 6 and under, do not expect their memories to distinguish dates, times, or events. Finally, remember that the clinical interview is an assessment method for gathering information and is time consuming for the interviewee as well, so thanking him or her for his or her time and information is warranted.

Figure 21.1 provides a set of common elements that should be present in a best practice clinical interview, regardless of the informant (Sattler & Hoge, 2006;

Figure 21.1. Clinical Interview Commonalities and Differences by Informant

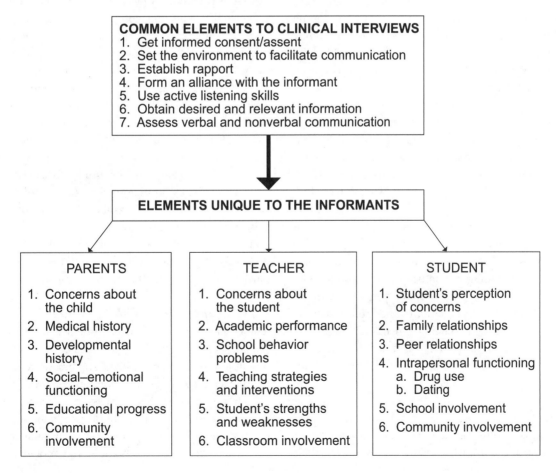

Whitcomb & Merrell, 2012). Figure 21.1 also shows the unique or cross-domain questions that an effective clinical interview should cover. For example, conducting a clinical interview with a student should include the ontogenic characteristics as well as the microsystem-level environmental factors, meaning asking questions about his or her relationship with parents, school, and peers. Details of the unique questions/domains for each informant are discussed in separate paragraphs below. It should be noted that Figure 21.1 is simply a guideline and that answers to some questions may direct the inquiry of the clinical interview to an area not represented in the figure. Thus, each clinical interview is likely to be unique, and a one-size-fits-all approach does not lend itself well to best practices in clinical interviewing.

Clinical Interview With Parents

The clinical interview with parents provides the school psychologist with an opportunity to get the parental perspective of the current situation as well as developmental information. Information that should be assessed in the clinical interview of parents includes the following (Whitcomb & Merrell, 2012): First, questions should cover parents' concerns about their child and what issues their child is currently struggling with. This provides the school psychologist not only with the identified problem or concern but also with nonverbal information (i.e., distress, anxiety, frustration, anger, and helplessness) through the parents' tone, pitch, and loudness. The second area to cover with parents is their child's medical history. Questions in this area should focus on any past or current medical issues that required intervention, especially regarding medications. The third is developmental history. This area examines the milestone developments such as when their child first began walking, talking, and reading as well as any complications during pregnancy and birth. The fourth area is social–emotional functioning, which is a broad category that includes such things as mental health issues, intimacy/dating relationships, drug and alcohol use, peer relationships (including bullying or victimization), and family involvement and relationships. Therefore, the school psychologist needs to assess each of these specific areas within the broader domain of social–emotional functioning. The fifth area is educational progress. Although this area will also be assessed by the teacher, the parent interview should cover questions regarding their child's attitude toward homework, difficulties in any classes or in completing school work, the parents' perception of how well their child is performing in school, and any future academic ambitions. Finally, the area of community involvement should be assessed. Questions in this area should include the student's involvement in any community sports teams or clubs, part-time jobs (for adolescents), volunteer work, religious activities, and relationships with extended family.

Clinical Interview With Teachers

The clinical interview with the student's teacher is also composed of multiple domains or areas of interest. Similar to the parent interview, the first area of questioning involves concerns about the student. Because the teacher sees the student in a different environment than the parents and often includes highly structured activities and rules of compliance, this line of questioning is likely to produce different information than that of the parent interview. The second area is academic performance, where the questions concentrate on different academic skills, abilities, and work completion. If academic issues are identified, follow-up questions determining if they are due to ability deficits or performance issues are important. The third area of questions focuses on the broad domain of school behavior problems. Questions in this domain should include discipline and compliance issues, relationships with classmates, peer group at school or lack thereof, and aggressive or antisocial behavior (i.e., bullying and bullying victimization). The fourth area is teacher strategies, and this would include interventions or strategies that have been implemented to address the student's difficulties or issues. In addition, the school psychologist needs to inquire about what interventions worked and which ones did not. The fifth area focuses on questions regarding the student's strengths and weaknesses. These questions assess academic areas or issues as well as listening skills, effort put forth in the classroom, and respect for teachers and fellow classmates. Finally, classroom involvement is a key domain to assess. Questions in this area involve classroom participation and volunteering to assist others.

Clinical Interview With Students

The clinical interview with a student is multifaceted in domains that are similar and unique compared to the parent and teacher interviews. The first area or domain of the clinical interview focuses on the student's perception of his or her own issues or concerns. This line of questions helps school psychologists gain a perspective of how the student views himself or herself and his or her current situation. It is not unusual for parents and teachers to identify concerns or problematic behaviors while the student perceives something completely different. The second area of inquiry revolves around family relationships. In this domain, questions include the quality of relationships with parents, siblings, and extended members; family routines and responsibilities; perceived family support; and perceived conflicts within the family. The third area to assess involves peer relationships, and this includes questions pertaining to the student's close friends and the activities they do together, perceived conflict with peers, ability to meet and maintain new friends, peer rejection (i.e., social isolation and loneliness), and perceived bullying. The fourth domain is interpersonal functioning, which is a broad category covering social–emotional well-being as well as developmental issues. The clinical interview questions for this area need to account for the student's developmental age, and thus questions for adolescents would likely look different than those for an elementary or preschool student. Questions in this area should address the student's perception of attributional strengths and weaknesses, emotional well-being (i.e., self-confidence, depression, anxiety, fears, anger, anti-social behavior), peculiar experiences if any (i.e., hearing voices or hallucinating), and identification of issues that are currently causing stress or emotional discomfort. For adolescents, additional questions should include topics of romantic relationships, dating, and drug and alcohol use. The fifth area revolves around school involvement such as current relationships to teachers (favorite and least favorite), attitudes toward school, interest in participating in school activities, impressions about academic performance (strengths and weaknesses), and any perceived issues or concerns at school. The last significant domain is community involvement. In this domain, questions should pertain to community sports or clubs, participation in any community volunteer experiences, engagement in any religious activities, part-time employment (for adolescents), and relationships with any community members.

Cross-Informant Disagreement

With three informants representing three sets of lenses and the interaction of the microsystem environments, it is not surprising that the amount of agreement among the informants is small to moderate. Achenbach, McConaughy, and Howell (1987) examined the amount of agreement or lack thereof across informants, and found that agreement across informant types was higher for elementary children than for adolescents and found

that undercontrolled (i.e., externalizing) behaviors had higher rater informant agreement than overcontrolled (i.e., internalizing) behaviors. Overall, across informant type agreement was low, especially with the student and other types of informants. These findings have been reproduced by subsequent work by Rønning et al. (2009). Taken together, these findings suggest that although agreement across informants can be minimal, the clinical relevancy of their information remains important and that the different informants can be accurate in their answers to the clinical interview questions even when the answers do not agree with each other.

The importance of cross-informant agreement and the lack thereof holds importance, especially in different contexts and across mental health issues. Several of the findings noted by Achenbach et al. (1987) deserve further discussion due to their importance in designing and implementing intervention programs.

The low relationship among informants compared to the student regarding concerns or behaviors that are considered internalizing disorders or symptomatology (i.e., depression, anxiety, and suicidal behavior) should not be too surprising. Given that internalizing disorders and symptomatology by nature cannot be seen or observed readily by others, it would make clinical sense that parent and teacher reports of such behaviors may not agree with what the student reports. In situations like these, the information gleaned from the student would likely be weighted more regarding developing and implementing intervention programs that would be based on the student-reported frequency, severity, and chronicity. This overweighting of the student's report becomes very important when the identified concern is depression and suicidal behavior (Mazza & Reynolds, 2008). Interestingly, experts in the field of assessment via clinical interviews have special protocols and follow-up questions that are student focused when the issue or concern is suicidal behavior (Miller & McConaughy, 2013; Whitcomb & Merrell, 2012). From a suicidal behavior perspective this is important, not only ethically but also in determining the suicidal risk and level of intervention that is required (Mazza & Reynolds, 2008).

In contrast, information provided by students regarding externalizing-type behaviors or symptomatology, such as conduct disorder, oppositional defiant disorder, and bullying behavior, tend to be underreported (McConaughy, 2013). Thus, parent and teacher information from the clinical interviews tends to be weighted more for intervention programming and determining what level of intervention is needed. One explanation for this finding may be that parents and teachers have a better understanding of what is considered appropriate behavior compared to students. In addition, teachers often have a good perspective of what range of behaviors are considered acceptable, as they have between 15 and 25 students of the same age in their classrooms and have multiple years of experience in working with students of this age.

Thus, the overall finding regarding cross-informant agreement suggests that the lack of agreement from the different informants/raters is more likely expected than not, especially when the issue or concern is behavioral (McConaughy, 2013). This is important to remember once all the data have been collected and the school psychologist is trying to synthesize the information.

Selected Clinical Interviews

Table 21.2 provides a list of clinical interviews that were selected based on their clinical importance, their psychometric characteristics, their use in schools, and

Table 21.2. Selected Clinical Interviews for Practicing School Psychologists

Name of Clinical Interview	Informant	Interview Type	Purpose	Domains
Semistructured Parent Interview	Parent	Semistructured	Tier 2 and Tier 3 reevaluation of the problem and intervention	• Concerns regarding child • Behavioral and emotional problems • Social functioning • School functioning • Medical and developmental history • Family relationships
Semistructured Teacher Interview	Teacher	Semistructured	Tier 2 and Tier 3 intervention evaluation and revisions for higher level of services	• Concerns regarding the child • School behavioral issues • Academic performance • School intervention for behavioral issues • Special services
ASEBA: Semistructured Clinical Interview for Children and Adolescents (parent and teacher interviews also available)	Student	Semistructured	Tier 2 and Tier 3 intervention evaluation and revisions for higher level of services, examines clinical syndrome scales and DSM-oriented scales	• Activities, school, job • Friends • Family relationships • Fantasies • Self-perception • Parent/teacher issues • Academic achievement • For ages 6–11: fine and gross motor skills • For ages 12–18: somatic complaints
Diagnostic Interview Schedule for Children–IV	Student/ parent	Structured	Tier 3, diagnostic	Assesses 30 different DSM diagnoses
Diagnostic Interview for Children and Adolescents–IV	Student/ parent	Structured	Tier 3, diagnostic	Assesses 28 different DSM diagnoses
K-Schedule for Affective Disorders and Schizophrenia–Present State	Student/ parent	Semistructured	Tier 3, diagnostic	Assesses 33 different DSM diagnoses
Autism Diagnostic Interview–Revised	Parent	Structured	Tier 3, diagnostic for autism	• Reciprocal social interactions • Communication and language • Repetitive, restricted
Suicidal Behavior Interview	Student	Semistructured	Tier 3, level of suicide risk	• Psychological distress • Presence of suicidal thoughts • Past suicide attempt

Note. ASEBA = Achenbach System of Empirically Based Assessment; DSM = *Diagnostic and Statistical Manual of Mental Disorders.*

their focus on different topics that are relevant to practicing school psychologists.

Semistructured Parent Interview

The Semistructured Parent Interview (McConaughy, 2004a) is a broadband, semistructured clinical interview that is composed of six domains that parents complete on their child. The domains are concerns about the child, behavioral or emotional problems, social functioning, school functioning, medical and developmental history, and family relations and home situation (McConaughy, 2004a, 2013). There are specific questions within each domain that provide structure for the administrator to assess the range of behaviors that comprise that domain. The domain of social functioning contains categorical items that examine mental health issues and antisocial behavior. For adolescents it contains issues of romantic relationships, drug/alcohol use, and trouble with the law. If items in this domain are positively endorsed, the interviewer is prompted to follow up with more detailed questions that are provided regarding the specific behavior area. The medical and developmental history domain items are also categorical, and if endorsed, follow-up questions are provided on the Child and Family Information Form (McConaughy & Achenbach, 2004). The Semistructured Parent Interview does not provide domain scores or an overall score, and thus is viewed as a guide to obtain important clinical information from the parent. This author did not find any psychometric data on the Semistructured Parent Interview, nor was it expected given the lack of quantitative scoring. The Semistructured Parent Interview does not require training, though McConaughy (2013) recommends that administrators be familiar with semistructured clinical interviewing techniques and standardized assessment procedures. McConaughy (2004a) suggests that interviewers select the domains of interest based on the referral issues and the areas not covered by the other assessment instruments (i.e., rating scales). The completion time is based on the number of domains selected by the administrator and the complexity of the issues being examined.

Semistructured Teacher Interview

The Semistructured Teacher Interview (McConaughy, 2004b) is a semistructured clinical interview that assesses six domains of a student from the teacher's perspective. The domains are concerns about the child, school behavior problems, academic performance, teaching strategies, school interventions for behavior problems, and special help/services (McConaughy, 2004b, 2013).

Within each domain are specific questions that guide the administrator through various topics. Items in the domains of teaching strategies, school interventions for behavior problems, and special help/services are categorical, with the teaching strategies domain seeking information regarding the impact of teaching strategies, the school interventions for behavior problems domain evaluating the use of current/future interventions, and the special help/services domain examining the presence or absence of specific special education and mental health services (McConaughy, 2004b, 2013). The Semistructured Teacher Interview does not provide domain scores or an overall score, and is viewed as a guide to obtain important clinical information from the teacher's perspective. This author did not find any psychometric data on the measure, nor was it expected given the lack of quantitative scoring. The administration time varies based on the number of domains being selected and the severity/complication of the concerns.

Semistructured Clinical Interview for Children and Adolescents

The Achenbach System of Empirically Based Assessment: Semistructured Clinical Interview for Children and Adolescents (McConaughy & Achenbach, 2001) is a broadband, semistructured clinical interview administered to the student that examines clinical syndrome scales as well as DSM-oriented scales. The Semistructured Clinical Interview for Children and Adolescents is part of a multiaxial approach that includes parent reports, teacher reports, cognitive assessment, physical assessment, and direct assessment of the child, which is where the Semistructured Clinical Interview for Children and Adolescents comes in. The Semistructured Clinical Interview for Children and Adolescents assesses nine different broad areas: activities, school and job; friends; family relations; fantasies; self-perception and feelings; parent/teacher-reported problems; achievement tests; for ages 6–11, fine and gross motor abnormalities; and for ages 12–18, somatic complaints, drug/alcohol use, and trouble with the law. The achievement test and screen for fine and gross motor skills are optional (McConaughy & Achenbach, 2001). The protocol provides structured questions that are asked of students (ages 6–18), with the interviewer recording responses on the protocol in the designated column. In addition, a second column on the protocol allows clinical observations to be recorded. Once the Semistructured Clinical Interview for Children and Adolescents is complete, the interviewer completes the observation and self-report forms based on the answers that were provided in the clinical interview. Thus, the protocol form itself is not scored but rather is used to obtain information that addresses behavioral issues and mental health concerns that correspond with items on the observation and self-report forms. The psychometric properties are well established and have been examined extensively and are reported in the manual (McConaughy & Achenbach, 2001). There is no formal training required. However, administrators should be trained in clinical interviewing techniques for children and adolescents and be well versed in standardized assessment procedures (McConaughy & Achenbach, 2001). The average administration time is 60–90 minutes, with additional time required to complete the follow-up observation and self-report forms.

Diagnostic Interview Schedule for Children–Version IV, Diagnostic Interview for Children and Adolescents–IV, and Schedule for Affective Disorders and Schizophrenia–School Age–Present State Version

The Diagnostic Interview Schedule for Children–Version IV (Shaffer et al., 2000), the Diagnostic Interview for Children and Adolescents–IV (Reich et al., 1999), and the Schedule for Affective Disorders and Schizophrenia–School Age–Present State Version (Ambrosini & Dixon, 1996) are clinical interviews that are based on DSM-IV (APA, 1994) and used to assess mental health symptomatology in children and adolescents. With the recently released DSM-5 (APA, 2013), these measures are likely to be updated to correspond to the new version. The Diagnostic Interview Schedule for Children–Version IV and the Diagnostic Interview for Children and Adolescents–IV are structured clinical interviews that follow standardized procedures in obtaining clinical information. The Schedule for Affective Disorders and Schizophrenia–School Age–Present State Version is a semistructured clinical interview that obtains similar diagnostic information. The Diagnostic Interview Schedule for Children–Version IV is composed of items that assess 30 different DSM-IV diagnoses, the Diagnostic Interview for Children and Adolescents–IV covers 28, and the Schedule for Affective Disorders and Schizophrenia–School Age–Present State Version covers 33. A noted feature of the Diagnostic Interview for Children and Adolescents–IV is the Stein-Reich Critical Items listing, which helps to identify students who are engaging in high-risk behaviors such as drug abuse, violent behaviors, and suicidal ideation (Reich et al., 1999).

The three clinical interviews share similarities regarding their use and application. The Diagnostic Interview for Children and Adolescents–IV and the Diagnostic Interview Schedule for Children–Version IV have computerized versions to aid in administration and scoring. All three interviews are designed to assess the child or adolescent as well as obtain information from the parent. Similarly, all three interviews (and their earlier versions) have been widely used in research studies with various clinical and nonclinical populations. Along with their use in research studies, the psychometric properties of each interview have extensive support and have been used with school-based samples. All three interviews require formal training and are time consuming to administer, with an average range of 60–90 minutes to complete (Reich et al., 1999), with some assessments taking 2 hours or longer depending on the amount of comorbidity.

Autism Diagnostic Interview–Revised

The area of autism and autism spectrum disorders (ASD) has gained a great deal of attention since 2000 (Gray, Tonge, & Sweeney, 2008) and has become a primary area of focus for preschool and elementary school assessment and interventions (Lecavalier et al., 2006). Because of the increased prevalence of ASD in children and subsequent increased responsibility for school psychologists in this area, ASD was identified as one domain that deserved additional attention.

Best practice in assessing ASD is usually conducted with two measures (Gray et al., 2008): an observation measure (e.g., Autism Direct Observation Scale; Lord et al., 2000) and a clinical interview (Autism Diagnostic Interview–Revised; Rutter, LeCouteur, & Lord, 2003). The clinical interview is of interest here, and in particular the Autism Diagnostic Interview–Revised, which is widely accepted as the gold standard clinical interview in assessing ASD (Gray et al., 2008). The Autism Diagnostic Interview–Revised is a semistructured clinical interview that focuses on three primary domains: quality of reciprocal social interactions; communication and language; and repetitive, restricted, and stereotyped patterns of behavior (Gray et al., 2008). Scores are based on the Receiver Operating Characteristics for each domain with different cutoff scores for individuals with speech and without it. The psychometric data are excellent with children ages 5 and older (Lecavalier et al., 2006), with some limitations of its use for children under age 4.5 (Gray et al., 2008). On the challenging side, it does require formal training, with interrater reliability coefficients between .69 and .95

across different domains being cited in research studies (Lecavalier et al., 2006). In addition, completing it is time consuming, with studies reporting between 1.5 and 3 hours (Lecavalier et al., 2006).

Suicidal Behavior Interview

The area of youth suicidal behavior was selected given that suicides rank as the third leading cause of death among high school adolescents (15–19 years old) and fourth leading cause of death among middle school students (10–14 years old; Centers for Disease Control and Prevention, 2013), yet school psychologists receive little if any training in talking to or assessing suicidal youth (Mazza & Reynolds, 2008). Although the problem of adolescent suicidal behavior has not gone unnoticed, the problem persists that very few school psychologists have received formal training in conducting risk assessments using clinical interviews and/or working with suicidal youth.

There have been numerous instruments that have been developed to assess youth suicidal behavior (Reynolds, 1989), with the vast majority being self-report measures. Of the few clinical interviews that have been developed, only a small portion has been tested on school-based populations (Goldston, 2003). Goldston provides an extensive review of suicidal behavior assessment instruments that have been administered to children and adolescents. According to this review, the Suicidal Behavior Interview (Reynolds, 1989) was identified as the one semistructured clinical interview that focused on the continuum of suicidal behavior and reported strong psychometric data among school-age children and adolescents. It is composed of three different domains: general psychological distress, presence of suicidal thoughts (i.e., plan, intent, and steps toward making an attempt), and seriousness and recency of a past suicide attempt. Formal training is required in using the Suicidal Behavior Interview, with interrater reliabilities of .95–.99 being reported in research studies (Reynolds & Mazza, 1999). The time to complete the Suicidal Behavior Interview varies based on the level of severity of suicidal behavior. However, most interviews can be completed within 15 to 25 minutes (Reynolds & Mazza, 1999).

SUMMARY

The use of clinical interviews to obtain information from parents, teachers, and students is an important tool for school psychologists to learn and use as part of conducting comprehensive assessments. This chapter explained the situational context in which to use clinical interviews within a multitiered system and how that information should be viewed within a multidimensional assessment approach. The unique information that can be gathered by using clinical interviewing methodology is extremely important and cannot be overstated.

REFERENCES

Achenbach, T. M., McConaughy, S. H., & Howell, C. T. (1987). Child/adolescent behavioral and emotional problems: Implications of cross-informant correlations for situational specificity. *Psychological Bulletin, 101,* 213–232.

Ambrosini, P. J., & Dixon, J. F. (1996). *Schedule for Affective Disorders and Schizophrenia for School Aged Children-Present version, Version IVR (K-SADS-P IVR)*. Unpublished instrument. Philadelphia, PA: Medical College of Pennsylvania, Eastern Pennsylvania Psychiatric Institute.

American Psychiatric Association. (1994). *Diagnostic and statistical manual of mental disorders* (4th ed.). Washington, DC: Author.

American Psychiatric Association. (2013). *Diagnostic and statistical manual of mental disorders* (5th ed.). Arlington, VA: Author.

Belsky, J. (1980). Child maltreatment: An ecological integration. *American Psychologist, 35,* 320–335.

Bronfenbrenner, U. (1977). Toward an experimental ecology of human development. *American Psychologist, 32,* 513–531.

Busse, R. T., & Beaver, B. R. (2000). Informant report: Parent and teacher interviews. In E. S. Shapiro & T. R. Kratochwill (Eds.), *Conducting school-based assessments of child and adolescent behavior* (pp. 235–273). New York, NY: Guilford Press.

Centers for Disease Control and Prevention. (2013). *Injury prevention and control: Data and statistics.* Atlanta, GA: Author. http://www.cdc.gov/injury/wisqars/LeadingCauses.html

Cook, C. R., Burns, M. K., Browning-Wright, D., & Gresham, F. M. (2011). *A guide to refining and retooling school psychological practice in the era of RTI.* Palm Beach, FL: LRP.

Goldston, D. B. (2003). *Measuring suicidal behavior and risk in children and adolescents.* Washington, DC: American Psychological Association.

Gray, K. M., Tonge, B. T., & Sweeney, D. J. (2008). Using the Autism Diagnostic Interview–Revised and the Autism Diagnostic Observation Schedule with young children with developmental delay: Evaluating diagnostic validity. *Journal of Autism and Developmental Disorders, 38,* 657–667.

Lecavalier, L., Aman, M. G., Scahill, L., McDougle, C. J., McCracken, J. T., Vitiello, B., … Kau, A. S. M. (2006). Validity of the Autism Diagnostic Interview–Revised. *American Journal on Mental Retardation, 3,* 199–215.

Lord, C., Risi, S., Lambrecht, L., Cook, E. H., Leventhal, B. L., DiLavore, P. C., … Rutter, M. (2000). The Autism Diagnostic Observation Schedule-Generic: A standard measure of social and communication deficits associated with the spectrum of autism. *Journal of Autism and Developmental Disorders, 30,* 205–223.

Mazza, J. J., & Reynolds, W. M. (2008). School-wide approaches to intervention with depression and suicide. In B. Doll & J. A. Cummings (Eds.), *Transforming school mental health services: Population-based approaches to promoting the competency and wellness of children* (pp. 213–241. A joint publication with the National Association of School Psychologists). Thousand Oaks, CA: Corwin Press.

McConaughy, S. H. (2004a). *Semistructured Parent Interview*. Burlington, VT: University of Vermont, Research Center for Children, Youth, and Families.

McConaughy, S. H. (2004b). *Semistructured Teacher Interview*. Burlington, VT: University of Vermont, Research Center for Children, Youth, and Families.

McConaughy, S. H. (2013). *Clinical interviews for children and adolescents: Assessment to intervention* (2nd ed.). New York, NY: Guilford Press.

McConaughy, S. H., & Achenbach, T. M. (2001). *Manual for the Semistructured Clinical Interview for Children and Adolescents* (2nd ed.). Burlington, VT: University of Vermont, Research Center for Children, Youth, and Families.

McConaughy, S. H., & Achenbach, T. M. (2004). *Child and Family Information Form*. Burlington, VT: University of Vermont, Research Center for Children, Youth, and Families.

McConaughy, S. H., & Ritter, D. R. (2008). Best practice in multimethod assessment and emotional and behavioral disorders. In A. Thomas & J. Grimes (Eds.), *Best practice in school psychology V* (pp. 687–715). Bethesda, MD: National Association of School Psychologists.

Miller, D. N., & McConaughy, S. H. (2013). *Assessing risk for suicide. In S. H. McConaughy, Clinical interviews for children and adolescents: Assessment to intervention (2nd ed.)*. New York, NY: Guilford Press.

National Association of School Psychologists. (2010). *Model for comprehensive and integrated school psychological services*. Bethesda, MD: Author. Retrieved from http://www.nasponline.org/standards/2010standards/2_PracticeModel.pdf

Overstreet, S., & Mazza, J. J. (2003). An ecological-transactional understanding of community violence: Theoretical perspectives. *School Psychology Quarterly, 18*, 66–87.

Reich, W., Welner, Z., & Herjanic, B. (1999). *Diagnostic Interview for Children and Adolescents–IV*. North Tonawanda, NY: Multi-Health Systems.

Reynolds, W. M. (1989). *Suicidal Behavior Interview. Unpublished instrument*. Madison, WI: University of Wisconsin.

Reynolds, W. M., & Mazza, J. J. (1999). Assessment of suicidal ideation in young inner-city youth: Reliability and validity of the Suicidal Ideation Questionnaire-JR. *School Psychology Review, 28*, 17–30.

Rønning, J. A., Sourander, A., Kumpulainen, K., Tammien, T., Niemela, S., Moilanen, I., … Almqvist, F. (2009). Cross-informant agreement about bullying and victimization among eight-year-olds: Whose information best predicts psychiatric caseness 10–15 years later? *Social Psychiatry and Psychiatric Epidemiology, 44*, 15–22.

Rutter, M., Le Couteur, A., & Lord, C. (2003). *Autism Diagnostic Interview–Revised*. Los Angeles, CA: Western Psychological Services.

Sattler, J. M., & Hoge, R. D. (2006). *Assessment of children: Behavioral, social, and clinical foundations* (5th ed.). San Diego, CA: Sattler.

Sattler, J. M., & Mash, E. J. (1998). Introduction to clinical assessment interviewing. In J. M. Sattler (Ed.), *Clinical and forensic inter viewing of children and families* (pp. 2–44). San Diego, CA: Sattler.

Shaffer, D., Fisher, P., Lucas, C. P., Dulcan, M., & Schwab-Stone, M. E. (2000). NIMH Diagnostic Interview Schedule for Children–Version IV: Description, differences from previous versions, and reliability of some common diagnoses. *Journal of the American Academy of Child & Adolescent Psychiatry, 39*, 28–38.

Whitcomb, S., & Merrell, K. W. (2012). *Behavioral, social, and emotional assessment of children and adolescents* (4th ed.). Mahwah, NJ: Erlbaum.

22 Best Practices in Identification of Learning Disabilities

Robert Lichtenstein
Massachusetts School of Professional Psychology

OVERVIEW

School psychologists provide services across a wide range of domains, the breadth and depth of which are ever expanding. Yet data-based decision making and accountability continues to top the list of the National Association of School Psychologists (NASP) Practice Model domains in the NASP *Model for Comprehensive and Integrated School Psychological Services* (NASP, 2010b) and to claim a disproportionate share of school psychologists' time and effort. Identification of children with learning disabilities is a topic of paramount importance to school psychologists. School psychologists contribute unique expertise to the process of determining the eligibility and educational needs of children with disabilities, of which specific learning disabilities is, far and away, the most prevalent.

This chapter frames the objectives and challenges of learning disabilities identification, with a particular focus on the parameters imposed by federal laws and regulations. Leading models of learning disabilities identification are described and analyzed. Practical issues involving data collection and decision making are addressed, and recommendations are provided as to how school psychologists can enhance their professional skills and advocate for school practices and procedures that are in keeping with best practice.

As of 2007, the most recent year for which federal data are available, more than 2.3 million children in the United States received special education services under the learning disabilities category (U.S. Department of Education, 2012), which represents 44% of school-age children with disabilities. (Notably, this figure has decreased from a high of 51% in the late 1990s.) Prevalence rates for learning disabilities were not consistent across racial groups. The learning disabilities prevalence rate was 3.9% for the overall population ages 6–21, but the prevalence rate was 5.3% for African American children and 4.6% for Hispanic children.

Learning disabilities have been recognized as an entity for more than a century. The term *learning disabilities*, coined by Samuel Kirk, has become well established in the field of education since the early 1960s (Hallahan & Mercer, 2002). Learning disabilities have been a topic of great interest, and our understanding of how to address them has progressed in step with the ever-increasing literacy demands of U.S. society.

In spite of research, legislation, and improved intervention practices in recent years, what has not occurred is greater clarity and consistency in identifying children with learning disabilities. If anything, questions and controversies have redoubled, as the 2004 reauthorization of the Individuals with Disabilities Education Act (IDEA) introduced significant changes in how educators identify children with learning disabilities. In this time of transition, school psychologists play a critical role in reshaping service delivery systems to promote better outcomes for children. As has been long advocated by leaders in the field, the shift away from traditional approaches to learning disabilities identification offers school psychologists the opportunity to expand their roles as consultants, team collaborators and facilitators, data-based decision makers, and intervention specialists.

BASIC CONSIDERATIONS

A valid and functional definition of a disorder is a prerequisite to establishing valid identification procedures, and herein lies much of the problem.

Nature of Learning Disabilities

Learning disabilities, by their very nature, are not susceptible to sharply defined identification procedures. The more we learn about learning disabilities, the better we understand the difficulties of establishing clear and consistent diagnostic criteria.

Characteristics of Learning Disabilities

A central defining characteristic is that learning disabilities affect specific aspects of formal learning while general cognitive functions such as problem solving and understanding concepts remain basically intact. Thus, the learning-disabled child's school performance is perceived as unexpected underachievement.

The interference with specific learning tasks is understood to be the result of impaired cognitive processes at the neurobiological level. Further complicating this picture, the neurobiological aspects of learning disabilities interact with environmental factors in complex ways. Consistent with this causally complex nature, learning disabilities are dimensional, a continuously distributed, rather than categorically distinct, entity. Accordingly, it can be difficult to distinguish between a weakness, a difficulty, and a disorder or disability.

Learning disability is a heterogeneous condition. The manifestation of learning disabilities varies in nature and in severity from child to child. There is no single symptom or cognitive pattern that is necessary (i.e., always present in children with learning disabilities) or sufficient (i.e., by itself, enough to result in the presence of a learning disability). These and other widely accepted characteristics of learning disabilities were summarized in the NASP position statement, *Identification of Students With Specific Learning Disabilities* (NASP, 2011; see Table 22.1).

A detailed review of the cognitive processes presumed to characterize learning disabilities is beyond the scope of this chapter and would largely serve to illustrate the difficulty of diagnosing a heterogeneous syndrome. There are, however, particular cognitive skills that play such a central role that school psychologists must understand these skills well and routinely consider these skills when designing an evaluation.

While reading disabilities do not encompass the entirety of learning disabilities, the great majority of children with learning disabilities—estimated at more than 80%—experience difficulty with reading. Accordingly, the mechanisms involved in reading, early literacy in particular, have been the most intensively studied and are the best-known aspects of learning disabilities. Research on learning disabilities increased dramatically in the 1980s and 1990s as reading problems reached epidemic levels. Congress, recognizing this as a public health issue, devoted major funding to a multisite program of research through the National Institute of Child Health and Human Development (NICHD), under the direction of Reid Lyon. Lyon (1998) summarized key findings of the NICHD research program in a report to Congress:

> For 90–95% of poor readers, prevention and early intervention programs that combine instruction in

Table 22.1. The Nature of Learning Disabilities

- Specific learning disabilities are endogenous in nature and are characterized by neurologically based deficits in cognitive processes.
- These deficits are specific; that is, these deficits have an impact on particular cognitive processes that interfere with the acquisition of academic skills.
- Specific learning disabilities are heterogeneous. There are various types of learning disabilities, and there is no single defining academic or cognitive deficit or characteristic common to all types of learning disabilities.
- Specific learning disabilities may coexist with other disabling conditions (e.g., sensory deficits, language impairment, behavior problems) but are not primarily due to these conditions.
- The great majority of children identified as having specific learning disabilities (more than 80%) have a disability in the area of reading.
- The manifestation of a specific learning disability is contingent to some extent upon the type of instruction, supports, and accommodations provided and the demands of the learning situation.
- Early intervention can reduce the impact of many specific learning difficulties.
- Specific learning disabilities vary in their degree of severity, and moderate to severe learning disabilities can be expected to have an impact on performance throughout the life span.
- Multitiered systems of student support have been effective as part of a comprehensive approach to meet students' academic needs.

Note. From *Identification of Students With Specific Learning Disabilities,* by National Association of School Psychologists, 2011, Bethesda, MD: Author. Copyright 2011 by National Association of School Psychologists. Reprinted with permission.

phoneme awareness, phonics, fluency development, and reading comprehension strategies, provided by well-trained teachers, can increase reading skills to average reading levels. However, if we delay intervention until age 9 (when most children with reading difficulties receive services), approximately 75% will continue to have difficulties learning to read throughout high school.

Research on mathematics and writing disabilities has lagged behind that of reading but is receiving increased attention. There has been good progress in mapping the key functional skills for proficient writing: spelling, handwriting, and composition (Berninger, 2009). Various cognitive processes are involved in writing, most notably working memory and other executive functions. Functional skills involved in mathematics include math-fact retrieval, computation, procedural knowledge, understanding of number sets, estimation, and problem solving. A number of cognitive process areas are suspected to underlie math disabilities, including processing speed, spatial abilities, number sense, memory, attention, and monitoring (Geary, Hoard, Byrd-Craven, Nugent, & Numtee, 2007; Johnson, Humphrey, Mellard, Woods, & Swanson, 2010). Research findings to date, however, are far from definitive.

Research findings on learning disabilities and reading problems have had a major influence on recent directions in national education policy. The 2001 reauthorization of the Elementary and Secondary Education Act (better known as No Child Left Behind) and the 2004 reauthorization of IDEA, in concert, established an infrastructure that shifted the focus to prevention and blurred the once-bright line between general and special education. The cornerstone of these reforms is response to intervention (RTI), a prevention-oriented multitiered system of service delivery that has shifted attention from assessment to intervention, with a corresponding impact on the role of school psychologists. An annual national survey has shown a steady increase in the frequency and extent to which school districts are adopting an RTI model: As of 2011, 68% of districts were reportedly in full implementation or in the process of district-wide implementation (SpectrumK12, n.d.).

Definitions of Learning Disabilities

Although definitions of learning disabilities have not provided the kind of specificity needed to guide identification procedures, there is fairly high correspondence among the more widely used definitions of learning disabilities. The most frequently cited definition is the one that appears in IDEA:

> The term "specific learning disability" means a disorder in one or more of the basic psychological processes involved in understanding or in using language, spoken or written, which disorder may manifest itself in the imperfect ability to listen, think, speak, read, write, spell, or do mathematical calculations. Such term includes such conditions as perceptual disabilities, brain injury, minimal brain dysfunction, dyslexia, and developmental aphasia. Such term does not include a learning problem that is primarily the result of visual, hearing, or motor disabilities, of mental retardation, of emotional disturbance, or of environmental, cultural, or economic disadvantage. (Sec. 602(30)(A-C))

This definition has remained constant since its initial adoption by the U.S. Office of Education in 1968 and its inclusion in the precursor to IDEA, the Education for All Handicapped Children Act of 1975.

Another frequently cited definition is the one adopted by the National Joint Committee on Learning Disabilities (1990). While similar to the federal definition, this definition explicitly recognizes that learning disabilities are heterogeneous, not limited to language-related processes, and often comorbid with other disabling conditions.

Operational Definition and Federal Regulations

It was apparent soon after federal special education law was first enacted in 1975 that the definition of learning disabilities was insufficient to guide clear and consistent eligibility determinations. The U.S. Office of Education tried to address this concern as it issued the first set of special education regulations in 1977 and introduced additional criteria specific to determining learning disabilities eligibility. Thus, learning disabilities became the only special education disability category with extensive requirements, above and beyond the definition itself, for determining eligibility.

The critical new element of the 1977 learning disabilities eligibility regulations was the introduction of the ability–achievement discrepancy as one of three eligibility criteria:

- Underachievement in one or more of the specified academic areas (oral expression, listening comprehension, written expression, basic reading skill, reading comprehension, mathematics calculation, and mathematics reasoning)

- Severe discrepancy between achievement and intellectual ability
- Exclusionary clause, which disallowed learning disabilities eligibility if underachievement was primarily the result of visual, hearing, or motor disabilities; mental retardation; emotional disturbance; or environmental, cultural, or economic disadvantage

Because the ability–achievement discrepancy criterion provided a specific and measurable means of distinguishing children with learning disabilities from other underachieving students, it served as the key determinant of eligibility. The discrepancy criterion became even more dominant and rigidly applied as the majority of states adopted formulas to fix the magnitude of a discrepancy that qualified as "severe" (most commonly, a difference of 1.5 standard deviations).

Under the weight of countervailing scientific evidence, the ability–achievement discrepancy criterion was eclipsed with the introduction of the following rule in the 2004 reauthorization of IDEA:

(A) When determining whether a child has a specific learning disability as defined under this Act, the local educational agency shall not be required to take into consideration whether the child has a severe discrepancy between achievement and intellectual ability…

(B) In determining whether a child has a specific learning disability, a local educational agency may use a process which determines if a child responds to scientific, research-based intervention as part of the evaluation procedures. (Sec. 614(b)(6))

This has resulted in renewed concern and controversy as to how best to identify children with learning disabilities.

In 2006, the U.S. Department of Education issued new regulations that provided additional guidance on how to interpret the learning disabilities eligibility language in IDEA. In allowing for a choice among approaches, the regulations perpetuated, rather than resolved, the question of a preferred learning disabilities identification model. As before, the 2006 regulations specify three criteria that must be met: (a) verification of underachievement, (b) an inclusionary criterion attesting to the presence of learning disabilities, and (c) an exclusionary criterion ruling out other explanations as the primary cause of learning problems (see

Table 22.2). While the achievement criterion and exclusionary criterion underwent modest revisions, changes in the inclusionary criterion have been the main focus of attention, as well as controversy and confusion. (See Lichtenstein & Klotz, 2007, for a detailed analysis of the 2006 learning disabilities eligibility regulations.)

With the addition of reading fluency skills in the 2006 regulations, there are now eight academic areas that are considered in the underachievement criterion (as listed in Table 22.2). What constitutes "inadequate" achievement is determined in relation to the child's age or to "state-approved grade level standards" (300.309(a)(2)(ii)), implicitly giving weight to state curriculum frameworks. The underachievement criterion also includes the stipulation that the child has been provided with appropriate instruction. This language closely corresponds to the requirement, applicable to all disability categories, that lack of appropriate instruction in reading or math cannot be the "determinant factor" of a finding that a child has an educational disability.

The exclusionary criterion stipulates that various factors that may interfere with education performance must be ruled out as the determinant of a learning disabilities finding. Most of these exclusionary factors are referenced in the federal definition of learning disabilities: "visual, hearing or motor disabilities, mental retardation, emotional disturbance, and environmental, cultural and economic disadvantage" (Sec. 602(30)(C)). In addition, the regulations cite "lack of appropriate instruction in reading or math" and "limited English proficiency" as exclusionary factors (300.309(a)(3)) Consequently, the regulations direct evaluation teams to consider data that (a) demonstrate that the child received appropriate instruction in regular education, either prior to or as part of the referral process, and (b) document repeated assessment of student progress during instruction (see Table 22.2). These aspects of a multitiered service delivery system must be addressed regardless of whether or not an RTI model of learning disabilities identification is in use.

Typology

As noted, learning disabilities are highly variable in nature and in severity. It is not possible to establish universally applicable identification procedures that cover specific cognitive abilities, academic skills, or behavioral characteristics. To increase diagnostic clarity, researchers have sought to map out learning disabilities subtypes that have a higher degree of coherence.

Table 22.2. Learning Disabilities Eligibility Criteria in Federal Special Education Regulations

§ 300.309 Determining the existence of a specific learning disability

(a) The group described in § 300.306 [i.e., the evaluation team] may determine that a child has a specific learning disability, as defined in § 300.8(c)(10), if—

(1) The child does not achieve adequately for the child's age or to meet State-approved grade-level standards in one or more of the following areas, when provided with learning experiences and instruction appropriate for the child's age or State-approved grade-level standards:

(i) Oral expression.

(ii) Listening comprehension.

(iii) Written expression.

(iv) Basic reading skill.

(v) Reading fluency skills.

(vi) Reading comprehension.

(vii) Mathematics calculation.

(viii) Mathematics problem solving.

(2) (i) The child does not make sufficient progress to meet age or State-approved grade-level standards in one or more of the areas identified in paragraph (a)(1) of this section when using a process based on the child's response to scientific, research-based intervention; or

(ii) The child exhibits a pattern of strengths and weaknesses in performance, achievement, or both, relative to age, State-approved grade-level standards, or intellectual development, that is determined by the group to be relevant to the identification of a specific learning disability, using appropriate assessments, consistent with § 300.304 and 300.305; and

(3) The group determines that its findings under paragraphs (a)(1) and (2) of this section are not primarily the result of—

(i) A visual, hearing, or motor disability;

(ii) Mental retardation;

(iii) Emotional disturbance;

(iv) Cultural factors;

(v) Environmental or economic disadvantage; or

(vi) Limited English proficiency.

(b) To ensure that underachievement in a child suspected of having a specific learning disability is not due to lack of appropriate instruction in reading or math, the group must consider, as part of the evaluation described in § 300.304 through 300.306—

(1) Data that demonstrate that prior to, or as a part of, the referral process, the child was provided appropriate instruction in regular education settings, delivered by qualified personnel; and

(2) Data-based documentation of repeated assessments of achievement at reasonable intervals, reflecting formal assessment of student progress during instruction, which was provided to the child's parents.

Note. From U.S. Department of Education (2006), pp. 46786–46787.

Pennington (2009) has been a major contributor to this effort. In establishing a taxonomy of neurodevelopmental disorders that interfere with learning, he proposed criteria that must be met to constitute a *valid syndrome*: "groups of symptoms that reliably co-occur, are associated with functional impairment, are theoretically meaningful, and are not redundant with an already validated disorder" (p. 23). Applying these criteria, he identified eight distinguishable neurodevelopmental disorders: four that are recognizable as learning disabilities subtypes (reading disability, mathematics disorder, speech sound disorder, and language impairment) and four that are diagnostically distinguishable from learning disabilities (autism spectrum disorder, attention deficit hyperactivity disorder, developmental coordination disorder, and intellectual disability).

The recently revised *Diagnostic and Statistical Manual* (5th ed.; DSM-5) of the American Psychiatric Association (2013) departed from educational terminology and used the term *specific learning disorder*, instead of specific learning disabilities, as one of six identified "neurodevelopmental disorders." The other five closely align with the disorders in Pennington's taxonomy: intellectual development disorders, communication disorders, autism spectrum disorder, attention deficit hyperactivity disorder, and motor disorders. In DSM-5, a specific learning disorder is characterized by persistent difficulties in one or more of three academic domains: reading, written expression, and mathematics. DSM-5 classifies communication disorders as a separate entity from specific learning disorders. IDEA, by comparison, does not make this distinction because it includes underachievement in oral expression and listening comprehension among the eight underachievement areas of learning disabilities, even though there is a separate disability category of speech or language impairment.

The term *dyslexia* is often used interchangeably with reading disability. However, neither IDEA nor DSM-5 employs this term. Dyslexia is a term most often found in the scientific literature. Some researchers use the term to refer specifically to an impairment in accurate and fluent word-level reading while others use the term interchangeably with reading, disabilities in general. To avoid confusion and to ensure consistency with federal education mandates, school psychologists are advised to use the term *reading disability* rather than dyslexia and to inform parents and other stakeholders that dyslexia, or reading disability, is encompassed within the IDEA category of specific learning disability.

Beyond Typology

Waber (2010), in formulating a developmental model of learning disabilities that recognizes the many factors that contribute to a learning disability, concluded that the learning disabilities construct has outlived its usefulness. Like Pennington, she rejected a "modular" model of learning disabilities, whereby the cognitive deficits are focal, self-contained, and sufficient targets for assessment and diagnosis. Waber noted that social, emotional, and environmental variables interact with cognitive ones and are necessary considerations in diagnostic formulation and in intervention planning. Consequently, Waber

espoused a problem-solving approach to diagnostic and intervention efforts that would "shift the focus of effort and resources from identification of a learning disability to solving the student's problem—arguably the correct goal of the exercise" (Waber, 2010, p. 215). Mellard, Deshler, and Barth (2004) verified that a number of environmental factors, such as degree of parental involvement and availability of services for at-risk students, do indeed influence educators as they make learning disabilities identification decisions. Hence, conceptualizing learning disabilities in strictly cognitive and academic terms is an oversimplification that can interfere with both identification and educational planning.

Alternative Approaches to Learning Disabilities Identification

For a child to qualify for special education under the learning disabilities category, three criteria must be met: low achievement, evidence of learning disabilities, and absence of exclusionary factors (see Figure 22.1). As two of these criteria—low achievement and the exclusion of other determining factors—are applicable in all cases, what distinguishes alternative approaches is the inclusionary criterion: the evidence indicating that learning disabilities are the source of academic difficulties.

Much of the recent professional literature has reduced the learning disabilities identification process to a choice between two methods: ability–achievement discrepancy

Figure 22.1. Summary of Learning Disabilities Eligibility Criteria

Finding 1: **Underachievement**	**Finding 2:** **Evidence of Learning Disabilities**	**Finding 3:** **Exclusion of Other Factors**
Child does not achieve adequately … in one of more of the following achievement areas when provided with [appropriate] learning experiences and instruction: • Oral expression • Listening comprehension • Written expression • Basic reading skill • Reading fluency skills • Reading comprehension • Mathematics calculation • Mathematics problem solving	Child does not make sufficient progress to meet age or grade standards, in response to scientific, research-based intervention. **OR** Child exhibits a relevant pattern of strengths and weaknesses in performance and/or achievement, relative to age, grade, or intellectual development.	Findings 1 and 2 are not primarily the result of: • Visual, hearing, or motor disability • Mental retardation • Emotional disturbance • Cultural factors • Environmental or economic disadvantage • Limited English proficiency **AND** A child shall not be determined to have a disability if the determinant factor is lack of appropriate instruction in reading or math.

or RTI. Similarly, many states, in updating their learning disabilities eligibility criteria to be consistent with federal regulations, have focused primarily on these two methods. This, however, is a misleading over-simplification. Although IDEA 2004 offered RTI as an additional method for consideration, this did not prohibit other approaches that have been traditionally used or more recently proposed. In fact, neither ability–achievement discrepancy nor RTI reflect the manner in which school personnel typically approach learning disabilities identification.

The traditional approach, as described in assessment texts such as Sattler (2008), is to collect psychoeducational assessment from multiple data sources (i.e., records, interviews, observations, and tests), with an emphasis on intelligence tests and other norm-referenced measures, and to interpret findings using clinical judgment. While not always recognized as a distinct method of learning disabilities identification, clinical judgment invariably plays a significant part and is often the primary means of determining whether assessment findings are consistent with a diagnosis of learning disabilities. Even in the era when ability–achievement discrepancy was the predominant method of learning disabilities identification, 32 states formally recognized the role of clinical judgment in their learning disabilities eligibility procedures (Reschly & Hosp, 2004).

As shown in Figure 22.2, there are four approaches to learning disabilities identification that merit discussion and analysis: ability–achievement discrepancy,

intra-individual differences, clinical judgment, and RTI. Table 22.3 summarizes the underlying philosophy, key concepts, and characteristics associated with each of these approaches. Although each approach is permissible under federal rules, each relates to a different part of the inclusionary criteria. The discrepancy model is sanctioned by the wording of the "pattern of strengths and weaknesses" passage in federal regulations (300.309(a)(2)(ii)), which allows for assessment of achievement, relative to intellectual development. The intra-individual differences approach follows from the IDEA definition of learning disabilities as a disorder in psychological processes that interferes with academic performance. Clinical judgment is supported by the regulatory language that allows the evaluation team to determine whether a pattern of strengths and weaknesses is "relevant" to a diagnosis of learning disabilities. The RTI model has its origins in the IDEA 2004 language that allows for the use of "a process which determines if a child responds to scientific, research-based intervention" (Sec. 614(b)(6)).

Ability–Achievement Discrepancy

Learning disabilities identification has long been plagued by the operational definition that, ironically, was introduced in an effort to make identification decisions more consistent, objective, and scientifically based. Soon after the federal special education law was first enacted in 1975, it became apparent that the lack of clear, objective criteria for learning disabilities eligibility

Figure 22.2. Learning Disabilities Identification Approaches

Traditional Assessment (Battery of Psychoeducational Assessment Measures)		Response to Intervention
Psychometric Models	Clinical Judgement	Dual Discrepancy
Ability–achievement discrepancy Intra-individual differences	Evaluator interprets findings from multiple data sources	• Underachievement, relative to peers • Insufficient response to intervention, relative to peers
Key data sources: Cognitive ability tests, achievement tests	*Key data sources:* Records/history, tests, observation, rating scales, interviews	*Key data sources:* Progress-monitoring data (e.g, curriculum-based measures), classroom observation

Note. This figure shows different approaches to meeting the inclusionary criterion (i.e., the basis for determining the presence of a learning disability). The underachievement and exclusionary criteria are applicable to all approaches.

Table 22.3. Comparison of Learning Disabilities Identification Approaches

	Ability–Achievement Discrepancy	Intra-Individual Differences	Clinical Judgment	Response to Intervention
Guiding principle	Learning disabilities as unexpected underachievement	Learning disabilities definition as a disorder in basic psychological processes	Diagnostic-prescriptive analysis of suspected learning disabilities	Prevention and early intervention
Underlying philosophy	Entitlement: eligibility criteria as a means of rationing limited resources	Medical model: objective diagnosis of a measurable intrinsic condition	Functional model: consider benefit of special education for the individual child	Systemic model: effective use of system resources
Basis for decision making	Psychometric pattern: comparison of two test scores	Psychometric pattern: profile analysis of multiple test scores	Subjective integration of assessment data	Dual discrepancy: underachievement and insufficient progress relative to peers
Most applicable language in federal law	"The child exhibits a pattern of strengths and weaknesses in performance, achievement, or both, relative to ... intellectual development" Federal regulations, §300.309(a)(2)(ii)	"The term 'specific learning disability' means a disorder in 1 or more of the basic psychological processes involved in understanding or in using language, spoken or written ..." IDEA 2004, Sec.602(30)(A)	"The child exhibits a pattern of strengths and weaknesses ... that is determined by the group to be relevant to the identification of a specific learning disability" Federal regulations, §300.309(a)(2)(ii)	"... may use a process which determines if a child responds to scientific, research-based intervention" IDEA 2004, Sec.614(b)(6)(B)
Time frame	Fixed point in time	Fixed point in time	Considers both history and current performance	Multiple assessments over time
Key assessment data	Intelligence test scores; achievement test scores	Cognitive ability and achievement measures	Integration of multiple sources (R-I-O-T)	Achievement measures, especially curriculum-based measurement

was resulting in inconsistent decision making and unexpectedly high prevalence rates. The U.S. Office of Education, with ostensible support from an epidemiological study by Rutter and Yule (1975), introduced in the 1977 special education regulations the eligibility requirement that "the child has a severe discrepancy between achievement and intellectual ability" (U.S. Office of Education, 1977, p. 65083). The rationale underlying the discrepancy model is the concept of an learning disabilities as unexpected underachievement. The ability–achievement discrepancy represented an objective way to apply this concept.

Scientific support for the ability–achievement discrepancy approach has been conspicuously lacking while evidence to the contrary has been plentiful. The shortcomings of the discrepancy model have been widely documented. Many these shortcomings involve technical issues, as psychometric problems abound in reducing complex constructs to a simple formula (see Table 22.4). While the use of ability–achievement discrepancy formulas has fallen into disrepute, some researchers have suggested that it is premature to jettison the ability–achievement discrepancy model (Kavale, 2002; Scruggs & Mastropieri, 2002). Kavale (2002) asserted that the problems with the discrepancy model ensue from overreliance on the use of a formula.

Bright, motivated students with learning disabilities who make optimal use of remedial instruction and accommodations may raise their achievement scores to a level that does not meet the discrepancy criterion, but they need ongoing support of a type not routinely available through general education. Two of the most significant problems with the discrepancy model, however, are conceptual and inherent in the very nature of learning disabilities. First, efforts to sort children into distinct categories of learning disabled and nondisabled are prone to error because learning disabilities are dimensional, as are the ability and achievement measures that the discrepancy model relies on for diagnosis. Many low-achieving children will fall close to the cutoff used to differentiate between learning disabilities and non-learning disabilities, and, consequently, a weighty categorical distinction is made between children with similar characteristics. Moreover, this category assignment is not stable over time, resulting in a significant number of false negatives and false positives (Francis et al., 2005). Francis and colleagues (2005) found that approximately one third of the children in a large-scale longitudinal study of children with suspected learning disabilities changed classification—in both directions— over a 2-year interval.

Second, it is a faulty assumption to expect that children with low IQ scores will not attain basic academic skills (Siegel, 1989). Children with low cognitive ability are often ruled out of consideration when the discrepancy approach is employed, and characterized as slow learners, on the basis that their underachievement is expected. However, cognitive ability is not a good indicator of the capacity to read and acquire other basic academic skills. It is diagnostically significant when low-ability students fail to acquire basic literacy skills despite appropriate instruction and remedial supports. The cognitive deficits associated with learning disabilities interfere with learning in a similar manner, regardless of whether measured intelligence is high or low. In comparing students with low achievement and those who have a discrepancy-based learning disabilities, researchers have found that both groups exhibit similar deficits in critical cognitive skills (i.e., phonological processing, rapid naming, and verbal memory), respond equally well to specialized instruction, and demonstrate a similar

Table 22.4. Technical Problems Associated With the Discrepancy Model

- The psychological processes associated with learning disabilities often compromise performance on measures of cognitive ability, thereby reducing the ability–achievement discrepancy for children with learning disabilities.
- Measures of intellectual ability incorporate aspects of achievement, such as prior learning of vocabulary and general information, which reduces the ability–achievement discrepancy for children with learning disabilities.
- Measurement error is inherent in both ability and achievement measures, therefore difference scores are particularly prone to error.
- Measurement error is compounded when an ability score is compared to multiple measures of achievement (e.g., of basic reading skills, reading comprehension, reading fluency, and written expression), thereby increasing the probability of a significant difference occurring by chance.
- Measures comparing ability and achievement are often not conormed.
- Various measures of intellectual ability can be used, each of which will produce different results.
- There is no objective way to separate out the effects of environmental, sensory, cultural, and emotional factors, which may contribute to learning problems but fail to meet the exclusionary criterion that they are the primary cause of underachievement.

trajectory of academic progress over time (Francis, Shaywitz, Stuebing, Shaywitz, & Fletcher, 1996; Lyon et al., 2001). The strict requirement of an ability–achievement discrepancy is problematic because it rules out many children with distinct processing difficulties and a genuine need for specialized instruction. Notably, children who exhibit the psychological processing difficulties that are characteristic of learning disabilities and who have lesser cognitive abilities with which to compensate for learning difficulties are even more at risk and in need of specialized instruction. To rule them out of consideration for specialized instruction is at odds with scientific research, is counterproductive, and is unfair.

There are significant liabilities to the discrepancy approach. Most notably, the use of the discrepancy model has engendered a wait-to-fail phenomenon, whereby educators wait to see whether learning difficulties meet the discrepancy criterion rather than implement timely preventive and remedial strategies (Lyon et al., 2001). Many referrals for learning disabilities take place at the upper elementary grades or later, which is beyond the critical point for intervention. This is the rationale for using universal screening measures in the primary grades to identify children who need additional general education supports. Otherwise, in the absence of timely and effective intervention, academic performance may deteriorate to the point that the child qualifies as having a disability.

While the discrepancy model reduces the problems of inconsistent identification procedures and high learning disabilities identification rates, it has proven to be a miscalculation in applying empirical research to practice. NASP (2003), in its recommendations to Congress on the reauthorization of IDEA, proposed that it "eliminate use of the scientifically unsupported ability–achievement discrepancy requirement" (p. 2). The discrepancy model, rigidly applied, has proven to be little more than an administrative, economic, and procedural convenience for simplifying a complex decision process. It has allowed school districts to rely on a seemingly objective, bright-line decision rule, backed by federal mandate, as a basis for granting or (more to the point) denying special services to a child.

Despite the contraindications, the discrepancy model continues to be widely used. This presents a dilemma for the school psychologist as, per NASP (2010a) ethical principles: "School psychologists use assessment techniques and practices that the profession considers to be responsible, research-based practice" (Standard II.3.2). When a discrepancy model is required by school district

policy, school psychologists should advocate for an alternative method.

Intra-Individual Differences

The intra-individual differences approach follows from the premise that certain patterns of strengths and weaknesses in a child's cognitive functioning are indicative of a "disorder in basic psychological processes," as per the definition of learning disabilities in federal law (Public Law 108-446, Sec. 602(30)(A)). Rather than consider intellectual ability holistically, as is the case with the ability–achievement discrepancy, the crux of this model is the analysis of specific cognitive functions in relation to educational performance. Proponents of the intra-individual differences approach regard standardized, norm-referenced measures as essential for making learning disabilities eligibility determinations in a consistent and objective manner. Psychoeducational testing completed within a limited time period provides the critical data for determining eligibility. Assessing a child in a context that is separate from the child's instructional and social environment (i.e., a testing room) is in keeping with this model because it regards a disability as a condition inherent in the child.

Several intra-individual differences models have been proposed as a way of operationalizing learning disabilities eligibility procedures. Three similar models are concordance-discordance (Hale, Wycoff, & Fiorello, 2011), discrepancy/consistency (Naglieri, 2011), and CHC-based operational definition of specific learning disabilities (Flanagan, Alfonso, & Mascolo, 2011). The common feature of these models is that they imply existence of a learning disability from a profile of norm-referenced cognitive and academic achievement measures in which a relative weakness among cognitive functions is empirically linked to an area of academic deficiency (see Figure 22.3). As an example, a relative weakness in phonological processing might be linked to difficulty with basic reading skills. These models are sometimes described as third method approaches (Hale et al., 2011), in reference to the passage in the federal regulations (Sec. 300.307(a)(3)) that allows states to use "alternative research-based procedures," rather than ability–achievement discrepancy or RTI for learning disabilities identification.

Caution must be used in interpreting any relative cognitive weaknesses as diagnostically relevant. The low point in an individual's cognitive profile does not necessarily imply functional impairment that significantly interferes with academic performance. For

Figure 22.3. Intra-Individual Differences Models

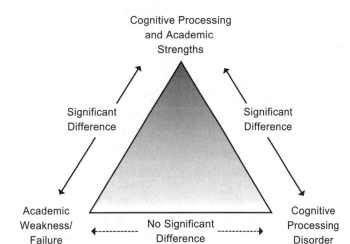

Note. From "Alternative Research-Based Methods for IDEA (2004) Identification of Children With Specific Learning Disabilities," by J. B. Hale, D. P. Flanagan, and J. A. Naglieri, 2008, *Communiqué, 36*(8), pp. 1, 14–17. Copyright 2008 by the National Association of School Psychologists. Reprinted with permission.

example, a bright child may have a relative weakness in visual–spatial ability that falls within the low average range but does not interfere with academic performance.

Fletcher et al. (2005) challenged the assumption that a flat profile—one lacking relative strengths in cognitive functions—is an appropriate basis for ruling out learning disabilities. Some children with overall below average range intellectual abilities are hampered by dysfunctional cognitive processes that significantly interfere with formal learning, consistent with the definition of learning disabilities, while other children with below average intelligence are not so affected. Fletcher and colleagues (2005) cited evidence suggesting that children with flat profiles are at least as likely to experience severe learning problems. They also challenged the assumption that analysis of intra-individual differences provides added value in developing beneficial interventions.

The U.S. Department of Education (2006) does not regard cognitive profile analysis as an appropriate application of the "pattern of strengths and weaknesses" language in the federal regulations:

The Department does not believe that an assessment of psychological or cognitive processing should be required in determining whether a child has a [specific learning disability]. There is no current evidence that such assessments are necessary or sufficient for identifying [specific learning disabilities] … The regulations, however, allow for the assessment of intra-individual differences in

achievement as part of an identification model for [specific learning disabilities]. (p. 46651)

Consistent with this guidance, Mather and Gregg (2006) propose a learning disabilities identification model that relies on establishing concordance between an area of relative academic weakness and cognitive or linguistic deficiency that is related to that academic area without the stipulation that the cognitive deficiency is a relative weakness within the cognitive profile. Under this model, a child with pronounced difficulty in basic reading skills and a corresponding deficit in phonemic awareness need not have a pattern of significant cognitive scatter to qualify as having a learning disability.

Response to Intervention

RTI is a contextualized approach to learning disabilities identification that has been elevated by changes in public policy and corresponding shifts in practice. The report of the President's Commission on Excellence in Special Education (2002), which significantly shaped IDEA 2004, provided significant support for the RTI approach with its three major recommendations: (a) focus on results, not on process; (b) embrace a model of prevention, not embrace a model of failure; and (c) consider children with disabilities as general education children first.

RTI actually has two related, but distinct, connotations. RTI in the broad sense refers to a prevention-oriented multitiered system that systematically implements high-quality classroom instruction, identifies children who are not meeting academic standards, and provides remedial supports for these children within general education. Commonly cited advantages of a systemic RTI approach include (a) improved instructional practices for students in general education, (b) timely assistance to children experiencing learning difficulties as an alternative to wait-to-fail, (c) assurance that lack of appropriate instruction is not the reason for a student's poor academic performance and eligibility for special education, and (d) linking of assessment and intervention so that assessment data inform and improve instruction (Fuchs, Mock, Morgan, & Young, 2003). RTI, in this broad sense of a service delivery system, can be implemented regardless of the learning disabilities identification approach in use. Researchers with diametrically opposed views on learning disabilities identification are in agreement that a multitiered RTI approach should be routinely used to improve educational outcomes (Gresham, Reschly, & Shinn, 2010; Hale et al., 2011).

RTI is also used in the narrow sense to refer to an approach to learning disabilities identification. This approach follows from the aspect of a multitiered system that involves monitoring a child's performance over time to determine the effect of an educational program. Within a multitiered service delivery system, assessment occurs at all levels, beginning with universal screening of educational progress in the classroom and followed by more frequent progress monitoring for those children who need additional supports and strategies at Tier 2. Evidence of responsiveness, or the lack thereof, to general education interventions then contributes a significant part of the assessment data for a referral for special education. Positive response to favorable instructional conditions serves as an indicator that the child's underachievement had been the result of lack of appropriate instruction or environmental obstacles rather than a disability inherent in the child. Conversely, the finding that a child who has received quality instruction and appropriate interventions within a multitiered service system and not made sufficient progress may constitute evidence of learning disabilities.

An RTI model is well suited to a noncategorical system of special education identification, such as the one pioneered in Iowa's Heartland Area Educational Agency (Grimes, 2002). In the Iowa model, a child's insufficient response to intervention at successively more intensive levels of support in general education can serve as in vivo evidence of the need for special education. This largely eliminates the need for cognitive assessment to determine learning disabilities eligibility and also enables children to be served without assigning a disability label. The Heartland model could be characterized as an RTI-only approach in that RTI data are sufficient for making a disability determination. While supporters regard it as an outcome-based approach that is responsive to student needs, RTI-only has been criticized for failing to meet the federal requirements for comprehensive evaluation (Hale et al., 2011). Hale and colleagues contest that overreliance on RTI data is problematic because a child may show insufficient RTI for any of several possible reasons.

The RTI approach uses a dual discrepancy model to make the determination that a child requires an increased level of support and may have a learning disability (Fuchs & Fuchs, 1998). The two elements of the dual discrepancy criterion are that (a) the child exhibits a level of academic performance that is below expectations for the instructional setting and (b) the child's rate of learning lags behind that of peers, despite appropriate instruction and interventions in general education. As conceived by Fuchs and Fuchs (1998), RTI data after a child is placed in special education would be relevant as well because failure to benefit from specialized instruction may be an indicator that the child's academic difficulties are the result of something other than an educational disability.

The logistics of using repeated assessments to gauge responsiveness call for an economical way of screening and monitoring academic performance. Curriculum-based measurement (CBM) has gained prominence as an effective method of doing so, using brief (typically 1–2 minute) probes of various academic tasks to assess basic literacy skills. Repeated administration of CBM probes can serve as evidence of whether a child meets the sufficient response criterion of the dual discrepancy model.

RTI is more widely used at the elementary level (O'Donnell & Miller, 2011) where it is aligned with the early literacy research that gave rise to this approach. School psychologists contribute significantly to RTI implementation by knowing how to compile and interpret CBM findings because these data are used to inform classroom instruction, identify children who need additional supports and strategies, and determine the effectiveness of intervention efforts. Elementary schools are also well served by the availability within general education of standard protocol interventions to address commonly occurring problems with emerging literacy. Thus, school psychologists provide valuable service as they plan, coordinate, and evaluate preventive services and programs.

CBM is less readily applicable to the learning objectives at upper grades, which emphasize more complex and multifaceted skills such as reading comprehension, math problem solving, expository writing, and understanding of scientific and social phenomena. Given the multifaced nature of these academic areas and of the executive functions and language impairments that affect them, it is difficult to identify discrete skills that can be administered repeatedly in a cost-effective manner for progress-monitoring purposes. Secondary-level educational goals and interventions are more likely to be student specific and generated by a problem-solving process. This calls for school psychologists to be skilled at consultation, collaboration, and team facilitation.

A particular challenge for school psychologists is to know how to interpret RTI data in making a determination of learning disabilities eligibility, particularly with respect to determining whether or not a student's responsiveness to intervention is satisfactory. In reviewing the research literature, Fuchs (2003) identified various methods that researchers have used in making these categorical distinctions. Approaches that analyze slope—a statistical method for quantifying rate of improvement—are the most promising but leave unanswered the questions of which peer group to use as the basis for comparison (same class, same grade, same school district, or same state) and what standard to apply for sufficient progress (improving at the same rate as peers or catching up to peers).

The lack of a clear-cut, objective decision rule for determining a sufficient level of response can result in uncertainty and inconsistency in decision making. The greater obstacle, however, is ensuring that reliable and valid RTI data are routinely available in the first place. This depends not only on careful selection of measures and good data collection techniques but also on assurance that interventions have been implemented with integrity. When reliable and valid RTI data are available, visual inspection of charted gains over time (essentially, eyeballing the data) may be as useful a technique as any. Determining sufficiency of response is also made less subjective by considering curricular standards, classroom expectations, and progress rates of other children who have received similar interventions.

If RTI data are to be of value, then the multitiered service delivery system in which it is embedded must be effective. Otherwise, the key assumptions of appropriate instruction and efficacy of scientific research-based intervention may not be met. In the absence of such conditions, a child's academic difficulties may reflect an instructional causality rather than an inherent disability. Experience has shown that a number of key variables such as administrative supports, professional development, and resources must be in place in order to have reasonable expectations of a well-functioning RTI system. School psychologists may need to advocate for such practices and policies to ensure that a multitiered system works as intended so that instructional causalities are not misidentified as children with learning disabilities.

Clinical Judgment

Clinical judgment—the application of professional knowledge and skill on a case-by-case basis—is instrumental in every aspect of learning disabilities identification. Evaluation team members apply clinical judgment in determining whether a child meets the criterion of underachievement as team members (a) reconcile multiple measures of achievement (e.g., state mastery tests, class performance, and individually administered achievement tests) or (b) consider whether a child is performing at the expected level given his or her learning experiences and history of instruction. Clinical judgment is also employed in determining whether exclusionary factors are the cause of learning difficulties. The exclusionary criterion directs teams to make a simple determination of whether some other factor other than learning disabilities is the primary determinant of learning problems. However, given the frequent co-occurrence and complex interaction of cognitive and environmental factors, there is nothing simple about this task. There is no well-defined rule to determine whether factors such as sensory impairment, emotional disturbance, language differences, and lack of appropriate instruction are primary contributors to underachievement or are secondary to learning disabilities. Clinical judgment is the usual arbiter.

Clinical judgment can also be the primary method for addressing the inclusionary criterion (i.e., evidence for the existence of a learning disability) and therefore merits the status of a leading approach to learning disabilities identification. Learning difficulties are typically a manifestation of multiple interacting factors, including but not limited to intrinsic cognitive abilities. Contributing factors may be related to a child's instructional environment (e.g., curriculum, methods of instruction, instructional level, availability of remedial services, reinforcement schedule, academic level of classmates), personal and social circumstances (e.g., mobility, cultural and language differences, parental pressures and expectations, emotional stressors), or prior educational experiences. This requires clinical interpretation of qualitative and nonstandardized assessment data from various sources, including school records, parent and child interviews, classroom observations, and behaviors observed during standard testing. Similarly, clinical judgment is used in interpreting quantitative psychoeducational assessment data. Test scores must be interpreted in light of such factors as educational, cultural, and linguistic background; motivation, effort, and anxiety; and family and peer group influences.

While clinical judgment carries much weight, it is not without hazards. Clinical judgment has long been called into question with respect to objectivity, reliability, and accuracy. There are striking differences among school psychologists not only with regard to their assessment methods and skills but in their theoretical orientations and their perspectives on learning disabilities identification. Lichtenstein (2002), in polling school psychologists for NASP input on IDEA 2004, documented striking lack of agreement on issues concerning learning disabilities definition and identification methods. In the absence of such agreement, wide variation can be expected in the measures and interpretation approaches used by school psychologists as they assess children with suspected learning disabilities.

Given the significant role of clinical judgment, school psychologists are relied upon for considerable expertise about learning disabilities diagnosis. For school psychologists whose learning disabilities expertise is still evolving, an advisable validity check on the use of clinical judgment is to seek out supervision from colleagues who have a wealth of experience and knowledge.

Comparison of Alternative Approaches

Comparing RTI to psychometric models that emphasize norm-referenced testing (i.e., ability–achievement discrepancy and intra-individual differences) is like comparing apples and avocados. The nature of these divergent approaches reflects the context in which each is embedded. They are associated with distinctly different service delivery systems and consequently operate under distinctly different assumptions and objectives.

Psychometric models place major emphasis on making a diagnostic decision about special education eligibility. Psychometric models are aligned with the medical model that has long been inherent in the special education system, which makes sharp distinctions between children with and without documented disabilities. Psychometric models rely on standardized, norm-referenced tests to ensure objectivity and consistency in

identifying the children who are the "rightful recipients" of special education. Underlying assumptions of this approach are that (a) a condition inherent in the child is the cause of learning difficulties, (b) the condition can be accurately diagnosed, and (c) there is a critical need for specialized instruction to remedy the condition. The assumptions of a medical model may hold true for severe disabilities of an endogenous nature, such as deafness or orthopedic impairment, but are less tenable with respect to learning disabilities.

In contrast, RTI is a systemic model, one that matches system resources with the educational needs of children who are experiencing difficulty irrespective of the disability label. The RTI approach to learning disabilities identification is embedded within a multi-tiered service-delivery system (RTI in the broad sense) that reduces the need to make the weighty and difficult decision about special education eligibility. A multitiered system is predicated upon systematic implementation of high-quality classroom instruction, targeted remedial instruction, and other strategies in general education that benefit children with and without learning difficulties. A continuum of supports and services that spans both general and special education is thereby established.

A distinctive element of an RTI approach to learning disabilities identification is the systematic collection of achievement data at multiple points in time to determine whether appropriate instruction or additional supports or interventions have produced the intended gains. Data of this type may figure into a traditional psychoeducational assessment as part of the child's educational history, but it is not obtained in a consistent manner. In an RTI model, however, repeated assessment of academic progress is routinely and systematically conducted.

The discrepancy model of learning disabilities identification is a particularly limited and limiting means of interpreting psychoeducational assessment results because it applies a standard statistical procedure for making a diagnostic determination of learning disabilities. In doing so, it minimizes the relevance of assessment findings from sources other than standardized tests (i.e., history and records, observations, ratings scales, and interviews). These other data sources are presumably considered in the investigation of exclusionary factors but in the context of a simplified binary decision; that is, each possible exclusionary factor (emotional disturbance, environmental disadvantage, limited English proficiency) is determined to either be or not be the primary cause of underachievement. Once exclusionary factors are ruled out, they are no longer regarded as relevant to determining the presence or the severity of a learning disability.

For the intra-individual differences approach, a critical assumption is that certain cognitive deficits are causally and predictably linked to learning disabilities and that these deficits are relevant to educational planning (Floyd, 2010; Hale, Kaufman, Naglieri, & Kavale, 2006). Such a relationship is well established between the cognitive skills of phonological processing, fluency, and verbal memory and the early acquisition of basic reading skills. Researchers have proposed other such links, but the evidence to date is too weak for this model to be universally applied as a requisite condition for verifying the presence of a learning disability. This is the rationale for the position taken by the U.S. Department of Education (2006) in discouraging intra-individual differences models that rely on assessment of cognitive processing.

Our understanding of how cognitive processes are associated with learning disabilities and with interventions will continue to evolve, as this is an active area of research. At present, however, given the limited extent of scientific research linking cognitive processes to academic achievement, an intra-individual differences approach must rely on the individual evaluator's knowledge of cognitive processes and educational interventions to fill in the gaps. Accordingly, the federal regulations allow evaluation teams to determine whether a pattern of strengths and weaknesses is relevant to learning disabilities identification.

Just as a critical mass of empirically established links between specific cognitive processes and areas of underachievement is critical to the use of the intra-individual differences model, the effective operation of a multitiered service delivery system is critical to the use of the RTI model. To prevent learning disabilities eligibility decisions from foundering on the shortcomings of a general education support system, the federal learning disabilities eligibility requirements established procedural safeguards to ensure that appropriate instruction has been provided and the child's progress has been assessed repeatedly over time. Otherwise, key assumptions regarding appropriate instruction and the use of scientific research-based intervention may not be met.

The clinical judgment model of interpreting assessment findings employs a balanced use of multiple sources of data, particularly in order to understand the relative and complex influence of exclusionary factors. Special education law provides a well-defined framework within which clinical judgment operates, with

guidance in the form of disability definitions, requirements for evaluation procedures, and the purposes that an evaluation must address (i.e., levels of performance, eligibility determination, and educational needs). Nevertheless, studies have shown that eligibility decisions by school-based professionals are significantly influenced by factors extraneous to federal and state mandates, such as the perceived needs of the individual child in a particular educational setting (Bocian, Beebe, MacMillan, & Gresham, 1999; Mellard et al., 2004).

An RTI model, with educational performance as the ultimate concern, relies largely on the achievement aspects of the eligibility criteria, thereby placing emphasis on direct measurement of academic achievement and educationally related behaviors. Research to date regarding the accuracy of RTI for making learning disabilities eligibility decisions has been more lacking than negative. What is clear is that an RTI approach and a discrepancy approach will identify distinctly different sets of children (Vellutino, Scanlon, & Lyon, 2000). Studies have also investigated the effect of RTI approaches on prevalence rates. Findings from RTI implementation studies have shown that school psychologists and other evaluation team members devote increased time to intervention and decreased time to assessment and that special education identification rates tend to remain stable or to decrease (Marston, Muyskens, Lau, & Canter, 2003; VanDerHeyden, Witt, & Gilbertson, 2007).

The distinction between alternative approaches to learning disabilities identification is as much a philosophical one as a scientific one. The traditional psychoeducational assessment approach is founded upon the premise that special education services should be reserved for children with neurobiologically based disorders. In comparison, the RTI approach is more concerned with ensuring appropriate services and supports for underperforming children, irrespective of etiology.

A related philosophical issue is whether the limited and valuable time of school psychologists and other educators is more productively used for screening, prevention, and intervention than for extensive assessment and gate keeping (Lyon et al., 2001). It has been proposed that efficient, focused evaluations that analyze a child's school-related performance and functional problems, and the factors that influence the child's performance yield relevant and valuable findings (Floyd, 2010; Gresham et al., 2004) and that using these findings would allow more time for problem solving and other important professional functions.

BEST PRACTICES IN LEARNING DISABILITIES IDENTIFICATION

School psychologists play a key role in helping educators, parents, and students understand the interplay between academic, cognitive, and behavioral factors and in devising plans and strategies to promote healthy development and positive learning outcomes. In doing so, school psychologists must navigate a number of clinical, legal, and practical issues. The role of the school psychologist in identifying and serving children with learning disabilities begins well before a referral to special education.

Prior to Referral

Regardless of the learning disabilities identification model used, school systems must have mechanisms in place to intervene with learning difficulties at an early stage. Early intervention is essential not only to promote positive educational outcomes but to address the rule that excludes from eligibility students whose underachievement is the result of lack of appropriate instruction in reading or math. Timely and effective general education interventions are particularly important for students who experience environmental disadvantage or cultural or language differences. As emphasized by the National Research Council report on disproportionate representation in special education (Donovan & Cross, 2002), providing supplemental instruction and implementing evidence-based interventions before a referral is an effective and socially responsible way to reduce bias and disproportionality in making eligibility decisions about minority students.

Referral and Evaluation Design

A referral for special education evaluation is initiated when it is determined that (a) a child's response to general education interventions has been insufficient or (b) when there is overwhelming evidence to suggest that a child may have a disability. Within a multitiered service delivery system, insufficient response to intervention may necessitate different, or more intensive, supports and strategies in general education depending upon why the intervention has fallen short. In the event of strong suspicion of a disability, however, a special education referral should be initiated without delay.

Upon referral, a comprehensive evaluation should be strategically designed to address both the general question of eligibility and the educational functioning and needs of the specific child. Every referral will have unique issues and questions to be addressed. As per IDEA requirements, educational evaluations are designed on an individualized basis. There is no standard battery for determining the presence of a learning disability. The evaluation design is initially based on referral information. A better sense of what assessment data are needed may evolve, however, as hypotheses are tested in the course of the evaluation or as screening (e.g., of social–emotional functioning) reveals the need to probe further in a particular area.

There are several aspects of evaluation design that school psychologists should routinely consider when a child is referred for a suspected learning disability: (a) functional assessment, (b) the role of home environment, (c) social–emotional factors, (d) collaboration with other professionals, (e) documentation procedures, and (f) feedback to the parent and child.

Functional Assessment

Given the many factors that affect learning, it is essential to obtain assessment data from multiple sources. Accordingly, IDEA 2004 requires that evaluations "use a variety of assessment tools and strategies to gather relevant functional, developmental, and academic information" (Sec. 614(b)(2)(A)). Functional information—how the child actually performs in school—is especially important. The nature and severity of a learning disability is best understood by its behavioral manifestation in the educational setting. The child's school performance is influenced by the demands, expectations, and supports of that setting. Some considerations for gathering functional information are listed in Table 22.5.

Home Environment

Parent information, obtained by interview or rating scales, may provide important data about the influence of the home upon learning. What are expectations for academic performance, and how are they conveyed? What is the child's attitude toward school and his or her capacity to learn? How does the child approach homework or prepare for a test? Does the child have access to a computer, and, if so, how is it used?

Social–Emotional Factors

Given the requirement to assess "all areas related to the suspected disability," school psychologists should routinely consider social and emotional factors. Emotional stress or dysregulation, peer group influences, parental pressures or lowered expectations, victimization, peer

Table 22.5. Functional Information Relevant to Learning Disabilities Identification

Direct observation
- How does the child perform academically and behaviorally in the classroom? (Consider effort, affect, time on task, level of independence, frustration.)
- How does the child's performance compare with the other children in the class?
- Is instruction differentiated and at an appropriate level of difficulty for the child?
- What are the environmental conditions, academic demands, and behavioral expectations associated with learning tasks?
- What are the rewards or consequences for successful and for unsuccessful performance?
- What stressors or distractions appear to affect the child?

Teacher report
- What is the child's typical performance pattern in the classroom? Can the child work independently? Can the child work for a sustained period of time? At what rate does the child work? How often does the child complete assignments satisfactorily?
- What is the child's attitude toward academic tasks? Does it vary by type of task or subject area?
- What strategies and interventions have been tried? For how long? With what degree of intensity and fidelity?
- What was the result of these strategies and interventions? How systematically were outcome data collected?
- What does the teacher believe to be the obstacles to learning?
- How does the child interact with peers? Is the child sensitive to ridicule or embarrassment regarding poor academic performance?

Work samples
- Inspect the child's academic work in both weak and strong subject areas.
- Compare work samples with those of classmates.
- Have the child read aloud from reading material used in class.

group distractions, and antisocial behavior are among the many factors that may interfere with learning. Conversely, learning problems can have a devastating effect on a child's personal, social, and emotional well-being. A learning disability may undermine a child's motivation and self-concept as a learner and lead to avoidance and other behaviors that escalate the negative effects on learning. It is often difficult to determine whether, or to what extent, social and emotional factors are secondary to a learning disability, especially if behavioral interventions and supports are not implemented before referral. A comprehensive psychoeducational assessment must explore these dynamics. The school psychologist is the educational specialist who is best prepared to understand the interaction between cognitive and social–emotional functions, interpret these findings to others, and design effective strategies to counter negative influences.

Collaboration With Other Professionals

As multiple factors contribute to learning problems, a school psychologist's assessment is interdependent on the expertise of other members of the evaluation team. Given the prominent role of language in learning disabilities and the overlap between the educational disability categories of learning disabilities and speech and language impairment, the school psychologist must often compare notes with a speech and language pathologist who has conducted a concurrent assessment of the child.

The evaluation responsibilities of public schools are broad and inclusive. Consequently, a multidisciplinary evaluation may require input from professionals outside the school team, such as a physician (e.g., neurologist, psychiatrist), neuropsychologist, occupational therapist, or physical therapist.

Documentation Procedures

Just as there are special rules for learning disabilities eligibility in federal regulations, there are documentation requirements that are unique to learning disabilities. According to federal special education regulations (Sec. 300.311), a determination of learning disabilities eligibility requires that the evaluation team generate a written statement—typically included in the Individualized Education Program (IEP)—that provides explicit assurance that the team has found each of the learning disabilities eligibility requirements to be met. In addition to referencing the learning disabilities eligibility criteria, the documentation statement must include a report of (a) relevant behavior noted during an observation of the child as it relates to academic functioning and (b) any educationally relevant medical findings. Each evaluation team member must attest to his or her agreement with the conclusions of the written statement or else submit a separate statement of the member's conclusions.

With the 2006 federal regulations, the documentation requirements were expanded to include additional items that must be addressed when using an RTI model of learning disabilities identification: (a) instructional strategies used, (b) the student-centered data collected, and (c) parent notification of the following (Sec. 300.311(a)(7)): (a) the state's policies regarding the amount and nature of student performance data to be collected and the general education services to be provided, (b) strategies for increasing the child's rate of learning, and (c) the parents' right to request an evaluation. Presumably, this is applicable when an RTI model has been used as the primary basis for determining the presence of a learning disability rather than any implementation of a multitiered system (i.e., RTI in the broad sense) that generates relevant data.

Feedback to Parent and Child

A key aspect of the evaluation process is informative and respectful feedback of evaluation results to the parent and child. Considerable thought and care is needed when a disability determination is first conveyed to the family. The school psychologist should offer a clear explanation of learning disabilities and an overview of educational and procedural implications. In providing recommendations, it is advisable to emphasize how to reduce the impact of the disability—such as with specialized instruction, use of accommodations and assistive technology, and self-advocacy—rather than the limitations the disability may impose.

What Constitutes a Comprehensive Evaluation

Special education laws require that a comprehensive evaluation be conducted when a child is suspected of having a learning disability. Proponents of both an RTI approach and a psychoeducational testing approach endorse this principle (Fletcher, Lyon, Fuchs, & Barnes, 2007; Gresham et al., 2004; Hale et al., 2006), but there are striking differences in how they conceptualize what appropriately comprises a comprehensive evaluation.

Federal regulations are not prescriptive about the specific measures or assessment procedures that constitute a comprehensive evaluation but do offer some guidance about what is required. The evaluation team must first review existing data (including evaluations and information provided by the parents of the child),

current assessments, and observations by teachers and service providers. Given this information, the evaluation team determines what additional data are needed to determine (a) whether the child has a disability, (b) what are the educational needs of the child, (c) what are the present levels of academic achievement and related developmental needs, and (d) whether the child needs special education and related services. [The first (a) and fourth (d) points may appear to be redundant; however, there are two elements to the federal definition of a child with a disability: the child qualifies under one of the 14 federal disability categories *and* "by reason thereof, needs special education and related services" (Sec. 602(3)(A)(ii)). Therefore, a child with a mild learning disability who can be appropriately served in general education would not qualify under IDEA.] Assessment measures must adhere to certain procedural safeguards, for example, using "technically sound instruments" that are "selected and administered so as not to be discriminatory," "administered in the child's native language or other mode of communication" if feasible, and "administered by trained and knowledgeable personnel" (U.S. Department of Education, 2006, Sec. 300.304). The regulations also include the following requirements concerning evaluation content:

> [Evaluators must] use a variety of assessment tools and strategies to gather relevant functional, developmental, and academic information about the child, including information provided by the parent.... (Sec. 300.304(a)(1))
>
> Assessments and other evaluation materials include those tailored to assess specific areas of educational need and not merely those that are designed to provide a single general intelligence quotient.... (Sec. 300.304(c)(2))
>
> The child is assessed in all areas related to the suspected disability, including, if appropriate, health, vision, hearing, social and emotional status, general intelligence, academic performance, communicative status, and motor abilities.... (Sec.300.304(c)(4))
>
> [T]he evaluation is sufficiently comprehensive to identify all of the child's special education and related services needs, whether or not commonly linked to the disability category in which the child has been classified.... (Sec. 300.304(c)(6))
>
> Assessment tools and strategies that provide relevant information that directly assists persons in determining the educational needs of the child are provided.... (Sec. 300.304(c)(7))

This language can be interpreted as reason to favor norm-referenced tests of cognitive abilities, neuropsychological processes, learning efficiency, and academic achievement (Flanagan et al., 2011; Hale et al., 2006). In contrast, Gresham and colleagues (2004) maintain that the federal regulations regarding comprehensive evaluation can be met by an RTI approach that emphasizes direct measures of achievement, behavior, and the instructional environment; analysis of academic skills in areas of critical deficits; and progress-monitoring data. Noting the "if appropriate" qualifier regarding the various areas to be assessed (per Sec. 300.304(c)(4), above), Gresham and colleagues (2004) propose that screening is an efficient way to address areas such as hearing, vision, intelligence, and emotional status, with more in-depth assessment conducted on an as-needed basis.

Applying the Federal Eligibility Criteria

As illustrated in Figure 22.1, the 2006 federal special education regulations specify three criteria that must be met for IDEA eligibility as a child with learning disabilities: underachievement, inclusionary evidence of a learning disability, and exclusionary factors.

Underachievement

It has been said by educators, only half-jokingly, that one cure for learning disabilities is to move to another school district, as children who are underachieving relative to an advantaged peer group will not meet the underachievement standard in a lower-performing school district. Although quality of instruction and the availability of resources in general education are factors that affect special education referrals and eligibility decisions, it is inconsistent with the goals and principles of special education for disability status to be determined by the performance of the classroom or school district peer group. The federal regulations reject a peer group basis for determining underachievement (U.S. Department of Education, 2006):

> The performance of classmates and peers is not an appropriate standard if most children in a class or school are not meeting state-approved standards. Furthermore, using grade-based normative data to make this determination is generally not appropriate for children who have not been permitted to progress to the next academic grade or are otherwise older than their peers. (p. 46652)

Although underachievement would appear to be the most readily operationalized aspect of learning disabilities identification, exclusive reliance on standardized achievement test scores is problematic. Waber (2010) makes the case for the need to consider functional skills—actual class performance—in establishing underachievement:

> Standardized achievement tests, which typically measure discrete learned skills, can often fail to capture the problems with which these children contend. These problems tend to involve fluency, efficiency, output, and (for want of a better word) integration, and are remarkably similar in both adequate and low achievers. These associated problems can interfere with the child's ability to implement his or her skills and to meet academic demands. (p. 103)

Evidence of Learning Disabilities

The second criterion, which calls for evidence of learning disabilities as the cause of underachievement, is complex and multifaceted. As discussed above, the regulations allow for the use of any of the four models discussed above: ability–achievement discrepancy, intra-individual differences (with certain qualifications), clinical judgment, or RTI.

Exclusionary Factors

Alternative explanations for underachievement must routinely be investigated so as to determine whether sensory, emotional, environmental, cultural, language, or educational factors, rather than learning disabilities, are the cause. The exclusionary criterion is intended to rule out learning disabilities when some other disability category is applicable (e.g., hearing impairment or emotional disturbance). However, school psychologists must use caution in applying exclusionary factors because these exclusionary factors can coexist with learning disabilities.

A prime example of this is early exposure to language. As documented by the landmark study of Hart and Risley (1999), children from impoverished language environments are exposed to about half as many words as children from an enriched language environment during the preschool years, and this significantly interferes with educationally relevant verbal skills. The resulting deficits—and the consequent need for specialized instruction to address them—are indistinguishable from manifestations of learning disabilities due to other causes. As another example, emotional problems may result from communication difficulties or other frustrations associated with having a learning disability. Thus, environmental factors can have substantial impact on the manifestation of the psychological process referenced by the federal definition of learning disabilities.

As explained by Fletcher and colleagues (2007), there is little discernible difference in the cognitive functioning of children with academic deficits that are attributed to environmental, emotional, and instructional factors, as compared to "true learning disability" cases of neurobiological origin. The educational needs of these two groups and the types of interventions that effectively address them are similar as well. Fletcher and colleagues (2007) cited research studies to support the argument that environmental factors are not just causes of underachievement but also of learning disabilities and concluded that "many of the conditions that are excluded as potential influences on [learning disabilities] interfere with the development of cognitive and linguistic skills that lead to the academic deficits that in turn lead to [learning disabilities]" (p. 59). School psychologists must be especially cautious in ruling out learning disabilities because of language, cultural, and environmental factors. Evaluation teams may be predisposed to rule out eligibility for disadvantaged, minority, and culturally or linguistically different children with learning disabilities.

What further complicates assessment is that intrinsic and external causes typically co-occur and interact (Fletcher et al., 2007; Waber, 2010), and there is no way to parse out the relative influence of these multiple contributing factors. Thus, the determination of learning disabilities eligibility may require clinical judgment to interpret the totality of assessment findings. What can help to assess the relative influence of environmental stressors and other external factors is to conduct a thorough history and look for patterns where educational performance has varied in step with greater or lesser influence of such factors. Prevention-oriented approaches use a similar paradigm, as the child's response to interventions and strategies that reduce the impact of external factors provides a basis for gauging the relative contribution of different factors.

Reevaluations

The procedural requirements for a reevaluation, according to federal regulations, are essentially the same as for an initial evaluation: to determine continued eligibility, current levels of academic performance, and educational needs. An additional requirement, if the child continues to need special education and related services, is to determine whether any additions or modifications to the special education program are needed for the child to meet IEP goals and participate in the general education curriculum. To address these points, a reevaluation need not be as comprehensive as the initial evaluation. This is especially true if the child's academic progress and educational needs have been routinely assessed as part of the special education program.

In conducting a reevaluation, the school psychologist cannot apply the same learning disabilities identification criteria as in the initial evaluation because it is to be expected that the child has made improved academic progress in special education. The question, then, is not whether the child is underachieving but whether the child would be underachieving if not for special education and related services. This is not something that can be determined from a battery of tests. Alternative strategies are (a) to conduct child and teacher interviews and classroom observations to determine how much the child relies upon specialized supports and strategies and (b) to implement a trial reduction in the level of services to see if the child's performance level is maintained.

In the event that the child has not been making expected gains in special education, the reevaluation is more critical and may be more comprehensive. The reevaluation would need to investigate hypotheses as to why educational gains have been limited, which may include an assessment of the instructional environment.

Use of Formulas for Learning Disabilities Determination

Strict use of a formula to interpret a pattern of strengths and weakness is problematic. While norm-referenced cognitive and achievement measures facilitate objective comparisons among children, the circumstances of a particular case often dictate against blind application of a formula. Consider, for example, a formulaic model that sets one standard deviation below the mean (16th percentile) as the criterion for underachievement. A child who, in spite of severe educational deprivation, obtains an achievement score of 84 would be considered for learning disabilities eligibility, but an educationally advantaged child who, after extensive remedial instruction, obtains an achievement score of 86 would not. This example also illustrates that an effective multitiered system may confound the use of a formula, as gains resulting from effective general education interventions may lift the child's performance above the cutoff point for underachievement.

Formulas are also limiting in that they fail to address relevant aspects of learning disabilities. Formulas do not consider variables such as instructional level, opportunity for practice and drill, curriculum materials, personal and social distractions, performance feedback, positive reinforcement, and the teacher's skill and willingness in making accommodations. Formulas also disregard background and history factors, such as attendance, mobility between schools, exposure to rich language, and family support for education.

An unfortunate consequence of a formula-based discrepancy model is that when a school psychologist primarily functions as a psychometrist, it can come at the expense of developing expertise in diagnostics and intervention strategies. School psychologists who rely on manipulation of test scores to determine the presence or absence of a learning disability have little impetus to keep abreast of learning disabilities research.

Intra-individual difference models vary in their reliance on formulas to analyze patterns of strengths and weaknesses. Hale and colleagues (2011), while noting that "clinical significance and ecological validity of findings must accompany statistical significant in [specific learning disabilities] identification" (p. 191), prescribe statistical procedures for establishing evidence of learning disabilities. Flanagan and colleagues (2011), while describing the comparisons to be made among test scores, are explicit about the need to consider multiple sources of assessment data and qualitative findings, in effect recognizing the role of clinical judgment in profile analysis.

Computer-Generated Reports

The use of computer software to interpret assessment results is similar to the use of a formula, one that is provided by an external source and that considers test scores while disregarding other data that are unique to the child. While computer software and other reference materials can be helpful in generating hypotheses, these materials should not be relied upon to make eligibility determinations or recommendations. The *Standards for Educational and Psychological Testing* (American Educational Research Association, American Psychological Association, & the National Council on Measurement in Education, 1999) provide apt guidance in cautioning against overreliance on computer-generated test interpretations because the interpretations fail to consider context and the full complement of assessment data.

Linking Assessment With Intervention

Identifying a child's educational needs is of paramount importance. Evaluations should be of value in guiding recommendations about the kind of instructional and behavioral supports needed as well as environmental conditions at school—and possibly at home—that are conducive to the child's learning. This presumes an extensive body of empirical evidence for assessment–intervention links, covering the many manifestations of learning disabilities. However, such a database does not exist at present. Consequently, clinical judgment is the primary basis for translating psychoeducational assessment findings into educational interventions. Sattler (2008), in his textbook on cognitive assessment, recognizes this point:

> It is a complex and difficult task to design interventions to ameliorate a child's problems and to foster behavioral change, learning, social adjustment, and successful participation in the community. Still, we need to use our present knowledge to design interventions, apply them carefully and thoughtfully, and then evaluate their effectiveness. … Currently, developing interventions is as much an art as it is a science" (p. 17)

Integration of Identification Models

Each learning disabilities identification model has both advantages and disadvantages. No model, used in isolation, is clearly superior. Consequently, school psychologists should consider a hybrid approach that integrates the best aspects of the multiple models. An integrated approach is implicitly supported in the commentary of the federal special education regulations:

> An RTI process does not replace the need for a comprehensive evaluation. A public agency must use a variety of data gathering tools and strategies even if an RTI process is used. The results of an RTI process may be one component of the information reviewed as part of the [required] evaluation procedures...." (U.S. Department of Education, 2006, p. 46648)

Fletcher and colleagues (2007) advocate for a hybrid model that combines curriculum-based assessments and evaluation of appropriate instruction in general education with norm-referenced achievement tests to confirm underachievement and investigate intra-individual differences in achievement. They propose that other sources of data be used selectively, with an emphasis on use of screening measures, to rule out causes of underachievement other than learning disabilities, to explore contributing factors, and to investigate referral questions.

Another way of combining methods is to rely on RTI findings of insufficient response to signal the need for a special education referral to evaluate for a suspected learning disability. As proposed by Hale and colleagues (2006), the comprehensive assessment at this stage would include norm-referenced measures of cognitive abilities and academic achievement, among other sources of information, as standard inputs for eligibility determination and educational planning.

As noted earlier, an RTI approach is compromised if an effective multitiered model is not in place. This may be a reason to rely on a traditional psychoeducational assessment battery. A psychoeducational assessment battery, however, can be supplemented with RTI data generated during the special education evaluation period. This would involve a trial period of well-designed interventions and progress monitoring. These interventions should be of the type that can be delivered within general education. If trial period interventions are more characteristic of "specialized instruction," as defined in special education law, a child's positive response may be evidence that the child is actually in need of special education and related services.

Although primary reliance on a discrepancy model is strongly discouraged, school psychologists may conduct assessments in which an ability–achievement discrepancy is a meaningful indicator of underachievement resulting from learning disabilities. This is more likely to be the case when (a) the child is intellectually capable and motivated to achieve, (b) there is a history of good instruction and educational opportunity, and (c) there is an absence of extenuating (e.g., exclusionary) factors.

Similarly, intra-individual difference models may be combined with the use of clinical judgment. The underlying principle of the intra-individual differences approach may be useful when applied selectively, giving careful consideration to patterns that yield meaningful evidence of a learning disability. For example, cognitive deficits in phonological processing, rapid naming, or verbal memory for rote information may be indicators of learning disabilities in a child with significant difficulty in basic reading skills. In order to judiciously apply an intra-individual differences approach, school psychologists must be knowledgeable about the nature and taxonomy of learning disabilities, the relationship between cognitive functions and academic skills, and the constructs underlying the assessment measures school psychologists use.

Recognizing that certain patterns of performance (i.e., ability–achievement discrepancy or intra-individual differences in cognitive abilities) are sometimes, but not always, indicators of learning disabilities calls for clinical judgment. Clinical judgment may also serve as a check, or balance, in deciding whether to downplay or apply an alternative interpretation of norm-referenced scores, such as when inattention or maladaptive behavior compromise a child's performance on cognitive tests. Also, as noted earlier, clinical judgment may be required to interpret RTI data, such as in judging whether appropriate instruction has been provided or whether an intervention has been implemented with fidelity.

Eligibility Versus Identification

While a major focus of this chapter is eligibility for special education and related services, it is important to remember that a child may have a learning disability but fail to meet eligibility criteria. It is possible that a child with a mild learning disability may be appropriately served in general education without specialized instruction or related services and therefore not meet the eligibility requirement of having a disability for which special education is needed. This is more likely to occur in schools using a multitiered model that offers high quality, differentiated instruction at Tier 1 and effective supports and strategies at Tier 2. In such circumstances, the child may still qualify as having a disabling condition under Section 504 and be entitled to accommodations.

SUMMARY

No single method of learning disabilities identification has been demonstrated to be sufficient or superior. It is clear, however, that the ability–achievement discrepancy approach is highly problematic when used as the primary determinant of learning disabilities identification rather than as a noteworthy finding. Because IDEA 2004 no longer requires an ability–achievement discrepancy as a criterion for learning disabilities eligibility, attention has shifted to alternatives methods.

Co-occurrence of deficits in cognitive functions and related achievement areas—the focus of intra-individual differences models—can be a useful indicator. Cognitive processes such as rapid naming, phonological processing, verbal memory, and executive functions have been shown to be related to particular aspects of academic achievement. However, school psychologists must have sound knowledge of cognitive science and learning disabilities in interpreting such relationships so as not to apply this model when the research evidence is limited or lacking.

There is overwhelming support for using a multitiered RTI approach that delivers appropriate instruction and other supports within general education. This reduces the likelihood of inappropriate referrals due to short-comings of general education and also produces valuable data for identification purposes. An RTI model is most practical and effective when embedded within a well-designed and effectively implemented multitiered service delivery system.

Clinical judgment plays a role to a greater or lesser degree in every learning disabilities identification model. Reliance upon clinical judgment to interpret assessment results is heavily dependent upon the expertise of the individual school psychologist.

In using any model, clinical judgment in particular, school psychologists are strongly advised to know the research literature on learning disabilities and learning problems, to make use of clinical supervision and other resources, and to follow up on their assessments to evaluate the appropriateness of eligibility decisions and recommendations.

REFERENCES

American Educational Research Association, American Psychological Association, & National Council on Measurement in Education. (1999). *Standards for educational and psychological testing*. Washington, DC: Author.

American Psychiatric Association. (2013). *Diagnostic and statistical manual of mental disorders* (5th ed.). Washington, DC: Author.

Berninger, V. W. (2009). Highlights of programmatic, interdisciplinary research on writing. *Learning Disabilities Research & Practice, 24*, 69–80. doi:10.1111/j.1540-5826.2009.00281.x

Bocian, K. M., Beebe, M. E., MacMillan, D. L., & Gresham, F. M. (1999). Competing paradigms in learning disabilities classification by schools and the variations in the meaning of discrepant achievement. *Learning Disabilities Research & Practice, 14*, 1–14.

Donovan, M. S., & Cross, C. T. (2002). *Minority students in special and gifted education*. Washington, DC: National Academies Press. doi:10.1111/j.1467-9280.2006.01685.x10.1111/j

Flanagan, D. P., Alfonso, V. C., & Mascolo, J. T. (2011). A CHC-based operational definition of SLD: Integrating multiple data sources and multiple data-gathering methods. In D. P. Flanagan & V. C. Alfonso (Eds.), *Essentials of specific learning disability identification* (pp. 233–298). Hoboken, NJ: Wiley. doi:10.1044/1092-4388(2012/10-0335)

Fletcher, J. M., Denton, C., & Francis, D. J. (2005). Validity of alternative approaches for the identification of LD: Operationalizing unexpected underachievement. *Journal of Learning Disabilities, 38*, 308–312.

Fletcher, J. M., Lyon, G. R., Fuchs, L. S., & Barnes, M. A. (2007). *Learning disabilities: From identification to intervention*. New York, NY: Guilford Press. doi:10.1177/1087054707305354

Floyd, R. G. (2010). Assessment of cognitive abilities and cognitive processes: Issues, applications and fit within a problem-solving model. In G. G. Peacock, R. A. Ervin, E. J. Daly, & K. W. Merrell (Eds.), *Practical handbook of school psychology: Effective practices for the 21st century*. New York, NY: Guilford Press. doi:10.1007/s10864-011-9141-x

Francis, D. J., Fletcher, J. M., Stuebing, K. K., Lyon, G. R., Shaywitz, B. A., & Shaywitz, S. E. (2005). Psychometric approaches to the identification of LD: IQ and achievement scores are not sufficient. *Journal of Learning Disabilities, 38*, 98–108.

Francis, D. J., Shaywitz, S. E., Stuebing, K. K., Shaywitz, B. A., & Fletcher, J. M. (1996). Developmental lag versus deficit models of reading disability: A longitudinal, individual growth curves analysis. *Journal of Educational Psychology, 88*, 3–17.

Fuchs, D. J., Mock, D., Morgan, P. L., & Young, C. L. (2003). Responsiveness to intervention: Definitions, evidence, and implications for the learning disabilities construct. *Learning Disabilities Research & Practice, 18*, 157–171.

Fuchs, L. S. (2003). Assessing intervention responsiveness: Conceptual and technical issues. *Learning Disabilities Research & Practice, 18*, 172–186.

Fuchs, L. S., & Fuchs, D. (1998). Treatment validity: A unifying construct for reconceptualizing the identification of learning disabilities. *Learning Disability Research & Practice, 13*, 204–219.

Geary, D. C., Hoard, M. K., Byrd-Craven, J., Nugent, L., & Numtee, C. (2007). Cognitive mechanisms underlying achievement deficits in children with mathematical learning disability. *Child Development, 78*, 1343–1359.

Gresham, F., Reschly, D., & Shinn, M. R. (2010). RTI as a driving force in educational improvement: Research, legal, and practice perspectives. In M. R. Shinn & H. M. Walker (Eds.), *Interventions for achievement and behavior problems in a three-tier model including RTI* (pp. 47–77). Bethesda, MD: National Association of School Psychologists.

Gresham, F., Reschly, D., Tilly, W. D., Fletcher, J., Burns, M., Crist, T., … Shinn, M. R. (2004). Comprehensive evaluation of learning disabilities: A response-to-intervention perspective. *Communiqué, 33*(4), 34–35.

Grimes, J. (2002). Responsiveness to interventions: The next step in special education identification, service, and exiting decision making. In R. Bradley, L. Danielson, & D. P. Hallahan (Eds.), *Identification of learning disabilities: Research to practice* (pp. 531–547). Mahwah, NJ: Erlbaum.

Hale, J. B., Flanagan, D. P., & Naglieri, J. A. (2008). Alternative research-based methods for IDEA (2004) identification of children with specific learning disabilities. *Communiqué, 36*(8), *1*, 14–17.

Hale, J. B., Kaufman, A., Naglieri, J. A., & Kavale, K. A. (2006). Implementation of IDEA: Integrating response-to-intervention and cognitive assessment methods. *Psychology in the Schools, 43*, 753–770.

Hale, J. B., Wycoff, K. L., & Fiorello, C. A. (2011). RTI and cognitive hypothesis testing for identification and intervention of specific learning disabilities: The best of both worlds. In D. P. Flanagan & V. C. Alfonso (Eds.), *Essentials of specific learning disability identification* (pp. 233–298). Hoboken, NJ: Wiley.

Hallahan, D. P., & Mercer, C. D. (2002). Learning disabilities: Historical perspectives. In R. Bradley, L. Danielson, & D. P. Hallahan (Eds.), *Identification of learning disabilities: Research to practice* (pp. 1–67). Mahwah, NJ: Erlbaum.

Hart, B., & Risley, T. R. (1999). *Meaningful differences in the everyday experience of young American children*. Baltimore, MD: Brookes. doi:10.1007/s00431-005-0010-2

Johnson, E. S., Humphrey, M., Mellard, D. F., Woods, K., & Swanson, H. L. (2010). Cognitive processing deficits and students with specific learning disabilities: A selective meta-analysis of the literature. *Learning Disabilities Quarterly, 33*, 3–18.

Kavale, K. A. (2002). Discrepancy models in the identification of learning disability. In R. Bradley, L. Danielson, & D. P. Hallahan (Eds.), *Identification of learning disabilities: Research to practice* (pp. 369–426). Mahwah, NJ: Erlbaum.

Lichtenstein, R. (2002). *NASP input on LD identification and eligibility for the NJCLD workgroup*. Unpublished document.

Lichtenstein, R., & Klotz, M. B. (2007). Deciphering the federal regulations on identifying children with specific learning disabilities. *Communiqué, 36*(3), Retrieved from http://www.nasponline.org/publications/cq/mocq363regs.aspx

Lyon, G. R. (1998). *Overview of reading and literacy initiatives*. Prepared statement to the U.S. Senate Committee on Labor and Human Resources. Retrieved from http://www.reidlyon.com/edpolicy/5-OVERVIEW-OF-READING-AND-LITERACY-INITIATIVES.pdf

Lyon, G. R., Fletcher, J. M., Shaywitz, S. E., Shaywitz, B. A., Torgesen, J. K., Wood, F. B., … Olson, R. (2001). Rethinking learning disabilities. In C. E. Finn Jr., A. J. Rotherham, & C. R. Hokanson Jr. (Eds.), *Rethinking special education for a new century* (pp. 259–287). Washington, DC: Thomas B. Fordham Foundation. Retrieved from http://www.dss.nrru.ac.th/download/ld/SpecialEd_ch12.pdf

Marston, D., Muyskens, P., Lau, M., & Canter, A. (2003). Problem-solving model for decision making with high-incidence disabilities: The Minneapolis experience. *Learning Disabilities Research & Practice, 18*, 187–200.

Mather, N., & Gregg, N. (2006). Specific learning disabilities: Clarifying, not eliminating, a construct. *Professional Psychology: Research and Practice, 37*, 99–106.

Mellard, D. F., Deshler, D. D., & Barth, A. (2004). LD identification: It's not simply a matter of building a better mousetrap. *Learning Disability Quarterly, 27*, 230–242.

Naglieri, J. A. (2011). The discrepancy/consistency approach to SLD identification using the PASS theory. In D. P. Flanagan & V. C. Alfonso (Eds.), *Essentials of specific learning disability identification* (pp. 145–172). Hoboken, NJ: Wiley.

National Association of School Psychologists. (2003). *NASP recommendations for IDEA reauthorization: Identification and eligibility determination for students with specific learning disabilities*. Bethesda, MD: Author. Retrieved from http://www.nasponline.org/advocacy/LDRecs_042803.pdf

National Association of School Psychologists. (2010a). *Ethical and professional practices for school psychologists*. Bethesda, MD: Author. Retrieved from http://www.nasponline.org/standards/ethics/ethical-conduct-professional-practices.aspx

National Association of School Psychologists. (2010b). *Model for comprehensive and integrated school psychological services*. Bethesda, MD: Author. Retrieved from http://www.nasponline.org/standards/2010standards/2_PracticeModel.pdf

National Association of School Psychologists. (2011). *Identification of students with specific learning disabilities* (Position Statement). Bethesda, MD: Author. Retrieved from http://www.nasponline.org/about_nasp/positionpapers/Identification_of_SLD.pdf

National Joint Committee on Learning Disabilities. (1990). *Learning disabilities: Issues on definition*. Retrieved from http://www.ldonline.org/about/partners/njcld/archives

O'Donnell, P. S., & Miller, D. N. (2011). Identifying students with specific learning disabilities: School psychologists' acceptability of the discrepancy model versus response to intervention. *Journal of Disabilities Policy Studies, 22*, 83–94.

Pennington, B. F. (2009). *Diagnosing learning disorders: A neuropsychological framework* (2nd ed.). New York, NY: Guilford Press.

President's Commission on Excellence in Special Education. (2002). *A new era: Revitalizing special education for children and their families*. Washington, DC: Office of Special Education and Rehabilitative Services, U.S. Department of Education.

Reschly, D. J., & Hosp, J. L. (2004). State SLD identification policies and practices. *Learning Disability Quarterly, 27*, 197–213.

Rutter, M., & Yule, W. (1975). The concept of specific reading retardation. *Journal of Child Psychology and Psychiatry, 16*, 181–197.

Sattler, J. M. (2008). *Assessment of children: Cognitive foundations* (5th ed.). San Diego, CA: Jerome Sattler.

Scruggs, T. E., & Mastropieri, M. A. (2002). On babies and bathwater: Addressing the problems of identification of learning disabilities. *Learning Disabilities Quarterly, 25*, 155–168.

Siegel, L. S. (1989). IQ is irrelevant to the definition of learning disabilities. *Journal of Learning Disabilities, 22*, 469–486.

SpectrumK12. (n.d.). *2011 RTI implementation report*. Towson, MD: Author. Retrieved from http://www.spectrumk12.com/rti/the_rti_corner/rti_adoption_report

U.S. Department of Education. (2006). 34 CFR Parts 300 and 301: Assistance to states for the education of children with disabilities and preschool grants for children with disabilities; Final rule. *Federal Register, 71*(156).

U.S. Department of Education, Office of Special Education and Rehabilitative Services. (2012). *31st annual report to Congress on the implementation of the Individuals with Disabilities Education Act, 2009*. Washington, DC: Author.

U.S. Office of Education. (1977). Assistance to states for education of handicapped children: Procedures for evaluating specific learning disabilities. *Federal Register, 42*(250), 65082–65085.

VanDerHeyden, A. M., Witt, J. C., & Gilbertson, D. A. (2007). Multi-year evaluation of the effects of a Response to Intervention (RTI) model on identification of children for special education. *Journal of School Psychology, 45*, 225–256. doi:10.1016/j.jsp.2006.11.004

Vellutino, F., Scanlon, D., & Lyon, G. R. (2000). Differentiating between difficult-to-remediate and readily remediated poor readers: More evidence against the IQ-achievement discrepancy definition of reading disability. *Journal of Learning Disabilities, 33*, 223–238.

Waber, D. P. (2010). *Rethinking learning disabilities: Understanding children who struggle in school*. New York, NY: Guilford Press.

23

Best Practices in the Assessment and Remediation of Communication Disorders

Melissa A. Bray
Thomas J. Kehle
University of Connecticut
Lea A. Theodore
College of William and Mary (VA)

OVERVIEW

Taking into consideration the National Association of School Psychologists (NASP) *Model for Comprehensive and Integrated School Psychological Services* (NASP, 2010) and the domain Data-Based Decision Making and Accountability and how this relates to a multitiered system of supports (e.g., response to intervention [RTI]), the fields of school psychology and speech pathology are ideally suited for collaboration. With respect to this framework, school psychologists and speech–language pathologists may provide children and adolescents with services in the following general areas: (a) service delivery, such as outcome-driven decisions, accountability, and consultation; (b) practices that affect student-level services, such as collaboration during assessment and intervention for academic and social functioning; (c) practices that affect systems-level services, such as the implementation of school-wide practices for the promotion of learning, prevention, and family–school collaboration; and (d) collaboration with regard to issues that are related to individual differences, research, and program evaluation.

Traditionally, school psychologists have viewed communication disorders as falling within the area of speech and language pathologists. Similarly, speech pathologists often defer mental health and academic problems to school psychologists. This thinking is erroneous and not beneficial to schoolchildren because collaboration between both disciplines is integral to promoting positive student outcomes.

In addition to the NASP Practice Model (NASP, 2010), other factors support the collaboration of the disciplines of school psychology and speech–language pathology. These include shortages in both fields; the specific implementation of the RTI approach that necessitates a cross-disciplinary structure; and current emphasis on prevention, data-based outcomes, and the implication of language disorders in the identification of learning disabilities, along with the interplay between communication and educational functioning. Additional support is derived from the fact that children with communication disorders often experience emotional, social, and academic deficits, which strengthens the argument that school psychologists and speech pathologists should work together on assessment and intervention issues.

School psychological practices that affect student-level services during assessment and interventions for academic issues (e.g., learning disabilities, intellectual disorders, gifted behavior) and social functioning issues (e.g., internalizing and externalizing disorders) is where collaborative efforts should be placed (NASP, 2010). Collaboration about children with communication challenges fits within the practice of speech pathology, which

> … is responsible for the diagnosis, prognosis, prescription, and remediation of speech, language, and swallowing disorders. A speech-language pathologist evaluates and treats children and adults who have difficulty speaking, listening,

reading, writing, or swallowing. The overall objective of speech-language pathology services is to optimize individuals' ability to communicate and swallow, thereby improving quality of life. (American Speech-Language-Hearing Association, 2013, para. 2)

Thus, school psychologists should understand the relevant communication disorders in terms of categorization into speech, language, and hearing. (See Table 23.1.)

Speech disorders may be categorized as articulation, voice, and fluency. An articulation disorder is defined as the mispronunciation of sounds, and is characterized by substitutions, omissions, additions, or distortions that affect the listener's understanding. A voice disorder, or dysphonia, is defined by abnormalities of vocal quality relative to the features of pitch, loudness, duration, and resonance. Stuttering is a primary fluency disorder that involves repetitions or prolongations of sounds, words, or phrases. It also includes blocking, which is the freezing of the lips, tongue, or vocal folds when attempting to produce speech.

Language disorders are bifurcated into receptive (listening and reading comprehension) and expressive (speaking and writing). Expressive and receptive language disorders generally include deficits in form (grammar) and function (meaning and social use). Specifically, the areas of phonology (sound system of language), morphology (smallest units of language that carry meaning), syntax (grammar), semantics (meaning), and pragmatics (social language) can be affected. With respect to phonological problems, the areas that affect reading are rhyming, letter recognition, letter–sound pairing, sound, and syllable segmentation are the areas that affect reading. Morphology, by definition, addresses the smallest parts of words that contain meaning, and these may not be understood by those with language disorders (e.g., big, bigg*er*, bigg*est*). Syntax (punctuation and grammar) may also be impaired. Importantly, semantics or word knowledge, involving vocabulary and basic concepts, is linked to academic achievement, social behavior, and communication. Therefore, it is important to make note of vocabulary errors during testing. In addition, pragmatics or social language, is associated with social skills and various associated disorders such as autism spectrum disorder. Finally, memory and word-finding errors many times accompany language disorders but are difficult, unfortunately, to remediate.

Hearing is divided into peripheral and central disorders. Peripheral hearing includes middle ear/conductive and inner ear/sensorineural impairments, whereas central disorders include auditory processing disorder, which is related to brain or neuropsychological functioning.

In summary, communication is separated into three broad areas: speech (articulation, voice, and fluency), language (expressive and receptive), and hearing (peripheral and central). Swallowing disorders are also included, but primarily fall within the expertise of the communication specialist. The intent of this chapter is to present areas of collaboration in terms of specific assessment tools and treatment options with respect to communication issues and cognitive, academic, and social functioning. The rationale is that collaboration is the best practice and as such will substantially benefit school children in promoting positive student outcomes.

Table 23.1. Definition of Communication Disorders

Speech disorders
- Articulation: Misarticulation of sounds, syllables, or words; characterized by substitutions, omissions, additions, or distortions
- Voice: Qualitative disturbance of pitch, loudness, duration, and/or resonance
- Fluency: Stuttering, or repetition or prolongation of sounds, words, or phrases; also may include blocking or a freezing of the lips, mouth, or vocal folds

Language disorders
- Expressive: Deficit in speaking or writing
- Receptive: Deficit in listening or reading comprehension
- Mixed or global: Combination of expressive and receptive disorders

Hearing disorders
- Peripheral: Middle or inner ear impairment
- Central auditory processing disorder: Auditory processing problems due to neurological causes not related to middle or inner ears
- Swallowing difficulty or dysphagia: Difficulties moving food from the mouth to the stomach

BASIC CONSIDERATIONS

The theoretical relationship among students' emotional, academic, and communication dysfunctions is such that it may be beneficial to consider the three issues as a unitary concept. In other words, the association among the three areas is clear, and thus promotes collaboration. Employing collaboration through RTI and the NASP Practice Model (NASP, 2010) should lead to improved academic, communication, and social outcomes for students.

Peer acceptance of children with communication disorders is inversely related to the severity of the disorder. Early language disorders appear related to the initiation and maintenance of friendships that endure throughout life and are also associated with both internalizing and externalizing behavioral problems. Students who lack meaningful social relationships with peers tend to evidence myriad emotional and communication/language disorders. Most students with language dysfunctions may even experience elevated bullying behavior or may be the recipient of the bullying behavior. Further, language disorders may persist into adolescence, and these adolescents are generally not as socially skilled, less well liked, and more often rejected. Further, Thatcher, Fletcher, and Decker (2008) argued that children with communication disorders, in addition to exhibiting dysfunctional social behavior, are also likely to experience academic difficulty, particularly learning disabilities. They also may exhibit deficits in speech perception and short-term memory. Consequently, according to Thatcher et al. (2008), a multidisciplinary approach to assessment and intervention with communication, academics, and mental health is warranted.

The prevalence of communication disorders is high in criminal offenders. The relationship is pronounced, and not uncommonly these problems persist throughout adulthood. Further, the relative inability to initiate and maintain friendships, as evidenced in some children with communication disorders, tends to predict a higher probability of adult mental health and communication problems. Specifically, with respect to language disorders, there is a higher incidence of not only academic and social difficulties, but also occupational disturbances.

Overall, students with insufficient language skills struggle with developing friendships because of their inability to interact and communicate socially. These children also may have poor pragmatic skills, difficulty with negotiating conflict, and trouble analyzing social situations. Children with language disorders typically use aggressive nonverbal behaviors to negotiate with peers or withdraw and become socially isolated. Research findings have shown that over half of children with behavioral issues also seem to have associated language deficits. Males with language and learning disorders also seem to have a somewhat higher risk of run-ins with the law. Children with autism spectrum disorders, due to pragmatic language deficits, are also more likely to experience poor social peer acceptance. Countless school psychologists come across students diagnosed with autism spectrum disorders, and the impact it has on academics and social relationships is substantial. For enriched student results, it is critical that collaboration occur between school psychologists and speech–language pathologists on the development, application, and evaluation of school-based supports to aid students with autism spectrum disorders and other types of communication disorders.

There is evidence to support a relationship between speech and language disorders and academic competence, particularly with language and reading. It has been found that in about half of children with reading disorders, these children also have impaired speech, language, and writing, and this is supported by genetic evidence. Consequently, it may be assumed that reading and speech and language impairments may have the same genetically based etiology. Further, in support of this finding is that, during early toddlerhood, speech and language disorders predict poor reading. Overall, deficits in these areas are associated with a commensurate lack of competence in academic skills.

BEST PRACTICES IN THE ASSESSMENT AND REMEDIATION OF COMMUNICATION DISORDERS

Assessment and intervention of children with communication disorders will be presented in terms of addressing the areas most relevant to speech–language pathologists and school psychologists. Collaborative assessment in the areas of academic, cognitive, and psychological functioning as well as communication will be discussed, followed by best practices in interventions designed for the major communication areas of speech, language, and hearing.

Assessment

The assessment results of children with communication and psychological and academic disorders lend themselves to efficacious and enduring interventions. Obviously, the psychometric soundness of indices and the interpretation of the results relative to the design of treatment strategies are most important. Typically, school psychologists and speech pathologists formulate a hypothesis of the likely causes of the student's problematic behavior. However, in some cases the causes are either unknown or mistakenly identified and thus not necessarily needed to effect meaningful and enduring positive change. Nonetheless, on most occasions, assessment results are helpful in determining the course of treatment, and taking the most informative parts of various tests given by different professionals leads to best practices.

It is important to recognize the value of language to better understand the close relationship between school psychology and speech–language pathology. That is, language supports reading. Therefore, if a student has a language disorder, there is a greater likelihood that that student also has reading problems. Other connections between the two fields, as theoretically discussed above, include the findings that students with many types of communication disorders have not only academic problems but psychological difficulties as well (e.g., internalizing behaviors, especially anxiety and depression, and externalizing behaviors, such as disruptive behaviors). Children with an autism spectrum disorder are an excellent example of those who have impairments in social/pragmatic communication, behavior, and academic functioning, and thus, collaboration is warranted. In addition, stuttering and some voice problems can involve learning factors, and collaboration is also beneficial. Finally, central auditory processing disorder, typically diagnosed by speech–language pathologists and audiologists, can be another area of collaboration.

Generally, however, the primary areas of overlap between the two professions are likely related to an academic problem in reading or writing (mostly reading) with implicated language deficits. Thus, the diagnostic outcome many times is a language-based learning disability. This is why the academic area of reading and not mathematics are typically affected in children with language disorders. This is not to say that math is never affected. As math skills evolve from basic calculations in elementary school to higher order thinking in later elementary grades and subsequently middle and high school, students are required to understand the meaning of mathematical vocabulary and word problems. In other words, students need to understand the language of math, which is why students may struggle academically in this area.

In light of the overlap between school and speech–language pathologists, these school-based professionals should work collaboratively in the assessment of communication and psychological and academic disorders. Assessment is crucial as the pooling of results leads to a better description of the student. The RTI type of model works best because here professionals can collaborate at various levels of service delivery. Collaboration can occur in the classroom or in intensive treatment situations. Minimally, assessments of academic, cognitive, psychological, and speech–language functioning should be employed, especially when a formal diagnosis is being sought. Informal assessment at lower tiers would most likely involve curriculum-based assessment for academic issues and direct observation for communication and social–emotional concerns. Academic, cognitive, psychological, and speech–language functioning are the areas most important to collaboration in order to better understand a child's overall deficits. There are numerous indices that purport to adequately measure these areas. The following assessment instruments are considered to be the most appropriate and adequate measures and appear best suited to the RTI type of collaborative model. Most of these tests may not be needed until Tier 3, with the exception of the curriculum-based and direct observational measures that are well suited for Tiers 1 and 2. However, when a diagnosis is reached through the collaborative problem-solving process, these tests are imperative. School psychologists must be aware of what tests are suitable for these students.

Academic Skills

The Wechsler Individual Achievement Test–Third Edition (Wechsler, 2009), based on its excellent psychometric characteristics, should be considered in the assessment of academic skills in individuals ages 4–51. The subtests are useful not only in diagnosing academic issues but also in diagnosing language disorders. The most useful subtests for doing so are listening comprehension, early reading skills, oral expression, written expression, and reading comprehension. In addition, the Woodcock-Johnson III Tests of Achievement (Woodcock, McGrew, & Mather, 2007) are also an acceptable measure for the same reasons. When assessing academic achievement, students with language disorders often have difficulty with the reading and writing portions of the instrument.

Therefore, school psychologists should pay close attention to students' performance in the administration of the following subtests: picture vocabulary, letter–word identification, story recall, understanding directions, writing fluency, passage comprehension, oral comprehension, word attack, and sound awareness. Each of these subtests is useful for diagnosing problems with both receptive (oral and written comprehension/reading) and expressive language (speaking and writing). The math subtests should also be inspected for language implications relative to word problems or memory issues.

There are narrow-band instruments that are useful in diagnosing a language disorder. Of particular benefit are those for reading and written expression. The Gray Oral Reading Test–Fourth Edition (Wiederholt & Bryant, 2001) and the Wechsler Reading Mastery Test–Third Edition (Wechsler, 2011) not only are psychometrically sound but also have great precision in identifying deficits in reading fluency and comprehension deficits related to language skills. Written expression may be evaluated using the Test of Written Language–Fourth Edition (Hammill & Larsen, 2006).

Cognitive Skills

When developing a test battery, it is important to include an overall measure of cognitive functioning. This is because such measures will not only provide school psychologists with information about a student's overall level of functioning but also give a picture of his or her language ability. With regard to the necessity of ascertaining the student's level of general cognitive ability on a standardized test, and in consideration of its excellent psychometric properties, the Wechsler Intelligence Scale for Children–Fourth Edition (WISC-IV; Wechsler, 2003) and Woodcock-Johnson III Tests of Cognitive Abilities (WJ III-Cognitive; Woodcock, McGrew, & Mather, 2009) are appropriate measures of cognitive functioning as well as language skills. Both of these indices provide psychometrically sound evidence for language disorders.

In particular, when administering a cognitive measure, school psychologists should take note of low verbal performance scores. Cognitive tests are most relevant for diagnosing expressive and receptive language disorders and language-based learning disabilities, particularly in relation to reading and writing outcomes. Individual state regulations should be taken into account to be sure guidelines for learning disabilities are being followed. These tests are also helpful in looking at memory, processing speed, and visual–spatial skills. In particular, the WISC-IV cognitive subtests of vocabulary, similarities, and information, and the verbal cluster on the WJ III-Cognitive provide school psychologists with valuable opportunities to note signs of a language disorder. For example, if vocabulary is weak or word analogies are difficult to make, then this would point to a language issue.

In addition, processing speed and memory scores are relevant to the speech and language diagnosis of a central auditory processing disorder. The Peabody Picture Vocabulary Test–Fourth Edition (Dunn & Dunn, 2007) is an excellent assessment instrument that can be used as a short and easily administered evaluation of receptive vocabulary and is considered to be tantamount to a measure of cognitive ability.

Psychological Functioning

The psychological areas of most relevance to school psychology and speech–language pathology are in the areas of learning factors, anxiety, depression, and disruptive and pragmatic behaviors. A broadband assessment taps an array of behaviors. Areas that are identified as at risk or clinically significant may then be addressed more specifically by a narrow-band test if needed. The broadband Behavior Assessment System for Children–Second Edition (BASC-2; Reynolds & Kamphaus, 2004) provides a multimethod, multidimensional assessment of personality and behavioral functioning derived from self, parent, and teacher perspectives. BASC-2 has acceptable psychometric properties and provides beneficial differential diagnostic information and classification of academic functioning and emotional–behavioral disorders. Another psychometrically sound broadband instrument is the Achenbach System of Empirically Based Assessment (Achenbach, 2010). Overall, both instruments yield data that address behavioral and social–emotional functioning and are considered to be an important component of the assessment battery. The appeal is the focused information that they provide, which facilitates the development of specifically designed, evidence-based interventions for children with communication and/or psychological disorders.

As mentioned previously, if administration of a broadband measure can be done at Tiers 1 and 2, results of at-risk or clinically significant findings would be appropriate to further investigate and follow up using a narrow-band instrument. Narrow-band tests measure internalizing disorders (e.g., anxiety and depression), externalizing disorders (attention deficit hyperactivity disorder, oppositional defiant disorder, conduct disorder), social skills, and factors that influence learning. One of the primary areas of overlap between school psychology and speech–language pathology is that of social skills functioning. This is because children with language disorders and learning disabilities have concomitant social skill deficits. The lack of ability to verbally negotiate can also lead to disruptive behavior. Therefore, a thorough assessment of pragmatic language or social skills is essential. The psychologically based narrow-band test most relevant to communication disorders for pragmatic language or social skills is the Social Skills Improvement System (Elliot & Gresham, 2008). This provides both assessment information and suggestions for intervention that are especially useful for children with language-based learning disabilities or autism spectrum disorder, where social skill issues are implicated.

The Behavior Observation of Students in Schools (BOSS; Shapiro, 2008) is a psychometrically sound measure that yields valuable information regarding classroom disruptive behaviors and is easily implemented during the early tiers. More specifically, BOSS provides information regarding both active and passive behaviors that can relate to various communication disorders. For anxiety, the narrow-band Revised Children's Manifest Anxiety Scale–Second Edition (C. R. Reynolds & Richmond, 2004) is an excellent assessment instrument, and the Reynolds Adolescent Depression Scale–Second Edition (W. Reynolds, 2002) is ideally suited to evaluate depression. Finally, in order to better understand factors that influence student learning, it is considered best practice to interview the child, teachers, and, if appropriate, parents and conduct observations in different demand-context centers. The goal is to determine if the behaviors were learned through modeling or operant or classical conditioning paradigms.

Communication Disorders

School psychologists are capable of both formal and informal assessment of communication disorders specifically in the areas of language, stuttering, articulation, and central auditory processing.

Language. School psychologists should include classroom observation of language skills, in conjunction with collaboration with the speech pathologist, in their evaluations, which may include oral and written communication, auditory discrimination, following directions, pronunciation, grammatical usage, phonological skills, and pragmatic or social language. Language is the backbone of reading. Therefore, most individuals with a learning disability have reading and language difficulties. Specifically, phonological processing problems are highly implicated in poor readers and those with language-based learning disabilities. Phonological awareness training is an area that can be strengthened once identified as a weakness.

When conducting a language evaluation or observation, it is important to take into account whether the child speaks another language. This is because speaking another language has an impact on language skill, as these skills relate to phonological awareness and reading. If the student is an English language learner, then it may take longer for fluent phonological awareness to be achieved. Perhaps a bilingual speech pathologist would be helpful in these cases.

Instruments that specifically assess phonological awareness include the Phonological Awareness Test 2 (Robertson & Salter, 2007), which is intended for children ages 5–9 and measures phonological knowledge, specifically letter–sound correspondence. The Test of Phonological Awareness–Second Edition: PLUS (Torgesen & Bryant, 2004) is an individualized or group administered test of phonemic awareness for children ages 5–8 and identifies at-risk children for language and reading disorders. The Yopp-Singer Test of Phoneme Segmentation (Yopp, 1995) measures a child's capability to isolate, segment, and pronounce phonemes in children ages 5–7. The Khan-Lewis Phonological Analysis Test–Second Edition (Khan & Lewis, 2002) assesses phonological processing in individuals ages 2–21. The Comprehensive Test of Phonological Processing (Wagner, Torgesen, & Rashotte, 2004) is normed for individuals ages 5–25. It is one of the few phonological processing tests that extend into adulthood and assesses phonological knowledge (sound matching, blending, and segmenting with nonsense words and real words, and phoneme reversal) and phonological memory (memory for numbers, nonsense repetition, and rapid labeling of colors, numbers, items, and letters). It has solid reliability estimates (.78–.95) and a relatively reduced standard error of measurement. The Lindamood Auditory Conceptualization Test–Third Edition (Lindamood & Lindamood, 2009) is a test of phonological awareness. This test assesses speech–sound discrimination, auditory perception, and the ability to make comparisons of sound patterns.

The school psychologist may also evaluate a student's receptive and expressive vocabulary. Tests that the school psychologist may employ to address this include the Peabody Picture Vocabulary Test–Fourth Edition (Dunn & Dunn, 2007), which is appropriate for individuals 2½–90+, and the Receptive One-Word Picture Vocabulary Test–Fourth Edition (Brownell, 2010b) for individuals 2–80+ years of age and is a companion test to the Expressive One-Word Picture Vocabulary Test–Fourth Edition (Brownell, 2010a). Both are excellent measures of vocabulary and include Spanish versions.

The Test of Language Development–Fourth Edition (Hammill & Newcomer, 2005) measures language development in children ages 4–9. The Clinical Evaluation of Language Fundamentals–Fifth Edition (Semel, Wiig, & Secord, 2013) is an excellent assessment of receptive and expressive language and has solid psychometric properties. The Dynamic Indicators of Basic Early Literacy Skills–Next (Kaminski & Good, 2009) may also be used by school psychologists, especially at Tiers 1 and 2, to identify school-age students who may be at risk for reading problems related to myriad language-based reading skill precursors. It assesses such areas as phoneme segmentation fluency, rhyming, and onset recognition fluency and letter-naming fluency. With regard to written language, the Test of Written Language–Fourth Edition (Hammill & Larsen, 2006) is the best psychometrically and one of the very few narrow-band instruments in this area.

School psychologists should also consider providing a pragmatic language assessment when conducting an evaluation. There are many assessment measures, including the Pragmatic Language Skills Inventory (Gilliam & Miller, 2006), which is appropriate for children ages 5–13. It assesses interpersonal skills, social communicative skills, and classroom interaction. The Test of Pragmatic Language–Second Edition (Phelps-Terasaki & Phelps-Gunn, 2007) is appropriate for individuals ages 6–19 and specifically assesses pragmatic or social language skills, using pictorial dilemmas.

Speech pathologists are uniquely suited to conduct observations of speech and language at the lower tiers. Mean length of utterance is one example of what they may do. School psychologists could aid this process with their expert knowledge of how to conduct direct observations in classrooms and in progress monitoring techniques.

Stuttering. There are many reasons why individuals stutter: language disorders, psychopathologies, and learning factors. Therefore, scores on language skills testing should be considered when assessing a student for a stuttering disorder. This is because language issues and language development can lead to stuttering and are particularly important to address for children of approximately 3–4 years of age who may stutter during critical language acquisition periods. As mentioned previously, it is important to ask if the student speaks another language, because children who learn two languages simultaneously have a greater likelihood of stuttering. Speech pathologists will conduct the testing to specifically evaluate stuttering, but school psychologists will hear the dysfluencies during testing, and may provide language-related testing scores. In addition, school psychologists can also aid in the collection of direct observational data of stuttering in various demand-center contexts. If language is deemed to be the cause, then the speech–language pathologist can address this underlying problem.

The school psychologist may conduct direct observations in various demand-center contexts to identify whether stuttering occurs in certain situations (e.g., when talking to a teacher or authority figure and not to a friend). If so, behavior modification and social learning strategies (e.g., video self-modeling) could be recommended and implemented with the school psychologist's assistance. Also, since various psychopathologies are related to stuttering (mainly depression, panic, and anxiety), these emotional test scores are helpful for intervention planning. Therefore, it is important to stress that speech–language pathologists either consult with or refer students who stutter to the school psychologists.

Articulation. Since most school psychologists do not have expertise in articulation, they will not administer articulation tests as part of their overall assessment battery. However, it is important for school psychologists to be aware of such indices that assess articulation, such as the Goldman-Fristoe Test of Articulation–Second Edition (Goldman & Fristoe, 2000). This instrument evaluates consonant sound production in both children and adults. School psychologists can also work with speech–language pathologists to collect direct observational data in this area. In addition, school psychologists may assist speech–language pathologists in developing and implementing behavioral evidence-based interventions designed to improve articulation and speech production.

Central auditory processing disorder. Central auditory processing disorder involves deficits that are considered to be related to brain functioning. It is typically diagnosed by a speech–language pathologist or audiologist. Deficits in the processing of auditory information may be manifested in terms of attention, memory, word retrieval, auditory discrimination, perception, sound blending, and sequencing problems. These types of deficits have an impact on oral/listening comprehension, reading, and written expression. The school psychologist has the opportunity to observe these deficits during standardized testing. Assessment measures that specifically address auditory processing issues are instruments such as the Comprehensive Test of Phonological Processing (Wagner et al., 2004) or the Lindamood Auditory Conceptualization Test–Third Edition (Lindamood & Lindamood, 2009; see Table 23.2).

Table 23.2. Assessment Interface of Speech Pathology and School Psychology

Test	Information Provided
Academic broad bands	
• Wechsler Individual Achievement Test (3rd ed.)	• Reading and writing subtests
• Woodcock-Johnson III Tests of Achievement	• Aids in language-based learning disabilities diagnosis
Academic narrow bands	
• Gray Oral Reading Test (4th ed.)	• Reading and writing tests
• Wechsler Reading Mastery Test (3rd ed.)	• Reading and writing tests
• Test of Written Language (4th ed.)	• Reading and writing tests
Cognitive	
• Wechsler Intelligence Scale for Children (4th ed.)	• IQ test, language-based learning disabilities diagnosis
• Woodcock-Johnson III Tests of Cognitive Abilities	• IQ test, language-based learning disabilities diagnosis
• Peabody Picture Vocabulary Test (4th ed.)	• Receptive vocabulary
Broadband psychological	
• Behavior Assessment System for Children (2nd ed.)	• Behavioral issues
• Achenbach System of Empirically Based Assessment	• Behavioral issues
Narrow-band psychological	
• Revised Children's Manifest Anxiety Scale (2nd ed.)	• Anxiety inventory
• The Reynolds Adolescent Depression Scale (2nd ed.)	• Depression inventory
• Social Skills Improvement System	• Social/pragmatic language
• Behavior Observation of Students in Schools	• Disruptive behavior
Communication/language	
• Phonological Awareness Test 2	• Assesses phonological skills
• Test of Phonological Awareness 2 Plus	• Assesses phonological skills
• Yopp-Singer Test of Phoneme Segmentation	• Assesses phoneme usage
• Khan-Lewis Phonological Analysis Test (2nd ed.)	• Assesses phonological processing
• Comprehensive Test of Phonological Processing	• Assesses phonological and auditory processing
• Lindamood Auditory Conceptualization Test (3rd ed.)	• Auditory skills
• Expressive One-Word Picture Vocabulary Test (4th ed.)	• Expressive vocabulary
• Peabody Picture Vocabulary Test (4th ed.)	• Receptive vocabulary
• Receptive One-Word Picture Vocabulary Test (4th ed.)	• Receptive vocabulary
• Test of Language Development (4th ed.)	• Language test
• Clinical Evaluation of Language Fundamentals (5th ed.)	• Language test
Assessment interface of speech pathology and school psychology	
• Dynamic Indicators of Basic Early Literacy Skills	• Reading fluency
• Test of Written Language (4th ed.)	• Writing
• Pragmatic Language Skills Inventory	• Pragmatic language
• Test of Pragmatic Language (2nd ed.)	• Pragmatic language
Communication: Articulation	
• Goldman-Fristoe Test of Articulation 2	• Articulation of sounds
• Frequency Counts	• Counts of misarticulations
Communication: Stuttering	
• Frequency Counts	• Stuttered sounds, syllables, or words
Hearing/central auditory processing disorder	
• Comprehensive Test of Phonological Processing	• Auditory processing
• Lindamood Auditory Conceptualization Test (3rd ed.)	• Auditory processing

Interventions for Communication Disorders

Nippold (2012) supported Brandel and Loeb's (2012) argument that the pullout model of service delivery for speech–language interventions, where children are treated outside their classrooms, is relatively ineffective. However, the pullout model is the most commonly employed school-based intervention with an individual student or small groups of students. The problem with it is that it is "routinely employed regardless of the type or severity of a child's communication disorder" (Nippold, 2012, p. 117). However, the RTI method of service delivery that provides strategies and interventions for students in a three-tiered model is ideally suited for addressing communication disorders.

Specifically, and with respect to efficacious interventions, Nippold (2012) presented an argument that different service delivery models, including in-class and pullout, should be designed and implemented to address communication disorders depending on severity. This notion aligns well with RTI and school psychology's view on service delivery, especially because communication and emotional and behavioral disorders more often than not coexist. Further, interventions are most likely to succeed if the interventions focus on the multiplicity of factors affecting the student's social, communication, and academic functioning found in the classroom and other environments, and not just in isolation. Consequently, it is reasonable that school psychologists and speech pathologists should collaborate on the design of treatment for these students and implement them carefully.

To summarize, the four broadly based recommendations for academic, social, and communication interventions include (a) remediation strategies that are implemented early and before the student evidences severe educational failure; (b) a multidisciplinary approach where interventions designed to address communication disorders and their concomitant academic, social, and behavioral deficits are frequent and intense, in concert with an RTI model of service delivery where interventions should be implemented in the classroom setting, with students being pulled from their classroom only when necessary; (c) evidence-based interventions that are grounded in sound learning principles, including promoting of attention, corrective feedback, and reinforcement of correct responses; and (d) incorporation of both individualized and classroom-based components in the intervention (Nippold, 2012).

Case Study: Selective Mutism

Selective mutism is a low-incidence disorder that is highly unaffected by intervention. It is defined as an individual speaking in some environments (e.g., home) but not in others (e.g., school). It affects academic and social functioning and is associated with shyness, social withdrawal, negativism, compulsive traits, tantruming, anxiety, diurnal enuresis, and oppositional behavior.

This case study is about a 9-year-old female, Jessie (pseudonym), who was diagnosed with selective mutism at age 4 in preschool. She was previously treated with numerous interventions without success. Following this, video self-modeling was employed to treat the behavior (Kehle, Madaus, Baratta, & Bray, 1998). "Self-modeling is defined as the attitudinal and behavioral gains made as a result of repeated and spaced viewings of oneself on edited video that depict only appropriate or exemplary behaviors" (p. 248).

As described by Kehle et al. (1998), a 7-minute-long, edited self-modeling video was shown to Jessie, of her speaking in class. However, in reality this video was constructed after school hours to make it look like she was actually talking. Further, a mystery motivator was also used to increase her motivation to speak. Following five viewings of the video, Jessie's verbal behavior, for the first time in more than 5 years, "increased to a level that was indistinguishable from her classmates" (Kehle et al., 1998, p. 253). The social learning that occurred as a result of watching herself on video was powerful. In addition, the mystery motivator served to reinforce the behavior once she spoke.

This is an excellent example of where school psychologists and speech pathologists can work together using psychological treatments with a communication disorder.

Case Study: Stuttering

Similar to the augmented self-modeling treatment for selective mutism, Bray and Kehle (1998) developed an intervention to effect change in stuttering in elementary school children. This case study involved four students. The video self-modeling lasted for 6 weeks, where the children viewed their videos on seven separate occasions. After the intervention, all four children achieved fluent speech. It has been suggested that video self-modeling is a solid treatment choice for learned dysfluencies. In addition, self-modeling is simple and efficient to implement. Thus, using video self-modeling for stuttering, when it is a learned behavior, is an excellent treatment option and a best practice involving speech pathologists and school psychologists.

Speech: Articulation, Voice, and Stuttering

Specific treatments that have been found useful for articulation, that is, voice (e.g., vocal nodules) and swallowing, are behaviorally based and designed to reinforce correct speech production. This is something that school psychologists may do to assist in the treatment of children with speech disorders. Stuttering can be effectively treated, with collaboration between the two professionals, not only with video self-modeling but also with behavior modification (e.g., reinforcement, successive approximations, differential reinforcement of other behaviors, and response–cost strategies). Also, biofeedback, relaxation, systematic desensitization, and habit reversal have been effective treatments for stuttering disorder.

Language Disorders

Interventions with language disorders include strategies to promote social and pragmatic language; phonological processing; direct reading and writing instruction; behavioral programs for disruptive behavior; and traditional cognitive–behavioral counseling for social skills, underlying anxiety, or depression issues when present. Social language skills can specifically be taught through modeling, coaching, and behavioral techniques. Social stories can be used to reinforce appropriate social language by having the student read the dialogue and model after it. These pragmatic skills can be addressed in social skills groups focusing on such targets as eye contact, giving and receiving a compliment, topic maintenance, and initiation of conversation. The social use of language has also been targeted for remediation with video self-modeling. The videos show appropriate social and pragmatic language. This is another intervention area that both school psychologists and speech–language pathologists can work together with the focus being on improved communication skills.

Phonological training should highlight the acquisition of letter–sound correspondence, ear training with respect to environmental sounds then moving to speech sounds, auditory detection and discrimination, rhyming, segmentation, and sight-word reading to complement the phonological code. Reading comprehension can be improved using cuing, story mapping, paragraph restatements, study skills, and creative dramatics. Reading fluency can be achieved with repeated readings, listening previewing, and cuing. Vocabulary instruction is important to improving both expressive and receptive language skills. Behavioral strategies can also be used to reinforce these skills. The school psychologist working with the speech pathologist can team teach many of these behaviors.

Peripheral Hearing and Central Auditory Processing Disorder

Hearing problems affect speech and language performance. Audiologists and speech and language pathologists are those most likely in charge of assessment and intervention. However, coordination and collaboration with school psychologists may encourage best practice. Hearing aids, FM auditory trainers, and cochlear implants may be used to promote better hearing. School psychologists can provide counseling to those having difficulty adjusting to using the technology. Also, school psychologists should be aware that early hearing loss leads to language deficits and concomitant reading and writing problems. This includes early hearing loss due to middle ear infections.

There is a relative lack of agreement between speech–language pathology and school psychology as to the definition and existence of the central auditory processing disorder, and this has precluded effective intervention. Further, making differential diagnostic distinctions difficult are the behavioral deficits of inattention, impulsivity, distractibility, and inability to effectively process auditory stimuli that are observed across other disabilities (e.g., attention deficit hyperactivity disorder). Therefore, the result is some confusion over what the best practices for treatment are. In the majority of cases, traditional therapies for promoting auditory processing are employed. This includes the use of electronic devices such as an FM auditory trainer to help focus the listener on relevant information only, the use of compensatory strategies such as visual cuing, and the use of direct auditory training using various computer software approaches. Further research is needed in this area. (See Table 23.3.)

SUMMARY

Current research continues to establish and emphasize the relationship among communication, academic, and psychological or social disorders. School psychologists need to be aware of the need for comprehensive and collaborative assessment with speech–language pathologists, given the overlap between these two professions. The ultimate goal is for the interpretation of the assessment data to promote the design of evidence-based interventions that are meaningful and enduring. The most appropriate areas for collaboration are stuttering, language and learning disabilities, and central auditory processing disorders. There are many assessments that provide insight into these areas in terms of collaboration. Likewise, there are interventions, such as video self-modeling or behavioral paradigms, that can be effectively and more efficiently implemented through collaborative efforts.

Table 23.3. Intervention Interface of Speech Pathology and School Psychology

Area	Primary Treatment Collaboration
Speech • Articulation • Voice • Fluency or stuttering	• Behavior modification • Behavior modification • Behavior modification, video self-modeling, relaxation training
Language	• Strategies to promote social and pragmatic language, phonological processing, direct reading and writing instruction, behavioral programs for disruptive behavior, and traditional cognitive–behavioral counseling for social skills, and underlying anxiety and/or depression
Hearing • Peripheral • Central auditory processing disorder	• Hearing aids, FM trainer, cochlear implants • FM trainer, auditory training

REFERENCES

Achenbach, T. (2010). *The Achenbach System of Empirically Based Assessment*. Burlington, VT: University of Vermont, Research Center for Children, Youth, and Families.

American Speech-Language-Hearing Association. (2013, March 1). *Definitions of the professions*. Rockville, MD: Author. Retrieved from http://www.asha.org/div40/definitions.htm

Brandel, J., & Loeb, D. F. (2012, January 17). Service delivery in schools: A national survey. *The ASHA Leader*. Retrieved from http://www.asha.org/Publications/leader/2012/120117/Service-Delivery-in-Schools–A-National-Survey.htm

Bray, M. A., & Kehle, T. J. (1998). Self-modeling as an intervention for stuttering. *School Psychology Review, 27*, 587–598.

Brownell, R. (2010a). *Expressive One-Word Picture Vocabulary Test–Fourth edition*. San Antonio, TX: Pearson Assessment.

Brownell, R. (2010b). *Receptive One-Word Picture Vocabulary Test–Fourth edition*. San Antonio, TX: Pearson Assessment.

Dunn, L., & Dunn, D. (2007). *Peabody Picture Vocabulary Test–Fourth edition*. San Antonio, TX: Pearson Assessment.

Elliot, S., & Gresham, F. (2008). *Social Skills Improvement System*. San Antonio, TX: Pearson Assessment.

Gilliam, J., & Miller, L. (2006). *Pragmatic Language Skills Inventory*. Austin, TX: PRO-ED.

Goldman, R., & Fristoe, M. (2000). *Goldman-Fristoe Test of Articulation–Second edition*. San Antonio, TX: Pearson Assessment.

Hammill, D., & Larsen, S. (2006). *Test of Written Language–Fourth edition*. Torrance, CA: Western Psychological Services.

Hammill, D., & Newcomer, P. (2005). *Test of Language Development–Fourth edition*. San Antonio, TX: Pearson Assessment.

Kaminski, R., & Good, R. (2009). *Dynamic Indicators of Basic Early Literacy Skills–Next*. Longmont, CO: Sopris West.

Kehle, T. J., Madaus, M. M. R., Baratta, V. S., & Bray, M. A. (1998). Augmented self-modeling as a treatment for children with selective mutism. *Journal of School Psychology, 36*, 247–260.

Khan, L. M., & Lewis, N. P. (2002). *Khan-Lewis Phonological Analysis–Second edition*. Circle Pines, MN: American Guidance Services.

Lindamood, P., & Lindamood, P. (2009). *Lindamood Auditory Conceptualization Test–Third edition*. San Antonio, TX: Pearson Assessment.

National Association of School Psychologists. (2010). *Model for comprehensive and integrated school psychological services*. Bethesda, MD: Author. Retrieved from http://www.nasponline.org/standards/2010standards/2_PracticeModel.pdf

Nippold, M. A. (2012). Different service delivery models for different communication disorders. *Language, Speech, and Hearing Services in the Schools, 43*, 117–120.

Phelps-Terasaki, D., & Phelps-Gunn, T. (2007). *The Test of Pragmatic Language–Second edition*. Greenville, SC: Super Duper Publications.

Reynolds, C. R., & Kamphaus, R. W. (2004). *Behavior assessment system for children–Second edition*. Circle Pines, MN: American Guidance Service.

Reynolds, C. R., & Richmond, B. (2004). *Revised Children's Manifest Anxiety Scale–Second edition*. Torrance, CA: Western Psychological Services.

Reynolds, W. (2002). *Reynolds Adolescent Depression Scale–Second edition*. Torrance, CA: Western Psychological Services.

Robertson, C., & Salter, W. (2007). *Phonological Awareness Test 2*. East Moline, IL: Lingui Systems.

Semel, E., Wiig, E. H., & Secord, W. A. (2013). *Clinical Evaluation of Language Fundamentals–Fifth edition*. San Antonio, TX: Pearson Assessment.

Shapiro, E. S. (2008). *Behavioral Observation of Students in Schools*. San Antonio, TX: Pearson Assessment.

Thatcher, K. L., Fletcher, K., & Decker, B. (2008). Communication disorders in the school: Perspectives on academic and social success–An introduction. *Psychology in the Schools, 45*, 579–581.

Torgesen, J., & Bryant, B. (2004). *Test of Phonological Awareness–Second edition: PLUS*. Torrance, CA: Western Psychological Services.

Wagner, R., Torgesen, J., & Rashotte, C. (2004). *Comprehensive Test of Phonological Processing*. North Tonawanda, NY: Multi-Health Systems.

Wechsler, D. (2003). *Wechsler Intelligence Scale for Children–Fourth edition*. San Antonio, TX: Pearson Assessment.

Wechsler, D. (2009). *Wechsler Individual Achievement Test–Third edition*. San Antonio, TX: Pearson Assessment.

Wechsler, D. (2011). *Wechsler Reading Mastery Test–Third edition*. San Antonio, TX: Pearson Assessment.

Wiederholt, J., & Bryant, B. (2001). *Gray Oral Reading Test–Fourth edition*. San Antonio, TX: Pearson Assessment.

Woodcock, R., McGrew, K., & Mather, N. (2007). *Woodcock-Johnson III Tests of Achievement*. Rolling Meadows, IL: Riverside.

Woodcock, R., McGrew, K., & Mather, N. (2009). *Woodcock-Johnson III Tests of Cognitive Abilities*. Rolling Meadows, IL: Riverside.

Yopp, H. K. (1995). A test for assessing phonemic awareness in young children. *The Reading Teacher, 49*, 20–30.

24

Best Practices in Multimethod Assessment of Emotional and Behavioral Disorders

Stephanie H. McConaughy
University of Vermont
David R. Ritter
Burlington (VT) School District

OVERVIEW

This chapter describes best practices in assessing emotional and behavioral disorders using a multisource, multimethod approach. The chapter begins with a case study to illustrate the problem-solving approach to assessment across a three-tiered service delivery system and then moves to basic considerations and detailed discussion of measures and procedures. This chapter aligns with the domain of Data-Based Decision Making and Accountability in the National Association of School Psychologists (NASP) *Model for Comprehensive and Integrated School Psychological Services* (NASP, 2010a). The following examples of professional practices from the NASP Practice Model are relevant for this chapter (NASP, 2010a, p. 4):

- School psychologists use a problem-solving framework as the basis for all professional activities.
- School psychologists systematically collect data from multiple sources as a foundation for decision making and consider ecological factors (e.g., classroom, family, community characteristics) as a context for assessment and intervention in general and special education settings.
- School psychologists, as part of an interdisciplinary team, conduct assessments to identify students' eligibility for special education and other educational services.

Case Illustration

The central question before the school's instructional support team (IST) was whether to continue with current classroom-based strategies and interventions for the referred student or to conduct a comprehensive evaluation to determine eligibility for more intensive special education services. As a core member of the IST, the school psychologist had already helped to design and implement a sequence of classroom-based accommodations and student-centered interventions. Unfortunately, the outcomes of those interventions were less than desired.

It was 4 months ago that Ms. Thurlow, a sixth-grade teacher, first expressed her concerns to the IST about her student, Cassandra, who was exhibiting fluctuating moods and disruptive behavior. On good days, Cassandra seemed reasonably happy, but she was often inattentive and disrupted class activities. On her so-called bad days, Cassandra came to school seeming angry and sullen or worried and depressed. Regardless of her mood, she often refused to do academic work and when approached about her poor productivity, she either responded in a disrespectful and defiant manner or just shut down. Whenever Cassandra's behavior seemed unmanageable, Ms. Thurlow resorted to sending her to a neighboring classroom for a paired-teacher time-out, hoping that a change of scenery would be helpful, or she sent her to the principal's office for disciplinary action. Mrs. Thurlow also reported that Cassandra seemed to have few friends. Most of the time she kept to herself at recess or hung out on the fringe of group activities.

The school psychologist was aware that most educational problems are first identified by teachers when they find a student's behavior distressing and/or when the student's performance falls below age and grade expectations (Kwon, Kim, & Sheridan, 2012; Mychailyszyn, Mendez, & Kendall, 2010). Thus, in our case, it came as no surprise when the teacher noted that Cassandra was behind in most academic subjects, which was attributed to refusals to do academic tasks and failure to complete assignments or homework. Cassandra also missed instructional time due to a high number of time-outs and administrative referrals, not to mention school absences. The school psychologist acknowledged Ms. Thurlow's concern that Cassandra's behavior did not seem normal and, as is often the case, that the teacher did not feel sufficiently trained or skilled to cope with abnormal displays of emotion and behavior (Egyed & Short, 2006). The school psychologist knew it was important to address all of Ms. Thurlow's concerns right away, before Cassandra's behavior became more problematic and less amenable to intervention.

Tier Intervention

Fortunately, the school already utilized a three-tiered service delivery model that included universal conditions to promote school success for all students at Tier 1, targeted small group interventions at Tier 2, and intensive interventions for individual students at Tier 3. As a first step in responding to the initial IST referral, the school psychologist had interviewed the teacher, using the problem-solving method to learn what specific behaviors were of most concern and identify antecedents and consequences of those behaviors. The school psychologist also sought to learn what universal conditions (Tier 1) were already in place that might help ease Cassandra's academic and behavioral challenges. For example, were explicit instructions provided for academic assignments? Were the rules and expectations for classroom behavior clear to all students? Could students work with others in class when they were having difficulty with a task or assignment? Since Cassandra's academic skills were also in question, the school psychologist reviewed findings from curriculum-based measures (CBM) and classroom work samples to estimate the extent of any skill delays. This information provided a broader perspective on the nature and severity of the difficulties and also served as a

baseline for subsequent progress monitoring in Tier 2 interventions.

As a second step, the school psychologist collaborated with Ms. Thurlow to develop Tier 2 interventions, which included classroom accommodations to increase on-task behavior (a self-monitoring system) and academic productivity (a signal system to ask for help, peer tutoring, preferential seating), a home–school note system, and reduced homework assignments. Academic and behavior goals were also identified, and the school psychologist helped Ms. Thurlow identify ways that the school's positive behavior support system (Sugai & Horner, 2006) could be used to recognize and reward Cassandra's progress toward her goals. Finally, the adults collaborated on ways to monitor progress, gather and analyze progress data with reasonable ease, assure fidelity of implementation, and evaluate outcomes of Tier 2 interventions (Gresham, 2009).

After 4 weeks of Tier 2 interventions, Cassandra showed some improvement in on-task behavior and academic productivity, but she still refused to do many academic tasks and remained disruptive in class. She also continued to experience bouts of depression and displayed problems getting along with classmates. Additional direct classroom observations revealed that reading and writing tasks were consistent antecedents of work refusals and disruptive behavior. Further CBM probes of Cassandra's reading and writing skills suggested below-average reading comprehension in spite of average decoding skills and labored word-per-minute rate in writing. It then became apparent that the initial Tier 2 review of CBM data was misleading, both in terms of the nature and extent of the student's reading and writing skills. What had been assumed to be a performance deficit (failure to complete tasks) was re-hypothesized as a skill-based academic deficit. Linking assessment to intervention, the school psychologist assisted Ms. Thurlow and other school staff in designing and implementing more intensive Tier 2 academic interventions (small group remedial instruction in reading comprehension and writing fluency) and creating a positive behavior plan aimed at improving work completion and reducing disruptive behavior. After a month of these more intensive Tier 2 interventions, Cassandra showed some gains in her reading and writing skills, but still exhibited behaviors indicative of depression. Her intrusive behavior with classmates also continued to have an impact on peer interactions and relationships.

Selected Tier 2 interventions were adapted so they were delivered with an even greater intensity, and Tier 3 student-centered interventions were added (individualized remedial reading and writing instruction, explicit instruction in social skills, and a modified positive behavior plan that had more powerful incentives). Interventions were implemented with fidelity for a number of weeks, but progress monitoring still showed only limited success. Cassandra's parents reported that their daughter's negative attitude toward school had not eased in any noticeable way and she still feigned being ill in an effort to avoid going to school. Cassandra's limited progress toward academic and behavioral goals, despite Tier 2 and Tier 3 interventions delivered with fidelity, suggested that the next step was a referral for a comprehensive multimethod assessment of Cassandra's emotional and behavioral functioning and cognitive ability to determine what further interventions would be appropriate to address her needs. However, before doing so, the school psychologist obtained permission from Cassandra's parents to review her case with a peer consultation group.

Consistent with best practice in ongoing supervision and consultation, the school psychologist for this district had joined with school psychologists from neighboring districts to form a peer consultation group that met biweekly for the purpose of reviewing challenging cases and discussing assessment methodology and intervention strategies. In effect, the peer consultation group served as a forum through which everyone involved could learn from his or her colleagues and assess the effectiveness of his or her own practice. The consensus of the consultation group was that Cassandra's limited progress to date warranted a comprehensive multimethod assessment to determine how best to meet her needs.

The next sections discuss basic considerations regarding multimethod assessment of children's emotional and behavioral disorders and specific instruments and procedures available to school psychologists for such assessments. For brevity, we use the terms *child* and *children* to refer to the entire school-age population, including adolescents. At the end of this chapter we will then return to our case example to illustrate how the multimethod assessment was integrated with the three-tiered service delivery system to address to address Cassandra's emotional and behavioral problems and academic skill deficits.

BASIC CONSIDERATIONS

The first issue facing the school psychologist is to determine whether reported emotional and behavioral problems qualify as disorders. Two approaches have been taken toward classifying children's emotional and behavioral disorders: empirically based taxonomies and categorical systems (Achenbach, 2009; Achenbach & McConaughy, 1997). In empirically based taxonomies, no initial assumptions are made about what types of emotional or behavioral problems represent disorders. Instead, research data on large samples of children are used to derive groupings of different patterns of problems. Then normative standards are applied to determine whether the patterns of problems for an individual child are deviant from what would be typically expected for the child's age and gender. In categorical classification systems, committees of experts determine what patterns of emotional and behavioral problems are deviant enough to be considered disorders. Each of these approaches is discussed in the next sections.

Empirically Based Taxonomies

As a first step in developing empirically based taxonomies, researchers gathered data from knowledgeable adult informants (parents and teachers) about children's problems that were of concern to them. Data were also gathered from the children's self-reports. Using rating scales, informants scored lists of problem items according to the degree to which a particular child manifested each problem. That is, rather than judging whether a particular problem was present or absent, informants rated each problem on quantitatively graded scales that represented frequency, duration, and/or intensity. Researchers then applied statistical procedures (exploratory and confirmatory factor analyses) to these data sets to derive syndromes or groupings of behavioral and emotional problems that tended to co-occur. The statistical analyses of large samples of such ratings thus identified different syndromes or patterns of problems (e.g., aggressive behavior, attention problems, anxiety, or depression) reported for large samples of children. The second step was to determine how severe an individual child's pattern of problems was compared to other children. To do this, an informant's ratings of problem items for an individual child were summed to produce an overall raw score for each syndrome. Using large nationally representative samples, standard scores were then derived for each syndrome to indicate how severe an individual child's syndrome score was compared to children of the same gender and age range. Standard scores were also derived for total problems and broad groupings of internalizing problems (e.g., withdrawal/depression, anxiety, and somatic complaints) versus externalizing problems (e.g., aggressive behavior and rule-breaking behavior).

The Achenbach System of Empirically Based Assessment (ASEBA; Achenbach & Rescorla, 2001) is an example of an empirically based taxonomy. The ASEBA is an integrated system of rating scales for assessing competencies, adaptive functioning, and problems of individuals ages 1½ to 90. (The ASEBA adult forms are not a focus of this chapter.) For school-age children, the ASEBA includes the Child Behavior Checklist for Ages 6–18 (CBCL/6-18) for parents, the Teacher's Report Form (TRF), and Youth Self-Report Form (YSR). The ASEBA school-age forms are scored on similar profiles of empirically based syndrome scales. In the ASEBA taxonomic system, the names of the syndrome scales are not considered diagnostic labels, but instead simply describe types of problems that tend to co-occur. Other ASEBA forms are available for parent and teacher/caregiver ratings of preschool children (Achenbach & Rescorla, 2000), test examiners' ratings of observations of children's behavior during test sessions (McConaughy & Achenbach, 2004b), and observers' ratings of children's behavior in school classrooms and other group settings (McConaughy & Achenbach, 2009). The ASEBA also includes a protocol and rating forms for conducting semistructured clinical interviews with children and adolescents (McConaughy & Achenbach, 2001). Details of relevant ASEBA forms and profiles are discussed in later sections.

The Behavior Assessment System for Children-Second Edition (BASC-2; Reynolds & Kamphaus, 2004) and Conners Comprehensive Behavior Rating Scales (CBRS; Conners, 2008) are two additional examples of empirically based taxonomies. Like the ASEBA, the BASC-2 and CBRS have separate rating forms for parents and teachers and child self-reports. Each BASC-2 or CBRS form is scored on profiles of empirically based syndromes that measure co-occurring problems. Details of the BASC-2 and CBRS scales are discussed in later sections.

Categorical Classification Systems

Categorical classification systems classify problems in a dichotomous present versus absent or yes/no fashion. In a categorical classification system, specific criteria describe problems and other features of each disorder. If all of the required features are met, an individual is judged to have the disorder. If all the required features are not met, the individual is judged not to have the disorder.

DSM Classification System

The American Psychiatric Association's *Diagnostic and Statistical Manual of Mental Disorders* (5th edition; DSM-5; American Psychiatric Association, 2013) and its precursor, the *Diagnostic and Statistical Manual of Mental Disorders* (4th edition, text revision; DSM-IV-TR; American Psychiatric Association, 2000), is one of the most widely used categorical systems for classifying adult and childhood emotional and behavioral disorders. The DSM-5 lists specific symptoms and diagnostic criteria for numerically coded disorders. In the organizational structure for the DSM-5, disorders of infancy, childhood, and adolescence are listed under several different broad categories. Many of the DSM-IV-TR childhood diagnoses have been retained in the DSM-5 but, for some, modifications have been made for certain symptoms or criteria. For example, both DSM-5 and DSM-IV-TR include diagnoses of intellectual development disorders, communication disorders, attention deficit hyperactivity disorder (ADHD), specific learning disorder, motor disorders, separation anxiety disorder, oppositional defiant disorder (ODD), and conduct disorder (CD). Other DSM-5 diagnoses that can be applied to adults and children include major depressive disorder, dysthymia (a chronic form of sad affect), obsessive compulsive disorder, generalized anxiety disorder, social anxiety disorder, specific phobias (which can include school phobia), and schizophrenia. The DSM-5 also includes diagnoses of autism spectrum disorder (which combines DSM-TR-IV diagnoses of autism, Asperger's syndrome, and pervasive developmental disorders), and a newly defined disruptive mood dysregulation disorder (for children who show severe recurrent temper outbursts that are grossly out of proportion to the intensity or duration of a situation), plus proposed criteria for nonsuicidal self-injury disorder and suicidal behavior disorder.

To make a DSM diagnosis, evaluators must judge whether the defined symptoms are present or absent over a specified time period (e.g., the past 6 months) and whether the symptoms produce "clinically significant impairment" in social, academic/educational, or occupational functioning. They must also rule out other diagnoses with similar symptoms. Some disorders, such as ADHD, also have specific criteria for age of onset (age 7 for DSM-IV-TR, age 12 for DSM-5).

The DSM is commonly used to classify disorders of individuals referred for mental health treatment. DSM diagnoses provide standard descriptions of disorders for communicating about children's problems and developing treatment plans. A DSM code number is commonly required for third-party insurance reimbursement and other mental health administrative purposes. Knowledge of the DSM system can help school psychologists understand when a child may be manifesting symptoms of psychiatric disorders and thereby facilitate communication with mental health professionals and other nonschool mental health and social service providers. DSM diagnoses can also help guide treatment decisions and can help access financial resources for the child and family (e.g., insurance reimbursement, Medicaid). Since 2000 or more, evidence-based treatments, including school-based interventions, have been developed targeted on specific DSM disorders (see Weisz & Kazdin, 2010). For these reasons, school psychologists should familiarize themselves with the DSM classification system.

At the same time, school psychologists should be aware that DSM diagnoses, other than schizophrenia, are not required by federal law for determining eligibility for special education services in schools, although some states have incorporated certain DSM diagnoses into their special education rules and regulations. It is important to note that some experts in school psychology have also questioned the utility of psychiatric diagnoses for special education and school psychological services (Gresham & Gansle, 1992).

IDEA 2004 Classification System

The disability categories of the Individuals with Disabilities Education Improvement Act (IDEA 2004; 2004, Public Law 108-446) represent another form of categorical classification system. IDEA 2004 lists 13 disability categories that can entitle children to special education services. The federal law provides a general description of each disability. Children with emotional and behavioral disorders are most likely to qualify for special education under the category of emotional disturbance (ED), defined as follows:

(c) (4) (i) Emotional disturbance means a condition exhibiting one or more of the following characteristics over a long period of time and to a marked degree that adversely affects a child's educational performance:

(A) An inability to learn that cannot be explained by intellectual, sensory, or other health factors;

(B) An inability to build or maintain satisfactory interpersonal relationships with peers and teachers;

(C) Inappropriate types of behavior or feelings under normal circumstances;

(D) A general pervasive mood of unhappiness or depression;

(E) A tendency to develop physical symptoms or fears associated with personal or school problems;

(ii) Emotional disturbance includes schizophrenia. The term does not apply to children who are socially maladjusted unless it is determined that they have an emotional disturbance under paragraph (c)(4)(i) of this section. (20 U.S.C. 1401 (3); 34 C.F.R Part 300 subpart A §300.8(c)(4)(i))

To meet the criteria for ED according to the above definition, a child must exhibit one or more of the five characteristics (A through E) *or* have a psychiatric diagnosis of schizophrenia. In addition, all three qualifying conditions listed in paragraph (c)(4)(i) must apply to at least one of the identified characteristics. That is, the characteristic(s) must exist over a long period of time, to a marked degree, and adversely affect the child's educational performance. A child who exhibits at least one of the five characteristics, or has a diagnosis of schizophrenia, and who also meets all three qualifying conditions, is judged to have ED. A child who does not meet criteria for ED is deemed to be ineligible for special education on the basis of an emotional and behavioral disorder. Like the DSM system, special education classification requires a categorical yes/no decision as to the presence or absence of a disability.

The IDEA 2004 definition of ED has retained similar wording since enactment of the Education of All Handicapped Children Act in 1975. Professionals and advocacy groups have criticized the definition of ED as being overly restrictive and not supported by legal precedent or educational and clinical research (Forness, 1992; Skiba & Grizzle, 1992). Despite an effort to change the ED definition in the early 1990s, however, Congress opted to retain the content of the definition, except to remove the word *serious* from the name of the category. Many states have adopted the federal definition of ED, while other states have framed their own definitions modeled on the federal definition. A few states have opted not to require any categorical classification for special education, including emotional and behavioral disorders. School psychologists must follow the rules and regulations for their own particular state. In subsequent sections, we will use the IDEA 2004 definition of ED as a guideline for discussing multimethod assessment of children's emotional and behavioral disorders. For consistency, we will use ED to encompass all terms used by the 50 states for eligibility for special education services.

Children with emotional and behavioral disorders may also qualify for special education under other IDEA 2004 categories, such as Specific Learning Disability, if they meet the requisite criteria. Children with a DSM diagnosis of ADHD may qualify for special education services under the IDEA 2004 category of Other Health Impaired because of their difficulties in alertness and attention.

Categorical classification systems, like IDEA 2004 or the DSM, are not incompatible with the empirically based taxonomies discussed earlier. The difference is that empirically based taxonomies do not assume a particular syndrome represents a distinct or separate disorder or disability. Instead, in an empirically based taxonomy, different patterns of problems are reflected in profiles of high and low scores across a set of syndromes. In this way, empirically based taxonomies offer a more differentiated picture of children's problems than do categorical classification systems. In addition, cut-points on empirically based problem scales define normal, borderline, and clinical range scores that can be used for judging the severity of a child's patterns of problems relative to nationally representative normative samples. For these reasons, we recommend incorporating empirically based taxonomies into all multimethod assessments of children's emotional and behavioral disorders. School psychologists can then integrate data-based evidence from empirically based taxonomies with other data to decide whether a particular child's pattern of problems fits the descriptive criteria of the DSM diagnostic categories and/or IDEA 2004 special education eligibility categories, as appropriate. As indicated earlier, in many cases, the DSM may not be very relevant or useful for determining the need for more intensive school-based interventions in a three-tier service delivery system. However, DSM diagnoses can be helpful for communicating with mental health practitioners who collaborate with school practitioners or provide additional services outside of school.

BEST PRACTICES IN MULTIMETHOD ASSESSMENT OF EMOTIONAL AND BEHAVIORAL DISORDERS

School psychologists have key roles in assessing emotional and behavioral disorders at both Tier 2 and Tier 3 of the service delivery model, as illustrated in our case example at the beginning of this chapter.

Professional ethics require that school psychologists be familiar with the relevant instruments and procedures and select only those they can administer and interpret with confidence (Jacob, Decker, & Hartshorne, 2011; NASP, 2010b). It is especially important to understand the limits of reliability and validity of each instrument or procedure. School psychologists must also be cognizant of the advantages and limitations of various assessment procedures and report findings accordingly. Not all procedures are standardized, nor do they all yield quantitative data. However, whenever possible, standardized norm-based instruments are preferred over nonstandardized procedures. Standardized instruments can be used in conjunction with nonstandardized procedures. No single measure or procedure should be considered definitive in yielding evidence of an emotional and behavioral disorder. Instead, data must be gathered and integrated across multiple methods and sources, as discussed in the next sections.

Multimethod Assessment

Children's behavior often varies from one setting to another, including home versus school and one classroom versus another. Perspectives or judgments of children's behavior can also vary from one child to another. Therefore, agreement between informants in different situations is likely to be moderate at best (Achenbach, McConaughy, & Howell, 1987). Differing views about children's behavior do not mean that one informant is right and others are wrong. Instead, differing perspectives underscore the need for multiple information sources to assess children's functioning across settings. For best practice in assessing emotional and behavioral disorders, information should be obtained from at least three major sources, as outlined in Table 24.1: parent reports, teacher reports, and direct assessment of the child. The next sections describe instruments and procedures for each of these data sources.

Standardized Parent and Teacher Rating Scales

Standardized rating scales provide efficient methods for obtaining parent and teacher reports of children's problems and competencies. Numerous rating scales have been developed for this purpose. The ASEBA school-age forms, BASC-2, and CBRS represent omnibus measures that assess a wide range of potential problems. Table 24.2 lists features and publishers of each of these sets of instruments.

Table 24.1. Components of Multimethod Assessment of Emotional and Behavioral Disorders

Parent Reports	Teacher Reports	Direct Assessment of the Child
Standardized rating scales Parent interview: • Concerns about the child • Behavioral or emotional problems • Social functioning • School functioning • Medical and developmental history • Family relations and home situation	Standardized rating scales Teacher interview: • Concerns about the child • School behavior problems • Academic performance • Teaching strategies • School interventions for behavioral problems • Special help/services	Standardized self-reports Child/adolescent interview: • Activities and interests • School and homework • Friendships and peer relations • Self-awareness and feelings • Adolescent issues (alcohol and drugs, antisocial behavior, trouble with the law, dating and romances, sexual identity, cell phones, and social networking) • Home situation and family relations
Developmental history questionnaires	School records	Direct observations

On the ASEBA CBCL/6-18, parents rate their child on 120 problem items for how true the item is over the past 6 months. Each problem item is rated on a 3-point scale: 0 = not true (as far as you know), 1 = somewhat or sometimes true, and 2 = very true or often true. Parents also provide information on their children's activities, social involvement, and school functioning. On the Teacher's Report Form (TRF), teachers rate a child on 120 problem items over the past 2 months. Ninety-seven TRF items are similar to those on the CBCL/6-18. The CBCL/6-18 and TRF are scored on similar profiles for eight empirically based syndrome scales and six DSM-oriented scales, plus Internalizing, Externalizing, and Total Problems. In 2007, multicultural norms were developed for the CBCL/6-18, TRF, and Youth Self-Report (YSR) and three clinical scales were added in the computer-scoring software (Achenbach & Rescorla, 2007).

On the BASC-2 Parent Rating Scale (PRS), parents rate their child on 160 items for ages 6–11 and 150 items for ages 12–21. On the BASC-2 Teacher Rating Scale (TRS), teachers rate the child on 139 items for ages 6–11 and 12–21. Each problem item is rated on a 4-point scale: 0 = never, 1 = sometimes, 2 = often, and 3 = almost always. The BASC-2 PRS and TRS are scored on 10 empirically based syndromes and seven content scales, plus Internalizing, Externalizing, and a total Behavioral Symptoms Index. On the CBRS, parents and teachers rate the child on 203 items that are scored on seven empirically based problem scales and 14 DSM-IV-TR disorders.

Along with the omnibus measures, other parent and teacher rating scales narrow the focus to certain types of problems. Examples are the ADHD Rating Scale-IV (DuPaul, Power, Anastopoulos, & Reid, 1998) and the Conners Rating Scales (Conners, 1997), which assess

problems associated with ADHD. Narrow measures can be used in conjunction with omnibus measures to assess particular patterns of problems.

In addition to assessing problems, school psychologists should also consider children's competencies or strengths. The Behavioral and Emotional Rating Scale-Second Edition (BERS-2; Epstein, 2004) is an example of an instrument designed to assess emotional and behavioral strengths. The BERS-2 is scored on six empirically based competency scales (Interpersonal Strengths, School Functioning, Intrapersonal Strengths, Family Strengths, Affective Strengths, Career Strengths) plus Total Strengths. The ASEBA CBCL/6-18 and TRF and the BASC-2 PRS and TRS can also be scored on competency and adaptive scales, as listed in Table 24.2. Assessment of competencies is important for identifying positive behaviors to reinforce in interventions while trying to reduce problem behaviors.

Advantages of Standardized Rating Scales

Best practice encourages school psychologists to select standardized rating scales with empirically based syndromes and large normative samples that cover a wide age range for both genders. Standardized rating scales meeting these criteria have the following advantages:

- Information is quantifiable and thus amenable to psychometric tests of reliability and validity.
- Multiple items on omnibus measures provide data on a broad range of potential problems, rather than limiting the focus only to referral concerns or behaviors in one area.
- Information is organized in a systematic way by aggregating problems into groupings of syndromes and broad scales.

Table 24.2. Examples of Standardized Parent and Teacher Rating Scales

Instrument	Items and Scales	Normative Samples	Publisher
ASEBA CBCL/6-18, TRF	120 problem items *Empirically based problem scales* Withdrawn/Depressed, Somatic Complaints, Anxious/Depressed, Social Problems, Thought Problems, Attention Problems, Rule-Breaking Behavior, Aggressive Behavior *DSM-oriented scales* Affective Problems, Anxiety Problems, Attention Deficit Hyperactivity Problems, Oppositional Defiant Problems, Conduct Problems *Clinical scales* Obsessive Compulsive Problems, Post Traumatic Stress Problems, Sluggish Cognitive Tempo Total Problems, Internalizing, Externalizing *Competence/adaptive scales* CBCL/6-18: 20 items, Total Competence, Activities, Social, School TRF: Academic Performance, Adaptive Functioning	Separate norms for boys and girls, ages 6–11 and 12–18 Multicultural norms	Research Center for Children, Youth, and Families, Inc. One South Prospect Street Burlington, VT 05401-3456 (802) 656-5130 www.aseba.org
BASC-2 PRS, TRS	139–160 items *Empirically based problem scales* Hyperactivity, Aggression, Conduct Problems (ages 6–18), Anxiety, Depression, Somatization, Attention Problems, Atypicality, Withdrawal *Content scales* Anger Control, Bullying, Developmental Social Disorders, Emotional Self-Control, Executive Functioning, Negative Emotionality, Resiliency Behavioral Symptoms Index, Internalizing, Externalizing *Competence/adaptive scales* Adaptive Skills Composite, Adaptability, Social Skills, Leadership (ages 6–18), Activities of Daily Living, Functional Communication	Separate norms for boys and girls, ages 2–5, 6–11, 12–18	Pearson 19500 Bulverde Road San Antonio, TX 78259 (800) 627-7271 www.psychcorp.com
CBRS (parent version, teacher version)	203 items *Empirically based problem scales* Emotional Distress, Academic Difficulties, Defiant/Aggressive Behaviors, Hyperactivity/Impulsivity, Perfectionistic and Compulsive Behaviors, Violence Potential Indicator Physical Symptoms 14 DSM-IV-TR Disorders *Validity scales* Positive Impression, Negative Impression, Inconsistency Index	Separate norms for boys and girls, ages 6–11 and 12–18	MHS P.O. Box 950 North Tonawanda, NY 14120-0950 (800) 456-3003 www.mhs.com

Note. ASEBA CBCL/6-18, TRF = Achenbach System of Empirically Based Assessment, Child Behavior Checklist for Ages 6–18, Teacher's Report Form; BASC-2, PRS, TRS = Behavior Assessment System for Children-Second Edition, Parent Rating Scale, Teacher Rating Scale; CBRS = Conners Comprehensive Behavior Rating Scales; DSM-IV-TR = *Diagnostic and Statistical Manual of Mental Disorders* (4th edition, text revision).

- Empirically based syndromes are composed of problems that co-occur in large samples of referred children, rather than being based on hypothetical constructs or assumed diagnostic categories.
- Norms provide a standard for judging the severity of problems for a child compared to large general population samples of the same gender and age range.
- Rating scales are economical and efficient, since most can be completed by the relevant informant in 10–15 minutes and can be scored quickly by hand or computer.
- Sets of related rating scales can be used to compare similar data from multiple informants, such as parents, teachers, children themselves, and observers.

When choosing a standardized rating scale, it is important that the scale meet acceptable psychometric standards of reliability and validity. Good reliability is indicated when scale scores on the instrument do not change substantially across short periods of time (test–retest reliability) and when there is reasonably good agreement between raters in the same situation (inter-rater reliability). There are many different ways to test validity. Construct validity indicates that the instrument measures what it is supposed to measure. Predictive validity indicates that scores on the instrument are associated with, or predict, other relevant variables (e.g., elevated behavior problem scores predicting poor social skills or poor school adjustment). Discriminative validity indicates that scores on the instrument differentiate between appropriate groups (e.g., clinically referred versus nonreferred children; children with ADHD versus those without ADHD).

In addition to meeting psychometric standards, it is equally important that a rating scale provide useful information for assessing emotional and behavioral disorders and planning appropriate interventions. To accomplish these goals, the following criteria should be considered:

- Do the items on the instrument pertain directly to the child's observable behavior (e.g., gets into fights, restless, or hyperactive) rather than broader inferences about the behavior (e.g., lacks social skills) or judgments about the situational context of the behavior (e.g., comes from dysfunctional family, has depressed parent, lives in violent neighborhood)?
- How are the items scored? Simple yes/no scores are less effective than multipoint scales, since most behaviors vary in degree. In general, 3- or 4-point

scales have shown better discriminatory power than dichotomous scales (e.g., yes/no or true/false).
- Are the items on the instrument appropriate for the particular situation? For example, some behavior is more likely to be observed by teachers (e.g., cannot follow directions) while other behavior is better observed by parents (e.g., has nightmares).
- Can the scores for an individual child be compared to normative samples to determine whether identified problems or competencies are unusually high or low?
- Do the forms and scoring procedures allow comparisons among multiple raters who observe the child under different conditions inside and outside of school?

Limitations of Standardized Rating Scales

While standardized rating scales provide useful quantitative data on children's problems and competencies, they also have limitations:

- Rating scales do not identify the etiology or causes of children's problems. Most rating scales assess current functioning over a limited time frame, such as 2 or 6 months. To identify factors that may precipitate and sustain identified problems, evaluators must obtain additional information on the antecedents and consequences of specific types of problems, as well as environmental circumstances and other factors (e.g., developmental problems, biological conditions) contributing to the problems.
- Rating scales do not dictate choices for interventions. While results are useful for identifying specific areas of concern, additional data are necessary to determine and design appropriate and feasible interventions.
- Rating scales are not objective measures of children's problems. Scores derived from rating scales are based on a particular informant's perceptions of children's problems. Perceptions can vary from one informant to the next and can be influenced by the informant's memory, values, attitudes, and motivations, as well as situational factors.
- Rating scales are decidedly more complex instruments than one may realize, and ease of administration and scoring does not always mean ease of interpretation.

Standardized parent and teacher rating scales are most appropriate for Tier 3 assessments of an individual child's problems and competencies. However, they may also be used as Tier 2 assessments to help determine need for group interventions for specific types of problems. As best practice, an omnibus standardized rating scale should be obtained from at least one teacher who knows the child well and at least one parent. If a child has multiple teachers, it is useful to obtain ratings from several teachers in order to compare patterns of behavior across different school environments. For comprehensive assessments, rating scale results should be integrated with data from other procedures, including standardized self-reports, interviews, and direct observations, as discussed in subsequent sections. Once specific patterns of problems have been identified and targeted in interventions, school psychologists can use more narrowly focused parent and teacher rating scales, and direct observations, to monitor progress and assess short-term outcomes. For long-term outcome evaluation (e.g., 6 months, 1 year, 3 years), omnibus measures can be used again to assess targeted problems along with other potential problems that may or may not have changed as a result of a specific intervention.

Standardized Self-Reports

Standardized self-reports can be used to obtain children's own views of their problems and competencies. The ASEBA YSR (Achenbach & Rescorla, 2001), BASC-2 Self-Report of Personality (SPR; Reynolds & Kamphaus, 2004), and CBRS-Self-Report (CBRS-SR; Conners, 2008) are examples of omnibus self-report scales. The ASEBA YSR has 105 problem items for ages 11–18 comparable to those of the CBCL/6-18, plus 14 socially desirable items. The YSR problem items are scored on eight syndrome scales, six DSM-oriented scales, Internalizing scales, Externalizing scales, and Total Problems scales, all similar to those of the CBCL/6-18 and TRF. The YSR profile also provides scores for Activities, Social, and Total Competence scales, and the three 2007 clinical scales. The BASC-2 SPR contains 139 items for ages 8–11 and 176 items for ages 12–21. (There is also a 185-item form for college students ages 18–25.) The SRP is scored on 14 empirically based problem scales: Anxiety, Attention Problems, Attitude to School, Attitude to Teachers, Atypicality, Depression, Hyperactivity, Locus of Control, School Adjustment, Sensation Seeking, Sense of Inadequacy, Social Stress, Somatization, and Substance Use. The SRP has four scales for positive behaviors: Interpersonal Relations, Relations With Parents, Self-Esteem, and Self-Reliance. The CBRS-SR contains 179 items that are scored on six empirically based problem scales and 12 DSM-IV-TR disorders similar to the CBRS parent and teacher forms.

Several other standardized self-report scales focus on particular types of problems, such as depression. Examples

are the Child Depression Inventory-2 (Kovacs, 2010), Reynolds Child Depression Scale-Second Edition (Reynolds, 2010), and Reynolds Adolescent Depression Scale-Second Edition (Reynolds, 2002).

When interpreting results from self-report scales, school psychologists should consider how responses might be affected by a child's reading ability, insight, motivation, and willingness to disclose sensitive personal information. It is also important to consider age and cognitive ability. In general, older children are better able to reflect on their own emotions and behavior than are younger children. For this reason, most standardized self-reports are usually not appropriate for children under age 8. However, even some adolescents may have difficulty adopting a personal perspective on their functioning.

Cross-Informant Comparisons

To gain a comprehensive and integrated picture of children's functioning, school psychologists should compare scores on self-report scales to similar scores obtained from parent and teacher rating scales. The ASEBA computer-scoring program facilitates such comparisons for the CBCL/6-18, TRF, and YSR for up to eight informants. The ASEBA software provides printouts of cross-informant comparisons for 89 common problem items across the three forms, as well as cross-informant comparisons of syndrome and broad-scale scores. The program also provides Q correlations for judging the level of agreement between pairs of informants, such as two parents, a parent and a teacher, or the child and a teacher or parent. A 2007 version of the ASEBA computer-scoring program also provides scores for comparing a child's pattern of problems to multicultural norms, based on data from 34 different geographical regions around the world (Achenbach & Rescorla, 2007).

Research has revealed low agreement between informants in different situations or different relations with a child, as well as low agreement between children's self-ratings and ratings from other informants (Achenbach et al., 1987; Achenbach & Rescorla, 2001). With this in mind, school psychologists should not be surprised when rating scales reveal different patterns of problems reported by parents versus teachers or by children versus their parents or teachers. Teachers may also report different patterns of problems in their particular classrooms. When problem reports vary across informants, it is important to investigate environmental circumstances, relationships, or other factors that may have an impact on a child's behavior. For example, higher problem ratings by one teacher versus another might be associated with different classroom rules or expectations, difficulty of the academic subject being taught, or different groups of peers in one classroom versus another. As an another example, lower problem scores from a child's self-ratings, in contrast to higher problem scores from parent and/or teacher ratings, may indicate that the child is unaware of his or her problems or is unwilling to disclose the problems. Higher problem scores on self-ratings, in contrast to lower scores from parents and/or teachers, could reflect the child's heightened sensitivity to problems that are not apparent to adult informants. By contrast, similarity in problem patterns and competencies reported by different informants indicate areas of consistency across environmental circumstances and relationships.

Comparing scores from standardized parent and teacher rating scales and standardized self-reports can provide quantitative evidence of the extent to which a child exhibits the characteristics and qualifying conditions of the IDEA 2004 definition of ED. To illustrate this process, Appendix A outlines applications of the IDEA 2004 ED criteria to scale scores obtained from the ASEBA and BASC-2 parent, teacher, and self-report instruments. Appendix A also shows applications of the IDEA 2004 ED criteria to scale scores obtained from a semistructured child clinical interview (McConaughy & Achenbach, 2001), as discussed in a later section.

Interviews

In both clinical and school settings, interviews are a time-honored method for assessing children's emotional and behavioral problems (Busse & Beaver, 2000; McConaughy, 2013; Merrell, 2008). Problem-solving interviews with teachers, and perhaps similar interviews with a parent, can help identify specific problems to target in Tier 2 interventions. For a comprehensive assessment of emotional and behavioral disorders at Tier 3, interviews should be conducted with parents (or parent surrogates), teachers, and the child, whenever possible. Interviewing guidelines and procedures in the next three sections apply to comprehensive assessments of emotional and behavioral disorders at Tier 3, while some procedures are also applicable at Tier 2.

Parent Interviews

Communication with parents, or parent surrogates, is essential for comprehensive assessment of children's emotional and behavior disorders. Parents have unique relationships with their children that cannot be duplicated by other informants. Semistructured interviews are especially appropriate for use with parents (Busse & Beaver, 2000). If parents have already completed standardized rating scales, the interview can focus on key problem areas revealed by rating scale scores along with other information not readily assessed by those instruments. To facilitate parent interviews, McConaughy (2013) provides a reproducible protocol for a semistructured parent interview that covers the six topic areas listed in Table 24.1. After discussing confidentiality, the parent interview begins with questions regarding details of the child's presenting problems. Once specific behavioral or emotional problems have been identified, the interviewer then asks about the duration and frequency of the problems and the antecedent, sequential, and consequent conditions that precipitate and sustain the problems. Interviewers should also inquire about parents' feelings regarding targeted problems, their usual responses to the problems, and their expectations and preferences regarding their child's behaviors. If not covered already, interviewers can then move to the parents' views on their child's social functioning (e.g., friends, social groups, problems getting along with peers, fighting, or social withdrawal or rejection) and their child's school performance. Many children with emotional and behavioral problems have trouble completing assignments. Homework is often a source of potential conflict between parents and children and sometimes conflict between parents and teachers. Therefore, it is important to learn what supports are available in the home to facilitate completion of homework assignments. To assess the feasibility of interventions, interviewers should ask parents about their typical strategies for coping with identified problems, such as rules at home, rewards, and punishments.

Parents should also be asked about family factors and stressors that may precipitate or exacerbate their child's problems:

- Changes in family structure or relationships, such as divorce or a death in the family
- Upsetting events or changes at home or school for the child, including changes in residence
- Psychological or psychiatric problems of family members and mental health services for such problems
- Significant losses experienced by the child, such as death or loss of a loved one, loss of a pet, or breakup of peer or romantic relationships
- Medical traumas, hospitalizations, or serious illnesses of the child or family members

- Alcohol or drug use/abuse by the child or family members
- Traumatic episodes experienced by the child or family members, such as a suicide attempt, sexual or physical abuse, violence, or a serious accident
- Trouble with the law or involvement with the justice system or social service agencies by the child or family members

To reduce time requirements, some information on developmental history and family circumstances can be obtained by asking parents to complete questionnaires ahead of time. The Child and Family Information Form (McConaughy & Achenbach, 2004a; reprinted in McConaughy, 2013) and the BASC-2 Structured Developmental History (Reynolds & Kamphaus, 2004) are examples of such forms. Before sending home background questionnaires, school psychologists should consider parents' educational level and potential reading difficulties. If there is a possibility that a parent cannot read the questionnaire, then relevant questions should be covered in the interview instead. For non-English speaking parents, it may be necessary to use an interpreter for the parent interview, as discussed in a later section.

Teacher Interviews

It is teachers who most often initiate referrals for Tier 2 and Tier 3 assessments and interventions, in part because teachers have multiple opportunities to observe a child's behavior and social interactions. As teachers become more experienced, they gain knowledge of what behavior may be atypical for one child when compared to other children. Teacher interviews are key features of school-based problem-solving consultation. To facilitate teacher interviews, McConaughy (2013) provides a reproducible semistructured teacher interview that covers the six topic areas listed in the second column of Table 24.1. Other interview formats focus specifically on academic problems and wider aspects of the school environment. Examples are the Teacher Interview Form for Academic Problems (Shapiro, 2011) and the Academic Intervention Monitoring System (Elliott, DiPerna, & Shapiro, 2001).

As a general rule, interviews should be conducted with teachers who know the student best or who spend the most time with the student. For elementary students, this includes the current classroom teacher and perhaps one or more teachers of special subjects (e.g., art, music, physical education). For junior high or high school students, teachers of several academic and/or elective subjects can be interviewed. Other school staff, such as the guidance counselor, principal, or school nurse, can also be interviewed if he or she has sufficient involvement with the student. Another approach is to interview one or two teachers and then gather information from other school staff via standardized rating scales and questionnaires.

Owing to time constraints, it may not be practical to conduct individual interviews with multiple teachers. An alternative approach is to interview several teachers simultaneously in a round-robin fashion. However, this runs the risk of missing information if certain teachers fail to express their views in a group and runs the risk of reinforcing negative views of the child if a group interview degenerates into a mutual complaint session. To avoid this, interviewers should cultivate a positive problem-solving approach that involves an open exchange of information without pejorative judgments of the child or teachers involved.

The teacher interview begins with questions regarding teachers' current concerns about the child. After identifying specific emotional and behavioral problems, teachers may need to prioritize problems to focus on key areas of concern. Following the problem-solving model, interviewers should ask about the duration and frequency of key problems and the antecedent, sequential, and consequent conditions surrounding the problems. Answers to these questions can lead to hypotheses for a functional behavioral assessment (FBA; Stage et al., 2006). Teachers should also be queried about the child's academic performance, even when the primary concerns are about behavioral, emotional, or social functioning. Teacher reports about academic performance are essential to determine whether emotional and behavioral problems have an adverse effect on the child's educational performance, as required by the IDEA 2004 definition of ED. Interviewers should also ask teachers what instructional strategies they typically use, what interventions for academic or behavioral problems have already been tried in their classroom, and what special services have already been provided to the child. It is also important to query teachers about the types of interventions they feel are feasible in their classrooms. These questions can help identify Tier 2 interventions that have had limited success as well as other Tier 2 and Tier 3 interventions that might still be tried.

Child Interviews

Semistructured formats are usually most appropriate for interviewing children. Unstructured interviews are the least useful, because clinicians vary widely in their questioning strategies and interpretations of responses. Structured diagnostic interviews are also not recommended for interviewing children, since the interviews are often too long and tedious and the information provided can be obtained more reliably from parents (see McConaughy, 2000b).

Semistructured interviews offer unique opportunities for evaluating children's patterns of problems, their coping strategies, and their perceptions of significant persons and events related to their problems (McConaughy, 2000a, 2013). Child interviews also provide opportunities for direct observation of children's behavior, affect, and interaction styles, especially behavior that may impinge on different intervention options. Observations of a child's behavior and responses during the interview can then be compared to reports from other informants, such as parents and teachers. A well-conducted child interview can also help establish rapport and thus build a bridge from assessment to intervention.

The ASEBA Semistructured Clinical Interview for Children and Adolescents-Second Edition (SCICA; McConaughy & Achenbach, 2001) is an example of a standardized interview for children ages 6–18. The SCICA utilizes a semistructured protocol covering topic areas similar to those listed in the third column of Table 24.1. A unique feature of the SCICA is the use of structured rating scales for scoring the interviewer's observations of the child's behavior and problems reported by the child during the interview. The SCICA rating scales contain 120 observation items and 114 self-report items to be scored on a 4-point scale for ages 6–18, plus 11 self-report items scored for ages 12–18. Interviewers' ratings are scored on eight empirically based syndrome scales, plus broad scales for Internalizing, Externalizing, Total Observations, and Total Self-Reports. The SCICA profile offers the advantage of separate syndromes for scoring observations (Anxious, Withdrawn/Depressed, Language/Motor Problems, Attention Problems, and Self-Control Problems) and the children's self-reports (Anxious/Depressed, Aggressive/Rule Breaking, and Somatic Complaints). The SCICA scoring profile also provides scores for six DSM-oriented scales (Affective Problems, Anxiety Problems, Somatic Problems, Attention Deficit Hyperactivity Problems, Oppositional Defiant Problems, and Conduct Problems). Quantitative scores on the SCICA scales can be compared to similar scale scores on the CBCL/6-18, TRF, and YSR profiles.

Besides assessing problems from the child's perspective, the child interview can be a key source for assessing

feasibility of different interventions and deciding whether to refer a child for mental health or social services outside of school. Along with questions related to the topics listed in Table 24.1, other questions can be added to address specific referral issues, such as possible physical or sexual abuse, risk for suicide and threats of violence. For in-depth discussion of school-based assessments of these special issues, see Halikias (2013), Horton and Cruise (2001), and Miller (2011, 2013).

Developmental Considerations

Children's thinking and behavior change over the course of development. School psychologists need to keep this in mind when assessing emotional and behavioral disorders. For example, on the CBCL/6-18, parents scored children 6–11 years old significantly higher than those 12–18 years old on 47 problem items (e.g., can't sit still, demands attention, whining); whereas, parents scored children 12–18 years old significantly higher than those 6–11 years old on 35 problem items (e.g., hangs around with others who get into trouble, poor school work, truant, unhappy, sad, or depressed). There were also significant age differences in certain problems reported by teachers on the TRF (Achenbach & Rescorla, 2001). Standardized parent and teacher rating scales adjust for developmental differences in behavior by providing standard scores for problem scales based on large normative samples for different ages and gender. Using standard scores, school psychologists can then make evidence-based judgments about whether particular patterns of problems are deviant for a particular child's age or gender. Such developmental adjustments in scoring procedures are a major reason that we recommend standardized rating scales as key instruments for assessing emotional and behavioral disorders.

Developmental differences are also important to consider when conducting clinical interviews with children and their parents and teachers. Table 24.3 summarizes some key developmental characteristics of children in middle childhood (ages 6–11) and adolescence (ages 12–18) in terms of cognitive development, social reasoning, and typical peer interactions. For example, as noted in Table 24.3, 6–11 year old children tend to be more concrete in their cognitive functioning in contrast to adolescents who can think more abstractly and hypothetically. In their social reasoning, 6–11 year old children tend to judge right and wrong in terms of rules and social conventions (e.g., fighting on the playground is wrong because it is against school rules),

Table 24.3. Developmental Characteristics of Middle Childhood and Adolescence

Period	Cognitive Functioning	Social–Emotional Functioning	Typical Peer Interactions
Middle childhood (ages 6–11)	• Concrete operations stage • Can reason logically about objects and events • Can engage in concrete problem solving (e.g., math problems, role playing) • Can engage in conversations and clinical interviews	• Can think about another person's point of view • Conventional moral reasoning: sense of right or wrong based on rules and social conventions • Understands and complies with rules of a game • Has a developing sense of self-competence • Can regulate affect in competition	• Structured board games, group games, and team sports with complex rules • Squabbles about rules • Stable best friendships, usually with same-sex peers • Aggressive or socially withdrawn peers are generally disliked • Friendly, helpful, and supportive peers are generally liked • Peer status defined by classroom group or structured activities (e.g., clubs, teams)
Adolescence (ages 12–18)	• Formal operations stage • Can reason abstractly and hypothetically • Can engage in systematic problem solving • Has increased ability to engage in conversations and clinical interviews	• Can take a third-person point of view about social interactions • Postconventional moral reasoning: sense of right or wrong based on principles of conscience or ideals • Can be confused about self-identity • Often experiences intense and labile emotions • Is self-conscious and concerned about social interactions • Very concerned about peer group acceptance and social status	• Hanging out and communicating with peers (e.g., talking, notes, phone calls, e-mail, texting) • Intimate self-disclosure, especially among girls • Squabbles about relationship issues (e.g., gossip, secrets, loyalty issues) • Romantic partners • Aggressive and antisocial peers are generally disliked • Cooperative, helpful, and competent peers are generally liked • Peer status defined by norms for various groups, cliques, or clubs

Note. From *Clinical Interviews for Children and Adolescents: Assessment to Intervention* (2nd ed.), by S. H. McConaughy, 2013, New York, NY: Guilford Press. Copyright 2013 by Guilford Press. Reprinted with permission.

in contrast to adolescents who are able to appeal to abstract principles (e.g., stealing is wrong because it violates a person's property rights). Friendships and peer status in middle childhood generally involve other children of the same gender and the same peer group (though there can always be exceptions). Friendships and peer interactions among adolescents often become more complicated because of competing or changing loyalties, greater intimacy, and their intense and labile emotional reactions to social interactions.

Table 24.3 describes typical developmental trends for middle childhood and adolescence. However, some of those suffering from emotional and behavioral disorders may show delays in certain areas of development. For example, some 6–11 year olds may judge right versus wrong more in terms of consequences for their actions (e.g., fighting on the playground is wrong because you will be sent to the principal's office), which is more typical of younger children. Some adolescents may also

become stuck at earlier stages of social and moral reasoning (e.g., identifying wrong behavior according to punishments or rule violations rather than violations of abstract principles). Delays in social problem solving and social interaction styles are also not uncommon in children and adolescents with emotional and behavioral disorders. Readers are referred to McConaughy (2013), Merrell (2008), and scholars in developmental psychology for more in-depth discussion of these issues.

Direct Observations

Direct observations are another essential data source for multimethod assessment of children's emotional and behavioral disorders. Direct observations form the foundation for FBA and progress monitoring at Tier 2 in the three-tiered service delivery model. At Tier 3, additional direct observations should be conducted as part of a comprehensive assessment of emotional and behavioral disorders. Observations can be conducted by the school psychologist or by other school staff who have appropriate training. Observations should occur in relevant settings where problems are evident. It may also be useful to observe the child in other less problematic settings and more structured situations, such as test sessions (McConaughy & Achenbach, 2004b).

Because children's behavior is apt to vary from day to day, it is important to obtain more than one observation over several different days. It is also better to conduct observations over relatively short time periods (e.g., 10–20 minutes) across different days than to rely on one single lengthy observation. Observing one or two randomly selected control children in the same setting can also be useful for peer comparisons. Finally, the validity of direct observations may become suspect if the target child is aware of being observed. This problem can be reduced by using a trained observer who is unknown to the child or who is a regular visitor to the classroom. If the evaluator conducts the observations, then it is advisable to observe the child prior to interviewing or testing.

The two most commonly used methods for direct observations are narrative recording or systematic direct observations. To obtain narrative recordings, an observer writes a description of events that occurred within a given time frame. Methods for narrative recording include descriptive time sampling, antecedent-behavior-consequence analysis, or daily logs. Narrative recordings are then used to operationally define behaviors that can be targeted for intervention. Most often, an anecdotal descriptive report is the product of narrative recordings. While anecdotal reports are common practice, they have several disadvantages, including a lack of standardization, the potential for bias in recording, and no guarantees of reliability and validity across observation sessions, settings, and observers.

Systematic direct observation methods share the following features: (a) They measure the occurrence of specific target behaviors; (b) the target behaviors are operationally defined in a manner that makes them readily observable with a minimum of inference; (c) the observations are conducted according to standardized procedures; (d) the times and places for observations are specified; and (e) observations are scored and summarized in a standardized manner that does not vary from one observer to another (Volpe & McConaughy, 2005). Moreover, systematic direct observations provide quantitative data that can be tested for reliability and validity and can be easily compared to data obtained from other sources, including parents and teachers.

Once operational definitions of target behaviors have been established, several different techniques can be employed. For continuous recording, the observer counts the number of times a behavior (or event) occurs within a given time period or records the duration of time in which the behavior (or event) was observed. Continuous recording is most effective when behaviors have discreet beginnings and ends, low to moderate rates of occurrence, and are present only briefly. For time sampling, the observer records the presence or absence of operationally defined behaviors within short specified time periods. Time sampling is useful when multiple simultaneous target behaviors hinder continuous recording or when samples of behavior are observed across different settings.

The Direct Observation Form (DOF; McConaughy & Achenbach, 2009) is an observational system that combines narrative recording with rating scale technology. To use the DOF, an observer writes a narrative description of the child's behavior, affect, and interactions over a 10-minute period and rates the child for being on task or off task for 5 seconds at the end of each 1-minute interval. At the end of a 10-minute observation, the observer rates the child on 88 specific problem items and one open-ended item, using a 4-point scale: 0 = no occurrence; 1 = very slight or ambiguous occurrence; 2 = definite occurrence with mild or moderate intensity/frequency and less than 3 minutes duration; and 3 = definite occurrence with severe intensity, high frequency, or 3 or more minutes total duration. Ratings on the 89 items are then scored via computer on a profile of five empirically based syndromes (Sluggish Cognitive Tempo, Immature/Withdrawn, Attention Problems, Intrusive, and Oppositional), plus a DSM-oriented Attention Deficit Hyperactivity Problems scale with Inattention and Hyperactivity-Impulsivity subscales, and a Total Problems score. In addition to raw scores for each scale, the DOF profile provides *T* scores and percentiles for judging the severity of observed problems compared to normative samples of boys and girls ages 6–11. Scale scores on the DOF can also be compared to similar scale scores on the CBCL/6-18, TRF, and YSR profiles. The reliability and validity of the DOF is well established (McConaughy & Achenbach, 2009), including its validity for discriminating children with ADHD versus other referred children without ADHD and normal controls (McConaughy, Ivanova, Antshel, Eiraldi, & Dumenci, 2009; McConaughy et al., 2010). The ASEBA also includes a similar instrument, the Test Observation Form, for rating observations of children's behavior during test sessions (McConaughy & Achenbach, 2004b).

Social Skills and Social Reasoning

Many children with emotional and behavioral problems have difficulties in social interactions. Assessing social skills and social reasoning can add important information when evaluating emotional and behavioral disorders and designing interventions. Several standardized rating scales have been developed to measure social skills. Examples are the Home and Community Social Behavior Scales (Merrell & Caldarella, 2002), School Social Behavior Scales-Second Edition (Merrell, 2002), and Social Skills Improvement System (SSIS; Gresham & Elliott, 2008). The SSIS has separate forms for parents, teachers, and youth self-reports, which are scored on eight competence/adaptive scales (Total Social Skills, Communication, Cooperation, Assertion, Responsibility, Empathy, Engagement, and Self-Control), plus six problem scales.

Observations of children's behavior with peers and adults in natural settings, such as the general education classroom or the playground at recess, can also provide information about social skills and relationships. Leff and Lakin (2005) reviewed observation systems for playgrounds. Observing a child's behavior during social skills instruction or role-play situations is another way to assess specific areas of social reasoning, such as empathy or problem solving, as well as specific social behaviors, such as giving and receiving praise or criticism. Sociometric techniques may also be useful, such as asking groups of children to identify peers with specific traits, such as most liked or least liked (Merrell, 2008).

Co-Occurring Conditions

Emotional and behavioral disorders can overlap or co-occur with other types of problems. Children with ADHD or specific learning disabilities, for example, often display emotional and behavioral problems (Barkley, 2006). Children with chronic or acute medical conditions, such as allergies, seizure disorders, traumatic brain injury, or Tourette's syndrome, may exhibit co-occurring emotional and behavioral problems, as can children with intellectual or communication impairments. In certain cases, children with other identified disabilities may also be found to have ED based on IDEA 2004 criteria. Knowledge of the child's educational and medical history, coupled with direct observations, should help school psychologists judge the presence or absence of co-occurring conditions.

Achievement and Educational Performance

All special education evaluations require the assessment of a child's current academic achievement and educational performance. For ED classifications under IDEA 2004, there must be evidence that the identified emotional and behavioral problems adversely affect the child's educational performance. Standardized tests, CBM, grade reports, and work samples can all provide evidence regarding current academic achievement. Evaluation of broader educational performance can focus on school adaptive functioning and academic behaviors, such as motivation, study skills, productivity, and engagement. The Academic Competence Evaluation Scales (DiPerna & Elliott, 2000) and Academic Performance Rating Scale (DuPaul, Rapport, & Perriello, 1991) are examples of standardized instruments for this purpose. Standardized teacher rating scales, such as the ASEBA TRF, BASC-2 TRS, and the SSIS-Teacher Form, also provide scores for academic performance and/or school adaptive functioning. Evaluators can use these measures in conjunction with other academic achievement data to determine adverse effects on educational performance. For special education evaluations, Tier 2 and Tier 3 progress-monitoring data can also be cited as evidence that identified emotional and behavioral problems are having adverse effects on educational performance.

Social Maladjustment

Paragraph (ii) of the IDEA 2004 definition of ED specifically excludes "children who are socially maladjusted, unless it is determined that they have an emotional disturbance." The social maladjustment clause was added to the definition of ED to exclude adjudicated delinquents from special education (see Skiba & Grizzle, 1991). Accordingly, certain authors (e.g., Slenkovich, 1992a, 1992b) have argued that externalizing disorders, or psychiatric diagnoses of ODD and CD, constitute social maladjustment, and thereby disqualify children from special education under the ED category. Others disagree, arguing that there is no theoretical or empirical basis to exclude children with externalizing disorders from special education (Forness, 1992; Skiba & Grizzle, 1991, 1992). Research studies have also shown high co-occurrence or comorbidity of externalizing and internalizing problems (McConaughy & Skiba, 1993).

All of the above issues muddy interpretations of the social maladjustment clause. To guide best practice, school psychologists are encouraged to focus first on assessing the IDEA 2004 (and state defined) characteristics of ED. If a child exhibits one or more of the five defined ED characteristics, plus all three qualifying conditions, then that child can be considered to have ED (assuming other possible explanations for the problems have been ruled out). Once ED criteria are met, any evidence of social maladjustment is irrelevant for purposes of determining eligibility for special education. The presence of social maladjustment along with ED, however, is an important factor to consider when planning interventions, since children with externalizing problems (e.g., aggressive and delinquent behavior) often require mental health treatment and/or social services outside of school, along with special education.

Need for Special Education Services

To qualify for special education services under IDEA 2004, it is not sufficient that a child exhibit a specific disability, such as ED. Need for special education must also be demonstrated. This means that the multidisciplinary team must conclude that the child needs specially designed instruction or other interventions that cannot be accomplished through remedial education or related services alone. As indicated earlier, many children with emotional and behavioral problems are likely to have participated in Tier 2 interventions prior to any referral for evaluation of ED. If these interventions have shown limited effectiveness in reducing identified problems or improving academic performance, then such poor response to intervention can be used as evidence of need for more intensive services. School psychologists who have been actively involved in Tier 1 prevention programs and Tier 2 targeted interventions can play key roles in assisting multidisciplinary teams with decisions regarding need for special education services or other more intensive Tier 3 interventions.

Multicultural Competencies for Assessing Emotional and Behavioral Disorders

According to the 2010 U.S. census, of the total U.S. civilian population (estimated 307,006,550), 79.6% identified themselves as White (65.1% as White–not Hispanic), 15.8% identified themselves as Hispanic or Latino, 12.9% as Black or African American, 4.6% as Asian, and 1% as American Indian or Alaska Native. The 2010 U.S. census also showed that 11.1% of the population was foreign born and 17.9% spoke a language other than English at home (U.S. Census Bureau, 2010). These statistics highlight the great ethnic, cultural, and linguistic diversity of our country. The diversity of the U.S. population is also reflected in the number of children who have limited English language skills or are bilingual, termed *limited English proficient* (LEP) in the No Child Left Behind Act (NCLB). In the 2007–2008 school year, the number of LEP students in the 50 states and the District of Columbia totaled approximately 4.7 million, or close to 10% of the K–12 enrollment in public schools nationwide (Ramsey & O'Day, 2010). California had more than 1.5 million students identified as LEP (24% of the K–12 population), and New Mexico, Texas, Florida, Illinois, New York, and South Carolina had more than 100,000 LEP students. While the majority of LEP students speak Spanish as their dominant language, a 2002 survey identified more than 400 other languages that were dominant among LEP students (Kindler, 2002).

Recognizing the diversity of the U.S. population, the NASP 2010 *Model for Comprehensive and Integrated School Psychological Services* (NASP, 2010a) stresses multicultural competence as a key foundation for the delivery of school psychological services:

School psychologists demonstrate skills to provide effective professional services that promote effective functioning for individuals, families, and schools with diverse characteristics, cultures, and backgrounds and across multiple contexts, with recognition that an understanding and respect for diversity in development and learning and advocacy for social justice are foundations for all aspects of service delivery. (p. 7)

The NASP 2006 *School Psychology: A Blueprint for Training and Practice III* also stresses multicultural competence as a foundational domain: "School psychologists must be able to recognize when issues of diversity affect the manner and nature of interactions with other people and organizations. They must have the ability to modify or adapt their practices in response to those being served" (Ysseldyke et al., 2006, p. 16).

Multicultural competence goes beyond notions of cultural awareness and sensitivity. Cultural awareness is the ability to recognize similarities and differences among cultural groups. Cultural sensitivity is the ability to understand and empathize with the emotional needs of individuals from other cultural groups. Cultural awareness and sensitivity are necessary components of multicultural competence. However, multicultural competence, as conceptualized by the NASP 2010 Practice Model, requires the ability to recognize when cultural differences affect interactions with other people and requires the ability to modify or adapt practices accordingly to meet the needs of those being served. It is beyond the scope of this chapter to discuss multicultural competence in detail. Rhodes, Ochoa, and Ortiz (2005) provide an excellent discussion of the complexities of assessing culturally and linguistically diverse students.

Three professional practices are especially relevant for school psychologists in assessing emotional and behavioral disorders in LEP children and children from nonmainstream cultural and ethnic backgrounds.

The first professional practice concerns use of interpreters for interviewing children and their parents. The NASP ethical principles have a specific standard regarding the use of interpreters: "When interpreters are used to facilitate the provision of assessment and intervention services, school psychologists take steps to ensure that the interpreters are appropriately trained and are acceptable to clients" (Standard II.3.6; NASP, 2010b). Rhodes et al. (2005) and McConaughy (2013) provide guidelines for use of interpreters. What follows are some key recommendations:

- The interpreter should be equally fluent in English and the native language of the child or parent being interviewed or tested.
- Friends and family members should not be used as interpreters because this would likely involve a breach of confidentiality for the child and/or parent.
- Interpreters should have at least a high school diploma and should be trained in communication skills adequate for the task, including ability to accurately convey meaning from one language to another, knowledge about the cultures of the people for whom they are interpreting, familiarity with educational or psychological terminology, and understanding of the function and role of interpreter.

While school psychologists may not be the ones who hire interpreters for their assessments, they can and should insist that interpreters meet the above standards and they can instruct interpreters about what is expected of them in the assessment process.

A second professional practice concerns the interpretation of data obtained from various assessment procedures. As pointed out earlier, along with clinical interviews, standardized parent and teacher rating scales and self-report scales are the instruments of choice for assessing

emotional and behavioral disorders. For LEP children and their parents, school psychologists can seek non-English translations of such forms. The ASEBA, BASC-2, and CBRS all provide Spanish translations of their parent and self-report instruments. The ASEBA school-age forms have also been translated into more than 85 different languages, copies of which can be obtained by contacting the publisher listed in Table 24.2. If an appropriate non-English translation is not available, then the school psychologist can work with an interpreter to administer the parent rating scale and/or child self-report. A much more complex issue, however, concerns the interpretation of the scoring profiles obtained from such instruments. Most standardized parent rating scales and child self-report forms are scored on normative samples from the U.S. mainstream culture. Appropriate interpretation of scores for individuals from different cultural or societal groups must take into account differences in cultural values and the individual's unique experiences that may impinge upon emotional and behavioral functioning. To adjust for differences in problems and competencies reported by informants from different societies or cultures, the ASEBA computer-scoring program provides options for obtaining scoring profiles based on normative samples from different societal and cultural groups other than the U.S. mainstream normative sample (Achenbach & Rescorla, 2007; readers can learn more about multicultural scoring of the ASEBA forms by visiting the website www.aseba.org).

A third professional practice concerns the ability to recognize one's own limitations and potential biases in assessing individuals from different cultures or ethnic backgrounds. As an example of professional practices to respect diversity, the NASP Practice Model (NASP, 2010a) states: "School psychologists recognize in themselves and others the subtle racial, class, gender, cultural and other biases they may bring to their work and the way these biases influence decision making, instruction, behavior, and long-term outcomes for students" (p. 8). When school psychologists recognize such biases in themselves, they should seek supervision or peer consultation and further education, as appropriate. If a school psychologist has strong negative views, prejudices, or stereotypes about a particular cultural or ethnic group that cannot be resolved in supervision or peer consultation, then he or she should request that another person conduct the assessment.

Self-Evaluation of Effectiveness

Conducting a multimethod assessment of emotional and behavioral disorders is an individual endeavor. Rarely do two or more school psychologists collaborate in the evaluation process. Therefore, it is essential that school psychologists evaluate their own practice. Appendix B lists a series of questions school psychologists can ask themselves about their assessment. The central question is this: If this were your child, would you have wanted the school psychologist to have done anything more or anything different to best understand your child and formulate a working hypothesis about your child's emotional and behavioral functioning? If the answer to that question is "no," then there is reasonable assurance that the school psychologist adhered to best practice in conducting the assessment. That being said, self-evaluation of practice involves more than asking and answering that one core question. It is also essential to ask specific questions about instruments and procedures; the way results, findings, and information were integrated; and how all of this information was explained in a final report. Fortunately, most assessments conducted by school psychologists fall well within their range of expertise. Sometimes, however, information arises that is beyond one's normal scope of experience. Assessment results may conflict rather than align, a difficult issue may present itself, a positive or negative bias may be triggered, or something may arise that challenges one's scope of knowledge, breadth of expertise, or multicultural competence. In such situations, reviewing the assessment with a supervisor or engaging in peer consultation, as the school psychologist did in our case example, is a requisite step. Self-evaluation of effectiveness is a reflective process. Asking oneself the essential questions is only the first part of that process. Answering those questions openly and honestly is where self-evaluation truly occurs.

SUMMARY

Best practice procedures were presented for assessing emotional and behavioral disorders. A multimethod assessment approach was recommended, which requires gathering and integrating information from multiple data sources across multiple settings. Multimethod assessment assumes that no single method or informant can capture all relevant aspects of a child's emotional and behavioral functioning. Procedures were described for obtaining parent reports, teacher reports, and direct assessment of the child. As best practice, some combination of the following procedures is recommended: standardized parent and teacher rating scales, standardized self-reports, parent and teacher interviews, child interviews, systematic direct observations, and

reviews of relevant background information (family, medical, educational, cultural). Some cases may require additional assessment of intellectual ability, executive functions, communication skills, social skills, or broader aspects of personality. While much of the assessment of emotional and behavioral disorders focuses on problems, it is also important to assess strengths and competencies. Coupling knowledge of strengths with identification of specific problems should lead to more effective individually targeted interventions. Last, but certainly not least, understanding of relevant cultural factors is essential, because a behavior deemed aberrant in one culture may be deemed normal in another, even though that same behavior may be posing a problem in the school setting.

A return to the case example at the beginning of this chapter illustrates the problem-solving model, the three-tiered service delivery system, and the multimethod assessment process, and how these can be integrated in an effort to best understand and effectively address a child's emotional and behavioral problems and academic difficulties. In the case example, the school psychologist used progress monitoring and other data to assess Cassandra's emotional and behavioral problems and academic difficulties at each tier of the three-tiered service delivery model. Cassandra's developmental history also raised concerns about delays in her social development. Therefore, in the child interview, the school psychologist tailored questions to assess Cassandra's level of social and moral reasoning, her social problem-solving skills, and her ability to understand the perspectives of other people. The school psychologist also assessed Cassandra's strengths and competencies via standardized rating scales and interviews to identify positive behaviors that could be marshaled to bolster interventions. In this case example, circumstances were ideal, in that the school psychologist who consulted with the teacher and IST and Tier 1 through Tier 3 was the same person who conducted the Tier 3 comprehensive evaluation, thereby affording continuity throughout the assessment and intervention process. When there is a break in such continuity, it is essential that there be adequate communication and documentation of efforts by teachers and other school staff who have been actively involved at different service levels, so the individual who is conducting the comprehensive evaluation understands what has already occurred and can make use of data gathered during the three-tiered process to inform the evaluation.

In this example, the results of the Tier 3 comprehensive evaluation supported eligibility for special education under the IDEA 2004 ED disability category, an eligibility that opened the door for even more intensive individually based Tier 3 interventions (e.g., evidence-based treatments for anxiety and depression, social skills training, and specialized instruction in reading comprehension and written language). For students with emotional and behavioral disorders, intensive interventions may take the form of special education services or other programs in the local school, regional programs at the district level, referral for mental health treatment, or even placement in intensive hospital-based or residential programs.

The blending of the traditional school psychologist role of assessment with effective use of a problem-solving model and three-tiered service delivery model represents best practice for multimethod assessment of emotional and behavioral disorders. Many of the same assessment procedures discussed in this chapter can also be used for outcome evaluations to determine when it is appropriate for students to exit Tier 3 interventions, including special education.

AUTHOR NOTE

Disclosure: Stephanie H. McConaughy has a financial interest in books she authored or coauthored referenced in this chapter. She is also a faculty member of the ASEBA research team at the University of Vermont and has a financial interest as a developer of several ASEBA instruments reviewed in this chapter.

REFERENCES

Achenbach, T. M. (2009). *The Achenbach System of Empirically Based Assessment (ASEBA): Development, findings, theory, and applications.* Burlington, VT: University of Vermont, Research Center for Children, Youth, and Families.

Achenbach, T. M., & McConaughy, S. H. (1997). *Empirically based assessment of child and adolescent psychopathology: Practical applications.* Thousand Oaks, CA: SAGE.

Achenbach, T. M., McConaughy, S. H., & Howell, C. T. (1987). Child/adolescent behavioral and emotional problems: Implications of cross-informant correlations for situational specificity. *Psychological Bulletin, 101,* 213–232.

Achenbach, T. M., & Rescorla, L. A. (2000). *Manual for the ASEBA preschool forms and profiles.* Burlington, VT: University of Vermont, Research Center for Children, Youth, and Families.

Achenbach, T. M., & Rescorla, L. A. (2001). *Manual for the ASEBA school-age forms and profiles.* Burlington, VT: University of Vermont, Research Center for Children, Youth, and Families.

Achenbach, T. M., & Rescorla, L. A. (2007). *Multicultural supplement to the manual for the ASEBA school-age forms and profiles.* Burlington, VT: University of Vermont, Research Center for Children, Youth, and Families.

American Psychiatric Association. (2000). *Diagnostic and statistical manual of mental disorders* (4th ed., text rev.). Washington, DC: Author.

American Psychiatric Association. (2013). *Diagnostic and statistical manual of mental disorders* (5th ed.). Washington, DC: Author.

Barkley, R. A. (2006). *Attention deficit hyperactivity disorder: A handbook for diagnosis and treatment* (3rd ed.). New York, NY: Guilford Press.

Busse, R. T., & Beaver, B. R. (2000). Informant report: Parent and teacher interviews. In E. S. Shapiro & T. R. Kratochwill (Eds.), *Conducting school-based assessments of child and adolescent behavior* (pp. 235–273). New York, NY: Guilford Press.

Conners, K. C. (1997). *Conners' Rating Scales-Revised technical manual.* North Tonawanda, NY: MHS.

Conners, K. C. (2008). *Conners' Comprehensive Behavior Rating Scales manual.* North Tonawanda, NY: MHS.

Diperna, J. C., & Elliott, S. N. (2000). *Academic Competence Evaluation Scales.* San Antonio, TX: The Psychological Corporation.

DuPaul, G. J., Power, T. J., Anastopoulos, A. D., & Reid, R. (1998). *ADHD Rating Scale-IV.* New York: Guilford Press.

DuPaul, G. J., Rapport, M. D., & Perriello, L. M. (1991). Teacher ratings of academic skills: The development of the Academic Performance Rating Scale. *School Psychology Review, 20,* 284–300.

Egyed, C. J., & Short, R. J. (2006). Teacher self-efficacy, burnout, experience, and decision to refer a disruptive student. *School Psychology International, 27,* 462–474. doi:10.1177/0143034306070432

Elliott, S. N., Diperna, J. C., & Shapiro, E. S. (2001). *Academic Intervention Monitoring System guidebook.* San Antonio, TX: The Psychological Corporation.

Epstein, M. H. (2004). *Behavioral and Emotional Rating Scale: A strength-based approach to assessment* (2nd ed.). Austin, TX: PRO-ED.

Forness, S. (1992). Legalism versus professionalism in diagnosing SED in the public schools. *School Psychology Review, 21,* 29–34.

Gresham, F. M. (2009). Evolution of the treatment integrity concept: Current status and future directions. *School Psychology Review, 38,* 533–540.

Gresham, F. M., & Elliott, S. N. (2008). *Social Skills Improvement System manual.* San Antonio, TX: Pearson.

Gresham, F. M., & Gansle, K. A. (1992). Misguided assumptions of the DSM-III-R: Implications for school psychological practice. *School Psychology Quarterly, 7,* 79–95.

Halikias, W. (2013). Assessing youth violence and threats of violence in schools: School-based risk assessments. In S. H. McConaughy (Ed.), *Clinical interviews for children and adolescents: Assessment to intervention* (2nd ed., pp. 228–252). New York, NY: Guilford Press.

Horton, C. B., & Cruise, T. K. (2001). *Child abuse and neglect: The school's response.* New York, NY: Guilford Press.

Individuals with Disabilities Education Improvement Act of 2004. Pub. L. 108–446. 20 U. S. C. §§ 1400 et seq. (2004). Amendments to Individuals with Disabilities Education Act of 1990. Pub. L. 101–476. 20 U.S.C. §1401 et seq.

Jacob, S., Decker, D. M., & Hartshorne, T. S. (2011). *Ethics and law for school psychologists* (6th ed.). New York, NY: Wiley.

Kindler, A. L. (2002). *Survey of the states' limited English proficient students and available educational programs and services 1999–2000 summary report.* Washington, DC: National Clearinghouse for English Acquisition and Language Instruction Educational Programs.

Kovacs, M. (2010). *Children's Depression Inventory 2.* North Tonawanda, NY: MHS.

Leff, S., & Lakin, R. (2005). Playground-based observational systems: A review and implications for practitioners and researchers. *School Psychology Review, 34*, 475–489.

Kwon, K., Kim, E., & Sheridan, S. (2012). Behavioral competence and academic functioning among early elementary children with externalizing problems. *School Psychology Review, 41*, 123–140.

McConaughy, S. H. (2000a). Self-report: Child clinical interviews. In E. S. Shapiro & T. R. Kratochwill (Eds.), *Conducting school-based assessments of child and adolescent behavior* (pp. 170–202). New York, NY: Guilford Press.

McConaughy, S. H. (2000b). Self-reports: Theory and practice in interviewing children. In E. S. Shapiro & T. R. Kratochwill (Eds.), *Behavioral assessment in schools: Theory, research, and clinical foundations* (pp. 323–352). New York, NY: Guilford Press.

McConaughy, S. H. (2013). *Clinical interviews for children and adolescents: Assessment to intervention* (2nd ed.). New York, NY: Guilford Press.

McConaughy, S. H., & Achenbach, T. M. (2001). *Manual for the Semistructured Clinical Interview for Children and Adolescents* (2nd ed.). Burlington, VT: University of Vermont Research Center for Children, Youth, and Families.

McConaughy, S. H., & Achenbach, T. M. (2004a). *Child and Family Information Form*. Burlington, VT: University of Vermont, Research Center for Children, Youth, and Families.

McConaughy, S. H., & Achenbach, T. M. (2004b). *Manual for the Test Observation Form for Ages 2–18*. Burlington, VT: University of Vermont, Research Center for Children, Youth, and Families.

McConaughy, S. H., & Achenbach, T. M. (2009). *Manual for the ASEBA Direct Observation Form*. Burlington, VT: University of Vermont, Research Center for Children, Youth, and Families.

McConaughy, S. H., Harder, V. S., Antshel, K., Gordon, M., Eiraldi, R., & Dumenci, L. (2010). Incremental validity of test session and classroom observations in a multimethod assessment of attention deficit hyperactivity disorder. *Journal of Clinical Child and Adolescent Psychology, 39*, 650–666. doi:10.1080/15374416.2010.501287

McConaughy, S. H., Ivanova, M., Antshel, K., Eiraldi, R., & Dumenci, L. (2009). Standardized observational assessment of attention deficit hyperactivity disorder combined and predominantly inattentive subtypes: II: Classroom observations. *School Psychology Review, 38*, 362–381.

McConaughy, S. H., & Skiba, R. (1993). Comorbidity of externalizing and internalizing problems. *School Psychology Review, 22*, 419–434.

Merrell, K. W. (2002). *School Social Behavior Scales-Second edition*. Eugene, OR: Assessment-Intervention Resources.

Merrell, K. W. (2008). *Behavioral, social, and emotional assessment of children and adolescents* (3rd ed.). New York, NY: Taylor & Francis.

Merrell, K. W., & Caldarella, P. (2002). *Home and Community Social Behavior Scales*. Eugene, OR: Assessment-Intervention Resources.

Miller, D. N. (2011). *Child and adolescent suicidal behavior: School-based prevention, assessment, and intervention*. New York, NY: Guilford Press.

Miller, D. N. (2013). Assessing risk for suicide. In S. H. McConaughy (Ed.), *Clinical interviews for children and adolescents: Assessment to intervention* (2nd ed., pp. 208–227). New York, NY: Guilford Press.

Mychailyszyn, M. P., Mendes, J. L., & Kendall, P. C. (2010). School functioning in youth with and without anxiety disorders: Comparisons by diagnosis and comorbidity. *School Psychology Review, 39*, 106–121.

National Association of School Psychologists. (2010a). *Model for comprehensive and integrated school psychological services*. Bethesda, MD: Author. Retrieved from http://www.nasponline.org/standards/2010standards/2_PracticeModel.pdf

National Association of School Psychologists. (2010b). *Principles of professional ethics*. Bethesda, MD: Author. Retrieved from http://www.nasponline.org/standards/2010standards/1_%20Ethical%20Principles.pdf

Ramsey, A., & O'Day, J. (2010). *ESEA evaluation brief: The English Language Acquisition, Language Enhancement, and Academic Achievement Act*. Washington, DC: U.S. Department of Education. Retrieved from http://www.air.org/files/Title_III_State_of_the_States_043010_r1.pdf

Reynolds, C. R., & Kamphaus, R. W. (2004). *Behavior Assessment System for Children-Second edition (BASC-2)*. San Antonio, TX: Pearson.

Reynolds, W. M. (2002). *Reynolds Adolescent Depression Scale manual* (2nd ed.). Odessa, FL: Psychological Assessment Resources.

Reynolds, W. M. (2010). *Reynolds Child Depression Scale manual* (2nd ed.). Odessa, FL: Psychological Assessment Resources.

Rhodes, R. L., Ochoa, S. H., & Ortiz, S. O. (2005). *Assessing culturally and linguistically diverse students: A practical guide*. New York, NY: Guilford Press.

Shapiro, E. S. (2011). *Academic skills problems: Direct assessment and intervention* (4th ed.). New York, NY: Guilford Press.

Skiba, R., & Grizzle, K. (1991). The social maladjustment exclusion: Issues of definition and assessment. *School Psychology Review, 20*, 577–595.

Skiba, R., & Grizzle, K. (1992). Qualifications vs. logic and data: Excluding conduct disorders from the SED definition. *School Psychology Review, 21*, 23–28.

Slenkovich, J. (1992a). Can the language of "social maladjustment" in the SED definition be ignored? *School Psychology Review, 21*, 21–22.

Slenkovich, J. (1992b). Can the language of "social maladjustment" in the SED definition be ignored? The final words. *School Psychology Review, 21*, 43–44.

Stage, S. A., Jackson, H. G., Moscovitz, K., Erickson, M. J., Thurman, S. O., Jessee, W., & Olson, E. M. (2006). Using multimethod-multisource functional behavioral assessment for students with behavioral disabilities. *School Psychology Review, 35*, 451–471.

Sugai, G., & Horner, R. (2006). A promising approach for expanding and sustaining the implementation of school-wide positive behavior support. *School Psychology Review, 35*, 245–259.

Volpe, R. J., DiPerna, J. C., Hintze, J. M., & Shapiro, E. S. (2005). Observing students in classroom settings: A review of seven coding systems. *School Psychology Review, 34*, 454–474.

Volpe, R. J., & McConaughy, S. H. (2005). Systematic direct observational assessment of student behavior: Its use and interpretation in multiple settings: An introduction to the miniseries. *School Psychology Review, 34*, 451–453.

Weisz, J. R., & Kazdin, A. E. (2010). *Evidence-based psychotherapies for children and adolescents* (2nd ed.). New York, NY: Guilford Press.

U.S. Census Bureau. (2010). *State and county quick facts*. Washington, DC: U.S. Department of Commerce. Retrieved from http://quickfacts.census.gov/qfd/states/00000.html

Ysseldyke, J., Burns, M., Dawson, P., Kelley, B., Morrison, D., Ortiz, S., …Telzrow, C. (2006). *School psychology: A blueprint for training and practice III*. Bethesda, MD: National Association of School Psychologists. Retrieved from http://www.nasponline.org/resources/blueprint/FinalBlueprintInteriors.pdf

APPENDIX A. APPLICATIONS OF IDEA 2004 ED CRITERIA TO ASEBA AND BASC-2 SCALES

IDEA 2004 Criteria for ED	ASEBA CBCL/6-18 and TRF	ASEBA YSR	ASEBA SCICA	BASC-2 PRS & TRS	BASC-2 SRP
Inability to learn	• Attention Problems • DSM: Attention Deficit Hyperactivity Problems	• Attention Problems • DSM: Attention Deficit Hyperactivity Problems	• Attention Problems[OB] • DSM: Attention Deficit/Hyperactivity Problems	• Attention Problems • Learning Problems	• Attention Problems • Attitude to School
Inability to build or maintain relationships	• Withdrawn/Depressed • Social Problems	• Withdrawn/Depressed • Social Problems	• Withdrawn/Depressed[OB]	• Withdrawal	• Attitude to Teachers • Social Stress
Inappropriate types of behaviors or feelings	• Aggressive Behavior • Thought Problems • DSM: Conduct Problems • DSM: Oppositional Defiant Problems	• Aggressive Behavior • Thought Problems • DSM: Conduct Problems • DSM: Oppositional Defiant Problems	• Aggressive/Rule Breaking[SR] • Self-Control Problems[OB] • DSM: Conduct Problems • DSM: Oppositional Defiant Problems	• Aggression • Conduct Problems • Atypicality	• Sensation Seeking • Atypicality
General pervasive mood of unhappiness	• Anxious/Depressed • DSM: Affective Problems	• Anxious/Depressed • DSM: Affective Problems	• Anxious/Depressed[SR] • DSM: Affective Problems	• Depression	• Depression
Tendency to develop physical symptoms or fears	• Anxious/Depressed • Somatic Complaints • DSM: Anxiety Problems • DSM: Somatic Problems	• Anxious/Depressed • Somatic Complaints • DSM: Anxiety Problems • DSM: Somatic Problems	• Anxious[OB] • Anxious/Depressed[SR] • Somatic Complaints[SR] • DSM: Anxiety Problems • DSM: Somatic Problems	• Anxiety • Somatization	• Anxiety • Somatization
Long period of time	• History • Progress monitoring	• History • Progress monitoring	• History • Progress monitoring	• History • Progress monitoring	• History • Progress monitoring
Marked degree	• High scores for Total Problems, Internalizing, Externalizing, and/or specific problem scales	• High scores for Total Problems, Internalizing, Externalizing, and/or specific problem scales	• High scores for Total Observations, Total Self-Reports, Internalizing, Externalizing, and/or specific problem scales	• High scores for Behavioral Symptoms Index, Internalizing, Externalizing, and/or specific problem scales	• High scores for Emotional Symptoms Index, Internalizing, Externalizing, and/or specific problem scales
Adverse effects on educational performance	• Low scores for CBCL/6-18 School, TRF Academic Performance, and/or TRF Adaptive Functioning		• Low SCICA achievement screening test scores	• Low scores for Adaptive Skills Composite	• High scores for School Problems and School Maladjustment

Note. CBCL/6-18 = Child Behavior Checklist/6-18; ED = Emotional Disturbance; PRS = Parent Rating Scales; SCICA = Semistructured Clinical Interview for Children and Adolescents; TRF = Teacher's Report Form; TRS = Teacher Rating Scales; YSR = Youth Self-Report. [OB] refers to SCICA observation scales; [SR] refers to SCICA self-report scales.

APPENDIX B. SCHOOL PSYCHOLOGIST SELF-EVALUATION OF EFFECTIVENESS IN THE ASSESSMENT OF EMOTIONAL AND BEHAVIORAL DISORDERS

Specific questions regarding assessment process:

- Did I use instruments with well-documented reliability and validity for identifying emotional and behavioral problems?

- Did I obtain reports from at least one parent or guardian on a standardized parent rating scale? Do I know how to interpret the results on the rating scale's scoring profile?

- Did I obtain reports from one of more teachers on standardized teacher rating scales? Do I understand how to interpret the result on the rating scale's scoring profile?

- Did I include appropriate standardized self-report scales to assess suspected areas of emotional and behavioral problems? Do I know how to interpret the results of these self-report scales?

- Did I conduct an informative and sensitive clinical interview of the student? Did I use a semistructured format when conducting the student clinical interview? Did I allow enough time for the student clinical interview (typically 1–1 ½ hours)?

- Did I interview the student's parent(s) or guardian(s)? Did my interview cover all areas of concern as well as relevant background information about the student's living situation and family circumstances? Did I ask the parent(s) or guardian(s) for their perspective(s) on possible interventions for the student?

- Did I interview appropriate teachers who have knowledge of the student's current school functioning? Did I ask teachers for their perspectives on possible interventions for the student?

- Did I review school records and gather other relevant background information about the student, including medical history, peer/social information, and cultural factors? Do I have sufficient knowledge and multicultural competence to understand this information?

- If I were unsure of my knowledge, understanding, or multicultural competence, did I seek assistance from another person who possesses such knowledge, understanding, or competence?

- Did I write an evaluation report that integrated assessment findings in a manner that was understandable to parents or guardians and school staff?

- Did my evaluation report include statements regarding eligibility for Tier 3 interventions? Did I offer practical recommendations for Tier 2 and Tier 3 interventions, progress-monitoring methods, and need for ongoing consultation, as appropriate?

- Did I meet with the student's parent(s) or guardian(s) and the student's teachers to discuss my findings and recommendations?

Core questions:

- Did I take the necessary time to conduct a thorough assessment of the student and all of the circumstances that might possibly have an impact on the student's functioning?

- Did I seek supervision or peer consultation for aspects of the assessment about which I felt uncertain or for emotions or behaviors for which I could hypothesize multiple antecedents, triggers, or bases?

- If this were my child, would I have wanted the school psychologist to have done anything more or anything different to best understand my child and his or her circumstances?

Best Practices in the Assessment of Youth With Attention Deficit Hyperactivity Disorder Within a Multitiered Services Framework

25

Renée M. Tobin
W. Joel Schneider
Steven Landau
Illinois State University

OVERVIEW

Historically, the pharmacological treatment of attention deficit hyperactivity disorder (ADHD; formerly known as ADD from 1980 to 1987) evoked considerable controversy. Presently, this controversy has extended to the assessment of ADHD as well. Because ADHD is a complex disorder that affects multiple domains of functioning, it is widely recognized that there is no single empirically established test of ADHD. However, the combination of several assessment methods selected to determine the child's history, current functioning, and nature of impairment can represent an evidence-based approach. Even so, this information is valuable only to the extent that it informs an evidence-based treatment. We should not ask, "Does Chris have ADHD?" Instead, we should ask, "What can be done to ameliorate Chris's failure to finish schoolwork, loss of emotion regulation while playing games with peers, and violation of classroom rules?"

Although the formal medical diagnosis was recently updated (i.e., *Diagnostic and Statistical Manual of Mental Disorders*, 5th ed. [DSM-5]) and progress has occurred in the development of neuroimaging techniques, few changes relevant to the practice of school psychology have emerged. However, a broad change across all services for children is the increased professional endorsement of services within a multitiered services framework. This chapter builds on this framework to provide school psychologists with a step-by-step, evidence-based guide to conducting assessment that will lead to evidence-based interventions for ADHD using a data-based problem-solving model. The approach to ADHD assessment detailed here is consistent with the National Association of School Psychologists (NASP) *Model for Comprehensive and Integrated School Psychological Services* (NASP, 2010), which calls for school psychologists' services in the domain of Data-Based Decision Making and Accountability.

There are multiple objectives that drive the assessment of a child suspected of experiencing ADHD. These objectives include assessment for *diagnosis* (i.e., the categorical/psychiatric determination), *assessment of impairment* (i.e., specification of impaired domains of functioning), *assessment for intervention planning*, and *outcome evaluation of treatment*. According to Pelham, Fabiano, and Massetti (2005), these objectives differ in their respective levels of empirical support. It is our contention that the penultimate objective of ADHD assessment is to describe the topography of a student's strengths and limitations, and identify areas of functional impairment relevant to the design of an individualized plan within the multitiered model of service delivery. From this perspective, the psychiatric diagnosis of ADHD per se is irrelevant and unnecessary. Just as there is no single evidence-based test of ADHD, best practice clearly indicates that a single efficacious and effective intervention has not been found for all students with ADHD.

This chapter addresses recent methods touted as central to the design of classroom-based, individualized interventions for children with ADHD and provides a best practices approach for situating assessment and intervention planning of ADHD within a multitiered services framework. Although we present the most current assessment information, there are numerous assessment considerations for the practicing school psychologist to keep in mind.

BASIC CONSIDERATIONS

A comprehensive, cross-cultural review of the studies examining the core symptoms of ADHD found support for a clear two-factor model of the disorder (inattention plus the combination of hyperactivity and impulsivity) for school-age children across cultures but not for preschool children (Bauermeister, Canino, Polanczyk, & Rohde, 2010). DSM-5 (American Psychiatric Association [APA], 2013) is consistent with these findings. That is, DSM-5 maintains that presenting symptoms of ADHD are organized into three different presentations (i.e., combined, predominantly inattentive, and predominantly hyperactive/impulsive), indicating the degree to which these two core factors are displayed.

Two Factors of ADHD

When examining the actual DSM-5 diagnostic criteria for ADHD, it is easy to infer that, as was the case in the fourth edition (DSM-IV-TR), symptoms of impaired attention are the same for the predominantly inattentive and combined ADHD presentations. This inference is based on the fact that the DSM-5 diagnostic criteria for inattention are the same for these two presentation categories. Even so, there is mounting evidence that children with ADHD who are impaired because of inattention only evince a different form of inattention. This presentation may involve a more sluggish cognitive tempo, a slow-moving response style, and greater drowsiness and lethargy (Skirbekk, Hansen, Oerbeck, & Kristensen, 2011). In addition, children with inattention exclusively tend to have higher scores on internalizing symptoms and disorders, and they are more likely to be female. In contrast, children with the significant symptoms of hyperactivity and impulsivity are typically extroverted, active, boisterous, and prone to externalizing disorders (Barkley, 2006).

Most children with ADHD tend to have problems with peer relationships, but reasons differ as a function of presentation. Children with predominantly hyperactive/impulsive and combined presentations often alienate potential friends because of poor emotion regulation, difficulties with turn taking in games, interrupting during conversations, failing to consider the feelings of others, and being too intrusive. In addition, they tend to evoke a high number of most-disliked nominations from classmates. In contrast, children whose symptom problems involve inattention exclusively tend to be socially isolated and ignored because they may be shy, passive, and withdrawn, and have difficulty attending to social cues (King et al., 2009).

Children with predominantly hyperactive/impulsive and combined presentations tend to have academic difficulties related to a low level of productivity (i.e., they complete fewer assignments and with poor accuracy), whereas the academic difficulties of children without major concerns involving hyperactivity and/or impulsivity seem related to problems in cognitive functioning, daydreaming, and forgetfulness. In addition, children with significant inattention symptoms tend to have slow processing speed, whereas children with hyperactivity/impulsivity problems show inconsistent and inadequate response inhibition. Even though there is debate regarding presentation differences in the biological causal processes of ADHD, there is no controversy that children with problems resulting primarily from inattention have different treatment needs than children with problems resulting from disinhibited and under-controlled behaviors.

Developmental Considerations

As children mature, concerns about hyperactivity decline, but the impairing consequences of inattention become more obvious (Miller, Nevado-Montenegro, & Hinshaw, 2011). Problems with inattention also seem to affect interpersonal relationships, motor vehicle operation, job performance, and, most obviously, grade point average in high school. At follow-up, the typical person with ADHD has shown less educational and occupational attainment (Miller et al., 2011). Thus, the purposes of assessment change as the individual progresses through different developmental stages.

Symptoms of inattention may not be apparent until children enter school, whereas symptoms of hyperactivity and impulsivity are seen earlier in the developmental process, and it is these symptoms that may lead to referral for the preschool-age child. During the elementary school years, disruptive behaviors tend to continue and the risk of academic and behavior problems emerges. These areas should become a focus of assessment.

As children mature, there are additional assessment considerations that should be applied to middle school and high school students with ADHD. For example, school psychologists should be sensitive to the increased prevalence of risk-taking behaviors that include unprotected sex, drug and alcohol use, and nicotine addiction (Barkley, 2006). In addition, high school students with ADHD may benefit from assessment focused on vocational planning, because many of these students will not go on to college and will be at risk for experiencing employment problems.

Gender Considerations

As one of the most common disorders of childhood, ADHD presents in approximately 5% of school-age children (APA, 2013). Sex ratios range from 2:1 in community samples to 9:1 in clinic samples (APA, 2013). There are multiple explanations for the greater male prevalence among children with ADHD. Some accounts reflect gender effects on etiological processes, and some reflect assessment bias. For example, the DSM-5 (APA, 2013) diagnostic criteria are the same as they were in the previous edition; these criteria were principally derived from field trials featuring samples with few girls and therefore represent the prototypic conception of boys with ADHD. Because of these factors, girls who meet criteria for ADHD may appear to be engaging in less gender-typical behavior than their male counterparts and may have crossed a higher threshold for diagnosis. One consequence of this gender-norm violation for girls is that their peer relations may be more impaired than those found with their male counterparts. For example, Tseng et al. (2012) found that inattention led to less optimal peer functioning, but only for girls with ADHD.

In a similar vein, most rating scales currently used by teachers to assess ADHD focus on disruptive classroom problems more typical of male students (e.g., rule violations), thereby leading to more symptomatic ratings of boys with the disorder. Indeed, evidence indicates there are many girls with ADHD who are truly impaired but have not met the formal diagnostic criteria (Waschbusch, King, & Northern Partners in Action for Children and Youth, 2006). In addition, there are data indicating that adolescent girls with ADHD are at particularly high risk for suicidal ideation and suicide attempts during their teen years, and exhibit high rates of self-harm behavior (Miller et al., 2011). These results have implications for the practicing school psychologist, who is advised to assess for these self-harm concerns when working with adolescents with ADHD.

Cultural Considerations

There are no known cultural effects on the epidemiology of ADHD (Bauermeister et al., 2010). However, culture may influence parents' referral practices and which child behaviors they consider most troubling. As with any assessment, cultural competence of the school psychologist is essential in ADHD assessment (APA, 2013). The effects of cultural/ethnic group identity and social class on the epidemiology of ADHD remain unclear. In terms of social class, most investigations have determined that ADHD is equally prevalent across socioeconomic strata. However, those studies that report ADHD to be more heavily concentrated among lower socioeconomic status children may be best explained by downward social mobility in the families of these children, and not by elevated risk because these children reside in the lower strata.

Legal Considerations

ADHD is a psychiatric designation that alone does not inform the nature and intensity of intervention services, particularly in the school setting. Through a multitiered system of supports, children displaying symptoms of ADHD may be offered interventions as part of general education without a diagnostic label. If the interventions provided in general education are not effective in addressing the behavioral and learning needs of children with ADHD symptoms, readers are encouraged to consult current local, state, and federal guidelines and regulations. Generally, more intensive accommodations and intervention services fall under two legal umbrellas: Section 504 of the Rehabilitation Act of 1973, as amended (Section 504), or the 2004 Individuals with Disabilities Education Improvement Act (the IDEA reauthorization). Section 504 addresses general education accommodations provided when impairments to learning are deemed significant. Under Section 504, receiving these accommodations requires a diagnosis. If these accommodations are not regarded as adequate to address the child's needs, it is possible for a child to qualify for special education services, typically under the IDEA category of Other Health Impaired, and to receive both accommodations and more intensive intervention services. Thus, the legal underpinnings of the system are consistent with a dimensional approach to the assessment and treatment of ADHD with different opportunities to address the child's symptoms with increasingly intensive interventions and supports at each tier (e.g., positive behavioral intervention supports).

BEST PRACTICES IN ASSESSMENT OF ADHD

In many settings, the purpose of ADHD assessment is limited to the assignment of a formal DSM-5 (APA, 2013) diagnosis to determine eligibility for needed services and/or third-party reimbursement. In contrast, children with attention problems in school settings, including those with ADHD, are assessed and treated within a multitiered service framework. In these cases, diagnosis is less relevant than the child's response to intervention. As mentioned previously, four purposes drive the assessment of ADHD: diagnosis, assessment of impairment, assessment for intervention planning, and outcome evaluation of treatment.

Purposes of Assessment

Given that ADHD is a psychiatric disorder, its diagnosis must depend on criteria specified in the psychiatric taxonomy (i.e., DSM-5). There are times when practicing school psychologists may be asked to generate a diagnosis, such as when a pediatrician is considering the administration of psychopharmacological agents. However, an ADHD diagnosis is not required for the provision of school-based supports and services.

Formal Diagnosis of ADHD

Although the DSM-5 diagnostic criteria for ADHD remain the same as they appeared in DSM-IV-TR, there are a few diagnostic changes, and they have implications for practicing school psychologists. For example, the age of onset criterion expressed in DSM-IV-TR (i.e., symptoms that caused impairment were present before age 7) has now been changed to 12 years in DSM-5. As noted by Frances (2010), this change did not reflect a risk–benefit analysis. The benefit of increasing the age is that it will reduce false negatives, but there is considerable risk of a significant increase of false positives in the diagnosis of ADHD. Frances (2010) also noted that among adolescents and adults, real or perceived inattention is so common and nonspecific to ADHD that further overdiagnosis will occur. Finally, moving onset age from under 7 years to under 12 years involves crossing a significant stage of development (i.e., childhood to adolescence). As mentioned previously, there is considerable evidence that as children with ADHD mature, some symptoms diminish (e.g., hyperactivity), whereas other symptoms (e.g., inattention) play a more prominent role in impairment over time (Miller et al., 2011). School psychologists should be sensitive to

this issue when considering the age of the student at the time of assessment. Other changes include (a) more frequent and different exemplars to clarify the denotation of the diagnostic criteria, (b) the disorder's placement in the neurodevelopmental disorders section of the DSM-5 (as opposed to its former location in the section of the DSM-IV-TR on disorders usually first diagnosed in infancy, childhood, or adolescence), and (c) the designation of the presence of an autism spectrum disorder as no longer an exclusionary criterion.

Assessment of Impairment

There is an important distinction between a focus on the core symptoms of ADHD and a focus on the peripheral features of the disorder. The core symptoms—inattention, impulsivity, and hyperactivity—are presumed to be the direct manifestations of underlying neurobiological dysfunctions, whereas the peripheral symptoms—academic/occupational underachievement, family and peer relationship difficulties, elevated risk of injuries, and so forth—are various functional consequences of the core symptoms. These so-called peripheral symptoms are only peripheral to the diagnosis of ADHD. With respect to assessment, broadly conceived, they are central concerns. Case conceptualization and treatment planning are not only incomplete, but grossly inadequate, if these areas of impairment are not also considered. Indeed, most psychosocial treatments of ADHD are rightly focused on the so-called peripheral features of ADHD (Pelham et al., 2005). When assessment of impairment and outcome evaluation come together, the assessment and treatment of ADHD may be situated within a multitiered services framework, as will be discussed later.

Functioning within the school. The list of academic problems common among children with ADHD is long and varied (Barkley, 2006). This list does include deficient academic skills (e.g., reading, writing, calculating) compared with those of same-age peers of comparable cognitive ability. However, it is much more likely for students with ADHD to have academic performance problems than it is for them to have academic skill deficits. That is, they are more likely to fail to do what they know than not know what to do.

Teachers are faced with the extremely difficult task of providing high-quality instruction while keeping order in the classroom, enforcing high standards of conduct, and maintaining warm relationships with the children they teach. Their task becomes much more challenging with children who are restless, impulsive, and easily bored, and who require multiple prompts. Justified or not, frequent redirection takes a toll on the warm, respectful relationship most children with ADHD would otherwise have with their teachers. In addition, these repeated teacher prompts usurp teacher attention from the other students in the classroom. This dynamic should also be the focus of assessment. Teachers of students with ADHD may benefit from additional supports from the school psychologist, such as assistance in developing coping and stress reduction skills. Within a multitiered model, identified educational needs of a student with ADHD must be considered when matching the teacher's and school's level of resources.

Functioning within peer relationships.

Consistent peer rejection is a risk factor for many current and future negative life outcomes, including delinquency, school maladjustment, later psychiatric disorders, job dismissals, bad conduct discharge from the military, police contact and incarcerations, and psychiatric hospitalizations. Unfortunately, children with combined presentation of ADHD tend to be viewed as bossy, loud, intrusive, immature, domineering, disruptive, aggressive, and easily frustrated in play situations. Frequently argumentative, explosive, defiant, and unpredictable, these children often establish negative reputations with unfamiliar children very quickly, and these negative reputations become durable and follow the disliked child for years (Ronk, Hund, & Landau, 2011).

Given the high stakes involved, an assessment of the child's peer relationships is essential, especially if interventions to facilitate improved peer relations are to be attempted. Parents and teachers may have good insights about a child's peer relationship problems, but direct observations of peer interactions during free play are probably necessary to form accurate and useful case conceptualizations that lead to effective interventions.

Functioning within the family.

It is well known that relationships within families of children with ADHD are, on average, disrupted on multiple levels. One of the most important insights to emerge from robust empirical findings is not only that poor parenting affects children's behavior but also that children's misbehavior worsens parenting style (e.g., Hawes, Dadds, Frost, & Hasking, 2011). Parents of children with ADHD, for a variety of reasons, tend to have more negative thoughts and feelings about their children and about their own approach to parenting. Perhaps because these children tend to be less compliant, parents of children with ADHD tend to employ more authoritarian parenting strategies. Not surprisingly, families of children with ADHD tend to exhibit higher rates of divorce, marital discord, and sibling conflict than families without a child with ADHD. Because ADHD also tends to run in families, these problems may be exacerbated by the presence of ADHD in the parent (e.g., Murray & Johnston, 2006). Even so, mothers who themselves have ADHD tend to be more tolerant of the behavior of their children with ADHD than the non-ADHD siblings of the child (Psychogiou, Daley, Thompson, & Sonuga-Barke, 2008). Therefore, information on specific family characteristics, including parenting skills, may provide the school psychologist with valuable information that guides the planning of intervention strategies that cross from home to school.

Comorbidity.

Although rates of overlap vary across studies, more than one half of all children with ADHD present comorbid oppositional defiant disorder and/or conduct disorder diagnoses (APA, 2013). Early toddler-age symptoms of ADHD (specifically hyperactivity) may predate the onset of these other disruptive disorders. Thus, many children with ADHD can become extremely stubborn, noncompliant, and hostile, and ultimately engage in rule violations, stealing, lying, and aggressive acts. This is significant, as follow-up studies of children with comorbid ADHD and conduct disorder indicate they are at great risk for more serious adolescent and adult adjustment problems (APA, 2013). Children with ADHD are also at risk for low self-esteem, depression, and substance use disorders as they mature. These symptoms should also be considered during the assessment process.

Assessment for Intervention Planning

To be relevant to the evidence-based design of interventions, the ideal ADHD assessment battery should focus on specific behaviors of high social validity, as well as areas of impairment that compromise the child's daily adaptive functioning. An evidence-based assessment approach to treatment planning should include a history, broadband and narrowband (i.e., ADHD symptom specific) rating scales, interviews, global measures of adaptive functioning/impairment, and direct observation methods. In addition, the assessment battery should include functional behavioral assessment and assessment of domain-specific areas of impairment, as well as academic achievement.

Outcome Evaluation of Treatment

This fourth objective in the assessment of ADHD involves progress monitoring or evaluation of the child's response to intervention. Assessment at this stage includes many of the same methods applied during earlier stages of assessment; these will be discussed in greater detail in the context of ADHD assessment vis-à-vis a multitiered services framework.

Specific Assessment Methods

The procedures described in this chapter have been used in a traditional, diagnosis-driven approach to the assessment of ADHD. However, these procedures are also appropriate for use in a dynamic and fluid problem-solving approach within a multitiered services framework. This approach specifically focuses on assessing the child's areas of impairment at school, in peer relations, in the family, and in the community. In line with the goals of multitiered service delivery, these methods are intended for use within the context of ongoing, appropriate interventions. Thus, we recommend pairing best practices in intervention with best practices in assessment within the multitiered framework.

The assessment methods detailed are readily available to the practicing school psychologist. The difference between what we prescribe here and the traditional, diagnosis-driven assessment of ADHD does not involve a difference in methods selected, but a difference in the questions to be addressed throughout the assessment process. Although there are no established guidelines for integrating assessment data across sources and methods or for resolving informant discrepancies, the systematic approach detailed in this chapter allows for more frequent examination of the assessment data informing decisions to remove interventions that are no longer necessary as well as those involved in exiting children from services. Table 25.1 presents a summary of select methods for assessing children with ADHD.

Rating Scales

As with the assessment of other disorders affecting children at schools, rating scales are fundamental in the assessment of ADHD. Unlike a DSM diagnosis that involves a categorical perspective derived from a symptom present/symptom absent approach, rating scales reflect a dimensional perspective that establishes the degree to which a child exhibits certain problem behaviors relative to same-age and same-gender students (i.e., symptom severity from a normative perspective). In addition, they provide information from various adult informants (i.e., parents and teachers) about how a child functions in naturalistic contexts over extended periods of time, and provide insight into concerns experienced by those who work and live with the child. They also permit a cost-effective method of data collection on low base-rate behaviors that may be missed by other methods (e.g., direct observations). Rating scales also provide a means of conducting outcome evaluation by assessing clinically significant

Table 25.1. Select Methods for the Assessment of ADHD Symptoms Within a Multitiered Framework

Method	Tier	Examples
Rating scales		
Screening instruments	1	Achenbach System of Empirically Based Assessment, Brief Problem Monitor; Behavior Assessment System for Children–Second Edition, Behavioral and Emotional Screening System
Progress monitoring	1–3	Achenbach System of Empirically Based Assessment, Brief Problem Monitor; Behavior Assessment System for Children–Second Edition, Progress Monitoring
Broadband measures	2	Achenbach System of Empirically Based Assessment, Child Behavior Checklist, Teacher Report Form; Behavior Assessment System for Children–Second Edition, Teacher Rating Scales, Parent Rating Scales
Narrowband measures	3	Conners–Third Edition; ADHD Rating Scale-IV
Direct observations	2	Individualized Target Behavior Evaluation; Test Observation Form
Functional behavioral assessments	3	Gresham, Watson, & Skinner (2001)
Interviews	3	Unstructured format
Cognitive	3	Wechsler scales; Woodcock-Johnson tests; Kaufman scales
Educational	3	Curriculum-based assessment
Computer-based	3	Continuous performance tests

change (e.g., dropping from the clinical range to the at-risk range on the inattentive subscale of the Behavior Assessment System for Children–Second Edition [BASC-2]). There are four types of rating scales (i.e., screening instruments, broadband, narrowband, and progress monitoring) relevant to the assessment of ADHD.

Screening instruments. Although not recommended for diagnostic purposes, screening instruments are essential tools for a school psychologist practicing within a multitiered services framework. These methods have long been in place for academic concerns and have more recently been used for school children's social, emotional, and behavioral concerns. For example, social–emotional screening instruments were recently added to two of the most commonly used assessment systems, providing opportunities for wide-scale, school-based screenings of children in line with a multitiered services approach to assessment and intervention. Specifically, the Behavioral and Emotional Screening System (Kamphaus & Reynolds, 2007), a new portion of the second edition of the BASC, was released in 2007. For a modest additional charge, this screener can be an integrated part of the AIMSweb benchmark and progress monitoring system for grades K–8. In 2011, the Achenbach System of Empirically Based Assessment (ASEBA; Achenbach, 2009) released a similar screening tool, the Brief Problem Monitor (Achenbach, McConaughy, Ivanova, & Rescorla, 2011). Through the use of social, emotional, and behavioral screening instruments, the school psychologist is able to identify efficiently children at risk for nonacademic problems, including ADHD, in a cost- and time-effective manner. These or similar measures (e.g., BASC-2 Progress Monitor; Kamphaus & Reynolds, 2009) can also be used to monitor a student's progress in response to interventions throughout the multitiered system.

Omnibus or broadband rating scales. Like screening instruments, broadband rating scales are also not recommended for diagnostic purposes, but they do provide the school psychologist with a means to assess for comorbid problems and disorders associated with ADHD. The ASEBA (Achenbach, 2009) and the BASC (Reynolds & Kamphaus, 2004) are two of the most widely used in school and clinical research. These scales differ in their respective methods of derivation, and neither is based on actual DSM-5 diagnostic criteria. The ASEBA is empirically derived, whereas the BASC is rationally derived. However, both systems provide an attention problems subscale that corresponds significantly with ratings on narrowband ADHD symptom scales described below. In addition, each system has extensive norms across age and gender, and a detailed manual.

Narrowband or ADHD symptom rating scales. There are several rating scales that focus directly on the core symptoms of ADHD. Although items differ across these scales, each presents a DSM structural view of the disorder. The Conners–Third Edition (Conners, 2008) and the ADHD Rating Scale-IV (DuPaul, Power, Anastopoulos, & Reid, 1998) are two of the most popular among these scales. ADHD-specific symptom ratings can assist school psychologists in determining if the child meets DSM diagnostic criteria for the disorder, and represent an excellent way to provide the physician or child psychiatrist with information about the nature and severity of school- or home-based concerns using diagnostic criteria familiar to medical professionals. These scales have a lengthy history of use and have proved to be an efficient way to separate clinical from nonclinical groups and to clarify an ADHD presentation among referred children. According to the test makers, the more reliable ADHD scales are highly sensitive to both psychosocial and psychopharmacological interventions, and make excellent response-to-treatment measures.

Progress monitoring. In addition to using narrowband rating scales, progress monitoring rating scales can also be used to assess attention and behavior problems over time. The measures allow school psychologists to monitor progress in response to intervention efficiently throughout the multitiered system. These measures include screening instruments intended for this purpose (e.g., Brief Problem Monitor; Achenbach et al., 2011), as well as other brief measures designed to assess inattention specifically (e.g., BASC-2 Progress Monitor; Kamphaus & Reynolds, 2009).

Direct Observation

Systematic direct observation in naturalistic settings is an essential component in evidence-based assessment of ADHD. Direct observation is distinctive, as it represents the only method to quantify current, ongoing behavioral events and the bidirectional relationship between behavior and setting. From the perspective of content and ecological validity, the school psychologist is in a unique position to assess children's functioning using this in vivo method, which is unavailable to those who work in the clinic setting.

However, direct observations should not be used for diagnostic purposes. Data from ratings and interviews are considered more efficient for classification purposes (Pelham et al., 2005). Direct observations can be extremely time consuming, and resulting data may have reliability problems. For example, the behavior of children with ADHD is notoriously variable across settings and time, leaving one to wonder if the results of direct observation on a given day are representative of the child's veritable functioning. In addition, the validity research on direct observations is sparse compared to psychometric studies involving the other methods of ADHD assessment. Because of these concerns, direct observations are better suited to describing the precise nature of the child's difficulties, and are an essential ingredient in the functional behavioral assessment of problem behaviors. Fine-grained, clinically rich, and subtle processes of interpersonal interaction (e.g., negative reinforcement traps), that are easily missed by other methods, can be noted by the school psychologist and used to formulate treatment plans.

The Individualized Target Behavior Evaluation is a simple, fast, and reliable method that allows teachers to track behaviors of concern systematically (Pelham et al., 2005). Practical and relevant target behaviors such as homework completion, desk organization, and preparation for class can be rated once each day. Relatively infrequent behaviors, such as aggression, can be more reliably tracked using daily Individualized Target Behavior Evaluations than with time-sampling observation systems. Thus, the Individualized Target Behavior Evaluation is an economical, effective method of assessing a child's ADHD-related behavior in school and peer relations. Observations may also be shared with parents through parent daily reports to facilitate parental communication and involvement. In addition, if rating scale data indicate the child with ADHD is experiencing problems in the peer group, direct observation of free play behavior may also be warranted.

Finally, the child's test-taking behavior during psychoeducational assessment, plus his or her demeanor during interviews, can provide rich data for observational coding (McConaughy, 2005). For example, using the Test Observation Form (McConaughy & Achenbach, 2004), McConaughy, Ivanova, Antshel, and Eiraldi (2009) found meaningful differences between children with and without ADHD-Combined presentation based on observations during standardized test administration. Therefore, school psychologists can improve upon the unreliable method of anecdotal note

taking during testing by systematically collecting data using these methods, and these data can be used to inform treatment.

Functional Assessments

Valid measurements and descriptions of problem behaviors associated with ADHD are important in the assessment process. Functional assessment moves beyond description and focuses instead on how and why the problem behaviors occur. Functional assessment is not a specific technique or method. Rather, it is a conceptual framework based primarily on behaviorist principles that encourages the school psychologist to use multiple sources of information to determine the purpose or function of a behavior for the individual (Gresham et al., 2001).

Once the function of an undesirable behavior has been identified, interventions can be devised that directly address the nature of that problem. Such an approach will be more effective than one based on trial and error or inference.

Interviewing

Interviews are necessary to clarify and contextualize behavior rating scale data. Interviews also allow for direct observation of the informant (i.e., teacher, parent, child) during the interview process. One of the most important functions of the interview process is to rule out other conditions that produce ADHD-like symptoms (e.g., thyroid problems, sleep apnea and other sleep disorders, seizure disorders, lead poisoning, chronic fatigue, sensory impairments, hypoglycemia, fetal alcohol syndrome, traumatic brain injuries, substance abuse, mood disorders, anxiety disorders, thought disorders, conduct disorder, autism, learning disorders, and low cognitive ability; see Wodrich, Pfeiffer, & Landau, 2008).

In terms of format, evidence-based assessment in the schools typically does not involve structured or semi-structured interviews because the interviews are time consuming and add little incremental validity. However, unstructured interviews are advantageous for several reasons. They provide valuable data on all three major areas of impairment (i.e., school, peer relations, and family) while glossing over or skipping irrelevant domains and covering a wide range of issues without constraints. Unstructured interviews facilitate opportunities for the school psychologist to display accurate empathy that strengthens the therapeutic alliance and allows the family to feel comfortable sharing potentially embarrassing aspects of the child's problems. Interviews also provide information regarding the informants' priorities for socially valid intervention alternatives.

Unstructured interviews are best used in combination with parent and teacher rating scales and direct observations. For school-based interventions targeting ADHD and related deficits, teacher interviews are especially useful in designing, implementing, and monitoring treatment over time.

Cognitive, Educational, and Computer-Based Assessment

Because many school psychologists simultaneously assess for learning disorders and ADHD, cognitive ability/intelligence tests are often part of a full assessment battery. The presence of ADHD may have some implications for the child's level of intelligence (APA, 2013). There is evidence that children with ADHD score, on average, approximately 0.6 standard deviations lower than age mates on IQ tests (Frazier, Demaree, & Youngstrom, 2004), but this information is not diagnostically meaningful at the individual level.

There are good reasons to administer a cognitive assessment to a child, but ADHD diagnosis is not one of them. It is true that people with ADHD are a bit more likely to have certain cognitive profiles than those without ADHD. For example, students with ADHD, on average, tend to score slightly lower on tests of working memory, processing speed, and verbal fluency than on tests of visual–spatial reasoning, fluid reasoning, and crystallized intelligence (Schwean & Saklofske, 2005). However, most people with ADHD do not have this particular profile, and most people with this profile do not have ADHD. In the end, ADHD cannot be ruled in or out by any particular cognitive profile.

Although cognitive ability data are of limited diagnostic value, knowledge of the child's cognitive ability can and should play an important role in case conceptualization and functional analysis (e.g., some children are bored and misbehave in class because the tasks are too easy, whereas others are bored and misbehave because the work is too difficult). In addition, validity data linking children's cognitive abilities with important life outcomes are extremely robust. Thus, cognitive ability data should be interpreted in roughly the same way for children with and without ADHD.

It is well known that children with ADHD have academic difficulties, but the nature of these difficulties is often misunderstood. In general, children with ADHD do not have academic skill deficits, but rather academic performance or productivity deficits (Barkley, 2006). That is, on their best days and under certain conditions,

students with ADHD may be as likely as other children to perform well on academic tests. However, it is often difficult to get those with ADHD to engage in skill-building seatwork and homework. Often, students with ADHD display performance deficits upon reaching school age, but skill deficits may result due to diminished focus on academic work and fewer practice opportunities with the skills if not corrected through interventions. As is the case with cognitive ability testing, academic achievement testing is an important component of the assessment process because it informs case conceptualizations and helps identify treatment goals. Although achievement testing may not be used for diagnostic purposes, as delayed achievement is not a criterion for the DSM-5 ADHD diagnosis, it can be useful in meeting eligibility criteria for services in the schools. School psychologists may find curriculum-based assessment of academic skills to be particularly useful in measuring intervention effectiveness for children with ADHD, and it is well suited for the multitiered services approach to ADHD assessment advanced in this chapter.

Within schools, there is growing interest in the formal assessment of executive functions deficits. In many cases, school psychologists are being asked to recommend commercially prepared, computer-based training programs to ameliorate executive functions deficits. To date, the evidence supporting the effectiveness of these training programs is lacking, and children seem to improve only in the tasks for which they were trained (i.e., there is no transfer).

ADHD Assessment and the Multitiered Services Model

Within a multitiered services framework, a team of professionals, including school psychologists, addresses the specific learning and behavioral needs of the student, not the student's ADHD diagnosis. Thus, a school psychologist may serve as a leader in improving the academic, behavioral, and social impairments affecting the child's functioning at school. In terms of the application of a multitiered services model, a sizable body of literature supports its implementation for academic concerns relative to social, emotional, or behavioral ones such as ADHD. However, discussion of applying a multitiered services approach to concerns like ADHD is growing (e.g., Haraway, 2012).

As noted previously, a multitiered services approach to assessment relies on many of the same evidence-based assessment methods also used in a traditional approach. Differences lie in the questions school psychologists strive to answer. If the intervention produces a desirable change in behavior at one of the lower tiers of intervention and returns the child's behavior to within normal limits, the child will no longer require intervention. If, however, the child progresses through the three-tiered model of evidence-based interventions and significant progress is not apparent, the child becomes a candidate for more intensive intervention, ultimately at the level of special education services. Thus, these methods capitalize on the school psychologist's training in continuous hypothesis generation and testing throughout the process. Further, embedding evidence-based assessment within ongoing treatment delivery saves time and resources. An assessment through the multiple tiers of services ensures treatment validity and the ability to evaluate treatment outcomes easily in a progress monitoring system. It is important to note, however, that this application of the multitiered services framework to social, emotional, and behavioral concerns is an extension of the approach described for a strictly academic concern. We advocate that school psychologists implement a multitiered services approach as it pertains to assessment and intervention planning for all students with ADHD whose needs go beyond academic functioning.

On the basis of findings from more than 30 years of research on the topic, Pelham et al. (2005) provide guidelines for best practices in assessment of ADHD, and these guidelines map readily onto the multitiered services model presented in this edition of *Best Practices*. In this chapter, we aligned traditional and contemporary methods of assessment for ADHD with the current multitiered approach to service delivery. Here, we update the integration of these bodies of literature to present a best practice multitiered services approach to the assessment of ADHD, as shown in Figure 25.1.

Tier 1: Universal Interventions

At the first tier, preventive interventions and universal screening are conducted for children at risk for problems associated with ADHD. In terms of academic assessment, screenings of reading, mathematics, and writing problems are conducted at this tier to identify students (including those with ADHD) who may be functioning below expected levels. School psychologists are then able to provide additional interventions to these children using a multitiered services approach. Thus, relative to other areas of intervention, those aimed directly at the academic functioning of a student with ADHD have already been aligned with a multitiered services approach. In contrast, the assessment of behavioral

problems at school is not as well developed within a multitiered services approach, but the research literature offers suggestions. School psychologists can use screening instruments, including ADHD symptom-specific rating scales reflecting DSM diagnostic criteria, to identify potential problems with core ADHD symptoms (i.e., inattention, impulsivity, and hyperactivity), as well as related cognitive, academic, and social concerns.

Within Tier 1 of a multitiered services approach, school psychologists may organize, facilitate, and examine rating scale data from screening instruments completed by parents and teachers to identify children at risk for problems related to ADHD. Screening instruments, such as the Brief Problem Monitor scales from the ASEBA (Achenbach et al., 2011) and the Behavioral and Emotional Screening System from the BASC-2 (Kamphaus & Reynolds, 2007), help to identify children at risk for internalizing and externalizing concerns with minor time and financial costs in much the same way academic screening instruments have been implemented in the schools. Students should also be screened for problems in academic work completion and accuracy. Moreover, teachers should be sensitized to the developmental importance of children's peer relations, and screening for those at risk for these problems should use these methods.

Tier 2: Targeted Group Interventions

At the second tier, children identified as at risk should be assessed using omnibus or broadband ratings to obtain a more comprehensive baseline assessment of social, emotional, behavioral, and adaptive functioning that informs intervention. Children identified with ADHD-related problems should receive accommodations from their teachers within the general education curriculum. Changing the seating location of the student with ADHD, repeating instructions, implementing behavior modification plans, and reducing assignment length are suitable examples. At this stage, school psychologists should facilitate communication between less and more experienced teachers to provide teachers with assistance in developing appropriate accommodations using curricular modifications.

Using a multitiered services approach, teachers should be guided in carefully tracking specific behaviors of these students in response to the intervention efforts. At this level of intervention, school psychologists can assist teachers in defining specific behavioral targets. This process will contribute to the social validity of interventions because it reflects the teacher's most immediate concerns. In addition, school psychologists

Figure 25.1. Assessment of ADHD Within a Multitiered System of Supports

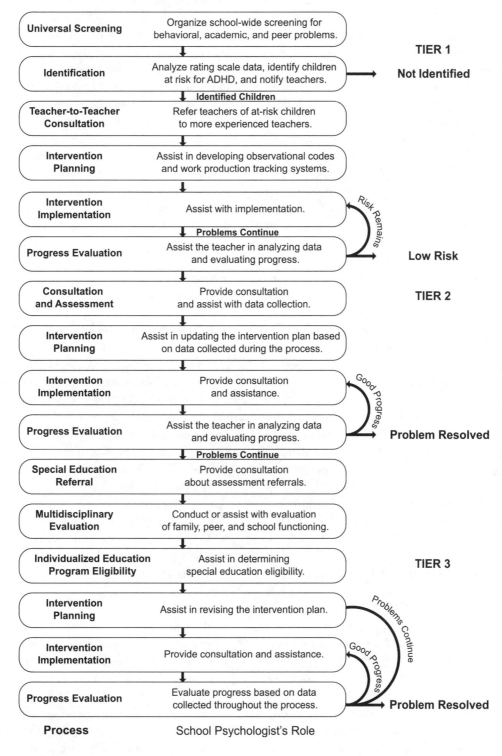

Process	School Psychologist's Role	
Universal Screening	Organize school-wide screening for behavioral, academic, and peer problems.	**TIER 1**
Identification	Analyze rating scale data, identify children at risk for ADHD, and notify teachers.	**Not Identified**
Identified Children		
Teacher-to-Teacher Consultation	Refer teachers of at-risk children to more experienced teachers.	
Intervention Planning	Assist in developing observational codes and work production tracking systems.	
Intervention Implementation	Assist with implementation.	*Risk Remains*
Problems Continue		
Progress Evaluation	Assist the teacher in analyzing data and evaluating progress.	**Low Risk**
Consultation and Assessment	Provide consultation and assist with data collection.	**TIER 2**
Intervention Planning	Assist in updating the intervention plan based on data collected during the process.	
Intervention Implementation	Provide consultation and assistance.	*Good Progress*
Progress Evaluation	Assist the teacher in analyzing data and evaluating progress.	**Problem Resolved**
Problems Continue		
Special Education Referral	Provide consultation about assessment referrals.	
Multidisciplinary Evaluation	Conduct or assist with evaluation of family, peer, and school functioning.	
Individualized Education Program Eligibility	Assist in determining special education eligibility.	**TIER 3**
Intervention Planning	Assist in revising the intervention plan.	*Problems Continue*
Intervention Implementation	Provide consultation and assistance.	*Good Progress*
Progress Evaluation	Evaluate progress based on data collected throughout the process.	**Problem Resolved**

can assist in developing observational codes and establishing a method for tracking the student's work production. These efforts will allow teachers to collect meaningful observation data, to examine the student's work accuracy and productivity relative to classmates, and to evaluate the quality of work relative to other students. School psychologists will likely need to assist with data analysis and progress monitoring.

Observational data should be collected using an Individualized Target Behavior Evaluation (Pelham et al., 2005). Therefore, teachers should establish a short list of prioritized problem behaviors (e.g., blurting out answers, running in the hall, off-task behavior during seatwork), and then tally the rates of occurrence of these problems on a daily basis. These data also help facilitate collaboration with parents, as they can serve as a parent daily report sent home at the end of each day or week. Collecting data throughout the intervention allows school personnel to graph data and track changes over time. Thus, improvement of a student with ADHD could be empirically evaluated. If the child's behavior does not improve in response to these interventions, teachers may also seek consultation with other teachers to develop a revised intervention plan. Again, the school psychologist can help the teacher in analyzing the data to determine whether the intervention is leading to improved functioning over time for the child with ADHD.

If the intervention is not leading to the desired effects, teachers may also consult with support service personnel, including the school social worker, the school counselor, the special educator, and the school psychologist. At this point, the school psychologist should conduct interviews with teachers and parents and complete a functional behavioral assessment. Collecting these data will allow the school psychologist to identify controlling variables that inform intervention planning. These data should be used to inform improvements in the intervention plan. Teacher tracking of Individualized Target Behavior Evaluation categories and work production should continue throughout the intervention. At this stage, the school psychologist may continue to facilitate data collection, update the intervention plan, and evaluate the student's progress based on data collected throughout the process.

Tier 3: Intensive, Individual Interventions

If escalating the intervention plan to this level, it is assumed that the child with ADHD was not responsive to the interventions initiated by the general education teacher in consultation with other teachers and support personnel, including the school psychologist. Thus, there is a need for more intensive interventions to address impairments presented by the student with ADHD. At this point in the process, the child may be referred for a full multidisciplinary evaluation to determine eligibility for special education services. The person coordinating this evaluation, often the school psychologist, must assess the three major areas of potential impairment common among children with ADHD (i.e., academic functioning, peer relations, and family relations), collect observational data, and compare results with previously collected data. For example, the BASC-2 rating scales

include a scale assessing relations with parents. Thus, the multidisciplinary team would have access to baseline data from initial screening, as well as data collected at each of the previous steps in the process.

Based on data collected throughout the process, the school psychologist is positioned to provide the team with results from earlier intervention plans and to serve a primary role in the development of an intensive Individualized Education Program if deemed necessary. Regardless of the eligibility decision, the school psychologist should continue to provide consultation to the child's general education teacher in implementing intervention plans, collecting data, and evaluating progress in response to treatment. In cases where the child with ADHD is prescribed medication for symptoms related to ADHD, the school psychologist may also serve as a consultant to the prescribing physician by providing data from a school-based drug evaluation (Volpe, Heick, & Guerasko-Moore, 2005).

Guidelines for Implementation

The following guidelines are suggested for implementing a multitiered services approach to the assessment of children with ADHD. These guidelines should not be considered a rigid chronology for the assessment process, but instead be a flexible, iterative model for decision making to be linked directly to the planning and evaluation of interventions. These guidelines are also presented as a flowchart in Figure 25.1.

- The school psychologist organizes a school- or class-wide screening for academic, social, emotional, and behavioral concerns using parent and teacher screening instruments.
- The school psychologist analyzes the screening data, identifies children at risk for problems associated with ADHD, and notifies teachers of the students' status.
- The school psychologist should also administer a more thorough baseline assessment using rating scales for children who screen positive for ADHD problems or related deficits. This includes assessment of the core diagnostic criteria of inattention, impulsivity, and hyperactivity and related impairments in school, peer, and family functioning. These rating scales should include both narrowband measures to assess ADHD symptoms (e.g., Conners–Third Edition and ADHD Rating Scale-IV) and broadband measures to assess comorbid impairments and adaptive functioning (e.g., rating scales from the ASEBA and the BASC).

- Once a child is identified as at risk for ADHD-related problems, the school psychologist may serve as a consultant to the teacher in several ways. First, the school psychologist may suggest that the teacher of an at-risk child consult with other teachers who have experience instructing children with ADHD-related problems. Next, the school psychologist may help the teacher define specific target behaviors to be tracked over time in the Individualized Target Behavior Evaluation categories, and establish a coding system for these observations. The school psychologist may also assist the teacher in establishing a time-efficient method of tracking the child's academic work production relative to the child's classmates. Finally, the school psychologist may help the teacher analyze the data and evaluate progress.

- If problems continue, the school psychologist may increase the level of assistance provided to the teacher. To inform changes in the intervention plan, the school psychologist is likely to conduct interviews with teachers and/or parents of the child to examine more closely the child's functioning in school, peer relations, and family.

- Regarding problem behaviors, the school psychologist should also conduct a functional behavioral assessment to identify antecedents, settings, and consequences of the target behaviors. These methods allow the school psychologist to identify controlling variables that inform the design of interventions.

- Based on data collected throughout the process, the school psychologist assists in revising the intervention plan and the means to monitor progress. Typically, the evaluation plan will specify the behavioral and work production data to be collected by the teacher over time (e.g., Individualized Target Behavior Evaluation category tallies).

- The school psychologist then assists in evaluating the intervention's effectiveness based on ongoing data collection (e.g., Individualized Target Behavior Evaluation category tallies, work production, readministration of rating scales, follow-up interviews) relative to data collected earlier in the process. School psychologists can also encourage additional home–school collaboration through the use of daily report cards.

- The school psychologist also assesses treatment integrity of interventions using direct observations or collaboratively developing a treatment integrity checklist with the classroom teacher and other support personnel. If problems persist, the child with ADHD may be referred for a full multidisciplinary evaluation to establish eligibility for special education services. The school psychologist may coordinate, conduct, or assist with this evaluation as needed. At this stage, the assessment should again focus on eligibility criteria as they pertain to special education law. An important part of this process is comparing data collected during this evaluation with data that were collected throughout the process.

- The multidisciplinary team, including the school psychologist, then determines whether the student with ADHD is eligible for special education services.

- Regardless of the decision, the school psychologist then updates the intervention plan to address the child's problems and continues to evaluate its effectiveness.

SUMMARY

The purpose of this chapter is to guide school psychologists in implementing assessment of ADHD within a multitiered services framework. This chapter covers basic considerations, including potential developmental, gender, and cultural issues with a focus on assessing three main areas of impairment and their influence on the child's functioning. Even though the response-to-intervention literature was not written with children's behavior disorders in mind, its application to the assessment of ADHD is a natural extension of the current best practices approach developed for children with learning disabilities. Traditional assessment methods can be used as before, but the methods should be applied within a fluid problem-solving approach designed to answer different questions, assess areas of impairment, and evaluate the child's response to intervention.

REFERENCES

Achenbach, T. M. (2009). *The Achenbach System of Empirically Based Assessment (ASEBA): Development, findings, theory, and applications.* Burlington, VT: University of Vermont Research Center for Children, Youth, and Families.

Achenbach, T. M., McConaughy, S. H., Ivanova, M. Y., & Rescorla, L. A. (2011). *Brief Problem Monitor manual.* Burlington, VT: University of Vermont Research Center for Children, Youth, and Families.

American Psychiatric Association. (2013). *Diagnostic and statistical manual of mental disorders* (5th ed.). Arlington, VA: Author.

Barkley, R. A. (2006). *Attention deficit hyperactivity disorder: A handbook for diagnosis and treatment* (3rd ed.). New York, NY: Guilford Press.

Bauermeister, J. J., Canino, G., Polanczyk, G., & Rohde, L. A. (2010). ADHD across cultures: Is there evidence for a bidimensional organization of symptoms? *Journal of Clinical Child and Adolescent Psychology, 39*, 362–372.

Conners, C. K. (2008). *Conners Comprehensive Behavior Rating Scale manual*. Toronto, ON, Canada: Multi-Health Systems.

DuPaul, G. J., Power, T. J., Anastopoulos, A. D., & Reid, R. (1998). *ADHD Rating Scale–IV: Checklists, norms, and clinical interpretation*. New York, NY: Guilford Press.

Frances, A. (2010). Increasing the age at onset for ADHD? *American Journal of Psychiatry, 167*, 718.

Frazier, T. W., Demaree, H. A., & Youngstrom, E. (2004). Meta-analysis of intellectual and neuropsychological test performance in attention deficit hyperactivity disorder. *Neuropsychology, 18*, 543–555.

Gresham, F. M., Watson, T. S., & Skinner, C. H. (2001). Functional behavioral assessment: Principles, procedures, and future directions. *School Psychology Review, 30*, 156–172.

Haraway, D. L. (2012). Monitoring students with ADHD within the RTI framework. *The Behavior Analyst Today, 13*, 17–21.

Hawes, D. J., Dadds, M. R., Frost, A. D. J., & Hasking, P. A. (2011). Do childhood callous-unemotional traits drive change in parenting practices? *Journal of Clinical Child and Adolescent Psychology, 40*, 507–518.

Kamphaus, R. W., & Reynolds, C. R. (2007). *BASC-2 Behavioral and Emotional Screening System*. Minneapolis, MN: Pearson.

Kamphaus, R. W., & Reynolds, C. R. (2009). *Behavior Assessment System for Children–Second edition (BASC-2): Progress Monitor (PM)*. Bloomington, MN: Pearson.

King, S., Waschbusch, D. A., Pelham, W. E., Jr, Frankland, B. W., Andrade, B. F., Jacques, S., & Corkum, P. V. (2009). Social information processing in elementary-school aged children with ADHD: Mediator effects and comparisons with typical children. *Journal of Abnormal Child Psychology, 37*, 579–589.

McConaughy, S. H. (2005). Direct observational assessment during test sessions and child clinical interviews. *School Psychology Review, 34*, 490–506.

McConaughy, S. H., & Achenbach, T. M. (2004). *Manual for the Test Observation Form for ages 2–18*. Burlington, VT: University of Vermont Research Center for Children, Youth, and Families.

McConaughy, S. H., Ivanova, M. Y., Antshel, K., & Eiraldi, R. B. (2009). Standardized observational assessment of attention deficit hyperactivity combined and predominantly intattentive subtypes. 1. Test session observations. *School Psychology Review, 38*, 45–66.

Miller, M., Nevado-Montenegro, A. J., & Hinshaw, S. P. (2011). Childhood executive function continues to predict outcomes in young adult females with and without childhood-diagnosed ADHD. *Journal of Abnormal Child Psychology, 40*, 657–668.

Murray, C., & Johnston, C. (2006). Parenting in mothers with and without attention deficit hyperactivity disorder. *Journal of Abnormal Psychology, 115*, 52–61.

National Association of School Psychologists. (2010). *Model for comprehensive and integrated school psychological services*. Bethesda, MD: Author. Retrieved from http://www.nasponline.org/standards/2010standards/2_PracticeModel.pdf

Pelham, W. E., Jr., Fabiano, G. A., & Massetti, G. M. (2005). Evidence-based assessment of attention deficit hyperactivity disorder in children and adolescents. *Journal of Clinical Child and Adolescent Psychology, 34*, 449–476.

Psychogiou, L., Daley, D. M., Thompson, M. J., & Sonuga-Barke, E. J. S. (2008). Do maternal attention-deficit/hyperactivity disorder symptoms exacerbate or ameliorate the negative effect of child attention-deficit/hyperactivity disorder symptoms on parenting? *Development and Psychopathology, 20*, 121–137.

Reynolds, C. R., & Kamphaus, R. W. (2004). *Manual of the Behavior Assessment System for Children–Second edition*. Circle Pines, MN: American Guidance Service.

Ronk, M. J., Hund, A. M., & Landau, S. (2011). Assessment of social competence of boys with attention-deficit/hyperactivity disorder. *Journal of Abnormal Child Psychology, 39*, 829–840.

Schwean, V. L., & Saklofske, D. H. (2005). Assessment of attention deficit hyperactivity disorder with the WISC-IV. In A. Prifitera, D. H. Saklofske, & L. G. Weiss (Eds.), *WISC-IV clinical use and interpretation: Scientist-practitioner perspectives* (pp. 235–280). San Diego, CA: Elsevier.

Skirbekk, B., Hansen, B. H., Oerbeck, B., & Kristensen, H. (2011). The relationship between sluggish cognitive tempo, subtypes of attention-deficit/hyperactivity disorder, and anxiety disorders. *Journal of Abnormal Child Psychology, 39*, 513–525.

Tseng, W., Kawabata, Y., Gau, S. S., Banny, A. M., Lingras, K. A., & Crick, N. R. (2012). Relations of inattention and hyperactivity/impulsivity to preadolescent peer functioning: The mediating roles of aggressive and prosocial behaviors. *Journal of Clinical Child and Adolescent Psychology, 41*, 275–287.

Volpe, R. J., Heick, P. F., & Guerasko-Moore, D. (2005). An agile behavioral model for monitoring the effects of stimulant medication in school settings. *Psychology in the Schools, 42*, 509–523.

Waschbusch, D. A., King, S., & Northern Partners in Action for Children and Youth. (2006). Should sex-specific norms be used to assess attention deficit hyperactivity disorder or oppositional defiant disorder? *Journal of Consulting and Clinical Psychology, 74*, 179–185.

Wodrich, D. L., Pfeiffer, S. I., & Landau, S. (2008). Contemplating the new DSM-5: Considerations from psychologists who work with school children. *Professional Psychology: Research and Practice, 39*, 626–632.

26 | Best Practices in Early Identification and Services for Children With Autism Spectrum Disorders

Ilene S. Schwartz
Carol A. Davis
University of Washington

OVERVIEW

Since the 1980s autism spectrum disorder (ASD) has evolved from being a rare disorder that was thought to be difficult if not impossible to treat to a relatively common disorder that, in many cases, is very responsive to early intensive behavioral intervention and continued educational programming. With the current prevalence of ASD being in 1 in 88 (Centers for Disease Control and Prevention [CDC], 2012), almost every school will have some children with ASD in the student body, and every educator will encounter a student with ASD in his or her classroom. Given the diversity of the strengths and needs of students with ASD, one very clear statement to make about best practices for this population is that there is no one right way to educate a child with ASD. Stahmer, Schreibman, and Cunningham (2011) sum up current treatment for children with ASD by saying, "No treatment method completely ameliorates the symptoms of ASD and no specific treatment has emerged as the established standard of care for all children with ASD" (p. 230).

Although there are still many questions that need to be answered, the field of assessment and intervention for children with ASD has made tremendous advances. There may not be a list of instructional practices that are effective for all children, but what does exist is a burgeoning literature about a range of practices that are effective with children with ASD. This growing body of research allows school psychologists to use the general problem-solving skills that are foundational to their practice to develop individualized programs for children with ASD that are effective, sustainable, culturally responsive, and acceptable to their consumers. Implementing best practices for young children with ASD requires school psychologists to work with their school-based interdisciplinary teams and families to ensure that children have access to high-quality early-learning curricula and environments and the differential amounts and types of services and supports that they need to be successful.

This chapter reviews current research and proposes a framework that school psychologists can use to evaluate the adequacy of programs for children with ASD. It is the implementation of this framework, rather than any specific instructional practice, that represents best practices for young children with ASD. The chapter applies basic principles of the Data-Based Decision Making and Accountability domain of the National Association of School Psychologists (NASP) *Model for Comprehensive and Integrated School Psychological Services* (NASP, 2010) for children with ASD.

Evaluation of the extant research about ASD may be viewed through the lens of this statement: A child with ASD is a child first. This statement is important for a number of reasons. First, it helps the team recognize and respect that every child is an individual and that the diagnosis of ASD is not the child's most important defining characteristic. It helps the team remember to consider the cultural background and family history that every child brings with him or her to school. It also helps the team to remember to consider issues of typical child development when working with a child with ASD. Considering what type of behavior a typically developing child demonstrates and what types of activities he or she may be involved in helps the educational team develop and implement a better intervention program for a child with ASD.

BASIC CONSIDERATIONS

Given the increased prevalence of ASD, most school psychologists will have on their caseloads students whom parents and school teams suspect of having ASD or who are already diagnosed with ASD. The information provided in this section deals with some of the basic background that a school psychologist should have to be able to be a good advocate for students with ASD. Four main areas of information are essential: (a) basic information about symptoms, range of abilities with which students with ASD present, and how these areas of core deficit may interact with participation in early learning and school settings; (b) understanding of the difference between educational determination of autism and a medical diagnosis of ASD; (c) a working knowledge of applied behavior analysis and an understanding of how behavioral principles can be implemented in school settings; and (d) basic understanding of the efficacy studies on early intervention for children with ASD.

Basic Diagnostic Information

Autism was initially described by Kanner (1943) as a rare disorder in which children were drawn into themselves and relatively uninterested in social interaction. Kanner described the children in his study with the three primary behavioral characteristics still used to describe this disorder: disturbances of social relationships, limited use of language to communicate, and fixed repetitive interests and routines (Kanner, 1943).

The *Diagnostic and Statistical Manual of Mental Disorders*, Fifth Edition (*DSM-5*; American Psychiatric Association, 2013) presents a major change in how ASD will be described and diagnosed. First, the primary diagnoses of ASD, autism disorder and Asperger's syndrome, are being combined into one diagnostic category of autism spectrum disorder. The other significant change is that the three areas of deficit long associated with ASD have been collapsed into two areas: social communication impairment and repetitive/restricted behaviors. It is important to note that the goal behind the changes in diagnostic criteria is not to limit service, but rather to ensure that

students with neurodevelopmental disabilities are diagnosed accurately and receive appropriate services (e.g., Huerta, Bishop, Duncan, Hus, & Lord, 2012). It was the intent of the committee revising the DSM that no one lose their current diagnosis due to a change in the diagnostic criteria. Any person currently diagnosed with ASD will retain that diagnosis after the new criteria go into effect.

Educational Determination Versus Medical Diagnosis

Most children with ASD will receive both an educational determination of autism and a medical diagnosis of ASD, and both are important, but they help children and their families access different types of services. A medical diagnosis of ASD is made by a licensed physician or psychologist and is based on the criteria listed in the DSM. An educational determination of a disability is made by a multidisciplinary team and is required to access early intervention and special education or Individuals with Disabilities Education Act (IDEA)–funded programs. It is based on the regulations governing IDEA and in most cases does not make students eligible for any services other than special education.

To qualify for special education services, a student must have an assessment conducted by a multidisciplinary school team that determines the presence of a disability and documents that the disability interferes with the student's ability to access and succeed in the general education curriculum. Once a child qualifies for special education, an Individualized Education Program (IEP; or an Individualized Family Service Plan [IFSP] if the child is under age 3) is developed based on the child's current educational needs, not the diagnostic category. School psychologists do and should play an active role in making educational determinations.

While a medical diagnosis is not necessary for a student to receive special education services, a medical diagnosis is necessary for a child to benefit from state programs (e.g., respite care) or health insurance benefits for autism-related behavioral intervention.

Basics of Applied Behavior Analysis

Applied behavior analysis is an academic discipline that studies the principles of behavior (e.g., reinforcement; Baer, Wolf, & Risley, 1968). Behaviorally based intervention strategies have long been recognized as the most effective strategies for teaching students with

ASD. It should be noted that applied behavior analysis is not one strategy or intervention but represents a group of interventions that uses the principles of behavior to effect change. In the *Journal of Applied Behavior Analysis* alone, there are well over 1,000 data-based articles in which the intervention of study was with a participant with ASD, and most autism advocacy groups and reports describing effective practices for ASD list behaviorally based interventions as the cornerstone of effective intervention for students with ASD. School psychologists must have a basic understanding of behavioral principles and strategies to help a school team design, implement, and evaluate effective services for a child with ASD.

It is clearly beyond the scope of this chapter to provide even a primer on applied behavior analysis, but three key components will be highlighted. The first is that positive reinforcement may be one of the most effective tools that a school team has available to it in working with children with ASD. Reinforcement is the process through which a behavior is strengthened by the immediate presentation of a consequence. Therefore, positive reinforcement is the application of a consequence contingent on a desired behavior that results in the increased probability of the behavior happening again in the future.

The second key component is that behavior serves a function. The function of a behavior is addressed most often when considering challenging behavior, but it is important to remember that all behavior serves a function. A child engages in a behavior because it enables the child to access a reinforcer or perhaps to avoid a less preferred consequence. Understanding the functional relationship between behavior and its consequences is essential when planning effective school programs for children with ASD. For example, when presented with a group project where four children must work collaboratively with one set of materials, a child with ASD may engage in mildly disruptive behaviors. The teacher removes the child from the group and lets the child work independently with his or her own set of materials. If the function of the behavior was to avoid social interactions with peers, then the teacher may be reinforcing the challenging behavior. Understanding the function of behavior is a necessary first step in developing appropriate interventions.

The final key component is the importance of collecting data and using these data in the decision-making process. Data collection and analysis is a cornerstone of applied behavior analysis. Without careful definition of the target behaviors and ongoing observation to assess the frequency, rate, duration, or other appropriate dimension of the behavior, it is impossible to make instructional decisions for students with ASD.

Efficacy Studies of Autism Treatment

In the years since Kanner (1943) identified autism, the majority of intervention studies have been done by applied behavior analysts, primarily using single-case research design. This changed when Lovaas (1987) published his seminal paper describing the effects of the Young Autism Program at UCLA. In this paper he described the results of a home-based intervention program for very young children with ASD in which children received at least 40 hours a week of behavioral therapy in their homes for a minimum of 2 years. Lovaas found that 9 of the 19 children (47%) in his experimental group entered first grade and were "indistinguishable" from their typically developing peers. Lovaas referred to these participants who achieved the best outcomes as being "recovered." Only 1 of the 39 children in the two control groups achieved this best outcome. The results of this study changed the way that researchers, educators, policy makers, parents, and advocates viewed autism treatment.

In the years following Lovaas's (1987) paper, the field of early intervention for children with ASD has been reinvented. Rather than assuming that ASD was a disability that was impervious to intervention, approximately 50% of the children make significant gains and some children make truly remarkable gains when provided with high-quality early intensive behavioral intervention. The effects of early intensive behavioral intervention have been replicated and the results of these studies have been reviewed by a number of meta-analyses (e.g., Reichow & Wolery, 2009). In addition, the number of programs that can be used to provide comprehensive treatment to children with ASD has increased. Odom, Boyd, Hall, and Hume (2010) identified 30 comprehensive treatment models. For a school psychologist working with young children with ASD, it is essential to know that there is no one best way to educate children with ASD. Impressive research on intervention in recent years shows that, with a well-designed early intensive behavioral intervention program, many children with ASD will make impressive gains across developmental domains, and some may even lose their diagnosis of ASD (Fein et al., 2013).

Thus, the educational team needs to look beyond name brand and prepackaged programs for children with ASD and figure out how to match specific evidence-based interventions to the unique needs presented by individual children. This requires that educational teams have a knowledge of evidence-based practices and, more importantly, data-based decision making. Strategies for how school psychologists can work with their team members to create truly individualized and effective interventions for young children with ASD are presented in the next section.

BEST PRACTICES IN EARLY IDENTIFICATION AND SERVICES FOR CHILDREN WITH AUTISM SPECTRUM DISORDERS

Although the formal diagnostic criteria for ASD are changing with the *DSM-5*, the heterogeneity of children diagnosed with this disorder and the specific challenges that these children present for educational programs will not change. Children with ASD range in abilities from those who are academically gifted to those with severe intellectual impairments. Children with ASD may be quite verbal, especially about a topic of special interest, or be nonverbal and need an augmentative device to help them acquire a functional communication system. They may require intensive support in a classroom or be able to be very successful in a general education classroom with limited, but individualized, supports and modifications.

The defining characteristics of ASD are especially challenging in school settings. Classroom settings, especially those for young children, are inherently busy and often unpredictable environments requiring a great deal of sophisticated social and communicative behavior to succeed. Despite these challenges, many children with ASD succeed and thrive at school when their educational teams identify and provide the range of supports and specially designed instruction that they need.

Best practices for school psychologists who work with young children with ASD include early identification, early referral to high-quality services, and continued monitoring to ensure that the services being provided are meeting the needs of the individual child and family. In the section below, best practices in early identification and interventions for children with ASD are reviewed. Components of a high-quality intervention program for young children with ASD are outlined, including a detailed discussion of each element and some guiding questions that school psychologists can use to ensure that these components are being implemented.

Early Identification

The ability to accurately identify young children with ASD has improved dramatically since 2000. Assessment practices now exist that can reliably make accurate assessments of children with ASD during their second year of life (Steiner, Goldsmith, Snow, & Chawarska, 2012). Although early diagnosis is possible, most children with ASD are not diagnosed until preschool and identification is often even more delayed for ethnic-minority children (Mandell, Listerud, Levy, & Pinto-Martin, 2002).

Early and accurate identification is the first step toward achieving optimal outcomes for children with ASD. There are four components to implementing effective early identification for children with ASD, and school psychologists should take an active role in each step: (a) awareness, (b) screening, (c) timely access to a high-quality assessment, and (d) beginning of appropriate intervention as soon as possible.

Awareness

An important first step in early identification of children with ASD is community awareness. A school psychologist can play an important role in making sure that members of the school community have materials explaining ASD and identifying the red flags associated with this disorder. The medical and public health community has been extremely active in working on the issues of awareness and early identification, and as a result there are excellent materials that are available free of charge to help with this awareness effort.

The important message from these awareness campaigns is that "let's wait and see" is not an appropriate approach to take about developmental concerns. These campaigns ask parents and providers to be aware of their children's communicative, social, and behavioral development in the same way they are about their child's physical development. The following behaviors have been suggested by the American Academy of Pediatrics (2012) and others as red flags for ASD in the first two years of life: (a) lack of appropriate gaze; (b) lack of warm, joyful expressions with the gaze; (c) lack of sharing enjoyment or interests; (d) lack of alternating to-and-fro vocalizations with parents; (e) lack of response to his or her name; (f) delayed onset of babbling past 9 months of age; (g) decreased or absent use of prespeech gestures (waving, pointing, showing); (h) no single words by 16 months; (i) no two-word utterances by 24 months; (j) repetitive movements or posturing of body, arms, hands, or fingers; and (k) loss of language or social skills at any age.

Two websites provide materials that can guide efforts to increase public awareness of the school community, including families and early care and learning programs that feed into the school: CDC, http://www.cdc.gov/ncbddd/actearly/index.html, and First Signs, http://www.firstsigns.org. Both of these websites provide excellent information for school psychologists to share with parents and community partners about the importance of early developmental screening, tips for parents about how to talk to a pediatrician about concerns they may have about their child's development, and screening tools that they can use. The CDC website also includes important information for parents about overall child development and strategies that they can use to promote healthy child development.

Screening

An important message to share with families about developmental screening is that it is an essential component of healthcare for all children. The American Academy of Pediatrics (2012) recommends that all children be screened for ASD at 18 and 24 months during their well-child visit. It is helpful to view developmental screenings as services that produce positive and helpful outcomes. If the result is that the child is on track developmentally, then that is good news. If the result is that the child demonstrates behaviors of concern, then the family can seek early intervention services, which are important for improved outcomes. If families have concerns about their child's development or concerns that developmental screenings are not being conducted, then they should share those concerns with their physicians. School psychologists can work with families to help them share these concerns in an effective manner. First Signs (http://www.firstsigns.org/concerns/parent_doc.htm) provides information for parents to use when talking to their healthcare professional about their concerns about their child's development. They recommend that parents:

- Be prepared with concrete examples of the behaviors that are of concern.
- Express concerns clearly and ask for a developmental screening.
- Ask questions if there are terms that are not understood and ask what the next steps will be.
- Follow up either with the next scheduled visit if development is on track or with appropriate referrals for more detailed assessment and early intervention services if there are developmental concerns.

Developmental screening should be a two-level process. First, all children should be screened using a measure of general developmental progress, such as the Ages and Stages Questionnaire (Squires, Bricker, & Mounts, 2009). If indicators of ASD are found on the general screen, or if parents express concern about ASD, then an autism-specific screening tool should be used. Although there are a number of ASD screening tools available that are demonstrated to be effective with young children, the American Academy of Pediatrics (2012) recommends the Modified Checklist for Autism in Toddlers (Robins, Fein, Barton, & Green, 2001). It is designed to be used with children from 16 to 48 months of age. The checklist consists of 23 *yes/no* items that are completed by the parents and includes a follow-up interview that providers can use to get more in-depth answers on the questions for which parents have concerns. There are six critical items. Children who "fail" two critical items or any three items total should be referred for further evaluation. The Modified Checklist for Autism in Toddlers is available at http://www.m-chat.org.

Timely Access to a High-Quality Assessment

When children are identified as at risk with an autism screening tool, they should be referred to an assessment team that includes professionals who have specialized training in diagnosing ASD in young children. These teams may include school psychologists, clinical psychologists, and physicians. Long wait times exist in many locations for this type of specialized diagnostic evaluation. Therefore, as soon as children are identified with a developmental or autism screen or the parents or providers have a serious concern that the child may have ASD, the child should also be referred to his or her local early intervention provider (if under age 3) or his or her local school district (if age 3 and above) to receive an educational determination and begin to receive special education services. In most communities, children can qualify for and begin to receive special education services (including speech therapy, occupational therapy, and physical therapy as needed) before they can receive a full diagnostic assessment. The school psychologist plays an essential role in guiding parents through this confusing maze of conducting assessments, receiving diagnoses/determinations, and getting qualified for services. Helping parents understand that there may be parallel processes at school and in the community because different service systems require different types of assessments is an important job for the school psychologist.

One of the pressing questions about best practices in diagnostic assessments for children who are suspected to have ASD is who should conduct these assessments. The distinction between a medical diagnosis of ASD and an educational determination of autism becomes very important at this point. Best practice suggests that assessments for both a medical diagnosis and educational determination should be conducted by a multidisciplinary team. For a medical diagnosis the team should include parents, pediatrician, psychologist, speech and language pathologist, and occupational therapist. For an educational determination the team should include parents, school psychologist, speech and language pathologist, occupational therapist, and other relevant educational professionals (e.g., teachers). It is also important that the members of the assessment team have specialized training and experience working with children with ASD. This is especially important when diagnosing toddlers with ASD, since this is a relatively new practice and requires specialized training and experiences.

There is no medical test for ASD. Identification of ASD is based on information gathered from a careful history collected from family members, other caregivers (e.g., child-care providers or teachers), behavioral observations across environments, and systematic testing. Systematic testing should include information from all domains, including overall development, adaptive behavior, motor, communication, social interaction, and the presence of autism-related symptoms (see Steiner et al., 2012, for a thorough description of assessment tools that can be used in this process). One important purpose of this assessment is to help identify goals and objectives for intervention. It is imperative to link the assessment and intervention processes. This means that when a school psychologist or other practitioner identifies an area of deficit during an assessment, he or she should work with the interdisciplinary team to ensure that the child's IFSP or IEP has a corresponding learning goal.

Although there is no definitive behavioral assessment for ASD, the most widely used assessments for autism-related symptoms are the Autism Diagnosis Observation Schedule (Lord et al., 2000) and the Autism Diagnostic Interview–Revised (Rutter, Le Couteur, & Lord, 2003).

Beginning of Appropriate Interventions as Soon as Possible

If a child is identified to have a medical diagnosis of ASD, an educational determination of autism, or any other type of developmental delay, then it is essential to refer the child to the appropriate agency and help the family get the child enrolled in services as soon as possible. Parents often report that assessment teams tell parents the results of the assessment, but they do not provide them with adequate information about how to get their child enrolled in services (Braiden, Bothwell, & Duffy, 2010). It is extremely important to provide parents with written information about how to access services, including the necessary phone numbers and websites parents will need. It is also recommended to follow up with parents soon after they have been told about the diagnosis to answer any questions, provide more information about service options, and provide support to the family. School psychologists need to be informed about what services are available for the child and family through the school district, but also what services the family may be eligible for in the community.

If the child receives an educational determination of autism, or any other disability category for which he or she qualifies for special education services, and has not yet received a medical diagnosis of ASD, then the school psychologist should follow up with the family in two ways. First the school psychologist should work with the IFSP or IEP team to ensure that appropriate school-based services, including appropriate related services, are being provided. The National Research Council (NRC; 2001) suggests that young children with ASD should be placed in autism-related services as soon as the team has a credible suspicion that the child has ASD. The NRC does not recommend waiting for a formal diagnosis to begin specialized services. In addition, the school psychologist should refer the family to a clinic, hospital, or practice where the child can be evaluated by a team that can provide the medical diagnosis. This medical diagnosis is necessary for the child and family to receive noneducational services (e.g., respite care, in-home behavioral support) and be eligible for medical insurance benefits for autism-related behavioral services.

Early Services for Young Children With ASD

The outlook for a young child with ASD who is beginning early intervention services has never been brighter. The number of different treatment options continues to increase, and the data from research on early intervention continue to show that most children who participate in high-quality intervention make progress and approximately 50% of the children achieve very good outcomes across a number of different intervention models. Research on autism intervention over recent years identifies core components shared by the most effective intervention programs. These components provide an overarching view of best practices for intervention for young children with ASD.

As school psychologists work to develop interventions for individual children with ASD it is important to remember that ASD is a lifelong neurodevelopmental disorder that has an impact on children's social–communication skills and results in restricted, repetitive, and stereotyped patterns of behavior, interests, and activities. This disorder can have a significant impact on children's abilities across developmental domains and affect how children interact in the numerous contexts (e.g., school, home, community) in which they spend time. Recognizing that ASD is a spectrum disorder is also essential when planning interventions. Acknowledging that the symptoms of this disorder will affect different children in different ways requires that interventionists work to match the strengths and needs of every child with the supportive components of comprehensive intervention (Delmolino & Harris, 2012;

Odom, Hume, Boyd, & Stabel, 2012). This means that there is no one program or collection of services that will meet the needs of every child with ASD. Rather, it is the responsibility of school psychologists to lead intervention teams through the problem-solving process to individualize services for children with ASD based on the research, child characteristics (including developmental differences), and family characteristics and preferences. The first step in this process of individualization, however, is to identify program components that are common among the most effective approaches to intervention, and these program components can then guide planning for children and their families. Based on research literature, it is best practice for programs for young children with ASD to consider and address the following components (see Table 26.1 for the list of components accompanied by guiding questions for implementation): (a) comprehensive intervention planning across contexts and domains, (b) use of evidence-based instructional practices, (c) data-based decision making to ensure progress, (d) technical and social

Table 26.1. Guiding Questions to Implement Best Practices for Young Children With ASD

Comprehensive intervention planning across domains:
- Does the program address all identified needs from the assessment in areas of social, play/leisure, adaptive skills, cognitive, communication?
- Is the planned intervention or specially designed instruction across all levels of learning (e.g., acquisition, fluency, maintenance, generalization)?
- Is the planned intervention or specially designed instruction implemented at the level of intensity that progress can be determined?

Use of evidence-based instructional practices:
- Is the chosen intervention for a particular skill considered an evidence-based practice?
- Have the context, child characteristics, or family preferences been considered when choosing a particular practice/intervention?
- Does the team have appropriate training and adequate resources to implement the practice with fidelity?

Data-based decision making:
- Are data being collected on a frequent enough basis to determine progress on a particular skill?
- Is the data collection system likely to be implemented and does it provide a measure of progress for the particular skill?
- Are the data reviewed frequently (at least twice monthly) and are instructional decisions made, communicated to the team, and implemented as a result of the data reviews?

Technical and social support for family members:
- Has the family's input during the assessment process been solicited?
- Has the family's need for technical support (e.g., parenting classes) been assessed and have these services been provided?
- Have the family's needs regarding social support been assessed and suggestions provided?

Access to typically developing peers:
- Does the program provide the children with ASD opportunities to interact with typically developing peers at least 3 days a week?
- Does the program staff use appropriate classroom activities, room arrangement, and instructional strategies to promote positive social interactions between children with ASD and typically developing children?

Access to a quality of life influenced curriculum:
- Are family members involved in setting the goals for intervention?
- Do intervention goals align with parents' values, preferences, and identity?
- How will the targeted skills and behaviors increase the child's independence and increase his or her overall quality of life?

support for family members, (e) access to typically developing peers, and (f) access to a quality of life influenced curriculum.

Comprehensive Intervention Planning

Although the defining deficits in ASD are in the area of social communication and restricted, repetitive patterns of behavior, interests, or activities, these deficits often have an impact on children's abilities to acquire and demonstrate skills across all developmental domains. This means that in order to be effective, intervention for children with ASD needs to address the child's needs across developmental domains and ensure that the child learns how to use his or her skills in an appropriate manner across activities, settings, and people. These areas include communication and social, cognitive, play/leisure, and adaptive behavior. All areas should be assessed and considered for specialized, systematic instruction.

Children with ASD are also more likely than children with other developmental disabilities to demonstrate uneven profiles of behavior. In other words, children with ASD may demonstrate average or above average cognitive skills, but have significant delays in social behaviors. This uneven behavioral profile may have an impact on a child's ability to demonstrate the skills the child knows in the ways that typically developing children do and may require levels of instruction and support that do not fit into existing school programs. For example, a child with ASD may be placed in a gifted classroom based on an IQ test, but he or she still needs explicit instruction on social skills and a structured reinforcement program to maintain appropriate behavior in the classroom. Traditionally when thinking about teaching and learning, interventionists identify four phases of learning: acquisition, fluency, generalization, and maintenance. Comprehensive intervention planning for children with ASD requires that instruction occur across all four phases of learning, with a level of intensity that, when progress monitoring data are collected, ensure that children can demonstrate the skills targeted by the intervention in a generalized manner. That means intervention on a targeted skill continues until the child can apply the skill whenever and wherever it is needed.

The pervasiveness of the delays associated with ASD suggests that children need programs that start early, are comprehensive, and are of sufficient intensity to result in behavior change. Although there has been a great deal of discussion about defining the comprehensiveness or intensity of a program for children with ASD by the number of hours of services that a child receives every week (e.g., the NRC suggests that children with ASD from 3 to 8 years old should receive a minimum of 25 hours a week of therapeutic intervention), a more functional approach to defining these important concepts (Strain & Bovey, 2011; Strain, Schwartz, & Barton, 2011) may be used. Intensity is a multidimensional individually determined concept. To determine the intensity of a program, these must be examined: what is being taught, how it is being taught, the progress that the child is making in the program, and the fit of the program with the family priorities and values. To define the intensity and comprehensiveness of a program functionally, child outcome, rather than number of hours of instruction, is the key variable.

Use of Evidence-Based Instructional Practices

The need for evidence-based practices is axiomatic in special education and in the field of autism intervention (Odom, Collet-Klingenberg, Rogers, & Hatton, 2010). Although there is consensus about the need to use evidence-based practices, it is a much more complex discussion to determine how to identify evidence-based practices. In this discussion, distinction between a focused intervention (e.g., use of reinforcement) and a comprehensive treatment model (e.g., Project DATA; see Schwartz, Sandall, McBride, & Boulware, 2004) is important.

Many lists of evidence-based practices for children with ASD exist. The most authoritative list is the 24 evidence-based practices compiled by the National Professional Development Center on Autism Spectrum Disorders (see http://autismpdc.fpg.unc.edu). This list of practices was developed after a careful and comprehensive review of the literature. The literature review supporting this list includes both group design and single-subject design research. This inclusion is vital given the preponderance of research in the area of autism that has been conducted by applied behavior analysts using single-subject research.

This list of practices is a useful starting place for school psychologists developing intervention programs for children with ASD. It provides a list of instructional strategies that have been demonstrated to be effective for some people with ASD under some conditions. What it does not provide is information about whether or not the instructional strategy will be effective to teach the individual child, the specific skills being taught, in the specific settings in which they are taught. This list of interventions also does not provide any information on whether these interventions are a good match with children given family preferences, beliefs, and attitudes toward intervention. Finally, no evidence-based practice works if it is not implemented with high fidelity. This list of practices can be used by school psychologists as a starting point and a reference for the inclusion of particular practices or instructional strategies in an overall program for working with children with ASD. The role of a school psychologist and educational professional, however, is to use his or her professional expertise to know when and where to use an evidence-based practice (Cook, Tankersley, & Harjusola-Webb, 2008). To move beyond textbook use of these practices to strategic use, a school psychologist must work with a team to match a specific practice to a specific child, context, and learning objective. It is only when the data on that specific child's learning are evaluated will the team know if that instructional strategy is evidence based for a specific child, to teach a specific skill, in a specific context.

Data-Based Decision Making to Ensure Progress

The majority of the evidence-based practices that have been identified for children with ASD come from the field of applied behavior analysis. A guiding principle of applied behavior analysis is ongoing measurement (Cooper, Heron, & Heward, 2007). Data collection and evaluation to make changes in the instructional procedures is a critical and necessary component of any program for children with ASD. Without data collection, the team is unable to decide the appropriate strategy and conditions to provide instruction and whether or not those instructional procedures are effective.

Child data should be collected frequently and evaluated regularly to demonstrate that progress is being made. The frequency with which data are collected on an instructional objective should be determined by the skill to be taught or changed and the nature of the skill. School psychologists can play an important role in providing guidance to the educational team regarding the frequency of data collection and the analysis of the data. Data must be collected frequently enough so that child progress can be evaluated in a timely manner. If it is assumed that three data points are necessary to see a trend, then data collected weekly will take the minimum of 3 weeks to produce information that can be used to evaluate child learning. If this is too long, then data need to be collected more frequently. While success or effectiveness of any one intervention for any specific child cannot be guaranteed, it is incumbent on the educational team and school psychologist to collect data frequently enough to determine if progress is being made and, if not, then change the instructional strategy being implemented.

A school psychologist should also consider the type of data being collected. Teachers have the knowledge to collect data, but many data systems are cumbersome and difficult to implement in the classroom, thus decreasing the likelihood that data will be collected. Data systems must be easy to implement while managing the instructional demands of a classroom. Moreover, the data must be meaningful enough to ensure that what is intended to be measured is what is being measured. Sometimes it is helpful to reframe data collection from a compliance activity to an act of scientific inquiry. School psychologists need to help educational teams think of data as the answers to questions about child behavior that they want to know more about. The team needs to determine the child's active participation, rate of challenging behaviors, or amount of social interaction. It is not likely that a teacher can collect data on the length of every social interaction in which a child engages, but the teacher could place a check next to the names of the peers with whom the child interacted and rate the overall length of interactions during free choice. Instructional decisions about what strategies are being used to teach specific skills, how often instruction is occurring, and where instruction is occurring must be made using the data from instructional sessions.

Technical and Social Support for Family Members

Support for family members of children with ASD is an essential component of a high-quality program. The distinction between technical and social support is that family members need specific information and help with instructional and behavior management techniques that may best be provided by educational professionals (i.e., technical support), as well emotional and social support that may best be provided by other parents of children with disabilities. Technical support begins by obtaining the family's input during the assessment process and the determination of appropriate learning objectives for a child. School psychologists should continue to get this input when determining the evidence-based practice chosen for a particular skill. Buy-in from parents is important when wanting to increase the likelihood that parents will use a particular evidence-based practice in the home. For young children in particular, choosing a practice that is a good fit with the home, community, and family is important as young children spend the majority of their time in the home and community setting.

School psychologists should also support parents by identifying helpful resources providing social support. Parents of children with ASD report extreme levels of chronic stress (Smith, Greenberg, & Seltzer, 2012). Parents of children with ASD report spending up to 2 hours per day more than the parents of typically developing children on basic caregiving responsibilities and that the need for basic caregiving and supervision continue long beyond that required by typically developing children. The need for family support extends far beyond parents. Other family members, especially siblings, benefit from clear information (i.e., technical support) and the opportunity to share their experiences with others who are also living with a brother or sister with ASD or a related disability. One informal assessment practice for identifying the possible social supports for families is the use of person-centered plans or futures planning. This method is often also a part of the functional behavior assessment process. Person-centered plans can be used to determine what supports are necessary for the family to be able to provide the most nurturing environment for their child with ASD.

Access to Typically Developing Peers

Children with ASD make gains in language, social skills, cognition, engagement in routines, and reductions in ASD symptoms when they receive intervention in inclusive settings (Strain et al., 2011). The opportunity to interact successfully, not just be in the same room, with typically developing peers on a regular basis is a necessary component of effective intervention programs for all children with ASD, especially young children. This requirement for successful social interaction with typically developing children as an ongoing part of intervention is essential for children with ASD from the time of diagnosis, so even toddlers with ASD need opportunities to participate in inclusive programs. ASD is a primarily social–communicative disorder, so it makes sense that access to and opportunities to interact with peers who demonstrate typical social–communication skills is key to successful intervention. Access to peers should not be limited to social situations, but the educational team should ensure that young children also have the opportunity to engage in learning activities that include peers and provide the opportunity for joint attention and social referencing.

Access to a Quality of Life Influenced Curriculum

Evaluating outcomes for children with disabilities, especially children with ASD, is complex. The overarching question, of course, is what is a meaningful outcome for a young child with ASD. Is a meaningful outcome the ability to sit with his or her family during a family meal, or attend a religious service with the family, or enter first grade indistinguishable from his or her peers after increasing his or her IQ score by 20 points? There is clearly no right answer to this question. Carr (2007) suggested that the central dependent variable of positive behavioral support interventions should be quality of life, and perhaps should be adopted as the primary outcome for comprehensive interventions for children with ASD as well. Quality of life encompasses issues of happiness, accomplishment, social relationships, and family values. When quality of life influenced curriculum is considered, it is not to take away from the importance of the hundreds of discrete social, communicative, cognitive, play, and self-care skills that children with ASD need to learn. Rather, it is to embed these discrete skills in a context of meaning, family values, and community participation.

Using a quality of life influenced curriculum requires that school psychologists work closely with family members at the beginning of the intervention process to identify priorities and continue to work closely with them to ensure that priorities are being meet and new concerns are being woven into the intervention program. This requires school psychologists to integrate issues of family preference, belief, cultural and linguistic identities, and dreams and goals for this child into intervention planning and assessment. More importantly, it requires all members of the intervention team to repeatedly ask questions about goals and objectives such as: Why are we teaching this skill or behavior? In what context will the child be able to use this skill and behavior? How will this skill and behavior help the child be more independent? How will this skill and behavior improve the quality of the child's and family's life?

Implementing a high-quality, comprehensive program for young children with ASD requires school psychologists and the other members of the team to do more than check items off a list or pull recommended practices off a list. It requires team members, including the child's family, to work together to ensure that children have access to appropriate curricular content, that they are taught using evidence-based instructional strategies, and that the result of the teaching is evaluated using data-based decision making. Providing these services requires school psychologists to apply the problem-solving frameworks that are inherent throughout their practice to the specialized set of knowledge around autism intervention. It also requires that school psychologists and other members of the team know when they need to ask for consultation or technical assistance. Understanding, as a professional, when additional training or even just another set of eyes is needed for a challenging behavior or set of data is important when dealing with complex neuro-developmental disabilities like ASD.

SUMMARY

The landscape of best practice in assessment and intervention for young children with ASD has changed dramatically over recent years. ASD has gone from a relatively low incidence disability to a disability with a prevalence of 1 in 88. The postintervention outlook for children with ASD has also changed dramatically. As a result of early intensive behavior intervention, most children make meaningful progress toward important developmental outcomes, and some children make truly remarkable progress, to the point where the children who demonstrate best outcomes may no longer be identified as having ASD. Not all children demonstrate best outcomes, and even after many years of high-quality behavioral intervention and special education programming, some children leave secondary school still requiring a high level of support.

There is not a simple list of instructional practices that can be identified as the comprehensive set of best practices for young children with ASD. Implementing an intervention program that utilizes best practices requires school psychologists to use their problem-solving skills and professional judgment to match the needs of individual children and families to the practices that have been validated by the research. They need to ensure that they use guidelines provided by the research to create intervention programs that are reflective of the values and preferences of individual families, while meeting the needs of the children receiving the intervention.

Best practice for young children with ASD involves early and accurate diagnosis, timely referral to appropriate services, delivery of comprehensive early intervention services that address the core deficits of ASD as well as other important developmental outcomes, use of evidence-based instructional strategies as part of the comprehensive treatment program, and data-based decision making on the part of the intervention team.

REFERENCES

American Academy of Pediatrics. (2012). *Autism: Caring for children with autism spectrum disorders: A resource toolkit for clinicians.* Elk Grove Village, IL: Author.

American Psychiatric Association. (2013). *Diagnostic and statistical manual of mental disorders* (5th ed.). Washington DC: Author.

Baer, D. M., Wolf, M. M., & Risley, T. R. (1968). Some current dimensions of applied behavior analysis. *Journal of Applied Behavior Analysis, 1,* 91–97.

Braiden, H., Bothwell, J., & Duffy, J. (2010). Parents' experience of the diagnostic process for autistic spectrum disorders. *Child Care in Practice, 16,* 377–389.

Carr, E. G. (2007). The expanding vision of positive behavior support: Research perspectives on happiness, helpfulness, hopefulness. *Journal of Positive Behavioral Interventions, 9,* 3–14. doi:10.1177/10983007070090010201

Centers for Disease Control and Prevention. (2012). Prevalence of autism spectrum disorders—Autism and developmental disabilities monitoring network, 14 sites, United States, *MMWR Surveillence Summary, 61,* 1–19.

Cook, B., Tankersley, M., & Harjusola-Webb, S. (2008). Evidence-based special education and professional wisdom: Putting it all together. *Intervention in School and Clinic, 44,* 105–111.

Cooper, J. O., Heron, T. E., & Heward, W. L. (2007). *Applied behavior analysis* (2nd ed.). Columbus, OH: Pearson.

Delmolino, L., & Harris, S. L. (2012). Matching children on the autism spectrum for classrooms: A guide for parents and professionals. *Journal of Autism and Developmental Disorders, 42,* 1197–1204.

Fein, D., Barton, M., Eigsti, I. M., Kelley, E., Naigles, L., Schultz, R. T., ... Tyson, K. (2013). Optimal outcome in individuals with a history of autism. *Journal of Child Psychology and Psychiatry, 54,* 195–205.

Huerta, M., Bishop, S. L., Duncan, A., Hus, V., & Lord, C. (2012). Application of DSM-5 criteria for autism spectrum disorder to three samples of children with DSM-IV diagnoses of pervasive developmental disorders. *American Journal of Psychiatry, 169,* 1056–1064. doi:10.1176/appi.ajp.2012.12020276

Kanner, L. (1943). Autistic disturbances of affective contact. *Nervous Child, 2,* 217–250.

Lord, C., Risi, S., Lambrecht, L., Cook, E. H. Jr., Leventhal, B. L., DiLavore, P. C., ... Rutter, M. (2000). The Autism Diagnostic Observation Schedule–Generic: A standard measure of social and communication deficits associated with the spectrum of autism. *Journal of Autism and Developmental Disorders, 30,* 205–223.

Lovaas, O. I. (1987). Behavioral treatment and normal educational and intellectual functioning in young autistic children. *Journal of Consulting and Clinical Psychology, 55,* 3–9.

Mandell, D. S., Listerud, J., Levy, S. E., & Pinto-Martin, J. A. (2002). Race differences in the age at diagnosis among Medicaid-eligible children with autism. *Journal of the American Academy of Child and Adolescent Psychiatry, 41,* 1447–1453.

National Association of School Psychologists. (2010). *Model for comprehensive and integrated school psychological services.* Bethesda, MD: Author. Retrieved from http://www.nasponline.org/standards/2010standards/2_PracticeModel.pdf

National Research Council. (2001). *Educating children with autism.* Washington, DC: National Academies Press.

Odom, S. L., Boyd, B., Hall, L. J., & Hume, K. (2010). Evaluation of comprehensive treatment models for individuals with autism spectrum disorders. *Journal of Autism and Developmental Disorders, 40,* 425–436.

Odom, S. L., Collet-Klingenberg, L., Rogers, S., & Hatton, D. (2010). Evidence-based practices in interventions for children and youth with autism spectrum disorders. *Preventing School Failure, 54,* 275–282.

Odom, S. L., Hume, K., Boyd, B., & Stabel, A. (2012). Moving beyond the intensive behavior treatment versus eclectic dichotomy: Evidence-based and individualized programs for learners with ASD. *Behavior Modification, 36,* 270–297. doi:10.1177/0145445512444595

Reichow, B., & Wolery, M. (2009). Comprehensive synthesis of early intensive behavioral interventions for young children with autism based on the UCLA Young Autism Project model. *Journal of Autism and Developmental Disorders, 39,* 23–41.

Robins, D., Fein, D., Barton, M., & Green, J. (2001). The Modified-Checklist for Autism in Toddlers (M-CHAT): An initial investigation in the early detection of autism and pervasive developmental disorders. *Journal of Autism and Developmental Disorders, 31,* 131–144.

Rutter, M., Le Couteur, A., & Lord, C. (2003). *Autism Diagnostic Interview–Revised.* Los Angeles, CA: Western Psychological Services.

Schwartz, I. S., Sandall, S. R., McBride, B. J., & Boulware, G. L. (2004). Project DATA (Developmentally Appropriate Treatment for Autism): An inclusive, school-based approach to educating children with autism. *Topics in Early Childhood Special Education, 24,* 156–168.

Smith, L. E., Greenberg, J. S., & Seltzer, M. M. (2012). Social support and well-being at mid-life among mothers of adolescents and adults with autism spectrum disorders. *Journal of Autism and Developmental Disorders, 42,* 1818–1826.

Squires, J., Bricker, D., & Mounts, L. (2009). *Ages and Stages Questionnaire: A parent completed child monitoring system* (3rd ed.). Baltimore, MD: Brookes.

Stahmer, A. C., Schreibman, L., & Cunningham, A. B. (2011). Toward a technology of treatment individualization for young children with autism spectrum disorders. *Brain Research, 1380,* 229–239.

Steiner, A. M., Goldsmith, T. R., Snow, A. V., & Chawarska, K. (2012). Practitioner's guide to assessment of autism spectrum disorders in infants and toddlers. *Journal of Autism and Developmental Disorders, 42,* 1183–1196.

Strain, P. S., & Bovey, E. (2011). Randomized controlled trial of the LEAP model of early intervention for young children with autism spectrum disorders. *Topics in Early Childhood Special Education, 31,* 133–154.

Strain, P. S., Schwartz, I. S., & Barton, E. (2011). Providing interventions for young children with ASD: What we still need to accomplish. *Topics in Early Childhood Special Education, 33,* 321–332. doi:10.1177/1053815111429970

27

Best Practices in Assessment and Intervention of Children With High-Functioning Autism Spectrum Disorders

Elaine Clark
University of Utah
Keith C. Radley
University of Southern Mississippi
Linda Phosaly
University of Utah

OVERVIEW

Data from the Centers for Disease Control and Prevention (CDC; 2012) show that 1 in 88 eight-year-olds in the United States likely has an autism spectrum disorder (ASD). These data represent a 78% increase in the overall prevalence rate for ASD since the last CDC study published in 2002. Unlike prior surveillance studies showing a majority of cases with intellectual disability, 62% of the cases identified in this study were thought to have normal or near normal intelligence (otherwise referred to in this chapter as a high-functioning ASD [HFASD]). Most of the autism intervention research to date has been conducted with very young children and/or those with significant developmental disability such as intellectual disability. Although researchers have found early intensive behavioral interventions such as applied behavior analysis to be very effective with many young children who have ASD and other significant developmental disabilities such as intellectual disability, it is not clear how well the same methods will work with children who have HFASD, who often manifest autistic symptoms differently and a lot later than cases of ASD with comorbid intellectual disability. What is clear is that interventions are needed for these students, and school psychologists can play a critical role in early identification (even if

early means late elementary) and empirically based interventions.

There are only a few long-term outcome studies to date that have included individuals with HFASD. One by Farley et al. (2009), though, found that the majority of adults they studied were unemployed or underemployed and were living with family or in situations where they received support. Very few had close friends or relationships outside the family, and a surprising number had serious physical and mental health problems and histories of committing criminal offenses. Core symptoms associated with HFASD (i.e., impairment in social communication and social interaction as well as restricted interests and repetitive behaviors) often impair a person's ability to function in everyday life regardless of how well he or she performs on IQ tests or how talented he or she is in a particular area (e.g., science, technology, engineering, and mathematics). Other problems associated with HFASD that can impair a student's functioning in school include a lack of motivation and focus to sustain attention and complete tasks as well as anxiety and low mood.

Comorbid diagnoses of attention deficit hyperactivity disorder (ADHD), generalized anxiety disorder, and major depression are fairly common. Backner et al. (2013) found that nearly 50% of the adolescents in their study with HFASD who had received psychological or psychiatric treatment had ADHD, and more than half had internalizing disorders and externalizing disorders. A large number had histories of property destruction, physical assault (often toward a female teacher or parent), and threatened or attempted suicide. Although substance use was not found to be a factor in these behaviors, anger and impulsivity were. According to the adolescents' reports, they were extremely frustrated by the fact that they had been bullied for years and did not have social support from peers. These types of reports are not uncommon. The undergraduate math and science majors with HFASD at University of Cambridge in England who Baron-Cohen, Wheelwright, Skinner, Martin, and Chubley (2001) studied also reported being miserable in primary and secondary school because of peer bullying and rejection. It was only in college that these talented young men found a place where they felt accepted for their differences and respected for their interests and skills. None, though, had been identified with HFASD until college, unfortunately, not that uncommon a situation.

School psychologists with in-depth knowledge about HFASD and advanced assessment and intervention skills can play a critical role in helping to identify students with HFASD as early as possible so that interventions can be designed to better meet these students' needs and reduce the likelihood that these students will be mistreated (see Cappadocia, Weiss, & Pepler, 2012, for discussion of bullying) and increase the chances they will have positive peer interactions. School psychologists can also help ensure that all students with HFASD are better prepared for transition from high school to college or other types of education and work.

Although the Cambridge students may appear to be an anomaly given their success at getting into a top university, like others with HFASD they still face the challenge of getting a job and being independent. As Farley et al. (2009) showed, very few (19%) of the 68 adults with HFASD in their study were independent. According to Shattuck et al. (2012), core autistic traits likely play a role in the problems young adults have with employment (e.g., not understanding another person's thoughts or intentions and not responding in appropriate ways, being inflexible in terms of procedures, and focusing on irrelevant details). However, the researchers have also concluded, after studying the problems that vocational counselors have placing adults in job sites, that some of this is a function of the schools not adequately preparing students for the post-high school experiences (education and jobs).

Although offering a wider range of vocational classes and more supervised work experiences in the community may help, so might better assessments of students' aptitudes and vocational interests that will offer guidance. Although school psychologists are not necessarily the best persons in the schools to consult with students and parents about careers and college educations, school psychologists who are knowledgeable about HFASD can provide important information to school counselors and families about issues that have a potential impact on success in careers and college and the resources that are available that may help (e.g., legal and advocacy services, services for people with disabilities, and support groups).

In this chapter, information is provided to help prepare school psychologists to work with students who have HFASD, including their role as a consultant, assessor, and decision maker. To do this, this chapter applies the Data-Based Decision Making and Accountability domain of the National Association of School Psychologists (NASP) *Model for Comprehensive and Integrated School Psychological Services* (NASP, 2010) and starts this next section with basic information about HFASD.

BASIC CONSIDERATIONS

This section serves as a review of information that school psychologists may lack knowledge in: core ASD symptoms and the manifestations of HFASD, and current criteria for diagnosis of ASD using the fifth edition of the *Diagnostic and Statistical Manual of Mental Disorders* (DSM-5; American Psychiatric Association 2013) and the autism classification under the 2004 Individuals with Disabilities Education Act; challenges in identifying HFASD, including in females and ethnic minorities; complexity and outcomes of HFASD, including associated learning and psychiatric problems; and implementation of evidence-based practices and data-based decision-making methods.

HFASD Symptoms and Systems for Diagnosis and Classification

To best understand HFASD, it is helpful to understand current diagnostic criteria for ASD, since HFASD is not a diagnosis but rather a descriptor of individuals who have ASD but have normal or higher intellectual ability. In order to receive a diagnosis of ASD in the DSM-5, a person is required to display the following:

- Persistent deficits in social communication and social interaction across multiple contexts that cannot be accounted for by general developmental delays and are manifested by deficits in the following three areas: social–emotional reciprocity, nonverbal communication in social interaction, and development and maintenance of relationships appropriate to developmental age
- Restricted, repetitive patterns of behaviors, interests, or activities manifested currently or by history of two of the following: stereotyped or repetitive speech, motor movement, or use of objects; excessive adherence to routines or ritualized patterns of nonverbal or verbal behavior (e.g., resistance to or distress caused by change); highly restricted, fixated interests that are abnormal in focus or intensity; and unusual response to sensory stimuli (hyperreactivity or hyporeactivity) or unusual interest in sensory aspects of the environment
- Symptoms that are present since early childhood (recognizing, however, that the disorder may not be apparent until social demands exceed the child's capacity)
- Symptoms that limit and impair everyday functioning

In order to receive a diagnosis of ASD, the aforementioned disturbances cannot be better explained by an intellectual disability or other general delay in development. Further, the individual's social communication needs to be below the expected developmental level. To help distinguish individuals who have social problems because of early communication problems from those who have social problems because of ASD, a new category has been added to the DSM-5: Social (Pragmatic) Communication Disorder. In addition, a singular term, Autism Spectrum Disorder, is used in the DSM-5, with no separate diagnostic categories (i.e., autistic disorder, Asperger's, and pervasive developmental disorder not otherwise specified). The DSM-5 has also added severity specifiers that denote the level of support that is needed for a person with ASD across the two primary domains: social communication and restricted, repetitive behaviors. The range of support goes from Level 1 (requires support) to Level 3 (requires very substantial support). A student, for example, may need only Level 1 support to help with social initiation, but need more substantial Level 2 support to address verbal communication with peers and the highest Level 3 support for their resistance to change and insistence on doing things the same way. The DSM-5 also includes specifiers to

identify potential compounding problems, such as genetic disorders (e.g., Fragile X) and other neurodevelopmental problems (e.g., ADHD), medical conditions, and the like. Specifiers are intended to help identify interventions and set priorities, and are not to be used to determine eligibility for services.

As school psychologists know, a DSM diagnosis is not sufficient to ensure special education services under any classification, including Autism. According to IDEA, in order to receive services there must be evidence that a student's *educational performance* is being adversely affected, in the case of ASD by core autistic symptoms (i.e., verbal and nonverbal communication and social interaction). Core symptoms have to have been present since early childhood (i.e., 3 years of age; 34 CFR 300.8(c)(i) (ii)). IDEA does not require evidence of repetitive, restrictive behaviors or unusual sensory interests. However, these problems are described as common features of ASD. Given the differences in IDEA and DSM-5, school psychologists may find themselves in situations where they need to explain why a student may have been "diagnosed" with ASD by a psychiatrist or psychologist outside the schools but does not meet criteria for special education services under Autism due to a lack of evidence of poor educational performance. Similarly, school psychologists may be asked to explain the reverse; that is, a student who is determined to be eligible for special education services under Autism but who does not get a "diagnosis" of ASD because of a lack of evidence for restricted, repetitive behaviors. The DSM-5 places greater emphasis on restricted, repetitive behaviors, and it is thought that this emphasis, along with the system's dimensional structure (i.e., no separate categories), will result in improved diagnostic reliability and sensitivity across various populations, in particular, those who were often not identified using the old system (i.e., females and ethnic and racial minorities).

Challenges of Identifying HFASD

As previously mentioned, HFASD is often identified much later than cases of ASD and associated intellectual disability. Wanzek et al. (2013) found that the average age of diagnosis in their study of adolescents and adults with HFASD was 10 years, 8 months. One of the challenges that school psychologists will face in identifying HFASD is the lack of reliable reporting of early symptoms by parents, especially symptoms that occur during the first year of life (Ozonoff et al., 2010).

Reliance on Informant Reports

As Ozonoff et al. (2010) point out, parents are often poor observers of ASD symptoms, including symptoms that represent developmental regressions such as reduced eye contact, less frequent smiling, and diminished social responsiveness. Identification of HFASD in older children and adolescents, like in younger children, though, requires evidence that autistic symptoms were present in early childhood. This, and the fact some children with HFASD show improvement in core autistic symptoms with age, makes it difficult to make a firm diagnosis at times.

Although in 2010 the American Academy of Pediatrics developed guidelines for ASD screening during well-baby checkups at 18 and 24 months of age, researchers have found that the amount of time pediatricians and their staff spend with the child is too short to observe symptoms. According to Gabrielsen (2012), even trained observers cannot reliably identify young children with ASD within the typical time frame of a routine examination. The problem of early reliable identification of HFASD symptoms can be expected to be much worse in cases where social interactions are hampered by delayed language development or a social communication disorder (American Psychiatric Association, 2013). Other groups of children who are more difficult to identify, however, include females and children from diverse ethnic and linguistic backgrounds.

Females and Ethnic and Linguistic Minorities

Females with HFASD are at greater risk than males for being missed at young ages given their early language development and tendency to use social communication more for interaction with peers (males using objects more). Basically, using language more and having better language skills as very young children mean females with HFASD may mask their symptoms. Wanzek et al. (2013) found that parents of females with HFASD reported first noticing symptoms at an older age than parents of males; that is, parents of females first noticed symptoms around 30 months of age whereas parents of males noticed symptoms at 18 months. These researchers also found that parents of females did not report concerns to their pediatricians as soon as the parents of males. Since autism was first described by Kanner in 1943, a significantly greater number of females have been identified with ASD, and this includes findings from the last CDC (2012) study showing an overall prevalence of 18.4 in 1,000 males and 4 in 1,000 females.

Data from the CDC (2012) study further show that more Caucasian children than non-Caucasian children were identified with ASD. Whereas the prevalence was 12 in 1,000 Caucasian children, it was 7.9 in 1,000 Hispanic children. The difference between Caucasians and African American children was not as great; that is, for African Americans it was 10 in 1,000. Studies have consistently shown fewer Hispanic children with ASD being identified, and being identified at much older ages. This is thought to be due, in part, to linguistic and cultural differences. However, further research is needed to better understand the differences.

School psychologists with a well-trained eye play a critical role in the identification of HFASD, including among preschoolers. School psychologists have unique educational backgrounds in assessment and disabilities and have experience working with a wide range of children, including those with low-incidence disabilities that may present differently depending on age, gender, ethnicity, and context. The problem, though, is often a matter of time. School psychologists typically do not have assistants and are solely responsible for evaluations that include multiple measures. As a result, practices are often not as comprehensive as expected, and school psychologists end up relying on screening methods instead of more timely face-to-face meetings with parents and direct assessment of children using state-of-the-art direct observation diagnostic measures. It is, therefore, critical that school psychologists conduct thorough evaluations of students suspected of having HFASD, or other disorders that might be similar, to ameliorate problems that are likely to have a negative impact on learning and social–emotional development of the child or adolescent.

BEST PRACTICES IN ASSESSMENT AND INTERVENTION IN HFASD

Schools psychologists can help teachers and other school personnel to identify students with HFASD who are struggling and may need further assistance. Students with HFASD, or those suspected of having the disorder, are referred by a variety of individuals, including teachers, counselors, administrators, and parents concerned about poor academic progress and disruptive behaviors. Figure 27.1 shows a step-by-step procedure for school psychologists responding to referrals of students with HFASD and the various considerations that must be made for assessment and intervention development and evaluation.

Figure 27.1. School Psychologist Response to Referral for HFASD Assessment or Intervention

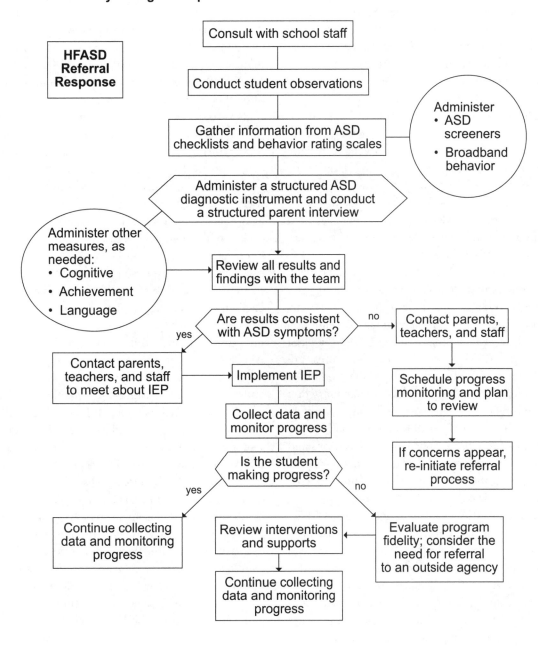

When a referral is made, regardless of the source, school psychologists should be the ones who are in a leadership role on a multidisciplinary team so they can help determine if observed problems are associated in some way with HFASD or something else. The school team, however, must decide what services will be most likely to address the student's educational and social–emotional needs. The ASD referral response flowchart in Figure 27.1 draws attention to the multiple steps involved in identifying ASD and the need for careful follow-up on evaluation findings (e.g., false negative error made and student with ASD missed).

Figure 27.1 should also serve as a reminder to school psychologists about the need to conduct comprehensive assessments of academic, cognitive, and psychological functioning and to monitor the student's response to interventions to inform changes to interventions and resource needs.

Assessments of HFASD

Best practice for assessing HFASD includes at a minimum the following: (a) a structured or semistructured interview with parents, (b) autism checklists completed by parents and teachers, and (c) the Autism Diagnostic Observation Schedule–Second Edition (ADOS-2; Lord et al., 2012) or a similar structured autism observation method. Similar procedures and some of the same measures are used to assess for HFASD as ASD with associated intellectual disability or other developmental disability. However, some tests include different forms and/or norms to be used for HFASD identification. Below is a description of measures that have been shown to have strong psychometric properties for use with HFASD, including properties such as scale sensitivity (accuracy in HFASD identification) and specificity (accuracy in distinguishing HFASD from other disorders). Steps that are suggested for interpreting data from these and other scales are provided at the end of the section.

ADOS-2 (Lord et al., 2012) is a standardized behavioral observation that can be used with all ages, starting at 12 months of age. It takes about 1½–2 hours to administer and score (formal training is required). ADOS-2 allows calculations to be made that are consistent with DSM-5 criteria, that is, scores are computed for social affect, which is the combined communication and reciprocal social interaction score; restricted and repetitive behaviors; and total. Sensitivity is reported to be in the upper .90s and specificity in the upper .80s to lower .90s. Supplemental observations and assessments are needed to collect data on children's peer interactions and the child and family history (e.g., development, medical).

Autism Diagnostic Interview–Revised (ADI-R; Rutter, Le Couteur, & Lord, 2003) is a standardized 93-item parent/caregiver structured interview that can be used for any child with a "mental age" of at least 2 years. It takes about 2½–3 hours to administer and score (formal training is required). Developmental and other history data are collected to determine if the person meets ASD criteria. Given the amount of time it takes to conduct the ADI-R, however, adapted versions and other checklists are often used by professionals in schools and clinics.

Social Communication Questionnaire (Rutter, Bailey, & Lord, 2003) is a parent checklist that includes 40 items selected to address the three ADI-R domains: reciprocal social interaction; communication; and restricted, repetitive, and stereotyped patterns of behavior. The questionnaire is intended for all ages. However, questions in the Lifetime version pertain to the period between 4 and 5 years of age, whereas the Current form pertains to a period within 3 months of testing. It takes approximately 10 minutes to fill out and a couple of minutes to score. The suggested cutoff score is 15 for ASD. However, a lower score can often denote ASD. The sensitivity is reported to be .96 and specificity .80.

Social Responsiveness Scale–Second Edition (Constantino & Gruber, 2012) is a 65-item parent and teacher informant rating scale intended for preschoolers and school-age children (forms for 2½- to 4½-year-olds and 4- to 18-year-olds). For adults 19 years or older, there is a separate informant (e.g., parent) and self-report form. Scores are consistent with the DSM-5 criteria, with scores calculated for social communication and interaction, restricted and repetitive behaviors, and total. There are also five treatment subscales: social awareness, social cognition, social communication, social motivation, and restricted, repetitive behaviors. Sensitivity is reported to be between .78 and .91 and specificity .41 to 1.0 (setting dependent).

Steps that need to be used to determine HFASD and eligibility for special education services, or 504 Plan accommodations, include (a) analyzing scores from measures administered directly to the child (e.g., ADOS-2) and checklists completed by parents or other informants (e.g., ADI-R, Social Responsiveness Scale, and Social Communication Questionnaire) to determine if HFASD cutoffs are met and (b) reviewing all data (e.g., observed behaviors and endorsed items) and deciding if symptoms meet diagnostic criteria for ASD using the DSM-5 or some other widely accepted system such as the International Classification of Diseases. Deficits in social communication and interaction and restricted, repetitive behaviors must be evident and a determination made that HFASD symptoms were present since early childhood and have caused functional impairment. If HFASD is identified, the assessor should determine if the student's cognitive and language skills are within the normal or near normal range and if the student's educational performance is below the expected level by administering standardized tests and curriculum-based measures or reviewing recent test data. The assessor also should conduct psychological testing of social–emotional functioning to design interventions.

Assessments of Learning Problems and Psychological Issues

Not all students with HFASD have significant academic skill deficits. However, many have pragmatic and structural language deficits that impair reading comprehension. Despite relative strength in decoding words, their text comprehension is often poor if the text is abstract or overly complex (e.g., use of compound sentences and advanced vocabulary and inference are required). Deficits in what is referred to as theory of mind, that is, not understanding well the thoughts and intentions of the writer, also have an impact on the comprehension of what the person is reading. Often, individuals with HFASD focus too much on minor details and not so much on the big picture (referred to in autism literature as *weak central coherence*) to attempt to comprehend what they are reading, just as they struggle to understand what another person is trying to communicate verbally to them. Their own expression, though, is also impaired at times. This includes verbal and written communications. Although graphomotor problems are often found, children with HFASD tend to have difficulty putting into words their thoughts and, eventually, writing these thoughts down.

Scores on achievement and intelligence tests often overestimate what a student with HFASD will actually do in the classroom. The more subtle the deficits, and the more strengths the student has (e.g., extensive vocabularies), the harder it is for teachers to understand what is actually causing poor performance. Psychiatric problems, including anxiety disorders and depression, however, often complicate the student's ability to fully participate and perform up to his or her own expected level in school. School psychologists can be very helpful in assessing psychological problems and communicating this information as well as other information about a student's academic strengths and weaknesses to teachers and parents so problems are better understood and appropriate interventions are planned. Although for some students with HFASD using more regular external reinforcements and/or instructional materials that are intrinsically reinforcing (e.g., consciously embedding basic math instruction into computer class curriculum) are sufficient, in many cases further support services are needed. This includes tutoring, resource classes, and psychological services to address the complex and oftentimes serious needs of the students. Since core autistic features are often a primary cause of problems for students with HFASD, however, it is critical that when planning interventions core deficits are thoroughly evaluated.

Intervention-Focused Assessments of Social Deficits and Challenging Behaviors

Impaired understanding of verbal and nonverbal communications of others (e.g., conversation, facial expression, and gesture), misunderstanding of intentions and social rules and social protocols, and failure to accept different perspectives and respond in a socially acceptable manner often result in inappropriate social interactions, noncompliance, and aggressive acting out on the part of students with HFASD. Given how idiosyncratic some skills deficits and challenging behaviors are, individualized assessments must be conducted to determine specific skill deficiencies as well as environmental setting events and antecedents and consequences of behaviors that lead to poor educational performance and poor social and behavioral adjustment.

Intervention-focused assessments should, therefore, include focused interviews, rating scales, and direct behavioral observations.

Interviews

Given the fact that many behaviors and social interactions vary depending on the setting and person (e.g., classroom, students, teachers, playground, and lunch room), focused interviews need to be conducted with students, parents, teachers, and other relevant parties. Interviews provide a means to describe skills and behaviors that need to be more extensively studied using quantitative methods (e.g., rating scales and direct observation). Interviews with different people also provide an opportunity for school psychologists to gain familiarity with the student, other family members (parents and siblings), and school staff (teachers, office staff, lunchroom and playground supervisors) in order to decide on interventions, including what, when, and how these interventions should be introduced.

Rating Scales

Behavior rating scales take a lot less time than interviews and behavioral observations and can provide information otherwise unobtainable (e.g., behaviors that occur in different environments with different people, as well as environments where direct observations are impossible or impractical to conduct). Two examples of informant rating scales that have been used for school-age children with HFASD include the Autism Social Skills Profile (Bellini, 2008) and the Repetitive Behavior Scale–Revised (Bodfish, Symons, Parker, & Lewis, 2000). The Autism Social Skills Profile identifies specific social skill deficits and yields a total score and three subscale scores: social reciprocity, social participation and avoidance, and detrimental social behaviors. The Repetitive Behavior Scale–Revised identifies repetitive and restricted behaviors and yields a total score and six subscale scores (stereotyped, self-injury, compulsive, ritualistic, sameness, and restricted behaviors), and is useful for determining different types of repetitive and restricted behaviors and intervention effectiveness. Both the Autism Social Skills Profile and Repetitive Behavior Scale–Revised are useful in designing interventions to address core autistic deficits by identifying target deficits, monitoring progress, and assessing response.

It should be noted that few rating scales have been specifically designed to assess challenging behaviors associated with autism for intervention purposes. The Pervasive Developmental Disorder Behavior Inventory (Cohen, 2003) is one exception in that it uses informants (parent and teacher) to assess responses and behaviors that are maladaptive (e.g., problems with sensory/perceptual approach, fears, arousal, aggression, and both social and semantic pragmatic problems) and adaptive (e.g., social approach and receptive/expressive social communications).

Direct Observations

Direct observation methods allow for information to be incorporated from interview, rating scales, and other sources so that operational definitions of behaviors are constructed and relevant observations are made in the different environments. Neither a rating scale nor a focused interview can replace direct observations of behaviors that warrant intervention (e.g., repeatedly resisting teacher requests, inappropriate comments to peers while passing in the hallway, aggression on the playground). Observations also allow for information to be collected on unaffected peers in similar situations and in interaction with the student who has HFASD. Obviously, without installing a video camera at all points in a school building and running it all day, it is not possible to capture all critical moments. However, observations designed to take place in environments where the student is more likely to have difficulty, or function well, are still very important.

Functional behavioral assessments are especially important for assessing restricted, repetitive behaviors. However, information about the functions of these behaviors may also be obtained through modification of direct observation procedures. For example, conditional probability observations allow for the calculation of conditional probabilities that an antecedent is related to a target behavior and that a particular consequence is contingent on that target behavior. The analysis of quantitative data (i.e., antecedents, target behaviors, and consequences) helps identify reinforcing events so interventions can be designed to include the correct amount/intensity and timing of reinforcements as well

as contributory deficits such as problems with social interactions.

Skill Deficit Assessment

The last step in assessment of target behaviors is determination of type of skill deficit. School psychologists must determine whether the target behavior identified through interviews, checklists, and direct observation is the result of a skill acquisition deficit (i.e., child does not know how to correctly perform the target behavior), a performance deficit (i.e., child does not demonstrate the desired behavior due to factors such as anxiety or motivation), or a fluency deficit (i.e., child performs the target behavior awkwardly). Inaccurate conceptualization of deficit type may result in implementation of an intervention that is ineffective in addressing the needs of the child with HFASD. For example, an acquisition deficit that requires teaching steps to a target behavior is unlikely to improve by addressing only motivation to perform a behavior (performance deficit) or by providing the child with additional opportunities to utilize the target behavior (fluency deficit).

Direct observation is likely to provide data essential to the determination of deficit type, although interviews and checklists may also yield useful information. School psychologists should consider the following in determining deficit type: (a) whether the child demonstrates the target behavior across multiple settings and with multiple persons, (b) if the child does not require prompting to demonstrate the target behavior, (c) if the child performs the behavior contingent upon reinforcement, (d) if the child demonstrates little effort or awkwardness in performance of the behavior, and (e) if the child performs the behavior following modifications to the environment. If the child with ASD meets all of these criteria, then a performance deficit likely exists and school psychologists should seek to utilize interventions that remove barriers to performance of the behavior (e.g., motivation, anxiety). If the child does not meet the aforementioned criteria, then school psychologists should consider the presence of an acquisition or fluency deficit and identify intervention strategies appropriate for teaching steps for performance of the target.

Interventions for Targeted Behaviors

Interventions that specifically target core deficits associated with HFASD need to be implemented and monitored in school. Researchers studying social skills in this population have found that setting up occasions where students with HFASD interact with unaffected peers has helped, but it is not sufficient. Other methods need to be used, in particular those that have empirical support. Many of the positive effects that are found, though, are short lived; that is, they do not stick. Therefore, the skills that are learned are not used in other situations (sometimes not even with a different group of peers). School-wide programs, including those that reward positive behaviors and have in place positive behavioral supports, are important, and so are public awareness campaigns. However, the effectiveness of these types of interventions tends to rely more on other people behaving differently rather than the person with ASD.

When selecting interventions to target challenging behaviors associated with HFASD, it is important to understand that there is no single procedure for addressing all areas of concern. Interventions, then, must be comprehensive—targeting antecedents to behavior, addressing the behavior itself, and modifying consequences—and include progress monitoring. For evidence-based practices the National Autism Center (2009) requires regular progress monitoring, which at times requires continuous data collection and evaluation in order to assess intervention needs and modifications to programs and Individualized Education Program goals. As research has yet to identify one intervention strategy that may be considered universally effective, school psychologists must be aware of multiple approaches that have been found to be beneficial for addressing social skill deficits and challenging behaviors.

The interventions discussed in this chapter do not provide an exhaustive list of all practices with empirical support for children with HFASD, but this chapter should serve as an overview of several effective practices, particularly those that have been identified as "established treatments" by the National Autism Center (2009). (See Table 27.1 for a step-by-step guide for the intervention approaches discussed below, including types of deficits and examples of behaviors addressed.)

Video Modeling

Video modeling is an intervention strategy that utilizes videos to provide models of target behaviors (Bellini & Akullian, 2007). Video modeling should be utilized as an intervention approach to address acquisition, performance, and fluency deficits for social skills, communication skills, daily living skills, and play skills. Video models that incorporate the skills of students with HFASD (video self-modeling) and those of others have been found to be efficacious. Setting up a video modeling intervention involves several simple steps:

identify target behaviors, produce videos demonstrating successful demonstration of the target behavior, and have students with HFASD view the videos on a regular basis (e.g., daily). School psychologists may consider video modeling as an intervention strategy applicable for most students with HFASD, as it has been found to be effective in addressing social deficits and reducing problem behaviors, with improvements being maintained over time.

Social Scripts

School psychologists should consider utilization of social scripts, or social stories, in cases of acquisition, performance, or fluency deficits and when target behaviors are behavioral, social, or communication skills. A social script is an individualized intervention strategy that provides a child with HFASD with a guide for responding to various situations. Social scripts are written from the perspective of the child and should include sentences that describe the situation, provide directives for behaviors, and explain perspectives of others in the situation. While social scripts have been found to be helpful in addressing both social skills and problem behaviors, school psychologists should be aware that research suggests that social stories may be ineffective when utilized as the sole intervention strategy (Kokina & Kern, 2010). Therefore, utilization of social scripts should be done in conjunction with additional intervention strategies (e.g., video modeling).

Self-Monitoring

Self-monitoring describes the process of discriminating between occurrences and nonoccurrences of target behaviors (Lee, Simpson, & Shogren, 2007). The judgment of occurrence and nonoccurrence may be cued by a temporal (e.g., after recess), verbal (via teacher or peer), or physical cue (e.g., MotivAider), at which time the child records whether he or she is engaged in a behavior. Self-monitoring is effective in improving both challenging behaviors and social skills, and has the benefit of requiring minimal teacher, parent, and school psychologist involvement. Similar to video modeling, self-monitoring interventions are simple to implement: determine if students can perform target behaviors, select an achievable goal, and provide reinforcement for meeting goals while monitoring progress over time.

Peer-Mediated Interventions

Peer-mediated interventions are useful in addressing performance and fluency deficits of children with ASD. Peer-mediated interventions employ peers as change

Table 27.1. Evidence-Based Intervention Strategies for Students With HFASD

Strategy	Steps to Implementation	Types of Deficits Addressed	Examples of Behaviors to Be Addressed
Video Modeling	1. Identify potential target behaviors. 2. Consult with special education team members to select socially valid behavior to be targeted. 3. Create three to five video models of the target skill, demonstrating skill use with a variety of individuals in multiple settings. 4. Edit videos to show the best demonstration of the target skill in 30-second segments to 5 minutes. 5. Identify a time and location to view videos. 6. Student views the video models *at least* once daily. 7. Student role-plays the target skill after viewing the video model.	• Acquisition deficits (e.g., does not know how to join in) • Performance deficits (e.g., joins in only with one specific peer) • Fluency deficits (e.g., is awkward in joining in)	• Social skills (e.g., perspective taking, problem solving, eye contact) • Communication skills (e.g., greeting others, maintaining a conversation) • Daily living skills (e.g., washing hands, brushing teeth) • Play skills (e.g., turn taking, joining in a game, participating in a group)
Social Scripts	1. Identify potential target behaviors. 2. Consult with special education team members to select a socially valid behavior to be targeted. 3. Write social narrative using sentences that describe the social setting, direct appropriate behaviors, describe feelings and reactions of others, and provide cues to remember the social script. 4. Incorporate photos, icons, or drawings when appropriate. 5. Identify a time when the social script may be read with the child. 6. Utilize the social script on a daily basis, either read independently or with assistance of an adult or a peer.	• Acquisition deficits (e.g., does not know steps to making a request) • Performance deficits (e.g., makes requests only when reinforced) • Fluency deficits (e.g., long pauses before requests)	• Problem behaviors (e.g., talking out of turn, tantruming) • Social skills (e.g., making eye contact, getting someone's attention, dealing with rumors, responding to bullies) • Communication skills (e.g., making requests, asking questions, talking about interests of others)
Self-Monitoring	1. Identify potential target behaviors. 2. Consult with school team members to select a socially valid behavior to be targeted. 3. Identify reinforcers to be utilized. 4. Determine a self-monitoring device for recording (e.g., sticker chart). 5. Determine need for auditory or physical (e.g., MotivAider) tools needed for self-monitoring. 6. Teach the student to discriminate between occurrence and nonoccurrence of behavior. 7. Teach the student to utilize the self-monitoring recording device in conjunction to record his or her own behavior; model correct examples. 8. Set the goal and provide reinforcement for meeting goals (e.g., tangible, attention).	• Acquisition deficits (e.g., does not maintain a topic) • Performance deficits (e.g., only maintains a topic when prompted) • Fluency deficits (e.g., requires effort to talk about unfamiliar topics)	• Problem behaviors (e.g., out of seat, off-task behaviors, aggression) • Social skills (e.g., following directions, managing anxiety, respecting personal space) • Communication skills (e.g., responding to others, maintaining topic, asking follow-up questions)
Peer Mediated	1. Identify potential target behaviors. 2. Consult with special education team members to select a socially valid behavior to be targeted. 3. Identify peers who demonstrate age-appropriate play and social skills, have regular attendance, and would be willing to participate in an intervention. 4. Select the type of peer-mediated intervention to be utilized: peer modeling, in which peers demonstrate appropriate target behavior; peer initiation/response training, in which peers are taught strategies for interacting with the student with HFASD; or target student initiation/response training, in which the student with HFASD is taught strategies and reinforced for peer interactions. 5. Identify setting in which peer-mediated intervention needs implementation (minimum of 10 minutes). 6. Implement the intervention.	• Performance deficits (e.g., only engages with peers with provided reinforcement) • Fluency deficits (e.g., interactions with peers are awkward)	• Social skills (e.g., sharing, helping others) • Communication skills (e.g., commenting, requesting information) • Play skills (e.g., following rules, dealing with losing, joining in a game)

National Association of School Psychologists

agents, and they are particularly effective as they allow children with HFASD increased access to social situations and promote generalization of target behaviors (Zhang & Wheeler, 2011). Peer-mediated interventions may take the form of utilizing peers as models to demonstrate appropriate target skill use, training peers to better initiate and respond to children with ASD, or training initiation and response skills in children with ASD and reinforcing interaction with peers. While peer-mediated interventions may be utilized as the only means of intervention, it is recommended that the utilization of typically developing peers in the intervention process be done in conjunction with other evidence-based practices. When utilizing peer-mediated interventions, it is essential that peers selected be good models of the target behavior and be willing to participate in the intervention. As with other intervention strategies, peer-mediated interventions should be implemented regularly, and each session should last a minimum of 10 minutes.

Comprehensive Social Skills Programs

Although the previously mentioned intervention strategies may be utilized to produce clinically significant improvements in target behaviors, comprehensive social skills programs are often more easily implemented due to their being curriculum based. While a number of different comprehensive programs are available, school psychologists are encouraged to consider the following programs due to empirical support. The Social Thinking (Winner, 2000) curriculum was designed to help children with HFASD understand the importance of socialization and understand that other people have thoughts that differ from one's own. Social Thinking places an emphasis on teaching children with ASD how their own behaviors may influence the thoughts, feelings, and actions of those around them. Although the curriculum does not explicitly train discrete social skills or incorporate reinforcements for demonstration of target skills, it has been shown to be effective for increased social initiations, improved on-topic remarks, and joint attention.

The Superheroes Social Skills (Jenson et al., 2011) program is also intended for school-age children who have HFASD. The program trains discrete skills ranging from basic communication skills to how to respond to bullying through incorporation of several evidence-based practices and high-interest media. It has been shown to improve social engagement and at the same time reduce unwanted behaviors, and it can be implemented with fidelity in various settings (e.g.,

school, home, clinic, and summer camp) and by different professionals and nonprofessionals (e.g., school psychologists, teachers, aides, and parents; e.g., Radley, Jenson, Clark, & O'Neill, 2014).

Fewer manualized treatment programs can be found for adolescents and young adults with HFASD. The UCLA Program for the Education and Enrichment of Relational Skills, however, is one that has been found to be effective in improving social skills and decreasing ASD-related mannerisms (Laugeson, Frankel, Gantman, Dillon, & Mogil, 2012). The program focuses on skills essential to social functioning in adolescence, such as electronic communication, choosing appropriate friends, and conversation skills. Similar to Superheroes Social Skills, this program utilizes role-playing and homework components to promote acquisition and generalization of target social skills.

Interventions for Noncompliance

Modification of assignments may reduce challenging behaviors found to occur following task demands. However, high-probability command sequences may also be necessary as they are a type of antecedent intervention that has been found to increase compliance in this group. Based on behavioral momentum theory, the intervention consists of delivery of multiple high-probability requests prior to delivery of low-probability requests. A similar approach, errorless compliance training, has been effective in decreasing noncompliance in children with ASD. Errorless compliance interventions begin by encouraging parents and teachers to only utilize commands that are likely to be complied with and gradually introducing lower probability commands. This practice ensures that children are exposed to high levels of reinforcement for compliance. In addition to managing antecedent events, it is important that behaviors be taught in a way that allows the person to become more competent. This means intervention strategies need to provide consequences and thus prevent reinforcement from inappropriate problem behaviors but at the same time maximize reinforcements for competing behaviors using methods such as token economies.

Coordinating and Collaborating on Interventions

In order to ensure that interventions are actually implemented and expected outcomes achieved, there needs to be coordination and collaboration among school staff. Efficient use of everyone's time needs to be assessed, and the methods of assessment and intervention that are used need to be as economical as possible. But to ensure efficiency and adequate resource allocation requires a case manager. A case manager not only serves to monitor these types of things, but facilitates communication with all parties who are involved in the intervention. To address the needs of students with HFASD, regularly scheduled team meetings are needed to ensure that staff are following up on assignments and data are collected to ensure steps are being followed. These data reviews should also include those that evaluate fidelity of the intervention as well as the student's response to the intervention. Although school psychologists may find this to be part of their regular routines when participating on a team working on an intervention for students, many of the intervention plans for students with HFASD require more personnel and often involve the parents and other professionals working outside the school (e.g., pediatricians). Even interventions involving these larger groups can be implemented reliably and with high levels of satisfaction by those who facilitate and benefit from intervention (e.g., students, teachers, and parents). To ensure that everyone is on board, however, and not confused about his or her responsibilities, it is important to use some type of framework or model to guide the process. Magyar and Pandolfi (2012) proposed the ASD Support Model.

The ASD Support Model incorporates components of a multitiered problem-solving approach and is consistent with the NASP Practice Model (NASP, 2010). For example, the model includes components that address problems at a student and systems level, involve a multidisciplinary team that is held accountable for assigned tasks, and use data-based assessments and a data-driven method for decision making. As with other multitiered problem-solving protocols, Magyar and Pandolfi (2012) recommend standardized assessments for assessing student needs, interventions that are evidence based, professional development incorporated to build personnel capacity in the schools, and activities that help to ensure fidelity of the methods and desired outcomes. Using a standardized assessment protocol is important in that it provides a comprehensive multi-method procedure for assessing a student's unique strengths and weaknesses as well as an assessment of contextual factors that may affect, negatively or positively, the student's response to intervention. Protocols also serve as a means to get feedback about the implementation of the intervention, a student's response, and need for modification. These methods basically serve as a feedback loop so that interventions

can be modified to increase the chances of a positive effect (e.g., changing the level of support students receive).

School teams need to pay attention to intervention hierarchies so that different levels of support can be provided simultaneously to students with HFASD who show higher levels of variability in their performance. Progress monitoring should include data on the levels of support that are needed and provide information about particular contexts where a different level of support might be required. Included below are examples of primary, secondary, and tertiary supports that may be used with all students, including those with HFASD.

Primary-level supports. These are intended to help all students to be engaged and perform at the expected level in the classroom. Students with HFASD often need clearly defined classroom routines and behavior management systems in place to ensure they remain focused, are organized, and can complete their work (e.g., visual prompts, organizers, and continuous reinforcers). Direct instruction is another example of a primary-level support that most students need to ensure skill acquisition in subjects such as reading and math and for desired behaviors. Students with HFASD, however, often need more supports and more opportunities to make choices that help to promote self-determination, independence, and responsibility. Many students with HFASD struggle when routines are interrupted and transitions are required (e.g., changing classes, teachers, classmates, and schools). The fact that this seems to get more difficult with each passing year requires not only individual support but also system-wide practices that ensure students are prepared for transitions through activities and opportunities that support developing better skills for self-management, goal setting, decision making, problem solving, and assertiveness (all tasks that students with HFASD tend to struggle with).

Many students with HFASD want to go on to college and complete an undergraduate and graduate education. Secondary school programs that provide more intensive educational experiences that match the student's interests or allow students to take more classes off campus may help. Some families may debate whether to have their children attend a charter school, and school psychologists and other school personnel can provide parents with information that can help them make this decision so that the student is able to have choices in terms of the types of classes and opportunities to interact with peers. Charter schools, however, are not necessarily better, and some students end up back at their neighborhood school because of the resources.

Secondary-level supports.

These are intended to provide more intensive supports such as small group instruction, but they ensure that students with HFASD have opportunities to interact and learn from typically developing peers (e.g., learn ways to demonstrate social skills, socioemotional and coping skills, problem-solving skills, independent living skills, and self-regulation). Parents, however, play an important role at this level, making parent training an important part of secondary supports. Not only does parent training help augment training for skill acquisition, it also helps to ensure that students with HFASD actually get to school and have consistency of behaviors across home and school and it promotes generalization elsewhere.

According to Johnson et al. (2007), parent training must ensure that certain skills are developed, such as behavior management. First, parent training curricula need to focus on teaching antecedent strategies (i.e., proactive strategies to prevent problem behaviors), teaching strategies (i.e., strategies to teach new behaviors and skills), and consequence strategies (i.e., strategies for responding to problem behavior). Basic skills that parents need to develop include learning how to effectively deliver instructions, appropriately provide reinforcement, and consistently apply rules and consequences. Second, parent training curricula need to teach parents when and how to apply prompting, shaping procedures, and task analysis strategies. Basically, parent training needs to provide instruction to parents (e.g., defining strategies and when to apply strategies), model strategies for the parents, provide opportunities for guided practice (i.e., parent implements strategies in the presence of the trainer), and give parents feedback on their implementation of newly acquired strategies.

Methods that address social skills deficits and transitions should also be included in parent training curricula. Parents of younger students with HFASD may need to learn how to help their children practice basic skills of initiating and responding to play dates, joining peer groups, and engaging in reciprocal conversation. In addition, parents may need to learn how to identify whether their children are victims of bullying and how to respond in these situations. Even parents of older students may need to engage their children in conversations about how they are being treated by peers and how they should respond to difficult situations, and about their own feelings of rejection and loneliness. In addition,

these parents may need help initiating conversations about topics such as dating and sexual relationships. School psychologists can play an important role in helping parents learn more about these issues and allowing them opportunities to talk about other concerns that they have for their child. Since this level of support can be very time consuming, and thus costly in terms of personnel resources, offering parent-training workshops through the district may work well.

Tertiary-level supports.

These are provided when students do not respond to other levels of support and need a lot more individualized attention and instruction. In these cases, the school psychologist's role may be that of a team leader for reviewing data and helping to determine what modifications need to be made and additional assessments and/or interventions to add. The intensity and frequency of tertiary interventions vary somewhat but often require an individualized behavior support plan that involves professionals from multiple disciplines. Considerations must be made for referral and collaboration with outside agencies, such as mental health facilities or social service agencies, and for whether more restrictive or specialized placement settings may be necessary.

Resources to Support Consultation and Intervention

There are several national autism organizations that serve as important resources and a clearinghouse for information to diverse groups. This includes Autism Speaks (http://www.autismspeaks.org), which provides information about ongoing research and developments related to autism. Autism Speaks offers legal news, resource guides, toolkits, and technology applications useful for educators and families, and it provides links to state Autism Speaks chapters that can be helpful to professionals and parents.

Each state has autism councils that help disseminate information about ASD, including local resources. Another important resource for school psychologists is the National Conference of State Legislatures, which provides a directory of state autism councils, a database that tracks autism-related legislation in all 50 states and territories (e.g., insurance coverage for autism), and a description of task force activities involving the evaluation of services within each state and territory (http://www.ncsl.org/issues-research/health/autism-task-forces-commissions-and-councils.aspx).

There are organizations that provide critical support to parents of children with HFASD and are often founded by parents. School psychologists will find these organizations to be especially important when discussing with parents what it means for a person to have HFASD, what types of services are available, and how they can get involved themselves with various organizations, including state autism groups. Parents play a critical role in providing resources to other parents, including referring parents to professionals other parents have found helpful in the community (e.g., pediatricians and psychiatrists) and connecting them with state leaders in various organizations and groups that are involved in advocacy and provide information about services (e.g., disability, legal, and vocational services and mental health).

There are a number of applications available for Apple and Android tablets that are being used in classrooms and with individuals who have ASD. Autism Speaks provides a list of applications that are easy to access and can be customized to help improve academics, behaviors, language, and functional skills. With so many applications available, however, parents may want to use i.Am Search, a free application that examines research-driven technological tools for individuals with ASD.

SUMMARY

School psychologists play a critical role in ensuring that psychometrically sound assessment measures are used and procedures are followed to ensure the earliest possible identification of HFASD. Often, HFASD is not identified at younger ages and is misdiagnosed. Although adding a category to the DSM-5 for Social (Pragmatic) Communication Disorder is expected to help, multiple methods need to be used to gather information from multiple informants (e.g., the student, parents, teachers, and other school staff), and direct observations need to be made in different situations where students are able to interact with peers (e.g., classroom, hallway, and playground).

School psychologists who have in-depth knowledge about HFASD and have specialized skills in autism assessment and interventions are in one of the best positions to work with students who have HFASD. They also can help other school staff to determine what services are needed and what can be provided within the school (e.g., classroom behavior management, social skills training, parent education, guidance counseling, and programs that target bullying behaviors). School psychologists can also provide an invaluable service to parents by informing them about outside resources and helping them locate services for their child and themselves (e.g., autism support groups, legal assistance, advocacy services, and psychiatric evaluations). It is not clear how many children and adolescents in the United States have HFASD. However, what is clear is that the core deficits cause serious impairment in everyday functioning, and this is made worse by a number of associated problems, including internalizing and externalizing disorders.

AUTHOR NOTE

Disclosure. Elaine Clark and Keith Radley have a financial interest in a social skills program they coauthored and referenced in this chapter.

REFERENCES

American Psychiatric Association. (2013). *Diagnostic and statistical manual of mental disorders* (5th ed.). Arlington, VA: American Psychiatric Association.

Backner, W., Clark, E., Jenson, W., Gardner, M., & Kahn, J. (2013). An investigation of psychiatric comorbidity and symptom awareness among male adolescents with autism spectrum disorder. *International Journal of School & Educational Psychology, 4,* 259–268. doi:10.1080/21683603.2013.845737

Baron-Cohen, S., Wheelwright, S., Skinner, R., Martin, J., & Chubley, E. (2001). The Autism Spectrum Quotient (AQ): Evidence from Asperger syndrome/high-functioning autism, males and females, scientists and mathematicians. *Journal of Autism and Developmental Disorders, 36,* 5–17.

Bellini, S. (2008). *Building social relationships: A systematic approach to teaching social interaction skills to children and adolescents with autism spectrum disorders and other social difficulties.* Shawnee Mission, KS: Autism Asperger Publishing.

Bellini, S., & Akullian, J. (2007). A meta-analysis of video modeling and video self-modeling interventions for children and adolescents with autism spectrum disorders. *Council for Exceptional Children, 73,* 264–287.

Bodfish, J., Symons, F., Parker, D., & Lewis, M. (2000). Varieties of repetitive behavior in autism: Comparisons to mental retardation. *Journal of Autism and Developmental Disorders, 30,* 237–243.

Cappadocia, M. S., Weiss, J. A., & Pepler, D. (2012). Bullying experiences among children and youth with autism spectrum disorders. *Journal of Autism and Developmental Disabilities, 42,* 266–277.

Centers for Disease Control and Prevention. (2012). Prevalence of autism spectrum disorders: Autism and developmental disabilities monitoring network, 14 sites, United States, 2008. *Morbidity and Mortality Weekly Report: Surveillance Summaries, 61,* 1–19. Retrieved from http://www.cdc.gov/mmwr/preview/mmwrhtml/ss6103a1.htm?s_cid=ss6103a1_w

Cohen, I. (2003). Criterion-related validity of the PDD behavior inventory. *Journal of Autism and Developmental Disorders, 33,* 47–53.

Constantino, J., & Gruber, C. P. (2012). *Social Responsiveness Scale* (2nd ed.). Los Angeles, CA: Western Psychological Services.

Farley, M., McMahon, W. M., Fombonne, E., Jenson, W. R., Miller, J., Gardner, M., & Coon, H. (2009). Twenty-year outcome for individuals with autism and average or near-average cognitive abilities. *Autism Research, 2*, 109–118.

Gabrielsen, T. (2012). *Autism symptom presentations in toddlers during brief observations* (Unpublished doctoral dissertation). University of Utah, Salt Lake City, UT.

Jenson, W., Bowen, J., Clark, E., Block, H., Gabriensen, T., Hood, J., … Springer, B. (2011). *Superheroes Social Skills*. Eugene, OR: Pacific Northwest.

Johnson, C. R., Handen, B. L., Butter, E., Wagner, A., Mulick, J., Sukhodolsky, D. G., & Smith, T. (2007). Development of a parent training program for children with pervasive developmental disorders. *Behavioral Interventions, 22*, 201–221.

Kokina, A., & Kern, L. (2010). Social story interventions for students with autism spectrum disorders: Meta-analysis. *Journal of Autism and Developmental Disorders, 40*, 812–826.

Laugeson, E., Frankel, F., Gantman, A., Dillon, A., & Mogil, C. (2012). Evidence-based social skills training for adolescents with autism spectrum disorders: The UCLA PEERS program. *Journal of Autism and Developmental Disorders, 42*, 1025–1036.

Lee, S., Simpson, R., & Shogren, K. (2007). Effects and implications of self-management for students with autism: A meta-analysis. *Focus on Autism and Other Developmental Disabilities, 22*, 2–13.

Lord, C., Rutter, M., DiLavore, P., Risi, S., Gotham, K., & Bishop, S. (2012). *Autism Diagnostic Observation Schedule (ADOS-2): Modules 1–4*. Los Angeles, CA: Western Psychological Services.

Magyar, C. I., & Pandolfi, V. (2012). Establishing a multitiered problem-solving model for students with autism spectrum disorders and comorbid emotional-behavioral disorders. *Psychology in the Schools, 49*, 975–987.

National Association of School Psychologists. (2010). *Model for comprehensive and integrated school psychological services*. Bethesda, MD: Author. Retrieved from http://www.nasponline.org/standards/2010standards/2_PracticeModel.pdf

National Autism Center. (2009). *National standards report*. Randolph, MA: Author.

Ozonoff, S., Iosif, A. M., Baguio, F., Cook, I. C., Hill, M., Hutmam, T., … Young, G. S. (2010). A prospective study of the emergence of early signs of autism. *Journal of the American Academy of Child and Adolescent Psychiatry, 49*, 256–266.

Radley, K., Jenson, W., Clark, E., & O'Neill, R. (2014). The feasibility and effects of a parent-facilitated social skills training program on social engagement of children with autism spectrum disorders. *Psychology in the Schools*. Advance online publication. doi:10.1002/pits.21749

Rutter, M., Bailey, A., & Lord, C. (2003). *The Social Communication Questionnaire*. Los Angeles, CA: Western Psychological Services.

Rutter, M., Le Couteur, A., & Lord, C. (2003). *Autism Diagnostic Interview* (rev.). Los Angeles, CA: Western Psychological Services.

Shattuck, R., Narendorf, S., Cooper, B., Sterzing, P., Wagner, M., & Taylor, J. (2012). Post-secondary education and employment among youth with an autism spectrum disorder. *Pediatrics, 129*, 1042–1049.

Wanzek, M., Clark, E., Farley, M., Connelly, J., Gardner, M., Pompa, J., & Goldman, S. (2013, August). *Symptom manifestation and trajectory in females with ASD*. Paper presented at the annual meeting of the American Psychological Association, Honolulu, HI.

Winner, M. (2000). *Inside out: What makes the person with social cognitive deficits tick?*. San Jose, CA: Think Social.

Zhang, J., & Wheeler, J. (2011). A meta-analysis of peer-mediated interventions for young children with autism spectrum disorders. *Education and Training in Autism and Developmental Disabilities, 46*, 62–77.

28 Best Practices in Writing Assessment Reports

Robert Walrath
John O. Willis
Rivier University (NH)
Ron Dumont
Fairleigh Dickinson University (NJ)

OVERVIEW

It has been estimated that school psychologists on average complete about 27 initial special education evaluations and 33 special education reevaluations each year (Castillo, Curtis, & Gelley, 2012). To write an effective and useful report, school psychologists must develop a number of professional skills. They must formulate and complete an assessment, which itself includes skills such as attaining and maintaining rapport with clients, selecting tests and procedures that will address the referral issues, flawlessly administering and scoring educational and psychological tests and questionnaires, performing useful school observations, productively interviewing relevant individuals, and integrating and interpreting the findings. Once the assessment is completed, they must decide upon the best method and style to use for communicating their ideas effectively.

There are two very important skills that can lead to professional success in writing assessment reports. First, a school psychologist must have a specific knowledge base not only as an expert in assessment and in understanding both the technical aspects of assessment materials and the results obtained from them, but in the areas of child development, various disabilities, cultural and linguistic diversity, special education law, consultation, intervention, and how schools work. Second, and at least equally important, is the ability of the school psychologist to communicate that knowledge in a clear and precise manner that is suitable and understandable to the intended audience. It is clearly not enough to have knowledge if it cannot be communicated in a clear

and understandable way. Skills in writing assessment reports are an integral part of the domain of Data-Based Decision Making and Accountability, found in the National Association of School Psychologists (NASP) *Model for Comprehensive and Integrated School Psychological Services* (NASP, 2010a).

This chapter suggests best practices in writing assessment reports that are clear, effective, and useful. In the following sections, salient aspects of effective report writing will be described that address helpful hints and potential pitfalls in effective report writing. NASP's *Principles for Professional Ethics* (NASP, 2010b) provides some useful guidelines to aid school psychologists in the areas of assessment interpretation, report writing, and sharing of findings, which will also be cited in relevant sections.

It is impossible to prescribe a single set of best practices for writing reports beyond a few very basic considerations, such as obey the law, do not lie, answer referral questions, be accurate, be useful, and write understandably. School psychologists write evaluation reports for many purposes in many settings and what might be best practice in one circumstance might not even be good practice in another. In some instances there are two or more approaches that could share the mantle of best practice, so the school psychologist must choose one that appears to be most appropriate.

BASIC CONSIDERATIONS

School psychologists should always strive to accomplish several purposes with their assessment reports. Among these purposes are the following ones: answer referral questions as clearly and explicitly as possible; provide meaningful data for evaluating future progress after interventions have been implemented; and combine relevant observations, background information, multidisciplinary results, and other pertinent data. Unfortunately, this may not always be the case. As Willis (2011) has noted:

> A passion for parsimony, efforts to save time and control costs, and complacency about offering nothing more than diagnoses with only minimal, vague, generic, or one-size-fits-all recommendations often lead to evaluation reports that are neither very comprehensive nor especially helpful to examinees, parents, teachers, therapists, and other consumers of our reports. (p. xix)

Harvey (2006) explains that, among other things, there are typically several functions that assessment reports should serve. Reports should increase the understanding of clients (e.g., students, parents, and teachers) about specific issues related to the reason for referral, reports should provide realistic recommendations for accommodations and interventions based upon the results of the assessments, and these recommendations should be presented in a way that can be understood and appreciated by the clients. All of this is most useful when reported within the context of the individual student's history and current difficulties (Weiner & Costaris, 2012) and in keeping with the overarching purpose of all assessment reports: informing the school, parents, and others about the child's skills, needs, and appropriate interventions. This purpose keeps the report student focused rather than label focused.

BEST PRACTICES IN WRITING ASSESSMENT REPORTS

In the following sections, guidelines for major characteristics of effective assessment reports are presented, including clarity, readability, and organization. Suggestions are offered for writing each specific section of an assessment report.

Clarity and Readability

NASP *Principles for Professional Ethics* (NASP, 2010b) state that "[s]chool psychologists adequately interpret findings and present results in clear, understandable terms so that the recipient can make informed choices"

(Standard II.3.8). Brenner (2003) suggests that, to increase the relevance of psychological assessments, psychologists should (a) eliminate jargon, (b) focus on referral questions, (c) individualize assessment reports, (d) emphasize client strengths, and (e) write concrete recommendations that can be used to inform instructional practices. Given the amount of time and effort spent specifically on communicating, in writing, to parents, teachers, and administrators the results and interpretation of assessments, it seems reasonable to expect that these reports would be clear, concise, and informative. Despite the availability to evaluators of many excellent resources, wide variability exists in school psychologists' ability to communicate their results clearly enough to be useful to program planning. If what is written is not written well, then the exercise is a waste of time.

A good assessment report should provide accurate assessment-related information to the relevant parties (e.g., referral source, parent, school); serve as the basis for generating clinical hypotheses and interpretations, appropriate interventions, and information for program evaluation; provide meaningful baseline data for evaluation of student progress after interventions have been implemented; and act as a legal document (Sattler, 2008, p. 705).

In order to follow the NASP standard for presenting results that are written in "understandable terms so that the recipient can make informed choices" (Standard II.3.8), readability can be key. In regard to readability, features that many document software programs (e.g., Microsoft Word) provide should be used, not only to spell and grammar check the entire document but to get a rough estimate of the readability of assessment reports. That is, readability level should be kept below grade 10.5 at the highest, taking into account parents' levels of education. Although the report might be written for what is thought to be a high school reading ability, actual readability might be beyond college.

All spell-checking corrections and suggestions should not be simply accepted. Sometimes the program does not know the context for what has been written and, in its attempt to be helpful, may change the meaning of a sentence. Errors of grammar and punctuation can alter the meaning of what is written and even trivial typos annoy readers and undermine credibility of reports.

Ethical and Legal Standards and Safeguards

When completing a report, the school psychologist may be governed by different laws, regulations, policies, or supervisor directives, so the report must differ with the situation. For example, an issue with which many school psychology students and novice practitioners struggle is whether to include a diagnosis in a final report. There is no definitive answer for this, since, again, the type of report and the conclusions drawn may be dependent on the purpose of the report and the audience for whom the report is written. Sometimes assessment reports can serve two (or more) purposes. For example, the Office for Civil Rights (n.d.) has advised that school districts may meet their legal obligation to provide evaluations for children with disabilities under Section 504 of the Rehabilitation Act either by having a separate process or by using the same procedures they use for determining eligibility under the Individuals with Disabilities Education Improvement Act of 2004 (IDEA). Among the procedures used for IDEA is the provision of a report.

There is, however, a significant difference between IDEA and 504 procedures and consequently there may be two options for the resulting report. As stated earlier, NASP's *Principles for Professional Ethics* (NASP, 2010b) provides guidelines for school psychologists in the areas of assessment interpretation, report writing, and sharing of findings.

It is important to distinguish between the team's evaluation report and the separate reports of the evaluations by the individual evaluators. The evaluation report is a summary of all the screenings and evaluations used in making an eligibility determination. Parents must be given a copy of the evaluation report (Assistance to States, 2006, 34 CFR 300.321, p. 46786). The 2006 Final Regulations also require that, if the parents ask to see any education records, "each participating agency must permit parents to inspect and review any education records relating to their children that are collected, maintained, or used by the agency under this part" (§ 300.321(a)). Schools are obliged to let parents inspect evaluations that have been completed, but schools usually are not (under federal law) obliged to provide copies of those evaluations (state laws may differ, so state laws and regulations should be checked). However, schools often do provide parents with copies of the individual reports (whether requested or not), particularly in situations where the parents want to share the reports with other professionals such as a family doctor. Regardless of school policies, school psychologists should always assume that their reports will be read by parents (and perhaps by students) and should write the reports so that the reports will be understandable and useful for parents.

It is important to mention that lying is never best practice, no matter how pure the author's intent. There are times when school psychologists are sorely tempted to deliberately report misinformation in what they consider the best interests of the child. Never do that.

Given the wide range of computer technology available to the school psychologist, including software to score many of the commonly used assessment measures and report writing programs that significantly automate the report writing process itself, specific ethical requirements must be abided by. For example, for computer-generated materials, NASP (2010b) Standard II.3.2 explains that:

> When using computer-administered assessments, computer-assisted scoring, and/or interpretation programs, school psychologists choose programs that meet professional standards for accuracy and validity. School psychologists use professional judgment in evaluating the accuracy of computer-assisted assessment findings for the examinee.

Although there are legitimate reasons for relying on computer technology when formulating and writing a psychological report (e.g., scoring tests that cannot be scored without the computer program; helping to analyze data; generating reasonable, statistically sound hypotheses about test results), best practice would recommend strongly against any overreliance on these tools. Not only is cutting and pasting from these reports not recommended, there are ethical concerns in engaging in this practice (Walrath, 2001). Reports must include adequate interpretation of the assessment results, as seen in the following standard (NASP, 2010b):

> School psychologists maintain school-based psychological and educational records with sufficient detail to be useful in decision making by another professional and with sufficient detail to withstand scrutiny if challenged in a due process or other legal procedure. (Standard II.4.2)

School psychologists are also expected to take full responsibility for any document they produce and to review all written work. Standard II.2.1 states: "School psychologists [should] review all of their written documents for accuracy, signing them only when correct. They may add an addendum, dated and signed, to a previously submitted report if information is found to be inaccurate or incomplete."

Objectivity Versus Subjectivity

Sattler (2008) warns us that:

> No report can be completely objective … you introduce subjectivity with each word you use to describe the child, each behavior you highlight or choose not to discuss, each element of the history you cite, and the sequence you follow in presenting the information. (p. 705)

While it can be argued that reporting standardized test scores is an objective measure of a child's performance on some task, the choice of the test; the decision to report a standard score, a percentile rank, and/or some other statistic; and proper reporting in the context of pertinent history, of test behaviors, and even in the consideration of the referral question, can introduce necessary subjectivity. For example, suppose Catherine is thought to have generally average abilities except for a possible weakness in processing speed. The examiner, when choosing an assessment battery, might select the Weschler Intelligence Scale for Children-Fourth Edition (WISC-IV; Wechsler, 2003), on which 3 of 10 subtests would probably be affected by the processing speed weakness; or the Differential Ability Scales-Fourth Edition (DAS-II; Elliott, 2007) with the standard Pattern Construction, on which only one of six subtests that contribute to the overall score would probably be affected; or the DAS-II with the alternative Pattern Construction, on which none of the six subtests that contributes to the overall score would be likely to be affected; or the Woodcock-Johnson III (Woodcock, McGrew, Schrank, & Mather, 2001, 2007), on which one seventh of the tests would be directly affected; or the Reynolds Intellectual Assessment Scales (Reynolds & Kamphaus, 2003), on which none of the four subtests would be affected.

Writing Style

As Sattler importantly noted, "Attend carefully to grammar and writing style" (2008, p. 735). In general, reports should use fairly short sentences. Allyn (2012) provides a detailed discussion of the elements of attitude, tone, style, and voice for clear communication in psychological report writing. She advocates for a narrative approach to writing assessment report and suggests

> … an assessment report can be viewed as a story. You will write about a series of happenings: referral questions, history, interviews with concerned parties, prior assessments, current testing, results, and recommendations … style begins in the sentence and grows out of the snowball effect by which sentences become paragraphs. No sentence can hitch along just for the ride in order to fill space; each must contribute to the overall sense and impact of the whole. (pp. 33–34)

In addition, the sixth edition of the *Publication Manual of the American Psychological Association* (American Psychological Association, 2010) offers, in addition to technical details needed for submitting articles for publication, two valuable chapters, "Writing Clearly and Concisely" and "The Mechanics of Style," both of which provide clear and concise writing guidance for psychological reports.

Avoiding Abbreviations and Jargon

As a general principle, school psychologists should strive to "[c]ommunicate clearly, and do not include unnecessary technical material in the report" (Sattler, 2008, p. 731). To achieve this goal, it is best not to get too folksy in assessment reports. For example, language such as "the subtests hung together" should not be used since only assessment insiders can guess what that slang expression implies. The most important readers (parents) may not know what a confidence interval is, may have no concept of a percentile rank, and probably will not appreciate the importance of a standard error of measurement. In assessment reports, such terms should be used sparingly and only with clear definitions.

To ensure the valuable contributions of parents, teachers, and students to program planning, evaluation results must be as clear as possible. Jargon and statistics, if used, must be defined very clearly. Avoid as much as possible abbreviations, acronyms, and jargon.

Abbreviations and local names are especially confusing when an assessment report is read outside the school in which the evaluation was conducted. If the child moves to another state, readers may not know that an ARD is an Admission, Review, and Dismissal meeting, known in most places as an Individualized Education Program (IEP) team meeting. The first time an abbreviation or acronym in used in a report, the full term should be spelled out with the abbreviation in parentheses.

Some terms will need to be explained. Readers in another district will not know whether "Anne's transfer from Happy Hollow to Sunnyvale" was a normal progression from the district elementary school to the district middle school or an emergency placement in a secure, residential facility. The consulting neuropsychologist probably does not know whether the Special Learning Individualization Program is designed for children with severe disabilities or for gifted children.

Jargon, in the case of assessment reports, is probably best defined as the technical terminology or characteristic idioms of testing, psychology, or special education. Common examples of jargon include the unexplained insertion of such terms as "double-deficit," "fluid reasoning," or "phonemic awareness," or references to details of neuroanatomy that do not contribute to an understanding of the examinee.

Readers of assessment reports may not be familiar with terminology that school psychologists know and use. Specific subtest names such as "Matrices" or "Similarities" should not be mentioned without explaining and describing the subtests. If such specific material about a test is to be included, it is often best practice to include with the report an appendix with helpful descriptions of the tests and subtests. A file of test descriptions can be copied and pasted into reports. The practices of providing an appendix describing test score statistics, descriptions of tests and subtests, and other technical information are not excuses from explaining things in the narrative of the report.

Decide whether specifics are necessary and relevant to the understanding of the report itself. Does the material add something so meaningful and specific that is must be included? Does the description of any of the technical aspects of a test help the reader understand the results?

Writing for the Audience

One of the greatest challenges in writing evaluation reports is the audience for whom the school psychologist is writing. These include parents and students, classroom and special education teachers, administrators, psychologists, and therapists and physicians of various specialties. Their needs and background knowledge are widely varied. Because of the often contradictory demands of these various readers, be cognizant of, and sensitive to, the readers of their reports.

For example, an examinee's parent might have dropped out of high school, might have a PhD in statistics, or might have worked for a decade as a special education attorney. The levels of interest and background knowledge among classroom teachers vary widely. Some veterans of multiple evaluation team meetings may be extremely sophisticated about assessment. Other staff may

have little relevant knowledge or interest and may bring a significant fund of misinformation to the meeting. Parents, teachers, and the students themselves make important contributions to the evaluation and they will be among those who are called upon to implement the interventions the school psychologist or a team might give, so they must be included in the process. Without clarity, parents cannot provide useful or complete information to support answering the referral question, and if they cannot understand results, they will have difficulty supporting recommendations and IEPs.

Clarity in reporting may be necessary to disabuse participants of misconceptions as much as to provide correct information. Therapists and physicians, as well as many independent evaluators, may be unfamiliar with school settings and have tendencies to both misunderstand what reasonable interventions are possible for a school and offer recommendations that are less than helpful.

Many special education teachers quote the assessment report in the IEP to demonstrate the student's current level of functioning. In this case, clear narrative regarding the evaluation results may be helpful and the use of specific test scores should be discouraged. IEP authors appreciate clear statements.

A good practice is to provide an appendix with complete tables of scores with standard scores, confidence bands, and percentile ranks. In those tables, all the technical information can be provided that an expert might demand without overburdening other readers with those details. This practice also allows narratives to be written without citing every subtest score.

The persons responsible for allocating school resources need clear, persuasive information on which to base their decisions. For example, assessment results often support (or negate) recommendations for serious and expensive decisions such as out-of-district placements, one-to-one paraprofessional support, and even suspension or expulsion from school. Administrators may prefer strong statements and recommendations in these cases. If identification of a disability is being argued for in spite of fairly high test scores or fairly good class grades, then the argument must be clear, strong, and based on objective information.

Organization of Reports

Regarding what might reasonably be included in a school psychologist's report, NASP (2010b) Standard II.4.3 states that "[s]chool psychologists include only documented and relevant information from reliable sources in school psychological records." Determine the organization and sequence of information in an assessment report; that is, whether to place information in the text or in appendices, and whether to use narrative or tabular presentations. There is no single best practice. Although a boilerplate report outline can be set up, be prepared to alter it to meet the demands of a particular evaluation.

The final responsibility for what goes into any report and the sequence of that information rests with the individual writer. Always write in ways that are comfortable. For example, one of this chapter's authors discovered that, when he shared his reports with many special education teams or parents, often the readers would jump quickly to the "Summary" section, because that was the point that they really felt was most important and relevant for them. To aid those readers, the report format was reordered, with the "Summary of Findings" coming very early in the report, often immediately after the "Reason for Referral" section. In this way the two areas ("Reason for Referral" and "Summary") were very closely connected.

Basic Elements for Effective Report Writing

Different sources provide different opinions about what should be included in any assessment report (e.g., Bradley-Johnson & Johnson, 1998; Lichtenberger, Mather, Kaufman, & Kaufman, 2004; Mather & Jaffe, 2011; Sattler, 2008). However, there does seem to be some agreement that a well written report should include, to some extent, and in varying sequence, the following elements (we have added specific comments to some, but not all points).

Identifying Information

As a minimum, the examinee's name and birth date, the dates of the evaluation, and the date of the report should be listed. Age, grade placement, parents' names and addresses, teacher's name, and school name could also be listed. Do not use abbreviations, such as DOB, CA, DOE, and DOR. This section may also include a brief statement of identifying characteristics, special or notable events surrounding the assessment, or any other information deemed crucial to understand the context of the evaluation and report before the reader moves on. The examiner and the examiner's role with the examinee may also be described here. The time between dates seen and the report date should be as short as possible. The best report in the world is of little use if it arrives after decisions have had to be made about the examinee.

Reason for Referral

Elicit genuine referral questions (not just issues) to be answered by the evaluation. Interviews and questionnaires are essential parts of a complete evaluation. "Referral questions are often a lost opportunity" (Farrall, 2012, p. 75). Try to extract explicit, potentially answerable referral questions from parents, teachers, therapists, and the student, and enter the questions into the "Referral" section so that the questions can be copied and pasted into a "Conclusions" or "Recommendations" section. Try to encourage questions that are definable, measurable, and relevant. This is key to connecting the purpose of the assessment, the report, and the probable educational outcomes. For example, a referral such as, "John is not doing well in class so I would like him evaluated," is not useful. However, if a referral notes that "John is doing his homework, passing it in, contributing in class, but failing tests and quizzes, so I would like him evaluated," then there is the basis for a much better referral question that allows tailoring the evaluation and results. Even better is "John is not fluent with oral reading and has problems decoding individual words. His comprehension seems adequate, but he has specific difficulty understanding word problems in math lessons. While his spelling is fine, he does have difficulty getting his thoughts on paper without individual help from the teacher to organize his work. I would like him evaluated."

Background Information

The NASP (2010b) professional ethics states that school psychologists should include only documented and relevant information from reliable sources in school psychological records (Standard II.4.3). Under this fairly broad topic are several important subtopics, including information about a child's family history; health and developmental milestones and issues; educational history, both past and present; previous evaluations; and behavioral history.

The depth of information reported will vary from student to student. In one case, it might unfortunately be essential to quote large portions of a previous evaluation report verbatim, but in another a one-sentence summary might be more than enough (especially when trying not to perpetuate misinformation). At times, there is so much history available on a particular student that to try to describe everything known would be confusing and too lengthy. Often, depending upon the age of the child being assessed and that child's history of involvement with special education, a cumulative file alone can run hundreds of pages. Sifting through all this information and determining what is and is not important can seem a daunting task. Simply reading through a file, no matter how conclusive and thorough it may seem, is usually not sufficient to fill in the information needed to report conclusively on the matters. Parent and teacher interviews are often added to the information gathering. History pertinent to the referral question or that has direct bearing on the circumstances of the testing, interpretation of results, or recommendations should always be described as concisely as possible. After completing a review and having determined what will be used in the report, some information should be provided about where, or from whom, the background information was obtained. Did it come from the file (and if so, be specific about the source and date and whenever possible, verify it), an extensive structured interview, a semistructured interview, or a phone conversation with a grandparent? When determining whether or not to include certain facts in a report, consider issues such as datedness and relevance.

Datedness. When gathering and then reporting on history, always balance the datedness of the information with the usefulness or importance of the information. For example, a lengthy recitation of a student's history may be important in an initial evaluation but may add little substance to a second or third reevaluation. If there is an older report, anybody can read it, including the reader of the assessment report. Sometimes simply referring to the place where historical information can be found might suffice. However, include any information that is needed to make sense of current findings and conclusions. For example, a long-ago history of serious otitis media might still be important for the assessment of a child with reading problems, but not for a child with weak math calculation skills. A family history of psychiatric problems might not have much bearing on the assessment of a well-adjusted child with an intellectual disability, but would be germane for a child referred for social and emotional issues. For some disabilities, such as autism and intellectual disability, early history, including the ages at which symptoms appeared, is essential for the diagnosis or identification. The key here is deciding what is pertinent to the referral question and evaluation, highlighting it to provide the important context for the interpretation of current results, and avoiding confusing the reader with unnecessary information.

In general, very old information may be less relevant to present concerns than newer information, but there are many exceptions to that idea. For example, a severe head injury in infancy might still be very important in

understanding the educational performance of a high school student.

Relevance and need to know. "Include only relevant information in the report; omit potentially damaging material not germane to the assessment" (Sattler, 2008, p. 717).

Family issues are always tricky for reports. Be sure not to break confidences, not to upset families unnecessarily, not to omit information that is essential for understanding the student's needs, and not to be misled by biased reports. Each case is a unique problem. A report that adequately describes a child's entire situation as a student is much more than test scores. If the information is recorded elsewhere, refer the reader to those sources. Sometimes just summarizing by writing that there are issues in whatever category applies and explaining the effect on the child without specifying the actual events is all that is needed. Provide enough information to help staff understand and do what the child needs and enough to support the recommendations. For example, there may be a good reason the child cannot do homework at home. It might not be necessary to tell what the reason is, but it is necessary to help teachers understand that the inability is legitimate. Before writing the report, it is best practice to talk with the family, even if by telephone. It is not possible to always know what is private.

Consider the impact on the child as well. Is there a risk of embarrassing information being leaked? Confidentiality in schools is not what it should be. Is there information that might prejudice staff against the child or the family? It does not, for example, help a student's cause to quote sarcastic comments about a teacher. Also, be aware of state laws regarding confidentiality of certain types of information.

Previous Evaluations and Results

Be careful to fact check what is being put into a report. Simply copying what someone else has written in prior reports is often not useful (writers may make mistakes) and can, at times, lead to total misinformation. The false assignment of a diagnosis could lead to inappropriate and ineffective services for the child. An integrated history emphasizing relevant information can sometimes be as helpful as any new evaluation findings, but gather this historical information carefully and skeptically.

Behavioral Observations

There are two reasons for reporting the examinee's behavior during evaluation sessions. First, some behaviors might offer clues about the examinee's personality or learning difficulties and might even suggest appropriate interventions. A second reason for describing test behaviors is, of course, that some behaviors may affect test scores, requiring the evaluator to explain any likely threat to validity. Observations of any behaviors, attitudes, response styles, or mannerisms that may affect any specific test responses or findings should be reported. Report genuinely germane observations from test sessions, but be clear that behavior in a test session may be unique to that test session and may never be seen in any other context.

The frequency of a behavior also needs to be compared to what is typical of children of the same age in test sessions. This judgment will depend largely on the school psychologist's experience except in rare instances, such as when using the WISC-IV Integrated (Wechsler et al., 2004), which includes norms for base rates for "I don't know" responses, no responses, self-corrections, and other behaviors on some of the Integrated subtests.

Whenever describing test behaviors that might affect test scores (e.g., slow responding, difficulty understanding questions, a tendency to drop pencils and test materials on the floor, refusals to elaborate minimal responses, hearing or vision problems, and problems with attention and distractibility), explain the probable effect on test scores or the reason for asserting that "the test scores are reasonably valid indications of the child's current educational functioning levels." Sometimes it is important to explain that the scores do not reflect the child's potential, but do reflect current functioning levels because the same behaviors seen in the test session have also been observed to interfere with classroom performance. If there is a reason to question a score or add context, do so both in the text of the report and in any tables in which the score appears.

Assessment of the Validity of Results and Test Conditions

Pay close attention to observations. If citing the student's boredom or fatigue, then explain why shorter test sessions were not used. If describing situations that suggest that an evaluation may have been compromised, then explain if the evaluation in whole or in part holds validity.

Typically, all test scores should be reported so that they may be used as the basis for reference by future readers or evaluators. However, best practice dictates that if it is believed that a score is not accurate, or for some reason is not reflective of the child's actual ability (or whatever construct was measured), this belief must be acknowledged and the invalid score not reported.

Description of Assessment Materials

To help the reader of assessment reports understand the assessment, it certainly helps to inform the reader about the tests and procedures used for evaluation. Providing the specific names, versions, editions, and norms of the components of the assessment battery, and providing an appendix that has full descriptions of the tests, may be considered best practice. This approach provides full disclosure to the parent, school, and others of how the assessment was conducted. Omitting the form (e.g., A or B) of a test may have an impact on future retesting. If a child has skipped or repeated a grade, then it is especially important to specify age-based or grade-based norms. (Best practice would be to report scores by both sets of norms if they are provided.)

There should be total agreement between any sources listed in this section and any references made to specific tests in the body of the report. A test report that lists procedures used with no mention of results, or that provides results from a test not listed as administered, is considered suspect. Suspicious readers search for evidence that parts of a report were copied and pasted from a report on some other student.

Examiners must use the best and most up-to date-instruments available when important decisions, such as eligibility for services, are at stake. The Flynn Effect (e.g., Flynn, 2007; Kaufman, 2010) dictates that recently normed tests of cognitive abilities must be used because older norms may yield scores that are not only inflated, but inflated to different degrees across various cognitive abilities. The pattern of norm changes over time is more complex for tests of academic achievement.

The one exception is the rare case in which the new edition of a test is clearly inferior in some important respect (e.g., norming sample, number of subtests, or test content) to the previous edition. In such cases, another recent test must be used that accomplishes the same purpose or, if there is no such test, then the older edition should be used with a very clear explanation of the reason. Meanwhile, the search for a better test must continue.

Results and Interpretation

It is best to report test scores in the past tense to emphasize the fact that they are the scores the student happened to earn that day. The scores would probably have been different on a different day. For example, Arnold's Full Scale IQ on the WISC-IV (Wechsler, 2003) *was* 87 (percentile rank 19) last Tuesday, but it is not known that his intellectual ability *is* in the 19th percentile. Guidepost words can help the reader navigate findings in an assessment report. For example, use words and phrases such as *also, similarly, but, however, in contrast to,* and *on the other hand* to guide the reader. For example, it can be written that one score was higher or lower than another, not just that the scores were different.

Inferences should be drawn with appropriate caution in assessment reports. For example, a low score on the WISC-IV Verbal Comprehension Index might suggest a weakness in oral language (although there are many other possibilities). Jorja's performance on the Perceptual Reasoning Index does not "suggest" that her standard score was 117. Valid or not, her score simply was 117 (108–123).

Assessment results should include detailed descriptions of actual skills, gaps, strengths, and weaknesses. It is useless to print a table of test scores and then repeat the same scores in words as if simply reading the table aloud. "Interpret the meaning and implications of a child's scores, rather than simply citing test names and scores" (Sattler, 2008, p. 723). Here is an example of reporting scores that provides the reader with almost no information about a student's actual performance (and nothing beyond the information in the table of test scores): Mort scored 73 for reading. His reading score was below average. Mort scored 75 for written language. His written language score was below average. Mort scored 72 for math. His math score was below average. Mort scored 77 for oral language. His oral language score was below average.

A more helpful explanation of these scores might look like this: Mort achieved a standard score of 73 in the broad area of reading, which falls in the below average range. This score was based on very poor performance in reading words (Word Reading) and sounding out nonsense words (Pseudoword Decoding) with many errors on vowel sounds, in contrast to average Reading Comprehension. Mort had difficulty reading and decoding individual words, but he was able to comprehend meaning from longer passages.

While attention should be paid to the referral questions (such as the child's level of skill in math computation), with results described as they relate specifically, often other important and unexpected issues (e.g., suicidal ideation) emerge. These findings should

not be ignored, but should be reported in the context of understanding the student as a whole.

Test Scores

It is best to cite only scores that convey useful information about the examinee's performance, such as standard scores, scaled scores, T scores, percentile ranks, stanines, and Relative Proficiency Index scores. There is no reason to report scores that are used only by the evaluator, such as raw scores, sums of scaled scores, or W scores.

There are a number of different formats in which results could be presented and discussed. It is usually necessary to include scores somewhere in the report (however, see Dumont, 2011, for a largely number-free sample report). Some include scores in the narrative. Others prefer putting them in an addendum to the report. A few do both, collecting all scores in an appended table that includes any necessary technical footnotes and copying and pasting parts of the table into relevant sections of the text. Test scores should always be reported with some brief explanation of what the scores mean and how they are derived. For example, the first time mentioning a percentile rank in a report (which may be in the history section), add a footnote such as, "Percentile ranks tell what percentage of other same-age students scored the same as or lower than Keesha. For example, a percentile rank of 36 would mean that Keesha scored as high as or higher than 36% of students her age and lower than the other 64%." Similarly, a footnote to the first citation of a confidence interval may read: "Even on the very best tests, scores can never be perfectly reliable. This interval shows how much scores are likely to vary randomly 95% of the time." Another example footnote is, "A 'statistically significant' difference between scores is one that is too large to occur just by random variation more than, for instance, 5 times in 100." And another is, "Even significant differences may not be unusual. Human abilities vary. In this report, an 'uncommon' difference is a significant difference so large that fewer than 10% of persons taking the test would show such a large difference." If a description of all the test statistics used is appended, then the reader can be referred to that appendix.

A statistically significant difference that is not uncommon may still be important, but a difference that is not significant should not be treated as a difference at all. A nonsignificant difference, by definition, could have occurred by pure chance. It is not good practice to write,

"There was a nonsignificant difference between ..." When discussing significant differences, indicate which is the higher score.

Many school psychologists use a test-by-test presentation of findings, building to a conclusion that integrates the commonalties or agreement in findings across tests. Others may prefer to use an approach that presents more general results based on specific areas of functioning that may be assessed with multiple procedures (e.g., cognitive versus social–emotional functions). While individual preferences are often a matter of training in writing assessment reports, IDEA (§ 300.304) does have language specifying the variety and appropriateness of tests used and the requirements that results describe what the child can do academically, developmentally, and functionally, and that results provide information that assists in determining the educational needs of the child. Best practice would suggest that a test-by-test presentation of results would best demonstrate that these criteria are met.

Most test authors and publishers provide somewhere in the test manual an explanation of how a test score might be described narratively. Include these descriptions in reports. Using narrative descriptions allows the report to be free of some of the technical jargon that so often confuses the lay audience. However, caution must also be used. Since test authors or publishers can arbitrarily choose whatever narratives they wish for their tests, narratives from one test do not always align with narratives from another test. The arbitrarily chosen labels applied to a test's results can lead to problems. While the various Wechsler Intelligence Scales (e.g., Wechsler, 2003) currently utilize the narrative term "average" for scores from 90 to 109, the Woodcock-Johnson III (Woodcock et al., 2001, 2007) extends that same narrative label to scores of 90–110. The Kaufman Assessment Battery for Children-Second Edition (Kaufman & Kaufman, 2004) and—especially confusingly—the Wechsler Individual Achievement Test-Third Edition (WIAT-III; Pearson, 2009) refer to scores of 85–115 as "average." Readers of the report might reasonably wonder why the school psychologist was concerned about average achievement (WIAT-III, 85) and average ability (WISC-IV Full Scale IQ, 109) on two current Wechsler instruments.

If the publisher's narrative labels are being used for a test, then identify for the reader (maybe in a footnote or at least in the appendix) exactly what the narrative labels are. If the results for various tests that utilize differing narrative labels are being reported, then strongly consider (following the recommendations of Kamphaus, 2001) choosing one set of labels, explaining it, and sticking to it for all tests with repeated reminders that classification labels are being used that differ from those supplied by the publisher. If all the various labeling schemes of the different publishers are being used, then keep reminding the reader that the same score may have different labels on different tests.

"Be extremely cautious in making interpretations based on a limited sample of behavior" (Sattler, 2008, p. 718). Some readers may not realize that observations and a child's performance on a standardized test are being reported, which is not necessarily representative of the child's performance in the classroom, ability to do homework at the kitchen table, or even test performance at another time of day. School psychologists should be careful to describe their observations and interpretations in this context. These observations and interpretations are a slice-of-time measure and how findings may or may not be generalized to other situations should be carefully stated.

Summary/Conclusions/Recommendations

Here, results of the evaluation described in the previous section should be distilled into their most important details and described in terms of the answers to the referral questions. New information should not be introduced here. If there is something to add, then go back and add it to the body of the report. It may be difficult to strike a balance between too much restatement of the details of the report and too little reporting of the most salient details. Summary statements about levels of ability, behavioral observations, validity of scores, and generalizability to other aspects of the student's life and skills may strike the best balance. Ask what is the essential information readers should take from the report.

Recommendations

As Sattler notes, "Make recommendations carefully, using all available sources of information" (2008, p. 730). Concrete recommendations, individually planned for the student based upon the information obtained by an evaluation, are an important goal of the evaluation. Stock, boilerplate recommendations are not much help. A useful evaluation with recommendations does not cost much more than a useless one without recommendations. Mather and Jaffe (2004) provide useful forms, sample reports, specific and practical recommendations, and detailed explanations of teaching strategies that evaluators can use in their reports. To make recommendations more persuasive, better understood, and more likely to be reasonable, provide a rationale for each recommendation and consider preceding them with "because" statements, such as "Because Samantha's low average Verbal Comprehension score was significantly and uncommonly lower than her high average Perceptual Reasoning score, her Oral Language score was significantly lower than her Comprehensive Achievement Composite, and her Listening Comprehension (lower extreme) was significantly lower than her Reading Comprehension (below average), the team should consider referring her for a speech and language evaluation to further investigate concerns with language comprehension and expression."

Regardless of how it is decided to offer recommendations, best practice demands that the evaluation process must produce useful recommendations. Some administrators hold to the mistaken belief that recommendations should not be permitted in reports or even in meetings because the school district would be held liable for following all recommendations made by all evaluators. First, this idea is not found anywhere in the federal regulations and rules for IDEA. Second, it is logically impossible. Suppose one evaluator recommends that the child be taken out of regular class for 90 minutes a day of intensive, individual, Orton-Gillingham reading instruction. Another evaluator on the team insists that the child must be sent to a private, special education boarding school. A third evaluator is adamant that the child must have full inclusion with whole language reading instruction, never setting foot outside the regular classroom and never working in a group of fewer than five children. Obviously, the school cannot possibly follow the three sets of mutually exclusive recommendations. Therefore, it is equally obvious that the school cannot be required to follow any of them.

Unless there is a specific reason for using only a particular brand-name program, indicate clearly that examples are simply being given. If a program is not familiar to the report author then it is best not to recommend it. Since the results from other evaluators may not be known until the report is presented in a team meeting, recommendations may best be viewed and presented as flexible and fluid. For example, a school psychologist, speech and language pathologist, and occupational therapist may all present reports that overlap to some degree but create a database of student information from which specific and noncontradictory recommendations can be created. It is helpful to disseminate reports among all the evaluators prior to

the IEP meeting to compare results, and it is best practice, providing that this does not involve a formal process that excludes parents. Technically, the assessment report could be considered a draft (and only one piece of a body of evidence used to develop the educational plan) until it is reviewed by the parents and the rest of the school team. Occasionally, such review will require corrections or additions to the original report. The revised report must show both report dates, must have a new title indicating it is a revision, and must explain the revision and the reason for it.

We believe very strongly that recommendations should be offered by at least one of these three ways. The first recommendation is that the evaluator could perform a sufficiently comprehensive evaluation (or has the chance to review prior to writing the report a sufficiently comprehensive set of concurrent evaluations) to permit the evaluator to provide useful recommendations in the evaluation report. However, for example, if an evaluator has been permitted to do only a cognitive assessment and has never heard the child read and has not even seen a concurrent reading evaluation, then he or she probably cannot, and therefore should not, offer anything very useful about reading instruction. Similarly, if an evaluator has assessed only reading and not phonological awareness, listening comprehension, oral vocabulary, other verbal abilities, rapid naming, and various aspects of memory, then the evaluator's ability to offer useful recommendations is severely constrained. Also, an evaluator needs to know something about, for example, reading and reading instruction if the evaluator is to have much to say about reading. Do not make recommendations outside an area of competence without first seeking advice and counsel from those who do possess such knowledge. A brief consultation with a reading specialist on methods of remediating decoding weaknesses, for example, will most likely lead to solid and pragmatic recommendations. In addition to the risk of the evaluator not having access to sufficient information about the child before writing the report, there is also the problem that the people who will have to carry out the recommended activities may not be thrilled to have such demands imposed on them by the consultant who has worked with the student for a few hours, disappeared, and issued a long series of instructions. In these situations, it is of paramount importance to offer clear recommendations, or perhaps a range of potential recommendations, for consideration by other team members.

The second recommendation is that many evaluators could work collaboratively in the meeting with parents, teachers, specialists, and administrators to cooperatively develop a comprehensive and detailed set of recommendations based on all of the information that has become available. This working-group approach usually leads to a rich discussion of both implications of results and recommendations, but there is the potential for valuable insights to be lost. It is absolutely essential that the recommendations be recorded in specific detail, that they be preserved where they will remain accessible, and that they are incorporated completely in the meeting minutes and/or the Written Prior Notice and in the IEP.

The third recommendation is that some evaluators could write a preliminary report for the meeting and a final report based on the information revealed and the recommendations developed in the meeting. This method tends to yield a better report, and recommendations can be explicitly attributed to the persons who offered them, who may be the same persons who will be implementing them. The disadvantages to this approach are that the second report may not be perceived as fully independent, that the second report may not be distributed and preserved, and that, absent a deadline, the second report may not be written quickly or at all.

Mallin, Beimcik, and Hopfner (2012) found that teachers tend to prefer highly specific recommendations in reports for student planning purposes and suggest "the school psychologist should feel comfortable in providing detailed recommendations" (p. 258). With this in mind, it is valuable, if not best practice, to include with these recommendations the rationales for them. An evaluator or other team member simply stating that some accommodation or method of special instruction "should" be used is not very persuasive.

SUMMARY

Overall, the successful writing of assessment reports does not have to be daunting or an anxiety-provoking task. Efficient and effective report writing begins well before the actual assessment process, with the clarification of the referral question, careful consideration of assessment materials, review and evaluation of pertinent history and prior testing, and includes close attention of the student's behavior and comments throughout the assessment process. These are the necessary components for the context of a useful report.

Clear and careful reporting of scores in both narrative and tabular formats, interpretation of results that clearly relate to referral questions, and sensitivity to the need for recommendations that connect results to practical interventions complete the process. Remember that templates, formulaic interpretations, and boilerplate language are never a substitute for individualized clinical judgment.

Allyn's (2012) advice should be followed on treating a report as a narrative and "knowing how and where your report begins, what you wish to cover in the middle, and how you will tie it off at the end.... . Say all that needs to be said—no more, no less" (pp. 33–34). When all is said and done, best practice is to treat every assessment report as the most important document ever created by a school psychologist.

REFERENCES

Allyn, J. B. (2012). *Writing to clients and referring professionals about psychological assessment results*. New York, NY: Routledge.

American Psychological Association. (2010). *Publication manual of the American Psychological Association* (6th ed., 2nd printing). Washington, DC: Author.

Assistance to States for the Education of Children With Disabilities and Preschool Grants for Children With Disabilities, 34 CFR Parts 300 and 301. (IDEA Final Regulations, August 14, 2006). Retrieved from http://idea.ed.gov/download/finalregulations.pdf

Bradley-Johnson, S., & Johnson, C. M. (1998). *A handbook for writing psychoeducational reports*. Austin, TX: PRO-ED.

Brenner, E. (2003). Consumer-focused psychological assessment. *Professional Psychology: Research and Practice, 34*, (pp. 240–247).

Castillo, J. M., Curtis, M. J., & Gelley, C. (2012, June). School psychology 2010—Part 2: School psychologists' professional practices and implications for the field. *Communiqué, 40*(8), Retrieved from http://www.nasponline.org/publications/cq/40/8/school-psychology-demographics-2.aspx

Dumont, R. (2011). ADHD: To be or not to be? That was the question. In N. Mather & L. E. Jaffe (Eds.), *Comprehensive evaluations: Case reports for psychologists, diagnosticians, and special educators* (pp. 450–462). New York, NY: Wiley.

Elliott, C. D. (2007). *Differential Ability Scales-Second edition*. San Antonio, TX: The Psychological Corporation.

Farrall, M. L. (2012). *Reading assessment: Linking language, literacy, and cognition*. New York, NY: Wiley.

Flynn, J. R. (2007). *What is intelligence? Beyond the Flynn Effect*. New York, NY: Cambridge University Press.

Harvey, V. S. (2006). Variables affecting the clarity of psychological reports. *Journal of Clinical Psychology, 62*, 5–18.

Kamphaus, R. W. (2001). *Clinical assessment of child and adolescent intelligence* (2nd ed.). Boston, MA: Allyn & Bacon.

Kaufman, A. S. (2010). "In what way are apples and oranges alike?" A critique of Flynn's interpretation of the Flynn Effect. *Journal of Psychoeducational Assessment, 28*, 382–398. doi:10.1177/0734282910373346

Kaufman, A. S., & Kaufman, N. L. (2004). *Kaufman Assessment Battery for Children-Second edition*. Circle Pines, MN: American Guidance Service.

Lichtenberger, E. O., Mather, N., Kaufman, N. L., & Kaufman, A. S. (2004). *Essentials of assessment report writing*. New York, NY: Wiley.

Mallin, B., Beimcik, J., & Hopfner, L. (2012). Teacher ratings of three school psychology report recommendation styles. *Canadian Journal of School Psychology, 27,* 258–273. doi:10.1177/0829573512449999

Mather, N., & Jaffe, L. E. (2004). *Woodcock-Johnson III: Reports, recommendations, and strategies.* New York, NY: Wiley.

Mather, N., & Jaffe, L. E. (Eds.). (2011). *Comprehensive evaluations: Case reports for psychologists, diagnosticians, and special educators.* New York, NY: Wiley.

National Association of School Psychologists. (2010a). *Model for comprehensive and integrated school psychological services.* Bethesda, MD: Author. Retrieved from http://www.nasponline.org/standards/2010standards/2_PracticeModel.pdf

National Association of School Psychologists (NASP). (2010b). *Principles for professional ethics.* Bethesda, MD: Author. Retrieved from http://www.nasponline.org/standards/2010standards.aspx

Office for Civil Rights. (n.d.). *Frequently asked questions about Section 504 and the education of children with disabilities.* Washington, DC: Author. Retrieved from http://www2.ed.gov/about/offices/list/ocr/504faq.html

Pearson. (2009). *Wechsler Individual Achievement Test-Third edition.* San Antonio, TX: Author.

Reynolds, C. R., & Kamphaus, R. W. (2003). *Reynolds Intellectual Assessment Scales.* Lutz, FL: Psychological Assessment Resources.

Sattler, J. M. (2008). *Assessment of children: Cognitive foundations* (5th ed.). La Mesa, CA: Sattler.

Walrath, R. (2001). Psychological assessment. In S. Cullari (Ed.), *Counseling and psychotherapy: A practical guidebook* (pp. 217–239). Boston, MA: Allyn & Bacon.

Wechsler, D. (2003). *Wechsler Intelligence Scale for Children-Fourth edition.* San Antonio, TX: The Psychological Corporation.

Wechsler, D., Kaplan, E., Fein, D., Kramer, J., Morris, R., Delis, D., & Maerlender, A. (2004). *Wechsler Intelligence Scale for Children-Fourth edition: Integrated.* San Antonio, TX: The Psychological Corporation.

Weiner, J., & Costaris, L. (2012). Teaching psychological report writing: Content and process. *Canadian Journal of School Psychology, 27,* 119–135. doi:10.1177/0829573511418484

Willis, J. O. (2011). Foreword. In N. Mather & L. E. Jaffe (Eds.), *Comprehensive evaluations: Case reports for psychologists, diagnosticians, and special educators* (pp. xix–xxii). New York, NY: Wiley.

Woodcock, R. W., McGrew, K. S., Schrank, F. A., & Mather, N. (2001, 2007). *Woodcock-Johnson III Normative Update.* Rolling Meadows, IL: Riverside.

Section 3
Consultation and Collaboration

Best Practices in School Consultation

William P. Erchul
Arizona State University
Hannah L. Young
Alfred University

OVERVIEW

Reschly (1976) famously posed the query, is consultation in school psychology "frenzied, faddish, or fundamental?" (p. 105). This question came at a time when consultation was evolving and its identity and definition within school psychology were far less clear than today. Consultation is indeed fundamental to school psychology, and a clear testament to this is the listing of Consultation and Collaboration as a separate domain in the National Association of School Psychologists (NASP) *Model for Comprehensive and Integrated School Psychological Services* (NASP, 2010) with the statement that it reflects "practices that permeate all aspects of service delivery" (p. 2). Furthermore, the practice of school consultation exemplifies problem solving (Erchul & Martens, 2010), and general problem solving constitutes one major unifying theme of this edition of *Best Practices*. Another theme, multitiered systems of support, is frequently initiated and sustained through the consultative practices described in this chapter and in others found in this section of *Best Practices*.

Zins and Erchul (2002) define consultation as

a method of providing preventively oriented psychological and educational services in which consultants and consultees form cooperative partnerships and engage in a reciprocal, systematic problem-solving process guided by ecobehavioral principles. The goal is to enhance and empower consultee systems, thereby promoting clients' well-being and performance. (p. 626)

More specifically, Erchul and Martens (2010) define school consultation as

a process for providing psychological and educational services in which a specialist (consultant) works cooperatively with a staff member (consultee) to improve the learning and adjustment of a student (client) or group of students. During face-to-face interactions, the consultant helps the consultee through systematic problem solving, social influence, and professional support. In turn, the consultee helps the client(s) through selecting and implementing effective school-based interventions. In all cases, school consultation serves a remedial function and has the potential to serve a preventive function. (pp. 12–13)

The research base that informs the practice of school consultation has grown through the years despite the inherent difficulties in undertaking such investigations and the methodological problems with studies that have been conducted (Erchul & Sheridan, 2014). Despite these shortcomings, several meta-analyses and literature reviews examining consultation (e.g., Reddy, Barboza-Whitehead, Files, & Rubel, 2000; Sheridan, Welch, & Orme, 1996) provide support for its effectiveness. Sheridan et al. (1996), for example, conducted a comprehensive analysis of 46 school consultation outcome studies published between 1985 and 1995. They found that consultation produced some positive effect in 67% of the studies reviewed, while 28% were neutral and the remaining 5% were negative. They also noted that advances had been made in the use of experimental designs, multiple outcome measures, and attention to social validity. More recently, randomized control trials of consultation have begun to appear (e.g., Cappella et al., 2012; Fabiano et al., 2010), and these hold even greater promise for promoting consultation as an evidence-based practice in schools.

The primary purpose of this chapter is to delineate the fundamental best practices in school consultation. Although one may question the necessity of including a chapter in this edition of *Best Practices* that emphasizes the basics of school consultation, we believe that some school psychologists either may have forgotten, or may not readily see the relevance of, this content in the era of response-to-intervention (RTI) multitiered systems of support (Erchul, 2011). After offering several basic considerations of and prerequisite competencies for school consultation, we examine consultation in the contemporary context of RTI and problem-solving teams. We then offer some best practices and explore multicultural considerations and the evaluation of effectiveness in school consultation.

BASIC CONSIDERATIONS

It remains a common practice to organize the literature of school consultation by model, and here we discuss three of the most common models of consultation used by school psychologists.

Major Models of Consultation

The three most common models are behavioral, mental health, and organizational or systems consultation. Other models, such as collaborative, conjoint, instructional, Adlerian, process, and rational–emotive, have been advanced, but they share many of the same basic characteristics and appear to be far more similar to than different from one another.

Behavioral Consultation

Behavioral consultation is based on theories of learning and behavioral psychology, although more recently ecological and social learning theories have been integrated into the model. Consequently, the terms *ecobehavioral* (Gutkin, 1993) and *ecological* (Gutkin & Curtis, 2009) consultation are sometimes used. Landmark texts on behavioral consultation (e.g., Bergan & Kratochwill, 1990), however, focus largely on proximal environmental variables and give far less consideration to more distal events and systems issues.

Behavioral consultation involves the well-known problem-solving steps that are conducted during structured interviews: problem identification, problem analysis, treatment implementation, and evaluation. In a variant of this model, conjoint behavioral consultation, Sheridan and Kratochwill (2008) proposed following the same steps but conducting the entire process with parents and teachers together. A key contribution of the behavioral consultation model is its adherence to methodological rigor and scientific precision. For this reason, the majority of the research in consultation has focused on this model (Sheridan et al., 1996). Behavioral consultation has been promoted as a viable means of delivering psychoeducational services in schools through RTI models (Kratochwill, Clements, & Kalymon, 2007).

Mental Health Consultation

Mental health consultation and its related focus on prevention has its roots in the work of community psychiatrist Gerald Caplan, as reflected in his classic text, *The Theory and Practice of Mental Health Consultation* (Caplan, 1970), and follow-up work (Caplan & Caplan, 1999). Caplan's name is virtually synonymous with mental health consultation, but almost all consultation models have been influenced by his pioneering work. He is also recognized for having introduced the public health terms of primary, secondary, and tertiary prevention into the field of mental health (Erchul, 2009).

Theoretically, mental health consultation has close ties with psychoanalytic theory, which accounts for its focus on more intrapersonal or person-centered issues. There are four types of mental health consultation: client-centered case consultation, consultee-centered case consultation, program-centered administrative consultation, and consultee-centered administrative consultation. As suggested by these terms, the four types differ depending on whether the focus is on individual cases or programs. Similarly, they vary in terms of their emphasis on prevention or remediation. For instance, consultee-centered case consultation is directed toward "elucidating and remedying the shortcomings in the consultee's professional functioning ... [so as to] ... lead to an improvement in the consultee's professional planning and action, and hopefully to improvement in the client" (Caplan & Caplan, 1999, p. 101). Though conceptually rich, mental health consultation lacks strong empirical support. Consultee-centered consultation (Knotek & Hylander, 2014) holds promise as an updated variation of mental health consultation, especially for school-based practice.

Organizational or Systems Consultation

There has been less written about consultation targeting large groups within an organization or the entire organization, either of which could be the focus of organizational or systems consultation. School psychologists utilize this approach when implementing programs dealing with school-wide positive behavior interventions and supports and RTI, as just two examples. Organizational or systems consultation has the advantage of allowing school psychologists to share their skills and knowledge with a larger number of individuals, thereby expanding their impact.

This consultation approach draws on several theoretical perspectives ranging from general systems theory (von Bertalanffy, 1968) to those specifically developed for use in human service organizations (e.g., French & Bell, 1999). It involves a planned, systematic process of introducing new principles and practices into an organization, with the goal of enhancing organizational effectiveness and competence. Consultants can use diagnostic, process, individual, and/or technostructural interventions to assist the organization, or they can apply consultative principles to implement new programs (Illback, 2014).

Fundamental Characteristics of School Consultation

This section, based on Zins and Erchul (2002), presents the major characteristics most models of consultation share. It does, however, primarily reflect ecobehavioral (Gutkin, 1993) or ecological consultation (Gutkin & Curtis, 2009), an orientation that is highly appropriate for school psychologists.

Preventive orientation: From its inception, consultation has had a dual focus. First, it provides a mechanism through which current problems can be identified, addressed, and resolved. Second, it is also intended to increase consultees' skills so that they can be proactive and more effectively solve similar problems in the future and/or prevent their reoccurrence. Likewise, consultation may serve to alter environmental variables and setting events that elicit and maintain an individual's problem behaviors or it can be focused on systems-level concerns. All in all, consultative procedures are intended to resolve current problems while at the same time preventing them from becoming more severe and keeping additional ones from arising. Consultation may also address larger scale issues. Unfortunately, consultation's potential and promise as a primary (i.e., universal/Tier 1) prevention strategy has yet to be fully realized; that is, most school consultation remains in the service of secondary (i.e., targeted/Tier 2) and tertiary (i.e., indicated/Tier 3) prevention (Zins, 1995).

Cooperative partnership: In contrast with the types of interactions that characterize many professional exchanges in which an expert primarily provides advice to another person or group without much involvement on his or her part, school psychologists and their consultees work together as partners to solve problems. Consequently, both are able to take advantage of the knowledge and expertise that each possesses, and thus address problems more skillfully. Consultants and consultees must establish relationships characterized by trust, openness, genuine regard, and a sharing of responsibilities and expertise, as the success of the entire process depends on the ability of participants to interact and communicate effectively.

Reciprocal interactions: The functioning of consultants, consultees, and clients results from the continuous and reciprocal interactions among behavioral, personal, and environmental factors. Throughout the process, participants influence, and are influenced by, one another. During the interpersonal exchanges of consultation, consultants and consultees draw from available power bases (e.g., positive expert, positive referent, direct informational) and exert influence on one another, and subsequently alter beliefs, attitudes, and behaviors (see Erchul, Grissom, Getty, & Bennett, 2014).

Ecological/systems perspective: Typical preservice training within school psychology has a person-centered focus. As a result, many school psychologists give minimal consideration to addressing systems-level concerns that may be affecting problems brought to consultation. However, a broader range of factors may contribute to the development and maintenance of problems; therefore, ecological/systems theories are applicable for school consultation (Illback, 2014). For example, larger factors such as school climate, federal laws, community support, and teachers' instructional style may influence student academic performance. Ecological/systems perspectives in particular have been used to expand on traditional approaches in behavioral and organizational consultation (Gutkin & Curtis, 2009).

Means of empowerment: Consultants explicitly recognize that consultees and consultee systems already possess or can readily develop most competencies necessary to deal with child- and system-related problems when they are given the right opportunities and knowledge of available resources (Rappoport, 1981). Thus, professionals who view their work as helping to empower others must change (i.e., expand) some of their long-standing beliefs about help giving as it applies to case-centered problem solving. Empowerment can take on many forms, but one view holds that consultants need to harness their own power and influence to enable consultees to become more powerful and influential in their work with clients (Erchul & Martens, 2010).

Enhancement of client well-being: Although consultation often focuses on improving consultees' skills and performance, changing their attitudes and behavior, or modifying some aspect of the environment, the ultimate beneficiary of the efforts is always intended to be the client. The client could be an individual student, a classroom of students, or the entire school organization (Zins & Erchul, 2002).

Systematic problem-solving process: Consultation mainly involves having participants engage in joint problem solving. During this process, they proceed through an orderly, systematic sequence of steps as discussed in the best practices section of this chapter. Although the steps logically proceed in sequence, there is some flexibility in the order in which they occur. It is essential for all school psychology consultants to be skilled in these techniques.

Other Process Issues

Several other aspects of the school consultation process deserve mention. First, issues discussed during consultation should remain confidential—or, more realistically, the limits of confidentiality should be carefully specified—if consultees are to develop a high level of trust in consultants. Interestingly, with the increasing adoption of RTI/multitiered systems of support models, confidentiality may well vanish as a core characteristic of school consultation because considerable information is now shared freely among participants (Erchul, 2011).

Second, consultants can be internal or external to the schools they serve. Most schools, for example, employ staff members (e.g., school psychologists) who may serve as consultants to general education teachers. In contrast, community agencies may employ consultants on a contractual basis to help the agencies deal with various organizational issues, implement new programs, and so on. Internal consultants tend to understand the workings of the organization and the people within it much better because of their more frequent interactions and continuous involvement. On the other hand, external consultants may have the advantage of being more objective in their perceptions of problems and may be less likely to feel pressured by organizational members to make certain decisions. School psychologists acting as consultants are often difficult to categorize as strictly

internal or external and thus may be best described as falling somewhere on an internal–external continuum (Alpert & Silverstein, 1985).

Prerequisite Competencies

To be effective, school psychology consultants must have very good interpersonal communication skills, in part because consultation requires using strategic communication to accomplish its goals (Erchul & Martens, 2010). Consultants need to be active listeners and utilize effective questioning techniques to extract necessary information from consultees in order to develop accurate conceptualizations of problems and persuade consultees to endorse and then implement evidence-based interventions. The establishment of warm, caring, understanding relationships is very important to the consultant role.

School psychology consultants also should have a keen sense of self-awareness, particularly with respect to feelings, beliefs, thoughts, and their potential impact on others. Thinking clearly about one's core values and theoretical bases is also helpful. Because a significant part of the consultation process hinges on interpersonal interactions, consultants must be aware of their interpersonal styles, biases, and values, and of how these can affect their perceptions of problems as well as influence consultees and the problem-solving process (Zins & Erchul, 2002).

A subtheme of self-awareness relates to cultural, racial, ethnic, socioeconomic, and gender issues. Effective school psychology consultants must be sensitive to these and other aspects of diversity, particularly because they exert a considerable impact on the communication process, development of trust, shared understanding, and overall relationship development (Ramirez, Lepage, Kratochwill, & Duffy, 1998). Also, multicultural factors can affect the power–authority dimension of consultation, especially when one participant is a member of a minority and the other is of a majority group (Ingraham, 2014). Owing to their significance, we return to other multicultural considerations later in the chapter.

Because of the importance placed on evidence-based interventions within contemporary school psychology (Kratochwill & Stoiber, 2002), consultants must possess an advanced knowledge of scientifically based interventions and how they can be implemented with maximum integrity within consultation. Fortunately, there are many helpful resources available (e.g., published meta-analyses, What Works Clearinghouse [http://ies.ed.gov/ncee/wwc], Intervention Central [http://www.interventioncentral.org], and Collaborative for Academic, Social, and Emotional Learning [http://www.casel.org]). The brainstorming of interventions—a time-honored practice within consultation—is no longer considered a best practice; today, consultants ideally assist consultees in selecting and implementing evidence-based interventions (Erchul & Martens, 2010).

Finally, given our emphasis on an ecological/systems orientation, effective school psychology consultants need to display an understanding of schools as organizations. School psychologists' training and daily practice often focus on the assessment and remediation of individual student-related problems, and consequently more global and macrolevel variables that exert significant influence do not receive adequate attention. Thus, "consultants need an understanding of the workplace [school] not only as a technological system but also as a complex social organization" (Gallessich, 1982, p. 5). School norms, values, philosophy, and organizational climate can greatly facilitate or impede the consultative process (Zins & Erchul, 2002).

Relationship to RTI/Multitiered Service Delivery

RTI and school consultation have several key elements in common, and yet at the same time the research on each of these two service delivery models rarely builds off the other (Erchul, 2011). The prevention of academic and behavioral difficulties for students, however, is of prime importance for those implementing both RTI and school-based consultation. The amelioration of problems before they manifest as well as the remediation of burgeoning problems are the basis for the promotion and development of both of these service delivery models. In addition, school consultation and RTI utilize problem solving or a problem-solving process in the delivery of the model. Using a problem-solving approach, both methods place importance on identifying the problem, analyzing data, implementing evidence-based interventions, and evaluating the effectiveness of the evidence-based interventions. Last, both emphasize the importance of implementing evidence-based interventions with high integrity and fidelity (Erchul, 2011; Reschly & Bergstrom, 2009).

Although there are several points of commonality for these two approaches, there are also several important differences. Among these, Erchul (2011) noted that the focus of these service delivery models is different, with RTI having primarily a student focus and consultation,

varying its focus between the system, classroom, consultee, and student. Some other differences include terminology within the fields (even when describing similar concepts), confidentiality within the process, and primary contributors to the two fields of research. Perhaps the two most striking differences, however, are that (a) RTI consistently involves systematic data collection, whereas the same cannot be said for consultation, and (b) unlike traditional consultation, RTI does not allow a consultee an individual choice to participate because evidence-based interventions must be implemented with integrity (Erchul, 2011).

There are several ways that school consultation can be used to enhance the process of RTI. Perhaps the most obvious is through the connection of RTI and behavioral (Bergan & Kratochwill, 1990) and instructional (Rosenfield, Gravois, & Silva, 2014) consultation models. These specific school consultation models are often implemented within the RTI framework through the use of problem-solving teams (Reschly & Bergstrom, 2009). Because the RTI approach is largely a team-based approach, the group consultation and prereferral intervention team literature could potentially help school personnel improve the RTI process by placing importance on best practices in group dynamics or group functioning (Erchul, 2011).

Team-Based Consultation

In addition to the traditional consultation dyadic structure (i.e., consultant and consultee) or triadic structure (e.g., conjoint behavioral consultation, with consultant, consultee, and parent), consultation can also be a service delivery model used with larger teams. Prereferral intervention teams were the first widely used team-based consultation service delivery models (Graden, Casey, & Bonstrom, 1985; Graden, Casey, & Christenson, 1985). Prereferral intervention teams were developed to help teachers develop, implement, and document the effectiveness of interventions in the general education setting in order to help teachers teach students who have academic or behavioral difficulties and to prevent similar problems in the future.

Team-based consultation approaches vary in composition, model of consultation utilized, and even in the name used to characterize the teams. However, they are founded in consultation theory and have prevention as a core goal. Over the years, as special education laws have evolved and new regulations have been adopted, problem-solving teams have been used to implement RTI. Although founded in the same basic consultation principles, these teams usually adopt a behavioral consultation perspective and place importance on data-based decision making (Burns, Wiley, & Viglietta, 2008).

Though membership can vary, team-based consultation involves a multidisciplinary team consisting of general and special education teachers, school counselors, social workers, specialists (e.g., speech, occupational therapy, physical therapy), administrators, parents, and school psychologists. School psychologists often play a key role, as they are uniquely trained in consultation and assessment. The advantage of the multidisciplinary structure is that members bring unique training experiences and professional perspectives to bear on the problems at hand. In order to be effective, teams must be trained in consultation principles (i.e., indirect service delivery, collaboration, ecological/systems perspective) as well as the importance of following a specific problem-solving model (Fuchs & Fuchs, 1989). Although the specific problem-solving models and stages may vary, it is important for the teams to spend time accurately identifying problems, utilize data to analyze problems, develop or select interventions, monitor the effectiveness of those interventions, and adjust interventions when needed.

BEST PRACTICES IN SCHOOL CONSULTATION

"Problem solving is the essence of consultation" (Zins & Erchul, 2002, p. 631). Consultation therefore incorporates a series of steps, including relationship development and identification and analysis of the problem; intervention development/selection; intervention implementation; assessment of intervention effectiveness; and planning for generalization, maintenance, and follow-up (Bergan & Kratochwill, 1990; Erchul & Martens, 2010). As described in this section, it is necessary for the school psychologist to engage in multiple levels of problem analysis and intervention development during consultation. Because consultation is an indirect service, it requires that changes be achieved on more than just the individual student level. Thus, it is essential to remain aware of the link between changes in the environment or in consultees' behavior and changes in the target student (Truscott et al., 2012). Finally, it should be noted that although consultative interventions may involve multiple consultants and consultees and can take place on several organizational levels, the primary focus of our presentation below is on individual consultants, consultees, and students rather than on these broader levels of change.

Establishing a Cooperative Partnership

As noted, prerequisites to effective problem solving within consultation include adequate communication skills and development of a trusting partnership. Participants must be able to interact effectively and build trust in one another before they can solve problems. The overall consultation process begins with establishing a cooperative partnership (see Table 29.1).

Relationship building is a critical element of school consultation, beginning with initial entry into the school and/or classroom and continuing throughout the process. When school psychology consultants and consultees meet initially, each participant tries to become better acquainted with the other, and together they strive to create an atmosphere of mutual respect and trust. They discuss and negotiate a working contract, which is a basic oral or written understanding of what will occur during consultation. The contract minimally specifies the roles and responsibilities of each participant as well as expected activities and anticipated timeline for the consultation (Zins & Erchul, 2002).

Key to the establishment of a cooperative partnership is for the school psychology consultant to avoid the "egalitarian virus." Barone (1995) coined this phrase after lamenting his failure as a consultant to challenge a teacher's misguided statement that "peanut butter cures attention deficit hyperactivity disorder" (p. 35). The egalitarian virus can paralyze otherwise competent consultants who mistakenly think that (a) the specialized expertise of one professional is directly interchangeable with that of any other professional and (b) consultees' opinions always should be given equal rather than due consideration.

Identifying and Clarifying the Problem

Once problem solving begins, the first task is to identify/clarify the problem and have consultant and consultee agree on the resulting definition (Bergan & Kratochwill, 1990). Problems should be identified and defined in clear, concise, objective, and measurable terms to the extent possible so that the progress made in solving them can be assessed. Consultees often do not have clear conceptualizations of problems and thus present information in vague, global terms. Through skillful questioning, paraphrasing, and summarizing, various aspects of the problem can be brought to their attention and then defined in measurable terms. Once accomplished, participants can then generate specific goals for change.

Table 29.1. Essential Tasks Within the Consultation Process

Establishment of Cooperative Partnerships
- Develop facilitative, respectful relationships with consultees
- Establish a relational framework in which consultees are free to respond to and elaborate on issues of mutual concern
- Attend to relevant multicultural considerations throughout the consultative process
- Promote an understanding of and obtain agreement on each participant's roles and responsibilities
- Avoid the egalitarian virus

Problem Identification/Clarification and Analysis
- Define the problem and goal for change in measurable, operational terms and obtain agreement with consultees
- Collect baseline data on problem frequency, duration, and/or intensity
- Collect curriculum-based measurement data and conduct functional behavior assessment and/or brief experimental analysis as necessary
- Identify antecedents that may trigger or cue the behavior
- Identify consequences that may maintain the behavior
- Assess other relevant environmental factors
- Identify resources available to change behavior

Intervention Selection and Implementation
- Identify evidence-based interventions appropriate for the identified problem
- Evaluate positive and negative aspects of the proposed evidence-based interventions before implementation
- Select evidence-based interventions for implementation from alternatives identified
- Clarify implementation procedures and responsibilities with consultees
- Support consultees in implementing the chosen evidence-based interventions through demonstration, training, and ongoing feedback
- Assess intervention plan integrity
- Increase intervention plan integrity using performance feedback with graphed implementation rates

Intervention Evaluation and Follow-Up
- Use collected data to inform further problem solving and decision making
- Evaluate outcomes and any unintended effects of the evidence-based interventions
- Assess intervention transfer/generalization, maintenance, and need for continuation
- Recycle and follow up as necessary

Note. Based on information from Bergan and Kratochwill (1990), Erchul and Martens (2010), Harvey and Struzziero (2008), and Zins and Erchul (2002).

If a problem is not identified accurately, efforts may be directed toward solving the wrong problem. On the other hand, once a problem is identified accurately, this meets the necessary, but not always the sufficient, conditions to solve a problem or promote some desired goal. It often takes a good amount of time to complete this assessment process because a variety of contextual factors need to be understood (Zins & Erchul, 2002).

Analyzing the Problem

During this step, participants try to understand the forces that are causing and maintaining the problem as well as those that may be available to solve it. Participants work to develop the best possible hypotheses about the problem, collect baseline data (i.e., frequency, duration, intensity), and identify temporal and situational antecedents and consequences that are contributing to it. Adopting an ecological/systems perspective is important because problems usually are the result of a complex interaction of multiple factors. Unless these factors are considered, it is probable that a simplistic, ineffective solution will be applied. All resources that potentially could be utilized in the development and implementation of interventions must be identified at this step. These include student strengths, system characteristics that help the student be successful in other situations, and material and human resources (e.g., teachers, parents, peer and volunteer tutors, community support systems) available for intervention (Zins & Erchul, 2002). During problem analysis, it is increasingly important (and common) for school psychology consultants to employ curriculum-based measurement, functional behavior assessment, and/or brief experimental analysis rather than rely exclusively on consultees' verbal reports and observations of client behavior, previously considered best practices (Erchul & Martens, 2010).

Selecting an Intervention

Once a list of appropriate evidence-based interventions is developed, participants need to evaluate each for its feasibility, acceptability, cost, likelihood of success, effectiveness, consequences, and so on. In an earlier time, acceptability was a top consideration in intervention selection, but because the hypothesized connection between high acceptability and high implementation has not been demonstrated consistently through research (Noell & Gansle, 2014), the issue of intervention effectiveness is a much higher priority. As mentioned earlier, resources such as meta-analytic reviews, What Works Clearinghouse, Intervention Central, and the Collaborative for Academic, Social, and Emotional Learning are helpful in locating evidence-based interventions.

As significant as the problem identification stage is to the ultimate success of consultation, a recent study highlights the importance of the problem analysis and intervention selection stage. Erchul et al. (2009) coded consultant and teacher statements in problem analysis interviews using a relational communication coding system that included measures of attempted influence (i.e., domineeringness) and successful influence (i.e., dominance). Results indicated (a) teacher domineeringness correlated −.66 with teachers' treatment integrity, (b) teacher dominance correlated −.63 with teachers' ratings of intervention acceptability, (c) teacher dominance correlated −.61 with teachers' ratings of intervention effectiveness, and (d) consultant dominance correlated .59 with teachers' treatment integrity. Thus, a general pattern is that teachers' influence at the problem analysis and intervention selection stage was related to several negative outcomes, but consultants' influence was related to at least one positive outcome.

Clarifying Implementation Procedures and Responsibilities

A frequently observed obstacle to successful consultation is that intervention implementation procedures are not always specified in sufficient detail. As a result, an intervention found to be effective in one instance may not work in another. It is not that the wrong treatment was implemented; rather, it was implemented incorrectly and/or was in place for an insufficient amount of time. Consequently, developing a written plan of action specifying the steps of the intervention, plans to follow up once the intervention has been implemented, and a strategy for monitoring the implementation process can create greater opportunities for success. Participants should put in place an approach to monitor intervention plan integrity (i.e., the degree to which the intervention has been implemented as planned), which has significant implications with respect to interpreting treatment outcomes. Prior to implementation, it is advisable for the school psychology consultant to demonstrate the intervention and/or directly train consultees on implementation procedures.

Implementing the Intervention

The selected strategy now can be put into action according to the plans and timelines developed. Consultants need to be available to consultees to assist in the event that unforeseen problems arise or any changes in the environment occur. Also, school psychologists provide support for consultees' efforts, as consultees initially may not receive much positive feedback in terms of seeing improvements in the problem situation. The assessment of intervention plan integrity needs to occur during this step, and this can proceed using direct observation, self-report, and/or permanent product methods. There is an established body of research indicating that intervention plan integrity is enhanced when consultees receive feedback on their intervention implementation performance, and the consistency of this effect is increased when the data are presented in graph form (Noell & Gansle, 2014).

Evaluating Intervention Effectiveness and Follow-Up

There are several interrelated aspects in this stage, including determination of intervention effectiveness, generalization/transfer, fading, and follow-up. First, it is generally the case that the same data collection procedures used to obtain baseline information will be applied again as a means of evaluation. Evaluation procedures (e.g., single-subject designs) may suggest that (a) the intervention resulted in attainment of desired goals, thereby indicating that follow-up monitoring and/or generalization and fading procedures are needed, or (b) the intended outcomes were not reached entirely, suggesting the need to recycle through earlier problem-solving steps (Zins & Erchul, 2002).

Generalization or transfer may be achieved in several ways. Selected reinforcers, for instance, should be naturally occurring events when possible, and techniques should be implemented that lend themselves to fading or to greater transfer of control to the student (i.e., self-management approaches). When possible, students (and parents) should take an active role in intervention development, and efforts should be made to train and help them understand the usefulness and relevance of the intervention to their lives. Training ideally should take place in a number of settings using multiple tasks and trainers. Also, opportunities to confront and deal positively with failure or mistakes should be built into intervention procedures (Zins & Erchul, 2002).

Interventions that include specific prompts or reinforcement contingencies need to be faded systematically once a student is performing at desired levels. It is important to withdraw prompts or reinforcement incrementally rather than suddenly to ensure maintenance of treatment gains. Finally, modifications to the existing plan suggested through corrective feedback often are all that are necessary to increase ease of implementation, improve intervention effectiveness, or counteract unintended consequences. If the alterations do not result in better outcomes, new strategies should be pursued by revisiting appropriate steps of the problem-solving process (Zins & Erchul, 2002).

Including Multicultural Considerations

Multicultural considerations are also necessary components of best practices in consultation for school psychologists. It is imperative that the powerful influence of culture in its variety of forms (e.g., race, ethnicity, language, socioeconomic status, sexual orientation, age, religious/spiritual) be acknowledged and the potential impact of these factors understood during the consultative process.

Multicultural consultation is not a separate model of consultation, but rather it was developed as an approach that could be adapted to different models of consultation in order to emphasize the role that culture plays in the process and ensure that cultural variables are a central aspect of consultation (Ingraham, 2014; Tarver Behring & Ingraham, 1998). Within this method, "culture is defined broadly to include an organized set of thoughts, beliefs, and norms for interaction and communication, all of which may influence thoughts, behaviors, and perceptions" (Ingraham, 2000, p. 325). From this perspective, culture can vary between consultant, consultee, and/or client (cross-cultural consultation), or culture can be a key variable that is embedded within the environmental context (i.e., family, classroom, school, community). At the same time that culture is being emphasized, it is important for the consultant to

be able to recognize that cultural variables are not always part of the problem and be able to balance an understanding of the role of individual differences as well as group cultural variables.

Based on the philosophy and underpinnings of multicultural consultation, Ingraham (2000) proposed multicultural school consultation as a comprehensive framework having five key domains of knowledge and skill development for best practices in the schools: (a) consultant learning and development, (b) consultee learning and development, (c) cultural variation in the consultation constellation, (d) contextual power influences, and (e) hypothesized methods for supporting consultee and client success.

The multicultural school consultation framework provides school psychologists with best practice competencies for understanding and applying multicultural considerations within the consultative relationship. First, and arguably most important, is that a consultant needs to have a level of self-awareness regarding his or her own cultural background, knowledge and biases toward other groups, respect and appreciation for cultural diversity, awareness of the cultural context of the consultative environment, and an understanding of how all of these will have an impact on the consultation relationship in order to choose and implement effective interventions. The second element emphasizes the importance of using the consultation process to improve the consultee's (i.e., at an individual, group, or systemic level) knowledge, skills, objectivity, and confidence related to multicultural competence. This element of the multicultural school consultation framework is similar to Caplan's (1970) consultee-centered case consultation, as the focus of the consultation is helping the consultee in order to indirectly improve the situation for the students. The third domain addresses the unique cross-cultural compositions that are most likely to occur within consultation settings. This element of the framework emphasizes the need for effective consultants to understand cultural saliency, defined as "cultural similarities or differences perceived by consultation members" (Ingraham, 2000, p. 334), and how to use this knowledge to build confidence and trust where differences are identified. Consultants following best practices also need to understand how the larger context (e.g., community, region, or society) of the consultative setting plays a role in the consultative process by imposing values, norms, traditions, and hierarchies of importance on the problem at hand. In addition, consultants should be aware of the ideas of privilege and oppression among different cultural groups and how these concepts affect the power a person may be granted or denied within a setting. The final element of the multicultural school consultation framework for school psychologists to incorporate in consultation is the ongoing challenge of improving consultee development in the area of diversity and appreciation of multiculturalism.

Evaluating the Effectiveness of School Consultation

There are multiple ways to evaluate the effectiveness of consultation. Effectiveness can be monitored at the level of the referring problem, the consultee or consultant, or the system. School psychology consultants can use data from the records of the consultative process and aggregate the type of referral problems (i.e., academic, behavioral) and outcomes. Consultee changes can be used to monitor the effectiveness of consultation. Consultee satisfaction with the process, types of future referrals, and/or knowledge of interventions can be used to show changes in consultees. Consultant skills or perceptions of the process can be monitored through the use of surveys (Flugum & Reschly, 1994; Knoff, Hines, & Kromrey, 1995). Although changes at the systems level take time to demonstrate and are difficult to pinpoint to a single cause, changes such as decreases in inappropriate referrals for special education, decreases in discipline referrals, or increases in academic performance can also be monitored.

Conclusion

Following a problem-solving model is a major element of school consultation, but it is not sufficient in and of itself to ensure its effective practice. The effective school psychologist not only has to include the ingredients of the consultation process (problem-solving stages) but also has to do this while maintaining collaborative, open, and collegial consultative relationships. At the same time, cultural variables are integral to any situation. Therefore, the culturally laden variables of consultant, consultee, client, and system also demand attention. Finally, a school psychologist following best practices also has to ensure adequate fidelity of the intervention and follow up on successful and unsuccessful interventions. If prevention is to occur in the form of a consultee utilizing a newly learned skill or intervention in the future, it is imperative that the school psychology consultant provide adequate professional support as well as data on the effectiveness of the selected intervention.

SUMMARY

Consultation is a model of indirect service delivery that has been widely embraced by school psychologists, and school psychologists are in the unique position to be one of the few school professionals who are trained specifically in consultation methods. The current educational environment demands quality instructional methods, a focus on prevention, and the use of interventions that possess documented effectiveness. Consultation is well suited to meet these needs. School-based consultation is a method for solving problems using a preventive, collaborative, and flexible approach that keeps cultural variables at the forefront. School psychology consultants using best practices are able to target problems on an individual, classroom, or systems level. For example, the adaptable nature of consultation allows a consultant to work with one consultee to remediate an individual student concern or participate as a member of a problem-solving team to identify a systems-level variable to target for change. The variety of consultative models and logistics of indirect service delivery have made it difficult to conduct methodologically sound research. However, there is a sizable literature that provides promising evidence for the effectiveness of school consultation.

The goal of this chapter is to orient school psychologists to the importance of consultation, provide an understanding of the basic considerations and competencies of consultants, and then outline the best practice elements within school consultation. In the current educational climate, there is a demand for using evidence-based interventions to remediate problems. Consultation can provide the ability for individuals or teams to identify the need for such interventions, assist in selecting and implementing them, and monitor and evaluate their effectiveness. Ultimately, we hope that by reviewing the fundamentals of the consultation process, school psychologists will be better equipped to serve children, teachers, and schools both now and in the future.

AUTHOR NOTE

The authors would like to acknowledge the influence of Joseph E. Zins (1949–2006), who coauthored chapters on this topic appearing in previous editions of *Best Practices in School Psychology*. The current chapter remains true to his vision of school consultation.

Disclosure. William P. Erchul has a financial interest in books he authored or coauthored referenced in this chapter.

REFERENCES

Alpert, J., & Silverstein, J. (1985). Mental health consultation: Historical, present, and future perspectives. In J. R. Bergan (Ed.), *School psychology in contemporary society: An introduction* (pp. 281–315). Columbus, OH: Merrill.

Barone, S. G. (1995, March 1). The egalitarian virus. *Education Weekly*, 35.

Bergan, J. R., & Kratochwill, T. R. (1990). *Behavioral consultation and therapy*. New York, NY: Plenum Press.

Burns, M. K., Wiley, H. I., & Viglietta, E. (2008). Best practices in implementing effective problem-solving teams. In A. Thomas & J. Grimes (Eds.), *Best practices in school psychology V* (pp. 1633–1644). Bethesda, MD: National Association of School Psychologists.

Caplan, G. (1970). *The theory and practice of mental health consultation*. New York, NY: Basic Books.

Caplan, G., & Caplan, R. B. (1999). *Mental health consultation and collaboration*. Prospect Heights, IL: Waveland Press.

Cappella, E., Hamre, B. K., Kim, H. Y., Henry, D. B., Frazier, S. L., Atkins, M. S., & Schoenwald, S. K. (2012). Teacher consultation and coaching within mental health practice: Classroom and child effects in urban elementary schools. *Journal of Consulting and Clinical Psychology*, *80*, 597–610. doi:10.1037/a0027725

Erchul, W. P. (2009). Gerald Caplan: A tribute to the originator of mental health consultation. *Journal of Educational and Psychological Consultation*, *19*, 95–105. doi:10.1080/10474410902888418

Erchul, W. P. (2011). School consultation and response to intervention: A tale of two literatures. *Journal of Educational and Psychological Consultation*, *21*, 191–208. doi:10.1080/10474412.2011.595198

Erchul, W. P., DuPaul, G. J., Bennett, M. S., Grissom, P. F., Jitendra, A. K., Tresco, K. E., ... Mannella, M. C. (2009). A follow-up study of relational processes and consultation outcomes for students with attention deficit hyperactivity disorder. *School Psychology Review*, *38*, 28–37.

Erchul, W. P., Grissom, P. F., Getty, K. C., & Bennett, M. S. (2014). Researching interpersonal influence within school consultation: Social power base and relational communication perspectives. In W. P. Erchul & S. M. Sheridan (Eds.), *Handbook of research in school consultation* (2nd ed., pp. 349–385). New York, NY: Routledge.

Erchul, W. P., & Martens, B. K. (2010). *School consultation: Conceptual and empirical bases of practice* (3rd ed.). New York, NY: Springer.

Erchul, W. P., & Sheridan, S. M. (2014). Overview: The state of scientific research in school consultation. In W. P. Erchul & S. M. Sheridan (Eds.), *Handbook of research in school consultation* (2nd ed., pp. 3–17). New York, NY: Routledge.

Fabiano, G. A., Vujnovic, R. K., Pelham, W. E., Waschbusch, D. A., Massetti, G. M., Pariseau, M. E., ... Volker, M. (2010). Enhancing the effectiveness of special education programming for children with attention deficit hyperactivity disorder using a daily report card. *School Psychology Review*, *39*, 219–239.

Flugum, K. R., & Reschly, D. J. (1994). Prereferral interventions: Quality indices and outcomes. *Journal of School Psychology*, *32*, 1–14. doi:10.1016/0022-4405(94)90025-6

French, W. L., & Bell, C. H. (1999). *Organization development: Behavioral science interventions for organization improvement* (6th ed.). Upper Saddle River, NJ: Prentice-Hall.

Fuchs, D., & Fuchs, L. S. (1989). Exploring effective and efficient prereferral interventions: A component analysis of behavioral consultation. *School Psychology Review*, *18*, 260–283.

Gallessich, J. (1982). *The practice and profession of consultation*. San Francisco, CA: Jossey-Bass.

Graden, J. L., Casey, A., & Bonstrom, O. (1985). Implementing a prereferral intervention system: Part II: The data. *Exceptional Children*, *51*, 487–496.

Graden, J. L., Casey, A., & Christenson, S. L. (1985). Implementing a prereferral intervention system: Part I: The model. *Exceptional Children*, *51*, 377–384.

Gutkin, T. B. (1993). Moving from behavioral to ecobehavioral consultation: What's in a name? *Journal of Educational and Psychological Consultation*, *4*, 95–99. doi:10.1207/s1532768xjepc0401_6

Gutkin, T. B., & Curtis, M. J. (2009). School-based consultation theory and practice: The science and practice of indirect service delivery. In C. R. Reynolds & T. B. Gutkin (Eds.), *The handbook of school psychology* (4th ed., pp. 591–635). Hoboken, NJ: Wiley.

Harvey, V. S., & Struzziero, J. A. (2008). *Professional development and supervision of school psychologists* (2nd ed.). Bethesda, MD: National Association of School Psychologists.

Illback, R. J. (2014). Organization development and change facilitation in schools: Theoretical and empirical foundations. In W. P. Erchul & S. M. Sheridan (Eds.), *Handbook of research in school consultation* (2nd ed., pp. 276–303). New York, NY: Routledge.

Ingraham, C. L. (2000). Consultation through a multicultural lens: Multicultural and cross-cultural consultation in schools. *School Psychology Review*, *29*, 320–343.

Ingraham, C. L. (2014). Studying multicultural aspects of consultation. In W. P. Erchul & S. M. Sheridan (Eds.), *Handbook of research in school consultation* (2nd ed., pp. 323–348). New York, NY: Routledge.

Knoff, H. M., Hines, C. V., & Kromrey, J. D. (1995). Finalizing the Consultant Effectiveness Scale: An analysis and validation of the characteristics of effective consultants. *School Psychology Review*, *24*, 480–496.

Knotek, S. E., & Hylander, I. (2014). Research issues in mental health and consultee-centered approaches. In W. P. Erchul & S. M. Sheridan (Eds.), *Handbook of research in school consultation* (2nd ed., pp. 153–179). New York, NY: Routledge.

Kratochwill, T. R., Clements, M. A., & Kalymon, K. M. (2007). Response to intervention: Conceptual and methodological issues in implementation. In S. R. Jimerson, M. K. Burns, & A. M. VanDerHeyden (Eds.), *Handbook of response to intervention: The science and practice of assessment and intervention* (pp. 25–52). New York, NY: Springer.

Kratochwill, T. R., & Stoiber, K. C. (2002). Evidence-based interventions in school psychology: Conceptual foundations of the Procedural and Coding Manual of Division 16 and the Society for the Study of School Psychology Task Force. *School Psychology Quarterly*, *17*, 341–389.

National Association of School Psychologists. (2010). *Model for comprehensive and integrated school psychological services*. Bethesda, MD: Author. Retrieved from http://www.nasponline.org/standards/2010standards/2_PracticeModel.pdf

Noell, G. H., & Gansle, K. A. (2014). Research examining the relationships between consultation procedures, treatment integrity, and outcomes. In W. P. Erchul & S. M. Sheridan (Eds.), *Handbook of research in school consultation* (2nd ed., pp. 386–408). New York, NY: Routledge.

Ramirez, S. Z., Lepage, K. M., Kratochwill, T. R., & Duffy, J. L. (1998). Multicultural issues in school-based consultation: Conceptual and research considerations. *Journal of School Psychology*, *36*, 479–509. doi:10.1016/S0022-4405(98)00014-4

Rappoport, J. (1981). In praise of paradox: A social policy of empowerment over prevention. *American Journal of Community Psychology*, *9*, 1–25.

Reddy, L. A., Barboza-Whitehead, S., Files, T., & Rubel, E. (2000). Clinical focus of consultation outcome research with children and adolescents. *Special Services in the Schools*, *16*, 1–22. doi:10.1300/J008v16n01_01

Reschly, D. J. (1976). School psychology consultation: "Frenzied, faddish, or fundamental?" *Journal of School Psychology*, *14*, 105–113. doi:10.1016/0022-4405(76)90045-5

Reschly, D. J., & Bergstrom, M. K. (2009). Response to intervention. In T. B. Gutkin & C. R. Reynolds (Eds.), *Handbook of school psychology* (4th ed., pp. 434–460). Hoboken, NJ: Wiley.

Rosenfield, S. A., Gravois, T. A., & Silva, A. (2014). Bringing instructional consultation to scale: Research and development of IC and IC teams. In W. P. Erchul & S. M. Sheridan (Eds.), *Handbook of research in school consultation* (2nd ed., pp. 248–275). New York, NY: Routledge.

Sheridan, S. M., & Kratochwill, T. R. (2008). *Conjoint behavioral consultation: Promoting family–school connections and intervention* (2nd ed.). New York, NY: Springer.

Sheridan, S. M., Welch, M., & Orme, S. F. (1996). Is consultation effective? A review of outcome research. *Remedial and Special Education*, *17*, 341–354.

Tarver Behring, S., & Ingraham, C. L. (1998). Culture as a central component to consultation: A call to the field. *Journal of Educational and Psychological Consultation*, *9*, 57–72. doi:10.1207/s1532768xjepc0901_3

Truscott, S. D., Kreskey, D., Bolling, M., Psimas, L., Graybill, E., Albritton, K., & Schwartz, A. (2012). Creating consultee change: A theory-based approach to learning and behavior change processes in school-based consultation. *Consulting Psychology Journal: Practice and Research*, *64*, 63–82. doi:10.1037/a0027997

von Bertalanffy, L. (1968). *General systems theory*. New York, NY: Braziller.

Zins, J. E. (1995). Has consultation achieved its primary prevention potential? *Journal of Primary Prevention*, *15*, 285–301. doi:10.1080/10474410701413079

Zins, J. E., & Erchul, W. P. (2002). Best practices in school consultation. In A. Thomas & J. Grimes (Eds.), *Best practices in school psychology IV* (pp. 625–643). Bethesda, MD: National Association of School Psychologists.

30

Best Practices in School-Based Problem-Solving Consultation: Applications in Prevention and Intervention Systems

Thomas R. Kratochwill
Margaret R. Altschaefl
Brittany Bice-Urbach
University of Wisconsin–Madison

OVERVIEW

Consultation continues to be a major approach for providing mental health and educational services to children and adolescents, and behavioral consultation has been identified as a practice guideline for problem solving and the delivery of evidence-based interventions (Frank & Kratochwill, in press; White & Kratochwill, 2008). Traditionally, consultation was recognized as the most preferred and satisfying function of school psychologists (Gutkin & Curtis, 1999; Sheridan & Walker, 1999; Sheridan, Welch, & Orme, 1996), and it has become a major part of response to intervention (RTI; Kratochwill, Clements, & Kalymon, 2007). Consultation's linkage to RTI is particularly important in that consultation can play a major role in the problem-solving process needed for the provision of prevention services. The purpose of this chapter is to review some of the fundamental features of school psychologists' problem-solving consultation and its relationship to prevention and intervention and to multitiered services in particular.

The content and practice recommendations in this chapter fall under the Consultation and Collaboration domain in the National Association of School Psychologists (NASP) *Model for Comprehensive and Integrated School Psychological Services* (NASP, 2010). The consultation and collaboration practices related to the model that are addressed in the chapter include engaging in a consultative problem-solving process; addressing needs at the individual, family, and systems levels; and applying psychological and educational principles.

BASIC CONSIDERATIONS

Three major models of consultation have been featured in the professional literature and include mental health consultation, organizational development consultation, and behavioral consultation (labeled *problem-solving consultation* in this chapter), but many more have been identified over the years. It is beyond the scope of this chapter to review these and other models of consultation, and the reader is referred to other sources for this information (see Brown, Pryzwansky, & Schulte, 2011). Although differences exist among these models, all emphasize problem-solving expertise of the consultant within a triadic relationship (consultant–consultee–client). The behavioral model of consultation emerged as an alternative to traditional service delivery approaches in applied settings (Reschly, 1988) and historically has strong ties to applied behavior analysis and behavior therapy (e.g., Bergan & Kratochwill, 1990). Nevertheless, the model has expanded, primarily in the theoretical foundations that underlie the interventions, and, consequently, new names have been invoked to describe the evolution in research and practice (see Gutkin & Curtis, 1999). The term *problem-solving consultation* is adapted here to replace the term *behavioral*, but other terms could be used as well (e.g., solution oriented, ecobehavioral). Many of the problem-solving models presented in this edition of *Best Practices* can be traced to the problem-solving features of behavioral consultation (Bergan, 1977; Bergan & Kratochwill, 1990).

Consultation can be distinguished from the assessments and interventions that are used as part of the problem-solving process (Frank & Kratochwill, in press; White & Kratochwill, 2005). Consultation is the process that defines the interactions that constitute the identification, analysis, intervention implementation, and evaluation that occur between a consultant and a mediator/consultee. Although problem-solving consultation traditionally has been affiliated with behavior modification and intervention techniques derived from this theoretical school, a more current focus is to use a wide range of assessment and intervention technologies from diverse theoretical origins embedded within an evidence-based practice framework (see Gutkin & Curtis, 1999; Sheridan & Kratochwill, 2008). For example, school psychologists may apply more traditional behavioral principles and techniques (e.g., functional assessment and analysis) in developing intervention programs and use behavioral assessment methodologies to evaluate the effectiveness of these services. Likewise, school psychologists also may apply evidence-based instructional principles such as pause time, pacing, teacher feedback, and homework instruction when developing an intervention plan to enhance the academic performance of students who are underachieving (Gettinger & Stoiber, 2009). Whereas specific intervention strategies may vary across presenting problems, two identifiable features are most frequently associated with problem-solving consultation: (a) indirect service delivery and (b) a problem-solving approach. Each of these features extends into its use within prevention and intervention services and, in particular, with multitiered service.

The most widely recognized feature of consultation is its indirect service delivery approach. Services can be delivered by a consultant (e.g., school psychologist) to a consultee (e.g., teacher and/or parent), who, in turn, provides services to a child in the school and/or community setting. Services can also be rendered to a group of teachers, administrators, or a problem-solving team, although the research base on teams is far less developed than on single-mediator approaches. The indirect approach to service delivery generally is regarded as a distinct advantage of consultation, since it allows the school psychologist to have an impact on many more mediators, and especially children, than could be served by a direct service approach. In fact, the centrality of consultation in linking assessment and intervention practices is making consultative models increasingly prominent as a component of solution-focused, multitiered prevention service delivery systems such as RTI (see National Association of State Directors of Special Education [NASDSE], 2005).

Consultation involves a collaborative relationship in which the consultant is viewed as a facilitator. Emphasis is placed on the collaborative problem-solving process that occurs during a series of interviews and related assessment and intervention activities. Throughout this process, the school psychologist's role is to elicit a description of the problem, assist in analyzing the problem, construct a plan for intervention, and establish a monitoring system once the program is implemented. The consultee's role is to clearly describe the problem, work with the consultant to implement the intervention program with integrity, observe progress, periodically evaluate the plan's effectiveness, and monitor the intervention outcomes. For the consultation process to be effective, both consultant and consultee should bring the following dispositions to the consultation process: (a) a sense of preparedness and clear expectations, (b) a willingness to participate actively and openly in a collaborative work environment, and (c) a capacity to assume a proactive role, especially with prevention programs and services.

Goals of Consultation

Problem-solving consultation has two important goals: (a) to provide methods (prevention and intervention) for changing a system, classroom, or child's behavioral, academic, or social problem; and (b) to improve the system and/or a consultee's skills so it, he, or she can prevent or respond effectively to future problems or similar problems in other children. Given these goals, consultation can be both a proactive (prevention) and a reactive (intervention) service. Although consultation-based interventions often have changed children's problem behaviors successfully (Sheridan et al., 1996; White & Kratochwill, 2008), the proactive goal of influencing a consultee's ability to handle future problems has not been observed consistently in research (Coffee & Kratochwill, 2013). Plus, the role of consultation in prevention systems is really in its infancy compared to work in developing interventions for existing problems. The accomplishment of these goals requires consultees to participate in a general process for analyzing conditions that result in an effective plan to prevent and resolve the problems. Successful school psychology consultants must demonstrate expertise in coordinating and facilitating the problem-solving process, demonstrating a strong knowledge of prevention and intervention practices, and implementing methods for monitoring whether the intervention is working.

In the remainder of this chapter, the basic components of problem-solving consultation, relationship variables that may influence the consultation process, and school psychologists' use of consultation with systems, groups, and/or teachers and parents are discussed.

Expansion of Structure and Process of Consultation: Applications for the Individual, Group, and System

Consultation has been conceptualized as a series of stages that structure and focus the problem-solving interactions between consultant and consultees (Bergan & Kratochwill, 1990; Sheridan & Kratochwill, 2008). This series of stages and their corresponding interviews define consultation as separate from more generic problem-solving approaches as recently presented in the literature (e.g., Brown-Chidsey & Andren, 2013). A heuristic five-stage framework for consultation can be applied to a system, group, or individual problem-solving process.

Work With Special Education Teachers

Traditionally, school psychologists have implemented consultation with classroom teachers in an effort to establish intervention programs in the regular classroom. This emphasis on interventions with teachers also advanced the development of a knowledge base to prevent more serious behavioral problems in children and is one reason why the approach is recommended in RTI models (Gresham, 2006; NASDSE, 2005). School-based consultation services have expanded to include work with special education teachers, particularly teachers of students with emotional disturbance and teachers from early intervention programs for preschool-age children. In addition, consultation also has been used for many years to successfully remediate academic and socialization difficulties in school settings. Applications such as these have presented unique opportunities for school psychologists to increase contact with special education teachers while generally addressing more severe presenting problems in special needs

children who often experience multiple difficulties. Hence, school psychologists' roles as consultants have become increasingly complex, with unique time demands and prevention and intervention foci that may vary according to the child's presenting problems and the teacher's level of expertise in areas such as behavior management and individualized instruction.

A Focus on Promoting Competencies

Problem-solving consultation can focus on prevention by linking the process to a multitiered system such as RTI. However, prevention can move beyond the deficit RTI model and include promoting social competency skills in clients. In this regard, case-based problem solving can extend to a focus that also includes building social competencies to prevent more serious problems from developing (Stoiber & Kratochwill, 2000). For example, during the problem analysis phase, the school psychologist can ask teachers and parents to complete measures on the academic functioning of students, such as the Academic Competence Evaluation Scales (DiPerna & Elliott, 2000), to target academic enablers or skills development. Figure 30.1 provides an illustration of the subscales of the Academic Competence Evaluation Scales. This assessment tool can help the school psychologist identify skills for development and promotion at a primary or secondary level of services.

Parent–Teacher Pairs / Conjoint Consultation

Another method of expanding consultation services entails involvement of parent–teacher pairs in problem solving. Although consultation with teachers (regular and special education) to deal with problem reduction is an effective method of remediating school-based problems, this traditional focus often fails to address the broader context and focus within which the child's problems may occur (Kratochwill & Pittman, 2002). For example, a withdrawn child who exhibits an absence of peer interactions at school likely would be unable to develop and maintain positive social relationships with neighborhood peers. Focusing exclusively on this child's social withdrawal in the school setting through teacher-only consultation may restrict conceptualization, analysis, and intervention of the problem to a single target domain and setting. Thus, the broader behavioral interrelationships across environments may not always be considered, which may have important implications for practice. Thus, problem-solving consultation can be extended to serve as a link among the significant settings in a child's life, primarily, the home, school, and community environments (Sheridan & Kratochwill,

Figure 30.1. The Clusters of Skills, Attitudes, and Behaviors Contributing to Academic Competence

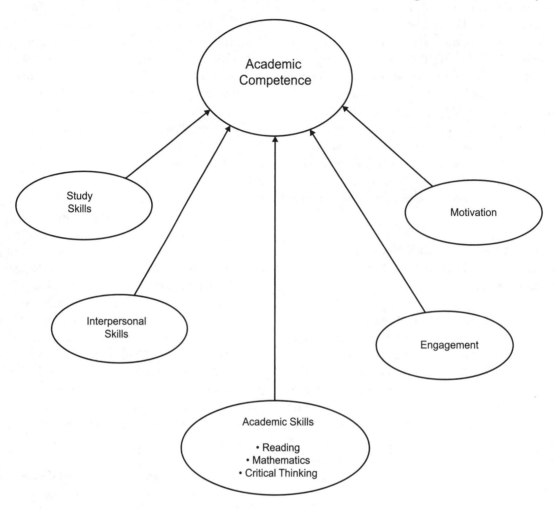

Note. From *The Academic Competence Evaluation Scales* by J. C. DiPerna and S. N. Elliott, 2000, San Antonio, TX: The Psychological Corporation. Copyright 2000 by The Psychological Corporation. Reprinted with permission.

2008). This approach facilitates a comprehensive conceptualization of the needed services while involving primary caretakers in the prevention and intervention processes. In addition, although few investigators have assessed the generalization of intervention effects across settings, the potential benefits of broadening the focus of problem-solving consultation to encompass the interacting system in the child's life are apparent.

In conjoint consultation, parents and teachers together serve as consultees (Sheridan, Eagle, & Doll, 2006; Sheridan & Kratochwill, 2008). The primary goals of this approach are to bridge the gap between home and school settings, maximize positive intervention effects within and across settings, and promote generalization of intervention effects over time. Continuous data collection and consistent programming across settings are also inherent

with this approach. Conjoint consultation has been found to be an effective method of service delivery in enhancing social and academic competencies across home and school settings (see Sheridan & Kratochwill, 2008, for a comprehensive review). In a recent study, Sheridan et al. (2012) conducted a randomized trial of conjoint consultation focused on promoting behavioral competence and decreasing problem behavior of students referred by their teachers. In comparison to students in the control group, students in the conjoint consultation condition demonstrated greater increases in adaptive behaviors and social skills. Moreover, teachers in the conjoint condition demonstrated greater change in their relationships with parents. This change in parent–teacher relationship mediated the effects of conjoint consultation on positive changes in the child's behaviors.

Parent Consultation

Use of problem-solving consultation also has been extended beyond schools to address problems with individuals other than teachers, such as with parents only (Kratochwill & Pittman, 2002). Parent-only consultation may be applicable when a child's problematic behaviors are observed predominantly in the home and/or community settings but are not evident (or cannot be treated) in the school environment. For example, parent consultation has been used to decrease the noncompliant behaviors of school-age children whose difficult behaviors were displayed at home and in public places but were not observed in the more structured classroom setting (e.g., Carrington Rotto & Kratochwill, 1994). In parent-only consultation, the traditional problem-solving consultation framework provides structure for involving the parent in the process of identifying and analyzing the problem, as well as observing and evaluating intervention effects over time. Use of parent training provides structure for teaching parents specific skills that enhance plan implementation. Necessary preparations for plan implementation include teaching parents specific behavior management skills and ensuring that they are adept at implementing these skills. Specific methods of promoting generalization of parent behaviors (i.e., skill implementation) across settings and situations to enhance specific child behaviors need to be implemented.

Teleconsultation

A recently developed option for problem-solving consultation is the use of teleconsultation within the school setting. Teleconsultation is one aspect of telepsychology, telehealth, and the use of other technologies to deliver psychological services (see Maheu, Pulier, McMenamin, & Posen, 2012). In our context, teleconsultation refers to the utilization of videoconferencing methods to increase access to consultation services (Glueckauf, Pickett, Ketterson, Loomis, & Rozensky, 2003; McGinty, Saeed, Simmons, & Yildirim, 2006). This method can be especially useful within rural communities, where access to knowledgeable consultants is scarce (Brownlee, Graham, Doucette, Hotson, & Halverson, 2010). There are many possibilities that teleconsultation offers, including accessing expert school psychologists to improve systems-level processes, reducing travel constraints for including parents within consultation services, and providing more thorough school psychologist feedback and support for teachers (Myrick & Sabella, 1995).

Although teleconsultation has been explored more thoroughly in the areas of medicine and psychiatry (e.g.,

Germain, Marchand, Bouchard, Guay, & Drouin, 2010; Glueckauf & Ketterson, 2004; Novotney, 2011), it has also been used in the school setting to monitor the integrity of teacher-implemented interventions for students with autism (Machalicek et al., 2009; Rule, Salzberg, Higbee, Menlove, & Smith, 2006). These initial studies suggest a promising solution for addressing some of the limitations of the traditional problem-solving approach to consultation. As technology continues to improve, teleconsultation will most likely become an increasingly viable option for delivering consultation services in the school setting.

Problem-Solving Teams

Problem-solving consultation can be extended to working with school-based teams. Such teams may involve building-level problem-solving teams, RTI teams, or positive behavior support teams. Since school teams frequently struggle to successfully adopt multitiered prevention and interventions due to lack of knowledge and skills, students often do not receive adequate support with evidence-based practices (Doll, Gaack, Kosse, Osterloh, & Siemers, 2005). Direct consultation with the team can be used to improve the likelihood that team members choose evidence-based interventions and implement them with integrity (Doll et al., 2005; Gravois, Groff, & Rosenfield, 2009). Consultants can also address other issues, such as a lack of resources and inadequate use of the problem-solving approach. When school psychologists are able to target the needs of the team, there is a greater likelihood that students will have access to evidence-based programs, a multitiered system of support, and better academic and/or behavioral outcomes (Glisson, 2002, 2007; Rosenfield & Gravois, 1996).

Systems-, Organization-Level Consultation

Another application of problem-solving consultation is at the systems level and allows consultation services to occur with a wide variety of stakeholders who may be involved in implementation of a prevention system such as single and/or multitiered programs (see Kratochwill & Pittman, 2002). With implementation of a multitiered model where RTI has been integrated into the process, consultants must be knowledgeable about prevention science approaches as well as methods of progress monitoring (see Kratochwill, Volpiansky, Clements, & Ball, 2008). Most importantly, school psychologists should understand the limitations of a multitiered approach as currently being advocated in much of the school psychology literature (e.g., the focus on a deficit approach as opposed to a proactive social–emotional learning approach; see Kratochwill et al., 2008).

As schools attempt to implement multitiered models, there are many barriers that hinder the delivery of these programs and the implementation of evidence-based practices. The school psychologist engaging in problem-solving consultation should be aware of barriers, including, for example, a lack of time for proper teacher involvement, inadequate training or knowledge about potential prevention programs, insufficient funding for program development, limited staff buy-in, and minimal administrator support (Doll et al., 2005; Kincaid, Childs, Blase, & Wallace, 2007). Therefore, it is important to examine potential barriers and determine how these barriers can be addressed.

BEST PRACTICES IN THE DELIVERY OF PROBLEM-SOLVING CONSULTATION

Problem-solving consultation is a model for delivering assessment, prevention, and intervention services to children and schools via consultees through a series of structured meetings. Although the problem-solving structure is sequential, it should not be interpreted as inflexible or irreversible. The activities of school psychologists and consultees are multifaceted, involving interviews, functional assessments, selection and implementation of evidence-based interventions, and evaluation of the interventions. Such activities generally require several interactions between the school psychologist and consultee, as well as ongoing consultee and client collaborative interactions.

Problem-solving consultation consists of a series of stages or phases that are used to implement the process of consultation, and each of these steps, with the exception of plan implementation, can involve a formal interview with specific objectives to guide the interactions between school psychologist and consultee. Best practices in problem-solving case consultation suggest that school psychologists adhere to specific objectives and activities within each phase, as each of these steps can be conceptualized as a practice guideline with evidence for its components (Frank & Kratochwill, in press). The major components for each of these phases include establishing a consultant–consultee relationship, problem identification, problem analysis, plan implementation, and plan evaluation.

Stage 1: Establishing of Relationships

The interpersonal relationship between a school psychologist and consultees can play a major role in the use and effectiveness of consultation services. Thus, as with psychotherapy, issues of trust, genuineness, and openness have been deemed important qualities for both consultants and consultees. Although competencies in problem identification and plan implementation are necessary conditions of problem-solving consultation, they may not be sufficient to facilitate effective consultative interactions. Integration of positive interpersonal skills and understanding with technical expertise is equally important to maximize consultant–consultee effectiveness. For example, characteristics such as acceptance through nonjudgmental statements, openness, nondefensiveness, and flexibility positively affect the interaction among school psychologists and consultees. These qualities are magnified in a consultative model of service delivery due to the predominance of an interview or verbal mode of information gathering and sharing. The dynamics of communication, both talking and listening, are the medium through which school psychologists display their attitudes and beliefs about consultees. Personal characteristics, professional competencies, and modeling are all important elements in establishing and maintaining constructive and professional interactions in an individual and/or a group relationship.

Consultation should begin with the development of a relationship between the school psychologist and the consultee. Collaborative school psychologists who develop positive working relationships with consultees may (a) experience less resistance to the consultation process and intervention, (b) find their suggestions are readily accepted by consultees, (c) increase the probability that consultees will follow through on an intervention, and (d) increase the effectiveness of the consultation process for the consultee and clients. During this stage, it is critical that the school psychologist and consultee embrace a shared need or goal to focus the consultation process and develop an intervention (e.g., developing a classroom management program for an individual child, setting up a multitiered prevention model). It is also during this stage that the school psychologist discusses with the consultee the stages of the consultation process, school psychologist and consultee roles, and shared responsibilities and ownership of the consultation outcomes such as systems change.

Issues of Importance to Consultees
Sensitivity to issues of importance to consultees also contributes to the development of a positive consulting relationship. Variables commonly examined in intervention acceptability research (e.g., Elliott, 1988a; Witt

& Elliott, 1985) and dimensions of helping emphasized by empowerment theorists (e.g., Dunst & Trivette, 1988; Witt & Martens, 1988) provide variables to consider consistent with consultation that are relevant to the enhancement of relationships with individuals (e.g., teacher, parents) or groups (e.g., problem-solving teams). For example, acceptability researchers repeatedly have found that administration/management time and fairness of the intervention are important themes virtually to all teachers, and nonaversive approaches to intervention are valued highly by most teachers. Work by empowerment theorists applied to consultation suggests that (a) help is more likely to be perceived positively if it is offered proactively, (b) competence within teachers is best promoted by building upon their existing child management strengths rather than remediating deficits, and (c) use of existing resources in the school environment is preferred over the intervention or purchase of new resources (Witt & Martens, 1988). Thus, it is concluded that effective consultants (a) overtly communicate awareness of these issues that are central to teachers' daily functioning and (b) act cooperatively to design interventions. Such consultative actions may overcome many potential sources of resistance.

Consultee Resistance

Resistance is a topic of considerable concern to practitioners and researchers alike and often has been conceptualized as something negative that resides within a person and/or institution. Yet, as observed by Wickstrom and Witt (1993), such a view of resistance may be overly simplistic and unnecessarily negative. Within the context of a consultant–consultee relationship, they define resistance as "including those system, consultee, consultant, family, and client factors which interfere with the achievement of goals established during consultative interactions making the construct very relevant to multi-levels of prevention" (p. 160). Resistance, then, is "*anything* that impedes problem solving or plan implementation and ultimately problem resolution" (p. 160). This definition stresses that resistance is part of a system context and is multidirectional; that is, it does not reside in only one part of the system.

Having reviewed the theoretical and empirical reports on resistance to intervention in both the psychotherapy and consultation literature, Wickstrom and Witt (1993) recommended two general tactics to respond to resistance that remain important today. The first tactic they call "joining the consultee" and the second tactic they refer to as "emphasizing referent power." Joining

the consultee involves understanding a consultee's attribution system for explaining a problem of concern and then using that attributional framework to build a link to an intervention. Emphasizing referent power involves a school psychologist working to become more similar to consultees. This tactic can be accomplished by using nonauthoritarian and noncoercive means of control, using cooperative modes of interaction, asking questions, and making suggestions for change in a tentative manner (Parsons & Meyers, 1984). Efforts to use the consultee's existing skills and preferences for interaction activities, thereby reducing the number of new aspects of an intervention, also is likely to make suggestions more acceptable, and thus less resisted.

Resistance at the systems level requires that the school psychologist address a wide range of practical and logistical variables. For example, school psychologists must have the skills to consult and develop interventions, and this role requires training. Administrators must support the role of the consultant through public endorsement and resources. Alternate models of special education service delivery such as RTI approaches may need to be embraced by the district and state. This process will require considerable effort on the part of the school psychologist to change the student service system.

System Impacts

Implementation of consultation in a multitiered system raises special issues in terms of having an impact on the school system as well as on key stakeholders in the process. Fortunately, a growing body of literature has provided some guidance on increasing the probability that the multitiered system of prevention services can be implemented through a consultation process. For example, in the prevention science literature, the *Blueprints for Violence Prevention* (hereinafter called *Blueprints*) was initiated with the goal to identify research-based violence prevention programs and to replicate these programs in a dissemination project (see Mihalic, Irwin, Fagan, Ballard, & Elliott, 2004). During the process of implementing these various programs, important issues came to the fore, including conducting a site assessment; creating an effective organizational structure; having qualified staff, including program champions, in the effort; integrating the program into existing structures; ensuring implementation fidelity; and providing training and technical assistance. Especially relevant in this process was the professional development effort (see Kratochwill et al., 2008, for further information on professional development issues). Specifically, among the important issues learned from implementation of *Blueprints*, a number of important findings related to training teachers occurred (see Mihalic et al., 2004, pp. 7–8). The authors found that (a) trained teachers were more likely to implement, and implement more of, the prevention program than untrained teachers; (b) fully trained teachers completed a greater percentage of programs with fidelity; (c) trained teachers reported greater preparedness to teach the programs, teach it with greater fidelity, and achieve better student outcomes than untrained teachers; (d) trained teachers were more effective and had more favorable student outcomes than untrained teachers; and (e) teachers without follow-up and support over time failed to fully implement or continue to use the program. These findings have important implications for technology-training consultation and, specifically, for multitiered models. The lesson is that effective professional development must be part of a consultation process for implementation of single-focused and/or multitiered prevention and intervention school psychological services (see Kratochwill et al., 2008).

Stage 2: Problem Identification

Problem identification is the most critical stage of consultation because it results in the design and implementation of an effective plan. Traditionally, in case-centered behavioral consultation, the focus was exclusively on identification of a target problem and elimination of that problem. More recently, an intervention emphasis has been placed on teaching social and academic competencies in addition to dealing with a target problem (DiPerna & Elliott, 2000; Stoiber & Kratochwill, 2000). The interview represents a primary assessment technology for defining the problem and developing an understanding of the needs in social and academic competencies, although numerous other strategies may assist in defining the problem or issue (e.g., tests, rating scales and checklists, functional assessment, direct observations; Hurwitz, Rehberg, & Kratochwill, 2007).

Operational Definition of Concerns
During the problem identification interview, the school psychologist and consultee focus on describing and operationally defining concerns. In consultation, a problem is a relative concept that becomes operationalized when consultees report a significant discrepancy between current and desired levels of performance or circumstances. The determination of whether a significant discrepancy exists is not examined initially.

However, once the current and desired levels of performance are defined objectively, this significant discrepancy becomes the focus. This approach to problem identification is based on the assumption that problems are the result of unsuccessful or discrepant interactions between and among persons and/or systems (e.g., child and teacher; child and parent; teacher, parent, and child; parent and school). Functional assessment strategies may be conducted to focus attention on the academic and social competencies that need to be taught and on the ecological context surrounding the concern, especially in the most intense level of services in a multitiered model. Thus, the school psychologist and consultee first analyze the issues within the ecological context. When baseline data support the existence of the specific problem, the school psychologist and parent or teacher begin to jointly identify variables that might lead to problem resolution.

Consultation can involve a developmental or problem-centered focus. In developmental consultation the school psychologist establishes general, subordinate, and performance objectives. Usually these are obtained over a long period of time and in several series of interviews and are especially relevant to system change issues. In contrast, problem-centered consultation involves specification of problems that are specific and relate to one or a few primary concerns or goals. Relative to the developmental consultation process, problem-centered consultation is more time limited. Whether the nature of consultation is developmental or problem centered, the school psychologist needs to achieve clear specification of problems, competencies, and goals. Typically, this process involves generating precise descriptions of the situation, carefully analyzing the conditions under which the problems occur, and establishing some indication of the level of persistence or strength of the problems.

Goals of Consultation
During the problem identification phase, the goals of consultation should be established. One tool that can be helpful to establish goals and benchmarks is Outcomes: Planning, Monitoring, Evaluating (Stoiber & Kratochwill, 2002). Outcomes: Planning, Monitoring, Evaluating includes five steps that are featured in Figure 30.2. The system embraces a focused goal setting and goal attainment scaling framework in which up to three goals and corresponding benchmarks are established. The system also includes a convergent evidence scaling format so that multiple outcome measures can be examined for correspondence on intervention effectiveness. Outcomes: Planning, Monitoring, Evaluating is a

Figure 30.2. Steps and Objectives for Outcomes: Planning, Monitoring, Evaluating

Outcomes: Planning, Monitoring, Evaluating Procedural Checklist
Check All Steps Completed

1. *Describe and establish baseline of the behavioral or academic concern.*

    1. Behavioral or academic concern defined in observable, measurable terms.
    2. Baseline established on behavioral or academic concern.
    3. Situational analysis of concern conducted (e.g., routines, expectation–skill match, contingent relationships, adult/teacher support required).
    4. Student and situational assets to build on identified.
    5. Parental input about behavioral or academic concern obtained.

2. *Set meaningful goals and benchmarks.*

    6. Goal statement focusing on controllable, measurable behaviors written.
    7. Benchmarks specifying standard against which to compare and scaling format selected.
    8. Target date for goal attainment established.
    9. Standard or social-comparison criterion against which to measure progress selected.

3. *Plan the intervention and specify progress-monitoring procedures.*

    10. Intervention with empirical support or functional basis identified.
    11. Intervention strategies/steps developed and reviewed with the change agent(s) or interventionist(s), such as parent, teacher, language specialist, psychologist.
    12. Context, frequency, and resources needed to implement intervention determined.
    13. Progress-monitoring procedures specified, including individual responsible for implementing progress monitoring and individual responsible for collecting progress-monitoring data.

4. *Monitor progress and analyze data.*

    14. Goal scaled at beginning point, intervention with specified strategies implemented for specified time, goal scaled at ending point.
    15. Progress-monitoring data and goal-attainment data plotted.
    16. Evidence in support of child's progress documented.
    17. Reasons for positive and/or negative progress review.

5. *Evaluate intervention outcomes and plan next steps.*

    18. Based on convergent-evidence procedures, consensus on progress toward goal occurred.
    19. Intervention-quality and intervention-integrity data reviewed.
    20. Discrepancy between expected change and postintervention examined for significance.
    21. Sufficient monitoring data and convergent data established.
    22. Intervention goals and strategies revised, if indicated (e.g., due to poor progress).

Note. From *Outcomes: Planning, Monitoring, Evaluating,* by K. C. Stoiber and T. R. Kratochwill, 2001, San Antonio, TX: The Psychological Corporation. Copyright 2001 by The Psychological Corporation. Reprinted with permission.

useful tool for structuring and facilitating productive problem solving in consultation at both the case and system level.

The Academic Competence Evaluation Scales (DiPerna & Elliott, 2000) and its corresponding intervention system, the Academic Intervention Monitoring System (DiPerna, Elliott, & Shapiro, 2000), are other examples of an approach to assessment intervention that is consistent with, but is not, a consultative problem-solving model. The Academic Competence Evaluation Scales and the Academic Intervention Monitoring System utilize teachers as the primary assessment and intervention agent for children experiencing difficulties with academic skills (reading, language arts, mathematics, and critical thinking) and academic enablers (interpersonal skills, engagement, motivation, and study skills). Both the Academic Competence Evaluation Scales and the Academic Intervention Monitoring System emphasize behavior rating and goal attainment scaling technology to identify and monitor behavior. Figure 30.3 provides an overview of the use of both the Academic Competence Evaluation Scales and the Academic Intervention Monitoring System to facilitate enactment of a five-step problem-solving process. The Academic Competence Evaluation Scales has been supplemented with a Brief Academic Competence Evaluation Screening System (see Elliott, Huai, & Roach, 2007). The Brief Academic Competence Evaluation Screening System is especially useful in a multitiered system, as it can be used to screen at the universal or primary level and identify students in need of early interventions for academic skill problems.

Establishment of Assessment Techniques

Another important objective of problem identification is establishing assessment techniques. Together, the consultees and school psychologist agree on the type or kind of measures to be used, what will be recorded, and how this process will be implemented. There are a growing number of progress monitoring tools that can be used to screen, assess baseline performance, and assess intervention outcomes (e.g., Albers, Glover, & Kratochwill, 2007; Albers, Kratochwill, & Glover, 2007; Kratochwill et al., 2009).

Procedural Objectives

Certain procedural objectives must be met during the problem identification phase. One of the first objectives involves establishing times, dates, and formats for subsequent interviews and/or contacts with consultees to examine procedural aspects of the consultation process. For example, the school psychologist may agree to contact the parent/teacher weekly or biweekly to determine whether data are being gathered properly or if any unique barriers have occurred.

Stage 3: Problem Analysis

Problem analysis, the third major stage of consultation, focuses on the variables and conditions that are hypothesized to influence the system and/or the child's prosocial and challenging behaviors. Case-centered problem analysis is a natural extension of the problem identification stage in that it essentially begins with the behaviors and prosocial competencies of concern and focuses on establishing functional relationships between it and the functions of behavior. Questions about who, what, where, when, and under what conditions or contingencies are all considered relevant and generally facilitate a better understanding of the problem behavior. In many cases, the problem analysis stage will require the school psychologist to collect additional data about the child's challenging behaviors and social competencies. Thus, problem analysis may enhance refinement and, consequently, redefinition of the problem and the factor or factors that influence it.

Factors That Might Lead to Resolution

After baseline data are collected on the areas of concern, the school psychologist and consultees meet to decide jointly on factors that might lead to some resolution of the problem. In this regard, the consultation process will focus on variables that may be relevant to case or system change. The problem analysis interview includes five major steps: (a) choosing analysis procedures, (b) determining the conditions and/or skills analysis, (c) developing plan strategies, (d) developing plan tactics, and (e) establishing procedures to evaluate performance during implementation of any intervention program. Within the context of these phases, the school psychologist might first analyze the variables that lead to potential solution of the problem and then develop a plan to solve the problem.

Conditions for Goal Attainment

The school psychologist focuses on conditions that facilitate attainment of the mutually agreed upon goals at the individual and/or system level. Generally, the following steps are necessary: (a) specifying whether the goal of intervention is to increase, decrease, or maintain conditions of the target issue and determining what

Figure 30.3. The Use of Academic Competence Evaluation Scales, Goal Attainment Scale, Academic Intervention Monitoring System, and Academic Intervention Monitoring System Forms Within a Five-Step Problem-Solving Process

---

Step 1. Identify academic concern(s)

- Student completes Academic Competence Evaluation Scales

Step 2. Analyze academic concerns with the instructional environment

- Score Academic Competence Evaluation Scales–College and analyze behaviors using Academic Competence Evaluation Scales–Behavior Classification Framework
- Student College Intervention Form

Step 3. Plan for intervention

- Determine desired behavior(s)
- Determine intervention goal
- Develop goal attainment scale to monitor intervention

Step 4. Implement intervention and monitor student progress

- Specify strategies to change target behavior
- Student completes goal attainment scale daily or weekly

Step 5. Evaluate intervention

- Student completes Academic Competence Evaluation Scales a second time
- Review goal attainment scale and Academic Competence Evaluation Scales data

---

Note. From *The Academic Competence Evaluation Scales,* by J. C. DiPerna and S. N. Elliott, 2000, San Antonio, TX: The Psychological Corporation. Copyright 2000 by The Psychological Corporation. Reprinted with permission.

conditions will be assessed; (b) identifying setting events and antecedent/consequential conditions associated with conditions; (c) determining what current conditions affect the goal by comparing the existing situation to related evidence-based prevention/intervention; and (d) identifying conditions that are not currently associated with the target issue but that nonetheless could influence solving the issue.

Through mutual problem-solving efforts, the school psychologist and consultees must analyze the kinds of conditions necessary to achieve the goals of consultation during the problem analysis phase. In case-centered consultation this process includes analyzing skills that the child does not possess, and it can include academic and/or social performance. In a multitiered system model, this process involves an analysis of system variables to put a prevention program in place (e.g., resources, staff time, and professional development). Basically, the school psychologist must work with consultees to identify psychological and educational principles that relate to attaining the goals of consultation. It is beyond the scope of this chapter to outline these procedures in great detail. Rather, the reader is referred to a number of sources that can be useful to analyze behavioral and cognitive features that relate to system, instructional, and social functioning (e.g., DiPerna et al., 2000; Ysseldyke & Christenson, 2002).

Plan for Intervention

The outcome of successful problem analysis is a plan to put into effect during the intervention implementation process. Development of this plan includes first specifying broad strategies that can be used to achieve the mutually agreed upon goals. The plan typically indicates sources of action to be implemented. Second, plan tactics are used to guide implementation of the strategy and outline principles to be applied during the intervention. For example, if professional development is to be used, the person responsible for carrying out the plan and the conditions under which they will occur should be specified. During this phase school psychologists might also assess prevention/intervention acceptability prior to its implementation. A number of scales have been developed for assessment of pretreatment acceptability, and readers are encouraged to consult this material (Elliott, 1988b; Witt & Elliott, 1985). The appendix includes copies of two scales that can be used in the assessment of acceptability.

Performance and Assessment Objectives

During problem analysis the school psychologist and consultees must establish performance and assessment objectives that will be used during plan implementation. Typically, this procedure follows from a conditions analysis and involves specification of an assessment procedure previously used during baseline. For example, when plan implementation involves skill development, some agreed-upon format for collection of data on performance related to the final objectives achieved is necessary.

Stage 4: Plan Implementation

Plan implementation follows the problem analysis stage and has dual objectives of (a) selecting an appropriate prevention and/or intervention and (b) implementing the program or procedures. Procedural details are essential at this stage, such as assigning individuals to various roles, gathering or preparing specific materials, or training individuals to implement the plan. The design and selection of appropriate interventions should be based on evidence-based interventions or practices and requires attention to issues of intervention acceptability, effectiveness, and consultee skills and resources (Kratochwill & Shernoff, 2004). Many consumers and providers of psychological services are also demanding that interventions also be acceptable (i.e., time efficient, least restrictive, fair and/or low risk to the child; Elliott, 1988a, 1988b). Likewise, interventions that are consistent with the teacher's and parent's child management philosophy and compatible with existing resources and skills of the individual delivering the intervention have also recently gained consumer interest and empirical support (Witt & Martens, 1988).

Plan implementation also involves discussing and actually carrying out the selected intervention. This substage may consume several weeks or months and is characterized by interactions between the school psychologist and consultees. These interactions may occur through brief contacts in which the school psychologist monitors intervention integrity and side effects (Sanetti & Kratochwill, 2013) and possibly brainstorms with the consultee ways to revise the plan and its use. For case-centered consultation, DiPerna and Elliott (2000) developed a series of Intervention Record forms for teachers, parents, and students. These Intervention Record forms are based on the effective teaching literature and provide respondents opportunities to indicate how helpful and how feasible specific intervention tactics are likely to be with a given student. These Intervention Record forms are an example of trying to enhance the likelihood that the interventions selected are acceptable and that a consultee will be able to implement them. The school psychologist's role may also involve observations to monitor child and consultee behaviors or training sessions to enhance the skills of the individual who is executing the intervention plan.

Major Tasks of Implementation

During plan implementation, the three major tasks that must be accomplished include skill development of consultees (if necessary), monitoring of the implementation process, and plan revisions. Typically, the school psychologist must determine whether the consultee has the skills to carry out the plan. If skill development is required, the consultee must be offered some type of professional development or guidance (Kratochwill et al., 2008). Skill development might be offered through direct instruction by the school psychologist, modeling of the intervention, videotaping, Web-based instruction, self-instructional materials, and/or formal training offered by others. Many evidence-based interventions are accompanied by a manual or protocol that can be used to train consultees or engage them in a self-instructional process of training.

A second task is to monitor data to determine if assessment and implementation are occurring as intended. Consultee records usually are examined to assess child outcome. This process usually will indicate to the school psychologist when progress-monitoring data are being gathered, how the performance of the child is being assessed, and what behaviors are being observed.

Treatment Integrity

Plan implementation must also be monitored. Assessment of plan implementation is referred to as treatment integrity and corresponds to the degree to which intervention components are delivered to the student as planned (Sanetti & Kratochwill, 2014). Several proposed dimensions of treatment integrity can be assessed during the plan implementation stage of consultation.

Adherence is related to the intervention steps delivered to a student in an intervention session. Quality refers to a rating of the qualitative aspects of intervention delivery. Exposure is related to the quantitative side of the interventions, such as the number of intervention sessions the student receives or the duration of an intervention session. Program differentiation is important for examining whether the intervention components constitute unique strategies different from those the student is receiving elsewhere in the classroom. Finally, student

responsiveness, or engagement in the intervention sessions, may also be a critical dimension to assess throughout the plan implementation stage (Dane & Schneider, 1998; Sanetti & Kratochwill, 2014). The school psychologist and parent or teacher should decide the dimensions that are most critical to effective intervention implementation.

The goal of monitoring treatment integrity in consultation is to determine whether the student consistently receives the plan developed in the problem analysis stage. This information is integrated with student progress monitoring data on the areas of concern. The school psychologist can combine treatment integrity and student data to inform decision making in hopes of helping the student reach intervention goals. The decision will involve continuing the intervention as planned, or only currently implemented steps that are demonstrating effectiveness; providing additional implementation support to the parent or teacher to implement the plan as originally intended; or changing the intervention plan to improve student progress (Sanetti, Fallon, & Collier-Meek, 2011). Table 30.1 outlines these decisions on the basis of treatment integrity and student data.

Monitoring of treatment integrity and student data is helpful in determining whether the intervention was actually responsible for any changes seen in the student, and thereby concluding that there was a functional relationship between the intervention components and the area of concern for the student (Sanetti, Gritter, & Dobey, 2011; Sanetti & Kratochwill, 2014). It is important to know the intervention components that are believed to improve the student's academic or behavioral concern. As a result, the intervention could be used in the future for a problem recurrence or setting generalization with the same student, or with a new student demonstrating similar concerns (Lane, Bocian, MacMillan, & Gresham, 2004; Sanetti, Gritter, et al., 2011).

Intervention Integrity and Accountability

Treatment integrity evaluation during consultation is also an important consideration for accountability

Table 30.1. Decisions for Combining Student Outcome and Treatment Integrity Data

	Improved Student Outcomes	No or Insufficient Progress Toward the Goal
High treatment integrity	Continue implementation of the current intervention plan.	Change the intervention plan by selecting an alternative evidence-based practice appropriate for the student.
Low treatment integrity	Change the intervention plan to reflect effective components.	Identify a strategy to increase treatment integrity for the current intervention plan.

related to federal legislation and RTI. The provision of evidence-based interventions to students is a requirement in the 2001 No Child Left Behind Act and the 2004 Individuals with Disabilities Improvement Act. The inclusion of treatment integrity assessment plans is a key step in accounting for mandated access to interventions that are effective. The information regarding whether an intervention was implemented is a component used in the RTI decision-making process for individual students. Without data to verify that an intervention was implemented, it cannot be confirmed that the intervention was implemented as intended. Thus, lack of progress may unfairly be attributed to a failure of true response rather than the lack of intervention implementation (Noell & Gansle, 2006). Thus, the validity of intervention decisions in RTI can be compromised if treatment integrity data are not collected.

Methods for Monitoring Treatment Integrity

Several methods of data collection have been proposed to assist in the measurement of treatment integrity in consultation for the purposes of decision making. These methods include self-report, direct observation, and permanent products (Sanetti, Fallon, et al., 2011). It is recommended that data collection be continuous throughout the plan implementation stage. Furthermore, it should include assessment of all relevant dimensions to treatment integrity as logistics and resources of the intervention permit (Sanetti & Kratochwill, 2014). The data collected through these methods can inform decisions made about student RTI across tiers of support.

Revision of the Intervention

Changes should be made in the intervention plan when necessary. If circumstances and/or the program are not changing in the desired direction and treatment integrity is low, plan revision should occur. Generally, this outcome will require the school psychologist and consultees to return again to the problem analysis phase to further analyze variables such as the setting, intrapersonal child characteristics, skill deficits or social competencies, or system barriers. Likewise, it may be necessary to return to the problem identification stage if it is determined that the nature of the problem has changed.

Stage 5: Plan Evaluation

Plan evaluation is the final stage of consultation with the objective of establishing a sound basis for interpreting outcomes of the intervention for the targeted issue or problem and providing a forum for evaluating plan effectiveness. The rigor of evaluation involved in research may not be used consistently in practice, but good evidence to verify outcomes should be routine in case consultation efforts. The use of single-case research designs, as recommended in some approaches to evaluation of RTI (e.g., Brown-Chidsey & Steege, 2006), are very difficult to use in practice as they are quite complex (Kratochwill & Piersel, 1983). The procedures involving case study evaluation and discussed by Stoiber and Kratochwill (2002) and Kratochwill (1985) are recommended as an option and are discussed below.

Case Study Evaluation Methods

One approach that can be used by the school psychologist to evaluate consultation outcomes is to use case study methods that involve elements of single-case research design but do not use the replication features that are required in these methods (Kratochwill, 1985). This process typically involves using a basic AB design framework where a baseline assessment (A) is followed by the intervention (B). A variety of strategies can be invoked to improve the inferences that can be drawn from the outcomes assessment, including, for example, consideration of the history of the problem, quality assessment methods that are used repeatedly, the size of the effect, and monitoring of the integrity of the treatment. With quality indicators as part of the process, such practice-based evidence can even be used to inform the field about the elements of how certain evidence-based interventions are effective in school settings (Kratochwill et al., 2012).

Outcome Criteria

When the reported discrepancy between the child's behavior and the desired level of functioning is reduced significantly or eliminated, when academic and/or social competencies have been acquired, and when the intervention is acceptable to both the parent/teacher and child, the school psychologist and consultee decide whether consultation should be terminated. Outcome criteria should include maintenance of the desired behavior over time and generalization across multiple settings and conditions. In theory, consultation is not concluded until the discrepancy between the existing and desired circumstances are addressed substantively and an acceptable maintenance plan is in place. Criteria such as overall improvement in the quality of life (social and academic) and system change can also be invoked but may require a developmental focus in case consultation. Therefore, it is often necessary to recycle through previous stages of consultation and reevaluate refined or newly implemented interventions.

Evaluation Interview

Plan evaluation can be implemented through a formal plan evaluation interview and typically is undertaken to determine whether the goals of consultation have been attained. The process of evaluation includes assessment of goal attainment, plan effectiveness, and implementation planning. The first major step in plan evaluation is to decide whether the actual goals previously agreed upon have been met. This decision is determined through discussion with the consultee and observation of the client's behavior. Again, the goal attainment framework of Outcomes: Planning, Monitoring, Evaluating can be very useful in making decisions about the goals of consultation and can be continued during this phase. The process of evaluating goal attainment was first initiated during problem identification, where the objectives and procedures for measuring mastery were specified. When Outcomes: Planning, Monitoring, Evaluating is used, specific benchmarks for each consultation goal are indicated. The data gathered subsequent to the problem identification phase should provide some evidence as to whether there is congruence between objectives and the problem solution. Basically, this step occurs on the basis of the data collected, but additional strategies might be invoked as well, such as social validation criteria specified in Outcomes: Planning, Monitoring, Evaluating. That is, the school psychologist will want to know, for example, whether the child reached some clinically established level of change and whether the intervention program brought the child's performance within a range of acceptable behavior as compared to typical peers. Determination of the congruence between behavior and objectives generally leads the school psychologist to conclude that no progress was obtained, some progress was made, or the actual goal was attained.

Goal Attainment Scaling

Advances in the evaluation of intervention effects and consultation outcomes continue to appear in the research literature. Several of these advances have been used in the evaluation of community mental health services and supplement the case study and social validation strategies that have traditionally been used by school psychologists. One of the most practical strategies is goal attainment scaling (see Stoiber & Kratochwill,

2002). Briefly, there are several different approaches to using a goal attainment framework. The basic tactic, however, is one in which a consultee would be asked to describe five to seven levels of intervention outcome. The most unfavorable outcome described is given a -2 or -3 rating, a no change outcome is given a 0 rating, and the most favorable outcome is given a $+2$ or $+3$ rating. Ratings of -1 to -2 and $+1$ to $+2$ are ascribed to benchmark descriptions of outcomes that are situated between the most unfavorable and expected outcome and the most favorable and expected outcome, respectively. Outcomes: Planning, Monitoring, Evaluating can be used to obtain daily or weekly measures on intervention progress, as well as final outcome perceptions from a consultee. Goal attainment scaling is a sensitive system since both overattainment and underattainment of objectives can be rated. Outcomes: Planning, Monitoring, Evaluating has specific application to prevention program application and can be very useful in RTI multitiered model implementation and evaluation.

Postimplementation Planning

Once it has been determined that the problem has been solved, post-implementation planning occurs to help ensure that the particular problem does not occur again. There are some alternatives available for the school psychologist and parent/teacher in designing postimplementation plans. One strategy is to leave the plan in effect. Typically, however, a plan that is put into effect will need to be modified (another alternative) to facilitate maintenance of program outcomes over time. There is considerable evidence in the intervention literature that specific tactics are needed to facilitate maintenance and generalization of intervention outcomes, and these tactics must be accomplished during this phase of consultation. Generalization may occur naturally, but more likely it will need to be programmed. Several factors have been identified that have a bearing on the generalization of skills (Haring, 1988; White et al., 1988). White et al. (1988) lists the strategies for facilitating generalization, along with a definition and example. The summary is based on the seminal work of Stokes and Baer (1977) and can serve as a useful guideline for school psychologists.

Another major objective that should occur during the plan evaluation interview is discussion of postimplementation recording. Generally, this procedure refers to the process of continuing record-keeping activities to determine whether the problem occurs in the future. Usually, the school psychologist and consultee select periodic measures that are convenient to use and may maintain specific features of the original plan to facilitate this data collection process. The school psychologist should consider conducting postplan implementation acceptability assessment as well. These procedures can be implemented informally or more formally with acceptability instrumentation (Elliott, 1988b). The parent or teacher should notify the school psychologist of any reoccurrence of the problem behaviors that might be indicated. These issues usually can be brought to the school psychologist's attention and specific tactics set up to establish a system to analyze the problems.

Consultation With Culturally and Linguistically Diverse Populations

Student demographics within U.S. schools continue to increase in diversity. Over a period of 13 years, the number of Caucasian students within the school population has decreased by 10%, while the percentage of students from a Hispanic background increased by 8% (Snyder & Dillow, 2011). Not only are the numbers of minority students growing, but the number of students with English as a second language also continues to grow. It is predicted that 40% of the student population will speak English as a second language by the year 2030 (U.S. Department of Education & National Institute of Child Health and Human Development, 2003). With the increasing diversity of the student population within schools, it is essential for consultants to understand the most appropriate manner to work with teachers, families, and students from culturally and linguistically diverse backgrounds.

Best practices for the delivery of consultation services to culturally and linguistically diverse teachers, students, and families suggest the need to strengthen consultant knowledge of the attitudes, values, customs, languages, and behaviors of diverse cultures (Jones & Florell, 2009; Whaley & Davis, 2007). When working with teachers and families regarding a culturally and linguistically diverse student, there are a number of specific factors to examine that may inform decisions on the identification of academic or behavioral problems. Albers, Mission, and Bice-Urbach (2013) suggest that the English proficiency of the child, the type of instruction the student is receiving, the mobility of the student, the quality of prior schools, the attendance at school, and the ecological variables that have an impact on behavior are all important factors to consider when working with

diverse populations. These variables are especially important when engaging in the problem identification stage of problem-solving consultation.

When engaging in a problem-solving approach, it is important to understand that each consultation brings unique and diverse factors that must be considered on an individual basis. Although group differences may exist between diverse cultures, students and families tend to be highly heterogeneous (August & Shanahan, 2006). Owing to both between-group and within-group differences for culturally and linguistically diverse students, the problem-solving process needs to emphasize appropriate assessment for identifying a problem and useful adaptations when choosing and implementing an appropriate intervention.

Currently, consultants must be mindful of the appropriateness of assessments, measurement tools, and interventions for diverse populations. When identifying the problem in a consultation for a culturally and linguistically diverse student, not only is it important to consider cultural factors that may have an impact on student behavior, but it also is important to consider the appropriateness of the assessments. One challenge in providing consultation services to these populations is that many assessments and interventions have not been thoroughly evaluated for work with diverse populations (Ortiz, Flanagan, & Dynda, 2008; Whaley & Davis, 2007). Once a problem has been accurately identified, consultants must help consultees find an evidence-based intervention that is appropriate for the cultural differences of the students. This process often requires cultural adaptations in an intervention (Wood, Chiu, Hwang, Jacobs, & Ifekwunigwe, 2008). Specific culturally responsive elements that could be utilized within an intervention include involving family within the intervention; being aware of the influence of culture, ethnicity, and spirituality on behavior; providing culturally specific examples within intervention; using consultants from a similar ethnic background; and emphasizing that the interventionist should act as a coach instead of as a teacher (Huey & Polo, 2008).

Given the likelihood of working with teachers, families, and students from culturally and linguistically diverse backgrounds, consultants must continually engage in reflection of how their own cultural background has an impact on their practice and how cultural differences have an impact on the utility of assessments and interventions. By engaging in this continual reflection, consultants can ensure that they are practicing in a culturally competent manner. This process therefore ensures that consultees and students are being provided with the best consultation services for their unique needs.

Some Final Perspectives

Research documenting the effectiveness of consultation has been organized around four areas of investigation: (a) outcome research, (b) process research, (c) practitioner utilization, and (d) training research (White & Kratochwill, 2008). To these considerations we add a perspective on developmental considerations in this practice and how school psychologists can evaluate their own effectiveness, or outcomes, when providing consultation services.

Outcome Research

Overall, problem-solving consultation is a rapidly growing area with increasing empirical support (e.g., Sheridan et al., 2012). Research addressing outcomes of consultation documents the effectiveness of consultation in remediating academic and behavior problems manifested by children in school settings. Likewise, these same studies suggest that changes result in the teacher's and parent's behavior, knowledge, attitudes, and perceptions. Although consultation traditionally has been directed toward a single client (i.e., teacher), it can also be applied successfully with a number of mediators (e.g., peer consultation, conjoint consultation; see Kratochwill & Pittman, 2002) and formats (e.g., teleconsultation). A collaborative problem-solving model whereby the school psychologist, teacher, and parent share information, value each other's input, and incorporate each other's perspective in developing the intervention plan is considered to afford great benefits. Yet, little outcome research has been conducted on consultation problem-solving applications with groups and systems (Kratochwill & Pittman, 2002) and especially with multitiered models of prevention. Research in the area of teleconsultation is in its infancy.

Process Research

Typically, process research has focused on case-focused problem identification, since the consultant's ability to elicit a clear description of the problem has been identified as the best predictor of plan implementation and problem solution (e.g., Bergan & Tombari, 1975, 1976). Studies in this area also have focused on comparing consultation effectiveness with other forms of service delivery (Medway, 1979). Yet, it remains difficult to draw conclusions from the studies addressing variables associated with the process of consultation due to limitations in scope, theoretical base, and research methodology (Gresham & Kendell, 1987; Frank & Kratochwill, in press).

Practitioner Utilization

Traditionally, studies on practitioner utilization have suggested that school-based case consultation is a preferred activity for school psychologists (e.g., Gutkin & Curtis, 1981; Meacham & Peckham, 1978). Many school psychologists have traditionally engaged in consultation activities (Curtis, Walker, Hunley, & Baker, 1999), but many practitioners identify limitations to implementing consultation due to time constraints and lack of consultee commitment (Gresham & Kendell, 1987). Both individual consultant–consultee and system issues must be addressed to deal with those constraints.

Practitioner Self-Assessment

Careful self-evaluation of consultation services will have an impact on their future use as an alternative to traditional assessment and intervention practices in educational settings and may result in an increased emphasis on the development of formalized training in school psychology programs. The quality of consultation services can be evaluated in several ways. One important indicator of the effectiveness of consultation services is the client outcome that is achieved through the problem-solving process. Actual client improvement in academic and/or behavioral areas is possible to document through the plan evaluation strategies noted above. Second, consultee and client satisfaction with the intervention and services can be used to self-assess the quality of problem solving. Third, the school psychologist can use various record forms and protocols that structure each component of the consultation problem-solving process. Protocols for this process are available for both case-centered (Kratochwill & Bergan, 1990) and conjoint consultation (Sheridan & Kratochwill, 2008). These self-assessment strategies can contribute to the evidence-based practice of school psychology and have a positive impact on the quality of consultation services.

SUMMARY

There has never been a time in the history of the field of school psychology when consultation has been more relevant and appropriate for the provision of prevention and intervention services. Problem-solving consultation can be conceptualized as a five-stage approach that uses broad-based behavioral, evidence-based interventions or practices, and collaborative methods as the basis for the consultation process. The major features of consultation include its indirect service delivery approach and problem-solving focus. Consultation has two principal goals. The first goal is to produce positive outcomes for a system, consultees, and clients indirectly through collaborative problem solving between a consultant (school psychologist) and consultee (e.g., parent/teacher, problem-solving team, peers, administrators). A second, yet equally important, goal of consultation is to empower consultees with skills that will enable future independent problem solving at the system, classroom, and individual levels. In this regard, the consultation approach outlined in this chapter can be thought of as a practice guideline for school psychologists.

A growing body of research has accumulated on the positive outcomes of problem-solving consultation, including approaches that involve conjoint consultation between school and home. Additionally, the practice of problem-solving consultation is expanding rapidly. In particular, there is a strong movement toward problem-solving consultation in school settings at the systems level to the exclusion of traditional refer–test–place practices largely due to the RTI movement. Building the consultation skills of current school psychologists and developing skills of those in graduate programs will have an impact on its future use as an alternative to traditional assessment and intervention practices in educational settings. In turn, these developments would contribute to the practice of school psychology and affect the children, teachers, parents, and systems receiving psychological and educational services.

AUTHOR NOTE

Disclosure. Thomas R. Kratochwill has a financial interest in books he authored or coauthored that are referenced in this chapter.

REFERENCES

Albers, C. A., Glover, T. A., & Kratochwill, T. R. (2007). Introduction to the special issue: How can universal screening enhance educational and mental health outcomes? *Journal of School Psychology, 45*, 113–116.

Albers, C. A., Kratochwill, T. R., & Glover, T. A. (2007). What we are, and where do we go now? Universal screening for enhanced educational and mental health outcomes. *Journal of School Psychology, 45*, 257–263.

Albers, C. A., Mission, P. L., & Bice-Urbach, B. (2013). Considering diverse learner characteristics in problem-solving assessment. In R. Brown-Chidsey & K. J. Andren (Eds.), *Assessment for intervention: A*

problem-solving approach (2nd ed., pp. 101–122). New York, NY: Guilford Press.

August, D., & Shanahan, T. (2006). *Developing literacy in second-language learners: Report of the National Literacy Panel on language, minority children and youth.* Hillsdale, NJ: Erlbaum.

Bergan, J. R. (1977). *Behavioral consultation.* Columbus, OH: Merrill.

Bergan, J. R., & Kratochwill, T. R. (1990). *Behavioral consultation in applied settings.* New York, NY: Plenum Press.

Bergan, J. R., & Tombari, M. L. (1975). The analysis of verbal interactions occurring during consultation. *Journal of School Psychology, 14*, 3–14.

Bergan, J. R., & Tombari, M. L. (1976). Consultant skill and efficiency and the implementation and outcome of consultation. *Journal of School Psychology, 14*, 3–14.

Brown, D., Pryzwansky, W. B., & Schulte, A. C. (2011). *Psychological consultation and collaboration: Introduction to theory and practice* (7th ed.). Boston, MA: Pearson.

Brown-Chidsey, R., & Andren, K. J. (2013). *Assessment for intervention: A problem-solving approach* (2nd ed.). New York, NY: Guilford Press.

Brown-Chidsey, R., & Steege, M. W. (2006). *Response to intervention: Principles and strategies for effective instruction.* New York, NY: Guilford Press.

Brownlee, K., Graham, J. R., Doucette, E., Hotson, N., & Halverson, G. (2010). Have communication technologies influenced rural social work practice? *British Journal of Social Work, 40*, 622–637.

Carrington Rotto, P., & Kratochwill, T. R. (1994). Behavioral consultation with parents: Using competency-based training to modify child noncompliance. *School Psychology Review, 23*, 669–693.

Coffee, G., & Kratochwill, T. R. (2013). Examining teacher use of praise taught during behavioral consultation: Implementation and generalization considerations. *Journal of Educational and Psychological Consultation, 23*, 1–25.

Curtis, M. J., Walker, K. J., Hunley, S. A., & Baker, A. C. (1999). Demographic characteristics and professional practices in school psychology. *School Psychology Quarterly, 28*, 104–116.

Dane, A. V., & Schneider, B. H. (1998). Program integrity in primary and early secondary prevention: Are implementation effects out of control? *Clinical Psychology Review, 18*, 23–45.

DiPerna, J. C., & Elliott, S. N. (2000). *The Academic Competence Evaluation Scales.* San Antonio, TX: The Psychological Corporation.

DiPerna, J. C., Elliott, S. N., & Shapiro, E. S. (2000). *The Academic Intervention Monitoring System.* San Antonio, TX: The Psychological Corporation.

Doll, B., Gaack, K., Kosse, S., Osterloh, M., & Siemers, E. (2005). The dilemma of pragmatics: Why schools don't use quality team consultation practices. *Journal of Educational and Psychological Consultation, 16*, 127–155.

Dunst, C. J., & Trivette, C. M. (1988). Helping, helplessness, and harm. In J. C. Witt, S. N. Elliott, & F. M. Gresham (Eds.), *The handbook of behavior therapy in education* (pp. 343–376). New York, NY: Plenum Press.

Elliott, S. N. (1988a). Acceptability of behavioral treatments: A review of variables that influence treatment selection. *Professional Psychology: Research and Practice, 19*, 68–80.

Elliott, S. N. (1988b). Acceptability of behavioral treatment in educational settings. In J. C. Witt, S. N. Elliott, & F. M. Gresham

(Eds.), *The handbook of behavior therapy in education* (pp. 121–150). New York, NY: Plenum Press.

Elliott, S. N., Huai, N., & Roach, A. T. (2007). Universal and early screening for educational difficulties: Current and future approaches. *Journal of School Psychology, 45*, 137–161.

Frank, J. L., & Kratochwill, T. R. (in press). School-based problem-solving consultation: Plotting a new course for evidence-based research and practice in consultation. In W. C. Eurchl & S. M. Sheridan (Eds.), *Handbook of research in school consultation: Empirical foundations for the field*. Mahwah, NJ: Erlbaum.

Germain, V., Marchand, A., Bouchard, S., Guay, S., & Drouin, M. (2010). Assessment of the therapeutic alliance in face-to-face or videoconference treatment for posttraumatic stress disorder. *Cyberpsychology, Behavior, and Social Networking, 13*, 29–35.

Gettinger, M., & Stoiber, K. C. (2009). Excellence in teaching: Review of instructional and environmental variables. In C. R. Reynolds & T. B. Gutkin (Eds.), *The handbook of school psychology* (4th ed., pp. 769–790). Hoboken, NJ: Wiley.

Glisson, C. (2002). The organizational context of children's mental health services. *Clinical Child and Family Psychology Review, 5*, 233–253.

Glisson, C. (2007). Assessing and changing organizational culture and climate for effective services. *Research on Social Work Practice, 17*, 736–747.

Glueckauf, R. L., & Ketterson, T. U. (2004). Telehealth interventions for individuals with chronic illness: Research review and implications for practice. *Professional Psychology: Research and Practice, 35*, 615–627.

Glueckauf, R. L., Pickett, T. C., Ketterson, T. U., Loomis, J. S., & Rozensky, R. H. (2003). Preparation for the delivery of telehealth services: A self-study framework for expansion of practice. *Professional Psychology: Research and Practice, 34*, 159–163.

Gravois, T. A., Groff, S., & Rosenfield, S. (2009). Teams as value-added consultation services. In T. B. Gutkin & C. R. Reynolds (Eds.), *The handbook of school psychology* (4th ed., pp. 808–820). Hoboken, NJ: Wiley.

Gresham, F. M. (2006). Response to intervention. In G. G. Bear & K. M. Minke (Eds.), *Children's needs III: Development, prevention, and intervention* (pp. 525–540). Bethesda, MD: National Association of School Psychologists.

Gresham, F. M., & Kendell, G. K. (1987). School consultation research: Methodological critique and future research directions. *School Psychology Review, 16*, 306–316.

Gutkin, T. B., & Curtis, M. J. (1981). School-based consultant: The indirect service delivery concept. In M. J. Grimes & J. E. Zins (Eds.), *The theory and practice of school consultation* (pp. 219–226). Springfield, IL: Charles C. Thomas.

Gutkin, T. B., & Curtis, M. J. (1999). School-based consultation theory and practice: The art and science of indirect service delivery. In C. R. Reynolds & T. B. Gutkin (Eds.), *The handbook of school psychology* (3rd ed., pp. 598–637). Hoboken, NJ: Wiley.

Haring, N. G. (1988). A technology for generalization. In N. G. Haring (Ed.), *Generalization for students with severe handicaps: Strategies and solutions* (pp. 5–11). Seattle, WA: University of Washington Press.

Huey, S. J., & Polo, A. J. (2008). Evidence-based psychosocial treatments for ethnic minority youth. *Journal of Clinical Child and Adolescent Psychology, 37*, 262–301.

Hurwitz, J. T., Rehberg, E. A., & Kratochwill, T. R. (2007). Dealing with school systems and teachers. In M. Hersen & J. C. Thomas (Eds.), *Comprehensive handbook of interviewing: Vol. 2. Interviewing children, their parents, and teachers* (pp. 95–114). Thousand Oaks, CA: SAGE.

Jones, J., & Florell, D. (2009, April). *NASP dialogues: Interview with Janine Jones* [Audio podcast]. Retrieved from http://www.nasponline.org/resources/podcasts/multiculturalism.aspx

Kincaid, D., Childs, K., Blase, K. A., & Wallace, F. (2007). Identifying barriers and facilitators in implementing school-wide positive behavior support. *Journal of Positive Behavior Interventions, 9*, 174–184.

Kratochwill, T. R. (1985). Case study research in school psychology. *School Psychology Review, 14*, 204–215.

Kratochwill, T. R., & Bergan, J. R. (1990). *Behavioral consultation in applied settings: An individual guide*. New York, NY: Plenum Press.

Kratochwill, T. R., Clements, M. A., & Kalymon, K. M. (2007). Response to intervention: Conceptual and methodological issues in implementation. In S. R. Jimerson, M. K. Burns, & A. M. VanDerHeyden (Eds.), *The handbook to response to intervention: The science and practice of assessment and intervention* (pp. 25–52). New York, NY: Springer.

Kratochwill, T. R., Hoagwood, K. E., Kazak, A. E., Weisz, J., Vargas, L. A., & Banez, G. A. (2012). Practice-based evidence for children and adolescents: Advancing the research agenda in schools. *School Psychology Review, 41*, 215–234.

Kratochwill, T. R., Hoagwood, K. E., White, J., Levitt, J. M., Romanelli, L. H., & Saka, N. (2009). Evidence-based interventions and practices in school psychology: Challenges and opportunities for the profession. In T. Gutkin & C. Reynolds (Eds.), *Handbook of school psychology* (4th ed., pp. 497–521.). Hoboken, NJ: Wiley.

Kratochwill, T. R., & Piersel, W. C. (1983). Time-series research: Contributions to empirical clinical practice. *Behavioral Assessment, 5*, 165–176.

Kratochwill, T. R., & Pittman, P. (2002). Defining constructs in consultation: An important training agenda. *Journal of Educational and Psychological Consultation, 12*, 65–91.

Kratochwill, T. R., & Shernoff, E. (2004). Evidence-based practice: Promoting evidence-based interventions in school psychology. *School Psychology Quarterly, 18*, 389–408.

Kratochwill, T. R., Volpiansky, P., Clements, M., & Ball, C. (2008). Professional development in implementing and sustaining multitier prevention models: Implications for response to intervention. *School Psychology Review, 36*, 618–631.

Lane, K. L., Bocian, K. M., MacMillan, D. L., & Gresham, F. M. (2004). Treatment integrity: An essential—but not forgotten—component of school-based interventions. *Preventing School Failure, 48*, 36–43.

Machalicek, W., O'Reilly, M., Chan, J. M., Rispoli, M., Lang, R., Davis, T., … Langthorne, P. (2009). Using videoconferencing to support teachers to conduct preference assessments with students with autism and developmental disabilities. *Research in Autism Spectrum Disorders, 3*, 32–41.

Maheu, M. M., Pulier, M. L., McMenamin, J. P., & Posen, L. (2012). Future of telepsychology, telehealth, and various technologies in psychological research and practice. *Professional Psychology: Research and Practice, 43*, 613–621.

McGinty, K. L., Saeed, S. A., Simmons, S. C., & Yildirim, Y. (2006). Telepsychiatry and e-mental health services: Potential for improving access to mental health care. *Psychiatric Quarterly, 77,* 335–342.

Meacham, M. L., & Peckham, P. D. (1978). School psychologists at three-quarters century: Congruence between training, practice, preferred role, and competence. *Journal of School Psychology, 16,* 195–206.

Medway, F. J. (1979). How effective is school consultation? A review of recent research. *Journal of School Psychology, 17,* 275–282.

Mihalic, S., Irwin, K., Fagan, A., Ballard, D., & Elliott, D. (2004). *Successful program implementation: Lessons from Blueprints* (No. NCJ 204273). Washington, DC: U.S. Department of Justice, Office of Justice Programs, Office of Juvenile and Delinquency Programs.

Myrick, R. D., & Sabella, R. A. (1995). Cyberspace: New place for counselor supervision. *Elementary School Guidance and Counseling, 30,* 35–44.

National Association of School Psychologists. (2010). *Model for comprehensive and integrated school psychological services.* Bethesda, MD: Author. Retrieved from http://www.nasponline.org/standards/2010standards/2_PracticeModel.pdf

National Association of State Directors of Special Education. (2005). *Response to intervention: Policy considerations and implementation.* Alexandria, VA: Author.

Noell, G. H., & Gansle, K. A. (2006). Assuring the form has substance: Treatment plan implementation as the foundation of assessing response to intervention. *Assessment for Effective Intervention, 32,* 32–39.

Novotney, A. (2011). A new emphasis on telehealth: How can psychologists stay ahead of the curve—and keep patients safe? *Monitor on Psychology, 42*(6), 40–44.

Ortiz, S. O., Flanagan, D. P., & Dynda, A. M. (2008). Best practices in working with culturally diverse children and families. In A. Thomas & J. Grimes (Eds.), *Best Practices in School Psychology V* (pp. 1721–1738). Bethesda, MD: National Association of School Psychologists.

Parsons, R., & Meyers, J. (1984). *Developing consultation skills: A guide to training, development, and assessment for human services professionals.* San Francisco, CA: Jossey-Bass.

Reschly, D. K. (1988). Special education reform: School psychology revolution. *School Psychology Review, 17,* 465–481.

Rosenfield, S. A., & Gravois, T. A. (1996). *Instructional consultation teams: Collaborating for change.* New York, NY: Guilford Press.

Rule, S., Salzberg, C., Higbee, T., Menlove, R., & Smith, J. (2006). Technology-mediated consultation to assist rural students: A case study. *Rural Special Education Quarterly, 25*(2), 3–7.

Sanetti, L. M. H., Fallon, L. M., & Collier-Meek, M. A. (2011). Treatment integrity assessment and intervention by school-based personnel: Practical applications based on a preliminary study. *School Psychology Forum: Research in Practice, 5,* 87–102.

Sanetti, L. M. H., Gritter, K. L., & Dobey, L. M. (2011). Treatment integrity of interventions with children in school psychology literature from 1995 to 2008. *School Psychology Review, 40,* 72–84.

Sanetti, L. M. H., & Kratochwill, T. R. (2013). Treatment integrity assessment within a problem-solving model. In R. Brown-Chidsey & K. J. Andren (Eds.), *Assessment for intervention: A*

problem-solving approach (2nd ed., pp. 304–325). New York, NY: Guilford Press.

Sanetti, L. M. H., & Kratochwill, T. R. (2014). *Treatment integrity: Conceptual, methodological, and applied considerations for practitioners and researchers.* Washington, DC: American Psychological Association.

Sheridan, S. M., Bovird, J. A., Glover, T. A., Garbacz, A., Witte, A., & Kwon, K. (2012). A randomized trial examining the effects of conjoint behavioral consultation and the mediating role of the parent–teacher relationship. *School Psychology Review, 41,* 23–46.

Sheridan, S. M., Eagle, J. W., & Doll, B. (2006). An examination of the efficacy of conjoint behavioral consultation with diverse clients. *School Psychology Quarterly, 21,* 396–417.

Sheridan, S. M., & Kratochwill, T. R. (2008). *Conjoint behavioral consultation: Promoting family–school connections and interventions.* New York, NY: Springer.

Sheridan, S. M., & Walker, D. (1999). Social skills in context: Considerations for assessment, intervention, and generalization. In C. R. Reynolds & T. B. Gutkin (Eds.), *The handbook of school psychology* (3rd ed., pp. 686–708). Hoboken, NJ: Wiley.

Sheridan, S. M., Welch, M., & Orme, S. F. (1996). Is consultation effective: A review of outcome research. *Remedial and Special Education, 17,* 341–354.

Snyder, T. D., & Dillow, S. A. (2011). *Digest of education statistics 2010* (NCES 2011-2015). Washington, DC: U.S. Department of Education, National Center for Education Statistics, Institute of Education Sciences.

Stoiber, K. C., & Kratochwill, T. R. (2000). Empirically supported interventions in schools: Rationale and methodological issues. *School Psychology Quarterly, 15,* 75–105.

Stoiber, K. C., & Kratochwill, T. R. (2001). *Outcomes: Planning, Monitoring, Evaluating.* San Antonio, TX: The Psychological Corporation.

Stokes, T. F., & Baer, D. B. (1977). An implicit technology of generalization. *Journal of Applied Behavior Analysis, 10,* 349–367.

U.S. Department of Education & National Institute of Child Health and Human Development. (2003). *National symposium on learning disabilities in English language learners: Symposium summary.* Washington, DC: Author.

Whaley, A. L., & Davis, K. E. (2007). Cultural competence and evidence-based practice in mental health services: A complementary perspective. *American Psychologist, 62,* 563–574.

White, J. L., & Kratochwill, T. R. (2005). Practice guidelines in school psychology: Issues and directions for evidence-based interventions in practice and training. *Journal of School Psychology, 43,* 99–115.

White, J. L., & Kratochwill, T. R. (2008). School-based problem-solving consultation: Plotting a new course for evidence-based research and practice in consultation. In W. C. Erchul & S. M. Sheridan (Eds.), *Handbook of research in school consultation: Empirical foundations for the field* (pp. 13–30). Mahwah, NJ: Erlbaum.

White, O. R., Liberty, K. A., Haring, N. G., Billingsley, F. F., Boer, M., Burrage, A., ... Sessoms, I. (1988). Review and analysis of strategies for generalization. In N. G. Haring (Ed.), *Generalization for students with severe handicaps: Strategies and solutions* (pp. 15–51). Seattle, WA: University of Washington Press.

Wickstrom, K. F., & Witt, J. C. (1993). Resistance within school-based consultation. In J. Zins, T. R. Kratochwill, & S. N. Elliott (Eds.), *Handbook of consultation services for children* (pp. 159–178). San Francisco, CA: Jossey-Bass.

Witt, J. C., & Elliott, S. N. (1983). Assessment in behavioral consultation: The initial interview. *School Psychology Review, 12*, 42–49.

Witt, J. C., & Elliott, S. N. (1985). Acceptability of classroom intervention strategies. In T. R. Kratochwill (Ed.), *Advances in school psychology* (Vol. 4, pp. 251–288). Hillsdale, NJ: Erlbaum.

Witt, J. C., & Martens, B. K. (1988). Problems with problem-solving consultation: A reanalysis of assumptions, methods, and goals. *School Psychology Review, 17*, 211–226.

Wood, J. J., Chiu, A. W., Hwang, W., Jacobs, J., & Ifekwunigwe, M. (2008). Adapting cognitive-behavioral therapy for Mexican American students with anxiety disorders: Recommendations for school psychologists. *School Psychology Quarterly, 23*, 515–532.

Ysseldyke, J., & Christenson, S. (2002). *Functional assessment of academic behavior: Creating successful learning environments.* Longmont, CO: Sopris West.

APPENDIX. BEHAVIOR INTERVENTION RATING SCALE AND THE CHILDREN'S INTERVENTION RATING PROFILE

Behavior Intervention Rating Scale

You have just read about a child with a classroom problem and a description of an intervention for improving the problem. Please evaluate the intervention by circling the number which best describes *your* agreement or disagreement with each statement. You *must* answer each question.

	Strongly Disagree	Disagree	Slightly Disagree	Agree	Strongly Agree
1. This would be an acceptable intervention for the child's problem behavior.	1	2	3	4	5
2. Most teachers would find this intervention appropriate for behavior problems in addition to the one described.	1	2	3	4	5
3. The intervention should prove effective in changing the child's problem behavior.	1	2	3	4	5
4. I would suggest the use of this intervention to other teachers.	1	2	3	4	5
5. The child's behavior problem is severe enough to warrant use of this intervention.	1	2	3	4	5
6. Most teachers would find this intervention suitable for the behavior problem described.	1	2	3	4	5
7. I would be willing to use this intervention in the classroom setting.	1	2	3	4	5
8. The intervention would *not* result in negative side effects for the child.	1	2	3	4	5
9. The intervention would be appropriate for a variety of children.	1	2	3	4	5
10. The intervention is consistent with those I have used in classroom settings.	1	2	3	4	5
11. The intervention was a fair way to handle the child's problem behavior.	1	2	3	4	5
12. The intervention is reasonable for the behavior problem described.	1	2	3	4	5
13. I liked the procedures used in the intervention.	1	2	3	4	5

Continued

Continued

	Strongly Disagree	Disagree	Slightly Disagree	Agree	Strongly Agree
14. The intervention was a good way to handle this child's behavior problem.	1	2	3	4	5
15. Overall, the intervention would be beneficial for the child.	1	2	3	4	5
16. The intervention would quickly improve the child's behavior.	1	2	3	4	5
17. The intervention would produce a lasting improvement in the child's behavior.	1	2	3	4	5
18. The intervention would improve the child's behavior to the point that it would not noticeably deviate from other classmates' behavior.	1	2	3	4	5
19. Soon after using the intervention, the teacher would notice a positive change in the problem behavior.	1	2	3	4	5
20. The child's behavior will remain at an improved level even after the intervention is discontinued.	1	2	3	4	5
21. Using the intervention should improve the child's behavior not only in the classroom, but also in other settings (e.g., other classrooms, home).	1	2	3	4	5
22. When comparing this child with a well-behaved peer before and after use of the intervention, the child's and the peer's behavior would be more alike after using the intervention.	1	2	3	4	5
23. The intervention should produce enough improvement in the child's behavior so the behavior no longer is a problem in the classroom.	1	2	3	4	5
24. Other behaviors related to the problem behavior also are likely to be improved by the intervention.	1	2	3	4	5

The Children's Intervention Rating Profile

	I agree				I do not agree
1. The method used to deal with the behavior problem was fair.	+	+	+	+	+
2. This child's teacher was too harsh on him.	+	+	+	+	+
3. The method used to deal with the behavior may cause problems with this child's friends.	+	+	+	+	+
4. There are better ways to handle this child's problem than the one described here.	+	+	+	+	+
5. The method used by this teacher would be a good one to use with other children.	+	+	+	+	+
6. I like the method used for this child's behavior problem.	+	+	+	+	+
7. I think that the method used for this problem would help this child do better in school.	+	+	+	+	+

Note. From "Assessment in Behavioral Consultation: The Initial Interview," by J. C. Witt and S. N. Elliott, 1983, *School Psychology Review, 12,* 42–49. Copyright 1983 by National Association of School Psychologists. Reprinted with permission.

31

Best Practices in Behavioral/ Ecological Consultation

Tammy L. Hughes
Jered B. Kolbert
Laura M. Crothers
Duquesne University (PA)

OVERVIEW

This chapter describes the behavioral and ecological consultative models, including the basic assumptions in using behavioral and ecological consultation, the best practices in implementing behavioral and ecological consultation, and a summary regarding finding more detailed information. The purpose of the chapter is to briefly present the theories that underpin the behavioral and ecological consultative models, explain the process for using these consultative approaches, and review the research that supports the use of these practices. As described in the National Association of School Psychologists (NASP) *Model for Comprehensive and Integrated School Psychological Services* (NASP, 2010), consultation skills are essential to all service delivery in schools. Moreover, because school psychologists are part of interdisciplinary school teams and work with parents and teachers on behalf of children in order to find real-world solutions that prove useful in a variety of contexts, the knowledge, skills, and dispositions needed for behavioral/ecological consultation are fundamental for all school psychologists.

Consultation in schools is a service delivery model in which a school psychologist (serving as a consultant) uses problem-solving strategies in order to alter an existing set of circumstances to become a desired set of circumstances to address the needs of a consultee (often teachers or parents) and a client (students; Kratochwill & Bergan, 1990). Consultation is both a time- and cost-efficient way to provide service to a large number of clients (e.g., children, families) and allows school psychologists to work with teachers and other educators

who, guided by treatment plans, in turn work with children and their families. Consultants and consultees work collaboratively to help solve the academic, behavioral, and social–emotional problems children exhibit. Thus, consultation is an indirect vehicle through which school-based educational and mental health professionals can combine their expertise to positively affect children's development and functioning.

A historic problem in schools is the schools' failure to consistently and accurately implement evidence-based practices. One reason posited as to why evidence-based practices are not sufficiently used in schools is a research-to-practice gap, in which research-driven empirically based interventions have limited transportability to the school setting (Hoagwood, Burns, Kiser, Ringeisen, & Schoenwald, 2001). Consultation can increase the use of evidence-based practices by facilitating the transmission of information from consultants to other school-based professionals, as well as reducing barriers to evidence-based practice implementation, such as intervention complexity, since school psychology consultants can provide training, guidance, and supervision to consultees to improve intervention integrity (Auster, Feeney-Kettler, & Kratochwill, 2006). In following the consultative process, school psychologists use persuasion, facilitated through the bond of relationships (e.g., referent power), to work collaboratively to meet the needs of children and their families. In doing so, school psychologists can encourage the use of empirically sound practices to help improve children's academic and behavioral functioning. Since consultation can, in the short term, improve the academic, behavioral, and social functioning of specific students and, in the long term, increase consultees' competence to positively affect a greater number of children and adolescents, thereby assisting districts in meeting multiple goals, including the demonstration of improvement in students' annual progress, it is a valuable practice in school systems.

BASIC CONSIDERATIONS

The consultant, the consultee, and the client are the three main individuals involved in the consultative process. However, the use of the words consultant, consultee, and client become awkward reading very quickly, as do the repeated caveats that the consultee can be parents, principals, and other educators depending upon the nature of the problem and its location in a school system. As such, in order to improve the readability of the text, we will use school psychologist to mean the consultant, the teacher to mean the consultee, and the student to mean the client.

In contrast to other disciplines in which consultation is simply advice seeking, consultation in the schools is generally defined as a nonhierarchical problem-solving relationship between the teacher and the school psychologist. The goal of the consultative relationship is to improve the teacher's skills so that the teacher will be able to provide services independently to other students in the future (Caplan, 1970; Zins & Erchul, 2002). Gains in teachers' skills have led researchers to emphasize that the consultation is not only designed to help solve an immediate problem but ultimately serves as a preventive approach in meeting the needs of children, families, and schools (Meyers, Meyers, & Grogg, 2004; Zins & Erchul, 2002).

Consultation is conceptualized as an indirect service because the improvement in the functioning of the student is linked to the school psychologist through the consultation with the teacher rather than through direct school psychologist-to-student contact. It should be noted that although consultation is an indirect service, it may be used in conjunction with direct services. Furthermore, consultation may be used to determine the next steps that should occur when reviewing postintervention outcomes (Zins & Erchul, 2002).

Behavioral Consultation

One of the models of consultation most frequently used in school systems is behavioral consultation. Consultants using a behavioral consultation model start with a structured and systematic problem-solving method whereby the school psychologist and teacher collectively identify, define, and analyze the problem. An intervention is identified and implemented, after which the teacher and school psychologist together evaluate its effectiveness. Although Akin-Little, Little, and Delligatti (2004) suggest that behavioral consultation can be used to assist teachers in learning strategies to prevent and manage behavior problems in students, behavioral consultation is often principally used in order to help a teacher cope with an acute student behavioral difficulty.

Using the tenets of behaviorism, early examples of behavioral consultation used a behavior-operant model developed by Bergan (1977). In 1990, Bergan and Kratochwill broadened the scope of Bergan's original model and in the process the new model became one of the most well-known and empirically supported consultative models in school psychology. Their model continues to be grounded in behavioral psychological principles, such as systematic problem solving. However, in addition to the teacher applying behavioral techniques as a result of behavioral consultation, behavioral principles are used throughout the consultative process.

In the behavioral consultation model, the school psychologist consultant's role is structured and directive in nature. While the teacher is expected to take an active role in describing the nature of the presenting problem, the school psychologist considers the relevant psychological principles driving or influencing the problem. The school psychologist uses verbal structuring techniques to gain information from the teacher and to increase the possibility of the teacher accepting intervention recommendations proposed by the school psychologist. As a relevant part of the student's environment, it is anticipated that there will also need to be a change in the teacher's behavior. Ultimately, the teacher is responsible for implementing the selected intervention. Together, the teacher and school psychologist measure behavioral changes and evaluate the effectiveness of the intervention.

The behavioral consultation model focuses on current or proximal influences on the student's behavior. Antecedents or prompts are considered and changed during intervention. The success of behavioral consultation is in part due to its reliance on defining observable and measurable behaviors that can be compared both preintervention and postintervention, thus providing teachers with real-time data regarding the student's response to the intervention. Charting student improvement is an excellent way to document the use of evidence-based practices in the schools.

One drawback to using behavioral consultation is the opportunity for the consultation relationship to feel manipulative, whereby the teacher can perceive the school psychologist's questioning and guidance as coercive. Another drawback is that some student problems do not have a proximal cause and will not be amenable to behavioral consultation interventions alone (Miller, Tansy, & Hughes, 1998).

Behavioral Consultative Processes: Details

The behavioral consultation process includes problem identification, problem analysis, plan implementation, and evaluation. The school psychologist and teacher determine (a) the desired student behavioral goals, (b) who will deliver the intervention, (c) when and where strategies and reinforcements will occur, and (d) the expected date for behavior change. What follows is a detailed description of the steps unique to the behavioral consultation process.

Problem identification. The purpose of this step is for the school psychologist to better understand the needs of the teacher with respect to the student difficulty (Bergan & Kratochwill, 1990). In order to begin to establish the objectives of consultation, all student test data, formal and informal observations, records, and interviews are reviewed. Next, the school psychologist and the teacher work together to define the student's problem behavior in succinct, objective, and observable terms.

It is important to note that, at times, teachers have difficulty describing the problem in clear and specific terms. Instead, teachers may use vague or nonspecific terms and phrases, such as, "He is out of control and his behavior is off the wall." As such, the initial task is to assist the teacher in accurately describing the behavior in measurable terms (Gutkin & Curtis, 1999). Formally, the verbal communication process is one in which the school psychologist uses elicitors, emitters, paraphrasing, and summarizing to improve problem identification. In the end, everyone should be able to identify the presenting problem behavior so that it can be accurately recorded. For example, what was once described as a classroom disruption may be redefined as "the number of times the student speaks without being called upon by the teacher." In this way, the target behavior is specific and easily measured.

Problem analysis. In this stage, the school psychologist seeks to identify the environmental and student variables that are contributing to the maintenance of the problem behavior. By observing the student, the target behavior baseline is established and the antecedents and consequences of the behavior over time are considered (Zins & Erchul, 2002). Observations, along with an examination of work samples and interviews, can also help to identify a student's skill deficits (Bergan & Kratochwill, 1990). Identified skill deficits may require specific supplemental teaching. During this step, school psychologists should also encourage teachers to identify their own strengths and other supports they may find useful (Zins & Erchul, 2002).

After the target problem has been identified and analyzed, the school psychologist and the teacher should consider possible interventions in order to prepare for implementing the intervention plan. In general, preference should be given to strategies aimed at increasing positive student behaviors rather than techniques used to reduce behavior unless the behavior is extreme. Interventions that are less intrusive and complex are also favored. When students must learn new skills, strategies should complement existing classroom routines and supplemental community support, such as tutoring, should be used as needed. Additionally, school psychologists should support and reinforce teacher efforts, since teachers too are learning new ways to interact with the student. In the end, interventions that are time efficient, are nonintrusive, are perceived to be effective by teachers, and have a sound evidence base are best. It is important to note that all intervention efforts should be targeted at the highest level of the organization as possible. For example, antibullying efforts on behalf of the school building have more impact than those aimed at a small group.

Implementation. This stage includes the following steps: (a) establishing objectives, (b) selecting interventions, (c) considering any barriers to the implementation of the intervention, and (d) selecting appropriate assessments. The teacher is expected to carry out the intervention plan during this implementation stage. The school psychologist is expected to provide support and reinforcement to the teacher, coaching behavior monitoring, modeling intervention adjustments, and reviewing the intervention effectiveness to ensure that the student is benefiting from the intervention plan.

Evaluation. In this stage, the data are reviewed in order to determine the effectiveness of the intervention. If the intervention resulted in the established behavioral goals, then follow-up monitoring is initiated, generalization (using skills acquired and demonstrated across settings) is promoted, and supports are gradually diminished. Reinforcers that occur naturally in the environment, especially those that encourage student independence, such as self-monitoring or self-management (Meichenbaum & Turk, 1987), often result with the most success. At this point, the consultation relationship is terminated (Bergan & Kratochwill, 1990). In the case of unsuccessful interventions, a new plan may need to be made and implemented (Zins & Erchul, 2002).

Effectiveness of Behavioral Consultation

There is substantial empirical evidence to show the effectiveness of behavioral consultation. However, the majority of these studies use single-case study designs (Brown, Pryzwansky, & Schulte, 2001; Guli, 2005; Kratochwill & Van Someren, 1995; Sheridan, Welch, & Orme, 1996; Wilkinson, 2005; Zins & Erchul, 2002). Although single-subject design procedures are helpful in informing decision making about the usefulness of the intervention for a single case, these small sample sizes limit the generalizability of the research findings. Simply stated, while there have been documented previous successes, how this evidence is related to the next case trying to be solved may be unclear. Additionally, the modification to intervention plans in real time interferes with the ability to replicate successes, to infer the level of treatment integrity, and to clearly identify pertinent procedures (Guli, 2005; Wilkinson, 2005).

Behavioral Consultation: Transitions

The behavioral consultation model has evolved from the assumption that behavior is a function of proximal reinforcement of behaviors (Bergan, 1977) to include a more expansive worldview whereby behavioral consultation acknowledges that student–teacher characteristics and dynamics are relevant in understanding the expression of behaviors (Bergan & Kratochwill, 1990; Zins & Erchul, 2002). Today, researchers continue to explore the dynamics within the multiple environments of children's functioning in order to determine the range of influences on children's behavior, acknowledging that all of these systems are likely influential upon children.

Ecological Consultation

The practice of ecological consultation has successfully capitalized on the strengths of behavioral consultation while expanding the understanding about the broad environmental contexts that influence student learning and behavior. Ecological consultation is informed by Bronfenbrenner's (1979) original work describing the overlapping levels of the environment, which is described in detail below. It is important to note that Bronfenbrenner's (1979) work has been combined with several other theories over the years, including general systems theory (von Bertalanffy, 1968), which rejects the simple cause-and-effect link in explaining behavior. Furthermore, subcomponents of Bronfenbrenner's work have been used in family-centered services (Dunst, Trivette, & Deal, 1988), which explains the strong influence of the family subsystem. School psychologists may be familiar with conjoint behavioral consultation (Sheridan & Kratochwill, 1992), which acknowledges the special role of the family and school as the primary contexts for influencing student behaviors, a theoretical orientation that is situated within the broad Bronfenbrenner context.

Ecological Consultation: The Framework

The reason that it is useful to continue to focus on the ecological consultation model rather than some of the subcomponents is that the ecological consultation model encourages incisive explanations of student behavior and allows practitioners to use similar consultation strategies in a variety of contexts (e.g., family, school, community, society). As such, the ecological consultation model provides the greatest number of leverage points to deliver effective interventions (Gutkin, 2012). Furthermore, the ecological consultation model is consistent with the push toward public health strategies in which prevention at the macrosystems level is fostered and efforts can then be coordinated to the individual student (Ysseldyke et al., 2006).

Bronfenbrenner (1979) describes multiple embedded systems that influence student learning and behavior. These systems are described as inseparable and interacting where each influences and is influenced by the other. The classic four overlapping circles are pictured in Figure 31.1.

Microsystem. The microsystem is the innermost part of the circle and is the most immediate or most proximal environmental context. As described in ecological consultation, the primary contexts are the student's home and school and their influence is bidirectional. Essentially, parents who support school tasks influence how the child functions in the school context. Other microsystems may be more temporary, such as peers in a karate or ballet class or intermural teams. All microsystems have direct contact with the student even if the influence is temporary.

Figure 31.1. Bronfenbrenner's Model

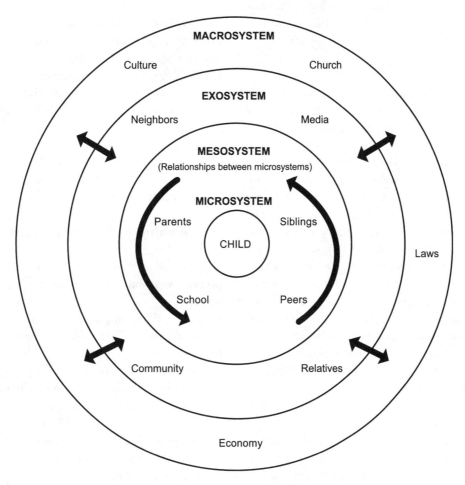

Mesosystem. The mesosystem is composed of the relationships between the microsystems. Some relationships are critical, such as the bridge between home and school. Others are less influential, such as coming together for a summer camp or field trip. What is important about the mesosystem is the pattern of functioning within the contexts. How we communicate, trust, and respect the microsystems around us teaches the child a pattern of expectations the child will reference as he or she learns. Like microsystems, mesosystems directly affect the functioning of a student.

Exosystem. The exosystem offers an indirect influence on the student but its impact is felt at the microsystem or mesosystem level. For children, parent issues trickle down to influence their world. For example, parents' work demands may keep them from attending and supporting their children at school events. A new job farther from home may require a longer commute time, which indirectly diminishes support for homework or lessens family social support.

Macrosystem. The macrosystem is described as the broadest experience that colors or influences a student's learning or functioning at school. Religious backgrounds, socioeconomic statuses, and experiences with poverty or privilege, for example, all come together to form a contextual lens whereby such experiences shape a student's values and how he or she comes to approach and appreciate the world. Although macrosystems are also indirect influences on student behavior, their impact can be profound.

Ecological Consultative Processes: Details
There are three overarching goals of the ecological consultation model: collect relevant data that can be used to generate solutions, implement effective intervention plans that result in student-focused outcomes, and effect change that is longstanding. Although the identification of specific behaviors, data collection, and analyses are not detailed in the same manner as behavioral consultation, the ecological consultation model addresses the bidirectional interactions of the

student's biology, the student's environmental contexts, and the reciprocal influences on the student's learning. Furthermore, ecological consultation is thought to best explain the complexity of influences upon an individual's behavior (Gutkin, 2009).

Effectiveness of Ecological Consultation

There are many studies detailing the effectiveness of ecological consultation and its application to practice (Chess & Thomas, 1999; Conyne & Mazza, 2007; Gutkin 2009). However, the ecological consultation model has not been detailed as a practical plan for service delivery. That is, there are so many potential opportunities for intervention that how, when, and where to direct resources may not be easy to determine. Additionally, it is difficult to compare outcomes when interventions are implemented at different system levels. In explanation, the strength of the intervention impact may differ depending upon whether the intervention was initiated from a microsystem or mesosystem level. While microsystem interventions may be easier and more directly measured, mesosytem effects may be more long lasting. As always, it is difficult to measure problems that have been prevented.

Ecological Model: Transitions

By combining the structured and practical model of behavioral consultation with the expanding opportunities for intervention found in ecological consultation, school psychologists have more opportunities to effect change and to show that that change is measurable and meaningful. Indeed, school psychologists are uniquely situated to have a positive impact not only on the primary microsystems (school and home experiences) but also to promote positive prevention by working with the cultural contexts of the larger (macrosystem) influences.

BEST PRACTICES IN BEHAVIORAL/ ECOLOGICAL CONSULTATION

Behavioral/ecological consultation is a hybrid of behavioral consultation and ecological consultation, combining the essential and most efficacious components of each model. Behavioral/ecological consultation provides a problem-solving framework in which there are structured, distinct stages, although the order of these stages is not necessarily rigid. Instead, the school psychologist and teacher may revisit a previous stage without damaging the integrity of the relationship or intervention outcomes (Brown et al., 2001).

Formal Entry

For most school psychologists employed by a school district, entering into a classroom or school building occurs without difficulty because the service is internal to the organization. Nonetheless, it is important to explain the details of the consultative process in a formal meeting with all involved in the implementation of the intervention. Such a discussion should address, for example, the goals of consultation, confidentiality and its limits, a time frame for service, when the school psychologist will be available, and the best methods of communication (Brown et al., 2001).

Establishing an Effective Relationship

One of the most important steps in the consultative process is establishing a good working relationship. A "cooperative partnership" (Zins & Erchul, 2002, p. 627) is one in which all parties understand their roles and responsibilities and are actively pursuing a common goal for the student to achieve. The nonhierarchical relationship is characterized by equality rather than a power differential. Thus, the school psychologist, teacher, and family offer unique perspectives regarding the student's presenting problem.

School psychologists draw upon their expertise in child development, psychological theory, and research-based practices that assist in determining and defining the presenting problem. The teacher might offer information regarding classroom contexts, teaching styles, behavior management techniques, and classroom observations. Similarly, parents or families may reveal relevant family practices, contextual stresses, and the broad cultural frame that influence the child's functioning at school.

Assessment

During the assessment stage of the consultative process, student characteristics, teacher characteristics, and the immediate and larger environment are considered in conceptualizing and defining the presenting problem (Brown et al., 2001). It is anticipated that school psychologist, teacher, and family may have varying perspectives regarding the nature of the problem. For example, a teacher may view the problem as largely child based; the school psychologist may place more emphasis on the distal environmental variables, such as family strain; and the family may believe that the school and other community support systems are underperforming in assisting the child in succeeding at school (Athanasiou, Geil, Hazel, & Copeland, 2002). The problem definition can affect the selection and perceived efficacy of the interventions. It is important, then, to consider these differences at the outset of the consultative process, so that the school psychologist, teacher, and family can better understand how their unique perspectives of the problem behavior might improve the selection of an intervention (Bergan & Tombari, 1976).

Defining the Problem and Setting Goals

We provide a problem identification data review sheet (see Figure 31.2) to aid school psychologists in systematic data collection. This tool helps school psychologists organize a strategy for approaching teachers to determine how teachers define problematic behavior, the contextual variables that precede problematic behavior, and the settings where the problem behavior persists.

Figure 31.2. Problem Identification Interview Data Sheet for Behavioral Consultation

Date: _____   Observer: _____

Client: _____   Reliability: _____

Consultee: _____   Observer: _____

Consultant: _____   Session #: _____

Interview Objective: *Occurrence:*   *Response:*

1. Opening salutation
2. General statement
3. Behavior specification
   a. Specify examples
   b. Specify priorities
4. Behavior setting
   a. Specify examples
   b. Specify priorities
5. Identify antecedents
6. Identify sequential conditions
7. Identify consequences
8. Summarize and validate
9. Behavior strength
10. Summarize and validate
11. Tentative definition of goal
12. Assets Question
13. Question about existing procedures
14. Summarize and validate
15. Directional statement about data recording
16. Data collection procedures
17. Summarize and validate
18. Date to begin data collection
19. Establish date of next appointment
20. Closing salutation

Note. From *Behavioral Consultation in Applied Settings: An Individual Guide* (pp. 107–108), by T. R. Kratochwill and J. R. Bergan, 1990, New York, NY: Plenum Press. Copyright 1990 by Springer Science and Business Media. Reprinted with permission.

For example, when a school psychologist is faced with a teacher report that "a child is out of control," it is useful to determine what that description may mean (e.g., out of the seat, roaming the classroom without purpose, leaving the class without permission). This is consistent with the behavioral consultation approach.

Additionally, details regarding when the behavior has been observed, how long the behavior persists, the level of classroom (context) disruption that occurs when the behavior is present, and a systematic consideration of the relevant forces contributing to the maintenance of the problem behavior is recorded in order to consider (positive or negative) consequences. This is consistent with the ecological consultation approach.

Perhaps the most useful consideration detailed on the Problem Identification Interview Data Sheet is the child's strengths in order increase prosocial actions. This is blending the behavioral consultation (reinforcement) and ecological consultation (contextual rewards) approaches.

Intervention or Strategy Selection

When selecting interventions, it is important to recall that there are several avenues through which a problem may be solved, a phenomenon known as equifinality (Katz & Kahn, 1978). It is appropriate to begin by brainstorming possible interventions that may be effective in targeting the problem. It is likely useful to be open to the teacher's suggestions since the suggestions are based on the teacher's wealth of classroom experience. It is appropriate to consult with the family about how the family may be willing to support interventions delivered at school in the home. The school psychologist's contribution to brainstorming should start with a reference to evidence-based practices while keeping in mind that pertinent local contexts, including teacher and family preferences and student characteristics, may require changes to the known strategies. All these must be considered when selecting an intervention: (a) strategy integrity, the extent to which interventions can be changed or adapted without affecting intervention effectiveness (Reynolds, Gutkin, Elliot, & Witt, 1984); (b) strategy acceptability, the extent to which the teacher believes that intervention is acceptable (Reimers, Wacker, & Koeppl, 1987; Witt, Elliot, & Martens, 1984); and (c) feasibility, the extent to which interventions are time efficient, nonintrusive, and viewed as effective (Brown et al., 2001; Elliott, 1988).

Implementation

It is helpful to review a written outline of the intervention plan before the intervention begins. The plan should include (a) roles and responsibilities of the student, family, teacher, and school psychologist; (b) how baseline data will be collected; (c) day, time, and the duration of the intervention; (d) reinforcers, reinforcement schedules, and how the distribution of reinforcers can be coordinated across the home–school environment; (e) type and frequency of data collected; and (f) when data should be reviewed and modifications made if needed. Once the intervention begins, the school psychologist should be in frequent contact with the whole team to ensure treatment integrity and to provide support for any difficulties (Brown et al., 2001; Zins & Erchul, 2002).

Evaluation

Baseline data should be collected before the intervention starts. This allows the school psychologist to measure the frequency, duration, and intensity of the problematic behavior as well as to establish a plan for how often the data should be collected in order to measure changes. Once the intervention is started, the ongoing data comparisons are used to determine if the intervention needs to be adjusted and if the intervention can be terminated. Single-subject methodologies, such as single phase, reversal, or multiple baseline designs, are an easy way to illustrate findings (Zins & Erchul, 2002) and may prove useful for decision making.

Termination

Although school psychologists expect to have ongoing relationships with teachers in the building and families in the community, it is useful to formally terminate the consultative relationship when the teacher, family, and the school psychologist agree that the student has attained the established goals or when the teacher and family are effective in the implementation of the intervention. One goal of the consultation is to improve teacher independence and effectiveness. Therefore, school psychologists should expect to gradually diminish direct support once the teacher is self-sufficient in managing the intervention process. Another goal is to improve home–school communications and partnerships. Thus, the school psychologist should expect to diminish support once positive communication patterns are established.

Multicultural Competence

Given the changing demographics of children in schools as well as the growing diversity within the U.S. population, cultural awareness and cultural sensitivity becomes an ever-important skillset for school psychologists. All professionals within the schools need to attend to the risk of individuals feeling judged based on their background. Culturally diverse youth need to feel that they are equally valued within the school context and that the perspectives their families bring will be respected (Nuijens & Klotz, 2004).

Sheridan (2000) points out that much of the research on behavioral consultation has focused on the structures and procedures required to implement this model. However, it is helpful to remember that consultation occurs within a relationship. The cultural variables that affect the relationships within behavioral consultation, or the implications of working in a behavior consultative relationship in which one or member is culturally diverse, is not well understood. It is partly for this reason that the merging of ecological consultation with behavioral consultation (the behavior/ecological consultation model) will help to remedy the tendency for behavioral consultation models to be focused exclusively upon the structures and procedures of the consultative process and instead recognize that utilizing the knowledge gleaned from examining the spheres of influence that have an impact on the child's functioning at school (microsystem, mesosystem, exosystem, and macrosystem) will likely result in a richer, more nuanced, and incisive identification of the problems that child may be experiencing. This will also help to develop interventions designed to be used at the level of multisystems points in order to increase the likelihood that change will be authentic and generalizable to other contexts besides school.

Measuring Usefulness: School Psychologists' Impact

School psychologists interested in determining the usefulness of implementing a behavioral/ecological consultation model will find that there are limited assessment strategies that help to show the impact of the work. As stated, it is easier to show student progress and teacher or parent satisfaction than it is to show how the school psychologist's use of the behavioral/ecological consultation model advances the effectiveness of school teams. However, given the continued interest in demonstrating behavioral change, alongside the reality

of the ever complex, multicultural, and multisystematically informed context that is the school setting, and the regulatory push for schools to explain and evidence how they improve outcomes for children, it is anticipated that school psychologists will lead the effort to show how their work measurably improves student outcomes and the systems that serve them.

SUMMARY

Consultation is an indirect service model that allows school psychologists to work collaboratively to improve the skills of teachers and families in order to positively affect a large number of students. Consultation is particularly effective when it considers the immediate or proximal influences upon behavior while simultaneously addressing situational and contextual variables. Families and schools are primary systems where students spend most of their day growing and learning. However, the bigger picture contextual influences, ranging from the amount of parent time spent with children working on school projects to the broad influences of religion, poverty, and other factors, accumulate to result in influences upon children that will last a lifetime. How a student comes to understand his or her world and take up the challenges of growing, learning, developing, and maturing provides opportunities for support and, at times, intervention. Ultimately, effective schools are collaborative in using student, family, school, community, and social realities to find real-world solutions for children.

REFERENCES

Akin-Little, K. A., Little, S. G., & Delligatti, N. (2004). A preventative model of school consultation: Incorporating perspectives from positive psychology. *Psychology in the Schools, 4*, 155–162. doi:10.1002/pits.10147

Athanasiou, M. S., Geil, M., Hazel, C. E., & Copeland, E. P. (2002). A look inside school-based consultation: A qualitative study of the beliefs and practices of school psychologists and teachers. *School Psychology Quarterly, 17*, 258–298. doi:10.1521/scpq.17.3.258.20884

Auster, E. R., Feeney-Kettler, K. A., & Kratochwill, T. R. (2006). Conjoint behavioral consultation: Application to the school-based treatment of anxiety disorders. *Education and Treatment of Children, 29*, 243–256.

Bergan, J. R. (1977). *Behavioral consultation*. Columbus, OH: Merrill.

Bergan, J. R., & Kratochwill, T. R. (1990). *Behavioral consultation and therapy*. New York, NY: Plenum Press.

Bergan, J. R., & Tombari, M. L. (1976). Consultant skill and efficiency and the implementation and outcomes of consultation. *Journal of School Psychology, 14*, 3–14. doi:10.1016/0022-4405(76)90057-1

Bronfenbrenner, U. (1979). *The ecology of human development: Experiments by nature and design.* Cambridge, MA: Harvard University Press.

Brown, D., Pryzwansky, W. B., & Schulte, A. C. (2001). *Psychological consultation: Introduction to theory and practice* (5th ed). Boston, MA: Allyn & Bacon.

Caplan, G. (1970). *The theory and practice of mental health consultation.* New York, NY: Basic Books.

Chess, S., & Thomas, A. (1999). *Goodness of fit: Clinical applications from infancy through adult life.* Philadelphia, PA: Brunner/Mazel.

Conyne, R. K., & Mazza, J. (2007). Ecological group work applied to schools. *The Journal for Specialists in Group Work, 32,* 19–29. doi:10.1080/0193392060097749

Dunst, C. J., Trivette, C. M., & Deal, A. G. (1988). *Enabling and empowering families: Principles and guidelines for practice.* Cambridge, MA: Brookline Books.

Elliott, S. N. (1988). Acceptability of behavioral treatments: Review of variables that influence treatment selection. *Professional Psychology: Research and Practice, 19,* 68–80. doi:10.1037/0735-7028.19.1.68

Guli, L. A. (2005). Evidence-based parent consultation with school-related outcomes. *School Psychology Quarterly, 20,* 455–472. doi:10.1521/scpq.2005.20.4.455

Gutkin, T. B. (2009). Ecological school psychology: A personal opinion and a plea for change. In T. B. Gukin & C. R. Reynolds (Eds.), *The handbook of school psychology* (4th ed., pp. 463–496). New York, NY: Wiley.

Gutkin, T. B. (2012). Ecological psychology: Replacing the medical model paradigm for school-based psychological and psychoeducational services. *Journal of Educational and Psychological Consultation, 22,* 1–20. doi:10.1080/10474412.2011.649652

Gutkin, T. B., & Curtis, M. J. (1999). School-based consultation theory and practice: The art and science of indirect service delivery. In C. R. Reynolds & T. B. Gutkin (Eds.), *The handbook of school psychology* (3rd ed., pp. 598–637). New York, NY: Wiley.

Hoagwood, K., Burns, B. J., Kiser, L., Ringeisen, H., & Schoenwald, S. K. (2001). Evidence-based practice in child and adolescent mental health services. *Psychiatric Services, 52,* 1179–1189. doi:10.1176/appi.ps.52.9.1179

Katz, D., & Kahn, R. L. (1978). *The social psychology of organizations* (2nd ed.). New York, NY: Wiley.

Kratochwill, T. R., & Bergan, J. R. (1990). *Behavioral consultation in applied settings: An individual guide.* New York, NY: Plenum Press.

Kratochwill, T. R., & Van Someren, K. R. (1995). Barriers to treatment success in behavioral consultation: Current limitations and future directions. *Journal of Educational and Psychological Consultation, 6,* 125–143. doi:10.1207/s1532768xjepc0602_3

Meichenbaum, D., & Turk, D. C. (1987). *Facilitating treatment adherence: A practitioner's guidebook.* New York, NY: Plenum Press.

Meyers, J., Meyers, A. B., & Grogg, K. (2004). Prevention through consultation: A model to guide future developments in the field of school psychology. *Journal of Educational and Psychological Consultation, 15,* 257–276. doi:10.1080/10474412.2004.9669517

Miller, J. A., Tansy, M., & Hughes, T. L. (1998). Functional behavioral assessment: The link between problem behavior and effective intervention in schools. *Current Issues in Education, 1*(5), Retrieved from http://cie.ed.asu.edu/volume1/number5/

National Association of School Psychologists. (2010). *Model for comprehensive and integrated school psychological services.* Bethesda, MD: Author. Retrieved from http://www.nasponline.org/standards/2010standards/2_PracticeModel.pdf

Nuijens, K. L., & Klotz, M. B. (2004). *Promoting cultural diversity and cultural competency: Self-assessment checklist for personnel providing services and supports to children and their families.* Bethesda, MD: National Association of School Psychologists. Retrieved from http://www.nasponline.org/resources/culturalcompetence/checklist.aspx

Reimers, T. M., Wacker, D. P., & Koeppl, G. (1987). Acceptability of behavioral treatments: A review of the literature. *School Psychology Review, 16,* 212–227.

Reynolds, C. R., Gutkin, T. B., Elliott, S. N., & Witt, J. C. (1984). *School psychology: Essentials of theory and practice.* New York, NY: Wiley.

Sheridan, S. M. (2000). Considerations of multiculturalism and diversity in behavioral consultation with parents and teachers. *School Psychology Review, 29,* 344–353.

Sheridan, S. M., & Kratochwill, T. R. (1992). Behavioral parent-teacher consultation: Conceptual and research considerations. *Journal of School Psychology, 30,* 117–139. doi:10.1016/0022-4405(92)90025-Z

Sheridan, S. M., Welch, M., & Orme, S. F. (1996). Is consultation effective? A review of outcome research. *Remedial and Special Education, 17,* 341–354. doi:10.1177/074193259601700605

von Bertalanffy, L. (1968). *General system theory: Foundations, development, applications* (Rev. ed., p. 90). New York, NY: George Braziller.

Wilkinson, L. A. (2005). Bridging the research-to-practice gap in school-based consultation: An example using case studies. *Journal of Educational and Psychological Consultation, 16,* 175–200. doi:10.1207/s1532768xjepc1603_3

Witt, J. C., Elliott, S. N., & Martens, B. K. (1984). Acceptability of behavioral interventions used in the classrooms: The influence of amount of teacher time, severity of behavior problem, and type of intervention. *Behavioral Disorders, 9,* 95–104.

Ysseldyke, J., Burns, M., Dawson, P., Kelley, B., Morrison, D., Ortiz, S., … Telzrow, C. (2006). *School psychology: A blueprint for training and practice III.* Bethesda, MD: National Association of School Psychologists.

Zins, J. E., & Erchul, W. P. (2002). Best practices in school consultation. In A. Thomas & J. Grimes (Eds.), *Best practices in school psychology IV* (pp. 625–643). Bethesda, MD: National Association of School Psychologists.

Best Practices in School-Based Mental Health/Consultee-Centered Consultation by School Psychologists

32

Jonathan Sandoval
University of California, Davis

OVERVIEW

The objective of this chapter is to illuminate best practice in consultation based on an approach imported into school psychology from public health. Consultation is, of course, a key domain (Consultation and Collaboration) in the National Association of School Psychologists (NASP) 2010 *Model for Comprehensive and Integrated School Psychological Services* (NASP, 2010). Many of the methods and techniques used by school psychologists adhering to mental health consultation theory are similar to those practiced by adherents to other models in other consultation chapters in this edition of *Best Practices*. This chapter will emphasize those practices that are particularly characteristic of consultee-centered consultation, a modern approach to mental health consultation. These practices have been derived from theory, a long history of case study, and empirical investigation as well as qualitative research (e.g., Hylander, 2000).

School-based consultee-centered consultation takes place when school psychologists enter into conversations with teachers or other professional educators about difficulties or questions the educators have concerning their clients. Clients are typically children who are not thriving in school or are otherwise causing concern. Issues may be academic or behavioral in nature. In the case of school administrators, clients may be children, staff, or parents. These conversations may occur once or several times over the course of several weeks. The process is flexible and must be adapted to the particular school context. Consultees range from experienced

professionals who seek the perspective of a school psychologist in thinking through a classroom problem to novice educators struggling with a new role and desiring support and insights from the member of another profession. Many of these conversations will take place prior to a formal referral and the involvement of school-based multidisciplinary teams and often obviate their need.

This chapter will describe best practices for conducting these conversations. By adopting these practices the school psychologist should be able to structure and facilitate creative problem solving among school personnel.

Historical Sources

Mental health consultation began as a part of the early effort by psychiatrists to move away from traditional psychotherapeutic approaches to mental health and toward prevention. The fusion of public health and psychiatry began in the 1940s when mental health resources were overwhelmed by the circumstance of the Great Depression of the 1930s and World War II. It became necessary to use scarce resources to focus on populations and institutions and on methods to promote emotional wellness rather than on individual treatment. A number of primary institutions such as hospitals, churches, and schools became the target for attention from mental health professionals coming from outside the system.

An early pioneer in these efforts was Gerald Caplan, who chronicled 2 decades of work in his landmark 1970 text, *The Theory and Practice of Mental Health Consultation* (Caplan, 1970). His book has become a major source of ideas about best practice in consultation. Another key figure, Irving Berlin (1977), began similar work in bringing outside psychiatric consultation to teachers and school administrators. He too worked extensively with schools as an outside consultant from a mental health center.

Caplan, Berlin, and others' descriptions of their work soon came to the attention of prominent school psychologists such as Judith Alpert (1976), Nadine Lambert (1974), and Joel Meyers (Meyers, Freidman, & Gaughan, 1975), who sought to apply these external mental health experts' work to school psychologists working in the schools. The major issue facing applications to the schools is the difference between coming from the outside as a consultant and working as an employee of the school system (i.e., as an inside consultant).

Caplan's seminal work influenced others around the world who also believed his ideas could influence practice in the schools. In Scandinavia, particularly, where school psychologists are explicitly prepared as consultants to preschools and schools, his ideas were accepted and extended (Lambert, Hylander, & Sandoval, 2004). Over the past 50 years, the field of mental health consultation has continued to evolve. In the years before his death, Caplan commented that it was interesting that his ideas had been most accepted and appreciated by school psychologists (Caplan & Caplan-Moskovich, 2004; Erchul, 2009).

Caplan and Caplan (1993) identified four types of mental health consultation: (a) client-centered case consultation, (b) consultee-centered case consultation, (c) program-centered administrative consultation, and (d) consultee-centered administrative consultation. Of those, consultee-centered consultation captured the goals of many school psychologists' consultation activities in school settings.

Consultee-centered mental health consultation focuses on the characteristics and ideas of the consultee that are contributing to his or her work difficulty and involves little or no direct assessment of the client. The goal is to assist the consultee in working productively with the client and future clients; that is, the consultee voluntarily enters into the relationship, the consultant has no administrative responsibility for the consultee, the consultation is time limited, and the consultee is free to accept or reject any client interventions generated by the process. Thus, mental health consultation is distinguished from supervision, counseling, therapy, education, and collaboration.

In contrast, Caplan's client-centered case consultation is more related to school psychologists implementing ecological and behavioral consultation. In client-centered consultation, "[t]he consultant helps by bringing his specialized knowledge and skills to bear in making an expert assessment of the nature of the client's problem and in recommending how the consultee should deal with the case" (Caplan, 1970, p. 32).

The descriptor *mental health* in mental health consultation and the psychiatric background of its pioneers has led to some misconceptions about this model of consultation. First, because Caplan was psychoanalytically trained, many assumed that Freudian theory is the main underpinning for this process. Although Freud's ideas have value in the consultation process, other psychological theories also have an important place in understanding the work problems of a consultee. Current conceptions of consultee-centered consultation emphasize the use of a multitude of behavioral, cognitive, and developmental theories to understand consultees and clients.

Second, the term mental health in the label implies that the consultee is not mentally healthy and that the consultee is receiving a psychological treatment. In fact, Caplan meant that the ultimate outcome of consultation was mental health promotion; that is, to improve mental health and educational outcomes for future clients of the consultee. Caplan's public health background led to his hope in making institutions like the school more effective in promoting healthy mental and physical development by assisting key personnel in becoming more successful with their clients.

In spite of these misconceptions and the difference between being an outside consultant and being employed by the consultee's institution, consultants in the United States, Scandinavia, Europe, and Israel have continued to develop the practice and theory of consultee-centered consultation (Lambert et al., 2004). To avoid some of the past misconceptions and to capture some new ideas from contemporary practice, many school psychologists following this model have chosen to use the label *consultee-centered consultation* rather than the more generic label *mental health consultation*.

Definition of Consultee-Centered Consultation

As of 2013, four international conferences have been held to discuss continuing developments in consultee-centered consultation since the publication of Caplan's book in 1970. Participants including Caplan developed the following definition in 1999 (Lambert, 2004):

Consultee-centered consultation emphasizes a nonhierarchical, nonprescriptive helping role relationship between a resource (consultant) and a person or group (consultee) who seeks professional help with a work problem involving a third party (client)....

This work problem is a topic of concern for the consultee who has a direct responsibility for the learning, development, or productivity of the client....

The primary task of both the consultant and consultee is to choose and reframe knowledge about well-being, development, intrapersonal, interpersonal, and organizational effectiveness appropriate to the consultee's work setting....

The goal of the consultation process is the joint development of a new way of conceptualizing the work problem so that the repertoire of the consultee is expanded and the professional relationship between the consultee and the client is restored or improved. (Lambert, 2004, pp. 11–12)

Parameters of Consultee-Centered Consultation

According to Caplan, in consultee-centered consultation the consultant has no administrative responsibility for the consultee's work and no professional responsibility for the outcome of the client's case. The consultant has no authority to modify the consultee's behavior toward the client. Similarly, the consultee has no need to accept the consultant's ideas or suggestions. There is a coordinate relationship between the consultant and consultee and an understanding that together they will discuss the work problem and share respective views of the problem from their own perspectives. The discussion about the client occurs between two professional equals. The consultant, being a member of another profession, fosters this coordinate relationship.

Further, the consultant has no predetermined body of information that is to be imparted to the consultee. The consultant acknowledges that the consultee has relevant expertise about the client's work problem. The consultant hopes to help the consultee improve the handling or understanding of the current work problem with the goal of assisting the consultee in managing similar problems in the future. The aim is to improve the consultee's job performance and not necessarily his or her general sense of well-being. Consultee-centered consultation does not involve the discussion of personal or private material, and the consultation process is understood to be a privileged communication on the part of the consultant. The primary responsibility for the outcome with the client remains with the consultee.

NASP Practice Model, Problem-Solving, and Multitiered Services

Consultee-centered consultation is one of the models school psychologists should have some familiarity with. Historically, it was one of the first approaches developed when working with a significant adult who influences a child's cognitive, social, and emotional development. When adults, such as teachers, turn to school psychologists for help with a behavioral, social, or academic work problem, the processes, procedures, and techniques generated from this consultation approach will be of use.

Consultee-centered consultation has at its heart a problem-solving process in common with other models of consultation and collaboration. Because of the emphasis on problem solving, it has many implications for the school psychologist's role on teams implementing multitiered initiatives or generating individual educational plans. One of the outcomes of consultee-centered consultation is new ways of understanding a problem and the development of interventions to address it.

Since an emphasis on prevention is implicit in the NASP Practice Model (NASP, 2010), consultee-centered consultation also relates to the domain of Preventive and Responsive Services. The intent is for consultees to expand their repertoire of skills to be able to work more effectively with future clients. Consultees may include other adults who have influence over children beside teachers. When consulting with school administrators, for example, system level change may result.

Finally, consultee-centered consultation is related to additional domains of the NASP Practice Model in that it is a process for developing interventions to respond to problems in teaching and learning and to facilitate social–emotional functioning and mental health. Consultation may be considered an intervention in its own right or be a delivery system for developing interventions.

BASIC CONSIDERATIONS

A number of prerequisite skills and background knowledge are needed prior to implementing best practices in consultee-centered consultation. First, a school psychologist needs excellent interviewing skills, which include active listening and responding. These skills are typically acquired by taking courses on counseling with adults and children. A second skill set is an appreciation for the role of emotion and unconscious motivation in human affairs. School psychologists should be comfortable with emotionally laden topics and be able to respond in ways that facilitate coping in others. A third set of skills is an ability to apply a number of insights from psychological theories of human development, learning, motivation, and social interaction. School psychologists need a thorough grounding in psychology and the ability to switch theoretical frameworks in thinking about problems.

Training in consultee-centered consultation should include didactic instruction in the underlying theory of consultee-centered consultation expressed by Caplan and others. Training should also include practice in providing consultation in the school setting with supervision from an experienced consultant with opportunities to review cases and to examine the process. Another useful training experience is to receive consultation (in addition to supervision) during fieldwork from a mental health professional who is not a school psychologist but is trained in consultee-centered consultation (Lambert, Sandoval, & Yandell, 1975). Evidence suggests, however, that training in consultation is not very comprehensive in many school psychology programs (Rosenfield, Levinsohn-Klyap, & Cramer, 2010).

Caplan (1970) has also raised the question of whether a consultee-centered consultant should go through personal psychotherapy. This idea is based on a tradition in psychoanalysis that self-knowledge is necessary for the consultant to be able to identify his or her own psychological issues that may interfere with the consultation process. Such a requirement is beyond most school psychology training, but may be useful background experience.

BEST PRACTICES IN CONSULTEE-CENTERED CONSULTATION

As mentioned, many of the best practices in consultee-centered consultation are similar to those in other consultation models. However, there are differences once the definition of consultee-centered consultation, derived from a number of parameters set by Caplan and other pioneers, is studied and is a first source of best practices. Although these early mental health practitioners consulting in community mental health settings were primarily clinicians, they were disciplined in case-study methods and introduced principles based on long and careful observation.

A second way to identify best practices is to examine the stages through which consultee-centered consultation proceeds. Most problem-solving consultation models identify five stages: relationship building, problem identification, problem analysis, intervention implementation, and program evaluation. However, after careful consideration of the writings of Berlin, Caplan, and others, we developed additional phases. See Table 32.1. (See also Sandoval & Davis, 1984.) Because the process seldom proceeds linearly, we will use the term *phases* instead of *stages* since stages implies a process that does proceed linearly. Many of these additional phases are elaborations of the basic five, but represent important practices in consultee-centered consultation. Each phase and the related declarative knowledge and procedural knowledge is listed. This division between declarative and procedural knowledge is between what the school psychology consultant must know and be able to do. Consequently, the best practices spring from procedural knowledge.

A third source of best practices originates from research on the process of interaction during consultee-centered consultation that leads to changes or shifts in the consultee's understanding and behavior toward the client. Research on school-based consultation generally has been criticized on the grounds that students or beginning consultants are used as the consultant, consultation consists of a relatively brief consultation with a single teacher concerning a single behaviorally defined problem, client outcomes are short term with little follow up data, system and other outcomes are missing, and the consultant and researcher are often the same person (Hughes, Loyd, & Buss, 2008). To examine the process, qualitative research may provide more evidence about what is effective in naturalistic settings with practicing school psychologists.

Working in Sweden, Hylander (2000, 2012) has undertaken such research. She created a grounded theory based on what skilled, effective consultants trained in Caplan's model actually do in practice. She explicated how three modes of interaction characterize consultee-centered consultation at different times. The skilled use of these modes results in conceptual change in the consultant and the consultee. Hylander describes the *approach* mode, the *free neutral* mode, and the *moving away* modes.

The approach mode involves the consultant helping the consultee describe the dilemma (presentation),

Table 32.1. Important Declarative and Procedural Knowledge in Consultee-Centered Consultation

Phase	Declarative Knowledge	Procedural Knowledge
Orientation and relationship building	• Features of consultation • What consultation is not	• Establishing proximity • Establishing a contract • Using active listening and attending skills
Maintaining rapport and responding to cultural issues	• Appropriate self-disclosure • Principles of establishing rapport • Multicultural awareness • Consultation ethics	• Communicating openness nonverbally • Using appropriate, professional friendliness • Being direct with respect to cultural issues
Problem exploration	• Types of questions • Critical listening skills • Idea of presentations and representations • Hylander consultation mode of approach, free neutral	• Using open and indirect questions • Using reflection • Using restatement • Using summarization • Asking what has been tried • Saying "I don't know" • Avoiding premature suggestions
Gathering data	• Measurement techniques across domains, sources, and methods	• Assigning mutual homework • Planning and executing client and system assessment
Sharing information	• Issues of cognitive bias • Need to verify understandings	• Expressing results and ideas tentatively • Looking for confirmatory and disconfirmatory information • Examining one's own representations
Problem analysis and reframing	• Applying Caplan's diagnostic taxonomy (lack of skill, knowledge, self-confidence, objectivity) • Understanding lack of objectivity • Attribution theory • Cognitive dissonance theory • Conceptual change theory • Hylander consultation mode of moving away	• Using theme interference reduction • Avoiding blind alleys • Challenging representations and facilitating conceptual change
Generating interventions	• Psychological theory • Educational practice • Evidence-based interventions • Treatment acceptability	• Applying theory to generate interventions • Identifying resources for training • Providing accessible reasoning
Supporting experiments and interventions	• Facilitating treatment integrity	• Providing ego support • Generating formative evaluation feedback • Facilitating treatment validity
Evaluating interventions	• Evaluation methods and procedures	• Generating summative evaluation • Inculcating the experimental attitude • Conducting action research
Follow up and disengagement	• Need for feedback • Need to retain professional relationship	• Using informational interviewing skills • Facilitating transfer to new clients

Note. Copyright 2012 by Jonathan Sandoval. Used with permission.

seeking to understand underlying thoughts about the causes of the problem (representations), and allowing the consultee to discharge feelings and express negative thoughts. In this mode, school psychologists demonstrate they can understand and appreciate the point of view of the consultee.

The free neutral mode involves the school psychologist and the consultee freely exchanging thoughts and ideas about the dilemma. The school psychologist provides structure and focus through asking questions and sharing different perspectives. In this mode, the consultant and the consultee generate hypotheses about what might be happening and then examine the situation in multiple ways.

The moving away mode gets its name from both the consultee and consultant moving away from the old ways of understanding the problem toward new ways of intervening with the client based on a shift in the consultee's (and consultant's) representation. The consultant is challenging the old ideas by introducing new information, more satisfactory explanations for behavior, and perspectives from psychological theory. The consultee and the consultant are discovering a new way to frame the dilemma.

Hylander's (2012) is not a stage theory. She notes that the process of consultation involves shifting back and forth between the modes, but never directly between the approach mode and moving away mode without going through the free neutral mode. In her grounded theory, she points out how the process may result in change and how it may fail, either because the consultee or the consultant gets stuck in a blind alley. Hylander's theory provides many insights into best practices.

Best Practices Based on Definition and Parameters

In what follows, school psychologists' best practices in consultee-centered consultation are identified along with their sources. Assigning a practice to a specific source is artificial in that most of the best practices may be derived from any of the three sources.

Maintaining a Nonhierarchical Relationship
The definition of consultee-centered consultation includes the concept of a nonhierarchical relationship. Consultants and consultees view each other as peers, although coming to the relationship with different professional background and expertise. To maintain the relationship, best practice for a school psychologist is to avoid elevating his or her status on the one hand or to allow the consultee to become deferential or overly modest on the other. One technique, called one-downsmanship, involves purposely being modest about oneself while at the same time acknowledging and complimenting the knowledge and skill of the consultee. For example, if the teacher compliments the school psychologist on an idea, the school psychologist might reply that the teacher will know best how to use or modify the idea in the classroom. The school psychologist must listen at all times for flattery or dismissal or other attempts to change the coordinate status of the relationship and be prepared to counter attempts to

elevate his or her status by pointing out valuable skills and knowledge possessed by the consultee.

Besides one-downsmanship, another practice is self-disclosure about one's own shortcomings in doing professional work. This disclosure, aside from lifting oneself off of a pedestal, if done correctly, can free the consultee to examine failure as an opportunity to reflect and learn from the experience. The consultant's self-disclosure should be accompanied by a sober analysis of what occurred and the lesson learned, modeling a positive use of failure.

Supporting Consultee Responsibility for the Client
In consultee-centered consultation the school psychologist has no direct responsibility for the learning, development, or productivity of the client, although as employees of the school system they have indirect responsibility. Best practice is to avoid assuming a direct role in working with the client (i.e., usurping the teacher's role) and to support the consultee in assuming his or her responsibility in a professional way. The school psychologist might help collect new information by observation or other means, but not by means easily available to the teacher. Consultation is not supervision.

Avoiding Personal Issues
Consultee-centered consultation focuses on the work problems of the consultee. As a result, best practice is to be aware of when the focus shifts to personal difficulties or problems the consultee wishes to solve. Best practice is to move the conversation back to the work problem and to gently refuse to enter into a counseling role with the consultee. Consultation is not counseling.

Acknowledging Consultee Freedom of Choice
School psychologists are not coercive in the consultee-centered consultation role; that is, they cannot impose consultation. Best practice is for the school psychologist to acknowledge and accept the voluntary nature of the process and to use the existence of a problem as motivation to enter into consultation and to use any consultee frustration in productive ways. The school psychologist must present consultation as a viable method for problem solving and find ways to make consultation convenient and attractive. Because it is voluntary, the consultee is free to accept or reject any suggestions or new ideas that are generated by the consultation process. Further, since only the consultee can decide what action to take following consultation,

issues of intervention acceptability will be important (Frank & Kratochwill, 2008).

Having No Predetermined Agenda Except Change

Best practice in consultee-centered consultation is to enter consultation with no set agenda for how a problem will be solved. School psychologist consultants are knowledgeable about and committed to a process that will result in a conceptual change but not what that change will be. They hope to contribute insights from psychological theory but have in mind no particular theory in advance. They may offer ideas from behavioral theory in one case and do behavioral problem solving but in another case may introduce ideas from Vygotsky about the need for social interaction with a skillful tutor at the zone of proximal development. Consultee-centered consultation is not prescriptive and does not follow a strict protocol.

Facilitating Conceptual Change

As the school psychologist and consultee explore the consultation problem, the consultee will likely reveal some thoughts or theories about the client and the causes of the problem. The school psychologist will begin to form ideas or theories (representations) as well. Best practice is to bring those representations out into the open during consultation and examine the representations for validity and utility in generating interventions. As the process proceeds, the school psychologist and consultee will likely explore how the consultee's construction is inadequate to explain this and other cases. By the presentation of anomalous data—pointing out where the theory does not work and by highlighting dissonant evidence not predicted by the consultee's framework—the school psychologist helps build dissatisfaction with the current explanatory theory (representation; Sandoval, 1996, 2003). Should this dissatisfaction occur, best practice then is for the school psychologist and consultee to coconstruct a new hypothesis or theory to be tested via intervention.

The source of the new conception may be the school psychologist or the consultee (or consultees, if it is a group consultation). The new theory must be an understandable substitute for the old. It must be intelligible, coherent, and internally consistent and seem like a plausible explanation for what is occurring in the classroom. Finally, the hope is that the new idea will seem to have widespread applicability; that is, it should be elegant, parsimonious, and have a high probability of being efficacious in working with the current client and

problem as well as with future clients and problems. It should explain more of the observed facts of the case than the previous theory.

In order to test and validate the original conception, the school psychologist turns to data elicited from the consultee, discovered in archival records, or newly collected with the consultee's input and sanction. The school psychologist looks and listens for discrepancies in what has been said or comes from other sources. These discrepancies produce cognitive dissonance, which is an excellent source of motivation for individuals to change conceptions. The focus will be on anomalies (i.e., how existing notions about the problem fail to explain the situation or produce successful interventions).

Often analogies and metaphors will be used to introduce the new ideas and conceptualization and make them intelligible to both the school psychologist and consultee. Although analogies may be useful initially, it is important to be sure that the correct features are abstracted from the analogy and transferred to the new theory. For example, one teacher saw a child in a new light after the school psychologist brought up a character in the movie *Little Miss Sunshine*. Instead of viewing the child as strange and inattentive, the teacher began to appreciate how driven the child was to succeed in an unusual domain.

The concept of conceptual change is central consultee-centered consultation. It will be discussed again in the section on best practices based on modes of interaction.

Best Practices Based on Phases

Here will be discussed best practices based on phases rather than based on stages. Remember that because the process seldom proceeds linearly we use the term phases instead of stages since stages implies a process that does proceed linearly.

Beginning the Process Carefully

A best practice in beginning the process of consultation involves establishing a closeness with consultees. For example, the school psychologist should spend time in the teachers' lounge or join teachers on yard duty or other school events but should not engage in gossip. It will take time to establish both trust and credibility with consultees. The school psychologist will need to find ways to be seen as reliable and competent. To this end, the school psychologist needs to respond to needs in the school and classroom and be seen as a professional. Best practice is to be useful in as many ways as possible and available, trusting that in time he or she will be approached with a request for consultation.

Another best practice during this phase is establishing a clear contract. The school psychologist must be clear about what consultation can do, what the parameters are, and what the responsibilities of each party are. The school psychologist must explain confidentiality and attend to it scrupulously.

Exploring Consultee Conceptualizations of the Dilemma

Consultee conceptions must be openly examined, and then tested, and then falsified if found to be inadequate. To be tested, however, the conceptions must first be organized in hypothetical form, such as "This is what we think is going on." Once made explicit, conceptions may be tested. Testing may range from recollections, thought experiments, and actual trials of interventions with the client. For example, after a teacher noted a girl's engagement problems during arithmetic instruction, attributing it to attention deficit disorder, further observation in other settings indicated the child was able to work independently on a demanding social studies assignment. What was found was the girl had been absent from school because of an extended illness and thus did not have fundamental arithmetic skills. Simply put, a different way of thinking about the girl's problems had to be discovered.

The information used to test conceptions must be valid and objective. The discussion and testing must be done in a way that is neutral and does not put the consultee or consultant on the defensive. Such a discussion requires great interpersonal skill.

Asking Questions to Illuminate Conceptions

At the beginning of the process, school psychologists should ask a number of questions to understand the consultee's representation of the problem and should ask what the consultee has done to address the problem and how well it worked. Guvå (2004) has suggested a number of questions to help clarify the consultee's understanding of and theory about the consultation dilemma. To focus on the consultee's explanations a school psychologist might ask, "Why do you think this is so? Is there something than can help us understand the client? What do you think is going on?" To focus on the consultee's picture of the client, the consultant might ask, "What does the client look like?" To focus on the consultee's fantasies about the future, the consultant might ask, "What do you think will happen if nothing is done?" To focus on other imagined scenarios of importance, the consultant might ask, "Have you met a similar problem before and what was the cause?" Questions such as these are very helpful in illuminating the consultee's initial theory (or theories) of human behavior in general, and specific theory of what is causing the consultation predicament. Most of the school psychologist's questions are open ended in nature.

Challenging Attributions

The consultant should be aware of several errors known to occur in individuals' explanations of the behavior of others. Attributions may involve internal factors such as ability or external factors such as circumstances. One bias, the fundamental attribution error, is the tendency to overestimate the internal and underestimate the external factors when explaining the behaviors of others. Another bias, the self-serving bias, is the tendency to equate one's own successes to internal factors and failures to external attributes. Questions to understand attributions are: "What is it about the client's makeup/abilities/personality that seems to be causing this?" "What might be going on in the client's world or environment that might be causing this?" By asking both questions, the school psychologist may open new possibilities.

Avoiding Some of the Dangers in Using Questions

Using the same format of open-ended questions repeatedly or only open questions can result in stilted conversation, and consultants should vary question formats. A temptation to be avoided is asking questions to satisfy curiosity rather than to help the consultee to explore. Asking too many questions in a short period can be perceived as grilling by the consultee. "Why" questions need to be used carefully, since consultees may view them as accusatory and judgmental rather than as simple requests for information. School psychologists should also avoid asking rhetorical questions (i.e., questions to which they know the answer) as this communicates superiority.

Differentiating the Four Common Reasons for Work Difficulty

Caplan (1970) pointed out that consultees come to consultation for one or more of four underlying reasons that the relationship with the client has deteriorated. A work difficulty can come from (a) lack of knowledge, (b) lack of skill, (c) lack of self-confidence, or (d) lack of professional objectivity. Best practice involves the school psychologist determining to what extent each source is having an impact on the consultee's professional functioning with the client. Such a determination is important since each implies a different approach to consultation. Table 32.2 lists Caplan's four sources of consultee difficulty, a description, signs of the difficulty during consultation, and the best practice in dealing with it.

Responding to the Consultee's Lack of Knowledge

Sometimes a consultee's difficulties of lack of knowledge are because the consultee has no theory or conception of what is occurring. But some consultees

may be a tabula rasa and need to be helped to gain knowledge. Whether or not the school psychologist supplies the needed knowledge or refers the consultee to other sources depends on many factors having to do with the organizational structure of the institution in which the consultee works. The school psychologist in this situation is in the position of explaining aspects of psychological theory or finding ways for peers or the system to provide the needed information about, for example, available curricular resources. The consultant is not teaching the consultee information in his or her professional domain (e.g., pedagogy) but rather providing information from psychology. Since many school psychologists have previously been teachers

Table 32.2. Best Practices Based on Caplan's Category of Consultee Difficulty

Consultee Difficulty	Description	Signs Emerging During Consultation Interview	Best Practice
Lack of knowledge	Knowledge about psychology or mental health	Verbal acknowledgment; errors in descriptions	Provide psychological knowledge to the system directly or indirectly; offer group consultation
Lack of skill	Consultee understands causes of the problem and principles underlying intervention but executes poorly	Skill deficits revealed in the interview and what has been done previously with the client	Avoid assuming supervisory role; facilitate exposure to role model
Lack of self-confidence	Reluctance to engage with or change modes of working with the client	Anxiety avoidance	Provide peer support through group consultation; provide nonspecific ego support
Lack of objectivity	Direct personal involvement	Client is the object for the satisfaction of personal needs	Support professional identity and ethics; replace personal need with the satisfaction of professional goal achievement; discuss client's parallel needs; self-disclosure
	Simple identification	Similarity between consultee and client; consultee taking sides	Provide a role model by being empathetic with all relevant actors in the consultation dilemma; consider multiple perspectives
	Transference	Consultee imposes on the dilemma a pattern of roles from previous life experiences or fantasies; strong emotion	Reality testing through careful observation; consider a reversal of roles or cause and effect
	Characterological distortions	Minor disorders evidenced: consultee has strange affect	Support defenses and lower anxiety; increase intellectual understanding; remain task oriented; provide group consultation
	Theme interference	Special type of transference; suddenly occurs in otherwise effective professional; theme takes the form of a syllogism; stereotyping	Demonstrate that an inevitable outcome is only one possibility; Cardinal error: Remove client from initial category

Note. Copyright 2012 by Jonathan Sandoval. Used with permission.

and most have had coursework in education, it may be difficult to resist slipping into the role of supervisor. Nevertheless, the school psychologist's role in the partnership is to bring psychological theory and knowledge to the conversation so it can be used in the classroom.

Responding to the Consultee's Lack of Skill

Best practice in responding to lack of skill in a consultee is to avoid assuming a supervisory role and to locate and encourage the use of models with whom the consultee can identify and who can illustrate the needed skill. The school psychologist can, however, provide emotional support and encourage practice of the new skill through role playing.

Responding to the Consultee's Lack of Self-Confidence

Best practice in addressing a consultee's lack of self-confidence is to provide nonspecific ego support. School psychologists accomplish this by being an empathetic listener and responding verbally and nonverbally with calmness and optimism. The school psychologist can probe for mistaken ideas and fears so those ideas and fears may be examined by testing them against reality. Sometimes a comment such as "What is the worst thing that can happen" is helpful. Attending carefully to issues of treatment acceptability is particularly important. In consultation with groups of consultees, peers can also provide encouragement and help the consultee believe an intervention he or she is considering has a reasonable probability of success.

Reducing the Impact of the Consultee's Lack of Objectivity

When a consultee has no conceptualization or has a naïve, but not strongly held, idea about the causes of the problem with a client, the issue is lack of knowledge. However, a consultee may have a conceptualization clouded by personal subjective factors that is emotionally charged and thus leads to the consultee's being professionally too close or too distant from the client's situation. As listed in Table 32.2, overlapping categories include direct personal involvement, simple identification, transference, characterological distortions, and theme interference. The table includes suggestions for addressing each (see also McCready, 1985).

Caplan is best known for his thoughts on theme interference reduction. However, he acknowledged that many consultants, particularly school-based practitioners, have not endorsed this technique (Caplan, Caplan, &

Erchul, 1995). A theme is, "A conflict related to actual life experience or to fantasies that has not been satisfactorily resolved [and that] is apt to persist in a consultee's preconscious or unconscious as an emotionally toned cognitive constellation" (Caplan & Caplan, 1993, p. 122). Caplan suggested that in many cases themes, like neutrally toned schema, interfere with effective problem solving but are even more difficult to address because of the negative affect. He described how themes may be understood as syllogisms the consultee has constructed consisting of an initial category and an inevitable outcome. In consultation, these themes must be shown to be inadequate before new ways of working with and of conceptualizing the client will emerge. Theme interference techniques include (a) demonstrating that the inevitable outcome is only one logical possibility and that other outcomes are more likely than the dreaded one and (b) avoiding giving nonverbal validation to the theme outcome. These techniques of theme interference reduction are attempts at conceptual change inasmuch as they attempt to influence syllogisms constructed by the consultee. It contributes to prevention by reducing the chance the theme will be applied to future clients.

Instead of offering a different conceptualization, however, the aim of consultee-centered consultation is to elaborate the theme in such a way as to make membership in the initial category imply a number of different outcomes and to complicate the picture. The resulting changed syllogism will suggest that many outcomes are possible and that none is inevitable. The revised theme will be more plausible and fruitful for working with other clients. One approach is to bring in anomalous data to indicate how the initial category did not lead to the inevitable outcome.

As Caplan suggested, the emphasis should be on how the initial theory is inadequate and not on how the theory is inapplicable to the particular client (i.e., by removing the client from the initial category). There will be no motive to change the theory if it is perceived as not applying to the client.

Distinguishing Themes From Cultural Values

Many ideas that a consultee may have about a client may stem from the cultural background of the consultee, which may be different from that of the consultant or the client. In the consultee, these ideas may be stereotypes of the client (or the consultant; Ingraham & Meyers, 2000). Typically, stereotypes lack the strong emotional tone of the theme and may be addressed more easily. Nevertheless, the school psychologist must challenge cultural stereotypes when encountered.

Being Multiculturally Competent

Best practice in consultee-centered consultation involves working cross culturally with consultees and clients coming from backgrounds different from one's own. Ingraham (2003, 2004) pointed out that there are threats to consultant and consultee objectivity from filtering perceptions through stereotype, from overemphasizing the role of culture, or from being insensitive to cultural norms and values operating in the consultation situation. She also describes intervention paralysis, a threat to consultee self-confidence, where the consultee is aware of cultural differences but fearful of being inappropriate and considered a racist. Best practices include valuing and soliciting multiple perspectives, creating an emotionally safe environment where culture and race can be discussed, supporting cross-cultural awareness and learning, and seeking cultural guides and teachers. School psychologists must model comfort in discussing cultural issues in consultation.

Exploring and Monitoring the Ecological Field

The consultation problem exists in a complex field consisting of the classroom, the school, the consultee's personality, the client, and the client's family and community. In addition, historical, sociocultural, and psychosocial forces will be at work. The influence of all of these factors must be taken into account, particularly in generating interventions that will be acceptable, feasible, and capable of being implemented with integrity in the consultee's unique setting.

Using Multiple Theories to Understand and Generate Intervention

There is little question that behavioral theory has yielded a powerful technology for changing client behavior and that this technology can used by consultees with the help of consultants. Best practice in consultee-centered consultation is to be open to multiple theoretical ways to understand a classroom situation and to generate ideas that might be helpful in changing the dynamic between the consultee and the client. Developmental theory may be helpful, for example, when a teacher has mistaken expectations for a child. Social psychology may suggest ways to deal with destructive group processes in the classroom. Instructional psychology might suggest ways to modify the curriculum. A school psychologist adhering to consultee-centered consultation must be able to shift from one psychological paradigm to another during the course of consultation.

Supplying Ego Support During Intervention

Making changes in one's professional practices, either modifying old ones or adopting new ones, is not easy and can generate anxiety. Caplan and Caplan (1993) observed that consultees are often in a crisis state. Best practice is to supply emotional support during the intervention period by supplying accurate feedback, along with optimism about eventual success. School psychologists use data from multiple sources to help the consultee see progress, even if it is a small amount at first. In addition, by remaining calm and unruffled the consultant communicates confidence in the consultee.

Inculcating an Experimental Attitude

There is usually a hope in consultation that a new solution will emerge quickly and that the client will change overnight. Unfortunately, human problems are seldom easy to solve and change takes place gradually and requires constant monitoring. The consultant must address the expectation of getting it right the first time. The school psychologist must be positive and realistically optimistic but help the consultee appreciate a process that is experimental. The consultant might say, "This seems like one plausible change you can make in your classroom that will address the problem, but we won't know until we try it." Hypotheses are generated and tested, and information can be gained from failure as well as success. Based on data, the consultee must be willing to go back to the beginning and modify plans built on what has been learned.

Carefully Evaluating Consultation Outcomes

In most forms of consultation, a change in the client is considered the primary goal. In consultee-centered consultation it is also important to examine the effect of the consultation process on the whole range of clients who are the responsibility of the consultee. If a target behavior has been identified, then the school psychologist and teacher should look for changes over baseline. These changes may also be reflected in institutional data such as absences and test scores.

In consultee-centered consultation, a key outcome is restoring the relationship between the teacher and the child or between an administrator and the staff. If consultation results in a reestablished positive working relationship and mutual respect between the consultee and client, typically the client's behavior will improve. Improvement in the relationship can be captured by self-report or by an analysis of the consultation process based on the school psychologist's notes, logs, or other records of the process. There are many dangers in relying on the self-report of consultee change or of satisfaction with consultation, but they have a place along with other data in the evaluation process (Sandoval, 2004). One of the barriers to a positive relationship between a teacher and a child is anxiety on the part of the consultee. When the anxiety is gone as a result of talking about a case in consultation, the relationship often improves. As a result, measures of degree of concern about a client might also be useful.

Because consultee-centered consultation has a goal of prevention, another outcome that should be reviewed and fostered is the transfer of learning to new clients and settings. Transfer is facilitated by directly examining applications to other clients and situations by asking, for example, "Could this intervention be effective with other children in your classroom?" If the prevention goal of consultation is attained, measures of the system should show improvement. Following consultation, a teacher might eventually bring fewer cases of the same type to consultation, student performance in academics and decorum will improve, special education referrals will decline, and teachers will show fewer signs of burnout.

Working in Groups When Feasible

Followers of consultee-centered consultation have been particularly interested in working with groups of teachers where feasible (Babinski & Rogers, 1998; Sandoval, 1977; Wilcox, 1980). Often this has occurred with groups of new teachers, teachers in training, or small groups assigned to a school or a disciplinary department at the secondary level. Best practice involves using group process skills to guide problem solving and develop group cohesion. An advantage of groups is that members can supply fresh perspective and support for change, as well as make suggestions for intervention based on their experience.

Caplan and Caplan (1993) added the concept of mental health collaboration to capture the work school psychologists do when they work as members of interdisciplinary teams. Distinctions implied by the term interdisciplinary teams include the shared responsibility for the outcome of the process, the required participation in the team, the lack of freedom to reject team decisions, and more direct involvement with the client and, possibly, with parents. As a member of the team, the school psychologist can participate by complicating the thinking of the team and soliciting alternative conceptualization of the problem being addressed (Knotek, Sauer-Lee, & Lowe-Greenlee, 2009).

Best Practices Based on Modes of Interaction

Hylander's (2000, 2012) grounded theory of consultee-centered consultation also suggests best practices. She argues that school psychologists should be able to move flexibly from a nondirective stance in interactions to a directive stance and back without being prescriptive or coercive.

Dealing Skillfully With Emotion

An important assumption in a consultee-centered consultation is that consultee emotion is almost always involved in the consultation process. Emotion might spring from challenges to professional self-concept, for instance, or from frustrations in failing to work with a client or from fears for the client's future. Best practice is for the school psychologist to respond to the consultee in a calm, friendly, and deliberate manner. The consultant uses nonverbal means as well as realistic reassurance to communicate that human problems are often difficult to solve. The consultant uses the approach mode, helping the consultee discharge emotion and confirming that he or she can understand the depth and extent of the problem the consultee faces.

Willingness to Change Conceptualizations

One of the assumptions of consultee-centered consultation is that the consultee will have a basic idea of what the dilemma is about. Hylander (2012) calls this initial conceptualization a representation. Other terms for the consultee's understanding might be schema or scenario. The consultee's articulation of the representation is called the presentation, which may or may not clearly reveal the underlying representation. After listening to the consultee's presentation and exploring it, the school psychologist will also form an initial representation of the problem. The consultant's representation may or may not match that of the consultee. Best practice for the consultant is to be open to shifting representations including his or her own. School psychologists must be able to identify the initial representation of the consultee and to shift from an understanding of the consultee's representation to their own representation to another based on theory and evidence collected during consultation. School psychologists must also be able to create an environment or conversation in which the consultee feels comfortable making a presentation that is accurate and close to their representation (approach). The representation will have a cognitive component, an affective component, and a motivational component. That is, the representation reflects what the consultee thinks the problem is, how he or she feels about it, and what he or she is willing to do about it. The consultee's thoughts, feelings, or willingness to act may not be socially acceptable and cause the presentation to be too vague or too stereotyped. When this occurs, the school psychologist will never know the representation unless he or she can ask questions and sharing thoughts in a calm, supportive, and nonjudgmental fashion.

Making Reasoning Accessible

In consultee-centered consultation, a key skill of the school psychologist is to make explicit to the consultee his or her own conceptualization of the problem drawn from the information that has emerged from the consultation interview (moving away mode). That is, the school psychologist makes his or her reasoning accessible to the consultee (Monson & Frederickson, 2002) and, more importantly, offers up the conceptualization for discussion and debate. One practice that is valuable is following up on a question or observation and then adding the reasoning behind the question. The school psychologist might say, "I am asking that question because I was wondering what behavior is tolerated in his home." By explicitly talking about one's own representation one can model the process of sharing. On the other hand, the school psychologist must be willing to challenge his or her own representations and return to the neutral position to evaluate them.

Examining Turnings

Hylander (2012) discussed five kinds of shifts in understandings that may occur in consultation. These are distinct turnings, magic turnings, weathercock turnings, false turnings, and continuous turnings. Best practice consists of distinguishing between them. A distinct turning occurs when the consultee adopts a different explanation for the client's behavior. The school psychologist hopes there will be a distinct change in the understanding the teacher has about the dilemma. However, a distinct turning should be distinguished from a false turning, where there has been no change, and from weathercock turnings, where there are shifts back and forth between old conceptions and new ones. The school psychologist should be aware of and comfortable with the idea that changes in conceptions may take place gradually and that it may be a continuous process. When a conceptual shift is gradual, it is continuous turning. The consultant must also recognize shifts may occur without awareness, as if by magic. These magic turnings occur when the consultee makes a spontaneous change in the relationship with the client after simply initiating the

consultation process but not completing it. Taking the first step and beginning to talk about the issue can be helpful in and of itself, and lead to new ideas away from the session, or a reduction in the level of anxiety on the part of the consultee that is responded to by the client.

Although difficult, the consultant can also monitor the turning or conceptual process by periodically checking the teacher's representation of the problem. This evaluation can be done by asking, "At this point, what do you think is the most likely explanation for the child's behavior?" Another device is to graphically represent the problem at multiple times during consultation (Sandoval, 2004).

SUMMARY

School-based consultee-centered consultation is a method of interacting with a significant adult in a child's life to help the adult improve his or her work relationship with the child in the present and in the future. It is chiefly distinguished from other problem-solving models of consultation in its emphasis addressing emotion and affect as well as exploring underlying ideas the consultee may have about the causes of the problem. It is a voluntary relationship between peers, albeit practitioners coming from different professions. It is nonprescriptive in that there is no set agenda or psychological theory to be used. Consultants following this model use practices aimed at problem solving and responding to both the emotional and motivational components of the consultation dilemma. Many consultee-centered consultation best practices are directed at facilitating the process of conceptual change. Most models of consultation hope to bring about conceptual change. But in this model the school psychologist does not have a particular change (e.g., framing a problem as one of contingency management) in mind at the beginning of the process but is confident a new conception will develop spontaneously and organically. In addition, school psychologists following this model should work from the assumption that different approaches are called for depending if the problem is a lack of knowledge, lack of skill, lack of self-confidence, or lack of objectivity. School psychologists should also understand that consultants can be both nondirective and directive at different times during a complex process.

AUTHOR NOTE

Disclosure. Jonathan Sandoval has a financial interest in books he authored or coauthored referenced in this chapter.

REFERENCES

Alpert, J. L. (1976). Conceptual bases of mental health consultation in the schools. *Professional Psychology*, *7*, 619–626. doi:10.1037/h0078612

Babinski, L. M., & Rogers, D. L. (1998). Supporting new teachers through consultee-centered group consultation. *Journal of Educational and Psychological Consultation*, *9*, 285–308. doi:10.1207/s1532768xjepc0904_1

Berlin, I. (1977). Some lessons learned in 25 years of mental health consultation to schools. In S. C. Plog & P. I. Ahmed (Eds.), *Principles and techniques of mental health consultation*. (pp. 21–48). New York, NY: Plenum Press.

Caplan, G. (1970). *The theory and practice of mental health consultation*. New York, NY: Basic Books.

Caplan, G., & Caplan, R. (1993). *Mental health consultation and collaboration*. San Francisco, CA: Jossey-Bass.

Caplan, G., Caplan, R. B., & Erchul, W. P. (1995). A contemporary view of mental health consultation: Comments on "Types of mental health consultation" by Gerald Caplan. *Journal of Educational and Psychological Consultation*, *5*, 23–30. doi:10.1207/s1532768xjepc0601_2

Caplan, G., & Caplan-Moskovich, R. (2004). Recent advances in mental health consultation and mental health collaboration. In N. M. Lambert, I. Hylander, & J. Sandoval (Eds.), *Consultee-centered consultation: Improving the quality of professional services in schools and community organizations*. (pp. 21–35). Mahwah, NJ: Erlbaum.

Erchul, W. P. (2009). Gerald Caplan: A tribute to the originator of mental health consultation. *Journal of Educational and Psychological Consultation*, *19*, 95–105. doi:10.1080/10474410902888418

Frank, J. L., & Kratochwill, T. R. (2008). School-based problem-solving consultation. In W. P. Erchul & S. M. Sheridan (Eds.), *Handbook of research in school consultation*. (pp. 13–30). Mahwah, NJ: Erlbaum.

Guvå, G. (2004). How to respond to teachers who ask for help but not for consultation. In N. M. Lambert, I. Hylander, & J. Sandoval (Eds.), *Consultee-centered consultation: Improving the quality of professional services in schools and community organizations*. (pp. 257–266). Mahwah, NJ: Erlbaum.

Hughes, J. N., Loyd, L., & Buss, M. (2008). Empirical and theoretical support for an updated model of mental health consultation for schools. In W. P. Erchul & S. M. Sheridan (Eds.), *Handbook of research in school consultation*. (pp. 343–360). Mahwah, NJ: Erlbaum.

Hylander, I. (2000). *Turning processes: The change of representations in consultee-centered case consultation*. (Unpublished doctoral dissertation). Linköping, Sweden: Linköping University, Department of Behavioural Science. Retrieved from http://urn.kb.se/resolve?urn=urn:nbn:se:liu:diva-33180

Hylander, I. (2012). Conceptual change through consultee-centered consultation: A theoretical model. *Consulting Psychology Journal: Practice and Research*, *64*, 29–45. doi:10.1037/a0027986

Ingraham, C. L. (2003). Multicultural consultee-centered consultation: When novice consultants explore cultural hypotheses with experienced teacher consultees. *Journal of Educational and Psychological Consultation*, *14*, 329–362. doi:10.1207/s1532768xjepc143&4_7

Ingraham, C. L. (2004). Multicultural consultee-centered consultation: Supporting consultees in the development of cultural competence. In N. M. Lambert, I. Hylander, & J. Sandoval (Eds.), *Consultee-centered consultation: Improving the quality of professional services in schools and community organizations*. (pp. 133–148). Mahwah, NJ: Erlbaum.

Ingraham, C. L., & Meyers, J. (Guest Eds.). (2000). Multicultural and cross-cultural consultation in schools: Cultural diversity issues in school consultation [Special issue]. *School Psychology Review*, *29*(3).

Knotek, S., Sauer-Lee, A., & Lowe-Greenlee, B. (2009). Consultee-centered consultation as a vehicle for knowledge diffusion and utilization. In S. Rosenfield & V. Berninger (Eds.), *Implementing evidence-based academic interventions in school settings*. (pp. 233–252). New York, NY: Oxford University Press.

Lambert, N. M. (1974). A school-based consultation model. *Professional Psychology*, *5*, 267–275.

Lambert, N. M. (2004). Consultee-centered consultation: An international perspective on goals, process, and theory. In N. M. Lambert, I. Hylander, & J. Sandoval (Eds.), *Consultee-centered consultation: Improving the quality of professional services in schools and community organizations*. (pp. 3–19). Mahwah, NJ: Erlbaum.

Lambert, N. M., Hylander, I., & Sandoval, J. (Eds.). (2004). *Consultee-centered consultation: Improving the quality of professional services in schools and community organizations*. Mahwah, NJ: Erlbaum.

Lambert, N. M., Sandoval, J. H., & Yandell, G. W. (1975). Preparation of school psychologists for school-based consultation. A training activity and a service to community schools. *Journal of School Psychology*, *13*, 68–75.

McCready, K. F. (1985). Differentiation of transference versus theme interference in consultee-centered case consulation. *School Psychology Review*, *14*, 471–478.

Meyers, J., Freidman, M. P., & Gaughan, E. J. (1975). The effects of consultee-centered consultation on teacher behavior. *Psychology in the Schools*, *12*, 288–295. doi:10.1002/1520-6807(197507)12:3<288::AID-PITS2310120308>3.0.CO;2-O

Meyers, J., Parsons, R. D., & Martin, R. (1979). *Mental health consultation in the schools*. San Francisco, CA: Jossey-Bass.

Monson, J. J., & Frederickson, N. (2002). Consultant problem understanding as a function of training in interviewing to promote accessible reasoning. *Journal of School Psychology*, *40*, 197–212. doi:10.1016/S0022-4405(02)00097-3

National Association of School Psychologists. (2010). *Model for comprehensive and integrated school psychological services*. Bethesda, MD: Author. Retrieved from http://www.nasponline.org/standards/2010standards/2_PracticeModel.pdf

Rosenfield, S., Levinsohn-Klyap, M., & Cramer, K. (2010). Educating consultants for practice in the schools. In E. Garcia-Vasquez, T. Crespi, & C. Riccio (Eds.), *Handbook of education, training, and supervision of school psychologists in school and community: Vol. 1. Foundations of professional practice*. (pp. 259–278). New York, NY: Routledge.

Sandoval, J. (1977). Mental health consultation for teachers in preservice training. *California Journal of Teacher Education*, *3*, 110–124.

Sandoval, J. (1996). Constructivism, consultee-centered consultation, and conceptual change. *Journal of Educational and Psychological Consultation*, *7*, 89–97. doi:10.1207/s1532768xjepc0701_8

Sandoval, J. (2003). Constructing conceptual change in consultee-centered consultation. *Journal of Educational and Psychological Consultation*, *14*, 251–261. doi:10.1207/s1532768xjepc143&4_3

Sandoval, J. (2004). Evaluation issues and strategies in consultee-centered consultation. In N. M. Lambert, I. Hylander, & J. Sandoval (Eds.), *Consultee-centered consultation: Improving the quality of professional services in schools and community organizations.* (pp. 393–400). Mahwah, NJ: Erlbaum.

Sandoval, J., & Davis, J. M. (1984). A school-based mental health consultation curriculum. *Journal of School Psychology, 22,* 31–43.

Wilcox, M. R. (1980). Variables affecting group mental health consultation for teachers. *Professional Psychology, 11,* 728–732. doi:10.1037/0735-7028.11.5.728

33 Best Practices in Instructional Consultation and Instructional Consultation Teams

Sylvia Rosenfield
University of Maryland

OVERVIEW

Consultation and collaboration are domains that permeate all aspects of school psychology service delivery, according to the National Association of School Psychologists (NASP) *Model for Comprehensive and Integrated School Psychological Services* (NASP, 2010). One practice within those domains is Instructional Consultation, enabling school psychologists to work with school staff on the most basic goal of schooling, enhancing the academic achievement of students. In the context of the 2004 reauthorization of the Individuals with Disabilities Education Act and the No Child Left Behind Act (NCLB), there is an increased emphasis on achieving academic outcomes for all students, including those who are often considered at risk for meeting standards. Instructional Consultation (Rosenfield, 1987), and its systemic delivery system, Instructional Consultation Teams (Rosenfield & Gravois, 1996; Rosenfield, Gravois, & Silva, in press), focuses on the ecology in which the student and teacher interact as the most direct way for all students to reach the goals of schooling.

Instructional Consultation is a consultee-centered approach to problem solving (Knotek, Rosenfield, Gravois, & Babinski, 2003; Sandoval, in press). As such, the focus of problem solving is on the consultee, typically the teacher. The goal is to reconceptualize the problem so that the teacher-consultee can gain new knowledge to be used not only with the referred student but potentially with other students of the teacher as well. The larger objective of Instructional Consultation Teams is improving and enhancing staff competence as a route to both systems improvement and positive individual student outcomes.

Instructional Consultation can play a role in school psychologists' multitiered system of service delivery, but in Tier 1, the classroom is the primary site for consultation and collaboration. Given the accountability of the classroom teacher for student outcomes, Instructional Consultation provides a structure that enables a teacher to problem solve for those at risk, but it also enhances the teacher's skills for the benefit of all the students in the classroom. It is consistent with research documenting the importance of the classroom teacher, situated professional development of school staff (i.e., professional development within the context of their work), and consultation and collaboration among school professionals (e.g., Hawley, 2007).

In this chapter, the essential assumptions of Instructional Consultation and Instructional Consultation Teams will be presented as basic considerations. The need for systematic training in consultation, academic assessment and intervention, and problem-solving skills will be reviewed. The best practices section describes the process for school psychologists conducting Instructional Consultation, focusing on three central elements: (a) communication and relationship skills, (b) problem-solving stages, and (c) use of evidence-based assessment and intervention strategies. Next, best practices in conducting Instructional Consultation Teams, the school-based delivery system for Instructional Consultation, are described, including the team structure, functions of the team, and the referral system. The role of the Instructional Consultation Team facilitator is addressed. Best practice also requires that any model of service delivery attends to issues of training and implementation. Thus, the approaches to the use of these components are included, as well as issues of multicultural competencies and evaluation of outcomes. A review of research supporting Instructional Consultation and Instructional Consultation Teams can be found in Rosenfield et al. (in press).

BASIC CONSIDERATIONS

Instructional Consultation is a problem-solving model that is closely related to multiple components of the NASP Practice Model (NASP, 2010). It is specifically related to the practices that permeate all aspects of service delivery; that is, consultation and collaboration and data-based decision making and accountability. The focus is also on student- and system-level indirect service delivery, which are additional aspects of the NASP model. One of the special aspects of Instructional Consultation is the emphasis on assessment and interventions to develop academic skills.

Components

As an indirect service delivery model, Instructional Consultation (Rosenfield, 1987), and its integration into a school-wide delivery system as Instructional Consultation Teams (Rosenfield & Gravois, 1996), provides support to staff and students. Components of the model include (a) a collaborative stage-based problem-solving process that integrates relationship and communication processes; (b) assessment strategies, including a specific academic assessment process, instructional assessment; and (c) academic and behavioral interventions. Instructional Consultation Teams embed the instructional consultation process within an implementation design that supports schools and school districts in facilitating change from initiation through to the institutionalization phase. Training a skilled facilitator to manage the change is a central aspect of the model. Additionally, a formative and summative evaluation of the training, the implementation, and the outcomes, based on a causal model, reflect the ongoing commitment of the developers (Gravois & Rosenfield, 2002; Rosenfield et al., in press) to evidence-based practice.

Importance of Underlying Assumptions

Instructional Consultation is, however, more than a set of procedures and activities. The underlying assumptions are central to the integrity of the model's implementation. Failure to accept the assumptions leads

to problems in the successful implementation of any service delivery or intervention model, especially when the model challenges traditional beliefs. Instructional Consultation challenges the traditional deficit models that have been central to the training and practice of many school psychologists. Thus, a discussion of assumptions is the starting point for the practice of Instructional Consultation.

One basic assumption is that the consultant and consultee actively construct and resolve the problem through their interaction: "The facts of a particular case are but a reflection of the values and prejudices of those persons describing that situation" (White, Summerlin, Loos, & Epstein, 1992, p. 350). This contrasts with the assumption that there is a problem to be diagnosed through the use of instruments (e.g., intelligence and processing tests) designed to examine and describe the student. In reflecting on what we observe and pay attention to, Horowitz (2013), a cognitive scientist, notes that "there is a certain bias in everyone's perspective," and for professionals there is "the tendency to look at every context from the point of view of one's [professional expertise]" (p. 8). In seeking answers to questions about whether, for example, the child has a condition such as attention deficit hyperactivity disorder or has a learning disability, teachers, parents, and school psychologists may not recognize that the questions asked and instruments used frame the type of problem that can be found.

The ecological perspective of school psychologists who adopt Instructional Consultation is framed around the importance of a flexible or dynamic approach to performance in which context matters, rather than a fixed approach in which permanent traits of individuals explain behavior. Based on the work of Carol Dweck and her colleagues, Johnston (2012) supported the importance of viewing students' concerns from a flexible perspective so that ability or intelligence is seen "as something that grows with learning and depends on the situation" (p. 11). Creating conditions for learning is at the heart of Instructional Consultation. The alternative of a fixed perspective is basic to a deficit orientation, in which once a student is viewed as lazy or as a student with a learning disability, "we start to see evidence of it everywhere in their behavior" (p. 19). The student's situation, the context for the student's learning, is not seen as part of the problem. For school psychologists engaging in Instructional Consultation, the dynamic perspective guides how teachers' concerns about students in their classrooms are addressed: (a) the school's mission is to support learning, not sort learners;

(b) support should be provided at the classroom level; (c) the focus is on the instructional triangle (see below), not just the student; and (d) embedded professional development is best practice.

Supporting Learning

Under NCLB, schools became increasingly accountable for outcomes for all students. In this culture, school psychologists have a valuable contribution to make at the classroom and system levels rather than serving as the gatekeepers for special education. Instructional Consultation is a form of response to intervention (RTI) and comprehensive, integrated multitiered service delivery. However, in this form of RTI, the primary goal is for the school psychologist to collaborate with the classroom teacher in assessing, intervening, and evaluating student progress in the regular classroom, rather than to focus on whether the student is a nonresponder and should be considered for additional services outside the classroom or be assessed for special education. When RTI is interpreted as a problem-solving approach to finding the most effective way to enhance student learning within the classroom, Instructional Consultation can be considered a response-to-instruction approach.

Support at the Classroom Level

Given that the mission of Instructional Consultation and Instructional Consultation Teams is to support learning in the least restrictive environment, it follows that support at the classroom level is a core value. Evidence confirms that early intervention and prevention for both academic and behavioral concerns are more effective and preferable to waiting until the problem requires intervention at more intensive levels. This is appropriate, moreover, "for children of any race or ethnic group, and children with or without an identifiable 'within-child' problem" (Donovan & Cross, 2002, p. ES-5). Further, this support should be provided within the setting in which the concerns first appear, usually the classroom.

However, there is increasing recognition that teachers cannot do this alone and that support systems need to be in place for the classroom teacher (see, e.g., Adelman & Taylor, 2012). The classroom teacher is a critical resource in enabling students to close gaps in achievement or behavior. As a consultee-centered consultation model that enhances teacher knowledge and skills, Instructional Consultation provides an important

resource to the teacher. It should be noted, however, that special education teachers and instructional specialists also use Instructional Consultation and that teachers and specialists continue to have concerns about students even when students are provided services. For example, in one case a teacher of a self-contained class for students diagnosed with autism was able to work with a school psychologist to resolve a concern that had an instructional rather than a behavioral cause (Pas, 2012). This case is especially notable as the original referral was for behavior assumed to reflect the autism diagnosis, and it was through careful reflective problem solving that the instructional concern was identified. As in all cases, the focus of the service is to enable the staff to support students more effectively.

Focus on the Instructional Triangle

An academic concern about a student or group of students is analyzed through the instructional triangle (see Figure 33.1); that is, the interactions between the student's entry-level skills, the instructional design or format, and the actual task with which the student is presented. It is ecologically based and is focused on alterable variables. The instructional triangle is a shift from the traditional assessment paradigm that focuses predominantly on student characteristics. Even when the focus is on student entry-level skills, the target is alterable learner variables, such as the prior knowledge of the student rather than IQ test scores. An instructional assessment (see Gickling & Gravois, in press) evaluates the entry-level skills of the student in the domain of concern. Even when the presenting concern of the teacher is behavior, the Instructional Consultation process includes an evaluation of whether

Figure 33.1. The Instructional Triangle

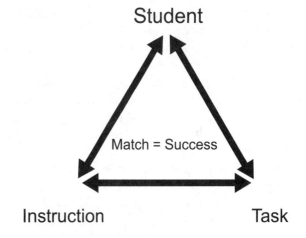

students are able to engage successfully with classroom tasks and instructional methods. Frustration caused by student–task mismatch can be the source of a behavior problem, such as inattention or failure to complete work.

Teachers operationalize curriculum objectives into classroom materials and tasks, and their expectations for the students in their classroom are based on their evaluation of the students' work on these materials and tasks. Students who are unable to complete the work successfully are considered to be at risk or in need of additional support. In Instructional Consultation, an instructional assessment examines the gap between the task and the learner's skills. (The term *instructional assessment* has now replaced the former label of *curriculum-based assessment*). Instructional assessment is first used as a formative assessment in the problem identification stage of Instructional Consultation, and its purpose is to assess the instructional level of the student. An instructional assessment enables the teacher to gain an understanding of what skills the student has and where the student can enter the curriculum at an instructional level. The goal is to improve the match between the learner's skills, instructional methods, and the task, so that the student can engage successfully with classroom material.

It is essential to differentiate the instructional assessment method used by instructional consultants from curriculum-based measurement (CBM). Screening and monitoring students using CBM does not target the specific instructional needs of the students. Decisions based on CBM, such as Tier 2 placement, may continue to reflect poor instructional matches unless additional assessments are done. For example, screening students for reading problems using fluency measures or instruments that measure level of skill is not sufficient to determine the specific academic needs of the student in the classroom curriculum materials. In addition, sending students to specialists in reading may not resolve the students' reading concerns unless both classroom teacher and reading specialist are providing an instructional match in the students' lessons. Without the specificity of an instructional assessment of entry-level skills, implementing even an evidence-based program may not result in students' progress if the level of the materials and instruction are not matched to the students' instructional levels.

The third point of the triangle is the instructional and management strategies that are implemented. Because Instructional Consultation is a consultee-centered model that focuses on building teacher knowledge and skills, it provides an opportunity for school psychologists to introduce evidence-based interventions to the teacher through the collaborative process and to support teachers in their use. There is growing recognition of how difficult it is to move interventions from research to practice, and consultee-centered consultation is viewed as one way to address this concern (Forman et al., 2013; Rosenfield, 2000). In all situations, whether or not an evidence-based intervention is adopted, an outcome evaluation is conducted to determine effectiveness of interventions, recognizing that even evidence-based interventions do not work in every situation and with every student.

The consultation process should result in classroom-based change, so that the student gains the benefit of productive engaged time in the classroom setting. Sending the student for interventions outside the classroom, without affecting and coordinating with the instructional methods within the classroom, can result in overloading the student with multiple objectives and materials. What is equally problematic, as has been noted above, is that some portion of the tasks in the multiple settings might not be at the assessed instructional level of the student. Further, valuable instructional time is lost as the student moves back and forth between instructional settings. Thus, Instructional Consultation emphasizes developing a good instructional match for the student in the classroom setting as a first priority.

Embedded Professional Development

Providing support to the classroom teacher also means that professional development is a key aspect. Current best practice in professional development values creating learning communities for teachers as a prerequisite for building learning communities for students. However, the learning community must also be implemented effectively in order to embed best practices. Benn (2004) found, in a qualitative study of the implementation of a new problem-solving model, that teachers in grade-level teams created shared meanings that further entrenched their commitment to previous practice, rather than adopting the new model. However, with support, teacher reflective activities can enable teachers' skills to grow and improve student outcomes (Rosenfield et al., in press). Referrals by teachers are viewed by school psychologists serving as instructional consultants as opportunities for teachers to consult and collaborate with colleagues about the problems of practice.

BEST PRACTICES IN INSTRUCTIONAL CONSULTATION

Instructional Consultation can be implemented at the individual school psychology practitioner level, but it is also at the core of the Instructional Consultation Team. Additional components of the team model are considered below, but even in the team model, the consultation process is conducted between the teacher-consultee and the consultant rather than by the teacher and the team. Conducting the process (termed *case management* in the Instructional Consultation Teams model) requires skill in the essential components, training to facilitate integrity of implementation, and ongoing evaluation to ensure that the outcomes are being achieved.

Core Components of Instructional Consultation as a Process

Three components are central to the consultation process: (a) capacity to build a collaborative working relationship, requiring effective use of communication skills; (b) ability to implement the steps of the problem-solving stages; and (c) knowledge of and skill in implementing the assessment and intervention strategies to address learning and behavior concerns.

Consultation Relationship

The process of consultation is between a teacher and a school psychology consultant, termed a *case manager* in Instructional Consultation Teams. The dyadic relationship at the heart of the process is essentially an "interchange between two or more professional colleagues, in a nonhierarchical relationship, working together to resolve a problem" (Rosenfield, 1987, p. 21). The relationship provides a space for teachers to reflect on their practice in a supportive environment and opens the opportunity for them to examine the instructional environment for the student in a risk-free setting. Schein (2007) makes the critical point that a consultant needs to build enough of a relationship "to stimulate the client to reveal what is really the problem and what kind of help is really needed" (p. 19), and goes on to point out that those we work with in consultation are "notoriously reluctant to reveal what is really bothering them until they have a feeling that the consultant is really trying to help" (p. 19). For example, in one consultation case, a skilled and caring teacher was able to reflect with the school psychology consultant on her interactions with a

child. The teacher could comment at the conclusion of the process on the benefit of the interaction in reframing her understanding of the problem and her own part in both creating and resolving the concern that brought her to the problem-solving process. In front of a team there is often not the time to build this supportive environment for a teacher to be reflective.

Further, when the team is used for implementing the problem-solving steps, there is usually not sufficient time to engage fully in all of the process. There is often a press to develop interventions in the time allotted at a team meeting for any individual case. When dyadic case management is not available, teams may move too quickly to the intervention stage without adequate attention to definition and analysis of the problem.

Because of the focus on the classroom as the site for change and the intent to support the teacher, building a working relationship is critical. Teachers are informed from the beginning about the instructional triangle, making it clear that the process directly involves the teacher's work with the student. Without a working relationship in place, it is difficult to examine and change the curricular, assessment, instructional, and management issues that surface during the process. In one consultation case (Newman & Rosenfield, 2008), the teacher reflected on how difficult it was for him to acknowledge that the source of the academic concerns in his classroom was his instruction. Without a solid working relationship with a school psychologist skilled in building this relationship, the teacher would likely to have continued to view the problem as deficits in the students in his classroom.

The relationship in Instructional Consultation is collaborative, with the partners working shoulder to shoulder to resolve the concerns of the teacher rather than the school psychologist shouldering the problem. A working relationship allows school psychologists and teachers to continue to work collaboratively in the face of potential differences that may arise in how the problem should be conceptualized and the intervention implemented. The consultant is, however, responsible for monitoring the quality of the relationship and for ensuring that the stages of the problem-solving process are completed with integrity. A solid working relationship enables difficult situations to be negotiated, such as those described above.

Communication Skills

The school psychologist's communication skills are essential to the quality of the relationship, as consultation is largely conducted through verbal exchanges

(Rosenfield, 2004). It is through dialogue that the problem and solution are constructed. School psychologists in training as instructional consultants become aware during supervision of how much their language affects the relationship and problem solving, and they develop skills in using language to facilitate the process (see multiple examples in Rosenfield, 2012). During training consultants are asked to record their sessions with teachers. In listening to themselves on these recordings, many novice consultants recognize for the first time that the teacher's willingness to collaborate on problem solving is, in part, a function of the verbal interchanges during the sessions. Thus, consultants learn that when problems arise in the process, attention must be paid to the quality of the communication, and there is a need for support to help them examine the language used.

Listening skills. Communication strategies that are particularly useful for school psychologists during Instructional Consultation, and likely familiar to school psychologists from the helping skills literature, are listening skills such as clarifying, paraphrasing, and perception checking (Rosenfield, 1987, 2004). These skills help school psychologists to understand the teacher's perception of the problem rather than develop and pursue hypotheses about problems based on their own interpretations. For example, if teachers say that they think a child has a learning disability, school psychologists with a deficit model orientation will begin to frame questions and conduct assessments to explore that possibility. On the other hand, during Instructional Consultation, the school psychologist explores with the teacher the underlying behaviors that have led the teacher to that inference. The instructional consultant will look for conditions under which the student is successful and determine whether the work is at the instructional level of the student. Using clarifications and paraphrases, as well as instructional assessments, school psychologists as consultants would check to be sure that they are congruent with the teacher in their understanding of the behavior.

In another example, a teacher was concerned that the school psychology consultant would increase her, the teacher's, work. It became important for the consultant to clarify with the teacher what the term *work* meant to the teacher. Until that conversation was held, it was not possible to move into the intervention phase.

Early in their training as consultants, school psychologists often find the focus on using clarification and paraphrasing irritating, believing that it is time consuming and does not get them anywhere in diagnosing the "real" problem, which they could do more efficiently by asking questions. With increasing practice, however, school psychologists can come to recognize the value of communication skills and become more automatic in their use. Such skill development, however, does require specific attention to the language used in consultation, including hearing their recording sessions and receiving feedback from supervisors or peers.

Defining the problem using behavioral language. One of the key roles of the school psychologist as consultant is to support the teacher in constructing a problem definition that the teacher views as connected to the concern, but that is also potentially resolvable within the classroom. If the teacher views the problem as stemming from a potential disabling condition in the student, then the school psychologist needs to help the teacher reframe the concern in terms of what the student is actually doing in the classroom to generate that perception. When a problem is defined in terms of learning and behavior rather than child deficit language, the teacher is more empowered to address the problem within the classroom (Rosenfield, 2004).

For example, a second-grade teacher brought a case to the school psychologist for problem solving because he believed that the student had both behavioral and learning problems, including distractibility, off-task behavior, and below-grade-level skills in reading and math (Barrett, 2012). At the time of referral, the student was receiving supplemental reading instruction with the reading specialist, with different materials and objectives, creating additional learning objectives for the student. Conducting an instructional assessment to find the student's instructional level was the first step. In neither the reading program nor the general education classroom was the student being taught at instructional level, and a critical aspect of the intervention was assuring that the student was and remained at instructional level during instruction in the classroom. The student advanced to grade-level material and became invested in his work. The behavior problems diminished as his success increased. At the conclusion of the case, the teacher went from viewing the problem from a deficit perspective (off task and distractible) to seeing the importance of matching classroom instructional material, student entry-level skills, and instruction.

Problem-Solving Stages

The school psychologist and teacher engage together on a set of structured problem-solving stages. Each stage has specific tasks that need to be completed before moving to the next stage. Without the scaffold of the stages and the work that each stage requires, many consultation interactions lack focus and accountability. Although conversations with teachers in the hallway and in other informal settings are typical regularities for school psychologists, such interactions are a limited vehicle for best practice in Instructional Consultation.

The stages of problem solving are (a) entry and contracting, (b) problem identification and analysis, (c) intervention design and planning, (d) intervention implementation and evaluation, and (e) closure. While the stages are linear, in that the business of each stage must be conducted before moving on to the next one, at any time it might be necessary to cycle back to an earlier stage. For example, a teacher may express concern about some aspect of the consultation process and it might be necessary to contract again to determine if the teacher is clear about the process or committed to continuing. Or, if additional information in the intervention stage is needed, it might require a new analysis of the problem such that the problem identification stage may need to be reinstituted. The stages are similar to those of behavioral consultation, but there are differences as well. Because these stages are so central to Instructional Consultation, a description of each stage follows.

Entry and contracting. Introduction of Instructional Consultation is done at two levels: at the school level through entry and at the individual teacher level through contracting. In entry, the school community is provided a basic awareness of Instructional Consultation as a component of the school psychologist's service delivery. Presentations at staff meetings and written materials, including brochures and newsletters for teachers and parents, are common formats for this process. During this stage, information about referral procedures is disseminated so that staff can easily access consultation services. A simple one-page request for consultation with an indication of when the teacher is available to meet enables staff to access the process.

However, no group presentation or written material absolves the school psychologist from the requirement of contracting with the individual teacher to obtain informed consent from the teacher to engage in the consulting process. Contracting informs the teacher about the collaborative nature of the consultation relationship and the stages of the problem-solving process. The teacher can then make an explicit decision about whether or not to engage in the problem-solving

process. This stage can be especially important for school psychologists, as the teacher may not really be clear about what is involved and may expect the school psychologist to assess the student in the more traditional assessment-oriented type of service delivery.

The information that the school psychologist presents during contracting includes the following:

- Informs the teacher about the stages of the problem solving process
- Explains the instructional triangle (with its focus on alterable student variables, instructional methods, and tasks in the classroom)
- Clarifies the collaborative nature of the relationship
- Discusses time involvement
- Explains data collection that is typically involved
- Introduces the Student Documentation Form that is used to guide and document the process
- Discusses the limits of confidentiality and the non-evaluative nature of the process (before engaging in consultation, it is critical for the school psychologist to clarify the school and school district policy on student and teacher confidentiality, so that the teacher can be accurately informed)
- Discusses the function of the team in relation to the consulting process if there is an Instructional Consultation Team in the school.
- Concludes with a joint decision to move forward, including scheduling time and place, or concludes with a joint decision not to move forward but to leave the door open for a possible later collaboration

Problem identification and analysis. After the school psychologist and teacher contract to move forward with problem solving, the problem identification and analysis stage begins. Although the teacher's initial description of the concern serves as a starting point, and is captured on the front page of the Student Documentation Form (see Figure 33.2), it is assumed that the participants will construct the problem through their dialogue and data collection. The problem will be framed in terms of the gap between current and desired performance and is defined in relation to the instructional triangle. A problem meaningful to the participants and respectful of their perspectives is expected to emerge from this stage. The collaborative interactions between teachers and school psychologists during the problem identification stage, and later the intervention implementation stage, may help teachers gain a more objective perspective on the concern and better value the data gathered.

Figure 33.2. Student Documentation Form, Cover Page

Student's Name_____ Grade _____ Date of Birth_____ Date Started _____

Teacher's Name_____ Case Manager _____ School _____

Goal Attainment Scale (GAS)

Step 1: Initial description of concern				
Step 2: Prioritize	**Importance 1 2 3 4** (Student at instructional level? Y N)	**Importance 1 2 3 4** (Student at instructional level? Y N)	**Importance 1 2 3 4** (Student at instructional level? Y N)	**Importance 1 2 3 4** (Student at instructional level? Y N)
Step 3: Observable/measureable statement of current performance (following baseline)	Date collected _____	Date collected _____	Date collected _____	Date collected _____
Step 4: Short-term goal: Expected performance in ___ weeks (4–6 weeks)	Date consistently attained _____	Date consistently attained _____	Date consistently attained _____	Date consistently attained _____
Step 5: Interim goal: Expected behavior in ___ weeks	Date consistently attained _____	Date consistently attained _____	Date consistently attained _____	Date consistently attained _____
Step 6: Long-term goal: Expected behavior in ___ weeks	Date consistently attained _____	Date consistently attained _____	Date consistently attained _____	Date consistently attained _____

Communication skills, as described above, play a major role in problem construction. The school psychologist avoids diagnostic and clinical jargon, focusing instead on the presence or absence of behaviors that led the teacher to decide that a referral was needed. Since speakers attune their concerns to their listeners (Rosenfield, 2004), teachers may focus when speaking to school psychologists on disorders such as learning disability rather than academic concerns or specific classroom behaviors. Teacher concerns typically need to be reframed from initial, often high inference, within-child concerns to specific behaviors within the ecology of the classroom, so that teachers feel more empowered to intervene.

The work of this stage is often completed over several sessions, depending upon the information that the consultee brings to the session and the complexity of the concerns. However, in some schools, principals and staff have implemented schedule and staff time so that there is opportunity provided for the teacher and school psychologist to have sufficient time to conduct the problem identification in one longer session.

Within whichever time frame, this work is done at the dyadic level rather than at the team level, even if there is a team in place. The quality of the assessment information obtained by teams is often fairly limited, a function of their time constraints. The team-generated data are often less useful for setting specific goals or targeting interventions in relation to student instructional needs. Moreover, the dyadic consultation model allows teachers time to reflect on the problem within a collaborative, nonjudgmental relationship, especially critical when the classroom ecology needs change.

The following tasks are required to complete the stage: (a) Specify the teacher's concerns in observable and measurable terms, defined as a gap between current and expected performance. (b) Select and implement a data collection method to establish the entry-level skills of the student and the expected instructional level in the curriculum materials. (c) Address the issue of instructional level as a contributor to behavior if there is a behavioral concern. If instructional level is not the issue, select and implement a data collection method to establish a baseline of the identified behavior. (d) Identify the context of the problem within the instructional triangle. (e) Decide if the gap is significant and requires intervention. (f) Establish short-term, intermediate-term, and long-term goals for the student.

Assessment strategies, usually instructional assessments and behavioral observation as well as discussion with the teacher, are designed to supply information about the student's entry-level skills or baseline behaviors, the task, and the instructional or management strategies in use. An essential aspect is the requirement that an instructional mismatch be ruled out even when the teacher's presenting concern is behavior, based on the assumption that the student who is working at his or her frustration level in the classroom instructional setting can be prone to behave inappropriately as well. For example, even if the teacher's initial concern is a student's lack of work completion or constant interruptions of other students during reading lessons, the first hypothesis to be explored is the appropriateness of the reading tasks assigned in relation to the student's skills. Instructional assessment helps to identify whether a mismatch is present.

Instructional assessment. Instructional assessment is a system of formative evaluation that helps the teacher identify the skills needed by a student for successful completion of an academic task. It also identifies the appropriate level of challenge within the task for the student to be at instructional level. The instructional assessment yields data useful for aligning priorities and interventions with goals that are consistent with required classroom curriculum standards.

Stiggins and Conklin, back in 1992, lamented that many "teachers either do not take the time or do not know how to make good use of assessment in presenting instruction, in evaluating it, and in making it more effective and meaningful" (Stiggins & Conklin, 1992, p. 148). Strikingly, Popham (2013) still finds meager use of formative assessment in American classrooms, in spite of calls for the classroom teacher to engage in this form of effective assessment for instruction. As a result, the implementation of instructional assessment often introduces teachers to a valuable tool.

The five basic instructional assessment questions are: What does the student know? What can the student do? What does the student think? How does the student approach what he or she is unsure of? What can the teacher do next? A more extensive view of instructional assessment is provided by Gickling and Gravois (in press).

Behavioral observation. School psychologists are typically skilled in behavioral observation techniques, which are also tools for the instructional consultant. However, the consultation process provides teachers opportunities for designing an observation in relation to their concerns and jointly interpreting the data gathered during the observation.

Student Documentation Form use in problem identification. The Student Documentation Form serves several functions during the problem identification stage. The front page (Figure 33.2) of this form provides a place for up to four initial statements of concern, a checkmark to ensure that instructional match has been evaluated, the concern that will be addressed, and short-term, intermediate-term, and long-term goals, with a time line for achieving the goals. Inside the form (Figure 33.3) are two graphs on which baseline and later intervention data can be entered for two concerns. Additional graphs can be added on separate sheets, if more than two concerns are being addressed.

Technical perfection in data collection may not be achieved in all cases, but over time teachers seem to develop a healthy respect for the data on the form. They also recognize that the graphing of this case-specific data is valuable to their decision making. The inside pages also contain a place to record the specifics of the intervention design. The back cover, not presented here, provides a place for documenting the dates of consultant–teacher meetings, with space for a brief summary of what occurred and next steps planned. Use of the form requires training in the Instructional Consultation process and by itself does not provide all the necessary skills to conduct Instructional Consultation.

Intervention planning. The next stage is for the school psychologist and teacher jointly to plan the intervention, based on the information gained during problem identification. The specificity of the Instructional Consultation problem definition process enables the consultant and teacher to design a targeted intervention. Sometimes this stage is easily completed. Teachers often can plan an intervention in their classroom once the initial concern that seemed unsolvable at the classroom level has been reframed through problem identification. If the instructional assessment results document that work is not at instructional level for a student who was referred for being off task much of the time, then the intervention is targeted to developing tasks that better match the student's skills rather than

Figure 33.3. Student Documentation Form, Center Page

Operational Definition of Academic/Behavioral Performance   Priority # _____
on GAS

What specific academic/behaviors will be recorded? _____

_____

When will the behavior be recorded? _____

Where will the behavior be recorded? _____

KEY
☐ _____
☐ _____
☐ _____

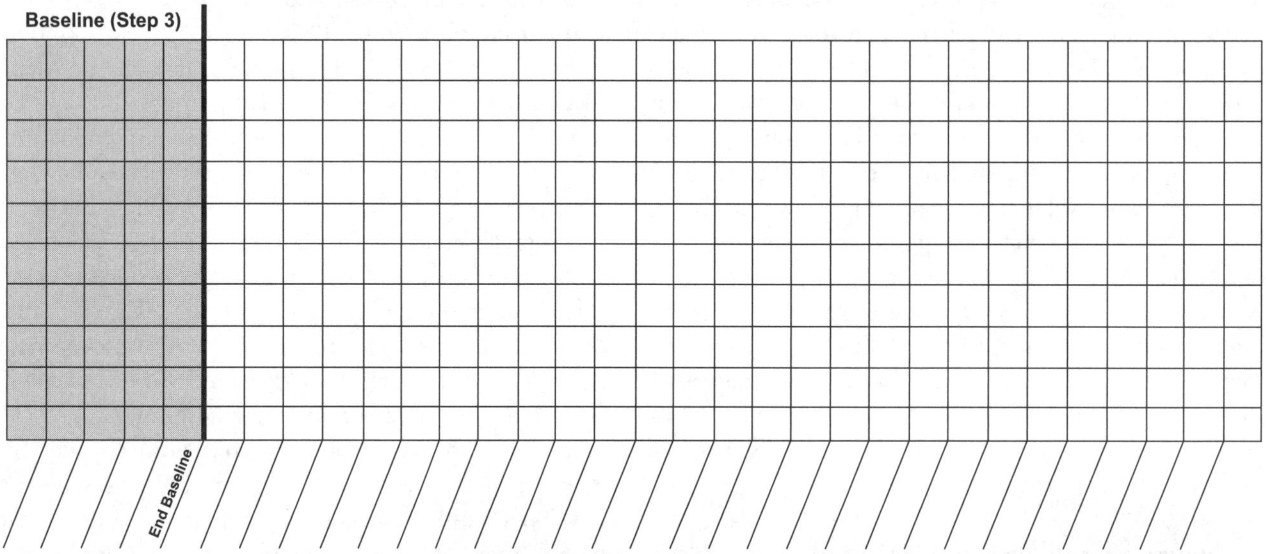

Baseline (Step 3)

End Baseline

Describe intervention design and materials	When and how often?	Persons responsible?	Motivational strategies?

focus on the behavior. Alternatively, collaborating with the teacher to clarify that a reading concern is a problem with comprehension skills might provide an opportunity for the teacher to learn new empirically supported strategies to teach comprehension to the target students and others in the classroom. Such strategies can be tailored to fit that teacher's classroom context.

This stage is completed when the details of the intervention are described and the intervention is perceived as doable by those responsible for implementation. The following questions must be answered: (a) What is the description of the strategy or intervention? (b) When and how often will the strategy or intervention be implemented? (c) Who will implement the intervention? (d) What materials are required and are the materials currently available? If not, how will the materials be obtained? (e) What data collection methods will be used to evaluate progress toward the student's goals? (f) When and how often will progress be

monitored? The Student Documentation Form (Figure 33.3) provides a place for documenting the intervention design.

Selecting a research-based intervention is the goal whenever possible. Research supports instructional strategies rather than interventions designed to fix processes that are deficient (e.g., Kavale & Forness, 1999). The interventions typically involve classroom personnel (teachers, aides, peers), since the classroom is the level at which the intervention will be conducted. Interventions need to be tailored to the demands of a particular classroom setting or student situation. Conditions that increase treatment integrity include ensuring that teachers have the necessary materials, are clear about the intervention design, and that those designated to deliver the intervention are available.

Research-based interventions may still need to be modified in a particular case (Forman et al., 2013; Rosenfield, 2000). For example, behavioral contracting is a research-based intervention, but an effective contract may not be constructed on the first attempt. That is, building a student's alphabet knowledge may require modification of the number of new letters introduced per lesson or the type of reinforcement used. Pickering (2012) documented the different outcomes of a kindergarten child's ability to learn alphabet letters, depending upon the number of new letters introduced in the intervention design. School psychologists and teachers need to share the understanding that intervention plans may need to be modified based on progress-monitoring data.

Intervention implementation. Classrooms are complex places. It is during implementation that the feasibility and effectiveness of an intervention become clear. The collaborative working relationship allows the consultation dyad to continue to problem-solve during the uncertainty of the treatment implementation stage. This includes resolving the inevitable practical problems that arise during implementation, coping with treatment integrity issues, and supporting data collection on the effectiveness of the intervention. School psychologists should be prepared for problems in these areas, rather than view them as evidence of teacher resistance or failed problem solving. Consultation sessions are typically less frequent during this stage, but meetings to evaluate progress and treatment integrity should be scheduled at regular intervals.

During this stage, data continue to be collected, and evaluation of progress toward goal attainment is monitored. As short-term goals are attained within the designated time period, progress toward longer term goals can be addressed. If goals are not attained in a timely way, treatment integrity problems can be addressed or the intervention can be changed or modified. Sometimes the problem identification stage needs to be revisited.

Resolution/termination. The last stage is formal closure of the problem-solving process and the working relationship with the teacher. Accountability requires a resolution or termination stage, culminating in a decision to continue or terminate working together. If the goals have been achieved and the problem is resolved to the partners' satisfaction, then the achievement can be celebrated. It should be clear to the teacher–consultee that the consultation process can be reengaged should new concerns emerge.

If the data indicate that progress toward goals is unsatisfactory, it may be necessary to recycle back through the stages. A more clearly defined behavior or additional data collection may be needed. Alternatively, the teacher–school psychologist dyad can ask for support from the building-level team or other resources, including other professionals (either internal to the school or in the community), or family members. In some cases, referral to special education becomes appropriate when general education and remedial services do not have the resources to meet the instructional or behavioral needs of the student. However, labeling students does not guarantee that appropriate services will follow. Much of the problem solving done during Instructional Consultation helps to focus the Individualized Education Program team on intervention planning when that service is needed.

If the teacher decides not to continue in the relationship, formal termination of the process should occur. One hazard of consultation is that the relationship may fade away through the press of time, personal concerns (e.g., an illness in the teacher's family or other major life event), unwillingness by one or both parties to confront relationship issues, or perceived or real lack of progress in resolving the referral concern(s). Explicitly addressing the reason for the teacher's withdrawal makes it possible to terminate the process while leaving the door open for future opportunities to consult on the current or other concerns.

Consultation Across Tiers of Services

It is not unusual for instructional consultants to provide consultation to teachers of students receiving additional services, whether with instructional specialists, such as reading teachers, or with special educators, bringing all those working with the student together to ensure alignment and address concerns. General education teachers often request consultation, even when the student is receiving additional services. It is essential to recognize that Tier 1 and Tier 2 services for students need to be coordinated. Without addressing the student's instructional needs within the general education classroom, Tier 2 services may not provide sufficient support for students at risk (Gravois, 2012). Further, most students who are receiving special education services spend a majority of their time in regular education. Data confirm that 95% of students, ages 6–21 who are served in special education were enrolled in regular schools, and approximately 59% of these students, including 63% of those with specific learning disabilities, spent more than 80% of their school day in general education classes (National Center for Education Statistics, 2012). Even within self-contained special education settings, Instructional Consultation can play a role in supporting teachers and students (e.g., see Pas, 2012; Tsakiris, 2012). Tsakiris (2012) documents how often special education teachers feel excluded from supportive consultation services, and she has found that they would appreciate the same type of services provided to general education teachers.

Documentation

Documentation should be incorporated into any consultation service delivery system to demonstrate accountability. While this can be handled differently at the local level, documentation should provide a brief summary of the concern, relevant assessment data, a description of the interventions implemented, and the results. A summary form with instructional and management recommendations can be prepared for the student's next teacher. Maintaining records is important in the event of future concerns about a particular student, and outdated records should be culled when appropriate. For individual accountability, school psychologists should examine how many consultee concerns are successfully addressed during the school year so they can evaluate the effectiveness of their practice and target appropriate professional development.

A central document for accountability is the Student Documentation Form, which has been discussed earlier in relation to the stages. Part of training involves use of the form, which structures the process and provides a document for accountability. The format was designed in collaboration with school staff that had experience in implementing Instructional Consultation.

Fidelity in documentation is one measure of integrity in completing the steps of the problem-solving stages. In program evaluation, the completed Student Documentation Forms are scored for completeness and accuracy. Goal attainment scaling, based on actual data on students' progress in relation to goals set, is used to evaluate the effectiveness of their work.

Training and Evaluation of Competency as an Instructional Consultant

Training in and evaluating consultation skills constitute an essential but complex process. There is limited consensus about the necessary skills and knowledge to be taught, and evaluating skill growth in such a complex activity is challenging. For individual practitioners and consultation course instructors interested in further information on training, Rosenfield (2012) provides a series of chapters on learning instructional consultation and ways to evaluate effectiveness and outcomes. Burkhouse (2012) has organized the key skills of Instructional Consultation into a scale for use in evaluating growth. Further, she provides a series of recommendations and strategies for training and evaluating instructional consultation skills, including simulations, recording and recording analysis, and logs. Of course, self-assessment is valuable, but supervision and supervisor assessment of skills provide important strategies for evaluating growth. Newman (2012) describes concerns of novice consultants and supervision strategies to address those concerns.

Best Practices in Instructional Consultation Teams

It is possible for an individual school psychologist to adopt Instructional Consultation as a service delivery system. However, as noted elsewhere in this chapter, the process has also been embedded in a school-wide delivery system, the Instructional Consultation Team (Rosenfield & Gravois, 1996). The core component of this model is a multidisciplinary team, each member of which is trained in the process and is expected to serve as an instructional consultant (called a case manager in the model) to classroom teachers. The team, led by a trained facilitator, consists of major building stakeholders, including general education teachers, administrators, special educators, and pupil services staff.

The facilitator has often been a school psychologist, although other professionals can undertake this role. In such cases, the school psychologist should become a member of the team. Facilitation is typically a half-time role in a school, although some schools have full-time facilitators, and, in some cases, a facilitator has worked in two different schools. Generally, the facilitators have additional responsibilities in their schools.

Team members volunteer to serve on the team, although in some schools those with specific roles, such as the reading support teacher, are expected to be team members. Since most team members are volunteers, they can cycle off the teams, usually at the end of a school year. As team members receive training in multiple components of problem solving, assessment, and intervention, team membership results in professional development for school staff.

The team meets weekly to assign new cases, monitor case progress, discuss cases that are not making progress, engage in embedded professional development, and attend to maintenance activities, including team evaluation. Part of a school's commitment when adopting the model is to ensure that time is available for team meetings and for teacher/case manager sessions. The hundreds of Instructional Consultation Teams in operation have developed creative arrangements for meetings. These include many of the same strategies used by other school teams, including schedule changes so that time for meetings is available, early school day meetings, and in some cases use of substitute teachers to provide coverage.

As has been mentioned above, a central defining feature of Instructional Consultation Teams that differentiates it from many other team models is that the team members do the majority of problem-solving work in dyadic consultation sessions with teachers separate from the team meetings. The rationale for using a case management system is that team meetings provide insufficient time for the work of the problem-solving stages. In addition, large team meetings are not conducive to building high-quality working relationships with teachers. However, the team can provide consultation to the teacher–consultant dyads when they need additional support or are not able to make progress together.

Instructional Consultation Teams have been implemented in multiple types of schools, geographically and demographically (urban, suburban, rural, and with different ethnicities; see Rosenfield et al., in press, as well as http://www.icatresources.com for current information on school sites). Although Instructional Consultation Teams have been implemented in middle and high schools, elementary schools have been the site of most implementations. When implemented in secondary schools, case management with individual teachers appears to be more effective than grade-level meetings for similar reasons to their effectiveness in elementary schools. The teacher is the primary consultee for the process, so the age and grade level of the students about whom the teachers are concerned vary widely. Ability to conduct the problem-solving stages and instructional assessment at varying grade levels benefits from familiarity with an understanding of school culture, differences between elementary and secondary school structures, and curriculum goals at different grade levels.

Systems-Level Entry

When introduced to a school or school district, systems-level entry is also advised (Rosenfield & Gravois, 1996; see http://www.icatresources.com/icteams/developing.

cfm for the steps to prepare for introducing Instructional Consultation Teams into a school district). This involves working with key administrators to ensure clarity about the resources and time commitments involved. As with other major school change models, consulting with certified trainers is recommended.

Training of Instructional Consultation Teams

One critical component of effective implementation is comprehensive training in the intervention (Gravois, Knotek, & Babinski, 2002; Rosenfield, 2002). An intensive training program has been designed to enable team members to grow from novice to competent consultants. Additional training is provided to team facilitators, who must acquire not only competence in the instructional consultation process, but also skill in team facilitation (Rosenfield et al., in press). A team can be implemented with integrity only when a skilled facilitator leads it.

One competence required for facilitators, and for all instructional consultants, is skill in case management. Each new team facilitator attends a 20- to 24-hour training session and is then coached through a consultation case. Novice facilitators record each consultation session of their first case in a school and then send the recording to a coach. The coach responds by e-mail, using a structured coaching process. The novice consultants have been shown to reach a criterion level of skill on the core process dimensions of Instructional Consultation (McKenna, Rosenfield, & Gravois, 2009).

After developing basic consultation process skills, the facilitator-in-training receives an additional 2-day training session in the skills of facilitation, including school change issues. Facilitators then attend a training session with their new teams. The facilitator guides team members through the problem-solving stages with practice cases in their home school (see Rosenfield et al., in press, for additional information about coaching and team training; also see http://www.icatresources.com).

Program Evaluation

Program evaluation is integrated into every step of implementation. There is an emerging evidence base, including evidence demonstrating that Instructional Consultation Teams can be scaled up for use in schools in different geographic and demographic settings (Rosenfield et al., in press). Training is evaluated for skill development of participants. Treatment fidelity of the process and team functioning is measured by the Level of Implementation Scale (Fudell, 1992), revised by

Rosenfield and Gravois (1996), and evaluated by McKenna et al. (2009). Outcome research has documented the effect of Instructional Consultation Teams on teacher satisfaction and professional development, student goal attainment, and special education referrals and placements (Rosenfield et al., in press).

Instructional Consultation and Instructional Consultation Teams have been used with multicultural populations as well. The impact on disproportional placement of minority students in special education is presented in Gravois and Rosenfield (2006). Use of Instructional Consultation with a bilingual population has been demonstrated by Silva (2005) and Lopez and Truesdell (2007). Schussler (2012) provides a case example of instructional consultation with a fifth-grade teacher to support the social studies achievement of a bilingual student. Instructional assessment revealed considerable vocabulary problems, and the impact of vocabulary instruction made a positive impact on student learning, not only for the bilingual student but for all the students in the classroom. In addition, the teacher reported that she had learned a valuable new set of strategies.

Role of Parents in Instructional Consultation

A frequently asked question concerns the role of parents in the process. Since the use of Instructional Consultation Teams is based on consultee-centered consultation principles, the major focus is on building the skills and knowledge of teacher-consultees to more fully support student growth. School staff are encouraged to view consultation as providing an opportunity for teachers to reflect on their practice and obtain support for improving aspects of the instructional triangle in their classroom, not just with the student whose concerns bring the teacher to the process but with other students with whom the teacher works. Building a working relationship so that teachers feel comfortable in examining their practice is more difficult when parents, whose major concern is naturally their own child's progress, are present.

In most cases, communication with parents remains the function of the classroom teacher. As a result of engaging in the consultation process, teacher-consultees can base their discussions with parents on specific academic and behavioral goals, will gain useful data to share, and may have introduced instructional modifications matched to the student's skill level. With these specifics in place, teachers report being able to provide recommendations to parents that are based on data. In some cases, family members provide additional structured practice activities that support the classroom interventions.

Challenge of Implementation

School psychologists have the opportunity to become instructional consultants and facilitators of Instructional Consultation Teams. However, the first requirement is to understand and accept the basic assumptions of the model, including a belief in the relationship of academic and behavioral issues to the ecology of the classroom. For some school psychologists trained in more traditional models, who may have strong beliefs about fixed characteristics (Johnston, 2012), that is a difficult set of assumptions to accept; for others, it is a great relief to be able to work with teachers in the classroom setting to enable both teachers and students to learn. Second, it is essential to develop the skills to become an instructional consultant. Learning the skills requires practice and the opportunity to use skills in applied settings under supervision. This is as true for practicing school psychologists as it is for novices, since consultation training is often limited in preservice programs (e.g., Hazel, Laviolette, & Lineman, 2010).

The challenge of becoming a facilitator includes developing and implementing additional skills, such as those of systems-level consultation. Successful facilitators develop and coach their teams and engage in administrative consultation. Some facilitators move out of their school and become district-level facilitators for the project. A career ladder for trainers allows some to develop the skills to train facilitators and help bring Instructional Consultation Teams into the state or district.

SUMMARY

Instructional Consultation, based on a consultee-centered consultation framework, is designed to enhance teacher capacity to address student academic and behavioral concerns in the classroom. Ecological assumptions focus on the instructional triangle: alterable student variables, instructional tasks, and instructional design. Variables are assessed to determine if there is an instructional match that facilitates student learning and if there is a gap between the student's current and expected performance that requires intervention. School psychologists and teachers evaluate student progress and make decisions about additional resources needed.

Training of skills in collaborative problem solving includes (a) ability to build a working relationship with the teacher and use good communication strategies and (b) ability to conduct problem-solving stages (entry or contracting, problem identification, intervention planning, intervention implementation, and resolution or termination). Instructional assessment is a key skill. For concerns not resolved, stages can be recycled or additional resources accessed. Instructional consultants are competent in instructional and behavioral assessment and intervention. Documentation of processes and outcomes is critical for accountability. The Student Documentation Form structures the problem-solving stages and is integrated into evaluation of fidelity and effectiveness.

Instructional Consultation Teams provide a structured school-based service delivery system for Instructional Consultation. Case problem solving continues to be implemented at the dyadic level. The team serves other functions: providing professional development of team members, working on cases not making progress, examining school-wide problems identified through individual cases, and evaluating implementation effectiveness. The multidisciplinary team, led by a skilled facilitator, includes stakeholders who represent administration, regular and special education, pupil services, and others determined by school leadership.

Research (Rosenfield et al., in press) has evaluated training, technical assistance, treatment integrity, and outcomes for students and teachers. Implementation of Instructional Consultation and Instructional Consultation Teams enables school psychologists to provide services that have an impact on the positive development of both teachers and students.

AUTHOR NOTE

Disclosure. Sylvia Rosenfield has a financial interest in books she authored or coauthored that are referenced in this chapter.

REFERENCES

Adelman, H., & Taylor, L. (2012). *Teachers can't do it alone!* Los Angeles, CA: Author. Retrieved from http://smhp.psych.ucla.edu/pdfdocs/alone.pdf

Barrett, C. (2012). Instructional match: Making the match salient for teachers. In S. Rosenfield (Ed.), *Becoming a school consultant: Lessons learned* (pp. 127–138). New York, NY: Routledge.

Benn, A. (2004). *Communities of practice: Study of one school's first year of implementation of a new problem-solving model* (Unpublished doctoral dissertation). University of Maryland, College Park, MD.

Burkhouse, K. S. (2012). Educating a reflective school consultant: Multi-faceted techniques. In S. Rosenfield (Ed.), *Becoming a school consultant: Lessons learned* (pp. 25–48). New York, NY: Routledge.

Donovan, S., & Cross, C. (Eds.). (2002). *Minority students in special and gifted education.* Washington, DC: National Academies Press.

Forman, S. G., Shapiro, E. S., Codding, R. S., Gonzales, J. E., Reddy, L. A., Rosenfield, S., … Stoiber, K. C. (2013). Implementation science and school psychology. *School Psychology Quarterly, 28,* 77–100. doi:10.1037/spq0000019

Fudell, R. (1992). Level of implementation of teacher support teams and teachers' attitudes toward special needs students. *Dissertation Abstracts International, 53*(05), 1399A.

Gickling, E. E., & Gravois, T. A. (in press). *Instructional assessment: The essential path to effective instruction.* Clearwater, FL: ICAT Resources.

Gravois, T. A. (2012). Aligned service delivery: Ending the era of triage. In L. C. Burrello, W. Sailor, & J. Kleinhammer-Tramill (Eds.), *Unifying educational systems* (pp. 109–134). New York, NY: Routledge.

Gravois, T. A., Knotek, S., & Babinski, L. (2002). Educating practitioners as instructional consultants: Development and implementation of the IC team consortium. *Journal of Educational and Psychological Consultation, 13,* 113–132. doi:10.1080/10474412.2002.9669456

Gravois, T. A., & Rosenfield, S. (2002). A multidimensional framework for the evaluation of instructional consultation teams. *Journal of Applied School Psychology, 19,* 5–29. doi:10.1300/J008v19n01_02

Gravois, T. A., & Rosenfield, S. (2006). Impact of instructional consultation teams on the disproportionate referral and placement of minority students in special education. *Remedial and Special Education, 27,* 42–52. doi:10.1177/07419325060270010501

Hawley, W. D. (2007). *The keys to effective schools: Educational reform as continuous improvement.* Thousand Oaks, CA: Corwin.

Hazel, C. E., Laviolette, G. T., & Lineman, J. M. (2010). Training professional psychologists in school-based consultation: What the syllabi suggest. *Training and Education in Professional Psychology, 4,* 235–243. doi:10.1037/a0020072

Horowitz, A. (2013). *On looking: Eleven walks with expert eyes.* New York, NY: Simon & Schuster.

Johnston, P. H. (2012). *Opening minds: Using language to change lives.* Portland, ME: Stenhouse.

Kavale, K. A., & Forness, S. R. (1999). *Efficacy of special education and related services.* Washington, DC: American Association on Mental Retardation.

Knotek, S. E., Rosenfield, S., Gravois, T. A., & Babinski, L. (2003). The process of orderly reflection and conceptual change during instructional consultation. *Journal of Educational and Psychological Consultation, 14,* 303–328.

Lopez, E. C., & Truesdell, L. (2007). Multicultural issues in instructional consultation for English language learning students. In G. B. Esquivel, E. C. Lopez, & S. Nahari (Eds.), *Handbook of multicultural school psychology: An interdisciplinary perspective* (pp. 71–98). New York, NY: Routledge.

McKenna, S. A., Rosenfield, S., & Gravois, T. A. (2009). Measuring the behavioral indicators of Instructional Consultation: A preliminary validity study. *School Psychology Review, 38,* 496–509.

National Association of School Psychologists. (2010). *Model for comprehensive and integrated school psychological services.* Bethesda, MD: Author. Retrieved from http://www.nasponline.org/standards/2010standards/2_PracticeModel.pdf

National Center for Education Statistics. (2012). *The condition of education.* Washington, DC: Author. Retrieved from http://nces.ed.gov/pubsearch/pubsinfo.asp?pubid=2012045

Newman, D. (2012). Supervision of school-based consultation training: Addressing the concerns of novice consultants. In S. Rosenfield (Ed.), *Becoming a school consultant: Lessons learned* (pp. 49–70). New York, NY: Routledge.

Newman, D., & Rosenfield, S. (2008, August). *Supervisee-centered training of consultee-centered consultants.* Paper presented at the International Seminar on Consultee-Centered Consultation, Boston, MA.

Pas, E. T. (2012). Case metamorphosis through consultation. In S. Rosenfield (Ed.), *Becoming a school consultant: Lessons learned* (pp.195–209). New York, NY: Routledge.

Pickering, C. (2012). Relationship building and objectivity loss: The importance of the process in consultation. In S. Rosenfield (Ed.), *Becoming a school consultant: Lessons learned* (pp. 111–124). New York, NY: Routledge.

Popham, W. J. (2013, January 9). Waving the flag for formative assessment. *Edweek.* Retrieved from http://www.edweek.org/ew/articles/2013/01/09/15popham.h32.html

Rosenfield, S. (1987). *Instructional consultation.* Mahwah, NJ: Erlbaum.

Rosenfield, S. (2000). Crafting usable knowledge. *American Psychologist, 55,* 1347–1355. doi:10.1037/0003-066X.55.11.1347

Rosenfield, S. (2002). Developing instructional consultants: From novice to competent to expert. *Journal of Educational and Psychological Consultation, 13,* 97–111.

Rosenfield, S. (2004). Consultation as dialogue: The right words at the right time. In N. M. Lambert, I. Hylander, & J. H. Sandoval (Eds.), *Consultee-centered consultation: Improving the quality of professional services in schools and community organizations* (pp. 337–347). Mahwah, NJ: Erlbaum.

Rosenfield, S. (Ed.). (2012). *Becoming a school consultant: Lessons learned.* New York, NY: Routledge.

Rosenfield, S., & Gravois, T. A. (1996). *Instructional Consultation Teams: Collaborating for change.* New York, NY: Guilford Press.

Rosenfield, S., Gravois, T., & Silva, A. (in press). Bringing Instructional Consultation to scale: Research and development of IC and IC Teams. In W. Erchul & S. Sheridan (Eds.), *Handbook of research in school consultation: Empirical foundations for the field.* (Rev. ed.). New York, NY: Routledge.

Sandoval, J. (in press). *An introduction to consultee-centered consultation in the schools: A step-by-step guide to the process and skills.* New York, NY: Routledge.

Schein, E. H. (2007). Coaching and consultation revisited: Are they the same? In M. Goldsmith & L. Lyons (Eds.), *Coaching for leadership* (2nd ed., pp. 17–25). New York, NY: Wiley.

Schussler, L. (2012). Improving an English language learner client's comprehension through consultee-centered consultation. In S. Rosenfield (Ed.), *Becoming a school consultant: Lessons learned* (pp. 139–159). New York, NY: Routledge.

Silva, A. E. (2005). *English language learner special education referral and placement outcomes in instructional consultation teams schools.* (Unpublished master's thesis). University of Maryland, College Park, MD.

Stiggins, R. J., & Conklin, N. F. (1992). *In teachers' hands: Investigating the practices of classroom assessment.* Albany, NY: State University of New York Press.

Tsakiris, E. (2012). Leaving no teacher behind: Widening the view and changing the perspective. In S. Rosenfield (Ed.), *Becoming a school consultant: Lessons learned* (pp. 211–231). New York, NY: Routledge.

White, L. J., Summerlin, M. L., Loos, V. E., & Epstein, E. S. (1992). School and family consultation: A language-systems approach. In M. Fine & C. Carlson (Eds.), *The handbook of family-school intervention: A systems perspective* (pp. 347–362). Boston, MA: Allyn & Bacon.

Best Practices in Facilitating Consultation and Collaboration With Teachers and Administrators

34

Robin S. Codding
University of Massachusetts Boston
Lisa M. Hagermoser Sanetti
University of Connecticut
Florence D. DiGennaro Reed
University of Kansas

OVERVIEW

According to the National Association of School Psychologists (NASP) *Model for Comprehensive and Integrated School Psychological Services* (NASP, 2010), the domain Consultation and Collaboration is a cornerstone of school psychology practice. With the increasing prevalence of and support for prevention models such as multitiered services, problem solving, and school-wide positive behavior supports, the nature of consultation and collaboration is evolving away from the traditional, voluntary, triadic model. Within schools an array of internal and external consultants are likely present with external consultants serving the temporary role of training internal consultants and/or coaches who will gradually take on full responsibility for supporting school-wide multitiered systems of service delivery through building teams. Success within the consultation process will require school psychologists to have working knowledge of and skills pertaining to (a) schools as organizational systems, (b) ecological/behavioral school-based consultation models, and (c) evidence-based assessment and intervention.

A central feature of the effectiveness of consultation is the extent to which changes in student, teacher, and administrator beliefs, attitudes, and behaviors occur in the expected direction (Raven, 2008). In order for students to benefit from individual interventions, secondary supports, or universal prevention, evidence-based practices must be implemented by the adults within the school setting. Unfortunately, the gap between availability of evidence-based practices and implementation is well documented, and novel educational practices are rarely sustained (Fixsen, Blasé, Naoom, & Wallace, 2009). Research has suggested that integration of evidence-based practices necessary to maintain multitiered systems of service delivery requires the development of support from administrators, particularly principals, and teachers (Forman, Olin, Hoagwood, Crowe, & Saka, 2008).

Although school psychologists spend approximately one third of their time facilitating and delivering services consistent with a multitiered framework and 16% of that time in roles devoted to problem solving and systems/organizational consultation, the majority of hours continue to be allocated to traditional assessment and special education activities (Castillo, Curtis, & Gelley, 2012). These data are not commensurate with a national survey on response to intervention that found that 68% of respondents indicated full or partial district-wide implementation (Spectrum K-12 School Solutions, 2011).

Differences between desired and expected time spent in consultation is remarkably consistent (e.g., Mägi & Kikas, 2009) and historically has been attributed to teacher and administrator resistance. Fortunately, a pilot survey conducted by Gilman and Gabriel (2004) indicated that teachers (62%) and administrators (63%) would prefer school psychologists to spend more time providing teacher-related consultation, suggesting a consensus for the necessity of consultation services.

The purpose of this chapter is to provide school psychologists with commonly identified teacher and administrator barriers to consultation, an overview of various cross-disciplinary theoretical models of behavior change, and corresponding action steps to facilitate consultation and collaboration.

BASIC CONSIDERATIONS

Change is difficult for individuals and organizations. Consequently, resistance might be considered a ubiquitous aspect of the process. Rather than be considered an impediment to consultation, resistance might be reframed as an opportunity to begin collaboration by determining the underlying reasons for resistance. Within their consultative role, school psychologists can facilitate collaboration by recognizing existing barriers, selecting corresponding strategies to mitigate the source of those barriers, assisting teachers and administrators to operate as effectively as possible within these constraints, and empowering consultees by providing the necessary tools and resources to develop already existing skills (Erchul & Martens, 2010).

Common barriers facing teachers and administrators are described below and summarized into three broad categories: perceptions, knowledge and skills, and resources.

Teacher Barriers

Teachers have a deep dedication to facilitating their students' academic achievement and social–emotional–behavioral development. As such, it seems intuitive that teachers will readily engage in consultation focused on addressing student issues. Despite their dedication to students, however, there are numerous contextual factors that may hinder such collaboration (Long, Sanetti, Gallucci, Collier-Meek, & Kratochwill, 2012).

Perceptions

Teachers' perceptions of the problem to be addressed, role compatibility, intervention alignment with current practices, and intervention outcomes can be barriers to collaboration and consultation. Consultation may be initiated due to a request for assistance originated by the teacher or from another stakeholder (e.g., principal, parent). When a teacher requests consultation, it is clear that the teacher perceives the problem as severe enough to benefit from support, which will likely facilitate

consultation and collaboration. When another stakeholder requests support for a teacher, it may not be evident whether the teacher perceives a need for consultation. In addition, a teacher must also believe that the target behavior to be addressed is aligned with his or her role as an educator. For example, a teacher may believe that engaging in consultation to address a student's academic deficits is well aligned with his or her role as an educator, but that an intervention related to a student's mental health is solely the purview of the school psychologist (Reinke, Stormont, Herman, Puri, & Goel, 2011). A teacher may perceive milder academic, behavioral, and social–emotional issues as appropriate for classroom-based intervention, and thus within his or her role as an educator, but may perceive intervening with more severe issues to be outside his or her role.

It has been suggested that teachers are more likely to find an intervention acceptable and implement the intervention (Durlack & DuPre, 2008) if it is compatible with their teaching philosophy and classroom routines. Research consistently indicates that teachers are more likely to perceive an intervention as aligned with their philosophy when the intervention is described using philosophy-relevant terminology (e.g., behavioral, humanistic, pragmatic). Teachers may find positive interventions (e.g., praise, differential reinforcement) more acceptable and affiliated with their role as an educator than punishment-based interventions (e.g., time-out, response cost). Further, teachers are more likely to implement interventions that fit within, or can be adapted to fit within, the consultee's already present classroom routines (Durlack & DuPre, 2008).

A teacher's outcome expectations, or beliefs about how effectively an intervention will remediate a student's target behavior, can influence intervention acceptability (Forman et al., 2008). Outcome expectations may be informed by a teacher's previous experience with the same intervention ("The Good Behavior Game worked very well in my classroom last year."), or an intervention with a similar label ("I've tried planned ignoring and it doesn't work."). Outcome expectations may be influenced by a teacher's perception of the student, which can facilitate or hinder intervention implementation (Long et al., 2012). For example, if a teacher believes the student just needs additional structure and support to be successful, then the teacher may be more likely to engage in consultation and collaboration than a teacher who does not believe the student can benefit from a school-based intervention. Likewise, a teacher who is requesting assistance with the expectation that it will become someone else's role to intervene may be less willing to engage in consultation than a teacher seeking support with the intention of being the intervention agent.

Knowledge and Skills

The quantity and quality of the preservice training and professional development teachers receive related to academic, behavioral, and social–emotional interventions and data-based decision making is highly varied (Reinke et al., 2011). Professional development opportunities in schools typically only occur a few times per year and are not aligned with best practices. Considering the myriad topics that could be covered in these infrequent professional development opportunities in combination with the ineffectiveness of traditional professional development sessions, it is likely that many teachers will not have exposure to evidence-based interventions recommended via consultation. Without an understanding of the theoretical underpinnings of the intervention a teacher is asked to implement, he or she may perceive the intervention as less acceptable and be more likely to inappropriately modify intervention steps. When a teacher has had previous exposure to an intervention, it is important to consider the amount of exposure and skill level.

Resources

Teachers' resources related to time, competing priorities, as well as psychological resources such as self-efficacy and burnout can be barriers to collaboration and consultation. Teachers consistently report time and competing priorities as barriers to engaging in consultation and implementing interventions (Long et al., 2012). For example, teachers are regularly responsible for creating and executing differentiated lesson plans, formatively assessing student achievement, managing student behavior, implementing several Individualized Education Programs, serving on multiple committees, maintaining regular communication with all parents and more regular communication with parents of struggling students, attending to their personal obligations, and engaging in consultation. At any given point, a teacher may perceive any one of these activities to be more important, urgent, or rewarding than ongoing consultation-related activities and thus may choose to spend his or her limited time focused on that priority. Research suggests that when presented with several interventions that are relatively similar in effectiveness and complexity, teachers prefer the most time-efficient intervention (Erchul & Martens, 2010). Teachers will, however, find a more time-intensive intervention acceptable if the student's problem is perceived to be severe.

Two psychological resources, self-efficacy and burnout, have been widely associated with teachers' job performance and may serve as barriers to collaborative consultation. Self-efficacy refers to teachers' confidence in their ability to influence students' academic and behavioral outcomes (Ransford, Greenberg, Domitrovich, Small, & Jacobson, 2009). Low levels of teacher self-efficacy related to delivering instruction and managing student behavior have been associated with poorer job performance. Highly efficacious teachers are more likely to set challenging goals for themselves and their students, accept responsibility for student outcomes, as well as adopt and maintain new intervention and prevention programs (Ransford et al., 2009).

Burnout refers to a teachers' affective reaction to ongoing exposure to workplace stress (Fernet, Guay, Senecal, & Austin, 2012). It emerges over time and is characterized by (a) emotional exhaustion, or a feeling of chronic fatigue from overtaxing work; (b) depersonalization, or a cynical or detached attitude toward teaching, colleagues, or students; and (c) reduced personal accomplishment, or a decrease in feelings of achievement at work. Teacher burnout has been associated with perceptions of high job demands, little job control, and absence of job resources. Students' behaviors, administrative leadership, and classroom overload are particularly important predictors of teacher burnout and motivation (Fernet et al., 2012).

Administrator Barriers

Administrators shape a school's mission and goals and consequently dictate the type of climate that will develop. School administrator commitment to school-wide activities, such as consultation, may have an impact on educator buy-in, investment in the consultative process, and job satisfaction. Thus, identifying administrator barriers to effective consultation and collaboration is a worthwhile endeavor. Barriers may reflect a lack of (a) perceptions of the role of school psychologists and evidence-based practice (Gilman & Gabriel, 2004), (b) administrator knowledge and skills (Woodruff & Kowalski, 2010), and (c) school resources (Kensler, Reames, Murray, & Patrick, 2012).

Regardless of the reasons for resistance, a lack of administrator commitment has the potential to hinder innovative educational practices. Through consultation with administrators, school psychologists can apply their expertise in assessment, intervention, and evaluation to influence the adoption and maintenance of such practices. Consequently, it is important for school psychologists to consider the factors that influence administrator decision making.

Perceptions

Administrators play an important role in determining the activities of a school psychologist and continue to place greater emphasis on traditional assessment activities (Mägi & Kikas, 2009). Despite recent changes in the role of school psychologists, thus expanding consultation services in schools, the expectations of administrators and school personnel often make it challenging for psychologists to participate in consultative problem solving, prevention activities, and systems-level intervention (Mägi & Kikas, 2009). That is, a mismatch between the perceptions of an administrator who values assessment and special education placement and those of a school psychologist who values consultation, intervention, and prevention could serve as a barrier to implementation of multitiered systems of service delivery (Gilman & Gabriel, 2004). Moreover, administrators' views on evidence-based practice, the value of data-based decision making, and the consultative process—separate from the role of the school psychologist—will likely have an impact on the effectiveness of consultation and collaboration and contribute to administrator resistance (Kowalski, 2009).

Knowledge and Skills

Administrators' knowledge and skills related to data analysis and management as well as quality professional development can be barriers to consultation and collaboration. A number of administrator skills are relevant to the collaborative process, quality improvement, and school-wide change, which may be important indicators in the implementation of evidence-based practice and, subsequently, effective consultation (Kensler et al., 2012). These skills include data management, data analysis, and a systems-level approach to decision making and collaboration. Unfortunately, administrators may lack these and other prerequisite or requisite skills to manage or analyze data produced by the consultation process. Research has shown that administrators often have inadequate skills regarding data analysis, data-based assessment, and information technology (Kowalski, 2009). As a result, administrators and educators may experience challenges with making informed decisions about particular cases, systems variables, and processes. To complicate matters further, variations within and among states with respect to academic preservice preparation and licensing influences the extent to which administrators have the

skills and experience necessary to make data-based decisions (Woodruff & Kowalski, 2010).

Research has shown that improvement in educator skills, and subsequently student performance, is associated with access to high-quality professional development opportunities. Effective professional development incorporates active educator learning and engagement, a focus on addressing content relevant to the profession and to the goals and issues of the school, and repeated exposure over time (Kensler et al., 2012). The behavioral skills training literature provides an empirically supported model for developing effective educator training opportunities. Important training components include sharing written information/content to develop knowledge, demonstrating the skills educators are expected to perform, and educator practice with peer coaching (Joyce & Showers, 2002).

Unfortunately, the educational system has historically provided professional development that differs substantially from best practices in training and commonly entails single-session didactic workshops that lack practice opportunities and active learning (Webster-Wright, 2009). This traditional approach to professional development is unsuccessful in producing meaningful change in educator skills and knowledge (Desimone, 2009). Given the role administrators have in shaping the culture of a school and adherence to best practices as well as their involvement in collaborative leadership teams and school-based intervention teams, the importance of administrator professional development cannot be overemphasized. The same principles of effective training and professional development apply to educational administrators, though the content might differ. The likelihood that administrators regularly access high-quality training and professional development is low given the current state of training practices.

Resources

The infrastructure of and resources available within a school may have an impact on administrator commitment to consultation and evidence-based practice (Kowalski, 2009). These may include (a) physical resources (e.g., space, technology); (b) time and availability of administrators and other school personnel; (c) access to data, up-to-date literature, and relevant information (Kowalski, 2009); and (d) open communication (Kensler et al., 2012). The availability of adequate resources contributes to a community of practice and/or school culture that could either facilitate or hinder evidence-based consultation practices. Acknowledging that inadequate resources may serve as a barrier to effective practice (and subsequently impede student progress) places administrators and school psychologists in a better position to recognize when these barriers are present and take action to prevent or remediate their role as barriers.

BEST PRACTICES IN FACILITATING CONSULTATION AND COLLABORATION

Several general approaches are important for school psychologists to consider when engaging in consultation and collaboration. First, development of a positive, collaborative school environment provides a foundation for consultation with teachers and administrators. Also essential is establishing respectful, responsive, and trustworthy partnerships among school professionals. Second, establishing clear communication regarding the consultation process including the purpose of and goals for consultative services as well as defining roles and responsibilities of all parties will help facilitate compatibility between teacher and administrator expectations (Jacob, Decker, & Hartshorne, 2011). Third, consistent findings have suggested that school psychologists' availability is essential for consultation (e.g., Gilman & Medway, 2007). Building-based school psychologists tend to have greater influence on individual problem solving and systems change. However, ensuring that school psychologists are immediately responsive to teacher and administrator requests for assistance as well as provide consistent and reliable follow through is also beneficial. Fourth, it is important for school psychologists to reframe their definition of success and recognize small gains when implementing new practices given the constant requirement for adjustments in prevention and intervention programming.

Theories of Change

Barriers to consultation and collaboration are a typical part of practice, but consideration of change theories within a consultation framework can assist school psychologists with (a) understanding the mechanisms of change for both individuals and organizations, (b) facilitating and evaluating the acceptance and use of new practices, and (c) providing a basis for promoting individual and organizational change.

Understanding Change Mechanisms

There are a number of relevant change theories but description of all of these extends beyond the scope of this chapter. Therefore, we will focus on a few representative models. Within a multitiered system of service delivery, it is important to consider the characteristics of the individuals, organization, and the innovative practice or intervention.

With regard to characteristics of the individuals, numerous theories suggest teachers and administrators need to be aware of the need for an impending change, be knowledgeable about the innovative practice or intervention, decide to buy-in to the innovative practice or intervention, use the innovative practice or intervention, and incorporate the innovative practice or intervention into the typical routine.

The Concerns-Based Adoption Model (Hall & Hord, 2011) provides one such example of teacher and administrator experiences with change in educational contexts. Based on the results of the Stages of Concern questionnaire, a professional's concern is determined to be in one of seven stages: (a) awareness ("I am not concerned about an intervention."), (b) informational ("I would like to learn more about the intervention."), (c) personal ("How will this affect me?"), (d) management ("How will I manage the materials?"), (e) consequence ("How is my use affecting the students? How can I change it to be more effective?"), (f) collaboration ("How can I relate what I am doing to what others are doing?"), or (g) refocusing ("I have some ideas about an intervention that might have an even greater impact."). School psychologists can use these stages to make data-based decisions about the individualized supports a consultee needs as he or she progresses through the change process.

It is important for school psychologists to realize that individuals within a school system may proceed through the change process differently (Rogers, 2003). Some individuals will be *innovators* who seek out and embrace change immediately. Others will be *early adopters* who are open to change and closely connected to the social system, albeit less risky in their adoption decisions. One third of members will be *early majority adopters*, accepting innovations just before the average member. *Late majority* individuals also represent a third of an organization's members, are more skeptical and therefore slower to adopt. *Laggards* might be described as traditionalists and are the last to adopt an innovation, if at all.

With regard to characteristics of the organization, in this case, the broader school system, change may progress through six nonlinear stages (Fixsen et al., 2009): (a) exploration and adoption, which constitutes evaluation of the match between school needs and resources with various evidence-based practices and also reflects the decision to implement selected practices;

(b) program installation, which refers to developing an organizational structure to support implementation of the selected evidence-based practices such as securing resources, personnel, and achieving stakeholder buy-in; (c) initial implementation, which is a stage where the practices are actually employed and new learning is occurring; (d) full operation, within which the practices are integrated and accepted into daily routines, policies, and practices; (e) innovation, which is a stage that describes naturally occurring and desirable adaptations to the selected practices that improve contextual fit; and (f) sustainability, which refers to continued successful implementation of effective practices over time.

With regard to characteristics of the innovation, part of an individual's readiness to accept or adopt a new practice is also going to depend on the innovation itself. The Diffusion of Innovation Theory (Rogers, 2003) postulates that five innovation characteristics might account for the rate of adoption: (a) relative advantage, the extent to which an innovative practice offers improvement over the current practice; (b) compatibility, how much the innovative practice aligns with an individual's values, experiences, and beliefs; (c) complexity, how difficult the practice is to understand or use; (d) trialability, whether the innovative practice can be tested and evaluated on a trial basis; and (e) observability, whether the outcome of the innovative practice is noticeable.

Although an increase in all of these characteristics (except for complexity where a decrease is desirable) improves the rate of adoption, relative advantage and compatibility might be the most important. School psychologists can facilitate support for a new practice by explicitly highlighting its advantages in trainings and presentations to teachers and administrators (relative advantage) or by illustrating the connection between the theory underlying the new practice and teachers' beliefs, school mission, and values (compatibility).

Facilitating and Evaluating Acceptance

Changing the behavior of teachers and administrators also necessitates that school psychologists use influence strategies. In particular it is useful for school psychologists to consider ways to facilitate change as well as understand whether teachers and administrators are actually implementing a new practice.

Social power is described as a means through which change in behaviors, attitudes, and beliefs can be generated (Raven, 2008). Teachers and school psychologists perceive the following five noncoercive power strategies as preferable and effective in school settings:

informational (direct), reward (personal), expert (positive), referent, and legitimacy of reciprocity (Erchul & Martens, 2010). Informational power consists of presenting teacher or administrator consultees with new information (e.g., handout, article, tip sheet) or explanations pertaining to recommendations. Reward power occurs when the consultee believes that the consultant can provide a reward if he or she complies with the request. School psychologists can generate reward power by providing praise and positive feedback to teachers for participating in a new building team or implementing a treatment plan. Expert power results from the consultee's belief that the consultant maintains specialized knowledge in a designated area. A school psychologist interested in using expert power may first need to convey to teachers his or her previous expertise with, for example, designing class-wide behavior plans. Referent power occurs when the consultee identifies with or wants to identify with the consultant. Referent power might be facilitated by developing rapport with a teacher, asking a teacher to present his or her experiences with the new problem-solving team to other school professionals, or collaborating on intervention plan development (Erchul & Martens, 2010). Legitimacy of reciprocity suggests that if the consultant does something beneficial for the consultee, the consultee will feel obliged to reciprocate. Reciprocity might occur when a school psychologist develops the materials required for a behavior plan and in turn the teacher implements the plan.

School psychologists' use of these social power strategies can be useful to influence a teacher to adopt or implement a new practice. However, these strategies do not provide information about the extent to which that practice is implemented.

The Levels of Use framework within the Concerns-Based Adoption Model includes a standardized interview protocol to identify to what extent an intervention is implemented (Hall & Hord, 2011). Intervention use is categorized in one of seven stages based on the results of the interview: (a) nonuse, no interest in intervention; (b) orientation, taking an initiative to learn more about intervention; (c) preparation, has definite plans to use intervention; (d) mechanical, making changes to facilitate use of intervention; (e) routine, demonstrating an established pattern of use; (f) refinement, making adjustments to improve outcomes; (g) integration, coordination with others; and (h) renewal, seeking even more effective alternatives. If, for example, results of the Stages of Concern questionnaire indicate that most of a teacher's concerns are related to how that teacher will manage the materials (management), and the Levels of Use indicates that the teacher has plans to implement the intervention but has not (preparation), a school psychologist might provide consultation about how the teacher can manage intervention materials within current routines to move the teacher toward implementation.

Promoting Individual and Systems Change

Evaluation of the ecological environment is necessary to determine how to promote desired practices. Functional assessment consists of a problem-solving process that traditionally has been applied to students experiencing behavior challenges in order to define problem behavior, identify antecedents that trigger problem behavior, document setting events that make it more likely the problem behavior will occur, and determine consequences that maintain problem behavior. Accordingly, intervention plans can be developed to minimize the problem by addressing antecedents and to alter the problem behavior by rearranging reinforcing contingencies. An interesting extension of this logic is to apply these activities to other behaviors requiring remediation, such as administrator or teacher resistance to consultation.

At the organizational level, Austin (2000) described a four-stage adapted model useful for consulting school psychologists evaluating school-wide barriers and strengths: Evaluation of antecedents, equipment and process, knowledge and skills, and consequences. Evaluation of antecedents includes determining if (a) instructions were explicit; (b) appropriate attainable goals were generated; (c) simple, specific prompts evoked performance; and (d) rules were established and understood. Equipment and process requires an evaluation of physical infrastructure that could be impeding behavior change as well as lack of resources and political constraints. Knowledge and skills represents whether teachers or administrators have the skill to engage in the required tasks. Consequences consists of determining the amount of performance feedback and reinforcement provided, response effort required, as well as the aversive stimuli and competing contingencies present.

School psychologists could take a proactive approach by addressing antecedents through the development of clearly written protocols, explicit definition of role responsibilities, and pairing of paraprofessionals with teachers to implement an innovative task. Likewise, school psychologists may be able to address equipment and processes by actively considering what resources are needed for an intervention to be successfully implemented and ensuring the resources are secured prior to implementation. When addressing consequences, evidence has accrued that performance feedback increases teachers' adherence to treatment protocols (e.g., Solomon, Klein, & Polityло, 2012) and permitting teachers to cancel consultation meetings contingent on successful treatment implementation also results in behavior change (e.g., DiGennaro, Martens, & Kleinmann, 2007).

Consistent with knowledge and skills discussed above is the consideration of teacher and administrator proficiency with the skills required to implement an intervention at the individual or systems level. The Instructional Hierarchy (Haring & Eaton, 1978) is a heuristic for skill development consisting of four stages: (a) acquisition, which refers to the time when an individual has recently learned a skill and is working to develop accurate performance; (b) fluency, which refers to the development of rapid and accurate skill performance; (c) generalization, which refers to the maintenance of the skill across time, as well as the demonstration of the skill in other settings, with other people, and toward other related behaviors; and (d) adaption, which refers to the novel application of skills. This heuristic can be applied as a change theory for the consultative process by assessing the stage of teachers' and administrators' skill development and applying an appropriate strategy for improvement.

If school professionals are learning a skill for the first time and in the acquisition stage of development, sufficient opportunities for modeling, guided practice, behavioral rehearsal, immediate feedback, and reinforcement within the intervention setting that the skill needs to be applied are important. However, if school professionals are accurate but not fluent with skill implementation, then frequent opportunities for practice using newly acquired skills with reinforcement provided by the school psychologist might be programmed. Although successful generalization may not take place until after accuracy and fluency are achieved, incorporating strategies to facilitate generalization should happen as early as possible during consultation.

School psychologists can facilitate generalization by (a) generating scripts, protocols, or intervention manuals that illustrate highly specific treatment steps; (b) helping teachers' identify self-instructional strategies, such as cues or signals; and (c) setting goals such as time allocated to transition versus instruction. Another option is to provide generalization prompts and training by encouraging teachers or administrators to identify other students who might benefit from a previously implemented successful intervention, reviewing the intervention process and steps from that case, and developing an application for use with the identified students (Riley-Tillman & Eckert, 2001).

Addressing Teacher and Administrator Barriers

It is possible to design strategies that address barriers associated with perceptions of an intervention, roles, and the problem to be addressed.

Perceptions

When addressing perceptions of the intervention itself, the following three barriers should be considered: (a) the value of evidence-based practices, (b) alignment with current practices, and (c) outcomes (see Figure 34.1). Inadequate understanding of best practices can be addressed by creating a culture of evidence-based practice. This may be accomplished by developing educational policies and practices that promote or require the use of evidence-based practice. School psychologists can help school professionals remain abreast of evidence-based practice and research surrounding assessment and intervention by disseminating information at faculty meetings, making resources available and easily accessible, or by arranging professional development workshops consistent with best practices in training.

Aligning interventions with current school practices results in improved collaboration. School psychologists can facilitate such an alignment by engaging in collaborative intervention development, offering choices of appropriate evidence-based options, discussing adaptations of evidence-based interventions, and mapping potential teacher-generated barriers to implementation and associated strategies to overcome such barriers.

Instilling confidence in positive outcome expectations can be accomplished by ensuring a match exists between a problem and identified solution and providing local or research-based examples of how the proposed intervention is appropriate to address the identified student's problem. Inviting teachers to share treatment successes may help to address barriers. Treatment matches can be facilitated by using screening and additional data to generate hypothesized reasons for the problem and then linking those reasons to evidence-based solutions. Treatment trials can also be offered through brief experimental analysis whereby different strategies are directly evaluated, by supporting teacher implementation

on a brief basis and reviewing outcomes before fully committing to a treatment, or by establishing more frequent consultation meetings to ensure continued progress. School psychologists are also encouraged to assess the acceptability of adopted or proposed interventions as part of the consultation process.

The respective roles of school psychologists, teachers, and administrators in a multitiered system of service delivery are likely novel to many school professionals. Therefore, school psychologists and administrators can collaborate to define building-wide roles and responsibilities and disseminate these expectations through flyers, parent and teacher information sheets, and the school website. It is incumbent upon the school psychologist to directly inform teachers, staff, principals, and superintendents of the range of skills they possess, particularly in the domains of consultation, coaching, and data-based decision making. School psychologists may also find it helpful to emphasize the advantages of preventive approaches on valued outcomes as well as how these approaches align with the school mission.

Given the complexity of consultation within multitiered systems of service delivery, disconnect among professionals regarding the existence or nature of a problem experienced by an individual student or a school is likely. Fortunately, data can be used to illustrate discrepancies between teacher and administrator expectations and actual performance. School psychologists can use these data to facilitate a discussion of benefits and challenges to proceeding as usual or intervening by highlighting evidence-based practices, connecting practices to relevant state and local laws, and describing valued outcomes. School psychologists might have different conversations regarding benefits of an innovative practice with teachers, principals, and superintendents. For example, discussing reduction of office referrals, gains in instructional time, and improvement in high-stakes testing as outcomes of implementing positive behavior supports might appeal to principals. School psychologists might also minimize jargon and define necessary terms to promote understanding and buy-in.

Case application: Consider a scenario in which a school administration decides that a social–emotional learning curriculum is going to be implemented in all fifth- and sixth-grade classrooms. To support this initiative, the principal directs the school psychologist to provide consultation support to all fifth- and sixth-grade teachers. Some teachers perceive the intervention as meeting an important need in their classroom, others perceive it to be redundant as they are already infusing

Figure 34.1. Link Between the Specific Barriers Associated With Perceptions and Action Steps to Address Those Barriers in Practice

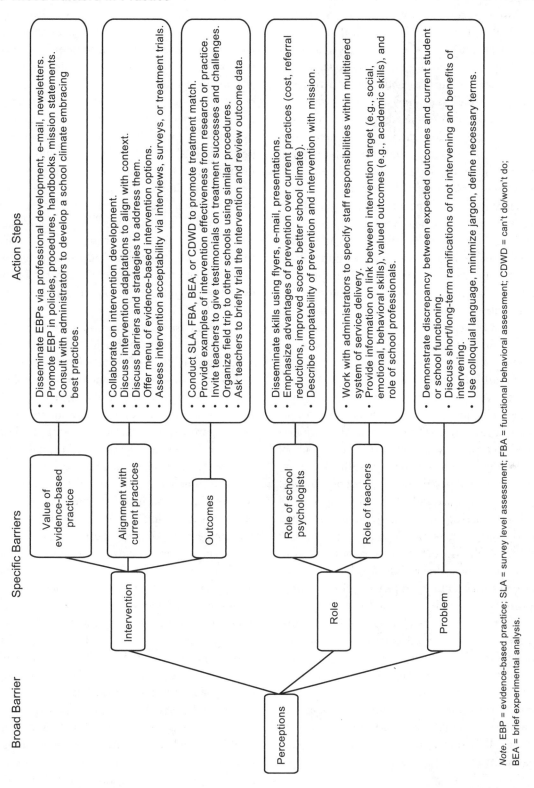

Note. EBP = evidence-based practice; SLA = survey level assessment; FBA = functional behavioral assessment; CDWD = can't do/won't do; BEA = brief experimental analysis.

social–emotional learning content into their lessons, and still others perceive it to be unnecessary as the students in their classroom do not appear to need explicit instruction related to social–emotional learning. Teachers who perceive the intervention as important are more likely to readily engage in a collaborative consultation process, whereas teachers who perceive it as redundant or unnecessary may be more reticent as they do not perceive an urgent need for the intervention.

This scenario identifies barriers associated with perceptions of the problem and the intervention. There are several strategies a school psychologist might employ to address these barriers. First, to illustrate need for the intervention, the school psychologist might present local school screening data and/or national data describing the benefits and ramifications for providing a whole school socioemotional curriculum, taking care to highlight areas where the current fifth- and sixth-grade students may not be meeting expectations. Second, the relationship between social–emotional learning and academics might be highlighted to facilitate buy-in as academic outcomes are most clearly associated with teachers' roles and valued outcomes. In addition, common ground might be found by discussing the importance of prevention. Third, to promote a culture of evidence-based practices, the school psychologist could work with the principal to ensure that promotion of evidence-based practices is included across all school policies, procedures, and materials. Fourth, to ensure alignment with current practices, the school psychologist might facilitate review and discussion of several preselected evidence-based social–emotional learning curricula so that teachers can identify strengths and limitations of each as well as correspondence with ongoing practices and subsequently develop consensus about the best curriculum to implement. Fifth, rather than require the teachers to make a long-term commitment, the school psychologist and principal might suggest that the selected curricula is trialed for one marking period after which acceptability of the curricula, ability to integrate with typical routines, and adaptations to the standard protocol are discussed. School psychologists might also be sure to check in with teachers weekly to provide any identified support to teachers and collect student data to evaluate outcomes of the treatment.

Knowledge and Skills

A cornerstone of the NASP Practice Model (NASP, 2010) is data-based decision making, which represents a potential challenge when teachers and administrators are unaware of associated best practices, data collection sources and procedures, and evaluation. Consequently, school psychologists will need to disseminate their knowledge in this area as well as assist administrators with identification and evaluation of current and potential additional sources of data for promotion of effective program evaluation. School psychologists will be in a position to collaborate with administrators to develop a sequence of ongoing professional development training that meets the needs of all school professionals (see Figure 34.2). To facilitate collaboration, a communication system could be developed so that school professionals might also make training recommendations. For example, teachers might convey interest for specific content or type (e.g., information sharing, peer coaching, testimonials from another school, skill rehearsal) of professional development experience through collection of quarterly surveys or by regular use of a suggestion box placed in a central building location.

A critical aspect for promoting knowledge and skills is for the school psychologist to assess teachers' and administrators' level of skill development. Identification of key topics to address can be accomplished initially through needs assessments that generate both system-wide and individual skill gaps. Evaluation of the nature of skill gaps can be achieved by using the instructional hierarchy. A skill assessment can be conducted through interviews, needs assessment surveys, and direct observation of practices to determine skill exposure and use. As a result, professional development opportunities can be specified so that new skills are facilitated through comprehensive training whereas supervised rehearsal and coaching are arranged for skills that have been previously introduced but lack fluent implementation. Arranging professional development within collaborative groups of educators can maximize benefits (Kensler et al., 2012). Content learned within varied professional development experiences can be retained and generalized through the purchase and maintenance of intervention/program manuals as well as development of intervention scripts and protocols.

Case application: Consider a scenario in which a new principal is assigned to a school that has a large number of office discipline referrals and suspensions as well as a history of failing to meet annual yearly progress. The principal, eager to address these problems, collaborates with interested parties from national technical assistance centers, the state department of education, and a local university to provide new programs and services. As a result, there is now an array of programs implemented

Figure 34.2. Link Between the Specific Barriers Associated With Knowledge/Skills and Action Steps to Address Those Barriers in Practice

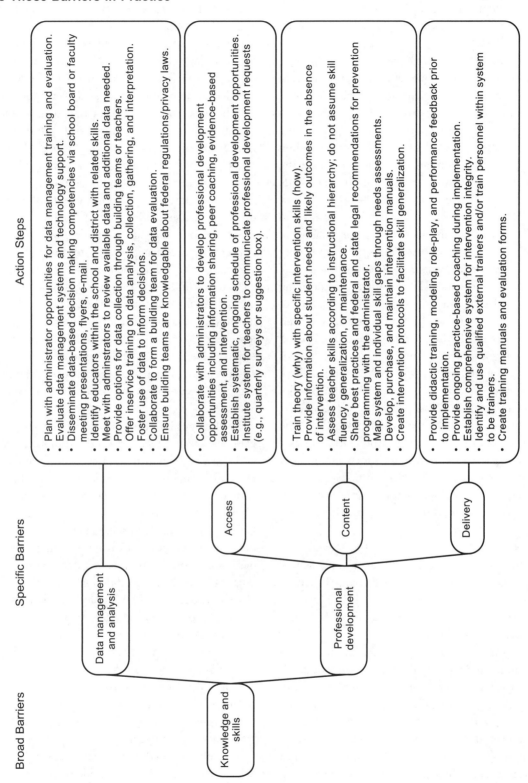

without coherence. In addition, the principal is having difficulty locating all relevant school data and has focused on student demographics and teacher assignments as primary sources for evaluating school-wide problems.

In this example, the principal is not exhibiting direction in leadership style and appears to lack knowledge in data management and evaluation. First, the school psychologist might arrange one-to-one meetings directed at building rapport with the new principal on a weekly basis. This might include understanding the school vision, expectations, and staff roles from the principal's perspective as it relates to improving school outcomes. Second, once rapport has been developed, discussion of the manner in which data can be used to determine the needs of the school could be facilitated. The school psychologist can provide specific examples of the currently available data such as the number of students referred to special education or receiving suspensions and subsequent costs to the system. Third, the school psychologist might convey knowledge and skills in the areas of system change and data-based decision making and discuss data management systems that could be selected by the principal that also adhere to federal and privacy laws. Fourth, the school psychologist might offer to assist with the development of a school-based team for data evaluation. Fifth, the school psychologist could move from brief weekly meetings to providing the principal with coaching, brief updates, and/or reminders on different tasks related to the implementation of data analysis and evaluation (Lohrmann, Forman, Martin, & Palmeiri, 2009).

Resources

Through effective and creative collaboration, school psychologists can uncover unidentified resources within their school and surrounding community to address infrastructure, competing priorities, and psychological and time barriers (see Figure 34.3).

Securing administrator support surrounding infrastructure is fundamental to successful implementation of multitiered systems of service delivery. To accomplish this, the school psychologist could work with the administrator, potentially through brief 15-minute weekly meetings, to (a) secure meeting space, (b) work with the information technology department to establish a computerized communication network for collecting and evaluating data, (c) train designated personnel or volunteers on intervention procedures, (d) ensure that schedules allocate time to consultative support, and (e) convey commitments in the school mission and

improvement plan. School psychologists can assist the principal with (a) identification of low-cost evidence-based intervention options that require minimal training and (b) development of an inventory of existing resources, such as underutilized intervention programs in the storage closet, free gym time for use as a reward, or teachers willing to have lunch with students.

Advertising school- and teacher-level successes to key stakeholders, such as parents and school board members, might lead teachers and administrators to rearrange priorities. Identifying teacher, student, and school goals for change as well as providing feedback and reinforcement can help establish importance of consultative tasks. This can be accomplished in a variety of ways, for example, through public recognition of teacher efforts through monthly raffles, certificates of appreciation, offering access to priority parking, or escape from bus duty. School psychologists are encouraged to use individualized rewards based on the values and preferences of each teacher. The same reward will not have the same effect for another teacher and could inadvertently interfere with collaboration and consultation. Thus, school psychologists should avoid a one-size-fits-all approach and instead ask teachers directly, through surveys, or using reward menus what types of activities they value.

Psychological barriers and time constraints commonly experienced by teachers and administrators can be addressed in several integrated ways. School psychologists and principals could collectively distribute a school climate survey to all stakeholders as a means for identifying sources of satisfaction and concern. Consequently, findings will generate areas to prioritize for change. Offering to assume primary responsibility over some intervention tasks such as material development, schedule coordination, and data collection, especially during initial implementation phases, may reduce the psychological and time resource barriers and facilitate intervention implementation. To accommodate limitations in teachers' schedules, school psychologists might generate tip sheets that are distributed on a regular basis or organize workshops that address common classroom problems. If a teacher is experiencing burnout, then offering choices could increase perceptions of control, providing an empathetic ear might offer needed emotional support, and utilizing brief, simple intervention options might address the feeling of being overwhelmed.

Case application: Consider a scenario where the principal of a school with high needs but low resources is interested in providing funding to invest in universal

Figure 34.3. Link Between the Specific Barriers Associated With Resources and Action Steps to Address Those Barriers in Practice

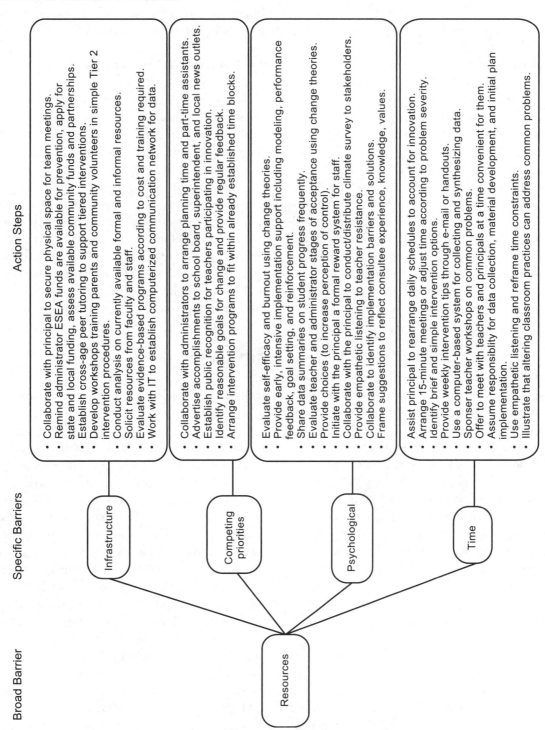

Note. ESEA = Elementary and Secondary Education Act

and Tier 2 programming to address reading and socioemotional skills. Screening data had been collected over the previous year under the direction of the school psychologist, and the building leadership team, composed of teachers and administrators, has a clear understanding of the needs and goals for improvement. Buy-in among school staff of organizational change is more than 80%. However, the school has no additional curricula or standard protocol interventions.

This is an example where implementation of universal and selected interventions has been prioritized and time has been allocated to establishing the foundation for these supports. Given the establishment of a leadership team and acceptance among school professionals, psychological barriers do not appear to be evident. The primary barrier is related to physical infrastructure, a common challenge. The school psychologist and leadership team develop a comprehensive plan to identify resources. The principal allocates the 15% of funds offered through the Elementary and Secondary Education Act for prevention toward purchasing evidence-based Tier 2 reading programs and investigates available local grant funding opportunities. The school psychologist generates a list of other low-cost or free research-supported programs and presents the list to the principal and leadership team. The leadership team decides to institute school-wide positive behavior supports, a low-cost but evidence-based alternative. In doing so, the team establishes local community partners to donate materials to facilitate the initiative. The school psychologist generates a building-level survey to identify formal and informal resources that may already be present and asks building staff whether the staff can donate time or other existing resources to offer rewards to students. The leadership team decides that to support Tier 2 intervention implementation, a cross-age peer tutoring program will be established. The school psychologist organizes formal professional development opportunities for current building paraprofessionals. Collaboratively, the school psychologist and principal also reach out to local universities with school psychology training programs to develop a partnership that might result in shared resources.

Multicultural Competencies

When addressing teacher and administrator barriers and assessing status within the process of change, school psychologists need to consider the specific cultural and sociopolitical backgrounds of the school, student, and consultees. Cross-cultural competencies for conducting consultation include (a) working with others, (b) demonstrating sensitivity toward the culture of all parties involved in consultative services, (c) identifying a range of potential solutions that are cross-culturally responsive, and (d) being aware of culturally related factors that could have an impact on accurate problem identification (Lopez & Rogers, 2001).

Clear communication regarding all parties' expectations, goals, ensuring mutual participation, and establishing rapport at the outset of relationship building can universally support collaboration.

Evaluation of Effectiveness

Outcomes pertaining to school psychologists' goals for promoting collaborative consultation that yield changes in service delivery reflecting best practices will range in scope from achieving buy-in with 80% of school professionals to securing an administrator at building team meetings. Formally, evaluation of implementation is necessary through the development of a multifaceted and comprehensive intervention integrity system. For example, the following combination of sources could be used to evaluate implementation integrity: direct observations of the new skill being performed, self-evaluation by school professionals using protocol checklists, periodic consultation meetings, and review of permanent products generated by the procedure.

SUMMARY

Collaboration and consultation with teachers and administrators is evolving with movement toward prevention and early intervention programming. As school psychologists lead their schools in developing and refining multitiered systems of service delivery, resistance will surface and underlying barriers such as perceptions, knowledge and skills, and resources will need to be addressed. Although teachers and administrators will each face these barriers, manifestation will differ according to the independent responsibilities of these school professionals. It is incumbent upon the school psychologist to recognize and acknowledge these barriers, using these challenges as a platform to establish the groundwork for change. Knowledge of a variety of theories that describe how individuals and organizations experience change can help school psychologists recognize where in this process their colleagues are operating and engage in different strategies to enhance consultation.

Being aware of the numerous potential barriers to consultation and collaboration as well as strategies to address these barriers proactively should, in concert with (a) established models of ecological/behavioral and school-based consultation, (b) knowledge of data-based decision making, and (c) evidence-based assessment and intervention, facilitate all aspects of school psychologists' service delivery.

REFERENCES

Austin, J. (2000). Performance analysis and performance diagnostics. In J. Austin & J. E. Carr (Eds.), *Handbook of applied behavior analysis* (pp. 321–349). Oakland, CA: Context Press.

Castillo, J. M., Curtis, M. J., & Gelley, C. (2012). School psychology 2010–Part 2: School psychologists' professional practices and implications for the field. *Communiqué, 40*(8), 4–6.

Desimone, E. (2009). Improving impact studies of teachers' professional development: Toward better conceptualizations and measures. *Educational Researcher, 38*, 181–199. doi:10.3102/0013189X08331140

DiGennaro, F. D., Martens, B. K., & Kleinmann, A. E. (2007). A comparison of performance feedback procedures on teachers' treatment implementation integrity and students' inappropriate behavior in special education classrooms. *Journal of Applied Behavior Analysis, 40*, 447–461. doi:10.1901/jaba.2007.40-447

Durlack, J. A., & DuPre, E. P. (2008). Implementation matters: A review on the influence of implementation on program outcomes and the factors affecting implementation. *American Journal of Community Psychology, 41*, 327–350.

Erchul, W. P., & Martens, B. K. (2010). *School consultation: Conceptual and empirical bases of practice* (3rd ed.). New York, NY: Springer. doi: 10.1007/978-1-4419-5747-4

Fernet, C., Guay, F., Senecal, C., & Austin, S. (2012). Predicting intra-individual changes in teacher burnout: The role of perceived school environment and motivational factors. *Teaching and Teacher Education, 28*, 514–525.

Fixsen, D. L., Blasé, K. A., Naoom, S. F., & Wallace, F. (2009). Core implementation components. *Research on Social Work Practice, 19*, 531–540. doi:10.1177/1049731509335549

Forman, S. G., Olin, S. S., Hoagwood, K. E., Crowe, M., & Saka, N. (2008). Evidence-based interventions in schools: Developers' views of implementation barrier and facilitators. *School Mental Health, 1*, 23–36.

Gilman, R., & Gabriel, S. (2004). Perceptions of school psychological services by education professionals: Results from a multistate survey pilot study. *School Psychology Review, 33*, 271–286.

Gilman, R., & Medway, F. J. (2007). Teachers' perceptions of school psychology: A comparison of regular and special education teacher ratings. *School Psychology Quarterly, 22*, 145–161. doi:10.1037/1045-3830.22.2.145

Hall, G. E., & Hord, S. M. (2011). *Implementing change: Patterns, principles, and potholes* (3rd ed.). Upper Saddle River, NJ: Pearson.

Haring, N. G., & Eaton, M. D. (1978). Systematic instructional technology: An instructional hierarchy. In N. G. Haring, T. C. Lovitt, M. D. Eaton, & C. L. Hansen (Eds.), *The fourth R: Research in the classroom* (pp. 23–40). Columbus, OH: Merrill.

Jacob, S., Decker, D., & Hartshorne, T. S. (2011). Indirect services I: Ethical-legal issues in working with teachers and parents. In, *Ethics and Law* (6th ed., pp.191–203). Hoboken, NJ: Wiley.

Joyce, B., & Showers, B. (2002). *Student achievement through staff development* (3rd ed.). Alexandria, VA: Association for Supervision and Curriculum Development.

Kensler, L. A. W., Reames, E., Murray, J., & Patrick, L. (2012). Systems thinking tools for improving evidence-based practice: A cross-case analysis of two high school leadership teams. *The High School Journal, 95*(2), 32–53.

Kowalski, T. J. (2009). Need to address evidence-based practice in educational administration. *Educational Administration Quarterly, 45*, 351–374. doi:10.1177/0013161X09333623

Long, A. C. J., Sanetti, L. M. H., Gallucci, J., Collier-Meek, M. A., & Kratochwill, T. R. (2012). *Perceptions of barriers to intervention implementation: A teacher survey.* Manuscript in preparation

Lohrmann, S., Forman, S., Martin, S., & Palmeiri, M. (2009). Understanding school personnel's resistance to adopting school-wide positive support at a universal level. *Journal of Positive Behavior Interventions, 10*, 256–269.

Lopez, E. C., & Rogers, M. (2001). Conceptualizing cross-cultural school psychology competencies. *School Psychology Quarterly, 16*, 270–302.

Mägi, K., & Kikas, E. (2009). School psychologists' role in school: Expectations of school principals on the work of school psychologists. *School Psychology International, 30*, 331–346. doi:10.1177/0143034309106943

National Association of School Psychologists. (2010). *Model for comprehensive and integrated school psychological services.* Bethesda, MD: Author. Retrieved from http://www.nasponline.org/standards/2010standards/2_PracticeModel.pdf

Ransford, C. R., Greenberg, M. T., Domitrovich, C. E., Small, M., & Jacobson, L. (2009). The role of teachers' psychological experiences and perceptions of curriculum supports on the implementation of a social and emotional learning curriculum. *School Psychology Review, 38*, 510–532.

Raven, B. H. (2008). The bases of power and the power/interaction model of interpersonal influence. *Analyses of Social Issues and Public Policy, 8*, 1–22.

Reinke, W. M., Stormont, M., Herman, K. C., Puri, R., & Goel, N. (2011). Supporting children's mental health in schools: Teacher perceptions of needs, roles, and barriers. *School Psychology Quarterly, 26*, 1–13.

Riley-Tillman, T. C., & Eckert, T. L. (2001). Generalization programming and school-based consultation: An examination of consultee's generalization of consultation related skills. *Journal of Educational and Psychological Consultation, 12*, 217–241.

Rogers, E. M. (2003). *Diffusion of innovations* (5th ed.). New York, NY: The Free Press.

Solomon, B. G., Klein, S. A., & Politylo, B. C. (2012). The effect of performance feedback on teachers' treatment integrity: A meta-analysis of the single-case literature. *School Psychology Review, 41*, 160–175.

Spectrum K–12 School Solutions. (2011). *Response to intervention adoption survey 2011.* Towson, MD: Author. Retrieved from http://www.spectrumk12.com/rti/the_rti_corner/rti_adoption_report

Webster-Wright, A. (2009). Reframing professional development through understanding authentic professional learning. *Review of Educational Research, 79*, 702–739. doi:10.3102/0034654308330970

Woodruff, S. B., & Kowalski, T. J. (2010). Problems reported by novice high school principals. In A. R. Shoho, B. G. Barnett, & A. K. Tooms (Eds.), *The challenges for new principals in the twenty-first century: Developing leadership capabilities through professional support.* Charlotte, NC: Information Age Publishing.

35 Best Practices in School Psychologists' Promotion of Effective Collaboration and Communication Among School Professionals

Tanya L. Eckert
Natalie Russo
Bridget O. Hier
Syracuse University (NY)

OVERVIEW

The National Association of School Psychologists (NASP) *Model for Comprehensive and Integrated School Psychological Services* (NASP, 2010), emphasizes the importance of school psychologists promoting effective collaboration and communication between school professionals in order to improve the educational, behavioral, and mental health outcomes of all students. Promoting effective communication between school psychologists, teachers, administrators, and other professionals requires consideration of several inter- and intrapersonal factors and dynamics. These include making deliberate choices in communication style that are reflective of an understanding of the specific audience with which one is communicating, the goal of the communication from the perspective of both the school psychologist and the school professional, the style of communication that will be most effective, and, more broadly, the culture of the school. An awareness of these considerations is essential to promoting effective communication among school professionals. Put another way, these considerations allow the school psychologist to provide the right information in the right way to the right school professional.

It is important to highlight that, although each school professional presumably has the best interest of the child

in mind, school professionals differ with respect to how best to manage those interests. For example, teachers want to do what they can to help their students learn and develop into strong students and citizens. However, teachers do not always have the time or resources to provide undivided attention to one student when they must consider the whole class. On the other hand, school principals must balance the needs and resources provided to one student with broader budgets, and administrative pressures of which school psychologists are not always aware. School psychologists are in a unique position to serve as the child's advocate.

The goal of this chapter is to highlight how to most effectively communicate and support consultation across both horizontal (other professionals) and vertical (teachers and administrators) lines. By developing effective communication skills, school psychologists will be better positioned to consult with school personnel using consultee-centered consultation, problem-solving consultation, school-based consultation, instructional consultation, or behavioral–ecological consultation. Further, effective collaboration and communication are essential as school psychologists engage in problem solving and multitiered service delivery, both of which serve as foundations for practice in the school and are emphasized in the NASP Practice Model (NASP, 2010). Though the literature emanating from the field of school psychology will be reviewed, it is fairly sparse, and, thus, we borrow from other fields in which effective communication is essential to supplement and extend our discussion. This includes areas such as industrial and organizational psychology, education, management, and the medical literatures.

BASIC CONSIDERATIONS

Communication is defined as "imparting or interchanging thoughts, opinions, or information by speech, writing, or signs" (Mishra & Mishra, 2009, p. 438), and, ideally, "the message should be received and understood as intended" (Guo, 2009, p.16). Within the context of this chapter, the goal of a school psychologist's communication with other professionals is to arrive at a mutual understanding of a particular situation and to come to a consensus on the best course of action. Although this seems rather obvious, successfully achieving this goal requires a specific set of skills that school psychologists are particularly well suited to provide as a result of their training and experience. In this way, school psychologists are in a unique position to bridge language and communication barriers among and between school professionals in order to promote the well-being of children. Further, given that effective communication is the central construct in the consultation process (Daniels & DeWine, 1991), school psychologists can increase their effectiveness as consultants.

Elements of Effective Communication

Following a review of business and healthcare fields (Victorian Government Department of Health, 2010), five basic principles of effective communication were identified: (a) complete, (b) concise, (c) concrete, (d) clear, and (e) accurate. Although these principles seem intuitive and somewhat obvious, effective communication requires the ability to flexibly apply these principles across the broad contexts for communication relevant to school psychologists. Despite their simplicity, findings from medical literature suggest that adhering to these simple communication principles is linked to improved patient care and outcomes, decreased length of patient stay, and increased job satisfaction (Griffin et al., 2004; Stewart, 1991), all considerations that are relevant to the school psychologist. Indeed, in the medical literature, research has shown that effective communication between professionals tends to lead to fewer medical errors and improved client safety (Cameron, Jelinek, Kelly, Murray, & Brown, 2009; McCallin, 2001; Pfrimmer, 2009).

Conversely, as highlighted in a 2002 Institute of Medicine report on health communication (Institute of Medicine, 2002), ineffective communication can contribute to poor client outcomes and inconsistent care. It is important to note that the medical field is a forerunner regarding the dissemination of research examining effective collaboration and communication skills. Specifically, a plethora of medical researchers have examined (a) effective means of communicating information regarding disease and treatment options to concerned parties and (b) the promotion of collaboration between and among medical professionals.

Elements of Effective Collaboration

Despite the implications these findings pose for school professionals, research examining effective collaboration skills has largely been reserved for the business, management, and industrial/organizational fields. Similar to many businesses, schools are bureaucratic organizations (Erchul & Martens, 2010). Thus, findings from these fields can be readily applied to school settings given their similar organizational structure. For example, industrial/organizational research suggests that collaboration tends to be effective when it incorporates tasks focused on both the individual and group levels (Mishra & Mishra, 2009). Within the school setting, this may look like various professionals (e.g., school psychologist, occupational and physical therapists, counselor) working to complete independent evaluations in their respective areas of expertise, and integrating their findings to develop one cohesive report. The findings from business, management, and industrial/organizational research and their application to the school setting are further discussed below in the Best Practices section.

The shortage of research in school psychological and educational literature suggests that school psychologists may not have ready access to research-based strategies for effective communication and collaboration. Thus, school psychologists may lack knowledge of empirically supported strategies to promote effective collaboration and communication between school professionals. Further, school psychologists may not be aware of some of the common barriers to communication and how those barriers ultimately have an impact on student outcomes.

Common Barriers to Communication and Collaboration

Why do conflicts arise when school personnel share the common goal of helping children achieve their potential? How can school psychologists promote an atmosphere where different school professionals are invested and feel supported and important? Examining barriers to effective communication can provide information about common pitfalls that school psychologists can work to avoid. These pitfalls include human factors, such as attitudes, cultural and linguistic differences, stress, fatigue, and the verbal and nonverbal messages that speakers and listeners convey to one another during communicative acts. They also include broader institutional or contextual factors, such as role definition and the organizational culture of the school. Borrowing from the social psychology literature, we will further examine these implicit and explicit factors and their impact on collaboration and communication among school professionals.

Social psychologists have long studied how different human factors have an impact on individuals and groups and the judgments that are made. These factors can be directly applied to promoting effective communication and collaboration in the schools. Much of the research has revolved around how subtle and implicit biases affect how individuals, and hence the messages they are trying to convey, are perceived. This chapter discusses these implicit biases as they directly affect efforts to promote effective communication pathways among school professionals. Specifically, the fundamental attribution error (Jones & Harris, 1967) and the elaboration likelihood model (Petty & Cacioppo, 1986) serve as important social–psychological phenomena that can be applied to address subtle and implicit biases that affect communication and collaboration processes among school psychologists and other school personnel. Practical solutions to altering these biases (e.g., Biernat & Dovidio, 2000; Devine, 1989) have been proposed to result in more effective communication and collaboration.

Fundamental Attribution Error

The fundamental attribution error refers to the notion that people tend to place more importance on dispositional factors (i.e., personality traits) when explaining an individual's behaviors than on situational factors (e.g., fatigue, stress). However, people tend to explain their own behaviors using situational factors rather than personality factors. This discrepancy, called the actor–observer bias, is particularly relevant to the school psychologist–teacher relationship. An example might be a situation in which a school psychologist is describing to a teacher an intervention that will help facilitate a child's academic success. When communicating this message, the school psychologist notices that the teacher appears distracted. The fundamental attribution error would predict that the

school psychologist would be more likely to interpret the teacher's behavior as being a reflection of dispositional factors (e.g., disrespectfulness, disinterest, uncaring) rather than recognizing situational factors (e.g., stressful day, has another meeting scheduled, not understanding the intervention) that may be affecting the teacher's appearance of being distracted.

The actor–observer bias, where a person explains his or her own behavior primarily as the result of situational factors, but explains the behavior of others as the result of internal causes, can have significant repercussions on the efficacy of communication between school psychologists and other school professionals. More importantly, the actor–observer bias can lead to lost opportunities to help children, because communications are being misinterpreted or ignored. For example, Kennedy (2010) argues that conclusions regarding teacher quality are predominately based on teacher characteristics. As a result, situational factors (e.g., time, materials, work assignments, student characteristics, school incursions into student life, educational reform efforts) that affect teaching practice and student learning are largely overlooked. By addressing these factors, more meaningful changes in teaching practices might be observed, thereby improving student outcomes.

Interestingly, the social psychology literature also suggests that overcoming or minimizing the actor–observer bias requires only that people feel as though they are part of the same team (Jones & Nisbett, 1972). Thus, creating and fostering a team atmosphere among all school professionals and instilling a feeling of group membership among all school professionals can go a long way in improving communication and collaboration among school psychologists and other school professionals. Some practical tips regarding how school psychologists can foster an environment of mutual support among teachers and other school professionals will be presented later in the Best Practices section.

Elaboration Likelihood Model

Perhaps the most central topic in the discussion regarding implicit human factors that impede communication relates to the elaboration likelihood model, which is a framework that attempts to explain the probability that an individual will change his or her attitude or be persuaded by an argument (Rucker & Petty, 2006). For school psychologists, this model can help them understand how to persuade others. The central tenet of this model is that communications are processed by one of two pathways and that these pathways affect whether a message is persuasive or not.

The two pathways by which a communicator can convince a listener are the central and peripheral routes, which reflect the mind-set of the listener and influence the depth of message processing as well as the change in attitude or behavior that may result from a communication. The central processing route to attitude change requires the communicator to put the listener in a position whereby the listener relies on cognitive processes, such as drawing from experiences and knowledge, to make a decision regarding whether or not the listener supports the message being presented. This arduous processing requires a set of necessary characteristics, which the school psychologist can make explicit prior to, or during, the communication.

In order to process information centrally, a listener must be (a) motivated, (b) invested, and (c) able to think about the merits of a particular change. For example, for a teacher to be on board with an intervention, the teacher must be motivated to help change a behavior in a child, be invested in doing so, and be able to understand and think about the potential benefits of an intervention. It is thus up to the school psychologist to explain the importance of an intervention to a teacher using language that is easily understood so that the benefits are clearly evident to both the teacher (e.g., how will implementing this intervention make it easier for the teacher to have this child in his or her classroom) and the child (e.g., how will this help the child succeed in the classroom).

In contrast to central processing, behavior and attitude change can also be arrived at via the peripheral processing route. In this pathway, external cues, rather than cognitive processes, lead to an attitude or behavior change. That is, external factors such as the way one dresses, one's perceived expertise, or the mood of the listener have more of an impact on whether the listener will be persuaded by an argument than do the merits of the argument itself. Other factors of influence include more personal and contextual factors, such as whether the listener enjoys engaging in this kind of thinking and whether there are distractions in the environment that impede thinking (Cacioppo, Petty, & Morris, 1983; Rucker & Petty, 2006).

It is important to note that although the peripheral route can lead to behavior or attitude change in the listener, the changes incurred via central processing tend to be longer lasting and more profoundly internalized than changes incurred via peripheral processing. According to Petty and Cacioppo (1986), listeners who are both capable and motivated to think about the merits underlying a particular argument and are thus convinced by it will internalize the arguments and believe in the arguments strongly. Thus, in promoting effective communication and collaboration among school-based professionals, school psychologists should do what they can to ensure that the listener is processing information centrally.

School psychologists are frequently in a position where they need to effectively persuade teachers, administrators, and other professionals regarding what they believe to be the best course of action, be it at the level of the student (e.g., behavioral intervention to improve on-task behavior) or at the institutional level (e.g., the school should invest in a bullying prevention program). It may appear deliberate and manipulative to exploit the elaboration likelihood model in order to convince school-based professionals to do what school psychologists think is best. However, bearing in mind professional ethics, the welfare of the child should help guide the goals of any persuasive argument championed by the school psychologist. Knowledge regarding the dynamics of persuasion can help the school psychologist be aware of what communication barriers may be operating in a school and how best to mitigate those barriers. Further, by planning appropriately and making strides to engage the listener using central processing strategies, the school psychologist can increase the likelihood that the changes are maintained over time and generalized to other situations, children, or programs.

BEST PRACTICES IN PROMOTING COMMUNICATION AND COLLABORATION

In the scholarly literature, definitions of collaboration emphasize the act of individuals working together to accomplish a common goal. This may occur through interacting with, sharing information with, and coordinating activities with other professionals (Jassawalla & Sashittal, 1998). Additionally, collaboration often requires the group to work together to solve difficult, complex problems (Mishra & Mishra, 2009), with the expectation that collaborators will come to a shared decision and will be equally responsible for task outcomes (Friend & Cook, 2002). Because collaboration depends on the efforts of the individuals within the group as well as the group as a whole, each member of the group should fulfill a relevant, meaningful role (Fulk, 2011) and should receive individually focused tasks that contribute to interactive group work (Mishra & Mishra, 2009). Given the interindividual context that collaboration necessitates, effective collaboration among school professionals requires the use and promotion of effective communication skills (see

Table 35.1. Best Practice Guidelines for School Psychologists in Promoting Communication and Collaboration

Effective Communication Skills	Best Practice Guidelines
Written communication	• Use sparingly • Supplement with face-to-face communication • Provide brief, factual information
Face-to-face communication	• Convey interest and investment • Provide encouragement • Clarify ambiguous information
Professional investment	• Avoid jargon and technical language • Discuss mutual goals • Emphasize personal relevance
Jargon-free and clear language	• Use short conversational words and phrases • Reframe communications so they are colloquial • Make messages personally relevant
Vocal tone and speech	• Use vocal volume to emphasize key points • Alter word rate to emphasize key points • Alter tone of speech to emphasize key points
Repetition of key words	• Repeat and emphasize key points • Reduce distractions that inhibit the listener • Provide written follow-up communications
Nonverbal communication	• Directly face the listener • Provide the listener with equal distribution of gaze • Maintain facial expressions that convey interest • Use affirmative responses to convey interest
Listening skills	• Provide attentive body posture • Engage in impartial listening • Avoid patronizing or judgmental expressions

Table 35.1 for a summary of best practice guidelines for school psychologists that are discussed in the subsequent section of this chapter). Not only will effective communication have an impact on school-based consultation outcomes, but effective communication can also be helpful in establishing effective helping relationships among school professionals and in promoting systems-level change.

Effective Communication

In any communication attempt there is the possibility for miscommunication, which may lead to a spectrum of problems ranging from inefficient interactions to the more dire circumstance of disservice to students. Effective communication strategies increase the likelihood that the message being communicated is received and understood as intended, thus limiting the problems that may arise from miscommunication.

Written Communication

Several avenues through which information may be communicated exist within the school setting, including the posting of information on bulletin boards, the insertion of fliers in staff mailboxes, and the increasingly popular use of electronic communication such as e-mail, wiki pages, and Google docs. Given the importance of efficiency for time-strapped school-based professionals, some may hypothesize that these low-effort means of communication are favored and perhaps overused within the school setting in lieu of face-to-face communication. Indeed, these low-effort communication tools can be fine options when disseminating factual information that does not require further analysis (e.g., the date of a parent–teacher conference, the time of a meeting; Mishra & Mishra, 2009). In summary, best practice guidelines for written communication include (a) using it sparingly, (b) supplementing it with face-to-face communication in chaotic circumstances (e.g., noisy hallway), and (c) providing brief, factual information (e.g., confirming appointment time).

Face-to-Face Communication

Face-to-face communication is one of the most effective means of transmitting information, as this allows individuals to (a) supplement information with verbal (e.g., voice inflection) and nonverbal cues (e.g., body language) that will likely aid in the transmission of the message, (b) receive immediate mutual feedback, and (c) immediately clarify instances of ambiguity (Allen, 1971; Daft, Lengel, & Trevino, 1987). Simply put, face-to-face communication also helps to build the relationship between professionals. Thus, information that is anything but purely factual is more efficiently communicated face-to-face. In this sense, there are numerous types of information that should not be communicated via low-effort means (e.g., e-mail) but should rather be reserved for in vivo interactions. For school psychologists, these include information related to assessment or intervention planning, the communication of assessment results, and consultation.

Face-to-face communication requires a broad and diverse set of both verbal and nonverbal skills. When speaking to other professionals, it is important that information be relayed in a clear, concise manner that is free of jargon (Petty, Heesacker, & Hughes, 1997). For example, informing an occupational therapist that Johnny is demonstrating attention-maintained problem behavior is not likely to have its intended effect. In fact, Petty and Cacioppo (1986) would predict that using jargon would increase the likelihood that the occupational therapist would process the message using the peripheral route, decreasing the chances for long-term persuasion or attitude change. Alternatively, putting this information into a statement that the occupational therapist can easily understand and use (e.g., "It looks like Johnny is engaging in off-task behavior to get your attention") would more likely result in a correct interpretation of the message. In summary, best practice guidelines for face-to-face communication include (a) using verbal and nonverbal skills to convey interest and investment in the communication, (b) providing encouragement during the communication, and (c) clarifying ambiguous messages or content.

Professional Investment

Research suggests that presenting information as described above (i.e., condensing information into an organized, clear argument that does not include technical language) is particularly important when the professional with whom one is communicating is highly invested in the issue (Rhoades & Kratochwill, 1992), as high levels of personal investment increase the likelihood for central route processing of information (Petty et al., 1997). Among a team of school-based professionals, investment in the issue is likely to be high much of the time, as these individuals often have high stakes regarding student outcomes. For example, although school psychologists and counselors are largely respon-

sible for maintaining the social–emotional and behavioral well-being of their students, speech–language therapists have a responsibility to ensure that their students' speech is developing adequately. Teachers have a similarly high investment in their students' academic outcomes.

Conversely, when the issue at hand has low personal relevance to the listener, the information has a higher likelihood of being peripherally processed. In this case, the use of jargon may actually increase the acceptability of that message (Rhoades & Kratochwill, 1992), possibly because it appeals to low-effort heuristics (e.g., "The expert must be right"). As previously mentioned, although peripheral route processing has the potential to produce reformed attitudes, its effects are often short lived (Petty et al., 1997). For this reason, encouraging central route processing in communication endeavors is recommended for longer term effectiveness.

In addition to avoiding technical language, another way to encourage central route processing is to increase the listener's investment in the issue by ensuring the message is personally relevant to the audience. This may be done by making general, simple statements that reference the listener at the onset of the communication session. For instance, saying, "Dave, I have some information that may make your reading class more manageable," may prompt the listener to elaborate on the information provided in the communication. Providing more specific references to the individual listener may make the personal relevance of the message more obvious (e.g., "Cindy, I know you have been looking for more cost-effective ways to provide services to students. Let me tell you about some ideas I have for doing this."). In summary, best practice guidelines for professional investment include (a) avoiding jargon and technical language, (b) discussing mutual goals, and (b) emphasizing personal relevance.

Jargon-Free and Clear Language

Not only is the use of jargon-free language and personal relevance of the message important in the listener's likelihood of elaborating upon the communicated information, but providing necessary background information so the listener has enough information to understand the message is also likely to increase the occurrence of central route processing. For example, describing the functions of a student's behavior to other professionals is not likely to be effective unless those individuals have basic, prerequisite knowledge about operant conditioning principles. Thus, providing a very brief and basic overview of the theoretical underpinnings of the message or why the information being communicated is important will likely result in improved elaboration. In summary, best practice guidelines for jargon-free and clear language include (a) making the message personally relevant; (b) reframing communications such that a layperson can understand the concept; and (c) using short conversational words, phrases, and expressions.

Vocal Tone and Speech

In addition to attempting to increase elaboration on the part of the listener when speaking with other professionals, literature from the counseling field suggests that vocal tone and speech rate are important aspects of effective communication (Ivey, Ivey, & Zalaquett, 2010). For example, consider the different ways that one could say, "Let's meet about that later," simply by altering the rate or tone of speech. Thus, awareness about one's own vocal qualities and appropriateness to the situation is crucial. Additionally, Ivey et al. (2010) recommend verbally underscoring key words or points to ensure that central aspects of the message are recognized by the audience. This may be done by using emphasis or varying the vocal volume level when presenting key components of the message. In summary, best practice guidelines for vocal tone and speech include (a) emphasizing key points with increasing vocal volume and (b) altering word rate or tone of speech to highlight key points.

Repetition of Key Words

Another technique to ensure that the most important parts of the message are received as intended involves the repetition of key words, phrases, and points. Cognitive research suggests that the human working memory has a limited capacity and that its ability to hold units of information can be constrained by a variety of factors (e.g., heavy cognitive load, less time for rehearsal of information; e.g., Cowan, 2001; Cowan, Rouder, Blume, & Saults, 2012). Thus, situational factors are important to consider in professional, school-based communication. For instance, reducing distractions is likely to result in improved retention of the central ideas of the communication. Given that, it would be best for communication to occur when school professionals are in a quiet setting rather than during a chaotic moment in the hallway or classroom. In this sense, it may be beneficial to schedule a before- or after-school meeting rather than attempting to catch another professional during the school day. However, in many instances, communication cannot wait and information must be delivered within the context of a chaotic or

distracting environment. Given those circumstances, it is recommended that information be repeated via written correspondence that summarizes the main points of the original face-to-face communication (Petty et al., 1997). Best practice guidelines for repetition of key words include (a) reducing distractions that will inhibit communication, (b) repeating and emphasizing key points central to communication, and (c) providing written follow-up communication to emphasize key points.

Nonverbal Communication

Nonverbal communication skills are considered to be an important means of providing context in a verbal interaction and of clarifying a message's content and intent. Indeed, several nonverbal characteristics have been shown to have an impact on the acceptability of an interaction. For example, maintaining a facial expression that is appropriate given the topic and tone of the conversation, using affirmative gestures (e.g., head nodding), and restricting the use of random movements and hand gestures are all positively related to perceptions about the quality of the interaction and competency in communication skills (Collins, Schrimmer, Diamond, & Burke, 2011). Additional factors that are related to positive perceptions of communication skills include providing an equal distribution of gaze when talking and listening and directly facing the listener (Ishikawa et al., 2006). Best practice guidelines for nonverbal communication include (a) directly facing school professionals during communication, (b) providing equal distribution of gaze to school personnel during communication, (c) maintaining facial expressions that convey interest, and (d) using affirmative responses to convey interest and agreement.

Listening Skills

Although the use of effective verbal and nonverbal communication strategies is useful when conveying a message, it is important to use effective listening skills when collaborating with other professionals. Specifically, because a component of effective communication includes accurately understanding others' messages, working in teams with other school-based professionals requires the ability to listen effectively. Several recommendations for appropriate listening strategies have emerged from the counseling literature. For example, Ivey et al. (2010) recommended providing the speaker with eye contact, facing the speaker while leaning forward slightly, and using facilitative gestures that encourage the speaker to continue talking. This attentive body language is more likely to convey a message of interest in and understanding of the speaker's message.

Not only do effective listening skills show that one is listening, these skills also attempt to limit intentional or unintentional biases. For instance, when listening to another professional's message, it is important not to disregard unfavorable information that does not align with one's own theoretical orientation, opinions, or values (Kinicki & Kreitner, 2008), as this would likely increase potentially negative effects of the confirmation bias (i.e., interpreting information that confirms pre-conceptions). Instead, taking notes on the speaker's central ideas and actively attempting to be impartial may limit emotional reactions that hinder an ability to correctly interpret the content of the message. Thus, by saving judgments for after the speaker's delivery of the content, it is more likely that potentially important information will not be dismissed. In summary, best practice guidelines for listening skills include (a) providing attentive body posture, (b) engaging in impartial listening, and (c) avoiding the use of patronizing or judgmental expressions.

Promoting Effective Collaboration and Communication Among School Professionals

The various components of effective communication skills mentioned above should be considered founda-tional skills that are the basis for any professional interaction within the school setting. In terms of promoting these skills within a collaborative context among school professionals, it is important to consider the various needs and perspectives of each professional. Specifically, effective communication in a collaborative context revolves around balancing what kind of information each professional wants to gain from one another and what each professional wants to contribute to the interaction.

Communicating and Collaborating With Teachers

Given that teachers are typically the professionals who have the most contact with students within the school setting, are often associated with students' success or failure, and experience high rates of burnout, it is crucial for school psychologists to take on a supportive role when collaborating with teachers and promoting collaboration between teachers. Additionally, as tea-chers are frequently expected to enact change in their classroom routines at the suggestion of the school

psychologist, building rapport with these professionals is critically important. Rather than simply asking teachers to comply with demands, school psychologists should take the time to (a) allow teachers to express their scopes of concern and (b) provide empathic listening and responses, which may reduce negative perceptions that teachers may hold of school psychologists. Additionally, in collaborating with teachers, if the school psychologist provides additional supports or resources that benefit the teachers, then it is more likely that the teachers will reciprocate in the future (Gregory, Cialdini, & Carpenter, 1982). Although many factors have an impact on teacher communication and collaboration, it is important for school psychologists to continually evaluate their effectiveness when communicating and collaborating with teachers. Adopting a social validity perspective may be an important approach for school psychologists to evaluate their effectiveness in this area (Eckert & Hintze, 2000).

Communicating and Collaborating With Administrators

In most schools it is imperative for communication with administrators to be effective and meaningful. However, collaborating with administrators is likely to require a vastly different repertoire than collaborating with teachers. It is important for school psychologists to consider the vast array of issues that school adminis-trators face on a daily basis (e.g., improving student achievement, creating school organization to support student learning, promoting parent and community partnerships, creating educational change, working with declining state and federal resources). Consideration of these issues may be helpful in building rapport with school administrators. In addition, given the bureau-cratic climate of the school system, administrators are frequently hurried, pressured to make quick decisions, and required to ensure the cost-effectiveness of pro-grams. Thus, school psychologists should be prepared to quickly relay the main points to administrators as well as any benefits or limitations associated with the informa-tion being communicated. Additionally, having brief weekly meetings with the school principal in which the school psychologist presents himself or herself as a source of expertise regarding building-related issues may have a beneficial effect for both professionals (Curtis & Stollar, 2007). Finally, school psychologists should continually evaluate their effectiveness when commu-nicating and collaborating with school administrators from a social validity perspective (Eckert & Hintze, 2000).

Communicating and Collaborating Within Teams

Building teams of specialists (e.g., multidisciplinary teams, eligibility teams, multitiered services teams) within the school setting has been a common practice for decades and is gaining renewed interest with response-to-intervention initiatives (Nellis, 2012). Specialists who serve on multidisciplinary teams may include the teacher, parent, school principal, school psychologist, counselor, social worker, occupational therapist, physical therapist, speech–language therapist, special education teacher, and school nurse. In addition, building teams may also involve the inclusion of professionals who are not from the school, including parents or caregivers, community members, and parent and child advocates. Although collaboration between all professionals within the school building is an important component for student success, collaboration with other specialists and nonschool personnel is necessary for ensuring that, when appropriate, students receive additional services and supports.

Effective collaboration requires the fostering of mutual support through teamwork. Teams have typically been conceptualized as multiple individuals working cohesively and interdependently to achieve a common goal (Friend & Cook, 2002). Small teams made up of 2–10 individuals are most effective in aspects related to coordination, communication, and collaboration (Curtis, Curtis, & Iscoe, 1988), particularly when addressing complex problems (Mishra & Mishra, 2009). When building or restructuring a team, it is important for group members to have complementary skills and expertise (Katzenbach & Smith, 2001). For instance, although a school psychologist may have the tools and skills to assess a child's social–emotional strengths and needs, a school counselor may be well suited to intervene based on the results of the psychologist's assessment.

As teams begin working to address the needs of individual students or classrooms, the greatest improvements will likely result if accountability is promoted (Katzenbach & Smith, 2001). Thus, at each team meeting, it may be helpful for school psychologists promoting the teacher to complete the following: (a) set measurable goals for each team member, (b) set measurable goals for the team, and (c) review the progress toward these goals. Providing feedback is often a popular and effective means of evaluation. Also, school psychologists reinforcing the accomplishments of both individuals within the team and the team as a whole can be incorporated into professional development workshops or other institutional seminars.

With respect to interactions between multidisciplinary team members, it is important that school psychologists promote team members by providing information in a nonthreatening manner and use areas of disagreement as an opening for communication rather than conflict (Fulk, 2011). Asking for and providing clarification are necessary components in effective collaboration, and they should be frequently employed by school psychologists serving on a multidisciplinary team (Fulk, 2011). When team members inhabit offices that are in proximity to one another, there is an increased likelihood of communication. Although this is not always feasible in schools, it is important to consider if team members are in a position to negotiate office locations with administrators. Finally, encouraging the participation of all team members is an important assurance that all team members' opinions are adequately represented (Guo, 2009). In this sense, it may be necessary to directly ask for the opinions of team members who may be passive and/or quiet.

Using Culturally Competent Practices

As school psychologists collaborate and communicate among school professionals, it is important to utilize culturally competent practices. Relying upon these resources is critical, as school psychologists work with school personnel and families who are addressing students from culturally and linguistically diverse backgrounds. Further, it is important for school psychologists to evaluate their own effectiveness in providing culturally competent practices.

Several general multicultural competencies are needed by school psychologists as they engage in effective communication and collaboration among school professionals. At the individual level, it is important for school psychologists to understand their own culture and how it affects others (Rogers, 2000). When engaging in communication and collaboration among school professionals, school psychologists need to engage in mutual respect and value of other cultures and to build bridges when cultural differences exist (Nuijens, 2004). At the school level, it is important for school psychologists to understand the culture of the school as well as commonly held beliefs and attitudes regarding students from culturally and linguistically diverse backgrounds (Nuijens, 2004). Given that culturally and linguistically diverse students will often receive educational services from a vast array of school personnel, it is important for school psychologists to advocate that all school personnel engage in culturally competent practices.

More specific factors are important for school psychologists to consider as they engage in effective communication and collaboration among school professionals. School psychologists should be aware that cultural clashes can impede communications with school professionals. As noted by Ingraham (2000), attentiveness and responsiveness to cultural and ethical issues during communications and collaborations with school professionals can increase effectiveness. For example, school psychologists should consider engaging in the following practices to ensure multicultural sensitivity during communication and collaboration: (a) create informal and formal opportunities for school professionals to communicate and develop trust (Sheridan, 2000), (b) maintain positive rapport with school personnel representing diverse backgrounds (Sheridan, 2000), (c) frame communications to value multiple perspectives held by school personnel representing diverse backgrounds (Maital, 2000), and (d) examine barriers that may negatively affect communications among school professionals (Maital, 2000; Nuijens, 2004).

SUMMARY

The culture of a school will affect the type of communications that are acceptable and how those communications are initiated and received. Together, the fundamental attribution error and the elaboration likelihood model provide a framework from which to understand how other factors, external to the school psychologist, play a role in supporting collaboration and communication between school professionals. For example, the fundamental attribution error suggests that in order for school psychologists to have meaningful communications with school professionals, situational factors should be prioritized and emphasized at the expense of personal character traits associated with a situation. The elaboration likelihood model suggests that school psychologists will be more effective in their communications when school personnel are motivated and able to process information directly. In addition, using team building and helping each individual see the personal relevance of a persuasive message can also increase the likelihood of central processing. Further, schools that promote an inclusive or egalitarian perspective may increase the likelihood that messages will be perceived centrally because school professionals will feel that they are invested and are working toward a common goal. In such circumstances, the focus should be on providing logical, accessible information that is presented using easily understood language that focuses on mutual goals and interests. Making deliberate choices in communication style is essential to promoting effective collaboration and communication among school professionals.

REFERENCES

Allen, T. J. (1971). Communications networks in R&D laboratories. *R&D Management, 1*, 14–21.

Biernat, M., & Dovidio, J. F. (2000). Stigma and stereotypes. In T. F. Heatherton, R. E. Kleck, M. R. Hebl, & J. G. Hull (Eds.), *The social psychology of stigma* (pp. 1–28). New York, NY: Guilford Press.

Cacioppo, J. T., Petty, R. E., & Morris, K. (1983). Effects of need for cognition on message evaluation, recall, and persuasion. *Journal of Personality and Social Psychology, 45*, 85–818. doi:10.1037/0022-3514.45.4.805

Cameron, P., Jelinek, G., Kelly, A., Murray, L., & Brown, A. (2009). *Textbook of adult emergency medicine* (3rd ed.). New York, NY: Elsevier.

Collins, L. G., Schrimmer, A., Diamond, J., & Burke, J. (2011). Evaluating verbal and non-verbal communication skills, in an ethnogeriatric OSCE. *Patient Education Counseling, 83*, 158–162. doi:10.1016/j.pec2010.05.012

Cowan, N. (2001). The magical number 4 in short-term memory: A reconsideration of mental storage capacity. *Behavioral and Brain Sciences, 24*, 87–114. doi:10.1017/S0140525X01003922

Cowan, N., Rouder, J. N., Blume, C. L., & Saults, J. (2012). Models of verbal working memory capacity: What does it take to make them work? *Psychological Review, 119*, 480–499. doi:10.1037/a0027791

Curtis, B., Curtis, H., & Iscoe, N. (1988). A field study of the software design process for large scale systems. *Communications of the ACM, 31*, 1268–1287.

Curtis, M. J., & Stollar, S. A. (2002). Best practices in system-level change. In A. Thomas & J. Grimes (Eds.), *Best practices in school psychology IV* (pp. 223–234). Bethesda, MD: National Association of School Psychologists.

Daft, R. L., Lengel, R., & Trevino, L. K. (1987). Message equivocality, media selection, and manager performance: Implications for information support systems. *MIS Quarterly, 11*, 355–366. doi:10.2307/248682

Daniels, T., & DeWine, S. (1991). Consultancy intervention: Rethinking a hackneyed theme. *Journal of Educational and Psychological Consultation, 2*, 303–322. doi:10.1207/s1532768xjepc0204_1

Devine, P. (1989). Stereotypes and prejudice: Their automatic and controlled components. *Journal of Personality and Social Psychology, 56*, 5–18. doi:10.1037/0022-3514.56.1.5

Eckert, T. L., & Hintze, J. M. (2000). Behavioral conceptions and applications of acceptability: Issues related to service delivery and research methodology. *School Psychology Quarterly, 15*, 123–148. doi:10.1037/h0088782

Erchul, W. P., & Martens, B. K. (2010). *School consultation: Conceptual and empirical bases of practice* (3rd ed.). New York, NY: Springer.

Friend, M., & Cook, L. (2002). *Interactions: Collaboration skills for school professionals* (5th ed.). White Plains, NY: Longman.

Fulk, B. M. (2011). Effective communication in collaboration and consultation. In C. G. Simpson & J. P. Bakken (Eds.), *Collaboration: A multidisciplinary approach to educating students with disabilities* (pp. 19–30). Waco, TX: Prufrock Press.

Gregory, W. L., Cialdini, R. B., & Carpenter, K. M. (1982). Self-relevant scenarios as mediators of likelihood estimates and compliance: Does imagining make it so? *Journal of Personality and Social Psychology, 43*, 89–99. doi:10.1037/0022-3514.43.1.89

Griffin, S. J., Kinmonth, A. L., Veltman, M. W., Gillard, S., Grant, J., & Stewart, M. (2004). Effect on health-related outcomes of interventions to alter the interaction between patients and practitioners: A systematic review of trials. *Annals of Family Medicine, 2*, 595–608. doi:10.1370.afm.142

Guo, K. L. (2009). Effective communication in healthcare: Strategies to improve communication skills for managers. *The Business Review, Cambridge, 12*, 8–17.

Ingraham, C. L. (2000). Consultation through a multicultural lens: Multicultural and cross-cultural consultation in schools. *School Psychology Review, 29*, 320–343.

Institute of Medicine. (2002). *Speaking of health: Assessing health communication strategies for diverse populations.* Washington, DC: National Academies Press.

Ishikawa, H., Hashimoto, H., Kinoshita, M., Fujimori, S., Shimizu, T., & Yano, E. (2006). Evaluating medical students' non-verbal communication during the objective structured clinical examination. *Medical Education, 40*, 1180–1187. doi:10.1111/j.1365-2929.2006.02628.x

Ivey, A. E., Ivey, M. B., & Zalaquett, C. P. (2010). *Intentional interviewing and counseling: Facilitating client development in a multicultural society.* Belmont, CA: Brooks/Cole.

Jassawalla, A. R., & Sashittal, H. C. (1998). An examination of collaboration in high technology new product development processes. *Journal of Product Innovation Management, 15*, 237–254. doi:10.1111/1540-5885.1530237

Jones, E. E., & Harris, V. A. (1967). The attribution of attitudes. *Journal of Experimental Social Psychology, 3*, 1–24. doi:10.1016/0022-1031(67)90034-0

Jones, E. E., & Nisbett, R. E. (1972). The actor and the observer: Divergent perceptions of the causes of the behavior. In E. E. Jones, D. E. Kanouse, H. H. Kelley, R. E. Nisbett, S. Valins, & B. Weiner (Eds.), *Attribution: Perceiving the causes of behavior* (pp. 79–94). Morristown, NJ: General Learning Press.

Katzenbach, J. R., & Smith, D. K. (2001). *The discipline of teams: A mindbook-workbook for delivering small group performance.* Hoboken, NJ: Wiley.

Kennedy, M. M. (2010). Attribution error and the quest for teacher quality. *Educational Researcher, 39*, 591–598. doi:10.3102/0013189X10390804

Kinicki, A., & Kreitner, R. (2008). *Organizational behavior: Key concepts, skills and best practices.* Boston, MA: McGraw-Hill Irwin.

Maital, S. L. (2000). Reciprocal distancing: A systems model of interpersonal processes in cross-cultural consultation. *School Psychology Review, 29*, 389–400.

McCallin, A. (2001). Interdisciplinary practice: A matter of teamwork: An integrated literature review. *Journal of Clinical Nursing, 10*, 419–428. doi:10.1046/j.1365-2702.2001.00495.x

Mishra, D., & Mishra, A. (2009). Effective communication, collaboration, and coordination in eXtreme programming: Human-centric perspective in a small organization. *Human Factors in Ergonomics in Manufacturing, 19*, 438–456. doi:10.1002/hfm.20164

National Association of School Psychologists. (2010). *Model for comprehensive and integrated school psychological services.* Bethesda, MD: Author. Retrieved from http://www.nasponline.org/standards/2010standards/2_PracticeModel.pdf

Nellis, L. M. (2012). Maximizing the effectiveness of building teams in response to intervention implementation. *Psychology in the Schools, 49*, 245–256. doi:10.1002/pits.21594

Nuijens, K. L. (2004). *Culturally competent consultation in schools: Information for school psychologists and school personnel.* Bethesda, MD: National Association of School Psychologists. Retrieved from http://www.nasponline.org/resources/culturalcompetence/cc_consultation.aspx

Petty, R. E., & Cacioppo, J. T. (1986). The elaboration likelihood model of persuasion. In L. Berkowitz (Ed.), *Advances in experimental social psychology* (pp. 123–205). San Diego, CA: Academic Press.

Petty, R. E., Heesacker, M., & Hughes, J. N. (1997). The elaboration likelihood model: Implications for the practice of school psychology. *Journal of School Psychology, 35*, 107–136. doi:10.1016/S0022-4405(97)00003-4

Pfrimmer, D. (2009). Teamwork and communication. *Journal of Continuing Education in Nursing, 40*, 294–295.

Rhoades, M. M., & Kratochwill, T. R. (1992). Teacher reactions to behavioral consultation: An analysis of language and involvement. *School Psychology Quarterly, 7*, 47–59. doi:10.1037/h0088247

Rogers, M. P. (2000). Examining the cultural context of consultation. *School Psychology Review, 29*, 414–418.

Rucker, D. D., & Petty, R. E. (2006). Increasing the effectiveness of communications to consumers: Recommendations based on elaboration likelihood and attitude certainty perspectives. *Journal of Public Policy & Marketing, 25*, 39–52.

Sheridan, S. M. (2000). Considerations of multiculturalism and diversity in behavioral consultation with parents and teachers. *School Psychology Review, 29*, 389–400.

Stewart, M. A. (1991). Effective physician–patient communication and health outcomes: A review. *Canadian Medical Association Journal, 152*, 1423–1433.

Victorian Government Department of Health. (2010). *Promoting effective communication among healthcare professionals to improve patient safety and quality of care.* Melbourne, Victoria, Australia: Hospital and Health Service Performance Division, Department of Health.

36 Best Practices as an Internal Consultant in a Multitiered Support System

Kathy McNamara
Cleveland State University

OVERVIEW

Multitiered systems of support (MTSS), response to intervention (RTI), and positive behavior supports are systems to which most schools now subscribe, in which students receive increasingly more intensive academic and behavioral support on the basis of performance data that are collected on a routine basis (O'Connor & Freeman, 2012). According to Greenwood and Kim (2012), the purpose of MTSS is to address known causes of school failure by providing protection against the onset of problems through evidence-based instructional and behavior management practices (Tier 1, or primary prevention), by accelerating progress in learning a skill when delays are evident (Tier 2, or secondary prevention), and by preventing existing problems from becoming worse (Tier 3, or tertiary prevention).

A recent RTI implementation survey conducted by Spectrum K12 School Solutions (2011) reported that 94% of schools responding to the survey are at some stage of implementation, and that in an estimated 24% of schools, an MTSS model is operational as "routine practice." Elsewhere, systems of multitiered services are still aspirational in nature, or lacking consensus on the form or features of the model, and are often characterized by uneven implementation of practices (Fuchs, Fuchs, & Compton, 2012; O'Connor & Freeman, 2012). Despite these issues, there is general agreement that an MTSS model, properly implemented, holds considerable promise as an efficient framework for a data-driven approach to providing more effective solutions to children's school problems, an objective that is consistent with the contemporary mission of school psychology, as articulated in the NASP *Model for Comprehensive and Integrated School Psychological Services* (NASP, 2010).

School psychologists have been urged to contribute their knowledge, skills, and expertise to the problem-solving activities comprising MTSS (i.e., assessment and intervention). They also are uniquely positioned to serve as consultants supporting the implementation process itself. The NASP (2010) Practice Model suggests services within the domain of Consultation and Collaboration as competencies permeating all aspects of service delivery and this accurately describes the nature of school psychologists' role in MTSS implementation.

As in-house or internal experts (Dougherty, 2009; Sugai, Horner, Fixsen, & Blase, 2010), school psychologists benefit from knowledge of institutional history. From the perspective of teachers and administrators, school psychologists also are regarded as experts with access to information and resources, maintaining a relatively objective stance in relation to administration and staff. While school psychologists may not possess the authority to mandate adoption of MTSS practices, they can use both expert (information based and skill based) and referent (relationship based) power to influence and help shape the form and progress of MTSS in settings.

In this chapter we highlight issues that schools encounter as they introduce and scale up MTSS, and offer advice to school psychologists as internal consultants uniquely positioned to advocate for the adoption and maintenance of best practices.

BASIC CONSIDERATIONS

Graduate educators are familiar with the sight of newly minted school psychology interns returning to campus

553

after their first weeks or months in schools, reeling from their exposure to what is euphemistically described as the "research-to-practice gap" or, less charitably, the myopic view from the ivory tower. Having received on-campus instruction in the techniques, efficiency, and benefits of a multitiered, prevention-oriented approach to service delivery, interns sometimes are dismayed—or at best confused—by a seeming lack of enthusiasm for this approach in the field. Among seasoned practitioners, complaints more often reflect frustration with the mandate to satisfy the ever-present demands of a traditional, well-established role (e.g., administering tests and completing paperwork) despite knowing that there may indeed be a better way to address children's academic and behavior problems.

School Psychologist's Role in MTSS

We recently conducted a survey in a midwestern state where the state education agency has identified RTI/MTSS implementation as a priority for schools, including it in its school improvement initiatives (McNamara, York, Kubick, McMahon, & Clark, 2013). The survey examined a variety of employment phenomena, but of particular interest were relationships between self-reported engagement in specific MTSS-oriented activities and characteristics of school psychologists and their work settings. For this purpose, although more than one third of approximately 1,500 school psychologists who received a link to the survey (from the state's professional school psychology association) completed the survey, only the responses of full-time school-based practitioners ($N = 379$) were analyzed. While generalizability of findings may be limited, several themes emerged that shed some light on the nature and extent of school psychologists' engagement in MTSS activities.

School Psychologists' Knowledge and Skills
Replicating earlier reports, practitioners in our survey (McNamara et al., 2013) reported having received most of their preparation for MTSS-oriented activities from conference presentations and local, on-site inservice programs, a finding of some concern because these exemplify a relatively ineffective train-and-hope approach to skill development (Kratochwill, 2007; Sullivan, Long, & Kucera, 2011). School psychologists reported the greatest skill in consulting with teachers about the performance of students at risk for failure, but have far less confidence in their data management and analysis skills, especially with respect to school-wide academic and social–emotional performance indicators.

Other surveys of practicing school psychologists have documented deficits in knowledge and skills (Machek & Nelson, 2010), and these effects are exacerbated by an absence of consensus among educators not only about what, exactly, MTSS is but also what contributions school psychologists can and should make to MTSS implementation. Certainly, school psychologists need a broad understanding of MTSS, including its structures and processes focused on effective, increasingly intensive instruction. In the absence of this understanding, practitioners are likely to settle for training in discrete skills and procedures without a rationale and context for why, how, and when these skills and procedures should be used.

Professional Identity of School Psychologists
While many school psychologists surveyed seemed to celebrate the prospect of the redefined role available with MTSS, others were less enthusiastic, perhaps because of concern that they are being stretched too thinly. Still others question the wisdom of straying too far from a traditional diagnostician role, since there is little competition for this role in schools (unlike other roles, such as mental health or instructional consultants), and the legal guarantee of appropriate, individual evaluation of students for special education eligibility represents a source of job security. The association between school psychology and special education extends beyond funding considerations, however. Many school psychologists identify closely with special education not only in practice but in advocacy and research efforts as well. Some school psychologists question the desirability of identifying with the mission and routines of general education (such as academic screening and developing academic interventions, which are major features of MTSS models) since it is an enterprise in which a broad array of educators can claim expertise, and for which many school psychologists do not feel adequately prepared (Machek & Nelson, 2010).

Situational Barriers
According to Machek and Nelson (2010), school psychologists' eagerness to engage in MTSS may be outpaced by limitations on financial and personnel resources, time, and actual and perceived abilities. Our survey (McNamara et al., 2013) revealed that, while workplace features are related to school psychologists' engagement in MTSS activities, some—including the size of student enrollments—appear to be less influential than others, such as administrator buy-in and clearly conveyed expectations for school psychologists' involvement.

As Don Deshler observed in remarks to a national conference on RTI implementation (National Center for Learning Disabilities, 2010), numerous factors and forces interfere with the quality and fidelity of MTSS implementation, increasing the risk that MTSS will be relegated to an unacceptably lengthy (and growing) list of failed educational initiatives. These factors include political pressure to quickly generate measurable improvements in student performance, increasing demands on limited and shrinking economic resources, entrenched bureaucracies and routines that are resistant to change, absent or inadequate provisions for planning and management, and ineffective, revolving-door leadership, most of which are beyond school psychologists' ability to control. Nevertheless, Machek and Nelson (2010) note that school psychologists "who have incorporated the model have been somewhat successful in navigating these … pitfalls" (p. 241) and that school psychologists already working within an MTSS framework report such concerns to a significantly lesser degree.

Notwithstanding these limitations and obstacles, however, our data and that reported in other studies suggest that school psychologists are frequently regarded as potential leaders and/or integral resources in MTSS implementation. (In our survey, approximately one third of full-time practitioners reported playing a leadership role.) That school psychologists can and should play a key role in MTSS is evidenced by the fact that school psychologists comprised the second-largest number of respondents reporting on behalf of schools and districts in the most recent Spectrum K12 School Solutions (2011) RTI survey. Moreover, O'Connor and Freeman (2012) report that many MTSS initiatives are succeeding precisely because of the contributions made by school psychologists.

On what issues, then, should school psychologists focus in their efforts to support MTSS implementation in schools? To answer this question it is helpful to examine where and how implementation efforts are likely to stumble and perhaps fail. There appear to be three general categories of problems that impede implementation efforts: perspectives on MTSS purpose and mission, shortcomings in MTSS planning and management, and MTSS structures and processes that fall short of best practice standards.

MTSS Purpose and Mission

An important source of implementation vulnerability lies in the manner in which schools construe the purpose of MTSS. This frames the process, as perceived and then enacted by all members and stakeholders in the system. In some settings, MTSS is narrowly construed in context of its relationship to special education, frequently operationalized through centralized teams that plan general education interventions for referred students before testing is authorized. (See Table 36.1.)

MTSS as Special Education Prerequisite or Substitute

The earliest attempts to implement a system-level problem-solving approach were framed as prereferral intervention, wherein attempts were made to create and deliver interventions whose success could reduce the need for special education eligibility evaluations. In many settings, this orientation to MTSS persists, supported by federal legislation (the 2004 Individuals with Disabilities Education Improvement Act) permitting the use of information about a child's "responsiveness to scientifically-based instruction" to identify specific learning disabilities.

While more judicious use of special education and assessment resources (and a reduction in unnecessary labeling of children as disabled) is a demonstrated and commendable outcome (McNamara & Hollinger, 2003; Spectrum K12 School Solutions, 2011), the larger purpose of MTSS—to enhance the success of all children—is often minimized or overlooked when MTSS provisions are viewed as prerequisites or substitutes for special education and related services. In many systems, the emphasis is on *resistance* rather than *responsiveness* to evidence-based instruction and interventions, with the former being interpreted as evidence of the inadequacy of any service other than special education. This is most likely to be the case when the foundation for MTSS (primary prevention, or core instruction, and/or secondary prevention, or supplemental instruction targeting areas of skill deficiency) is weak, and stakeholders view special education as the only viable form of meaningful intervention.

Data from our survey (McNamara et al., 2013) indicated that a greater-than-expected number of schools assign responsibility for MTSS implementation to general education, or responsibility is shared by general and special education administrative units. Similarly, 24% of respondents in the most recent Spectrum K12 School Solutions (2011) survey identified general education as the unit leading MTSS implementation in their school buildings and districts, with only 19% reporting that special education units held primary responsibility. Even more encouraging was the

Table 36.1. MTSS Purpose and Mission

Issue	Possible Indicators or Red Flags	Implications and Consequences	School Psychologist as Internal Consultant
MTSS as special education prerequisite or substitute	• Concern or questions about the number of interventions expected or about the period of time over which interventions must be sustained before students can be evaluated for a suspected disability • Oversight or responsibility for MTSS assigned to or originating in a special education unit • Explaining high rates of student failure as result of unidentified (or untreated) disabilities, rather than of inadequate instruction	• Common and persistent view of MTSS as a creature of special education, rather than as an undertaking from which both general and special education benefit • Inadequate general education teacher buy-in for MTSS implementation • Persistence of notion that special education is the most appropriate intervention for difficult-to-teach students	• Adopt the language of "effective intervention" in place of "disability determination" as the goal of the problem-solving process • Assist teachers in using screening and other data to evaluate and improve core instruction
MTSS as a problem-solving intervention team	• References to RTI team referral as the primary problem-solving resource for students • Absence of structured sequence of increasingly more intensive interventions • Reliance on opinion (rather than data) to identify students needing more intensive intervention • Teachers make direct referrals of individual students to a centralized problem-solving team or every student who fails universal screening is referred to a centralized team for individualized intervention planning	• Failure to develop an adequate foundation of primary and secondary prevention for academic and social–behavior problems • Bias in referral practices and elevated rate of false positives and false negatives of students identified for intervention • Invalid decisions regarding levels of risk and degree of intervention intensity required for referred students • Inability to properly apply an individualized problem-solving procedure with an unnecessarily inflated number of students	• Assist in selecting evidence-based interventions (standard protocol/commercially available programs, or a set of strategies indexed to skill deficiency areas) • Offer valid and reliable data collection alternatives that can be repeatedly administered and whose results can be graphed for analysis across time and settings • Help planners understand how normative, benchmark, and criterion-predictive cut scores can be used to establish degree of risk for failure

finding that 57% of respondents work in schools or districts in which general and special education units collaborate on MTSS initiatives (Spectrum K12 School Solutions, 2011). These trends signal progress among educators in understanding the broad relevance of MTSS to both general and special education.

MTSS as a Problem-Solving Intervention Team

In many schools, MTSS is synonymous with a procedure in which a building-level team is convened to gather and review information about referred students. The team then recommends instructional modifications or interventions to be implemented by general education teachers or, if necessary, by instructional or behavioral specialists. While this method can result in improved student performance, its intensity of effort and the degree of expertise required for its use make it impractical for use with more than the estimated 5–10% of students who will not have responded satisfactorily to less intensive intervention (Hunley & McNamara, 2009).

Several concerns are associated with a conceptualization of MTSS primarily as a problem-solving process focused on the needs of individual students. First, it is reactive rather than preventive, since the process is typically activated via referral; that is, students who enter the process do so as a result of already-existing academic or behavior problems, and there are few or inadequate provisions for identifying risk rather than failure. Second, its reliance on teacher referral virtually guarantees bias in the selection of students as candidates for more intensive intervention; that is, some students needing intervention (especially those who do not engage in disruptive behavior) will be overlooked, others will receive unnecessarily intensive levels of support, and referrals will be subject to bias across demographic variables such as gender and race (VanDerHeyden, Witt, & Gilbertson, 2007). Third, in many schools the problem-solving procedure itself is poorly understood; that is, the choice of interventions is typically determined (and limited) by team members' particular expertise or experience; the fidelity with which interventions are implemented is typically poor; progress monitoring, if it occurs, often uses inappropriate measures, leading to invalid decisions; and decision rules are neither clearly articulated nor psychometrically sound (Telzrow, McNamara, & Hollinger, 2000; Ball & Christ, 2012). Fourth, apart from the impracticality of addressing the needs of so many children, the one-student-at-a-time focus of the problem-solving team fails to differentiate levels of risk or to consider the potential for responsiveness to evidence-based standard protocol or other targeted interventions of lesser intensity (Shapiro, 2000).

MTSS Planning and Management

A second general set of concerns is presented in Table 36.2. These reflect a failure to plan and manage MTSS in a way that anticipates and addresses the relatively predictable issues and needs associated with its course of implementation (Schaughency, Alsop, & Dawson, 2010). In a study of three schools implementing MTSS, where two of three schools demonstrated significantly improved student outcomes, Clemens, Shapiro, Hilt-Panahon, and Gischlar (2011) traced the third school's lack of improved student outcomes to inconsistent and unclear communication about model implementation and procedures, absence of authoritative leadership, and minimal training, follow up, and accountability, all of which are features of the planning and management process.

Absent or Inadequate Centralized Long-Term Planning

MTSS succeeds or fails not only on the basis of the quality of its components and their implementation as recommended by Keller-Margulis (2012) and others, but

also as a function of the attention paid to process aspects of implementation, such as planning, obtaining stakeholder buy-in, and maintaining implementation progress and momentum (Curtis, Castillo, & Cohen, 2008). Given the magnitude of change in attitudes and practices that accompanies successful MTSS implementation in schools, a mechanism for planning and monitoring overall progress is essential. This mechanism often takes the form of a centralized planning team or appointment of an implementation coordinator.

Lack of Consistency or Compliance With System-Wide Routines

While it is important for schools to adapt MTSS structures and processes to better fit their unique circumstances (Burns & Gibbons, 2008), there are elements and procedures that are essential to the model, and some of these should be centrally designated and uniformly implemented across classrooms, grade levels, and buildings within a school district.

Agreement on system-wide routines encourages the adoption of evidence-based practices, makes it possible to monitor fidelity of implementation, legitimizes comparisons of students' performance across school buildings, and promotes the use of resources in ways that best match system-wide priorities. Importantly, adherence to system-wide routines also enables decision makers to rule out issues of quality (of measurement and instruction/intervention) as plausible explanations for poor student performance, an issue of particular concern to school psychologists in evaluating students for special education eligibility.

Inadequate Monitoring or Accountability for Fidelity

A pattern that sometimes emerges and impedes MTSS implementation is one in which initial enthusiasm fuels the adoption of universal screening and preliminary intervention plans, followed by a plateau period in which further progress stalls, often because there is no long-term implementation plan or impetus to continue moving forward. As a consequence, teachers and others come to define MTSS primarily in terms of screening activities, but little or no progress is made toward the meaningful use of screening data and intervention programs are hindered by a lack of attention to matters of resource allocation and the fine tuning of delivery systems.

Administrative endorsement and leadership are well established prerequisites for the success of any major educational initiative (Marzano, Waters, & McNulty,

Table 36.2. MTSS Planning and Management

Issue	Indicators or Red Flags	Implications	School Psychologist as Internal Consultant
Absent or inadequate centralized long-term planning	• Absence of a centralized planning team (representing all stakeholders) to consider options and make decisions or recommendations regarding MTSS policies and procedures • Splintered implementation of components across settings, with extreme variation in quality • False starts and plateau periods in which forward movement is suspended or halted • Protracted discussion, meetings, and guest presentations that lack follow up and yield no discernible signs of progress • Confusion among teachers regarding purpose, components, plan, and MTSS time line	• Vulnerability to shifting priorities, resulting in failure to sustain efforts when there is a change in environment or administration • Objections or resistance from stakeholders who were not included in the planning process • Poor understanding of the overall MTSS framework on the part of stakeholders and constituencies • Frustration and loss of momentum and enthusiasm on the part of supporters • Nobody to champion to ensure that implementation efforts are sustained over time • Predictable obstacles and challenges overwhelm and defeat implementation efforts	• Volunteer to assist or serve as MTSS coordinator or assume responsibility for discrete aspects of planning and implementation • Encourage planners to adopt and monitor long-term plans and draw attention to milestones and successes as they are achieved
Lack of consistency or compliance with system-wide routines	• Overreliance on local entities (school buildings or individual principals) to make decisions, select techniques or resources, coordinate activities, and monitor/evaluate MTSS • Adoption of nonevidence-based (or poorly conceived and managed) practices in some settings • Wide variation among grade levels and/or buildings in MTSS practices	• Stakeholder frustration over absence of prescription/direction regarding screening and intervention selection, personnel and other resource allotments, and data decision rules • Critical MTSS components are sacrificed, overlooked, or compromised because their importance is not clearly conveyed and understood • Inconsistent MTSS practices make it impossible to tie student outcomes to MTSS implementation.	• Use assignment to multiple schools as a vantage point for assessing differences in implementation, noting effective versus ineffective practices • Create flowcharts and forms to document sequences of MTSS problem-solving activities • Utilize local, state, and national school psychology resource networks to bring attention to successful MTSS routines enacted elsewhere
Inadequate monitoring or accountability for fidelity	• Differences among administrators (especially building principals) in priority given to MTSS activities, often resulting from weak mandates and lack of oversight from central administration • No consequences for individual units' failure to implement agreed-upon MTSS procedures • Absence of forum or procedure for evaluating progress toward full MTSS implementation • Assessment, instruction, and intervention implemented, but no method for ensuring fidelity	• MTSS shortcomings not recognized, increasing likelihood that within-child factors will be blamed for students' nonresponsiveness • Needed changes in MTSS policies and practices (based on feedback from ongoing monitoring) are not made • Absence of accountability signals that MTSS initiative is unimportant, further weakening commitment and effort • Poor quality MTSS, lacking effectiveness in improving student outcomes	• When reviewing data, confirm intervention fidelity before applying decision rules • Find ways to utilize MTSS outcome data to highlight system-level issues, needs, and priorities (e.g., identifying students at risk of failure on high-stakes tests) • Volunteer to monitor assessment and intervention fidelity and to give performance feedback

2005), and MTSS implementation is no exception. A centralized mandate for implementation conveys a clear message that MTSS is a priority and that compliance with its provisions is expected. In contrast, a lukewarm administrative endorsement—or infrequent and minimal references to MTSS in administrative communications regarding district priorities and plans—will provide skeptics with justification for relegating MTSS to low priority status.

Finally, planners must include provisions for ongoing monitoring of the fidelity with which various components of the model (such as intervention delivery, screening activities, and use of data for decision making) are implemented.

Shortcomings in MTSS Components and Practices

Most school psychologists are familiar with the essential or basic components of MTSS implementation, which include the following structures and processes:

- A comprehensive, preplanned sequence of progressively more intensive, evidence-based academic and/or behavioral instruction/interventions, with an adequate supporting infrastructure
- Universal screening of students' academic (and/or behavioral) performance through the use of appropriate measures that predict meaningful student outcomes
- Analysis of screening data by teachers, administrators, and MTSS planners to evaluate the effectiveness of current practices and to identify students who are at elevated risk for failure
- Systematic and routine student progress monitoring to document adequate or inadequate responsiveness to early (moderate intensity) intervention, with valid decision rules for making this determination
- Provisions for intensifying intervention when students demonstrate inadequate responsiveness within a given tier of support
- Structure and procedures for analyzing persistent nonresponsiveness to high-quality intervention (i.e., inadequate level of performance or rate of improvement) to plan interventions targeting factors contributing to or maintaining problematic performance (Tier 3)
- Guidelines for assessing students' responsiveness to high-intensity interventions to assist in determining the existence of a disability that might explain inadequate levels of performance and rates of progress toward prescribed goals

It is probably safe to say that all schools have in place some of the above-listed MTSS elements, but that their form, as well as the degree to which they are integrated in a coherent system of instruction and assessment, vary considerably. There are three typical patterns in schools that are struggling with MTSS implementation efforts. (See Table 36.3.)

Universal Screening Data Are Not Used for Decisions

Assessment should be purpose driven; that is, data collection is undertaken to answer particular questions. Unfortunately, in many schools teachers are hard pressed to explain why tests are given other than in response to some state- or district-level mandate. Most schools now conduct some form of universal screening, typically through the use of repeated measures of academic skills such as curriculum-based measurement, managed through commercially available systems such as DIBELS or EasyCBM (University of Oregon), and AIMSweb. A growing number employ social–emotional screening measures such as the School-Wide Information System (which tabulates office disciplinary referrals; Irvin, Tobin, Sprague, Sugai, & Vincent, 2004) or the Early Warning System (which tracks factors such as school attendance that are predictors of outcomes such as high school graduation; Allensworth & Easton, 2005). However, schools have not necessarily articulated the questions that these assessments are meant to answer, the uses to which results will be put, or the manner in which decision-making rules will be applied to the data. Consequently, schools are data rich but information-poor, with data being relegated to folders stored on computer hard drives or, at best, reported to parents by mail. In these instances, schools miss valuable opportunities to use data to inform important decisions about the overall effectiveness of core instruction or to identify students in need of early intervention.

Inadequate Support or Accountability for Teachers to Implement Interventions

While much has been written about the importance of taking specific steps to promote intervention adherence (Telzrow & Beebe, 2002), it is not unusual to find schools in which responsibility for implementation falls almost exclusively on classroom teachers. In some schools, problem-solving teams have compiled a handbook of intervention strategies (sometimes accompanied by scripts) from which they make prescriptions or from which teachers are invited to choose. Not surprisingly, this practice typically results in conclusions that

Table 36.3. Commonly Observed Shortcomings in MTSS Components and Practices

Issue	Indicators or Red Flags	Implications	School Psychologist as Internal Consultant
Universal screening data are not used for decisions	• Routine collection of data, typically through test administration, with little or no follow-up discussion or use of data to make decisions • Inability of teachers or administrators to articulate the questions to be answered by the data • Tendency to add new tests, without also eliminating existing tests • No consensus or common understanding of how results can or should be used, beyond identifying at-risk students	• Purpose of universal screening is unclear, exacerbating teacher resistance and increasing chances that it will be neglected or eliminated as an unnecessary, costly, and time-consuming activity • Valuable information about the effectiveness of curriculum/instruction is overlooked, making it more likely for within-child factors to be blamed for performance problems • Increased risk of test fatigue and resentment of time needed for testing activities	• Use individual consultation to help teachers understand screening data and set class-wide performance goals • Review individual students' screening results only after discussing class-wide results and instructional implications • Adopt a script for conducting data analysis meetings
In adequate support or accountability for teachers to implement interventions	• Classroom teachers assigned interventions to use in the classroom, with little or no detail, training, or resource support (including scheduled time) • Variation in intervention practices (altered intervention protocols, inconsistent or infrequent delivery of interventions, use of strategies based on familiarity or availability) and confusion about frequency and duration of interventions	• Students do not receive interventions as prescribed • Credibility of system and experts is undermined by ineffective interventions and absence of support, resulting in loss of teacher confidence and buy-in • Intervention failure is likely to be attributed to the intractability of the child's problem (within-child factors) rather than to the inadequacy of interventions	• Encourage adoption of a standard, prescriptive plan for interventions • Advocate for adoption of a "no new instruction" (intervention) period in school schedules • Help narrow the range of students and interventions for which specific teachers are responsible by facilitating grade-level deployment of resources
Inadequate or improper progress-monitoring practices	• Inadequate training, guidance, or support for appropriate progress-monitoring practices • Progress monitoring not conducted with all students receiving Tier 2 and Tier 3 services or conducted using inappropriate methods or schedules • Failure to adopt valid decision rules that are correctly applied to progress-monitoring data	• Decisions about intervention continuation, modification, or termination are not informed by appropriate progress-monitoring data, resulting in failure to provide interventions of appropriate intensity • Unable to use intervention data to make special education eligibility decisions, since reliability and validity of such data cannot be verified	• Review technical adequacy of progress-monitoring measures for various decisions • Discourage the use of common (yet questionable) decision rules • Consult current research for guidance in recommending decision rules and illustrating problems with those currently in use • Supplement curriculum-based measurement general outcome measures with other valid and reliable data for high-stakes decisions

interventions did not work, typically because the selected interventions were not well matched to the student's problem, were of inappropriate intensity, or were not properly administered. Adequate infrastructure must be provided (including scheduled time for intervention, as well as instructional materials and personnel), and preliminary and ongoing support (in the form of training, scripts, coaching, and performance feedback) are essential to the delivery of high-quality instruction and intervention.

Inadequate or Improper Progress-Monitoring Practices

Compounding the problems created by multiple assessments is growing concern about the validity of decisions that are being made with data generated in MTSS frameworks. For example, a recent meta-analysis and review of decision-making practices using oral reading fluency measures (R-CBM) advised extreme caution in using R-CBM data for decisions, especially those of a high-stakes nature (Ardoin, Christ, Morena, Cormier, & Klingbeil, 2013). This finding highlights the importance of understanding the differences among measures and their appropriate uses, as well as the need for school psychologists to evaluate the technical adequacy of various outcome evaluation procedures and rules for making both low- and high-stakes decisions.

BEST PRACTICES AS AN INTERNAL CONSULTANT IN A MULTITIERED SUPPORT SYSTEM

The great advantage of learning from others who are further along in the process is the potential not only to avoid their mistakes but also to apply recommendations arising from their successes. Therefore, this section first offers general advice to school psychologists, gleaned from the experiences of implementers who have encountered both setbacks and successes in MTSS design and implementation. Then, specific advice targeting each of the problem areas identified above is provided.

School Psychologists Serving as Internal MTSS Consultants

Get on the train before it is too far down the tracks. In accepting a school psychologist practitioner award from her peers, Dana M. described the transition from being head-quartered in a school closet "stacked with wet mops and cardboard boxes" to a central office suite, and from a job consisting of writing reports "whose due dates were more important than their content" to lead facilitator for MTSS in her district (McNamara, 2008, p. 10). Throughout this transition, Dana managed to keep up with testing and paperwork demands while cultivating a relationship with an administrator who shared Dana's suspicion that there were better ways to address children's school problems. Slowly and without fanfare (and carefully avoiding "RTI jargon"), Dana and similar

MTSS-pioneering school psychologists in other settings began to change the language used during team meetings, introduced more intervention-friendly assessment practices, encouraged the adoption of standard evidence-based interventions, and showed how screening data could be used to identify important trends in student performance. Undoubtedly, the workdays of these school psychologists were a bit longer, and weekend hours were probably spent reading and planning, but their efforts made possible the eventual emergence of the comprehensive MTSS models that are currently in place in their schools.

As internal consultants, school psychologists are more likely to understand the politics and decision-making hierarchy within a building, and are familiar with historical events (such as previous initiatives that succeeded or failed) that may be pertinent to MTSS implementation. They also have established trust and credibility with administrators and teachers, and know which teachers are considered to be opinion leaders (who have earned others' respect, and whose endorsement leads to broader acceptance of an initiative). On the other hand, since school psychologists are typically attached to school buildings only on a part-time basis and are not part of the instructional staff, they also function as external consultants. As outsiders, school psychologists can adopt a more objective and neutral stance, which positions them to bring together likely supporters within the system and to identify problems and priorities in the implementation process. In a best-case scenario, combining the internal and external consultancy roles can yield superior results. For example, a school psychologist may have become aware of a pattern of ineffective behavior management practices at a particular grade level (internal consultant knowledge) and, as a member of the school district's MTSS implementation team (external consultant influence), ensure that the district plan includes provisions for a program of positive behavior supports.

At times, however, it may be necessary to call for the services of an external consultant who is not employed by the school or district, particularly in politically charged settings. External consultants are in a better position to chart a big-picture, multiyear course for implementation and to call attention to counter-productive aspects of the implementation process and also are less likely to be troubled by the byproducts of implementation, such as stress, ambiguity, and conflict (Dougherty, 2009). External MTSS consultants have the most beneficial impact when they are used to (a) familiarize faculty, staff, and administrators with the essential structures and components of the MTSS framework, often through one or more large-group presentations designed to promote understanding and buy-in, and (b) meet with the MTSS implementation team periodically, helping them to discern priorities and assess progress, and troubleshooting problems and challenges encountered along the way. External consultants also can introduce ideas or resources that might not have been considered by an internal team and serve as a nexus for networking with other schools and districts that are farther along in the implementation process.

Pay attention to process issues. Although technical understanding of various MTSS components is essential, implementation efforts are probably more often derailed by a failure to understand and accommodate process considerations such as stakeholder inclusion and buy-in; the need for comprehensive, multiyear planning; and periodic reviews of implementation progress. Too many MTSS initiatives have fallen victim to unanticipated stakeholder resistance (e.g., a labor union's objections to perceived unacceptable changes in teachers' working conditions, leading to rejection of the plan), changes in leadership (e.g., resignation of a student services director who had been solely responsible MTSS implementation), or lost momentum (e.g., a school board's refusal to authorize the purchase of a proposed data management system that was treated by planners as a defeat that could not be overcome).

With respect to process, experience shows that it is especially important to disseminate information at every step along the way so that MTSS is kept in the spotlight (e.g., regular updates at monthly faculty meetings) and stakeholders know that progress is occurring even though it may not be visible from their vantage point. Experienced implementers also have learned the importance of an ongoing training plan that offers learning opportunities tailored to needs as they emerge and change over time (e.g., a guest speaker to introduce MTSS framework, but small group coaching later, to practice generating data reports).

Encourage planners to choose a good data management and reporting system. Commercially available data systems enable school personnel to generate reports along multiple dimensions, including local and national normative comparisons, performance levels and growth rates of subgroups within and across school years, and proportions of students in high- and low-risk categories. Not all measures and systems are created equal, however, so it is important to carefully review options that will meet a school district's decision-making needs in the most cost-efficient manner. Educators sometimes

fail to draw distinctions between measures in terms of the questions they can answer, resulting in the unfortunate discovery that the system they have adopted cannot provide all of the information needed for data-based decision making. The National Center on Response to Intervention conducts periodic reviews of screening and progress-monitoring tools (http://www.rti4success.org), presenting information about different types of measures and their usefulness for various MTSS-related applications.

Do what school psychologists do best: Help teachers understand and use data. Giving teachers access to data, and creating opportunities for them to study and use it, creates far more enthusiasm and buy-in than even the most inspiring guest speaker. The ability to print graphs displaying students' performance over time gives teachers an invaluable tool for conversations with parents, and pointing out accelerated rates of growth bolsters the credibility of interventions. Both are available with good data management systems. It is not surprising that Burns and Gibbons (2008) recommend that the entire first year of MTSS implementation be devoted to the adoption and assimilation of a screening system into teachers' routines, and this phase offers school psychologists a critical opportunity for participation.

MTSS procedures should include a forum in which instructional personnel review reports following each screening event, using them to discuss the effectiveness of curriculum and instruction, and to identify students who require more intensive forms of support. Monthly review of progress-monitoring data by all teachers involved with a given student also is recommended, using graphed data. Kovaleski and Pedersen (see Chapter 6) offer an excellent model for conducting and documenting these data analysis team meetings, and readers can use this model as a protocol for meetings to review, interpret, and apply screening and progress-monitoring data.

Develop a continuum of interventions as a priority, but not the first priority. When teachers and administrators were asked to share their priority interests, they invariably cited a desire to build an intervention program or to learn about interventions that they can use in their classrooms the very next day. Of course, they want improved student outcomes to occur as soon as possible, and it seems reasonable to expect that this will happen as soon as the correct interventions are put into place. However, there are many issues related to intervention development that must be considered, starting with an awareness that primary prevention—or high-quality core instruction and/or behavior supports at Tier 1—

is an essential foundation for manageable and effective secondary (Tier 2) and tertiary (Tier 3) prevention.

Tier 3 is perhaps the most variable of the three levels of intervention intensity, with some arguing for a standard protocol of higher intensity than Tier 2; others arguing for an individually planned set of interventions based on a comprehensive assessment; and still others arguing for Tier 3 as special education (Hunley & McNamara, 2009; Fuchs et al., 2012). While there are differences in how schools conceive and deliver Tier 3 interventions, experience suggests that planners should devote effort first to building a system of efficacious practices at Tiers 1 and 2, relying on the wealth of research that is now available to inform the selection process.

Adopt (and then consistently use) valid decision rules. As recent publications make clear (Ball & Christ, 2012; Fuchs et al., 2012), MTSS decision making can be of a low- or high-stakes variety, ranging from low-stakes classification of students as at risk (and therefore in need of moderate-intensity intervention), through specification of appropriate intervention intensity (with more intensive intervention being made immediately available to students in higher grade levels), to evaluating responsiveness as part of a high-stakes special education eligibility determination. While screening decisions are understood to tolerate some degree of error, there is no room for foreseeable error in deciding whether or not a child has a disability requiring special education, and this principle is especially important for school psychologists as key contributors to the decision-making process.

With an increased amount of attention being paid to MTSS decision rules (using criteria such as slope of trend lines, percentage of nonoverlapping data points, effect sizes, and position of data points relative to goal lines) and their appropriateness for various decisions, school psychologists who are familiar with emerging research findings will be well equipped to guide teams as they formulate decision rules about the adequacy of students' responsiveness to instruction and intervention. Once formulated, rules can be embedded in a flowchart or diagram that shows how to use screening and progress-monitoring data to make decisions about whether to introduce, maintain, intensify, fade, or discontinue current levels of instruction and intervention.

Addressing Problems Impeding Implementation

Returning to Tables 1, 2, and 3, which present several categories of problems that commonly impede MTSS implementation efforts, we turn our attention to the role

that school psychologists might play as internal consultants addressing these problems.

MTSS Purpose and Mission
The first of these categories (Table 36.1) includes problems in the purpose and mission of MTSS as conceived by school personnel when it is viewed as a substitute or prerequisite for special education or as a vehicle in which a centralized team recommends prereferral interventions to be delivered in general education. In settings where these misconceptions exist, there is likely to be inadequate attention to the need for a foundation of evidence-based instruction in general education (primary prevention), along with routine evaluation of the effectiveness of such instruction. Without this foundation, secondary and especially tertiary prevention are either similarly under-developed (lacking an adequate infrastructure) or over-whelmed by the sheer number of students whose poor performance creates a demand for them.

MTSS as a special education prerequisite or substitute. To facilitate the paradigm shift away from a special education emphasis in MTSS perspectives, school psychologists can change their language, using informal conversations and meetings as opportunities to stress effective intervention rather than eligibility determination as the goal of problem-solving efforts. To assist in strengthening core instruction (Tier 1) as a foundation for more intensive tiers of service, school psychologists should consider joining teachers' data analysis meetings, helping them to review universal screening data in terms of class-wide (not individual student) outcomes, and to set goals based on these data (i.e., a designated proportion of students who will attain the criterion score at the next screening event).

To the extent that school psychologists are able, they should attempt to engage upper- and mid-level school administrators in announcing, endorsing, and making frequent references to MTSS as a general education initiative in meetings and presentations. Many school psychologists have close consultative relationships with principals, whose support is crucial to acceptance on the part of classroom teachers, and therefore to the success of MTSS implementation efforts. School psychologists also are often members of special education admin-istrative units, where they can encourage collaboration with general education administrators in convening and supervising the planning process.

MTSS as a problem-solving intervention team. In schools where references to the RTI team exemplify teachers' understanding of MTSS, the team may be valued (and sometimes resented) as the sole route through which (what is perceived as) meaningful intervention in the form of special education eventually can be attained. A preventive, system-oriented response to this phenomenon is the construction of a sound platform for supplemental (Tier 2) instruction. Planning for Tier 2 might seem a daunting prospect to many school psychologists who, according to our survey (McNamara et al., 2013), do not see themselves as experts in instructional methods. However, skills in consultation and collaboration can be used to help planners choose and then build a supporting structure for a program of evidence-based practice.

Planners can choose to adopt commercially available packages, or assemble a limited number of evidence-based strategies from a review of the research literature and from an inventory of those currently available in the school. School psychologists can help with selection decisions by consulting the research literature for relevant evidence-based strategies and by introducing planners to resources, including websites sponsored by the Institute for Education Science (What Works Clearinghouse) and the National Center for Response to Intervention, which evaluate and report features of intervention programs. School psychologists also can volunteer to write scripts detailing intervention procedures and contribute to protocols for training, coaching, monitoring, and providing feedback to interventionists (Noell & Gansle, 2006).

To facilitate appropriate matching of students to interventions, planners can organize interventions into subskill domains. In reading, the areas of instruction recommended by the National Reading Panel (phonemic awareness, fluency, vocabulary, and comprehension) might be used (National Reading Panel, 2000). School psychologists also can recommend the instructional hierarchy proposed by Haring, Lovitt, Eaton, and Hansen (1978) as a helpful framework to classify interventions according to the type of problem they address: acquisition, fluency, generalization, or adaptation. Once interventions have been selected and categorized, planners can turn their attention to an infrastructure that specifies who will deliver interventions, when, using what materials, and to which groups of students.

In working with schools where MTSS is equated with an intervention team, consultants might be tempted to recommend that intervention teams be disbanded, because their existence maintains the status quo, circumvents the need for a tiered system of evidence-based instruction and intervention, and reinforces the tendency to focus on only the most recalcitrant performance problems. On the other hand, there is a subset of students requiring intensive intervention, and their needs cannot be ignored while the school builds a more appropriate MTSS framework. Moreover, it is almost never advisable to dismantle a structure on which teachers have come to rely without replacing it with a credible alternative.

Ultimately, it has been most effective for school psychologists to pursue a compromise strategy that improves problem solving through the gradual adoption of MTSS-friendly components. Such a strategy might introduce methods of data collection to substantiate referrals to the team and to monitor student progress. For example, school psychologists can show teachers how to document performance problems and monitor progress using curriculum-based measurement (indexed to national norms for level of performance and rate of improvement) or user-friendly procedures such as Direct Behavior Ratings (Chafouleas, Riley-Tillman, & Christ, 2009).

MTSS Planning and Management

The second category of problems characterize planning and management efforts (Table 36.2), including absent or inadequate centralized planning; absent or inconsistent compliance with system-wide routines; and inadequate monitoring or accountability for implementation.

Centralized long-term planning. Some schools lack a centralized mechanism for initial and ongoing MTSS planning and monitoring, whether in the form of an appointed coordinator or a team representing experts and stakeholders. Coordinators who have administrative responsibility for MTSS implementation must possess a variety of consultative and collaborative skills, in addition to knowledge of MTSS structures and procedures. By virtue of these competencies, school psychologists are qualified to serve as implementation coordinators and many do so, but, at minimum, they can and should contribute as members of district planning teams.

Organizers who convene planning teams should ensure that the team is neither too large as to be unwieldy nor too small as to exclude important stakeholders, and that the responsibilities of the team are clearly articulated (Sugai, Horner, Fixsen, & Blase, 2010). For example, a leadership team might be given responsibility for setting goals and adopting a multiyear timetable for implementation; coordinating a plan for staff development and buy-in; setting policy, garnering resources, and articulating procedures for district-wide routines; and monitoring progress toward implementation goals. Additional teams might be given responsibility for more discrete tasks, such as coordinating district-wide universal screening activities and data management or for researching and planning a program of evidence-based, multitiered interventions, and then coordinating teacher preparation and integrity monitoring for such interventions.

By formulating a multiyear implementation plan, planners present a big-picture perspective within which specific objectives (such as selecting and piloting an intervention program) can be pursued, without risking a loss of commitment to MTSS should a particular objective encounter unforeseen obstacles. Burns and Gibbons (2008) present a 4-year implementation plan that reinforces not only the long-range nature of proper implementation but also the need to gradually and sequentially introduce various components of the model. The specification of short-term objectives that are linked to a timetable also enables planners to acknowledge and celebrate progress, sustaining effort and contributing to an atmosphere of enthusiasm and shared purpose. The RTI Action Network (http://www.ritnetwork.org) offers a series of brief yet practical papers written by Susan Hall, entitled *Create Your Implementation Blueprint*, addressing each of six stages: exploration, installation, initial implementation, full implementation, innovation, and sustainability. School psychologists might recommend the use of this series as a guide for planning and monitoring implementation efforts.

System-wide routines.
While decision makers should solicit and consider the ideas and concerns raised by all stakeholders, they must ultimately decide on a set of routines to which everyone must adhere, and these routines should be constructed around evidence-based practice. In some schools, concern for ensuring that stakeholders have opportunities for input into decisions leads to seemingly unending rounds of discussion and debate, stalling the implementation process and creating frustration among those who are eager to move forward.

Examples of routines that should be considered are (a) administration of screening measures by an itinerant team, within a set period of weeks in the fall, winter, and spring; (b) presentation of local norms in reporting data for grade levels, school buildings, and classrooms; (c) adoption of a schedule providing a common time for Tier 2 interventions within each grade level, although specific times will vary among grade levels and across buildings; (d) specification of curricula or intervention programs for core (Tier 1) and supplemental (Tier 2)

instruction; and (e) administration of progress-monitoring measures by teachers on a weekly basis to all students receiving instruction or intervention at Tiers 2 and 3 (including special education). Although school psychologists cannot mandate district-wide routines, they can focus planners' attention on the standardized assessment and intervention practices employed in neighboring districts, illustrating how these practices have enabled officials to enhance, track, and demonstrate progress toward important objectives.

Inadequate monitoring or accountability for fidelity of implementation.
The greatest implementation success has occurred when planners create a time line that they use to index overall progress (and periodically report this progress to administrators and staff) and to identify problems that may be interfering with successful implementation. This practice reinforces the continued priority and relevance of MTSS, draws attention to milestones achieved along an intentional multiyear implementation plan, and highlights problems as they surface. It also affords some protection from the disruption that can be caused by political forces and changes in leadership, particularly when planners can show how MTSS milestones correspond with improvements in organizational functioning and student outcomes.

VanDerHeyden (2010) notes that a narrow focus on screening and intervention selection activities can be averted in systems where there are provisions for management of ongoing training, progress monitoring, and contingencies for correct implementation of MTSS procedures. Recognizing the importance of delivering interventions as planned, school psychologists can volunteer to develop observation or checklist protocols to monitor fidelity. In fact, some districts cite school psychologists' relative objectivity as the basis for their appointment as observers who provide subsequent nonevaluative feedback to implementers. As Keller-Margulis (2012) explains, other MTSS components that require monitoring include assessment practices (screening, instructional placement, and progress monitoring); instruction (core curriculum adherence, student attendance, and appropriate scheduling); and decision-making procedures (appropriate and timely interpretation of data; rules for determining adequacy of students' responsiveness).

Commonly Observed Shortcomings in MTSS Components and Practices
A final set of recommendations pertains to several commonly observed shortcomings in MTSS initiatives (Table 36.3).

Universal screening data are not used for decisions. When too many data gleaned from multiple assessments are considered, the validity of educational decisions is impaired, rather than enhanced, particularly when results are inconsistent or contradictory, or when assessments have not been matched to specific questions.

Moreover, many educators lack an understanding of how different measures are designed to answer different questions and how to interpret them accordingly. For example, classroom teachers have questioned the use of curriculum-based measurement, citing its failure to provide more detailed information about qualitative aspects of students' performance, especially in reading. For teachers accustomed to administering diagnostic reading tests, it is easy to understand how curriculum-based measurement's use of a 1-minute oral reading probe seems inadequate. However, when reminded that curriculum-based measurement is considered to be only an indicator of overall skill, and that the purpose of screening is to assess the effectiveness of a curriculum and to identify students who may be at risk for failure—and to do so with a minimum of time and effort—teachers are more likely to accept curriculum-based measurement as a screener, especially if they know that diagnostic measures can be employed when other assessment questions must be answered.

Some educators criticize screeners for incorrectly classifying some students with respect to their risk for academic failure. However, a certain degree of error is understood to exist when a cutting score is established on a screening measure (i.e., some students will be incorrectly classified as being at risk when they are not and others will be incorrectly classified as not being at risk when in fact they are), and this error is regarded as acceptable when making low-stakes decisions. Similarly, criterion-referenced measures designed to evaluate whether a particular body of knowledge has been learned (such as proficiency measures administered by state mandate) should not be used as screeners, although teams can use these measures to better understand the areas in which an at-risk student is experiencing difficulty.

School psychologists' expertise in assessment is perhaps their greatest asset in selling themselves as valuable contributors to MTSS planning and implementation. In place of the more typical role of inservice presenters to after-school audiences, school psychologists can volunteer to serve as data coaches during teacher team meetings, using graphs and reports to illustrate the ways in which actual data can be used to answer questions and make instructional decisions.

Inadequate support for teachers to implement interventions. Especially in problem-solving (versus standard protocol) MTSS intervention models, it is not uncommon for teachers to express frustration or confusion about how and when to deliver recommended interventions. School psychologists need not exacerbate this problem by compiling reference binders filled with intervention strategies. Instead they can help guide planners to consult resources for standardized, evidence-based strategies (such as the What Works Clearinghouse, at http://ies.ed.gov/ncee/wwc/), and lead discussions about ways to build and, later, to troubleshoot supporting infrastructure. Adequacy of intervention infrastructure does not necessarily mean that schools must incur additional expense, although it might mean that existing resources need to be deployed more strategically. At a given grade level, for example, one of three classroom teachers might be assigned to provide Tier 2 instruction to a group of students drawn from across all three classrooms, while the remaining teachers supervise other students during a no new instruction period.

Most successful interventions are those that have been planned and specified in advance rather than selected on a case-by-case basis. Such interventions are more likely to benefit from an adequate infrastructure of scheduled time, adequate resources, and appropriate training of implementers. As internal consultants, school psychologists can use their routine presence in school buildings to informally monitor and support teachers' learning, offering intervention demonstrations, coaching, and performance feedback.

Inadequate or improper progress-monitoring practices. General outcome measures (e.g., R-CBM) are probably the most commonly used instruments for assessing students' levels of performance and progress toward academic goals. However, other measures have emerged as valuable resources, including skills-based and subskill mastery measures, and the use of these and other data sources has been encouraged in recent publications (Fuchs et al., 2012). These recommendations merit serious consideration in light of findings that, while R-CBM is a valid and reliable screening measure that also can be used for monitoring progress relative to normative standards, it has serious limitations as an ipsative (within-student) measure of progress, especially when decisions are based on data collected over limited time periods (Ardoin et al., 2013).

Students whose progress is routinely monitored include those who ultimately will be evaluated for special education eligibility, placing them at high risk for improper decisions. As experts in assessment and data interpretation, school psychologists—perhaps alone among school personnel engaged in MTSS activities—have a unique and critical role to play in recommending valid progress-monitoring measures, schedules, and decision rules.

SUMMARY

The notion of best practice is especially challenging when attempting to translate into daily practice all that has been learned from the research on components of high-quality MTSS. For example, while some standard protocol intervention packages have been judged to meet best practice evidence standards, their cost may put them beyond the reach of a small, rural school district. And, although MTSS can lead to improved student performance outcomes, the field of education does not always welcome initiatives requiring a dramatic shift in attitudes and practice. However, as the trend toward adoption of MTSS moves inexorably forward in schools across the country, school psychologists are faced with decisions about how they can best participate in and contribute to successful implementation.

We have suggested that school psychologists' education and expertise (especially in assessment) places them in positions of potential MTSS leadership as internal consultants while acknowledging that limitations on skills and opportunities exist and must be addressed or accommodated. The principal of a school building will not necessarily think to invite into the MTSS planning process a school psychologist who has long been regarded as the person who tests children for special education eligibility, and while much can be done to persuade this principal otherwise, personnel shortages and legally mandated service priorities are less amenable to change, so must be accommodated.

In this chapter we examined a number of counterproductive trends and predictable obstacles to MTSS, including poorly conceived purposes and mission, inadequate planning and management of the implementation process, and the use of questionable or ineffective components and procedures. We offered a set of five general recommendations for school psychologists' involvement, and specific advice for responding to challenges, based on the experiences of internal and external consultants.

AUTHOR NOTE

Disclosure. Kathy McNamara has a financial interest in books she authored or coauthored referenced in this chapter.

REFERENCES

Allensworth, E., & Easton, J. (2005). *The on-track indicator as a predictor of high school graduation.* Chicago, IL: Consortium on Chicago School Research.

Ardoin, S. P., Christ, T. J., Morena, L. S., Cormier, D., & Klingbeil, D. (2013). A systematic review and summarization of the recommendations and research surrounding curriculum based measurement of oral reading fluency (CBM-R) decision rules. *Journal of School Psychology, 51,* 1–18. doi:10.1016/j.jsp.2012.09.004

Ball, C. R., & Christ, T. J. (2012). Supporting valid decision making: Uses and misuses of assessment data within the context of RTI. *Psychology in the Schools, 49,* 231–244. doi:10.1002/pits.21592

Burns, M., & Gibbons, K. (2008). *Implementing response-to-intervention in primary and secondary schools: Procedures to assure scientific-based practices.* New York, NY: Routledge.

Chafouleas, S. M., Riley-Tillman, T. C., & Christ, T. J. (2009). Direct Behavior Rating (DBR): An emerging method for assessing social behavior within a tiered intervention system. *Assessment for effective intervention, 34,* 195–200. doi:10.1177/1534508409340391

Clemens, N., Shapiro, E., Hilt-Panahon, A., & Gischlar, K. (2011). Student achievement outcomes. In E. Shapiro, N. Zigmond, T. Wallace, & D. Marston (Eds.), *Models for implementing response to intervention.* (pp. 77–96). New York, NY: Guilford Press.

Curtis, M., Castillo, J., & Cohen, R. (2008). Best practices in system-level change. In A. Thomas & J. Grimes (Eds.), *Best Practices in School Psychology V.* (pp. 887–902). Bethesda, MD: National Association of School Psychologists.

Dougherty, A. M. (2009). *Psychological consultation in school and community settings.* (5th ed.). Belmont, CA: Brooks-Cole.

Fuchs, D., Fuchs, L. S., & Compton, D. L. (2012). Smart RTI: A next-generation approach to multilevel prevention. *Exceptional Children, 78,* 263–279.

Greenwood, C. R., & Kim, J. M. (2012). Response to intervention (RTI) services: An ecobehavioral perspective. *Journal of Educational and Psychological Consultation, 22,* 79–105. doi:10.1080/10474412.2011.649648

Haring, N. G., Lovitt, T. C., Eaton, M. D., & Hansen, C. L. (1978). *The fourth R: Research in the classroom.* Columbus, OH: Merrill.

Hunley, S., & McNamara, K. (2009). *Tier 3 of the RTI model: Problem-solving through a case study approach.* (A joint publication with the National Association of School Psychologists). Thousand Oaks, CA: Corwin.

Irvin, L., Tobin, T., Sprague, J., Sugai, G., & Vincent, C. (2004). Validity of office discipline referral measures as indices of school-wide behavioral status and effects of school-wide behavioral interventions. *Journal of Positive Behavior Interventions, 6,* 131–147. doi:10.1177/10983007040060030201

Keller-Margulis, M. (2012). Fidelity of implementation framework: A critical need for response to intervention models. *Psychology in the Schools, 49,* 342–352. doi:10.1002/pits.21602

Kratochwill, T. (2007). Preparing psychologists for evidence-based school practice: Lessons learned and challenges ahead. *American Psychologist, 62*, 843–845. doi:10.1002/pits.20524

Machek, G., & Nelson, J. (2010). School psychologists' perceptions regarding the practice of identifying reading disabilities: Cognitive assessment and response to intervention considerations. *Psychology in the Schools, 47*, 230–245. doi:10.1002/pits.20467

Marzano, R. J., Waters, T., & McNulty, B. A. (2005). *School leadership that works: From research to results*. Alexandria, VA: Association for Supervision and Curriculum Development.

McNamara, K. (2008, Summer). Dana Marolt wins OSPA's best practices award. *The Ohio School Psychologist, 53*, p. 10.

McNamara, K., & Hollinger, C. (2003). Intervention-based assessment: Evaluation rates and eligibility findings. *Exceptional Children, 69*, 181–194. doi:10.1111/1540-5826.00072

McNamara, K., York, J., Kubick, R., McMahon, C., & Clark, P. (2013). [Ohio School Psychologists Association omnibus survey]. Unpublished raw data.

National Association of School Psychologists. (2010). *Model for comprehensive and integrated school psychological services*. Bethesda, MD: Author. Retrieved from http://www.nasponline.org/standards/2010standards/2_PracticeModel.pdf

National Center for Learning Disabilities. (2010). *RTI leadership forum.* Washington, DC: Author.

National Reading Panel. (2000). *Teaching children to read: An evidence-based assessment of the scientific research literature on reading and its implications for reading instruction.* Washington, DC: U.S. Department of Health and Human Services, National Institutes of Child Health and Human Development.

Noell, G., & Gansle, K. (2006). Assuring the form has substance: Treatment plan implementation as the foundation of assessing response to intervention. *Assessment for Effective Intervention, 32*, 32–39. doi:10.1177/15345084060320010501

O'Connor, E. P., & Freeman, E. (2012). District-level considerations in supporting and sustaining RTI implementation. *Psychology in the Schools, 49*, 297–310. doi:10.1002/pits.21598

Shapiro, E. S. (2000). School psychology from an instructional perspective: Solving big, not little problems. *School Psychology Review, 29*, 560–572.

Schaughency, E., Alsop, B., & Dawson, A. (2010). The school psychologist's role in assisting school staff in establishing systems to manage, understand, and use data. In G. Gimpel-Peacock, R. Ervin, E. J. Daly, III., & K. Merrell (Eds.), *Practical handbook of school psychology.* (pp. 548–565). New York, NY: Guilford Press.

Spectrum K12 School Solutions. (2011). *Response to intervention adoption survey 2011.* Towson, MD: Author. Retrieved from http://www.spectrumk12.com

Sugai, G., Horner, R., Fixsen, D., & Blase, K. (2010). Developing systems-level capacity for RTI implementation. In T. Glover & S. Vaughn (Eds.), *The promise of response to intervention: Evaluating current science and practice.* (pp. 286–309). New York, NY: Guilford Press.

Sullivan, A., Long, L., & Kucera, M. (2011). A survey of school psychologists' preparation, participation, and perceptions related to positive behavior interventions and supports. *Psychology in the Schools, 48*, 971–985. doi:10.1002/pits.20605

Telzrow, C. F., & Beebe, J. (2002). Best practices in facilitating intervention adherence and integrity. In A. Thomas & J. Grimes (Eds.), *Best Practices in School Psychology IV.* (pp. 503–516). Bethesda, MD: National Association of School Psychologists.

Telzrow, C. F., McNamara, K., & Hollinger, C. (2000). Fidelity of problem-solving implementation and relationship to student performance. *School Psychology Review, 29*, 443–461.

VanDerHeyden, A. (2010). Analysis of universal academic data to plan, implement, and evaluate school-wide improvement. In G. Gimpel-Peacock, R. Ervin, E. J. Daly, III., & K. Merrell (Eds.), *Practical handbook of school psychology.* (pp. 33–47). New York, NY: Guilford Press.

VanDerHeyden, A., Witt, J., & Gilbertson, D. (2007). A multi-year evaluation of the effects of a response to intervention (RTI) model on identification of children for special education. *Journal of School Psychology, 45*, 225–256. doi:10.1016/j.jsp.2006.11.004

37

Best Practices in Implementing School-Based Teams Within a Multitiered System of Support

Matthew K. Burns
Rebecca Kanive
Abbey C. Karich
University of Minnesota

OVERVIEW

Decisions in K–12 schools are made by teams. Teaming has been a common practice within schools for decades, but many school-based teams (e.g., problem-solving teams, multidisciplinary evaluation teams, individualized educational planning teams) are linked to special education services. The focus of recent educational reforms, including response-to-intervention frameworks (RTI), is on improving the learning outcomes of all children. Thus, the focus of various school-based teams has recently expanded to address the needs of all children.

School psychologists are uniquely qualified to facilitate effective teaming given their training in consultation, problem analysis, and educational systems; and participating on various school-based teams could allow school psychologists the opportunity to lead efforts to address bigger systems issues. School psychologists often participate on problem-solving teams, but they may not be fully participating in teams that address the needs of all children (e.g., grade-level team). Moreover, there is a well-documented history of implementation difficulties for problem-solving teams (Burns & Symington, 2002). Therefore, the goal of this chapter is to describe basic considerations, potential barriers, and best practices for grade-level teams and problem-solving teams, and to contextualize both within an RTI model.

The chapter aligns with the National Association of School Psychologists (NASP) *Model for Comprehensive and Integrated School Psychological Services* (NASP, 2010) because it addresses skills that school psychologists can use within various consultation settings, which aligns with the Consultation and Collaboration domain. Moreover, school psychological services are best delivered through a three-tiered model (Ysseldyke et al., 2006), and the skills discussed in this chapter cut across various tiers. Decisions made by grade-level teams most often have implications for Tiers 1 and 2, but problem-solving team decisions are most often implemented within Tier 3.

Schools utilizing well-functioning teams foster an environment that lends itself to a multitiered model of support services such as RTI and positive behavioral intervention and supports (PBIS). There is empirical support for school teaming approaches (Solomon, Klein, Hintze, Cressey, & Peller, 2012), but some educational experts have voiced concern about teams, paying heed to the importance of varied types of staff assignment, structure, training, and processes in place that make a particular team successful (Burns, Vanderwood, & Ruby, 2005). Vantour (1975) cautioned that simply bringing together a number of different staff members will not ensure that appropriate processes are followed and subsequent informed decisions made, which remains a relevant admonishment today. For example, recent research found poor implementation integrity of the team process among problem-solving teams (Burns, Peters, & Noell, 2008) and PBIS teams (Newton, Horner, Algozzine, Todd, & Algozzine, 2012).

Two commonly implemented teams within an RTI and PBIS framework are grade-level teams, which frequently engage in collaborative decision making at the school and classroom levels, and problem-solving teams, which tend to address issues for individual students. School psychologists likely participate in problem-solving teams with some consistency, and the school psychology literature consequently examines the effectiveness of those teams (Burns et al., 2008; Burns & Symington, 2002; Newton et al., 2012). However, school psychologists likely do not participate in grade-level teams, which is unfortunate given that issues addressed by grade-level teams are more systemic in nature than the ones discussed at problem-solving team meetings. Grade-level team meetings could provide a venue for school psychologists to engage in a systems-oriented service-delivery model, which is clearly desirable (Shapiro, 2000).

BASIC CONSIDERATIONS

For change to have an impact on learning, it must be collaborative and embedded, not independent and fragmented. School-based teams are consistent with current approaches to school reform and allow for reflective dialog, collaboration, collective responsibility, and embedded professional development that can lead to positive school reform (Shernoff, Marinez-Lora, Frazier, Jakobsons, & Atkins, 2011). Thus, school psychologists should be knowledgeable about reform process and should also recognize the potential role that school-based teams could play within reform efforts.

Many grade-level teams have adopted a professional learning community (DuFour, Eaker, & DuFour, 2005) model because it focuses on student outcome data and creating a culture of collaboration to enhance student learning. Moreover, grade-level teams that structure meeting time to discuss student achievement are more apt to focus attention toward improving instruction. Collaboration without structured reporting of student achievement does not lead to insights into how to achieve higher gains, and the level of training that school psychologists receive regarding collaboration and data-based decision making is unique among educational professionals.

Educators who engage in effective teaming focus on student achievement, identify and share goals, assess progress toward the goal, make necessary adjustments to instructional plans, and hold all members of the team accountable toward improving instruction (McLaughlin & Talbert, 2010). Moreover, professional development content directly addresses student learning difficulties, and teachers can then focus on acquiring the necessary skills to address student deficits using responsive and targeted instruction.

Previous research in school psychology literature that examined the effectiveness of problem-solving teams found large effects when the model was consistently implemented, but only moderate effects when the level of implementation integrity was less clear (Burns & Symington, 2002). However, fewer than 20% of articles regarding problem-solving teams included enough data to compute effect sizes, which suggested a need for additional empirical research regarding the effectiveness of problem-solving teams.

More recent research on problem-solving teams focused on increasing the integrity with which teams followed the problem-solving process. Two studies examined problem-solving teams associated with PBIS and found that training in a team-initiated problem-solving protocol with coaching led to consistently improved implementation (Newton et al., 2012; Todd et al., 2011), and Burns et al. (2008) found that providing performance feedback increased implementation integrity of the problem-solving process. Thus, there seems to be a research base to support school-based teams, but implementation integrity remains a concern for problem-solving teams. Further research is warranted within the grade-level team framework, considering the lack of studies examining such integrity.

Grade-Level Teams and Problem-Solving Teams in RTI

Effective problem-solving teams are an important component of any RTI model. However, schools that begin an RTI implementation initiative by relying solely on a problem-solving team are likely to experience failure. Consider a hypothetical elementary school with 500 students. If 20% of students experience academic difficulties and are referred for additional academic support in a school with 500 students, then approximately 100 students will require additional support. If the school is attempting to engage in an effective in-depth problem analysis and subsequent individualized interventions for 100 students, then the school will quickly exhaust its resources and declare the model a failure. Thus, an effective grade-level team should drive the RTI process, rather than a problem-solving team, which also transforms the RTI initiative into a multitiered system of support. A multitiered system of support is a general education initiative, and RTI is conceptually aligned with special education, which suggests that focusing on the former rather than the latter would integrate the decision-making framework into school practice and not be seen as a step in the process for referring a student for special education.

Grade-level teams should meet on a consistent basis and follow a specific agenda for each meeting. One meeting each month is dedicated to looking at student data. Immediately following the collection of screening data (three times per year), the grade-level team meets to gauge the progress of all students and identify class-wide gaps. The other six monthly data meetings are dedicated to examining data that are collected to monitor progress of students receiving Tier 2 or Tier 3 interventions. Thus, grade-level teams decide who needs intervention, whether the intervention should have a systemic focus, what type of Tier 2 intervention is needed, and if the students are making sufficient progress. A problem-solving team is brought in when a student is not making sufficient progress within Tier 2 (as determined by the grade-level team) and a more intensive and individualized intervention is needed. Grade-level teams engage in many additional activities, but the focus of this chapter is on the role of grade-level teams within a multitiered system of support. We address only those activities that occur during the monthly meetings in which student screening and monitoring data are examined, because those are the meetings at which the school psychologist is most needed.

Potential Barriers

Although grade-level teams and problem-solving teams are being implemented with increasing frequency, several barriers to implementation occur. As stated earlier, the implementation integrity of various team processes is critically important (Burns et al., 2005). Problem analysis does not always come naturally. Grade-level teams often adopt a professional learning community model, which relies heavily on student data.

However, teams need data-driven dialogue that focuses on current student learning, and many school-based teams struggle to identify common assessments, criteria with which to judge student proficiency, and a process to collaboratively analyze data and improve student learning (DuFour et al., 2005). Thus, school psychologists could collaborate with grade-level teams to help maneuver various assessment issues.

The ideal format of school-based teams is not widely agreed upon. A survey that investigated problem-solving team leadership across several states found that 59% of the respondents reported the case managers to be general education personnel, 47% reported case managers to be special education teachers, and 31% reported case managers to be school psychologists (Buck, Polloway, Smith-Thomas, & Cook, 2003). Respondents to this survey frequently reported more than one professional as team leaders, which makes the role of school psychologists, special education teachers, and other specialists within the problem-solving team meetings unclear.

Effective problem solving relies on a system of school organization that provides a context in which problem solving is integrated into school-wide communication and decision making. Therefore, grade-level teams and problem-solving teams should be conceptually linked and differentiated within any model that uses RTI or a multitiered system of support, but the role of each is often not clear among practitioners, which results in mismatched analyses and personnel. For example, we have frequently found schools that utilize a problem-solving team to determine Tier 2 interventions, engage in Tier 3-level analyses for Tiers 1 and/or 2, or make Tier 3 decisions with grade-level teams based on a level of analysis that is often associated with Tiers 1 or 2. Table 37.1 displays the types of analyses required at each tier and which team should be conducting the

Table 37.1. Analyses Conducted at Each Tier of Intervention and Who Conducts Them

	Analysis	Data	By Which Team
Tier 1	Is there a class-wide problem?	• Universal screening data	• Grade-level team
Tier 2	• Who needs intervention?	• Universal screening data	• Grade-level team
	• What is the category of the problem?	• Comparisons of data from core instructional components	• Grade-level team
	• Is the student making adequate progress?	• Monitoring with a general outcome measure and a skill measure	• Grade-level team
Tier 3	• What is the causal variable?	• Relevant student outcome and environmental data	• Problem-solving team
	• Is the student making adequate progress?	• Monitoring with a general outcome measure and a skill measure	• Grade-level team

analysis and making the resulting decision. However, school psychologists could serve on both teams and could therefore be the liaison between them.

Teachers today need a different skill set to engage in successful teaming than what was previously required, due to the implementation of RTI frameworks. Collaboration is often not reinforced in the schools, and only approximately 33% of those teachers surveyed indicated that they adequately understood how to access student data within the school's electronic data warehouse system (Means, Padilla, DeBarger, & Bakia, 2009). School psychologists are well trained in consultation and data-based decision making, but teachers also need basic skills in these important areas.

Finally, teacher acceptance can be slow, but buy-in is a critical component of successful implementation. Simply involving staff in the selection of programs within school reform by itself may not lead to buy-in without training, support, administrator buy-in, and control over classroom implementation. However, teacher buy-in remained a concern throughout several large-scale reform efforts (e.g., Bryk, & Schneider, 2003), and school-based teaming is no exception.

BEST PRACTICES IN SCHOOL-BASED TEAMS

There are substantial barriers for schools to overcome if grade-level teams and problem-solving teams are to be effective and if school psychologists are to consistently participate in them. Fortunately, there are many well-conceptualized and empirically supported components of an effective team, including data-based decision making, collaboration, problem analysis, parental involvement, and implementation integrity. Below we discuss the five aspects of effective teams and how to implement teams in schools to best address the barriers identified above.

Data-Based Decision Making

Former approaches to grade-level team meetings and professional learning communities involved having teachers self-select a topic of interest, and then discuss common resources pertaining to that topic. There were also thematic professional learning communities that cut across grade levels (e.g., reading comprehension instruction, assessment). Current approaches to grade-level teams are based on the current professional learning community model in which student outcome data are used to identify instructional targets and interventions (DuFour et al., 2005). Teachers within a grade-level team may select a common resource on a given topic, but the topic would be selected with data, instructional practices would change based on the information, and the effects would be closely monitored. Thus, data-based decision making is a core component of an effective grade-level team, and we refer to this team as a grade-level team rather than a professional learning community to avoid confusion with how the term was previously used. The importance of data-based decisions within a problem-solving team framework is well defined.

School psychologists could collaborate with grade-level teams to collect instructional data to help identify academic and behavioral needs of students, to develop interventions for small groups of children, and to monitor student progress. All three of these activities (identify needs, develop interventions, and monitor progress) should occur within effective grade-level teams and problem-solving teams. Thus, we will discuss them in more detail below.

Identifying Student Needs

Many schools are periodically screening all students each year and identifying difficulties by comparing student performance to currently accepted criteria. School psychologists should work with school personnel to identify psychometrically sound measures that can be used to screen students and help to develop acceptable criteria. Grade-level teams would then identify students who score below the accepted criterion (e.g., 25th percentile) as requiring additional intervention. However, grade-level teams should examine all relevant areas of student learning in order to determine what and how to teach. Certainly the Common Core Standards for language arts and math should be considered, and assessments should align with those standards. However, "the Standards focus on what is most essential, they do not describe all that can or should be taught" (National Governors Association Center for Best Practices, Council of Chief State School Officers, 2010, p. 5). Therefore, school psychologists should be sure that assessments that are used to identify student need also address the major instructional targets for reading and for math.

Determining Instruction and Intervention

Data are also needed to decide what to teach and how to intervene. Thus, school psychologists should be knowledgeable in assessment systems to identify instructional needs and intervention targets and to examine systems data. Gickling's model of curriculum-based assessment (Gravois & Gickling, 2002) seems ideally suited to address instructional planning in the grade-level team or problem-solving team process. Data obtained from curriculum-based assessments to determine interventions led to increased student skills in reading (Burns, 2007) and mathematics (Gickling, Shane, & Croskery, 1989).

Data regarding individual students are an obvious assessment focus for school-based teams, but data that reflect a systemic perspective on education are also required. For example, problem-solving teams may collect data on students regarding the number of disciplinary infractions during recess, the total number of student absences within a particular grade, or the location of the school in which most of the reported incidence of student physical aggression occur. Other useful systems data to consider could include the percentage of students who score within the proficient range on state tests, group-administered and interpreted measures of reading and math skills, number of children retained in a grade each year, number of discipline referrals to the school office, frequency of severe behavioral incidents (e.g., student fights), course grades in high schools, and measures of school climate.

Monitoring Progress

Curriculum-based measurement seems ideally suited to monitor progress for groups and individual students. Thus, school psychologists should also be knowledgeable about using curriculum-based measurement to monitor the progress of small groups and individual students. The research regarding curriculum-based measurement is extensive and the procedures are well described. Moreover, there are a variety of curriculum-based measurement packages, many of which provide free assessment materials: Dynamic Indicators of Basic Early Literacy Skills (http://dibels.uoregon.edu), AIMSweb (http://www.aimsweb.com), Easy CBM (http://www.easycbm.com), and Computer-Based Assessment System for Reading (http://www.faip.umn.edu). A thorough review of various screening measures can be found at the National Center on Response to Intervention website (http://rti4success.org/screeningTools).

Collaboration

Collaboration is a continuous process in which educators work together to develop instruction to address student academic needs, check indicators of progress, and revise instruction as necessary until a desired outcome is met (Saunders, Goldenberg, & Gallimore, 2009). Participation in collaborative activities such as sharing lessons, using protocols for decision making, investigating problems, and collectively generating new ideas for practice has a positive impact on teaching practice (Vescio, Ross, & Adams, 2008) and is an important role for school psychologists.

Grade-Level Team

Decisions are better made and enacted when they are contextualized within group synergy, perhaps because of the built-in accountability. Thus, it is preferable for the grade-level team to include all teachers from that grade and all school personnel engaged in the learning process for the children in that grade. However, if there is only one teacher for each grade within the building, then group synergy and accountability can be created by collapsing the team across grades (e.g., K–1, 2–3, and 4–5). At the secondary level, grade-level teams are often replaced by departmental teams (e.g., English department) or by teachers within a given small learning community model. The functional activities of the secondary teams would be the same, but the members might be somewhat different.

Grade-level teams within a multitiered system of support examine student data each month to make screening decisions and to judge adequate progress. We suggest that every educational professional who is working with students in that grade participate in the meeting. Thus, for example, special education teachers, Title I teachers, and speech and language pathologists should participate, especially when examining student progress. We suggest that each elementary school have a data management team that is responsible for ensuring that all data are ready to be consumed at the grade-level team screening and student progress meetings. Moreover, the members of the data management team should be highly trained in problem analyses and should attend the monthly grade-level team meeting that examines either screening or student progress data.

Data management teams usually consist of two members, both of whom are highly skilled in data analysis. The school psychologist is often one of the two members of the data management team, along with reading teachers, math specialists, Title I teachers, and other personnel who specialize in data-based decisions. A representative of the data management team would attend the one grade-level team meeting each month that examines screening and intervention effectiveness data. If supporting a K–5 elementary school, then each member of the data management team would have to attend three meetings each month to support data consumption. Thus, a school psychologist would only add three meetings each month to his or her busy schedule, which will likely reduce future evaluation activities due to the preventive nature of the multi-tiered system of support model while providing an opportunity to address systems issues. The main reason to have multiple personnel on the data management team is in case multiple grade-level teams have simultaneous meetings, but in that case the school psychologist should work closely with the other members of the team to ensure an adequate skill base and effective process.

The grade-level team meeting each month that examines screening or intervention effectiveness data should only require 20–30 minutes to complete. We will discuss the activities that occur within those meetings below, but readers are referred to the Minnesota Center for Reading Research website (http://www.cehd.umn.edu/reading/PRESS/resources/videos.html) for a video demonstrating grade-level team meetings in which screening data are examined and another video in which intervention effectiveness is reviewed.

Problem-Solving Team

Collaboration in most problem-solving teams is limited to the interactions that occur between professionals during a problem-solving team meeting, which is too limiting of a role. The standard procession of consultation within a problem-solving team process involves a frustrated teacher seeking consultation from the problem-solving team, which then suggests interventions for the already frustrated teacher to attempt, followed by a referral to the school psychologist to determine special education eligibility and needs. This process involves a shift in responsibility from the teacher to the team, back to the teacher, and then temporarily to the school psychologist. The results of the special education evaluation determines where the responsibility eventually ends in that if the child is determined to require special education services then the responsibility is shifted to the special education teacher, but a conclusion of ineligibility for special education results in a shift back to the referring and now hopelessly discouraged teacher.

Unlike the sequence described above, the problem-solving team process should involve a collaborative sharing of responsibility rather than a shift. This is best accomplished with immediate, supportive, effective, and lasting collaboration through the problem-solving team process shown in Table 37.2. It is important that the referring teacher feel sufficiently supported in the implementation process. Moreover, collaborative efforts before and after the conference reduce the length of time required at the meeting. The actual problem-solving team conference should require no more than 10–15 minutes for each child, as any additional time is usually spent "admiring" the problem rather than solving it (Allen & Graden, 2002, p. 568).

Although the number of professionals involved in a problem-solving team could vary among individual problem-solving team schools, key personnel to involve include the referring teacher, school psychologist, at least one other general education teacher, a special

Table 37.2. Problem-Solving Team Activities for Each Step in the Process

Event	Personnel	Activity	Time Line
Referral to problem-solving team	Grade-level team	Identify students not making adequate progress with Tier 2 interventions	Monthly grade-level team meeting that examines intervention data
Initial consultation	Student's teacher and consultant	Behaviorally define problem; collect baseline data	Within 2–5 days of initial request for assistance
Problem-solving team conference	Problem-solving team	Conduct problem analysis; brainstorm interventions; assign implementation responsibilities to specific personnel	Within 2 weeks of request for assistance
Follow-up consultation	Student's teacher and consultant	Assess teacher's understanding of the intervention; assess intervention integrity; problem-solve unforeseen difficulties	Within 3–5 school days after the problem-solving team conference
Review effectiveness	Grade-level team	Examine intervention effectiveness data to determine if student needs are being met	Subsequent grade-level team meetings that examine intervention data
Follow-up conference	Problem-solving team	Report on effectiveness and identify different interventions as needed	Approximately 2 weeks after follow-up consultation

education teacher, and specialized personnel as needed (e.g., social worker, speech and language pathologist). While administrative support is an important variable for problem-solving teams, it may not be necessary for the building principal to be a member of the team to obtain that support. It is highly preferable for the principal to be an active member of the problem-solving team, but the principal should be an active supporter if not an actual member.

We also suggest that the school psychologist, a special education teacher, and one general education teacher be standing members of the problem-solving team. Thus, the problem-solving team would have four standing members (school psychologist, a general education teacher, special education teacher, and principal) in addition to the student's referring teacher and any specialized personnel. However, the general education teacher aside from the student's teacher may not always be the same person. We recommend that one teacher from each grade (or each grade group for a small school) be trained in the problem-solving team process and that that teacher attend the meeting if a student from that grade is being discussed. For example, we suggest that a kindergarten, first-, second-, third-, fourth-, and fifth-grade teacher be trained in the problem-solving team process; and if a third-grade student is being discussed, then the third-grade representative of the problem-solving team would attend that meeting but would not attend meetings in which students from other grades were discussed. If the grade-level representative to the problem-solving team was also the student's teacher, then a different grade-level problem-solving team member would also attend, preferably a teacher who may have taught the student in an earlier grade.

Perhaps more important than the professional positions of the problem-solving team member is the role of each in the problem-solving team process. We advocate for identifying (a) a system facilitator who organizes meetings and monitors the steps of the process, (b) a problem-solving facilitator who leads the brainstorming process within a problem-solving team conference, and (c) a consultant who meets with the referring teacher before and after the conference. It is not necessary for the same person to always be the problem-solving facilitator or consultant, but one person should be designated as the system facilitator. Assignment of personnel to these roles should be dependent on skill rather than position, but school psychologists are ideally suited to serve as the consultant because of training in consultation, data collection, and behaviorally defining problems.

Problem Analysis

Problem solving can be described as the attempt to eliminate the difference between "what is" and "what should be" (Deno, 2002, p. 38). Once identified, this difference represents the magnitude of the problem. Problem analysis seeks to determine reasons for the discrepancy and identify deficits that contribute to lower outcomes so as to inform instruction. The necessary precision of the analysis depends on the decision being made. Decisions made within Tiers 1 and 2 may be made with group data and may only suggest hypotheses. However, decisions made within Tier 3 should be made with individual student data and should lead to specific interventions for individual students.

The problem analysis process within a multitiered system of support focuses on one specific question for each tier of intervention, which is detailed in Table 37.1. The primary problem analysis question for Tier 1 is: Is there a class-wide problem? For Tier 2 the question is: What is the category of the problem? For Tier 3 the question is: What is the causal variable? We discuss these questions in more detail elsewhere, but will use them as the framework to discuss problem analysis here.

Tier 1: Class-Wide Problem

If core instruction is effective, it is expected that the majority of students would respond favorably and reach end-of-the-year goals. VanDerHeyden, Witt, and Naquin (2003) called Tier 1 problems class-wide problems because the data are analyzed by classroom and the resulting intervention usually focuses on a classroom. Class-wide problems are identified by computing a class median for the benchmark data and comparing the median to a standard (e.g., target for seasonal benchmark assessment), and indicate that individual student difficulties are the result of a potential systems issue (Tier 1 problem) rather than individual students with low skills.

For example, consider a hypothetical third-grade classroom with 25 students in it. Each student is screened with oral reading fluency. Of the 25 students screened on the winter benchmark assessment, 14 scored below the winter benchmark criterion of 91 words read correctly per minute and were identified as needing an intervention. The median for this hypothetical group of 25 students was 87 words read correctly per minute. Thus, the class median fell below the fall benchmark criterion and indicated a class-wide problem.

In the above scenario, it would be more efficient to apply an intervention for the class than it would be to pull students out individually for Tier 2 interventions. It would be beyond the scope of the current chapter to discuss instructional practices and interventions that occur when a class-wide problem occurs, but readers are referred to the Scientifically Based Research website (sponsored by iSTEEP; http://www.gosbr.net) and the Minnesota Center for Reading Research website (http://www.cehd.umn.edu/reading/PRESS/resources/interventions.html) for class-wide intervention protocols. Research has consistently demonstrated the effectiveness of identifying and remediating class-wide problems before beginning Tier 2 interventions (VanDerHeyden et al., 2003). In addition, determining aspects of instruction that are ineffective allows a team to address the needs within core curriculum and instruction and to understand why the core instruction being implemented is insufficient.

Tier 2: Category of the Problem

Once class-wide problems are remediated or not needed, students who are struggling are then identified as needing a Tier 2 intervention. Tier 2 interventions generally target the same skills that are targeted in Tier 1 instruction, align with the benchmarking measures used for that grade, and address components of effective instruction for the content (reading: phonemic awareness, phonics, reading fluency, comprehension, and vocabulary; math: conceptual understanding, procedural fluency, and application).

The components of effective instruction provide a useful intervention heuristic in that students who struggle with one area (e.g., phonics for reading or procedural fluency for math) are grouped and a standardized intervention for that area is delivered. Curriculum-based measurements can directly assess different areas of reading, such as phoneme segmentation fluency being an indicator of phonemic awareness, nonsense word fluency of decoding, and oral reading fluency of reading fluency. Alternatively, the percentage of words read correctly falling below 93% could also suggest a potential difficulty with decoding. Most curriculum-based measurement systems provide words read correctly per minute and errors per minute. Practitioners can determine the percentage of words read correctly by dividing the words read correctly per minute by the words read correctly plus the errors per minute (total words). For example, if a student read 40 words read correctly with 5 errors per minute, that would be 40/45 or 89% and would suggest that the student struggled to break the code while reading. Comprehension is more difficult to measure and practitioners may rely on group-administered measures

of comprehension such as the Measures of Academic Progress for Reading (Northwest Evaluation Association, 2010; http://www.nwea.org/node/98) or the Standardized Test for the Assessment of Reading (Renaissance Learning, 2006; http://www.startest.org).

Grade-level teams could examine measures of reading skills to identify the category of the problem and target interventions. If a student scores low in more than one area, then the intervention would target the more foundational skill. For example, if a student scored low in comprehension and fluency, then the intervention would start with fluency, but a student who also scored low in decoding would likely receive a phonics intervention.

Tier 3: Causal Variable

The first step in the problem-solving process within Tier 3 is to adequately define the problem for which the student has been referred to the problem-solving team. The problem must be defined in a way that clearly directs the team to interventions. In a sense, the problem is often obvious to the team upon referral, but until the problem is operationally defined in meaningful and measurable terms, it is inappropriate and unwise to begin considering interventions.

In order to determine the "what is" aspect of the problem, it is important to obtain quantitative data regarding a student's performance. For example, instead of simply stating that a student is facing difficulty in reading and math, the general education teacher could report the average number of words per minute that the student reads, or the student's average scores on math homework, both of which could be compared to a standard derived from meaningful criteria or normative data.

Although the difference between "what is" and "what should be" defines the magnitude of the problem, it may not necessarily define the relative importance of the problem. It is crucial to remember that this difference has its roots in academic and social expectations (Deno, 2002). Depending on a variety of individual student characteristics, normative goals in some areas may not be realistic for some students, and may be less important than other goals. For example, a student referred for behavioral problems may have fewer positive peer relationships than what is considered normative. However, if the student's classroom behavior is extremely inappropriate, this behavior problem may bear more relative importance than does the student's number of friends. Once analyzed in relation to a student's individual characteristics and environmental surroundings, a problem may appear more or less relevant to the individual student's welfare.

The causal variable within Tier 3 analysis is defined as the environmental variable that is both malleable and most closely related to the problem. There are many student-level variables that are relevant, but not malleable. For example, the limits of a student's working memory may be directly related to an academic deficit, but a recent meta-analysis found that

> … training generalizes to other equivalent measures of working memory, but in no case is there evidence of a transfer to other less directly related tasks. This pattern of near-transfer effects in the absence of more general effects on cognitive performance (such as attention or nonverbal ability) or measures of scholastic attainment (reading or arithmetic ability) suggests that working memory training procedures cannot, based on the evidence to date, be recommended as suitable treatments for developmental disorders (such as ADHD or dyslexia). (Melby-Lervåg & Hulme, 2013, p. 270)

Therefore, working memory difficulties would not be considered a causal variable because of the lack of research demonstrating that working memory interventions affect academic skills and because it is not an environmental variable that is within the control of school personnel.

Parental Involvement

Communication with parents throughout the entire multitiered system of support process is vitally important. Every parent within the school should be sent a letter each fall that describes the process. A second letter should be sent to parents of students who are indicated as needing a Tier 2 intervention. School personnel do not need informed parental consent to conduct Tier 2 interventions, but school personnel should discuss what the intervention is with parents and how parents can support the intervention efforts.

When a child is first referred to the problem-solving team because he or she needs a Tier 3 intervention, the parents should be made aware that their child is experiencing difficulty at school if the parents have not already been contacted. Parents should be invited to participate in meetings, share strategies that they have seen work with their child, and have a say in the intervention that is selected for implementation. Though

not all parents will choose to participate in team meetings, they should be welcomed, listened to, and considered equal partners if they do attend. If parents do not attend, then either the teacher or related service provider should interview the parents before the conference, and follow up to inform the parents of what was discussed and what intervention was selected. Parents should then be told how long the intervention will be conducted before the team will reconvene to evaluate the student's progress.

It is important that teams allow parents to exercise their due process rights and request a traditional evaluation if the parents feel that one is necessary if and available data support the validity of such a request. Many parents are supportive of problem-solving strategies and prefer to first try to intervene within the general education setting before considering special education services.

In addition to individual interventions and assessments, parents should also be involved in systemic interventions developed through the multitiered system of support process. Schools should invite parents to meetings in which systemic issues are discussed, obtain data from parent perspectives when analyzing the problem and solution, and share the results of the intervention with all parents. Finally, any district- or building-level task force should include parents.

Implementation Integrity

It is important to implement interventions with integrity. Implementation integrity provides the foundation for assessing student response within RTI (Gansle & Noell, 2007) and should be examined for every component of the multitiered system of support. Agendas are important for various grade-level team and problem-solving team meetings because they help organize the meeting and can be used to document integrity of the process. As outlined in Table 37.1, we suggest using the following agenda, listed as questions to answer, for the three grade-level team meetings each year that examine universal screening data (e.g., September, January, and May): (a) Is there a class-wide problem? (b) Who needs a Tier 2 intervention? (c) What is the category of the problem? (d) Is there anyone who should immediately receive a Tier 3 intervention?

The remaining grade-level team meetings each year (October, November, December, February, March, and April) are dedicated to examining the effectiveness of Tier 2 and Tier 3 interventions. The agenda for the intervention meetings consist of these three questions:

Figure 37.1. Problem-Solving Team Sample Request for Assistance and Documentation Form

Student name:	Grade:	Gender: ❏ Female ❏ Male	Date of referral:
Parent(s):	Referring teacher:		Best time to meet:

Teacher concern:

Summary of data that the grade-level team used to identify need:

Tier 2 intervention (include frequency and duration):

Date of initial consultation:	Consultant:

Behaviorally defined problem:

Relevant information from the cumulative file:

Relevant information obtained from the student:

Relevant information obtained from the parents:

Baseline data:

Interventions attempted before the problem-solving team conference:

Date of problem-solving team conferences: First_____ Second_____ Third_____

Second intervention:

Person responsible and time line:

Intervention integrity:

    Permanent product:

    Observation:

    Self-report:

Date of first follow up:

Third intervention:

Person responsible and time line:

Intervention integrity:

    Permanent product:

    Observation:

    Self-report:

Date of second follow up:

(a) Which students are making adequate progress? (b) Which students are not making adequate progress? (c) Are there any new students who may need Tier 2 intervention that we have yet to discuss?

The questions listed above can be used at the respective grade-level team meeting to organize the meeting. We suggest developing a note-taking sheet that the teachers and the data management team member can complete during the meeting as a method to record action plans. However, those note-taking sheets can also be compiled as documentation that the problem analysis process was followed.

Because a successful problem-solving team process should closely follow problem analysis procedures, specific steps are necessary and should be documented. A consultant should meet with the referring teacher before and after the problem-solving team conference. In order to facilitate and document the process while enhancing communication through the problem-solving stages, we suggest using a form like the one presented in Figure 37.1. Although the proposed form is based on forms used in practice, individual districts may need to make modifications based on their unique systems and needs.

In addition to implementing problem-solving team-developed interventions with integrity, teams should also examine the process with which interventions were developed by conducting a self-assessment. In other words, it is important to adhere to both the intervention as designed and the problem-solving process as intended. Figure 37.2 represents a 20-item self-evaluation in which items are endorsed as *yes* if the team consistently engages in this activity and *no* if not. Next, the team could examine the items listed as inconsistently implemented or absent and decide if and how it could address implementation difficulties. We suggest that the team complete this entire worksheet as a self-assessment at least once each quarter, but also identify four or five items from the checklist (most important items or items with which the problem-

Figure 37.2. Problem-Solving Team Implementation Integrity Checklist

Item	Yes	No
1. Team meets on a consistent (e.g., weekly) basis.		
2. A Request for Assistance form is used to identify the problem and provide data before the meeting.		
3. The Request for Assistance form is brief, but provides adequate information about the problem.		
4. Documentation of consultant meeting with teacher prior to the problem-solving team meeting.		
5. Baseline data are collected and presented.		
6. Data are objective and empirical.		
7. Selected interventions are research based.		
8. Selected intervention is directly linked to assessment data.		
9. Start with interventions that have a high probability of success.		
10. Consulting personnel assist with implementation of the intervention.		
11. Team develops specific implementation plan with the teacher.		
12. Parent information is discussed.		
13. Data collection plan is developed to monitor effectiveness and progress.		
14. Monitoring data are objective, empirical, and directly linked to the problem.		
15. A plan is developed to assess implementation integrity of the intervention.		
16. Follow-up consultation is scheduled between the teacher and one problem-solving team member.		
17. Follow-up meeting is scheduled.		
18. A case documentation form is used to track the team's activities.		
19. The building principal or administrative designee is present at the meeting.		
20. Problem-solving team members have designated roles (e.g., note taker, discussion facilitator).		

solving team has particular difficulty) and complete a self-assessment of how well it implements those items after each meeting. Moreover, an independent observer should observe the problem-solving team with the checklist at least twice each year to provide feedback. Previous research found that using a checklist to assess adherence of the problem-solving team process increased the fidelity with which it was implemented (Burns et al., 2008; Newton et al., 2012; Todd et al., 2011), and adhering to the problem-solving team process with fidelity will likely enhance the outcomes associated with it.

Adherence to an educational practice requires that all involved understand it, which makes successful professional development a critical component of problem-solving teams. We fully support the need for ongoing inservice development for teachers and school psychologists, and preservice instruction in school psychology training programs. Training should be directed toward using collaborative techniques, performing problem analysis, establishing intervention goals, generating practical intervention plans that are directly linked to data, communicating effectively, and managing the process in team meetings.

Multicultural Competence

There is an extensive research literature regarding school psychological consultation, and a smaller but considerable research base for multicultural consultation. The seminal paper by Rogers and Lopez (2002) outlined four multicultural competencies for consultation: (a) knowledge of cultural influences of the process and outcome of consultation, (b) experience collaborating with diverse families and school personnel, (c) skills using a variety of culturally and linguistically sensitive approaches to collecting data across the consultation process, and (d) awareness of prejudice and obstacles to consultation. The four competencies for multicultural consultation apply to school-based teaming as well.

Evaluating Practice and Outcomes

School psychologists should examine both the process and outcomes of school-based teaming. As mentioned above, the agenda provided for the grade-level team meetings can serve as implementation integrity checks because school psychologists can use those agendas to focus the meeting and to determine if the necessary steps to the meetings are occurring. Moreover, the checklist provided in Figure 37.2 can be used to assess the problem-solving team process. We suggest recording

those data and keeping them as a means to demonstrate that process goals are being met.

Outcomes should also be measured to evaluate the effectiveness of school-based teams. Practitioners should examine both systemic and student variables. Systems variables include things such as number of students referred for special education identification evaluation, number of students receiving special education services, number of students retained in grade, and percentage of students who score within the proficient range on a state accountability tests. Student variables are specific to the student receiving support within the multitiered system of support and include, for example, increased academic skills and decreased behavioral difficulties. Thus, school psychologists should record both types of data, but we encourage practitioners to focus on proficiency rather than reductions in special education referrals and placements. Moreover, school psychologists should monitor the reduced frequency of class-wide problems and growth of students receiving a Tier 2 intervention as evidence for effectiveness of grade-level teams, and could record the percentage of students for whom a successful outcome is reached by the problem-solving team process as evidence for effectiveness of the team.

SUMMARY

Problem-solving and RTI/multitiered systems of support are often used synonymously, but the application of the two may not result in equal processes and results. Some school psychologists could implement a problem-solving team to develop interventions about individual students and assume that they have implemented an RTI/multitiered system of support framework, but RTI/multitiered system of support is much more. In order to fully mesh the two complementary concepts, problem-solving teams and the resulting data should be used for many types of decisions including, but not limited to, special education eligibility. Combining both functions would likely assist in meeting the diverse needs of students while enhancing student learning, improving the resulting accountability data, directly linking research to practice in K–12 schools, and providing school psychologists with a venue to engage in desirable professional activities.

AUTHOR NOTE

Disclosure. Matthew Burns has a financial interest in books he authored or coauthored that are referenced in this chapter.

REFERENCES

Allen, S. J., & Graden, J. L. (2002). Best practices in collaborative problem solving for intervention design. In A. Thomas & J. Grimes (Eds.), *Best practices in school psychology IV* (pp. 565–582). Bethesda, MD: National Association of School Psychologists.

Bryk, A. S., & Schneider, B. (2003). Trust in schools: A core resource for school reform. *Educational Leadership, 60*(6), 40–45.

Buck, G. H., Polloway, E. A., Smith-Thomas, A., & Cook, K. W. (2003). Pre-referral intervention processes: A survey of state practices. *Exceptional Children, 69,* 349–360.

Burns, M. K. (2007). Creating an instructional level for reading by preteaching unknown words to children identified as learning disabled: Potential implications for response-to-intervention. *School Psychology Quarterly, 22,* 297–313. doi:10.1016/j.jsp.2008.001

Burns, M. K., Peters, R., & Noell, G. H. (2008). Using performance feedback to enhance implementation fidelity of the problem-solving team process. *Journal of School Psychology, 46,* 537–550. doi:10.1016/j.jsp.2008.04.001

Burns, M. K., & Symington, T. (2002). A meta-analysis of pre-referral intervention teams: Student and systemic outcomes. *Journal of School Psychology, 40,* 437–447.

Burns, M. K., Vanderwood, M., & Ruby, S. (2005). Evaluating the readiness of prereferral intervention teams for use in a problem-solving model: Review of three levels of research. *School Psychology Quarterly, 20,* 89–105.

Deno, S. L. (2002). Problem solving as "best practice." In A. Thomas & J. Grimes (Eds.), *Best practices in school psychology IV* (pp. 37–55). Bethesda, MD: National Association of School Psychologists.

DuFour, R., Eaker, R., & DuFour, R. (2005). *On common ground: The power of professional learning communities.* Bloomington, IN: Solution Tree.

Gansle, K. A., & Noell, G. H. (2007). The fundamental role of intervention implementation in assessing response to intervention. In S. R. Jimerson, M. K. Burns, & A. M. VanDerHeyden (Eds.), *Response to intervention: The science and practice of assessment and intervention* (pp. 244–251). New York, NY: Springer. doi:10.1007/978-0-387-49053-3_18

Gickling, E. E., Shane, R. L., & Croskery, K. M. (1989). Developing math skills in low-achieving high school students through curriculum-based assessment. *School Psychology Review, 18,* 344–356.

Gravois, T. A., & Gickling, E. E. (2002). Best practices in curriculum-based assessment. In A. Thomas & J. Grimes (Eds.), *Best practices in school psychology IV* (pp. 885–898). Bethesda, MD: National Association of School Psychologists.

McLaughlin, M. W., & Talbert, J. E. (2010). Professional learning communities: Building blocks for school culture and student learning. *Voices in Urban Education, 27,* 35–45.

Means, B., Padilla, C., DeBarger, A., & Bakia, M. (2009). *Implementing data-informed decision making in schools: Teacher access, supports, and use.* Washington, DC: U.S. Department of Education, Office of Planning, Evaluation, and Policy Development.

Melby-Lervåg, M., & Hulme, C. (2013). Is working memory training effective? A meta-analytic review. *Developmental Psychology, 49,* 270–291. doi:10.1037/a0028228

National Association of School Psychologists. (2010). *Model for comprehensive and integrated school psychological services.* Bethesda, MD: Author. Retrieved from http://www.nasponline.org/standards/2010standards/2_PracticeModel.pdf

National Governors Association Center for Best Practices, Council of Chief State School Officers. (2010). *Common core state standards.* Washington, DC: Author. Retrieved from http://www.corestandards.org

Newton, J. S., Horner, R. H., Algozzine, B., Todd, A. W., & Algozzine, K. M. (2012). A randomized wait-list controlled analysis of team-initiated problem solving. *Journal of School Psychology, 50,* 421–441. doi:10.1016/j.jsp.2012.04.002

Northwest Evaluation Association. (2010). *Measures of Academic Progress.* Lake Oswego, OR: Author.

Renaissance Learning. (2006). *Standardized Test for the Assessment of Reading (STAR).* Wisconsin Rapids, WI: Author.

Rogers, M. R., & Lopez, E. C. (2002). Identifying critical cross-cultural school psychology competencies. *Journal of School Psychology, 40,* 115–142.

Saunders, W. M., Goldenberg, C. N., & Gallimore, R. (2009). Increasing achievement by focusing grade-level teams on improving classroom learning: A prospective, quasi-experimental study of Title I schools. *American Educational Research Journal, 46,* 1006–1033. doi:10.3102/0002831209333185

Shapiro, E. S. (2000). School psychology from an instructional perspective: Solving big, not little problems. *School Psychology Review, 29,* 560–572.

Shernoff, E. S., Marinez-Lora, A. M., Frazier, S. L., Jakobsons, L. J., & Atkins, M. S. (2011). Teachers supporting teachers in urban schools: What iterative research designs can teach us. *School Psychology Review, 40,* 465–485.

Solomon, B. G., Klein, S. A., Hintze, J. M., Cressey, J. M., & Peller, S. L. (2012). A meta-analysis of school-wide positive behavior support: An exploratory study using single-case synthesis. *Psychology in the Schools, 49,* 105–121. doi:10.1002/pits.20625

Todd, A. W., Horner, R., Newton, J. S., Algozzine, B., Algozzine, K., & Frank, J. (2011). The effects of using team-initiated problem solving on practices of school-wide behavior support teams. *Journal of Applied School Psychology, 27,* 42–59.

VanDerHeyden, A. M., Witt, J. C., & Naquin, G. (2003). Development of a process for screening referrals to special education. *School Psychology Review, 32,* 204–227.

Vantour, J. A. (1975). *Report of the study group on dissociation.* Ottawa, ON, Canada: Solicitor General.

Vescio, V., Ross, D., & Adams, A. (2008). A review of research on the impact of professional learning communities on teaching practice and student learning. *Teaching and Teacher Education, 24,* 80–91.

Ysseldyke, J. E., Burns, M. K., Dawson, M., Kelly, B., Morrison, D., Ortiz, S., … Telzrow, C. (2006). *School psychology: A blueprint for the future of training and practice III.* Bethesda, MD: National Association of School Psychologists. Retrieved from http://www.nasponline.org/resources/blueprint/finalblueprintinteriors.pdf

38

Best Practices in Providing Inservices for Teachers and Principals

Laura M. Crothers
Jered B. Kolbert
Tammy L. Hughes
Duquesne University (PA)

OVERVIEW

High-quality professional development, including planning inservice activities for teachers and principals, is a critical component in nearly all modern proposals for improving education. Its importance cannot be overstated, as policy makers have come to realize that schools cannot perform better than the teachers and administrators who staff them (Guskey, 2002). In this chapter, the information presented is designed to operationalize portions of the National Association of School Psychologists (NASP) *Model for Comprehensive and Integrated School Psychological Services* (NASP Practice Model; NASP, 2010) regarding consultation and collaboration, practices that permeate all aspects of school psychologists' service delivery.

Sections of the NASP Practice Model that refer to the domain Consultation and Collaboration state that "school psychologists have knowledge of varied models and strategies of consultation, collaboration and communication applicable to individuals, families, groups, and systems and methods to promote effective implementation of services" (NASP, 2010, p. 4). Arguably, planning inservice activities for teachers and principals is considered to be one of the areas of expertise held by school psychologists, who can use their consultative and communication skills to effectively plan and implement services for staff development.

Essentially, the task of planning inservice activities as performed by school psychologists is considered to be a data-driven, empirically supported process that (a)

includes measurements of the outcomes of the programming in order to determine whether or not the teacher development activities have been successful and (b) encourages the maintenance of the newly acquired behaviors.

It may be helpful to consider inservice activities within the larger framework of professional development and therefore to recognize that the learning happens most effectively over time and is enhanced by coaching (Joyce & Showers, 2002) and periodic booster sessions. Singh (2011) contends that effective professional development is embedded in the daily functioning of teachers' work and considers teacher input in its design. Professional development activities should allow for critical reflection, be internally coherent and vigorous, and be sustained over time. Furthermore, teachers and principals must see themselves as the owners of the activities, which should be relevant to all staff, enjoy administrator support, and be rooted in the culture of the organization. Finally, any professional development activity developed by school psychologists should be based upon a needs assessment of teachers' and principals' professional functioning (Singh, 2011; West, 1989).

In this chapter, the basic considerations for planning inservice activities for teachers and principals will be discussed. Following this section, the best practice procedures for school psychologists in planning inservice activities for teachers and principals will be presented. Finally, a summary will capture the most important points to consider when planning an inservice activity as a school psychologist.

BASIC CONSIDERATIONS

Some of the basic considerations that should be explored for planning inservice activities for teachers and principals include (a) acknowledging the federal legislation that is pertinent to the issue of teacher and principal inservice programming, (b) exploring the scope of the professional development activities for teachers and principals, (c) recognizing the nature of adult learning, (d) reflecting on school psychologists' expertise in planning inservice activities for teachers and principals, (e) ascertaining the multicultural competencies needed by school psychologists in planning inservice activities, and (f) investigating the typical problems faced in planning teacher development activities.

One of the major requirements of the 2001 No Child Left Behind Act (NCLB) is that states and school districts provide professional development activities that enhance teachers' knowledge regarding "the core academic subjects that the teachers teach" (20 USC § 1454). Another such requirement is that "effective instructional strategies, methods, and skills, and use of challenging [s]tate academic content standards and student academic achievement standards, and [s]tate assessments, to improve teaching practices and student academic achievement," is provided by states and school systems (20 USC § 1454). Improved student achievement is related to teacher quality, as high-quality teaching has been found to be one of the strongest predictors of students' academic achievement, among other school-based factors (Sanders & Rivers, 1996). Accordingly, considerable public funds have been devoted to professional development. For example, the federal government dispersed $2.5 billion in Title II state grants for enhancing teacher quality, which is the only source of federal funds for teacher training (U.S. Department of Education, 2012).

NCLB also emphasizes the use of evidence-based practice to improve students' achievement, including more than 100 references to "scientifically based research." In the era of accountability enforced by NCLB, schools are required to show that the experiences designed to educate children are selected because of the evidence base of such instructional activities and that the expected learning outcomes for students are meaningful and measurable (Felner, Seitsinger, Brand, Burns, & Bolton, 2008).

Scope of Professional Development Activities for Teachers and Principals

School-based professional developmental activities have traditionally varied in terms of duration, format, and activities (Hill, 2007). The duration of teacher inservice training ranges from one-time workshops to multiyear endeavors (Little, 1993). Formats include workshops, conferences, study groups, peer coaching, and collaborative groups (Garet, Porter, Desimone, Birman, & Yoon, 2001). Activities may use direct instruction in how to implement specific intervention strategies or an inquiry-based approach in which teachers' individual desires shape their professional development plans (Hill, 2007).

Hochberg and Desimone (2010) conducted a narrative review of the literature regarding the effectiveness of professional development activities and concluded that there is a general consensus concerning the essential features of effective professional development. These include "a focus on subject matter content, active learning opportunities, coherence, sustained duration, and collective participation" (p. 97). Furthermore, they concluded that the research suggests that professional developmental activities must enhance teachers' desire and self-efficacy for improving instructional practice. These conclusions were similar to those of Hill (2007), who stated that effective professional development must be of at least several days duration, focus on subject matter–specific instruction, and be closely aligned with the curriculum materials and instructional goals in teachers' schools.

Nature of Adult Learning

Much of the literature regarding professional development stresses the importance of designing activities that are compatible with the characteristics of adult learners (e.g., Moore, 1988). Although a full depiction of the fundamental principles of adult learning is beyond the scope of this chapter, interested readers are encouraged to consult resources written by Brundage and MacKeracher (1980); Donovan, Bransford, and Pellegrino (1999); and Mezirow (1991). Adult learners are more likely than children to be self-directed in that adults can identify their weaknesses and develop corrective plans of action. Thus, staff developers are encouraged to establish a collaborative environment that includes working with participants in constructing the goals and content of professional development activities and in providing opportunities for independent study. Adult learners have encountered numerous experiences and accumulated considerable resources, and they should be encouraged to relate their preexisting knowledge to the respective content or objectives.

For example, teachers can first be asked to identify the techniques they have found to be effective in working with at-risk children, or be asked to consider an at-risk child they worked with in the past, and their approaches to at-risk children can then be contrasted with the recommended approaches of the model being presented. Such an approach affirms that teachers have effective approaches for the respective issue, but also implies that through reflection and consideration of evidence-based practices they can improve. However, Moore (1988) cautions that one of the challenges of training adult learners is their tendency to adhere to their preferred ways of knowing and teaching and the corresponding resistance to self-evaluation. Staff developers can counter this tendency by normalizing adult learners' tendency to resist considering alternative perspectives while identifying the advantages of doing so.

School Psychologists' Expertise in Planning Teacher Development Activities

School psychologists are being recognized as essential personnel in developing programs to enhance schools' capacity to meet the needs of an increasingly diverse population by training teachers to use evidence-based practices (Wizda, 2004). The school psychology profession's adoption of the scientist–practitioner model (Mellott, 2007) and evidence-based practices (Kratochwill, 2007) long preceded the much more recent expectation, largely established by NCLB, that all educators use empirically validated interventions. School psychologists are likely to have earned advanced degrees that provide the necessary foundation for identifying, implementing, and evaluating evidence-based practices.

Multicultural Competencies Needed by School Psychologists in Planning Inservice Activities

In planning inservice activities for teachers and principals, school psychologists need to be aware of their role in helping to build schools' capacity to meet the needs of a progressively diverse population (Wizda, 2004). Regardless of the professional development topic, the content must explicitly address how the subject relates to students from diverse cultural and linguistic backgrounds and how the implementation of the new practice must consider the needs of diverse learners and their families. Moreover, school psychologists need to be aware of the specific skills and needs of school personnel (e.g., teachers' and principals' role-specific skills and needs, bilingual and racially diverse education issues, court rulings, and federal law), students, and their families so these school psychologists can aid in addressing potential barriers to program participation, help plan for student-specific program adaptations, and optimize programs of choice opportunities (Ochoa & Rhodes, 2005).

Typical Problems Experienced in Planning Inservice Activities

Although federal legislation in the form of the NCLB has been passed with an emphasis upon ensuring that all children, and, in particular, those who are vulnerable to unequal academic achievement outcomes, are taught by highly effective teachers, the mandate is less clear in identifying the ways in which states can ensure that teachers are indeed efficacious in their classrooms. Nevertheless, the literature suggests that state and local policy makers who focus on improving teacher quality should, among other efforts, support high-quality, coherent, and sustained professional development for teachers (Learning Point Associates, 2007).

Unfortunately, despite the acknowledgment that professional development is essential to improvement in teachers' and principals' skills, the professional development research suggests that most programs are ineffective (Wang, Frechtling, & Sanders, 1999). Although there are likely numerous contributors to this problem, the majority of programs appear to be unsuccessful because they fail to account for (a) what motivates teachers to engage in professional development and (b) the process by which change typically occurs (Guskey, 1986). Teachers appear to be attracted to professional development because of their belief that such activities will increase their knowledge and skills, assist them in growing as teachers, and increase their effectiveness with their students. Furthermore, teachers' pragmatism translates to a need for specific, concrete, and practical ideas that are directly translatable to their classrooms (Fullan & Miles, 1992; Guskey, 2002). Although teacher-driven interest may seem at the outset to be an area of strength, a waning interest often results in teachers quickly discarding learned strategies.

The second problem, that many professional development programs fail to consider the process of teacher change, may be tied to the inaccurate assumption that changes in teachers' attitudes and beliefs will lead to direct and specific changes in their classroom behaviors

Figure 38.1. A Model of Teacher Change

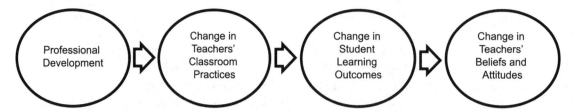

Note. From "Professional Development and Teacher Change" by T. R. Guskey, 2002, *Teachers and Teaching: Theory and Practice, 8,* 381–391. Copyright 2002 by Taylor & Francis. Reprinted with permission.

and practices, which in turn will result in improved student learning (Guskey, 2002). In recognition of this problem, Guskey (2002) has developed an alternative model to reflect the process of teacher change in order to help develop more effective professional development programs (see Figure 38.1).

Guskey's (2002) model stems from the concept that change is essentially an experientially based learning process for teachers that is cyclical, in that it is recursive, rather than linear. Practices that teachers find useful in helping students to attain their learning outcomes are incorporated into educators' skill repertoires while those that do not yield evidence of success are discarded. There is empirical support for this model (Guskey, 1982, 2002). However, there is also an acknowledgment that the process of teacher change is not solely a change in skill set but rather includes changes in attitudes and beliefs, which, when combined, likely lead to multi-faceted changes in practice that result in changes in student learning (Huberman, 1995). School psychologists may find Guskey's (2002) model to be helpful in planning inservice activities for teachers and principals,

recognizing that changes in teachers' and principals' attitudes and beliefs may actually follow changes in practice rather than precede them.

BEST PRACTICES IN PLANNING INSERVICE ACTIVITIES FOR TEACHERS AND PRINCIPALS

In planning an inservice activity, school psychologists will begin by identifying the staff needs and priorities, determining the relevant activities that promote adult learning, measuring the effectiveness of the programming, and designing strategies to promote skill maintenance (see Table 38.1).

Identifying Needs and Priorities

Prior to developing the content for an inservice activity, the school psychologist should determine the needs and priorities for the staff members. It is useful to recognize that individuals in different roles (e.g., administrators, teachers) may hold varying perspectives regarding what

Table 38.1. Summary of Best Practices in Providing Inservices for Teachers and Principals

Four Stages of Providing Inservices for Teachers and Principals	Secondary Components	Tertiary Components
Identifying needs and priorities	• Coming to agreement about the problem • Generating alternative paths • Identifying helping and hindering forces • Choosing action steps	
Leading teacher and principal professional development activities	• Understanding the culture of teaching • Understanding the culture of the school • Pitfalls to avoid • Strategies designed to engage	• Creating a positive professional development environment for teachers • Facilitation strategies
Evaluating outcomes		
Maintaining change		

would be most helpful for a planned inservice program. Nevertheless, it is important for the school psychologist to solicit the opinions of individuals in various roles in order to help create a sense of investment in the process and topics selected. What follow are the steps relevant to identifying needs and priorities (Green, 1994).

Coming to agreement about the issue or problem: School staff members convene to come to a consensus on the issue or problem. Questions that should be posed include whether or not there is a general consensus about the nature of the problem to be addressed and a shared definition of the problem. For example, are personnel all seeing the problem through the same lens, or are there disparate perspectives regarding the nature of the evolving situation or difficulty (e.g., is the problem the lack of specificity of the discipline policy or is it the implementation of that policy)? The school psychologist can identify feasible targets (what can be changed through intervention) by systematically gathering data (e.g., questionnaires, staff development interviews, group discussions) from the various staff members. It is also important to reach a consensus regarding the criteria for analyzing information and establishing priorities so that the process is seen as fair (Oldroyd & Hall, 1991).

Generation of alternative paths: When considering how to move from the current situation to the desired situation, have alternative pathways been considered? Are there other methods of implementing change in comparison to the path that enjoys the greatest support? Green (1994) recommends that brainstorming and using external resources can be particularly helpful in considering multiple ways to move from the status quo to the preferred state. For example, instead of trying to encourage teachers to learn a new curriculum without supervision or coaching, are there local resources that can aid in the learning and practice of these new skills?

Identifying helping and hindering forces: It is important to consider and describe those forces that will either facilitate or inhibit efforts to reach the target. Helpful forces would be those forces that facilitate the group's efforts to reach the target, such as consulting with local university experts or leveraging currently held skills. Conversely, hindering forces may include a lack of skills, a lack of administrative support, or an organizational climate that is not conducive to change.

Choosing action steps: School personnel should select those forces that will help to mobilize success and diminish impediments. An example of mobilizing success is setting the stage for change so that it is well received (e.g., gaining the support of stakeholders or administration before initiating the change). School

psychologists should consider not only the organizational climate and staff philosophies but also the impact of influential teachers or principals.

Leading Teacher and Principal Professional Development Activities

After identifying the needs and priorities of the school system, the school psychologist who is charged with leading teacher and principal professional development should consider the following areas before proceeding: (a) understanding of the culture of teaching, (b) understanding of the culture of the school, (c) pitfalls to avoid, and (d) strategies designed to engage. Since the late 1990s, researchers have studied "leaders of teachers" in schools, documenting what works best (and what tends to backfire) when working to change beliefs and practices.

Understanding the Culture of Teaching

A significant challenge in presenting new ideas to teachers with the ultimate hope of classroom-level implementation is situated in the history and culture of the teaching profession. Embedded in the history is (a) a general skepticism of outsiders disposed to advice giving, often described as telling teachers what to do; (b) an egalitarian ethic that tempers teachers' interest in experts (York-Barr & Duke, 2004); and (c) a sense that teacher professional development is cluttered by fads and trendy causes (e.g., that there is rarely a need to quickly adopt any new practice in teachers' professional development because if you wait it out, the latest educational fad will fade away). In fact, the history of school reform efforts is fraught with stories of teachers' resistance to change (see Cuban, 1993; Hatch, 2000). Additionally, more recently, many teachers have felt that they are under attack from local and federal entities seeking to control and monitor all aspects of their work. Finally, although change is hard and involves some discomfort for all involved (see Marris, 1986), change is particularly hard for teachers who tend to be invested in their work at a personal and emotional level (Evans, 1996). When combined, such factors render the facilitation of teacher professional development as a complex endeavor.

In an example from the authors' practice, a middle school undertook an initiative to implement teacher advisory practices (e.g., having teachers perform advisory activities for students in order to engage students in topics such as social development, career interests, and antibullying strategies). Understandably, many teachers felt uncomfortable with these new role responsibilities, and they were reluctant to engage in nondidactically structured activities that did not focus on an academic learning objective. Consequently, the school psychologist and school counselors, under the advisement of a teacher committee that raised these concerns, created video vignettes in which the most well-respected and well-liked teachers modeled some of the student-advising conversations that teachers would be responsible for handling as a part of their new responsibilities. This intervention immediately helped many of the teachers to feel more comfortable with the activities and therefore demonstrates greater positivity and buy-in to the idea of conducting advisory activities in their classrooms.

With this example in mind, the informed school psychologist can diffuse some of the challenges in the teaching culture. The following strategies, rooted in adult learning theory (Kegan, 1994), provide helpful guideposts regarding how to create a bridge for teachers by validating current beliefs and practices while simultaneously extending them in new directions:

- Ask teachers what they already know about—or want to know about—related to the teacher professional development topic.
- Survey teachers regarding both successes and challenges on the topic prior to the teacher professional development learning events.
- Invite teachers to share stories from their experiences, such as K–12 students or teachers of K–12 students, that connect with the teacher professional development topic.

These strategies require the school psychologist to devote additional time before and during teacher professional development sessions. However, the payoff is almost always worth it. Teachers bring decades of history with them, beginning with their apprenticeship of observation (Lortie, 1975) as K–12 students straight through to the class they just taught this morning. This significant amount of time spent in schools creates deeply rooted mental models for teachers in terms of what types of instruction and interaction with students are appropriate. Accessing those mental models and validating teacher experiences will put school psychologists in a much better position to meaningfully place newly created thoughts and experiences inspired by the teachers' professional development activities. This constructive developmental approach is particularly important when asking teachers to consider thinking and acting in ways that they themselves have never encountered as learners or facilitated as teachers.

Understanding the Culture of the School

In addition to understanding the culture of teaching, it is also important for the school psychologist, as the teacher professional development facilitator, to understand local school dynamics before planning the professional development session. These dynamics can include (a) issues related to power and control, (b) relationships that need to be facilitated or avoided, and (c) competing initiatives that may clash with or complement the specific topic or initiative.

The most successful teacher leaders have a capacity to connect the dots between the people and policies relevant in the teacher professional development activities (Margolis, 2012; Margolis & Huggins, 2012). That is, effective teacher professional development activities must clearly connect issues that relate to the who, how, and when of teachers acting on the new knowledge presented to them. Given that teachers are constantly bombarded by new information and mandates from multiple constituencies, a few suggestions for the teacher professional development initiative follow:

- *Name the ugly:* Teachers are already dancing with the elephant in the room, so do not be afraid to be explicit about the local challenges that will make the teacher professional development topic difficult to put into practice. Although this openness may be counterintuitive, such openness will resonate with teachers who already face the challenges of idea implementation minute to minute in classroom life.
- *Provide a cohesive frame:* Frame the teacher professional development initiative as connected to other work that teachers need to be doing anyway (e.g., use the Premack Principle, in which more probable behaviors will influence less probable behaviors). If teachers see some sort of systemic coherence between what they have to do and the teacher professional development activity, they are more likely to engage and follow through.
- *Create conversations:* Advance the teacher professional development topic as a chance to enhance relationships in the building between teachers, administrators, and students. Teachers work in a relationship-based profession. The more the school psychologist can demonstrate how the teacher professional development is ultimately about better relationships, the more open teachers will be to listening and, little by little, changing what they do. This approach fits well with the collaborative relationships that school psychologists hope to foster by conducting consultation in school systems.

Pitfalls to Avoid

Researchers who have studied how teachers change have documented specific approaches to teacher professional development that seem to work less well than others. Generally, these approaches neglect the nature of how teachers learn (Gallucci, 2008; Lave & Wenger, 1991) and the personal nature of how teachers' work evolves in relation to others (Korthagen, 2010). Specifically, as a school psychologist charged with leading teacher professional development, be wary of the following:

- *Overstating the usefulness of the teacher professional development information:* Teachers have seen many remedies that were supposed to fix all educational problems come and go before. The reality of day-to-day irregularities informs them that there are no grand solutions that will always work in every circumstance.
- *Failing to connect teacher professional development with the actual work of teachers and teaching:* If teachers are unable to see how the teacher professional development relates to their students and their classroom, then they will likely tune out and then move on.
- *Talking too much:* Teachers, like all learners, need to be engaged and motivated in order to learn. In other words, use the best teaching strategies when facilitating teacher professional development, many of which keep teachers active.

An example of a failed teacher development activity from the authors' own practice was at a district in which each year the school psychologist was instructed to provide a half-day workshop to all of the teachers to update them on their legal responsibilities regarding students with disabilities in their classrooms in accordance with state and federal mandates. Often, the mandates were contradictory to information that had been previously presented (e.g., a disability category of student exceptionality that had been phased out), which rendered the information suspect to the teachers. Many of the teachers could not see how this information fit with the actual work of teachers and teaching. Finally, the workshop was delivered in a didactic model that did not permit much feedback and discussion regarding the topics. The teachers typically left these sessions bored and demoralized about their new responsibilities.

Strategies Designed to Engage

The closer the teacher professional development mirrors the actual work of teaching, the higher the likelihood of its use (City, Elmore, Fiarman, & Teitel, 2009; Margolis

& Doring, 2012). Additionally, the more support that is provided within the school environment (e.g., school culture, administrative recognition), the greater the probability of achieving the desired results. With this in mind, below are suggestions for how the school psychologist can create a positive teacher professional development environment and facilitate engagement. To create a positive teacher professional development environment, consider the following:

- *Make the teacher professional development about the teachers:* That is, first be teacher centered and then be topic centered.
- *Integrate the strategic use of humor:* Research has shown that carefully planned levity can relax the teacher learning environment and pave the way for teachers to be able to grapple with more difficult and serious topics (Margolis, 2008).
- *Be humble:* Avoid the appearance of being the all-knowing expert. Use a collaborative approach by encouraging all to share knowledge, experiences, suggestions, fears, dilemmas, and even mistakes.

Consider the following strategies to increase engagement:

- *Connect the teacher professional development as much as possible to the actual work of teachers and teaching:* Artifacts of practice (e.g., student work) are good, videos that illustrate the topic used with students in classrooms are better, and in-classroom demonstrations are the gold standard. Such "existence proofs" (see Gallucci, 2008, pp. 555–565; Intrator & Kunzman, 2009) show real-life examples in a manner that is consistent with how teachers actually work. The training can then transcend the traditional limitations of the workshop model, which has been shown to have limited impact on teachers (Lee, 2011; Wilson & Berne, 1999).
- *Engage teachers in the ideas being presented through role-playing and model teaching:* Role-playing scenarios provide an opportunity to move through the logistics of the implementation of the teacher professional development activity. Furthermore, active engagement with the task will highlight both the pitfalls and possibilities of the new ideas.
- *Frame the ideas as adaptable, flexible, and connected to what teachers are already doing:* Communication should convey that idea implementation in teacher professional development is experimental and experiential, rooted in small trials in which all educators are working together to get gradually better at what they

do (Morris & Heibert, 2011). If it is emphasized that nobody has all the answers, and everyone makes mistakes when learning something new, teachers will likely be more open to giving the initiative a chance.

Although there will be significant challenges to facilitating a teacher professional development activity when working within a school system, there are also some advantages. The local school psychologist is less likely to be perceived as an outsider coming in to tell teachers what to do. Familiarity with the students, teachers, and daily routines in the district give credibility to the desire to provide information that is useful. Adept school psychologists will leverage this information and established relationships in service of improving the lives of teachers and the success of students. Reciprocally, teachers will then be more likely to respect what the school psychologist has to share, potentially even integrating this new information into their beliefs, and even their practices.

Evaluating Outcomes

Most inservice trainings focus on the criteria of teacher or principal satisfaction to evaluate inservice presentations. While this method is arguably important, it is also sorely inadequate to measure the effectiveness of inservice training activities. In reflection of Guskey's (2002) model of change, alterations in teachers' and principals' attitudes and beliefs are the final step in the process of new behaviors introduced through professional development activities. Guskey (1986) argues that satisfaction may follow behavior change when teachers become comfortable with a new technique or see improvements in the learning of their students.

Although there are other methods of measuring outcomes (e.g., peer evaluations, linking of instruction to state and federal standards), arguably the most important metric of change is improvements in students' classroom behavior and learning. Evaluations should include observations of teacher practice as well as documented improvement in students' learning and behavior (Harriott, 2004). However, a historic difficulty that educators, such as school psychologists, have encountered in conducting intervention research or evaluating intervention programs in school settings is that it is often impossible to meet the demands of the ideal experimental research design, which requires randomization and the use of a control group (de Anda, 2007). An alternative to the use of an experimental design is the use of quasi-experimental designs,

such as a paired comparison design, in which an individual serves as his or her own control, in conjunction with a separate-sample pretest–posttest control group design, in order to increase internal and external validity while overcoming the problems associated with implementing a true experimental design.

Another means of evaluating the effectiveness of inservice programming is to use curriculum-based measurement (CBM) to document changes in a student's performance in an academic subject. CBM involves a brief (1–5 minutes) weekly assessment in which the teacher counts the number of correct and incorrect responses made in the time allotted to find the child's score. For example, a child's reading fluency (e.g., reading speed and accuracy) may be assessed by having the child read aloud for 1 minute. The child's scores are then recorded on a graph and compared to the expected performance of a child of his or her age at that point in the school year. The graphing of the information is particularly valuable, as the child's performance may be quickly assessed to quantify the rate of improvement (slope), which can be used by an educator to assess the adequacy of the teaching (Fuchs & Fuchs, 2004).

An example of the use of CBM in documenting improvement in a child's reading skills can be provided through a case in which an elementary school student was receiving an empirically supported direct instruction reading curriculum, and was seeming to benefit, but the progress was not yet able to be observed through norm-referenced measures because of the once-a-year nature of these assessments. The school psychologist worked with the teacher to begin conducting weekly CBM probes with the whole class, so that the teacher could see the rate of improvement not only for the target student but for comparison peers as well. These CBM probes began taking the place of tests in the classroom, since these assessments were quick, done frequently, and yielded important data in determining whether the current instructional pace and delivery were adequate, or whether changes needed to be made so that the target student's aimline was narrowing the gap between the student's own projected progress and that of the student's peers.

Similarly, Evans and Owens (2010) describe tools to measure a student's response to behavioral intervention in a shorter period of time, known as short-cycle assessments. Such assessments may be more feasible (requiring less effort, training requirements, or time) or relevant (with an emphasis upon the demonstration of the association between assessment and practice, including academic outcomes; Evans & Owens, 2010).

In a special issue of *School Psychology Review* on using behavioral assessment within problem-solving models, a number of low-effort assessments that may be used to screen and monitor responses to intervention over time were presented (see Evans & Owens, 2010, for additional information). An example of a short-cycle assessment would be to take a few items from a published behavioral rating scale (e.g., the Social Skills Rating System–Teacher Form; Gresham & Elliott, 1990) that appear to be particularly sensitive to behavior change (e.g., "Disturbs ongoing activities"; Gresham et al., 2010) to use as a progress monitoring tool for behavior intervention. The items should be matched to the behavioral goal (the item provided as an example was used to assess changes in a student's social behavior).

Cigularov, Chen, Thurber, and Stallones (2008) similarly argue that nonexperimental designs can be a part of rigorous evaluation when random assignment control group designs are not feasible for practical and ethical reasons. These researchers utilized three methodological approaches (a rolling group design, an internal referencing strategy, and a minimum competency approach) to evaluate the efficacy of a school-based suicide education program, and they assert that their study demonstrates the utility and practicality of applying three methodological approaches under ethical challenges and practical restraints (Cigularov et al., 2008).

Therefore, although there are often statistical challenges to evaluating educational programs, there are opportunities for school psychologists to be creative and accountable in solving such dilemmas.

Another important consideration for school psychologists when evaluating the efficacy of an intervention is to incorporate measures of intervention fidelity—the degree to which the intervention is implemented as it is designed—as well as of the consistency of the intervention. Perhaps most important to recognize is that although measuring students' outcomes in the classroom may be difficult, it is the most valuable indicator of the success of an inservice program.

Maintaining the Change

One of the challenges that follow executing a professional development activity for teachers and principals is maintaining changes that occurred as a result of participating in the inservice programming. For this reason, change efforts must be well integrated in the school's organizational culture so that new behaviors are supported by the environment. Green (1994) discusses Killion and Kaylor's (1991) follow-up techniques involving regular group meetings designed to include problem solving, feedback, and assistance for those using new interventions. It is also important to have a committed, supportive administrator who provides leadership and exudes enthusiasm for the changes being made (Green, 1994).

Joyce and Showers (2002) advocate the use of coaching in contributing to the transfer of newly acquired knowledge and skills from teachers to their classrooms. They report that coached teachers, in comparison with teachers who are not coached but have identical initial training experiences, practice new strategies more frequently and adeptly, adapt the strategies more appropriately to their own goals and contexts, retain and increase their skills over time, are more likely to explain the new models of teaching to their students (thereby increasing their relevance), and demonstrate a clearer understanding of the purposes and uses of the new strategies (Joyce & Showers, 2002).

An example of this model is in a district in which all new teachers are assigned formal mentors to provide support in the district's goal areas: curriculum design, curriculum implementation, behavior management, and parent–teacher collaboration. In this model, new teachers are encouraged to meet with their mentors twice during the first week of each month regarding one of these four goal areas. The mentor observes the teacher in regard to the identified issue (e.g., behavior management), and the mentor and teacher meet to discuss the findings of the observation and develop a brief, empirically supported plan to remedy any weaknesses identified. The remainder of the month includes two meetings each week: one in which the mentor observes the teacher and one in which the mentor and teacher meet to discuss the findings of the observation as well as to tailor the intervention approach accordingly. Then, after the month concludes, the mentor and teacher move to another new goal and begin the process once again. Moreover, regular supervision and continued evaluation of student-level change are also critical in the maintenance phase of change.

Finally, celebration of the successes of the teachers' and principals' accomplishments by the school psychologist is a valuable way to validate efforts to improve the learning experience for children and their families. Honoring educators for helping to improve the education of children and adolescents is constructive and useful in the journey to sustain change efforts (Green, 1994).

SUMMARY

School psychologists are uniquely situated to design, implement, and evaluate professional development inservice activities for teachers and principals. Using consultation skills that are foundational to all of their professional interactions, school psychologists bring a knowledge base and conviction to increase the skill capacity of all educational staff (e.g., teachers, principals, administrators) in order to positively affect the lives of students. Specifically, using empirically informed learning processes and practices, school psychologists are able to design professional development activities that match the needs of the adult learners.

The commitment to evidence-based practices ensures that not only are the activities provided in the inservice programming evidence based, but so too is the commitment to evaluate the usefulness of teacher professional development. Furthermore, facility in establishing working relationships provides opportunities for the school psychologist to support real-time teacher professional development strategies with the teacher in the classroom.

For the local school psychologist, the inservice program provides a particularly compelling opportunity to effect change. The advantage is realized when the design, implementation, and evaluation of the inservice activity is steeped in the context that drives the need for the teacher professional development. The opportunity to provide teachers and principals with support through follow-up and maintenance strategies offers the best opportunity for success.

AUTHOR NOTE

The authors wish to thank Jason Margolis, Duquesne University, for his contributions to this chapter.

REFERENCES

Brundage, D. H., & MacKeracher, D. (1980). *Adult learning principles and their application to program planning.* Toronto, ON, Canada: Ontario Department of Education.

Cigularov, K., Chen, P., Thurber, B. W., & Stallones, L. (2008). Investigation of the effectiveness of a school-based suicide education program using three methodological approaches. *Psychological Services, 5,* 262–274. doi:10.1037/1541-1559.5.3.262

City, E., Elmore, R., Fiarman, S., & Teitel, L. (2009). *Instructional rounds in education: A network approach to improving teaching and learning.* Cambridge, MA: Harvard Education Press.

Cuban, L. (1993). *How teachers taught: Constancy and change in American classrooms 1890–1990* (2nd ed.). New York, NY: Teachers College Press.

de Anda, D. (2007). Intervention research and program evaluation in the school setting: Issues and alternative research designs. *Children and Schools, 29,* 87–94. doi:10.1093/cs/29.2.87

Donovan, M. S., Bransford, J. D., & Pellegrino, J. W. (Eds.). (1999). *How people learn: Bridging research and practice.* Washington, DC: National Academies Press.

Evans, R. (1996). *The human side of school change.* San Francisco, CA: Jossey-Bass.

Evans, S. W., & Owens, J. S. (2010). Behavioral assessment within problem-solving models [Special issue]. *School Psychology Review, 39,* 427–430.

Felner, R. D., Seitsinger, A. S., Brand, S., Burns, A., & Bolton, N. (2008). Creating a statewide educational data system for accountability and improvement: A comprehensive information and assessment system for making evidence-based change at school, district, and policy levels. *Psychology in the Schools, 45,* 235–256. doi:10.1002/pits.20294

Fuchs, L. S., & Fuchs, D. (2004). Determining adequate yearly progress from kindergarten through grade 6 with curriculum-based measurement. *Assessment for Effective Intervention, 29,* 25–37. doi:10.1177/073724770402900405

Fullan, M. G., & Miles, M. B. (1992). Getting reform right: What works and what doesn't. *Phi Delta Kappan, 73,* 745–752.

Gallucci, C. (2008). District-wide instructional reform: Using sociocultural theory to link professional learning to organizational support. *American Journal of Education, 114,* 541–581.

Garet, M. S., Porter, A. C., Desimone, L., Birman, B. F., & Yoon, K. S. (2001). What makes professional development effective? Results from a national sample of teachers. *American Educational Research, 38,* 915–945. doi:10.3102/00028312038004915

Green, S. K. (1994). Best practices in implementing a staff development program. In A. Thomas & J. Grimes (Eds.), *Best practices in school psychology III* (pp. 123–133). Bethesda, MD: National Association of School Psychologists.

Gresham, F. M., Cook, C. R., Collins, T., Dart, E., Rasetshwane, K., Truelson, E., & Grant, S. (2010). Developing a change-sensitive brief behavior rating scale as a progress-monitoring tool for social behavior: An example using the Social Skills Rating System–Teacher Form. *School Psychology Review, 39,* 364–379.

Gresham, F. M., & Elliott, S. N. (1990). *Social Skills Rating System.* Bloomington, IN: Pearson Assessments.

Guskey, T. R. (1982). The effects of change in instructional effectiveness upon the relationship of teacher expectations and student achievement. *Journal of Educational Research, 75,* 345–349.

Guskey, T. R. (1986). Staff development and the process of teacher change. *Educational Researcher, 15,* 5–12.

Guskey, T. R. (2002). Professional development and teacher change. *Teachers and Teaching: Theory and Practice, 8,* 381–391. doi:10.1080/135406002100000512

Harriott, W. A. (2004). Inclusion inservice: Content and training procedures across the United States. *Journal of Special Education Leadership, 17,* 91–102.

Hatch, T. (2000). What does it really take to break the mold? Rhetoric and reality in new American schools. *Teachers College Record, 102,* 561–589.

Hill, H. C. (2007). Learning in the teacher workforce. *Future of Children, 17,* 111–127. doi:10.1353/foc.2007.0004

Hochberg, E. D., & Desimone, L. M. (2010). Professional development in the accountability context: Building capacity to achieve standards. *Educational Psychologist, 45*, 89–106. doi:10.1080/00461521003703052

Huberman, M. (1995). Professional careers and professional development: Some intersections. In T. R. Guskey & M. Huberman (Eds.), *Professional development in education: New paradigms and practices* (pp. 193–224). New York, NY: Teachers College Press.

Intrator, S., & Kunzman, R. (2009). Grounded: Practicing what we preach. *Journal of Teacher Education, 60*, 512–519. doi:10.1177/0022487109348598

Joyce, B., & Showers, B. (2002). Student achievement through staff development. In B. Joyce & B. Showers (Eds.), *Designing training and peer coaching: Our needs for learning*. Alexandria, VA: Association for Supervision and Curriculum Development.

Kegan, R. (1994). *In over our heads: The mental demands of modern life*. Cambridge, MA: Harvard University Press.

Killion, J. P., & Kaylor, B. (1991). Follow-up: The key for training and transfer. *Journal of Staff Development, 12*, 64–67.

Korthagen, F. (2010). Situated learning theory and the pedagogy of teacher education: Towards an integrative view of teacher behavior and teacher learning. *Teaching and Teacher Education, 26*, 98–106.

Kratochwill, T. R. (2007). Preparing psychologists for evidence-based school practice: Lessons learned and challenges ahead. *American Psychologist, 62*, 829–843. doi:10.1037/0003-066X.62.8.829

Lave, J., & Wenger, E. (1991). *Situated learning: Legitimate peripheral participation*. New York, NY: Cambridge University Press.

Learning Point Associates. (2007). *Implementing the No Child Left Behind Act: Teacher quality improves academic achievement. Quick key 8 action guide*. Naperville, IL: Author.

Lee, I. (2011). Teachers as presenters at continuing professional development seminars in the English-as-a-foreign-language context: I find it more convincing. *Australian Journal of Teacher Education, 36*, 30–42.

Little, J. W. (1993). Teachers' professional development in a climate of educational reform. *Educational Evaluation and Policy Analysis, 9*, 133–152.

Lortie, D. (1975). *School teacher*. Chicago, IL: University of Chicago Press.

Margolis, J. (2008). When teachers face teachers: Listening to the resource "right down the hall." *Teaching Education, 19*, 293–310.

Margolis, J. (2012). Hybrid teacher leaders and the new professional development ecology. *Professional Development in Education, 38*, 291–315. doi:10.1080/19415257.2012.657874

Margolis, J., & Doring, A. (2012). The fundamental dilemma of teacher leader facilitated professional development: Do as I (kind of) say, not as I (sort of) do. *Educational Administration Quarterly, 48*, 859–882. doi:10.1177/0013161X12452563

Margolis, J., & Huggins, K. (2012). Distributed, but undefined: New teacher leader roles to change schools. *Journal of School Leadership, 22*, 953–981.

Marris, P. (1986). *Loss and change* (Rev. ed.). London, England: Routledge, Kegan and Paul.

Mellott, R. N. (2007). The scientist–practitioner training model for professional psychology. *American Behavioral Scientist, 50*, 755–757. doi:10.1177/0002764206296452

Mezirow, J. (1991). *Transformative dimensions of adult learning*. San Francisco, CA: Jossey-Bass.

Moore, J. (1988). Guidelines concerning adult learning. *Journal of Staff Development, 9*, 2–5.

Morris, A., & Heibert, J. (2011). Creating shared instructional products: An alternative approach to improving teaching. *Educational Researcher, 40*, 5–14. doi:10.3102/0013189X10393501

National Association of School Psychologists. (2010). *Model for comprehensive and integrated school psychological services*. Bethesda, MD: Author. Retrieved from http://www.nasponline.org/standards/2010standards/2_PracticeModel.pdf

Ochoa, S. H., & Rhodes, R. L. (2005). Assisting parents of bilingual students to achieve equity in public schools. *Journal of Educational and Psychological Consultation, 16*, 75–94.

Oldroyd, D., & Hall, V. (1991). *Managing staff development: A handbook for secondary schools*. London, England: Paul Chapman.

Sanders, W., & Rivers, J. (1996). *Research progress report: Cumulative and residual effects of teachers on future student academic achievement: Tennessee value-added assessment system*. Knoxville, TN: Value-Added Research and Assessment Center. Retrieved from http://www.cgp.upenn.edu/pdf/Sanders_Rivers-TVASS_teacher%20effects.pdf

Singh, S. K. (2011). The role of staff development in the professional development of teachers: Implications for inservice training. *South African Journal for Higher Education, 25*, 1626–1638.

U.S. Department of Education. (2012). *Improving teacher quality state grants*. Washington, DC: Author. Retrieved from http://www2.ed.gov/programs/teacherqual/index.html

Wang, Y. L., Frechtling, J. A., & Sanders, W. L. (1999). *Exploring linkages between professional development and student learning: A pilot study*. Paper presented at the annual meeting of the American Educational Research Association, Montreal, Canada.

West, P. (1989). Designing a staff development program. *Journal of Further and Higher Education, 13*, 8–11.

Wilson, S., & Berne, J. (1999). Teacher learning and the acquisition of professional knowledge: An examination of research on contemporary professional development. *Review of Research in Education, 24*, 173–209. doi:10.3102/0091732X024001173

Wizda, L. (2004). An instructional consultant looks to the future. *Journal of Educational and Psychological Consultation, 15*, 277–294. doi:10.3102/00346543074003255

York-Barr, J., & Duke, K. (2004). What do we know about teacher leadership? Findings from two decades of scholarship. *Review of Educational Research, 74*, 255–316.

39 Best Practices in Establishing Effective Helping Relationships

Julia E. McGivern
Corey E. Ray-Subramanian
University of Wisconsin–Madison
Elana R. Bernstein
University of Dayton (OH)

OVERVIEW

What contributes to the positive outcomes seen—sometimes, but not always—from interventions with children and adolescents? Researchers investigating factors that influence intervention outcomes with youth and adults have found that both relationship variables and specific intervention techniques influence outcomes (e.g., Kazdin & Durbin, 2012; Norcross, 2011). Research examining "common factors models" (Wampold, 2010, p. 53) has found that one of the common factors (factors at work in all theoretical perspectives and therapies) is the helping relationship (e.g., Norcross & Lambert, 2011; Shirk & Karver, 2011). Norcross and Wampold (2011), summarizing the results of research carried out by a 2009 task force commissioned by the American Psychological Association's (APA) Divisions of Psychotherapy and Clinical Psychology, defined the helping or therapy relationship as "the feelings and attitudes that therapist and client have toward one another, and the manner in which they are expressed" (p. 4).

Whereas the specific intervention is the "what" of helping, the relationship is the "how" of helping. The goal of building a helping relationship is to provide conditions that facilitate positive outcomes through the actions of a helper, such as a school psychologist, who develops a strong positive relationship with a student, based on that student's personality, culture, and preferences (Norcross & Lambert, 2011). As these authors and others (e.g., Hubble, Duncan, Miller, & Wampold, 2010) have noted, the intervention method

and the relational context in which it is applied are tightly bound. Think of a school psychologist asking an adolescent to put away her cell phone as they begin to talk. How might this interaction be affected by a positive relationship? A negative one?

This chapter will examine the elements that influence the helping relationship and will identify strategies for school psychologists to use to facilitate strong helping relationships with the goal of supporting positive student outcomes. After reading this chapter, it is hoped that school psychologists will understand the importance of developing strong helping relationships; will understand school psychologist behaviors and student, parent, and teacher factors that influence helping relationships; and will be able to identify specific strategies for maximizing the effectiveness of their helping relationships.

A note about terms used. We use the term *helping relationship* when discussing both direct services and consultation. We use the term *helper* when discussing research that addresses psychologists in general, but we use the term *school psychologist* when we are applying research findings specifically to psychologists in schools. We only use *patient* when quoting directly from a source. We use the term *parent* to refer to those responsible for the in-home care of children and adolescents, and we use the term *teacher* to refer broadly to educators, including, for example, related services providers.

BASIC CONSIDERATIONS

How does the relationship between a client (a student) or a consultee (a parent or a teacher) and a school psychologist affect student outcomes? Additional research is needed to refine our understanding of how the relationship exerts its influence in specific situations. Yet what is known is that the relationship is important to outcomes.

Helping Relationships and Evidence-Based Practice

Norcross and Wampold (2011) asserted that the therapeutic relationship is at least as important as the treatment method in explaining client outcomes. To maximize the effectiveness of practice, school psychologists must capitalize on the power of both evidence-based interventions and strong helping relationships. Some authors (e.g., McLeod, Southam-Gerow, & Weisz, 2009) have suggested that, because of their critical contribution to outcomes, relationship factors could be considered components of treatment integrity.

Helping Relationships and the School Context

School psychologists work at multiple tiers of service delivery to assist students, many of whom would not otherwise receive mental health services (e.g., Castro-Blanco, North, & Karver, 2010). Working at the universal or Tier 1 level, school psychologists can help all students understand the factors that facilitate positive mental health and academic achievement. At the more intensive second and third tiers of service, school psychologists can develop relationships with individual students to provide the mental health interventions students need. School psychologists, by building relationships with these students in need of more intensive services, can facilitate students' involvement in intervention and improve their likelihood of school success.

In addition to multitiered work with students, school psychologists work at multiple tiers with adults. School psychologists can work at the universal level with teachers and administrators. At more intensive levels, they can form helping relationships with individual parents and teachers through consultation to improve the mental health and academic outcomes of students. School psychologists who understand the importance of the helping relationship in consultation can have powerful effects on student outcomes (Kelley, Bickman, & Norwood, 2010; National Association of School Psychologists [NASP], 2010; Shirk & Karver, 2011).

School psychologists' professional associations recognize the importance of helping relationships. NASP's *Model for Comprehensive and Integrated School Psychological*

Services (2010) identified consultation and collaboration as specific domains in which school psychologists must develop competence. The American Psychological Association (APA), in the report of its *Presidential Task Force on Evidence-Based Practice* (APA, 2006), noted that "[p]sychological practice is, at root, an interpersonal relationship between psychologist and patient" (p. 277). Considering how best to form helping relationships within the context of the school environment is critical to the effective implementation of services (Atkins, Hoagwood, Kutash, & Seidman, 2010).

BEST PRACTICES IN ESTABLISHING EFFECTIVE RELATIONSHIPS

The main ingredients of helping relationships in school psychology are the participants. But the relationship is shaped by multiple factors as the helping process evolves (e.g., Shirk & Karver, 2006, 2011; see Figure 39.1):

- The participants in the relationship are the client (a student), the consultee (often a parent or teacher), and the school psychologist. These individuals bring specific characteristics into the relationship that influence its development.
- The processes of helping also influence development of relationships. Client and consultee engagement in intervention/consultation, the alliance that is developed between the client/consultee and school psychologist, and subsequent involvement in intervention or consultation tasks influence the developing relationship.

Examples

Below are examples of situations in which a school psychologist could work to develop helping relationships with students, parents, and teachers. The examples will be used throughout the chapter to illustrate application of research findings.

Lin (student): Lin is a tenth-grade girl whose grandparents immigrated to the United States from China. Lin has always been a hard-working student with good grades. However, this year her grades are dropping.

Ms. Jackson (parent consultee): Renee Jackson, a Caucasian woman, is concerned about her third-grade son, Andrew, who has refused to go to school this week, saying he is "afraid of going there."

Figure 39.1. Factors That Influence the Helping Relationship

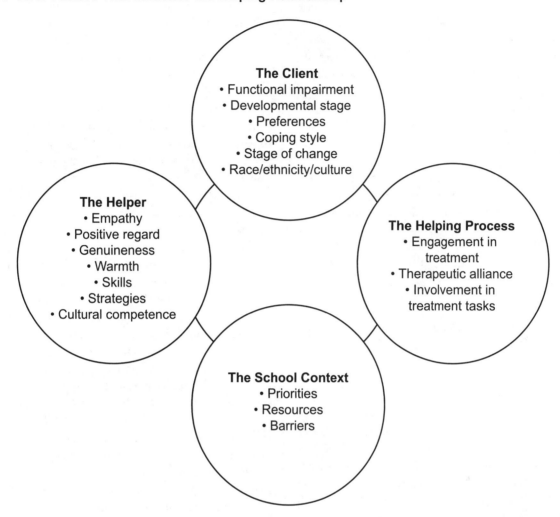

The Client
- Functional impairment
- Developmental stage
- Preferences
- Coping style
- Stage of change
- Race/ethnicity/culture

The Helper
- Empathy
- Positive regard
- Genuineness
- Warmth
- Skills
- Strategies
- Cultural competence

The Helping Process
- Engagement in treatment
- Therapeutic alliance
- Involvement in treatment tasks

The School Context
- Priorities
- Resources
- Barriers

Brad Shaver (teacher consultee): Brad Shaver is a Caucasian fifth-grade teacher who is concerned about T.J. Jones, a biracial boy in his class. Brad Shaver complained about T.J.'s disruptive behavior and said the intervention plan developed at a recent Problem-Solving Team meeting was "worthless." Brad Shaver said, "All that team ever does is make more work for teachers."

Helper Factors That Facilitate Effective Relationships

Helper factors that facilitate effective relationships and are often related to positive outcomes include the use of empathy, genuineness/congruence, and positive regard within the helping relationship (Cormier, Nurius, & Osborn, 2013; Norcross, 2011). Effectively utilizing these helper factors can be considered a necessary competency for school psychologists in all aspects of their work with students, parents, and other professionals. Although these concepts are historically rooted in the therapeutic approach advocated by Carl Rogers, they are now embraced either explicitly or implicitly by nearly all theoretical orientations toward therapy (Farber & Doolin, 2011). It has also been argued that these helper factors are interrelated rather than representing distinct constructs (e.g., Elliott, Bohart, Watson, & Greenberg, 2011). Research on helper factors has shown that the client's perception of these factors is often more important than the therapist's perspective (Elliot et al., 2011; Farber & Doolin, 2011). For example, it is not sufficient for a school psychologist to feel positive regard toward a student. This feeling must also be conveyed to the student through the psychologist's behavior.

Empathy

Simply put, empathy is "the ability to understand people from their frame of reference rather than your own" (Cormier et al., 2013, p. 86). Empathy can be conveyed verbally by (a) showing a desire to comprehend the student's perspective, (b) discussing what is important to the student, (c) referring to the student's feelings, and (d) adding to implicit student messages (Cormier et al., 2013). An empathic response is illustrated below using the example of Lin, a student.

> *Lin:* "I just can't stop worrying about everything that's going on at home. My dad lost his job recently. It's hard to even think about school."
>
> *School psychologist:* "I'm so sorry to hear this, Lin. I can see that you are very concerned about your family. Schoolwork may not be a top priority right now."

This response conveys empathy because the school psychologist referred to Lin's feelings (i.e., worry) and focused on what is most important to Lin now (i.e., her family).

The use of empathy can also be applied to school psychologists' role as consultants, particularly in the context of models such as conjoint behavioral consultation, a problem-solving framework designed to improve student academic, behavioral, and social–emotional outcomes and promote positive family–school relationships (Sheridan & Kratochwill, 2008). Closely related to empathy is the concept of perspective taking, which Sheridan and Kratochwill (2008) identified as a critical skill for effective consultants. Sheridan and Kratochwill maintained that consultants should listen to and acknowledge different perspectives and adopt a "nondeficit," or positively focused, approach toward consultees and students. Below is an example of an empathic response to Brad Shaver, T.J.'s teacher, and T.J.'s mother, Mrs. Jones, in the context of conjoint behavioral consultation.

> *Brad Shaver:* "Sometimes it feels like I'm putting all my energy toward managing T.J.'s behavior instead of teaching. It's not fair to the other students."
>
> *Mrs. Jones:* "T.J. said that he's always the one getting in trouble even if another kid is doing the same thing. Then he gets his recess taken away, which doesn't help. It just makes him mad and more likely to misbehave."

> *School psychologist:* "Brad, I understand that you are frustrated because you're spending too much time dealing with disruptions in the classroom. Mrs. Jones, it sounds like you are concerned that T.J. is being singled out and you may have some ideas for improving his behavior in the classroom."

This response by the school psychologist demonstrates empathy by addressing both the teacher's and parent's comments, discussing what is important to each person, referring to each person's feelings, and adding to implicit messages (e.g., Mrs. Jones might have some ideas for addressing T.J.'s behavior more effectively).

Genuineness

Also referred to as congruence, genuineness, particularly important in work with adolescents, can be conceptualized as both the helper's personal integration in the relationship with the client and ability to communicate his or her experience of the relationship to the client (Kolden, Klein, Wang, & Austin, 2011). Cormier et al. (2013) have identified four components of helper genuineness, including supporting nonverbal behaviors, role behavior, consistency, and spontaneity. Examples of supporting nonverbal behaviors include eye contact, facial expressions, and body posture. Role behavior refers to the helper refraining from overemphasizing his or her role, authority, or status as a helper. Consistency involves ensuring that words, actions, and feelings match. Finally, spontaneity refers to expressing oneself in a natural manner. Below are examples of responses by the school psychologist to Lin that would likely seem more genuine versus less genuine.

> *Lin:* "My parents don't want me to go to the concert. Why can't they just let me be myself? You know what I mean?"
>
> *School psychologist (more genuine response):* "I understand that it may be frustrating to want to pursue your interests and to feel like your parents are not allowing that."
>
> *School psychologist (less genuine response):* "I hear you. I'd like to go to that concert, too."

The first response is more likely to demonstrate genuineness than the second response, as a high school student may need empathy from a school psychologist but may not perceive as genuine comments by a school staff member who seems to be trying to fit in with the interests of adolescents (Creed & Kendall, 2005).

Positive Regard and Warmth

In the context of a helping relationship, positive regard refers to "a warm acceptance of each aspect of the client's experience as being part of that client" (Rogers, 1957, as cited in Farber & Doolin, 2011, p. 169). More specifically, Cormier et al. (2013) identified four aspects of positive regard: (a) demonstrating a sense of commitment to the client, (b) maintaining a nonjudgmental attitude, (c) showing competence and care, and (d) expressing warmth to the client. Below are examples of how the school psychologist could express positive regard and warmth to Ms. Jackson, the mother of Andrew.

- Keep scheduled appointments.
- Convey shared concern about Andrew's frequent absences from school.
- Ask about Ms. Jackson's understanding of why Andrew is staying home.
- Ask what aspects of the current situation are most important to Ms. Jackson.
- Do not make judgmental statements about Ms. Jackson's decision to allow Andrew to stay home from school frequently.
- Seek consultation as needed to meet Andrew's needs.
- Use nonverbal behaviors, such as eye contact and tone of voice, that convey warmth to Ms. Jackson.

Farber and Doolin (2011, p. 183) offered the following observations and recommendations based on their meta-analysis of this helper factor: (a) positive regard is "strongly indicated" in practice and should not be withheld, (b) it may serve many valuable functions across different types of therapy, (c) positive regard may be particularly important when a nonminority therapist is working with a minority client, (d) positive regard needs to be monitored by the helper and adjusted to match the needs of the client, and (e) positive regard needs to be clearly communicated to the client and not just felt internally by the helper.

Helper Behaviors That Interfere With the Helping Relationship

In contrast to the above factors that can facilitate development of effective helping relationships, there are helper behaviors that are generally ineffective and may negatively influence the relationship. In their review of the literature on problematic helper behaviors, Norcross and Wampold (2011) have identified specific behaviors that should be avoided. Below are examples of common errors a school psychologist might make, using the example of Brad Shaver, the teacher who is concerned about T.J.

School psychologist (being confrontational, critical, or blaming): "Brad, your classroom management techniques are not working, which is why T.J. is being disruptive."

School psychologist (making assumptions): "I know you will be happy with this intervention, Brad. Things are going to be so much better in your classroom now."

School psychologist (being overly rigid or inflexible): "I schedule all of my consultation meetings at 7:00 before school starts. That's just how I work."

School psychologist (adopting a one-size-fits-all approach): "I have the perfect intervention for T.J. I use it for all students who are being disruptive in classrooms."

See Table 39.1 for recommendations for using helper characteristics to build relationships.

Client/Consultee Factors That Influence the Helping Relationship

Client or consultee factors are those that are independent of the helper and the intervention; that is, the backpack of emotions, motivation, resources, demographic characteristics, social factors, and social support that clients/consultees bring to the helping relationship. These factors have been shown in multiple meta-analyses to account for more variance in treatment outcomes (approximately 30%) than any other factor (Bohart & Tallman, 2010; Norcross & Lambert, 2011).

In general, when developing helping relationships with students, school psychologists should consider a student's (a) age/developmental status, (b) important sociocultural factors (e.g., gender, race, and culture), (c) level of functioning and the severity of the presenting problem, (d) environmental context (e.g., stressors), (e) personal preferences (e.g., values and beliefs) and motivation, (f) readiness for change, and (g) family history (Hubble et al., 2010; Karver, Handelsman, Fields, & Bickman, 2005). Some of these factors, particularly the nature of the presenting problem, personal preferences, motivation, readiness for change, and sociocultural factors also influence consultation with teachers and parents (e.g., Newell, 2010). Given the complex nature of the factors listed above, it is likely that multiple client/consultee factors, or moderator variables, operate simultaneously and have an impact on intervention outcomes. In a helping relationship, consideration of these participant factors must begin

Table 39.1. Recommendations for Utilizing Helper Factors to Facilitate Effective Relationships

Empathy: Involves conveying understanding of the student's perspective to the student
- Respond to both the content and affect of the student's messages
- Be careful not to infer too much about how the student is feeling
- Discuss what is important to the student
- Seek clarification if there is uncertainty about what the student is conveying
- Use nonverbal behavior to convey empathy (e.g., body position, facial expression, eye contact, head nodding)
- Provide empathy to all persons in a conflict (e.g., student, parent, and teacher)

Genuineness/congruence: Involves the helper's integration into the relationship and ability to communicate his or her experience of the relationship to the student
- Use nonverbal behavior to convey genuineness
- Ensure that words, actions, and feelings match
- Try to talk to students in a natural, yet professional, manner
- Seek feedback from colleagues and supervisors to enhance authenticity in helping relationships

Positive regard and warmth: Involves demonstrating acceptance of and commitment to the student
- Be on time for meetings and keep appointments
- Follow through with promises (e.g., identifying community resources, making follow-up phone calls)
- Express warmth through nonverbal and verbal cues
- Be clear about areas of professional competence and utilize appropriate resources, consultation, or training for areas outside of defined competence
- Make a concerted effort to understand the student and his or her perspective (e.g., culture, values and beliefs, personal experiences)

Note. Based on information from Farber and Doolin (2011), Kolden et al. (2011), Cormier et al. (2013).

by meeting the client/consultee where he or she is, using an approach in which intervention strategies are tailored to the participant's unique needs and characteristics (Murphy & Christner, 2012).

Student Age/Developmental Status

School psychologists' clients are children and adolescents, so it is particularly important to consider clients' developmental status when establishing helping relationships. A working knowledge of influential developmental theories (e.g., Piaget, Maslow, and Erikson) is important when tailoring the helping relationship to a child's developmental level (Mennuti & Christner, 2012). The impact of development on student difficulties should be conveyed to parents and teachers in consultative relationships as well.

Development has an impact on biological, cognitive, emotional, and social aspects of children's functioning (Chu, Suveg, Creed, & Kendall, 2010), and student clients may demonstrate developmental strengths and weaknesses across these areas of functioning (Holmbeck, Devine, & Bruno, 2010). Consideration of developmental level will help guide the pace of an intervention and the language used during helper/client interactions (Murphy & Christner, 2012). It is important for school psychologists to consider a student's cognitive level, for example, when explaining the helping relationship. Below are examples of how the school

psychologist might explain his or her role to Lin, Grade 10, and Andrew, Grade 3.

School psychologist: "Lin, I work with students who have many types of difficulties—academic, social, emotional—a broad range. Your teachers are worried about your falling grades, and I'd like us to talk today to see if there is some way I can be helpful to you."

School psychologist: "Andrew, my job in our school is to help people. I've been talking with your mom, and she told me how scary it is for you to come to school right now. I've helped other children with these scary feelings, and I'd like to help you, too."

Many authors (e.g., Chu et al., 2010; Shirk & Karver, 2011) have suggested that forming helping relationships with adolescents is especially challenging. Changes occurring in adolescence, such as tension in the parent–child relationship, peer influences, emerging romantic interests, increased risk-taking behavior, and, in particular, a push toward more autonomy, can predispose adolescents to be reluctant to engage in or even to refuse interventions (Duncan, Williams, & Knowles, 2012; Shirk, Caporino, & Karver, 2010).

Table 39.2 provides considerations for school psychologists developing relationships with students at

Table 39.2. Suggestions for Building Helping Relationships Across Age Levels

Age Level	Recommendations for Establishing Helping Relationships
Preschool	• Recognize the child's language capacity and limited emotional vocabulary; use concrete terms and concepts; avoid asking strings of questions • Consider using more behavioral strategies (e.g., modeling, contingency management) because the child may struggle to maintain a sustained dialogue and may not benefit from insight-oriented intervention • Avoid strategies that require hypothetical or complex abstract thinking (e.g., role playing) • Recognize that the child may have difficulty taking others' perspectives • Remember that children at this age have a limited attention span; use multiple activities, change tasks frequently during sessions, and consider the length of the session • Provide choices during sessions to increase the child's level of perceived control • Use strategies that are appealing to the child: consider using games, toys, visual representations/manipulatives/movement during sessions (e.g., puppets, drawing) • Develop a therapeutic relationship with consultees (e.g., parents and teachers) because preschool children generally benefit from parental and/or teacher involvement in intervention • Demonstrate to the child that you are a trustworthy person by forming a working alliance with his or her parent and teacher • Sit at the child's level during sessions and provide a comfortable environment
Elementary and middle school	• Consider using some cognitive strategies with assistance in addition to behavioral strategies • Recognize the student's limited ability for abstract thinking; use examples when possible • Consider using games with structured rules when teaching new skills (e.g., social skills) • Incorporate the student's increased self-control and emotional regulation into intervention by gradually raising expectations, when appropriate • Note the increasing importance of the student's peer group; consider the influence of peers on intervention and including peers in intervention • Involve the student in discussion of interventions (e.g., explanation of intervention, discussion of stage of change) as the student develops logical thinking and reasoning • Remember that students at this age have a tendency to make assumptions and jump to conclusions while also developing more complex emotions (e.g., guilt shame, pride) • Consider developing helping relationships with other change agents (e.g., parent, teacher) in the student's life • Allow the student to make decisions regarding intervention (e.g., goal setting, scheduling) • Recognize that the student may experience increased self-consciousness and a decrease in self-esteem when beginning middle school
High school	• Demonstrate positive regard by establishing trust with the student; emphasize confidentiality in the helping relationship • Avoid confrontation and passing judgment on the student's decisions • Recognize that peers are very important and consider incorporating them in intervention • Respect the student's increasing need for autonomy; provide choices and multiple options when possible • Attend to issues of identity because race/ethnicity and culture can be especially influential as adolescents form identities; remember that adolescents will explore multiple roles; educate the parent/teacher about identity formation • Remember that adolescents have increased emotional vulnerability, so provide empathy and react with sensitivity; normalize common fears and anxiety, which are often related to the future • Do not belittle the student's problem and avoid providing false hope (e.g., "Every teenager goes through this, you will definitely get through it.") • Do not assume physical maturation is a sign of cognitive/social maturity • Limit use of self-disclosure as it may appear disingenuous in certain contexts • Determine whether the student may now be able to engage in more systematic problem solving and incorporate cognitively oriented intervention strategies; teach decision-making skills • Recognize that the student may be experiencing family conflicts and changing relationships with parents; determine the impact of involving the parent in the intervention • Involve the student in intervention planning and decisions (i.e., goal setting, structure, and scheduling) • Consider discussing the stage of change concept openly with the student; motivational interviewing strategies may be helpful • Use engaging/experiential strategies matched to the student's preferences (e.g., journal writing, role plays)

Note. Based on information from Holmbeck et al. (2010), Murphy and Christner (2006), and Vernon (2008).

various developmental stages. In addition to attending to students' developmental characteristics, school psychologists must recognize that development is a fluid process, be aware of students' evolving developmental capacity for certain techniques, and recognize that students may regress to an earlier developmental stage in times of stress and conflict (Murphy & Christner, 2006, 2012).

Functional Impairment

Functional impairment refers to the severity of a problem as well as the areas of a student's life in which there is diminished functioning (Beutler, Harwood, Alimohamed, & Malik, 2002). Interestingly, preliminary findings have suggested that functional impairment may be a more cross-cultural/universal concept than diagnosis/classification (Arcia & Fernandez, 2003; Bauermeister et al., 2005) as cultural factors may have an impact on the presentation of psychopathology in diverse populations (Haack & Gerdes, 2011). Functional impairment may be influenced by a number of factors: (a) level of social support, one of the most critical correlates; (b) problems with relationships at school and home; (c) comorbid conditions; (d) the length of time the problem has existed; and (e) cognitive impairment and difficulties with self-care (Beutler et al., 2002).

A student's level of functional impairment can influence the development of a helping relationship. For example, the student, Andrew, demonstrates a high level of functional impairment given that he has missed a significant amount of school; he has the support of his mother but lacks social relationships with other children his age; his school refusal is negatively affecting his academic achievement; and his anxiety may make him reluctant to engage in intervention. In developing a helping relationship with Andrew, the school psychologist might work to develop a positive relationship with Andrew's mother, a source of social support, and could enlist Andrew in planning intervention steps given his good cognitive skills and his anxiety about returning to school.

Some research suggests that children and adolescents with a high level of functional impairment, evidenced by multiple diagnoses, prolonged history of antisocial behavior, cognitive or academic problems, and/or negative peer influences, have more difficulty engaging in interventions and may drop out of interventions at a higher rate than other youth (Donaldson, Spirito, & Boergers, 2010). Additional research suggests that children and adolescents with different presenting problems (e.g., withdrawal because of anxiety versus aggression because of conduct problems) likely require relationship-building strategies that are unique to their situations (Levin, Henderson, & Ehrenreich-May, 2012). In cases where youth demonstrate severe impairments in functioning, outcomes may be improved at Tier 3 by using a comprehensive wraparound service model targeting multiple domains in the child's life (e.g., home, school, community; Painter, 2012). Table 39.3 presents suggestions for improving intervention outcomes for students with significant functional impairment.

Coping Styles and Preferences

Coping styles are defined as "recurrent patterns of behavior that characterize an individual when confronting new or problematic situations" (Beutler et al., 2011, p. 338). Based on early work by Eysenck (1967), coping styles are considered heritable and relatively stable, with roots tracing back to infancy and temperament (Beutler et al., 2011). Coping styles are thought to exist on a continuum from internalizing to externalizing, and students may display characteristics of both types. An internalizing coping style is typically marked by withdrawal, introspection, and self-blame, whereas an externalizing style is characterized by expressiveness, impulsivity, and a tendency to blame others. Internalizers are more easily overwhelmed by change, while externalizers seek stimulation and change (Beutler et al., 2011).

School psychologists can benefit from assessing a student's coping style early in the helping relationship, as the style will likely shape interactions with the student, the strategies used, and the outcomes attained. Beutler et al. (2011) point out that it is important to recognize that a diagnosis may not necessarily indicate a student's dominant coping style, and thus more specific assessment may be needed (e.g., talking to parents and teachers and using standardized tools that assess relationship factors). Finally, when children are faced with stress, they tend to observe the reactions of others to help them deal with the situation. Therefore, knowledge of a family's coping style can help in understanding a student's own reaction to a given situation (Murphy & Christner, 2006). In a consultative relationship, knowing the consultee's style of coping may assist the school psychologist in creating an acceptable intervention plan.

Another important factor, somewhat related to coping style, is the preferences a client or consultee brings into the helping relationship. Determining and accommodating student, parent, and teacher preferences regarding intervention factors, such as the helper's

Table 39.3. Factors That Influence Helping Relationships and Outcomes

Student, Parent, and Teacher Factors	Assessment Strategies	Intervention Strategies
Functional impairment (applies to students) *Definition:* The severity of the client's problem(s) and the degree to which the client exhibits diminished functioning in daily life (Beutler et al., 2002)	• Review records • Observe the student • Conduct interviews with the student, parent, teacher • Use norm-referenced measures (e.g., cognitive–academic assessment; social–emotional scales)	• Consider the need for longer intervention • Build home–school partnerships • Employ an interdisciplinary approach • Increase students' social support • Consider community referral
Coping style (applies to students, parents, and teachers) *Definition:* Habitual and enduring patterns of behavior that characterize the individual when confronting new or problematic situations; typically on a continuum of internalizing to externalizing (Beutler, Harwood, Kimpara, Verdirame, & Blau, 2011)	• Observe coping during work with the student • Interview the student, parent, and/or teacher regarding past reactions to difficulties • Use norm-referenced measures (e.g., Locus of Control scale on BASC-2)	• Model appropriate coping • Match intervention to coping style • Focus on interpersonal concerns with internalizing coping • Focus on action-oriented interventions with externalizing coping
Stage of change (applies to students, parents, and teachers) *Definition:* The client's/consultee's intention to change; may range from lack of awareness of a problem and no intent to change to active efforts to change (Prochaska, DiClemente, & Norcross, 1992)	• Ask the student, parent, or teacher about his or her commitment to change • Explore previous attempts to change behavior • Observe the student's, parent's, or teacher's actions to identify discrepancies between verbalizations and actions	• Assess decisional balance to determine pros and cons of the status quo • Use motivational interviewing • Increase self-efficacy beliefs • Affirm small successes
Expectations and preferences (applies to students, parents, and teachers) *Definition:* The outcomes of services anticipated by the client/consultee and the desires of the client/consultee about the types of services (Swift, Callahan, & Vollmer, 2011)	• Ask the student, parent, or teacher what he or she expects from the intervention or the consultation • Identify student, parent, or teacher preferences for types of services • Consider the types and outcomes of previous services to find indicators of expectations and preferences	• Facilitate positive expectations by addressing student, parent, or teacher goals • Address student, parent, or teacher preferences by providing the types of services desired • Reduce barriers to services

Note. BASC-2 = Behavior Assessment System for Children, Second edition.

style and role, type of intervention, and intervention logistics, have been shown to increase their intervention and consultation continuation (e.g., Sheridan & Kratochwill, 2008; Swift et al., 2011). See Table 39.3 regarding strategies for working with students, parents, and teachers with varied coping styles and preferences.

Race, Ethnicity, and Culture

With schools becoming increasingly diverse, it is essential for school psychologists to recognize that race, ethnicity, and culture may significantly influence a student's or a consultee's presentation of problem symptoms and the acceptability of certain interventions (APA, 2003; NASP, 2010). As noted by Smith, Domenick Rodrigues, and Bernal (2011), "In short, recognizing and aligning with client culture is not only best practice, it is ethical practice" (p. 316).

Developing cultural competence has come to be understood as a process a helper goes through to develop the skills necessary to maximize the positive outcomes of clients and consultees (Sue & Torino, 2005). School psychologists working with students, parents, and teachers must be aware of their own values and biases and develop knowledge about the populations they serve (APA, 2003). However, as Ortiz (2006) suggested, multicultural competence for school psychologists "lies not so much in understanding every unique or idiosyncratic characteristic of cultural groups, but more in the ability to recognize when and where cultural issues might be operating in any aspect of practice" (p. 159). It is also critical to be aware of research suggesting that family traditions, social norms, acculturation level, values, and mistrust of the healthcare system can significantly influence the helping relationship (Donaldson et al., 2010).

Discussion of differences in race, ethnicity, and culture can be difficult for helpers to introduce. However, indicating a willingness to discuss these topics can facilitate a stronger helping relationship. Questions to clients or consultees regarding their racial and cultural identities can facilitate discussion of critical issues that might have an impact on services (e.g., Cormier et al., 2013). For example, the school psychologist might say to Lin:

School psychologist: "Lin, is there a way in which your ethnic and cultural heritage contributes to your conflict with your parents?"

Researchers have attempted to determine whether matching clients and helpers by race/ethnicity and gender contributes to improved client outcomes. Cabral and Smith (2011), in a meta-analysis of more than 50 studies of clients' preferences for therapists of their own ethnicity/race, found that although clients preferred therapists of their own race/ethnicity and rated those therapists slightly more positively, client–therapist matching on race/ethnicity had virtually no impact on outcomes. However, it will be important for school psychologists to consider individual student and consultee factors (e.g., preferences and cultural affiliation) that might increase the likelihood that race/ethnicity matching will influence outcomes. Table 39.4 presents recommendations about building helping relationships with diverse students and families. Most of the suggestions also apply when working with consultees, such as teachers.

Socioeconomic Status and Sexual Orientation

Building consultation relationships with students and parents who are "nonmainstream," including families who are homeless or living in poverty, may require attention to special factors (Lott & Rogers, 2005). Some students and parents may be reluctant to question professionals' judgments and may feel (perhaps correctly) that their knowledge is devalued. As Lott and Rogers (2005) noted, "consultants need to function as

Table 39.4. Suggestions for Creating Relationships With Diverse Students and Families

Before intervention	• Be aware of your own race, ethnicity, culture, gender, socioeconomic status, and sexual orientation and how they influence your values, beliefs, and work • Learn about the populations with which you are working. • Learn about oppression, discrimination, and racism that students and families often face • Be aware of the complexity of constructs such as race, ethnicity, culture, gender, sexual orientation, and disability
Early in the intervention	• Determine whether race, ethnicity, culture, socioeconomic status, gender, or sexual orientation influence the presenting concern • Identify the student's and parent's conceptualization of mental health • Determine whether biases will influence your work with the student or family
Throughout the intervention	• Consider the cultural and linguistic context of the student, family, and school • Consider the sociopolitical context (e.g., immigration status and historical experiences) of the student and family • Become aware of how student acculturation interacts with intervention • Accept the student's and family's core cultural beliefs • Validate the student's and family's self-reported experiences of oppression, racism, and discrimination • Identify culturally related strengths, protective factors, and supports • Be willing to engage in important discussions of race, ethnicity, culture, gender, and sexual orientation • Use intervention methods that align with the student's and family's values and goals • Consider adapting interventions to align with cultural considerations and specific ethnic/racial groups while maintaining core elements of the intervention • Consider using culture-specific intervention strategies, if appropriate • Explore school psychologist–student and school psychologist–family differences if relevant to the intervention • Elicit feedback from the student and family about intervention • Share perceptions of the therapeutic alliance

Note. Based on information from APA (2003), Hays (2009), Newell (2010), and Smith et al. (2011).

facilitators for parents who are not accustomed to advocating for the interests of their children, feel ill-prepared and frustrated in their attempts to do so, and who have often had negative educational experiences themselves" (p. 12).

School psychologists today work with diverse families, including families with parents and/or children who identify as lesbian, gay, bisexual, or transgender, or who are questioning their sexual orientation (LGBTQ). To establish effective helping relationships with LGBTQ students and their parents, school psychologists must work at the system level to ensure that schools are inviting and safe places for all parents and children (Russell, Ryan, Toomey, Diaz, & Sanchez, 2011). In addition, school psychologists must examine their own individual practices to ensure the use of strategies, such as warmth, positive regard, appropriate language, and collaboration, to improve outcomes for children and adolescents. Consider, for example, the student Lin. In a meeting with the school psychologist the following exchange might take place:

Lin: "My parents just don't understand me. They want me to quit hanging out with my lesbian friends. I can't talk about any of my friends with them."

School psychologist: "I'm sorry you can't talk with your parents about such an important topic. We can think about how to change that, but first I'd like to talk with you about your friends. I can tell they are important to you. Why don't you tell me what you like about your friends?"

Client Stages of Change and Motivation

Research has demonstrated that an important factor that influences clients' outcomes from intervention is the attitude of the client/consultee toward change (Norcross, Krebs, & Prochaska, 2011). One of the most useful models developed to explain the change process is the transtheoretical model developed by Prochaska and colleagues (e.g., Prochaska et al., 1992). In the transtheoretical model, clients cycle through stages of change: (a) precontemplation, in which the client is not yet considering change; (b) contemplation, in which the client is thinking of changing; (c) preparation, in which the client is starting to plan for change; (d) action, in which the client is taking steps to change; and (e) maintenance, in which the client is working to preserve changes already made. A significant body of evidence

suggests that clients move through the stages in a spiral manner, with relapse and recycling through the stages common.

To address what has been determined as a significant factor influencing outcomes, Norcross et al. (2011) suggested that each stage of change should be accompanied by specific helper stances toward the helping relationship. Prochaska and colleagues (e.g., Norcross et al., 2011; Prochaska et al., 1992) warned against treating all clients as if they are in the action stage of change. Indeed, it is important for school psychologists to realize that many students are not committed to change, especially adolescents who might be referred for help by others. See Table 39.5 for recommendations for school psychologists' roles and strategies matched to specific stages of change.

Related to the concept of stage of change is the construct of motivation to change. Miller and colleagues (e.g., Miller & Rollnick, 2002) introduced a therapy approach called motivational interviewing, intended to increase client motivation to change. Over time, motivational interviewing has evolved through research and practice to encompass two critical active components (Miller & Rose, 2009). The first component is a relational component that centers on use of empathy and a strong interpersonal connection. The helper adheres to the spirit of motivational interviewing by invoking a style that is collaborative, eliciting the client's own motivation for change, and respecting the client's autonomy. Critical to motivational interviewing is the expression of the helper's genuine empathy toward the client. The second component involves "differential evocation and reinforcement of client change talk" (Miller & Rose, 2009, p. 527). The helper differentially reinforces change talk rather than talk that favors the status quo. As an example of the use of motivational interviewing and empathy early in the stage of work with T.J., the school psychologist might say:

School psychologist: "T.J., I hear you saying you really don't like your teacher, Mr. Shaver. I can understand that. He is a pretty strict teacher. Tell me the things you don't like about him."

Later in the session the psychologist might try to elicit positive talk about Mr. Shaver:

School psychologist: "That's quite a list of things you don't like. It helps me understand why you don't want to go to his class. So, is there anything at all you like about Mr. Shaver?"

Table 39.5. Stages of Change and Roles and Strategies for School Psychologists

Stage of Change	Role of the School Psychologist	Strategies for the School Psychologist
Precontemplation: The student, teacher, or parent has no intention to change behavior in the foreseeable future	*Acts as a nurturing facilitator:* • To understand why the student, parent, or teacher is not considering change • To help motivate the student, teacher, or parent to consider change	• Use empathy and reflective listening • Avoid arguments and advice • Identify pros and cons of the current situation • Provide a menu of options • Explore barriers • Instill hope; increase student, parent, or teacher self-efficacy
Contemplation: The student, teacher, or parent is aware a problem exists but is not yet committed to change	*Acts as a guide:* • To help the student, parent, or teacher understand problems • To help the student, parent, or teacher shift the decisional balance toward change • To help the student, parent, or teacher believe change is possible	• Ask questions to help clarify concerns • Assess how long the student, parent, or teacher has been contemplating change • Help the student, parent, or teacher identify risks and benefits of change • Provide accurate and relevant information and feedback • Affirm self-motivational statements • Help the student, parent, or teacher increase self-efficacy by emphasizing previous successes
Preparation: The student, teacher, or parent is intending to take action soon and has undertaken unsuccessful efforts in the past	*Acts as an experienced coach:* • To help the student, parent, or teacher anticipate or address barriers • To help the student, parent, or teacher believe change is possible	• Use careful listening and reflection • Help the student, parent, or teacher recognize ambivalence about change • Present a range of options to the student, parent, or teacher • Help the student, parent, or teacher evaluate options • Provide feedback on the student's, parent's, or teacher's choices • Instill hope and address self-efficacy
Action: The student, teacher, or parent has commitment to change and has taken overt behavioral action	*Acts as a consultant:* • To provide assistance as the student, parent, or teacher implements the change plan • To help the student, parent, or teacher maintain commitment to change	• Help the student, parent, or teacher recognize conflicting feelings about change • Evaluate/revise the student's, parent's, or teacher's change plan • Provide affirmation about the student's, parent's, or teacher's accomplishments • Continue to instill hope and address self-efficacy
Maintenance: The student, teacher, or parent is working to maintain gains and/or prevent relapse	*Acts as consultant or coach:* • To help prevent relapse • To increase the recommitment to change in the face of relapse	• Help the student, parent, or teacher be aware of relapse potential • Encourage ongoing commitment to change • Increase self-efficacy if a relapse occurs • Help the student, parent, or teacher understand the change cycle

Note. Based on information from Miller and Rollnick (2002), Norcross et al. (2011), and Prochaska et al. (1992).

See Table 39.5 for a summary of student factors that may influence the helping relationship and suggestions for addressing these factors.

Barriers to the Helping Relationship

Multiple layers of barriers may reduce school psychologists' opportunities to build helping relationships.

Helper and System Factors

Many school psychologists report having limited time to address students' academic and mental health concerns. In addition, some school psychologists need additional training regarding evidence-based relationship factors (e.g., Atkins et al., 2010). School scheduling and limited availability of parents and teachers can also present barriers to effective relationships. Reducing these barriers will require that school psychologists engage in system reform by working to create conditions that foster home–school partnerships (e.g., Atkins et al., 2010).

Client and Consultee Factors

Client resistance to change is often seen when the client is referred for help by someone else, as is often the case with children and adolescents; when others' goals of intervention are not shared by the client; when the client's problems are attributed to external sources; and when the client is satisfied or even pleased with the status quo (Shirk & Karver, 2011). These clients, from a stage of change perspective, could be thought of as in the precontemplation stage of change, in which the client has no intention to change (Miller & Rollnick, 2002). School psychologists working with students in the precontemplation stage can try to identify the reason a student has no intention to change and can tailor intervention to address the specific reason. For example, does the student disagree with the goals endorsed by his or her parent or teacher? If so, then the school psychologist can offer empathy and work to elicit student discussion of advantages and disadvantages of the status quo. Does the student feel that change is not possible? If so, then the school psychologist can offer empathy and work to increase the student's self-efficacy. Consultees also may be reluctant to engage in the change process. See Table 39.5 for recommendations for working with students, parents, and teachers in the precontemplation stage of change.

Developing Helping Relationships Throughout the Helping Process

There is growing understanding in psychology that there is within-intervention variability in outcomes (e.g., Shirk & Karver, 2011). This has led to examination of the process of intervention in attempts to refine understanding of what makes interventions effective. Shirk and Karver (2006) have proposed a temporal sequence

model of the helping relationship. First, the client must become engaged in the intervention process. Second, the experience of intervention allows the formation of an alliance in which the client perceives the helper as someone to be counted on. Third, the client is able to become involved, participating in the intervention tasks. (See Figure 39.2.)

Engaging Youth in Intervention

Engagement of students in the intervention process is the first step toward positive outcomes. Constantino, Castonguay, Zack, and DeGeorge (2010) asserted that "of the many process variables that have been investigated to date, the client's engagement in psychotherapy might safely be considered the most robust change mechanism" (p. 21).

Adolescents are considered some of the most challenging clients to engage in intervention. They might refuse or be reluctant to engage in interventions because they have been referred by someone else (e.g., parent or teacher); they might not agree with the referring party about target problems, the need for intervention, and the goals of intervention; they might attribute problems to external causes; they might lack awareness of the potential effects of problem behavior; they might be reluctant to look toward adults for help with problems; and they might fear the stigma still associated with help-seeing and mental illness (Castro-Blanco et al., 2010; Shirk et al., 2010). Barriers to engagement in intervention can also include practical obstacles, such as transportation and scheduling (Chu et al., 2010).

Gallagher, Kurtz, and Blackwell (2010) asserted that engagement in intervention, reflected, for example, by consistent attendance, can be influenced by multiple factors that might be overlooked in the helping process, such as the therapeutic setting and interactions with support staff. It is not difficult to imagine how such factors could influence the engagement of youth in schools. Where does the student go to meet the school psychologist? How helpful are the support staff

Figure 39.2. Temporal Sequence Model of the Helping Relationship

Note. Based on information from Shirk and Karver (2006) and Shirk, Karver, and Brown (2011).

members? For example, the student Lin might say to the school psychologist:

Lin: "I didn't like having to walk through the main office to come here. I felt like everyone was looking at me and wondering what is wrong with me."

Client predictors of high engagement in intervention have been identified, such as low functional impairment, positive expectations of and attitudes toward the intervention, hopefulness about positive outcomes, and realistic expectations (Chu et al., 2010). Sheridan and Kratochwill (2008) noted that encouraging parents to

identify their own strengths and needs can increase engagement in consultation.

Owing to the limited time window in which children and adolescents can be engaged in interventions (Castro-Blanco, 2010), school psychologists must work to engage students from their first interactions. Engagement can vary over time as students experience outcomes and changing perspectives on interventions (Chu et al., 2010). Researchers have identified some factors that have been associated with continued participation in interventions. From these factors, some recommended strategies for engagement can be distilled (see Table 39.6). Many of the strategies can also be effective with consultees.

Table 39.6. Behaviors That Facilitate and Interfere With Helping Relationships Across the Helping Process

Engaging Students in the Intervention Process	Building the Therapeutic Alliance	Involving Students in Intervention Tasks
Behaviors That Facilitate a Positive Helping Relationship		
• Explaining the intervention process to the student early in treatment; helping the student understand how intervention works • Presenting intervention as a collaborative effort • Setting positive but realistic expectations • Engaging the student in the process of providing assent • Explaining confidentiality and its limits • Listening to the student's perspectives on issues, especially early in the intervention • Addressing problems the student perceives to be most critical • Facilitating goal agreement between the student and parent	• Being honest and trustworthy • Treating the student with respect • Displaying warmth and confidence • Showing interest in the student • Being open to the student's perspectives • Exploring the student's perspectives on referral concerns • Reflecting on the student's statements and interpreting them accurately • Facilitating expression of affect • Attending to the student's experiences • Accepting responsibility for alliance ruptures • Remaining nondefensive in the face of student hostility	• Attending to the student's developmental levels throughout intervention • Addressing the adolescent's developmental needs • Allowing the adolescent more control of intervention tasks • Adapting materials to the student's developmental level while maintaining fidelity • Monitoring involvement in intervention tasks • Watching for decreased enthusiasm, self-disclosures, and withdrawal, which can indicate poor outcomes • Using engagement strategies if involvement decreases
Behaviors That Interfere With the Helping Relationship		
• Stressing goals supported by the parent and teacher but not the student • Adopting a confrontational style • Making critical or blaming statements • Being rigid and inflexible in structuring sessions • Attempting to emphasize common ground with the child and adolescent • Lecturing or being didactic • Being overly formal	• Being rigid • Appearing distant or distracted • Being tentative or uncertain • Appearing tense or nervous • Making inappropriate self-disclosures • Using silence too much • Adhering rigidly to theory in the face of alliance difficulties • Making assumptions about the student's perceptions of the helping relationship • Overemphasizing the helper's perception of the helping relationship • Pushing the student to talk about a problem	• Prescribing tasks the student does not perceive to be helpful • Ignoring the student's perspective on tasks • Choosing tasks related to goals endorsed by others but not by the student • Adopting a one-size-fits-all approach for the student • Being too directive, especially with adolescents • Using materials not appropriate for the student's developmental level • Neglecting to review homework after it is assigned

Note. Based on information from Campbell and Simmonds (2011), Creed and Kendall (2005), Constantino et al. (2010), and Shirk and Karver (2011).

Fostering the Therapeutic Alliance

A strong alliance is one of the best predictors of positive outcomes from therapy (e.g., Hubble et al., 2010; Kazdin & Durbin, 2012; Shirk et al., 2011). Kazdin and Durbin (2012) defined the therapeutic alliance as "the quality and nature of the client–therapist relationship, the collaborative interaction, and the bond or personal attachment that emerges during treatment" (p. 202). High-quality alliances are associated with higher rates of intervention completion, greater compliance with intervention demands, and greater therapeutic change (Kazdin & Durbin, 2012).

The alliance with children and adolescents.

The goal in forming a therapeutic alliance is to achieve the level of collaboration that is needed with a specific client in a specific context using a specific intervention. Agreement on intervention goals is critical for the alliance, especially with adolescents (Shirk & Karver, 2011). There is evidence also that therapist lapse behaviors, such as failing to acknowledge client emotions and criticizing the client, are negatively associated with the therapeutic alliance with adolescents (Karver et al., 2008). Creed and Kendall (2005) found that behaviors including "pushing the child to talk" contributed to lower child ratings of the alliance (p. 503). Below are examples of the school psychologist talking with Lin in ways that might harm and help the alliance.

Lin: "I know my grades have been dropping. There's just some stuff going on that I don't really want to talk about right now."

School psychologist: "Lin, I can't help you unless you tell me what is going on."

This response may interfere with the helping relationship if Lin were feeling forced to talk about something troubling beyond her comfort level. In this situation, the school psychologist may need to try a less direct approach by offering continued support until Lin appears to be ready to discuss her circumstances.

School psychologist: "Lin, it sounds like there are things going on in your life that are troubling and might be affecting your grades. When you feel ready to talk about them, I'd like to listen and help you in any way I can."

Helper characteristics and behaviors that can facilitate or interfere with development of therapeutic alliances are listed in Table 39.6.

Alliances with parents and teachers.

It is important for school psychologists to consider how relationships with adults (e.g., parents and teachers) influence youth outcomes and to identify factors that positively influence alliances with adults. Feinstein, Fielding, Udvari-Solner, and Joshi (2009) introduced the concept of the "supporting alliance" to characterize the secondary alliances that exist between those with primary relationships with the student who is the target of concern. In the Feinstein et al. (2009) model, these secondary alliances (e.g., parent–teacher, parent–school psychologist, teacher–school psychologist) support the alliance between the school psychologist and the student, facilitating positive outcomes.

Researchers have examined the influence of alliances with parents on child outcomes. Kelley et al. (2010) hypothesized that therapeutic alliances with parents may be important because "a parent who has a strong [therapeutic alliance] with the therapist is likely to convey hope and other positive attitudes about treatment that may generally encourage the child's participation in treatment, which then in turn may influence youth outcomes" (p. 336). For example, Ms. Jackson might say to her son, Andrew, who is reluctant to go to school:

Ms. Jackson: "I met with someone at your school today. She has some good ideas about how to help you go to school. She understands how scary it is for you now, and she says she has helped other kids who were scared, too."

When school psychologists work in consultation with teachers, they must engender an atmosphere of trust, and teachers must be confident that school psychologists will honor ethical mandates to maintain confidentiality (e.g., Jacob, Decker, & Hartshorne, 2011). Numerous authors (e.g., Sheridan & Kratochwill, 2008) have asserted that school psychologists should help enhance the connection between teachers and parents. For example, in working with Brad Shaver, T.J.'s teacher, the school psychologist might say:

School psychologist: "Brad, T.J.'s parents are pretty discouraged by the negative news they have gotten about his behavior. And I know you are frustrated, too. Could we talk about how we can present concerns about T.J. in a way that will help create a positive relationship with his parents?"

See Table 39.6 for suggestions for strengthening the therapeutic alliance and for factors and behaviors that might interfere with the alliance.

Involving Clients and Consultees in Intervention Tasks

Engagement in the intervention process and alliance development lead to greater involvement of clients in intervention tasks. Karver et al. (2008) described client involvement as "cooperating with, being involved in, making suggestions about, and/or completing therapeutic tasks" (p. 16). Client involvement in intervention tasks, such as homework and discussion of feelings, is facilitated by a strong therapeutic alliance; and while client involvement predicts outcomes, the association between alliance and outcomes is mediated by direct involvement in intervention tasks (Karver et al., 2008). Although child and adolescent involvement in intervention has a significant effect on outcomes, involvement may be more important in some disorders than others. For example, in anxiety interventions, client involvement in exposure activities is critical (Kendall, Settipani, & Cummings, 2012). The consultation literature indicates that consultants' direct instruction about interventions and feedback based on observations are critical to consultee intervention implementation (e.g., Noell & Gansle, 2009).

Adapting materials and tasks to be suitable for the developmental level of the student is critical to involving youth in intervention tasks. For example, Kendall, Choudhury, Hudson, and Webb (2002) made adaptations to the Coping Cat program for use with adolescents. The name was changed to the C.A.T. Project, and adolescents developed their own title for the program using the C.A.T. acronym, therapists described themselves as coaches rather than therapists to present themselves as collaborators rather than authority figures, psychoeducation was included, and the focus on cognitions was increased. See Table 39.6 for suggestions about involving clients in intervention tasks.

Goal consensus and collaboration.

There is evidence in the intervention and consultation literature that agreement about the goals of intervention and collaboration on tasks are critical to involving clients in intervention and facilitating positive outcomes (e.g., Creed & Kendall, 2005; Noell & Gansle, 2009; Tyron & Winograd, 2011). Goal consensus between a school psychologist and student results from negotiation about the goals and tasks of intervention. School psychologists' relationships with students, and particularly adolescents, can be furthered by stressing the collaborative nature of the school psychologist–student relationship.

Sheridan and Kratochwill (2008) noted that encouraging parents to identify their own needs and strengths can promote involvement in consultation. Yet Feinstein et al. (2009) warned that "drain"—the physical and emotional cost of collaboration that is not working—can occur (p. 333). School psychologists must consider whether collaboration costs are borne equally. For example, in an attempt to even the cost of collaboration, the school psychologist might say to the teacher, Brad Shaver:

> *School psychologist:* "Brad, I understand how frustrated you are with T.J.'s behavior during math. Why don't I come help out with the intervention plan for the next few days? Then we can put our heads together to find ways to make it more effective."

Strategies to increase goal consensus and collaboration are presented in Table 39.7.

Repairing Relationship Ruptures

Even the most skilled helpers can experience—and almost always play a role in—ruptures in their relationships with clients/consultees (e.g., Constantino et al., 2010). Ruptures occur along a continuum of severity, from minor tensions to ruptures that block communication and collaboration. If ruptures in the alliance occur, school psychologists must analyze the reasons for the ruptures and take actions to repair the relationship (Chu et al., 2010). In fact, acknowledging the negative feelings of the client can help the client feel that the helper understands and values both the client and the helping relationship.

Ruptures in alliances with adolescents can occur because of developmental factors such as a desire for autonomy and increased mood irregularities (Chu et al., 2010). Adolescents may be unwilling to raise issues of dissatisfaction because of the power differential between the client and helper and because of their still-developing skills in navigating interpersonal rifts (Chu et al., 2010). Table 39.8 identifies possible signs of alliance ruptures and provides suggestions for repairing ruptures in the alliance. Below is an example of how the school psychologist might discuss a rupture in the alliance with T.J.:

> *School psychologist:* "T.J., you have become very quiet today. In thinking about that I realized that you said something really important a while ago that I didn't pay enough attention to. You said I can't understand how it is for you, your having a Black mother and a White father. You are right. I can't understand. I've never had your experience. So I'm hoping you will help me understand how it is for you."

Table 39.7. Strategies to Increase Goal Consensus and Collaboration

Goal Consensus With Students, Parents, and Teachers	Collaboration With Students	Collaboration With Parents and Teachers
• Identify student, parent, and teacher concerns • Ask questions to ensure accurate understanding of the concerns • Attend to student's, parent's, and teacher's analyses of concerns • Explain the helping process • Address topics important to the student, parents, and teacher • Reach consensus on goals at the first interview, if possible, to facilitate engagement • Include the student in teacher and parent interviews when appropriate	• Establish a cooperative, friendly approach • Explain intervention as a collaborative effort • Discuss goals frequently • Respect the student's values, beliefs, and preferences • Use shared decision making with older students • Enlist active participation of the student • Focus homework on the student's concerns/problems • If assigning homework, review the homework regularly	• Establish a cooperative, friendly approach • Clarify consultation roles • Discuss goals frequently • Use shared decision making • Respect parents' and teachers' values, beliefs, and preferences • Respect the parents' and teachers' autonomy • Consider the parents' and teachers' preferences for collaborative or directive approaches • Avoid jargon • Schedule meetings at times and locations convenient for parents and the teacher

Note. Based on information from Lott and Rogers (2005), Newell (2010), Sheridan and Kratochwill (2008), and Tyron and Winograd (2011).

Table 39.8. Strategies for Strengthening Alliances and Repairing Ruptures With Clients and Consultees

Problem Examples	Strategies
Student, parent, or teacher does not attend sessions or meetings	• Examine barriers to services • Examine the student's, parent's, or teacher's expectations and preferences • Consider the referral issue: Is the appropriate issue identified? • Identify the student's, parent's, or teacher's stage of change • Focus on collaboration
Student, parent, or teacher is passive, does not participate actively	• Explain the intervention or consultation process • Identify the student's, parent's, or teacher's goals; increase the goal consensus • Examine the student's, parent's, or teacher's coping style • Use specific strategies to enlist commitment (e.g., motivational interviewing with adolescents) • Match interventions to the stage of change • Consider universal intervention if the problem is common in the population
Student, parent, or teacher is angry or resentful of referral for services or consultation	• Use empathy • Express positive regard; avoid blaming and rejecting • Address the alliance directly (parent and teacher) • Do not address the alliance directly (adolescent) • Examine the student's, parent's, or teacher's coping style • Match interventions to the stage of change • Model appropriate confrontation and compromise
Student, parent, or teacher does not follow through on homework or other goal-oriented actions	• Reexamine the goal consensus • Reexamine barriers • Clarify the referral issue • Identify the student's, parent's, or teacher's expectations and preferences • Obtain the student's, parent's, or teacher's perspective on the alliance

Note. Based on information from Beutler et al. (2002), Chu et al. (2010), Sheridan and Kratochwill (2008), Shirk and Karver (2011), and Shirk et al. (2011).

Evaluating the Helping Relationship in School Psychology Practice

School psychologists can determine whether they are developing strong helping relationships with children, adolescents, parents, and teachers by using both formal and informal assessment methods. Although a thorough discussion of alliance assessment is beyond the scope of this chapter, it is worth noting that there are rating scales available for use with youth (e.g., see Shirk & Karver, 2011). Some authors have suggested that honest discussions of alliances with children, adolescents, and adults could strengthen these relationships (e.g., Constantino et al., 2010). These authors noted that many helpers might not realize when they are failing to use strategies to support the alliance, such as empathy. However, by asking clients and consultees to talk about alliances, school psychologists may be able to identify and respond to differences in perceptions. For example, the school psychologist might ask the following questions to Lin; to Mrs. Jones, T.J.'s mother; to Brad Shaver, the teacher; and to T.J.:

To Lin: "Are we working on things that are important to you?"

To Mrs. Jones: "Are there things I could be doing that would be more helpful?"

To Brad Shaver: "Do you think I understand your perspective about T.J.?"

To T.J.: "Do you think I understand your feelings about Mr. Shaver's class?"

SUMMARY

To maximize the effectiveness of their services, school psychologists must consciously and strategically work to develop strong helping relationships with students, parents, and teachers and must evaluate those relationships throughout the helping process. A positive helping relationship provides the nurturing context within which evidence-based interventions can be delivered. Concurrent use of evidence-based therapeutic relationship factors and evidence-based interventions adapted to the client or consultee in a collaborative union is likely to yield the best outcomes for students.

REFERENCES

American Psychological Association. (2003). Guidelines on multicultural education, training, research, practice, and organizational change for psychologists. *American Psychologist, 58*, 377–402, Retrieved from http://www.apa.org/pi/oema/resources/policy/multicultural-guidelines.aspx

American Psychological Association. (2006). Evidence-based practice in psychology. *American Psychologist, 61*, 271–285. doi:10.1037/0003-066X.58.5.377

Arcia, E., & Fernandez, M. C. (2003). From awareness to acknowledgement: The development of concern among Latina mothers of children with disruptive behaviors. *Journal of Attention Disorders, 6*, 163–175. doi:10.1177/108705470300600403

Atkins, M. S., Hoagwood, K. E., Kutash, K., & Seidman, E. (2010). Toward the integration of education and mental health in schools. *Administration and Policy in Mental Health and Mental Health Services Research, 378*, 40–47. doi:10.1007/s10488-010-0299-7

Bauermeister, J. J., Matos, M., Reina, G., Salas, C. C., Martinez, J. V., Cumba, E., ...Barkley, R. (2005). Comparison of the DSM-IV combined and inattentive types of ADHD in a school-based sample of Latino/Hispanic children. *Journal of Child Psychology and Psychiatry, 46*, 166–179. doi:10.1111/j.1469-7610.2004.00343.x

Beutler, L. E., Harwood, M. T., Alimohamed, S., & Malik, M. (2002). Functional impairment and coping style. In J. C. Norcross (Ed.), *Psychotherapy relationships that work: Therapist contributions and responsiveness to patients* (pp. 145–174). New York, NY: Oxford University Press.

Beutler, L. E., Harwood, T. M., Kimpara, S., Verdirame, D., & Blau, K. (2011). Coping style. In J. C. Norcross (Ed.), *Psychotherapy relationships that work: Evidence-based responsiveness* (2nd ed., pp. 337–353). New York, NY: Oxford University Press. doi:1093/acprof:oso/9780199737208.003.0017

Bohart, A. C., & Tallman, K. (2010). Clients: The neglected common factor in psychotherapy. In B. Duncan, S. Miller, B. Wampold, & M. Hubble (Eds.), *The heart and soul of change: Delivering what works in therapy* (2nd ed., pp. 83–111). Washington, DC: American Psychological Association. doi:10.1037/12075-003

Cabral, R. R., & Smith, T. B. (2011). Racial/ethnic matching of clients and therapists in mental health services: A meta-analytic review of preferences, perceptions, and outcomes. *Journal of Counseling Psychology, 58*, 537–554. doi:10.1037/a0025266

Campbell, A. F., & Simmonds, J. G. (2011). Therapist perspectives on the therapeutic alliance with children and adolescents. *Counseling Psychology Quarterly, 24*, 195–209. doi:10.1080/09515070.2011.620734

Castro-Blanco, D. (2010). TEEN: Techniques for enhancing engagement through negotiation. In D. Castro-Blanco & M. S. Karver (Eds.), *Elusive alliance: Treatment engagement strategies with high-risk adolescents* (pp. 123–138). Washington, DC: American Psychological Association. doi:10.1037/12139-004

Castro-Blanco, D., North, K. K., & Karver, M. S. (2010). The problem of engaging high-risk adolescents in treatment. In D. Castro-Blanco & M. S. Karver (Eds.), *Elusive alliance: Treatment engagement strategies with high-risk adolescents* (pp. 3–19). Washington, DC: American Psychological Association.

Chu, B. C., Suveg, C., Creed, T. A., & Kendall, P. C. (2010). Involvement shifts, alliance ruptures, and managing engagement over therapy. In D. Castro-Blanco & M. S. Karver (Eds.), *Elusive alliance: Treatment engagement strategies with high-risk adolescents* (pp. 95–121). Washington, DC: American Psychological Association. doi: 10.1037/12139-003

Constantino, M. J., Castonguay, L. G., Zack, S. E., & DeGeorge, J. (2010). Engagement in psychotherapy: Factors contributing to the facilitation, demise, and restoration of the therapeutic alliance. In D. Castro-Blanco & M. S. Karver (Eds.), *Elusive alliance: Treatment engagement strategies with high-risk adolescents* (pp. 21–57). Washington, DC: American Psychological Association. doi:10.1037/12139-001

Cormier, S., Nurius, P. S., & Osborn, C. J. (2013). *Interviewing and change strategies for helpers* (7th ed.). Belmont, CA: Brooks/Cole.

Creed, T. A., & Kendall, P. C. (2005). Therapist alliance-building behavior within a cognitive-behavioral treatment for anxiety in youth. *Journal of Consulting and Clinical Psychology, 73*, 498–505. doi: 10.1037/0022-006X.73.3.498

Donaldson, D., Spirito, A., & Boergers, J. (2010). Treatment engagement with adolescent suicide attempters. In D. Castro-Blanco & M. S. Karver (Eds.), *Elusive alliance: Treatment engagement strategies with high-risk adolescents* (pp. 207–225). Washington, DC: American Psychological Association. doi:10.1037/12139-008

Duncan, R., Williams, B. J., & Knowles, A. (2012). Breaching confidentiality with adolescent clients: A survey of Australian psychologists about the considerations that influence their decisions. *Psychiatry, Psychology & Law, 19*, 209–220. doi:10.1080/13218719.2011.561759

Elliott, R., Bohart, A. C., Watson, J. C., & Greenberg, L. S. (2011). Empathy. In J. C. Norcross (Ed.), *Psychotherapy relationships that work: Evidence-based responsiveness* (2nd ed., pp. 132–152). New York, NY: Oxford University Press. doi:10.1093/acprof:oso/9780199737208.003.0006

Eysenck, H. J. (1967). *The biological basis of personality*. Springfield, IL: Thomas.

Farber, B. A., & Doolin, E. M. (2011). Positive regard and affirmation. In J. C. Norcross (Ed.), *Psychotherapy relationships that work: Evidence-based responsiveness* (2nd ed., pp. 168–186). New York, NY: Oxford University Press. doi:10.1093/acprof:oso/9780199737208.003.0008

Feinstein, N. R., Fielding, K., Udvari-Solner, A., & Joshi, S. V. (2009). The supporting alliance in child and adolescent treatment: Enhancing collaboration among therapists, parents, and teachers. *American Journal of Psychotherapy, 63*, 319–344.

Gallagher, R., Kurtz, S., & Blackwell, S. C. (2010). Engaging adolescents with disruptive behavior disorders in therapeutic change. In D. Castro-Blanco & M. S. Karver (Eds.), *Elusive alliance: Treatment engagement strategies with high-risk adolescents* (pp. 139–158). Washington, DC: American Psychological Association. doi:10.1037/12139-005

Haack, L. M., & Gerdes, A. C. (2011). Functional impairment in Latino children with ADHD: Implications for culturally appropriate conceptualization and measurement. *Clinical Child and Family Psychology Review, 14*, 318–328. doi:10.1007/s10567-011-0098-z

Hays, P. A. (2009). Integrating evidence-based practice, cognitive-behavior therapy, and multicultural therapy: Ten steps for culturally competent practice. *Professional Psychology: Research and Practice, 40*, 354–360. doi:10.1037/a0016250

Holmbeck, G. N., Devine, K. A., & Bruno, E. F. (2010). Developmental issues and considerations in research and practice. In J. R. Weisz & A. E. Kazdin (Eds.), *Evidence-based psychotherapies for children and adolescents* (2nd ed., pp. 28–39). New York, NY: Guilford Press.

Horvath, A. O., Del Re, A. C., Flückiger, C., & Symonds, D. (2011). Alliance in individual psychotherapy. In J. C. Norcross (Ed.), *Psychotherapy relationships that work: Evidence-based responsiveness* (2nd ed., pp. 25–69). New York, NY: Oxford University Press. doi:10.1093/acprof:oso/9780199737208.003.0002

Hubble, M. A., Duncan, B. L., Miller, S. D., & Wampold, B. E. (2010). Introduction. In B. L. Duncan, S. D. Miller, B. E. Wampold, & M. A. Hubble (Eds.), *The heart and soul of change: Delivering what works in therapy* (2nd ed., pp. 83–111). Washington, DC: American Psychological Association. doi:10.1037/12075-001

Ingraham, C. L., & Oka, E. (2006). Multicultural issues in evidence-based interventions. *Journal of Applied School Psychology, 22*, 127–149. doi:10.1300/J370v22n02_07

Jacob, S., Decker, D. M., & Hartshorne, T. S. (2011). *Ethics and law for school psychologists* (6th ed.). Hoboken, NJ: Wiley.

Karver, M. S., Handelsman, J. B., Fields, S., & Bickman, L. (2005). A theoretical model of common process factors in youth and family therapy. *Mental Health Services Research, 7*, 35–51. doi:10.1007/s11020-005-1964-4

Karver, M. S., Handelsman, J. B., Fields, S., & Bickman, L. (2006). Meta-analysis of therapeutic relationship variables in youth and family therapy: The evidence for different relationship variables in the child and adolescent treatment outcome literature. *Clinical Psychology Review, 26*, 50–65. doi:10.1016/j.cpr.2005.09.001

Karver, M., Shirk, S., Handelsman, J. B., Fields, S., Crisp, H., Gudmundsen, G., & McMakin, D. (2008). Relationship processes in youth psychotherapy: Measuring alliance, alliance-building behaviors, and client involvement. *Journal of Emotional and Behavioral Disorders, 16*, 15–28. doi:10.1177/1063426607312536

Kazdin, A. E., & Durbin, K. A. (2012). Predictors of child-therapist alliance in cognitive-behavioral treatment of children referred for oppositional and antisocial behavior. *Psychotherapy, 49*, 202–217. doi:10.1037/a0027933

Kelley, S. D., Bickman, L., & Norwood, E. (2010). Evidence-based treatment and common factors in youth psychotherapy. In B. L. Duncan, S. D. Miller, B. E. Wampold, & M. A. Hubble (Eds.), *The heart and soul of change: Delivering what works in therapy* (2nd ed., pp. 83–111). Washington, DC: American Psychological Association. doi:10.1037/12075-011

Kendall, P. C., Choudhury, M., Hudson, J., & Webb, A. (2002). *The C.A.T. Project workbook for the cognitive-behavioral treatment of anxious adolescents*. Ardmore, PA: Workbook. doi:10.1080/15374416.2012.632352

Kendall, P. C., Settipani, C. A., & Cummings, C. M. (2012). No need to worry: The Promising future of child anxiety research. *Journal of Clinical Child & Adolescent Psychology, 41*, 103–115. doi:10.1080/15374416.2012.632352

Kolden, G. C., Klein, M. H., Wang, C., & Austin, S. B. (2011). Congruence/genuineness. In J. C. Norcross (Ed.), *Psychotherapy relationships that work: Evidence-based responsiveness* (2nd ed., pp. 187–202). New York, NY: Oxford University Press. doi:10.1093/acprof:oso/9780199737208.003.0009

Levin, L., Henderson, H. A., & Ehrenreich-May, J. (2012). Interpersonal predictors of early therapeutic alliance in transdiagnostic cognitive-behavioral treatment for adolescents with anxiety and depression. *Psychotherapy*, *49*, 218–230. doi:10.1037/a0028265

Lott, B., & Rogers, M. R. (2005). School consultants working for equity with families, teachers, and administrators. *Journal of Educational and Psychological Consultation*, *16*, 1–16. doi:10.1207/s1532768xjepc161&2_1

McLeod, B. D., Southam-Gerow, M. A., & Weisz, J. R. (2009). Conceptual and methodological issues in treatment integrity measurement. *School Psychology Review*, *38*, 541–546.

Mennuti, R. B., & Christner, R. W. (2012). An introduction to cognitive-behavioral therapy with youth. In R. B. Mennuti & R. W. Christner (Eds.), *Cognitive-behavioral interventions in educational settings: A handbook for practice* (2nd ed., pp. 3–24). New York, NY: Routledge.

Miller, W. R., & Rollnick, S. (2002). *Motivational interviewing: Preparing people for change* (2nd ed.). New York, NY: Guilford Press.

Miller, W. R., & Rose, G. S. (2009). Toward a theory of motivational interviewing. *American Psychologist*, *64*, 527–537. doi:10.1037/a0016830

Murphy, V. B., & Christner, R. W. (2006). A cognitive-behavioral case conceptualization approach for working with children and adolescents. In R. B. Menutti, A. Freeman, & R. W. Christner (Eds.), *Cognitive-behavioral interventions in educational settings: A handbook for practice* (pp. 37–62). New York, NY: Routledge.

Murphy, V. B., & Christner, R. W. (2012). A cognitive-behavioral case conceptualization for children and adolescents. In R. B. Mennuti & R. W. Christner (Eds.), *Cognitive behavioral interventions in educational settings: A handbook for practice* (2nd ed., pp. 81–116). New York, NY: Routledge.

National Association of School Psychologists. (2010). *Model of comprehensive and integrated school psychological services*. Bethesda, MD: Author. Retrieved from http://www.nasponline.org/standards/2010standards/2_PracticeModel.pdf

Newell, M. (2010). The implementation of problem-solving consultation: An analysis of problem conceptualization in a multiracial context. *Journal of Educational and Psychological Consultation*, *20*, 83–105. doi:10.1080/10474411003785529

Noell, G. H., & Gansle, K. A. (2009). Moving from good ideas in educational systems change to sustainable program implementation: Coming to terms with some of the realities. *Psychology in the Schools*, *46*, 78–88. doi:10.1002/pits.20355

Norcross, J. C. (Ed.). (2011). *Psychotherapy relationships that work: Evidence-based responsiveness* (2nd ed.). New York, NY: Oxford University Press. doi:10.1093/acprof:oso/9780199737208.001.0001

Norcross, J. C., Krebs, P. M., & Prochaska, J. O. (2011). Stages of change. In J. C. Norcross (Ed.), *Psychotherapy relationships that work: Evidence-based responsiveness* (2nd ed., pp. 279–300). New York, NY: Oxford University Press. doi:10.1093/acprof:oso/9780199737208.003.0014

Norcross, J. C., & Lambert, M. J. (2011). Evidence-based therapy relationships. In J. C. Norcross (Ed.), *Psychotherapy relationships that work: Evidence-based responsiveness* (2nd ed., pp. 3–22). New York, NY: Oxford University Press. doi:10.1093/acprof:oso/9780199737208.003.0001

Norcross, J. C., & Wampold, B. E. (2011). Evidence-based therapy relationships: Research conclusions and clinical practices. In J. C. Norcross (Ed.), *Psychotherapy relationships that work: Evidence-based responsiveness* (2nd ed., pp. 423–430). New York, NY: Oxford University Press. doi:10.1093/acprof:oso/9780199737208.003.0021

Ortiz, S. O. (2006). Multicultural issues in school psychology practice: A critical analysis. *Journal of Applied School Psychology*, *22*, 151–167.

Painter, K. (2012). Outcomes for youth with severe emotional disturbance: A repeated measures longitudinal study of a wraparound approach of service delivery in systems of care. *Child Youth Care Forum*, *41*, 407–425. doi:10.1007/s10566-011-9167-1

Prochaska, J. O., DiClemente, C. C., & Norcross, J. C. (1992). In search of how people change: Applications to addictive behaviors. *American Psychologist*, *47*, 1102–1114. doi:10.1037/0003-066X.47.9.1102

Russell, S. T., Ryan, C., Toomey, R. B., Diaz, R. M., & Sanchez, J. (2011). Lesbian, gay, bisexual, and transgender adolescent school victimization: Implications for young adult health and adjustment. *Journal of School Health*, *81*, 223–230. doi:10.1111/j.1746-1561.2011.00583.x

Sheridan, S. M., & Kratochwill, T. R. (2008). *Conjoint behavioral consultation: Promoting family-school connections and interventions* (2nd ed.). New York, NY: Springer.

Shirk, S. R., Caporino, N. E., & Karver, M. S. (2010). The alliance in adolescent therapy: Conceptual, operational, and predictive issues. In D. Castro-Blanco & M. S. Karver (Eds.), *Elusive alliance: Treatment engagement strategies with high-risk adolescents* (pp. 59–93). Washington, DC: American Psychological Association. doi:10.1037/12139-002

Shirk, S. R., & Karver, M. (2006). Process issues in cognitive-behavioral therapy for youth. In P. C. Kendall (Ed.), *Child and adolescent therapy: Cognitive-behavioral procedures* (3rd ed., pp. 465–491). New York, NY: Guilford Press.

Shirk, S. R., & Karver, M. S. (2011). Alliance in child and adolescent psychotherapy. In J. C. Norcross (Ed.), *Psychotherapy relationships that work: Evidence-based responsiveness* (2nd ed., pp. 70–91). New York, NY: Oxford University Press. doi:10.1093/acprof:oso/9780199737208.003.0003

Shirk, S. R., Karver, M. S., & Brown, R. (2011). The alliance in child and adolescent psychotherapy. *Psychotherapy*, *48*, 17–24. doi:10.1037/a0022181

Smith, T. B., Domenick Rodrigues, M. M., & Bernal, G. (2011). Culture. In J. C. Norcross (Ed.), *Psychotherapy relationships that work: Evidence-based responsiveness* (2nd ed.; pp. 316–335). New York, NY: Oxford University Press. doi:10.1093/acprof:oso/9780199737208.003.0016

Sue, D. W., & Torino, G. C. (2005). Racial-cultural competence: Awareness, knowledge, and skills. In R. T. Carter (Ed.), *Handbook of racial-cultural psychology and counseling: Vol. 2. Training and practice* (pp. 3–18). Hoboken, NJ: Wiley.

Swift, J. K., Callahan, J. L., & Vollmer, B. M. (2011). Preferences. In J. C. Norcross (Ed.), *Psychotherapy relationships that work: Evidence-based responsiveness* (2nd ed., pp. 301–315). New York, NY: Oxford University Press. doi:10.1093/acprof:oso/9780199737208.003.0015

Tyron, G. S., & Winograd, G. (2011). Goal consensus and collaboration. In J. C. Norcross (Ed.), *Psychotherapy relationships that work: Evidence-based responsiveness* (2nd ed., pp. 153–167). New York, NY: Oxford University Press. doi:10.1093/acprof:oso/9780199737208.003.0007

Vernon, A. (2008). *Counseling children and adolescents* (4th ed.). Denver, CO: Love.

Wampold, B. E. (2010). The research evidence for common factors models: A historically situated perspective. In B. L. Duncan, S. D. Miller, B. E. Wampold, & M. A. Hubble (Eds.), *The heart and soul of change: Delivering what works in therapy* (2nd ed., pp. 49–81). Washington, DC: American Psychological Association. doi:10.1037/12075-002

Index

A

ability–achievement discrepancy, 334–339
academic and behavioral instruction and interventions, 81–82
academic competence, 464
Academic Competence Evaluation Scales, 463, 470, 471
academic data, 103, 106, 107, 109
academic dysfunctions, emotional and communication dysfunctions and, 357, 364
Academic Intervention Monitoring System, 470
academic interventions, communication disorders, 363
academic referrals, 153–154
academic skills, 16–17
    communication disorders and, 358–359
    low IQ scores, 339
acceptance, facilitating and evaluating, 530–531
accessibility, universal screening procedures, 126
accountability, 15–16
    data-based, 26
    movement, 76
    performance-based, 13
    service delivery, 13
accuracy, 288
    reading, 175
Achenbach System of Empirically Based Assessment (ASEBA), 294–295, 370, 372, 373, 374, 376, 384
achievement, 305
    educational performance and, 382
    test results, 75, 76
actor–observer bias, 543
adaptive reasoning, math, 235
ADD. See attention deficit disorder
ADHD. See attention deficit hyperactivity disorder

adherence, 134
administrator barriers, consultation, 527–529
adult learning, inservice activities, 584–585
advertising successes, 536
affective disorders, 328
agenda, predetermined, 499
aggregation, multiple levels of, 167
AIMSweb Oral Reading Fluency Scores, 3rd grade, 129
algebra, 233
    three-tiered model of instructional support, 240, 245
        cooperative learning, 243–244
        evidence-based practices, 241–244
        implementation fidelity, 244–245
        instruction, 241–242, 244–245
        order of operations problems, sample, 245
        visual representation, 242–243
alliances, 609, 611
Alpert, Judith, 494
alphabetic principle, 174–175, 176, 177
analysts, novice vs expert, 91
applied behavioral analysis, 92
    ASD, 406–407
apraxic dygraphias, 255
aptitude by treatment interaction (ATI), 73–74
articulation, 361, 363–364
ASD. See autism spectrum disorders
ASD Support Model, 428
ASEBA. See Achenbach System of Empirically Based Assessment
assessment reports, writing, 433–445
    abbreviations and jargon, 436–437
    results, summarizing, 165, 182
    writing, 436, 438–439
assessments, 16, 160, 274, 517
    additional, Tier 3, 109

computer-based, ADHD, 399
conducting, 317–330
data
 collecting, 165, 182
 linking to intervention, 284–285
drill-down, 101
early, 80
emotional and behavioral disorders, 372, 373
evidence-based, 291
instruction and, 172, 186
materials, 440
MTSS, 56, 59–60
planning, 181–182
types, 78–79
writing, 187–188
see also evaluation
assumed causes, 161, 164–165, 181, 185
at-risk students, identifying, 48–49
attention deficit disorder (ADD), interventions, 253–254
attention deficit hyperactivity disorder (ADHD), 287, 335, 373, 394–395
 assessment, 394–402
 at-risk child, 403
 comorbidity, 395, 417–418
 diagnosis, 372, 394
 interventions, 253–254
 multitiered services framework, 399–403
 peer relationships, 395
attitude change, 544
attributions, challenging, 500
Autism Diagnostic Interview–Revised (ADI-R), 328–329, 422
Autism Diagnostic Observation Schedule–Second Edition (ADOS-2), 422
Autism Speaks, 429
autism spectrum disorders (ASD), 328, 335, 405–416
 applied behavior analysis, 406–407
 assessment, 409–410
 checklists, 421–422
 diagnosis/identification, 406, 408, 409–410
 educational determination, 406, 410
 interventions, 406–408, 410–413, 415
 outcomes, 414–415
 peers, access to, 414
 postintervention outlook, 415
 progress monitoring, 413
 resources, 429–430
 support for family, 413–414
autism spectrum disorders, high-functioning (HFASD), 417–431

 assessments, 421–424, 430
 classification, 418–419
 comorbidity, 417–418
 diagnosis, 418–420
 interventions, 421, 424–430
 supports, 428–429

B

background information, 438–439
 datedness, 439
 recommendations, 442–444
 results and interpretation, 440–441
 summary/conclusions, 442
 test scores, 441–442
basic number operations, 228
behavior, 53, 407, 591
 antecedents, 276, 281
 biological bases, 247
 change, percentage from baseline to intervention (PEM), 155
 consultation, 450, 461, 484–486
 data, Tier 2, 106–109
 language, 514
 observations, 439–440, 517
Behavioral and Emotional Rating Scale-Second Edition (BERS-2), 373, 376
Behavioral and Emotional Screening System, 293
Behavior Assessment System for Children-Second Edition (BASC-2), 295, 370, 372, 373, 374
behavior rating scales, 287–304
 case example, 298–299
 classification and diagnosis, 296–297
 intervention planning and monitoring, 297–298
 problem-solving model, 299–302
 screening, 293–294
 usage, 288, 293–298, 303
Behavior Screening Checklist, 293–294
Bergan's behavior consultation, 71–72, 74
Berlin, Irving, 494
Best Practices in School Psychology, 1–3
 Data-Based and Collaborative Decision Making, 2
 Foundations, 2
 Student-Level Services, 2
 Systems-Level Services, 2
Bijou, 71, 72–73
Blueprints I, II, and III, 10–11, 77, 79, 82
broadband vs narrowband, universal screening approaches, 124–125
Bronfenbrenner's Model, 487
burnout, 527

C

can't do/won't do academic assessment, 305–316
    benefits and limitations, 312–314
    development and research evaluation, 306–307
    faculty and parents, 308
    instructional problems, 307–308
    instructions, math, 315
    materials to administer, 308–309
    performance, 305, 306, 311, 314
    proficiency, 313
    reading, 317
    record, summarize, and interpret, 310, 311
    roots, 306
    sensitivity, 313
    systems-level problem solving and, 310–312
    universal screening process and, 307
    writing, 315–316
Caplan, Gerald, 493–494
Cattell–Horn–Carroll Model, 250–251, 252
CBE. *See* curriculum-based evaluation
central auditory processing disorder, 361, 362, 364
central processing route, 544
change
    conceptual, 499
    maintaining, 591
    mechanisms, 529
    theories of, 529–531
Child Behavior Checklist, 294–295
child-initiated pretend play assessment (ChIPPA), 267, 268
child learning in play system (CLIPS), 265, 266–267
children, play assessment and intervention, 261–272
classification
    behavior rating scales, 294–297
    criteria, 78
    emotional and behavioral disorders, 370–371
    learning disabilities, 148–149
classroom-based change, instructional consultation, 512
classroom management strategies, 49
client
    consultation, 477
    helping relationship, 607
    influences, 599–607
    motivation, 605–606
    well-being, 452
Clinical Evaluation of Language Fundamentals–Fifth Edition, 361
clinical interviews, 316, 317–330
    conducting, 322–325
    informants

        disagreement, 325–326
        selection, 321–322
    interviews, 326–329
    parents, 324, 327
    school setting, structure, 321–322
    semistructured, 320, 327
    structured, 319–320
    students, 324–325, 327–329
    teachers, 324, 327
    unstructured, 320–321
clinical judgment, learning disabilities, 338, 343–344, 345, 352, 353
co-occurring conditions. *See* comorbidity
coaching, 34, 591
cognitive hypothesis testing (CHT) model, 250, 251–252
Cohen's *d*, 155
collaboration, 135, 274, 534
    administrators, 548
    barriers, 542–544
    communication and, 541–551
    communication disorders, 364, 365
    consultation and, 509, 525–539
    cooperative partnership, 451, 454, 488
    goal consensus and, 610, 611
    learning disabilities, 347
    teachers, 548
    teams, 549, 573–575
Common Core State Standards, 29, 219
    mathematics, 234
    writing and language, 200, 204
communication, 542
    administrators, 548
    barriers, 542–544
    collaboration and, 534
    consultation and, 541–542
    effective, 545–548
    face-to-face, 545–546
    nonverbal, 547
    professional, 19–20
    skills, 513–514, 516
    teachers, 548
    teams, 549
communication disorders, 335, 360
    assessment, 357–362
    case studies, 363–364
    definition, 356
    emotional and academic dysfunctions, and 357, 364
    interventions, 362–363
    prevalence, 357

comorbidity, 382
    ADHD, 395, 417–418
    HFASD, 417–418
    intervention effectiveness, 396, 403
competencies, 463, 464
    consultants, 452–453, 491
    school psychologists', 147
Comprehensive Behavior Rating Scales (CBRS), 370
Comprehensive Test of Phonological Processing, 360,
    361
conceptions
    changing, 504–505
    math, 235
    questions to illuminate, 500
Concerns-Based Adoption Model, 529, 530
conditional probability universal screening, 123–124,
    125
conjoint consultation, 463–464
Conners-Third Edition
    ADHD Index, 294
    Full Form, 295–296
    Full Parent Form, 296
    Full Teacher Form, 296
    Short and Global Index Forms, 298
consequences, 281
consultants, 452
    multitiered support system, 553–568
    prerequisite competencies, 452–453
consultation, 449–460, 483
    administrator barriers, 527–529
    assessment, 488–489
    barriers, 538
    behavioral and ecological models, 483–492
    benefits, 458
    changes, 525
    collaboration and, 4, 16–17, 462, 509
        teachers and administrators, 525–539
    competencies, prerequisite, 452–453
    concerns, definition of, 468
    consultee
        issues, 466–467
        resistance, 467
    defined, 449
    delivery steps, 466–476
    evaluations, 458, 490, 503
    goals, 462–463, 468–470, 478
    implementation, 489
    interventions, 472, 489
    mental health/consultee-centered, 493–507
    models, 450–451, 461–462
    MTSS, 53, 54
    multicultural competence, 491
    outcomes, 468–470
    performance and assessment objectives, 472
    plan evaluation, 474–476
    plan implementation, 472–474
    practice, 449–450
    presentation, consultee-centered, 496–498
    prevention and intervention systems, 461–482
    problem analysis, 470–471
    problem identification, 468, 489–490
    process, tasks, 455
    relationships, 466, 488
    RTI and, 461
    structure and process, 463–466
    teacher barriers, 526–527
    team-based, 453–454
    termination, 490
    time spent, 525–526
    usefulness, 491
consultation, instructional, 509–524
    assumptions, 509–510
    classroom-level support, 511
    components, 509, 513–519
    consultee-centered model, 512, 522
    defined, 509
    ecological perspective, 510–511
    instructional assessment method, 512
    instructional triangle, 511–512, 522
    supporting learning, 511
    teams, 513–519, 520–522
consultee-centered consultation
    definition, 494–495
    groups, 504
    practice model, 495
    stages/phases, 496, 497, 499–504
    understanding and behavior, 496
consultees
    conceptualizations, 500
    dilemma, description of, 496–498
    freedom of choice, acknowledging, 498–499
    knowledge, lack of, 501–502
    objectivity, lack of, 502
    responsibility, 498
    self-confidence, lack of, 502
    skill, lack of, 502
convergent evidence scaling (CES), 142–144
    rubric, 143
cooperative partnership, 451, 454, 488
    see also collaboration
core instruction, 48, 225–226
correlational model, 72

Cronbach, L. J., 71, 73
cross-informant comparisons, 376–377
cultural competence. *See* multicultural competence
cultural values vs themes, 502
culture, ADHD and, 393
curriculum
    map, 172, 173, 174, 175, 176, 177
    social–behavioral, 49, 51
    Tier 2, 50–51
curriculum-based evaluation (CBE), 93, 159–170, 306 590
    basics, 160–162
    checkpoints, 166
    defined, 160
    effectiveness in implementing, 169
    emotional and behavioral disorders, 368
    implementation, 185
    inquiry, process of, 162–167
    learning disabilities, 342–343
    literacy, 127
    math, 227–228
    multicultural competencies, 169
    multitiered system of supports and, 167
    process flowchart, 179
    reading, early, 171–186
        framework, 178–186
    review, 103–104, 106–107
    strengths and challenges, 168–169, 170
    writing, 190–195, 204, 205
        administration and scoring, 190–191, 192
        comparative data, 195
        elementary, early, later, middle, 191–193
        example, 195
        high school, 193
        multitiered model, 193–195
        preschool, 191
        racial and language group differences, 193

D

data
    collection, 33–34, 38, 100–101, 163
    ASD, 407
    displays, 101
    gathering, 180
    interpretation, 384
    intervention integrity and, 140
    management and reporting system, 562
    observational, 140
    patterns, 154
    review

    Tier 1, 103–104
    Tier 2, 106–107
    Tier 3, 109–110
data-analysis teams, 99–120
    operation, 101–113
data-based decision making and accountability, 3–4, 15–16, 82, 159, 172, 203, 247, 288, 413, 572–573
data-based problem solving, 38
    fidelity, 27
    historical perspective, 27–28
    MTSS, 36–37
    questions, 38
    school reform and, 25–27
decision-making, 80
    data-based, 15–16
    formative, 165–167
    structures, multiple, 167–168
    summative, 164–165
decision rules, valid, 563
delayed gratification, 305
Deno, S. L., 71, 72, 74
Deshler, Don, 555
development, 92
    ADHD and, 392–393
    emotional and behavioral disorders, 379–380
    helping relationships, 600–602
    neurocognitive deficits, 257
diagnosis
    errors, 148
    problem-solving approach, 156
Diagnostic and Statistical Manual (5th ed.; DSM-5), 335, 370
    ADHD, 391–392, 406
    HFASD, 418–419
Diagnostic and Statistical Manual of Mental Disorders (4th ed., text rev.; DSM-IV-TR), 370
Diagnostic Interview for Children and Adolescents–IV, 328
differentiated instruction, MTSS, 56, 57–59
direct assessment
    analytic scoring rubrics, 188–189, 189–190
    CBE, 190
    rubrics, 187
Direct Behavior Rating, 302–303
direct descriptive assessment, 277–278
direct observation, 280
    ADHD, 397–398
    emotional and behavioral disorders, 380–382
    HFASD, 424
Direct Observation Form, 381

disabilities, high-incidence, 76, 156
discrepancy model, 339–340, 344–345, 352
disruptive behaviors, 274
diversity in development and learning, 18
documentation procedures, learning disabilities, 347–348
dosage, 134
Dynamic Indicators of Basic Early Literacy Skills (DIBELS)
    Next, 176, 361
    Next Phoneme Segmentation Fluency, 111–113
    Next Tier 1, 103–104
    Oral Reading Fluency, 111–113
dyslexia, 336
dyslexic dysgraphias, 255

E

ecological consultation, 486–488
    effectiveness, 488
    exosystem, 487
    framework, 486, 487
    goals, 487–488
    macrosystem, 487
    mesosystem, 487
    microsystem, 486
    processes, 487–488
    transitions, 488
ecological environment, evaluation of, 531
ecological field, exploring and monitoring, 503
ecological/systems perspective, 451
ecological–transactional model, 317–318
education, graduate programs, 21
educational achievement, 75
educational assessment, ADHD, 399
Education of All Handicapped Children Act. *See* Individuals with Disabilities Education Act
educator characteristics, 135
effectiveness
    behavioral consultation, 486
    collaborative consultation, 538
    ecological consultation, 488
    estimates, 154–155
    evaluation of, 111, 113, 258, 538
    maximizing, 612
    neuropsychological, 258
ego support, 503
elaboration likelihood model, 543–544
Elementary and Secondary Education Act (ESEA), 26, 75, 76–77, 80
eligibility, 274

decision making, 66
    evaluations, 78
    federal, 349–350
    learning disabilities, 147–148, 333–334, 335, 336
    special education, 148, 336, 422
emotion, 504
emotional and behavioral disorders
    case illustration, 367–368
    multimethod assessment, 367–389
    RTI, 368
emotional disturbance/dysfunctions (ED), 371
    academic and communication dysfunctions and, 357, 364
    behavior problems vs, 150–151
    criteria for, 148
    IDEIA-defined, 150
empathy, 598
empowerment, 451–452
environment and plan implementation, 152–153
environmental support, 49
ethics, 19, 434
ethnic minorities, HFASD, 420
evaluation, 160
    behavioral consultation, 485, 490
    collaborative consultation, 538
    ecological consultation, 490
    effectiveness, 111, 113
    interviews, 475
    learning disabilities, 346, 348–349, 350
    practice and outcomes, teams, 580
    reevaluation, 350
    universal screening procedures, 122–124, 126
    written expression, 200
    see also assessment
evaluators, assessment reports, 443–444
evidence-based practice, 14
    ASD, 412–413
    HFASD, 426
    inservice programming, 592
    MTSS, 56, 62–64
    problem, 483–484
    research support for, 77
exclusionary factors, learning disabilities, 349–350
executive functions, interventions, 253, 254
experimental model/attitude, 72, 503
exposure, 134

F

fact finding, 178–181
    CBE, 162–164

false negatives, 148, 288, 289, 290
false positives, 148, 288, 289, 290
family
    ASD, support for, 413–414
    collaboration services, 18
federal eligibility criteria, applying, 349–350
feedback to parent and child, learning disabilities, 348
females, HFASD, 420
fidelity
    CBE, 169
    data, 35
First Sound Fluency, 176
fiscal support, 19–20
fluency, reading, 175, 176, 177
follow-up, evaluating, 456–457
formative assessment, 113, 238–239
    communication of assessment results, 238
    diagnosis, 238, 240
    framework, 238
    progress monitoring decisions, 238
    results interpretation, 239
    sample, 237
    secondary mathematics, 236–240
formative decision making, 182–184
formative-evaluation, 82
formative instructional decisions, 239–240
formulas, learning disabilities, 350–351
functional analysis, 277–279
functional assessment, 51–52
    ADHD, 398, 399–403
    learning disabilities, 346, 347
    multitiered services framework, 399–403, 401
functional behavioral assessment (FBA), 274–286
    case example, 280–281, 283
    conceptual foundation, 275–276
    contextual variables, 276
    defined, 274
    HFASD, 424
    hypothesis testing, 283
    practice guidelines, 274
    rating scale, 283–285
    requirements, 279
    school psychologists' effectiveness, 285
functional impairment, helping relationships, 602, 603
functional interventions, 153, 282
fundamental attribution error, 543

G

genuineness, 598
goals, 108, 470–472

assessment, 472
collaboration and, 610, 611
consultation, 468–470, 475, 478
ecological consultation, 487–488
identification, 32–33
Tier 1, 104
Tier 2, 108
Tier 3, 110
writing, 183
Good Behavior Game, 152–153
grade-level team, 570–571, 573–574
    barriers, 571–572
graphed data, visual inspection, 154
groups, consultee-centered consultation, 504

H

Hattie, J., 77
hearing disorders, 356, 364
    central auditory processing disorder, 361, 362, 364
    peripheral hearing, 364
helper factors, 595, 597–599, 606–607
helping relationships, 595–615
    barriers, 606–607
    client/consultee factors, 599–607
    coping styles, 602–603
    defined, 595
    evaluating, 612
    evidence-based practice and, 596
    examples, 596–597
    factors that facilitate, 597–599
    helper behaviors that interfere with, 599–607
    influences, 596, 597
    participants, 596
    processes, 596
    school context, 596
HFASD. *See* autism spectrum disorders, high-functioning
hypotheses, 31–32, 87–89, 90, 161–162
hypothesis-testing, 92–93
    examples, 93–95

I

IA. *See* instructional assessment
IDEIA. *See* Individuals with Disabilities Education Act
Identification of Students With Specific Learning Disabilities, 332
immediacy, 154
integrity, 33–34, 80
    teams, 577–580

implementation, 105, 109, 110, 456
    behavioral and ecological consultation, 489
    behavioral consultation, 485
    quality of, 141
    Tiers 1–3, 105–106, 109, 110
indirect assessment, 277
    standardized tests, 187
indirect service, consultation, 491
Individualized Target Behavior Evaluation, ADHD, 398
individuals
    behavior deficits, 276
    change, 531–532
    mediating variables, 276
Individuals with Disabilities Education Act (IDEA), 75, 76–77, 80, 371–372, 509
    learning disabilities, 331, 333, 148–149
Individuals with Disabilities Education Improvement Act (IDIEA 2004), 371–372
inference, 89–90, 96
informant reports, HFASD, 420
information, summarizing, 163, 180–181
information recording form. *See* Screening and Information Recording Form–Academics
inservices for teachers and principals, 583–593, 586
instruction
    appropriate, 334
    assessment and, 172, 186
    can't do/won't do assessment and, 307–308
    hierarchy, 92
    implementation, 166, 183–184, 185
    match, 207–208
    math, 229–230
    multiple tiers, 168
    program, 165–166, 183, 185
    secondary mathematics, 240–245
    support, 16–17
    teams, 572–573
    writing, 204, 209–210
instructional assessment (IA)
    method, 512, 517
    role and purpose, 204
    writing, 208–216
instructional consultation, 519–520
    teams, 520–522, 523
    parents' role, 522
    program evaluation, 521–522
    systems-level entry, 521
    training, 521, 522–523
instructional groups, 107–108
    sorting students into, 107–108

integrity, 134–136, 142–143
    see also intervention integrity
intellectual development disorders, 336
interaction, modes of, 504–505
interpreters, 384
interventions
    adaptation, 134
    ADHD, 396, 402, 403
    component, 136–138, 141
    consultation, 473–474
    delivery, 34
    evaluating, 456–457
    implementation, 29, 519
    MTSS, 56, 61–62
    teams, 572–573
intervention integrity, 133–134
    CES rubric, 143
    considerations, 139–144
    consultation, 138
    direct vs indirect measures, 141–142
    evaluating, 133–146
    observational data, 140
    performance feedback, 138–139
    promoting, 144
    rating scale, 136
    rubric, 137
    standardized interventions, 139
intervention monitoring
    behavior rating scale, 297–298
    Brief Problem Monitor, behavior rating scale, 297
intervention outcomes, 154
intervention planning, 33, 297, 412, 517–518
    behavior rating scale, 297
    consultation, 472
    identification, 108
    revision, 474
    Tier 2, 108
interventions, 16–17
    behavioral and ecological consultation, 489
    clients and consultees, 610
    complexity, 134
    continuum of, 562–563
    coordinating and collaborating, 427–428
    designing, 51–52, 53
    flexibility, 134–135
    functional, 282
    HFASD, 424–428
    implementing, 456
    MTSS, 53, 54
    multiple theories, 503
    multiple tiers, 168

noncompliance, 427
research-based, 518–519
selection, 274, 456
support or accountability, 34, 559–561
interviewing, 377–379
ADHD, 398–399
child, 378–379
HFASD, 421, 423
parent, 377–378, 421
teacher, 378
intra-individual differences, 338, 340–341, 345, 352
Iowa Test of Basic Skills (ITBS), 314
IQ, 339
achievement discrepancies, 149–150

K

key words, repetition of, 547
knowledge and skills, 531, 534–536
case application, 534, 536

L

Lambert, Nadine, 494
language
development, 360–361
disorders, 356, 356, 364
exposure to, 349
jargon-free and clear, 546–547
skills, 360, 361, 383
technical, 546
value of, 358
learning, 162
HFASD, 422–423
learning disabilities, 332–336
approaches, 336–345
characteristics, 332–333
definitions, 333
eligibility criteria, 147–148, 333–334, 335, 336
eligibility vs identification, 352
evaluation design, 346–348
evidence of, 349
exclusionary criterion, 334
federal regulations, 333–334, 335, 336, 349–350
high-incidence, 148–149
IDEIA-defined, 148–149
identification models, 351–352
identifying, 331–354
lower achiever vs, 148
NCJLD-defined, 149
prevalence, 331, 332–333

referral, 346–348
typology, 334–336
learn to play program, 267–268
legal considerations, 19
accountability, 26
ADHD, 393
assessment reports, 434
inservice activities, 584, 585
letter–sound correspondence, 174
Letter–Sound Fluency, 176
levels and objectives, 165
Levels of Use framework, 530
limited English proficient (LEP), 383
linguistic minorities, HFASD, 420
linguistically diverse populations, consultation, 476–477
listening skills, 514, 547–548
literacy, 171
difficulties, 171–172
teaching strategies, 51
universal screening approaches, 127–128
low achievement/achievers, 152
discrepant vs nondiscrepant, 149–150
learning disabled vs, 148

M

marshmallow studies, 305
mathematics
adaptive reasoning, 235
assessment and interventions
elementary, 219–232
national and international, 220
secondary, 233–246
Tier 1, 222–227
Tier 2 and Tier 3, 227–230
basic number operations, 226
CBM, 227–228
competence, 75–76
conceptual understanding, 235
content standards, 235
curriculum-embedded assessments, 227
disabilities, 333
explicit instruction, 229
focused content, 229
framework for advancing, 219–220
instructional intensity, 229–230
interventions, 256–257
number sense, 225–226
performance, 233
procedural fluency, 235

productive disposition, 235
proficiency, 220
progress, 75
rational numbers, 226
research base, 222
secondary, 236–245
   formative assessment, 236–240
   sample, 237
strategic competence, 235
trajectories, 221–222
universal screening approaches, 128
measurement, 160
mechanical or motor dysgraphia, 255
meetings, 111
   academic data, 106, 109
   assessments, 109
   behavioral data, Tier 2, 106–109
   data review, 103–104, 106–107, 109–110
   frequency and duration, 102
   goal setting, 104, 108, 110
   implementation, 105–106, 109, 110
   instructional groups, 107–108
   intervention packages, 108
   nonresponders, 110–111
   progress monitoring, 109–110
   record keeping, 102
   strategies, 104–105, 110
   team membership, 102
   Tier 1, 102–106
   Tier 2, 106–110
   Tier 3, 109–111
mental health problems
   consultation, 450, 461, 493–494
   diagnosis, 147–158
   incidence, 147
   services, 17
mentoring/mentors, 20, 591
Meyers, Joel, 494
Mischel, Walter, 305
mnemonic devices, 199
Model for Comprehensive and Integrated School
    Psychological Services, 9–23, 27, 100, 159, 172,
    203, 247, 288, 383, 391, 569, 583, 596
Modified Omnibus Rating Scales, 298
motivating operations, 275–276
motor disorders, 335
MTSS. *See* multitiered systems of support
multicultural competence, 503
   behavior rating scales, 301–302
   behavioral and ecological consultation, 491
   CBE, 169, 185–186

communication and collaboration, 549–550
consultation, 476–477, 457–458, 538, 491
emotional and behavioral disorders, 383–384
helping relationships, 603–604
inservice activities, 584, 585
neurocognitive deficits, interventions, 257–258
teams, 580
multitiered service delivery
   ADHD, 399–403
   consultation and, 454
   mathematics, 219–220
multitiered systems of support (MTSS), 27, 36, 46–54
   CBE and, 167
   conceptual model, 46
   defined and conceptualized, 45–47
   evidence-based and differentiated instruction, 50
   example, 46–47
   facilitating, 47, 54–66
   framework, 41–70
   impediments, 563–567
   implementation, 45–46, 55, 66
   improving outcomes, 56
   internal consultant, 553
      challenges, 567
      consistency or compliance, 557, 558
      fidelity, monitoring or accountability, 557, 558,
        559, 565
      management, 557–559, 558, 564
      planning, 557, 558, 564–565
      problem-solving intervention team, 556–557
      purpose and mission, 555–557
      school psychologist's role, 554–555
      shortcomings, 559–561, 565–567
      system-wide routines, 565
   problem-solving intervention team, 563–564
   purpose and mission, 563–564
   special education prerequisite/substitute, 563
   teams, 569–581
   Tier 1, 47–50, 55, 66
   Tier 2, 47–48, 50–52, 55, 66
   Tier 3, 47–48, 52–54, 55, 66
multitiered systems, 100
   mathematics, 230
   problem-solving, 151

N

narrative recording, 381
NASP
   standards development, 11
   website, 28

NASP Practice Model, 10–22
    professional practices, 15–16
    rationale for, 11–14
A Nation at Risk, 76
National Council of Teachers of Mathematics, *Focal Points*, 219
National Joint Committee on Learning Disabilities (NCJLD), 149, 333
National Mathematics Advisory Panel, 219
Nationally Certified School Psychologist (NCSP), 10, 13
NCLB. *See* No Child Left Behind Act
negative predictive value, 288–289
negative reinforcement functions, 153
neurocognitive deficits, interventions, 257
neurodevelopmental disorders, 247, 335
neuropsychology, 247–260
    assessment, 248–251, 258
    functioning, 247
    interventions, 252–257
        integrated, 250–251, 252
        evolution, 249–250
    school psychologist's roles and functions, 248
No Child Left Behind Act (NCLB), 26, 28, 42, 75, 333, 383, 509
    inservice activities, 584
nonresponders, identification, 110–111
Nonsense Word Fluency, 178
norm groups, selection, 289
number sense, 225–226

O

objectives. *See* goals
observational data, intervention integrity and, 140
operational definitions, 151–152
Oral Reading Fluency, 178
oral responding, 206–207
    reading and writing, link between, 206–207
    writing performance and, 206–207
organizational level, 531
    consultation, 451, 461, 465–466
    service delivery, 19
orthographic dysgraphia, 256
outcomes
    data, 35
    evaluating, 503–504, 580
    improving, 13–14
    school-level factors, 13
    student-level factors, 14
    teacher-level factors, 13–14
    teams, 580
overlap, 154

P

Parent Rating Scale (PRS), 295, 373
parents, 595
    consultation, 463–464, 465
    teams involvement, 577
parent–teacher pairs, consultation, 463–464
participant responsiveness, 134
patient, defined, 595
Peabody Picture Vocabulary Test–Fourth Edition, 360
peer relationships
    ADHD, 392
    communication disorders and, 357
    cultural considerations, 394
    gender, 394
    legal considerations, 393
peer-mediated interventions, HFASD, 425, 426, 427
percentage, change from baseline, 154
percentage of all nonoverlapping data (PAND), 154, 155
percentage of nonoverlapping data (PND), 154, 155
performance, 311
    skill problem vs, 31
    stability of, 312
    variables affecting, 305, 306
peripheral hearing, 364
peripheral processing route, 544
personal issues, avoiding, 498
Phoneme Segmentation Fluency, 176, 178
phonemic awareness, 173, 176
phonological awareness, 172–174, 360
Phonological Awareness Test 2, 360
phonological dysgraphia, 256
phonological training, 364
plan
    development, 32–35
    evaluation, 35
        consultation, 474–476
        evaluation interview, 475
        goal attainment scaling, 475
        methods, 474
        outcome criteria, 474–475
        postimplementation, 475–476
        RTI, 153–156
    implementation
        consultation, 472–474
        tasks, 472–473
        treatment integrity, 473, 474

postimplementation, consultation, 475–476
play, 261, 268
    case illustration, 268–270
    early childhood evaluation system, 265–266
    skills, 270
play assessment and intervention, 165, 261–272
    child learning in play system (CLIPS), 265, 266–267
    learn to play assessment and intervention system, 267–268
    learn to play program, 267–268
    RTI system, 262–264
    training, 262–263
    transdisciplinary play-based assessment and intervention, 264–267
play assessment and intervention system (PLAIS), 265
play in early childhood evaluation system (PIECES), 265–266
population, U.S., 383
positive behavioral support (PBS), 41–44
    implementation, 44
    indicators, 49
    internal consultant, 553
    intervention integrity and, 136
    pitfalls, 44
    positive behavior support
    ramifications, 44–45
    school-wide, 44
positive behavior interventions and supports (PBIS)
    system, 81–82
    teams and, 569–570
positive predictive value, 288
positive regard, 599
positive reinforcement
    applied behavior analysis, 407
    functions, 153
practitioners, 21
    self-assessment, consultation, 477
    utilization, consultation, 477
Pragmatic Language Skills Inventory, 361
preferences, helping relationships, 602–603
prevention
    identifying students in need, 122
    MTSS, 56, 60–61
    orientation, 451
    services, 17–18
problem
    agreement about, 587
    analysis, 31–32, 87–97, 455, 575–577
    assessment, 95–96
    attribution, 80

behavioral consultation, 485
    category of, 576
    causal variable, 576–577
    class-wide, 575–576
    consultation, 470–471
    definition, 162–163, 179–180, 185, 514
    identification, 29–31, 151–152, 454–455, 485
    interview, 470
    magnitude, 30–31
    progression, 96,
    standard protocol and, 92
    system, group, and individual levels, 92, 94
    today's, 80
    validation, 163–164
problem behaviors, chronic and resistant, 153
problem solving, 29–35, 82, 571–572
    barriers, 571–572
    consultation, 461, 462, 465–477, 478
    consultee-centered consultation and, 495
    data analysis, 36, 37
    entry and contracting, 515
    evolution, 113
    model, 72, 458
    multitiered systems of support, 92, 94, 96
    problem identification and analysis, 515–517, 518
    RTI, 74
    stages, 514–519
    teams, 465, 570–571, 574–575, 575–577
    Tier 1, 36–37
    Tier 2, 37
    Tier 3, 37
Problem-Solving Team Implementation Integrity Checklist, 579
Problem-Solving Team Sample Request for Assistance and Documentation Form, 578
procedural fluency, math, 235
procedural reliability, 134
process, 562
    research, consultation, 477
productive disposition, math, 235
professional development, 29, 583–593
    evaluating outcomes, 590–591
    instructional consultation, 512
    leading activities, 587–590
    MTSS, 56, 64–66
    pitfalls, 589
    strategies to engage, 589–590
professionals
    advocacy, 28–29
    associations in education, 27
    diversity, 384

standards, 20
proficiency strands, interconnectedness, 236
program
    differentiation, 134
    evaluation, 18–19
The Program Evaluation Standards, 142
progress monitoring, 82, 101, 166, 184, 185, 198, 560,
        561, 566–567, 573
    ADHD, 397
    measuring, 301
    MTSS, 56, 59–60
    planning for, 108–110
    reviews, 34–35
    tools, 240
    writing, 204
psychological issues
    barriers, 536–537
    communication disorders and, 359–360
    HFASD, 422–423
psychological services, model for comprehensive and
        integrated, 14–15
psychometric evaluation, 288–289

Q

questions, open-ended, 500

R

race and ethnicity, helping relationships, 603–604
    see also multicultural competencies
rating scales
    ADHD, 396–397
    behavior, 299–302
    HFASD, 423–424
rational numbers, 226
reading
    competence, 75–76
    disabilities, 332–333, 336
    early
        assessments, 175–178
        CBE, 171–186
        framework, 178–186
        troubleshooting, 184
    interventions, 254–255
    oral responding and, 206
    progress, 75
    teaching, 171
    writing and, 204, 206, 215–216
reasoning, accessible, 505

Receptive One-Word Picture Vocabulary Test–Fourth
        Edition, 360
reciprocity, 530
recommendations, assessment reports, 443–444
record keeping, Tier 1, 102
reevaluation, learning disabilities, 350
referent power, 530
referrals, 151–152, 321, 438
    learning disabilities, 346
reinforcement functions, positive and negative, 153
relationships
    nonhierarchical, 498
    repairing ruptures, 610, 611
    see also helping relationships
reliability, universal screening procedures, 122–123,
        126
reports, computer-generated, learning disabilities, 351
research
    dissemination, 82
    program evaluation, 18
research-based interventions, monitoring, 38
resilience, 80
resistance to intervention, 135
resolution, 519
resources, 34
    collaboration, case application, 536–538
    online, 82
response to intervention (RTI), 16, 36, 41–43, 99, 147,
        151
    behavioral, 302
    behavior rating scales vs, 299–302
    case example, 302
    collaboration and, 358
    communication disorder, 363
    consultation, 450, 553, 461, 478
    emotional and behavioral disorders, 368–369, 385
    framework, 292
    grade-level teams, 570–571
    identifying students in need, 122
    intervention integrity, 136
    learning disabilities, 333, 337, 338, 341–345, 351,
        352
    mathematics, 219–220
    pitfalls, 44
    play, 262–264
    problem-solving teams, 570–571
    ramifications, 44–45
    system, 262–264
    teams and, 569–570
responsiveness, 301
results

assessment of validity, 440
interpretation, 440–441
reward power, 530
rubrics example, 189–190

S

safeguards, assessment reports, 434
Schedule for Affective Disorders and Schizophrenia–
School Age–Present State Version, 328
schizophrenia, 328, 371
school, culture, 588
school psychologists, 595
assessment and instructional experts, 221
inservice activities, 585
knowledge and skills, 554
MTSS consultants, 561–563
number of, 71
professional identity, 554
self-evaluation of effectiveness, 389
situational barriers, 554–555
skill sets, 28–29
time spent, 525
training, 77, 82
school psychology
communicating the value of, 12–13
contemporary, 13, 28–29, 81
contextual factors, 74–79
evolution, 71–84
future, 81–82
growth, 72
paradigm shift, 71–74, 79
problem-solving foundations, 25–39
training and practice, 79–80
School Psychology: A Blueprint for Training and Practice,
10, 383
school-wide information system data, 104
school-wide practices, 17–18
scientific method, 87–89
screening
ADHD, 397
ASD, 409
behavior rating scales, 293–294
MTSS, 56, 59–60
Screening and Information Recording Form—Behavior
Tier 1, 118
Tier 2 and 3, 119–120
Screening Form and Information Recording Form—
Academics
Tier 1, 115
Tier 2 and 3, 116–117

secondary schools, data-analysis process, 113
selective mutism, case studies, 363
self-evaluation of effectiveness, 384–385
self-monitoring, HFASD, 425, 426
self-regulated strategy development, 196–198
service delivery, 18
indirect, 458, 462
rethinking, 66
services, developing effective ones, 300–301
setting, curriculum, instruction, learner (SCIL), 164
sexual orientation, helping relationships, 604–605
single-case design data, 154
skills
deficit assessment, HFASD, 424
development, 531
high-priority, 173
learning disabilities, 346
problem, performance problem vs, 31
SLD. *See* specific learning disability
social and life skills development, 17
social–behavioral referrals, 152–153, 154
Social Communication Questionnaire, 422
social competence goals, 52
social deficits, HFASD, 423
social–emotional concerns, 53
curricula, 49, 51
learning disabilities, 346–347
learning programs, 17, 49–50
universal screening approaches, 128–129
social interventions, communication disorders, 363
social maladjustment, 150–151, 382–383
social power, 530
Social Responsiveness Scale–Second Edition, 422
social scripts, HFASD, 425, 426
social skills and social reasoning, 382
Social Skills Improvement System (SSIS) Rating
Scales, 296
Social Skills Programs, HFASD, 427
social validation, 154, 155–156
socioeconomic status, helping relationships, 604–605
special education
effect, 77, 78
eligibility, 148, 336, 422
HFASD, 422
learning disabilities, 336
need for, 383
teachers, 463
specific learning disabilities (SLD), 74, 80, 333, 335
dilemma, 79
specificity, 288, 290
speech, 363–364, 547

disorders, 356, 362, 364, 365
speech and language pathologists, 358
    collaboration, 355–356
SSIS scores, 107
staffing, 19–20
Stages of Concern, 529
standardized mean difference, 154
standardized rating scales, 374
    advantages, 373, 375
    limitations, 375–376
    parent and teacher, 372–376
standardized self-reports, 376
Standards for Mathematical Content, 234
Standards for Mathematical Practice, 234, 235
state school psychology associations, 22
statewide assessment data, 100
Stiggins, R., 81
Strands of Mathematical Proficiency, 234, 235–236
strategic competence, math, 235
strategies
    Tier 1, 104–105
    Tier 3, 110
structured approaches, MTSS, 54
students
    characteristics, 135–136
    demographics, 476
    documentation form, 516, 517, 518
    helping relationships, 600–602
    outcomes, CBE, 169
    response, 590–591
    services, 16
    strengths and needs, 299–300
    teams identifying needs, 572
stuttering, 361
    case studies, 363–364
Suicidal Behavior Interview, 329
summative decision making, 181–182
Superheroes Social Skills, HFASD, 427
supervision/supervisors, 20, 21
supports, HFASD
    primary-level, 428–429
    secondary-level, 429
    tertiary-level, 429
symbolic and imaginative play developmental checklist (SIP-DC), 267, 268
systematic direct observations, 381
systematic problem-solving process, 452
systems
    can't do/won't do assessment and, 310–311, 531–532
    change, 531–532

consultation, 451, 465–466
factors, 606–607
services, 17–18

T

targeted group interventions, ADHD, 400–402
task analysis, 34
taxonomies, empirically based, 369–370
Teacher Rating Scale (TRS), 295, 373
Teacher Report Form (TRF), 294, 295, 373
teachers, 595
    change process, 585–586
    consultation barriers, 526–527
        expectations, 526
        knowledge and skills, 527
        perceptions, 526
        resources, 527
    understanding and using data, 562, 566
teachers and administrators
    consultation and collaboration barriers, 532–538
        case application, 532, 534
        knowledge and skills, 534–536
        perceptions, 532–534
        resources, 536–538
    proficiency, 531
teaching, culture of, 587–588
teams
    barriers, 571–572
    expertise, 32
    membership, Tier 1, 102
    multitiered system of support, 569
    mutual support, 549
    process, 38
teleconsultation, 465
temporal sequence model of the helping relationship, 607
termination, interventions, 519
    behavioral and ecological consultation, 490
Test of Language Development–Fourth Edition, 360–361
tests
    conditions, 440
    scores, 441–442
themes vs cultural values, 502
theoretical orientations, hypothesis-testing, 92–93
therapeutic alliance, fostering, 609
time constraints, 536–537
Tindal and Hasbrouck Analytical Scoring System, 189–190
training, HFASD, 418

transdisciplinary play-based assessment and intervention, 264–267
translations, 384
treatment
    acceptability, 33
    fidelity, 80, 134
    integrity, 473
    monitoring, 473
trend, 154
true negative, 288, 289, 290
true positive, 288, 289, 290
turnings, 505

U

underachievement
    federal regulations, 349
    learning disability, 334
universal interventions, ADHD, 400
universal screening, 121–131
    analysis, 102
    broadband vs narrowband, 124–125
    can't do/won't do assessments and, 310–312
    case example, 129–130
    conditional probability, 123–124, 125
    correlations, 125
    data, 100–101, 559, 560, 566
    evaluating, 122–124, 126
    literacy, 127–128
    mathematics, 128, 222–224
    measures, 48–49
    multiple-gate approaches, 125–126
    reliability, 122–123
    selecting, 126–130
    social, emotional, and behavioral, 128–129
    tools, 239–240
    validity, 123–124, 126
usefulness, measuring, 491

V

validity, universal screening procedures, 123–124, 126
variability, 154
    alterable, causal, and maintaining, 91
    rating scales, 291
video modeling, HFASD, 425, 426

vocabulary, receptive and expressive, 360
vocal tone, 547
voice, 363–364

W

warmth, 599
weak central coherence, 423
Witt, Joe, 306
Word Identification Fluency, 176, 178
work difficulty, differentiating the four common reasons, 500–501
working memory, interventions, 252–253
writing, 545
    prewriting activities, 198
writing assessment and intervention, 187–202
    challenges, 203–204, 208
    curricula, 198
    dimensions, 208–209, 210
    disabilities, 333
    instructional level, 209–210
    oral responding and, 206
    present levels, 183
    proficiency, 203
    reading and, 206, 215–216
    review, 211, 214–215
    samples, 210–211, 214
writing instruction, research-based elements, 198
    commercial interventions, 199
    example, 199–200
    mnemonic devices, 199
    Tier 2 and Tier 3, 198–199
writing instructional assessment, 203–217
    decision questions, 213–214
    match instruction, 213, 216
    sampling, additional, 211–213, 215
    snapshot, 210
writing intervention, 195–200, 255–256
    Tier 1 intervention, 196–200
    Common Core State Standards, 196–200

Y

Youth Self-Report Form, 294, 295
youth, helping relationships, 607–608

Best Practices in School Psychology: Series List

Best Practices in School Psychology: Data-Based and Collaborative Decision Making

INTRODUCTION AND FRAMEWORK

1. The National Association of School Psychologists Model for Comprehensive and Integrated School Psychological Services
   Rhonda J. Armistead and Diane L. Smallwood
2. Problem-Solving Foundations for School Psychological Services
   Kathy Pluymert
3. A Comprehensive Framework for Multitiered Systems of Support in School Psychology
   Karen Callan Stoiber
4. The Evolution of School Psychology: Origins, Contemporary Status, and Future Directions
   James E. Ysseldyke and Daniel J. Reschly

DATA-BASED DECISION MAKING AND ACCOUNTABILITY

5. Best Practices in Problem Analysis
   Theodore J. Christ and Yvette Anne Arañas
6. Best Practices in Data-Analysis Teaming
   Joseph F. Kovaleski and Jason A. Pedersen
7. Best Practices in Universal Screening
   Craig A. Albers and Ryan J. Kettler
8. Best Practices in Facilitating and Evaluating the Integrity of School-Based Interventions
   Andrew T. Roach, Kerry Lawton, and Stephen N. Elliott
9. Best Practices in Diagnosis of Mental Health and Academic Difficulties in a Multitier Problem-Solving Approach
   Frank M. Gresham
10. Best Practices in Curriculum-Based Evaluation
    Kenneth W. Howell and John L. Hosp

11. Best Practices in Curriculum-Based Evaluation in Early Reading
    Michelle K. Hosp and Kristen L. MacConnell
12. Best Practices in Written Language Assessment and Intervention
    Christine Kerres Malecki
13. Best Practices in Instructional Assessment of Writing
    Todd A. Gravois and Deborah Nelson
14. Best Practices in Mathematics Assessment and Intervention With Elementary Students
    Ben Clarke, Christian T. Doabler, and Nancy J. Nelson
15. Best Practices in Mathematics Instruction and Assessment in Secondary Settings
    Yetunde Zannou, Leanne R. Ketterlin-Geller, and Pooja Shivraj
16. Best Practices in Neuropsychological Assessment and Intervention
    Daniel C. Miller and Denise E. Maricle
17. Best Practices in Play Assessment and Intervention
    Lisa Kelly-Vance and Brigette Oliver Ryalls
18. Best Practices in Conducting Functional Behavioral Assessments
    Mark W. Steege and Michael A. Scheib
19. Best Practices in Rating Scale Assessment of Children's Behavior
    Jonathan M. Campbell and Rachel K. Hammond
20. Best Practices in Can't Do/Won't Do Academic Assessment
    Amanda M. VanDerHeyden
21. Best Practices in Clinical Interviewing Parents, Teachers, and Students
    James J. Mazza
22. Best Practices in Identification of Learning Disabilities
    Robert Lichtenstein
23. Best Practices in the Assessment and Remediation of Communication Disorders
    Melissa A. Bray, Thomas J. Kehle, and Lea A. Theodore
24. Best Practices in Multimethod Assessment of Emotional and Behavioral Disorders
    Stephanie H. McConaughy and David R. Ritter
25. Best Practices in the Assessment of Youth With Attention Deficit Hyperactivity Disorder Within a Multitiered Services Framework
    Renée M. Tobin, W. Joel Schneider, and Steven Landau
26. Best Practices in Early Identification and Services for Children With Autism Spectrum Disorders
    Ilene S. Schwartz and Carol A. Davis
27. Best Practices in Assessment and Intervention of Children With High-Functioning Autism Spectrum Disorders
    Elaine Clark, Keith C. Radley, and Linda Phosaly
28. Best Practices in Writing Assessment Reports
    Robert Walrath, John O. Willis, and Ron Dumont

CONSULTATION AND COLLABORATION

29. Best Practices in School Consultation
    William P. Erchul and Hannah L. Young
30. Best Practices in School-Based Problem-Solving Consultation: Applications in Prevention and Intervention Systems
    Thomas R. Kratochwill, Margaret R. Altschaefl, and Brittany Bice-Urbach
31. Best Practices in Behavioral/Ecological Consultation
    Tammy L. Hughes, Jered B. Kolbert, and Laura M. Crothers
32. Best Practices in School-Based Mental Health/Consultee-Centered Consultation by School Psychologists
    Jonathan Sandoval
33. Best Practices in Instructional Consultation and Instructional Consultation Teams
    Sylvia Rosenfield

34. Best Practices in Facilitating Consultation and Collaboration With Teachers and Administrators
    Robin S. Codding, Lisa M. Hagermoser Sanetti, and Florence D. DiGennaro Reed
35. Best Practices in School Psychologists' Promotion of Effective Collaboration and Communication Among School Professionals
    Tanya L. Eckert, Natalie Russo, and Bridget O. Hier
36. Best Practices as an Internal Consultant in a Multitiered Support System
    Kathy McNamara
37. Best Practices in Implementing School-Based Teams Within a Multitiered System of Support
    Matthew K. Burns, Rebecca Kanive, and Abbey C. Karich
38. Best Practices in Providing Inservices for Teachers and Principals
    Laura M. Crothers, Jered B. Kolbert, and Tammy L. Hughes
39. Best Practices in Establishing Effective Helping Relationships
    Julia E. McGivern, Corey E. Ray-Subramanian, and Elana R. Bernstein

Best Practices in School Psychology: Student-Level Services

INTERVENTIONS AND INSTRUCTIONAL SUPPORT TO DEVELOP ACADEMIC SKILLS

1. Best Practices in Instructional Strategies for Reading in General Education
   Rebecca S. Martinez
2. Best Practices in Increasing Academic Engaged Time
   Maribeth Gettinger and Katherine Miller
3. Best Practices in Fostering Student Engagement
   Amy L. Reschly, James J. Appleton, and Angie Pohl
4. Best Practices in Setting Progress Monitoring Goals for Academic Skill Improvement
   Edward S. Shapiro and Kirra B. Guard
5. Best Practices in Promoting Study Skills
   Robin Codding, Virginia Harvey, and John Hite
6. Best Practices in Homework Management
   Lea A. Theodore, Melissa A. Bray, and Thomas J. Kehle
7. Best Practices on Interventions for Students With Reading Problems
   Laurice M. Joseph
8. Best Practices in Oral Reading Fluency Interventions
   Edward J. Daly III, Maureen A. O'Connor, and Nicholas D. Young
9. Best Practices in Delivering Intensive Academic Interventions With a Skill-by-Treatment Interaction
   Matthew K. Burns, Amanda M. VanDerHeyden, and Anne F. Zaslofsky
10. Preventing Academic Failure and Promoting Alternatives to Retention
    Mary Ann Rafoth and Susan W. Parker
11. Best Practices in Services for Gifted Students
    Rosina M. Gallagher, Linda C. Caterino, and Tiombe Bisa-Kendrick
12. Best Practices in Planning for Effective Transition From School to Work for Students With Disabilities
    Fred Jay Krieg, Sandra S. Stroebel, and Holly Bond Farrell
13. Best Practices in Facilitating Transition to College for Students With Learning Disabilities
    Raymond Witte

INTERVENTIONS AND MENTAL HEALTH SERVICES TO DEVELOP SOCIAL AND LIFE SKILLS

14. Best Practices in Applying Positive Psychology in Schools
    Terry M. Molony, Maureen Hildbold, and Nakeia D. Smith
15. Best Practices in Social Skills Training
    Jennifer R. Frey, Stephen N. Elliott, and Cindy Faith Miller
16. Best Practices in Fostering Student Resilience
    Amity L. Noltemeyer
17. Best Practices in Assessing and Promoting Social Support
    Michelle K. Demaray and Christine K. Malecki
18. Best Practices in Classroom Discipline
    George G. Bear and Maureen A. Manning
19. Best Practices in Assessing and Improving Executive Skills
    Peg Dawson
20. Best Practices in Solution-Focused, Student-Driven Interviews
    John J. Murphy
21. Best Practices in Group Counseling
    Julie C. Herbstrith and Renée M. Tobin
22. Best Practices in Delivering Culturally Responsive, Tiered-Level Supports for Youth With Behavioral Challenges
    Robyn S. Hess, Vanja Pejic, and Katherine Sanchez Castejon
23. Best Practices in Classroom Interventions for Attention Problems
    George J. DuPaul, Gary Stoner, and Mary Jean O'Reilly
24. Best Practices in School-Based Interventions for Anxiety and Depression
    Thomas J. Huberty
25. Best Practices in Interventions for Anxiety-Based School Refusal
    Shannon M. Suldo and Julia Ogg
26. Best Practices in Promoting Appropriate Use of Restraint and Seclusion in Schools
    Brian M. Yankouski and Thomas Massarelli
27. Best Practices in Making Manifestation Determinations
    Robert J. Kubick Jr. and Katherine Bobak Lavik
28. Best Practices in Service Learning for School-to-Work Transition and Inclusion for Students With Disabilities
    Felicia L. Wilczenski, Paula Sotnik, and Laura E. Vanderberg

Best Practices in School Psychology: Systems-Level Services

SCHOOL-WIDE PRACTICES TO PROMOTE LEARNING

1. Best Practices in Systems-Level Change
   Jose M. Castillo and Michael J. Curtis
2. Best Practices in Strategic Planning, Organizational Development, and School Effectiveness
   Howard M. Knoff
3. Best Practices in Implementing Evidence-Based School Interventions
   Susan G. Forman, Audrey R. Lubin, and Alison L. Tripptree

4. Best Practices in Curriculum Alignment
    Bradley C. Niebling and Alexander Kurz
5. Best Practices in Facilitating Professional Development of School Personnel in Delivering Multitiered Services
    Melissa Nantais, Kimberly A. St. Martin, and Aaron C. Barnes
6. Best Practices in Decreasing Dropout and Increasing High School Completion
    Shane R. Jimerson, Amy L. Reschly, and Robyn S. Hess
7. Best Practices in Focused Monitoring of Special Education Results
    W. Alan Coulter
8. Best Practices in Supporting the Education of Students With Severe and Low Incidence Disabilities
    Franci Crepeau-Hobson
9. Best Practices for Working in and for Charter Schools
    Caven S. Mcloughlin

PREVENTIVE AND RESPONSIVE SERVICES

10. Best Practices in Developing Prevention Strategies for School Psychology Practice
    William Strein, Megan Kuhn-McKearin, and Meghan Finney
11. Best Practices in Population-Based School Mental Health Services
    Beth Doll, Jack A. Cummings, and Brooke A. Chapla
12. Best Practices in Developing a Positive Behavior Support System at the School Level
    Brian C. McKevitt and Angelisa Braaksma Fynaardt
13. Best Practices in the Use of Learning Supports Leadership Teams to Enhance Learning Supports
    Howard S. Adelman and Linda Taylor
14. Best Practices in School–Community Partnerships
    John W. Eagle and Shannon E. Dowd-Eagle
15. Best Practices in School Crisis Intervention
    Stephen E. Brock, Melissa A. Louvar Reeves, and Amanda B. Nickerson
16. Best Practices in School Violence Prevention
    Jim Larson and Sarah Mark
17. Best Practices in Bullying Prevention
    Erika D. Felix, Jennifer Greif Green, and Jill D. Sharkey
18. Best Practices in Threat Assessment in Schools
    Dewey Cornell
19. Best Practices in Suicide Prevention and Intervention
    Richard Lieberman, Scott Poland, and Cheryl Kornfeld
20. Best Practices in Crisis Intervention Following a Natural Disaster
    Melissa Allen Heath
21. Best Practices for Responding to Death in the School Community
    Scott Poland, Catherine Samuel-Barrett, and Angela Waguespack
22. Best Practices in Using the DSM-5 and ICD-10 by School Psychologists
    Susan M. Swearer, Kisha Radliff, and Paige Lembeck
23. Best Practices in Pediatric School Psychology
    Thomas J. Power and Kathy L. Bradley-Klug
24. Best Practices in Medication Treatment for Children With Emotional and Behavioral Disorders: A Primer for School Psychologists
    James B. Hale, Margaret Semrud-Clikeman, and Hanna A. Kubas
25. Best Practices in Assessing the Effects of Psychotropic Medication on Student Performance
    John S. Carlson and Jeffrey D. Shahidullah
26. Best Practices in Collaborating With Medical Personnel
    Sarah E. Glaser and Steven R. Shaw

27. Best Practices in Meeting the Needs of Children With Chronic Illness
    Cynthia A. Riccio, Jessica Beathard, and William A. Rae
28. Best Practices in Working With Children With Traumatic Brain Injuries
    Susan C. Davies
29. Best Practices in Responding to HIV in the School Setting
    Tiffany Chenneville

FAMILY–SCHOOL COLLABORATION SERVICES

30. Best Practices in Promoting Family Engagement in Education
    Susan M. Sheridan, Brandy L. Clarke, and Sandra L. Christenson
31. Best Practices in Systems-Level Organization and Support for Effective Family–School Partnerships
    Laura Lee McIntyre and S. Andrew Garbacz
32. Best Practices in Reducing Barriers to Parent Involvement
    Patricia H. Manz and Julie C. Manzo
33. Best Practices in Partnering With Parents in School-Based Services
    Dawn D. Miller and Nancy P. Kraft
34. Best Practices in Family–School Collaboration for Multitiered Service Delivery
    Gloria Miller, Cathy Lines, and Megan Fleming
35. Best Practices in Facilitating Family–School Meetings
    Kathleen M. Minke and Krista L. Jensen
36. Best Practices in Linking Families and Schools to Educate Children With Attention Problems
    Jennifer A. Mautone, Kristen Carson, and Thomas J. Power

Best Practices in School Psychology: Foundations

DIVERSITY IN DEVELOPMENT AND LEARNING

1. Best Practices in Increasing Cross-Cultural Competency
   Antoinette Halsell Miranda
2. Best Practices School Psychologists Acting as Agents of Social Justice
   David Shriberg and Gregory Moy
3. Best Practices in Primary Prevention in Diverse Schools and Communities
   Sherrie L. Proctor and Joel Meyers
4. Best Practices in Providing Culturally Responsive Interventions
   Janine Jones
5. Best Practices in Nondiscriminatory Assessment
   Samuel O. Ortiz
6. Best Practices in the Assessment of English Language Learners
   Catharina Carvalho, Andrea Dennison, and Ivonne Estrella
7. Best Practices in Assessing and Improving English Language Learners' Literacy Performance
   Michael L. Vanderwood and Diana Socie
8. Best Practices in School-Based Services for Immigrant Children and Families
   Graciela Elizalde-Utnick and Carlos Guerrero

9. Best Practices in Conducting Assessments via School Interpreters
   Emilia C. Lopez
10. Best Practices in Working With Children From Economically Disadvantaged Backgrounds
    Christina Mulé, Alissa Briggs, and Samuel Song
11. Best Practices in Providing School Psychological Services in Rural Settings
    Margaret Beebe-Frankenberger and Anisa N. Goforth
12. Best Practices in Working With Homeless Students in Schools
    Brenda Kabler, Elana Weinstein, and Ruth T. Joffe
13. Best Practices in Working With Children Living in Foster Care
    Tracey G. Scherr
14. Best Practices in Service to Children in Military Families
    Mark C. Pisano
15. Best Practices in Supporting Students Who Are Lesbian, Gay, Bisexual, Transgender, and Questioning
    Emily S. Fisher
16. Best Practices in Working With LGBT Parents and Their Families
    Julie C. Herbstrith
17. Best Practices in School Psychologists' Services for Juvenile Offenders
    Janay B. Sander and Alexandra L. Fisher
18. Best Practices in Planning Effective Instruction for Children Who Are Deaf or Hard of Hearing
    Jennifer Lukomski
19. Best Practices in School-Based Services for Students With Visual Impairments
    Sharon Bradley-Johnson and Andrew Cook

RESEARCH AND PROGRAM EVALUATION

20. Best Practices in Conducting School-Based Action Research
    Samuel Song, Jeffrey Anderson, and Annie Kuvinka
21. Best Practices Identifying, Evaluating, and Communicating Research Evidence
    Randy G. Floyd and Philip A. Norfolk
22. A Psychometric Primer for School Psychologists
    Cecil R. Reynolds and Ronald B. Livingston
23. Best Practices in Developing Academic Local Norms
    Lisa Habedank Stewart
24. Best Practices in Designing and Conducting Needs Assessment
    Richard J. Nagle and Sandra Glover Gagnon
25. Best Practices in Program Evaluation in a Model of Response to Intervention/Multitiered System of Supports
    Jose M. Castillo
26. Best Practices in the Analysis of Progress Monitoring Data and Decision Making
    Michael D. Hixson, Theodore J. Christ, and Teryn Bruni
27. Best Practices in Evaluating Psychoeducational Services Based on Student Outcome Data
    Kim Gibbons and Sarah Brown
28. Best Practices in Evaluating the Effectiveness of Interventions Using Single-Case Methods
    Rachel Brown, Mark W. Steege, and Rebekah Bickford

LEGAL, ETHICAL, AND PROFESSIONAL PRACTICE

29. Trends in the History of School Psychology in the United States
    Thomas K. Fagan
30. History and Current Status of International School Psychology
    Thomas Oakland and Shane Jimerson

31. Best Practices in Applying Legal Standards for Students With Disabilities
   Guy M. McBride, John O. Willis, and Ron Dumont
32. Best Practices in Ethical School Psychological Practice
   Susan Jacob
33. Best Practices in the Application of Professional Ethics
   Laurie McGarry Klose and Jon Lasser
34. Ethical and Professional Best Practices in the Digital Age
   Leigh D. Armistead
35. Best Practices in Using Technology
   William Pfohl and Susan Jarmuz-Smith
36. Best Practices in Using Technology for Data-Driven Decision Making
   Benjamin Silberglitt and Daniel Hyson
37. The Status of School Psychology Graduate Education in the United States
   Eric Rossen and Nathaniel von der Embse
38. Best Practices in Assessing Performance in School Psychology Graduate Programs
   Joseph S. Prus and Enedina Garcia-Vazquez
39. Best Practices in the Supervision of Interns
   Jeremy R. Sullivan, Nicole Svenkerud, and Jane Close Conoley
40. Best Practices in National Certification and Credentialing in School Psychology
   Eric Rossen
41. Best Practices in Early Career School Psychology Transitions
   Arlene E. Silva, Daniel S. Newman, and Meaghan C. Guiney
42. Best Practices in Supervision and Mentoring of School Psychologists
   Virginia Smith Harvey, Joan A. Struzziero, and Sheila Desai
43. Best Practices in School Psychologists' Self-Evaluation and Documenting Effectiveness
   Barbara Bole Williams and Laura Williams Monahon
44. Best Practices in the Professional Evaluation of School Psychologists Utilizing the NASP Practice Model
   Anastasia Kalamaros Skalski and Mary Alice Myers
45. Best Practices in Continuing Professional Development for School Psychologists
   Leigh D. Armistead
46. Best Practices in Using Technology for Continuous Professional Development and Distance Education
   Jack A. Cummings and Susan Jarmuz-Smith
47. Best Practices in Maintaining Professional Effectiveness, Enthusiasm, and Confidence
   Brian P. Leung and Jay Jackson

National Association of School Psychologists